LEGAL CONTROL

OF

WATER RESOURCES

CASES AND MATERIALS

Fourth Edition

By

Joseph L. Sax
James H. House & Hiram H. Hurd
Professor of Environmental Regulation Emeritus
Boalt Hall School of Law
University of California at Berkeley

Barton H. Thompson, Jr.
Robert E. Paradise Professor of Natural Resources Law
Stanford Law School
Director
Woods Institute for the Environment at Stanford University

John D. Leshy
Harry D. Sunderland Distinguished Professor of Law
University of California, Hastings College of the Law

Robert H. Abrams
Professor of Law
Florida A&M University College of Law

AMERICAN CASEBOOK SERIES®

THOMSON
WEST

Mat #40400839

American Casebook Series and West Group are trademarks
registered in the U.S. Patent and Trademark Office.

COPYRIGHT © 1986, 1991 WEST PUBLISHING CO.
© West, a Thomson business, 2000
© 2006 Thomson/West
        610 Opperman Drive
        P.O. Box 64526
        St. Paul, MN 55164–0526
        1–800–328–9352

Printed in the United States of America

ISBN–13: 978–0–314–16314–1
ISBN–10: 0–314–16314–X

 *TEXT IS PRINTED ON 10% POST CONSUMER RECYCLED PAPER*

To the Memory of

Benjamin H. Sax
Barton H. Thompson
John & Dolores Leshy
and
Hyman & Fay Abrams

*

Preface

Beginning with the first edition of this case book, the distinctive and fascinating character of water as property that is both public and private, individual and common, has provided a unifying theme. While much has changed in the water field since the first edition was published in 1986, these unique characteristics of water law have not.

In American law, property almost always means private property. Water law is (among other things) a branch of property law, but the first rule of water law is that water is not private property in the usual sense. Neither, however, is it public property. Water is different, and in that difference lies the charm, the interest, the fascination, and the complexity of water law as an area of study.

Because water has always been thought special, and specially precious, a central tenet of water law has been that no one can own water in the way that property is usually owned. The public retains an interest in practically every water right, and water rights are usually defined in terms of the public interest. The right one obtains is a right of use, and that use must be "reasonable" or "beneficial," which usually means that the water must be put to some use that benefits the community as a whole, rather than just the owner. Water law, moreover, discourages "wasteful" use. As Michael Meyer has noted, "[A] man might allow his crops to rot in the field while his neighbor went hungry and contravene no principle of property law, but he could not waste his water if his neighbor's fields were dry."[1] Water law also prohibits speculation: water may not be held unused as an investment with the hope that its value will rise in the future. Under western appropriation doctrine, water that is not put to a beneficial use is forfeited and goes back to the public. Some public rights are so strong that all private claims remain subservient to them: among these are the right of free public navigation and fishing, and (more recently) certain public claims to protection of natural ecosystems in water.

Water is also a shared property. Rights to sell or lease surface water, for example, are conditioned on the protection of the uses of others who have previously relied on a supply flowing down to them. The recreational interests of homeowners on a lake are defined in terms of the mutual interests of others on the lake.

In the pages that follow, you will see these and other rules about public rights in water, beneficiality, and sharing spelled out in great detail. While trying to illuminate the doctrines that you need to know as practic-

---

1. Michael Meyer, Water in the Hispanic Southwest 108 (1984).

ing lawyers, we have tried also to stimulate you to ask, again and again in different contexts, why water rights have evolved so differently from other property rights. Is it because water is physically distinctive, flowing from place to place, and reused many times? Is it because it is especially scarce? Because it is a fundamental necessity?

Or is water simply a setting in which the interests of the public were recognized earlier, and treated as more central, than in other areas of property law? Is water law at the leading edge of a new conception of property that is elsewhere only beginning to be recognized?

One useful way of bringing such broad inquiries down to earth is to ask, as to each case and doctrine you study, what the legal result would have been if the property in question was not water, but a sack of potatoes. Or, alternatively, to ask whether water should be considered as just another raw material for a business, like fertilizer or steel. By making these inquiries, you ultimately may be able to answer the following key questions: Is water really different from everything else? Does water law provide legal answers different from those given when other commodities or resources are in controversy? What interests and values are legislatures, executive branch officials, and judges trying to advance in formulating rules to govern the use of water? What sort of water policy is appropriate to a society that seeks to be prosperous, just, and protective of its natural endowment?

This edition is fully revised to include discussions of the most recent cases and issues in water law. Growing environmental concerns have increased the importance to water law of modern environmental statutes such as the Endangered Species Act and the Clean Water Act. New demands and worries have led to changes in the law of groundwater, water marketing, and other doctrines. As the law has evolved, water right holders in recent years have increasingly brought takings challenges, arguing that the changes in their rights are unconstitutional absent the payment of compensation. This edition delves in depth into such cutting edge issues.

We are grateful to many people who have helped us in the preparation of this edition and take this opportunity to acknowledge their special contribution. We particularly thank our student assistants: Heather Barnett (Boalt School of Law, University of California at Berkeley), who not only provided invaluable research assistance but checked all of the citations in this book for form; Chris Giovinazzo (Harvard Law School); Doug Obegi (U.C. Hastings School of Law); and Hobie Thompson (Occidental College). We also appreciate the comments and suggestions that we have received from faculty who used earlier editions of this book, and from consulting hydrologist Dan Luecke of Boulder, Colorado.

Special thanks are due to Professor Darin Jensen, of the Geography Department at the University of California at Berkeley, who designed and greatly improved many of the illustrations in this book. Legal texts are not traditionally known for the quality of their illustrations, and Darin has brought this book into the 21st century.

In editing excerpted materials we have in most cases retained without notation any errors in the original. The omission of text from excerpts is marked by ellipses, but the omission of footnotes and citations is typically not indicated. In some cases, we have also provided fuller citations in cases for clarity. Formatting sometimes has been changed.

We also have created a website for users of this book at www.lcwr4.org. At this site, you will find major updates and a selection of supplementary materials.

We continue to find that water law poses fascinating questions that never lose their importance and vitality. We hope that this book reflects the underlying excitement of the issues.

JOSEPH L. SAX
BARTON H. THOMPSON, JR.
JOHN D. LESHY
ROBERT H. ABRAMS

April 2006

*

Acknowledgements

We are indebted to the following authors and publishers for their generosity in giving us permission to reprint excerpts from copyrighted materials:

Robert Abrams, Setting Regional Policy on Diverting Great Lakes Water to the Arid West: Scaling Down the Myths, The Wayne Lawyer (Fall 1982).

Robert Abrams, Water Allocation by Comprehensive Permit Systems in the Eastern United States: Considering a Move Away From Orthodoxy, 9 Virginia Environmental Law Journal 255 (1990).

American Law Institute, Restatement of the Law Second, Torts (1979). Copyright © 1979 The American Law Institute. Reprinted with permission.

William Blomquist, Dividing the Waters: Governing Groundwater in Southern California (ICS Press 1992).

Jesse A. Boyd, Hip Deep: A Survey of State Instream Flow Law (2003). Reprinted by permission of the author and the Natural Resources Journal, University of New Mexico Law Review.

Williamson Chang, Water: Consumer Commodity or Government Subsidy?, in Water Values and Markets: Emerging Management Tools (Freshwater Foundation 1986).

Colorado River Users and Water Facilities, in Western Water (July/August 1985).

McKinley Conway and Linda L. Liston, eds., Normal Annual Total Precipitation, in the Weather Handbook (rev. ed., 1990).

The Regulated Riparian Model Water Code, Joseph Dellapenna, 1997, the American Society of Civil Engineers Press. Reprinted by permission of ASCE Press.

Charles DuMars and Michele Minnis, New Mexico Water Law: Determining Public Welfare Values in Water Rights Allocation, 31 Arizona Law Review 817 (1989). Copyright © 1989 the Arizona Board of Regents. Reprinted by permission.

P.H. Gleick, G. Wolff, E.L. Chalecki, R. Reyes (2002). The New Economy of Water: The Risks and Benefits of Globalization and Privatization of Fresh Water. A Report of the Pacific Institute for Studies in Development, Environment and Security, Oakland, California. Reprinted by permission.

Robert Glicksman and George Coggins, Groundwater Pollution I: The Problem and the Law, 35 University of Kansas Law Review 75

(1986). Copyright © 1986 by Kansas Law Review, Inc. Reprinted by special permission of Kansas Law Review, Inc.

Robert Gottlieb, A Life of Its Own: The Politics of Water (1988). Copyright © 1988 by Robert Gottlieb. Reprinted by permission of Harcourt, Inc.

Ellen Hanak, Water for Growth: California's New Frontier. Copyright 2005 by Public Policy Institute of California. Reprinted by permission.

Arthur Littleworth and Eric Garner, California Water (1995).

Edward Lotterman and John Waelti, Efficiency and Equity Implications of Alternative Well Interference Policies in Semi-Arid Regions, 23 Natural Resources Journal 323 (1983).

Michael McIntyre, The Disparity Between State Water Rights Records and Actual Water Use Patterns: "I Wonder Where the Water Went?", 5 Land & Water Law Review 23 (1970).

Taylor Miller, Gary Weatherford, and John Thorson, The Salty Colorado (World Wildlife Fund 1986).

A New Era for Irrigation (1996). Reprinted with permission. Copyright © 1996 by the National Academy of Sciences. Courtesy of the National Academy Press, Washington, D.C.

William Pedersen, Turning the Tide on Water Quality, 15 Ecology Law Quarterly 69 (1988). Copyright © 1988 by Ecology Law Quarterly. Reprinted from Ecology Law Quarterly, Vol. 15, No. 1, pp. 69–102, by permission.

Donald Pisani, From the Family Farm to Agribusiness (1984). Copyright © 1984 by the Regents of the University of California.

Leonard Rice and Michael D. White, Legal Doctrines for Surface Waters, in Engineering Aspects of Water Law (1987). Copyright © 1987 by John Wiley & Sons, Inc. Reprinted by special permission of John Wiley & Sons, Inc.

Ronald Robie, The Public Interest in Water Rights Administration, 23 Rocky Mountain Mineral Law Institute 917 (1977). Copyright © 1977 by Matthew Bender & Co., Inc. Reprinted with permission from Rocky Mountain Mineral Law Institute. All rights reserved.

Joseph Sax, The Constitution, Property Rights, and the Future of Water Law, 61 University of Colorado Law Review 257 (1990).

Joseph Sax, The Limits of Private Rights in Public Waters, 19 Environmental Law 473 (1989).

Joseph Sax, The Public Trust Doctrine in Natural Resource Law: Effective Judicial Intervention, 68 Michigan Law Review 471 (1970). Reprinted with permission of the Michigan Law Review.

Steven Shupe, Waste in Western Water Law: A Blueprint for Change, 61 Oregon Law Review 483 (1982). Reprinted by permission. Copyright © 1982 University of Oregon.

Jack Sterne, Instream Rights and Invisible Hands: Prospects for Private Instream Water Rights in the Northwest, 27 Environmental Law 203 (1997).

Barton Thompson, Institutional Perspectives on Water Policy and Markets, 81 California Law Review 671 (1993). Copyright © 1993 by California Law Review, Inc. Reprinted from California Law Review, Vol. 81, No. 2 (May 1993), pp. 671–764, by permission.

Barton Thompson, Water Markets and the Problem of Shifting Paradigms, in Water Marketing—The Next Generation, Terry Anderson & Peter Hill, eds. Reprinted with permission.

John Thorson, Water Marketing in Big Sky Country: An Interim Assessment, 29 Natural Resources Journal 479 (1989).

United States Water Supply and Consumption by Region, in America's Water: Current Trends and Emerging Issues (1984). Originally published by The Conservation Foundation. Copyright transferred to World Wildlife Fund.

Todd Votteler, The Little Fish that Roared: the Endangered Species Act, State Groundwater Law, and Private Property Rights Collide Over the Texas Edwards Aquifer, 28 Environmental Law 845 (1998).

Water Transfers in the West: Efficiency, Equity, and the Environment (1992). Reprinted with permission. Copyright © 1992 by the National Academy of Sciences. Courtesy of the National Academy Press, Washington, D.C.

Gary Weatherford and F. Lee Brown, New Courses for the Colorado River: Major Issues in the Next Century (1986). Copyright © 1986 University of New Mexico Press.

Stephen Williams, The Requirement of Beneficial Use as a Cause of Waste in Water Resource Development, 23 Natural Resources Journal 7 (1983).

Donald Worster, Rivers of Empire: Water, Aridity, & the Growth of the American West (1985).

*

Summary of Contents

Table of Contents

Table of Cases

The principal cases are in bold type. Cases cited or discussed in the text are roman type. References are to pages. Cases cited in principal cases and within other quoted materials are not included.

Table of Statutes

*

Table of Illustrations

*

LEGAL CONTROL
OF
WATER RESOURCES
CASES AND MATERIALS
Fourth Edition

*

Chapter 1

CURRENTS AND EDDIES: AN INTRODUCTION TO WATER RESOURCE ISSUES

POWER v. PEOPLE

Supreme Court of Colorado, 1892.
17 Colo. 178, 28 P. 1121.

Indictment against Mark Power for murder. Verdict of guilty, and judgment thereon. Defendant brings error. Affirmed.

ELLIOTT, J.

* * * The evidence shows that on July 2, 1890, late in the after-noon, Mr. and Mrs. Singledecker heard the report of a gun at a distance of 135 steps from their home in Montrose County, Colo., and, hastening to the spot, found Mr. Baer, wounded in the right leg, and in an unconscious condition. Mr. McLain, a physician and surgeon, who was called to attend Mr. Baer a few hours after the shooting, testified that he found a large gunshot wound in Baer's right thigh, caused by a large bullet, ranging upward, coming out back, and doing great damage [and] that there was no pulse in the wrist.

* * * It appears that the defendant, Power, and his sister had been involved in a controversy with Baer and others about an irrigation ditch. The ditch had been constructed by Baer and others, some years before; and Baer claimed the right to occupy, use, and maintain the same. Power claimed that the ditch interfered with his premises. Miss Power, it was said, had demanded certain water-rights in the ditch, which Baer had refused to concede; and thus the controversy had continued for several seasons. Baer, in the meantime, had maintained his occupancy of the ditch, and the Powers were very much dissatisfied. One witness testified that a few weeks before the homicide Power said that "he would settle the ditch controversy with Baer, and would take a rifle and shoot him." * * * On the day of the homicide, Power * * * approached Baer, and at a short distance, perhaps 40 steps, shot Baer with his rifle, inflicting the fatal wound, as heretofore stated.

1

Under such evidence, the important question to be determined on the trial was the nature of the homicide, whether justifiable or unlawful, and, if unlawful, the degree of the offense. The court charged the jury that the mere fact that Baer may have wrongfully or otherwise attempted to operate a ditch through defendant's or his sister's ranch would not justify the defendant in taking Baer's life. The instruction was proper. Human blood is more precious than water, even in this thirsty land.
* * *

A. AN OVERVIEW OF WATER RESOURCES

Despite the admonition of the Colorado Supreme Court and many others, people have been killing, maiming, fighting or just plain arguing over water for centuries.[1] Along with air, water is our most crucial natural resource. We obviously need water to survive, but the two quarts of water we drink each day are just the start. The average American uses about 120 gallons a day at home. Farms, industries, and commercial establishments required another 340 billion gallons of freshwater each day—or 1500 gallons per day for each American as of 1995, which is down from 1990 when per-capita use was 1620 gallons per day.[2] (To understand why these figures are nonetheless so large, consider that, counting the water needed to grow the feed, it takes about 3.5 million gallons of water to raise a 1000–pound steer—or over 3500 gallons per steak.) Table 1–1 shows how the nation uses the water that it withdraws for offstream use.

Nationwide, irrigated agriculture has traditionally used the most water. Agriculture accounts for over 80 percent of our total water consumption, as well as the highest percentage of withdrawals. The total number of irrigated acres increased about 7 percent from 1995 to 2000. In the eastern half of the United States total irrigated acres increased by 17 percent. During this same time period water withdrawals nationwide increased by only 2 percent. This gain in efficiency can be explained in part by the fact that in 2000 the number of acres irrigated using sprinkler or microirrigation systems was 25 percent more than during 1995.[3]

---

1. State reporters are filled with murder, homicide, and assault cases stemming from feuds over ditches, dams, and water rights. Not surprisingly, water disputes have also formed the grist for many movies from *The Winning of Barbara Worth* (a 1926 silent movie that told the perilous story of bringing water to California's Imperial Valley and introduced Gary Cooper in his first starring role) to *Chinatown* (the 1974 Jack Nicholson film centered around Los Angeles' celebrated taking of water from the Owens Valley) and the *Milagro Beanfield War*. For the current law on ditch rights see Roaring Fork Club v. St. Jude's Co., 36 P.3d 1229 (Colo. 2001).

2. Due to budget constraints, the U.S. Geological Survey did not collect consumptive use and other relevant data for the 2000 update of its report on consumption and withdrawals, infra p. 4. The 2005 update, not yet available at the time of this revision, should again have data for domestic consumption.

3. Susan S. Hutson et al., Estimated Use of Water in the United States in 2000 (U.S. Geological Survey Circular 1268, 2004); W.B. Solley, R.R. Pierce, and H.A. Perlman, Estimated use of Water in the United States in 1995 (U.S. Geological Survey Circular 1200, 1998).

Table 1–1
Comparative Freshwater Use (1995)

Type of Use	Percentage of Consumption [1]	Percentage of Withdrawals
Agriculture:	84 %	41 %
Irrigation	(81 %)	(39 %)
Livestock	(3 %)	(2 %)
Domestic	7 %	8 %
Thermoelectric	3 %	39 %
Industrial [2]	3 %	7 %
Commercial	1 %	3 %
Mining	1 %	1 %

[1] Because of rounding, columns may total more or less than 100 percent.
[2] Industrial figures do not include mining or thermoelectric power generation.

Source: U.S. Geological Survey, Estimated Use of Water in the United States in 1995 (1998).

Water also serves important instream needs. It is not accidental that the major cities in the United States grew up on waterways; since early colonial days, waterways have provided one of the central means of transportation. Hydroelectric facilities furnish about 10 percent of the United States' electric generating capacity (nuclear is about 20 percent), and are the primary source of electricity in the Pacific Northwest. The freshwater fishing industry depends for its livelihood on there being sufficient water in our rivers and lakes to support and promote fish populations. Many recreational activities, from fishing to sailing to swimming to canoeing, also rely upon adequate instream flows. Rivers, streams, lakes, and wetlands also form critical ecosystems for fish, wildlife, and flora. They are central features of many wilderness areas, forests, parks, and historic sites. Large streamflows also help dilute both natural and manmade contaminants in surface waters, and help prevent sediment buildup, which otherwise could result in flooding, erosion, and meandering of streambeds.

Current Offstream Consumption

The United States consumes, or uses up, less than 30% of the water that it withdraws from waterways and aquifers—with consumption varying considerably among uses and geographic regions. Thermoelectric power producers and irrigating farmers withdraw about the same quantities of water, but the power producers consume less than 3 percent of the water they withdraw, irrigating farmers some 60 percent. Because most farmers in the eastern United States do not need to irrigate their crops, these user differences also spill over into geographic differences. The eastern United States consumes only about 10 percent of the water that it withdraws, the West about 40 percent. Water that is not consumed often can be reused, assuming it is not too polluted, by the same or a different user. Many downstream consumers of water have long depended on the "return flow" from upstream users. Today the nation is taking steps to ensure that municipal and industrial effluent is of a quality capable of reuse. The country's use of reclaimed sewage water has been rising significantly over the past two decades.

Table 1–2
Estimated Freshwater Use in the United States

Type of Use	Withdrawals (in bgd [1])	Consumption (in bgd)	Percentage consumed
Domestic	26.1	6.68	25 %
Commercial	9.59	1.31	14 %
Agriculture:			
Irrigation	134	81.3	61 %
Livestock	5.49	3.2	58 %
Industrial [2]	25.5	3.37	13 %
Mining	2.56	0.78	30 %
Thermoelectric	132	3.31	3 %
TOTAL [3]	335.2	99.95	29.8%

[1] Billion gallons per day.
[2] Industrial figures do not include mining and thermoelectric power generation.
[3] Total figures also include public use and losses in the distribution systems.

Source: U.S. Geological Survey, Estimated Use of Water in the United States in 1995 (1998).

Consuming a high percentage of the water withdrawn, it should be emphasized, is not necessarily bad. To the extent that the nation can increase the efficiency with which it uses water, it can reduce the amount of water withdrawn (leaving more water for important instream needs). Total water withdrawals in the United States peaked in the late 1970s and early 1980s and has declined since. High costs and limited opportunities to further increase offstream water use encouraged water use efficiencies. Industry, for example, increased its water efficiency (measured by the ratio of the amount consumed to the amount withdrawn) by approximately 50 percent through such measures as internal recycling–and its withdrawals have accordingly fallen.

Regional Shortages of Water

Purely as a statistical matter, the nation has more than enough water to meet current offstream needs—while still retaining the vast majority of water instream. There are two principal sources of fresh water—the streams, rivers, lakes, and diffused runoff that form the earth's system of surface water, and the underground bodies of groundwater known as "aquifers."[4] In a typical year, rain and snow in the United States lead to average streamflows of 1380 billion gallons per day—nearly four times the amount of water currently withdrawn, and over 13 times the amount consumed. Another 60 billion gallons per day replenish the nation's groundwater aquifers, which already hold literally quadrillions of gallons laid down by nature from time immemorial.

The problem is that the water often is not in the place that people want to use it at the time they desire it. As shown in Figure 1–3, the amount of water available in the numerous regions of the United States varies tremendously. The Hundredth Meridian (which runs down through the middle of the Dakotas, Nebraska, and Kansas, separates the panhandle from the rest of Oklahoma, forms the border between Oklahoma and Texas, and then continues down through Texas) is a highly significant line. East of the Hundredth Meridian, the rainfall is usually generous enough that farmers can generally grow their crops without irrigation. Early nineteenth century maps labeled much of the flatlands west of the Hundredth Meridian as "The Great American Desert." Average precipitation in Baltimore exceeds 60 inches, in Chicago is about 40 inches per year, and in Phoenix barely reaches seven.

---

4. The Appendix contains a glossary of this and other common water resource terms. Because of the interrelated nature of water resources, the law should treat surface water and groundwater as a single system. As we shall see, however, the great majority of states still have separate legal systems for surface water and groundwater. Indeed, the law of most states breaks water resources up even more finely, treating under slightly different regimes: (1) confined surface waterways like rivers and lakes, (2) diffused surface water, (3) underground streams, (4) "percolating" groundwater, and (5) springs.

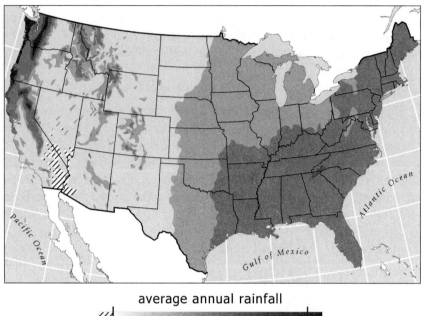

average annual rainfall

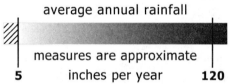

measures are approximate

5   inches per year   **120**

Figure 1–3
Average Annual Precipitation

Water planners frequently divide up the United States into 21 separate water-resource regions. Figure 1–4 shows the regions together with their annual renewable supplies of water (defined as the flow of water potentially available for use) and annual consumption. Do not be misled by the figures into believing water is plentiful in all regions except the Lower Colorado (which consumes more than its annual water supply by drawing down preexisting groundwater supplies). Other regions also suffer chronic shortages. As much as two-thirds of the annual renewable supply in a region may be unavailable for offstream use. Much of the annual supply must remain in rivers and lakes to meet diverse and important instream needs. To use every available gallon of the annual runoff, moreover, a myriad of reservoirs would be needed to capture and store the water. Although the United States has built literally thousands of reservoirs, numerous ecologic, topographic, geologic, hydrologic, and economic constraints prevent a region from capturing and using anywhere close to its entire annual runoff.

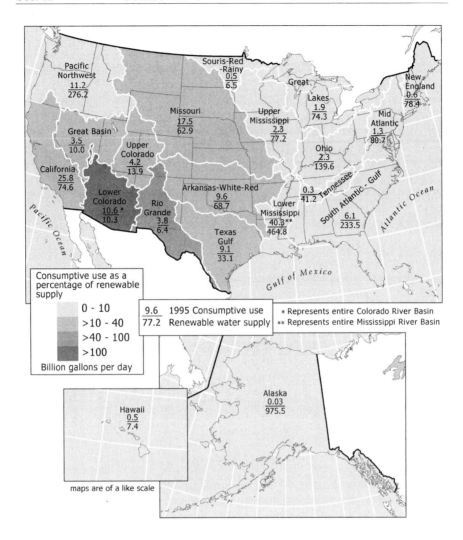

Figure 1–4

United States Water Supply and Consumption

Source: United States Geological Survey

There are great variations, moreover, even within regions. The Puget Sound area of Washington, for example, is quite humid with average precipitation exceeding 40 inches per year; only 100 miles away, on the other side of the Cascade Mountains, the average yearly precipitation drops to less than nine inches. In California, parts of the wine growing region of Napa Valley get as much rain as Washington. San Francisco averages about 20 inches per year, while Los Angeles gets only twelve. The greatest contrast in the United States is on the Hawaiian island of Kauai. The north side of Mount Waialeale is the wettest spot on earth, averaging about 450 inches per year; just a few miles away Kauai turns into a virtual desert.

We have made things more difficult by ignoring these natural variances in our quest to develop the United States. Deserts have been made into agricultural greenbelts ("reclaiming" the land is the typical misnomer). High percentages of various national crops are grown in areas of Arizona, California, and Colorado that once supported only sagebrush. Massive urban centers have blossomed in portions of the country baked in perpetual drought. Over half of California's population, for example, lives in the southernmost third of the state despite the fact that only three percent of its precipitation falls there. Even areas with relatively abundant water have often outstretched their supply. New York City, for example, has an average annual rainfall of 44 inches, but with a population of over 8 million people, each using an average of 150 gallons of water per day for domestic, commercial, and other purposes, the city cannot begin to meet its demand with its own local supplies.

Geographic imbalances are not the only problem. Some portions of the country (e.g., much of the Northeast and Midwest) enjoy ample precipitation—and thus river runoff—pretty much year-round. A significant portion of the United States, however, suffers from serious seasonal variations. The area around Tucson, Arizona, for example, gets almost 80 percent of its sparse rainfall during summer thunderstorms. Southern Florida similarly receives most of its rainfall in late summer. The Pacific Coast receives virtually all of its rainfall between November and April. Each of these areas need water all year.

Groundwater Overdraft

Confronted by scarce surface water and the high cost of storing and transporting water, many regions have increasingly turned to groundwater to meet their water supply needs. While total fresh surface water withdrawals varied less than 2 percent from 1985 to 2000 in the United States, groundwater withdrawals increased 14 percent. Groundwater supplies nearly half of the U.S population's drinking water and constitutes 24 percent of all freshwater used. The vast majority of groundwater withdrawals—74 percent—is used for irrigation while 21 percent is used for public water supply and 5 percent is used for self-supplied industrial purposes. Unfortunately, as reliance on groundwater has increased, the nation has begun extracting more groundwater each year than is replenished.

While the amount of groundwater storage in the United States is decreasing, the extent of the problem is difficult to determine. Data on groundwater overdraft is collected locally and no comprehensive national reporting network exists. For many aquifers, even basic local data does not exist. The U.S. Geological Survey, while unable to report national figures, has reported groundwater overdraft problems in several regions including the Atlantic Coastal Plain, West-central Florida, Gulf Coastal

Plain, High Plains, Chicago–Milwaukee area, Pacific Northwest and the Desert Southwest.[5]

The results of overdraft can be severe. Water that may be needed to meet critical future needs is permanently lost. As the water table falls, surface vegetation often dies, leading to desertification of the overlying land. Pumping costs increase, sea water can intrude into and pollute coastal aquifers, and other contamination problems can worsen. If an aquifer consists of poorly consolidated materials (like sand or gravel), severe overdrafts can also cause overlying land to subside. Land around Houston has dropped dramatically (resulting in millions of dollars in property damage); portions of California's Central Valley have dropped by nearly 30 feet. Once compacted, an aquifer's storage capacity is greatly diminished—reducing its utility to future generations as well.

A good case study of overdraft problems is the Ogallala (or High Plains) aquifer, perhaps the largest underground reservoir of fresh water anywhere in the world. Named after an Indian tribe which once roamed the High Plains, the Ogallala underlies large portions of Kansas, Nebraska, and Texas, and smaller portions of Colorado, New Mexico, Oklahoma, and Wyoming. It provides 30 percent of all irrigation water pumped within the United States and drinking water to 82 percent of the people who live within the aquifer boundary. Although the Ogallala contains trillions of gallons of water, there is virtually no recharge, due partly to the sparse rain that falls in the region, but more to the impervious layer that forms a watertight roof over most of the aquifer. Tapped by thousands of farmers and towns, portions of the aquifer are being quickly drained. Ogallala aquifer groundwater levels in Texas declined by an average of 1.35 feet per year between 1992 and 1997. Overall, the United States Geological Survey projected severe depletions in the high plains region by 2020, with Texas suffering the most. As the water runs out, millions of irrigated acres will have to find alternative sources of water or return to dryland farming and natural vegetation. The United States Geological Survey estimates that the irrigated acreage on the high plains of Texas will decrease by over 50 percent by 2050 due to groundwater shortages.[6] The USGS is also conducting extensive studies of water quality prompted by concerns that agricultural chemicals are polluting the aquifer.

Efforts to combat groundwater overdraft include aquifer storage and recovery projects, conjunctive use of ground and surface water resources (where surface water is injected into the ground during years of abundant flows, so it can be drawn out during dry periods), controlled groundwater pumping, and conservation and reuse of water. Groundwater withdrawals and recharge rates have been balanced in some aquifers due to a combination of these strategies. But groundwater overdraft continues to plague vast regions of the United States. Even in regions

5. U.S. Geological Survey, Fact Sheet 103–03, Ground–Water Depletion Across the Nation.

6. U.S. Geological Survey, Groundwater Atlas of the United States, Segment 4, Oklahoma and Texas, E12–13 (1996).

that recognize the need to manage groundwater pumping, net deficit use continues. For example, as of 2003 California continues to overdraw its groundwater by one million to two million acre-feet a year.[7] In Arizona, the Prescott Groundwater Management Area is not expected to achieve sustainable-yield use withdrawals until 2025.[8]

Droughts and Floods

Yearly variations in weather patterns add further problems. During this century, major multiyear droughts have hit large portions of the country in the 1930s, 1950s, 1970s, late 1980s, and early 2000s. Regional droughts scourge random segments of the United States at an even more frequent pace. The Northeast has suffered a number of local, but severe droughts over the last three decades supporting a growing conviction that it is far more prone to drought than once thought. California and the Southeast endured major droughts in the 1980s and early 2000's.

Too little water is not the only problem. Nature sometimes sends too much water our way. About six percent of the conterminous United States is inclined to floods, which kill ten times as many people as any other natural disaster and cause over one billion dollars in damages annually. The 1990's saw not only major droughts in the western United States and parts of the Northeast, but also disastrous flooding in the Midwest, the Mississippi valley, and the area surrounding Seattle, Washington. Even these floods seem small when compared to the devastating loss of life and property in Louisiana and Mississippi in flooding caused by hurricane Katrina in 2005. Here again, development policies have contributed to much of the problem. Rather than adapt to nature, Americans have built in flood plains and then attempted "structural" solutions to the flooding problem, constructing large storage reservoirs to collect storm waters, and levees and dikes to try to protect their property. Paradoxically, the presence of flood-control structures encourages more intense development in flood plains, so that when unexpectedly large floods occur (as they do), damage is even greater than before the area was "flood-proofed."

The Impacts of Global Warming on Water Supplies

There is little doubt that greenhouse gas emissions produced by human activities are starting to change the global climate. In the United States, the average temperature has increased by one degree Fahrenheit since 1900, permafrost in the Alaskan arctic is beginning to thaw, the mean sea level has risen between ten and twenty centimeters, mountain glaciers are melting at unprecedented rates and Arctic ice thickness is declining.[9] Projecting into the future, climate change models have pro-

7. California Department of Water Resources, Bulletin 118, California's Groundwater (2003).

8. Arizona Department of Water Resources, Third Management Plan for Prescott Active Management Area (1999).

9. Peter H. Gleick, Water: The Potential Consequences of Climate Variability and Change for the Water Resources of the United States 8 (Pacific Institute 2000).

duced a strong consensus around a range of expected changes. By the end of the 21st Century, global average temperature will increase by 2.5 to 10 degrees Fahrenheit from 1990 levels.[10] Melting polar ice caps and thermal expansion of ocean waters will raise sea levels by 0.2 to 2.8 feet by the end of the century (models project a median rise of 1.6 feet).[11] Global average precipitation will also increase and there will be changes in timing and patterns of precipitation. In high latitudes, average precipitation will increase. The frequency and severity of droughts are likely to increase in some regions and decrease in others.

Scientists have been studying the potential impacts of global warming on United States' water systems since the 1980s and water managers are beginning to take seriously the need to plan for climate change impacts. Climate change models are not yet able to predict regional changes in the United States with certainty. Whether and to whatever extent human-caused CO_2 emissions are altering the climate, information developed through dendrochronology and other means shows that the 20th century was among the wettest in many hundreds if not thousands of years.

In some regions climate change impacts may generate no, or even beneficial impacts. Effects on mountain and coastal water supplies are more certain and worrisome. Basins in the western United States depend in large part on mountain snowpack for their water supplies. Precipitation occurs primarily in the winter, and summers—when water is most needed—are dry. Mountain snowpacks store water through the winter and slowly release it in spring and early summer runoff. Temperature increases in mountain regions will disrupt this pattern. More precipitation will fall as rain instead of snow resulting in smaller snowpacks. Snowmelt and flooding will likely occur earlier in the year and reduce water runoff available in the spring and summer. Reservoirs may not be able to accommodate these changes and will be less reliable for water supplies.

Groundwater supplies may also decrease since snowpacks help recharge many groundwater aquifers (as much as 50–90 percent of western groundwater recharge may come from snowmelt). Recent studies suggest that temperature increases will be greater in winter and early spring, and in higher elevations, exasperating these implications.[12] Indeed, snowpacks may already be affected. A 2005 survey found that of the last 16 years snowpack levels have been below average for 13 years in the Columbia River basin, 11 years in the Colorado River basin, 14 years in the Missouri River basin, and 10 years in the Rio Grande basin. In each of these river basins the years 2000–2005 were the hottest in the past 110 years by 1.5 to 2.5 degrees, suggesting that the West may experience

10. Intergovernmental Panel on Climate Change, Climate Change 2001: The Scientific Basis.

11. Id.

12. Stephen Saunders & Maureen Maxwell, Less Snow, Less Water: Climate Disruption in the West 5 (The Rocky Mountain Climate Organization 2005).

higher temperature increases than the global average.[13] Studies have also shown that in many cases across the West, peak snowmelt periods advanced by 10 to 30 days.[14]

Sea level rise threatens saltwater intrusion in shallow inland aquifers such as those found in Hawaii and Nantucket and in coastal aquifers such as those that support populations in Long Island, New York and central and coastal California. Sea level rise will also increase pressure on coastal levee systems.

Freshwater ecosystems may also be impacted. Studies suggest changes in vegetation patterns, possible extinctions of fish species, and wetland and habitat loss.[15] Water quality may be impaired because of changing water temperatures and flows. Increased runoff rates and changes in timing may limit the ability of watersheds to assimilate wastes and pollutants. Higher temperatures would also increase evaporation from streams and reservoirs and increase soil dryness.

A 2002 study by the Scripps Institute of Oceanography concludes that by 2050 the Colorado River reservoir system, the Central Valley of California, the Columbia River system and smaller snowmelt-driven rivers will not be able to meet *current* demands on their water resources, much less demands of a larger population and economy.[16] Some researchers have suggested that demand management strategies and increased efficiency of water use provide the most flexibility for dealing with the uncertain consequences of climate change. Where new infrastructure is built, they suggest that engineers design structures to accommodate an expanded range of extreme scenarios.

Water Allocation Systems

The focus of this casebook is dominantly problems of scarcity, not overabundance. Wherever and whenever there is a shortage of water, society must decide how to allocate the available water among the competing uses and needs. State law provides the basic allocation system. As you will see in Chapters 2 through 4, states use two principal systems to allocate surface water among competing users. As shown in Figure 1–5, almost all of the states bordering on or east of the Mississippi River have adopted the *riparian* doctrine—under which the water in a river belongs, as a general rule, to the owners of land "riparian" to (i.e., including or bordering on) the waterway, with some modern inclination to allow non-riparians a subordinate right of use. Where there is insufficient water to meet all riparian needs, these states ration the water

---

13. Id. at 2.

14. I.T. Stewart, et al., Changes in Snowmelt Runoff Timing in Western North America Under a "Business as Usual" Climate Change Scenario, 62 Climate Change 217–232 (2004).

15. Gleick, supra note 9, at 62 (citing studies).

16. T.P. Barnett et al., The Effects of Climate Change on Water Resources in The West: Introduction and Overview 62 Climatic Change 1 (2004).

among the riparians according to a broad reasonableness standard. The dry inland states of the West follow the *appropriation* doctrine—under which available water generally is allocated on a first-come, first-served basis to anyone (whether riparian or not) who puts the water to a beneficial offstream use. Those conterminous states that border the Pacific Ocean or straddle the Hundredth Meridian adopted mixed appropriation-riparian systems, although riparian rights remain important today only in California, Nebraska, and Oklahoma. The other hybrid or mixed-system states initially adopted the common law but later abolished it, or essentially abandoned it, and appropriation predominates in them.

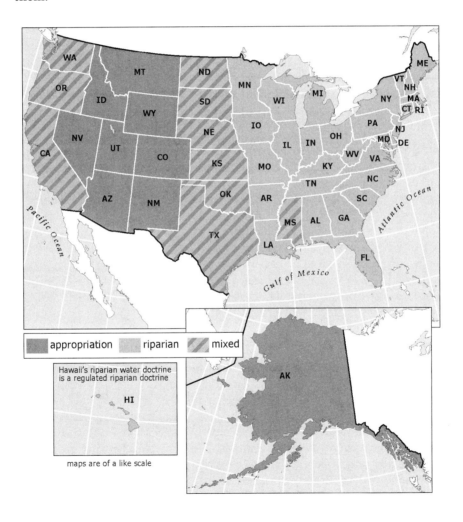

Figure 1–5

Legal Doctrines for Surface Waters

As you will see in Chapter 5, states have turned to a larger and more confusing number of doctrines to allocate groundwater—although the basic patterns remain the same. Most of the states bordering on or east of the Mississippi River have adopted systems under which only owners of lands that overlie an aquifer have a right to water from the aquifer. Most of the western United States allocate groundwater under some form of appropriation system (with California again following a mixed system). Few states anywhere in the country took significant steps to control groundwater overdraft until quite recently.

The Important Role of Institutions

Numerous governmental and non-governmental institutions play a central role in allocating water resources, and we shall examine them in Chapter 7. Almost all western states and a growing number of eastern states use permit systems, run by state agencies, to administer their allocation schemes for surface waters and sometimes groundwater. The permit agencies have considerable discretion in the administration of water rights and can have an important impact on who receives what water.

Most urban and suburban water users, moreover, depend on municipalities and public utilities for their water. The municipality or utility may in turn get its water from a governmental water agency. Over 130 California cities, for example, receive their water from the Metropolitan Water District of Southern California which serves over 18 million people. In the western United States, various special institutions also control and allocate vast quantities of water to farmers and ranchers. Of the over 46 million acres of land irrigated in the 17 western states, about a quarter receive water from local governmental units known as irrigation districts. Almost as many acres obtain water from so-called mutual water companies (private organizations in which each recipient of water owns a fractional interest).

Because water often has not been where people wanted it when they needed it, federal, state, and local governments have also taken massive steps to alter water availability. The nation as a whole has built over 50,000 reservoirs to store water when runoff is high and hold it until needed, and constructed thousands of miles of aqueducts to carry water to where people want it. Today, depleted aquifers are being used for storage under what are called conjunctive-use systems; during periods of high surface flows, excess water is used instead of groundwater, or is captured and allowed to replenish an aquifer.

The City of Los Angeles took an early step to transform the West when, near the beginning of the last century, it built an aqueduct 250 miles northeast to the Owens Valley, setting off perhaps the longest running and certainly one of the most famous water disputes in the United States. Today, many regions of the country import water from distant watersheds. California takes the lead in transbasin diversions; its

Federal Central Valley and State Water Projects transport water through 440 miles of aqueduct, lifting it over 3000 feet of hills and mountains, to the arid southern portion of the state. Other portions of the country, however, are not far behind. Denver tunnels water across the continental divide, Albuquerque has water exported from the Colorado River basin, and the Central Arizona Project moves water some 1800 feet up in elevation from the Colorado River and over 200 miles distant to Phoenix and Tucson. Every day the City of New York (which was one of the first cities to begin importing water) propels over 1.5 billion gallons of water through huge water tunnels from the Delaware River basin some 125 miles away to meet the demands of its population.

One of the major players in the transformation of the West has been the United States Bureau of Reclamation. For years, the Bureau has built massive dam and reservoir projects in the western United States to bring subsidized water to farming regions in need of more water. Since the federal reclamation program was begun in 1902, the Bureau has spent over $11 billion constructing dams, reservoirs, aqueducts, and distribution systems. Today, the Bureau is the largest water wholesaler in the country. It provides irrigation water to over 20 percent of the West's total irrigated acreage as well as to 31 million domestic users. Limitations on federal and state spending, as well as growing environmental concerns, have today slowed the construction of new projects to a snail's pace. The Bureau of Reclamation, for example, has not begun a major new water project for over two decades and has had to fight for the funds needed to finish projects currently under construction. While demands for new or enlarged facilities continue to be made (climate change seasonality impacts will create increasing demand to raise existing dams to increase reservoir capacity), and some new structures will undoubtedly be built, the "big dam" era has almost certainly ended.

Competing Values and Needs

Huge water projects were built to implement policies favoring offstream uses. Until the last third of the 20th Century, few policymakers expressed any need to preserve water instream for fish and wildlife, aesthetics, or recreation (although steps were taken to foster transportation and hydroelectric projects on many of our waterways, and to develop manmade lakes and reservoirs for recreational use). The focus instead was on furnishing the water demanded by agriculture, cities, and a growing economy. As a result, literally thousands of the country's waterways are totally drained of water at various points of the year, and others turn into mere trickles. The Colorado River today only reaches its mouth in the Gulf of California during very abundant flow years when excess water must be spilled from Lake Mead to meet flood control standards requiring that some empty space be reserved in reservoirs. Most years the river peters out some 14 miles from its destination in a saline pond. Natural wonderlands, like Glen Canyon and the Hetch Hetchy Valley, have been dammed and flooded.

This transformation has had its obvious costs. Important aesthetic resources have been lost, miles of vegetation have disappeared, and salinity and other water pollution problems have increased. Several decades ago, the National Fisheries Survey found that low water flows were injuring fish in almost 70 percent of inland waterways. In recent decades, however, stronger environmental values and laws have been generating major shifts in water policy. People are increasingly recognizing the value of keeping water in our rivers and lakes to preserve fish and wildlife, protect the ecosystem, enhance the environment, and promote recreation. Modern laws, especially the federal Endangered Species Act, have required restoration of instream flows and of riparian habitat to sustain threatened fish populations. In addition, to many preservation of free flowing waters is important for its own sake—part and parcel of a larger environmental ethic. As a result, government at all levels has taken steps to preserve and restore instream flows and riparian areas, and has authorized appropriations to be made for instream purposes, both recreational and environmental. These newer public use issues, and the conflicts they sometimes generate with riparian landowners and traditional diverters, are discussed in Chapter 6.

Increasing Water Use Efficiency

Many urban and suburban areas are growing at a rapid pace and placing increasing strain on the water resources available for offstream use—particularly in the water-poor West. Seven of the ten fastest-growing states in the nation in the 1990's were in the arid West, led by Nevada, Arizona, and Colorado, in that order. A 2003 Department of the Interior report concluded that, "in some areas of the West, existing water supplies are, or will be, inadequate to meet the water demands of people, cities, farms and the environment even under normal water supply conditions."[17]

Predictions of water shortages and calls for increased water supply infrastructure have been countered by researchers who urge that a more efficient use of water currently available could actually reduce future water demand, even in light of significant population increases in the arid regions of the country. They point out that development of traditional water supply infrastructure is extremely expensive and often environmentally damaging. Water use efficiency programs could be more cost-effective and often can be achieved with no new inventions or serious hardships on the economy.

Urban and suburban residents tend to use significantly more water for domestic purposes than do rural residents. Faced by temporary or permanent water shortages, many urban and suburban residents have reduced water consumption by 20 percent or more without radically changing their lifestyles. Water metering and economic incentives have encouraged the use of techniques such as setting water-efficiency stan-

17. U.S. Department of the Interior,
Water 2025: Preventing Crises and Conflict
in the West (2003).

dards, or offering rebates, for devices such as less-water-consuming dishwashers and toilets, and requiring that old homes be retrofitted with more efficient appliances before being sold. Some communities, such as Las Vegas, have successfully instituted programs to subsidize, and provide technical assistance to, homeowners by encouraging replacement of grass lawns with indigenous materials.

In the western United States, thirsty and growing metropolitan areas have begun to eye water being used by farmers and ranchers. Because agriculture uses such a high percentage of water in the West, relatively small conservation savings can free up sizable quantities of water. A 33 percent jump in Southern California's population could be met by either a 25 percent decrease in domestic water consumption or a four percent savings in agricultural use. Where it is economically feasible, farmers can conserve considerable amounts of water—by lining and covering canals, carefully scheduling and monitoring irrigation, grading their property with laser-guided equipment, switching to water-efficient crops, and adopting other conservation measures. Irrigation water use nationwide, which was 86 percent of total water use in 1960, declined to 81 percent in 1995, and is even lower in some parts of the West. These changes reflect both a decline in irrigated acreage and, even more importantly, a drop in the amount of water used to irrigate the average acre of land. A great deal of room still exists to improve the efficiency of agricultural irrigation, and some techniques that are not economically feasible for farmers can be financed by urban users in exchange for obtaining a share of the saved water. Some researchers suggest 50 percent efficiency gains are possible, primarily through expanding the use of drip irrigation systems and sprinklers that are low to the ground.[18] These irrigation techniques send water directly to the roots of plants and result in less wasted runoff than in traditional flooding or channeling techniques. In 2000, sprinkler and microirrigation systems accounted for 50 percent of total irrigated acreage.[19]

Industrial conservation can also free up water. Industry has already reduced its water withdrawals over the last decade to the lowest level since 1950. Spurred on by water quality laws that make recycling water cheaper than treating and discharging industrial effluent, industry reduced its water demand by 40 percent between 1980 and 1995. Changing production and consumption patterns can also produce hidden water savings. For example the amount of water it takes to make steel has decreased. But additional water savings have been had as many automakers switch to aluminum. Fuel efficiency increases in cars helps to save the hundreds of gallons of water required to produce, deliver and sell a gallon of gasoline.

Water reuse is another way to stretch water supplies. In Israel 70 percent of municipal water is treated and reused, mostly for nonfood

18. Sandra Postel, Growing More Food With Less Water, Scientific American, Feb. 2001, at 46.

19. Susan S. Hutson et al., Estimated Use of Water in the United States in 2000, U.S. Geological Survey Circular 1268 (2004).

crops. In the United States treated wastewater is reused for landscape irrigation of highway medians; golf courses and parks; supplying industrial processes; irrigating certain crops; and for recharging groundwater aquifers. Some office buildings also reuse water on site for flushing toilets. Figure 1–6 demonstrates that water reuse can be direct, sent through pipes directly to intended users; or it can be indirect, as when water is reused after passing through a natural body of water such as a river or groundwater aquifer. In order to augment water supply at a regional level, water recycling projects can focus on water that would not otherwise be reused indirectly downstream.

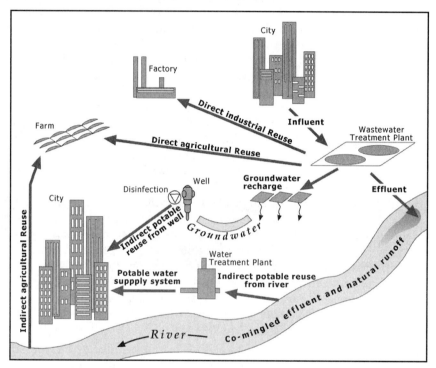

Figure 1–6
Direct and Indirect Recycled Water Use

Source: California Department of Water Resources, *Water Recycling 2030: Recommendations of California's Recycled Water Task Force* (2003).

The degree of treatment wastewater receives varies depending on the intended use. Groundwater recharge usually requires advanced treatment since the water will eventually reach municipal supplies. Despite advanced treatment, groundwater recharge proposals have routinely met with strong public opposition based on distrust of a process that is commonly labeled "toilet to tap". Other end uses require a lower level of treatment and generally command easier public acceptance. California currently recycles about 500,000 acre feet of water a year and a 2003 study predicted that by 2030 the state could recycle up to 1.5 million acre feet a year at a cost of $11 billion in additional infrastructure.[20] That would free up freshwater supplies to meet 30 percent of the projected increase in household needs.

Economic Proposals

Many economists and policymakers have advocated using market mechanisms to meet and reduce the demands of growing urban and suburban populations. The pricing of water supplies can strongly encourage conservation. Installation of water meters in cities previously without them has led to sharp declines in water use. Once water is metered, rises in water rates can also reduce water usage. Economic studies suggest that a ten percent increase in the price of water can produce anywhere from a two to 14 percent decrease in water consumption (with the greatest water savings coming in the summer). Current policies subsidize urban and agricultural water rates and simply removing these subsidies could reduce inefficient water use, but subsidies once in place prove very difficult to remove, and are often protected by contractual or statutory provisions.

Economists and policymakers have also urged the active development of water markets through which growing metropolitan areas can acquire water resources, primarily from agriculture. For many years, various legal, institutional, technological, and economic limitations prevented more than a handful of transfers from taking place. But in the western United States at least, the legal and institutional barriers are eroding. In recent years, many of the southwestern states have reported active markets in water rights. Market proposals, however, remain controversial. Transactions for water transfers are often complex, potentially threatening downstream uses dependant on return flows; and negatively impacting transferor communities, particularly if the transfer involves retirement of agricultural land (fallowing) rather than buyer-financed conservation techniques. Others fear that money-driven water markets will make it more difficult to enhance instream flows needed for ecosystem restoration.

Desalination

Desalination is the process of removing dissolved salts and other chemicals from water. Desalination for domestic consumption is a well established practice in the Middle East, Caribbean islands and areas bordering the Mediterranean Sea, although desalination accounts for only 0.2 percent of total global water withdrawals. In the United States, desalination has in the past been simply too expensive to compete with water from wells, reservoirs and rivers. A majority of the roughly 1,200 desalination plants in the United States are used for processing brackish

20. California Department of Water Resources, Water Recycling 2030: Recommendations of California's Recycled Water Task Force xi (2003).

groundwater, primarily for industrial operations that rely on highly purified water. This pattern is beginning to change. In the last decade, while traditional sources of water have become more expensive and less reliable, technological advances in desalination techniques have lowered the price and associated environmental damages. As a result, dozens of new desalination facilities are currently proposed to help meet domestic water demands in coastal regions of the United States as well as places such as New Mexico where basins of saline and brackish groundwater are located hundreds of feet below the surface.

Although there are a number of methods to desalt water, membrane and thermal distillation technologies are the most prevalent world-wide. The distillation process mimics nature's hydrologic cycle by heating salty water to produce water vapor that is then condensed to form fresh water. Distillation is a highly energy intensive process and is primarily used in the Middle East where surface water is at a premium and oil provides a cheap and abundant energy source. Membrane filtration is the exclusive desalination process used in the United States and looks to remain so. In these plants, ocean water is first pretreated to remove sand and other material. It is then forced at high pressure through layers of membranes that allow water molecules to pass through while trapping the larger salt molecules in a process termed reverse osmosis. Smaller private plants may produce 20,000 gallons per day while proposals for the largest desalination plants would produce as much as 50 million gallons per day.

Though desalination has become much less expensive as advances in membrane technology have decreased the amount of pressure needed by a half, reducing energy requirements, energy consumption still accounts for as much as 20 to 50 percent of total operating costs which makes the cost of desalinated water very sensitive to the cost of electricity. The true cost of desalinated water must also take into account the cost of treating it to reach potable standards, and distribution. Current estimates for desalination plants put the water costs to consumers at roughly between $800 and $1,500 per acre-foot. This is still four to five times the cost of agricultural irrigation water in most places, where such supplies are available in the marketplace. Proponents of desalination say it should be compared to the costs of traditional ways of increasing water supply, such as construction of dams, aqueducts and pipelines, instead of comparing it to prices of water from existing infrastructure. Even though desalination has yet to become a competitive source of water, the benefits of having a reliable and local source of water free of the legal and political complications of conventional water marketing are convincing some water agencies that it is worth the extra cost, at least for a fraction of its needs.

The environmental impacts of desalination have also improved in the last decade, although controversy remains. For every 100 gallons of seawater drawn in to a plant between 40 and 60 gallons of pure water is produced and the rest is returned to the ocean as brine, a discharge with concentrated levels of salt and organic materials that may harm ecosystems. A host of chemicals used to pre-treat water and clean and maintain the plant must also be managed properly. Technologies to prevent impingement of animals against fish screens are well developed but concerns remain regarding the large numbers of plankton and eggs and larva of fish and other aquatic organisms that slip through the fish screens and are killed due to high pressures or temperatures in the plant. Co-locating desalination operations at existing coastal power plants (which is economically attractive) has raised concerns about keeping old fossil fuel plants in operation indefinitely, rather than phasing them out over the coming years, as had been hoped by environmental advocates. The indirect impacts of desalination, primarily the growth inducing effects of increased water supply, have also risen to the fore in many desalination debates. If water from rivers and streams can be reserved for instream uses, desalination's indirect impacts could be beneficial. Desalination has also renewed debates about the use of public resources for private gain, and the appropriate role of private entities in the provision of water. While many of the proposed desalination plants would be owned and operated by government entities, some are wholly private ventures (though some public assistance is almost always present).

Pollution Problems

The quality of our water resources is an issue of ever growing importance, but one that for many years the law largely ignored. State governments played the principal role in addressing pollution until the passage of the federal Water Pollution Control Act Amendments of 1972 (now the Clean Water Act). Although states started to address the dangers from human wastes as early as the nineteenth century, the majority of municipalities still dumped raw, untreated sewage into our oceans and waterways as late as the 1960s. States did not even acknowledge the seriousness of industrial pollution until after World War II. The results were catastrophic. By the late 1960s, many unofficially pronounced Lakes Erie and Ontario to be dead, the country was dotted with "flammable rivers" like the Cuyahoga, and few major rivers were swimmable.

Today things have improved significantly, thanks primarily to the hundreds of billions of dollars that the nation has spent meeting the requirements of the Clean Water Act. The Clean Water Act provides for a direct assault on "point" (or confined) sources of pollution, such as sewage and industrial outfalls. This attack has been successful enough that Lakes Erie and Ontario are reviving and almost 75 percent of our inland waterways are clean enough to support sport fish.

While the quality of some waters is becoming cleaner, however, others are degrading—due partly to gaps and deficiencies in the Clean Water Act. "Nonpoint" sources of pollution such as agricultural runoff, for which the Clean Water Act still lacks effective provisions, remain a serious problem. Agricultural runoff highlights the close linkage between problems of quality and quantity. Merely diverting water from a river or lake can increase pollution by further concentrating natural contaminants in the waterway. The diversion of 10,000 acre-feet of water from the upper reaches of the Colorado River increases the salt content of the lower stretches by one milligram per liter and causes more than $250,000 in damage. Return flow from irrigated agriculture and other operations further pollutes waterways by carrying dissolved salts, suspended solids from eroding land, phosphates from fertilizers, and hazardous chemicals from pesticides. In the West, salinity levels have worsened significantly over the last several decades and now present a major water quality problem, though some salinity control programs are now in operation.

One of the newest pollution concerns is groundwater. Current efforts to use groundwater aquifers for storage to substitute for new dam and reservoir projects underlines the need to assure the safety of groundwater. The nation largely ignored groundwater contamination until the late 1970s. While the overall quality of our country's groundwater appears to be relatively good, many wells have had to be closed due to increasing contamination. Excessive pumping of coastal aquifers can lead to seawater intrusion and thus saline contamination of the groundwater. Wells in numerous coastal states have already had to be closed because of such intrusion. Where an aquifer is contaminated by man-made sources, moreover, heavy pumping can speed up the spread of the contamination. The United States is currently trying to address groundwater contamination through a diverse array of federal and state policies. The numerous and sundry sources of contamination (including landfills, septic systems, underground storage tanks, agriculture, mining wastes, and petroleum wells), however, complicate the task of preventing groundwater contamination. Once contaminated, moreover, groundwater is exceptionally difficult to clean up.

Interstate and International Complications

The interstate and international character of many of our water resources further complicates our efforts to address issues of both quantity and quality. Three states claim an interest in and draw water from the North Platte River; four states vie for the limited wealth of the Delaware River; seven states, as well as Mexico, fight over the scarce resources of the Colorado River, and the Rio Grande is also an international river flowing from Texas to Mexico and the back into Texas. The Great Lakes are largely international as well as interstate waters. Sewage dumped into Lake Michigan from Wisconsin can affect residents of Illinois, as well as Indiana and Michigan. Diversion proposals are a perennial source of anxiety to both U.S. and Canadian jurisdictions. Chapter 8 addresses our less than perfect means of resolving interjurisdictional disputes.

B. LOOKING AHEAD: THE BIG PICTURE

In 2003, the Department of the Interior published Water 2025: Preventing Crises and Conflict in the West. Water policy has been a governmental concern for well over a century, beginning with John Wesley Powell's classic Report on the Lands of the Arid Region of the United States (1879), and continuing with A Water Policy for the American People, Ten Rivers in America's Future (1950), the National Water Commission's Final Report (1973), and the Western Water Policy Review Advisory Commission's report entitled Water in the West: Challenges for the Next Century (1998).

In some respects, the theme is a constant: the inherent limitations imposed by aridity and the importance of managing water on a hydrologically rational basis. These two precepts are equally the central theme of Powell's 1879 report and of the Advisory Commission's recommendations in 1998. A cynic might say they are as much disregarded now as they were in Powell's time. Nonetheless, as you are about to see, water policy has undergone some dramatic and impressive changes in recent decades.

The long-standing assumption that meeting water demand was essentially an engineering problem—building dams and reservoirs, and transporting water to areas of use—has largely been supplanted by the assumption that new needs will be met primarily by conservation and by reallocation, the latter primarily meaning market transfers of water from agriculture to urban and industrial use. That new perspective has also focused attention on the desirability of integrating surface water and groundwater resources more effectively, using techniques like "conjunctive use," where surface water is injected into the ground during years of abundant flows, so it can be drawn out during dry periods.

Hydropower, once admired as a clean and cheap form of energy, is now seen as a significant cause of declining populations of species such as salmon; and under the prodding of laws like the Endangered Species Act, the traditional focus on damming up rivers has yielded significantly to pressures for restoration of natural (or at least more natural) conditions. Along with efforts to promote reallocation through marketing, perhaps the most significant change in water policy in recent years has been increasing concern with maintaining or restoring instream flows, as contrasted with the older notion that water was only beneficially used when it was diverted for irrigation or municipal use, or stored so it could be released to generate hydroelectric energy.

These changes have generated a number of new issues for water law. Increased pressure to restore instream flows raises questions about the rights of existing users who have relied on diversions. More broadly, how should scarce water be allocated between environmental and recreational (instream) claims, on one side, and conventional economic and out-of-stream uses on the other? For sharply contrasting views about where we ought to be going, see Report of the Long's Peak Working Group on National Water Policy, 24 Envtl. L. 125 (1994), drafted as a proposed water policy guidebook for the incoming Clinton Administration in 1993, and a critique (id. at 157) by Gregory J. Hobbs, Jr., a water lawyer of the traditional school and currently a Justice of the Colorado Supreme Court. The Report set out four general principles:

(1) Increased demand on water resources, rising costs for water treatment, and contemporary environmental values combine to make the efficient use of water resources a central aspect of all water policy.

(2) The federal government should provide leadership, making water conservation an explicit part of every water program and policy.

(3) Transfers of water from one use to another can contribute substantially to water use efficiency, and should be facilitated by the federal government, taking into account environmental and equity considerations.

(4) The efficient use and conservation of water will be optimized through cooperation among federal, state, local, and tribal governments, and by an open, participatory process.

Justice Hobbs' dissent described the Report as a "one-dimensional argument for the exercise of federal agency power over state and local planning * * * biased by its anti-storage, anti-use, anti-local-government agenda. The group's timely message about the need for water use efficiency, environmental protection, market mechanisms for water transfers, and community participation in water decision-making is lost in the strident din of preservationism." Id. at 158.

Reallocation through marketing not only raises concerns about the viability of agricultural communities, but also questions about who has (and should have) authority to sell water for use in distant places: an individual farmer, the agricultural water district that distributes water to the farms in a region, or the political entity, such as the local county where the water has been used? Should water be viewed as belonging to the area of origin in which it arises, or as a commodity that should be allowed freely to flow to areas where it is needed and wanted? Marketing also raises questions about growth management. Should public policy encourage or allow unrestricted water sales to cities in extremely arid places?

Water marketing raises a wide range of important issues. Traditionally, the water of interstate streams, such as the Colorado River, was apportioned among the states through which the river flowed, with each bordering state getting some portion of available water. Are such allocations an entitlement of the state, or should individual users of that water within the state be allowed to sell the water they have used (or even an unused entitlement, such as a number of Indian tribes hold) to buyers in another state, and pocket the proceeds?

These are just some of the perplexing issues we will encounter in the materials that follow.

C. WATER MEASUREMENT AND TERMINOLOGY

The Appendix contains a glossary of common water resource terms. Before embarking on our detailed study of water law, however, it is worth taking a moment more to discuss the typical fashions in which one measures water resources.

Whenever we have referred to a quantity of water in this introduction, we have usually talked in terms of gallons of water. Gallons are a familiar quantity to most of us (despite attempts to replace them with metric equivalents). Water law, however, rarely speaks in terms of gallons, except in referring to the rate of pumping for groundwater (gallons per minute). The measure is perhaps thought too small for the huge quantities involved. When people do speak in terms of gallons (e.g., in describing municipal water supply), they generally talk about "million gallons per day" ("mgd") or even "billion gallons per day" ("bgd").

Most of the time we will be talking about the "flow" of water—how much water is flowing in a river, or how much flow is being removed from a river. Flow is usually measured in "cubic feet per second" (or "cfs"). Most of us are accustomed to thinking in terms of total quantity, rather than flow. And, of course, a flow measure can be converted into a quantity measure. If you withdrew one cfs for 24 hours, for example, you would have 646,000 gallons of water (or enough water to supply a town of about 3500 residents for a day). In water law, however, we are not concerned simply with how much water we can take in total, but how much water we can take over various stretches of time. As previously explained, some periods of the year are wetter than others, and a water user wants to know what the flow of water is at each point in time and how much of that flow she can take.

When courts and others discuss rights in water that is stored in a reservoir, on the other hand, we do care about total quantities. In this context, the typical measurement unit is the "acre foot." One acre foot is enough water to cover one acre of land to a depth of one foot, and is equivalent to 325,851 gallons. For help in understanding this measurement, farmers usually apply between two and six acre-feet per year to each acre of irrigated crops (although the exact amount applied varies considerably among regions, soil types, and crops). Many municipal water suppliers estimate that they must provide one acre foot of water per year for every five persons in their service area.[21]

Table 1–7 on the next page gives some basic equivalents.

---

21. The latter figure is based on the assumption that a municipality needs about 180 gallons per person per day to meet its domestic, commercial, industrial, and public demands. As previously noted, cities vary tremendously in their actual per capita consumption.

Table 1–7
Common Water Measurements and Equivalents

FLOW MEASUREMENTS

1 cubic foot per second (cfs)	=	646,317 gallons per day
	=	448.8 gallons per minute
	=	7.48 gallons per second
1 million gallons per day (mgd)	=	1.55 cfs

QUANTITY MEASUREMENTS

1 acre-foot	=	325,851 gallons
1 million gallons	=	3.07 acre-feet

CONVERSIONS BETWEEN FLOW AND QUANTITY

1 cfs	=	1.98 acre-feet per day
	=	722.7 acre-feet per year
1 mgd	=	3.07 acre-feet per day
	=	1,120 acre-feet per year

Chapter 2

RIPARIANISM

A. THE BASIC TENETS OF RIPARIANISM

Riparian law and doctrine have legal significance throughout the United States. Riparianism is the governing law of the more humid areas of the United States, generally including those states along and to the east of the Mississippi River.[1] In most states of the non-mountain West and the Pacific tier, riparianism was initially adopted as the governing water law and later replaced by prior appropriation. Upon the change-over, most riparian water rights to use water were converted into appropriative rights so that riparianism as a water allocation system is of interest in those states primarily as an historical matter. In a very few states, riparianism and prior appropriation coexist today in what are called "mixed" or "dual systems." In the mountain West, led by Utah and Wyoming, riparianism has never been recognized as the basis on which water is allocated.[2] Even in states that reject any historic or continuing role for riparianism, precepts similar to those found in riparian doctrine states form the basis for non-water allocation matters, such as the right to wharf out and parcel boundary determinations. Beyond that, riparian principles, supplemented by doctrines relating to navigability and state ownership of water, control the availability of recreational use of water in all parts of the nation.[3]

Riparianism is a doctrine of ancient origin that defines water rights in terms of use of water in association with ownership of land. The traditional riparian right to use water is, in an important sense, derivative of ownership of land; the right inures to the benefit of owners of riparian parcels and does not depend for its continuing validity on actually initiating or continuing to make use of the water. With land

---

1. For the precise delineation of which states follow riparianism, see infra pp. 12–14.

2. See Joseph Dellapenna, Riparian Rights in the West, 43 Okla. L. Rev. 51, 53–54 (1990).

3. See, e.g., Snively v. Jaber, 48 Wash.2d 815, 296 P.2d 1015 (1956) (ripari-

an principles for private recreational use); Southern Idaho Fish & Game Ass'n v. Picabo Livestock, Inc., 96 Idaho 360, 528 P.2d 1295 (1974) (state ownership of water as basis for public use of recreationally valuable waters).

ownership as the fulcrum for the enjoyment of riparian rights, the two major undertakings of riparian doctrine are (1) the definition of what lands are riparian (thereby defining a potential user class) and (2) articulation of the rights of benefitted proprietors.

1. DEFINING THE RIPARIAN USER CLASS AND IDENTIFYING THE BENEFITTED PARCELS

While it borders on the tautological to say that only riparian land owners enjoy riparian rights, to do so highlights the importance of defining what land is riparian and what land is not. The simplest definition deems riparian those tracts of land that are contiguous with the water's edge. A parcel need not underlie a portion of that water surface to be riparian.[4] In general, the type of watercourse involved, be it river, stream, lake, or pond, is irrelevant.[5] Terminologically, a distinction exists between lands adjoining flowing waters and lands adjoining standing waters. The former are called riparian and the latter littoral. Nevertheless, the operative legal rules are virtually identical and go by the general name of riparianism. Traditional doctrine not only limited use of water to riparian landowners, but also limited riparian owners to using the water on the riparian tract itself. Further, the water had to be used in the watershed of origin.[6] Thus, if a single riparian parcel had portions that were situated in another drainage basin, water could not be used on those non-basin-of-origin portions of the tract.

There is a blend of logic and arbitrariness inherent in assigning rights of water use on the basis of ownership of tracts of land that are contiguous to the water and limiting the use to the boundaries of such tracts. Assignment of rights on that basis is an easily administrable tool for identifying the class of water users and transferring those rights to others. Recording systems for the ownership of land are an administrative staple of local governance throughout the nation and each state's rules for the transfer of land are well articulated. Likewise, markets for the transfer of land are well established. If, as is possible, the water supply can sustain some, but not all of the demands for use, the limitation of water rights to riparian parcels serves an important distributive function. Limiting uses to riparian tracts might even prove to be an elegant means of distribution insofar as those parcels, because of the

---

4. The question of where the precise property lines lie is discussed later at page 533.

5. Springs are a possible exception to the general rule stated above. Some jurisdictions hold that springs (places where water issues forth from the ground by natural causes) that do not become a part of a watercourse that flows off of the land on which they originate are the exclusive private property of the landowner. See, e.g., Boynton v. Gilman, 53 Vt. 17 (1880) (spring treated like diffused surface water); Blood-

good v. Ayers, 108 N.Y. 400, 15 N.E. 433 (1888) (spring not subject to law of riparianism).

6. The probable origin of the in-basin limitation is the desire to protect the established expectations of downstream riparians to continue to receive the benefit of the continued flow of the stream. See, e.g., Town of Gordonsville v. Zinn, 129 Va. 542, 106 S.E. 508 (1921). See also A. Dan Tarlock, Law of Water Rights and Resources § 3.10[2], at 3–56 to 3–57 (1988).

expense and loss of water inherent in water's conveyance, frequently will be the most efficient sites for water use.

Beyond fortuity and logic, there is also an historical component to the traditional American legal rule limiting water use to riparian tracts. America's early laws were inherited from England. The law of riparianism in pre-industrial England featured legal rules that facilitated use of the water in place, more as an amenity than as an instrument of economic significance. The legal doctrine, called the natural flow doctrine, assured each riparian owner of the right to receive the flow of the stream "undiminished as to quality or quantity" and provided a cause of action even in the absence of harm to the complaining riparian. Few, if any, off-tract or out-of-basin uses could be accomplished under such a regime. As a result, the doctrinal limitation of use to riparian parcels added little to the restrictiveness of the English law of that era; only in-basin lands immediately adjacent to the waters could feasibly be the situs of such uses. In the United States, the expanding water needs of industrialization, agriculture and growing cities quickly led to repudiation of the natural flow doctrine, but, as discussed more fully below, the in-basin and on-tract limitations lingered as part of the law in a number of riparian jurisdictions.[7]

From a modern perspective, the arbitrariness of limiting water rights to parcels adjoining the water is evident. First, there is no necessary correlation between contiguity of land to water and the ability of a parcel to benefit from use of the water. Use of water may be of greater value on non-riparian tracts than on riparian lands. For example, the riparian tracts in a steep-sided river valley might lack suitable level areas for agricultural use, while non-riparian benchlands might be very valuable for agriculture if irrigation water could be diverted from the stream. Second, the available water may be capable of supporting additional uses on parcels that are not riparian without a reduction in the benefits derived from the riparian parcels. Were that the case, the on-tract limitation would unduly restrict the benefits associated with full utilization of the water resource and be akin to a form of waste. Finally, the patterns of ownership that have evolved over the centuries of conveyancing have led to illogic regarding what lands are presently deemed riparian. A large single estate lying within a single drainage, only a small part of which is riparian, is considered riparian in its entirety. This is so even if the bulk of the land lies far from the water's edge. In contrast, a parcel, all of which is quite close to the water, but having no frontage on the watercourse, is entirely without riparian rights.

Legal rules delineating what parcels enjoy riparian rights changed little prior to the twentieth century. In the East, the use of water at locations remote from the watercourse was seldom significant, so there

7. See Joseph Dellapenna, The Right to Consume Water Under "Pure" Riparian Rights, in 1 Waters and Water Rights § 7.02(a)(2) (Robert Beck ed., 2001 replacement vol. & 2005 Cumm. Supp.).

was little foment for change of the rule that only tracts that touch the water enjoy riparian rights. Doctrinal development was limited to establishing rules for the transfer of the usufructuary rights associated with ownership of riparian land. In general, the operative principle is that severance of land not touching the water from a larger tract, part of which touches the water, destroys the riparian rights associated with the severed portion of the tract. Similarly, except for the advent of changes in law that permitted use of water off of the riparian tract, attempts to transfer water rights in gross, apart from the conveyance of riparian lands, were unsuccessful. In contrast, it is possible (although unusual) to transfer lands that do touch the watercourse without transfer of the riparian rights. This can be done by express reservation of riparian rights.

The most interesting legal question in regard to determining what lands are riparian is that of the status of reunited lands. For example, assume that AB is a single riparian tract from which part B, a non-riparian portion, is severed and sold. At some later point in time a single person becomes the owner of both portions A and B and seeks to have the "reunited" tract AB treated as riparian in its entirety. The question is handled in two principal ways.[8] A number of states hold that even if a severed non-riparian portion of a parcel is later reunited in unitary ownership with the riparian tract of which it was once part, the portion once severed is forever considered non-riparian. This doctrine, called the "source of title rule," limits riparian rights to the smallest contiguous riparian tract in the chain of title. A less harsh doctrine is the "unity of title rule." It grants riparian rights to the non-riparian portions of parcels that were at one time united if the title to the severed portion is again "unified" in the hands of one who simultaneously holds title to the riparian portion of the original tract. Most states following the stricter source of title rule are states that now permit the creation of appropriative water rights to benefit non-riparian parcels. As a result, the adherence to the source of title doctrine reflects the desire of those states to give primacy to their systems of appropriative rights.

Overall, the class of riparian lands tends to shrink. In source of title jurisdictions, each transfer of non-riparian portions of a riparian tract irreversibly reduces the stock of riparian lands. In unity of title jurisdictions, severed non-riparian portions of previously riparian tracts can regain their riparian status if they are reunited, but all non-reunited parcels have lost their riparian status. Thus, even in those states, the

---

8. Historically, there was a third view of the effect of transfer on riparian rights that is described by Professor Farnham as the "no limit rule." It "permits the increase in size of a riparian tract by the acquisition of additional land contiguous to it, even though the added land had been non-riparian ever since its passage from governmental to private ownership." See William Farnham, The Permissible Extent of Riparian Land, 7 Land & Water L. Rev. 31, 55–56 (1972). The view was supported by both judicial adoption and treatise writers. See, e.g., Jones v. Conn, 39 Or. 30, 64 P. 855 (1901); 1 Clesson Kinney, The Law of Irrigation and Water Rights 465 (2d ed. 1912). The rule was even given support in the first Restatement of Torts § 843 cmt. c (1939). Despite this heritage, the no limit rule has been eclipsed by the source of title and unity of title rules.

stock of riparian lands tends to decline over time. To the extent that the incidents of being riparian allow for more productive use of a tract of land and are not offset by the availability of other water rights, the shrinkage of the stock of available riparian lands threatens a loss of productivity.

Offsetting effects of the shrinkage of the corpus of lands that qualify as riparian is the fact that there is no definite limit on the ability of a riparian to divide a single riparian tract into two or more smaller tracts, each having some frontage on the water course. Upon transfer, each of the newly formed parcels will have riparian rights by virtue of the inclusion of some riparian land. Thus, the user class can be expanded, although the average parcel size declines. Importantly, each newly formed riparian tract enjoys the same usufructuary rights as every other riparian tract. The sum of rights possessed by the owners of the now-divided tracts is, in a sense, greater than the rights formerly held by the original owner. The fact that the frontage and parcel size of the resultant tracts will be less is relevant to the determination of what water uses will qualify as reasonable, but the law does not insist that the rights of use decline proportionately to the reduction in either frontage or parcel size.[9]

The expansion of the user class through the amoeba-like division of riparian parcels does nothing to address the water needs of non-riparian tracts. Given the futility of efforts to expand the user class by tinkering with the contours of the definition of what lands are riparian, it became inevitable that pressure would mount to discard the on-tract and even the in-basin limitations on the riparian right.[10] Here the law evolved.

The assault on the on-tract limitation was made possible by a change in a central aspect of the riparian right itself. In what is heralded as one of the more important breaks with English common law, the decision of Justice Story in Tyler v. Wilkinson, 24 F. Cas. 472 (C.C.R.I. 1827), rejected the English common law right of riparians to receive, without diminution, the natural flow of the stream. In effect, the English common law right of the lower owner acted as a prohibition on uses that diminished the flow of the stream, virtually banning all uses of water that required diversion of the water from the stream.[11] The American rule favored "reasonable use" of the water, allowing some diminution of flow as to both quantity and quality, so long as the challenged use was reasonable under the totality of the circumstances. While the American

---

9. There are limits to the "multiplication" of riparian parcels through subdivision. See, e.g., Thompson v. Enz, infra p. 577, and the materials discussed there.

10. William Farnham, The Permissible Extent of Riparian Land, 7 Land & Water L. Rev. 31 (1972).

11. The right of the lower owner might go unexercised allowing diminution in flow for a period of time, but that right retained

the potential to result in an injunction of the upper use, thereby providing a significant deterrent to off-tract uses that required any security of water supply. But see Carol Rose, Energy and Efficiency in the Realignment of Common-Law Water Rights, 19 J. Legal Stud. 261, 269 (1990) ("[P]ractical businessmen must have ignored the older doctrines * * * or must at least have found them inconsequential.").

rule did not abandon the on-tract limitation, it made steps in that direction conceivable for the first time.

Freed of the restrictive consequences of the natural flow doctrine, not all American states began to permit riparians to make off-tract uses. Those jurisdictions unwilling to move away from prior English common law on this point "allowed" off-tract uses only in the absence of objection by riparian proprietors. In effect, off-tract uses by riparians, or uses by non-riparians were permitted at sufferance of the class of riparians. Other jurisdictions, however, adopted a rule that uses on non-riparian lands could be enjoined only upon a showing of actual harm by adversely affected riparians.[12] In more modern times, a number of jurisdictions have abandoned totally the on-tract restriction, considering a use as permissible if reasonable.[13] The weakening of the on-tract limitation expands the potential water user class. Previously, only riparians were eligible; under the fully expanded view, anyone who can obtain lawful access to a point from which water may be diverted can participate in the competition for water.[14]

2. RIPARIAN RIGHTS OF USE AND INCIDENTS OF RIPARIAN OWNERSHIP

The rights of riparian landowners to use the water that adjoins or overlies a part of their parcels are several. The most elemental right of all is the right to use water for domestic purposes, such as drinking, bathing, and raising a small quantity of garden produce and livestock. This right to take water for domestic use is called natural use, in distinction to artificial use. It is an absolute right in the sense that the right may be exercised without regard to its effect on co-riparians. In pursuit of domestic use, a riparian may exhaust the entire stream even if it means that fellow riparians will receive no water whatsoever. The absolute nature of natural uses is exceptional; other usufructuary rights of riparians must be exercised with due regard for the effect on co-riparians.

Under modern doctrine, riparians also enjoy a host of additional rights to use the water for uses such as power generation, raising dairy and livestock herds, manufacturing, and recreation. The list of allowable artificial uses varies from state to state, usually reflecting the more common uses to which water is put in the jurisdiction. The list is non-

12. See, e.g., Stratton v. Mt. Hermon Boys' School, 216 Mass. 83, 103 N.E. 87 (1913). This latter view is adopted by the Restatement (Second) of Torts § 855.

13. See, e.g., Pyle v. Gilbert, infra p. 47.

14. The elimination of the on-tract limitation coupled with the non-exclusive nature of riparian rights of use creates the possibility of a tragedy of the commons problem. Even though the true riparian class, by virtue of trespass laws, can deny non-riparians lawful access to points of diversion, the individual self-interest of all riparians will be to gain the additional benefit of income derived from granting an easement to the non-riparian. The rights of the license granting riparian are diminished only to the extent that their former use is now less likely to be reasonable due to the increased demands being put on the water source, but that risk will be encountered without regard to whether they provide the access or another co-riparian provides it.

exclusive and changes over time to reflect the needs of the community. For example, in the mid-nineteenth century many states decided, contrary to prior law, that log floatation was a reasonable riparian use that previously was not deemed so. More recently, a number of states have ruled expressly that irrigation is a reasonable riparian use.[15] The word "reasonable" in this context indicates that the use is one that will not be enjoined by a court solely in virtue of the nature of the use. In terms of court decisions, uses that fail to meet this test of reasonableness are labeled "per se unreasonable." As discussed below, even artificial uses that are reasonable in this sense can be pursued in a fashion that is unreasonable under the particular circumstances.

In the taking of water for these artificial uses, riparians are constrained by the reasonable use doctrine. The use of a riparian must be reasonable with respect to the correlative ability of other riparians to make simultaneous reasonable use of the watercourse. To ensure that one riparian's uses do not interfere with equally protected uses of co-riparians, all of the fundamental riparian rights noted above, except domestic uses, are limited rather than absolute. An otherwise permissible use, carried to an extreme, can become unreasonable and therefore subject to legal abatement. For example, in a jurisdiction that recognizes irrigation of crops as a permissible riparian use, irrigation that so depletes the available supply of water as to prevent recreational use by a co-riparian will be enjoined as unreasonable.[16]

Substantial interference with the uses of others will be tolerated only if there is so little water available that neither of the competing uses can be pursued without harm to the other. In cases where all uses cannot go forward unhindered, courts muddle through by announcing circumstance-specific decisions that are then rationalized by reference to equitable principles. Generalizations are difficult. When the competing activities are scalable (i.e., when they can be reduced proportionately without becoming infeasible), a "share the shortage" philosophy can lead to pro rata reductions in water use. When that option is not available, courts may characterize one use as the "cause" of the interference to the other and require that user to make more substantial adjustments.[17] The lack of predictability of outcomes is an oft criticized aspect of riparian doctrine.[18]

A few states have adopted legislation that gives preference to some uses, thereby rejecting, in part, the "share the shortage" philosophy. These laws reflect recognition that the competing artificial uses are not necessarily of equal importance to the state. These laws have taken

15. See, e.g., Pyle v. Gilbert, infra p. 47; Harris v. Brooks, 225 Ark. 436, 283 S.W.2d 129 (1955).

16. See, e.g., Taylor v. Tampa Coal Co., 46 So.2d 392 (Fla. 1950). Under the common law of reasonable use, the courts do not appear to make explicit allowance for the relative benefits of the competing uses.

In states that now follow the Restatement (Second) of Torts, infra p. 57, the relative benefits of the competing uses are relevant to the reasonableness determination.

17. Mason v. Hoyle, 56 Conn. 255, 14 A. 786 (1888), described infra p. 45.

18. T. E. Lauer, Reflections on Riparianism, 35 Mo. L. Rev. 1 (1970).

various forms. A common preference in the nineteenth century favored milling operations and often took statutory form in laws that permitted entry on another's lands to construct a dam, or laws limiting riparian rights to enjoin interference with the flow of streams. These and similar laws made it far less costly for millers to obtain flowage easements (easements allowing the holder to cause water to overflow the land of another) for impounding the water that would drive their mills.[19] Later statutory forays into the preference arena include statutes favoring agricultural uses[20] and statutes favoring mining uses.[21] Thus, through legislative intervention, the classes of preferred riparian uses has grown from the traditional absolute preference for domestic ("natural") use to a variegated series of preferences reflective of state policy about the proper allocation of water resources among competing activities in the event of shortage.[22] Beneath it all, most courts, while recognizing and applying the statutory preferences, have otherwise adhered to the common law of riparianism that enshrines no preferences among competing artificial uses.

An alternative to preferences in combating the uncertain definition of what riparian uses are reasonable is to specify the factors that are relevant to the determination of reasonableness. Courts in several states have taken this approach that finds its clearest exposition in the Restatement (Second) of Torts. The Restatement propounds a complex set of factors that are used to judge the reasonableness of a riparian use,[23] but it does so without clear guidance as to how the several factors are to be weighed should they all fail to point to a single outcome.

Whether operating under the traditional common law or the Restatement (Second) approach, clear definition of the extent of riparian rights is elusive. The only path to certainty lies in expensive, highly fact-specific litigation that is of limited precedential value. Even litigated outcomes lack finality because the reasonableness of a particular mix of water uses can change over time, as co-riparians make changes in their uses, or as shifts in climate and overall patterns of regional development alter the flow or use characteristics of the water course. The lack of certainty regarding the extent of permissible riparian uses undoubtedly deters some water dependent economic development.

In addition to the allocation of water use in accordance with the reasonable use doctrine, riparians also hold the right to use the water surface for boating and allied pursuits, such as fishing and swimming.

19. See Joseph Dellapenna, Regulated Riparianism, in 1 Waters and Water Rights § 9.02 (Robert Beck ed., 2001 replacement vol. & 2005 Cumm. Supp.).

20. See, e.g., Ky. Rev. Stat. § 151.140.

21. See, e.g., Mich. Comp. Laws Ann. § 13.145(1), (3).

22. See, e.g., Minn. Stat. § 103G.261(a)(1)–(6). That statute assigns priorities respectively to (1) domestic use

and certain primary power generation covered by a contingency plan, (2) uses consuming less than 10,000 gpd, (3) irrigation and agricultural processing uses consuming less than 10,000 gpd, (4) other secondary power production under the contingency plan, (5) remaining power and agricultural uses, and (6) non-essential uses.

23. The relevant portion of the Restatement appears infra p. 57.

Riparian proprietors in many states have the right to use the entire surface of the water for navigation and recreation even though the lands beneath the water may in full, or in part, be owned by others.[24] This doctrine tends to maximize the utility of each riparian's use of the water by preventing subdivision of the surface into inconveniently small parcels of limited value. These riparian rights exist in addition to whatever other rights members of the general public may enjoy to use the water surface as a result of the water's definition as navigable under either state or federal law.[25] The right of surface use is not personal to the riparian, it extends to licensees and permitees, so long as the total use does not become unreasonable.[26] The riparian right of surface use, including water areas superjacent to another's beds, stands in derogation of the normal rules of real property law. The cases upholding this right tend to explain this divergence from the ordinary principles of real property law by reference to longstanding practice.

Allied with the right to make use of the water surface for boating, riparians, again as an incident of shore ownership, have a right to wharf out to deeper water in order to use the water for boating and navigation. The right to wharf out facilitates the ability of the upland proprietor to take advantage of the unique opportunities for water use provided by the riparian location. The right to wharf out, however, is limited in several regards. First and foremost, the wharves, piers and other structures cannot impede navigation. The extent of the right under the common law is described as, "the exclusive right to dig channels and build wharves from his land to reach deep water, so long as he does not interfere with free navigation."[27] The common law right is, in general, further encumbered by governmentally imposed permit requirements. In addition to navigation and permit concerns, the ownership of the subaqueous lands over which wharves, docks and piers are built is, at times, an issue. The general rule is that a pier or wharf must overlie beds owned by the riparian in question, or beds that are in public ownership. A final challenge to the right to wharf out can be posed by co-riparians whose waterborne access may be affected by the structure or whose view of the water is adversely affected.[28]

At times, riparian owners have sought to increase the utility of their parcels by extending the fast land portion waterward, usually by filling

---

24. See, e.g., Johnson v. Seifert, 257 Minn. 159, 100 N.W.2d 689 (1960). See also A. Dan Tarlock, supra note 6, § 3.17[4][b] at 3–47 (listing states that deny use of the entire surface but observing that "a majority of courts that have recently considered the question have adopted [a rule giving co-riparians use of the entire surface]"). See also, infra pp. 68–69 discussing the variability of positions on this issue in relation to state-law-non-navigable and artificial waters.

25. Navigability and the public rights of water use that surround a finding of navi-gability are complex and often confusing subjects. They are treated more fully in Chapter 6.

26. See, e.g., Snively v. Jaber, 48 Wash.2d 815, 296 P.2d 1015 (1956).

27. Shorehaven Golf Club v. Water Resources Comm'n, 146 Conn. 619, 624, 153 A.2d 444, 446 (1959).

28. Those owners would attack the wharfing out as an unreasonable riparian use. See, e.g., Hefferline v. Langkow, 15 Wash.App. 896, 552 P.2d 1079 (1976).

submerged lands. There is no riparian right to fill.[29] Today, most efforts at filling are heavily regulated by environmental laws and permit systems that limit the amount of filling allowed.[30] Likewise, in some states the recognition of the importance of shoreline areas has resulted in the imposition of public trust responsibilities that attach to those parcels and further restrict their waterward development[31] or use of the foreshore area.[32]

Few cases can be found that challenge filling as an unreasonable riparian use, but those challenges, when mounted, appear to have been successful in blocking non-water related developments. In one case, a riparian who had begun construction of an apartment building on fill in Bitter Lake in Seattle was enjoined to remove the structure and the fill. The landowner claimed that the use was riparian and should be judged by its reasonableness and further argued the grant of all needed city permits and approvals constituted a per se finding of reasonableness. In the key passage these arguments were soundly rejected:

> Mere proximity of the apartment to the water does not render it a riparian use. With respect to a structure, such a use must be so intimately associated with the water that apart from the water its utility would be seriously impaired. This is not the case with defendants' prospective use. The utility of the apartment is in no way dependent upon the waters of Bitter Lake, and its utility as an apartment would be in no way impaired apart from this lake. * * *

> All riparian owners along the shore of a natural, nonnavigable lake share in common the right to use the entire surface of the lake for boating, swimming, fishing, and other similar riparian rights so long as there is no unreasonable interference with the exercise of these rights by other respective owners. These rights are vested property rights, and may not be taken or damaged for public or private use without just compensation. It follows, therefore, that while the city of Seattle might regulate the exercise of these rights by means of its police power, it may not totally divest plaintiffs of them through the mechanisms of zoning. Indeed, the effect of this case, if we were to follow defendants' reasoning, would be to divest plaintiffs of valuable property rights for the private use and benefit of defendants. Such a result is clearly contrary to the law, and we are certain was not intended by the Seattle zoning authorities

29. See, e.g., Burt v. Munger, 314 Mich. 659, 23 N.W.2d 117 (1946).

30. See, e.g., Richard Bartke & Susan Patton, Water Based Recreational Developments in Michigan–Problems for Developers, 25 Wayne L. Rev. 1005 (1979) (noting five federal and four state statutes that might affect lakeshore development in Michigan). In general, permits for fill of wetlands that are part of the navigable waters of the United States are within Army Corps of Engineers jurisdiction. See infra p. 639. Concurrent state or local regulation has become increasingly common.

31. See, e.g., Marks v. Whitney, 6 Cal.3d 251, 491 P.2d 374 (1971), infra p. 597.

32. See, Glass v. Goeckel, 473 Mich. 667, 703 N.W.2d 58 (2005), involving rights of waterfront use, discussed more fully infra p. 592.

when the commercial general classification was placed on defendants' property.[33]

Notes and Questions

1. Riparianism has long been a favorite target for legal commentators who bemoan the indefinite and shifting nature of the usufructuary rights it awards. See, e.g., T. E. Lauer, Reflections on Riparianism, 35 Mo. L. Rev. 1 (1970). Is that criticism overstated, if, as it appears, there are relatively few situations calling for precise definition of rights? If riparianism fails to provide adequate certainty to would-be-users and thereby deters development, its longevity as a governing doctrine in the American East would be quite surprising. Why is the uncertainty of so little practical importance?

2. Are there more cogent criticisms of riparianism to be made? Professor Lynda Butler suggests that riparianism fails to provide reasoned allocations between public and private uses and targets the on-tract limitation, the definition of reasonable use with reference to low density domestic consumption and the restrictions on transferability of water as particularly central doctrinal problems. See Lynda Butler, Allocating Consumptive Water Rights in a Riparian Jurisdiction: Defining the Relationship Between Public and Private Interest, 47 U. Pitt. L. Rev. 95 (1985).

3. Would increases in water demand and decreases in the water supply threaten the survival of riparianism as the dominant water law of the East? Water demand is highly correlated with increasing population and the population of many riparian areas is growing rapidly. Climatic changes that are predicted to accompany the greenhouse effect and pollution of significant water sources portend possible reductions in water supply. For an analysis of riparianism's survivability in light of these and other predicted changes in water supply and demand, see Robert Abrams, Charting the Course of Riparianism: An Instrumentalist Theory of Change, 35 Wayne L. Rev. 1381 (1989). These issues are further explored at page 117.

B. THE COMMON LAW DEVELOPMENT OF RIPARIAN RIGHTS

The law of riparian rights has not been constant over time. The materials in this section chronicle the development of reasonable use riparianism as it replaced the natural flow doctrine. Apart from tracing the doctrinal changes in American riparianism that have occurred in the past two centuries, this section and the next also attempt to probe the animating forces behind those changes. What emerges is an overt, ofttimes explicit effort on the part of judges and legislatures, to make water law an instrument of pro-developmental policy.

1. CHALLENGING THE INHERITED ENGLISH COMMON LAW

American water law is historically an outgrowth of English water law. During the years before the American Revolution, the original colonies recognized water rights on the basis of the English common law

---

33. Bach v. Sarich, 74 Wash.2d 575, 579–80, 445 P.2d 648, 651–52 (1968).

as modified by royal grants, acts of Parliament, and the charters of the various colonies. Upon nationhood, the newly sovereign states continued the English common law of water rights as their own law. Under eighteenth century English law, the principal right of a riparian land owner was the right to have the water flow by his land, unimpaired as to quantity and quality, though the riparian owner was allowed to use the water for "domestic" purposes, including household uses and the keeping of domesticated animals. A clear judicial statement of the natural flow doctrine appears in an early New Jersey case, Merritt v. Parker, 1 N.J.L. 460, 463 (1795):

> In general it may be observed, when a man purchases a piece of land through which a natural water-course flows, he has a right to make use of it, in its natural state, but not to stop or divert it to the prejudice of another. *Aqua currit, et debet currere* is the language of the law. The water flows in its natural channel, and ought always to be permitted to run there, so that all through whose land it pursues its natural course, may continue to enjoy the privilege of using it for their own purposes. It cannot legally be diverted from its course without the consent of all who have an interest in it. If it should be turned into another channel, or stopped, I should think a jury right in giving almost any valuation which the party thus injured should think proper to affix to it. This principle lies at the bottom of all the cases which I have met with, and it is so perfectly reasonable in itself, and at the same time so firmly settled as a doctrine of the law, that it should never be abandoned or departed from.

The English regime of water rights was well suited to an agrarian society in which the major uses of water involved navigation and fishing. Professor Morton Horwitz said of natural flow riparianism and its anti-developmental consequences:

> The premise underlying the law as stated was that land was not essentially an instrumental good or a productive asset but rather a private estate to be enjoyed for its own sake. The great English gentry, * * * regarded the right to quiet enjoyment as the basic attribute of dominion over property. * * * [E]xploitation of water resources for irrigation or mill dams, which necessarily required significant interference with the natural flow of water, was thus limited to the lowest common denominator of noninjurious development * * *.[34]

Thus, although the Industrial Revolution and its initial reliance on water driven mills would, in time, see the modification of both the English[35]

---

34. Morton Horwitz, The Transformation in the Conception of Property in American Law, 1780–1860, 40 U. Chi. L. Rev. 248, 253 (1973).

35. The influential work of Chancellor Kent commented favorably on the American law insofar as it qualified the potential harshness of the natural flow doctrine: "Streams of water are intended for the use

and the American law of riparian rights, the inherited natural flow doctrine was an impediment to using water as an instrument of commercial activity.

a. Pro-Developmental Policy as Law

The English natural flow doctrine was rigid in a variety of ways. The only permissible uses of water were largely non-consumptive and had to be undertaken in a way that returned any withdrawn water to the stream before it left the riparian tract on which it was used. The on-tract limitation was a part of the English law: not only were non-riparian proprietors wholly debarred from obtaining any legal interests in water use in their own right, their ability to obtain rights from a riparian proprietor was also severely limited. If, for example, a riparian agreed to provide water to a non-riparian, the agreement was enforceable between the parties, but was subject to defeat on suit by any other riparian without a showing of actual damage.

In nineteenth century America the natural flow doctrine came under challenge. A new economic order was emerging that relied less on quiet enjoyment of land as the basis for productivity and lawsuits emerged that reflected the growing use of flowing water for powering mills. In some cases, mill use can be accommodated under a natural flow theory. Arguably, the driving of a mill does nothing to pollute the water[36] as it passes, nor does it remove water from the stream without returning it so as to reduce the quantity of water that proceeds to the land of the owners below.[37]

In a variety of cases, however, mill use was not readily accommodated by natural flow riparianism. On small streams mill seat operators might interdict the entire flow for hours at a time to fill a mill pond and produce a sufficient head to operate the machinery. Impoundment of water behind mill dams can cause substantial seepage and evaporation losses, sometimes reducing the flow to the lower owners. On some occasions, mill operators discharged water from their mills far downstream or into another watercourse, thereby bypassing some lower riparians or altering the flow to all downstream lands. In all of these instances, natural flow riparianism could not support the new water uses associated with the demands of the industries emerging in the northeast.

The early cases challenging mill use of water took two principal forms: conflicts among competing mills on the same stream and claims

and comfort of man; and it would be unreasonable and contrary to the universal sense of mankind, to debar every riparian proprietor, from the application of the water to domestic, agricultural, and manufacturing purposes * * *." 3 James Kent, Commentaries on American Law 440 (4th ed. 1896).

36. Saw mills and grinding mills do pollute the water, sometimes substantially.

37. Navigation was also an important use under English law, but the potentially adverse impact of mill dams on navigation in eighteenth and early nineteenth century America was non-existent. Most mills were located above the major navigable segments of the streams. Dams on rivers sizeable enough to be used extensively for navigation drew the water for mills by diverting a portion of the flow from the stream into a flume or wing dam without need of a dam that would interfere with navigation.

for inundation of upstream lands by the flowage of mill ponds. The common law approach of most states treated the two cases quite differently. Judges modified the venerable common law rules to resolve the rights of competing millers, but for the most part treated inundation cases as they would any other continuing trespass—an appropriate case for injunctive relief. In the flowage context, the millers more often won their concessions legislatively. The contrast in judicial attitudes toward the two types of cases is quite remarkable.

Reported cases involving conflicts between millers are quite common. For example, Merritt v. Parker, supra, involved a claim by a lower riparian mill owner that the plaintiff had altered the natural flow of the stream by discharging it into a new channel that bypassed the lower mill. Even though the nature of the conflicts among competing water users varied with the factual circumstances in which the cases arose, the cases exhibit two generic patterns. In one instance upstream millers are attacked by downstream riparians protesting either a diminution in flow that reduced power to downstream mills, or a diminution in quality that rendered the water unfit for the lower milling use. In the other pattern downstream millers are attacked by upstream proprietors when the lower mill dam raised the level of water in the stream reducing the operating head of an upstream dam.

MARTIN v. BIGELOW

Supreme Court of Vermont, 1827.
2 Aik. 184.

[Plaintiff Martin brought an action in trespass *quare clausem fregit* against defendant Bigelow. Both were mill operators on the same stream. Defendant had erected his mill several years before plaintiff's, but not so long before as to be able to claim any prescriptive rights. Plaintiff's mill was located upstream of defendant's, and its erection reduced the flow to the defendant's mill, reducing the power which the defendant derived from the mill. Defendant exercised a self-help remedy, entering plaintiff's land and removing the waste gate from plaintiff's mill dam, thereby restoring the stream's full flow to his mill. The fact that defendant exercised the self help remedy has the effect of reversing the usual party structure in these cases that finds the downstream first-in-time user complaining about reduced flow caused by operation of the upstream mill.]

HUTCHINSON J. pronounced the following opinion.

It appears by the case, that the defendant erected his mill before the plaintiff erected his, but it does not appear how long before; nothing shows it to have been fifteen years before. And the case negatives any wanton waste or obstruction on the part of plaintiff.

The decision of the county court which we now review, presents this question, merely, whether the defendant's having first appropriated the water of the stream to the use of his mill, entitled him to the water without such obstruction as was created by the plaintiff's use of the water at his mill? No objection is raised to the method used by the defendant to assert his right, if his right be as he contends for.

The common law of England seems to be, that each land owner, through whose land a stream of water flows, has a right to the water in its natural course, and any diversion of the same to his injury, gives him a right of action. He must have previously appropriated it to some use, before he can be said to sustain any damage. If this common law is to govern, it supports the defendant in his defence. But the Court consider it not applicable to our circumstances, and not of binding force here. There must have been a time when it was not applicable, so as to do justice in all cases, in England. Should this principle be adopted here, its effect would be to let the man who should first erect mills upon a small river or brook, control the whole and defeat all the mill privileges from his mills to the source.

I, for one, should like to see some old case in point; some case in which the injury complained of was merely the prudent use of the water, with machinery proportioned to the stream; after which use it flows down its natural channel.

Not only the interest of those who own water privileges, but of the surrounding inhabitants, seems to require that mills should be erected in suitable different places on the same stream. The cases cited at the bar seem all to be either diversions of the water out of its channel, or such obstructions, as effect a visible if not a wanton waste. At least none of them are like the present case, which negatives any imprudent use or wanton waste of the water. * * *

Questions relating to water privileges, of great importance to our citizens, must arise and be decided; and this court are disposed to be careful not to anticipate them before they come properly before the court; and while we are ready to decide in this case, that the mere prior occupancy of the water by the defendant does not give him a right to prevent the plaintiff from using the same water in a prudent way, as it flows down its channel, we wish it fully understood, that we give no intimation what our opinion would have been, had the defendant proved an occupancy of the water for his mills, more than fifteen years before the plaintiff erected his.

Notes and Questions

1. The opinion refers to "defendant's having first appropriated the water of the stream to the use of his mill" and whether that act "entitled him to the water without such obstruction as was created by the plaintiff's use of the water at his mill." The defendant may have been encouraged to make this priority argument by Blackstone. See 2 William Blackstone, Commentaries *402–03. If the court had accepted that argument based on priority of use, the result would strongly resemble the doctrine of prior appropriation, which is aptly summed up in the phrase "first in time is first in right." Why did the court decline to fully protect the prior occupant?

2. According to the opinion, the English common law on the subject granted the lower riparian "a right of action" against any upstream "diversion of [the stream] to his injury." The court adds that in its view the English common law required that the lower owner also be making some use of the water in advance of the change in flow in order to claim injury. This assertion may be in error. Here, recall the language of Merritt v. Parker, supra p. 38, clearly indicating that actual injury to a specific use of the stream is not required to state a cause of action; all that is required is diminution of flow. In any event, this distinction does not end up being highly important to the result in the case because Bigelow, the downstream miller, was there first and was adversely affected, but still loses the case. Why does Bigelow lose the case? The court has a very clear focus on the anti-developmental consequences of the natural flow doctrine. Is the rejection of natural flow made for the same policy reason that deterred the court from allocating rights of use on the basis of priority of use?

3. In Martin v. Bigelow, the court draws a distinction between a claim of right based on mere priority of occupancy and (in the last sentence) the possibility of a right based on prescription (longstanding prior occupancy). In Vermont, as in other eastern states, prescription proved successful. Although it was often difficult to adduce sufficient evidence of all its elements, once proven, priority of long duration was given legal protection. In American law, priority of use could not ripen into a prescriptive right if the activity involved was held to be a harmless use, but the actual injury requirement was modest. For example, in the event that an offending use resulted in any physical invasion of the property, as by inundation of land or alteration of the course of the stream, damage was presumed, even if the area affected was slight and not being used by the owner. See Norton v. Volentine, 14 Vt. 239, 245–46 (1842).

4. Cases such as *Martin* and its far more famous contemporary, Tyler v. Wilkinson, 24 F. Cas. 472 (C.C.R.I. 1827), authored by Justice Story as Circuit Justice, were hailed as having announced a new law of "reasonable use" riparianism. In fact, that conclusion is as much a distillation of the results as it is an accurate report of the content of the opinions. For example, the *Tyler* opinion is written in the language of natural flow riparianism, the result is based on prescription, yet the case was almost immediately heralded as announcing a major American departure from the English natural flow doctrine.

b. Water Quality Impacts and a More Comprehensive Form of Reasonable Use Riparianism

SNOW v. PARSONS
Supreme Court of Vermont, 1856.
28 Vt. 459.

REDFIELD, CH. J.

The important and, as I think, the only question in this case, is whether it is proper for extensive tanneries, upon moderate sized streams, to expend their refuse, or spent bark, into the stream. In regard to many uses of the water in streams, it has been so long settled by common consent, or is so obvious in itself, that it is determinable, as matter of law. Such are the uses for irrigation, for propelling machinery, and for watering cattle, and some others. And in regard to some debris or waste deposits in such streams, there would seem to be no question. The uniform practice, the convenience, and in some instances the indispensable necessity, would seem sufficiently to decide such cases. Among these may be named the infusion of soap dyes, and other materials used in manufacturing, into the streams by which the machinery is propelled. The deposit of saw-dust, to some extent, is nearly indispensable in the running of saw-mills, and most other machinery used in the manufacture of wood, and propelled by water power.

The reasonableness of such use must determine the right, and this must depend upon the extent of detriment to the riparian proprietors below. If it essentially impairs the use below, then it is unreasonable and unlawful, unless it is a thing altogether indispensable to any beneficial use at every point of the stream. An extent of deposit, which might be of no account in some streams, might seriously affect the usefulness of others. So, too, a kind of deposit, which would affect one stream seriously, would be of little importance in another. There is no doubt one must be allowed to use a stream in such a manner as to make it useful to himself, even if it do produce slight inconvenience to those below. This is true of everything which we use in common with others. The air is somewhat corrupted by the most ordinary use; large manufacturing establishments affect it still more seriously; and some, by reason of their vicinity to a numerous population, become so offensive and destructive of comfort, and health even, as to be regarded as common nuisances. Within reasonable limits, those who have a common interest in the use of air and running water, must submit to small inconveniences to afford a disproportionate advantage to others.

It seems to us that this question of the reasonableness of the use of a stream, when it is not settled by custom, and is in its nature doubtful, should always be regarded as one of fact, to be determined by the tribunal trying the facts. In the present case it does not seem to have been treated in that light, unless we regard the judgment of the county court in favor of the plaintiff, as determining it. And, as much of the testimony rejected might have had an important bearing upon this question, and no notice is taken of this point either in the report or the judgment, we must suppose it was not the purpose of the county court to decide the case upon that ground. Indeed, the report furnished no adequate materials for such a determination. That portion of the defendant's offer which tended to show that tanneries could not be operated to any useful purpose, without thus disposing of their waste bark, was almost a cardinal point, in determining the main question, and, if shown to the extent offered, might justify the court in finally requiring the proprietors below to submit to some inconvenience that those above might not be deprived of all benefit of the stream for this kind of manufacture. And the reasonableness of plaintiffs submitting to this inconvenience must depend upon its extent, and the comparative benefit to the defendants, to be judged of by the triers of the fact.

This must be determined upon general principles applicable to the entire business of tanning, and the importance of discharging its waste materials in this mode, and the probable inconvenience of those below. And if, in this view, they regard the use as an unlawful one, then surely the defendants are liable to all damage sustained by the plaintiff, whether he might have used a wheel less liable to such injury, or not.

But if the use is fairly to be regarded as a lawful one, then, probably, the plaintiffs should have conformed their machinery to the altered circumstances of the stream. And if the defendants use of the stream is a lawful and allowable one, it will make no difference that the plaintiff's mill was first erected, if it had not been in operation a sufficient length of time to acquire any prescriptive right to use the water in an extraordinary manner. And as the plaintiff's present wheel was put into his mill after the defendants' tannery was in operation, and his other wheel would not have been unfavorably affected by bark, nothing, by way of prescription, or license, or prior occupancy, can probably be claimed.

And upon the question of the reasonableness of the defendants' use of the stream, it seems to me the uniform custom of the country for generations, would be of some significance in determining its reasonableness. A uniform general custom upon this subject, ought, upon general principles, to have a controlling force. We think, therefore, the case should go back to be determined, upon the question of fact, of the reasonableness of the use by the defendants; 1st, upon general grounds; 2d, the peculiar facts, if any, affecting the reasonableness of the use in this particular case. [The opinion continued and catalogued the evidence that should be received in proof of the necessities of the tanning industry, including proof of custom, and testimony by experts in tanning describing industry practices.] * * *

Notes and Questions

1.   Does the court seem favorably disposed to the doctrine of *damnum absque injuria*? Essentially, that doctrine holds that property interests are not absolute, but must give way when some compromise of those interests offers a widespread benefit to the larger community of which the adversely affected owner also partakes. In a precursor to the modern economic analysis of law movement, the courts would find the "average reciprocity of advantage" sufficient to offset or justify the individual losses. This doctrine is at times discussed in "takings" cases. Does the court in Snow v. Parsons espouse that same attitude? Is the modification of rights that accompanies the shift from natural flow to reasonable use justified in that same manner?

2.   How far does the court move toward ruling that necessity of a particular manner of use is a complete defense to a claim of unreasonable use raised by an adversely affected co-riparian? Is judicial recognition of a water use as "reasonable because necessary" a thinly disguised means for encouraging economic development? In Sanderson v. Pennsylvania Coal Co.,

86 Pa. 401, 408 (1878), the Pennsylvania Supreme Court in a well-known passage stated:

> [T]he law should be adjusted to the exigencies of the great industrial interests of the Commonwealth, and that the production of an indispensable mineral, reaching to the annual extent of twenty millions of tons, should not be crippled and endangered by adopting a rule that would make colliers answerable in damages for corrupting a stream into which mine-water would naturally run. These are considerations that are entitled to be well weighed. In the trial of questions like this before a jury, they ought to be kept steadily in view. The proprietors of large and useful interests should not be hampered or hindered for frivolous or trifling causes.

Despite the tenor of that passage, the 1878 decision favored the plaintiffs and eventually led to a jury verdict of roughly $3,000 against the coal company. When that final judgment was appealed, however, it was reversed, adopting the perspective expressed in the passage, but not repeating the exact language. See, Sanderson v. Pennsylvania Coal Co., 102 Pa. 370 (1883). Eventually, after extensive litigation resulted in a verdict for slightly less than $3,000, that argument formed the basis for reversal denying all recovery. See, Pennsylvania Coal Co. v. Sanderson, 113 Pa. 126, 6 A. 453 (1886). That later decision has been repudiated and overruled. See Commonwealth v. Barnes and Tucker Company, 455 Pa. 392, 411, 319 A.2d 871, 881 (1974). Nevertheless, the question of the extent to which major projects and industrial uses should be limited by relatively smaller individual injuries remains an important legal issue in many water law contexts. Are damage awards and the attendant cost internalization that results a sufficient response? Compare, e.g., Smith v. Staso Milling Co., 18 F.2d 736 (2d Cir. 1927) (opinion by Judge Learned Hand, applying Vermont law issuing injunction) with Boomer v. Atlantic Cement Co., 26 N.Y.2d 219, 257 N.E.2d 870, 309 N.Y.S.2d 312 (1970) (balancing equities to deny injunction). Is governmental approval, regulation, or even sponsorship of a project, relevant or dispositive in common law litigation?

3.   The overall result that the court seems to be seeking in Snow v. Parsons is that of maximizing the total benefits obtained from the use of the stream. To accomplish that in the real world, the court's decision stresses accommodation. Any party to the dispute may be asked to alter their method of operating to enhance the overall good. Evidence that tends to show that tanning can be done without such destructive pollution is important to the court in attempting to decide what accommodation, if any, is possible. Likewise, that same focus leads the court to remark on the fact that plaintiff's former wheel was not as much affected by the debris. Part of the genius of reasonable use riparianism is its ability to devise case-by-case solutions for using the common resource that maintain an eye toward both maximization and fairness. The case that is often cited as the zenith of this quality of reasonable use riparianism is Mason v. Hoyle, 56 Conn. 255, 14 A. 786 (1888). Mason v. Hoyle adopted a famous set of factors for courts to consider in resolving user conflicts, factors that assist the court in measuring whether a use is reasonable: (1) the equal opportunity of all riparians to use the stream, (2) the maxim that no owner can use his own property so as to injure another, (3) the character and capacity of the stream, (4) foreseeable

shortages and apportioning them in a manner that permits all riparians to secure a fair proportion of the benefit, and, finally, (5) customary practices as an indicium of reasonableness.

4. Should the rights of use of each co-riparian be equal if their landholdings are unequal? Should a landholder with a large amount of frontage along the watercourse be limited to the same proportion of the benefit of the water as a landholder with only a few yards of frontage? One possible response is to take the relative size of the landholdings into account in determining what is reasonable.

5. Is the maxim that a property owner cannot use his property to injure another a throwback to natural flow, even if dressed in slightly different language? If taken literally, all property uses having effects that spill over onto a neighbor's land would be actionable. It is sometimes difficult to ascertain which of two competing users is committing the injurious act. For example, in Taylor v. Tampa Coal Co., 46 So.2d 392 (Fla. 1950), irrigation for a citrus farm and recreational use of a lake for water skiing and similar activities could not coexist. Is it clear that the irrigator is the one making the injurious use of the water? Are some uses afforded more protection than others? For example, inundated upper owners invariably obtain some relief, even in settings quite like that of Martin v. Bigelow. See, e.g., Johns v. Stevens, 3 Vt. 308, 316 (1830). The anti-developmental effects of that rule gave rise to the so-called Mill Act in many states, which, in general, immunized millers from injunctions at the behest of inundated owners, and often limited damages as well. The implications of such laws are considered at length in Morton Horwitz, The Transformation in the Conception of Property in American Law 1780–1860, 40 U. Chi. L. Rev. 248, 272 (1973).

6. In cases of mutually injurious use of riparian parcels, what will the courts do to resolve the conflict? Presumably, courts look to the other factors that go into a determination of reasonableness. To the extent that courts seem concerned with maximizing the benefit derived from the water (an efficiency concern), is it possible to identify what legal rules will more often achieve efficient results than other legal rules? The Law and Economics literature has devoted attention to this subject, with the work of Professor Ronald Coase, The Problem of Social Cost, 3 J. L. & Econ. 1 (1960), providing the usual starting point. Coase establishes that in the absence of transaction costs the rule of liability doesn't matter to efficiency as long as there is a clear and well-established rule. In essence, Coase argues that competing resource users will arrive at an optimal result by bargaining with reference to the rule of liability, but can do so only when the rule allows accurate prediction of who will win and who will lose if no bargain is made. Without regard to possible objections to Coase's position, does reasonable use riparianism provide the sort of predictability and certainty of outcome that will allow the bargaining to take place?

7. The limitation of use of water to the bounds of the riparian tract was one of riparianism's traditional limitations on use of water. As the reasonable use doctrine established itself as the successor to the natural flow doctrine, it became more inviting to revisit the per se rule that forbade off-tract use of water. If the measure of the riparian right was a question of

what was reasonable under the circumstances, in logic, at least, use off of the riparian tract could at times be reasonable. In Vermont the off-tract use issue was not finally decided in favor of allowing such use until early in the twentieth century. See Lawrie v. Sillsby, 82 Vt. 505, 511–12, 74 A. 94, 96 (1909). What should be the measure of reasonable off-tract use? Should the reasonableness of the off-tract use be reckoned as a subset of what is a reasonable use of the riparian parcel from which the water is diverted?

C. TWENTIETH CENTURY COMMON LAW REASONABLE USE

The doctrinal development of reasonable use riparianism slowed considerably in the twentieth century. In the first half of the century, the most critical water use issue in riparian jurisdictions was that of supporting municipal growth. That development is canvassed in Section D. In the second half of the twentieth century, the number of reported decisions presenting riparian issues dwindled to a few each year. Among these, the cases proving most numerous and ofttimes difficult for the courts are those involving intensive recreational water use on waterbodies of limited carrying capacity. A typical case is Thompson v. Enz, 379 Mich. 667, 154 N.W.2d 473 (1967), a "funnel development" case that added more than one hundred back lot owners to the user class of a lake via canals. There the court ruled that the back lot owners were not riparian to the lake and, therefore, enjoyed no riparian rights of surface use. That case is studied in the context of using water for navigational and recreational purposes, infra page 577.

This section takes up two distinct issues of modern riparian doctrine, how courts decide cases presenting truly incompatible uses and the increasingly common questions that arise when rights are asserted by riparians whose lands abut artificially created waters.

1. INCOMPATIBLE USES

PYLE v. GILBERT

Supreme Court of Georgia, 1980.
245 Ga. 403, 265 S.E.2d 584.

HILL, JUSTICE.

This is a water rights case involving a non-navigable watercourse. It presents a confrontation between the past and the present. Plaintiffs are the owners of a 140-year-old water-powered gristmill. They emphasize the natural flow theory. Defendants are upper riparians using water to irrigate their farms. They emphasize the reasonable use theory of water rights.

The plaintiffs, Willie and Arlene Gilbert, own property commonly known as Howard's Mill located on Kirkland's Creek, a non-navigable stream in Early County which goes into the Chattahoochie River. * * * Until August 31, 1978, the Gilberts owned and operated a water-powered gristmill on their property. They also rented boats for profit and permitted fishing and swimming in the 40-acre pond. (On August 31, 1978, the mill was destroyed by fire.)

On July 7, 1978, the Gilberts filed a complaint against Sanford Hill,[1] who is an owner of property that is upper riparian in relation to the Gilberts' property, alleging that since 1975 he has been diverting and using water from Kirkland's Creek for irrigation, and that he also has been trespassing and pumping water out of their mill-pond. This allegation of trespass by Hill for the purpose of taking water from the pond apparently was not pursued by the Gilberts. The Gilberts characterized Hill's diversion of waters from Kirkland's Creek for irrigation as both a nuisance and a trespass and sought injunctive relief as well as actual and punitive damages and attorney fees.

The testimony at a hearing on July 18, 1978, revealed to plaintiffs that other upper riparian owners also had irrigated with water from the creek. The plaintiffs subsequently added four defendants: George Edgar Pyle, Jimmy Doster, Phillip Buckhalter and Vinson Evans.[2] Following discovery, the trial court made an extensive examination of our water law and granted the plaintiffs' motions for summary judgment as to liability against all defendants, holding that the defendants' use of the water for irrigation constituted a diversion, a trespass, a nuisance and an unreasonable use as a matter of law, and enjoining any future use.[3] The issue of damages was reserved for trial. The defendants appeal.

1. Over 100 years ago, when this court first considered riparian rights in Hendrick v. Cook, 4 Ga. 241 (1848), several bedrock principles were established. First, the court firmly rejected the doctrine of appropriation and instead applied riparian principles to the dispute. And in stating the principles of riparian rights, the court also adopted the doctrine of reasonable use. As stated by the court (4 Ga. at 256): "Each proprietor of the land on the banks of the creek, has a natural and equal right to the use of the water which flows therein as it was *wont to run,* without diminution or alteration. Neither party has the right to use the water in the creek, to the *prejudice* of the other. The plaintiff cannot divert or diminish the quantity of water which would naturally flow in the stream, so as to prejudice the rights of the defendants, without their consent * * * Each riparian proprietor is entitled to a *reasonable* use of the water, for *domestic, agricultural* and *manufacturing* purposes; provided, that in making such use, he does not work a *material injury* to the

1. Sanford Hill and several others (who are not involved in this litigation) were the grantors of the property when it was conveyed in 1974.

2. Vinson Evans owns non-riparian property which he admits having irrigated with the alleged permission of a riparian owner.

3. The trial judge noted that the authorities point out conflicts as well as gaps in our water law. He observed that "Water rights are becoming more and more important with advancing techniques for its withdrawal and use, and there is a need for the courts or the legislature, or both, to further amplify and clarify equitable water rights between parties, particularly as those rights apply to irrigation."

other proprietors." (Emphasis supplied.)[5] The court also held that an injury to one's riparian rights gave rise to an action for damages for trespass even in the absence of proof of actual damage.[6]

Subsequently, two statutes were enacted and codified in the Code of 1863. Section 2206 of the Code of 1863 appears today almost verbatim at Code sec. 85–1301: "Running water, while on land, belongs to the owner of the land, but he has *no right to divert it* from the usual channel, nor may he so use or adulterate it as to interfere with the enjoyment of it by the next owner." (Emphasis supplied.) (See also Code sec. 85–1305.) Section 2960 of the Code of 1863 now appears at Code sec. 105–1407: "The owner of land through which non-navigable watercourses may flow is entitled to have the water in such streams come to his land in its natural and usual flow, subject only to such detention or diminution as may be caused by a *reasonable use* of it by other riparian proprietors; and the *diverting of the stream, wholly or in part,* from the same, or the obstructing thereof so as to impede its course or cause it to overflow or injure his land, or any right appurtenant thereto, or the pollution thereof so as to lessen its value to him, shall be a trespass upon his property." (Emphasis supplied.) * * *

Thus it is clear that under both court decisions and statutes, Georgia's law of riparian rights is a natural flow theory modified by a reasonable use provision. Kates, Georgia Water Law 1969, p. 63 (1969); Agnor, Riparian Rights in Georgia, 18 Ga. B. J. 401, 403 (1956). The reasons for the rule and its contradictory reasonable use provision were well stated by the court in Price v. High Shoals Mfg. Co., 132 Ga. 246, 248–249, 64 S.E. 87, 88 (1909): "Under a proper construction [of the pertinent Code sections], every riparian owner is entitled to a reasonable use of the water in the stream. *If the general rule that each riparian owner could not in any way interrupt or diminish the flow of the stream were strictly followed, the water would be of but little practical use to any proprietor, and the enforcement of such rule would deny, rather than grant, the use thereof.* Every riparian owner is entitled to a reasonable use of the water. Every such proprietor is also entitled to have the stream pass over his land according to its natural flow, subject to such disturbances, interruptions, and diminutions as may be necessary and unavoidable on account of the reasonable and proper use of it by other riparian proprietors. Riparian proprietors have a common right in the waters of the stream, and the necessities of the business of one can not be the standard of the rights of another, but each is entitled to a reasonable use of the water with respect to the rights of others." (Emphasis supplied.)

5. The facts in *Hendrick* involved raising the water level in the watercourse rather than diverting the water from the watercourse, but the court included diversion, albeit in dicta, in its discussion of riparian rights.

6. Whether a per se violation will authorize an injunction where water is in short supply, and the lower riparian is not using it, we do not here decide.

In this case, the trial court found that irrigation with modern equipment was a "diversion" which is entirely prohibited by Georgia law, Code secs. 85–1301, 105–1407, supra; i.e., the trial court found that irrigation with modern equipment constituted a trespass as a matter of law. We disagree. The use of water for agricultural purposes was recognized as a reasonable use along with domestic use in the first reported Georgia case on riparian rights. Hendrick v. Cook, supra. We realize, of course, that irrigation was not involved in that case. We also recognize that "There does not seem to be a Georgia case dealing with the consumption of water for irrigation. It is generally stated that a reasonable amount of water may be diverted for irrigation, under the general right of use for domestic and agricultural purposes." Agnor, supra, 405–406; Kates, supra, 35–36; see also 1 Clark, Waters and Water Rights 373, sec. 54.3(F); see also 45 Am.Jur.2d 951, 954, Irrigation, secs. 7, 14.

The first question, then, is whether the use of water for irrigation is a diversion under our laws and thus is prohibited. We find that it is not. When our riparian rights statutes were enacted, irrigation apparently was practiced only moderately here and in other "humid" states. Thus the General Assembly would not have contemplated prohibiting the use of water for irrigation in enacting these laws. This conclusion is buttressed by the absence of any litigation in Georgia on this topic. Additionally, the legislation largely tracks the case of Hendrick v. Cook, supra, and its progeny, and the court therein specified that a reasonable use of riparian water could be made for agricultural purposes. This use for agricultural purposes would have been primarily by some form of irrigation. * * *

2. * * * [T]he trial court also ruled that the uses at issue here were unreasonable as a matter of law. * * * [W]e do not find that the record supports the conclusion that the uses complained of were unreasonable as a matter of law. Whether the use of water for irrigation is reasonable or unreasonable presents a triable question. It was error to grant summary judgment to the plaintiffs.

3. In its detailed analysis of Georgia water law, the trial court had to apply Hendrix v. Roberts Marble Co., 175 Ga. 389, 394, 165 S.E. 223, 226 (1932), to the effect that " * * * riparian rights are appurtenant only to lands which actually touch on the watercourse, or through which it flows, and that a riparian owner or proprietor can not himself lawfully use or convey to another the right to use water flowing along or through his property * * * " Thus *Hendrix* held water could only be used on riparian lands.[9] Yet four years later, in reversing the denial of an injunction against the use of water on non-riparian land, the court did not rely heavily on *Hendrix*, supra. Instead the court (Russell, C.J., writing the opinion in both cases) based its decision more on general

9. It should be noted that the use of water in steam locomotives was a non-riparian use of that water unless the railroad right of way was considered riparian land wherever it went. See for example, Goodrich v. Georgia R. & Banking Co., supra, where such use apparently was approved.

riparian water law principles than on the non-riparian use. Robertson v. Arnold, 182 Ga. 664, 671, 186 S.E. 806 (1936). To the extent that Robertson v. Arnold might reflect ambivalence as to the rule announced in *Hendrix,* that concern is well-founded.

A major study of Georgia water law concluded that "Another disadvantage of this doctrine is that it permits the use of stream water only in connection with riparian land." Institute of Law and Government, University of Georgia Law School, A Study of the Riparian and Prior Appropriation Doctrines of Water Law (1955), p. 104. Likewise, the American Law Institute now recommends allowing use of water by riparian owners on non-riparian land, Restatement (Second) of Torts sec. 855, as well as allowing non-riparian owners to acquire a right to use water from riparian owners. Id., sec. 856(2), (see also 7 Clark, Waters and Water Rights 71–72, sec. 614.1 (1976)). The Restatement relies on two principles: that riparian rights are property rights and as such could normally be transferred, and that water law should be utilitarian and allow the best use of the water. Id., comment b. * * *

4. On remand, the issues must be tried in accordance with the foregoing decision, looking always to see if, insofar as injunctive relief is concerned, all uses of the creek and pond can be accommodated.[10]

Judgment reversed.

Notes and Questions

1. Georgia is one of several states that modified the common law of natural flow riparianism by statute, although the statute confirmed a change that had already been adopted judicially in Hendrick v. Cook, 4 Ga. 241 (1848).

2. In its discussion of the *Hendrick* case, the *Pyle* court, in footnote 6, suggested that the language that approves bringing a trespass damage action even absent proof of actual damage should not be viewed as applying to injunctive relief "where water is in short supply." The *Pyle* court declined to address that issue directly. Would it ever be sensible to issue an injunction against a water use that caused no actual damage? Under general equitable principles, no such injunction would issue because the party seeking the relief has not, and/or is not likely to suffer irreparable injury. What would be the relevance of the fact of water being in short supply? Possibly the court is hinting that the balance of equities (sometimes called balance of hardships) doctrine also would render injunctive relief inappropriate. If no actual harm is suffered by the one riparian, and the other is making a valuable use of a short supply, the latter use ought to prevail.

10. Kates, supra, 35–36; Oostanaula Mining Co. v. Miller, 145 Ga. 90, 88 S.E. 562 (1916). It would be inappropriate for us to undertake at this time to give other instructions as to how the case should be tried. However, lest the trial court feel that we have not provided sufficient guidance for such trial, we refer also the Rest. Torts 2d sec. 850A, p. 220. [The Restatement is reprinted infra p. 57 Eds.] While we cannot and do not here approve all that is said therein, we refer to it for whatever help it may be.

3. Is it surprising that the Georgia courts had never before been required to decide if irrigation was a reasonable use of water? Even in the East, irrigation of crops is a valuable (and increasing) agricultural technique, particularly irrigation devoted to ensuring an even supply of water to crops during periods of low rainfall.

4. Irrigation has been recognized expressly as a reasonable use in most riparian states. Even in those states where irrigation is a reasonable riparian use at law, the exercise of that right in context is still subject to review. The Wisconsin Supreme Court, in Omernick v. Department of Natural Resources, 71 Wis.2d 370, 238 N.W.2d 114 (1976), states the general rule:

> At common law, each riparian owner had the right, subject to the reasonable use doctrine, to use water from a natural waterway for the purpose of irrigating his lands. The reasonableness of the use depended upon the volume of water in the stream, seasons and climatic conditions and the needs of other riparian proprietors as well as the needs of the irrigator.[1]

5. *Pyle* also explores issues of the transferability of riparian rights. Evans, a defendant-appellant, owned no riparian land. That fact rendered it necessary for the court to consider whether water rights are appurtenant to the riparian tract. Prior Georgia law was ambivalent. The *Pyle* court adopts the Restatement (Second) of Torts view that water rights are not appurtenant to the riparian tract. Is this an important ruling? Does it affect cases raising different issues such as recreation?

6. After *Pyle* what will be the state of affairs in the market for transferring riparian rights separately from the riparian tract? As is evident from the ruling in favor of Evans, persons wishing to make use of waters can now seek to purchase water rights without the necessity of purchasing riparian lands. Riparian landowners can sell water rights without selling their lands and, thus, are in a position in which they need not alter their own use of their riparian land (or the water used on the riparian tract) in order to make a sale of water rights. Is there any incentive to refrain from selling water rights and the needed access for non-riparians to divert and convey the water to its intended situs of use?

———

California employs a unique water law system that melds riparian rights with the prior appropriation doctrine. The evolution of that dual system is studied at greater length in Chapter 4. A portion of the opinion that follows, however, provides a helpful introductory sketch. Although the case involves a conflict between an aggrieved riparian who asserts that an upstream use by an appropriator has infringed the downstream riparian right, the focus of the opinion is on the nature of the riparian

---

1. The case had an unusual twist. Under Wisconsin law, Omernick, in order to withdraw water for irrigation, was required to have a permit for the water use issued by the Wisconsin Department of Natural Resources (WDNR). By statute, however, the WDNR was required to refuse the permit if any other riparian objected, and a number of the other riparians filed objections. Omernick was left with a recognized usufructuary right, but without a legal means to exercise it because WDNR could not issue the requisite permit.

right rather than the legal basis upon which the interfering use is founded. The second major issue presented considers the impact on riparian rights of the 1928 amendment to the California Constitution that requires all uses of water be "reasonable and beneficial."

JOSLIN v. MARIN MUNICIPAL WATER DISTRICT

Supreme Court of California, 1967.
67 Cal.2d 132, 60 Cal.Rptr. 377, 429 P.2d 889.

SULLIVAN, Justice.

Plaintiffs, owners of lands riparian to Nicasio Creek in Marin County, appeal from a summary judgment for defendant entered in an action in inverse condemnation for damages resulting from defendant's construction of a dam across said creek at a point above plaintiffs' lands.

Plaintiffs' third amended complaint alleges that since March 1955 plaintiffs have been, and now are, the owners of a parcel of five acres of land; that a stream (Nicasio Creek) runs through their property; that the normal flow of the waters of the stream carried in suspension rock, sand and gravel which were deposited on plaintiffs' lands; that plaintiffs operated on their property a rock and gravel business in the course of which they sold and used the deposits of rock and gravel; that defendant is a municipal water district organized and existing under the Municipal Water District Act of 1911; that prior to May 1962 defendant constructed a dam across Nicasio Creek; that as a result the normal flow of waters in said stream was obstructed to such an extent that 'the normal and usual replenishment of rocks and gravel' upon plaintiffs' lands ceased; that the value of plaintiffs' lands was thereby diminished in the amount of $250,000, and that plaintiffs had been deprived of gravel and rock having an accrued value of $25,000 at the time of filing the complaint.

[Defendant moved for summary judgment. It argued that its use was pursuant to an appropriation permit for municipal supply purposes issued by the State Water Rights Board that allowed it to build a dam and divert water from Nicasio Creek. Defendant further argued] that defendant had no notice that plaintiffs claimed any right to use the waters of Nicasio Creek for the purposes stated in their complaint until plaintiffs' claim was presented to defendant on April 3, 1963; that plaintiffs' lands are approximately one mile downstream from defendant's dam with other riparian owners intervening; and that defendant did not physically enter upon or take by eminent domain any of plaintiffs' real property by constructing the dam or reservoir. * * *

The court granted defendant's motion for summary judgment "upon the ground there was no substantive right of plaintiffs violated by defendant."

With some variance in language the parties assert that the principal issue before us is whether defendant, an upstream appropriator of water, is liable in damages to plaintiffs, downstream riparian owners, by reason of having appropriated the waters of the creek under the above-mentioned circumstances. * * *

It was inevitable that the claims of appropriators and riparian owners would collide and that the legal principles upon which they were asserted would appear to be in conflict. Reconciling these principles, this court in the leading case of Lux v. Haggin, (1886) 69 Cal. 255, 10 P. 674, declared "that the rights of the riparian owners to the use of the waters of the abutting stream were paramount to the rights of any other persons thereto; that such rights were parcel of the land and that any diminution of the stream against the will of the riparian owner by other persons was an actionable injury. The question was settled by that case and the riparian right has never since been disputed." (Herminghaus v. Southern California Edison Co. (1926) 200 Cal. 81, 252 P. 607.) As a result the principle emerged that an upstream appropriator could not deprive a downstream riparian owner of his right to the use of the full flow of a stream, even though only a small percentage of the flow was utilized for the benefit the lands of the downstream riparian.

Thereafter, and in apparent response to the *Herminghaus* decision, the California Constitution was amended in 1928. (Art. XIV, § 3.)[5] The amendment was generally construed as applying a rule of reasonable use "to all water rights enjoyed or asserted in this state, whether the same be grounded on the riparian right or the right, analogous to the riparian right, of the overlying land owner, or the percolating water right, or the appropriative right." Thus the rule of reasonableness of use as a measure of the water right which had theretofore been applied as between other contesting claimants[6] but had been denied application as between

---

5. The amendment has not since been modified, altered or changed, and provides: "It is hereby declared that because of the conditions prevailing in this State the general welfare requires that the water resources of the State be put to beneficial use to the fullest extent of which they are capable, and that the waste or unreasonable use or unreasonable method of use of water be prevented, and that the conservation of such waters is to be exercised with a view to the reasonable and beneficial use thereof in the interest of the people and for the public welfare. The right to water or to the use or flow of water in or from any natural stream or water course in this State is and shall be limited to such water as shall be reasonably required for the beneficial use to be served, and such right does not and shall not extend to the waste or unreasonable use or unreasonable method of use or unreasonable method of diversion of water. Riparian rights in a stream or water course attach to, but to no more than so much of the flow thereof as may be required or used consistently with this section, for the purposes for which such lands are, or may be made adaptable, in view of such reasonable and

beneficial uses; provided, however, that nothing herein contained shall be construed as depriving any riparian owner of the reasonable use of water of the stream to which his land is riparian under reasonable methods of diversion and use, or of depriving any appropriator of water to which he is lawfully entitled. This section shall be self-executing, and the Legislature may also enact laws in the furtherance of the policy in this section contained." [In 1974, the section was renumbered and now appears unchanged at Article X, § 2—Eds.]

6. For example "as between riparian owners (Pabst v. Finmand, 190 Cal. 124, 211 P. 11); as between owners overlying an underground water supply (Katz v. Walkinshaw, 141 Cal. 116, 70 P. 663, 74 P. 766, 64 L.R.A. 236, 99 Am.St.Rep. 35); as between appropriators (Natoma W. & M. Co. v. Hancock, 101 Cal. 42, 31 P. 112, 35 P. 334); as between overlying owners and exporters from an underground basin to nonoverlying lands (Burr v. Maclay Rancho Water Co., 154 Cal. 428, 98 P. 260); and as between riparian owners and overlying owners under the doctrine of common source of sup-

riparian owners and appropriators was finally extended to include the latter. (Peabody v. City of Vallejo (1935) 2 Cal.2d 351, 367 40 P.2d 486). * * *

* * * It has been long and clearly settled in California that the effect of the passage of article XIV, section 3, "has been to modify the long-standing riparian doctrine * * * and to apply, by constitutional mandate the doctrine of reasonable use between riparian owners and appropriators, and between overlying owners and appropriators." (Tulare Irr. Dist. v.Lindsay–Strathmore Dist., supra, 3 Cal.2d 489, 524, 45 P.2d 972, 986.[7]) "The right to the waste of water is not now included in the riparian right." (Peabody v. City of Vallejo, supra, at p. 368, 40 P.2d at p. 492.) What is a reasonable use or method of use of water is a question of fact to be determined according to the circumstances in each particular case.

* * * [P]laintiffs have not shown how their claimed use of the stream in the instant case, when measured by the constitutional mandate, is a reasonable one. In essence their position is that such use is a beneficial one encompassed within their riparian rights and that all beneficial uses are reasonable uses. Such a position ignores rather than observes the constitutional mandate. Article XIV, section 3, does not equate "beneficial use" with "reasonable use." Indeed the amendment in plain terms emphasizes that water must be conserved in California "with a view to the reasonable *and* beneficial use thereof in the interest of the people," that the right to use water "shall be *limited* to such water as shall be *reasonably* required for the beneficial use to be served," and that riparian rights "attach to, but to *no more than so much of the flow*" as may be required "in view of such reasonable *and* beneficial uses." (Emphasis added.) (Cal.Const., art. XIV, § 3.) Thus the mere fact that a use may be beneficial to a riparian's lands is not sufficient if the use is not also reasonable within the meaning of section 3 of article XIV and, as indicated, plaintiffs' use must be deemed unreasonable. * * *

The judgment is affirmed.

Notes and Questions

1. In what way is Joslin's claim similar to that of the Gilberts? Both are dependent on a particular flow regime to effectuate their uses. In both cases the flow regime is being altered, at least in part, to support a non-

ply (Hudson v. Dailey, 156 Cal. 617, 105 P. 748); * * *." (Peabody v. City of Vallejo, supra, 2 Cal.2d 351, 367, 40 P.2d 486, 491.)

7. In Lindsay–Strathmore it was said: "Under this new doctrine, it is clear that when a riparian or overlying owner brings an action against an appropriator, it is no longer sufficient to find that the plaintiffs in such action are riparian or overlying owners, and, on the basis of such finding, issue the injunction. It is now necessary for the trial court to determine whether such owners, considering all the needs of those in the particular water field, are putting the waters to any reasonable beneficial uses, giving consideration to all factors involved, including reasonable methods of use and reasonable methods of diversion. From a consideration of such uses, the trial court must then determine whether there is a surplus in the water field subject to appropriation." (Tulare Irr. Dist. v. Lindsay–Strathmore Dist., supra, 3 Cal.2d 489, 524–525, 45 P.2d 972, 986.)

riparian use (i.e., municipal supply in *Joslin* and Evans' irrigation of a non-riparian parcel in Pyle v. Gilbert). Moreover, the competing use in both cases is a high quantity use having little or no return flow to the stream above the plaintiffs' riparian parcel. Is there any legitimate riparian expectation of an unchanged flow regime after the demise of the natural flow doctrine? Is there any certain protection at all after *Joslin*?

2. What aspects of the *Joslin* case are California-specific, and what aspects are applicable to any riparian jurisdiction? The fact that the alleged infringing use is made under an appropriation should not limit the cross-jurisdictional value of *Joslin* as a precedent, after all, the issue in pure riparian jurisdictions is the same: whether a use is reasonable under the circumstances. A somewhat more subtle question about cross-jurisdictional applicability is the role of the California constitutional provision in the decision. If the provision is used only to allow the break with older cases that had, in effect, granted legal protection to unreasonable uses, the precedent has force in helping courts in other jurisdictions determine what is reasonable. If, instead, the decision is seen as narrowly focused on the California Constitution and the phrase "reasonable and beneficial," the precedent is less readily transferrable.

3. The *Joslin* opinion foreshadows another major issue in water law, claims of takings of property in relation to legal evolution in the extent of allowable water rights. The court's opinion in commenting on Gin S. Chow v. City of Santa Barbara, 217 Cal. 673, 22 P.2d 5 (1933), freely admits, "that the [1928] constitutional amendment was adopted for the purpose of redefining water rights rather than merely of providing remedies for the invasion of such rights." Joslin, 429 P.2d at 897. Joslin's lawsuit sounded in inverse condemnation. Addressing that aspect of the case, the court quoted a passage from *Gin S. Chow*:

> There is a well recognized and established distinction between a "taking" or "damaging" for public use and the regulation of the use and enjoyment of a property right for the public benefit. The former falls within the realm of eminent domain, and the latter within the sphere of the police power. That the constitutional amendment now under consideration is a legitimate exercise of the police power of the state cannot be questioned. It is the highest and most solemn expression of the people of the state in behalf of the general welfare. * * * (T)he amendment purports only to regulate the use and enjoyment of a property right for the public benefit, for which reason the vested right theory cannot stand in the way of the operation of the amendment as a police measure. A vested right cannot be asserted against it because of conditions once obtaining. It has been long established that all property is held subject to the reasonable exercise of the police power and that constitutional provisions declaring that property shall not be taken without due process of law have no application in such cases.

22 P.2d at 16–17.

What in that passage, if anything, defends significant 'redefining' of riparian rights from being a taking of property rights? The solemnity and legitimacy of the constitutional process notwithstanding, those qualities do not address the substantive issue. The real force of the passage must be drawn from the reference to (1) 'conditions once obtaining' as insufficient to create vested entitlements and (2) the 'reasonable exercise' of the police power. Both of those ideas parallel closely the correlative nature of the rights created under reasonable use riparianism.

2. THE RESTATEMENT (SECOND) OF TORTS

The Restatement (Second) of Torts (1979) addresses the subject of "Interference with the Use of Water (Riparian Rights)." The principal features of the discussion are a series of definitions, followed by descriptions of the rules of liability for interference with use of a watercourse or lake, and rules of liability for interference with use of groundwater.[8]

In describing the general rules of reasonable use riparianism prevailing in the United States today, in its commentary the Restatement says, "There is, in its strictest application, no primary right in anyone to have the natural integrity of a stream or lake maintained for its own sake. The primary right of a riparian proprietor is to receive protection for his reasonable use of the stream or lake from an unreasonable use by another." Two of the Restatement's major provisions relating to riparian rights are set forth below.

Restatement (Second) of Torts (1979)

Section 850: Harm by One Riparian Proprietor to Another

A riparian proprietor is subject to liability for making an unreasonable use of the water of a watercourse or lake that causes harm to another riparian proprietor's reasonable use of water or his land.

Section 850A: Reasonableness of the Use of Water

The determination of the reasonableness of a use of water depends upon a consideration of the interests of the riparian proprietor making the use, of any riparian proprietor harmed by it and of society as a whole. Factors that affect the determination include the following:

(a) The purpose of the use,

(b) the suitability of the use to the watershed or lake,

(c) the economic value of the use,

(d) the social value of the use,

(e) the extent and amount of harm it causes,

(f) the practicality of avoiding the harm by adjusting the use or method of use of one proprietor or the other,

(g) the practicality of adjusting the quantity of water used by each proprietor,

---

8. A section discussing liability for pollution does so by relating pollution to the commission of other torts, to wit, trespass, nuisance, negligence and strict liability (abnormally dangerous activities).

(h) the protection of existing values of water uses, land, investments and enterprises, and

(i) the justice of requiring the user causing harm to bear the loss.

Notes and Questions

1. In illustrating section 850, an example is given of a country home-owner (A) making no use of the stream to which the parcel is riparian and an upstream co-riparian (B) who diverts the entire flow for irrigation so that A's parcel no longer obtains any of the amenity value of the stream. The value of the home is diminished. The illustration states "B is subject to liability to A." The "use" of A that receives legal protection is a passive use relating to the "natural integrity" of the riparian parcel rather than an instrumental use of the water itself. Does this belie the introductory comment that insists that the schema of riparian rights does not protect such interests? What is the proper measure of damage?

2. Is injunctive relief available? Section 850, comment b implies that an injunction will issue, noting that courts "have consistently required the defendant to leave a living stream on plaintiff's property or maintain an acceptable minimum water level in a lake." Why is a damage remedy inadequate?

3. Should the relative size of the riparian tracts involved be a factor in determining reasonableness? For example, can a riparian with minimal frontage make the same claims on a stream as a riparian with substantial frontage?

4. Drowning gophers by diverting the stream to flood the tract of land is given as an illustration of section 850A whereby an unreasonable riparian use fails in competition with an irrigation use. Is the example very helpful? While it no doubt portrays the easy case where an obviously unreasonable use is in competition with a reasonable use, the Restatement itself notes that the "typical case involves two riparians who are each making a beneficial use by suitable means and are each producing desirable values." § 850A cmt. a.

5. What guidance, if any, is provided for cases involving two competing uses that qualify as reasonable under the first four factors of section 850A? The remaining five factors come into play, with the initial stress on finding an accommodation of "as many reasonable riparian uses of a stream or lake as possible." § 850A cmt. a. The Michigan Court of Appeals recently reviewed Michigan law and found that it did not embrace the Restatement jot-for-jot, but instead applied "a reasonable use balancing test similar to the Restatement's rule." Michigan Citizens for Water Conservation v. Nestle Waters North America, Inc., 709 N.W.2d 174 (Mich. App. 2005).

The case is a highly controversial one in which riparians along a small stream fed by "spring water" sued for interference with their riparian rights caused by Nestle's pumping of the aquifer from which the spring is fed. The court approached the case under Restatement § 858 that describes unreasonable uses of groundwater. That section, however, adopts the § 850A factors as its test. In explaining why it adopted a balancing test the court said:

The Court in *Hart v. D'Agostini,* 7 Mich.App. 319, 321, 151 N.W.2d 826 (1967), observed, "[i]n our increasingly complex and crowded society, people of necessity interfere with each other to a greater or lesser extent." For this reason, the "right to [the] enjoyment of . . . water . . . cannot be stated in terms of an absolute right." Id. The reasonable use balancing test is best adapted to this reality. It recognizes that virtually every water use will have some adverse effect on the availability of this common resource. For this reason, it is not merely whether one suffers harm by his neighbor's water use, nor whether the quantity of water available is diminished, "but whether under all the circumstances of the case the use of the water by one is reasonable and consistent with a correspondent enjoyment of the right by the other." *Dumont v. Kellogg,* 29 Mich. 420, 423 (1874).

709 N.W.2d at 202. The appellate court upheld factual findings that Nestle's pumping had interfered with the rights of riparians on Dead Stream. It expressly found the plaintiffs' interests in "recreational, boating, wildlife observation, swimming, fishing, [and] aesthetic value" all to be reasonable uses under Michigan law. Similarly, looking especially at the economic benefits to the community, the court also found the pumping for bottled water to be a reasonable use, citing with favor Restatement (Second) of Torts § 850A cmt. f (1979). The court balanced the competing uses as follows:

While the balancing test is a case specific inquiry, there are three underlying principles that govern the process of balancing competing water uses. First, the law seeks to ensure a "fair participation" in the use of water for the greatest number of users. Hence, the balancing court should attempt to strike a proper balance between protecting the rights of the complaining party and preserving as many beneficial uses of the common resource as feasible under the circumstances. Second, the law will only protect a use that is itself reasonable. A plaintiff whose water use has little value or is excessive or harmful will be entitled to no protection. Third, the law will not address every harm, no matter how small, but rather will only redress unreasonable harms. Therefore, a plaintiff must be able to demonstrate, not only that the defendant's use of the water has interfered with the plaintiff's own reasonable use, but also that the interference was substantial.

[The court examined the three tests, frequently citing the Restatement factors and commentary, as well a factors noted in Michigan and other states' case law.] Although defendant should be permitted to have a "fair participation" in the common water resources of the area, if defendant is permitted to pump at the maximum permitted rate, it will effectively appropriate for its own needs approximately 24% of the base flow of the Dead Stream. This is more than a fair participation. While plaintiffs might properly be required to suffer some harm to their use of the Dead Stream, it would be unjust to permit defendant to shoulder plaintiffs with the entire burden of the harms created by the depletion of the Dead Stream's flow while retaining all the benefits. Furthermore, because defendant is in the best position to spread the costs incurred by a reduction in its use of the water from Sanctuary Springs, it is just that it should bear a greater portion of that burden. See Restatement, § 850A(i). Therefore, taking all of the above factors under consideration, we determine that defendant's proposed withdrawal of 400 gpm would be unreasonable under the circumstances.

709 N.W.2d at 202–207. The court found the record inadequate to set a level that fixed the right balance of interests and remanded, instructing the trial court "to determine what level of water extraction from Sanctuary Springs will provide defendant with a fair participation in the common water supply while maintaining an adequate supply for plaintiffs' water uses." The groundwater-surface water aspect of this case is addressed in Chapter 5. The Restatement approach applies the § 850A factors to both surface water and groundwater.

6.   Who should bear the costs of accommodation, assuming accommodation is possible? Is there any *a priori* reason that each user should bear his own costs? Consider, for example, a case like Mason v. Hoyle, supra p. 45. If the optimal conflict minimizing solution lay in increasing the reservoir capacity of the lower dams, is it clear that Hoyle, whose practices caused the lower dams to overflow by releasing periodic torrents of water, should not pay for any part of the improvements? Depending on the relative economic strength of the parties, the Restatement view seems to favor imposing the cost on Hoyle, "Later users with superior economic capacity should not be allowed to impose upon smaller water users costs that are beyond their economic reach or that will render their uses unprofitable." § 850A cmt. 2, illus. 6. Factors h and i are concerned solely with the problem of loss allocation in cases of irreconcilable conflict between competing reasonable uses. On what basis do they seek to allocate the loss?

7.   Is factor h a rule of priority? What sort of scenario is it apt to govern? Consider its application to the case of a long-time user of a mill seat in competition with an upper riparian who initiates a new and substantial irrigation use (or other use that is dependent on diversion of a substantial amount of the flow). Does this limited recognition of priority as a factor in resolving riparian disputes spur over-rapid development by riparians hoping to establish a use while dwindling supplies still remain? Does it stymie present and future development by locking in obsolete, but customary uses?

8.   In several of the section 850A illustrations, the Restatement places the costs of accommodation among reasonable uses on large, highly capitalized entities (such as electric companies and municipal water suppliers) who are (in the illustrations) putting the water to new uses. It seems to view the compensation issue in these cases as one to be governed by the "deep pocket" theory associated with the remedial goals of other branches of tort law, particularly that of reparations for personal injuries. Does importation of that theory to the riparian rights area demean the heritage of riparianism as a part of property law, a system of "rights"? Is it instead a reflection of the relative ability of those large entities to bear and spread the cost of accommodation.

9.   Is the need to assess which activity is causing the harm (factors e and i) a realistic undertaking? Mutually conflicting uses each cause harm to

the other in the cause-in-fact sense of the term. Does the causation inquiry permit a disingenuous application of the section 850A test that may mask the true basis for loss allocation?

10.   Consider the following hypothetical example. A, a lower riparian on a small, unusually pure stream, diverts the entire flow for beneficial irrigation. B, the *upstream* riparian owns a country home and enjoys the view.[1] Under section 850, A's use is not subject to liability because it is not unreasonable and causes no harm to B. A brewery that wishes to use one-half of the flow in the manufacture of its product is considering the purchase of B's parcel. How much will the brewer pay B for the purchase of his land? Will the amount be less than it would have been if A were not consuming the stream for irrigation? Will the brewer decide that A's interest so compromises the certainty that the water can be used to make beer, that the brewer will not purchase the parcel at all? What has happened to the value of B's riparian rights?

11.   The other major substantive riparianism sections of the Restatement are Section 855, "Nonriparian Uses by Riparian Proprietors," Section 856, "Harm by Riparian Proprietor to Nonriparian—Effect of Grants, Permits and Public Rights," and Section 857, "Harm by Nonriparian to Riparian Proprietor."

12.   The Restatement sums its own instrumentalist policies best in its Introductory Note to the topic of "Interference With The Use of Watercourses and Lakes by Use of the Water":

> By allocating the water to individuals who put it to use, private initiative is employed to increase the wealth of those individuals and the total wealth of society. By restricting its uses to those that are reasonable and beneficial, harmful and undesirable effects are minimized. By requiring users to share the resource and accommodate other users, successive and multiple uses are made possible. By giving security to water rights and protection to reasonable water uses, investments in water-resource development and enterprises dependent on water use are encouraged. By permitting grant and transfer of water rights, less valuable uses of water can be changed to higher and more beneficial uses through purchase by persons and entities for whom the water has greater value or productivity. By restricting water uses that interfere with public uses and have undesirable effects on the public at large, public rights are enforced and the public interest in environmental amenities may be promoted.

Is the product the equal of the promise? After studying prior appropriation law, compare the purposes of both systems and their success in achieving those purposes.

3.   SURFACE USAGE ON ARTIFICIALLY CREATED OR EN-LARGED WATERS

Legal definitions of artificial, as distinguished from natural, waters are usually stated in simple terms. For example, the Restatement of

---

1. The upstream position of the passive user in this case differentiates it from the hypothetical raised in the first Note and Question, where the relative positions of the passive and active users are reversed.

Torts states, "Artificial watercourses are waterways that owe their origin to acts of man, such as canals, drainage and irrigation ditches, aqueducts, flumes and the like." Likewise, Black's Law Dictionary simply defines artificial water courses as "formed by the work of man, such as a ditch or canal."

There are two common types of artificial waterbodies, lakes formed from dam and reservoir systems that enlarge the water surface of preexisting rivers or streams and excavations into which water flows by gravity or is introduced through human intervention.[2] Examples within everyday experience are so common that they are seldom noted. Dam and reservoir systems range from small millponds to the Hoover Dam and Lake Mead; excavations range from quarrying (and the formation of small pools often good for swimming), to retention ponds that are part of almost every commercial and subdivision development, to the Erie Canal. Especially in the modern era, as the possibility of recreational use of the water enhances the value of the adjacent lands, litigation has ensued.

The question arises, whether the ordinary rules of riparianism apply to artificially created waters. The conventional wisdom is that the normal rules of riparian rights do not attach to artificially created water bodies because the expectations of the abutting owners are not those of riparians along a natural watercourse.[3]

ANDERSON v. BELL

Supreme Court of Florida, 1983.
433 So.2d 1202.

ADKINS, JUSTICE.

* * * The facts which were stipulated to by counsel are as follows: The plaintiff below, Anderson, purchased a tract of land in 1965 from John Swisher. A small non-navigable creek traversed from north to south through the property. Anderson owned all lands contiguous to the creek, and it is not asserted that defendant had any interest in the water in its natural state. The plaintiff excavated the lowlands and constructed an earthen dam which resulted in a lake of substantial size. The construction, which began in 1966 or 1967, was completed in 1975.

As a result of the lake's creation, several parcels of land surrounding the lake were partially flooded. One of the flooded parcels was owned by

2. In many cases the water in these excavations is diverted from existing natural water courses. In some cases, the water is a combination of surface run-off and seepage of stored groundwater.

3. See, e.g., A. Dan Tarlock, Law of Water Rights and Resources § 3.08[1] at 3–23 (1988). Professor Tarlock also states, "However, because expectation is the basis for the denial of riparian rights in artificial bodies of water, it can also be the basis for recognition of rights in these waters; the particular character of the water body and circumstances surrounding its use may give rise to reasonable expectations. Thus, the simple rule that there are no riparian rights in artificial watercourses is often not a good guide to the results in the actual cases." Id. at 3–24.

Jessie Lewis and Madeline Watson who subsequently sold the tract to Sam Bell (defendant below). Prior to selling the land, Lewis and Watson brought an action against Anderson for damages incurred to their land as a result of the partial flooding. That action resulted in a settlement agreement whereby Lewis and Watson conveyed a flowage easement to Anderson in exchange for $10,000.

The easement, which describes the portion of land at issue, gives Anderson the right and privilege to flood the land, but expressly reserves title and beneficial use of the lands (except for the flowage rights) to the grantor. The easement also expressly reserves the grantee's right to discontinue the flowage at any time.

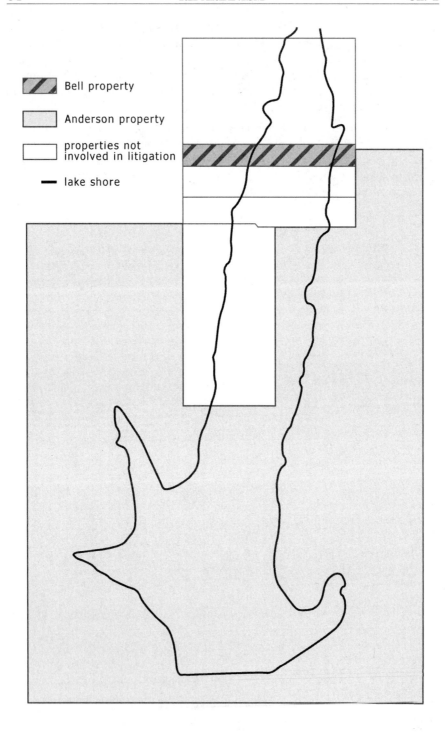

Bell property

Anderson property

properties not
involved in litigation

lake shore

Figure 2–1
Sketch of Bell's Land

The instant action was brought by Anderson against Sam Bell and two other individuals (who were guests of Bell's) to enjoin them from fishing and boating upon the surface waters that lie above the bottom land owned by Anderson.[a] Anderson does not contend, however, that Bell is precluded from using the lake surface above the land owned by Bell.

[A] scaled aerial photograph, which was stipulated as accurate by counsel, * * * reveals that the portion of bottom land owned by Bell appears to be over one acre. This amounts to only a small relative portion of the total lake area.

The trial court found for Bell, and refused to enjoin his use of the entire lake for fishing and boating. The first district affirmed, holding that there is no distinction between natural lakes and man-made lakes for purposes of determining the respective rights of adjoining landowners. They found that our decision in Duval v. Thomas, 114 So.2d 791 (Fla. 1959), was applicable in both cases, and that an adjoining landowner is entitled to the reasonable lawful use of the entire lake. * * *

For reasons that we will articulate, we now hold that the owner of property that lies adjacent to or beneath a man-made, non-navigable water body is not entitled to the beneficial use of the surface waters of the entire water body by sole virtue of the fact that he/she owns contiguous lands. * * *

Although this distinction is clearly marked in the decisional law and commentaries, the rationale for the dichotomy has not been clearly articulated. We believe, however, that sound policy reasons do exist which caution against the broad rule adopted by the district court in this case.

The first reason for this dichotomy pertains to a lake developer's expectations in his investment. Because the construction of a man-made water body often involves the expenditure of substantial sums of money and the expense is not, as a rule, divided proportionately among the various abutting owners, the individual making the expenditure is justified in expecting that superior privileges will inure to him in return for his investment. In contrast, the abutting owners to a natural water body probably invest proportionally equal amounts for the increased value of the water front property. While there are certainly exceptions to this general scenario, we believe that the district court's rule will more often result in an injustice, than in a correct decision.

The case *sub judice* presents the precise facts that demonstrate the injustice which would result from the approach taken by the lower court. Here Anderson expended substantial sums of money to improve his land; he also compensated the adjacent estate for damages and should be entitled to exercise exclusive dominion over the improvement.

a. Eds: The usual rule regarding use of the water surface by co-riparians bordering a natural lake is that each has the right to shared use of the entire surface area. This issue is discussed more fully at page 69.

The United States Supreme Court has recognized a distinction between public access to navigable waters and access to connected man-made alterations where substantial sums of money were expended to create the alteration. Kaiser Aetna v. United States, 444 U.S. 164 (1979). * * *

We note, further, that our holding today does not deprive the public of any right that they had previously possessed; therefore, our concern in *Duval* over the availability of lakes for tourism is not frustrated by this decision. Further, we believe a contrary rule may serve to dissuade Florida homeowners and investors from making improvements that not only increase property values but also aesthetically improve adjacent lands, since they would run the risk of losing some of their property rights to other people merely because the water body touches another's property. In the event that the water happens to take a course that would result in the flowage over public lands, the entire water body would become accessible to numerous piscators, bathers and boaters, thereby destroying the property owners' investment benefits. Under the district court decision, this would occur irrespective of whether or not reasonable compensation was paid by the developer to acquire the flowage easement.

Our apprehension in adopting the district court rule today is further based on our concern over the ramifications of such a broad rule and its effects in factual scenarios different from the case *sub judice*. Adherence to the district court's bright-line rule, in many situations, may lead to unjust results. One such consideration, as tailored to the facts in this case, would be the various riparian owners' rights to enjoin Anderson from reclaiming his land. If Bell has truly acquired "riparian rights" in the water, it seems apparent that these "rights" would include the right to enjoin Anderson from draining the lake. See Taylor v. Tampa Coal Co., 46 So.2d 392, 394 (Fla. 1950).

Another concern of ours involves the difficulty in limiting such a broad rule: Does an adjoining landowner to a drainage ditch have the right to follow the water surface and use all adjacent waters? Of equal concern would be the application of this rule to artificial alterations to water-courses. See generally Evans, Riparian Rights In Artificial Lakes And Streams, 16 Mo. L. Rev. 93 (1951). Although we need not answer the aforementioned questions, we remain cognizant of these hypotheticals in an effort to fashion a rule of law that will not result in untold horrors. Although we choose not to extend the *Duval* rule to man-made water bodies, this is not to say that rights to the beneficial use in these bodies cannot be acquired by other means. We believe that legal doctrines already in existence provide the flexibility necessary to achieve just results in a variety of factual contexts. See Farnham, Water Rights 2407.

In the first place, the respective parties are in a position to bargain for the rights obtained in the water body. These rights may be determined by express contract, such as covenants or easements. There was nothing to prevent Bell's predecessor in title from bargaining for an easement to use the water in exchange for the flowage right they granted to Anderson. However, the former owners chose to take monetary compensation for the "loss" of their property. When Bell took possession he did so with full knowledge that a flowage easement existed on the land, and with no reason to believe that the easement contract entitled him to a dominant tenancy with respect to the Anderson's property. In fact, the easement specifically states that Anderson has the exclusive right to discontinue the flowage if he so desires.

Further, we are concerned that a contrary rule would place the owners of adjacent land in an unequal bargaining position with respect to flowage rights sought by the person constructing the lake. Adjacent landowners would be in a position to set exorbitant prices for the flowage rights on their land knowing that they would receive full beneficial use of the lake irrespective of the price. This, we believe, may also frustrate the development of these waters, which is capital improvement we should not discourage.

We are aware that the ideal situation, where parties are able and willing to bargain for the respective rights in water bodies, does not always exist. There are, however, numerous legal doctrines that can be imposed to ascertain these rights without injustice. For example, in Walden v. Pines Lake Land Co., 126 N.J.Eq. 249, 8 A.2d 581 (N.J. 1939), the plaintiff had conveyed a flowage easement to the defendant who was constructing a dam to form a lake. The plaintiff also gave to defendant a pro-rata share of the cost of the dam. The court estopped the defendant from denying plaintiff from beneficially using the lake.

In another case, land adjoining an artificial lake was held in common ownership and was divided and sold to various purchasers, an implied easement was held to have been granted to the purchasers to use the lake and to prevent the defendant from draining the lake. Greisinger v. Klinhardt, 321 Mo. 186, 9 S.W.2d 978 (Mo. 1928). * * *

We hold today that an owner of lands that lie contiguous to or beneath a portion of a man-made lake has no right to the beneficial use of the entire lake merely by virtue of the fact of ownership of the land. Accordingly, we quash the decision of the district court of appeal and remand the cause to it with instructions to reverse the judgment of the trial court and remand with directions to issue the injunction requested by the plaintiff.

Notes and Questions

1. The *Anderson* opinion is the most thoughtful judicial exegesis of the law of recreational use of artificial lakes. Is its reasoning persuasive? Is it clear that purchasing a flowage easement from Bell's predecessor in interest establishes a presumption of an intention to withhold use of the entire surface? It appears that despite the existence of the easement, Anderson cannot exclude Bell from that portion of the surface overlying Bell's own land. Why is it so implausible that Bell should be able to enjoy the entire

surface if in so doing Bell's use does not unreasonably interfere with Anderson's use? What result would seem appropriate if no flowage easement had been purchased?

2. What motivates the court to decide in favor of Anderson? Is it a late twentieth century application of the same sort of instrumentalism that can be used to explain the developments of the nineteenth century? Arguably, for artificial waters, unlike natural waters, the utility maximizing principle requires rewards to the creators of the commodity. Human investment produces the artificial water and, like any other investment, the usual rules of property, not the special rules of riparianism, do more to protect and encourage persons to expend capital and/or labor to produce the good.

3. Is the court correct that its decision in this case promotes recreational development of artificial waters by reducing the bargaining power of the sellers of flowage easements? The owners of the newly flooded land retain the power to withhold a flowage easement and can therefore bargain over price in a way that satisfactorily compensates them for a lack of usufructuary rights. The assumption of cost shifting indulged by the court is likely to be accurate only when the developer has the power of condemnation, so that the price of the desired flowage easement will be set not by the affected landowner, but by a court. How close an analogy is this to the mill acts of the 19th century?

4. Does a rule that allows no riparian rights to parcels of land abutting an artificial lake create an unfair possibility of consumer surprise? Consider the scenario of remote purchasers of a retirement home in Florida who make no inquiry into their right to use the adjoining lake for recreational boating. Do these consumers need the protection of a favorable legal rule? Will lending institutions "protect" their borrowers by refusing to loan in the absence of express recreational use easements?

5. The issue of recreational use of artificial waters is by no means an issue that arises only in riparian jurisdictions. In Bijou Irr. Dist. v. Empire Club, 804 P.2d 175 (Colo. 1991), a similar issue was presented. There, the trial court denied an irrigation district a declaratory judgment that as holder of a flowage easement over defendants' lands and as holder of appropriative water rights to the water stored in the reservoir, it enjoyed an exclusive right to use the surface of the water for recreation. Prior Colorado precedents on the issue recognize the right of an owner of flowed lands to use the surface over those lands for recreational use as long as that use does not interfere with the rights of the holder of the flowage easement to do the same or to withdraw the water to be used for the purposes for which the water was appropriated. See Bergen Ditch & Reservoir Co. v. Barnes, 683 P.2d 365 (Colo. App. 1984). In *Bijou* the Colorado Supreme Court, in effect, found against both sides. It held that the irrigation district and the landowners were limited in their uses of the water by a federal law (Act of March 3, 1891, now codified at 43 U.S.C. § 946) under which the irrigation district had obtained rights of way for the project.

6. The creation of a unique jurisprudence for artificial waters appears to be a current trend among courts deciding the issue. In addition to the thoughtful discussion given to the problem in *Anderson,* in more conclusory opinions courts in Kentucky and Mississippi have

refused riparian rights to tracts made "riparian" by artificial increases in water level. See Rutledge v. Young, 646 S.W.2d 349 (Ky. App. 1982) and Black v. Williams, 417 So.2d 911 (Miss. 1982). Despite the modern trend, Richard Bartke and Susan Patton, in Water Based Recreation in Michigan—Problems of Developers, 25 Wayne L. Rev. 1005, 1009–10 (1979), urge that artificial waters should be treated identically with natural waters in regard to recreational use issues. They argue that adoption of the law of riparianism to resolve artificial waters recreational disputes would "apply a mature body of law to situations where conflicts exist over the access to and use of artificial waterbodies. Without the riparian doctrine the rights of those property owners abutting on artificial waterbodies are in legal limbo." A good summary of the governing legal principles that apply to surface use of artificial waters appears in James Corbridge, Surface Rights in Artificial Water Courses, 24 Nat. Resources J. 887 (1984). See also Jon Kusler, Artificial Lakes and Recreational Subdivision, 1971 Wis. L. Rev. 369.

7.   The extent of permissible surface usage by riparians on lakes, not only those whose levels are controlled by dams, is a topic fraught with considerable confusion and as to which jurisdiction-by-jurisdiction research is necessary to state accurately the governing rules. On artificial lakes, as in Anderson v. Bell, a different majority rule prevails— owners of the inundated lands, absent express contractual provisions, can use only the surface over their lands and are subject to use of that surface area by the dominant tenant. On larger natural lakes and rivers that are considered navigable under state law, the view is uniform that all riparians can use the entire surface. On state law non-navigable waters there is a split of jurisdictions, some follow the so-called 'civil law' view that on all natural lakes all riparians are deemed to enjoy the right to reasonably use the entire lake surface,[1] whereas others adhere to the so-called common law rule that traces to the '*ad coelum*' ownership rubric of ownership from the depths to the heavens in a column that includes the water surface. As noted earlier in the chapter, better reasoned newer cases seem to lean toward the civil law use of the entire surface while some of the contemporary common law rule cases conflate the artificial/natural waters distinction and the common law/civil law one. See, e.g., Ace Equipment Sales, Inc. v. Buccino, 273 Conn. 217, 869 A.2d 626 (2005).

8.   Does a dam owner have a common law duty to maintain the dam for the benefit of the artificial riparians? Can their reliance ripen into a prescriptive easement? See Kray v. Muggli, 84 Minn. 90, 86 N.W. 882 (1901). This issue is a bit of an artifact in light of the near-universal state regulation of dam operations now in place. The next case considers the respective riparian rights of littoral owners on a natural lake whose

---

1. "It is well established in Illinois that each owner of the bed of private non-navigable lake has the right to the reasonable use and enjoyment of the surface water of the entire lake." Hasselbring v. Lizzio, 332 Ill.App.3d 700, 704, 773 N.E.2d 770, 773–74 (2002) (quoting Beacham v. Lake Zurich Property Owner's Ass'n, 123 Ill.2d 227, 526 N.E.2d 154 (1988)).

level now is controlled by a dam and riparians on the river that flows from the lake's outlet.

4. MAINTAINING WATER LEVELS AND FLOWS

Dams, by their very nature, regulate water levels and water flows. In almost every case, dam operations are a potential conflict point because the dam's presence and its operations separate users of the larger resource complex into groups based on the effects of the dam's operations. Conflict over dam operations occurs in both large systems, such as the Missouri and Columbia Rivers,[2] and in small systems. Smaller dams, as in the case that follows, frequently generate conflict about environmental effects. The potential for conflict is widespread because in many Eastern states, where these small dams are most common, the annual hydrograph includes lower summer flows in the system at the time when demand is highest for both lake and stream recreation. Usually, the lakefront littoral owners want water retained in the lake in summer. That 'storage' causes a reduction in outflow at the time of year most likely to have more extreme downstream consequences because the system is already in a low flow stage due to smaller baseflow, higher summer evaporation, and lower precipitation. Add a touch of summer drought, or consumptive offstream uses such as irrigation, and the potential for conflict is complete.

The next case comes from a small basin and pits the interests of the lakeshore littoral owners against the riparians on the stream that carries the outflow from the lake. The case is decided by reference to a statute that regulates the dam and the riparian rights claim recedes into the background. In considering the case, ask in what respects, if any, the decision would be different under common law riparianism.

Michigan Compiled Laws Annotated
Chapter 324. Natural Resources and
Environmental Protection Act
Part 307. Inland Lake Levels

324.30701. Definitions

As used in this part: * * *

(d) "Dam" means an artificial barrier, structure, or facility, and appurtenant works, used to regulate or maintain the level of an inland lake.

(e) "Delegated authority" means the county drain commissioner or any other person designated by the county board to perform duties required under this part. * * *

---

2. The Missouri River disputes over management of the dams by the United States Army Corps of Engineers are a matter of intense conflict between the upstream and downstream states. See infra p. 838.

Columbia River hydropower dam operations have played havoc with anadromous fish spawning and migration, making dam management highly controversial.

(f) "Inland lake" means a natural or artificial lake, pond, impoundment, or a part of one of those bodies of water. * * *

(g) "Interested person" means the department [of Natural Resources] and a person who has a record interest in the title to, right of ingress to, or reversionary right to land that would be affected by a permanent change in the natural or normal level of an inland lake.

(h) "Normal level" means the level or levels of the water of an inland lake that provide the most benefit to the public; that best protect the public health, safety, and welfare; that best preserve the natural resources of the state; and that best preserve and protect the value of property around the lake. A normal level shall be measured and described as an elevation based on national geodetic vertical datum.

324.30707. * * * consideration of factors in determining normal level * * *

* * *

(4) In a determination of the normal level of an inland lake, the court shall consider all of the following:

(a) Past lake level records, including the ordinary high-water mark and seasonal fluctuations.

(b) The location of septic tanks, drain fields, sea walls, docks, and other pertinent physical features.

(c) Government surveys and reports.

(d) The hydrology of the watershed.

(e) Downstream flow requirements and impacts on downstream riparians.

(f) Fisheries and wildlife habitat protection and enhancement.

(g) Upstream drainage.

(h) Rights of riparians.

(i) Testimony and evidence offered by all interested persons.

(j) Other pertinent facts and circumstances.

(5) The court shall determine the normal level to be established and maintained, shall have continuing jurisdiction, and may provide for departure from the normal level as necessary to accomplish the purposes of this part. * * * The court may determine that the normal level shall vary seasonally.

GLEN LAKE–CRYSTAL RIVER WATERSHED RIPARIANS v. GLEN LAKE ASSOCIATION

Court of Appeals of Michigan, 2004.
264 Mich.App. 523, 695 N.W.2d 508.

BANDSTRA, J.

Defendant Glen Lake Association (GLA) appeals as of right the trial court order that modified the established normal level of Glen Lake under the inland lake levels part (ILLP) of the Natural Resources and Environmental Protection Act, MCL 324.30701 *et seq.* We conclude that the trial court had continuing jurisdiction to modify the lake level and that plaintiffs, private party riparian property owners, had standing to invoke that jurisdiction. Further, we do not conclude that the trial court's order was clearly erroneous on the merits and we affirm.

Glen Lake and the Crystal River are located in Leelanau County, immediately adjacent to the Sleeping Bear Dunes National Lakeshore. Water flows from Glen Lake over a dam into the Crystal River, which then meanders several miles before discharging into Lake Michigan. The dam controls the release of water from Glen Lake into the Crystal River. Therefore, any alterations in the height of the dam result in converse effects on the Glen Lake and Crystal River systems: increasing the height of the dam results in an increased height of Glen Lake, but a decreased instream flow for the Crystal River.

In the early 1940s, in response to concerns about erosion damage caused by high water levels in Glen Lake, the Leelanau County Board of Supervisors filed an action in the Leelanau Circuit Court under the statutory predecessor of the ILLP to determine the "natural height and level," now MCL 324.30702, of the water in Glen Lake. In 1945, the Leelanau Circuit Court entered an order setting the natural height and level of Glen Lake at 596.75 feet above sea level. * * * Since that time, the GLA has normally maintained the water level at or near 596.75 feet by inserting and removing dam boards. At various times of dry weather, the supervisory committee allowed the water level to drop below 596.75 feet to supplement flow to the Crystal River.

In 2000, the GLA contracted to have a new dam built to allow for more precise incremental control over the lake water level. In August 2001, plaintiffs, a small group of individual Crystal River riparian property owners and a canoe livery on the Crystal River, filed suit against the GLA, as the "delegated authority" to manage the dam. Plaintiffs also filed suit against Leelanau County. Plaintiffs sought to establish a new lake level, below the lake level set in 1945, to raise the height of the Crystal River. Plaintiffs alleged violations of the ILLP and the Michigan Environmental Protection Act (MEPA), MCL 324.1701 *et seq.* However, the trial court only addressed plaintiffs' petition for a modified lake level order, and the GLA challenges only that ruling on appeal. . . .

The GLA argues that the trial court erred in finding that the [1945] court-ordered lake level caused environmental harm to the Crystal River, and in entering a modified lake level order to remedy the damage caused by maintaining a lake level of 596.75 feet * * * We disagree. * * *

At trial, plaintiffs presented a management plan and regulation algorithms with the assistance of three expert consultants: Dr. Paul Moore, an associate professor in biology at Bowling Green State University, who was qualified as an expert in stream ecology; Dr. Roger Wallace, a professor in civil and environmental engineering at Michigan State University, who was qualified as an expert in hydraulics and hydrology; and Dr. Mark Luttenton, an associate professor of biology at Grand Valley State University and a research fellow with the Center for Integrated Limnology and Environmental Research at the University of Michigan, who was qualified as an expert in fresh water ecology, including limnology and stream ecology.

Dr. Moore visited the Crystal River on three separate occasions in August 2001, March 2002, and May 2002, during which he took photographs, field measurements, biological samples, and sediment samples. On the bases of his observations of the river and the organisms in the river, Dr. Moore determined that it was a benthic carbon driven river, meaning that "primary productivity" is generated by organisms living on the bottom of the river. Dr. Moore explained that it was important to determine where the primary productivity was occurring to "understand how flow is going to impact the system."

Dr. Moore identified three "critical habitats" within the river. First, because aquatic organisms need moist sediment, increasing the "wetted surface area" would result in more primary productivity. Second, the "emergent islands and microphytes," or reeds that have emerged out of the water, when wet, provide a larger surface area for increased marine algae growth, also resulting in more primary productivity. The emergent islands and microphytes also provide refuge to macroinvertebrates from predatory fish. Finally, fallen trees and debris, when submerged in water, provide areas where larval fish and minnows escape predation by waterfowl and fish.

Dr. Moore testified that on the basis of measurements taken from stream gauges, he was able to estimate the water levels necessary to maintain the key ecological functions of the river. Dr. Moore testified that a reading of 1.7 feet, which corresponded to a National Park Service (NPS) measurement at the same location, was a reasonable target level for the river, i.e., a water level at which the key ecological functions of the river could occur. Dr. Moore then extrapolated that 1.55 feet would be a level at which the key ecological functions of the river would be impaired, and 1.85 feet would be a high water level of the river at which the key ecological functions of the river would thrive.

Dr. Wallace then developed plaintiffs' regulation algorithms by incorporating consideration of the water level needs of the Crystal River and Glen Lake. Dr. Wallace explained that the water supply to the lake and the river came from precipitation minus evaporation. However, because of the historical practice of maintaining the court-ordered lake level by raising the dam, the river was doubly affected during periods of low precipitation. That is, not only would the river not receive water from precipitation, it also would not receive water from the lake, because the lake was being maintained at an artificially high level through the use of the dam. Dr. Wallace explained that the management plan was intended to "bring some balance back with the system more in line with the way it would be if it weren't so highly regulated [by using the dam to maintain the lake level set by the court in 1945]."

In developing plaintiffs' regulation algorithms, Dr. Wallace relied on the figures set out by Dr. Moore, i.e., 1.85 feet (normal), and 1.55 feet (low) for the water levels in the river. For the water levels in the lake, Dr. Wallace used the high water level for the lake that was set out in the pretrial stipulation, i.e., 596.90 feet above sea level. Dr. Wallace used the normal water level for the lake that was set out in the 1945 court order, i.e., 596.75 feet above sea level. Finally, Dr. Wallace determined the low level for the lake on the basis of historical data and a field analysis of lake ecology, i.e., 596.50 feet above sea level. The management plan explained that the algorithms "make decisions based on 3 index levels for Glen Lake and another 2 index levels for the Crystal River." Specifically,

> [t]he May algorithm focuses on how to raise the new control gates—this is equivalent to adding stop logs—to achieve summer lake levels while [e]nsuring adequate flow in the Crystal River during a biologically critical period of time. The June–August algorithm focuses on how to manage lake levels during the summer recreational season. The Fall–Winter algorithm provides guidance on how to drop the control surface at the end of the recreation season in order to prepare for the coming winter and spring.

Dr. Luttenton then testified regarding the potential effect plaintiffs' proposed regulation algorithm would have on Glen Lake, if implemented. Dr. Luttenton relied on a comprehensive study of Glen Lake by Dr. Timothy Keilty and determined that the primary potential effect of lowering the water level of Glen Lake would be on the fisheries and aquatic plant communities. In order to assess potential effects from a lower water level, Dr. Luttenton visited Glen Lake twice to develop a general impression of the lake in general and to confirm the information in the Keilty study. Dr. Luttenton assessed the basic characteristics of the lake and determined the habitat needs of the species of fish that inhabited the lake during each stage of their respective life cycles.

Dr. Luttenton testified that implementation of plaintiffs' regulation algorithm would not cause any problems for the species of fish that inhabited the lake. Indeed, Dr. Luttenton indicated that allowing the lake level to rise slightly in the spring would benefit two species at the egg stage in their life history. Dr. Luttenton testified that it was critical to maintain a high enough water level so that the fish could migrate out of wetland shore areas to deeper water during their transition from egg stage to juvenile stage. However, this typically happens by the end of June when the water levels are still high, and once migrated out, a drop in the water level of the lake would not affect the fish. Dr. Luttenton concluded that a drop in the water level of the lake three inches below the court-ordered level, as provided in the regulation algorithm, would result in shoreline exposure, but would not cause any detectable problems for the fish in Glen Lake.

The GLA presented a management plan and regulation algorithm with the assistance of Anthony Groves, a water resources director in the civil engineering division of Progressive Architecture and Engineering, who was qualified as an expert in limnology. On the basis of his computation of the long-term average water level of Glen Lake at 596.75 feet, Groves concluded:

> Maintaining a level above 596.75 feet in Glen Lake will exacerbate the potential for shoreline damage during periods of above-normal precipitation and high water. There appears to be a significant potential for erosion, and damage to shoreline structures and septic systems if a water level above 596.75 persists on Glen Lake. Conversely, maintaining a level significantly below 596.75 feet will create the potential for navigational difficulties in the lake during periods of below-normal precipitation and low water. It is important to note that lowering the water level of Glen Lake by only two or three inches could expose several feet of bottomland along the lake shoreline. Further, lowering the lake level would allow additional sunlight penetration to the lake bottom and expand the photic zone in which submersed aquatic plants can colonize.
>
> Maintaining a minimum flow of 18 cfs [cubic feet per second][a] in the Crystal River during the summer months will sustain a river stage of about 1 foot and a wetted perimeter of about 37 feet in the first straight river stretch below the dam. This minimum flow appears sufficient to protect and sustain the biological integrity of the Crystal River system.

Groves then recommended that no departure be made from the court-ordered lake water level of 596.75 feet, except during drought conditions during summer months. Groves proposed that to alleviate the potential for hardship to the Crystal River as the result of diminished outflow during the summer months, Glen Lake be temporarily lowered to a level not below 596.60 feet until the flow in the river equals or exceeds 18 cfs.

The trial court issued its decision and order, modifying the existing court-ordered lake level and adopting the regulation algorithms proposed

a. See Note 6 following the case for additional data regarding the flows in the   Crystal River system—Eds.

by plaintiffs. The trial court made the following findings of fact and conclusions of law:

The effects of low water on the river were discussed by a number of experts. Not surprisingly, they include damage to the fish population and rooted aquatic plant communities as well as loss of primary productivity in the river. Additional impacts are felt by the river's mussel and clam populations, its communities of benthic insects and a deleterious impact on other aquatic plants and animal communities. There are also harmful increases in water temperature. Naturally, reductions in flow also impair navigability which impacts the recreational public, including but not limited to visitors to the national lakeshore. Riparian owners along the river are also impacted by reduced navigability, impacts on the river's biology as well as loss of scenic and property values.

Recognizing a long tradition of balancing the needs of the lake and the river and mitigating the harm associated with erosion from high water on Glen Lake, the Court finds it necessary to institute a modified lake level order with regulation algorithms that will provide a more precise mechanism for managing the lake level and sharing the environmental burden of drought.

A key finding by this Court is that the Crystal River is not merely a tool used to maintain Glen Lake's water level. Rather, it is a viable part of the watershed, and, the management of Glen Lake's water level must be done so as to minimize environmental consequences to both the lake and the river.

* * * The focus of this Court's efforts are environmental and recreational. The Court is not motivated to maximize income to commercial canoe liveries or minimize the length of docks. There are a number of well-established criteria that must play a role in the determination of a lake level and in any subsequent determinations to modify it. These factors would certainly include a consideration of past lake level records and the normal seasonal fluctuations of lake level. In this process, ordinary high and low water marks have been determined and evaluated. Both the lake and the river have been the subject of substantial development. It is important in determining the levels of each that a consideration be given to septic tanks, drain fields, sea walls, docks and other physical features. . . .

There is a clearly established relationship between the lake and the river. The river provides upstream drainage from the lake and the stream has its own downstream flow requirements and impacts on downstream riparians. Property owners generally understand this relationship and historically managed the lake level with respect for it. Property owners on the lake and the river have well-recognized riparian rights which include but are not limited to recreational use of the surface waters, fishing and protection of wildlife habitat.

The trial court determined that plaintiffs presented more detailed and comprehensive evidence on the potential effect that modifying the lake level order might have on Glen Lake and the Crystal River and that the testimony of the GLA's lake expert was less convincing. The trial court considered the factors set out in MCL 324.30707(4), and properly entered a modified lake level order setting the "normal level" of the lake to "provide the most benefit to the public; best protect the public health, safety, and welfare; best preserve the natural resources of the state; and best preserve and protect the value of property around the lake." MCL 324.30701(h). The trial court's decision to adopt plaintiffs' regulation algorithms and management plan was supported by the evidence, and we find no clear error.

Notes and Questions

1. Glen Lake and the Crystal River are natural features where a dam has been introduced to regulate the system, presumably to mimic 'normal conditions' even in years of high or low precipitation. Although there may be good reasons to analyze artificial lakes and natural lakes differently in regard to lake surface usage by littoral/riparian owners, is there any reason to differentiate between dam operations on a natural lake and dam operations on an artificial lake when the complainant is the streamside riparian below the dam who claims injury as a result of the way the dam is being operated?

2. This case is decided on the basis of the governing statute. Not all states have statutes regulating dams, and most are more general. For example, the Wisconsin law provides that its administrative agency should regulate water levels 'in the interest of public rights in navigable waters or to promote safety and protect life, health and property * * *.' Wisc. Stat. Ann. § 31.02(1). Although the Michigan list of factors to be considered under section 324.30707(4) is quite extensive, it sets no hierarchy among those factors. As a practical matter, what does that mean for potential litigants? Does the presence of so many factors invite the possibility that the judge may stress one or another and thereby make the outcome somewhat unpredictable? In that light, the statute seems similar to the open-ended nature of the common law of riparianism. A conscientious judge is likely to rely heavily on expert testimony concerning the effects of proposed lake level management plans. That appears to be what happened in *Glen Lake* and the plaintiffs' experts were more convincing. In a far higher profile case from the same general part of Michigan, Michigan Citizens for Water Conservation v. Nestle Waters North America, discussed supra p. 58, very similar reliance on expert testimony about environmental impacts was pivotal in demonstrating an interference with riparian rights caused by a groundwater pumper whose pumping significantly reduced base streamflow by 24% in a small connecting waterway named Dead Stream. The 'significance' of the impacts, on a grand scale in both cases was not great, but within the system in Dead Stream, as

in Glen Lake/Crystal River, even small alterations in flow change the ecology and affect the ability of the riparians to enjoy the full use of their parcel.

3. Is it fair to criticize the law (whether a statute like section 324.30707(4) or common law riparianism) for demanding extensive modeling and competing expert testimony as the basis for resolving every altered streamflow case? In the Glen Lake setting, for example, the plaintiffs spent $110,000 on lawyers, experts, costs, and sampling, the defendants approximately three times that much, and the United States Park Service spent $252,000 on its three-year study of hydraulics, hydrology, and stream ecology. Looking at the costs and the small scale impacts, one partisan is rumored to have described both the *Glen Lake* and *Nestle* cases as 'Much Ado About Nothing.' Even if sound science is expensive, what other non-arbitrary basis for decision is available? It is important to remember that even in small systems, upstream-downstream conflicts affect littoral and riparian concerns that frequently touch upon a principal reason the property owners located there.

4. The Michigan statute in this case predates the passage of a state-level administrative procedure act. That may explain why the statute relies so heavily on the judiciary in setting and adjusting lake levels. Could greater reliance on an expert agency, vesting primary jurisdiction in the agency, allowing only deferential judicial review, etc., reduce cost and increase predictability in these disputes? Presumably, many of the same issues would be fought out in the agency, with an equal need for experts and costly studies. Agency rulings would be subject to judicial review, albeit deferential. Once an agency-set level is established, should it enjoy a presumption of continuing correctness as conditions in the basin change?

In the similar context of new development, developers try to enhance their projects with water-linked amenities, or provide their prospective purchasers with water supply by pumping surficial aquifers to which many small lakes and streams are linked. Predictably, these types of development are generating a number of small-scale water use conflicts. In some jurisdictions, regulatory burdens are being placed on the developers to show that their new uses do not affect the status quo. The burdens most often take one of two forms, obtaining a dam permit, or showing that a new development has an assured supply of water to meet its needs without interfering with the water rights and uses of others.

5. The Glen Lake–Crystal River system occupies the western part of the Leelanau Peninsula. This small drainage basin is dominated by Big Glen and Little Glen Lakes which together cover roughly 9,000 acres, about one-third of the entire basin.[1] Is it surprising that the physical management plans of the plaintiffs and defendants in *Glen Lake* seem to be so little different than one another, or that the argument seems to be about a few inches of lake level or river level? Topography is vitally important, and riparian impacts of slight changes in water levels are magnified in a relatively flat landscape like that involved on the *Glen Lake* case. On Glen Lake, a few inches down would considerably affect lake size and the accessibility of parts of the lake that have shallow spots separating them

1. For an interactive map and many details about the Glen Lake area, see http://www.leelanau.cc.

from the center of the lake. A few inches rise in water level coupled with a good wind might inundate near-lake septic fields with bad consequences for water quality. Scale and topography also affect the river. That same few inch difference in lake level proposed by the competing plans of plaintiff and defendant, when converted to flow in the Crystal River, translates to at least a 40% reduction in the river's flow.

6. As an experiment in getting comfortable with imagining what is meant by volume and flow measures, try to calculate the relationship between lake level and flow in the outlet stream. The parties in *Glen Lake* are fighting about retaining an extra 6 inches of water in Glen Lake rather than letting it flow out into the Crystal River over a four month period. To get a good feel for the comparative effect on flow of lowering the lake level requires a measure of what the flow is without the added water. For many systems, reliable data about the flows in the system is available from the United States Geological Survey (USGS). As of this writing, only a single year of streamflow data for the Crystal River is available from the USGS, see, http://waterdata.usgs.gov/nwis (then select surface water, streamflow, site number 04126802 Crystal River as partial name). For the period given that included Summer 2004, a relatively wet summer (using comparative USGS data from nearby watersheds for which more history was available), the average flow of the Crystal River in cfs dropped from a March high of 81.0 cfs to 64.1, 47.9, 56.5, 32.1, 35.0, in the May through August time frame (120 days). A low rainfall year would have less water entering the system and maintaining the lake level using smaller inputs would require discharging far less water at the dam. Next, refer back to the Table that appeared supra p. 25. Changes in water level in the lake can be equated with volumes of water, which in turn can be equated with flows in cfs over a period of time—e.g. 1 cfs flow = something very close to 2 acre-feet per day. So 6 inches of depth on an 9.000 acre lake, is 4,500 a.f. of water. If that water is discharged evenly over a 120–day period, the average flow needed to discharge it would be 18.75 cfs. Under those circumstances, lowering the lake level would make a huge impact on Crystal River flows, almost 20 cfs per day throughout the summer for a six inch drop in lake level. Recalling that the flows noted are wet-year flows, in a dry year the change in dam operations would account for more than half the summer flow of the Crystal River.

7. By now, it should be a familiar principle that the downstream proprietor under the reasonable use riparianism has no vested right to receive a particular amount of flow. How do plaintiffs translate the reduced flow into a claim that the upstream use is unreasonable and that injunctive relief is warranted? A key finding in this case for the plaintiffs was that the riparian zone of the downstream portion of the Crystal River was itself a resource of importance. Another powerful piece of evidence was a series of comparative photographs that gave unmistakable clarity that the ecological effects that the plaintiffs' experts were describing were, if anything, less than what might be expected. Selected photos utilized by plaintiff can be found at www.lcwr4.org.

D. MUNICIPAL WATER SUPPLY IN RIPARIAN JURISDICTIONS

Municipal water supply cases frequently spark controversial political questions. When the supply effort involves the transfer of large amounts of water from one basin to another, a host of policy issues come to the fore. Residents of the area of origin view the water as a local resource and object that the importing city has no legitimate claim to its use. They assert that the water is the underpinning of present and future economic well-being for their region and object to the transfer on that basis. Adding to the objections, the environmental costs of most water transfers are borne disproportionately by the area of origin. Running streams and fertile land in river valleys are submerged under reservoirs; canal and pipeline systems disrupt wildlife habitat and interfere with local amenity values. How these interests should be balanced with the need of cities for water is sometimes addressed legislatively, either through general authorizations to all cities, or ad hoc approvals for particular projects. The issues that surround the dispute between areas of origin and importing areas are studied later at page 234.

Even when only local water supplies are involved, municipal supply claims may cause friction among several constituencies. For example, as seen in the *Hudson River Fishermen's Association* case that follows, destruction of fisheries may be a part of the price of a water supply proposal. Likewise, the quality demands of municipal water supply reservoirs may lead to limitations on waterside development, thereby frustrating developmental aspirations of riparians.

The materials in this section attempt to survey the subject by first looking at the use of eminent domain to secure surface water for municipal use and then devoting attention to the policy issues that attend municipal supply decisions. In focusing on policy, the materials will start by reviewing the operation of New York's laws that govern municipal water supplies before turning to interbasin diversion issues, using the case of Virginia Beach, Virginia as the principal example.

1. USING EMINENT DOMAIN TO SECURE MUNICIPAL WA-TER SUPPLIES

Municipal water use needs are different in kind from those of most other water users. In serving concentrated populations, municipal water providers often must meet the domestic water and sewerage needs of large numbers of people as well as the important water needs of industry and commerce. Beyond conventional water supply needs, municipal sewerage puts demands on the receiving body to assimilate and transport wastes.

The common law of riparianism makes no special provision for municipal water use. Applying the reasonable use doctrine to a munici-pal user in the absence of special accommodation makes meeting munici-pal needs difficult indeed. Consider a municipality that owns a riparian tract on a relatively small stream from which it seeks to draw its supply or into which it seeks to discharge its waste. If no allowance is made for the public character of the uses of the municipal riparian, its withdrawal of large amounts of water to serve the domestic needs of its citizens might be enjoined as unreasonable. Likely, the municipal use would interfere with the (oft-times less important) uses of co-riparians, such as irrigation of fields, or the powering of mills. In states that hold off-tract uses per se unreasonable, the city, in using water to serve non-riparian tracts within its jurisdiction, would be enjoined routinely in the event of any interference with reasonable on-tract uses of co-riparians. Even the preferred status of domestic users does not aid the municipal supplier. Quite logically, the law considers the municipality (not its non-riparian domestic supply customers) to be the riparian when it withdraws water for municipal supply. The fact that some of those served might, in their own right, hold a preference for domestic uses is not relevant in determining municipal rights.

A representative statement of the law appears in Town of Purcellville v. Potts, 179 Va. 514, 19 S.E.2d 700 (1942), which, quoting from an earlier case said:

> It has been held with practical unanimity that a municipal corporation, in its construction and operation of a water supply system, by which it impounds the water of a private stream and distributes such water to its inhabitants, receiving compensation therefor, is not in the exercise of the traditional "right of a riparian owner to make a reasonable domestic use of the water without accountability to other riparian owners who may be injured by its diversion or diminution. The use of the waters of a stream to supply the inhabitants of a municipality with water for domestic purposes is not a riparian right." 67 C.J. 1120. * * * "A municipal corporation will be liable for diverting the waters of a stream or water course and depriving lower riparian owners of the use thereof." McQuillin, Municipal Corporations, Vol. 6, pp. 1251, 1252.

In *Potts,* the court went on to enjoin the town when its municipal supply diversions deprived a co-riparian farmer of accustomed opportunities to let his cattle drink from the affected stream. The court allowed the city time to commence condemnation proceedings against Potts before the injunction took effect.

By far, the most common provision for overcoming the problems of standard riparian doctrine as a means of assuring adequate municipal water is to clothe the municipal supplier with the power of eminent domain. This longstanding power is universally enjoyed and regularly employed by municipalities. See generally 2A Nichols on Eminent Domain § 7.39; 11 Eugene McQuillin, Municipal Corporations § 32.63. The power of condemnation of a municipality is derived from the state, usually via enabling legislation or a "home rule" provision. Enabling legislation will in most cases indicate whether the power to condemn is territorially limited to property within the municipality. If the power is limited in that way, lands lying outside of the municipality cannot be condemned, without special authorization. See 1A Nichols on Eminent Domain § 3.221[3], at 3–125; Wilbert Zeigler, Acquisition and Protection of Water Supplies by Municipalities, 57 Mich. L. Rev. 349, 352–56 (1959).

The condemnors need not take the entire parcel, they only condemn affected portions of the water rights of competing riparians in the targeted source of supply. At times, when a large project is involved, initiating condemnation proceedings against a large class of landholders will be difficult. See, e.g., Schroeder v. City of New York, 371 U.S. 208 (1962) (due process of law required more than mere posting on property as notice of condemnation proceeding).

For the most part, condemned riparians have no means to defeat the condemnation; the price to be paid is usually the most hotly contested issue. Meeting the domestic needs of inhabitants is universally viewed as a public use. The legal issues that arise in this context are, in general, quite tame ones that are addressed by the law of eminent domain rather than by distinctive water law doctrines. For example, local law and practice will determine the territorial extent of the condemnor's authority. The lawful exercise of the power of eminent domain requires that the property be taken only for public use. On the issue of public use, precedents from non-water rights eminent domain cases are relevant in determining if the water rights are being taken for a public use. The few cases that municipalities have lost occur when the water will be used by private firms located outside of the municipal boundaries.[1] See, e.g., Burger v. Beatrice, 181 Neb. 213, 147 N.W.2d 784 (1967). See also Richard Harnsberger, Eminent Domain and Water Law, 48 Neb. L. Rev. 325, 367–68 (1969).

2. CONTROLLING CONDEMNATION OF MUNICIPAL WATER SUPPLIES

New York Environmental Conservation Law Title 15—Water Supply

Section 15–0105

* * *

5. The acquisition, storage, diversion and use of water for domestic and municipal purposes shall have priority over all other purposes * * *.

Section 15–1501

Except as otherwise provided in this title, no person or public corporation who is authorized and engaged in, or proposing to engage in, the acquisition, conservation, development, use and distribution of water for potable purposes * * * shall have any power to do the following until

---

1. So narrow a concept of public use seems to be a bit anachronistic. That view is not required by the due process clause of the federal constitution, see, e.g., Berman v. Parker, 348 U.S. 26 (1954), although individual states can and sometimes do take a narrower view of what is a public use. Professor Tarlock suggests that the "public use" litmus in these cases is whether taking water to supply private non-domestic needs is merely incidental to the larger task of supplying domestic needs. The domestic needs preference in the law of riparianism is invoked to establish that portion of the municipal supply effort as a public use. See A. Dan Tarlock, Law of Water Rights and Resources § 3.12[3][b], at 3–61 to 3–62 (1988).

such person or public corporation has first obtained a permit from the department [of Environmental Conservation] pursuant to this title:

   a. To acquire or take a water supply or an additional water supply from an existing approved source; or

   b. To take or condemn lands for any new or additional sources of water supply or for the utilization of such supplies * * *.

Section 15–1503

* * *

   2. In making the decision to grant or deny a permit or to grant a permit with conditions, the department [of Environmental Conservation] shall determine whether the proposed project is justified by the public necessity, whether it takes proper consideration of other sources of supply that are or may become available, * * * whether the supply will be adequate, whether there will be proper protection of the supply and watershed or whether there will be proper treatment of any additional supply, whether the project is just and equitable to all affected municipalities and their inhabitants and in particular with regard to their present and future needs for sources of water supply, whether there is provision for fair and equitable determinations of and payments of any direct and indirect legal damages to persons or property that will result from the acquisition of any lands in connection with the proposed project or from the execution of the proposed project, and whether the applicant has developed and implemented a water conservation program in accordance with local water resource needs and conditions. * * *

Questions

   Are the criteria for determining whether to issue a permit sufficiently clear? Is the proper application of the criteria to a real-world case likely to be easy? Under standard principles of administrative law, an agency decision to issue (or deny) a permit is reviewable in court, but the standard of review is deferential. Is it appropriate to entrust these determinations to an administrative agency? Reconsider these matters after reading the case that follows.

HUDSON RIVER FISHERMAN'S ASSOCIATION v. WILLIAMS

New York Supreme Court, Appellate Division, 1988.
139 A.D.2d 234, 531 N.Y.S.2d 379.

YESAWICH, J.

   Respondent Spring Valley Water Company, Inc. (hereinafter Spring Valley) provides water for approximately 88% of the residents of petitioner Rockland County and various industrial users from four major sources: (1) 57 wells, (2) the Lake De Forest Reservoir and Filter Plant, (3) the Ramapo Valley Well Field, and (4) the Stony Point Reservoir and Filter Plant. In 1979, Spring Valley submitted a water supply application to respondent Department of Environmental Conservation (hereinafter

DEC) for permission to construct an additional water source named the Ambrey Pond project on a 364–acre site near the Town of Stony Point, Rockland County, including a reservoir with a nearly two-billion gallon capacity, a filtration plant, and a diversion pipeline to bring water to the reservoir from a nearby brook; acquisition of land to construct the reservoir and filtration plant is contemplated by the first stage of this multistage undertaking. The project, capable of adding a dependable yield of approximately 7.5 million gallons per day (mgd) to the utility's water distribution capacity, was sought to meet three perceived needs: (1) a present water supply deficit in the Haverstraw–Stony Point area of the Spring Valley system that is currently being met with releases of water from Lake Tiorati, pursuant to an agreement with the Palisades Interstate Park Commission, a circumstance which is not expected to continue, and by pumping water from lower elevations in the system at a substantial cost; (2) an anticipated inability to meet peak demand[1] throughout the system in the short-term future; and (3) a projected system-wide inability to meet average demand[2] further into the future. A primary factor requiring a new supply is the growth of Rockland County's population, though other factors include the contamination of six wells, the antiquation of the Stony Point treatment facility, the unavailability of water from the Ramapo Valley Well Field during periods of drought, and the aforementioned loss of water supply from Lake Tiorati.

During the course of extensive hearings, the inevitability of the need for an additional water supply became obvious; there was, however, a great deal of disagreement as to when this need would become manifest. The inherent uncertainty in determining precisely when the project would be necessary prompted Spring Valley and the Department of Public Service, which had expressed interest in increasing the peaking capacity of Spring Valley's system, to suggest that a "trigger mechanism" tying the date of the project's implementation to the demand for water be utilized. So that preliminary steps could be taken without authorizing premature construction and yet avoid a redundant new hearing which might perilously delay development of the proposed water supply, respondent Commissioner of Environmental Conservation (hereinafter the Commissioner) approved the project but "triggered" issuance of construction permits upon Spring Valley's experiencing an average demand of 27.9 mgd for two consecutive years. Although Spring Valley expects to reach its maximum peak demand capacity well before it approaches the limit of its average demand capacity, the "trigger mechanism" was linked to the average demand because it more accurately reflects the relatively smooth trend of increased demand than the erratic peak demand which is heavily influenced by such vagaries as the weather. The point at which Spring Valley's current peak demand capacity would be exhausted was approximated by divining an appropri-

1. "Peak demand" is the largest volume of water that is necessary in a single day during a year to meet both metered water use and unaccounted for water.

2. "Average demand" is the yearly amount of water pumped into the distribution system divided by the number of days in the year.

ate ratio between average and peak demands to determine at which average demand level the peak demand capacity would be exhausted; that average demand figure was then adjusted downwards to allow for the 3 to 4 years' construction time required for the project. A regrettable and apparently inescapable consequence of the Ambrey Pond project is the likely destruction of a major naturally reproducing trout population due to the diversion of most of the flow from Rockland County's best trout stream into the Ambrey Pond Reservoir.

Following adoption of the Administrative Law Judge's conditional approval of the Ambrey Pond project by the Commissioner, petitioners * * * challenged the Commissioner's determination as arbitrary and capricious, as an unlawful delegation of legislative authority to a private utility, and as being violative of the State Environmental Quality Review Act (hereinafter SEQRA) (ECL art. 8). * * *

Petitioners argue initially that Spring Valley failed to demonstrate the "public necessity" which ECL 15–1503(2) requires as a precondition to construction of a water supply project. Citing Matter of Country Knolls Water Works v. Reid, 52 A.D.2d 284, 383 N.Y.S.2d 661, they assert that because Spring Valley concedes that it does not have a present need for which the proposed source will be developed in the "immediate future," the application should have been denied. This argument is flawed in several respects. First, ECL 15–1503(2) authorizes the granting of permits based on a number of factors including "future needs for sources of water supply." It is also important to note the posture of the *Country Knolls* case. There we held that the DEC could deny a permit because a present need was not sufficiently shown; we did not concomitantly hold that the DEC must wait for the need to become dire and then only issue permits belatedly. Second, aside from the present water supply deficit in the Haverstraw–Stony Point area, there is substantial evidence of an unavoidable, if not imminent, necessity for greater peak demand capacity. Third, the trigger mechanism itself insures that the construction permits will not be issued until the need for an expanded water supply is close at hand, at least to the extent that such a demand can be foretold. The time required to construct dams, a filtration plant and a diversion pipeline necessitates that some sort of predictive mechanism be used. Given the many variables affecting the demand for water, it is hardly surprising that there was great divergence in the trigger proposals advanced by the various parties or that the figures relied upon have changed over the course of the long application process. Nevertheless, this does not equate to a showing of irrationality for the Commissioner's decision to conditionally authorize the project.

Petitioners maintain further that the Commissioner's choice of the crucial 27.9 mgd trigger which actuates the process for issuing the construction permits was irrational; specifically that there is no historical foundation for relying on average demand to forecast peak demand. Reliance on average demand is undeniably a logical indicator here because of its stability and, though not faultlessly predictive of peak demand, the ratio between the two has remained between 1.4 and 1.9, thus providing the Commissioner with a rational and not unreasonable means of judging when to authorize additional water supply construction.

We feel obliged to caution DEC, and Administrative Law Judges generally, to heed our concern that the basis for their core determinations be suitably explained. Here, for instance, petitioners justifiably complain that the rationale for choosing the figure 27.9 mgd is not fully elucidated. Nonetheless, because the approximate origin for the figure is discernible from the record and well supported therein and since this is a highly technical factor well within the agency's expertise, a remittal for elaboration is not appropriate in this instance. Viewed in the context of the problems facing Spring Valley and considering that the basic dispute is one of timing, the trigger mechanism was a particularly apt resolution, for it postpones costly construction if the water demand does not grow as expected while allowing Spring Valley to acquire property in the inevitable reservoir basin, and yet allows it adequate time to construct the project when the demand for water begins pressing the limits of the existing system. * * *

The last of petitioners' arguments, which though lacking in merit calls for comment, is their contention that compliance was not had with SEQRA. The fact that Spring Valley's offer to mitigate the damage to the trout stream by increasing the flow past its diversion structure from 0.3 mgd to 0.8 mgd was not given consideration in the final environmental impact statement is understandable inasmuch as there was expert testimony that a stream flow of 7.3 mgd was essential to sustain the trout. A flow of that level would effectively subvert the project. In light of the high priority of domestic and municipal water uses (see, ECL 15–0105[5]; see also, ECL 8–0103[7]), the trout stream must unfortunately give way to the predictable and unrelenting growth in human water demands.

Notes and Questions

1. The Department of Environmental Conservation (DEC) promulgated administrative regulations that further describe the material to be considered in acting on section 1501 permit applications. See N.Y. Admin. Code tit. 6, pts. 601 & 602. Section 601.5 explores in great detail the matters that must be presented in an application for a permit. Among the items that must be included are general and watershed maps, detailed engineering reports about the project, and the supply requirements. In section 601.6, the regulations track the requirements of the statute and offer no additional explication. Also prominent is a project justification requirement. The New York administrative requirements in this field are more highly articulated than those of most states.

2. Given the statutory direction that municipal use enjoys the highest priority, can DEC legally refuse a permit if the evidence supports the municipality's claim of inadequate supply? The short shrift given to the trout stream in *Fisherman's Association* case is an indication that courts will not impede municipal water supply efforts, but cf. City of Schenectady v.

Flacke, 100 A.D.2d 349, 475 N.Y.S.2d 506 (1984) (refusing to allow condemnation in the absence of full literal compliance with the requirements). The bulk of the directives to DEC in section 15–1503 point in the same direction, with the power of denial being held out primarily as a means to get the municipality to go about its project in the proper way.

3. How are conflicting claims to water sought by more than one municipal supplier to be resolved? Section 15–1503(2) makes the coordination of competing demands for water supplies DEC's responsibility, but offers no guidance as to how it is to be done.

4. How can an existing water supply be protected from adverse impacts that would be caused by changes in land use adjacent to the water? In one case, an attempted condemnation of lands to prevent siting of a solid waste management facility (i.e., a landfill) was held invalid in the absence of a section 15–1501 permit. See In re Acquisition of Real Property by the County of Fulton, 136 A.D.2d 115, 525 N.Y.S.2d 948 (1988). The general rule is that absent express legislative authorization, municipalities may not exercise police powers beyond their territorial limits to protect their water supplies. See Wilbert Zeigler, Acquisition and Protection of Water Supplies by Municipalities, 57 Mich. L. Rev. 349, 359–62 (1959). A majority of states have enacted legislation granting municipalities the necessary power to protect extra-territorial water supplies. See id. Land banks have also been effective in protecting water supplies against contamination. See Steven November, Groundwater and Open Space Protection: The New Land Bank and Land Acquisition Programs, 2 Hofstra Prop. L. J. 367 (1989).

5. Not all water suppliers are operated in the same fashion. Most fit into one of three categories, municipally-owned, investor-owned, and special utility districts. Is there any reason to expect differing performance as a function of organizational characteristics? For a study of comparative performance under drought conditions, see Ann Gellis, Water Supply in the Northeast: A Study in Regulatory Failure, 12 Ecology L.Q. 429 (1985).

6. The final paragraph of the excerpt summarily dispatches an attack on the project based on the failure of the environmental impact statement to consider the effects of allowing a slightly greater flow past the project. In this case, that result follows from the policy of section 15–0105 creating a "priority" in favor of municipal use that relegates all other concerns to a secondary status. In other settings, the impact of environmental concerns on water use may be more substantial. These matters are canvassed at page 639 and in Chapter 10.

7. Can one municipality or water supplier condemn water that is serving as another municipality's source of supply? The answer ought to be no, otherwise an unending tug-of-war might ensue. See, e.g., Town of Somerset v. Dighton Water Dist., 347 Mass. 738, 200 N.E.2d 237 (1964).

3. INTERBASIN DIVERSION TO PROVIDE MUNICIPAL WATER SUPPLY

Many of the larger cities in the eastern United States lack sufficient water available locally (for reasons either of quantity or quality) to meet their municipal supply needs. For some cities, the shortage of adequate supply stems from the ebb and flow of the ocean tides that render the nearby surface waters saline. For others, the problem may be more simple, not enough water to meet growing demand. The economic and strategic importance of these cities and their historic political clout invariably led to water being imported. For example, the State of Massachusetts has long exercised its authority and resources in efforts to provide sufficient water to meet the needs of the City of Boston. The plan ultimately relies on diversion and transportation of large amounts of water from the Connecticut River, a river to which the city is not riparian. The project was challenged by the State of Connecticut in a lawsuit heard and determined in favor of the Massachusetts diversion of the water in Connecticut v. Massachusetts, 282 U.S. 660 (1931).

In a similar fashion, the quest of New York City for adequate water supplies is a fascinating study in the range of devices that are potentially available to a large urban water supplier. The city's daily supply of water (now exceeding 1.5 billion gallons) comes from three major sources. The Croton watershed in nearby Westchester and Putnam counties provides about one-sixth of that water. Reservoirs in the Catskill mountains, roughly 100 miles from the city, provide about half of the remaining water and diversions from the Delaware River provide the remainder. The rights to the Croton and Catskill supplies were acquired by condemnation of lands for reservoir sites and payment of claims for impairment of riparian rights. Although those systems were completed more than 50 years ago, there is still on-going litigation regarding the riparian claims. The Delaware River water has twice been the subject of litigation in the United States Supreme Court and the Delaware River Basin Compact is among the most extensive interstate water management accords ever reached.[1]

Even smaller cities find themselves faced with mounting water supply problems. The materials that follow involve the efforts of the City of Virginia Beach to expand its water supply in response to growth induced increases in water demand. Virginia Beach, like many coastal communities, is particularly hard-pressed when it comes to expanding its water supply because local sources are unavailable. Surface water streams are affected by tidal action that powers the upstream advance of saltwater from the ocean; groundwater aquifers, if pumped too rapidly, are subject to damage by saltwater intrusion. To increase supply, Virginia Beach sought to import Roanoke River water from a point roughly eighty-five miles away. The controversy surrounding the Virginia Beach proposal is a case study of contemporary municipal supply efforts.

An important feature of these controversies captured in this example is that the issues of riparian rights play a scant role in deciding the case. Indeed, Virginia Beach is a bit unusual in that the riparian issues are the subject of a separate lawsuit that remained pending more than twenty years after being filed in 1984. See infra p. 97. The principal

---

1. See Joseph Sax, Water Law, Planning and Policy 151–85 (1968); Healy, New York City's Battle for Imported Water (paper presented at Natural Resources Law Cen-ter, Boulder Colorado, June 9, 1982). At the time Mr. Healy was General Counsel for the New York City Department Of Environmental Protection.

opinion from which the excerpts are drawn presents a potpourri of environmental and administrative law issues that have little in common with the "water law" issues of the case. This is typical and is therefore important in showing how disputes over interbasin transfer to support municipal growth are likely to progress.

Interbasin water import projects, involving dams and transmission facilities, virtually always require one or more administrative approvals or permits. The agencies charged with granting the needed approvals and permits operate pursuant to statutory mandates that often have little or nothing to do with the law of riparianism.[2] In litigation over agency action, the parties favoring the project and those opposed each try, within the confines of the statutes pertinent to the agency involved in the dispute, to force the agency to adopt a position that results in the outcome their side desires. Controlling agencies, like the United States Army Corps of Engineers in the earlier stages of the Virginia Beach case, often lack a clear water allocation mandate. For that reason, the litigation tends to be a stalking horse that hides important issues of water allocation policy behind legal niceties of statutory interpretation and administrative law. Even when a water planning agency is involved, the degree of deference normally shown by courts to agencies obscures and limits substantive review of policy and substitutes for it legal nit-picking about conformity to administrative procedure, or compliance with non-water policy statutes that erect specific statutory duties for the agency to discharge.

Do not be too concerned at this point with the substantive nuances of the environmental and administrative law doctrines that are discussed.[3] For now, focus more on matters of institutional control and process and the strategy of the various parties to the dispute.

STATE OF NORTH CAROLINA v. HUDSON

United States District Court, Eastern District of North Carolina, 1990.
731 F.Supp. 1261.

BRITT, CHIEF JUDGE.

The City of Virginia Beach, Virginia, is seeking permission from the United States Corps of Engineers (the Corps) to construct a sixty-inch pipeline some 84.5 miles across southern Virginia and withdraw up to 60 million gallons of water per day (mgd) from Lake Gaston for the purpose of meeting its municipal water supply needs. After the Corps made a decision to issue the permits needed by Virginia Beach to accomplish the project, this action was begun by the State of North Carolina, the

---

2. The ability of decisionmakers entrusted with power over non-water related issues to control water policy is not unique to riparian states. Cf. City and County of Denver v. Board of County Comm'rs, 782 P.2d 753 (Colo. 1989) (local land use control).

3. The substantive protection given to environmental concerns as a basis for altering water development projects is considered at page 639, and a more extensive consideration of pollution control and other water quality issues appears in Chapter 10.

Roanoke River Basin Association (RRBA) and several counties in Virginia and North Carolina for judicial review of the decision of the Corps. Thereafter, this court conducted a review of the Corps' decision under the Administrative Procedure Act, 5 U.S.C. § 706 (West 1977) and rendered a decision on 7 July 1987, State of North Carolina v. Hudson, 665 F. Supp. 428 (E.D.N.C. 1987).

I. PROCEDURAL HISTORY

After a thorough review of the Administrative Record and consideration of the arguments and briefs of all parties, the court remanded the matter to the Corps. The court's decision was very specific on the scope of the further review which was mandated:

On remand, the Corps shall:

1.   As a part of its NEPA [National Environmental Policy Act] review make an independent assessment of the effects of the proposed project on striped bass to determine whether the preparation of an EIS [Environmental Impact Statement] is required or whether any mitigative measures are necessary; and,

2.   As a part of its public interest review make a determination of the extent of Virginia Beach's water needs.

Hudson, 665 F. Supp. at 450.

All other objections by plaintiffs to the decision of the Corps were rejected. * * * The Corps has complied and the matter is now before the court for review of the supplemental record.

* * * The Corps concluded that Virginia Beach's withdrawal of water from Lake Gaston will have no significant impact on the human environment, that an environmental impact statement (EIS) is not necessary, and that the amount of the proposed withdrawal, 60 mgd, is needed.

[A detailed description of the dams controlling the Roanoke River and their effect on striped bass appears here. The Corps' Supplemental Environmental Assessment (SEA) concluded that the decline in striped bass was due to overfishing and that the diversion plan would have a negligible effect on the fishery. The court found the conclusion well supported in the record. The Corps nevertheless placed a condition on the permit that would assure water availability to augment flows in spawning season. The opinion then described what material the Corps had before it in determining the need for water.]

VI. APPLICABLE STATUTES AND REGULATIONS

As the court stated in its prior review, four statutes and their implementing regulations are pertinent: The Rivers and Harbors Appropriation Act of 1899, 33 U.S.C. § 403 (1986); the Clean Water Act, 33 U.S.C. §§ 1251–1376; the Water Supply Act of 1958, 43 U.S.C. §§ 390b–390f; and the National Environmental Policy Act of 1969 (NEPA), 42 U.S.C. §§ 4321–4347. Pursuant to section 10 of the Rivers and Harbors

Act of 1899, 33 U.S.C. § 403, the Corps of Engineers is responsible for evaluating proposed construction projects in the navigable waters of the United States. Section 404 of the Clean Water Act, 33 U.S.C. § 1344, gives the Corps jurisdiction to issue permits for the discharge of dredged or fill materials into the navigable waters of the United States. The Water Supply Act authorizes the Corps to reallocate water storage in federal reservoirs such as Kerr Reservoir. 43 U.S.C. § 390b. In exercising the authority granted by these three statutes, the Corps must also comply with the prerequisites of NEPA. * * *

B. Public Interest Review and Other Corps Regulations

In addition to the regulations implementing NEPA, the Corps has adopted regulations which serve as guidelines for the evaluation of all regulatory permit applications. 33 C.F.R. pt. 320. Chief among these regulations is 33 C.F.R. § 320.4(a) which requires the Corps to undertake a general "public interest review" to decide whether a permit should issue. In this review the Corps must evaluate a proposal's overall impact on the public interest, balancing the "benefits which reasonably may be expected to accrue * * * against its reasonably foreseeable detriments." 33 C.F.R. § 320.4(a).

The decision whether to issue the permit depends on the outcome of this balancing of factors. A permit is to be granted unless the district engineer determines that it will be contrary to the public interest. 33 C.F.R. § 320.4(a)(1). * * *

VII. CONTENTIONS

Both North Carolina and RRBA devote most of their arguments to the striped bass issue. Each contends that the Corps' analysis is flawed and not supported by expert opinion. They argue that the Corps failed to utilize data on a new flow regime using instead an outdated flow regime. The Corps' conclusions regarding the effect of fishing on the striped bass problem are disputed, and the Corps is taken to task for failing to consider cumulative impacts in its analysis. RRBA also contends that the Corps ignored important findings by the United States Congress. Additionally, both parties attack the Corps' determination of the extent of Virginia Beach's need.

VIII. STANDARD OF REVIEW

The applicable review standard is found in the Administrative Procedure Act which provides in pertinent part:

The reviewing court shall—

(2) hold unlawful and set aside agency action, findings, and conclusions found to be—

> (A) arbitrary, capricious, an abuse of discretion, or otherwise not in accordance with law; * * *

> (D) without observance of procedure required by law.

5 U.S.C. § 706(2)(A) & (D). Any interpretation of this standard must begin with the Supreme Court's decision in Citizens to Preserve Overton Park, Inc. v. Volpe, 401 U.S. 402 (1971). In *Overton Park* the Supreme Court made clear that the court's obligation pursuant to this statute is twofold. The court must consider, first, whether the agency acted within the scope of its authority and, second, whether the actual choice made by the agency was arbitrary, capricious, an abuse of discretion, or otherwise not in accordance with law. To make this finding the court must consider whether the decision was based on a consideration of the relevant factors and whether there was a clear error of judgment. This standard of review is highly deferential and the agency decision is "entitled to a presumption of regularity." *Overton Park,* 401 U.S. at 415.
* * *

IX. ANALYSIS

A. *Effect of the Project on Striped Bass*

* * * Dire consequences, particularly in the river flow, are forecast by North Carolina in the event of a severe drought. Whether that forecast or the Corps' forecast, that the project will have no impact on the river flow, is correct remains to be seen. This court is not an expert on that subject. Neither is North Carolina. The Corps is. And it is to the Corps that the Congress has entrusted the final decision. This court's sole function is to review the Corps' decision under the standard herein set out. Having done so, the court is convinced that the decision, insofar as it deals with striped bass, is not arbitrary and capricious. This is especially true considering the mitigative measure which was ordered.

B. *Virginia Beach's Need*

Plaintiffs contend that the Corps has not complied with the court's mandate to assess Virginia Beach's need. Specifically, they contend that population projections which have been used are too high and that other sources of water have not been adequately factored into the equation. The court disagrees. This court's 1987 Opinion upheld as reasonable the Corps' determination that Virginia Beach had a need for water and remanded only for a determination of the *extent* of that need. Upon remand the Corps sought input from all interested parties and all available sources. Its analysis of the projections of the amount of water Virginia Beach will need in 2030 and the amount which will be available may be flawed in some respects but is not arbitrary or capricious. Indeed, this court is convinced that 60 mgd in 2030 may be insufficient to meet the city's need after considering all other reasonably foreseeable sources of water. As Colonel Thomas stated:

> I am convinced that there will never be a consensus among experts, much less among those willing to offer an opinion, as to the extent of Virginia Beach's water needs. A cynic would say, ad hominem, that North Carolina and RRBA, as plaintiffs, are underestimating the need and Virginia Beach, as defendant, is overestimating it and, in fact those parties have said just those

things about each other. It is not sufficient to merely select a figure in the middle, though, because potable water is vital to human health and welfare and such decisions must not be made so lightly.

Colonel Thomas then very carefully analyzed the available information and contentions and concluded that "Virginia Beach needs this 60 mgd project." He reached this conclusion only after a searching analysis which complies with the requirement of an assessment of the public need for the project.

IX. Conclusion

As noted in this court's earlier opinion, the center of the controversy here is the *interbasin transfer* of water. The controversy is not state against state,[12] but basin against basin, the James River Basin against the Roanoke River Basin. This point is borne out by the fact that many of the plaintiffs are residents of the State of Virginia. The State of North Carolina is lead plaintiff but only because more of its citizens are involved.

It is quite natural for citizens to be concerned with the withdrawal of water from the basin in the area in which they live for use in another place. Interbasin transfer not only eliminates the availability of the water from the basin but it also has the potential to increase the degree of pollution of the water remaining in the basin. Nevertheless, whether to permit interbasin transfer of water is essentially a political decision.

Water is a necessity of life. It is a valuable resource which must be protected and conserved and shared by all. Congress has long recognized the importance of this natural resource and has passed many acts, some of which are relevant to this litigation, to conserve it and regulate its use. Primary responsibility for enforcement and implementation of the legislation pertinent here lies with the Corps. It has discharged that responsibility and concluded that the City of Virginia Beach should be allowed to withdraw up to 60 mgd from Lake Gaston. This court's review discloses that, in reaching its decision, the Corps has taken a "hard look" at the environmental consequences, including the potential effect on striped bass. Kleppe [v. Sierra Club], 427 U.S. at 410. The Corps' decision will be upheld. An appropriate order will issue.

Notes and Questions

1. North Carolina and the other plaintiffs unsuccessfully appealed the case. See Roanoke River Basin Assoc. v. Hudson (*Hudson III*), 940 F.2d 58 (4th Cir. 1991).

12. Such clashes are common within the State of North Carolina where fourteen interbasin transfers now divert about 40 mgd. One such dispute currently exists over the proposal of two Wake County towns, Cary and Apex, to withdraw water from Lake Jordan, in the Cape Fear Basin, and discharge it into the Neuse River Basin. The News and Observer, Raleigh, N.C., January 15, 1990, at 1B. Such transfers have served as a " 'lightning rod for disputes among water users in North Carolina and elsewhere.' " Id. (quoting from the fall issue of Popular Government magazine, a publication of the Institute of Government, Chapel Hill, North Carolina).

2. The National Environmental Policy Act (NEPA) requires that federal agencies complete an environmental impact statement (EIS) in regard to all major federal actions significantly affecting the environment. See 42 U.S.C. § 102(2)(c). The purpose of an EIS is to ensure that an agency has fully evaluated the impacts of its proposed action, but once an adequate EIS is filed, NEPA does not require that the agency abjure actions that would damage the environment. Some have termed it a full disclosure law and no more. Why is it a central issue in a water allocation case? The plaintiffs must hope that one of several things will happen, that the delay caused by preparing an adequate EIS somehow halts the project altogether, that the disclosure of negative environmental impacts creates enough political heat that the agency backs off, or that the agency is reined in by Congress. How much do any of these have to do with the "merits" of the water use at issue? As will be described later, North Carolina eventually was successful in obtaining an EIS and other studies of the project, but the studies were not undertaken by the Army Corps of Engineers.[1]

3. Why is the Army Corps of Engineers reviewing Virginia Beach's claimed water needs? Federal agencies are given their authority by statutes. The relevant statutes here are listed by the court. NEPA, as discussed in the prior note, gives the Corps no reason to concern itself with water supply and demand. None of the other three statutes listed grant the Corps jurisdiction over water allocation either. The Rivers and Harbors Act and Clean Water Act are (as relevant herein) concerned solely with water quality and, in particular, permits to place fill material into wetlands and/or the nation's navigable waters. The Water Supply Act of 1958, despite its name, gives the Corps an expressly secondary role in making municipal supply decisions:

> It is hereby declared to be the policy of the Congress to recognize the primary responsibilities of the States and local interests in developing water supplies for domestic, municipal, industrial, and other purposes and that the Federal Government should participate and cooperate with States and local interests in developing such water supplies in connection with the construction, maintenance, and operation of Federal navigation, flood control, irrigation, or multiple purpose projects.

43 U.S.C. § 390b(a).

The Corps had a role to play because the Lake Gaston Project required the Corps to take the diversion into account in managing dam operations of several dams on the Roanoke. The water demand issue was before the Corps only because the Corps by its own duly adopted regulations, undertakes "public interest review." That review, in turn, includes a benefit cost inquiry, to which Virginia Beach's water demand may be relevant. Recalling the specific language of the Water Supply act, did Congress intend to put the Corps in charge of approving or disapproving the Virginia Beach Lake

---

1. Procedurally, cases of this nature frequently follow a pattern. All federal agencies with project responsibilities are required by the statute to prepare an EIS in cases of significant environmental impact. Preliminarily, agencies do an "environmental assessment" (EA) that provides the basis for deciding to do an EIS or to issue a "finding of no significant impact." (FONSI) In this case, the Army Corps of Engineers' FONSI was upheld after it had produced a "supplemental environmental assessment" (SEA). See generally 40 C.F.R. pt. 1508.

Gaston project? If not, this effort is one that seeks to block a project by using a small, unintended legal handle, to defeat the project. That tactic is a common feature of environmental controversies. It is also a tactic that is finding its way into the water allocation arena with increasing frequency.

4. The Lake Gaston Project was fought on many fronts. North Carolina achieved a measure of success in slowing the project, particularly by obtaining a Congressionally required study of the fishery impacts[2] and an EIS to be prepared by the Federal Energy Regulatory Commission (FERC). FERC got involved in the case only because the pipeline needed an easement across the land of Virginia Electric Power Company's FERC-regulated damsite near the pipeline's intake point. These were Pyrrhic victories for North Carolina, as was any delay caused by additional skirmishes fought regarding the Coastal Zone Management Act and state authority over Clean Water Act discharge programs. The pipeline is built and has been delivering water since 1998. In total, there were eleven federal court decisions, two state court decisions, three published opinions of the Federal Energy Regulatory Commission, and one unpublished opinion of the United States Department of Commerce.

5. Notice how similar the *Hudson* case is to the *Fisherman's Association* case. In each an administrative body is making an important allocative decision about water in which riparian principles, and courts more generally, play a very limited role. Is it at all odd that in these important water allocation disputes there is no mention of the law of riparianism?

6. Judge Britt deems the question of interbasin diversions primarily a question for the political arena. What is the likely array of contending forces? See Robert Abrams, Interbasin Transfer in a Riparian Jurisdiction, 24 Wm. & Mary L. Rev. 591, 594–98 (1983). See also William Cox & Leonard Shabman, Virginia's Water Law: Resolving the Interjurisdictional Transfer Issue, 3 Va. J. Nat. Res. L. 181 (1984). William Walker, the Director of the Virginia Water Resources Research Center, is likewise critical of using courts to allocate water. In an editorial prompted by Judge Britt's ruling he wrote:

> If you combine the fact that water is not necessarily where there is the greatest geographic need, that "one person, one vote" is still the law of the land, and that the state [of Virginia] will redistrict its political boundaries next year, it becomes obvious that water will continue to "run to people" regardless of physical boundaries. * * * An administrative mechanism needs to be in place to balance the water needs of both importing and exporting regions so we have both water use efficiency and equity. By deferring to court systems, the people's representatives have abdicated their responsibility. We will have to live and relive most of our water supply problems in courts at great expense in time, money and uncertainty.

For a detailed account of the early stages of the Virginia Beach struggle and its history, see William Walker & Phyllis Bridgeman, Anatomy of a Water Problem: Virginia Beach's Experience Suggests Time for a Change (Va. Water Resources Research Center, Special Report No. 18, August 1985). Would conservation be a better solution to the problems of Virginia Beach?

---

2. See Pub. L. No. 100–589, 102 Stat. 2984 (1988); see also Water Resources De-velopment Act of 1990, § 407, 104 Stat. 4606, 4647 (1990).

See James Waite, Water Conservation: The Forgotten Solution to Water Supply Deficits in Southeastern Virginia, 9 Va. Envtl. L. Rev. 381 (1990).

7. A more recent rendition of the Virginia Beach tale is that of the City of Atlanta and other Georgia municipalities. Beginning in 1970s, Atlanta and a small number of other entities began receiving municipal water supply from Lake Lanier pursuant to interim contracts from the United States Army of Engineers Corps. The lake is created by the Buford Dam, which is located on the Chattahoochie River, in the upstream end of the Apalachicola–Chattahoochie–Flint (ACF) basin. The ACF basin covers parts of three states, Georgia, Alabama, and Florida.

The dam was expressly authorized to be built in 1945 for the purposes of flood control, navigation, and electric power generation. The Corps, however, delivered water to Atlanta and the others on the theory that municipal and industrial water use was an "incidental benefit." In 1989, with the municipalities seeking permanent contracts, the Corps announced plans to seek Congressional approval for the diversion of water to Atlanta and other Georgia communities under the Water Supply Act of 1958, 43 U.S.C. § 390b. In June, 1990, Alabama sued the Corps in the United States District Court for the Northern District of Alabama, seeking to enjoin the Corps from entering the contracts or enlarging the deliveries. In part, that suit alleged failure to comply with the National Environmental Policy Act ("NEPA"), 42 U.S.C. §§ 4321 et seq. Florida intervened as a plaintiff and Georgia intervened as a defendant.[3] Shortly thereafter, the case was stayed in hopes of reaching a negotiated settlement. The stay order contained a provision that forbade the Corps from entering long term contracts with municipalities for the water.

The highly politicized negotiation efforts continued for more than a decade. In 1997, the states even went so far as to enter into two interstate water compacts, one pertaining to the ACF basin and the other involving the Alabama–Coosa–Tallapoosa basin (ACT) a bit father west. Both compacts were of limited duration and their purpose was to reach an agreed allocation of the basins. Despite protracted efforts and two extensions of the compacts, both compacts failed and were terminated on August 31, 2003.

Adding to the complexity of the legal situation, in December of 2000, a consortium of electric power suppliers who purchased hydropower generated at Buford Dam on Lake Lanier, sued the Corps in the District of Columbia United States District Court. They claimed that the Corps was overcharging them for hydropower from the Burford Dam by failing to take into account the reduced flow caused by the diversions for municipal supply. See Southern Federal Power Customers, Inc. (SeFPC) v. Caldera, 301 F.Supp.2d 26 (D.D.C.2004). That case was settled on terms that obliged the Corps to take the steps that, arguably, violated the 1990 stay order, which had never been dissolved. Alabama and Florida revived the Alabama action and sought an injunction against the Corps for violating the stay order. That request was

---

3. Georgia later on filed a separate suit in the Georgia United States District Court, seeking a ruling that no Congressional action is needed for the Corps to enter into the permanent water supply contracts. That case was abated by the District Court, a ruling upheld on appeal. Georgia v. Corps. of Engineers, 144 Fed.Appx. 850 (11th Cir. 2005).

granted and the resulting injunction was appealed and overturned. Alabama v. Corps of Engineers, 424 F.3d 1117 (11th Cir. 2005). Importantly, however, the decisions in that case to date are not on the merits. The decisions in that case address only the alleged violation of the 1990 stay. Taking up that slack, Alabama and Florida have filed an amended complaint in the underlying action that includes claims under the Endangered Species Act and the Coastal Zone Management Act. The downstream states also are planning to file an original action in the United States Supreme Court. The most certain outcome in this matter is that there will be several more years of litigation, much of which will be collateral to the merits of the water allocation dispute that gave rise to the controversy in the first place.

Is this indirection in water allocation matters, involving major metropolitan supplies and significant downstream ecological concerns, tolerable? Litigation seems to go nowhere. Even when a decision is reached, it may control water allocation, but it is not bottomed on water allocation policy. Should the Corps of Engineers, an agency with so many mandates other than setting water supply policy, be the ultimate decision maker? Congress has shown little willingness to enter the fray in the absence of agreement by the states involved, so indirection seems likely to remain the only direction.

———

In the Virginia Beach setting, the riparian rights issue was brought to court. In 1984, the City of Virginia Beach filed a class action lawsuit seeking a declaration that the project would not infringe the rights of Roanoke River system riparians. That lawsuit, City of Virginia Beach v. Champion International Paper Co., Civ. 84–10–N, D. Va., was stayed with the possibility that it would be reopened after the permits were issued by the Corps and FERC and the CZMA issue also had been put to rest. The case was transferred to federal court in North Carolina for further proceedings and remained pending in that court until 2005, at which time it was voluntarily dismissed by plaintiff. A few of the key paragraphs of the complaint are excerpted below.

CITY OF VIRGINIA BEACH v. CHAMPION INTERNATIONAL CORP.

United States District Court, District of Virginia, 1984.
Civ. 84–10–N.

COMPLAINT FOR DECLARATORY RELIEF

Nature of the Case

1. This is a civil action by the City of Virginia Beach, Virginia ("Virginia Beach") against Champion International Corporation ("Champion") and Weyerhauser Company ("Weyerhauser") and the class comprising all owners of riparian lands on the Roanoke River below the Roanoke Rapids Dam. This action seeks a declaratory judgment that the defendants and the members of the class have no right to the use of the water that will be diverted from the Roanoke River by a pump

station and pipeline system constructed and operated to transport water for municipal use from a point on Lake Gaston in Brunswick County, Virginia to Virginia Beach, Virginia (the "Project"). * * *

Description and Interests of the Parties

4. Virginia Beach is a municipal corporation of the Commonwealth of Virginia. It is the most populous (290,000 permanent residents in 1983) municipal corporation in Virginia. Its population has almost doubled in each decade since 1940 at which time its population was 22,584. It is expected that the population served by the Virginia Beach water system will exceed 473,000 by the year 2030.

Virginia Beach currently furnishes its resident water customers with 23 million gallons of water per day (MGD) on an annual average basis, and is expected to need 48 MGD by 2030. [The paragraph went on to discuss that a portion of Virginia Beach's water supply is provided by the City of Norfolk, but that water is available only to the extent it is surplus to Norfolk's own needs. Droughts in 1977 and 1980 had shown that Norfolk's water supply was inadequate to meet its needs and those of Virginia Beach.]

[The interest of Champion was predicated on its announced intention to build a new paper mill on riparian land it owns on the Roanoke downstream of the diversion point. Public statements of state officials indicated that Champion will abandon the project if flows are reduced by diversion because the river will lack sufficient assimilative capacity. The interest of Weyerhauser, the operator of an existing paper mill drawing and returning 40–to–50 MGD from the lower Roanoke, lay in the fact that lower flows might force plant closure due to the loss of dilution of their effluent.]

7. The class comprising all owners of riparian property on the Roanoke River below the Roanoke Rapids Dam is so numerous that joinder of all members is impracticable, and there are questions of law or fact common to all members of the class, the defenses of Champion and Weyerhauser to this suit are typical of the defenses of all members of the class, and Champion and Weyerhauser will fairly and adequately protect the interests of all members of the class. The prosecution of separate actions by or against individual members of the class would create a risk of inconsistent or varying adjudications with respect to individual members of the class which would establish incompatible standards of conduct for Virginia Beach, and questions of law or fact common to the members of the class will predominate over any questions affecting only individual members and a class action is superior to other available methods for the fair and efficient adjudication of this controversy.

[The complaint described the existing waterworks on the Roanoke, stressing that the dam and reservoir systems were built for flood control purposes and describing the water impounded in the reservoirs as being "immense quantities of flood waters" with storage of 748 billion gallons in the Buggs Island Reservoir alone. The complaint alleged that, "Under normal conditions, there is a surplus of at least 350 MGD available for use after all downstream flow requirements are fulfilled." The complaint also described the project in some detail, noting that it would be sized to divert a maximum of 60 MGD and transport it 84.5 miles to Virginia Beach. The initial expectation was to take only 10 MGD beginning in 1990, with diversions increasing gradually over the next four decades.]

The Defendant Class Has No Right to the Diverted Water

* * *

30.   Champion and Weyerhauser and the class they represent own real property abutting the main stem of the Roanoke River below the Roanoke Rapids Dam, and therefore they have riparian rights under the law of North Carolina, and only under that law, in the flow of that river past their property.

31.   The water to be diverted by Virginia Beach is floodwater or surplus water to which no riparian owner * * * has any right.

32.   The amount of water to be diverted by Virginia Beach from the Roanoke River constitutes a minute fraction of its flow during any season of the year, and neither Champion, Weyerhauser, nor any riparian landowner in the class they represent will be damaged in any way by the diversion.

33.   The State of North Carolina has no right to the portion of the flow of the Roanoke River that Virginia Beach proposes to divert, and neither Champion, Weyerhauser, nor any riparian landowner in the class they represent has any right superior to that of the State of North Carolina, under whose law their riparian rights are created. * * *

Notes and Questions

1.   What would be the likely result of this suit based on common law riparianism principles alone? Under a traditional common law approach, an interbasin diversion might be deemed per se unreasonable, because the situs of use is, by definition, outside of the basin of origin. The origin of the per se rule is probably rooted in the rhetoric of the natural flow doctrine, and has long ago been discarded from the law of North Carolina. The reasonableness of an out of basin diversion for municipal use would, therefore, be a question of fact to be decided in the litigation.

Is there any doubt that municipal use, if viewed in isolation, would be found to be reasonable? The outcome of the litigation likely would turn on the severity of the impact of the municipal withdrawal on other riparian uses and, thereafter, on consideration of how to accommodate the uses or apportion the shortfall, if any should seem likely to occur. What would the analysis be in a state that follows the Restatement (Second) of Torts view? The Restatement appears to favor placing the costs of accommodation on large entities with cost spreading ability. That would point toward a ruling allowing the diversion to go forward with compensation by the municipality to basin of origin riparians suffering material injury.

2. Why did Virginia Beach seek to obtain a declaratory judgment? One possibility was that the legal issue was open to doubt and before spending many millions of dollars in pursuit of a water project, the city had hoped to be sure that no one could block the receipt of water based on a superior water right. A variant on this theme would be that bonds needed to be issued to support the project and the rating of the bonds (and therefore the interest rate that must be paid to attract investors) might be adversely affected by the threat of uncertain water rights. Could the case still be a victory for Virginia Beach if the court finds that the project adversely affects water rights that the defendant's enjoy under North Carolina law? Reconsider your answer after reading note 5 below.

3. Why does Virginia Beach select the class action device? Here, the most plausible answer is that the class action device offers the possibility of obtaining relief that will bind all downstream riparians in one lawsuit, a major efficiency gain. As a matter of procedure, it is not certain that result will obtain. This is a matter of some complexity involving difficult issues of the interpretation of the class action rule. See Fed. R. Civ. P. 23(b)(1)–(3). If the case is suitable for class action status only because "questions of law or fact common to the members of the class predominate over any questions affecting only individual members" then class members will be able to opt out of the litigation and preserve their individual claims for separate adjudication. The hope of Virginia Beach, apparent in the allegations of paragraph 7, is that the case will be certified for class action status under Rule 23(b)(1)(A) (cases where the party opposing the class will be subject to the threat of "incompatible standards of conduct"). In that event, subsection (c)(3) binds all those found by the court to be class members and does not allow for individuals to opt out. Judge Britt, to whom the case was transferred, had indicated that he would certify the class as appropriate under Rule 23(b)(1)(A) when the stay was lifted.

Are cases attempting to declare the rights of riparians cases in which commonality is likely to prevail over individual determinations? Both Champion and Weyerhauser will litigate the case vigorously because of their major investment in their facilities that might be injured if their ability to meet water quality laws is threatened. That interest seems to speak more to the likelihood that they will be zealous advocates than that their interest, using the flow of the river for the dilution of pollution, is typical of other downstream riparians. Is the interest of the paper companies in flow maintenance the same as that of downstream cities, irrigators and homeowners?

4. What facts would be most important to the outcome of the lawsuit? At least one key determination relates to whether the use of Virginia Beach is proportioned to the size and character of the watercourse. This means that items such as accurate histories of river flows would be vital. Likewise, a full inventory of downstream uses, both instream and consumptive, must be compiled. Virginia Beach characterized the water as "stored floodwater." Was this an attempt to deflect the inquiry away from adverse downstream impacts to an issue of water accounting? Isn't the stored water, without regard to when or why it was put in storage, available to support downstream flows on demand? In fact, the Roanoke is a highly regulated river and the FERC-licensed minimum flows are the only reliable flows in water short

years. These regulated minimum flows are not likely to be impaired by the Lake Gaston project. The post-project flows are more than double the 7Q10 dependable flows[4] of the river in the absence of flow regulation.

5.   What is the purpose of the allegation in paragraph 33? This much is clear: the allegation is correct when it alleges that the rights of the North Carolina riparians arise under North Carolina law, not federal law. Does the remainder of the paragraph imply that the water rights of the defendant class all arise as a subset of the rights that North Carolina might be able to assert? That is plausible insofar as there are numerous instances in which the use of an interstate water course is apportioned among the riparian states and each state's users are, in total, limited by their state's apportioned share. This topic is considered more fully in Chapter 8.

E.   RIPARIANISM'S REGULATED PRESENT AND POSSIBLE FUTURE

Beginning in the middle of the 20th Century, as populations grew and adopted a more affluent life style, per capita and aggregate water usage soared and water demand came within hailing distance of water supply in several parts of the Eastern United States. Droughts began to have a greater potential to cause dislocations in the economy and the way people lived. Riparianism came under attack because it was considered primarily a reactive doctrine that tried to resolve conflict only after the water shortage and its effects were already acute. The call of the critics was for a move to proactive managerial systems that could allocate water in a way that minimized the disruptive effects of water supply shortages.[5] In a number of states the call resulted in adoption of legislation that sought to superimpose an administrative management system on common law riparianism.[6]

Still more recently, the cycle of increased demand and drought intensified. Rapid population growth in some of the region's less water-rich areas, such as the middle and southern Atlantic coastal regions, stressed available water supplies. The economically beneficial development of those areas was put at risk by lack of secure water supplies. Severe droughts during the 1980's caused billions of dollars in crop losses in the East and led to increased irrigation water demand. The droughts and their severity rekindled the interest in managerial systems. As a further incentive to replace riparianism, some prominent scientists argued that in the future, summer drought and decreased soil moisture

---

4. The notation "7Q10" is a shorthand for the lowest 7-consecutive day flow expected in a ten-year period. For planning purposes it is used as a measure of a degree of low flow that should be anticipated as a worst case scenario.

5. See, e.g., Clyde Fisher, Western Experience and Eastern Proposals, in The Law of Water Allocation in The Eastern United States 75 (David Haber & Stephen Bergen, eds., 1958).

6. In a single state, Mississippi, reform went beyond the adoption of an administrative system and included a switch to appropriation as the basis of water rights. See 1956 Miss. Laws ch. 167. In 1983, Mississippi again changed its water system to a closely managed system of short-term permits. See Miss. Code Ann. §§ 51–3–1 to 51–3–55.

might become even more common as a consequence of the greenhouse effect. Under these pressures, the common law of riparianism, quietly, is waning and being replaced by administrative permit systems. This section explores those systems and the challenges they face.

ROBERT ABRAMS, WATER ALLOCATION BY COMPREHENSIVE PERMIT SYSTEMS IN THE EASTERN UNITED STATES: CONSIDERING A MOVE AWAY FROM ORTHODOXY

9 Va. Envtl. L.J. 255, 261–65 (1990).

It is not taxing to make the case in the abstract that a managerial system, such as a comprehensive permit system, is far preferable to continued adherence to riparianism or common law groundwater allocation rules. Three lines of argument predominate. First, private property rules are ineffective at producing the maximum set of benefits from a common pool resource. Second, managerial allocations offer the possibility of precise quantification of right and thereby the possibility for increased security of right. Third, managerial systems are proactive rather than reactive.

Water with its natural occurrence being in lake and stream systems that usually traverse property boundaries, is a quintessential common pool resource. Under riparianism, while one user's rights are bounded by a respect for the correlative rights of others, there remains an incentive for every user to increase use of the commons and thereby obtain as large a share of the resource as possible. The selfish incentive to overuse the commons is reinforced in riparian doctrine by the preference favoring existing uses expressed in factor h of Section 850A of the Restatement (Second) of Torts. Although not dispositive of all cases, that factor tacitly encourages a race to put as large a quantity of water to use as possible in hopes of winning judicial protection against subsequent water uses that would usurp the water supply of the first entrant.

In contrast to reliance on the common law, having an administrative body charged with allocational decision-making avoids such over-use. An example from the groundwater area in a jurisdiction that employs the traditional common law of reasonable use doctrine makes this point. Under the common law reasonable use doctrine [of groundwater law], an owner of land overlying an aquifer can pump with legal impunity as much water as desired provided that the water is devoted to a "reasonable use" on the overlying tract. * * * Consequently, a low value user, perhaps a gravel pit operator dewatering a pit, may deprive a high value user, such as a steel mill or other industrial facility, of its water. A managerial system for water allocation can avoid interference with high-value uses by limiting, denying, or conditioning permits issued for low-value uses.

The second advantage of regulatory intervention is the ability to overcome riparianism's lack of specificity regarding the extent of a water right. Riparian rights are not, by their nature, quantified rights that secure to their possessor a right to take water under all conditions. Rights are adjudicated infrequently and decrees in such cases are binding upon only the parties thereto and only so long as the underlying factual conditions remain unchanged. To illustrate, hypothesize that upon remand the trial judge in Pyle v. Gilbert [supra p. 47] holds in favor of the millpond use. That decision would be implemented by a decree forbidding Pyle and the other irrigating defendants from decreasing the flow into the pond below the rate sufficient to protect the Gilberts' use. Presumably, other upstream irrigators, although not bound by res judicata, would find their irrigation efforts blocked by stare decisis. In contrast, no similarly predictable fate necessarily follows for new upstream entrants making non-irrigation water uses such as for manufacturing or residential development. Should such additional competing uses be initiated, the rights of the Gilberts would have to be relitigated, leaving the mill pond operation again at risk despite the initial legal victory.

The characteristic uncertainty of riparian rights does not promote the establishment of security of right. Stated rhetorically, would a prudent bank or thrift institution lend large sums of money in reliance on the Gilberts' riparian right to receive sufficient flow to operate their enterprise? In contrast to riparianism, a permit system can provide certainty of right, as permits are usually quantified and normally will not be issued in the absence of available water sufficient to satisfy the entitlements of all permit holders.

The final attraction of a regulatory system is its ability to act before serious allocational problems mature into water crises. Riparianism in particular, and the common law in general, resolve legal disputes only after they have ripened sufficiently to allow either a concrete claim, or threatened infringement of right. The entire thrust of a permit system is a managerial approach that attempts to match allocation of available water supply with the state's discernable water needs. For example, rather than reacting to an overdraft situation, a state with a permit system can limit the total withdrawals from an aquifer to an amount equal to the average annual recharge of the aquifer, thereby avoiding the possibility of serious overdraft of the aquifer and reducing the possibility of widespread well interference claims. * * * Returning to the Pyle v. Gilbert setting as another example, a permit system can proactively mediate in-stream/off-stream user conflicts by prescribing as a permit condition for off-stream users a minimum streamflow that must be maintained.

The claimed advantages of the administrative allocation of water are not free goods. Offsetting the anticipated gains are predictable pitfalls of managerialism that can be lumped into two camps: monetary costs needed to support the operation of the system and inefficiencies resulting from administrative bad judgment. Importantly, the monetary costs extend beyond the salaries of the bureaucratic personnel it takes to staff the permit agency and the space required to house them. Rather, costs accrue to the permit applicants and other interested parties for the time and hired expertise that must attend their participation in the permit system. Additional monetary costs surely arise as a result of the delays inherent in the operation of any quasi-adjudicative body in which multiple perspectives are represented and administrative decisions are subject to several layers of agency and judicial review.

The costs associated with administrative bad judgments are harder to identify and assess.[27] In a farm belt state, for example, the administrative agency might be too generous with farm-related water use permits and too stingy with industrial permits despite the fact that in almost all instances the industrial uses will be of far higher value.[28] From an economist's perspective, this allocation of a scarce resource is inefficient and more likely to occur in a system that relies on a governmental, rather than on a market, allocation of the resource.

Questions

On balance, do comprehensive permit systems as a replacement for riparianism seem likely to obtain benefits that outweigh their costs? Will the answer depend on the frequency of water allocation conflicts? Can administrative systems be designed in a way that operates selectively, regulating those users only who are likely to contribute to water use conflicts, while leaving others free of the burdens of regulation?

———

A growing number of states in the East have adopted some sort of permit system.[1] The typical system allows all pre-existing uses to contin-

27. An intermediate form of inefficiency between administrative overhead and administrative malallocation is administrative overmanagement. In a basin with no foreseeable potential for shortage, to have any managerial system whatever is to overmanage and incur costs that produce no benefit. This problem is usually addressed by simple rules of exemption on the basis of low volume usage. More sophisticated rules of permit system inclusion and exclusion can be drawn that limit even further the cost of overmanagement.

28. The bad judgments may include bad judgments by the legislature in fixing policy guidelines for the administrative agency. The preference for a less valuable use over a more valuable use could issue from the legislature and be beyond the authority of the agency to change. See Iowa Code Ann. § 455B.266(2) (Supp. 1989) (preferring livestock production use to manufacturing and industrial or power generation use).

1. In recent years, the number appears to have grown from 12 to as many as 19. Compare Peter Davis, Eastern Water Diversion Permit Statutes: Precedents for Missouri?, 47 Mo. L. Rev. 429, 446 n. 76 (1982) with George Sherk, Eastern Water Law: Trends in State Legislation, 9 Va. Envtl. L. Rev. 287, 294 (1990). Sherk lists the states having permit systems for both groundwater and surface water use as Connecticut, Delaware, Florida, Georgia, Illinois, Indiana, Kentucky, Maine, Maryland, Mississippi, New Jersey, New York, North Carolina, Ohio, South Carolina, Tennessee, Virginia, West Virginia and Wisconsin. Several of the remaining riparian states have considered permit systems or statutory overlays to their underlying common law. It is important to observe that the scope of these statutes varies widely. See George Sherk, Eastern Water Law, 1 Nat. Resources & Env't 7 (1986).

ue on the condition that the riparians involved file a notice of their use and/or apply for and receive a permit under the new system. All prospective water users are required to apply for a permit, and, depending on the statute's provisions, may be denied a permit or have the permit granted but conditioned by the administrative body created by the statute. Denials can occur when the proposed use is inconsistent with the state's water management objectives.

As noted by Professor Davis, the permit systems have a variety of purposes and provisions:

> Those purposes include allocating water among competing users, promoting beneficial and efficient uses of water, assuring the best use of water in the public interest, dealing with water shortages, protecting public water supplies, protecting minimum streamflows, promoting flood control, promoting water conservation, and establishing state comprehensive water planning.[2]

Several of the individual state statutes have their roots in the Model Water Use Act (1958).[3] The Model Act relied on a powerful administrative agency that was given both the authority to make water policy and the power to implement the policy through the operation of the permit system and additional regulatory powers. Beyond comprehensive planning, the main thrust of the Model Act was to limit future uses by means of a permit system. The essentials of that system fell into three major categories: permitting domestic uses (§ 301), permitting continuation of existing uses with the possibility of allowing change of uses to more beneficial uses (§§ 303–305), and adopting prospectively a rigorous permit system that would scrutinize and, if needed, limit, the initiation of all non-domestic uses (§§ 401–415).

More recently, the Water Law Committee of the American Society of Civil Engineers, under the leadership of Professor Joseph Dellapenna, completed work on a new model code that reflects what has transpired in the states that have moved to regulatory codes to replace or supplement common law riparianism. The model also tries to synthesize and improve on the efforts to date. Selections from that work appear below and include portions of both the code's "Black letter" and its commentary.

THE REGULATED RIPARIAN MODEL WATER CODE

Water Laws Committee.
Water Resources Planning & Management Division
American Society of Civil Engineers (1997).

CHAPTER I: DECLARATIONS OF POLICY

§ 1R–1–01 Protecting the Public Interest in the Waters of the State

The waters of the State are a natural resource owned by the State in trust for the public and subject to the State's sovereign power to plan,

2. Peter Davis, Eastern Water Diversion Permit Statutes: Precedents for Missouri?, 47 Mo. L. Rev. 429, 446–47 (1982).

3. The Model Water Act, developed by the Commissioners on Uniform State Laws, is to be distinguished from the Model Water Code. The Model Water Code was developed later in time. See Francis Maloney, Richard Ausness & J. Scott Morris, A Model Water Code with Commentary (1972). Florida's statutory enactment is patterned on the Model Water Code.

regulate, and control the withdrawal and use of those waters, under law, in order to protect the public health, safety, and welfare by promoting economic growth, mitigating the harmful effects of drought, resolving conflicts among competing water users, achieving balance between consumptive and nonconsumptive uses of water, encouraging conservation, preventing excessive degradation of natural environments, and enhancing the productivity of water-related activities.

§ 1R–1–02 Assuring Efficient and Productive Use of Water

Pursuant to this Code, the State undertakes, by permits and other steps authorized by this Code, to allocate the waters of the State among users in a manner that fosters efficient and productive use of the total water supply of the State in a sustainable manner in the satisfaction of economic, environmental, and other social goals, whether public or private, with the availability and utility of water being extended with a view of preventing water from becoming a limiting factor in the general improvement of social welfare.

* * *

§ 1R–1–05 Efficient and Equitable Allocation During Shortfalls in Supply

The State, in the exercise of its sovereign police power to protect the public interest in the waters of the State, undertakes to provide, through this Code, an orderly strategy to allocate available water efficiently and equitably in times of water shortage or water emergency.

* * *

§ 1R–1–07 Flexibility through Modification of Water Rights

In order to attain contemporary economic, environmental, and other social goals, the State shall encourage and enable the sale or other voluntary modification of water rights subject to the protection of third parties and the public interest.

* * *

§ 1R–1–11 Preservation of Minimum Flows and Levels

The State shall preserve minimum flows and levels in all water sources as necessary to protect the appropriate biological, chemical, and physical integrity of water sources by reserving such waters from allocation and by authorizing additional protections of the waters of the State.

* * *

§ 1R–1–14 Regulating Interbasin Transfers

The State shall protect the reasonable needs of water basins of origin through the regulation of interbasin transfers.

* * *

CHAPTER II: GENERAL PROVISIONS

Part 1: General Obligations and Prohibitions

This Part reaffirms the basic rule of decision in riparian law that uses of water are lawful only if reasonable and also that vested property rights are to be protected. This Part, however, changes one feature of traditional riparian law that severely constrained the utility of the reasonability premise in operation: that uses on land that were not contiguous to the water source or within the same watershed were inherently unreasonable. See section 2R–1–02. This change, coupled with the addition of the requirement of a permit for most withdrawals of water provided in Chapters VI and VII, significantly transforms the manner in which the traditional criterion of reasonableness will be applied even while leaving its substantive content intact. * * *

§ 2R–1–01 The Obligation to Make Only Reasonable Use of Water.

No person shall make any use of the waters of the State except in so far as the use is reasonable as determined pursuant to this Code.

§ 2R–1–02 No Prohibition of Use Based on Location of Use

(1) Uses of the waters of the State on nonriparian or nonoverlying land are lawful and entitled to equal consideration with uses on riparian or overlying land in any administrative or judicial proceeding relating to the allocation, withdrawal, or use of water or to the modification of a water right.

(2) Nothing in this Code shall be construed to authorize access to the waters of the State by a person seeking to make a nonriparian or nonoverlying use apart from access otherwise lawfully available to that person.

§ 2R–1–03 No Unreasonable Injury to Other Water Rights

No person using the waters of the State shall cause unreasonable injury to other water uses made pursuant to valid water rights, regardless of whether the injury relates to the quality or the quantity impacts of the activity causing the injury.

* * *

Part 2: Definitions

* * *

§ 2R–2–11 Modification of a Water Right

A "modification of a water right" is any change in the terms and conditions of a permit, whether voluntary or involuntary on the part of the permit holder, including, without being limited to:

(a) exchanges of water rights; or

(b) changes in:

    (1) the holder of the permit,

    (2) the type, place, or time of use,

    (3) the point or means of withdrawal,

    (4) the place or manner of storage or application, or

    (5) the point of return flow, or

    (6) any combination of such changes.

* * *

§ 2R–2–14 Permit

A "permit" under this Code means a written authorization issued by the State Agency to a person entitling that person to hold and exercise a water right involving the withdrawal of a specific quantity of water at a specific time and place for a specific reasonable use as described in the written authorization.

* * *

§ 2R–2–18 The Public Interest

The "public interest" is any interest in the waters of the State or in water usage within the State shared by the people of the State as a whole and capable of protection or regulation by law, as informed by the policies and mandates of this Code.

* * *

§ 2R–2–20 Reasonable Use

"Reasonable use" means the use of water, whether in place or through withdrawal, in such quantity and manner as is necessary for economic and efficient utilization without waste of water, without unreasonable injury to other water right holders, and consistently with the public interest and sustainable development.

Commentary: "Reasonable use" has long been the criterion of decision under the common law of riparian rights. In that setting, the concept was strictly relational, with the court deciding whether one use was "more reasonable" than a competing or interfering use, except in the rare case when a particular use was "unreasonable *per se*." See generally Restatement (Second) of Torts ch. 41 (1979); [Joseph Dellapenna, Riparianism, in 2 Water & Water Rights §§ 7.02(d), 7.03 (Robert Beck, ed., 2d ed. 1991)]. The Regulated Riparian Model Water Code defines "reasonable use" in rather more abstract terms relating to the manner in which water is used, but also retains the relational concept that a reasonable use is one that does not unreasonably injure other uses. See Dellapenna, § 9.03(b)(1). The framework of analysis of whether a particular use is reasonable will be dictated by the goal of sustainable development. * * *

§ 2R–2–26 Unreasonable Injury

"Unreasonable injury" means an adverse material change in the quantity, quality, or timing of water available for any lawful use caused by any action taken by another person if:

(a) the social utility of the injured use is greater than the social utility of the action causing the injury; or

(b) the cost of avoiding or mitigating the injury is materially less than the costs imposed by the injury.

Commentary: * * * The Code incorporates the core of the common-law of riparian rights (and of some forms of the law of underground water) without necessarily accepting the particular details of the caselaw developed prior to the Code. The basic change introduced by the Code is that generally whether an injury is unreasonable will be determined by the State Agency rather than by a court. This not only means that the decision will be made by persons who better understand the hydrology of the dispute; it also means that, as the State Agency is charged with important and extensive responsibilities for gathering data and developing plans for water usage in the State, the persons making the decision are also likely to be better able to assess the competing social utilities of the two competing uses. As a result, the determination of whether an injury is unreasonable is likely to be somewhat more abstract than when the dispute is presented to a court. See Dellapenna, § 7.02(d)(1).

The basic notion is that an injury is unreasonable if the value or social utility of the prevailing use is less than the social value or utility of the impaired use. Another test is if the costs of avoiding or mitigating the injury through steps taken by those responsible for the action causing the injury would be less than the costs of the injury to the one responsible for the injured use. Often this second test will actually be a particular application of the first test of relative social utility, but this will not always be so. Consistent with riparian theory generally, this Code takes the position not only that a less socially valuable use of water should not interfere with a more socially valuable use, but that no injury should be caused to another lawful use of water if the costs of avoiding that injury are materially less than the losses (costs) caused by the injury. * * *

§ 2R–2–31 Water Shortage

(1) A "water shortage" is a condition, in all or any part of the State, where, because of droughts or otherwise, the available water falls so far below normally occurring quantities that substantial conflict among water users or injury to water resources are expected to occur.

(2) A "water shortage" is recognized in law only as declared by the State Agency.

* * *

CHAPTER IV: ADMINISTRATION

* * *

§ 4R–1–08 Water Use Fees

(1) The State Agency shall, by regulation of general application after public notice and hearings, establish a schedule of reasonable water use fees as compensation for the value of water used.

(2) The State Agency shall collect water use fees from every person withdrawing water under a permit issued pursuant to this Code.

(3) Water use fees shall vary only according to the class of use as determined by the purpose or quantity of use.

(4) Such fees shall be paid into the general funds of the State.

* * *

CHAPTER VI: ESTABLISHING A WATER RIGHT

* * *

Part 3: The Basis of a Water Right

This Part sets forth the standards to be used in evaluating a permit application. In particular, this Part specifies the factors relevant to determining whether a particular proposed use is reasonable. Certain limited preferences are provided for use in the permit process, but that are also relevant in times of water shortage or water emergency. Special standards are provided for interbasin transfers, including the power of the State Agency to provide for generalized compensation to the basin of origin for the secondary and tertiary effects of an interbasin diversion.

§ 6R–3–01 Standards for a Permit

(1) The State Agency shall approve an application and issue a permit only upon determining that:

(a) the proposed use is reasonable;

(b) the proposed withdrawal, in combination with other relevant withdrawals, will not exceed the safe yield of the water source;

(c) the proposed withdrawal and use are consistent with any applicable comprehensive water allocation plan and drought management strategies;

(d) both the applicant's existing water withdrawals and use, if any, and the proposed withdrawal and use incorporate a reasonable plan for conservation; and

(e) the proposed withdrawal and use will be consistent with the provisions of this Code and any order, permit term or condition, and regulation made pursuant to this Code or any other statute pertaining to the use of water.

(2) In any judicial review of the Agency's determination under subsection (1) of this section, the burden of proof shall be on the person challenging the Agency's determination.

Commentary: This section of the Regulated Riparian Model Water Code sets forth the standards that govern whether a permit shall be issued. Subsection (1)(a) sets forth the most basic standard, that any proposed use must be reasonable. The definition of a reasonable use requires that the use be efficient and not involve the waste of water, that the use will not unreasonably injure or otherwise burden any other individual water user or class of water user, that the use will not endanger the public health, safety or welfare or otherwise conflict with the public interest, and that the use is consistent with sustainable development. The public interest relative to the waters of the State, other than the immediate protection of public health, safety, and welfare, is found in the policies expressed in this Code. * * *

§ 6R–3–02 Determining Whether a Use Is Reasonable

In determining whether a use is reasonable, the State Agency shall consider:

(a) the number of persons using a water source and the object, extent, and necessity of the proposed withdrawal and use and of other existing or planned withdrawals and uses of water;

(b) the supply potential of the water source in question, considering quantity, quality, and reliability, including the safe yields of all hydrologically interconnected water sources;

(c) the economic and social importance of the proposed water use and other existing or planned water uses sharing the water source;

(d) the probable severity and duration of any injury caused or expected to be caused to other lawful consumptive and nonconsumptive uses of water by the proposed withdrawal and use under foreseeable conditions;

(e) the probable effects of the proposed withdrawal and use on the public interest in the waters of the State, including, but not limited to:

(1) general environmental, ecological, and aesthetic effects;

(2) sustainable development;

(3) domestic and municipal uses;

(4) recharge areas for underground water;

(5) waste assimilation capacity;

(6) other aspects of water quality; and

(7) wetlands and flood plains;

(f) whether the proposed use is planned in a fashion that will avoid or minimize the waste of water;

(g) any impacts on interstate or interbasin water uses;

(h) the scheduled date the proposed withdrawal and use of water is to begin and whether the projected time between the issuing of the permit and the expected initiation of the withdrawal will unreasonably preclude other possible uses of the water; and

(i) any other relevant factors.

Commentary: This section describes the factors that shall inform any decision by the State Agency regarding whether a proposed use is reasonable. Given the dual nature of the standard of reasonable use, the factors to be considered include both abstract questions of the social utility or value of the proposed use and also relational questions of the relative value of the proposed use compared to other existing or planned uses. This section also indicates that the question of reasonableness requires the Agency to consider impacts on users dependent on other hydrologically interconnected water sources, and on users in other water basins and in other States. * * *

Droughts will provide another occasion when the reasonableness principle will come into play. Existing permits can be restricted during water shortages and water emergencies. If there is a water shortage or water emergency, the Agency will restrict wells (or other withdrawals) more severely according to the reasonableness of the use. This last possibility arises even for wells or other withdrawals for which no permit is required. See section 7R–3–05. Shallow wells for domestic purposes might be protected to some extent given the priority given to the preservation of human life, yet those shallow wells will be most vulnerable to the effects of drought. The Agency will have to balance these concerns in order to manage the effects of drought reasonably. The Agency might, for example, authorize a competing deep, high pressure well to continue operating but require its owners to provide substitute water for domestic purposes to owners of shallow wells that go dry from the combined effects of the drought and the continued pumping from the deeper well. Other solutions might be found. Whatever the solution, it will be based upon reasonableness rather than upon temporal priority.

The list of factors to be considered in determining reasonableness is long, and involves features that relate to both the abstract and the relational aspects. The analysis rewards applications for permits that seek to minimize adverse impacts on other private and public values. No precise formula for combining these several factors can be devised, leaving considerable discretion in the Agency to weigh and balance these factors to determine whether a particular proposed use is reasonable. * * *

§ 6R–3–04 Preferences Among Water Rights

(1) When the waters available from a particular water source are insufficient to satisfy all lawful demands upon that water source, water is to be allocated by permits up to the safe yield or other applicable limit of allocation of the resource according to the following preferences:

(a) direct human consumption or sanitation in so far as necessary for human survival and health;

(b) uses necessary for the survival or health of livestock and to preserve crops or physical plant and equipment from physical damage or loss in so far as it is reasonable to continue such activities in relation to particular water sources; and

(c) other uses in such a manner as to maximize employment and economic benefits within the overall goal of sustainable development as set forth in the comprehensive water plan.

(2) In processing applications for withdrawals from water sources within the scope of subsection (1) of this section, the State Agency may determine whether applications are competing by aggregating the applications by periods of time, not to exceed one year, the periods to be set by regulation.

(3) Within each preference category, uses are to be preferred that maximize the reasonable use of water.

(4) Applications to renew a permit issued under this Code shall be evaluated by the same criteria applicable to an original application, except that renewals shall be favored over competing applications for new withdrawals if the public interest is served equally by the competing water uses after giving consideration to the prior investment pursuant to a valid water right in related facilities as a factor in determining the public interest.

＊ ＊ ＊

§ 6R–3–06 Special Standard for Interbasin Transfers

(1) In determining whether to issue a permit for an interbasin transfer of water, the State Agency shall give particular weight to any foreseeable adverse impacts that would impair the sustainable development of the water basin of origin.

(2) In addition to the factors set forth in sections 6R–3–01 to 6R–3–05 of this Code, in determining whether an interbasin transfer is reasonable the State Agency shall consider:

(a) the supply of water available to users in the basin of origin and available to the applicant within the basin in which the water is proposed to be used;

(b) the overall water demand in this basin of origin and in the basin in which the water is proposed to be used; and

(c) the probable impact of the proposed transportation and use of water out of the basin of origin on existing or foreseeable shortages in the basin of origin and in the basin in which the water is proposed to be used.

(3) When authorizing an interbasin transfer notwithstanding probable impairment to the existing or future uses of water in the basin of origin, the State Agency shall assess a compensation fee to be paid into

the Interbasin Compensation Fund by the person granted a permit for the interbasin transfer in so far as is necessary to compensate the basin of origin for generalized losses not attributable to injuries to particular holders of water rights in the basin of origin.

* * *

CHAPTER VII: SCOPE OF THE WATER RIGHT

Part 1: Extent of the Right

§ 7R–1–01 Permit Terms and Conditions

If the State Agency approves an application for a new, renewed, or modified permit, the Agency shall modify an existing permit or issue a new one, indicating in the permit the following terms and conditions:

(a) the location of the withdrawal;

(b) the authorized amount of the withdrawal and the level of consumptive use, if any, and required conservation measures, if any;

(c) the dates or seasons during which water is to be withdrawn, including any seasonal or shorter variations in the authorized withdrawals or level of consumptive use;

(d) the uses for which water is authorized to be withdrawn;

(e) the amount of return flow required, if any, and the required place of discharge, if any;

(f) the requirements for metering, surveillance, and reporting as the State Agency determines to be necessary to ensure compliance with other conditions, limitations, or restrictions of the permit, including consent to inspections or investigations as provided in section 4R–4–01 of this Code;

(g) the time within which all necessary construction authorized by the permit must be completed or within which the withdrawal or use of water must begin to be made, with the delay not to exceed one-half of the duration of the permit, subject to extension by order of the State Agency for cause shown;

(h) any extraordinary withdrawals of the waters of the State necessary for the construction of any facilities necessary to withdraw or use the water;

(i) any obligation to restore the lands or waters of the State to their condition prior to the issuance of the permit upon its expiration;

(j) the date on which the permit expires;

(k) payment by a holder of a water right involving an interbasin transfer of a withdrawal fee to be paid into Interbasin Compensation Fund; and

(*l*) any other conditions, limitations, and restrictions the State Agency determines to be necessary to protect the public interest, the environment and ecosystems, the public health, safety, and welfare, and to ensure the conservation, sustainable development, proper management, and aesthetic enhancement of the waters of the State.

§ 7R–1–02 Duration of Permits

(1) The State Agency shall issue permits for a period of time representing the economic life of any necessary investments not to exceed 20 years, except that permits may be issued for a period reasonable for the retirement of debt associated with the construction of related facilities by a governmental or other public body or public service corporation not to exceed 50 years.

  * * *

Part 3: Restrictions during Water Shortages or Water Emergencies

One of the central purposes of a regulated riparian system of water law is to enable a State to cope reasonably and effectively with the recurring shortfalls in water supply that are becoming more frequent in the humid parts of the nation. See Robert Abrams, Charting the Course of Riparianism: An Instrumentalist Theory of Change, 35 Wayne L. Rev. 1381 (1989). As a result, water conservation permeates the entire Regulated Riparian Model Water Code, and the Code is suffused by the goal of sustainable development. The dominant mode by which water is managed during periods of water crisis under a regulated riparian system is the pairing of a comprehensive information gathering system with legal authority in the state to restrict uses during periods of shortfalls of water supply notwithstanding the permits authorizing greater use during periods of normal supply. * * *

§ 7R–3–01 Authority to Restrict Permit Exercise

(1) The State Agency may restrict any term or condition of any permit issued under this Code for the duration of a water shortage or a water emergency declared by the Agency.

(2) The State Agency is to impose restrictions according to previously developed drought management strategies unless the Agency determines that the relevant drought management strategies are inappropriate to the actual situation.

(3) In implementing restrictions under this section, the State Agency shall comply with the preferences provided in section 6R–3–04.

Notes and Questions

1. The Model Code's commentary preceding its Chapter II points out that it "repeals any limitations on the use of water derived from the location of the use." The common law had gradually moved in that direction, but this stark declaration signals a near total severance of many usufructuary water rights from the riparian parcel. What is left that requires the ownership of riparian land? Two general categories come to mind, (1) uses that require proximity to the water, such as wharfing out and recreational use of non-navigable waters, and (2) control over access to initiate diversions, that is, a

non-riparian user is not able to take the water via a trespass, an easement must be obtained from a riparian. See § 2R–1–02. The latter power of "true" riparians to refuse access for diversions is reduced in two ways, some users will be clothed with the power of eminent domain and some users will be able to initiate their withdrawal by pumping hydrologically interconnected groundwater instead of making a surface water diversion.

2. What is the significance of erecting a permit requirement for the initiation of new and modified uses? Though it does not alter the measure of permissible uses from the reasonableness standard, it applies that standard before a use is initiated rather than in after-the-fact litigation. In practice, does that change add greater certainty to the rights of permit holders than that of common law riparian water users?

3. The permit granting agency appears to be quite powerful. Chapter V of the code subjects the agency to typical procedural requirements involving notice and opportunity to be heard, as well as typical administrative law modes requiring reasoned decisionmaking subject to judicial review.

4. Consider the fee system that the agency is required by section 4R–1–08 to erect. The fees are required to cover "the value of the water used." How does this alter past practice? What practical effects can be predicted if, as seems somewhat unlikely, the agency really charges fees based on value?

5. Read together, do sections 6R–3–01 and 6R–3–02 improve upon section 850A of the Restatement (Second) of Torts in describing what constitutes a reasonable use of water? Other approaches also are being explored. The trend toward regulated riparianism can also be seen at the regional and even international level. In 2001, the Governors and Premiers of the ten Great Lakes states and provinces signed a non-binding agreement that proposed three key standards for managing and regulating water withdrawals:

1. Preventing or minimizing [Great Lakes] Basin water loss through return flow and implementation of environmentally sound and economically feasible water conservation measures;

2. No significant adverse individual or cumulative impacts to the quantity or quality of the waters and water-dependent natural resources of the Great Lakes Basin; and

3. An improvement to the waters and water-dependent natural resources of the Great Lakes Basin.

The first standard is clearly based on well-established common law riparian principles favoring in-basin use and disfavoring wasteful water practices. The second standard incorporates environmental protection into riparianism, as does the Model Code. The third standard, requiring improvement to the environmental health of the water body as a condition of use, is a significant innovation. This standard can be justified as an emanation of trust principles, requiring current users of a public resource to ensure that the resource is left in better condition for future generations. It can also be seen as a recognition that environmental protection laws that only aim to prevent deterioration often allow a slow degradation over time. For a thorough description of the standard and its anticipated operation in the Great Lakes region, see Noah Hall, Towards a New Horizontal Federalism:

Interstate Water Management in the Great Lakes Region, 77 Colo. L. Rev. 405 (2006).

6.   How does water allocation under the code change in (1) predictable shortage and (2) emergency situations? The former is governed by section 6R–3–04 that limits permit allocations to safe yield and establishes preferences among uses in the event that there is not enough water to satisfy all users. Would the common law have done the same thing? Section 7R–3–06(3) indicates that the same preferences govern in emergency situations. Given their importance, are the preferences erected by section 6R–3–04 self-evidently correct for all states that might adopt the code?

7.   Assume an interbasin transfer for municipal supply purposes is proposed under the code. Compare the preferences material and section 6R–3–06 of the code with the municipal supply standards the New York's DEQ had to apply in the *Hudson River Fishermans* case. Which approach seems more likely to lead to sound, consistent decisionmaking? As a further comparison, under the code, would the Virginia Beach case have unfolded any differently? At least in regard to the array of "small handle" efforts to block the project, section 2R–1–02(2) makes it clear that the code would not prevent such attacks on the transfer.

8.   Assuming that common law riparianism would not be a suitable governing law in the event that water became a truly scarce resource in the East, would "regulated riparianism" succeed any better? What demands must a water law system satisfy? One of the authors has suggested the following:

> Here, the instrumentalist theory forms the basis for a reverse engineering project, identifying those water uses that are quintessentially important, and working back to legal mechanisms that promote them. Society demands that the water needed to fill the most critical uses—drinking, sewage, and ecosystem maintenance—be exempt from curtailment. To protect the security of use for the most important classes of use, the legal system can grant an enforceable preference to receive the water ahead of less vital uses. To protect the economies that surround those penultimate and other water dependent activities, the system must provide as much additional security of right as possible. An entire hierarchical system emerges as each class of use is identified in order of importance.

Robert Abrams, Replacing Riparianism in the Twenty–First Century, 36 Wayne L. Rev. 93, 124 (1989). In addition to protecting the most critical uses of water in time of shortage, what are other vital issues that an operative water law must address? Security of right that will promote water-dependant investment is also important, as is managerial flexibility that will allow water use patterns to change over time to reflect changing values of water in different uses. Are security of right and flexibility of use inherently inconsistent? See generally Richard Epstein, The Social Consequences of Common Law Rules, 95 Harv. L. Rev. 1717 (1982). Section 7R–1–102 has a subsection that provides a limited preference for renewals over new permit applicants. Does the combination of the relatively lengthy permit duration, renewal preferences, and special rules for permit modification in times of shortage strike a proper balance?

F. THE LAW OF DRAINAGE

Diffused surface waters are the subject of extensive definitions, but essentially, they are the run-off of precipitation before that run-off enters well defined streams and lakes. Historically, the law of all sections of the nation has segregated diffused surface water from flowing water or standing water, even though the physical realities of the hydrologic cycle do not offer any support for making such a distinction. Most of the cases involving diffused surface water relate to drainage rather than to the capture and use of the water. The upper owner of a parcel (not necessarily a riparian) seeks to throw the unwanted water down on a lower proprietor to that proprietor's detriment.

In the Eastern United States there are two traditional approaches to the legal governance of diffused surface waters, one deemed the civil law approach and the other colorfully referred to as the common enemy doctrine. "The civil law rule finds its origin in the maxim, *aqua currit et debet currere, ut solebat es juie naturae.*[4] In its purest form, the rule makes any diversion of surface water from its natural flow a tortious act."[5] As might be supposed, few states are willing to pay the anti-developmental consequences of so restrictive a rule, and the civil law rule has been modified to permit alterations in the flow of diffused surface waters, especially if the resultant damage to affected parcels is slight, and there is no alternative means of pursuing the developmental activity that preserves the natural pattern of run-off.

In contrast, the common enemy doctrine is based on the familiar *ad coelum* theory of absolute dominion of real property from the heavens to the depths. Viewing surface water as literally a common enemy of all landowners, each is entitled to do whatever is needed to protect her own parcel from damage caused by such waters. It matters not that one landowner's saving of her own property causes damage to another's property. The ameliorative sub-doctrines found in states following the common enemy doctrine resemble to some degree a requirement that in fighting the common enemy, a landowner must avoid active negligence that would damage another's lands. Thus, for example, if a landowner acts to collect surface water on her own land, she must take care in the manner of its subsequent discharge onto lower lying lands.

In recent times, nearly half of the states have moved from the civil and common law approaches to a so-called "reasonable use" rule, but it is not the same reasonable use rule that governs accommodation of competing riparian uses. Typical of these developments are McGlashan v. Spade Rockledge Terrace Condo Dev. Corp., 62 Ohio St.2d 55, 402

4. "Water runs and should run, as it is wont to do by natural right."—Eds.

5. Gwenn Rinkenberger, Landowner's Right To Fight Surface Water: The Applica-

tion of the Common Enemy Doctrine in Indiana, 18 Val. U. L. Rev. 481, 484 (1984).

N.E.2d 1196 (1980) and Hall v. Wood, 443 So.2d 834 (Miss. 1983). The *McGlashan* court stated:

> an analysis centering on the reasonableness of a defendant's conduct, in view of all the circumstances, is more likely to produce an equitable result than one based on arbitrary property concepts. It is true that the law should not inhibit reasonable land development, but neither should it allow a landowner to expel surface water without regard to the consequences. As eloquently stated by Justice Brennan in Armstrong v. Francis Corp. (1956), 20 N.J. 320, 330, 120 A.2d 4, 10, "no reason suggests itself why, in justice, the economic costs incident to the expulsion of surface waters in the transformation of the rural or semi-rural areas of our State into urban or suburban communities should be borne in every case by adjoining landowners rather than by those who engage in such projects for profit. Social progress and the common well-being are in actuality better served by a just and right balancing of the competing interests according to the general principles of fairness and common sense which attend the application of the rule of reason."

In *Hall* the court stated:

> we hold that upper landowners such as Hall are entitled to make reasonable use of their land. Where there is a reasonable likelihood of damage to the property of lower landowners, however, upper landowners are required to do whatever is reasonable to minimize the damage. The fact that some damage nevertheless occurs to the lower landowners does not render the upper landowner liable. On the other hand, where the upper landowner has done nothing in an effort to ameliorate the adverse effect on lower landowners and where the damage is in fact substantial, and further where the development activities of the upper landowner are a major proximate cause of that damage, the lower landowners are entitled to damages and/or injunctive relief as may be appropriate.

The following case provides a forum for discussion of the relative strengths and weaknesses of the competing doctrines.

ARGYELAN v. HAVILAND

Supreme Court of Indiana, 1982.
435 N.E.2d 973.

PRENTICE, JUSTICE.

[The Argyelans (defendants) developed their parcel in a way that increased the amount of area covered by buildings and parking lots. These changes increased the drainage of water onto the Havilands' (plaintiffs) adjoining lands. Thereafter, plaintiffs found that the surface water draining from defendants' property onto their property, was pooling there and causing substantial damage. More facts are mentioned in the opinion.]

Historically, two diametrically opposed but clear rules were consistently followed in the various states with respect to surface water, which must be distinguished from water flowing, even if not continuously, through established and defined channels. Through extensive modifications of both rules, a third doctrine emerged and has been adopted in approximately twenty of the states. These rules, their development and their application are extensively treated and annotated at 93 A.L.R.3d 1193 et seq.

In its most simplistic and pure form the rule known as the "common enemy doctrine," declares that surface water which does not flow in defined channels is a common enemy and that each landowner may deal with it in such manner as best suits his own convenience. Such sanctioned dealings include walling it out, walling it in and diverting or accelerating its flow by any means whatever.

The "civil law" doctrine, on the other hand, proscribes interfering with or altering the flow of surface water.

Both doctrines are harsh but have the common virtue of predictability. Under them, landowners know where they stand. They know what they may do and what they may not do without incurring severe risks. If at times the doctrines work to one's disadvantage, there are other times when he reaps its benefits. * * *

The common enemy and civil law rules are grounded upon real property concepts. The modifications engrafted upon them resulted from the use of tort law concepts used to mitigate the harsh results of the property law doctrines. The doctrine of "reasonable use," however, goes much further and focuses upon the results of the action and the consequent interference with another's use of his land. Its advantage is flexibility. Its disadvantage, obviously is its unpredictability.

Although Indiana doubtlessly would not permit a malicious or wanton employment of one's drainage rights under the common enemy doctrine, it appears that the only limitation upon such rights that we have thus far judicially recognized is that one may not collect or concentrate surface water and cast it, in a body, upon his neighbor.

Plaintiffs acknowledge the rule in Indiana to be as hereinbefore stated. They appear to argue, however, that by a combination of erecting downspouts directed towards the property line, paving a substantial portion of their land and erecting the aforementioned curb or retaining wall along the property line, the defendants somehow exceed the limits of what is permissible in fending off the surface water. It requires no reweighing of the evidence to determine that the evidence does not bear them out. There is simply no evidence that any surface water was ever channeled from Defendants' land onto that of the plaintiffs or cast in a body upon them.

Under the common enemy doctrine, it is not unlawful to accelerate or increase the flow of surface water by limiting or eliminating ground absorption or changing the grade of the land. These two things, we may concede, are shown by the evidence to have resulted from Defendants' improvements. However, the only evidence that water from the defendants' premises entered those of the plaintiffs' was testimony that, on occasions following sustained moderate to heavy rains, the water built up behind the wall and overflowed it. There was no showing whatever that the defendants, conducted the water "by new channels in unusual quantities onto particular parts of the lower field" as in Templeton v. Voshloe, (1880) 72 Ind. 134, or collected the water in a volume and cast it, as in Davis v. City of Crawfordsville, (1888) 119 Ind. 1, 21 N.E. 449, and in Patoka Township et al. v. Hopkins, (1891) 131 Ind. 142, 30 N.E. 896, or "shed the water from their building so as to *throw* it upon the appellant's lot" (emphasis added) as in Conner v. Woodfill et al, (1890) 126 Ind. 85, 25 N.E. 876.

We do not intimate, as Plaintiffs erroneously infer that the Court of Appeals did, that a distinction can be drawn between the case before us and the *Conner* case upon the basis that Defendants' downspouts are situated twenty feet from the property line whereas in *Conner* they were but eight feet removed. The distinction lies in the character of the flow as it entered the adjoining property. That water was once impounded or channeled can be of no moment if it is diffused to a general flow at the point of entering the adjoining land. * * *

To Judge Hoffman's comments we add that although the Common Enemy Doctrine may, at times, inflict hardships, it is as fair to one as it is to another—a guiding precept of the law. Additionally, it has worked satisfactorily in this State from the beginning, and it is well understood. There has been no change in the forces that cause water to run down hill since the problems caused thereby were first considered and resolved in this State; and there is no basis for assuming that a change in the rules for coping with such problems would, over-all, reduce their number or make them any more palatable.

Although courts should not be slow to respond to changing conditions, changes in the established law are not warranted simply because it is imperfect, and we should not feel compelled to join the ranks of greater numbers when it has not been demonstrated that their way is the better way.

DeBruler and Pivarnik, JJ., concur.

Hunter, J., dissents with opinion in which Givan, C.J., concurs.

Hunter, Justice, dissenting.

* * *

As it is, this jurisdiction is today presented with a rule of law and result so inimical to any sense of justice, be it lay or legal, that it offends our system of jurisprudence. Lest the legal and factual nuances involved in this cause obscure the import of the majority's decision, its ramifications for the homeowners of this state should be recognized from the outset. In its simplest terms, the majority of this Court has held that a landowner, in seeking to use property for a commercial purpose, may so alter the ground surface and natural drainage pattern that an adjacent landowner's existing usage of his property for residential purposes is rendered impossible by virtue of the resultant accumulation and run-off of surface water.

That is a proposition out of step with time and judicial logic, one which, as the majority tacitly concedes, is not and would not be followed by any other jurisdiction in this nation. Our law of surface water is today reduced to the rule of the jungle, where "might makes right" and the race belongs to the person who is last in time, elevates his land the highest, and paves the greater portion of his lot surface. It requires no resort to hyperbole to recognize that the ramifications for the home-owners of this state are unconscionable. * * *

Notes and Questions

1. One commentator takes a dim view of the *Argyelan* decision:

The rationale upon which the court based its conclusion is illusory and, as pointed out by Justice Hunter in his dissenting opinion, offensive to our system of jurisprudence. The use of the common enemy doctrine, which remains as that originally set forth in 1878, is a harsh rule requiring no balancing of interests and frequently leading to unjust results. The single modification to the rule, which states that a landowner has no right to collect surface water in a channel and cast it in a body upon another's land, is rendered virtually meaningless by the court in *Argyelan*, leaving the status of the law in Indiana truly archaic in form.

Gwenn Rinkenberger, Landowner's Right To Fight Surface Water: The Application of the Common Enemy Doctrine in Indiana, 18 Val. U. L. Rev. 481, 481–82 (1984). Is the court too stringent in applying the "channel and cast" modification to the *Argyelan* facts, too concerned about preserving crystals and avoiding mud? Is blacktopping a parking lot, and draining rainwater from a roof the sort of activity to which the channel and cast exception is addressed? See Bell v. Northside Finance Corp., 452 N.E.2d 951 (Ind. 1983).

2. The Ohio court in *McGlashan* praises the flexibility of its new rule, the precise quality that seemed so prominent in the Indiana rejection of the reasonable use doctrine in *Argyelan*. If one must choose between the two views, what are the relevant considerations? How do you measure the impact on would-be-developers of the "uncertainty" of the reasonable use rule? Does it seem likely that socially beneficial projects will be abandoned due to the uncertainty?

3. The importation of a tort standard to this property area is hardly remarkable. Nuisance, a most traditional of torts, has long protected real property interests against adverse impacts caused by property use on adjoining parcels. The move toward treating land/water issues along the lines of tort rather than property is also prominent in efforts to restate the princi-

ples governing riparian rights and groundwater use as a set of tort liability rules in the Restatement (Second) of Torts. See page 57.

4. On the assumption that *McGlashan* is essentially a nuisance case, and *Wood* is essentially a negligence case, which of the two doctrines is better adapted to the range of diffused surface water conflicts? See Donald Burnett, Surface Water And Nuisance Law: A Proposed Synthesis, 20 Idaho L. Rev. 185, 194 (1984) (proposing a nuisance approach in situations where the invasion of the lower property can be attributed to "an altered flow").

5. Is the "basic issue" as simple as the Ohio court in *McGlashan* would have it when it suggests that diffused surface water cases are in reality cost internalization problems? In a state of nature, when run-off causes damage to a lower owner, must the upper owner compensate injured lower owners so as to internalize costs? In that case a liability rule would seem to allow the lower owner to externalize the cost of protecting the lower parcel against damage. Even in the less striking context of requiring the upper owner to refrain from altering the run-off patterns, isn't the lower owner still externalizing a cost of her operation? See Joseph Sax, Takings, Private Property and Public Rights, 81 Yale L.J. 149, 152–53 (1971) (describing the mutual externalities caused by parcels that are "inextricably intertwined").

6. Not all cases involve simple damage caused by the invasion of water from the upper tract. The *Hall* case, supra p. 119, featured damage to a lake on which plaintiffs were riparians:

> Under the facts of this case, we do not hesitate to uphold the conclusions of the chancellor on the question of liability. The Plaintiffs in this case have important and viable property rights in Lake Catherine. That lake lies to the southeast and generally below Leo Hall's 20 acres. Hall stripped his land, albeit with legitimate development plans in mind. He reasonably should have known his actions would result in erosion which in turn would result in substantial silting, sedimentation and general pollution of Lake Catherine. When belatedly Hall attempted corrective actions, he was ineffectual. Without doubt there has been major damage to the ecology of the water of Lake Catherine, and without doubt, the culprit is Hall's skinned land. On the liability phase of this case, we affirm.

7. The law of drainage and the variety of approaches surveyed above is not limited to riparian jurisdictions. See, e.g., White v. Pima County, 161 Ariz. 90, 775 P.2d 1154 (App. 1989) (common enemy doctrine); Weaver v. Bishop, 206 Cal.App.3d 1351, 254 Cal.Rptr. 425 (1988) (reasonable use doctrine); Benton City v. Adrian, 50 Wash.App. 330, 748 P.2d 679 (1988) (nuisance).

Chapter 3

PRIOR APPROPRIATION

A. INTRODUCTION TO THE PRIOR APPROPRIATION SYSTEM

To understand the doctrines and controversies that arise in this section of the book, you first need a rudimentary overview of the functioning of the appropriation system. That is the goal of the following few pages.

The Elements of Appropriation Doctrine

In its pristine form, appropriation law operates as follows:

1. Mere ownership of land gives one no rights to the use of water.

2. Water flowing in a stream in its natural condition is unowned, and is held by the state for acquisition by users.

3. The water so held, known technically as the water of "natural streams", as a practical matter means rivers and lakes, but excludes most unconnected underground water. Even hydrologically connected underground water was traditionally dealt with by its own set of rules, administered separately from surface water. Excluded also are sources like rainwater and melting snow as they pass over the surface of the earth, and prior to the time that they appear in rivers and lakes.[1] These latter sources are technically known as "diffuse surface water."[2] While in that state, they can be captured by the

---

1. State v. Hiber, 48 Wyo. 172, 44 P.2d 1005 (1935) quotes the old, respected treatise, Kinney on Irrigation, §§ 302, 303: "A water course does not include surface water conveyed from higher to lower levels for limited periods, during the melting of snow, or during or soon after a heavy fall of rain, through hollows or ravines which at all other portions of the year are entirely dry.... [A]ccording to the great weight of authority, the essential characteristics of a water course are: A channel, consisting of a well-defined bed and banks, and a current of water."

2. Where such water is unwanted and floods a lower owner's land, the so-called "enemy waters" doctrine applies. A leading case is Keys v. Romley, 64 Cal.2d 396, 50 Cal.Rptr. 273, 412 P.2d 529 (1966). The owner of the upper (dominant) estate is entitled to discharge surface water from his land as the water naturally flows; but is liable if he causes the water to flow down in an unnatural manner, e.g., by channelizing it, or by changing the contour of his lands.

owner of the land over which they are flowing.[3] Once they enter natural streams, they change their legal character and become the water of "natural streams" such as watercourses, or lakes, and are subject to the law governing appropriation of water.

4. One acquires a property right (an appropriation) by taking the water of a natural stream and applying it to a "beneficial use" in a non-wasteful manner with due diligence.[4] That's all there was to the acquisition of a right in the pure appropriation system. Today in most states appropriative rights are acquired though an administrative permit system, and permits can be denied if the proposed use is not in the public interest. As you will soon see, it was traditionally the rule that one had to physically take the water out of the stream in order to put it to a beneficial use, a rule that has largely (but not entirely) been supplanted in favor of some arrangement that allows instream flows to be set aside for environmental purposes.

5. There are no limitations on the place of use. One can appropriate water from a river and carry it out of the watershed, or even out of the state (though modern laws sometimes provide protection for the future needs of areas of origin). It is often necessary to obtain legal access across other peoples' land to get to the water in order to appropriate it, and to carry it to the place of use. The law has allowed appropriators to acquire needed rights-of-way across private land by means of statutes authorizing private eminent domain, whose constitutionality has been sustained (Clark v. Nash, 198 U.S. 361 (1905)). Permits are required in order to convey water across public lands.

6. One cannot hold an appropriative water right merely as an investment for future use. While one acquires a right by applying it to beneficial use, one also loses the right by ceasing to make such a use. The common law doctrine dealing with this matter is called abandonment. Today, state statutes generally provide for loss of the right through forfeiture, which is usually defined as unexcused non-use for a certain period of years (often five years). Some modern statutes, however, provide that appropriators who cease to use some of their water as a result of conservation efforts will not lose that water through forfeiture (e.g., Cal. Water Code § 1011; Or. Rev. Stat. §§ 537.455–.500).

7. One's priority is determined by the date at which water was first applied to beneficial use; or, more commonly where a project takes

But see Grundy v. Thurston County, 117 P.3d 1089 (Wash. 2005), distinguishing the rule applying to surface water from that applying to "water flowing in its natural course or ... forming an identifiable body such as a lake or pond" or storm-driven waves of the ocean.

3. Note, however, that some states presume that all "flowing water, even diffuse runoff and seepage that is not in a defined channel, is presumed to be tributary to the river system." Ready Mixed Concrete Co. v. Farmers Reservoir and Irrigation Co., 115 P.3d 638, 642 (Colo. 2005).

4. The quantum of the right is measured by the amount actually applied to beneficial use, not by the physical capacity of the system. State of Washington v. Theodoratus, 957 P.2d 1241 (Wash. 1998).

time to complete, the priority is given ("relates back" to) the date on which the first work leading to application was begun.[5] The appropriator with the earliest date of appropriation is called the senior, and each person with a later date is junior to anyone with an earlier date. Often these appropriators are referred to by numbers. We speak of #1, #2 and #3, for example, to describe appropriators in the date order of their appropriation, with #1 having the earliest, most senior, appropriation.

8. When there is not enough water in the stream to meet the demands of all appropriators, the law requires that the most junior appropriator cease taking water in order to assure that water will be available to more senior appropriators. If the situation were such that the stream contained only enough water to satisfy the most senior appropriator, all junior appropriators would be required to terminate their uses completely, however severe the consequences for them. Pure appropriation doctrine rejects the notion of equitable sharing, or *pro-rata* reductions (though such arrangements are common among users within a water district or project who share common distribution facilities; there the appropriative right is held in the name of the district). That is why the appropriation system is often described with the phrase "first in time, first in right."

As you will see, almost all these rules have been subject to modification and controversy.[6] For example, modern efforts to promote water marketing may call for less stress on forfeiture for temporary non-use, and contemporary environmental needs have brought recognition that simply leaving water instream is a beneficial use. While important changes are occurring, the elements set out above describe the essential shape of the appropriation system.

1. HOW THE SYSTEM PHYSICALLY FUNCTIONS

With these basic rules in mind, you should next try to visualize the physical system that gives rise to them, and to which they are applied. Here, too, some radical simplification will help you to understand the cases. Figure 3–1 graphically illustrates an appropriation system, and shows how water is used and reused. Figure 3–2 illustrates the relationship between senior and junior appropriators resulting from their relative physical positions on the stream.

---

5. The so-called "first step" test required an overt act that shows intent to appropriate, is a substantial act that indicates something other than speculative interest, and that gives notice to others of the nature and extent of the proposed appropriation. In re Application of Vought v. Stucker Mesa Domestic Pipeline Co., 76 P.3d 906, 912–13 (Colo. 2003).

6. It has been suggested "that the classical principles of prior appropriation have never been applied as purely, as steadily, or as comprehensively as the popular understanding would have it." John Leshy, The Prior Appropriation Doctrine of Water Law in the West: An Emperor with Few Clothes, J. of the West, July 1990, at 5. True enough, but a precept of this book is that to understand how the doctrine has changed and continues to change, one must first understand its fundamental structure.

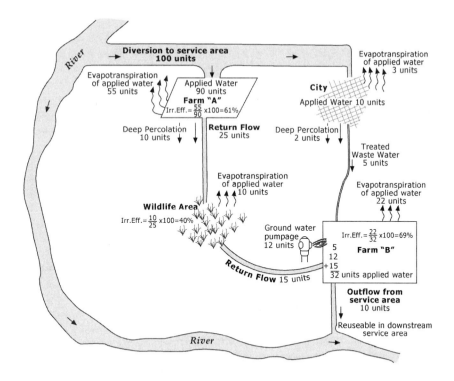

Figure 3-1

Water Use and Reuse

Source: Policies and Goals for California Water Management:
The Next 20 Years, A Joint Report of the State Water Resources Control
Board and the Department of Water Resources (Department of Water
Resources and the State Water Resources Control Board Bulletin No. 4,
January 1982).

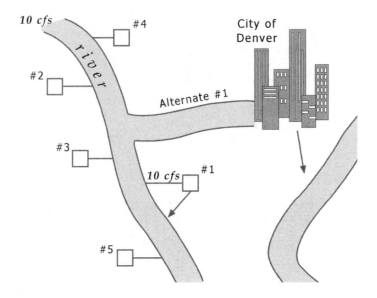

Figure 3–2

Rights to Return Flow

For the moment, forget about lakes (there are rather few natural lakes in the arid west) and think about the system as applying solely to flowing streams on the surface of the earth. Location on the stream can be critical to one's rights. The most senior appropriators are often downstream of some junior appropriators. Where that is the case, upstream junior appropriators may have to let water flow by their point of diversion in order to assure that sufficient water reaches the downstream senior rights. If the distance is great, transmission losses through evaporation and seepage may be considerable, and give rise to claims of inefficiency (or waste, as it is called in water law). If so much water is lost in transit that there would be nothing left for the downstream senior even if the junior ceased to divert, then under the "futile call" doctrine,[7] the senior cannot enjoin the junior's use (cannot "call" the river). This is a rule of simple common sense: the law will not require a futile act.

It also happens frequently that a very junior appropriator is located just downstream of a very senior appropriator. Since most uses of water are not wholly "consumptive," it is quite possible that there will be a "return flow" of water that comes back to the river after the senior has used his appropriation. In such a case (as illustrated in Figure 3–2), a seemingly paradoxical, but entirely logical, result ensues: the only people

---

7. For a statutory embodiment of the doctrine, see Colo. Rev. Stat. § 37–92–102(2)(d).

who are getting water in times of shortage are the most senior and the most junior appropriators.

How does this happen? Assume a river that presently has in it a flow of 10 cubic feet per second (10 cfs).[8] There are five appropriators on the river, each of whom has an appropriation of 10 cfs for the same period of time during the irrigation season. None has any capacity to store water off-season. How, then could all five appropriators have an appropriation for 10 cfs? This is possible because at one time—during some years of high flows—there was enough flow in the river to permit each of the five appropriators to take 10 cfs and to apply it to beneficial use. But now we are in a dryer period, and the total flow this year is only 10 cfs.

The location of the five appropriators, beginning at the most up-stream point on the river is as follows: #4, then #2, then #3, then #1, and finally, at the most downstream point on the river, #5, the most junior appropriator. The law requires that #4, #2 and #3 all let the 10 cfs flow downstream to #1, who takes it out of the river and uses it to irrigate his crops.

With traditional means of irrigation, usually about one-half the water is consumed by the crops, while the other half runs off the surface of the land and finds its way back into the river downstream of #1's farm, but still upstream of the point on the river where #5 diverts water for his farm. If you are unfamiliar with agricultural irrigation, just think of this situation in terms of watering a lawn. Undoubtedly you have seen lawn watering in which some of the water sprinkled on the grass runs off the surface and into the gutter of the street. From there it flows into a sewer and (usually) the sewer discharges this runoff back into a river downstream of the city. This is precisely what happens to much appropriated water in the West. And the result—depending on the location on the river of various appropriators' points of diversion—is that often not only the most senior, but also quite junior appropriators are the only ones who have water available during times of shortage.

There are several collateral points to observe based on this hypothetical example. First, note that whether the return flow in fact returns to the same river from which the appropriator took it depends on several factors. If the senior appropriator in our example has taken the water to a distant place of use out of the watershed, there will still be return flow, but it will return to a different river. For example, the city of Denver may appropriate water from the Colorado River on the west side of the continental divide and carry it over to the city on the east side of the divide (the continental divide, of course, is just a watershed line on a big scale). When Denver returns some percentage of its water after use, it will return it to a river in the watershed of use, rather than the watershed of origin where both #1 and #5 have their diversion facilities.

8. An older measure, rarely used anymore, is the miner's inch, the quantity of water that will flow through a one-inch square under certain pressure. Different states sought to standardize it, but not all used the same measure. It ranged from 38.4 to 50 miner's inches to the cfs.

Thus, if Denver were our hypothetical #1 senior, and the Colorado were our hypothetical river, with a #5 appropriator downstream of Denver's point of diversion, in such a case the downstream #5 junior would get no water, and would be as poorly off as the #2, #3 and #4 appropriators upstream of Denver's point of diversion. Since, as you learned a moment ago, the appropriation system does not prohibit out-of-watershed uses, a downstream junior in this hypothetical example would get no benefit from having its point of diversion located just below that of the senior.

Note also another factor that would prevent the downstream junior from getting the benefit of return flow. Sometimes, even though the place of use is within the same watershed as the point of diversion, the return flow will not go back into the river, but will seep into an underground water supply (called an aquifer). This is illustrated in Figure 3–1, where both some of Farm "A"'s and the City's return flows are lost to the underground, there described as "deep percolation." If this aquifer is not hydrologically connected to the river, then the return flow goes out of the appropriation system, and is dealt with by the separate regime of underground water. (When we get to underground water, you will see that many complex problems are raised by the interplay between surface and ground water systems. Don't worry about these problems now).

In describing the paradox of return flow, and the fact that sometimes very junior people get water while others more senior get none, we mentioned the fact that all five hypothetical appropriators got water rights during some previous period of high flows. This is a very important point, and one that is often found confusing. You need to keep in mind that the mere fact someone was at one time able to obtain an appropriation (at a period when there was much water available) does not mean that they have regularly been getting water from their appropriation. The flows of rivers are highly variable from year to year, with wet cycles and dry cycles. There are many junior appropriations, perfected in past times of abundance, that can be used only rarely because most years the flow of the river is scanty, and only very senior appropriators will be served. If there is no water available, juniors will not lose their rights by the abandonment or forfeiture doctrines mentioned earlier. They simply bide their time, awaiting years of more abundant flows, or abandonment by senior appropriators that will, in effect, move them up on the priority scale. How do such juniors survive in the meantime? They may be using other, more expensive sources, such as wells from which they have to pump. They may be irrigating less than their total acreage. They may be buying water from someone else at a high price, or they may shift to less water-consuming crops.

Note also that because return flow is common (few uses are 100% consumptive, and many appropriations are put to use within the watershed of origin), the same water is used and reused—often many times—as it goes down the river. As a practical matter this creates a serious problem of declining quality because in agricultural irrigation, which accounts for more than 80% of water use in most of the arid West, water picks up minerals from the soil each time it is used. The problem is intensified by the application of chemical fertilizers, fungicides and pesticides which are also swept into the stream by the return flow.

One final word about the matter of consumptive use and return flow mentioned in the hypothetical example. While the law only allows one to appropriate the amount that can be applied to beneficial use, this amount is often considerably more than the quantum actually consumed. Thus, if it is considered acceptable irrigation practice (usually measured by affordability and available technology) to apply 10 cfs to a crop, even though 5 cfs runs off the surface as return flow, or even if some of the water is lost in transportation by evaporation or seepage, then an appropriator is perfectly within his or her legal right to divert 10 cfs from the stream. You can easily imagine some of the issues that such uses raise, and that we shall soon consider. For example, what if our hypothetical #1 appropriator, diverting 10 cfs, and returning 5 cfs to #5 downstream, discovers a more efficient means of irrigation and could use the full 10 cfs to irrigate twice as much land as previously, without any return flow? May he implement such a new system, and cut off #5? Or is #2 entitled to the 5 cfs no longer needed by #1? Alternatively, what if #1, who has been irrigating within the watershed of the river, and returning one-half his appropriation as return flow to #5, now wishes to sell his right to a buyer whose place of use is outside the watershed and who will have no return flow to that stream? May he sell 10 cfs, cutting off #5 from the water #5 has been getting, or has he only 5 cfs to sell? Must he leave 5 cfs in the stream for #5, so that #5 won't be worse off than before? These are question we shall soon consider.

2. HOW THE SYSTEM IS ADMINISTERED

Modern appropriation law incorporates a rather complex administrative permit and management system in all the appropriation doctrine states except Colorado, which administers water rights through a comprehensive administrative apparatus within a system of state water courts. We shall soon take a look at contemporary permit systems. First, however, it is important to understand the rules under which the system operated in the old days when pure appropriation was still in flower. This point needs emphasis because there is a special fact about appropriation law that must always be kept in mind. The oldest rights are the most valuable, and much controversy still turns on the validity and status of rights acquired many years ago, often in the 19th Century. In western water law, age is not coextensive with obsolescence.

How were appropriative rights acquired in the old days? At first, one simply went down to a stream, put in a primitive dam of some sort to control the flow, dug a ditch and installed a device to regulate flow from the river into the ditch (called a "headgate"). The ditch then carried the water to the place of use. Even where there was some system for recording appropriations, the records were notoriously imprecise, and what records existed were not centralized. Wyoming adopted a permit system the year it became a state, in 1890. Montana did not enact such a system until 1973.

As noted earlier, an appropriative right (or priority) was vested simply by the act of applying the water to beneficial use, or complying with a simple filing or permit application requirement. The right was dated as of the beginning of work on the ditch, and was perfected upon application of the water. This dating back from actual application of the water to the date of first construction (or today to the date of a permit application) is called the doctrine of "relation back" and depends upon "due diligence" in bringing the work to completion.[9] The due diligence requirement operates to prevent one from speculatively holding a priority, thus abusing the legitimate right of relation back where some reasonable period of time necessarily elapses between the commencement of a project and the actual first application of the water to beneficial use. Thus, a New Mexico court reversed the assignment of a 1907 priority to an entire 84–acre parcel, where the evidence showed that only 20 acres had been irrigated back in that era, that the rest of the parcel had not been brought into cultivation until 1947, and that there was no good reason for such a delay.[10]

3. GENERAL ADJUDICATIONS AND "PAPER RIGHTS"

In the earliest prior appropriation systems, there was little or no governmental involvement and often no useful public record of appropriations. Even where some sort of filing requirement existed, no system existed to validate claimed rights, or to provide a consolidated record that revealed the relative rights of various appropriators. In the event of controversy, a lawsuit was filed and the claims of competing appropriators were worked out by the evidence adduced in the lawsuit. But even such litigation only involved the individuals in conflict at that time; it did not include others using the same river and dependent on the same water supply.

This was a very unsatisfactory system, and it did not take very long for states to try to deal with this defect. Some states rather early adopted primitive permit systems, which essentially operated as recording devices. This was useful, but far from curative, since it represented little more than the appropriator's own statement of what uses were being made. By contrast, the most efficient contemporary administrative systems regulate initial uses, maintain comprehensive tabulations of use, and keep track of actual diversions, abandonments, and changes of use, thereby greatly improving the task of administration.

A far more ambitious development was a new sort of statute which authorized the initiation of statutory class actions called "general adjudications." The idea was that the state would be divided up into river basins (which, unfortunately, were often not very accurate representa-

9. E.g., Colo. Rev. Stat. § 37–92–305(1); Dallas Creek Water Co. v. Huey, 933 P.2d 27, 35 (Colo. 1997).

10. State ex rel. Martinez v. McDermett, 901 P.2d 745 (N.M. Ct. App. 1995).

tions of all hydrologically interrelated waters) and all appropriators would come into court in a single consolidated proceeding for each basin and "prove up" their appropriations. The result would be a court decree that would list every appropriation, with the name of the appropriator, the date of the priority, the amount and purpose of the appropriation, the place of diversion, the dates and times of use and the place of use. General adjudications were ongoing lawsuits, and new appropriators could come in to court periodically and add themselves to the decree. Such decrees were used for the purpose of administering the water law system and for settling disputes without (or with a minimum of) litigation. An excerpt from an 1883 Colorado decree is printed below. Note that a given appropriator may have several appropriations, with different dates of priority, from the same river at the same point of diversion. That is because development was ongoing, and an irrigator might acquire and put into production new lands as time went on. To do so, the appropriator would enlarge his or her ditch and take additional amounts of water.

Frequently a number of different users shared an appropriation from the same ditch. Thus, as in the decree below, the appropriations were actually made by early water distribution organizations called mutual ditch companies, which were wholesalers to their stockholders. In those days the mutual ditch company offered a means for irrigators in a given area to share the cost of building the diversion facility and ditch. Among themselves, the stockholders in a mutual ditch company were not governed by the law of prior appropriation, but by whatever contractual arrangements they made among themselves to share their common appropriation, usually *pro rata* sharing in times of shortage. Of course, as among different appropriators (each of the different ditches mentioned in the decree) the law of prior appropriation applied.

One unusual feature of this decree is that the appropriations are described in cubic feet per *minute,* rather than cubic feet per second. Note also that this decree does not set out the seasons (e.g., March to September), or the times of flow (e.g., 24 hours a day for two days each week), often an essential element in settling disputes. Such omissions in old decrees have often been a source of litigation. As a practical matter irrigation water rights are time-based and appropriation rights are measured not only by amount, but by the time of year at which the water was originally appropriated. Farmers usually need water most during the dry season of the year, usually in mid-summer. A right from April to September is ordinarily much more valuable than a right from September to April. As streams began to be fully appropriated, reservoirs were constructed to hold winter flows, so that the stored water could be released during the irrigation season. Claims to these waters are known as storage rights and are also governed by the prior appropriation system.

IN THE MATTER OF A CERTAIN PETITION FOR ADJUDICATION OF RIGHTS TO THE USE OF WATER

District Court of the Second Judicial District of the State of Colorado.
Sitting in and for Arapahoe County, 1883.

Now, on this 28th day of April, A. D. one thousand eight hundred and eighty-three, this matter coming on for final hearing and adjudication upon the report of Isaac E. Barnum, Referee appointed herein, * * * it is by the Court, in consideration of all the premises, hereby ordered and adjudged and decreed * * *

7th. No part of this decree shall be taken or held as adjudging to any claimant * * * any water from any natural stream except to be applied to the use for which the appropriation was made, nor to allow any excessive use or waste of water whatever, nor to allow any diversion of water except for lawful and beneficial purposes.

* * * That said ditches be and the same are hereby numbered according to the date of their several and respective constructions, and said dates are hereby determined and decreed to be as follows: * * *

No. 1. Brantner Ditch, original construction * * *. April 1st, 1860

No. 2. The Platteville Irrigating and Milling Company's Ditch, original construction * * * July 1st, 1862

No. 3. Farmers' and Gardeners' Ditch, original construction * * * March 15th, 1863

No. 4. Brantner Ditch, first enlargement * * * May 1st, 1863

* * *

No. 52. The Brantner Ditch, third enlargement * * * January 15th, 1881 * * *

* * * And the amount of water adjudged to said ditches on their respective priorities per minute of time is computed as follows, to wit:

No. 1. Brantner Ditch

Priority No. 1— Cubic feet. 1,786
" " 4 " " 356
" " 27 " " 731
" " 52 " " 3,798
Total 6,671
. . . .

No. 2. The Platteville Irrigating and Milling Company's Ditch

Priority No. 2— Cubic feet. 2,873
" " 19 " " 315
" " 33 " " 5,655
Total 8,841
. . . .

No. 3. The Farmers' and Gardeners' Ditch

Priority No. 3— Cubic feet. 823

  "   " 34   "   "   617

Total 1,440

....

* * *

And the entire amount of water taken from said South Platte river under the priorities established by this decree is computed at 208,848 cubic feet of water per minute of time.

And more particularly in regard to said ditches and enlargements, respectively, as follows:

No. One.—The Brantner Ditch.—That said ditch is entitled to Priorities Nos. 1–4–27–52. The claimants are P.W. Snyder, Margaret Brantner, Maggie McCool, A.F. McCool, William Murry and William S. Lee; that it is a ditch used for the irrigation of lands, taking its supply of water from the South Platte river, and the headgate is located in Township 2 south, of Range 67 west, in Arapahoe county. And it is hereby adjudged and decreed that there be allowed to flow into said ditch from said river, for the use aforesaid and for the benefit of the parties lawfully entitled thereto, under and by virtue of appropriation by construction and priority: No. 1, so much water as will flow in said ditch, it being four feet wide on the bottom, depth of water flow two feet, slope of banks one to one, grade five and one-tenth feet per mile, computed at 1,786 cubic feet per minute; that there be further allowed to flow in said ditch as aforesaid, under and by virtue of Priority No. 4, so much additional water, for the purposes aforesaid, as will supply the increased flow thereof as enlarged one foot in width, the other dimensions remaining the same, computed at 356 cubic feet per minute; and that there be further allowed. * * * [A]nd the whole amount of water to which said ditch is entitled is computed at 6,671 cubic feet per minute. * * *

By the Court,
Victor A. Elliott,
Judge.

April 28, 1883.

————

The general adjudication system, though it did and still does serve as a basic tool for administering water rights, was deeply flawed in practice. Not all streams were adjudicated, and some were not adjudicated for many years. Much more importantly, the adjudications were often extremely inaccurate. People had to come to court at times when there was no ongoing controversy, and as a result the proceedings for many appropriators were not genuinely adversary. It was hardly worth the trouble and expense for each appropriator to hire experts to scrutinize the claims of all the other appropriators on the stream. There might be hundreds or even thousands of such appropriators in a single adjudication, separated by many miles, presenting very complex factual questions, such as how much return flow was available at a given place, or what uses someone actually made when her appropriation was initiated some decades earlier.

Moreover, it was in the interest of each of the participants in the general adjudication to claim as much water as possible for themselves. The result was that decrees were greatly inflated, routinely setting out amounts that vastly exceeded what the appropriators had actually used, and that—*in toto*—exceeded the total amount of water that had ever flowed in the stream. Such decreed amounts are called "paper rights," the implication correctly being that they do not describe the real water use situation.

Nonetheless, the decrees were the basis for day-to-day administration. They were usually administered by an individual called a ditch rider or commissioner who would keep track of all the users dependent on a given river (or a given stretch of the river and its tributaries). He would open and close the gates for each diversion ditch and maintain a record of the uses being made. When there was a shortage of water, an appropriator who was not receiving his full appropriation would notify the ditch rider (this was known as "making a call on the river"), and the ditch rider would proceed to close down diversions in inverse order of priority until no junior appropriator was taking water—other than return flow from an upstream senior—when anyone more senior was without it.

Another important limitation of the general adjudication is that the decrees are for some purposes subject to collateral attack. For example, if a senior appropriator wants to sell a right for 10 cfs that was adjudicated to him in 1883, it is open to other appropriators on the stream to assert that—despite the decree—the senior never actually appropriated and beneficially used that much water. Objectors can also claim abandonment or forfeiture of all or part of the 10 cfs. Obviously the possibility of thus attacking a decree creates some real confusion. The main points to keep in mind are: (1) that an appropriator cannot rest comfortably on the assumption that he owns and has available for sale the amount of water set out in a decree, and (2) that the vulnerability of a decree is not so surprising as it seems. First, everyone knows that the old decrees were routinely grossly inflated with "paper rights." Second, certain claims—such as abandonment sometime after the date of appropriation—certainly should be justiciable. Third, one who wants to sell her full decreed "paper right" may be creating a considerable change in the real *status quo ante* on the river if in fact she never appropriated a full 10 cfs, or abandoned all or part of it some years earlier. Finally, as we will see in learning about water marketing, transfers are subject to a no-injury rule, so that any purported sale of an existing water right must assure that others dependent on it (such as return-flow appropriators) are not disadvantaged by the proposed transfer.

In any event, the above description should give you a sense of what the traditional system looked like. Today, permit administration gives the state an opportunity to consider such issues as beneficial use before the fact, to provide public records of actual use, and to assure that there is unappropriated water available before anyone begins work on a diversion. It also permits a state to keep track of forfeitures and wasteful uses, and to keep the records up to date (though few states are as diligent as they might be about such matters). We will look at modern permit systems after considering the basic appropriation doctrines as they arise in litigation today. Again, keep in mind that however attractive a modern administrative system may be, it does not settle the very old, pre-permit system claims which are often the most important and valuable water rights.

This brief description of the system—which has here been simplified down to the bare bones—may nonetheless seem somewhat complicated and a bit mysterious. A complete view of appropriation law, however, is far more intricate than we have thus far indicated. For example, there are a variety of water rights that physically impinge on the system, but were not, and to a considerable extent still are not, administered with it. The list that follows identifies several of these complicating factors.

Mixed systems
: Some western states—California, Nebraska and Oklahoma—do not have pure appropriation, but combine appropriative rights with riparian rights, so that there are riparian claimants on the rivers whose rights must somehow be settled along with the competing claims of appropriators among themselves.

Groundwater
: Underground water was traditionally treated as a separate legal regime, and was not involved in general adjudications (unless it was, e.g., "a subterranean stream flowing through known and definite channels"[11]). Most groundwater is hydrologically connected to surface streams and lakes. Unless such groundwater is managed conjunctively in a unitary system with surface water, later in time groundwater pumpers (who may also be surface water junior appropriators not getting any water under their low priority) can pump water that decreases streamflow and effectively transgress the prior right of senior appropriators.[12] Most states have integrated groundwater and surface water management, at least to a substantial extent, but a few—notably California, Arizona and Texas—continue to resist integration.

---

11. Cal. Water Code § 2500.

12. See, e.g., John Leshy & James Belanger, Arizona's Law Where Ground and Surface Water Meet, 20 Ariz. St. L.J. 657 (1988).

Reserved rights

The federal government sometimes holds a special water right for its lands to fulfill the public purposes for which that land (such as Indian reservations, military enclaves, and national parks) was set aside. They are created under federal, rather than state, law and exist apart from state-created appropriative rights. Usually they are implied from the statutes, treaties or executive orders creating federal reservations as being necessary to carry out the congressional purpose in establishing the enclave. Reserved rights for Indian Reservations are the most important and controversial element of this system. But other federal lands, such as national parks, monuments and wildlife refuges may also have federal reserved rights. Until recently these claims could not be adjudicated because of federal sovereign immunity. Congress has abolished its immunity and opened itself to general adjudication of its rights in state courts.

Pueblo rights

Some cities in the Hispanic Southwest have water rights derived from Mexican law and granted prior to the Treaty of Guadalupe Hidalgo in 1848. These rights, based on the needs of a settlement to serve its inhabitants, expand with the growth of the municipality, and stand outside the priority system. Though once recognized in several states, now only California still has pueblo rights.

Prescriptive rights

In some states water rights may be obtained by prescription. These rights, by their very nature, arise outside of the public recording and permit systems. Although it seems reasonable to expect these rights to be incorporated into the list of appropriations at some point, or to be included in general adjudications, there is little evidence that this occurs.

4. WHERE APPROPRIATION LAW APPLIES

In considering appropriation in this part of the book, we deal only with surface waters. Ground water—where versions of appropriation doctrine increasingly apply—is considered in Chapter 5. There are nine pure appropriation doctrine states, though modern regulation has modified the pristine nature of the doctrine to a greater or lesser extent. These are: Alaska, Arizona, Colorado, Idaho, Montana, Nevada, New Mexico, Utah and Wyoming. California, Oklahoma, and to some extent Nebraska have mixed systems with both riparianism and appropriation side by side. Six other states did have riparian systems, but then switched to appropriation: Kansas, North Dakota, Oregon, South Dakota, Texas and Washington. In these states, riparian uses existing at the time of the changeover are recognized, but all rights acquired since that time, and presently, are appropriative rights. Hawaii has a regulated riparian system.

5. WESTERN WATER LAW IS STATE CONSTITUTIONAL LAW

While water rights are property rights protected by the due process clause of the federal constitution, one peculiarity of some western appropriation states is that a "right to appropriate" has been recognized explicitly in some state constitutions. It used to be argued that these state constitutional enactments prohibited state legislation from impairing or altering appropriation rights, e.g. by inserting a public interest standard on appropriations. Such arguments are almost certain to fail today in most places, but still seems to have some vitality in Colorado, which has never adopted an administrative permit system, and whose Constitution states in relevant part:

> Article XVI, Section 5. *Water of Streams Public Property.* The water of every natural stream, not heretofore appropriated, within the state of Colorado, is hereby declared to be the property of the public, and the same is dedicated to the use of the people of the state, subject to appropriation as hereinafter provided.

> Article XVI, Section 6. *Diverting Unappropriated Water—Priority Preferred Uses.* The right to divert the unappropriated waters of any natural stream to beneficial uses shall never be denied. Priority of appropriation shall give the better right * * *.

B. ACQUIRING APPROPRIATIVE RIGHTS: THE ELEMENTS

Colorado's constitutional provision that "the right to divert the unappropriated waters of any natural stream to beneficial uses shall never be denied" exemplifies the traditional law of appropriation. The provision literally establishes four requisites for an appropriation: (1) unappropriated water; (2) a natural stream; (3) diversion; and (4) application to beneficial use. The first two of these can be discussed in summary fashion, while the diversion requirement and application to a beneficial use require more extensive treatment.

1. UNAPPROPRIATED WATER

In the old days one who aspired to appropriate found out if there was unappropriated water when confronted by a suit to enjoin her use. Today, the availability of water for appropriation is usually left as a factual determination for a permit granting agency. One significant contemporary situation is that a state may refuse a permit for an appropriation even if water is available if it determines to reserve some unappropriated water to maintain instream flows for fish and wildlife.[13] Another contemporary issue is whether, in determining the existence of

---

13. See, e.g., Cal. Water Code § 1257.5.

unappropriated water, it must be assumed that all pending—but as yet uncompleted—pre-existing appropriation applications, will be successfully completed.[14] In effect, the question is whether a new applicant may raise due diligence, or speculation, issues as to others' pending applications (known as conditional water rights in Colorado).

2. NATURAL STREAM

The next issue is whether the water in question is that of a "natural stream," which is usually defined as:

> a stream of water flowing in a definite channel, having a bed and sides or banks, and discharging itself into some other stream or body of water. The flow of water need not be constant, but must be more than mere surface drainage occasioned by extraordinary causes; there must be substantial indications of the existence of a stream, which is ordinarily a moving body of water.[15]

As a practical matter, only two important sources are excluded from this definition; most ground water,[16] and such vagrant, diffused and occasional supplies as springs and seepage. Water originating in a spring that is now flowing in a defined channel toward a river is changing character and may be treated as a natural stream, a small tributary of a larger stream. At least two states—Oregon and Arizona—extend their appropriation laws to spring and seepage water, and Arizona's statute includes "intermittent, flood, waste or surplus water" as well as "springs on the surface".[17] Interpretation of the Arizona statute came into question when Phoenix sought to sell its treated sewage effluent, an increasingly important source. See Arizona Pub. Serv. Co. v. Long, infra p. 201. The rules relating to underground water and modern efforts to establish unitary, conjunctively-managed systems are discussed infra p. 411. The appropriability of seepage water—such as irrigation runoff flowing across the surface of the earth, but not, or not yet, back into a stream—is an important byway of appropriation doctrine. We consider it infra p. 197.

Some statutes, like Arizona's, explicitly make the water of lakes appropriable. Whether lakes are appropriable in states which have the

14. Board of County Comm'rs v. United States, 891 P.2d 952, 971 (Colo. 1995) ("Conditional water rights under which diversions have not been made or none are being made should not be considered in determining water availability"). See also Lower Colorado River Auth. v. Texas Dept. of Water Resources, 689 S.W.2d 873 (Tex. 1984) (unappropriated water is the amount remaining after taking into account all existing uncancelled permits and filings valued at their recorded levels). An Oregon court held it is unnecessary to determine if a river is fully appropriated since senior rights must always be first satisfied in any

event. Benz v. Water Resources Comm'n, 94 Or.App. 73, 764 P.2d 594 (1988).

15. Hutchinson v. Watson Slough Ditch Co., 16 Idaho 484, 488, 101 P. 1059, 1061 (1909).

16. Sometimes groundwater is claimed to be appropriable as the water of a subterranean stream, as in California's Pauma and Pala Basins. See SWRCB Draft Dec., Oct. 8, 2002.

17. Or. Rev. Stat. § 537.800. See Norden v. State, 329 Or. 641, 996 P.2d 958 (2000). Ariz. Rev. Stat. § 45–141A.

constitutional "natural stream" language is not easy to demonstrate,[18] although certainly the general presumption is that they are. In states where the constitution makes "all waters within the state" subject to appropriation, lakes are included.[19]

3. DIVERSION (INSTREAM FLOWS)

At one time it was considered a rather serious question whether one must physically remove water from the stream, or in some other way exercise physical dominion over it, in order to meet the "diversion" requirement. The classic example was the rancher who had regularly brought cattle to a stream for drinking, and the question was whether he actually had to remove water from the stream in order to perfect his appropriation. Montana, one of the last holdouts, has now reversed earlier decisions and held that no physical diversion was required in that state, even prior to the adoption of its permit system in 1973.[20] California is exceptional: it still holds that the absence of "actual diversion" prohibits the acquisition of an appropriation either by a private organization for preservation and enhancement of fish and wildlife, or by a state agency.[21] California law does, however, allow, anyone holding a conventional water right, with administrative approval, to convert it to an instream right.[22] Instream needs for fish and wildlife protection, and for water quality maintenance, are, however, taken into account in determining the amount of water available for appropriation, and permit provisions routinely require bypass flow schedules to protect instream values.[23] According to Professor Denise Fort, New Mexico has administratively determined that it would be legal for the state to grant an instream right.

The prospect of instream appropriations has created unease in many states. The basic concern is that recognition of instream rights would result in **insufficient supplies of water to meet future demand, whether municipal, agricultural, or industrial. For these reasons, most states have opted for other approaches to meeting instream needs.**[24] The

18. See Duckworth v. Watsonville Water & Light Co., 150 Cal. 520, 89 P. 338 (1907); Cole v. Richards Irr. Co., 27 Utah 205, 75 P. 376 (1904) (waters of a lake can be a running stream); Denver, T. & Ft. W.R. Co. v. Dotson, 20 Colo. 304, 38 P. 322 (1894) (appropriation of water not in a running stream valid under a statute permitting appropriation of springs and seeps).

19. See Proctor v. Sim, 134 Wash. 606, 236 P. 114 (1925).

20. In re Adjudication of the Existing Rights to the Use of All Water, 311 Mont. 327, 55 P.3d 396 (2002).

21. See California Trout, Inc. v. State Water Resources Control Bd., 90 Cal.App.3d 816, 153 Cal.Rptr. 672 (1979); Gregory Thomas, Conserving Aquatic Biodiversity: A Critical Comparison of Legal Tools for

Augmenting Stream Flows in California, 15 Stan. Envtl. L. J. 3 (1996). For a cogently argued plea to change the law, see Brian Gray, A Reconsideration of Instream Appropriative Water Rights in California, 16 Ecology L.Q. 667 (1989).

22. Cal. Water Code § 1707.

23. Id. §§ 1243, 1243.5, 1257.5, 1258.

24. See generally David Gillilan & Thomas Brown, Instream Flow Protection: Seeking a Balance in Western Water Use (1997); James Crammond, Leasing Water Rights for Instream Flow Uses: A Survey of Water Transfer Policy, Practices, and Problems in the Pacific Northwest, 26 Envtl. L. 225 (1996); Jack Sterne, Symposium on Northwest Water Law: Instream Rights and Invisible Hands: Prospects for Private In-

earliest device was statutory authority in a permit-granting agency to condition appropriation permits so as to require certain flows to be maintained,[25] or simply to cease granting permits at a certain point in order to assure a desired minimum of water flowing instream.[26] Under the federal Wild and Scenic Rivers Act[27] (and there are some similar state laws[28]), stretches of rivers may be put off limits to diverters or dam builders. The range of potential devices for imposing instream requirements is considerable. For example, a state agency setting water quality standards pursuant to the federal Clean Water Act may specify minimum stream flows that become mandatory conditions on any hydropower license sought for that body of water.[29] Federal land management agencies, such as the Forest Service, have been imposing so-called bypass flow requirements as conditions of granting or renewing right-of-way permits for appropriators who divert from federal lands (discussed infra p. 1004). Alternatively, a state may buy existing water rights and leave the water instream when such flows are required to comply with a regulatory law such as the federal Endangered Species Act.

The most common approach, illustrated by statutes in Alaska, Arizona, Idaho, Montana, Nebraska, Nevada, Oregon, Utah, Colorado and Wyoming, is to allow state agencies to appropriate water for instream flows.[30] Because these are recently enacted statutes, such appropriations tend to have very junior priorities. Some states also allow purchase or leasing of existing water rights for instream flow purposes.[31] Colorado requires private appropriations to be dedicated to the state.[32] Only Alaska and Arizona explicitly allow private individuals or organizations to hold appropriations for instream flows.

A number of places have also instituted willing-buyer, willing-seller acquisition programs, in which private non-profit organizations or governmental agencies buy up or lease existing senior water rights (usually

---

stream Water Rights in the Northwest, 27 Envtl. L. 203 (1997).

25. See, e.g., Hubbard v. State of Washington, 936 P.2d 27 (Wash. Ct. App. 1997); Cal. Fish & Game Code § 5937 ("The owner of any dam shall allow sufficient water at all times to pass * * * over, around or through the dam, to keep in good condition any fish that may * * * exist below the dam"); id. § 5946 ("No permit or license to appropriate water * * * shall be issued * * * unless conditioned upon full compliance with Section 5937"). See also Cal. Water Code §§ 1243, 1243.5, 1257.5, 1258.

26. See Louis Bonney, Oregon's Coordinated Integrated Water Resources Policy, 3 Willamette L.J. 295, 297–98 (1965).

27. 16 U.S.C. §§ 1271–1287.

28. See, e.g., Cal. Pub. Res. Code § 5093.50.

29. See PUD No. 1 v. Washington Department of Ecology, 511 U.S. 700 (1994), infra p. 1056.

30. The Arizona statute was sustained against challenge in a case allowing the U.S. Forest Service to make an instream appropriation. Phelps Dodge Corp. v. Arizona D.W.R., 118 P.3d, 1110 (Ct. App. AZ, 2005).

31. See generally Clay Landry, Saving Our Streams Through Water Markets (Pol. Econ. Res. Center 1998); Jason S. Wells, Leasing Water Rights for Instream Flow Protection: The Opportunities and Impediments to Improved Public Interest Involvement in Colorado's Instream Flow Protection Regime, 7 U. Denv. Water L. Rev. 309 (2004); Jesse A. Boyd, Hip Deep: A Survey of State Instream Flow Law from the Rocky Mountains to the Pacific Ocean, 43 Nat. Res. J. 1151 (2003); Barton H. Thompson, Jr., Markets for Nature, 25 Wm. & Mary Envtl. L. & Pol'y Rev. 261 (2000).

32. Colo. Rev. Stat. § 37–92–102(3).

agricultural), in order to restore instream values. While these programs are still in a relatively formative stage, and can be quite expensive, they appear very promising. However, even though they involve voluntary transactions, they remain controversial:

> In rural communities, concern about losing control of irrigation water (and ultimately of farmland) extends beyond farmers to other members of the community dependent on the agricultural economy. The local feed, farm implement and grocery store owners all share the concern that transfers of water rights from agricultural to instream use will cause a decline in the community's economy, reducing their income and job opportunities for their children. These concerns about the future of rural economies are the major reason that most * * * transfers have been temporary lease transactions rather than permanent acquisitions.[33]

JACK STERNE,
INSTREAM RIGHTS AND INVISIBLE HANDS: PROSPECTS FOR PRIVATE INSTREAM WATER RIGHTS IN THE NORTHWEST

27 Envtl. L. 203, 203–230 (1997).

When rivers and streams are deprived of adequate supplies of flowing water, the effects on wildlife are often devastating. In response to that problem, several states have created mechanisms that allow for the ownership of instream water rights. Unlike traditional water rights for consumptive uses, which allow the owner of the right to remove water, instream rights entitle the owner to have a quantity of water left in place to support wildlife and recreational uses of the river. Most of the programs currently in place provide primarily for state ownership of instream rights. Problems of funding and enforcement make those rights far less powerful than similar rights could be in the hands of private owners. While agricultural and development interests fear the possible consequences of privately owned instream rights, a well-developed program allowing those rights would improve the protection of Northwest rivers without depriving consumptive users of water for purposes such as irrigation.

* * * Even in Oregon, which established minimum streamflows in 1955, fish are frequently at the mercy of senior appropriators, whose rights often carry a much earlier priority date. Indeed, none of the instream rights established by state agencies or legislatures in the Northwest carry a priority date earlier than 1925, and the vast majority postdate 1955. * * *

33. Natural Resources Law Center, Univ. of Colo. School of Law, Restoring the Waters 19 (May 1997).

The most important issue for endangered fish populations, though, is not whether private parties may appropriate new instream flows, but whether they may acquire transfers of existing senior rights to instream uses. * * *

* * * [T]he Oregon legislature amended the water code in 1987 by authorizing the state to acquire senior rights for conversion to instream rights without loss of priority date. This statute * * * attempted to make instream rights more like diversionary rights and not merely rules that could be changed administratively. Specifically, the legislature declared that * * * "the in-stream right shall have the same legal status as any other water right for which a certificate has been issued."[94] * * * The statute is somewhat confusing [as to whether instream rights can be privately owned]. The department's position is that any person who leases, purchases, or receives as a gift a water right and converts it to instream flow must transfer the right to the department to hold in trust for the people of Oregon. [The Oregon Water Trust, a non-profit organization, purchases consumptive use water rights and transfers them to instream flow use.] * * *

Even under Oregon's law, publicly held instream rights can fail to protect fish populations. First, as a general rule, most publicly held instream rights have junior priority dates. Second, state legislatures have failed to adequately fund instream programs. Third, state agencies have not been vigorous enforcers of the instream rights they hold. Fourth, these agencies are saddled with highly inefficient and expensive bureaucratic processes for establishing instream rights. * * *

* * * In Idaho, * * * minimum streamflows have been subordinated to future stockwatering rights, unrecorded rights, junior rights, and future development. Moreover, because many instream flows are set by administrative rules, they can later be modified in response to political pressure * * *. These problems with publicly held instream rights suggest that revisions to state water laws to allow private parties to hold those rights may be appropriate * * *. [O]pposition is a function of three main concerns: 1) the fear that instream rights will harm * * * current consumptive rights by reducing the amount of water available in return flows; 2) the fear that instream rights will hamper future economic growth; and 3) the basic belief that water should be used 'on the land.' * * * Others worry that privately held instream rights might open the door to speculation in water and that the risk to the public trust is too high. If instream rights can be appropriated and transferred like consumptive rights, developers might file for instream rights and convert them to consumptive uses when development opportunities arise. Such a speculator is [also] likely to be much less concerned about illegal consumptive use of the instream right than is a party who holds the right for public benefit * * *.

94. Or. Rev. Stat. § 537–350. This section also provides that instream rights are subject to abandonment.

JESSE A. BOYD,
HIP DEEP: A SURVEY OF STATE INSTREAM
FLOW LAW FROM THE ROCKY MOUNTAINS
TO THE PACIFIC OCEAN

43 Nat. Resources J. 1151, 1211–13 (2003).

* * *

D. Private Ownership of Instream Rights

Across the West farmers and ranchers arc feeling the pinch of over appropriation. As water demand increases for municipal, industrial, and environmental purposes, agricultural water users are feeling pressure to transfer portions of their water rights, conserve water, and even fallow their land. Agriculture is bearing the brunt of calls for efficiency mainly because the sector represents 90 percent of the consumptive water use in the West.

Water that was initially meant for farmers has been co-opted in recent years to meet the requirements of the Endangered Species Act. Western state governments and water users alike fear federal intervention in western water law because it is seen as an infringement of state sovereignty and private property rights. However, unless state law provides a regime that allows increasing urban and environmental demands to be met, increased federal intervention is inevitable.

One way to lessen the risk of federal involvement is to encourage private involvement in habitat restoration and enhancement. Dozens of environmental organizations around the country are eager to secure instream flows, and they command millions of dollars to accomplish it. The money is there to lease and purchase water rights for instream purposes, but mandatory state ownership or trust status of the rights created severely limits the willingness of many consumptive users to participate. If the users themselves or the organization of their choice could control the instream rights, more people would be willing to transfer their rights instream.

One of the main arguments against private ownership of instream rights is that it would encourage speculation. An entity could purchase water rights, transfer them instream, wait for the price to rise, and then sell them to new consumptive users at a profit. This sort of speculation is contrary to the prior appropriation system and is indeed one of the reasons for a beneficial use requirement.

But a simple addition to state instream-flow law could largely alleviate speculation fears. Instream rights should only be transferable back to the land and purpose from which they originated. If such a reversionary transfer takes place, the right would have to be perfected again in order to be re-transferred. Though this might not stem all speculation, large-scale speculative endeavors through the holding of instream rights would be cumbersome and less attractive than purchasing and transferring existing consumptive rights.

The ability to privately hold instream rights in this manner would also encourage farmers to transfer water instream from economically marginal plots. They could fallow land that they would rather not cultivate (but continue to in order to avoid forfeiture of their water right), safe in the knowledge that if they ever wanted to farm the land again they could. Government and private entities could also contract for fallowing, which could be an additional source of income for the agricultural community—all without the farmer ever losing his right to farm.

Oregon has the most extensive private involvement in securing instream flows of any state surveyed for this article—and it does not have private ownership of instream rights. While Nevada allows private ownership of instream rights, it has seen little activity outside of the Truckee basin. The success of the Oregon instream flow program is due mainly to its comprehensive statutory and regulatory scheme. Participation in Oregon's instream-flow program would greatly increase if the law allowed private ownership of instream rights.

Oregon demonstrates that a functioning instream-flow regime can exist without private ownership, and Nevada shows that private ownership does not guarantee large-scale participation. However, private ownership provides considerable flexibility when developing strategies to deal with over appropriated streams.

Notes and Questions

1. While public agency acquisition of instream flows is important, it is insufficient, according to one study, which notes that the Colorado agency solely empowered to acquire and hold such rights "in 1999 * * * failed to file for a single ISF [instream flow] right; in 2000, [it] filed for eight; and in 2001, [it] filed for just one. * * * [L]oosening traditional prescribed obstructions and opening up instream water right transfers to the market economy represents the best way to meet the 'rapidly emerging market for environmentalists, agency officials, ranchers, farmers, and others interested in leasing or acquiring ISF rights.'" Jason S. Wells, Leasing Water Rights for Instream Flow Protection: The Opportunities and impediments to Improved Public Interest Involvement in Colorado's Instream Flow Protection Regime, 7 U. Denv. Water L. Rev. 309 (2004).

2. The fear that instream appropriations will lead to abuse, or tie up too much water, is not limited to private appropriators, and led to special legislation in Colorado in 2001. That law provided for adjudication of public agencies' instream recreational appropriations, e.g. for whitewater kayak courses. And it mandated that a determination must be made of "the minimum stream flow ... for a reasonable recreation experience in and on the water." The fear was that appropriations of high recreational flows could hinder the state's future development. One legislator even suggested that entities could "claim very high flows at the State borders to essentially export water to California, Kansas and other states ..." How should a state assure that instream appropriations will not unduly constrain future needs

for population and industry? The law and its background are discussed in Colorado Water Conservation Bd. v. Upper Gunnison River W.C.D., 109 P.3d 585 (Colo. 2005). See also Rebecca Abeln, Instream Flows, Recreation as Beneficial Use, and the Public Interest in Colorado Water Law, 8 U. Denv. Water L. Rev. 517 (2005).

3. Some states allow instream rights to be displaced if water is later needed for other more "economic" uses. Is there any reason to treat instream flow rights as of lesser status than other beneficial uses? Would (or should) an existing irrigation appropriative right be displaced by a later need for water by a municipality, for which use the water is much more economically valuable? Should the holder of an instream right, granted for recreational or fishery protection, be allowed to sell the right later, as agricultural users can, and increasingly do?

4. In general, appropriative rights are deemed abandoned or forfeited by non-use for a substantial period of time. How, if at all, would such doctrines be applied to instream appropriative rights? An interesting problem involving administration of instream rights arose in Colorado. Pursuant to statute (Colo. Rev. Stat. § 37–92–102(3)), a state agency appropriated an instream flow right. Subsequently it decided to abandon the right in part, apparently to make water available for appropriation by a ski resort. An organization called Aspen Wilderness Workshop sued to enjoin the partial abandonment of the instream right. The trial court held that the agency holding the right "was acting within its inherent power to rectify errors and its implied authority to modify its appropriation on Snowmass Creek; that the [agency], as any holder of a water right, need not enforce its rights and may voluntarily not use that portion of its decreed water rights in excess of the amount needed." Aspen Wilderness Workshop appealed. What result on appeal, and why? See Aspen Wilderness Workshop, Inc. v. Colorado Water Conservation Bd., 901 P.2d 1251 (Colo. 1995). What conclusions do you draw from this case about how states should deal with instream water needs? (The legislature later modified the law to allow the Board to decrease its appropriation (§ 37–92–102(4)(a), which it did at Snowmass Creek, assuring abundant artificial snow).

5. The preceding article seems to make a persuasive claim that private appropriative instream rights would generate more protection for environmental values? Why then is it that most states disallow private instream rights?

6. Existing uses may be restricted to meet legal requirements for instream flows, e.g., to maintain essential habitat for species listed under the federal Endangered Species Act: (1) Would such a compelled reduction in the exercise of an existing appropriative right constitute a taking of property for which compensation is constitutionally required? A very controversial decision in the Federal Court of Claims held that it was a physical taking of the water, though it left open the question whether a formal finding by the state that the use was not a reasonable and beneficial use would have prevented the restriction from being a compensable taking. Tulare Lake Basin Water Storage District v. United States, 49 Fed. Cl. 313 (2001). The Tulare decision is criticized in Klamath Irrigation District v. United States, 67 Fed. Cl. 504, 513 (2005). See infra pp. 653 et seq.

7. Assuming such restrictions can be imposed without triggering a right to compensation, must diversions be shut down in inverse order of priority, or may the burden be spread on some other equitable basis among all appropriators? Could a departure from the priority system be justified on the ground that no one has a legal right to endanger a listed species, in the same sense that no one has a legal right to pollute a stream? Is such a use not beneficial? Not in the public interest? You will encounter such questions again as we explore those doctrinal and statutory standards. See John Leshy, The Prior Appropriation Doctrine of Water Law in the West: An Emperor with Few Clothes, J. West, July 1990, at 5.

8. A review of ten years' experience in buying instream water rights by the private, non-profit Oregon Water Trust appears in Janet C. Neuman, The Good, The Bad, and The Ugly: Oregon Water Trust, 83 Nebr. L. Rev. 432 (2004). One unexpected finding was that when land is fallowed and its water sold, the owner often ceases to tend the land, opening the way for noxious weeds to proliferate and spread out of control. Neuman suggests the importance of stewardship of lands from which irrigation water has been withdrawn, and observes that the Trust, focused on water, has been resistant to "mission creep." Id. at 473.

4. STORAGE RIGHTS

The simplest model of the prior appropriation system assumes a diversion directly out of a river, carried through a ditch for immediate use upon land. In practice, however, a great deal of water is not diverted directly to use, but is captured behind a dam and stored in a reservoir prior to use. Storage offers several advantages. Storing Spring floodwaters for later seasonal use increases the total usable supply for irrigation. Urban and industrial users generally require steady supplies; storage offers them even flows throughout the year. Storage from one year to the next provides protection against drought periods. Reservoirs also have value in themselves: As lakes they serve recreation needs, and their unused storage capacity offers protection against floods. Dams permit the generation of hydroelectric power.

For our purpose the question is whether the law treats storage and direct use appropriations differently. In general the answer is no: Both direct diversion and storage rights are governed by the same general principles. There are, however, a few differences of which you should be aware. Let us first consider the various factual settings. In the simplest storage case, an appropriator diverts water from the river into a ditch, and then into an offstream reservoir, where it is held seasonally until it is needed for irrigation. Such an arrangement presents no legal issues different from those presented by a direct diversion. The storage will of course affect the flow of the river in time. If a prior appropriator is adversely affected, it is entitled to relief. Appropriators junior to the storage right must take subject to the changes it brings about. Nor is anything different if the reservoir is built in the stream channel, as most are, flooding the river and the land adjacent to it. So long as the appropriator permits all the water—except that to which it has a right of storage—to continue flowing downstream, the case is identical to that of the off-stream reservoir.

Most states require a special permit to build a dam and reservoir and to store water. There may, for example, be special provisions for dam safety or for the installation of ladders to permit the passage of fish past the dam. Because water rights are not perfected until water is applied to beneficial use, a right of storage is not ordinarily in itself sufficient to acquire a vested appropriative right. Water can be stored either in a surface reservoir or in an underground aquifer. Where water is appropriated to replenish depleted groundwater supplies (and thus, at least in the intermediate term, for the purpose of storage itself), special statutory authorization may be needed to classify the storage as a beneficial use. Section 1242 of the California Water Code provides that "the storing of water underground * * * constitutes a beneficial use * * * if the water so stored is thereafter applied to the beneficial purposes for which the appropriation for storage was made."

Insofar as the storer and the ultimate user are a single entity (typically a municipality), there is no special problem. The appropriative right is simply divided into separable time segments. The storage appropriator is, of course, entitled to prevent downstream appropriators from taking the stored water when it is released. Where the storer is not itself a user, the problem of speculative holding of water can arise. For example, proposals have been made for private ventures to store water behind levees on low-lying islands in the Sacramento River Delta, and sell it. See Delta Wetlands Properties v. County of San Joaquin, 121 Cal.App.4th 128,16 Cal.Rptr.3d 672 (Ct.App. 2004)(sustaining against a preemption claim a local zoning ordinance governing location of reservoirs).

Thus, to validate a storage right, there should be a definite plan of use and actual application within a reasonable time after the reservoir is completed. Among other purposes, a storage right can be acquired to capture and store flood waters.[1] To avoid speculative holding, Wyoming law provides that "the owner or owners of a reservoir impounding a greater quantity of water than the owner or owners thereof necessarily use * * * shall * * * furnish such surplus water at reasonable rates to the owners of lands * * * capable of being irrigated from such reservoir * * *." Wyo. Stat. Ann. § 41–3–325 (2005). Western water law provides for loss of water rights through abandonment for nonuse. In doing so it provides a way of protecting against "mere future speculative profit or advantage." Kearney Lake, Land & Reservoir Co. v. Lake DeSmet Reservoir Co., 475 P.2d 548, 551 (Wyo. 1970), opinion supplemented 487 P.2d 324 (1971). Storage projects are often large undertakings and may require some years to complete. The doctrines of due diligence and relation back apply to storage. These doctrines assure that a storage

1. Pueblo West Metro. Dist. v. Southeastern Colo. Water Cons. Dist., 689 P.2d 594 (Colo. 1984).

appropriation carries the date of commencement of the project, so long as the project is diligently carried to conclusion. Colorado has been especially active in enforcing due diligence. See Trans–County Water, Inc. v. Central Colorado Water Conservancy Dist., 727 P.2d 60 (Colo. 1986).

Things are a bit more complicated with a for-profit irrigation company, or with a state or federal water project which builds dams and transmission facilities and contracts with wholesalers or retail users. In such a case, usually both the storer and the ultimate user get appropriation permits. E.g., Wyo. Stat. Ann. § 41–3–302 (2005). The law is not entirely clear as to the relative status of the storer and the user. They are sometimes called joint appropriators. Board of Comm'rs v. Rocky Mountain Water Co., 102 Colo. 351, 79 P.2d 373 (1938). With a public project, it is probably best to think of the storer as having legal title to the water right, with the beneficial right in the ultimate user. The right cannot be perfected until it is put to beneficial use, and it is amenable to loss, as by forfeiture or abandonment, if use ceases. With some for-profit companies, it seems that the water right belongs to the company rather than to any particular users. The rights of the water company and its customers collectively, as against the rest of the world, are determined by the usual rules of water law. Internally, however, the ultimate users only have such rights as they contract for (or state law gives them) against the irrigation company. Often the users are shareholders in the company, and the number of their shares represents their entitlement to water. They may be free to sell or lease the water, and to move it around from one user to another within the project's service area. See Chapter 7 infra.

There is an oft-repeated rule to the effect that a storage appropriator is entitled to only one filling of its reservoir each year.[2] The rule arises from a misunderstanding. Assuming available water, beneficial uses, and circumstances under which it makes sense to fill the reservoir, empty it in part or whole, and then fill it again, there is no good reason to prohibit such a plan. Certainly it would be wasteful to build two reservoirs where one would do. There is dicta in the cases to the effect that "the appropriation for a reservoir is measured by the quantity of water it will hold at one filling." Orchard City Irr. Dist. v. Whitten, 146 Colo. 127, 132, 361 P.2d 130, 133 (1961); Windsor Reservoir & Canal Co. v. Lake Supply Ditch Co., 44 Colo. 214, 98 P. 729 (1908). A careful reading of the cases suggests no such flat rule. *Orchard City,* for example, seems to be a case where a storage appropriator was trying to enlarge its actual appropriation after the fact. It had an early appropriation for the capacity of its reservoir, but that appropriation didn't

---

2. See David Getches, Water Law in a Nutshell 188–89 (3d ed. 1997). But see Brian McCauley, The Nature of a Reservoir Right, 3 Land & Water L. Rev. 443, 460–61 (1968). The issue is raised and left rather unclear in Samuel Wiel, Water Rights in the Western States § 475, at 498 (3d ed. 1911). Water left over from the previous year is said to be counted against the reservoir owner's appropriation for the succeeding year. See Mark Squillace, A Critical Look at Wyoming Water Law, 24 Land & Water L. Rev. 307, 330 (1989).

regularly supply the full amount and so it later obtained a decree for additional water as a supplemental appropriation. The court held that the intent of the second appropriation was only as a supplement to augment shortfalls from the earlier appropriation, and not as a second filling.

There is no reason in theory (or policy) why one could not begin a storage project on Jan. 1, 1900 of a reservoir with 1,000 a.f. capacity. If the intent was to fill such a reservoir twice during the season, once in March, and again in June, that would be perfectly appropriate. Let us then say the reservoir was actually completed in 1903, and in March and June of that year was filled twice. In such a case the reservoir should have an appropriation dated Jan. 1, 1900 for 2,000 a.f., 1,000 to be taken in March of each year and 1,000 to be taken in June, after the first 1,000 a.f. had been removed and applied to beneficial use. Such a multiple-filling appropriation is not impossible either in fact or in law. For example, in City of Grand Junction v. City and County of Denver, 960 P.2d 675 (Colo. 1998), Denver sought a new appropriation to keep its reservoir at a fixed elevation despite losses from evaporation and seepage. For practical purposes this amounted to a refill of the reservoir. Denver's first fill was under a 1946 priority, and it sought a 1987 priority to refill the reservoir after its first fill if space was available. The original decree had limited Denver "to one fill in priority per year," which limit was not violated here, where "Denver * * * sought a refill right with a priority date of 1987 * * * *" that was concededly junior to all intervening priorities. 960 P.2d at 683.

———

Today the operation of storage facilities, or reservoir management, has taken on a public importance far beyond the merely technical questions of storing and releasing water. Reservoir re-operations can be essential to meeting contemporary instream flow goals, complying with requirements under laws such as the Endangered Species Act and Clean Water Act, and in restoring riparian areas.[3] Among the opportunities (and controversies) raised by such matters are releases of uncommitted or uncontracted-for water stored in reservoirs, changes in timing of releases to simulate natural pulse flows, and reservoir drawdowns to facilitate the movement of anadromous fish through reservoirs on their way to the ocean. Every such demand potentially affects existing uses such as hydropower production schedules, recreational use of surface waters, and the quantum of storage available to users such as irrigators and municipalities in the event of a series of dry years. Among the numerous unresolved legal questions these new developments raise is, for example, whether a federal agency that has appropriated water in accordance with state law for irrigation, industrial, and municipal use

3. See Lawrence MacDonnell, Managing Reclamation Facilities for Ecosystem Bene-   fits, 67 U. Colo. L. Rev. 197 (1996).

can release uncommitted water for fish protection without getting a modified permit from the state.

5. BENEFICIAL USE

a. *Quantum of Use*

Beneficial use is the basis, the measure and the limit of an appropriative right. The right vests when the water is actually applied to use. How, precisely, is the right measured? For example, let us assume that an irrigator diverts water in 1900 and in that year applies it to grow corn on 10 acres of land. She grows corn for two seasons and then switches to rice, which is a more water-demanding crop. May she take the additional water she needs to grow rice with a 1900 priority, or must she now make a new appropriation with a later date? Alternatively, assume she owns 50 acres of undeveloped land, which she intends to bring into use over time. She irrigates only 10 acres in 1900, but gradually cultivates the remaining acreage, and seeks to irrigate all 50 acres by 1910. Can she claim a 1900 date for sufficient water to irrigate the whole?

These problems have not been much litigated.[4] The answer both as to crop-switching and increased irrigation seems to be that one is entitled to increase use over time, and to date the total back to the original date, so long as there was an intent from the outset to change crops or to increase acreage or seasonal use, and the water was actually brought into use with due diligence. As one court put it, enlargement of use is permitted "only to the extent of use contemplated at the time of the appropriation."[5] Thus, if one had irrigated only one planting for many years, but then began also to grow a later-season crop, and sought water for a second irrigation season, such additional use would not be allowed with the date of the original appropriation. Similarly, an irrigator who had been using a certain amount of water seasonally could not sell a year-round priority for that amount. Of course, assuming water is still available, one can always seek a new appropriation with a current priority date, for the new or enlarged use.

In old-fashioned cases, such as the examples just given, the capacity of a ditch or reservoir, or the acreage owned, would be evidence of original intent. In modern cases, and with large projects such as water supply for a city, the applicant obtains a conditional decree, or a permit, for the total intended use, and then perfects it by due diligence. For a modern example of difficulties that persist in securing rights for long-term projects, see Water Supply & Storage Co. v. Curtis, infra p. 208.

Another issue is measurement of the water right. A right to 10 cfs is understood to be a right to divert 10 cfs at the appropriator's headgate. But loss through evaporation and seepage in lengthy ditch systems,

---

4. For a series of cases that illustrate various versions of the problem of what might be called "extended use," see McPhee v. Kelsey, 44 Or. 193, 74 P. 401 (1903); Foster v. Foster, 107 Or. 355, 213 P. 895 (1923); Oliver v. Skinner, 190 Or. 423, 226 P.2d 507 (1951).

5. Farmers Highline Canal & Reservoir Co. v. City of Golden, 129 Colo. 575, 584, 272 P.2d 629, 634 (1954).

especially in a hot and arid region, often means that considerably less than 10 cfs reaches the user's land. Moreover, not all water applied to use is consumed; some runs off as return flow or seeps into the ground. Which quantity measures the water right? Only the amount consumed is, literally, beneficially used. Nonetheless, the simple answer is that one's right is measured at the point of diversion. So long as the losses in transportation and application are not considered wasteful, those losses are an acceptable part of the beneficial use so long as they are consistent with industry practice and are economically and technologically reasonable. But as we shall see in considering transfers, efforts to *sell* more than the amount actually consumed are usually problematic. The reason is that those downstream who have appropriated return flows that come back into the stream are entitled to be protected when water rights are transferred under a "no injury" rule.

b. *Right to Quality*

Seniority protects quality as well as quantity, though this issue has not traditionally been much litigated. It has begun to be much more important as various sorts of exchanges are implemented, where a junior appropriator takes water out of priority, and then seeks to substitute other water to meet the entitlement of senior appropriators. The exchange water may come from another stream, or be pumped groundwater, or even recovered sewage effluent. The proposed exchange water may be cheaper, or it may be more efficient, avoiding transmission losses, etc. For a useful discussion of these techniques see Lawrence J. MacDonnell, Out-of-Priority Water Use: Adding Flexibility to the Water Appropriation System, 83 Nebr. L. Rev. 485,532–37 (2004).

In California such exchanges are sometimes imposed as litigation remedies under the rubric of a "physical solution."[6] A more pro-active version of the technique is specifically authorized in Colorado and known as Plans for Augmentation,[7] where someone who wants to make a new use that would interfere with vested prior rights is allowed to provide a substitute source to existing appropriators (e.g. ground water), the rule is that the substitute water must "be of a quality and continuity to meet the requirements of use to which the senior appropriation has normally been put."[8] In light of that rule, how would you expect courts to deal with the following situations:

    1. A Colorado statute first enacted in 1897 provides: "Whenever any person ... diverts water from one public stream and turns it into another public stream, such person ... may take out the same amount of water again, less a reasonable deduction for seepage and

6. Harrison C. Dunning, The 'Physical Solution' in Western Water Law, 57 U. Colo. L. Rev. 445 (1996).

7. Colo. Rev. Stat. § 37–92–103(9); See Michael F. Browning, Substitute Supply Plans: Recent Water Law Developments, 31 Colo. Law. 67 (Aug. 2002).

8. See Carmen Sower–Hall & Holly Holder, Water Quality Issues in Augmentation Plans and Exchanges, 1 U. Denv. Water L. Rev. 96 (1997), discussing Colo. Rev. Stat. § 37–80–120(3). The administration of augmentation plans is explained in Empire Lodge Homeowners' Association v. Moyer, 39 P.3d 1139, 1150–53 (Colo. 2002).

vaporation...." Colo. Rev. Stat. § 37–83–101. A city seeking an
xchange (taking new water upstream from a fully appropriated
iver, but replacing it with discharges downstream to fulfill seniors'
ights), proposes to discharge effluent from its treatment plant as
exchange water. The downstream senior complains that the quality
is lower than the water it previously got, but the city says its
discharges meet federal and state water quality standards for effluents and its discharge is in full compliance with its water quality
permits. See Colo. Rev. Stat. § 37–92–305(3), (5).

2.   A company discharges its treated wastes into a stream that has
long had certain flows coming down to its point of discharge. The
amount of treatment required of the company was limited because
the flows coming down to it diluted its discharges. Then a new
appropriation upstream of the company sharply reduced flows in the
stream. As a result a much higher (and more expensive) treatment
of wastes is now required of the company by the pollution control
authority. The company sues the new appropriator. The company is
the senior appropriator on the stream, but the new appropriation
does not deprive it of its quantitative rights as to the water it took
out of the stream for industrial use. It simply diminishes the dilution
of its subsequent discharges of the water it had diverted for industrial use. What result? See City of Thornton v. Bijou Irrigation Co., 926
P.2d 1, 93 (Colo. 1996).

3.   One important new technique for meeting demand is conjunctive use. During periods of high flows, surface water is captured and
used to recharge underground aquifers, where water is stored so
that it can be pumped during periods of low flow when there is not
enough water in surface streams. In a state where overlying landowners have a primary right to groundwater underlying their land,
there is concern about such groundwater recharge lowering the
quality of water in the aquifers. How can, and should, this concern
be addressed? This is one of the newer problems facing water
management.

c. *Permissible and Non–Wasteful Use*

The requirement that a use be beneficial has two quite distinct
elements, though they are not routinely distinguished in the cases. The
first is that the purpose for which the water is used is permissible. For
example, the question might be raised whether one should be permitted
to use water for ornamental fountains in a desert economy. In this
section we will consider only this aspect of beneficiality.

The second element of beneficiality—and by far the more important
one as far as litigated cases are concerned—is the requirement that uses
not be wasteful in amount, though the purpose is perfectly appropriate.
Natural overflow irrigation, transportation losses through leaky ditches,
and excessive application for irrigation are common illustrations of this
species of waste. We will consider this second aspect of beneficiality in

the following section. But first let us consider the role of the legal system in characterizing uses as beneficial or non-beneficial.

The rule that an appropriative right can be acquired only for a "beneficial use" has not been a prolific source of controversy. There has never been any serious doubt that the use of water for irrigation, manufacturing, power production, and domestic and municipal use is beneficial. Only where water was sought to be used for recreational or purely aesthetic reasons did the issue of beneficiality ordinarily come into question in times past, though a few uses are still defined by statute as non-beneficial.[9] Today a number of statutes explicitly include recreation as a beneficial use, and it is generally so regarded.[10]

Some state statutes are also explicit in identifying preservation of fish and wildlife and aesthetic values as beneficial.[11] The view expressed in old cases that "where water is so precious it should not be used for mere matters of taste and fancy [artificial ponds and fountains] while those who need it for useful purposes go without," is no longer consequential.[12] Colorado's "optimum use" doctrine has been tempered to require that "proper regard for all significant factors, including environmental and economic concerns be taken into account."[13] Draining a peat bog or wetland, or creating impermeable land surfaces by paving, have been disallowed as a means for increasing the amount of water available for consumptive use. In 2002, the Montana Supreme Court overruled a 1988 decision, and held that instream uses for fish, wildlife, and recreation were beneficial uses (despite the absence of a physical diversion), In re Adjudication of the Existing Rights to the Use of All Water, 311 Mont. 327, 55 P.3d 396 (2002).

The usual rule—indeed it has been the uniform rule to date—is "once beneficial, always beneficial." A use does not become non-beneficial at a later date simply because other new uses or needs appear to be more important. Whether that is in fact the law everywhere is at least debatable. Section 100.5 of the California Water Code sets the same standard for determination of the reasonableness of the use that it does for determining the reasonableness of the method of use, or method of

9. Using water in coal slurry pipelines (Okla. Stat. tit. 27, § 7.6); using geothermal water for other than heat value (Idaho Code § 42–233). Kansas now expressly defines evaporation of water from sand and gravel pits as beneficial (Kan. Stat. Ann. § 82a–734(b)).

10. See Frank Trelease, The Concept of Reasonable Beneficial Use in the Law of Surface Streams, 12 Wyo. L.J. 1 (1957); Comment, Water Appropriation for Recreation, 1 Land & Water L. Rev. 209 (1966). See also State v. Morros, 766 P.2d 263 (1988) (water for wildlife a beneficial use); DeKay v. U.S. Fish & Wildlife Serv., 524 N.W.2d 855 (S.D. 1995) (wildlife propagation a beneficial use). The Tenth Circuit said that diverting water to protect the

silvery minnow from jeopardy under the federal Endangered Species Act is a beneficial use under New Mexico state law, Rio Grande Silvery Minnow v. Keys, 333 F.3d 1109, 1132 (10th Cir. 2003).

11. Cal. Water Code § 1243; Wash. Rev. Code § 90.54.020.

12. City of Los Angeles v. Pomeroy, 124 Cal. 597, 650, 57 P. 585, 605 (1899), appeal dismissed, 188 U.S. 314 (1903); Empire Water & Power Co. v. Cascade Town Co., 205 Fed. 123 (8th Cir. 1913).

13. Gregory Hobbs, Colorado Water Law: An Historical Overview, 1 U. Denv. Water L. Rev. 1, 23 (1997).

diversion. Does this suggest that an established use—irrigation of golf courses in a desert community, to take one controversial example—could become unreasonable if there later arose other pressing needs for the water? Of course, building a new residential development in the desert might not be so reasonable either. But how about an extended drought, where the golf course was the most senior appropriator? (These days it is likely that recycled water would be used to irrigate many golf courses).

In any event, not everyone agrees with the "once beneficial, always beneficial" rule, at least as to some currently-beneficial uses. Some years ago, in a concurring opinion, a justice of the Idaho Supreme Court suggested that while an instream appropriation was presently a beneficial use,

> the concept of what is or is not a beneficial use must necessarily change with changing conditions. For example, if we were now presented with a question of whether or not using water to operate a public swimming pool, a fountain, or * * * a skating rink were beneficial uses, a good argument could be presented that such uses, although not [those specified by the State Constitution—domestic, agriculture, mining, manufacturing and power] were nonetheless beneficial. But we cannot say that such uses will always be beneficial * * * there is always the possibility that * * * uses beneficial in one era [such as instream uses for fish maintenance] will not be in another * * *.[14]

A similar theory about the impermanence of beneficiality was proffered, but for quite different reasons, by Professor Eric Freyfogle: "Beneficial use, as it stands today, is an affront to attentive citizens who know stupidity when they see it; who know, for instance, that no public benefit arises when a river is fully drained so that its waters might flow luxuriously through unlined, open ditches onto desert soil to grow surplus cotton and pollute the water severely."[15] Is Freyfogle suggesting a change in the "once beneficial, always beneficial" rule, or is he simply restating conventional views: that pollution is never a beneficial use, and that wasteful methods of use—which *are* judged by changing standards over time—are not beneficial? Perhaps the question can be put more starkly: would it be lawful for a legislatures to declare today that using water to grow grass lawns in cities with the aridity of Las Vegas or Phoenix is no longer a beneficial use, however efficiently done, in light of increasing demand by other more important uses?

Or consider the following situation. Many years ago, a hydropower appropriation was granted to store water behind a dam. At that time, the state imposed a release requirement for certain specified flows to be maintained at specified times for fish and recreation. Now, on the basis of new knowledge and data, it is determined that twice as much water

14. State, Dept. of Parks v. Idaho Dept. of Water Admin., 96 Idaho 440, 447, 530 P.2d 924, 931 (1974) (Bakes, J., concurring).

15. Eric Freyfogle, Water Rights and the Common Wealth, 26 Envtl. L. 27, 42 (1996).

must be released at those times in order adequately to protect the fish. To comply with the new release requirement would significantly diminish hydropower production. Could such a new requirement be imposed on the ground that the full original appropriation is no longer beneficial? Would such a finding undercut any claims that the enhanced regulatory requirement constitutes a compensable taking of property under the Constitution (that is, one only has a property right in beneficial use, and whether a use is beneficial can change over time).

Another interesting beneficiality question is why the legal system should have to deal with these matters at all, either through appropriation doctrine, or administrative allocation (under some sort of public interest test, see infra pp. 220–223). In general one's opportunity to obtain a property right is not constrained by legal rules requiring that the property be put to beneficial use. It is assumed that marketplace transactions will reallocate less useful, or less beneficial, applications to higher uses. It is often said, in this context as in others, that water is different because it is scarce. But might not one expect scarcity to work in favor of marketplace reallocation to more beneficial uses? For example, as oil becomes scarcer it becomes more expensive, and the "wasteful" uses of gasoline by large cars generates a market for smaller, less fuel-consuming cars. Why shouldn't a parallel process occur with water? Scarcity would presumably generate higher prices and less beneficial uses would then sell out to those that are more beneficial.

Economists have long urged that the distribution of water in arid regions should be submitted to market forces. They observe that a great deal of water is currently used in low value agriculture. As supply faltered, the federal government was persuaded to bring in new subsidized supplies so farmers could continue to obtain water at low cost. In such situations of scarcity, one possible solution is to let the cost of water rise and to price low value agriculture out of arid regions in favor of more valuable (more efficient? more beneficial?) uses.

Perhaps you are suspicious of this argument which assumes that the uses that can pay the most are the most "beneficial." If so, you must ask what was the justification for asking federal taxpayers to provide water at $15 per acre foot to farmers, when the real cost of supplying the water was $100 an acre-foot. To put the question another way, in another context, ask whether you would prohibit farmers from selling their water at an agreed-upon price to an energy company that wants to use the water in a coal slurry pipeline? Does the problem seem different if you think of it not as a prohibition upon sale, but as a problem for other farmers who want to acquire water for irrigation, but always find themselves outbid by energy companies?

Does the problem seem different in yet another way if we focus on unappropriated water. Would the issue change if the state auctioned off unappropriated water to the highest bidder, and used the proceeds to benefit all the people of the state? Would the agricultural irrigation community be satisfied with such a plan? If you are attracted by the auction approach, would you favor requiring environmentalists—who want to maintain instream flows of unappropriated water for recreation and ecosystem protection—to have to bid for that result as against farmers and energy companies who would like to assure that the water will be available to them for diversion when and if they need it?

One argument in favor of a beneficial use doctrine is that market transactions do not measure all the real costs and benefits of the allocation of water to the uses for which the bidders are bidding. To take a simple example, let us assume that energy companies voluntarily bought a good deal of the water now in agricultural irrigation use, with the result that many acres of farm land were retired from agricultural use. The farmers who owned the land thus retired might be perfectly satisfied, since by selling their water they were in effect selling their land at a price satisfactory to them. But how about the non land-owning employees who had worked for the farmers? Having nothing to sell, they would get no payment for the sale, and they would be left without jobs (assuming they could not simply switch over to working for the energy company). If these workers become welfare cases, their support will become a public obligation since, as a practical matter, the public is the employer and welfare provider of last resort. If one looks not only to the impacts on the seller and the buyer of water, but more broadly, it may turn out that the sale of water from agriculture to energy use, despite the high price the energy company is willing to pay, produces costs greater than its benefits. Is the answer that the market does not reflect these costs because neither the buyer nor the seller of the water has to pay them? If the law regulates sales of water in special ways (to protect the economy of the selling area, for example), it is imposing a sort of beneficiality doctrine, though without necessarily using that term. Note that the problem of community impacts from closing or relocation of businesses (the so-called runaway shop) is not specific to water, yet only water law has a beneficial use doctrine. Is there something special about the way water markets function? See infra pp. 264 et seq.

Precisely the same phenomenon may occur on the benefit side. If one goes back to the old Colorado waterfall case of Empire Water & Power Co. v. Cascade Town Co., 205 Fed. 123 (C.C.A. Colo. 1913), cited supra p. 155 n.12, it may now seem perfectly rational for the law to have determined that using water for a waterfall in a resort was not a beneficial use, even though that use had considerable economic value in that tourists were willing to pay to come to see it, and even though the amounts they were willing to pay might have been more than farmers (or even a hydropower company) could have paid to buy out the resort. Perhaps Colorado was right in believing that the provision of water power, or irrigated agriculture, would have more potential for the economic growth of the state in the long run than would the resort. With electricity and a prosperous agriculture, the state could grow, and cities like Denver could flourish. Yet the many people who would benefit from a much-enlarged Denver (even from such conventional benefits as increased real estate values in the city) would not contribute to the bids that Colorado farmers or electric companies would make to buy out the resort's waterfall. Or perhaps it is more accurate to say that even if in theory such beneficiaries could be expected to pay, the problems and costs of organizing them to pay their appropriate share would guarantee that too low a bid would be made.[11]

Is there after all a role for a beneficial use "legitimacy" doctrine where the public would articulate beneficial and non-beneficial uses even more than is now the case? Might a more active beneficiality doctrine be a key to the future prosperity and quality of life in the arid regions of the country?[12]

d. Waste

When the cases ask whether a use is beneficial, they usually are asking whether it is wasteful. Agricultural waste—on which most attention has been focused—is of two principal types: transmission losses, through leaky ditches or by evaporation; and excessive application of water to crops. As to the latter, some states impose a maximum duty of water, providing that no more than a certain number of acre feet of water per acre may lawfully be applied in irrigation.[13]

There is no dispute *in theory* about the basic rule. It is that one can acquire only the right to make a non-wasteful use and that all wasteful uses must be discontinued.[14] The practical question is to what extent appropriators should be required to bear the cost of modern facilities such as concrete-lined ditches, or drip irrigation, in order to free up water for new appropriators.

STEVEN J. SHUPE,
WASTE IN WESTERN WATER LAW:
A BLUEPRINT FOR CHANGE*

61 Or. L. Rev. 483, 486–95, 519–21 (1982).

* * * Under the traditional interpretation of the prior appropriation doctrine, no incentive to conserve existed at the time the initial diversion was made. Since the water was free, early appropriators found little reason to build efficient irrigation networks. If the ditch lost a high percentage of flow to seepage, more water could simply be diverted from

---

11. For a discussion of these considerations see Mancur Olson, The Logic of Collective Action (1974); Joseph Sax, The Claim for Retention of the Public Lands, in Rethinking the Federal Lands (Sterling Brubaker ed., 1984).

12. A good discussion of the underlying issues may be found in Arthur Maass, Benefit–Cost Analysis: Its Relevance to Public Investment Decisions, 80 Q.J. Econ. 208 (1966).

13. Some states fix a duty of water by statute. See, e.g., Neb. Rev. St. § 46–231; S.D. Codified Laws § 46–5–6. In others the

Water Board determines how much water may be applied by each applicant. 82 Okl. St. § 105.12. See also Nev. Rev. Stat. 533.070; N.M. Stat. Ann. § 72–5–18.

14. See In re Water Rights of Escalante Valley Drainage Area, 10 Utah 2d 77, 348 P.2d 679 (1960); George Pring & Karen Tomb, License to Waste: Legal Barriers to Conservation and Efficient Use of Water in the West, 25 Rocky Mtn. Min. L. Inst. 25–1 (1979).

* Reprinted by permission. Copyright © 1982 by the University of Oregon.

the stream. If two alternatives for irrigating were available, no impetus normally existed to choose the more efficient method. To the contrary, the doctrine actually encouraged the development of inefficient techniques in areas where greed and speculation were commonplace; the greater the appropriation, the greater the water right claimed.

Once a water right had been established, the prior appropriation doctrine continued to promote inefficient use of the resource. Courts commonly held that the doctrine protected the level of diversion, even after it had been established that the quantity of water withdrawn exceeded that reasonably needed under modern irrigation practices. Only in cases of extreme wastefulness have courts required that irrigation appropriations conform to the customary practices of the region. Most irrigators, therefore, faced no pressure to implement newly developed technologies. As a consequence, the inefficient irrigation methods of a previous era have persisted despite the growing strain on limited water supplies throughout the West. * * *

There can be little question that the prior appropriation system currently inhibits optimum utilization of western waters. It would be incorrect, however, to conclude that the doctrine is completely devoid of safeguards against irresponsible use of water. * * *

* * * Water may be applied only to the extent that it creates a benefit to the user. If a portion of an initial diversion is being wasted through inefficiency, it is not being put to such beneficial use and no right to that portion can be established. Furthermore, the courts have made clear that "no matter how great in extent the original quantity may have been, an appropriator can [claim] only the maximum quantity of water which he shall have devoted to a beneficial use. * * *"

Waste, as nonbeneficial use, consequently became an important element in initially determining and, in some extreme instances, modifying, the extent of water rights. Significantly, the concept now provides the means to update current water law to meet the need for conservation. Protection traditionally afforded inefficient irrigation appropriations can be overcome by a modern application of the policy against waste. * * *

Water waste in a particular irrigation operation can be considered as the volume of flow diverted from the natural water supply that is not consumptively used by the crop.[a] This waste derives from two areas: the losses in the conveyance system and waste in the field.

Conveyance losses result from evaporation from canals and ditches, consumption by phreatophytes growing along the channels, and seepage. Seepage that reaches an exploitable aquifer or that reemerges in surface waters is classified as return flow. The irretrievable portion of conveyance waste is deemed consumptive loss. Water waste in the irrigated field is likewise a combination of return flows and consumptive loss.

a. Note that this is not the legal definition of waste. As the author states elsewhere, legal waste is the "flow diverted in excess of reasonable needs * * *."—Eds.

Percolating moisture that reaches a usable water source constitutes return flow, as does surface runoff from the field. The main sources of field consumptive losses are evaporation and irretrievable percolation.

Nearly one-fourth of the streamflow withdrawn by a typical irrigation system fails to reach the farm boundary, while only fifty-three percent of the remainder is actually used by the crop. These figures for conveyance losses and onfarm efficiency mean that more than half the water diverted by the average western farmer constitutes physical waste. * * *

Most of the water physically wasted on a typical farm eventually journeys back to surface waters or the groundwater supply. It is estimated that these irrigation return flows amount to 92 million acre feet annually, as compared to the 79 million acre feet consumed by crops each year. Even though this return flow is commonly utilized downstream, it carries with it the problems of erosion and water quality degradation. Moreover, it results in increased operation costs to the wasteful irrigator.

Physical waste of water on farms also results in a significant volume of water irretrievably lost. More than 20 million acre feet of irrigation water diverted from western waters each year neither is used by the crops nor returns to local water supplies for reapplication. This vast quantity of irretrievable waste exceeds the total amount of water consumed in all municipalities and industries in the nation. * * *

In assessing the costs that would be created by a water conservation program, the federal government undertook a study of potential outlays for irrigation improvements. It was estimated that modernizing irrigation practices throughout the West would cost $14.6 billion (in 1977 dollars). Major components of this total included land leveling on 11.6 million acres (cost of $1.9 billion), changing the method of water application on 3.5 million acres ($1.1 billion), automating delivery on 20.6 million acres ($1.9), and recovering tailwater from 15.7 million acres ($0.75 billion). The largest expense would come from improving antiquated conveyance systems. The study estimated that over 30,300 miles of canals and laterals are "in such condition that lining or replacement with pipe would be needed to reduce seepage, evaporation, and phreatophyte consumption to a reasonable level." An additional 90,500 miles of onfarm ditches would likewise require lining or piping to reduce waste. The cost of improving the conveyance network would total $8.0 billion, with another $1 billion needed to install control structures to reduce spillage and to regulate flow. Finally, implementation of scientific irrigation scheduling for 28.4 million acres would have an annual cost of $0.14 billion.

The study concluded that with this conservation investment, overall irrigation efficiency would increase to fifty-eight percent from its current national average of forty-one percent. Consumptive waste reductions would amount to millions of acre-feet each year, with annual diversions reduced by tens of millions of acre-feet. The greatest improvement in efficiencies would result in the Northwest region, while the highest costs would be encountered in the Southwest. According to federal estimates, modernization of the irrigation network in the arid Southwest would cost $6.1 billion. The economic benefits resulting from this investment, however, would run into hundreds of millions of dollars annually. Also, the construction program itself would generate 90,000 person-years of employment, bringing in an additional annual payroll of $30 million.

Regional cost-benefit comparisons, although informative, provide little guidance in assessing the cost of modernizing particular irrigation systems. Depending upon the conditions met, conservation costs on a specific farm may range from $25 per acre for minor land leveling, to well over $1,000 per acre for a trickle irrigation network. Sprinkler systems, according to government statistics, cost from $350 to $900 (in 1977 dollars) to install on each acre. It is this kind of data, weighed against the benefits of incremental water savings, that will be critical in modifying individual water rights to reflect modern practices. Care must be taken to ensure that an unmanageable burden not be placed upon the agricultural community, particularly on the small family farm. The full cost of modernization may prove prohibitively high in some small-scale irrigation operations, and special dispensations may be required in order to prevent severe hardships. For example, it may prove necessary to give small farms preferential treatment in subsidy programs or to provide them with exemptions from certain modernization requirements.

Care must also be taken that a particular conservation effort is consistent with comprehensive resource management. For instance, some efficient irrigation systems require more energy than primitive alternatives. Additionally, an irretrievable commitment of resources will be made in lining thousands of miles of ditches and in producing new pipes, sprinklers, and pumps. The lining of ditches will also result in destruction of vegetative cover that has commonly grown along the earthen banks providing habitat for small mammals and birds. These resource tradeoffs must be considered in determining how best to implement a widescale conservation program in different regions of each state.

Notes and Questions

1. As Shupe notes, most wasted water gets back into use by others, as return flow, seepage, or recharge of groundwater supplies. Though there are some losses and inefficiencies, would it really be desirable to tighten up the system now, recognizing how disruptive it would be for all those who have for many years depended on the returns of unconsumed, "wasted" water? For a comprehensive analysis of waste, and a detailed plea for judicial, administrative, and legislative action, see Janet Neuman, Beneficial Use, Waste, and Forfeiture: The Inefficient Search for Efficiency in Western Water Use, 28 Envtl. L. 919, 985 (1998). The following brief excerpt gives the flavor of Professor Neuman's provocative article:

> Suppose an anthropologist from another galaxy sets his spacecraft
> down in an alfalfa field in the middle of Nevada * * *. Early the

next morning he greets an astonished farmer, out to clear vegetation from his irrigation ditch, with this question: What is the most
precious and scarce natural resource in this area? * * * [T]he
farmer * * * says "water". The anthropologist * * * says, "Ah, you
must have highly developed technology for measuring and rationing
this valuable resource. Will you show it to me?" When the farmer
gestures to the open ditch as the distribution device, and explains
that measurement is not required, it is the visitor's turn to be
astonished * * *. [I]t does not take an alien to see that earthlings
behave strangely at times. Is it not astounding that most of the
irrigation water diversions in the west are not measured in any
way?

2. As you will see in the discussion of salvage, infra p. 173, some states,
like California, now provide that water saved through conservation efforts is
deemed to be beneficially used, and thus not subject to forfeiture. Such laws
are designed to encourage water marketing. But if water from an existing
use can be conserved, doesn't that prove waste was occurring? Hint: Ask
who financed the conservation effort.

3. One interesting case study is the Imperial Irrigation District in
southernmost California (see illustration, infra p. 176). Large amounts of
water diverted for irrigation are not consumed and run off the District's
lands into the Salton Sea (which is formed by Imperial's agricultural runoff),
which provides significant recreational and fish and wildlife benefits. Moreover, as a dead end body of water in a desert climate, the Salton Sea would
become saltier and saltier, to the detriment of environmental values, and its
level would decline to the detriment of recreationists, if it was not constantly
refreshed by irrigation runoff from Imperial. Even if Imperial's irrigation
practices are determined to be wasteful by the usual legal rules, should such
practices be enjoined?[1] When Imperial made a deal to transfer some conserved irrigation water to San Diego, it turned out that the proposed
reduction of flows into the Salton Sea would create jeopardy to species listed
under the federal Endangered Species Act (ESA). Is it possible to have a
situation in which the discharges are both (1) wasteful and enjoinable and
(2) legally obligatory. Note that unlike most ESA situations, jeopardy would
be created not by disturbing a natural situation but by returning to it (that
is, by ceasing to dump waste water that was transported from a distant
watershed). For yet one more twist on the problem, see Cal. Water Code
§ 1013, enacted in 1987, some years before the agreement with San Diego
and before it was anticipated: "The Imperial Irrigation District * * * complying with an order.... to reduce through conservation measures, the
volume of the flow of water * * * into the Salton Sea, shall not be held liable
for any effects to the Salton Sea * * * resulting from the conservation
measures." The law was probably intended to insulate Imperial from claims
by homeowners and businesses such as marinas on the Salton Sea shoreline,
who were concerned about lowering water levels.

1. See Michael Cohen, et al., Haven or
Hazard: The Ecology and Future of the
Salton Sea (Pacific Institute 1999).

4. Conservation sometimes has unanticipated results. Texas, which provides low-interest loans to aid farmers in modernizing irrigation systems, has found that agricultural water use subsequently increased. Why? "The answer seem to be that farmers are finding they can grow higher water-using crops, and increase irrigated acreage, because adoption of water-saving technologies creates a 'new' water supply." Texas Water Resources, May 1999, at 2. Conversely, the City of El Paso found that a new pricing policy, charging higher prices for use above a specified baseline, and discounts for the use of reclaimed water, was highly successful in diminishing per capita use (the uniform experience of cities).

NATIONAL RESEARCH COUNCIL, A NEW ERA FOR IRRIGATION

104–05, 107–08 (1996).

Improvements in surface irrigation fall into two general categories: improvements in the delivery of water to the farm and improvements in on-farm practices.

Storage and Delivery Systems: The most significant changes in water delivery systems during this century are the incorporation of water-measuring devices such as metering turn-out gates and computerized flowmeters; the lining of porous earthen ditch systems with concrete and other impervious materials; the installation of "check" structures enabling better management of water in a canal or ditch; the use of reregulating ponds for the same purpose; the installation of debris collection systems; and the replacement of open ditches with pipes. All of these features tend to reduce the total quantity of water that must be diverted from a stream for delivery to farm headgates. Lining canals and installing pipelines can reduce the transmission losses. However, these "losses" act as a source of recharge for groundwater that is used for irrigation elsewhere or that supports wetlands or other instream uses of water.

On-Farm Systems: Surface irrigation systems such as flood and furrow systems are still the most widely used type of system. In areas with low-cost water, the typical surface irrigation system produces large quantities of runoff as the water flows across the field and infiltrates into the soil for use by the crop. Areas with more expensive water, such as the San Joaquin Valley, produce less runoff by using siphon tubes, which provide for a more uniform application into furrows of row crops. Land leveling, shorter furrow runs, and construction of borders and basins also provide more uniform irrigation. * * *

Sprinkler and microirrigation systems are designed to prevent surface runoff and apply the water uniformly to the entire field. Microirrigation applies water in a slow, precise manner. Water is delivered through a system of plastic tubes laid across or just under the surface and outfitted with special emitters designed to drip water into the soil at a rate close to the water consumption rate of the plant. Thus, rather than relying on maintaining soil moisture within the plant's root zone [the method of traditional furrow irrigation] drip systems seek to provide essentially a continuous supply of water (and other nutrients) directly to the plan. The range of on-farm efficiencies of alternative systems can be as great as 65–90 percent independent of the type of system.

* * * [S]urface systems still irrigate approximately 55 percent of the nation's total irrigated area, but continued reduction in use is expected. Microirrigation now represents approximately 5 percent of the total irrigated area * * * associated with high-value crops such as fruits and vegetables. Limited water availability and high costs are the driving forces for these conversions.

Notes and Questions

1. For a list of over 20 technological means of improving irrigation efficiency see Cal. Dept. of Water Resources, Agricultural Efficient Water Management Practices that Stretch California's Water Supply (1995).

2. Data on costs of conversion to more efficient systems is hard to come by. For one local study, see Irrigation System Costs and Performance in the San Joaquin Valley, prepared by CH2M Hill, for the Federal–State San Joaquin Valley Drainage Program (U.S. Bureau of Reclamation, et al., Sacramento, CA, Sept. 1989).

TULARE IRRIGATION DIST. v. LINDSAY–STRATHMORE IRRIGATION DIST.

Supreme Court of California, 1935.
3 Cal.2d 489, 45 P.2d 972.

An appropriator, as against subsequent appropriators, is entitled to the continued flow to the head of his ditch of the amount of water that he, in the past, whenever that quantity was present, has diverted for beneficial purposes, plus a reasonable conveyance loss, subject to the limitation that the amount be not more than is reasonably necessary, under reasonable methods of diversion, to supply the area of land theretofore served by his ditch. * * * The early cases measured the appropriator's right by the capacity of his ditch, but that rule has long since been repudiated in this state. As the pressure of population has led to the attempt to bring under cultivation more and more lands, and as the demands for water to irrigate these lands have become more and more pressing, the decisions have become increasingly emphatic in limiting the appropriator to the quantity reasonably necessary for beneficial use. * * * Insofar as the diversion exceeds the amount reasonably necessary for beneficial purposes, it is contrary to the policy of the law and is a taking without right and confers no title, no matter for how long continued. * * * However, an appropriator cannot be compelled to divert according to the most scientific method known. He is entitled to make a reasonable use of the water according to the general custom of the locality, so long as the custom does not involve unnecessary waste. * * *

We are also of the opinion that the evidence does not entirely support the findings that *all* the water that was used in the winter period (whatever the amount may have been) was put to beneficial uses. Preliminarily, it should be stated that, whatever quantity an appropriator has actually diverted in the past, he gains no right thereto unless such water is actually put to a reasonable beneficial use. * * * What is a beneficial use, of course, depends upon the facts and circumstances of each case. What may be a reasonable beneficial use, where water is present in excess of all needs, would not be a reasonable beneficial use in an area of great scarcity and great need. What is a beneficial use at one time may, because of changed conditions, become a waste of water at a later time.

On the subject of the purposes to which the winter water was put, there was considerable evidence introduced by respondents, the trial court, in fact, at least once suggesting that it had heard enough on this point.

Many of the witnesses produced by respondents were extremely vague as to the benefits of winter irrigation. One of them testified that winter irrigation "did not seem to hurt my alfalfa any and killed the gophers out; and I think where you irrigate early that way your alfalfa comes better." Another testified that from winter irrigation "the first benefit is you get rid of all your gophers, if you can irrigate in cold weather, or the spring—you get rid of your gophers and soak your land up thoroughly, and when the warm weather comes it starts the alfalfa to grow." Still another testified that he irrigated in December and January for the purpose of drowning out gophers and that such was the principal purpose of irrigating at that time, together with the purpose of starting the fox tail and wild feed. Another stated, "A man will always irrigate his alfalfa in the winter season if it is not raining, it helps to kill the gophers." * * *

Many other quotations could be made to the same effect. A great many of respondents' witnesses seemed to be of the opinion that the only reason they irrigated during the winter season was to exterminate these pests. It seems quite clear to us that in such an area of need as the Kaweah delta the use of an appreciable quantity of water for such a purpose cannot be held to be a reasonable beneficial use. This seems to us so self-evident that no further discussion of the point is necessary. We, therefore, hold that whatever quantity of water was used by respondents solely for this purpose during the winter period was not devoted to a beneficial use and that, in so far as the finding of the trial court now under discussion is based on such use, it is unsupported by the evidence. * * *

Notes and Questions

1. In the *Tulare* case, it was conceded that seepage loss through earthen ditches was between 40 and 45 percent. The court, after citing

evidence that other local ditch systems had losses averaging over 40 percent, and in some cases as high as 57 percent, refused to enjoin the use. This is the standard posture of the cases. See, e.g., A–B Cattle Co. v. United States, 196 Colo. 539, 589 P.2d 57, 69 (1978), noted in Stephen Brown, Maximum Utilization Collides With Prior Appropriation in A–B Cattle Co. v. United States, 57 Denv. L.J. 103 (1979); McDonald v. Montana, 220 Mont. 519, 722 P.2d 598, 605–07 (1986).

2. The Colorado statute defines beneficial use as the "use of that amount of water that is reasonable and appropriate under reasonably efficient practices to accomplish without waste the purpose for which the appropriation is lawfully made," Colo. Rev. Stat. § 37–92–103(4). California's Agricultural Water Suppliers Efficient Water Management Act defines "efficient water management practices" as "reasonable and economically justifiable programs to improve the delivery and use of water used for agricultural purposes." Cal. Water Code § 10902(b).

3. A 1980 amendment to section 100.5 of the California Water Code provides that "conformity of a * * * method of diversion of water with local custom shall not be solely determinative of its reasonableness, but shall be considered as one factor to be weighed * * *." How should one measure whether water is being wasted? For example, if like-positioned irrigators in an area could afford to line their ditches and still make some specified fair return, should they be obliged to do so, though none in fact do so? What if such improvements are affordable (in the sense just described), but the improvements would make water more expensive than available ground water which is now being used by other overlying owners, and thus create a shortage, or provoke overdrafting? As to municipalities, are they wasting water they are taking out of a fish-stressed river if they could recycle some of their existing supply and re-use it, for irrigating golf courses for example, even if not for potable purposes? Does it make any difference how much recycling costs (what does it mean to ask what Denver or Los Angeles can "afford")?

4. Though things are beginning to change, it was rare to find a case where nothing more than substantial transmission losses led to a holding of waste.[2] Most cases where a senior has been required to cease waste involved practices like natural overflow flood irrigation[3] or waste without benefit to the appropriator, as where water was allowed to flow uncontrolled day and night.[4] The *Tulare* standard, protecting beneficial use plus a reasonable transmission loss, is also applied in groundwater cases, where the question arises whether pumpers will be required to deepen their wells (to a "reasonable" depth) as new pumper-users in the aquifer lower the water table.

---

2. See, e.g., Doherty v. Pratt, 34 Nev. 343, 124 P. 574 (1912); Glenn Dale Ranches, Inc. v. Shaub, 94 Idaho 585, 494 P.2d 1029 (1972). For a detailed review of leading cases dealing with transmission losses, see Bruce Maak, Water Waste—Ascertainment and Abatement, 1973 Utah L. Rev. 449.

3. See, e.g., Joslin v. Marin Mun. Water Dist., 67 Cal.2d 132, 60 Cal.Rptr. 377, 429

P.2d 889 (1967) (water driven sorting of gravel); In re Silvies River, 115 Or. 27, 237 P. 322 (1925); Warner Valley Stock Co. v. Lynch, 215 Or. 523, 336 P.2d 884 (1959). This issue is sometimes posed as the question whether an appropriator has a right in her traditional means of diversion, a matter that most often arises with "pumping head" in groundwater. See infra p. 439.

4. See State ex rel. Erickson v. McLean, 62 N.M. 264, 308 P.2d 983 (1957).

5. The U.S. Supreme Court, in one of its rare discussions of waste doctrine (in an interstate equitable apportionment dispute), said that a user is required to take only conservation measures that are "financially and physically feasible" and "within practicable limits," and that the burden of showing financially and physically feasible means for eliminating or reducing inefficient use is on the challenger. Colorado v. New Mexico, 467 U.S. 310, 319 (1984). See infra p. 859).

ERICKSON v. QUEEN VALLEY RANCH CO.

California Court of Appeal, Third District, 1971.
22 Cal.App.3d 578, 99 Cal.Rptr. 446.

FRIEDMAN, ACTING PRESIDING JUSTICE.

Plaintiffs own 240 acres of ranch lands in Mono County. They seek to quiet title to the water of Morris Creek. In the early part of the century, plaintiffs' properties were owned by John Pedro, who established an appropriative right to the entire flow of Morris Creek. * * *

The headwaters of the creek are located in Nevada. In a state of nature the creek flowed into California, although John Pedro's ranch was not riparian to it. Commencing in 1902, Pedro acquired appropriative rights and built a diversion dam, which is located about one-half mile east of the present California–Nevada state line. From the dam he built a stone-lined diversion ditch, which conducted the entire flow of the creek by gravity to his ranch, about two and one-half miles distant. The ditch was about two feet deep and two feet wide. John Pedro died in 1916. The ranch was held by his widow and three sons until 1966, when it was sold to plaintiffs.

Some years after John Pedro's death, and over the protests of the Pedro family, defendants were issued appropriative permits by the Nevada state authorities, allowing them to transport up to five second/feet of Morris Creek by pipeline to irrigate Nevada property. The permits were expressly subordinated to any preexisting rights found by a court. At one point a contractor employed by defendants stopped the flow of water into the diversion ditch. Plaintiffs' protests caused partial restoration of the flow. Plaintiffs then instituted this action.

After considering evidence, the trial court found that John Pedro and his successors had continually put to beneficial use for irrigation and domestic purposes all the water of Morris Creek diverted to the land; that the Pedro family never abandoned or forfeited any right to the water; that, except for occasional storm runoffs, there is no surplus or unappropriated water; that evapo-transpiration losses occurred during the two and one-half miles of flow but these losses were not unreasonable and were similar to the custom or practice prevailing in the locality. The court entered a judgment quieting the title to plaintiffs as appropriative owners of all the water of Morris Creek diverted at the upper end of the ditch.

* * * Plaintiffs' existing appropriative right is measured not by the flow originally appropriated and not by the capacity of the diversion ditch, but by the amount of water put to beneficial use at the delivery point plus such additional flow as is reasonably necessary to deliver it. * * *

An appropriator cannot be compelled to divert according to the most scientific methods; he is entitled to make a reasonable use of the water according to the general custom of the locality, so long as the custom does not involve unnecessary waste. The trial court's finding included a formulary statement designed to satisfy this rule, declaring that evapo-transpiration losses in the course of the two and one-half miles of conveyance by ditch "are not unreasonable and are similar to the custom or practice of this locality."

According to measurements taken in August 1963, the Pedro ditch contained a flow of 2.585 cubic feet per second at a point 100 yards below the diversion dam, while only 0.424 cubic feet per second was delivered at the Pedro ranch. The major part, that is, five-sixths of the flow, was lost en route to the point of use. * * * Inferably, absorption into the sandy desert soil is a major loss factor, evaporation a relatively minor factor.

Article XIV, section 3, of the California Constitution declares the state's policy to achieve maximum beneficial use of water and prevention of waste, unreasonable use and unreasonable method of use. The constitutional policy applies to every water right and every method of diversion. It imposes upon trial courts an affirmative duty to fashion a decree which will simultaneously protect the paramount right of the established appropriator and prevent waste.

The findings and decree in this case fail to accomplish the second of these objectives. By holding that transmission losses amounting to five-sixths of the flow are reasonable and consistent with local custom, the court effectually placed the seal of judicial approval on what appears to be an inefficient and wasteful means of transmission. Such a holding is not in conformity with the demands of article XIV, section 3.

It is doubtless true that water in the arid desert areas of Mono County is frequently transported by open ditch; also, that much of the flow may be lost by absorption and evaporation. Moreover, an appropriator who has for many years conveyed water by earth ditches may not be compelled at his own expense to install an impervious conduit. Nevertheless, an excessive diversion of water for any purpose is not a diversion for beneficial use. Water of Morris Creek which is presently wasted becomes excess water available for appropriation. Another would-be appropriator may be willing to invest in a more efficient conveyance system in order to capture and use the water now lost en route. * * *

When the issue involves a possible surplus available to a later appropriator over and above the needs of the prior appropriator, a generalized finding of "reasonableness" at the point of diversion is inadequate. A finding of reasonableness which cloaks a transmission loss amounting to five-sixths of the diverted flow fails to respond to the demands of constitutional policy. That policy required the trial court to inquire and make findings in terms of the flow taken at the point of diversion; the flow delivered at the point of use; the flow, if any, made available to the later appropriator by a physical solution permitting maintenance of the flow delivered to the prior appropriator; and finally, to consider the retention of jurisdiction in order to accomplish maximum utilization of the water. In the light of constitutional policy, there were material issues on which the trial court did not find. * * *

Some enlightenment *dehors* the record turned up at oral argument. The attorneys were in apparent general agreement on the unrecorded circumstances; these circumstances do not affect our decision to reverse; their consideration may assist the trial court and parties. It appears that the two and one-half miles of ditch traverses land under the jurisdiction of the United States Forest Service. Over the years leakage from the ditch has generated vegetation. The water and vegetation support a population of deer and quail. Plaintiffs sought permission to replace the ditch with a pipeline but the Forest Service declined for the sake of the animal and bird life. As we pointed out earlier, plaintiffs are under no legal compulsion to install a pipe. Defendants, on the other hand, are under some economic compulsion, for their ability to segregate a surplus flow available for appropriation may depend upon a physical means of preventing transmission loss. Defendants may be able and willing to work out a solution with the Forest Service. Whether the federal agency has any proprietary interest in the water leakage is outside the present scope of this lawsuit. If a three-way extrajudicial solution is impossible, a three-way lawsuit in an appropriate forum may be necessary to resolve the problem. As between the present parties, in any event, the trial court is obliged to fashion findings and a judgment consistent with constitutional policy of water conservation.

Judgment reversed.

Notes and Questions

1. The appellate court reversed the trial court decision that had quieted title in the plaintiff to the entire flow of the Creek. So it seems the defendant won. If so, the plaintiff would presumably have to let some water, the amount over and above its reasonable diversion, be taken by the defendant. Yet in the last paragraph of its opinion, the court suggests that if the defendant wants to have water, it will have to pay to stop the leakage in the plaintiff's ditch. Why should that be the case under the court's ruling? On the contrary, isn't it the plaintiff who should be under "economic compulsion" if it wants to retain the quantum of water that has been reaching its ranch? We confess to puzzlement at the court's comment. Yet a similar rule is asserted in a law review article written by a Justice of the Colorado Supreme Court. He says "Indeed, an irrigator utilizing an inefficient surface diversion may be required to employ wells to effectuate the diversion *if a junior appropriator who might benefit undertakes to pay the expenses involved.*" Gregory Hobbs, Colorado Water Law: An Historical

Overview, 1 U. Denv. Water L. Rev. 1, 8 (1997) (emphasis added). For this proposition, Justice Hobbs cites Alamosa–La Jara Water Users Protect. Ass'n v. Gould, 674 P.2d 914, 935 (Colo. 1983). For a similar result, see Big Cottonwood Tanner Ditch Co. v. Shurtliff, 56 Utah 196, 189 P. 587 (1919). Along the same line, in 1903 the Nevada Supreme Court said "If waste by seepage and evaporation can be prevented * * * by substituting improved methods of conveying water * * * the desired improvement should be at the expense of the later claimant who is desirous of utilizing the water thereby to be saved." Tonkin v. Winzell, 27 Nev. 88, 99–100, 73 P. 593, 595 (1903). Why shouldn't the senior lose water wastefully taken? If he wants to keep getting the same net amount as before, shouldn't the senior pay to fix the system, and then only be able to take a non-wasteful amount?

2. In this sort of situation, California courts often invoke what is known as the "physical solution doctrine." It is not entirely clear what the "doctrine" is; whether it is simply a creative remedy, or whether it is a remedy that amounts to a departure from the ordinary rights between water users. For example, in City of Lodi v. East Bay Municipal Utility District, 7 Cal.2d 316, 60 P.2d 439 (1936), to assure a small amount of water to a downstream senior, junior municipal diverters upstream had been required to let huge quantities of water flow downstream where most of it was lost to use. The Court denied the senior the right to compel continuation of this wasteful situation, and required it to accept an alternative source of supply supplied by the junior (such as piped in water). In such circumstances the senior is denied the rigorous remedy that traditional doctrine would impose (e.g. a flat shutdown of the junior), but it is not clear to what extent the senior can be subjected to some disadvantage or cost in the name of this doctrine.[5] In the *Lodi* case, the senior was denied the right to maintain the status quo ante on the ground that to do so would violate the California Constitution's "reasonable and beneficial use" requirement (Art. 10, sec. 2), yet it did not simply have its pre-existing use cut off as invalid. See generally Harrison Dunning, The "Physical Solution" in Western Water Law, 57 U. Colo. L. Rev. 445 (1986). A downstream senior on a river where significant (but not all) water is lost in transit could traditionally enjoin upstream juniors to protect its senior rights. Can a court require the senior to pump available groundwater instead, at a considerably higher cost, and thus permit both the senior and upstream juniors to be served? Could such a result be imposed on the ground that the senior had been guilty of waste in not pumping groundwater instead of diverting from the river? Or would (should?) courts require the junior to pay the additional pumping costs?

3. In Krieger v. Pacific Gas & Elec. Co., 119 Cal.App.3d 137, 173 Cal.Rptr. 751 (1981), P.G. & E. sought to line its canal and prevent loss of water by seepage. The Court refused to allow it to do so, rejecting P.G. & E.'s assertion that ditch lining was consistent with the California Constitution's anti-waste policy. The Court found that the seepage supported non-indigenous vegetable growth and said, "One might reasonably conclude the seepage is beneficial within the intendment of [the anti-waste provision of the Constitution]." The case was instituted by a junior appropriator who was

5. See City of Los Angeles v. City of San Fernando, 14 Cal.3d 199, 290–91, 537 P.2d 1250, 1316, 1318 (1975); Cal. State Water Resources Control Bd. Water Right Dec. 1631 (Mono Lake), at 10–11 (Sept. 28, 1994).

also benefitting from some of the seepage and did not want to be cut off. Would the court have responded differently if an unsatisfied upstream junior had sued to compel P.G. & E. to line its ditch?

4. The leaky ditch problem presents four possibilities: (1) customary transmission losses could be accepted, leaving no new water available on fully appropriated streams; (2) the senior could be required to undertake repairs at his own expense, making newly saved water available at no expense to the new aspirant appropriator[6]; (3) the new appropriator could be permitted to repair the ditch at *his* expense if he wants to appropriate the water thereby saved; or (4) the public could pay for the repair, a commonplace practice in western states.[7] Each of these schemes raises problems.

5. If the public pays for ditch repair, who—under the theory of the *Erickson* case—gets the water produced, the original appropriator, or juniors who have been unable to fulfill their appropriations? See Interagency Task Force, U.S. Dep't of the Interior, U.S. Dep't of Agriculture & U.S. Environmental Protection Agency, Irrigation Water Use and Management 53 (1979).

6. What if the new appropriator says: "I will gladly pay to fix the ditch, so long as I can get the saved water. It will cost me $1,000 to repair the ditch, but the water I get will be worth $2000 to me." At this point the senior says, "Oh, no, I will repair the ditch, and sell you the water." You may ask why the senior appropriator didn't take this initiative in the first place. Experience shows that seniors often do not take such initiatives. Read on, and when you get to the cases on salvage, infra p. 183, you will know why.

7. What if the senior is willing to repair the ditch, but the leakage had been flowing back into the river at a point where it had been diverted for many years by a downstream junior? Is that downstream diverter entitled to protection? This is a question that arises in the setting of transfers of appropriative rights, infra p. 267. See also discussion of the right of recapture, infra pp. 197–209.

8. In an article entitled Western Water Rights: The Era of Reallocation, by Steven Shupe, Gary Weatherford, and Elizabeth Checchio, 29 Nat. Resources J. 413, 420 (1989), the following passage appears: "Another reallocation strategy for junior municipal and industrial users that need a more reliable supply is to make water conservation investments in a senior use. By financing the modernization of old irrigation systems, junior users may be able to make surplus water available for their use, while letting the senior user continue to irrigate the same amount of land with less water. * * * The City of Casper, Wyoming, applied this conservation strategy in the early 1980's in conjunction with the Alcova Irrigation District. The city financed canal lining and other means of reducing irrigation losses in the district, then diverted the salvaged water for municipal use * * * [as] the most cost-effective way to increase its water supply." Do you see any problem such arrangements might raise? What if the holder of priority #3 financed modernization of the system of priority #1, in a setting like that

6. See Basinger v. Taylor, 36 Idaho 591, 211 P. 1085, 1086 (1922).

7. See Steven Shupe, Waste in Western Water Law: A Blueprint for Change, 61 Or. L. Rev. 483, 511 (1982).

described in this note, and then priority #2 stepped in and claimed the saved water?

e. Regulating Waste, Encouraging Salvage

i. Waste

The two cases below, one judicial and one administrative, illustrate relatively rare modern instances of wasteful practices being restricted.

STATE DEPARTMENT OF ECOLOGY v. GRIMES

Supreme Court of Washington, 1993.
121 Wash.2d 459, 852 P.2d 1044.

Smith, J.

This matter is before the court upon direct review * * * raising the question of the legal definition of "reasonable use" of water as an element of "beneficial use" under the Water Code of 1917, the Water Resources Act of 1971, and other related statutes.

In September 1981, the Department of Ecology filed a petition in the Pend Oreille County Superior Court for clarification of existing rights to divert, withdraw, or otherwise make beneficial use of the surface and ground waters of the Marshall Lake and Marshall Creek drainage basin * * *.

The Grimeses submitted five claims for water rights, only the first of which is at issue in this appeal. This claim was for the use of waters for domestic supply, irrigation and recreational purposes. The Grimeses requested an instantaneous flow rate of 3 cubic feet per second (c.f.s.) for irrigation purposes, and a storage right of 1,520 acre feet of water in the Marshall Lake reservoir. The referee recommended that this claim be confirmed, but limited it to an instantaneous flow of 1.5 c.f.s. during irrigation season, and a storage right of 183 acre feet plus 737 acre feet for evaporative loss, for a total storage right of 920 acre feet.

* * * "Beneficial use" is a term of art in water law, and encompasses two principal elements of a water right. First, it refers to the purposes, or type of activities, for which water may be used. Use of water for the purposes of irrigated agriculture is a beneficial use. The Grimeses' use of water to irrigate alfalfa fields is not at issue in this case. Second, beneficial use determines the measure of a water right. The owner of a water right is entitled to the amount of water necessary for the purpose to which it has been put, provided that purpose constitutes a beneficial use. To determine the amount of water necessary for a beneficial use, courts have developed the principle of "reasonable use." Reasonable use of water is determined by analysis of the factors of water duty and waste.

In his findings establishing the measure of the Grimeses' water right, the referee * * * recommended that a right be confirmed to these defendants, with a July 13, 1906 priority for the irrigation of 73 acres from Marshall Lake. * * * [T]he Referee will allow the standard duty of water which would be 1.2 cubic feet per second plus an additional 25 percent for transportation loss, thus making an aggregate amount of 1.5 cubic feet per second identified with this right * * *. A second element concerning this right is the amount of storage of water to which these claimants are entitled * * *. [T]hese waters also have recreational benefits, not only to the riparian owners around the lake but also to the general public through the use of resort facilities located on the lake * * *. Therefore, the Referee recommends that a related but separate right be confirmed to these defendants for the storage of 920 acre-feet in Marshall Lake for irrigation and recreation purposes. The priority shall be fixed as of July 13, 1906. The period during which waters may be stored shall be identified as those periods of the year which do not include the April 1 to October 31 irrigation season * * *.

The Grimeses challenge the referee's "consideration of the evidence" and his application of the law in making these findings. We first consider the evidence used by the referee in establishing the factors of water duty and waste. We then consider the test of "reasonable efficiency" employed by the referee, and adopted by the Superior Court, to evaluate these factors. "[Water duty is] that measure of water, which, by careful management and use, without wastage, is reasonably required to be applied to any given tract of land for such period of time as may be adequate to produce therefrom a maximum amount of such crops as ordinarily are grown thereon. It is not a hard and fast unit of measurement, but is variable according to conditions. The referee based his determination of the volume of water necessary for irrigation in the Marshall Lake basin on a Washington State University Research Bulletin entitled 'Irrigation Requirements for Washington–Estimates and Methodology' " (Irrigation Report), and on the expert testimony of Jim Lyerla * * *.

Based on the testimony of Mr. Lyerla and the Irrigation Report, the referee determined that an irrigated alfalfa crop grown in the Marshall Lake area requires 21 inches or 1.75 acre feet of water per acre during the irrigation season. The referee then applied an efficiency factor and increased this water duty to 2.5 acre feet per acre per year. The referee found this water duty to be "approximately commensurate" with the duty utilized by the Department of Ecology in its quantity allocations in this geographic area under the water right permit system.

Because water rights are characterized in both total yearly allowance and instantaneous flow, the referee also established the maximum rate of diversion at 0.0166 c.f.s. per acre under irrigation. The referee first calculated a standard flow of 1 c.f.s. of water per 60 acres as a reasonable instantaneous flow for alfalfa irrigation in the Marshall Lake basin. In considering the Grimeses' claim, he determined that the Grimeses were entitled to sufficient flow to irrigate 73 acres, or a minimum of 1.21 c.f.s. He then calculated in an efficiency factor to increase this flow by 25 percent and awarded the Grimeses an instantaneous flow of 1.5 c.f.s.

The referee observed that a larger water duty could be awarded to any claimant with specific information proving a right to a larger amount. * * * The referee's determination of a generic water duty for irrigation of alfalfa in the Marshall Lake basin is supported by a preponderance of the evidence and will not be disturbed by this court.

Waste

From an early date, courts announced the rule that no appropriation of water was valid where the water simply went to waste. Those courts held that the appropriator who diverted more than was needed for the appropriator's actual requirements and allowed the excess to go to waste acquired no right to the excess. A particular use must not only be of benefit to the appropriator, but it must also be a reasonable and economical use of the water in view of other present and future demands upon the source of supply. The difference between absolute waste and economical use has been said to be one of degree only * * *. Appellant Clarence E. Grimes acknowledged in his testimony that his existing irrigation system required a water flow of up to 3 cubic feet per second in order to deliver 1 cubic foot per second to the field, and that this system was highly inefficient, causing one-half to two-thirds loss of water * * *.

While an appropriator's use of water must be reasonably efficient, absolute efficiency is not required * * *. Relying on a standard efficiency factor for irrigation sprinkler systems found in the Irrigation Report, he confirmed in the Grimeses a water right with one-fourth conveyance loss for a total of 1.5 cubic feet per second. There was at least sufficient evidence for the referee to determine * * * the allowable loss for system inefficiency in establishing their instantaneous flow.

The Reasonable Efficiency Test

In limiting the Grimeses' vested water right, the referee balanced several factors, including the water duty for the geographical area and crop under irrigation, the claimants' actual diversion, and sound irrigation practices. In his report, the referee described his method of calculating the Grimeses' water right as a "reasonable efficiency" test.

* * * This court has consistently held that rights of users of water for irrigation purposes are vested rights in real property. Amici curiae assert that the "local custom" test has been employed historically to determine whether given applications of water are wasteful, within the meaning of beneficial use, and that courts should now apply it in the setting of general adjudications * * *.

Decisions of courts throughout the western states provide a basis for defining "reasonable efficiency" with respect to irrigation practices.[64]

64. Tulare Irrig. Dist. v. Lindsay–Strathmore Irrig. Dist., 3 Cal. 2d 489, 546–47, 45 P.2d 972, 997 (1935); Hardy v. Beaver Cy. Irrig. Co., 65 Utah 28, 40–41, 234 P. 524, 529 (1924).

While customary irrigation practices common to the locality are a factor for consideration, they do not justify waste of water.

* * * [C]ustom can fix the manner of use of water for irrigation only when it is founded on necessity * * * [and] an irrigator is entitled to use only so much as he can put to a beneficial use, for the public policy of the people of the United States will not tolerate waste of water in the arid regions. * * *

In limiting the Grimeses' water use by a requirement of reasonable efficiency, the referee properly considered the Irrigation Report, the Grimeses' actual water use, and their existing irrigation system. The referee alluded to a test incorporating factors that consider impacts to the water source and its flora and fauna. While consideration of these impacts is consonant with the State's obligations under RCW 90.03.005 [reduce waste] and 90.54.010(1)(a) and (2)[beneficial use], these factors cannot operate to impair existing water rights. Other laws may, however, operate to define existing rights in light of environmental values.[69] * * *

The Takings Argument

Appellants Grimes argue that diminishment of their prior appropriation in any way is a "taking" of their property right for which they must be compensated or have the decision of the trial court set aside. A vested water right is a type of private property that is subject to the Fifth Amendment prohibition on takings without just compensation. Nevertheless, the concept of "beneficial use", as developed in the common law and as described earlier in this opinion, operates as a permissible limitation on water rights.

Conclusion

* * * Applying the concepts of "beneficial use" to water rights in this state, we rule on the merits and affirm the decision of the Pend Oreille County Superior Court, dated January 5, 1990, which substantially approved the conclusion of the referee relating to the water rights of Appellants Clarence E. and Peggy v. Grimes.

IMPERIAL IRRIGATION DISTRICT: ALLEGED WASTE AND UNREASONABLE USE OF WATER

California Water Resources Control Board, 1984.
Water Rights Decision Number 1600.

* * *

The Imperial Irrigation District (IID) is located in Imperial County between the southern end of the Salton Sea and the Mexican border. * * * [T]he Salton Sea is a natural sump. The IID encompasses 1,062,-290 acres, of which about 460,000 are irrigated each year. The main

69. See RCW 90.03.005; RCW 90.03.010.

crops grown in the Imperial Valley are alfalfa, wheat, cotton, sugar beets and lettuce. There are approximately 16,000 acres devoted to urban land use with a population of about 95,000 * * * [Figure 3–3 shows the IID in relation to its region.]

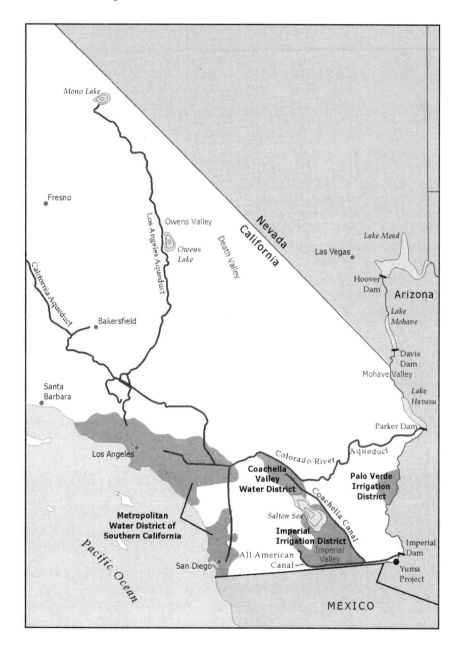

Figure 3–3

Colorado River Users and Water Facilities

The soils within the IID vary from Imperial Clays with a low permeability to highly permeable sandy soils. There is a high degree of unpredictable stratification of the soils within the District. This makes it difficult to apply water evenly and to obtain the necessary penetration for effectively leaching salts from the soil. Land leveling has helped in attaining water penetration of the soils with low permeability. Extensive tile drain installation has been required to keep the soil from becoming water logged and to attain the leaching needed because of salts in the soil and irrigation water. * * *

[In 1980, John Elmore, a farmer in the Imperial Valley, requested that the California Department of Water Resources (DWR) investigate alleged misuse of water by the IID. Elmore alleged that mismanagement by the IID led to a rise in the level of the Salton Sea which threatened his own farmland. In 1981, the DWR found that the IID was wasting water and requested the IID to submit a corrective conservation plan. Although IID initially agreed, in 1982 the District informed DWR that it considered its water use reasonable and refused to submit the plan. Elmore appealed to the California Water Resources Board in 1983, requesting a hearing on the issues. Elmore was joined in his request by other farmers in the area, 70 owners of Salton Sea property, and environmental groups including the Environmental Defense Fund. Elmore alleged that the following IID practices caused the rise in the level of the Salton Sea and constituted misuse of the water by the IID:]

a. Maintaining canals in overly full conditions causes frequent spills at the terminal end of the canals.

b. The absence of reservoirs for regulations of canal flows causes the unnecessary delivery of excess amounts of water. This results in canal spills and runoff into the Salton Sea.

c. Excess water is delivered to farmers' headgates resulting in excess tailwater.

d. There is an absence of tailwater recovery systems within the IID. Tailwater recovery systems would allow use of runoff for productive purposes.

e. Farmers are required to order water in 24-hour delivery intervals and the delivery cannot reasonably be terminated after sufficient water is received. Excess water from the deliveries drains unused into the Salton Sea. * * *

Other Potential Beneficial Uses for Conserved Water:

One of the most important factors to be considered in evaluating the reasonableness of IID's present use of water is identification of other beneficial uses to be made of water which could be conserved. In Joslin v. Marin Municipal Water District, [67 Cal. 2d 132, 60 Cal. Rptr. 377, 429 P.2d 889 (1967)], the court weighed the competing demands for water of a water district and the people it served against the demands of a riparian landowner who depended upon an unobstructed flow of water to replenish the rock and gravel which the landowner excavated from the streambed and sold. The Court concluded that the riparian's insistence on the full unobstructed flow was unreasonable. Similarly, in SWRCB Decision 1463 the Board concluded that filling a recreational lake during a drought was an unreasonable use of water since the same water could otherwise be used to reduce the need for water imports from Northern California where several areas were experiencing water shortages.

The position of IID is that "[i]f there are no competing users and some beneficial use is being made of the water, the water involved may be considered surplus water, but it is not 'wasted water'." (IID Brief 2/21/84, p. 26.) In reliance upon this position, the IID presented evidence intended to show that there have not been any shortages of water among diverters from the lower Colorado River in recent years.

Although evaluation of the alternative uses to be made of conserved water is an important aspect of evaluating the reasonableness of the District's water usage, a finding of unreasonable use or method of use does not require the existence of a dispute between competing users. For example, excessive diversion or an unreasonable method of diversion of water to the detriment of instream fish and wildlife uses may be wasteful even if there are no objections from competing consumptive users. Similarly, if other parties demonstrated an intention to utilize water which could be conserved through reasonable conservation measures, the failure to undertake such conservation may be found to be unreasonable. The parties interested in utilizing the conserved water are not required to file a lawsuit or an administrative complaint in order for the Board to acknowledge that there are other beneficial uses to be made of water which can be conserved.

Whether the Excess Water Now Serves a Reasonable and Beneficial Purpose:

Although there may be means for increasing the efficiency of water use by a particular water user, the availability of excess water for other beneficial purposes may serve to mitigate what might otherwise be an unreasonable situation. For example, if virtually all of an irrigator's tailwater reenters the steam where it is available for downstream use, and if the diversion has no adverse effect on instream uses, then it may not be unreasonable to allow large quantities of tailwater. Similar, if a water user's canal seepage contributed to the recharge of a groundwater basin, such seepage could be beneficial and considered reasonable in certain circumstances since underground storage of water for future use is recognized as a beneficial use. (Water Code Section 1242.) A third possibility * * * is the availability of irrigation return flow for the enhancement of fish and wildlife resources which is recognized as a beneficial use of water under Water Code Section 1243. * * *

Amount and Reasonableness of the Cost of Saving Water:

The fact that water conservation may require the water user to incur additional expense provides no justification to continue wasteful or unreasonable practices. In People ex rel. State Water Resources Control Board v. Forni, 54 Cal. App. 3d 743, 126 Cal. Rptr. 851 (1976), the court ruled that water users may properly be required to "endure some inconveniences or to incur reasonable expenses" in order to comply with the constitutional standard of putting the water resources of the state to maximum beneficial use. The decision in the *Forni* case indicates that the Board may require a water user to build water reservoirs or make other physical improvements if that is the only feasible method of achieving the constitutional mandate of reasonableness. (54 Cal.App.3d at 751–752.)

The determination of whether the cost of a particular conservation measure is reasonable must be made with respect to the resources available for financing water conservation efforts as well as the value of the water which would be conserved. Where outside parties are willing to finance improvements in exchange for conserved water, the availability of financing from those parties should also be considered.

Whether the Required Methods of Saving Water Are Conventional and Reasonable Rather Than Extraordinary:

Water Code Section 100.5, enacted in 1980, states:

> it is hereby declared to be the established policy of this state that conformity of a use, method of use, or method of diversion of water with local custom shall not be solely determinative of its reasonableness, but shall be considered as one factor to be weighed in the determination of the reasonableness of the use, method of use, or method of diversion of water within the meaning of Section 2 of Article X of the California Constitution.

Although this statute confirms the traditional view that local custom should be considered in evaluating reasonableness of water use, it clarifies that conformity with local custom alone does not foreclose a finding of waste and unreasonable use in appropriate circumstances. The Board also recognizes that determining the local custom with which the operations of an irrigation district should be compared is difficult if no closely comparable districts exist. This is a problem with respect to the IID where irrigation return flow is not available for further consumptive use. In contrast, the return flow from most districts eventually reenters a natural steam system and is available for further use. * * *

IRRIGATION PRACTICES AND OPPORTUNITIES FOR WATER CONSERVATION

Maintaining Canals in "Overly Full Conditions:"

The first allegation of the Elmore complaint states that in order to provide quick delivery service of irrigation water, canals are kept overly full to such an extent that overflow gates at the terminal ends of the canals frequently spill over into drains where the water is not subject to reuse. * * *

Since water spilled from the canals is lost without any beneficial consumptive use having been made, steps should be taken to improve the IID system so that operational flexibility can be provided without relying upon the storage capacity of the delivery canals. The regulatory reservoir program discussed below provides one means of increasing this flexibility.

Absence of Regulatory Reservoirs:

The second allegation of the Elmore complaint states that the absence of regulatory reservoirs causes unnecessary delivery of excess amounts of water producing spillovers and runoff into the Salton Sea.

The IID has constructed four regulatory reservoirs to date and pledged to construct one a year until a total of 20 to 22 reservoirs are in operation. Although the charge for water delivered by IID includes an assessment to generate the revenue for construction of reservoirs, reservoir construction was stopped because of economic problems.

Regulatory reservoirs would help to reduce canal spills by creating needed storage to allow a greater flexibility for the District's water delivery practices and for the farmer in ordering water. * * *

Lining Main Canals and Lateral Canals:

The estimates of net seepage from main canals and lateral canals range from a low of 97,000 afa [acre-feet per annum] by the consultants for John Elmore to a high of 200,000 afa by the Department of Water Resources. The District has been involved in a canal lining program since the early 1960s in cooperation with local farmers. The program has been criticized, however, because the priority for lining canals is established by those farmers who are willing to participate rather than by the District on the basis of seepage losses. The relatively high cost of canal lining appears to be the main reason that the program has not been accelerated.

The DWR estimates that the cost per acre-foot of water conserved by canal lining was $3 at 1981 price, or roughly double the cost of recovering an acre-foot of tailwater. One advantage of canal lining, however, is that the potential water savings can be determined with a relatively high degree of certainty. Canal lining also reduces the cost of weed control and canal maintenance. Therefore, an expanded canal lining program may be a likely candidate for financing by an outside party in exchange for conserved water. There was insufficient evidence, however, for the Board to conclude that the IID should be directed to change its present canal lining program at this time. * * *

Conclusion

Approximately one million acre-feet per year of Colorado River water enter the Salton Sea as irrigation return flow from IID. This large quantity of fresh water is lost to further beneficial consumptive use and has contributed to the flooding of property adjoining the Salton Sea. Following diversion of major quantities of water by the Central Arizona Project, which is scheduled to begin in late 1985 or 1986, there will be insufficient water available from the Colorado River to satisfy the existing level of demand of California water users. Although IID has taken some steps to conserve water, the evidence establishes that there are additional practical measures available to reduce the present losses of water within the District. Under the circumstances of this case, the Board concludes that the failure to implement additional water conservation measures at this time is unreasonable and constitutes a misuse of water under Article X, Section 2 of the California Constitution and Section 100 of the California Water Code. * * *

Notes

1. Elmore v. Imperial Irrig. Dist., 159 Cal.App.3d 185, 205 Cal.Rptr. 433 (1984) is a suit by a farmer alleging that waste by the IID caused flooding of his land. See also Imperial Irrig. District v. State Water Resources Control Bd., 186 Cal.App.3d 1160, 231 Cal.Rptr. 283 (1986). See Samantha Spangler, Imperial Irrigation District v. State Water Resources Control Board: Board as Arbiter of Reasonable and Beneficial Use of California Water, 19 Pac. L.J. 1565 (1988). In September, 1988 the Board issued a supplementary order, No. 88–20, mandating the IID to conserve 20,000 af/yr by 1991 and 100,000 af/yr by 1994.

2. Allegations of waste have continued to be an issue for Imperial. In 1998 Imperial executed an agreement with the San Diego County Water Authority (SDCWA) providing for up to 200,000 acre-feet of water to be conserved and transported to SDCWA. The Metropolitan Water District, of which San Diego is a member and which is junior to Imperial, insisted that Imperial was in effect seeking to sell water that it was wasting, as much as several hundred thousand acre-feet per year. Efforts to negotiate out a mutually agreeable outcome were led by the Department of the Interior and the State of California. The parties agreed that marketing of conserved water would be accepted, and Metropolitan and other juniors would agree for the contract period not to claim Imperial was wasting water. This approach is indicative of Imperial's bargaining position, resulting in part from Metropolitan's need to cut back its (California's) excess use of Colorado River water, and to find substitute supplies relatively promptly, an issue discussed infra in Chapter 8. It is also indicative, however, of a judgment about the difficulty of proving waste, notwithstanding the decisions excerpted above.

ii. Salvage

In ordinary circumstances the water saved by an appropriator who ceases wasteful use goes back into the river and is available for the next most senior appropriator who needs it. The reason is that an appropriator only has a right to water that he is using beneficially (non-wastefully). That may seem sensible enough. And perhaps it would be entirely appropriate if every appropriator were compelled to use just the amount needed, and not a drop more. As you now know, however, the system is often not very tightly administered and rules against waste are rarely rigorously enforced, leaving considerable leeway for appropriators to use their water much more efficiently. Even where there is no waste, imaginative users may be able to find ways to do more with less. For example, a modern method such as drip irrigation is more efficient than traditional flood irrigation. The problem is that since one is only entitled to the amount of water beneficially used, the less one needs, the less one is entitled to have. Insofar as that is the case, there is no incentive for an appropriator to use its water more efficiently. Any water saved will go back to the river for the benefit of a junior appropriator. That is precisely the lesson of the following decisions.

SOUTHEASTERN COLORADO WATER CONSERVANCY DISTRICT v. SHELTON FARMS, INC.

Supreme Court of Colorado, 1974.
187 Colo. 181, 529 P.2d 1321.

DAY, JUSTICE.

This is an appeal from two judgments and decrees awarding appellees Shelton Farms and Colorado—New Mexico Land Company ("the Company") water rights free from the call of any and all senior decreed water rights on the Arkansas River.

This case, so far as we are advised, is of first impression in the United States, dealing with whether the killing of water-using vegetation and the filling of a marshy area to prevent evaporation can produce a superior water right for the amount of water not transpired or evaporated. The Pueblo district court held it could, and granted both Shelton and the Company such a water right. * * *

We hold for the objectors, and reverse each judgment and decree.

To comprehend the importance of this lawsuit, it is necessary to understand the Arkansas River and its tributaries.

In 1863 there were virtually no "water-loving" trees along the banks of the river. Their growth was prevented when the great roaming buffalo herds ate the saplings, and the native Indians used most of the timber. In the next 40 years both the buffalo and the Indians were decimated. Phreatophytes (water consuming plants) and cottonwood began to appear along the Arkansas. After the great Pueblo flood of 1921 the river bottom became thickly infested with tamarisk or salt cedar, a highly phreatophytic growth.

Since 1863 all surface flow of the river has been put to beneficial use, until today the Arkansas is greatly over-appropriated. There is not enough flow to satisfy decreed water rights. The phreatophytes have hindered the situation, for they have consumed large quantities of subsurface water which would otherwise have flowed in the stream and been available for decreed use.

In 1940, appellee Shelton bought 500 acres of land on the Arkansas River. Since then, he has cleared two land areas of phreatophytes, and filled in a third marshy area. Shelton claimed he had saved approximately 442 acre-feet of water per year, previously consumed by phreatophytes or lost to evaporation, which is now available for beneficial use. Shelton had 8 previously decreed wells. He asked for the right to augment his previous water rights with the salvaged water, to use during those times when pumping is curtailed by the State Engineer.

The objectors Southeastern Water Conservancy District, and others, moved to dismiss the augmentation application. The motion was denied and trial was held. The lower court awarded Shelton [the salvaged] water, free from the call of the river. The lower court analogized to the law of accretion, stating that the capture and use by another of water which ordinarily would be lost is not detrimental to prior holders. * * *

[The Appellees] insist that but for their actions the salvaged water would have been available to no one, so now they may receive a water right free from the call of prior appropriators, who are in no way harmed. Appellees conclude that their actions provide maximum utilization of water, protect vested rights, and encourage conservation and waste reduction in the water-scarce Arkansas River Valley. * * *

The objectors assert that the lower court's resolution of the issue does violence to Colorado's firm appropriation doctrine of "first in time—first in right" on which the priority of previous decrees is bottomed. They point out that the existing case law in Colorado, which was not changed by statute, limits the doctrine of "free from call" to waters which are truly developed and were never part of the river system. They argue that appellees' claims were not for developed water, and thus must come under the mandates of the priority system. Furthermore, a priority date free from the call of the river will impinge the entire scheme of adjudication of water decrees as required by the Act.

There is no legal precedent squarely in point for either denying or approving these claims. The answer requires consideration of judicial precedent relating to "developed" and "salvaged" water, as well as consideration of the provisions of the Water Act. Also squarely before us is the equally serious question of whether the granting of such an unique water right will encourage denuding river banks everywhere of trees and shrubs which, like the vegetation destroyed in these cases, also consume the river water.

We first consider existing case law. There is no question that one who merely clears out a channel, lines it with concrete or otherwise hastens the flow of water, without adding to the existing water, is not entitled to a decree therefore. * * *

It is equally true and well established in Colorado that one who adds to an existing water supply is entitled to a decree affirming the use of such water. Strong evidence is required to prove the addition of the water. * * * There are three important situations, analogous to this case, when these rare decrees have been granted. The first is when one physically transports water from another source * * * The second is when one properly captures and stores flood waters. The third is when one finds water within the system, which would never have normally reached the river or its tributaries. An example is trapped water artificially produced by draining a mine. * * *

A thorough research by all parties, including the amicus, shows no Colorado case where a person has been granted a water right free from the call of the river for water which has always been tributary to a stream. If it is shown that the water would ultimately return to the river, it is said to be part and parcel thereof, and senior consumers are entitled to use it according to their decreed priorities. * * *

Thus, this case law draws a distinction between "developed" and "salvaged" water. Both terms are words of art. Developed implies new waters not previously part of the river system. These waters are free from the river call, and are not junior to prior decrees. Salvaged water implies waters in the river or its tributaries (including the aquifer) which ordinarily would go to waste, but somehow are made available for beneficial use. Salvaged waters are subject to call by prior appropriators. We cannot airily waive aside the traditional language of the river, and draw no distinctions between developed and salvaged water. To do so would be to wreak havoc with our water law. Those terms, and others, evolved specifically to tread softly in this state where water is so precious.

[handwritten margin note: SALVAGED – SUBJECT TO CALL BY PRIOR APPROPRIATORS]

The roots of phreatophytes are like a pump. The trees, which did not have to go to court or seek any right, merely "sucked up" the water from prior appropriators. Appellees now take the water from the trees. Therefore, appellees also are continuing to take from the appropriators, but seek a court decree to approve it. They added nothing new; what was there was merely released and put to a different use. To grant appellees an unconditional water right therefor would be a windfall which cannot be allowed, for thirsty men cannot step into the shoes of a "water thief" (the phreatophytes.) Senior appropriators were powerless to move on the land of others and destroy the "thief"—the trees and phreatophytes— before they took firm root. They are helpless now to move in and destroy them to fulfill their own decrees. The property (the water) must return from whence it comes—the river—and thereon down the line to those the river feeds in turn. * * *

Perhaps most important is the mandate of 1971 Perm. Supp., C.R.S.1963, 148C21C22. This sets up the priority system of "first in time—first in right" in Colorado:

> "* * * the priority date awarded for water rights * * * adjudged and decreed on applications for a determination of the amount and priority thereof * * * during each calendar year shall establish the relative priority among other water rights * * * awarded on such applications filed in that calendar year; *but such water rights* shall be junior to all water rights * * * awarded on such applications filed in any previous calendar year * * *." (Emphasis added.)

This section cannot be ignored, as it is part of the same overall Act. There is nothing in the plain language of the statute to exempt appellees' plans from the priority date system. Thus, we hold that all water decrees of any kind are bound to the call of the river, subject to any specific exemptions found within the law.

Notes

1. The *Shelton* case has effectively been "affirmed" by the legislature, Colo. Rev. Stat. §§ 37–90–103, 37–92–103(9), and it was followed in R.J.A., Inc. v. Water Users Ass'n, 690 P.2d 823 (Colo. 1984) (draining marsh, reducing consumption of tributary water) and Giffen v. Colorado, 690 P.2d 1244 (Colo. 1984) (removal of trees and replacement with nonirrigated grasses). For an in-depth study of the Colorado experience, see Comment, Phreatophyte Eradication as a Source of Water Rights in Colorado, 43 U. Colo. L. Rev. 473 (1972). Contrast Pomona Land & Water Co. v. San Antonio Water Co., 152 Cal. 618, 93 P. 881 (1908), where plaintiffs, under a contract with defendants, were entitled to one-half the natural flow of a stream as it reached a dam, and defendant saved water seeping out of the stream bed by impounding it upstream of the dam in a pipe, through which he brought the water to the dam. The court said that the waters saved "are essentially new waters and the right to use and distribute them belongs to the defendant." Montana authorizes the use of salvaged water. See 1991 Statement of Intent following Mont. Code Ann. § 85–2–402.

2. For an updated discussion of the issues raised by *Shelton* see Eli Feldman, Death Penalty for Water Thieves, 8 U. Denv. Water L. Rev. 1 (2004).

SALT RIVER VALLEY WATER USERS' ASSOCIATION v. KOVACOVICH

Court of Appeals of Arizona, 1966.
3 Ariz.App. 28, 411 P.2d 201.

EDWIN THURSTON, J.

* * * In essence this case involves the narrow issue of whether or not an owner of land having a valid appurtenant water right may through water-saving practices apply the water thus saved to immediately adjacent lands owned by that person, without need to apply for the right to use such additional waters under the State Water Code. * * *

It was argued that decision of this issue in favor of appellants would result in penalizing persons who, through their industry, effort and expenses, engage in water-saving practices. The water-saving practices here referred to include improvement of ditches and concrete lining of ditches. This court is of the opinion that the water-saving practices entered into by appellees not only result in conservation of water but also other benefits to appellees such as weed and vegetation growth control along such irrigation ditches and reduction of time and cost of maintenance of such ditches. Certainly any effort by users of water in Arizona tending toward conservation and more economical use of water is to be highly commended. However, commendable practices do not in themselves create legal rights. * * *

This Court is of the opinion that the Doctrine of Beneficial Use precludes the application of waters gained by water conservation practices to lands other than those to which the water was originally appurtenant. It has been argued that if the Court were to accept the position of appellees that appellees could allow the land to which the water right is appurtenant to lie fallow but continue to use the same quantity of water upon other adjacent lands owned by the same person. Again the need for land to lie fallow from time to time is a well recognized, beneficial need in order to preserve and maintain the proper fertility of the land. Although this may be a commendable practice, this is not sufficient to alter the established doctrine with respect to use of water. Under the doctrine of beneficial use, the appellees are not entitled under all circumstances to appropriate a given number of acre feet of water per year. Beneficial use is the measure and the limit to the use of water. * * * The appellees may only appropriate the amount of water from the Verde River as may be beneficially used in any given year upon the land to which the water is appurtenant even though this amount may be less than the maximum amount of their appropriation. They may not take a quantity of water in excess of their appropriation even though they could beneficially use the same upon water right land. If in a given year, this should constitute an appropriation and use of all the water available at that particular point on the Verde River, subordinate owners of water rights have no cause to complain. However, in those years when water in excess of that which appellees may beneficially use upon the appurtenant land to which their water right attaches, all water which may flow to lower and subordinate owners of water rights is no longer of concern to appellees. Any practice, whether through water-saving procedures or otherwise, whereby appellees may in fact reduce the quantity of water actually taken inures to the benefit of other water users and neither creates a right to use the waters saved as a marketable commodity nor the right to apply same to adjacent property having no appurtenant water rights. It is believed that any other decision would result in commencement of return to the very area of confusion and chaos which gave rise to the development and application of the concept of beneficial use. * * *

Notes and Questions

1. It is possible to read *Salt River Valley* quite narrowly: a water right is appurtenant to the specific tract of land for which it is appropriated, and may only be shifted to other land pursuant to an administrative application, as provided by statute. So construed, the case could be read as permitting salvaged water to be used as supplementary water on the original tract, but not shifted to another tract. Would such an interpretation result in less "confusion and chaos"?

2. The *Salt River Valley* case is noted critically at 46 Or. L. Rev. 243 (1967). See also Robert Clark, Background and Trends in Water Salvage Law, 15 Rocky Mtn. Min. L. Inst. 421 (1969).

3. It is not possible to proclaim the *Salt River Valley* case either a majority or minority view. Most states have no cases directly on point. See Water and Agriculture in the Western United States: Conservation, Reallocation and Markets 216–219 (Gary Weatherford et al., eds. 1982). Idaho in two early cases allowed a salvager to retain water saved. See Basinger v. Taylor, 36 Idaho 591, 211 P. 1085 (1922); Reno v. Richards, 32 Idaho 1, 178 P. 81 (1918). Utah has permitted an appropriator to put new lands under cultivation as a result of efficiency improvements, but it was understood that no harm would thereby come to juniors, and that no such savings would have been allowed to the salvager if a junior was injured. See Water and Agriculture in the Western United States, supra at 218; East Bench Irr. Co. v. Deseret Irr. Co., 2 Utah 2d 170, 271 P.2d 449 (1954).

4. It is possible, paradoxically, that while Kovacovich was unable to reap the benefit of reducing transmission losses by the salvage technique, he would have been able to reap the benefit of that water had he sold the total amount of his diversion (including the amount lost in transmission) *prior* to salvage. The reason is that under standard transfer doctrine, so long as junior appropriators are not made worse off by the transfer, the full amount of the water diverted can be sold. See infra pp. 275–276. Here, since juniors did not benefit from the water lost in transmission (it merely seeped into the ground), there would be no requirement to protect them in a sale. Only in the rare case where a statute prohibits one from selling more than his consumptive use would Kovacovich as a seller be in the same position he holds as a salvager. See Basin Elec. Power Coop. v. State Bd. of Control, 578 P.2d 557 (Wyo. 1978).

5. An "easy" solution to the *Salt River Valley* case would be a decision that the pre-salvage use is wasteful. Were that the holding of the courts, the appropriator would only be entitled to divert at the stream an amount that would—without wasteful transmission losses—reach the land to be irrigated. The appropriator could be required to improve his ditches at his own expense to preserve his consumptive use, the additional water thus saved going automatically to the next most senior appropriator after him; or, if he decided not to improve his ditches, he would lose to the person next in line all but the non-wasteful portion of his appropriation. Under Montana law, which allows junior appropriators to initiate an action to enforce adjudication decrees, and oversee the distribution of water through properly maintained ditches, a junior appropriator obtained a judgment ordering an upstream senior to remove phreatophytic trees and brush from along their irrigation ditches, and also allowing the juniors to repair and maintain the leaky ditch. Morrison v. Higbee, 204 Mont. 501, 668 P.2d 1029 (1983).

6. Courts do not usually take the position that uses such as that of Kovacovich are wasteful. Why not? One reason would be a fear that appropriators in his position could not afford to repair their ditches. Obviously that was not the case with Kovacovich himself, but it might well be the case for the majority of irrigators in his position. Would it not make sense to allow Kovacovich to capture the benefit of the water saved, contrary to what the court did in his case? After all, if he could get the benefit of water saved, he would be better off, those junior to him would be no worse off (since they weren't getting that water previously anyway), and one could not say that irrigators generally in his position were getting a windfall in being allowed to

commit waste. Is there any good argument to the contrary other than the formalistic one invoked by the court, that water saved "belongs" to the stream?

iii. The California Approach to Salvage

In contrast to the approach in the Colorado and Arizona cases set out above, California has sought to encourage users to conserve water by giving them the benefit of conservation. In essence it enacted laws providing that water conserved may be sold. The essential idea is that growing metropolitan areas can well afford to finance conservation programs for irrigators, and that water is more valuable economically in urban use than in agriculture. Thus, markets will develop to meet new urban needs without having to build environmentally destructive dams and reservoirs. The following excerpts reflect the major California laws enacted to facilitate this policy.

Water Code § 109:

(a) * * * It is hereby declared to be the established policy of this state to facilitate the voluntary transfer of water and water rights where consistent with the public welfare of the place of export and the place of import.

(b) * * * including, but not limited to, providing technical assistance to persons to identify and implement water conservation measures which will make additional water available for transfer.

Water Code § 1011:

(a) When any person entitled to the use of water under an appropriative right fails to use all or any part of the water because of water conservation efforts, any cessation or reduction in the use of the such appropriated water shall be deemed equivalent to a reasonable beneficial use of water to the extent of such cessation or reduction in use. No forfeiture of the appropriative right to the water conserved shall occur * * *. [T]he term "water conservation" shall mean the use of less water to accomplish the same purpose or purposes of use allowed under the existing appropriative right. * * *

(b) Water, or the right to the use of water, the use of which has ceased or been reduced as the result of water conservation efforts as described in subdivision (a), may be sold, leased, exchanged, or otherwise transferred pursuant to any provision of law relating to the transfer of water or water rights, including, but not limited to, provisions of law governing any change in points of diversion, place of use, and purpose of use due to the transfer.

(c) Notwithstanding any other provision of law, upon the completion of the term of a water transfer agreement, or the right to the use of that water, that is available as a result of water conservation efforts described in subdivision (a), the right to the use of the water shall revert to the transferor as if the water transfer had not been undertaken.

Water Code § 1244:

The sale, lease, exchange, or transfer of water or water rights, in itself, shall not constitute evidence of waste or unreasonable use, unreasonable method of use, or unreasonable method of diversion and shall not affect any determination of forfeiture applicable to water appropriated * * *.

This section does not constitute a change in, but is declaratory of, existing law.

Notes and Questions

1.   How can California simply legislate away the doctrines articulated in the Colorado and Arizona cases set out above? How can one who conserves water sell it, as against the claim of a junior appropriator on the stream who asserts a right to it?

2.   Do the California statutes allow one to cease waste, and then to sell the water previously wasted? Note the first phrase in section 1011(a) of the Water Code.

3.   Assume water has been leaking out of an unlined ditch, finding its way back into the river, and is being appropriated by someone (X) downstream. Does California law allow an appropriator to line the ditch, cut off that flow, and sell the water to a third party, to the detriment of X?

4.   Won't there be adverse environmental consequences from the California laws?[1] For example, if conserved water is sold to an entity that diverts it upstream from its previous point of diversion, won't there likely be harm to species in that stretch of the river below the new diversion point, as a result of diminished flows? An Oregon law permits irrigators to salvage and market conserved water under a plan that must be approved by the Water Resources Commission. It also establishes a guideline that 25% of the salvaged water should remain in the river to protect instream values. Or. Rev. Stat. §§ 537.455–500, 540.510(2)-(3) (1989). California has no such requirement, but Cal. Water Code §§ 386, 1725, 1736 provide that approval for a transfer may be granted only if it does not "unreasonably affect fish, wildlife, or other instream beneficial uses." Under these provisions, could the State condition salvage transfers on some degree of restoration of degraded instream habitats, i.e. on making things better than they were, rather than just preventing new harm?

f. Wasteful Use as a Constraint on New Appropriation

Traditionally waste doctrine has been employed (at most) to limit the amount an appropriator can use of his or her existing appropriation.

1.   Imperial Irrigation District's return flows go into the Salton Sea. A specific statute exempts it from responsibility for impacts on the sea as a result of any conservation measures. See Cal. Water Code § 1013. See also Haven or Hazard: The Ecology and Future of the Salton Sea (Pacific Institute, Feb. 1999).

The following case represents an effort to use the doctrine in a very unconventional way. The plaintiff Environmental Defense Fund (EDF) claimed that wasteful municipal uses by the defendant of its existing appropriations should bar it from being able to make new appropriations. EDF's concern was to save wild rivers by forcing existing appropriators to use their existing supplies more prudently. The California Court of Appeal's decision, which follows, was depublished by order of the California Supreme Court and therefore cannot be cited in California courts. Because of its interesting discussion of waste issues, however, we include it here for educational purposes.

ENVIRONMENTAL DEFENSE FUND v. EAST BAY MUNICIPAL UTILITY DISTRICT

Court of Appeal of the State of California, 1975.
125 Cal.Rptr. 601.[a]

LAZARUS, ASSOCIATE JUSTICE

Plaintiffs and appellants in this suit involving the interpretation of the basic water law of California are several nonprofit corporations dedicated to protecting and preserving the natural environment, joined by three individual plaintiffs. The latter are taxpayers and property owners within the area served by respondent East Bay Municipal Utility District. The utility district (hereinafter EBMUD) is the second largest distributor of water in the Western United States. * * *

Appellants brought this action for declaratory, mandatory and injunctive relief after EBMUD entered into a contract with the U.S. Bureau of Reclamation for the purchase of water to be diverted from the upper American River when the Auburn–Folsom unit of the Central Valley Project, now under construction by the federal government, is completed. EBMUD, which now gets most of its water from the Mokelumne River, insists that this supplemental water supply will be urgently needed by 1985 to meet its anticipated future requirements.

Plaintiffs and intervenor contend that this threatened diversion of water would substantially diminish the free flow of the lower American River to the extent that it would, *inter alia,* destroy all wildlife in the area, render it useless for boating, fishing and other recreational opportunities, and add to the pollution of San Francisco Bay. * * *

[P]laintiffs' claims are essentially that EBMUD's contemplated activities come within the purview of the constitutional ban on misuse of the state's water resources for the following reasons:

1. EBMUD's decision not to recycle or reclaim its waste water is an unreasonable and profligate wasting of water, and that its existing water supplies are therefore not being "put to beneficial use to the fullest extent of which they are capable." If it husbanded its available water resources, it would have relatively little need to look elsewhere.

a. This opinion is not citable in California courts as it was "depublished"—Eds.

UPSTREAM
RATHER
THAN
DOWNSTREAM
DIVERSION

2. By unreasonably threatening to divert their supplemental supply from an upstream rather than a downstream location, EBMUD will prevent multiple beneficial use of the waters of the lower American River for recreational and other purposes, thereby making it an "unreasonable method of use or unreasonable method of diversion of water." * * *

Is Preservation of the Environment Among the Interests Coming Within the Protection of Article XIV Section 3 of the Constitution[b]

PROPERTY
RIGHT

Article XIV, section 3, respondents say, has its roots in the law of real property. They therefore insist that its evolution is such that it was only meant to modify the rule followed in the 1926 *Herminghaus* case (Herminghaus v. South. California Edison Co. (1926) 200 Cal. 81, 252 P. 607) with respect to competing claims to *property right* in the water. They maintain that the fact that all water litigation since the enactment of article XIV, section 3, two years later, has so far involved traditional property claims to water between riparian owners and appropriators, or between prior and subsequent appropriators, or between competing riparian users, gives support to this view.

"GENERAL
WELFARE
MEASURE"
ALL RIGHTS
TO BENEFICIAL
USE

Appellants, on the other hand, assert that the constitutional provision was adopted as a general welfare measure to conserve California's rapidly diminishing water resources for the benefit of the public at large. It is therefore their contention that the constitutional mandate must be broadly construed to encompass all rights to the beneficial use of the rivers and streams of this state, including those of sportsmen and others who are still able to find opportunities to enjoy outdoor recreation.

The question as to whether or not article XIV, section 3, may be properly interpreted to encompass claims based upon environmental factors such as those involved here is therefore one of first instance that it is now the responsibility of this court to determine.

We begin by taking a closer look at the language of article XIV, section 3, having in mind the fundamental rule of interpretation that "constitutions, like laws, must be construed that full force and effect shall be given to every portion thereof. The legal intendment is that each and every sentence and clause has been inserted for some useful purpose, and when rightly understood has some practical operation." (People v. Zolotoff (1941) 48 Cal. App. 2d 360, 364, 119 P.2d 745, 747.)

Thus viewed, it would appear from the text of the amendment itself that it was not intended to be interpreted restrictively. Otherwise, as

b. Now Art. X, Section 2. The first two sentences of the provision states: "It is hereby declared that because of the conditions prevailing in this State the general welfare requires that the water resources of the State be put to beneficial use to the fullest extent of which they are capable, and that the waste or unreasonable use or unreasonable method of use of water be prevented, and that the conservation of such waters is to be exercised with a view to the reasonable and beneficial use thereof in the interest of the people and for the public welfare. The right to water or to the use or flow of water in or from any natural stream or water course in this State is and shall be limited to such water as shall be reasonably required for the beneficial use to be served, and such right does not and shall not extend to the waste or unreasonable use or unreasonable method of use or unreasonable method of diversion of water."—Eds.

pointed out by the Attorney General in his *amicus curiae* brief, the first two sentences focusing on the "use" of water would appear to be superfluous—a construction we are admonished to avoid. Furthermore, these are the two sentences that are incorporated alone in the Water Code as section 100, indicating that they are to be treated and considered separate and apart from the remainder. Riparian rights are mentioned only when we come to the third sentence, the language of which is isolated from the rest of the text to become section 101 of the Water Code. This dichotomy appears to be clear also from the very title given to the amendment: "Conservation of water resources; restriction of riparian rights." We must therefore construe this division as indicating that the first two sentences are to be applied without qualification to every right to the use of the diminishing water resources of this state.

Control of the use of all waters of the state for the benefit of the public at large is also spelled out in other provisions of the Water Code itself. For example, under the same heading, "General State Policy", section 104 provides, "It is hereby declared that the people of the State have a paramount interest in the use of all the water of the State and that the State shall determine what water of the State, surface and underground, can be converted to public use or controlled for public protection." A similar expression is found in section 105, which states: "It is hereby declared that the protection of the public interest in the development of the water resources of the State is of vital concern to the people of the State and that the State shall determine in what way the water of the State, both surface and underground, should be developed for the *greatest public benefit*." (Emphasis added.) * * *

We therefore have no difficulty in holding that article XIV, section 3, can only reasonably be interpreted as an unqualified expression of fundamental policy by the people of California that the general welfare requires that *all* of "the water resources of the State be put to beneficial use to the fullest extent of which they are capable."

FIRST HOLDING

IS RECYCLING WASTE WATER A TECHNIQUE THAT MAY BE REQUIRED UNDER THE AMENDMENT UPON A PROPER SHOWING AS A METHOD OF PREVENTING WASTE OR THE UNREASONABLE USE OF WATER?

* * *

We observe at the outset that appellants are not contending that the failure of EBMUD to adopt a program for recycling its water is *ipso facto* a violation of article XIV, section 3. What they do say is simply that they have set forth sufficient facts in their pleading to entitle them to proceed to trial so that the trial court can determine in the first instance whether or not its present water resources are indeed being "put to beneficial use to the fullest extent of which they are capable." * * *

The recycling or reclamation of water as a conservation measure is, of course, a relatively new concept. Its technological progress in recent years, however, has been of such significance that the Declaration of Policy in California's Water Reclamation Law (Wat. Code, sec 13500 et seq.) now includes the following Legislative finding: "sec 13511. The Legislature finds and declares that a substantial portion of the future water requirements of this state may be economically met by beneficial use of reclaimed water. The Legislature further finds and declares that the utilization of reclaimed water by local communities for domestic, agricultural, industrial, recreational, and fish and wildlife purposes will contribute to the peace, health, safety and welfare of the people of the state. Use of reclaimed water constitutes the development of 'new basic water supplies' as that term is used in Chapter 5 (commencing with Section 12880) of Part 6 of Division 6."

[margin note: RECLAMATION = DEVELOPMENT OF "NEW BASIC WATER SUPPLIES"]

More than forty years ago the Supreme Court, with considerable foresight, had this to say about the changing standards for determining whether water is being put to a beneficial use under article XIV, section 3: "What may be a reasonable beneficial use, where water is present in excess of all needs, would not be a reasonable beneficial use in an area of great scarcity and great need. What is a beneficial use at one time may, because of changed conditions, become a waste of water at a later time." (Tulare Dist. v. Lindsay–Strathmore Dist. (1935) 3 Cal.2d 489, 567, 45 P.2d 972, 1007.)

[margin note: BENEFICIAL USE CAN BECOME WASTE]

Appellants seek only to be permitted to proceed to trial in order that the trial court may determine from the evidence to be presented by both parties whether respondent, in refusing to reclaim its waste water, is making a reasonable or unreasonable use of its existing water resources in the face of today's changing conditions. Likewise, what is a reasonable or unreasonable use of water is a judicial question to be determined in the first instance by the trial court. There would seem to be no more difficulty in ascertaining what is a reasonable use of water than there is in determining probable cause, reasonable doubt, reasonable diligence, preponderance of evidence, a rate that is just and reasonable, public convenience and necessity, and numerous other problems which in their nature are not subject to precise definition but which tribunals exercising judicial functions must determine. * * *

It is our conclusion that appellants have therefore raised a justiciable issue in connection with their first cause of action. It may very well be, however, that at a trial they may not be able to offer sufficient evidence to demonstrate that recycling or reclaiming water has yet become an economically practical or feasible method of preventing waste in connection with respondent EBMUD's operations.

Elsewhere we pointed out that the judgment of dismissal in this case was based upon a general demurrer attacking the complaint as a whole. Since we now hold that there was at least one count in the complaint that was not vulnerable to objection, the demurrer should have been overruled. (Shook v. Pearson (1950) 99 Cal.App.2d 348, 221 P.2d 757; also see the authorities heretofore cited.) The judgment of dismissal as to plaintiffs' complaint must therefore be dismissed. * * *

Did the Trial Court Rule Properly That EBMUD's
Authority to Purchase Federal Project Water
Must Be Determined Under Federal Law?

The single cause of action asserted by intervenor and appellant County of Sacramento (as were the remaining causes of action in appellant's complaint) is based on EBMUD's future plans to divert water from the American River under contracts with the U.S. Bureau of Reclamation. * * *

The trial judge reached the conclusion however that the state law does not apply to the situation at all. "The factual setting for this question is that EBMUD has contracted with the U.S. Bureau of Reclamation to buy water in the future from a water project that the Bureau is in the process of constructing. The project has been authorized by Congress; the Bureau has obtained a permit for it from the State Water Resources Control Board; the legality of the project itself is not under attack here."

He therefore "somewhat reluctantly" agreed with the respondents that "under a line of U.S. Supreme Court decisions * * * the water that EBMUD will be buying is federal water and not subject to state law." * * *

From our own independent analysis, we necessarily conclude that the trial judge's ruling on this issue was correct. This is because, while the argument that the complaint in intervention stated a valid cause of action under state law may have been persuasive, we agree that federal law must govern here. * * *

Notes and Questions

1. On appeal, the California Supreme Court rejected the plaintiffs' claims on two grounds: (1) that the challenge to EBMUD's contract with the federal Bureau of Reclamation was preempted by federal law; and (2) that the demand for waste water reclamation was within administrative jurisdiction and thus was not properly before the court. 20 Cal.3d 327, 142 Cal.Rptr. 904, 572 P.2d 1128 (1977). The preemption determination was summarily reversed by the United States Supreme Court, 439 U.S. 811 (1978) on the basis of California v. United States, 438 U.S. 645 (1978), infra p. 753. On remand, the California court reaffirmed its view that on the waste water reclamation issue, the doctrine of primary jurisdiction counseled leaving the question initially to the State Water Resources Control Board for administrative determination. 26 Cal.3d 183, 161 Cal.Rptr. 466, 605 P.2d 1 (1980). The case was further remanded by the California Supreme Court to the Superior Court. EDF's demand for reclamation was not pursued any further and has faded away.

The case then took a new turn. It was urged that EBMUD should make its diversions lower down on the American River in order to protect riparian, recreational and fish and wildlife values upstream. The court permitted the upstream diversion but with rigorous flow maintenance requirements to protect those downstream values. Environmental Defense Fund v. East Bay Mun. Util. Dist. (No. 425955, Super. Ct., Alameda County, Cal., Jan. 2,

1990). Sacramento was not interested in partnering with EBMUD on an American River Project. However, after years of controversy EBMUD made an agreement with Sacramento County to take up to 133,000 af per year, in dry years, from a diversion downstream at Freeport on the Sacramento River, ten miles south of Sacramento, and build a structure to transport it to the Mokelumne River aqueduct. There will be mutual benefit: the groundwater under the growing southern part of Sacramento County needs replenishment, and the new west-east pipeline from Freeport can send water in wet years to south Sacramento while also connecting with EBMUD's Mokelumne system.

2. Recycled municipal water is becoming increasingly important. In 1997, San Diego announced a project to provide potable water from recycled sewage, a first for California, though such a use has been in place in Northern Virginia for several decades. So far the cost to San Diego is about 30% higher than the price for purchasing new potable water from the Metropolitan Water District. Altogether about 2% of California water use is from reclaimed sources, mostly for purposes such as golf course irrigation. Cal. Water L. & Pol'y, Oct. 1997, at 8. California law requires municipal water suppliers to prepare an urban water management plan which describes and evaluates practical and efficient use of the agency's supplies, including reclamation and conservation. Cal. Water Code §§ 10620 et seq.

3. The Oklahoma permit statute, 82 Okla. Stat. § 105.12(A)(2), provides that in determining whether to grant a permit, the agency shall determine whether there is unappropriated water available, and whether the applicant has a present or future need for the water. "In making this determination, the Board shall consider the availability of all stream water sources and such other relevant matters as the Board deems appropriate, and may consider the availability of ground water as an alternative source." Wouldn't this statute allow the Board to deny a new permit to a city that had declined to adopt recycling? If the principal case had arisen in the form of an application to appropriate under California's permit system, the Board would have had to consider the law's broad "public interest" standard. See Cal. Water Code §§ 1253, 1255. Note too that in considering whether to grant an application, the board is to consider "the reuse or reclamation of the water sought to be appropriated * * *." Id. § 1257.

4. Note that there is no one downstream to appropriate EBMUD's municipal wastes. Treated waste is discharged into San Francisco Bay. But what of a city that discharges into a stream where there are downstream appropriators? Can it reclaim and reuse its wastes even if it wants to do so, as against the claim of downstream appropriators? This has become an important practical issue in recent years. Is such a reuse within the scope of an original appropriation? One aspect of the question is treated in the next case, Bower v. Big Horn Canal. See also Stevens v. Oakdale Irrigation District, infra p. 211, and Arizona Public Service Co. v. Long, infra p. 201.

5. What advice would you give a legislator who sought to introduce a bill with the following text: "The Legislature hereby finds and declares that the use of potable domestic water for non-potable uses, including, but not limited to, cemeteries, golf courses, parks, highways, landscaped areas, and

industrial and irrigation uses, is a waste * * * of the water." Cf. Cal. Water Code § 13550.

g. *Rights of Recapture*

In the cases we are about to consider, an appropriator has been irrigating and, as is common with traditional irrigation techniques, a certain amount of water is not consumed, but drains off the land, or seeps into the ground where others use it. This situation may persist for years, after which the appropriator decides to recapture the runoff and to reuse it.[1] This is usually accomplished by building a ditch at the lowest point on the appropriator's land. Why does he do this? Sometimes he seeks a supplemental supply to replace groundwater he has previously pumped at high cost; sometimes he is augmenting his basic supply from the appropriation, which may be inadequate in dry periods; sometimes he wants to put new land under irrigation.

i. *The Special Doctrines Governing Seepage Appropriators*

One of the things that makes these cases special is that the person who has been benefitting from the runoff is usually not an appropriator from the stream where the appropriation was taken. She is what is called a "seepage appropriator". She has been capturing the runoff in the "vagrant" form known as diffused surface water. Of course the seepage appropriator opposes all recapture, arguing that she has depended on the runoff and should be treated just like any other appropriator. She argues that the senior's right is limited to the amount he originally beneficially applied and consumptively used on his land, that is, the amount received at his point of use, minus the runoff. As you have already seen, that is usually a successful argument. These seepage cases are an exception to the usual rule.

The following case is a leading example of the traditional approach to problems raised by seepage appropriators.

BOWER v. BIG HORN CANAL ASSOCIATION

Supreme Court of Wyoming, 1957.
77 Wyo. 80, 307 P.2d 593.

[Plaintiff sought to appropriate, and to condemn a right of way to carry water which seeped from defendant's land. Defendant resisted this action of condemnation on the ground that seepage water could not lawfully be appropriated in Wyoming and therefore the power of condemnation enjoyed by appropriators was not available to plaintiff. The court held for plaintiff.]

Parker, J.

---

1. The label that is applied to the scenario influences the legal analysis of the landowner's right. Runoff, especially if it is viewed as excessive, can be labeled just another version of waste. This seldom occurs.

Alternatively, the recapture problem can be deemed another version of the salvage issue, supra pp. 182–190. This view is also uncommon.

[P]laintiff cannot insist upon defendant's continuing to make the seepage available to him. On the contrary, defendant company may abandon its canal, relocate it, or line it with an impervious substance so that seepage ceases. But this does not mean that plaintiff is without right upon which to predicate his claim for condemnation of the right of way to take water in a pipe across defendant's canal. Nor does it mean that because water may not be available to him at all times that he may not be allowed to appropriate it for such times as it may be available. In the *Binning* case [Binning v. Miller, 55 Wyo. 451, 102 P.2d 54 (1940)], we said that seepage water which, if not intercepted, would naturally reach a stream is just as much a part of the stream as the water of any tributary. Were we now to hold that plaintiff is without right to such seepage water, which is a part of the stream, we would thereby allow later appropriators from the stream-proper to by-pass earlier beneficial users, who have made substantial investments in ditches, improvements, and equipment. Such is not and should not be the law where prior appropriation is the rule of water use. Not only would it be contrary to the expressed views of the framers of our constitution, but it would be in conflict with the greatest opportunity for full utilization.

In the *Binning* opinion, the importance of protecting water rights based upon return flows was repeatedly stressed. We would certainly discourage development and retard the full and efficient use of our precious water supply were we now to say that persons who save return flows and seepage before they reach a stream and put the water to beneficial use have no protection in law, that latecomers who subsequently seek rights from the stream itself can take the water as against the persons who have put it to beneficial use for years. Instead, we should here reiterate a principle announced in the *Binning* case, that water such as that in the Joint Ditch, which if not intercepted would naturally reach a stream, is appropriable. Additionally, it is equitable, in accordance with the constitutional provisions of this State, and in line with our previous holdings, that we here decree seepage water arising on Bower's land to be subject to appropriation by him (subject to prescribed procedures) for lands other than those upon which the seepage arises. Plaintiff's permit based on his October 6, 1952, application was properly granted; but any rights plaintiff secured thereby are subject, of course, to the right of defendant to terminate that source of the supply which seeps directly from defendant's canal and subject also to the rights of prior appropriators further down the stream, if they can prove that his interception of the water materially damages their prior rights. Plaintiff's right is, however, superior to any claims of subsequent appropriators; and it is a valid right upon which to base his claim for a right of way by eminent domain under Art. 1, sec. 32, of the constitution. Such a right is not affected by the fact that there exists no method of compelling the continuance of the source of the water. * * *

Notes and Questions

1. The *Bower* case is noted at 12 Wyo. L. J. 47 (1957). *Bower* states the general rule that an owner of land may always recapture waste and

seepage water as against an adjoining owner who has been taking that water from a source other than a natural stream, at least if it is captured and reused within the original land and for the original purpose of the right.[2] See also Cleaver v. Judd, 238 Or. 266, 393 P.2d 193 (1964) (citing authorities). That is also the situation on federal reclamation projects, so long as the water remains within the project boundaries. The Bureau of Reclamation was allowed to recapture irrigation water which had already been once used on the project. The Court said: "The seepage producing the artificial flow is part of the water which the [United States] * * * in virtue of its appropriation, takes from the Shoshone River and conducts to the project lands in the vicinity of the ravine for use in their irrigation. The defendants insist that when water is once used under the appropriation it cannot be used again—that the right to use it is exhausted. But we perceive no ground for thinking the appropriation is thus restricted. According to the record it is intended to cover, and does cover, the reclamation and cultivation of all the lands within the project. A second use in accomplishing that object is as much within the scope of the appropriation as a first use is." Ide v. United States, 263 U.S. 497 (1924). See also State Dept. of Ecology v. U.S. Bureau of Reclamation, 827 P.2d 275 (Wash. 1992). California v. United States, 438 U.S. 645 (1978), infra p. 753, suggests that state law will now govern recapture issues in federal projects.

2.   If recapture is attempted as against a user who got the seepage after it returned to the stream, rather than directly from the recapturer's land, as in *Bower*, the landowner may find his attempt to recapture unsuccessful. Jones v. Warmsprings Irr. Dist., 162 Or. 186, 198, 91 P.2d 542, 547–48 (1939); Northport Irr. Dist. v. Jess, 215 Neb. 152, 337 N.W.2d 733 (1983); Estate of Steed v. New Escalante Irrigation Co., 846 P.2d 1223 (Utah, 1992). Compare United States v. Haga, 276 Fed. 41 (D. Idaho 1921). There is also a possibility that the "right" of recapture may be thwarted by acquisition of a prescriptive right on the part of the seepage user. The Colorado Court so held in Lomas v. Webster, 109 Colo. 107, 122 P.2d 248 (1942), but the better view is that "as against the original appropriator and owner, an adjoining land owner cannot acquire a prescriptive right to waste or seepage water." Thompson v. Bingham, 78 Idaho 305, 302 P.2d 948 (1956); Burgett v. Calentine, 56 N.M. 194, 242 P.2d 276 (1951). The Colorado Court may have come to that view, Tongue Creek Orchard Co. v. Town of Orchard City, 131 Colo. 177, 280 P.2d 426 (1955).

3.   The Colorado court divides spring and seepage water into "tributary" and "nontributary" to distinguish that which is on its way to join the waters of a natural stream (appropriable waters) from that which is not on its way to, and will not reach, a natural stream. The court treats "tributary" seepage as a part of the water of a natural stream from the moment it begins its journey toward the stream, and all flowing water is presumed to be tributary. Ranson v. Boulder, 161 Colo. 478, 424 P.2d 122 (1967). This theory has led the court to a rather extreme anti-recapture position in regard to tributary seepage, even where recapture from a leaky reservoir was

2.   But see Krieger v. Pacific Gas & Elec. Co., supra p. 171.

promptly attempted while on the reservoir property and before anyone had come to rely on it, Fort Morgan Reservoir & Irr. Co. v. McCune, 71 Colo. 256, 206 P. 393 (1922). See also Lamont v. Riverside Irr. Dist., 179 Colo. 134, 498 P.2d 1150 (1972); Colo. Rev. Stat. § 37–82–102 (2004).

4. A plan to line the All–American Canal (see infra p. 809) has been challenged on the ground that it deprives users in Mexico of seepage they have received and relied on for decades. Consejo de Desarrollo Economico de Mexicali v. United States, CV–S–05–0870 KJD–PAL (D. Nev.).

5. The following is an excerpt from Rick Thompson, Reusing Irrigation Water on Different Lands: A Warning to Get a New Permit, 16 Land & Water L. Rev. 71, 74 (1981):

> [I]n the case of *Binning v. Miller,* it was decided that waste water could be appropriated. A qualifying requirement for this appropriation is that the seepage water would, if uninterrupted, flow into a natural stream. The court's rationale for this rule was that "seepage water which, if not intercepted, would naturally reach the stream, is just as much a part of the stream as the waters of any tributaries."
>
> The case of *Bower v. Big Horn Canal Association* further illustrated this idea when the court allowed Bower to intercept and appropriate seepage water flowing on his land which had been lost from defendant's canal. The seepage water in question did not form a channel, but was flowing toward a natural stream.
>
> However both *Binning* and *Bower* state that a seepage water appropriation is subject to the right of the owner of the land from which the seepage arose to use the water for beneficial purposes upon the land for which the water was originally appropriated. In other words, the lower land owner who appropriates waste water does not thereby secure a permanent right to continue to receive the water, he merely takes his chances that the supply will be kept up.

Note that this statement of the Wyoming case law raises several different issues:

• The first point deals with the rights between the original appropriator who wants to recapture, and the seepage appropriator. As to this point, you should ask yourself whether the appropriator-recapturer here is treated differently from an appropriator who wants to benefit from repairing a leaky ditch or from cutting down phreatophytes. If there is a difference in treatment, is there any reason for it? Hint: Consider how the respective objectors would fare in the different situations if the original appropriator simply abandoned his appropriation altogether and stopped diverting water from the stream.

• The second point made in the above law review note is that a recapturer can cut off a seepage appropriator only if he does so to "use the [recaptured] water for beneficial purposes upon the land for which the water was originally appropriated." Why this on-tract limitation? Note that in *Salt River Valley*, supra p. 186, the salvaged water was not applied to the original tract.

• A third point is that the seepage appropriator can only appropriate where it can be shown that the runoff would, if uninterrupted, find its way into a natural stream. Why this limitation?

• A final issue is whether the recapture is made before, or after, the runoff leaves the land of the appropriator-recapturer. Should the situs of recapture matter?

Do not feel alarmed if all this is less than perfectly clear. The cases themselves are not models of clarity. Moreover, none of them consider together the various rules relating to salvage, seepage recapture, waste and the original definition of the appropriative right, all of which are closely related.

ii. Selling and Re–Using Sewage: The New Wave

Water quality legislation has led to cleaner sewage effluent. "Advances in treatment technology have enabled agencies to re-use water that formerly would have been treated to acceptable standards and discharged to surface waters. Today, water is put back to work in several ways, from replenishing groundwater basins to irrigating golf courses to industrial applications." Western Water, May/June 2005, at 5. An important question is whether cities can sell (or re-use) their sewage.

ARIZONA PUBLIC SERVICE, CO. v. LONG

Supreme Court of Arizona, 1989.
160 Ariz. 429, 773 P.2d 988.

HOWARD, COURT OF APPEALS JUDGE.

[The cities of Phoenix and Tolleson, Arizona (the "Cities") for many years discharged treated sewage effluent into the Salt River. In the 1970s and early 1980s, however, the Cities entered into contracts agreeing to provide almost 80,000 acre-feet of sewage effluent each year to several utilities (the "Utilities") which planned to use the water to cool their power facilities. Two downstream appropriators, the A Tumbling T Ranches and the Gladdens (the "A Tumbling T parties"), objected. The A Tumbling T parties claimed that most of the water that they diverted to satisfy their appropriation rights was the Cities' effluent discharge.]

This case involves the sale by appellee Cities to the appellee Utilities of sewage effluent. Two questions are posed: (1) Can the Cities contract to sell sewage effluent for use on lands other than those involved in the original appropriation? And (2) once the Cities dump sewage effluent into a stream and such effluent is appropriated by downstream users, must the Cities continue such dumping ad infinitum? We answer the first question in the affirmative and the second in the negative.

* * * The A Tumbling T parties argue that allowing the Cities to sell appropriable water that is not consumed by the Cities' beneficial use departs from a basic premise of Arizona law governing appropriable surface waters. Citing A.R.S. § 45–141(A), they urge that appropriable surface waters belong to the public, and that the Cities by their appropri-

ation do not gain ownership of the appropriated waters so as to give them a right to sell the unconsumed effluent. Rather, it is urged that the Cities have only the right to the use of the water, limited by the purpose for which the appropriation was made, * * * and that any unused surface water must be returned to the river bed.

The Cities and Utilities argue that effluent is water which has essentially lost its character as * * * surface water and becomes the property of the entity which has expended funds to create it. The Cities and Utilities further argued that they are the owners of the effluent and may dispose of their property in any way they see fit.

EFFLUENT IS PRODUCT PROPERTY

The Department of Water Resources has filed an amicus brief in which it agrees with * * * A Tumbling T * * *.

A. THE VALIDITY OF THE CONTRACTS

In order to decide this issue we find it unnecessary to categorize sewage effluent as being * * * surface water * * *. Until such time as it is returned to the ground as either groundwater or surface water, it is nothing more than sewage effluent, which was described in City of Phoenix v. Long, [158 Ariz. 59, 63, 761 P.2d 133, 137 (App. 1988)], as "a noxious bi-product of the treatment of sewage which the cities must dispose of without endangering the public health and without violating any federal or state pollution laws." * * * A Tumbling T cites Pulaski Irrigation District Co. v. City of Trinidad, 70 Colo. 565, 203 P. 681 (1922), [which held that a city could not sell treated effluent, but instead must return it to the stream]. We are not persuaded by the analysis of that case. There the city had purified the sewage and was selling it. The court recognized that when the situation is such that the city cannot turn the sewage into the stream without causing a health hazard, the city must find some other way of disposing it. But, once the city purifies it, the water must be returned to the stream because the water element of the sewage always belongs to the public. It is not clear from the decision what the state of purity of the water was. In the case sub judice the water has been treated, but not puri and the discharge of such sewage effluent into a stream is subject to control by the state and federal government.

IN PULASKI CITY WAS PURIFYING SEWAGE & SELLING IT

↓

WATER ELEMENT ALWAYS BELONGS TO THE PUBLIC

We find the analysis in Wyoming Hereford Ranch v. Hammond Packing Company, 33 Wyo. 14, 236 P. 764 (1925), a case in which the issues are on all fours with ours, more persuasive. In discussing the validity of the city's contractual disposition of its sewage effluent, the court stated:

> It is well known that the disposition of sewage is one of the important problems that embarrass municipalities. In order to dispose of it without injury to others, a city may often be confronted with the necessity of choosing between several different plans, and in the selection of the plan to be followed we think it should be permitted to exercise a wide discretion. In determining how it will make proper disposition of that which

may be termed a potential nuisance, we think the city should not be hampered by a rule that would always require the sewage to be treated as waste or surplus waters. * * * It would often be considered the height of efficiency if it could be disposed of in some other manner than by discharging it into a stream. Even in this state, where the conservation of water for irrigation is so important, we would not care to hold that in disposing of sewage the city could not adopt some means that would completely consume it. It might, we think, be diverted to waste places, or to any chosen place where it would not become a nuisance, without any consideration of the demands of water users who might be benefitted by its disposition in some other manner. * * *

236 P. at 772. The Wyoming court held that the sale by Cheyenne of sewage effluent that was discharged directly into the buyer's ditch was valid, but that portion of the effluent that was discharged into a creek was public water subject to appropriation. However, the court did not discuss whether the City of Cheyenne was obliged to continue dumping part of its sewage into the creek in order to satisfy the needs of the plaintiff.

We hold that the Cities can put its sewage effluent to any reasonable use that it sees fit.[5] This will allow municipalities to maximize their use of appropriated water and dispose of sewage effluent in an economically feasible manner. It also provides a degree of flexibility that is essential to a city's ability to meet federal and state environmental and health standards.

C. Ownership of Effluent

We do not agree with the contention of the Cities and Utilities that the Cities own the sewage effluent. In Arizona, being a desert state, water is a precious commodity. One does not own water in Arizona. One only has the right to put it to beneficial use. * * * Thus the legislature has the right to control the use of sewage effluent. It has not restricted its use and, until it does, the Cities have the right to enter into contracts as they have done here.

Nor is the effluent "developed" water. "Developed" waters are not public waters, and generally are not subject to prior appropriation. * * * As applied to water in a stream system, "developed" water is that which has been added to the supply of a natural stream and which never would have come into the particular stream system in the absence of the effort of the developers. See Southeastern Colorado Water Conservancy District v. Shelton Farms, Inc., 187 Colo. 181, 529 P.2d 1321 (1974). Since a return of the effluent to the stream bed would not increase the flow of

5. Although the effluent is neither groundwater nor surface water, the common law requires, absent any legislative directive to the contrary, that even effluent be put to a reasonable use if it is not returned to the stream bed.

the water above that before it was diverted, the effluent is not developed water.

D. MUST THE CITIES CONTINUE DUMPING SEWAGE EFFLUENT IN ORDER TO SATISFY THE NEEDS OF DOWNSTREAM USERS?

We start with A.R.S. § 45–141(A) which states:

> The waters of all sources, flowing in streams, canyons, ravines or other natural channels, or in definite underground channels, whether perennial or intermittent, flood, *waste or surplus water,* and of lakes, ponds and springs on the surface, belong to the public and are subject to appropriation and beneficial use as provided in this chapter.

(Emphasis added.) A.R.S. § 45–151(A) provides that "[t]he person or the State of Arizona or a political subdivision thereof first appropriating the water shall have the better right."

Can a downstream user appropriate the sewage effluent component of water under A.R.S. § 45–141(A)? We hold that he can. The statute speaks of water "of all sources." It does not matter where the water came from. Once it is in one of the geological or topographical features enumerated by the statute it is subject to appropriation. See Wyoming Hereford Ranch v. Hammond Packing Company, supra. * * *

But does this mean that the Cities must continue to discharge sewage effluent into the river to satisfy the needs of these appropriators? Certainly there are no statutes which require the Cities to do so. The ramifications of such a doctrine are alarming. For example, if we follow the path urged by A Tumbling T * * *, the Cities would be unable to change the location of its point of discharge without risking a lawsuit.

Sewage effluent is water that is left over after having been put to use. A.R.S. § 45–402(6). Regardless of whether the water used to treat sewage was originally * * * surface water, the water remaining after treatment is waste water. Reynolds v. City of Roswell, 99 N.M. 84, 654 P.2d 537 (1982).

Two early Arizona cases dealt with the appropriation of waste waters. In Lambeye v. Garcia, 18 Ariz. 178, 157 Pac. 977 (1916) and Wedgworth v. Wedgworth, 20 Ariz. 518, 181 Pac. 952 (1919), this court considered issues relating to rights that might be obtained by subsequent users of irrigation waste waters (sometimes also referred to as "surplus" water in both decisions). Neither *Lambeye* nor *Wedgworth* involved an appropriator's right to divert and use waste waters from a natural channel. Instead, the waste water had been captured and used by a subsequent user who had no appropriative rights before it had returned to a natural channel. On these facts we held that the waste water was not subject to appropriation and that the subsequent user could obtain no vested rights in it. We noted that one who captures waste water may not insist that the initial appropriator continue to waste his irrigation water and, accordingly, that the supply of waste water could be discontinued or withdrawn at any time.

Our holdings in *Lambeye* and *Wedgworth* were codified shortly thereafter by an amendment of the Arizona statute governing surface waters so as to reflect that "waste or surplus waters" were subject to appropriation only when flowing in a natural channel. See 1921 Ariz. Sess. Laws, ch. 64 § 1. We do not believe that the amendment of A.R.S. § 45–141(A), considered in conjunction with 45–151(A), has changed the conclusion that we reached in Lambeye and Wedgworth concerning the right of the initial appropriator to discontinue or withdraw his waste. The very nature of waste water requires the application of different rules governing the rights of the junior appropriator. Waste water exists only as long as there is waste. No appropriator can compel any other appropriator to continue the waste of water which benefits the former. If the senior appropriator, through scientific and technical advances, can utilize his water so that none is wasted, no other appropriator can complain. See Reynolds v. City of Roswell, supra; Bower v. Big Horn Canal Association, 77 Wyo. 80, 307 P.2d 593 (1957). The junior appropriator, using waste water, "takes his chance" on continued flow. Thayer v. Rawlins, 594 P.2d 951 (Wyo. 1979). To hold otherwise and require the Cities to continue to discharge effluent would deprive the Cities of their ability to dispose of effluent in the most economically and environmentally sound manner, as discussed above. Moreover, such a holding would be contrary to the spirit and purpose of Arizona water law, which is to promote the beneficial use of water and to eliminate waste of this precious resource. * * *

Thus, the downstream appropriators such as A Tumbling T have limited rights as against the Cities. So long as the Cities choose to dispose of the effluent by discharge into the stream bed, the effluent becomes and is water "flowing in a stream" and under A.R.S. § 45–141 is subject to appropriation by downstream users. As between such appropriators, first in point of time is first in right under A.R.S. § 45–151(A), and A Tumbling T may well have appropriative rights as against any other junior appropriators. However, such downstream appropriators cannot force the Cities to continue to discharge the effluent at the same point in the stream or in the stream at all. The Cities may thus change the location of their sewer lines and of their water purification and treatment plants or dispose of their effluent in some other manner without violating any obligation or duty owed to the downstream appropriators.

FELDMAN, V.C.J., CAMERON, J., and LaCAGNINA, JUDGE, concur.

HAIRE, COURT OF APPEALS JUDGE, concurring in part and dissenting in part:

* * * The courts in other prior appropriation jurisdictions have reached inconsistent results when faced with questions involving the beneficial use by a municipality of its appropriated water insofar as concerns the use and disposition of sewage effluent. Thus, in Wyoming

Hereford Ranch v. Hammond Packing Co., 236 P. 764 (Wyo. 1925), the court considered whether the city of Cheyenne's "full beneficial use" of appropriated water included the right to sell the city's sewage effluent to the defendant in that case. The city had previously released part of the effluent directly into a ditch on the defendant's land and part into a creek from which the plaintiff's appropriated water was diverted. * * * [T]he Wyoming court upheld the sale by Cheyenne of the sewage effluent that was discharged directly into the buyer's ditch. However, as to that portion of the effluent that was discharged into the creek, the court held that these waters had again become public waters subject to appropriation. * * *

[In Pulaski Irrigation Ditch Co. v. City of Trinidad, 70 Colo. 565, 203 P. 681 (1922),] the city of Trinidad had discharged its sewage effluent directly into the Las Animas river. Eventually, the district court enjoined this practice, and the city then discharged the sewage into settling pits constructed on land adjoining the river. From these settling pits, a considerable part of the water content of the sewage then seeped or ran back into the river and became a part of the supply for appropriations below the point of discharge. Several years later, the city decided to build two water purification plants and, upon their completion, proposed to sell the effluent to its co-defendant, Model Land and Irrigation Company. The downstream appropriators sought to enjoin this proposed sale. In reversing the trial court's judgment in favor of the city, the Colorado Supreme Court rejected the city's contention that the sewage effluent was developed water, and held that the city could not sell the treated effluent, but rather must return it to the stream.

In its discussion, the Pulaski court emphasized that it was dealing with a fact situation in which the city was voluntarily purifying its effluent, thereby producing effluent which could be returned to the river. The court indicated that a different method of effluent treatment might well result in a total consumption of the effluent (e.g., evaporation), and suggested that the court's "return to the river" doctrine might not then be applicable. However, nothing in the opinion indicates a retreat from the court's position that in no event could the purified effluent be sold. * * *

I * * * agree with the majority * * * that the Cities may lawfully contract for the sale of sewage effluent without complying with statutory provisions regulating the change of use or place of use of surface or groundwater rights. My holding, however, would not be as broad as that embodied in either the majority's or the trial court's decision. * * *

[The Cities could have initially consumed all of their water.] However, the Cities did not do so. Rather their initial consumptive use was considerably less than total. They returned to the river a substantial part of the waters initially diverted. Under well established western water law principles, this lack of total consumptive use could subject the Cities to a loss of the right to later resume a total consumptive use. * * * As stated by a noted water authority:

Where, after use by a prior appropriator, water is discharged into a stream for the purpose of drainage or as a convenient method of disposing of it, * * * it works an abandonment of such water, and the water thus discharged becomes a part of the natural stream, and is subject to reappropriation and to the same rights as the water naturally flowing therein, and can not afterward be taken out by the original appropriator to the injury of other rights which have attached and vested to it. The authorities hold that in all cases where water formerly appropriated, or which has been under the control of any person, is permitted to flow down the natural channel of a stream below the point of diversion of the appropriator, * * * it works an immediate and express abandonment of all the water permitted so to escape; and subsequent appropriators can not be deprived of their rights in and to this water appropriated by them by an attempt upon the part of the first appropriator to shut off their supply by enlarging the amount diverted by him, or by any changes in the place or manner of use, which would injure the rights of such subsequent appropriators to the continuous flow of the stream as it was at the time that they made their appropriations.

Kinney, Irrigation and Water Rights, Vol. 2, Second Edition, § 1114.
* * *

For the reasons stated in this dissent, I would reverse the judgment entered by the trial court and remand for further consideration of the surface water abandonment issues. In view of my conclusion that the contracts for the sale of the sewage effluent do not per se violate Arizona groundwater or surface water law, injunctive relief would not be appropriate except to the extent that the A Tumbling T parties could show that they have obtained appropriative rights based on the historical discharge of the effluent into the river, and that the performance of the contracts would lessen that historical discharge so as to leave them with insufficient water to satisfy those rights.

Notes and Questions

1. In Arizona today, over 100,000 acre-feet of sewage effluent is used to water golf courses and parks, cool power plants, and irrigate agricultural land.

2. Did the Arizona Supreme Court reach its result more as a matter of policy than precedent? What would have been the policy implications of holding that the Cities had to continue to discharge their effluent into the Salt River?

3. In distinguishing the Colorado decision in *Pulaski*, the Arizona Supreme Court emphasizes that the effluent here had been treated, but was "not puri"—suggesting that the court might have reached a different result if the effluent had been cleaner. Is this an appropriate distinction? In a more recent case, under a plan of augmentation (see page 153 n.7 supra), Denver discharged treated effluent as a substitute for an out-of-priority diversion it

made upstream, and a downstream senior appropriator objected on grounds of reduced water quality. City of Thornton v. City and County of Denver, 44 P.3d 1019 (Colo. 2002).

4.   Montana has adopted the Arizona approach in an administrative opinion. See Final Order, In re City of Deer Lodge, B–No. 97514–76G (Mont. Dept. Natural Resources & Conservation, June 4, 1996).

5.   Both Colorado and Wyoming have held that a city may recapture *imported* water that has previously been discharged as waste water effluent, even though downstream appropriators have been relying on those discharges. See Denver Bd. of Water Comm'rs v. Fulton Irrigating Ditch Co., 179 Colo. 47, 506 P.2d 144 (1972); Thayer v. Rawlins, 594 P.2d 951 (Wyo. 1979). For the general doctrine governing recapture of imported water, see Stevens v. Oakdale Irrigation District, infra p. 211.

6.   In Boulder v. Boulder & Left Hand Ditch Co., 192 Colo. 219, 557 P.2d 1182 (1976), the Colorado Supreme Court drew a distinction in irrigation operations between "waste water" and "return flow." Waste water, according to the court, is the water that collects in ditches after irrigation, and can be captured and sold over the objections of downstream irrigators. Return flow is the water that seeps back into a stream after performing "its nutritional function" and is subject to the normal no-injury rule. Should "waste water" and "return flow" be treated differently? Is there any substantive difference between them? See also Metropolitan Denver Sewage Disposal Dist. v. Farmers Reservoir & Irrig. Co., 179 Colo. 36, 499 P.2d 1190 (1972) (holding that Denver could change the point at which it emitted sewage effluent into the South Platte River over the objections of an appropriator who had relied on the effluent but was upstream of the new point of discharge).

7.   A Texas court held that a city did not retain ownership of sewage effluent (originally pumped groundwater) after discharging it into a river. To divert it downstream, it would have to obtain a new appropriation permit. City of San Marcos v. Texas Comm'n on Env. Quality, 128 S.W.3d 264 (Tex. Ct. App. 2004), but new legislation authorizes reuse of discharged groundwater if prior authorization is obtained from the Commission. Tex. Water Code Ann. § 11.042(b).

Problem

A California city has for many years appropriated water from the Blue River that runs through the city, used it, treated it, and discharged it back to the Blue River downstream, where it was contributing to the support of a fish population. The city now has been ordered by pollution control authorities to treat the water to a much higher degree, which will make the water valuable for recreational use. The city wishes to cease discharging to the Blue River, and to discharge to another nearby stream, Canoe Creek, and to protect the new flows for the benefit of recreational users. However, there are also appropriators on Canoe Creek who have not been able to take their full appropriated amounts in most years, and who are delighted at the prospect of a new water supply. Can the city cut off the Blue River supply? Can it secure the water for recreationists against the appropriators on Canoe Creek? How would this problem be resolved under the common law of water rights? See Cal. Water Code §§ 1210, 1212; Dec. D–1638 (Cal. State Water Resources Control Bd. 1997); In the Matter of Treated Waste Water Change Petition WW–20 (Cal. State Water Resources Control Bd. 1995); Andrew H. Sawyer, Improving Efficiency Incrementally: The Governor's Commission Attacks Waste and Unreasonable Use, 36 McGeorge L. Rev. 210, 225–33 (2005) (Rights to Reclaimed Water).

iii. Appropriations for Use and Reuse

WATER SUPPLY & STORAGE CO. v. CURTIS

Supreme Court of Colorado, 1987.
733 P.2d 680.

LOHR, JUSTICE.

* * *

The applicant filed an application for a determination of a water storage right for Trap Lake II, a proposed reservoir on the side of the presently existing Trap Lake, claiming 4700 acre feet of storage for agricultural, industrial, municipal, and recreational, fisheries and other beneficial uses, and requesting a ruling "that the water may be used and reused and put to a succession of uses until totally consumed." The sources of the water were described as waters of Trap Creek, a tributary of the Cache La Poudre River, and waters of the Colorado River to be transported by the Grand Ditch across the continental divide. * * *

A.

The applicant recognizes that with respect to tributary waters, we have held that the owner of a water right may not reuse or make successive uses of return flow independent of the priority system. Pulaski Irrigating Ditch Co. v. City of Trinidad, 70 Colo. 565, 203 P. 681 (1922); see Comstock v. Ramsay, 55 Colo. 244, 133 P. 1107 (1913) (return flow is not subject to further appropriation independent of the priority system on the river). The applicant contends, however, that the basis for this principle is that after others have come to rely on return flows, the original appropriator should not be able to defeat that reliance by putting the return flows to use. Therefore, the applicant urges, if the waters are reused to extinction when first diverted, no reliance can arise and no expectation is defeated by permitting the original appropriator to reuse the water after it has first been employed for the decreed beneficial uses. As a result, the argument concludes, the original appropriator should be recognized to have the right to reuse and make successive uses of waters provided only that the further use be initiated immediately after the first beneficial use so that no expectations of others regarding return flow are permitted to arise.

The protestants argue that the right of reuse under these circumstances has never been recognized under our law. They contend that the applicant's plan is simply a form of speculation, permitting the applicant to reserve water for some undetermined future uses independent of the

SPECULATION

priority system on the river. We agree with the protestants, and therefore conclude that the water judge correctly denied the application for authorization to reuse and make successive uses of the tributary waters. * * *

The applicant does not base its asserted right to reuse and make successive uses of the return flow upon an appropriation of the return flow after initial use. Instead, the applicant argues that the right to reuse and make successive uses should be recognized as an incident of the conditional water right for storage in Trap Lake II Reservoir. The applicant contends that cases such as *Pulaski* and *Comstock* are based upon situations in which a return flow was permitted to occur for extended periods, and downstream appropriators came to rely upon that return flow. Although this was the factual situation present in *Pulaski* and *Comstock,* a more fundamental principle provides the foundation for those decisions. In each case, the return flow after use by the first appropriator became water tributary to natural streams and as such was subject to diversion and use under the appropriations and associated system of priorities existing on the streams. In *Pulaski,* as in the present case, the initial appropriator did not take those steps necessary to appropriate the return flow as part of its initial beneficial use. As a result, the return flow "became a part of the supply for the appropriations below the point of discharge." *Pulaski,* 70 Colo. at 567, 203 P. at 682.

* * * In the present case, then, the proper inquiry is whether the applicant has established a right in the return flow by appropriation, for that is the basis, if there is any, upon which its claim to that return flow must be founded. It is well settled that the initiation of an appropriation requires a concurrence of the intent to appropriate water for application to beneficial use and the performance of overt acts in furtherance of that intent.

The applicant here has not demonstrated the requisite intent to appropriate. "Intent to appropriate requires a fixed purpose to pursue diligently a certain course of action to take and beneficially use water from a particular source." City & County of Denver v. Colorado River Water Conservation District, 696 P.2d at 745. The applicant has not decided upon even the broadest outline of a plan for reuse or successive use of the water. The applicant's evidence was simply that it is too early to decide how the waters will be reused or successively used or even who will make such reuse or successive use. Although the applicant has many ideas, each differing markedly from the others, as to the best way to reuse or make successive uses of the water, it has no fixed purpose to pursue any particular one of them. Such a general and unfocused desire to use the return flow for undetermined uses is not the fixed purpose to apply water to beneficial use that has long been required as an essential element of a appropriation. * * *

We turn now to the question of the applicant's right to reuse and make successive uses of waters to be imported to the Cache La Poudre

River drainage from the Colorado River drainage for storage by exchange in Trap Lake II Reservoir. This right is established by both statute and case law. Section 37–82–106(1), 15 C.R.S. (1986 Supp.), provides:

> Whenever an appropriator has lawfully introduced foreign water into a stream system from an unconnected stream system, such appropriator may make a succession of uses of such water by exchange or otherwise to the extent that its volume can be distinguished from the volume of the streams into which it is introduced. Nothing in this section shall be construed to impair or diminish any water right which has become vested.

[handwritten margin note: FOREIGN WATERS CAN BE REUSED]

In City & County of Denver v. Fulton Irrigating Ditch Co., 179 Colo. 47, 506 P.2d 144 (1972), we noted this statute and also held that "[e]ven without the statute" Denver had the right to reuse and make successive uses of water imported to the eastern slope by transmountain diversions from the Colorado River basin. Ibid. at 52, 506 P.2d at 144. In arriving at this result, we considered it important that the Colorado River water would never have come into the South Platte River system except for the developer's efforts. The water judge in the present case erred, therefore, in deleting from the referee's ruling the right to reuse and successively use waters to be stored in Trap Lake II Reservoir pursuant to the decreed conditional water right to the extent that such waters have their origin in the Colorado River basin.

Notes and Questions

1. Was the court concerned that the applicant was simply speculating in water? If so, what exactly is the public policy that the court safeguards by prohibiting such efforts? See infra p. 284 n.2.

2. In light of the decision in the principal case is there any helpful advice one could give a Colorado city that sought to secure the right to reuse its non-imported effluent in the future if and when technology and economics make it desirable to do so? Would it help the city if it showed evidence of likely future growth, with concomitant increased future demand for water, and a city policy to avoid damming up any more natural rivers? See Environmental Defense Fund v. East Bay Mun. Util. Dist., supra p. 191.

iv. Recapture by Water Importers

STEVENS v. OAKDALE IRRIGATION DISTRICT

Supreme Court of California, 1939.
13 Cal.2d 343, 90 P.2d 58.

[Defendant, owning a tract of land in the watersheds of both the Stanislaus River and Lone Tree Creek, appropriated water from the Stanislaus and used it to irrigate his land, carrying some of the water over the watershed into that portion of his land within the watershed of Lone Tree Creek. Some of the runoff from defendant's irrigation then ran into Lone Tree Creek, where it flowed down to plaintiff's land, downstream on Lone Tree Creek. For 22 years plaintiff had used this runoff, which he diverted from Lone Tree Creek downstream from Defendant's land. Now defendant has begun to recapture the runoff out of Lone Tree Creek for his own reuse, diverting it from the Creek before it leaves his land. Plaintiff asserts that he is entitled to have the runoff continue to flow down to him as it has for the past 22 years.]

PER CURIAM.

* * * It is plaintiffs' theory that, regardless of whether a lower claimant may compel continuance of importation of a foreign water supply, once such water has actually been conducted into the foreign watershed and drained into a natural watercourse therein, the further interception or recapture of the flow by the producer may constitute an invasion of a right thereto acquired by the lower claimant—and this despite the fact that the retaking occurs before the water leaves the control of the producer or passes the boundaries of his land. Defendant, on the other hand, vigorously asserts that the lower appropriator of the foreign supply is not only without right to enforce continued importation of the water into the second watershed, but he is also without right to compel the producer to continue abandoning any particular portion of the flow. The status of the imported water is not changed, according to defendant, by the mere fact that the producer, upon his own property within the second watershed, uses the channel of a natural watercourse as a temporary conduit or drain, retaking the water therefrom for further beneficial application within his boundaries.

It is the general rule, probably subject to exceptions not here involved, that the producer of an artificial flow is for the most part under no obligation to lower claimants to continue to maintain it. At any time he may forsake the practice, and lower users will not have acquired a right against him, either by appropriation or prescription, to continued augmentation of the natural volume of the stream. While rights may be acquired by lower proprietors in and to such portions of the foreign flow as have been abandoned by the producer and thus made available for other use, these rights are always subject to the contingency that the supply may be intermittent or may be terminated entirely at the will of the producer. In other words, although the fact that the producer may discontinue the foreign supply does not preclude others from acquiring a right to it, when and if it exists, such fact does not affect the value of the right so acquired, in that its permanency is not assured. * * *

It follows that plaintiffs in this action cannot predicate their claims upon any acquired right to compel defendant district to continue the importation of water from the Stanislaus river into Lone Tree creek.

The problem then is to determine whether plaintiffs have acquired any lesser right against defendant which entitles them to the relief accorded by the trial court herein, such as a right to compel defendant, if and when it has imported the water, to maintain its past practice of abandoning in the channel of the creek within its boundaries, a sufficient supply to fill plaintiffs' requirements. Stating the question another way, where the producer of an artificial flow does not decrease it at the source, but after importing it, acts upon it a second time while it is still within his land and before it leaves his control, does the doctrine above set forth apply, or may lower proprietors assert a right to enjoin any decrease in the volume of abandoned water?

In finding the solution of this problem, the distinction must be observed between abandonment by one who creates an artificial flow, of his water right (the right to divert and use the water of the first stream), and abandonment of used water itself (the very body or corpus thereof), after it has been imported into the second watershed.

Waters brought in from a different watershed and reduced to possession are private property during the period of possession. When possession of the actual water, or corpus, has been relinquished, or lost by discharge without intent to recapture, property in it ceases. This is not the abandonment of a water right but merely an abandonment of specific portions of water, i.e., the very particles which are discharged or have escaped from control. So in the present case, for example, there has been no abandonment by defendant of a water right, but only an abandonment of those portions of the imported water which have actually been permitted to drain down to plaintiffs' land. As to this specific flow, discharged without intent to recapture, the abandonment has been complete, and plaintiffs have properly exercised a right to take the waters at their point of diversion. Defendant, having no further interest in the discharge, could not have stopped them from so doing. But this past abandonment by defendant of certain water, as distinguished from a water right, has not conferred upon plaintiffs any right to compel a like abandonment in the future, or to control defendant's use upon its own land of such water as it imports. * * *

While at first blush the above doctrine might seem a harsh one in its present application because plaintiffs here have expended a considerable sum for the construction of diversion works in the mistaken expectation that the foreign flow past their property would be permanent, upon mature consideration the injustice which would result if the rule were to the contrary is plainly to be seen. Defendant irrigation district has expended vast sums for the erection of the storage and diversion facilities which make possible the bringing of a continuous flow from the Stanislaus river to the Lone Tree creek watershed. The development of any irrigation district must necessarily be a gradual one. A perfection of the system to the point where fullest beneficial use is made of all water passing through the irrigation works is not attained in a day. As a district is brought to the peak of development, an increasing use of water may be anticipated, and also a more efficient method of use, with resultant decrease in the amount of abandoned waste, spill, and seepage. In this process of growth, the discharge of a considerable volume of artificial flow over a long period of formative years should not and does not invariably constitute an abandonment by the district of its right to such waters, or impose upon it a duty to always maintain the same volume of discharge. In this connection, the following observation made in a case concerning the government's right to recapture waste waters is pertinent: "One who by the expenditure of money and labor diverts appropriable water from a stream, and thus makes it available for fruitful purposes, is entitled to its exclusive control so long as he is able and willing to apply it to beneficial uses, and such right extends to what is commonly known as wastage from surface run-off and deep percolation, necessarily incident to practical irrigation. Considerations of both public policy and natural justice strongly support such a rule."

To summarize, one who produces a flow of foreign water for beneficial use and thereafter permits it to drain down a natural stream channel is ordinarily under no duty to lower claimants to continue importing the supply or to continue maintaining the volume of discharge into the second stream channel at any fixed rate. The rule may have exceptions, as perhaps where the artificial condition has become inherently permanent and there has been a dedication to the public use, or where the drainage is stopped wantonly to harm a lower party, without other object. But as a general proposition, an irrigation district, after importing water from one river, passing it through irrigation works, and discharging it into a natural creek bed in the second watershed, may change the flow of water imported or the volume of water discharged from its works into the second stream, or stop the flow entirely, so long as this is done above the point where the water leaves the works of the district or the boundaries of its land. An exception to the rule is not created by the fact that the district may act upon the water a second time while in its possession, by retaking it at a point of drainage for further beneficial application.

In the present case the recapture of the water from the stream channel by defendant district, upon its own land, and the use of the channel as a temporary drain, neither adds to nor detracts from plaintiffs' claims to the artificial flow. The right to use a natural channel as a temporary conduit or as a drain for artificial flow has been frequently upheld. There are cases where even after a foreign flow has left the land and control of its producer, he has been permitted to recapture it from the second stream, when it has been shown that such recapture was a part of his original project, and the water was discharged into the stream, not simply to be rid of it, but for the express purpose of retaking at a lower point. Where the recapture occurs before the foreign flow passes from the lands and control of the producer there can be no doubt of his right to make temporary use of a channel traversing his property, so long as normal conditions on the stream are not injuriously affected thereby. In such case the stream bed merely serves the purpose of the drainage ditch which might be constructed were no natural channel available.

Plaintiffs suggest, although with little vigor, that the doctrines of estoppel, adverse possession, or nonuser may be invoked to sustain their position. The findings of the court bearing on these subjects have already been set forth. The most that can be said on behalf of plaintiffs is that defendant, with knowledge of plaintiffs' construction of diversion works, stood silent. But in the absence of other essential elements neither expenditures by plaintiffs, defendant's knowledge thereof, nor its silence are sufficient to establish an estoppel. There is no showing whatsoever of any degree of turpitude in the conduct of defendant which would estop it from assertion of its title before a court of equity. As to adverse possession, it is apparent that plaintiffs' taking of the foreign water at its point of diversion was not hostile to defendant's title, but was a mere taking of certain water (the corpus as distinguished from the water right), to which defendant had relinquished all claim. * * *

Notes and Questions

1.   Colorado similarly holds that an importer of water has the exclusive right to use and reuse that water, regardless of whether the initial appropriation contemplated reuse, and whether any reuse of the water was ever made. Colo. Rev. Stat. § 37–82–106. City of Thornton v. Bijou Irrigation Co., 926 P.2d 1,74 (Colo. 1996). Since much of the water used by growing cities on Colorado's Front Range is imported water from the West Slope, it has been suggested that the right to re-use such imported water will be a boon to Colorado's burgeoning urban areas (at the expense of downstream agricultural irrigators who have been using it?).

2.   What rights are acquired by a user of discharged foreign water when the competing claimant is not the importer? An older Washington case, Elgin v. Weatherstone, 123 Wash. 429, 433, 212 P. 562 (1923), held that "foreign water, once abandoned by the developer, does not become part of the natural flow of the drainage area where it is discharged and may be used by the first person who takes it." See Dodge v. Ellensburg Water Co., 46 Wash.App. 77, 729 P.2d 631 (1986). In *Dodge* a later-in-time claimant of foreign source discharge prevailed by virtue of the physical capture of the water before it flowed down to the party who previously had been using the discharge.

3.   For a discussion of legal problems associated with recapture and reuse of water in riparian states, see Michael Baram & J. Raymond Miyares, In Order To Have Water: Legal, Economic and Institutional Barriers To Water Reuse in Northern New England, 17 N. Eng. L. Rev. 741 (1982).

4.   Consider this twist on the importation issue: In order to assist water-short farmers on River A, the government finances a project to import water from River B in another watershed. While entirely suitable for irrigation, the imported River B water is of lower quality than that on River A, and a city on River A complains that the imported water, now mixed with the natural flow, will adversely affect the quality of the River A water that it uses for drinking and bathing. Does the city have any remedy in terms of its water rights?

C.   MODERN ACQUISITION OF WATER RIGHTS: THE PERMIT SYSTEM AND ADMINISTERED WATER REGIMES

Wyoming instituted a permit system in 1890. Other Western States eventually followed her leadership. Today every prior appropriation state except Colorado provides for the acquisition of water rights through an administrative permit system. The basic elements of the system—appropriation of unappropriated waters of natural streams to beneficial use—remain in force, but with a significant change. Permitting is no longer treated as an essentially ministerial function, under which the applicant is entitled to obtain a permit so long as water is available and the use meets the rudimentary requirements of beneficiality. Today permitting agencies ordinarily have a much broader and more substantive role, granting and conditioning permits in light of reservations of water for instream use or future developments, coordinating permit applications with water quality criteria (and in some states, like California, administering pollution control laws), and determining whether the application is in "the public interest."[1] The implementation of this latter requirement is the principal question addressed in this section.[2]

In addition to its substantive significance, the permit system has indisputable administrative benefits. It provides a public record of uses sought to be made, permits beneficiality requirements to be ascertained in advance of investment, offers a means to assure diligence in construction of facilities and application of water to use, and allows for other important legal requirements (such as dam safety) to be enforced.

1. ADMINISTRATION OF THE PERMIT SYSTEM

ARTHUR LITTLEWORTH & ERIC GARNER, CALIFORNIA WATER
113–117 & 121–123 (1995).

Origin

The State Water Resources Control Board ("State Board") was formed in 1967 to replace the State Water Rights Board. [The new] State Board also assumed the water pollution planning and control duties of the State Water Quality Control Board. The integration of water rights and water quality authority was seen as a timely joinder as water quality and quantity issues steadily became more intertwined. * * *

The Appropriation of Water

Any person or entity wishing to appropriate water in California must file an application with the State Board. Water Code § 1252. This includes public agencies, cities, counties, and the state and federal governments. Before a permit can be obtained, several conditions must be met: (1) there must be a specific applicant or water user; (2) the applicant must file an application with the Board; (3) the applicant must intend to put the water to beneficial use; and (4) there must be enough

1. Cal. Water Code §§ 1253, 1255.

2. Note that appropriators may have to obtain other permits beyond the basic state authorization to appropriate dealt with here (see, e.g., South Florida Water Management District v. Miccosukee Tribe of Indians, infra p. 1032), as well as complying with laws such as the National Environmental Policy Act, 42 U.S.C.A. §§ 4321 et seq. and the Endangered Species Act, 16 U.S.C.A. §§ 1531 et seq. In California, permits include a standard condition that no construction may begin on a newly permitted project until all necessary federal, state and local approvals have been obtained.

unappropriated water to supply the proposed use. The appropriation system applies to surface waters flowing in any natural channel which are not needed to satisfy the reasonable needs of riparian landowners. Water Code § 1201. The appropriative process does not apply to riparian rights or to claims for percolating groundwater [nor do pre–1914 appropriators have permits, since there was no permit system prior to that time. Riparians and pre–1914 rights holders are supposed to file statements of diversion with the State Board, but there are no penal sanctions for failure to file.]

Only unappropriated waters are available for appropriation. These are defined in Section 1202 of the Water Code and include: (1) water which has never been appropriated; (2) water which has been appropriated and subsequently abandoned after the appropriator failed to put it to beneficial use; and (3) water which, once it has been appropriated, flows back into an underground channel or any surface water body.

After an application is filed, the Board is required to give notice of the application. Publication of notice triggers a protest period, during which any person with good cause may protest against the approval of the application. Water Code § 1330.[a] Under Section 1243 of the Water Code, the State Board is specifically required to notify the California Department of Fish and Game of all applications to appropriate water. The Department of Fish and Game then must recommend the amount of water, if any, required to preserve and enhance fish and wildlife resources. Water Code § 1243. * * *

If the application is not protested, no hearing is required. Water Code § 1351. If a protest is filed, applicants are entitled to an administrative hearing. Water Code §§ 1330, 1331, and 1340. After the State Board makes a decision, parties have several options if they wish to challenge the outcome. Within 30 days a petition may be filed with the State Board for reconsideration of its decision, and the State Board has 90 days to determine whether or not to grant the petition. Water Code § 1357. If the State Board grants the petition, it may reconsider its decision, and the Board has the option of asking the parties to submit new arguments and additional evidence. Water Code § 1358.

The parties may also seek a writ of mandate in the state Superior Court within 30 days of the State Board's decision. This option is available whether or not the parties petition the State Board for reconsideration. The court does not independently review the merits of the State Board's decision. Instead, the court examines the administrative record to determine if the decision was based on "substantial evidence." * * *

All water rights in California are subject to the state constitutional limitation of the principles of Article X, Section 2. These are embodied in Water Code Section 100. However, beyond these requirements, several other determinations must be made. First, the State Board must find

a. Colorado permits "any person" to protest an application for determination of   a water right. Colo. Rev. Stat. § 37–92–302(1)(b).—Eds.

that the proposed use of water will be beneficial. Water Code §§ 100, 1240, 1375. A list of beneficial uses is found in the California Code of Regulations, Title 23, Section 659 et seq. These uses are (1) domestic use; (2) irrigation; (3) power; (4) frost protection; (5) municipal; (6) mining; (7) industrial; (8) fish and wildlife preservation and enhancement; (9) aquaculture; (10) recreational; (11) water quality; (12) stockwatering; and (13) heat control. Additionally, the Water Code specifically identifies as a beneficial use the storing of water underground, the release of water to control water quality, and the use of water for recreation and the preservation of fish and wildlife. Water Code §§ 1242, 1242.5, 1243.

One clear requirement of beneficial use is that water must be diverted from the stream, or its flow in some way physically altered. Simply leaving water in a stream for instream use does not constitute a beneficial use. California Trout v. State Water Resources Control Board (1979) 90 Cal. App. 3d 816.

A second requirement is that unappropriated water must be available for the applicant's use. Water Code § 1375(d). The State Board has published a list of fully appropriated streams from which no further appropriations are allowed. * * * The Board must also determine if the water has been appropriated by someone else and whether other beneficial uses, such as the control of water quality, recreation, and the preservation of fish and wildlife, limit or preclude the appropriation. Finally, the State Board must consider the public interest in its decision to allow appropriations and must reject applications that are not in the public interest. Water Code §§ 1253, 1255.

Notes and Questions

1. A permit gives a conditional right to appropriate water. The permittee must act diligently to use the water in a beneficial manner (Cal. Water Code § 1396), and must comply with any conditions the Board has imposed. Prior to the time a license issues, the Board may reserve jurisdiction to change permit conditions (Cal. Water Code § 1394). In United States v. State Water Resources Control Bd., 182 Cal.App.3d 82, 227 Cal.Rptr. 161 (1986), the court invoked this provision to require salinity control releases by permittees holding reserved jurisdiction permits. Once water has been applied to a beneficial use, the right is perfected and the permit can be converted to a license, which remains in effect so long as the water is applied to reasonable and beneficial use (Cal. Water Code §§ 1600, 1627). The dual permit/license system is meant to assure that the permittee complies with the terms on which the permit was issued.

2. If all goes according to the rules, permits will either be perfected within the allotted construction time or will be invalidated. But things do not always work that way. In Wyoming, Professor Jackson Battle discovered in 1987 a number of decades-old, still-pending permits for uncompleted projects, as well as many applications for permits that had been filed but never acted upon, and were still pending. The practice of the Wyoming State Engineer was to grant extensions repeatedly so as to keep permits or

applications alive even though no action toward completion had been taken. Jackson Battle, Paper Clouds Over the Waters: Shelf Filings and Hyperextended Permits in Wyoming, 22 Land & Water L. Rev. 673, 680 (1987). The consequence was that holders of pure paper claims—such as permit applications that have never even been docketed for action—could demand to be bought out when a legitimate applicant for the same source later came along, and needed assurance of clear title. Fortunately, that issue has diminished in Wyoming, according to Jeff Fassett, the former State Engineer:

> To address this [problem] several things have happened. First, I have been more aggressive in making sure my staff follow up with the pending applications and we not let folks get away with just sitting on the applications to hold their date with no real intention of moving forward. This policy is flexible to allow for special considerations or factors of why time is needed. * * * Second, we've stiffened our enforcement of all the details needed to get in the door with a clean application and the maps/engineering work and have a Temporary Filing assigned. Lastly, we've passed some rules that provided a process for another applicant or appropriator or the State Engineer to * * * force an applicant holding a Temporary Filing to come forward and detail his/her diligence etc. in moving forward with a project. * * * Once a permit is issued then strict timelines are set to more closely follow a diligence standard to complete the project or to cancel the permit at a later time. I inherited a lot of old stuff that had been laying around. A lot has now been shoved out the door one way or the other. * * *[2]

3. In determining whether there is water available for appropriation, the California Water Board determines "the amount of water needed for protection of instream uses and other public trust uses." Dec. D–1638 (Cal. State Water Resources Control Bd. 1997). In determining the availability of water, Colorado does not assume that all conditional water rights will be become absolute, and that all such rights will, when they become absolute, divert to the full extent permitted under their conditional decrees, saying that such assumptions are "contrary to experience and are improbable." In re Application for Water Rights of Bd. of County Comm'rs, 891 P.2d 952, 958 (Colo. 1995).

4. In Colorado, where there is no permit system, new appropriators come into a water court (there is one for each basin in the state) and in effect announce that they have made, or intend to make, an appropriation. There is an opportunity for objectors to claim that no unappropriated water is available, that the proposed use is not beneficial or that existing priorities will be injured. The Colorado Supreme Court has refused to interpose a public interest test for conditional decrees, saying "a public interest theory is in conflict with the doctrine of prior appropriation because a water court cannot, in the absence of statutory authority, deny a legitimate appropriation based on public policy." In re Application for Water Rights of Bd. Of County Comm'rs, 891 P.2d 952, 972–73 (Colo. 1995). If the conventional

2. Email from Jeff Fassett, former State Engineer, State of Wyoming, to Joseph Sax, Oct. 14, 1999.

elements of an appropriation are present, the court will issue a decree. Since most applications are made at the beginning of projects, most decrees are in fact conditional, and the vesting of the water right depends upon sexennial showings of reasonable diligence in completion of the facilities and application of the water to beneficial use. Colo. Rev. Stat. §§ 37–92–301(4), 302(1)(a), 601. The Colorado court uses the due diligence requirement to weed out speculative applications. See Trans–County Water, Inc. v. Conservancy Dist., 727 P.2d 60 (Colo. 1986). An applicant for a conditional decree must show that it "can and will complete the appropriation of water with diligence" (Application of Hines Highlands Limited Partnership, 929 P.2d 718, 723 (Colo. 1996)), and must thereafter "in a diligence proceeding * * * prove that it has the intent to use the water and has performed concrete actions demonstrating diligent efforts to finalize its application. * * * Statutory law defines the measure of reasonable diligence to be the steady application of effort to complete the appropriation in a reasonably expedient and efficient manner under all the facts and circumstances" (Dallas Creek Water Co. v. Huey, 933 P.2d 27, 36 (Colo. 1997)). The "can and will" doctrine is based on Colo. Rev. Stat. § 37–92–305(9)(b). Cities are given considerable leeway, and need only show "reasonably anticipated requirements based on substantiated projection of future growth." City of Thornton v. Bijou Irrigation Co., 926 P.2d 1, 39 (Colo. 1996). Showing technical feasibility is sufficient despite evidence that the project "would be technically challenging and financially burdensome." City of Black Hawk v. City of Central, 97 P.3d 951 (Colo. 2004).

2. THE PUBLIC INTEREST STANDARD

a. Acquisition of Water Rights

RONALD B. ROBIE,
THE PUBLIC INTEREST IN WATER
RIGHTS ADMINISTRATION

23 Rocky Mtn. Min. L. Inst. 917, 935–938 (1977).

* * * As to initial allocation, present statutes and court decisions of some states still give little recognition to the public interest and hold that there is an absolute right of the first applicant to have an application approved if one has any economic use for the water. Also, since water rights permits are normally granted in perpetuity, procedures for reserving unappropriated water for future more beneficial uses generally are nonexistent.

In most states, the two most common criteria for approval of a new application are: is there unappropriated water available and does the proposed appropriation not interfere with vested water rights?

In California the courts have held that the "public interest is the primary statutory standard guiding the Water Rights Board (now the California State Water Resources Control Board) in acting upon applications to appropriate water.[80] Yet California law does not give the State

---

80. Johnson Rancho County Water District v. State Water Rights Board, 235 Cal. App. 2d 863, 874, 45 Cal. Rptr. 589, 596 (1965).

Water Resources Control Board specific guidelines in determining the public interest. The Model Water Code provides that as a condition for the issuance of a permit" the applicant must establish that the proposed use of water * * * (c) is consistent with the public interest.[81] These uses include: "protection and procreation of fish and wildlife, the maintenance of proper ecological balance and scenic beauty, and the preservation and enhancement of waters of the state for navigation, public recreation, municipal uses, and public water supply. * * * " Under these provisions, the state governing board has an affirmative duty to protect uses that are in the public interest and could reject an application to appropriate water which would otherwise be approved if, for example, it would have a harmful effect on fish and wildlife. The Alaska Statutes also provide specific guidance to the Commissioner of Natural Resources who must find that a proposed appropriation is in the public interest before issuing a water rights permit.[85]

Recently the California State Water Resources Control Board has taken steps to give itself greater flexibility in its administration of water rights. It has asserted a right to impose "a recapture clause" which would limit the right to appropriate water until a subsequent appropriator sought to put the water to a more reasonable use or a higher beneficial use.[86]

The California State Water Resources Control Board has a broad authority to impose terms and conditions on new permits to appropriate water. The California Water Code provides that "The board shall allow the appropriation for beneficial purposes of unappropriated water under such terms and conditions as in its judgment will best develop, conserve, and utilize in the public interest the water sought to be appropriated".[87]

Some have argued, however, that conditions such as a recapture clause should not be imposed by an administrative agency, but rather should be spelled out in statutory language and any conditions which apply to a water rights permit should be spelled out in the permit.[88] However, due to changing water conditions, these cannot be very specific. California uses standard terms which subject all rights under a permit to the continuing authority of the State Water Resources Control Board in the interest of the public welfare to prevent waste, unreasonable use, unreasonable method of use, or unreasonable method of diversion. The

81. A Model Water Code, [with commentary (1958)] at 179.

85. Alaska Stat. § 46.15.080(4) [now § 46.15.080(5), (8)—Eds.]. In determining the public interest, the commissioner is specifically directed to consider, among other things "the effect of loss of alternative uses of water that might be made within a reasonable time if not precluded or hindered by the proposed appropriation," and "the effect upon access to navigable or public waters."

86. This issue was raised in the case of Boyd Trucking Co. v. State Water Resources Control Board, 3rd Dist. Ct. App., 3 Civil 15626 (Cal.1976). However, a stipulation between the parties avoided a judicial ruling on that clause.

87. Cal. Water Code § 1253.

88. E. Clyde & D. Jensen, Administrative Allocation of Water (National Water Commission, Legal Study No. 3, 1971) at 65.

Board may impose specific requirements over and above those contained in the permit with a view to minimize waste of water. In addition the quantity of water diverted under the permit is subject to modification by the Board if it finds that this is necessary to meet water quality objectives under California water pollution control laws.[89]

The California State Water Resources Control Board (and similar boards or officials in other states) can determine, in granting new appropriations, what the public interest requires. Terms and conditions can be included in the permit that reflect the protection of this public interest.

To avoid locking in rights which should be flexible, such rights could also be granted for the term of the intended use only. Applications could be approved on a varying time span depending upon the specific project involved. For instance, in Utah, oil companies were given water permits after agreeing to relinquish all claims to the water when their project was over.[90] In another Utah example, an application was made to appropriate water to wash sands and gravel in a specific area. The right to the water will end when the sands and gravels are removed, and the water can be allocated to another use.[91]

Notes and Questions

1.   The public interest requirement demands a policy decision from the Board. Courts do not review the policy decision in itself, but only assure there is evidence to support the Board's decisions. There are certain standard conditions that the Board always imposes, such as where return flow must be returned to the stream. It will also define the service area (restricting the place of use), specify the type of use, the quantity to be stored at any given time, the quantity to be taken by direct diversion, and the amount that can be diverted month by month. The Board will also specify releases required to protect downstream uses and for pollution control, recreation and fish and wildlife.

2.   In the very controversial matter of the New Melones dam, the subject of California v. United States, infra p. 753, the Board imposed a requirement that water could not be impounded in the dam until there were contracts for its use. The Board sought to protect whitewater recreation uses as long as possible. If there had been no restraints imposed, the reservoir would have been filled in order to generate hydropower.

89.   23 Cal. Admin. Code § 780. § 780(a) provides: "Pursuant to California Water Code Sections 100 and 275 and the common law public trust doctrine, all rights and privileges under this permit and under any license issued pursuant thereto, including method of diversion, method of use, and quantity of water diverted, are subject to the continuing authority of the State Water Resources Control Board in accordance with law and in the interest of the public welfare to protect public trust uses and to prevent waste, unreasonable use, unreasonable method of use, or unreasonable method of diversion of said water."

90.   E. Clyde & D. Jensen, supra note 88 at 60.

91.   Ibid. at 61. The Utah State Engineer now has the explicit power to grant limited time permits when applications are made for industrial, power, mining development, or manufacturing purposes (Utah Code Ann. § 73–3–8 (1989).

3. For a critique of the Board's administration of the permit system, see Brian Gray, A Reconsideration of Instream Appropriative Water Rights in California, 16 Ecology L.Q. 667, 671–95 (1989).

CENTRAL DELTA WATER AGENCY v. STATE WATER RESOURCES CONTROL BOARD

Court of Appeal for the State of California, 2004.
124 Cal.App.4th 245, 20 Cal.Rptr.3d 898.

BLEASE, Acting P.J.

This action challenges the decision of the defendant State Water Resources Control Board (Board or Water Board) that issued permits for the appropriation of water for the Delta Wetlands Project (Project) and certified a final Environmental Impact Report (EIR).Proponents of the Project and real parties in interest are Delta Wetlands Properties, Delta Wetlands, and KLMLP, L.P., hereinafter referred to as DW. The Project involves the diversion of water from the San Francisco Bay/Sacramento–San Joaquin Delta Estuary (Delta) into reservoirs to be constructed on two islands in the Delta for later rediversion and sale to potential purchasers in amounts as yet unknown.

Notwithstanding the uncertain nature of the use, the Water Board approved the permits stating that a "potential exists for the DW Project water to be beneficially used because the existing demand for water in California is not met in most years." The permits do not specify the users or the quantity of water to be sold and the Decision states only that the Project could be economically feasible. Rather, these matters are made the subject of conditions attached to the permits. "The permits for the Project will require that it be adequately designed, impacts will be mitigated, and a market for its water supply exists so that it can continue to operate for the expected life of the project."

To this end the permits limit the amounts to be diverted from the Delta for storage and prohibit the filling of the reservoirs above mean sea level until DW has contracted for the purchase of the water, specified the use and place of use for each contract of sale, demonstrated that the water reliably can be wheeled,[2] and obtained a determination from the Chief, Division of Water Rights that the water will be used beneficially. The permits define beneficial use generally as "Domestic, Irrigation, Municipal, Industrial, and Fish and Wildlife" and the service area as the "Central Valley Project Service Area (CVP), State Water Project Service Area (SWP), and Bay–Delta Estuary," an area encompassing much of the state. (Wat.Code, §§ 1254 and 1257.) The Board's California Environmental Quality Act (CEQA) determination does not evaluate the environmental consequences of the potential uses of the appropriated water because they are speculative. * * *

2. "Wheeling" refers to the use of another's conveyance facility to transport water to the end user.

We conclude that under the state constitution and the Water Code an application for a permit to impound water in a reservoir must state, and the Water Board must determine, that an actual, intended beneficial use, in estimated amounts, will be made of the impounded waters. A general statement of potential beneficial use is insufficient and the Board may not satisfy its statutory and constitutional obligations by conditioning a permit on a particular use and in amounts to be specified at some later date. We also conclude the CEQA requires that the Water Board evaluate and condition the permits to mitigate the environmental consequences of the specific intended beneficial use of the impounded water before issuance of a permit.

We shall reverse the judgment and order the trial court to set aside the permits and direct the Board to require that DW amend the applications to specify an actual use of and the amounts of water to be appropriated consistent with the requirements of the Water Code and the implementing regulations. Before issuing revised permits, the Board shall evaluate the use or uses specified by an amended application, determine whether they are beneficial and whether the amounts to be used can be reliably wheeled and are reasonably required for the beneficial use specified. * * *

B. The Constitution and the Water Code

Appellants argue that the Board violated the Water Code by failing to investigate and evaluate the uses to which the appropriated water would be put before issuing the permits. They reason that because no actual purchasers for the Project water were identified the Board could not have analyzed the nature and impact of any specific use of the impounded water as required by the Water Code. We agree.

In the law of water rights two principles regarding the right to use water predominate. First, the right to use water is limited to the amount reasonably required for the beneficial use to be served. Second, the right to use water does not extend to waste or unreasonable use or method of use or diversion. These principles are set forth in the state constitution and are the basic policy of the Water Code.

The state constitution provides that the right to water or to use water is limited to such water as is "reasonably required for the beneficial use to be served," and does not extend to "the waste or unreasonable use or unreasonable method of use or unreasonable method of diversion of water." (Cal. Const., art X, § 2; *City of Barstow v. Mojave Water Agency* (2000) 23 Cal.4th 1224, 1242, 99 Cal.Rptr.2d 294, 5 P.3d 853; *Joslin v. Marin Mun. Water Dist.* (1967) 67 Cal.2d 132, 140–141, 60 Cal.Rptr. 377, 429 P.2d 889.) The Water Code replicates these provisions in stating that "[t]he right to water * * * in or from any natural stream or watercourse in this State is and shall be limited to such water as shall be reasonably required for the beneficial use to be served, and such right does not and shall not extend to the waste or unreasonable use or unreasonable method of use or unreasonable method of diversion of water." (§ 100.)[9]

The Water Code governs the exclusive means by which a right to appropriate water subject to appropriation may be acquired. It requires that the applicant set forth and the Board determine the beneficial purpose, place of use, amount of use and method of use to which the appropriated water will be put. The application must contain *inter alia* "(c) The nature and amount of the proposed use[,] * * * (f) The place where it is intended to use the water" (§ 1260) and, with respect to the storage of water in a reservoir, "the use to be made of the impounded waters...." (§ 1266). The application must set forth information appropriate to the use specified. (See e.g., §§ 1262 [agricultural], 1264 [municipal water supply]; see also Cal.Code Regs., tit. 23, §§ 659–670, 696.) It must contain maps, drawings and other data required by the Board. The map must show "the place of use, and any other features necessary for ready identification and understanding of the project." (Cal.Code Regs., tit. 23, § 715.) * * *

A statement of alternative, potential beneficial uses fails to meet these requirements. Since the DW applications fail to set forth the actual use or uses of the impounded water, it was not possible for the Board to estimate the reasonable amount of water that could be put to any specific beneficial use. The Board attempted to delegate its authority to the Chief, Division of Water Rights to determine these matters after the permits were issued and the Project constructed by a condition attached to the permits, but the authority is not delegable. Although the Board may employ personnel to assist it (§ 186), it may not delegate the authority to determine the merits of an application for a permit to appropriate water, except as provided by statute. * * *

The Water Board argues that "[t]he Water Code does not require that each and every end user be identified before a public interest determination can be made."[17] The argument is made in opposition to appellants' claim the Decision does not support the public interest as required by section 1253.[18] Although section 1253 gives the Water Board broad authority to condition a permit to meet the purposes served by the public interest, it does so within the procedural and substantive confines of the Water Code and the state constitution. The Water Board cannot ignore the detailed statutory and regulatory requirements it must meet in issuing a permit to appropriate water and cannot satisfy a duty

---

9. Section 275 directs that the Water Board and DWR take appropriate action to prevent waste and the unreasonable use of water.

17. It is true that if the water is sold to (say) a water district, the district's individual customers need not be specifically identified. But the district itself must be identified along with the amount of water it plans to use for the beneficial purposes of its customers.

18. Section 1253 provides: "The board shall allow the appropriation for beneficial purposes of unappropriated water under such terms and conditions as in its judgment will best develop, conserve, and utilize in the public interest the water sought to be appropriated." (§ 1253; see also §§ 1240, 1255, 1256.)

imposed on it by the state constitution and the Water Code in issuing a permit by placing it in a condition to a permit.

There is nothing in the public interest provisions of section 1253 that conflicts with the requirements of the Water Code. It authorizes the "appropriation for beneficial purposes of unappropriated water under such terms and conditions as in its judgment will best develop, conserve, and utilize" the water to be appropriated. Although the term "beneficial use" refers to the purpose to which the water to be appropriated will be put, when the phrase "appropriation for beneficial purposes" is used it means, in keeping with the policies of the state constitution and the Water Code, the amount of water that is "reasonably required for the beneficial use to be served...." (§ 100.) It presupposes an actual appropriation of a specified and reasonable amount of water for use for a beneficial purpose at a designated place.

Nor can the Water Board satisfy its responsibility on the view that since there is a general shortage of water in California all of the water impounded in the DW reservoirs could be put to beneficial use by someone for any of the beneficial purposes listed in the Decision. As noted, the statutes speak of actual, not potential uses. A contract or contracts for the sale of the impounded water to one or more of possible users of the water need not involve the use of all of the water that is available for appropriation and diversion from the Delta to the reservoirs or may involve an unreasonable use or means of use. If a choice of use is at issue the Board is enjoined to "consider the relative benefit to be derived from ... all beneficial uses" to which the water might be put. (§ 1257.) Lastly, in allowing the service area to be specified as the area served by the CVP and the SWP, the Board has done little more than say the water should be used in California. * * *

We conclude that DW failed to set forth in its application, and the Water Board failed to determine, the actual, intended use or uses of the water to be appropriated for any of the beneficial purposes listed in the Decision and consequently failed to meet the criteria of the Water Code and implementing regulations for determining the reasonable amount of water required for a specific beneficial use. * * *

Note

Following the above decision's reversal of the Board's grant of the permit, one Board member was quoted as saying "We believe that this decision ... will make it extremely unlikely that future groundwater banks or other future water-storage programs will go forward." San Joaquin Record, Dec. 8, 2004.

Problem

A major oil company obtained a conditional permit for water to process oil shale in Western Colorado 30 years ago. Vast amounts of oil shale are present, and huge sums have been invested over the years in trying to make shale profitable to mine, though so far without success. One of these days, because of a technological breakthrough or world political conditions, shale

may become marketable.[1] The oil company clearly believes this is an investment it should pursue for the long run, and it is willing to spend what is
necessary to maintain its land and water options. Still, decades have passed
and nothing is going on. Should the state invalidate the conditional permit
for lack of due diligence? In considering applications to appropriate from the
same source by others, who have live projects ready to go forward, how
should the permit granting authorities calculate whether there is water
available for appropriation? See Municipal Subdist., N. Colo. Water Conservancy Dist. v. Chevron Shale Oil Co., 986 P.2d 918 (Colo. 1999).

SHOKAL v. DUNN

Supreme Court of Idaho, 1985.
109 Idaho 330, 707 P.2d 441.

BISTLINE, JUSTICE.

On December 21, 1978, respondent Trout Co. applied for a permit to
appropriate 100 c.f.s. of waters from Billingsley Creek near Hagerman,
Idaho. Numerous protests were filed. * * * The Department of Water
Resources * * * issued Permit No. 36–7834 on November 14, 1979.
* * *

Some of the protestants sought judicial review. * * * On December
22, 1980, Judge Schroeder issued an opinion and order reversing the
decision of the Director of Water Resources. * * * He held that the
applicant for a permit had the burden of showing the impact of the
project on the public resource, whereas a party who claimed a harm
peculiar to himself had the burden of going forward to establish that
harm. Judge Schroeder also determined that Water Resources had failed
to properly evaluate the question of "local public interest," holding that
the applicant had the ultimate burden of proving that a proposed water
use was in the local public interest under I.C. § 42–203A. * * *

Under I.C. § 42–203A(5)(e), if an applicant's appropriation of water
"will conflict with the local public interest, where the local public
interest is defined as the affairs of the people in the area directly affected
by the proposed use," then the Director "may reject such application and
refuse issuance of a permit therefor, or may partially approve and grant
a permit for a smaller quantity of water than applied for, or may grant a
permit upon conditions." * * *

The authority and duty of the Director to protect the public interest
spring naturally from the statute; the more difficult task for us is to
define "the local public interest." Public interest provisions appear
frequently in the statutes of the prior appropriation states of the West,
but are explicated rarely. See e.g., Cal. Water Code § 1253; see generally

1. An AP story dated October 4, 2005,
datelined Meeker, Colorado says: "This is
ground zero for the latest push to unlock
shale oil, sometimes called the energy of the
future. Skeptics say it will always be the
energy of the future—a mirage that has led
to disappointing economic results for the
better part of a century. Yet oil shale is
looking more attractive. * * * [with] the
price of crude * * * holding above $60 a
barrel.* * * [Still] [t]echnological hurdles
remain daunting * * * "

1 R. Clark, ed., Waters and Water Rights, § 29.3 (1967). I.C. § 42–203A provides little guidance. Fortunately, however, the legislature did provide guidance in a related statute, I.C. § 42–1501.

In I.C. § 42–1501, the legislature declared it "in the public interest" that:

> the streams of this state and their environments be protected against loss of water supply to preserve the minimum stream flows required for the protection of fish and wildlife habitat, aquatic life, recreation, aesthetic beauty, transportation and navigation values, and water quality.

Not only is the term "public interest" common to both §§ 42–1501 and 42–203A, and the two sections common to the same title * * *, but also the legislature approved the term "public interest" in both sections on the same day, * * *. Clearly, the legislature in § 42–203A must have intended the public interest on the local scale to include the public interest elements listed in § 42–1501: "fish and wildlife habitat, aquatic life, recreation, aesthetic beauty, transportation and navigation values, and water quality." Accord, National Water Commission, New Directions in U.S. Water Policy 5 (1973) ("The people of the United States give far greater weight to environmental and aesthetic values than they did when the nation was young and less settled."), cited in R. Robie, The Public Interest in Water Rights Administration, 23 Rocky Mtn. Min. L. Inst. 917, 933 (1977).

In so intending, the legislature was in good company. Unlike other state public interest statutes, the Alaska statute enumerates the elements of the public interest. The public interest elements of I.C. § 42–1501 are almost precisely duplicated within the Alaska statute. * * *

Alaska Stat. § 46.15.080 provides:

(b) In determining the public interest, the commissioner shall consider

(1) the benefit to the applicant resulting from the proposed appropriation;

(2) the effect of the economic activity resulting from the proposed appropriation;

(3) the effect on fish and game resources and on public recreational opportunities;

(4) the effect on public health;

(5) the effect of loss of alternate uses of water that might be made within a reasonable time if not precluded or hindered by the proposed appropriation;

(6) harm to other persons resulting from the proposed appropriation;

(7) the intent and ability of the applicant to complete the appropriation; and

(8) the effect upon access to navigable or public waters.

The Alaska statute contains other elements which common sense argues ought to be considered part of the local public interest. These include the proposed appropriation's benefit to the applicant, its economic effect, its effect "of loss of alternative uses of water that might be made within a reasonable time if not precluded or hindered by the proposed appropriation," its harm to others, its "effect upon access to navigable or public waters," and "the intent and ability of the applicant to complete the appropriation." Alaska Stat. § 46.5.080(b).

Several other public interest elements, though obvious, deserve specific mention. These are: assuring minimum stream flows, as specifically provided in I.C. § 42–1501, discouraging waste, and encouraging conservation. * * *

The above-mentioned elements of the public interest are not intended to be a comprehensive list. As observed long ago by the New Mexico Supreme Court, the "public interest" should be read broadly in order to "secure the greatest possible benefit from [the public waters] for the public." Young & Norton v. Hinderlider, 15 N.M. 666, 110 P. 1045, 1050 (1910) (rejects considering only public health and safety; considers relative costs of two projects.). By using the general term "the local public interest," the legislature intended to include any locally important factor impacted by proposed appropriations.

Of course, not every appropriation will impact every one of the above elements. Nor will the elements have equal weight in every situation. The relevant elements and their relative weights will vary with local needs, circumstances, and interests. For example, in an area heavily dependent on recreation and tourism or specifically devoted to preservation in its natural state, Water Resources may give great consideration to the aesthetic and environmental ramifications of granting a permit which calls for substantial modification of the landscape or the stream.

Those applying for permits and those challenging the application bear the burden of demonstrating which elements of the public interest are impacted and to what degree. As Judge Schroeder correctly noted below, this burden of production lies with the party

> that has knowledge peculiar to himself. For example, the designer of a fish facility has particularized knowledge of the safeguards or their lack concerning the numbers of fish that may escape and the amount of fecal material that will be discharged into the river. As to such information the applicant should have the burden of going forward and ultimately the burden of proof on the impact on the local public interest. On the other hand, a protestant who claims a harm peculiar to himself should have the burden of going forward to establish that harm.

However, the burden of proof in all cases as to where the public interest lies, as Judge Schroeder also correctly noted, rests with the applicant: [I]t is not [the] protestant's burden of proof to establish that the project is not in the local public interest. The burden of proof is upon the applicant to show that the project is either in the local public interest or that there are factors that overweigh the local public interest in favor of the project. The determination of what elements of the public interest are impacted, and what the public interest requires, is committed to Water Resources' sound discretion. See 1 R. Clark, ed., Waters and Water Rights § 29.3, 170 (1967). In light of the preceding discussion, the district court admirably established some of the public interest elements which Water Resources must consider in this case. Judge Schroeder observed:

> First, as previously outlined, if the Department gives weight to the economic benefits of the project, it should also give consideration to the economic detriments. The effect of the project on water quality should be considered. It is not clear to what extent that was done in this case. The effect of the project on alternative uses of the watercourse should be considered—e.g., the impact on recreational and scenic uses. The effect on vegetation, wildlife, and other fish should be considered. This is not a catalogue of all factors that may relate to the public interest element, but is a suggestion of factors to be weighed in determining whether the project will or will not be in the public interest.

Notes and Questions

1. In a later case (Hardy v. Higginson, 123 Idaho 485, 849 P.2d 946 (1993)), the Court held that an application to amend an existing permit (to secure an additional point of diversion) was also subject to the "local public interest" standard, including elements of the permit the applicant had not sought to change. It rejected the applicant's claim that such action violated his vested right to divert water. The Court held that "water permits only give * * * an inchoate or contingent right to put the water to beneficial use [and that] it was not improper for the Director to impose conditions upon his whole permit based on the local public interest." 849 P.2d at 948. A permittee who finds the conditions unsatisfactory can withdraw his application for amendment and be left with what he had before. The Director had required that at one of the applicant's diversion points upstream of the place where the applicant sought an amendment, and which was above a fish pool of a species that requires cold, clean water, the applicant would henceforth be allowed to divert only to the extent that he would not decrease the water levels, temperature, quality and flow velocity within the pool. The Court said that "in an area heavily dependent on recreation and tourism * * * [the state water agency] may give great consideration to the aesthetic and environmental ramifications of granting or amending a permit which calls for substantial modification of the landscape or stream." Id.

2. The Supreme Court of Idaho sustained an administrative determination under Idaho Code § 42–203A that it was not in the public interest to use the water from a geothermal aquifer to irrigate crops, since the water

was more valuable for heating purposes. Collins Bros. v. Dunn, 114 Idaho 600, 759 P.2d 891 (1988).

3. In Stempel v. Department of Water Resources, 82 Wash.2d 109, 508 P.2d 166 (1973), the Court held that in considering an application for an appropriation to supply water to a residential subdivision the Department was obliged to take into account potential pollution resulting from further abstraction of water from the lake that was to be the source of the appropriation. The Department had claimed that its jurisdiction extended only to water supply and that issues of pollution, sanitation, sewage and health difficulties were the task of other agencies of government. The Court rejected this claim, holding that enactment of the state Environmental Policy Act (Wash. Rev. Code § 43.21C) and the Water Resources Act (Wash. Rev. Code § 90.54), by elevating the importance of environmental issues, had made environmental protection the mandate of every state and local agency and department.

4. California has a state water plan that sets out a general strategy for meeting future water needs. An appellate court has held that the plan is not binding in permit proceedings, but can be considered as a factor in the permit-granting decision. Johnson Rancho County Water Dist. v. State Water Rights Bd., 235 Cal.App.2d 863, 45 Cal.Rptr. 589 (1965). In United Plainsmen Ass'n v. North Dakota State Water Conservation Comm'n, 247 N.W.2d 457 (N.D. 1976), the Court held that permits for an energy production facility could not be granted until there was a comprehensive short and long term plan for the conservation and development of the State's natural resources. The court was a bit vague about the required planning: "The legislature has indicated its desire to see such planning take place, although not in mandatory language. Until the legislature speaks more forcefully, we think the Public Trust Doctrine requires * * * evidence of some planning by appropriate state agencies and officers * * *." Id. at 463. Texas provides that permits must be consistent with a regional water plan. See Tex. Water Code Ann. § 11.1501.

5. For a discussion of public interest criteria, see David Getches, Water Planning: Untapped Opportunity for the Western States, 9 J. Energy & Policy 1 (1988); Douglas Grant, Public Interest Review of Water Right Allocation and Transfer in the West: Recognition of Public Values, 19 Ariz. St. L.J. 681 (1987). Colorado continues to eschew a public interest standard. Aspen Wilderness Workshop v. Hines Highlands, 929 P.2d 718, 725 (Colo. 1996). For more expansive discussions of the public interest in water allocation, see A. Dan Tarlock & Sarah B. Van de Wetering, Growth Management and Western Water Law: From Urban Oases to Archipelagos, 5 Hastings W.-Nw. J. Envtl. L. & Pol'y 163 (1999); and David H. Getches, Changing the River's Course, Western Water Policy Reform, 26 Envtl. L. 157 (1996).

6. The Montana law sets different criteria for small and large appropriations:

85–2–311. Criteria for issuance of permit

(1) A permit may be issued under this part prior to the adjudication of existing water rights in a source of supply. In a permit proceeding under this part there is no presumption that an appli-

cant for a permit cannot meet the statutory criteria of this section prior to the adjudication of existing water rights pursuant to this chapter. In making a determination under this section, the department may not alter the terms and conditions of an existing water right or an issued certificate, permit, or state water reservation. Except as provided in subsections (3) and (4), the department shall issue a permit if the applicant proves by a preponderance of evidence that the following criteria are met:

(a) (i) there is water physically available at the proposed point of diversion in the amount that the applicant seeks to appropriate; and

(ii) water can reasonably be considered legally available during the period in which the applicant seeks to appropriate, in the amount requested, based on the records of the department and other evidence provided to the department. Legal availability is determined using an analysis involving the following factors:

(A) identification of physical water availability;

(B) identification of existing legal demands on the source of supply throughout the area of potential impact by the proposed use; and

(C) analysis of the evidence on physical water availability and the existing legal demands, including but not limited to a comparison of the physical water supply at the proposed point of diversion with the existing legal demands on the supply of water.

(b) the water rights of a prior appropriator under an existing water right, a certificate, a permit, or a state water reservation will not be adversely affected. In this subsection (1)(b), adverse effect must be determined based on a consideration of an applicant's plan for the exercise of the permit that demonstrates that the applicant's use of the water will be controlled so the water right of a prior appropriator will be satisfied;

(c) the proposed means of diversion, construction, and operation of the appropriation works are adequate;

(d) the proposed use of water is a beneficial use;

(e) the applicant has a possessory interest, or the written consent of the person with the possessory interest, in the property where the water is to be put to beneficial use;

(f) the water quality of a prior appropriator will not be adversely affected;

(g) the proposed use will be substantially in accordance with the classification of water set for the source of supply pursuant to 75–5–301(1); and

(h) the ability of a discharge permitholder to satisfy effluent limitations of a permit issued in accordance with Title 75, chapter 5, part 4, will not be adversely affected.

(2) The applicant is required to prove that the criteria in subsections (1)(f) through (1)(h) have been met only if a valid objection is filed. A valid objection must contain substantial credible information establishing to the satisfaction of the department that the criteria in subsection (1)(f), (1)(g), or (1)(h), as applicable, may not be met. For the criteria set forth in subsection (1)(g), only the department of environmental quality or a local water quality district established under Title 7, chapter 13, part 45, may file a valid objection.

(3) The department may not issue a permit for an appropriation of 4,000 or more acre-feet of water a year and 5.5 or more cubic feet per second of water unless the applicant proves by clear and convincing evidence that:

(a) the criteria in subsection (1) are met;

(b) the proposed appropriation is a reasonable use. A finding must be based on a consideration of the following:

(i) the existing demands on the state water supply, as well as projected demands, such as reservations of water for future beneficial purposes, including municipal water supplies, irrigation systems, and minimum streamflows for the protection of existing water rights and aquatic life;

(ii) the benefits to the applicant and the state;

(iii) the effects on the quantity and quality of water for existing beneficial uses in the source of supply;

(iv) the availability and feasibility of using low-quality water for the purpose for which application has been made;

(v) the effects on private property rights by any creation of or contribution to saline seep; and

(vi) the probable significant adverse environmental impacts of the proposed use of water as determined by the department pursuant to Title 75, chapter 1, or Title 75, chapter 20.

(4) (a) The state of Montana has long recognized the importance of conserving its public waters and the necessity to maintain adequate water supplies for the state's water requirements, including requirements for federal non-Indian and Indian reserved water rights held by the United States for federal reserved lands and in trust for the various Indian tribes within the state's boundaries. Although the state of Montana also recognizes that, under appropriate conditions, the out-of-state transportation and use of its public waters are not in conflict with the public welfare of its citizens or the conservation of its waters, the criteria in this subsection (4) must be met before out-of-state use may occur. * * *

7. *Shokal* sets out the provisions of the much-praised Alaska statute. The criteria of the new Montana statute appear in the preceding paragraph. How would the following cases be resolved under the Alaska law? Under the Montana law?

● A state agency granted a permit to divert water from a river and store it in a reservoir for subsequent irrigation and municipal use, but it imposed the following condition: "The reservoir shall be kept open to the public for recreational use subject to a reasonable charge for any services * * * provided by permittee * * *." The Agency claimed that the condition was a trade-off for diminished recreational value in the river from which the diversions were to be made, but the court held that the evidence did not support any such finding. A California court held such a condition impermissible, stating "While fully accepting the rule giving primacy to the public interest, * * * [the] condition constitutes an onerous burden. The Board * * * has the jurisdiction and the right to impose a condition requiring public access but only for precise and specific reasons founded on tangible record evidence." Bank of America v. State Water Resources Control Bd., 42 Cal.App.3d 198, 116 Cal.Rptr. 770 (1974).

● Thinking back to Environmental Defense Fund v. East Bay Mun. Util. Dist., supra p. 191, what if the Board had denied a permit under the public interest provision because it found that a city seeking new water could meet its asserted needs by reclamation of water it was already appropriating? If it found that the city could meet its needs by raising prices to residents, thus reducing demand for non-essential uses? Because it determined that preserving whitewater boating was more important than maintaining lawns in the city?

8. Whatever state statutes might provide, state officials often have shown themselves reluctant to implement the public interest standard. A 1994 decision of the New Mexico State Engineer decision, for example, concluded that "a statutorily recognized beneficial use of water is not against the public welfare of the state," cited in Consuelo Bokum, Implementing the Public Welfare Requirement in New Mexico's Water Code, 36 Nat. Res. J. 681, 691 n. 69 (1996). Similarly, though Nevada's statute commands the State Engineer to refuse to issue a permit where the proposed use "threatens to prove detrimental to the public interest" (Nev. Rev. Stat. § 533.370(4) (2004)), that official has taken a very narrow view of the statutory obligation—excluding consideration of economic factors or analysis of alternatives—and the State Supreme Court has sustained that position. Pyramid Lake Paiute Tribe v. Washoe County, 112 Nev. 743, 918 P.2d 697 (1996).

b. *Area of Origin Protection as a Test of the Public Interest*

In the preceding pages we have been considering the public interest as an issue in deciding whether to permit a particular use or a particular transfer of a water right. There is another "public interest" issue that arises on a much larger scale: Should water be exported from its area of origin at all for use in distant places? If such exports are permitted what, if any, protection or compensation ought to be given to the place of origin? These issues usually do not arise as claims of formal legal rights. They ordinarily appear as political conflicts between competing regions that lead to a statutory resolution. The materials that follow are meant to give you a sense of the nature and treatment of claims made on behalf of areas of origin.

You no doubt noticed that the Alaska permit statute (supra p. 228) addresses alternative uses of the water that might have been made but for the applicant's proposal, as well as harm to others. The most controversial version of each of these concerns is presented when a major trans-basin diversion is planned. There are a number of celebrated examples, some of them completed realities and others perennial proposals.[1] Denver transports water across the continental divide from western to eastern Colorado. New York City takes much of its water from the Delaware River. Southern California takes water both from the Sacramento and from the Colorado River Basins. In the most bitterly resented of all such developments, Los Angeles took water both from the Owens Valley and the tributaries of Mono Lake.

The element common to all such projects is that a highly developed and water-short area takes its supply from a less-developed and more water-abundant area. Put in terms of the material we have just studied, the question is whether such projects are in the public interest. Those who live in the areas of origin often do not think so. They feel strongly that the water belongs to them (it does not, according to appropriation doctrine theory). They tend to see water not just as property, but as their heritage, their opportunity for future growth and development. Moreover, they frequently view out-of-basin diversions as Robin Hood in reverse, uncompensated transfers from the poor to the rich. One obvious such example was the historic allocation of the Carson and Truckee Rivers in Nevada to irrigators at the expense of the Pyramid Lake Paiute Reservation Indians.

Traditionally local communities had no authority to constrain projects that transferred water to distant places. The assumption was, as Professor Dan Tarlock put it, "that the enactment of a statewide water code administered by a state official is good evidence of express intent to displace local regulation * * *. Because the assumption that the state had the exclusive authority to allocate the resource was so widely shared, local governments had little incentive to limit the exercise of state water rights and courts seldom had to preempt local efforts."[2] Yet communities in areas of origin have always intuitively viewed water arising locally as "theirs." In recent years area-of-origin protection has increasingly evidenced itself in legal form.

1. It has often been suggested that water be taken from the Columbia River basin, or even the Yukon, to the arid southwest (see Chapin Clark, Northwest–Southwest Diversion—Plans and Issues, 3 Willamette L.J. 215 (1965)); from the Great Lakes to the high plains of Texas; or from the Great Lakes via tankers to arid regions of the world. High costs and environmental concerns have put such schemes on the back burner.

2. Land Use L., Nov. 1998, at 4. However some state laws prohibit local water districts from exporting their water, even if they want to do so, which is an obstacle to voluntary marketing. See Alameda County Flood Control & Water Conservation Dist. Act, Cal. Stats. 1949, ch. 1275, at West's Ann. Cal. Water Code App. § 55–4.

A Colorado law demands that a "compensating" reservoir be built on the Western slope of the mountains when a trans-continental-divide diversion is made to serve the more populous Eastern slope. The Colorado Watershed Protection law requires exportations from the basin of the Colorado River to "be designed, constructed and operated in such manner that the present appropriations of water, and in addition thereto prospective uses * * * within the natural basin of the Colorado River * * * will not be impaired nor increased in cost at the expense of the water users within the natural basin." Colo. Rev. Stat. § 37–45–118(1)(b)(II). See Colorado River Water Conservation Dist. v. Municipal Subdistrict, 198 Colo. 352, 610 P.2d 81 (1979); City of Grand Junction v. City & County of Denver, 960 P.2d 675 (Colo. 1998). Colorado has sustained the authority of a west slope county to impose permit requirements on transbasin diversions, and to deny a permit where the diversion structure would impair a wetland. City of Colorado Springs v. Board of County Comm'rs, 895 P.2d 1105 (Colo. App. 1994).

Montana allows governmental entities to reserve water with a current priority date for anticipated future needs; need is established by showing that future in-state or out-of-state competing water uses would consume, degrade, or otherwise affect available water. Municipal reservations are given preferential status. Mont. Code Ann. § 85–2–316; see Mary McNally & Olen Matthews, Changing the Balance in Western Water Law? Montana's Reservation System, 35 Nat. Res. J. 671 (1995).

A California county asserting a right to prohibit the export of groundwater has prevailed on its preemption argument against a claim that the field was preempted by the state. Baldwin v. County of Tehama, 31 Cal.App.4th 166, 36 Cal.Rptr.2d 886 (1994)[3] as did a county zoning ordinance governing the location of reservoirs, Delta Wetlands Properties v. County of San Joaquin, 121 Cal.App.4th 128, 16 Cal.Rptr.3d 672 (Ct.App. 2004). Note how such decisions change the dynamics of a situation where an investor buys up substantial land areas overlying undeveloped groundwater supplies in order to sell that water at high prices to a thirsty city.[4] The problem has a public version as well. The Las Vegas area, running short of water to meet its fast-growing population, seeks to obtain and transport groundwater resources from distant rural counties, one of which was reportedly making uncommon cause with the Sierra Club to launch an environmental assessment of the project, according to the Las Vegas Review Journal of Apr. 30, 2005.

Contemporary water law evinces a deep tension between the tradition of export, on the one hand, and what Professor Tarlock calls a new

---

3. The California situation is complicated (or perhaps explained) by the fact that there is no statewide regulation of groundwater. See Antonio Rossman, County Groundwater Regulation: Half a Governor's Commission Legacy is Better than None, 36 McGeorge L.R. 457 (2005). California groundwater is discussed at length in chapter 5.

4. A much publicized proposal was one by Texas oil mogul T. Boone Pickens to transport water "from the arid Panhandle to fill swimming pools and irrigate golf courses in Dallas." Karen Breslau, Wildcatting for Water, Newsweek, Sept. 2, 2002, at 32.

western riparianism, on the other.[5] He points to a variety of modern devices calculated to keep water at home, such as instream flow appropriations, Indian water rights that claim water for reservations, public interest restrictions on appropriations, Endangered Species Act demands to restore aquatic ecosystems, and public trust claims. Ironically, considering its relative abundance, nowhere is water-possessiveness more deeply felt than in the Great Lakes States, where any whisper of export is viewed as a sort of regional treason.[6] A number of states have enacted legislation requiring the impacts of interbasin transfers to be assessed and areas of origin protected, as considerations in permit proceedings.[7]

The area of origin issue presents an intriguing question of public policy. Should water stay where it is, to be treated as an asset of the local people, or to protect natural values *in situ?* Or is it an asset of some larger community, to go where it is presently most needed? How should need be characterized in such controversies? Are the demands of recreational users for whitewater rivers in northern California more pressing than the needs of Los Angeles for drinking water, or lawn watering? If that is not the right comparison, how should the problem be stated? Would the problem be solved if water was sold to the highest bidder, or leased for a limited period of time? Is the answer to give compensation to the area of origin, or allow it to call back exported water if and when it needs it? Should environmental interests in Northern California be empowered to limit exports to the South in order to protect the natural values in the San Francisco Bay–Delta (see infra p. 628)?

We will later look at versions of this problem in several settings: public trust claims to protect natural conditions (infra p. 590); efforts of states to prohibit export of water beyond their boundaries (p. 880 infra); the allocation of interstate streams among different states (infra p. 835); and the U.S.-Mexico conflict over the Colorado River (infra p. 808). For the moment, we pause briefly to look at the response of one state, California, to the traumatic aftermath of Los Angeles' raid on the Owens Valley to slake its municipal thirst. You might ponder these two questions: (1) Was Los Angeles wrong to go far afield to serve its growing demands (and, if it was, what should it have done instead)? (2) Assuming an area of origin is entitled to some protection against other regions that want the water it contains, what sort of legal protections should it receive?

Some of the greatest area-of-origin battles have arisen in California. While there is a great deal of water in the state, from the perspective of human use it both originates in, and flows to, the wrong places. Most of

5. A. Dan Tarlock, New Water Transfer Restrictions: The West Returns to Riparianism, 27 Water Resources Res. 987 (1991).

6. See infra pp. 898–902.

7. See, e.g., Or. Rev. Stat. §§ 537.801 et seq.; Neb. Rev. Stat. § 46–289; Wy. Stat. § 41–2–121(a)(ii)(E)(VIII). A number of Eastern states also have interbasin transfer laws designed to protect future needs of the basin of origin. See, e.g., Minn. Stat. § 103G.265(2); Conn. Gen. Stat. § 22a–369(10); S.C. Stat. § 49–21–20; Mass. Gen. Laws ch. 21 §§ 8C–8D.

the water arises in the North Coastal (Trinity, Mad and Eel Rivers) and Sacramento Basins, and in its natural state flows out to the sea, either on the north coast or through San Francisco Bay via the "Delta," where the Sacramento and San Joaquin Rivers meet. The principal areas of need, both for agriculture and for municipal water supply, however, are in the Central Valley south of the Delta and in the Los Angeles and San Diego regions—which import water from elsewhere. The San Francisco Bay area also imports its water from mountain streams, rather than waiting until the water reaches the end of a "natural" pipeline. The reason is that water is usually of better quality upstream before it has been used one or more times. Figure 3–4 shows the sources of water for California cities and agriculture.

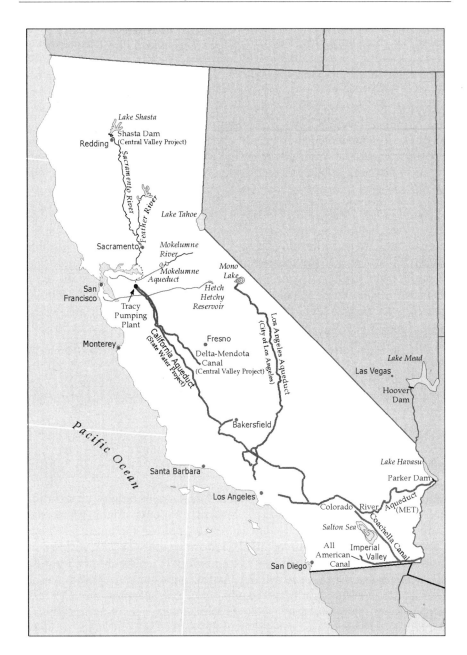

Figure 3–4

Major Water Conveyance Facilities in California

The Hetch Hetchy reservoir, which serves San Francisco, is in Yosemite National Park, and in the years before the First World War, was the source of a titanic conservation battle which led to establishment of the Sierra Club.[8] The East Bay, where Berkeley and Oakland are located, is principally served by the Mokelumne River, and the American River is sought as a supplemental source of supply. Both the Owens Valley aqueduct, and its extension to Mono Lake on the east side of Yosemite, which serve Los Angeles, have sparked bitter controversy. Los Angeles is now served by three import areas: Owens Valley/Mono Lake, the Colorado River, and the Sacramento River, through the California Aqueduct, in addition to its own limited local supplies. Also a good deal of water from the Colorado River is carried to the Imperial and Coachella irrigation districts in extreme south-central California via the Coachella and All–American Canals.

The Owens Valley controversy is the most celebrated area-of-origin battle in the history of water law. The history of Los Angeles' search for water in the Owens Valley on the east side of Mount Whitney, beginning around 1905, is one of the most dramatic stories anywhere generated by the problems of aridity. It even included bombings of the diversion works by outraged local citizens, and the calling out of the militia. The story has been frequently told, not only in scholarly books,[9] but in several novels,[10] and the popular movie Chinatown as well.

Put as succinctly as possible, Los Angeles, with the connivance of many local people and the federal Bureau of Reclamation, bought up riparian rights on the Owens River, and land and existing appropriation rights in the Owens Valley, thus gaining control over the river. The city built an aqueduct to Los Angeles (all by gravity flow, which also gave it the opportunity to generate power as the water flowed in the aqueduct), and as demand in the city and the San Fernando Valley grew, it gradually took all the Owens Valley land out of production, or the possibility of production. The story has usually been portrayed as one of totally unfeeling chicanery on the part of Los Angeles, and of devastation of a community's opportunity to develop. Without doubt there was cunning to spare on the part of the city and its allies, including a scheme to assure that the Bureau of Reclamation would not aid the Valley farmers in building the facilities they needed to cultivate their lands, thus in effect forcing them to sell out. At the same time, at least once the die was cast, Valley interests fought for and obtained considerable compensation for what they sold. The ultimate question—still being debated—is whether rural areas like the Owens Valley should be sacrificed, at any price or upon any terms, to advance the interests of modern cities. One irony of the Owens Valley history is that, as a result of Los

8. Holway Jones, John Muir and The Sierra Club: The Battle for Yosemite (1965).

9. The best and most recent recountings are William Kahrl, Water and Power (1982) and Marc Reisner, Cadillac Desert (1986). See also Vincent Ostrum, Water and Politics: A Study of Water Policies and Administration in the Development of Los Angeles

(1953); Abraham Hoffman, Vision or Villainy: Origins of the Owens Valley–Los Angeles Water Controversy (1981).

10. Frances Gregg & George Putnam, Golden Valley: A Novel of California (1950); Peter Kyne, The Long Chance (1914); Mary Austin, The Ford (1917).

Angeles' activities, the Valley has been returned to nature and has enjoyed some recent revival as a recreational destination.[11]

In any event, in reaction to Owens Valley, the California legislature declared the water rights of subsequent interregional projects, such as the Central Valley Project (CVP) and the State Water Project (SWP) to be subordinate to the rights of users within the areas from which the project water originates.[12] The history of these laws is detailed in Ronald B. Robie & Russell R.Kletzing, Area of Origin Statutes: The California Experience, 15 Idaho L. Rev. 419, 426–31 (1979). For many years these laws had never yet been invoked, but the Court of Appeals described them as "reserv[ing] to the areas of origin an undefined preferential right to future water needs."[13] Recently, however, they have been asserted in several settings, though there has not yet been any decisive litigation.1[14] In the Summer of 2000, the Westlands Water District, having experienced declared shortages in its imported northern California water from the federal Central Valley Project, asserted area-of-origin rights to San Joaquin River water which originates in Fresno County for its Fresno County lands (Water Code §§ 10504.01, 10505), and for its lands in the watershed of the San Joaquin (Water Code § 11460) against farmers on the east side of the Central Valley, who have long received water diverted out of the San Joaquin and transported to them. The claim, subsequently dropped, was described by the Fresno Bee newspaper at the time as "a choice to go nuclear in the state's long-running water wars."

A more interesting example arose in 2003 when a growing northern California city in the Sacramento area (Fairfield), anticipating a shortage to meet urban demand, decided to pursue the watershed-of-origin provision of Water Code § 11460,[15] rather than buying water from agricultur-

11. The battle over the Owens Valley has been fought on several fronts. Litigation challenged Los Angeles' pumping of groundwater in the Valley under California's environmental quality laws. See Antonio Rossmann & Michael Steel, Forging the New Water Law: Public Regulation of "Proprietary" Groundwater Rights, 33 Hastings L.J. 903, 914 (1982). The controversy appears to have been settled with an agreement not to increase exports and to manage pumping to control impacts on regulation and groundwater quality.

12. Cal. Water Code §§ 10505, 10505.5, 11128 (Central Valley Project); id. § 11460 (State Water Project); id. §§ 12200–12205 (Delta Protection Act).

13. United States v. State Water Resources Control Bd., 182 Cal.App.3d 82, 139, 227 Cal.Rptr. 161, 194 (1986).

14. The only extant authority is a 1955 California Attorney General Opinion which opines that those in the areas of origin could stop the exports and take the water at any time in the future that it was needed

for their reasonable uses—they could recapture the water. 25 Ops. Cal.Atty.Gen. 32. There is also an opinion finding the laws constitutional, id., at 8.

15. The 1933 statute provides, in relevant part: "In the construction and operation by the department of any project under the provisions of this part [,] a watershed or area wherein water originates ... which can conveniently be supplied with water therefrom, shall not be deprived by the department directly or indirectly of the prior right to all of the water reasonably required to adequately supply the beneficial needs of the watershed, area, or any of the inhabitants or property owners therein ... [§ 11460] The provisions of this article shall not be so construed as to create any new property rights other than against the department as provided in this part or to require the department to furnish to any person without adequate compensation therefor any water made available by the construction of any works by the department. [§ 11462]"

al sources. The cities were already getting some State Water Project water through one of its facilities, the North Bay Aqueduct, and in effect they claimed they were entitled to get additional water wheeled through that facility to them without further cost (claiming the Project had deprived them of the opportunity to build their own facilities), and in priority to those in the south who had been receiving water exported by the Project. The matter was ultimately settled without litigation, with the cities getting water but agreeing to some payment for it. The Department wanted to avoid a judicial decision on such questions as the claimants' priorities, their entitlement to wheeling through Project facilities, what if any payments the claimants would be obliged to make under the area-of-origin laws, and if the claimants bore any responsibility for mitigating the environmental impacts of their diversion.[16]

Notes and Questions

1. For background on the development of California export projects projects, see Erwin Cooper, Aqueduct Empire: A Guide to Water in California, Its Turbulent History and Its Management Today (1968). An economic study of the California water industry is Joe Bain, Richard Caves, Julius Margolis, Northern California's Water Industry: The Comparative Efficiency of Public Enterprise in Developing A Scarce Natural Resource (1966).

2. Here is a dissenting view of area-of-origin protections. "Guarantees of 'area of origin' protection rest fundamentally on the mistaken notion that water is a unique, special substance for which there is no substitute. Except in some physical sense, it is not; in an economic sense there are substitutes. It is very doubtful that any area will 'recapture' its water once it has been dedicated for another purpose. That a region has a stake in its water and therefore some right to compensation cannot be doubted; direct money payments by beneficiaries would of course provide the most flexible and economical system of exchange. * * * Hopefully, the pay-off will not be restricted to aqueous currency—leading to the authorization of ever more doubtful projects—but that the pay-off may come in some other form of public investment promising equal or greater return than the lost water. The foregone benefits associated with the export of water should be calculated, for which compensation should be provided either by the Nation or by those who profit directly and indirectly from the transfer." Dean Mann, Interbasin Water Transfers: Political and Institutional Analysis (report prepared for the National Water Commission, March 1972). Do you agree, either that guarantees are a mistake, or that the locals should be compensated for exports?

3. The people in the area of origin are not the only concern. Protection of natural resources in place may be required under the public trust doctrine. National Audubon Soc. v. Superior Court, infra p. 610.

The "project" applies both to the State Water Project and the Central Valley Project, and the "department" means both the State Department of Water Resources and the federal Bureau of Reclamation (federal law requires Reclamation projects to comply with state law, see California v. United States, infra p. 753).

16. The settlement is detailed in Richard L. Wood, Area-of-Origin Water Rights: A Promise Kept?, 14 Cal. Water Law & Policy Rptr. 291 (July 2004).

4. Why is water law the only resource-centered body of law that concerns itself with the area of origin? The residents of a forested area get no special compensation when trees are cut down and the logs exported. Nor do the residents of an area that is mined, where there is no regeneration of the exported wealth. Is the difference that water is not ordinary private property, and has no private owner, as oil and trees do? Is it that local residents benefit less from water exports than from log exports? Or is water law ahead of other fields in recognizing area of origin rights? Is there a theoretical link between area of origin laws, and the new ideas to compensate "origin" nations where plants are found that lead to development of valuable medicines?

5. Area-of-origin concerns ultimately relate to the issue of growth management. See generally A. Dan Tarlock & Sarah Van de Wetering, Growth Management and Western Water Law: From Urban Oases to Archipelagos, 5 West–Northwest 163 (1999). Importing water is said to facilitate urban sprawl, as well as denying future growth in places of origin. But no cities in the arid west rely exclusively, or even significantly, on indigenous supplies. Ending growth in such places has not been seen as a realistic solution. Instead, the concern is how to manage it effectively, and to assure that development permission is tied to assurance of adequate water supplies to support it, leading to what are known as "show me the water" laws.[1] One state's approach to the problem is illustrated in the following section.

c. Managing Growth by Water Availability: The California Example

ELLEN HANAK,
WATER FOR GROWTH:
CALIFORNIA'S NEW FRONTIER
Public Policy Institute of California (2005)

* * *

Finding enough water to support population growth has become a key resource management challenge for California and other western states. Historically, the region's development was predicated on harnessing water through the construction of large-scale dams, reservoirs, and conveyance facilities. However, over the past 25 years, water supply systems have come under increasing stress * * * seriously challenged on environmental and financial grounds. * * * Meanwhile, population is increasing rapidly. * * * In roughly half of California's cities and in most counties, water supply planning is further complicated by the fact that water utilities and general-purpose governments operate as separate

---

1. Arizona requires that a subdivider obtain a "certificate of assured water supply" from the Director of Water Resources before final plat may be approved—when the subdivision is located in a designated groundwater management area. Ariz. Rev. Stat. § 9–463.01. An assured water supply is defined as "[s]ufficient groundwater, surface water or effluent of adequate quality [that] will be continuously available to satisfy the water needs of the proposed use for at least *one hundred years*." Ariz. Rev. Stat. § 45–576 (emphasis added).

entities, whose physical boundaries only partly overlap. City and county governments are responsible for land-use decisions—general and specific plans, subdivision approval, and zoning—which critically affect community water demands. By the early 1990's, concerns over the water demand consequences of some large housing developments led the East Bay Municipal Utilities District (EBMUD) * * * to push for requirements that land-use authorities link their activities to the water planning process.

Over objections by associations representing cities and builders, Senate Bill (SB) 901 was passed in 1995, requiring that local governments conduct water supply assessments during the environmental review for large projects (above 500 units). In 2001, SB 601 strengthened these review requirements, and SB 221 made written verifications of long-term water supply a precondition of final subdivision map approval. * * * [T]hese laws rely largely on citizen enforcement by allowing the public to legally challenge a utility or local government that does not comply. * * *

* * * [These] "show me the water" laws continue to be the subject of considerable debate. * * * [Some] are wary that the new statutes may serve as a tool for antigrowth advocates, unreasonably blocking new housing in a state that already has a housing shortage. * * *

* * * There is * * * [also] surprisingly little discussion of the underlying premise of California's water planning system, which places ultimate responsibility with the local utilities. Yet it is the performance of these utilities, in conjunction with local land-use agencies, that will determine how well the state meets the water supply challenges of growth.

Notes and Questions

1. A series of interlocking laws now seek to deal with the water availability problem. The first tool was the California Environmental Quality Law (CEQA), enacted in 1970,[2] which has been vigorously used to challenge project approvals on the ground that environmental impacts and mitigation have not been adequately addressed, and that "no project" alternatives have not been evaluated. Among the issues have been failure to consider the impact of new water supply infrastructure where a project was planned before a future water supply had been assured;[3] failure to consider the interrelationship of growth and water;[4] or that the project was reliant on a supply that was unlikely to be available, and that "local decision makers are seduced by contractual entitlements [paper water] and approve projects dependent on water worth little more than a wish and a prayer."[5]

2. Cal. Pub. Res. Code § 21000 et seq., Cal. Code Regs. tit. 14 § 15000 et seq.

3. Santiago County Water District v. County of Orange, 118 Cal.App.3d 818 (1981); Stanislaus Natural Heritage Project v. County of Stanislaus, 48 Cal.App.4th 182 (1996).

4. County of Amador v. El Dorado County Water Agency, 76 Cal.App.4th 931 (1999).

5. Planning and Conservation League v. Department of Water Resources, 83 Cal. App.4th 892, 914, 915 (2000).

2. A number of other statutes seek to engage the water/land use problem more directly. In 1983 a law was enacted to require larger municipal supply agencies to prepare and update every five years an urban water management plan, analyzing water reliability and vulnerability under various hydrological conditions.[6] In 1995, the legislature sought to generate increased coordination between local governments and water agencies by requiring discussion and evaluation of water supply in general plans and in CEQA impact reports, though it has no substantive supply requirements.[7] In 2001, several new laws were enacted requiring, among other things, examination of groundwater reliability if a project is dependent on that source, and of water quality.[8]

Finally in a law known as S.B. 221, a substantive supply requirement was enacted.[9] For all residential developments exceeding 500 units, or where service connections are increased by 10% or more, each approval of a tentative subdivision map must be conditioned on a finding that a sufficient water supply will be available to serve the development, and such finding must be supported by written verification from the relevant water agency.

The measuring of sufficiency in the statute is defined as follows:

§ 66473.7. Sufficient Water Supply As Condition for Tentative Map [etc.]

(a) For the purposes of this section, the following definitions apply: * * *

(2) "Sufficient water supply" means the total water supplies available during normal, single-dry, and multiple-dry years within a 20–year projection that will meet the projected demand associated with the proposed subdivision, in addition to existing and planned future uses, including, but not limited to, agricultural and industrial uses. In determining "sufficient water supply," all of the following factors shall be considered:

(A) The availability of water supplies over a historical record of at least 20 years.

(B) The applicability of an urban water shortage contingency analysis prepared pursuant to Section 10632 of the Water Code that includes actions to be undertaken by the public water system in response to water supply shortages.

(C) The reduction in water supply allocated to a specific water use sector pursuant to a resolution or ordinance adopted, or a contract entered into, by the

6. Cal. Water Code § 10610.4 et seq.

7. Cal. Gov't. Code § 65302. This law is known as S.B. 901.

8. Cal. Water Code §§ 10910,10631. These laws are known as S.B. 610 and A.B. 901.

9. Cal. Gov't. Code § 66473.7 (the law does not apply to developments within urbanized areas, but is directed to leap-frog developments).

public water system, as long as that resolution, ordinance, or contract does not conflict with Section 354 of the Water Code.

(D) The amount of water that the water supplier can reasonably rely on receiving from other water supply projects, such as conjunctive use, reclaimed water, water conservation, and water transfer, including programs identified under federal, state, and local water initiatives such as CALFED and Colorado River tentative agreements, to the extent that these water supplies meet the criteria of subdivision (d).

(3) "Public water system" means the water supplier that is, or may become as a result of servicing the subdivision included in a tentative map pursuant to subdivision (b), a public water system, as defined in Section 10912 of the Water Code, that may supply water for a subdivision. * * *

(h) Where a water supply for a proposed subdivision includes groundwater, the public water system serving the proposed subdivision shall evaluate, based on substantial evidence, the extent to which it or the landowner has the right to extract the additional groundwater needed to supply the proposed subdivision. Nothing in this subdivision is intended to modify state law with regard to groundwater rights. * * *

In light of the above definition, could a sustainable finding of a sufficient supply be made in any, or all of the following circumstances, where the developer's water supply is:

a.   Acquired from a project subject to the area of origin laws;

b.   Contaminated groundwater that is the subject of an ongoing cleanup pursuant to a court order;

c.   Subject to call by an appropriator with a more senior priority;

d.   Subject to a shortage declaration, as is California's Colorado River Supply under a U.S. Supreme Court Decree, ¶ II(B)(3) [see infra p. 832];

e.   Acquired from agricultural use in another basin, where the physical facilities for moving the water have not yet been (i) permitted and/or (ii) constructed;

f.   Appropriated water from a river subject to future uses by riparians, or groundwater subject to future use by overlying landowners.

d. *Preferences*

Preference is one of the murkier concepts in water law. It sometimes refers to the ability of permit-granting agencies to favor one of several pending applications on the ground that it is more in the public interest, even though it wasn't first in date of filing, when there is not enough water available to satisfy all of them; or to provide in a permit that a use granted will be subordinate to an anticipated preferred use if and when it later arises. See East Bay Municipal Utility District v. Department of Public Works, 1 Cal.2d 476, 35 P.2d 1027 (1934).

Domestic use is another form of preference. It appears that domestic uses are served prior to all others, even though they are not senior. Some laws seem quite clear on this point. For example, the South Dakota statute provides: It is the established policy of this state: (1) That the use of water for domestic purposes is the highest use of water and takes precedence over all appropriative rights, if it is exercised in a manner consistent with public interest * * * "S.D. Codified Laws § 46–1–5. An uncompensated primacy for domestic uses, regardless of priority, seems to be a general practice even when the domestic preference is expressed more generally, as in California, e.g., Cal. Water Code § 106: "It is hereby declared * * * that the use of water for domestic purposes is the highest use of water and that the next highest use is for irrigation." As to irrigation preference, it is hardly imaginable that California farmers could demand that their unmet needs could displace free of charge senior urban appropriators. It is widely assumed that such laws grant a right of private eminent domain in favor of the preferred use, but there seems to be no explicit authority, statutory or judicial, to that effect. See Robert E. Beck, Use Preferences for Water, 76 N.D. L. Rev. 753, 776–77 (2000). See also Frank J. Trelease, Preferences to the Use of Water, 27 Rocky Mtn. L. Rev. 133 (1955).

There are other statutory preferences which could have significant impact. For example, § 6 of the Boulder Canyon Project Act (43 U.S.C. § 617e, infra p. 821, provides that Hoover dam and Lake Mead "shall be used: First for river regulation, improvement of navigation, and flood control; second for irrigation and domestic uses ... and third, for power." If a shortage were declared by the Secretary of the Interior during a drought (as in provided for under a U.S. Supreme Court Decree, infra p. 832), presumably the Secretary could not favor hydropower production to the disadvantage of irrigation, even though it is vastly more significant economically.

D. LOSS OF APPROPRIATIVE RIGHTS

1. ABANDONMENT AND FORFEITURE

By this point, it should not be surprising to learn that appropriative water rights can be lost by non-use. A system that prohibits speculation, defines beneficial *use* as the limit of the right, and deplores waste, can be expected to take water rights away from those who do not use what they have. What may seem surprising is how reluctant the courts have been to enforce abandonment and forfeiture laws. A dramatic example is a recent Colorado case where for nearly 30 years a company was unable to raise money to line its ditch and use the water it had appropriated. Then it sold the water, and the transaction was sustained, despite a claim of abandonment. Justice Hobbs issued a strong dissent: "We have considered economic difficulty a justifiable excuse for nonuse in very limited circumstances. We recognized the Great Depression, material and labor shortages during World War II. * * * However, run-of-the-mill economic difficulties are not recognized. * * * Without doubt, the investment partnership tried repeatedly to sell the ranch and the water rights. However * * * we [have] held that intent to sell a water right, including listing the right with a real estate agent, was not sufficient to overcome the presumption of abandonment raised by a long period of nonuse." East Twin Lakes Ditches and Water Works, Inc. v. Board of County Commissioners, 76 P.3d 918, 927 (2003).

On another front, new industry coming into arid places may have to think twice about getting the water it needs by buying up old, but doubtful, irrigation rights. In 1998 the State Engineer of New Mexico ruled that Intel Corp. had bought rights to water on land that had not been irrigated since 1941, and that therefore the landowners no longer owned the rights they wished to sell.[10]

The following excerpt is included as a descriptive statement of the two relevant doctrines, abandonment and forfeiture.

JENKINS v. STATE, DEPARTMENT OF WATER RESOURCES

Supreme Court of Idaho, 1982.
103 Idaho 384, 647 P.2d 1256.

SHEPARD, JUDGE.

* * * We note initially that care must be taken in this type of proceeding to distinguish between abandonment and forfeiture. Each is a related concept but each carries with it distinctive requirements. * * *

Abandonment is a common law doctrine involving the occurrence of (1) an intent to abandon and (2) an actual relinquishment or surrender of the water right. Forfeiture, on the other hand, is predicated upon the statutory declaration that all rights to use water are lost where the appropriator fails to make beneficial use of the water for a continuous five year period.

Intent to abandon must be proved by clear and convincing evidence of unequivocal acts, and mere nonuse of a water right, standing alone, is not sufficient for a per se abandonment. Intent to abandon is a question of fact to be decided by the trier of fact. * * * [T]here was no finding by the trial court, nor by the director of the Department, that Jenkins intended to abandon his Cottonwood water right. The record shows only non-use, disclosing no intent to abandon, and hence Jenkins did not lose his water right by common law abandonment.

---

10. High Country News, Feb. 16, 1998, at 6.

We then proceed to a determination of whether the findings are sufficient to support a determination of a statutory forfeiture. * * *

Statutory forfeiture is based upon the legislative declaration in I.C. sec. 42–222(2) that water rights may be lost if they are not applied to a beneficial use for a period of five continuous years. Gilbert v. Smith, 97 Idaho 735, 738, 552 P.2d 1220, 1223 (1976). Certain defenses to forfeiture have been recognized. Extension of the five year period may be made upon a showing of good cause, providing the application for extension is made within the first five-year period. I.C. sec. 42–222(2). Also wrongful interference with a water right or failure to use the water because of circumstances over which the water right holder has no control have been recognized as defenses. * * * Further, if use of the water right is resumed after the five year period, but before any third parties make a claim in the water, then the courts will decline to declare a forfeiture. * * *

Forfeitures are not favored, and clear and convincing proof is required to support a forfeiture. * * * Here it was found that Jenkins had not used his Cottonwood water right for 18 years i.e., 1961–1979. It is clear that the director of the Department of Water Resources relied on the forfeiture statute in his decision, and that decision was affirmed by the trial court "in all respects". While the record could have been made more clear by a specific conclusion of the trial court as to forfeiture, we do not deem such absence to be fatal here.

Question

Can a modern forfeiture statute constitutionally be applied to pre-code appropriation rights, acquired when only common law abandonment was the law? See Janet C. Neuman & Keith Hirokawa, How Good is an Old Water Right? The Application of Statutory Forfeiture Provisions to Pre–Code Water Rights, 4 U. Denver Water L. Rev. 1 (2000).

Problem

An owner of agricultural land owns stock in a water company holding an appropriation. The farmer/stockholder has taken none of the water to which it was entitled for 30 years, having used groundwater. The ditch through which it had received the water from the company is now unusable, yet the company continues to assess for operating costs. In order to avoid paying assessments, the farmer claims his water right has been forfeited. Is there a forfeiture? See Aberdeen–Springfield Canal Co. v. Peiper, 982 P.2d 917 (Idaho 1999).

BEAVER PARK WATER, INC. v. VICTOR

Supreme Court of Colorado, 1982.
649 P.2d 300.

HODGES, CHIEF JUSTICE.

In the District Court in and for Water Division No. 2 (water court), the plaintiffs-appellants sought a judgment declaring that the "Altman water rights'' located in Beaver Creek and now owned and used by the City of Victor, a defendant-appellee, were abandoned because of nonuse between the years 1957 and 1977, and an order restraining the appellees from extracting any water by virtue of these water decrees which had priority dates in 1861 and 1893. The plaintiffs-appellants are owners and lessees of certain water rights on Beaver Creek, a tributary of the Arkansas River. The water court found that the Altman water rights were not abandoned and entered judgment dismissing the appellants' complaint. We affirm.

The Altman water rights involve decreed surface water rights in Beaver Creek located in Water Division 2. From 1916, these rights were owned by the Altman Water Company. In 1933, the Southern Colorado Power Company (Power Company) acquired a three-fourths interest in these rights. The remaining one-fourth interest was purchased in 1975 by the Central Telephone & Utilities Corporation (the successor to the Power Company). The City of Victor purchased the Altman water rights from the Central Telephone & Utilities Corporation in February 1977.

In 1949, the Power Company leased the water rights to the Golden Cycle Gold Corporation (Golden Cycle) to mine and mill gold. At this time and for several years, gold was the principal basis for the economy of the area around the City of Victor. Later in the period the price of gold fell, causing the area's mining activity to decline. In the late 1950's, Golden Cycle's Carlton Mill was the last user of the Altman water rights. In 1957, the mill ceased using the Altman water rights and began drawing its water from the City of Victor's water system, which then had its source in the nearby Skaguay Reservoir. This continued from March 1957 until 1961 when the mill closed. Over a period of years, the Skaguay Reservoir began to run dry, which led to the City of Victor's purchase of the Altman water rights in 1977. It is undisputed that the Altman water rights remained unused from March 1957 to May 1977.

The water court concluded that the nonuse of the Altman water rights for twenty years created a rebuttable presumption of an intent to abandon on the part of prior owners and users. However, it also found that appellees had introduced sufficient evidence to overcome this presumption and to establish that the predecessor owners and users of the Altman water rights never intended to discontinue permanently the use of all or part of the water available under these rights. * * *

Under Colorado water law, abandonment of a water right requires a concurrence of nonuse and intent to abandon. However, intent is the very essence of abandonment. Allard Cattle Co. v. Colorado & Southern Railway Co., 187 Colo. 1, 530 P.2d 503 (1974). Intent may be shown either expressly or by implication, with nonuse for a long period of time being evidence of an intent to abandon. Upper Harmony Ditch Co. v. Carwin, 189 Colo. 190, 539 P.2d 1282 (1975). Nonuse alone will not establish abandonment where the owner introduces sufficient evidence to show that during the period of nonuse there never was any intention to permanently discontinue the use of the water. Upon a showing that there has been an "unreasonable" period of nonuse, a *prima facie* case of abandonment is made, which in turn, shifts the burden of going forward to the water rights' owner who may then introduce evidence sufficient to rebut the presumption established by nonuse. * * *

This uncontradicted evidence consisted of, inter alia, the following: First, former officers, directors and employees of the Power Company and Golden Cycle testified that the companies never intended to abandon the water rights during the period in question; second, the Altman pumping station remained operational until 1961, with the power line staying attached until 1965 when the station was removed; the station was dismantled because there was "no future load in sight," and because there was plenty of water available in the Skaguay Reservoir; and a replacement station could have been operational within thirty days of when the need arose; third, between 1958 and 1977, there was no need for diverting the Altman water since an adequate water supply was available from another source[1]; fourth, in 1949, the Power Company had leased the Altman water rights to Golden Cycle for fifty years, and Golden Cycle in turn had leased its rights to the City of Victor for twenty-five years as a "standby" or emergency source of water; fifth, the Power Company mortgaged its interest in the water rights in 1965; sixth, in 1974, the Power Company demanded that Golden Cycle convey title to the remaining one-fourth interest in the water rights pursuant to a 1933 agreement, and, accordingly, in 1975 Golden Cycle deeded this interest; and seventh, in 1972 or 1973, the Power Company and the City of Victor began negotiating about the purchase and sale of the Altman water rights.

Generally, this evidence shows, as indicated by the water court, that the Altman water rights were involved in constant activity during the twenty years of nonuse, all of which sufficiently reveals that there was never any intention to relinquish, surrender, or give up these water rights. In short, the intent to abandon was not established by the evidence.

Notes and Questions

1. The court in *Beaver Park* does not deal with statutory forfeiture because Colorado does not have an Idaho-type forfeiture law. Southeastern Colorado Water Conservancy Dist. v. Twin Lakes Associates, Inc., 770 P.2d 1231 (Colo. 1989). Colo. Rev. Stat. § 37–92–402(11) provides:

> For the purpose of procedures under this section [determining and decreeing water rights], failure for a period of ten years or more to apply to a beneficial use the water available under a water right * * * shall create a rebuttable presumption of abandonment * * *;

---

1. This evidence has only limited relevancy to the question of intent. While we recognize that reasonable justification may exist for excusing a period of nonuse, Hallenbeck v. Granby Ditch and Reservoir Company, 160 Colo. 555, 420 P.2d 419 (1966), acceptable justifications are extremely limited. See In re C.F. & I. Steel Corporation in Las Animas County, 183 Colo. 135, 515 P.2d 456 (1973). Generally, the reasons underlying the nonuse period are only relevant to the question of intent to abandon and will not alone rebut a prima facie showing of abandonment.

except that such presumption may be waived by the * * * state engineer if special circumstances negate an intent to abandon.

Washington and Montana also use rebuttable presumptions. See Okanogan Wilderness League v. Town of Twisp, 133 Wash.2d 769, 947 P.2d 732, 739 (1997); 79 Ranch, Inc. v. Pitsch, 204 Mont. 426, 666 P.2d 215 (1983) (40 years of nonuse raises a rebuttable presumption and shifts burden to the nonuser to explain why there was no intent to abandon). In the case of In re Clark Fork River, 274 Mont. 340, 908 P.2d 1353 (1995), the Court declared a mining right abandoned where the water had not been used for over 50 years and the current owner was not a miner. It rejected a claim in a mining industry amicus brief that long periods of dormancy are routine in the mining industry and do not denote an intent to abandon, characterizing that position as the "gleam-in-the-eye" theory. See generally Janet C. Neuman & Keith Hirokawa, How Good is an Old Water Right? The Application of Statutory Forfeiture Provisions to Pre–Code Water Rights, 4 U. Denv. Water L. Rev. 1 (2000).

2. The *Beaver Park* case reveals an interesting use problem. The city leases water from the owner as a standby source in case of emergency. The court says such a lease is evidence of an intent not to abandon. Quite so. Lease of a backup source may be very sensible for a city. In fact many water rights are supplemental, to be used only when water is not available from another appropriation. But in light of other doctrines requiring *use* of water, is a city permitted to acquire an appropriative right whose content is nothing more than the ability to demand water if and when its normal supply is cut off? See the provisions of the Utah statute in Note 5 below. Washington explicitly permits holding a standby water supply to be used in times of low flow as an exception to the forfeiture law. Wash. Rev. Code § 90.14.140(2)(b). Do cities need standby supplies any more than industries?

3. Abandonment and forfeiture cases rarely disclose what happened to unused water during the period of time in question. One might assume that it went to waste, but it seems often to be the case that a junior appropriator, who has been using the water herself, is the one who instigates the proceeding for abandonment or forfeiture.[1] If so, it was not being wasted. If water *was* being used all the time, why not simply let the senior reclaim it after a period of nonuse? The senior might sell the right to a non-profit as an instream flow, to the detriment of juniors who have been using it; see Kerivan v. Water Resources Comm'n, 188 Or.App. 491, 72 P.3d 659 (2003). Is some important policy advanced by taking water away from a senior who has not used the water for some years (though it was used by others) and who now wants to use it again, or market it? Are abandonment and forfeiture really just quiet title devices?

4. Why don't seniors who face abandonment and forfeiture claims avoid the problem by leasing their water to others during the years they are

---

1. The Wyoming Supreme Court had held that since junior appropriators benefitted—rather than being injured—from a senior's non-use, they lacked standing to bring a forfeiture action. The legislature promptly overruled this decision. Edward Harris, Forfeiture Proceedings in Wyoming Water Law: The Legislature Revives Private Standing, 20 Land & Water L. Rev. 459 (1985). But see Snider v. Kirchhhefer, 115 P.3d 1 (Wyo. 2005) (junior showed insufficient evidence of harm to invoke abandonment/forfeiture statute).

not using it? At least one old case held that leasing of a water right worked an immediate abandonment since leasing demonstrated an intent no longer to use the water. See Slosser v. Salt River Valley Canal Co., 7 Ariz. 376, 65 P. 332 (1901). It has been suggested that this view "is somewhat outdated and in all likelihood will not be followed in the future." Joseph Novak, Abandonment and Forfeiture: How To Hold A Water Right As Development Takes Place, 28 Rocky Mtn. Min. L. Inst. 1249, 1278 (1983). Some states statutorily permit water right leases. See N.M. Stat. Ann. § 72–6–3; Idaho Code § 42–108A—42–108B; S.D. Codified Laws §§ 46–5–30.3, 46–5–32, 46–5–34.1. Idaho and Texas also allow water to be deposited in a "water bank" and avoid forfeiture; such laws are designed to facilitate water marketing; Idaho Code § 42–1764(2) and Tex. Water Code § 15.701 to 15.708.

5. A number of states permit the owner of a water right to avoid statutory forfeiture by obtaining an extension from state officials, sometimes for a single five year period (as in Idaho), sometimes for successive five year periods (as in Utah). See Novak, supra note 4, at 1273. The Utah statute (Utah Code Ann. § 73–1–4–5(a)) provides that an extension shall be granted "upon a showing of reasonable cause for such nonuse. Reasonable causes for nonuse include financial crisis, industrial depression, operation of legal proceedings or other unavoidable cause, or the holding of a water right without use by a municipality * * * to meet the reasonable future requirements of the public." The Idaho statute simply provides that an extension may be made "upon proper showing * * * of good and sufficient reason for nonapplication to beneficial use * * *." Idaho Code § 42–222(3). Washington insulates a non-user from its five year forfeiture law if the unused water right "is claimed for a determined future development to take place * * * within fifteen years of * * * the most recent beneficial use." Wash. Rev. Code Ann. § 90.14.140(2)(c); see R.D. Merrill Co. v. State, 137 Wash.2d 118, 969 P.2d 458 (1999) (irrigation rights unused while seeking permission for a ski resort).

6. There seem to be no appellate cases interpreting the statutory "reasonable cause" or "good and sufficient reason" provisions noted in the preceding paragraph. How would you expect the following hypothetical cases to be resolved:

• A mining company interested in developing a promising new source, but one that is not yet economically practicable, buys up substantial water rights from irrigators, and takes them out of use. It reasonably believes that the cost of water rights will continue to rise rapidly. It knows the federal government has been interested in development of the mineral, and is considering substantial subsidies to companies willing to do exploration and development, but the federal money is not yet available. When and whether it will be available is uncertain. The company, anticipating a grant if the federal program goes through, applies under laws like that of Utah or Idaho, for an extension against application of the forfeiture law. Should an extension be granted in such circumstances? What standard ought to apply to such cases?

• An irrigator takes her land out of production pursuant to the federal Conservation Reserve Program (under which the government subsidizes farmers who leave land uncultivated to provide desired wildlife habitat), which results in a period of 17 years of nonuse of the irrigator's water right. The State Engineer is petitioned under North Dakota law which provides that if a water permit holder fails to apply water to a beneficial use for more than three successive years, the state engineer may cancel the water permit unless the failure is due to "good and sufficient cause." What result? See Order No. 95–3 (N.D. State Eng'r, May 31, 1995).

7.   Even in the absence of a statutory extension, there may be a defense to a claim of forfeiture. For example, the Arizona statute lists the following defenses: drought or other unavailability of water; duty in the armed services; operation of legal proceedings; legally imposed acreage or production quotas; and "any other reason that a court of competent jurisdiction deems would warrant nonuse." Ariz. Rev. Stat. Ann. § 45–189. See also N.M. Stat. Ann. § 72–5–28; Idaho Code § 42–222(2). In Rocky Ford Irrig. Co. v. Kents Lake Reservoir Co., 104 Utah 202, 135 P.2d 108, 111 (1943), the court held that "forfeiture will not operate in those cases where the failure to use is the result of physical causes beyond the control of the appropriator, such as floods * * * draughts, etc. * * *."

8.   "Jurisdictions are divided on whether, after the statutory period of non-use, the resumed use of water cures the forfeiture and revitalizes the right." Town of Eureka v. Office of State Engineer, 826 P.2d 948, 951 (Nev. 1992). A Washington court has held that automatic forfeiture, without notice and hearing, violates the appropriator's due process rights. Sheep Mountain Cattle Co. v. State, 45 Wash.App. 427, 726 P.2d 55 (1986). In Idaho "the forfeiture is not effective if, after the five year period, the original owner or appropriator [or a successor in interest]resumed the use of the water prior to the claim of right by a third party." Would such a common law doctrine prevail even in a state that had a statutory provision allowing extensions of the five-year period to be granted? See Sagewillow, Inc. v. Idaho Department of Water Resources, 138 Idaho 831, 70 P.3d 669 (2003).

9.   Is there a forfeiture if water is not used for the purpose for which the appropriation was made, even though it was used for some other beneficial purpose? Held, yes in Hennings v. Water Resources Dept., 50 Or.App. 121, 622 P.2d 333 (1981).

10.   The forfeiture/abandonment doctrines are supposed to serve in part as protection against speculation. Yet, as you have seen, courts are reluctant to take rights away even after long periods of non-use if they are being held with some future application in mind. Isn't that virtually a definition of speculation?[2] Consider the following excerpt from Steven Shupe, Gary Weatherford, & Elizabeth Checchio, Western Water Rights: The Era of Reallocation, 29 Nat. Resources J. 413, 426 (1989), and ask yourself whether the schemes described would (or should) be vulnerable to attack under any version of forfeiture or abandonment?

Not all water purchases are made to fulfill the needs of cities, developers, irrigators, and other end users. Many individuals and

---

2.   For a critical discussion of the policies underlying the anti-speculation rule see infra p. 302.

corporations have bought water rights simply because they believe the value of water rights will escalate. A typical investment transaction involves the purchase of irrigation water rights and a leasing back of the rights to the farmer for continued irrigation until the investor is ready to resell the rights. The lease-back provision can be critical, not only in order to create annual benefits from the water during the holding period, but also to continue the beneficial use of surface rights to protect them from forfeiture.

Past investments in water rights have typically involved individual investors purchasing a particular water right or district share. In recent years, however, major water right purchases have been made by investors pooling their money in collective transactions. For instance, private investors paid $7.8 million for an Arizona water ranch and are hoping to resell the associated 6,200 ac-ft groundwater rights for a profit. In Colorado, this concept was taken a step further by Western Water Rights Management, Inc., a corporation that raised $35 million in 1985 to purchase Colorado water rights on behalf of a small group of investors. The corporation has spent more than $10 million on senior irrigation rights that it believes Colorado cities and industries will buy in the future. The investment period for this package is 14 years, at which time the investors hope to realize a significant profit on the resale of the water rights.

11.   California uses the term "reversion" rather than forfeiture in its statute. See Cal. Water Code § 1241.

Problems

1.   In 1972 a land developer obtained a permit to change the use of an existing irrigation water right in order to serve a proposed residential project, conditioned on putting the water to beneficial use by 1977. In 1991, following 16 annual time extensions, the developer sought to change the point of diversion and place of use of the water to another proposed development. The State Engineer canceled the permit for lack of due diligence, and the Supreme Court sustained the cancellation. What happens then? Does the water revert to the public domain, or does the change permittee now have its irrigation water right back? What are the public policy issues in such a case? If the permittee continued to irrigate all those years, should we care how long he holds his change permit? If he was not irrigating, but held a change permit all those years, under what theory could his irrigation water right be taken away from him when the change permit is canceled for lack of due diligence, but there was presumably no violation of the irrigation water right? See Desert Irrig., Ltd. v. State, 113 Nev. 1049, 944 P.2d 835 (1997).

2.   You are a strategist for an environmental organization in a state where many old water rights are vulnerable to claims of abandonment or forfeiture. The question is whether the organization, which is eager to restore instream flows, would be likely to achieve instream flow gains even if it were to prevail in challenging these water rights?

3. You have no water rights yourself, but a neighbor has a ditch easement across your land to access its water right from a stream that runs across your land. The ditch and water right haven't been used for the statutory period, and you want to bring a forfeiture proceeding. Your goal is is to get rid of the ditch and free your land from the burden of the easement. Do you have standing? Cf. Snider v. Kirchhefer, 115 P.3d 1 (Wyo. 2005).

2. LOSS OF RIGHTS THROUGH PRESCRIPTION AND ADVERSE POSSESSION

Claims of prescription of water rights usually are allied in litigation with claims of abandonment and forfeiture. In a conventional case, an upstream junior who has been taking more than his or her decreed rights, and is challenged by the downstream senior, asserts an entitlement to the water on the ground that the senior has either abandoned or forfeited the right by nonuse and/or intention to abandon or, alternatively, the junior claims a right by prescription. In theory, at least, the two prongs of the attack fit nicely together. If there is abandonment or forfeiture, the junior wins. If not, then the junior's longstanding use may nevertheless meet the test of prescription as being adverse to the senior's claim of right. It would seem that the junior can hardly lose, but more often than not he does.[3] In Gilbert v. Smith, 97 Idaho 735, 552 P.2d 1220 (1976), the court found (1) no intent to abandon; (2) no "measurable" five year period of nonuse sufficient to sustain a statutory forfeiture; and (3) insufficient evidence of "open, hostile, exclusive, continuous [use] under a claim of right" for five years, which is the period required to obtain property by prescription in Idaho. Rather, the court found the junior's use to be "intermittent, interrupted, irregular and not wholly under an assertion of right." Mere use, even under a claim of right, is insufficient to give rise to a prescriptive right; the use must be proven to have "deprived" the prior appropriators of water at times when such prior appropriators actually needed the water.[4] A number of appropriation states have abolished prescription by statute, including Idaho, Montana, Nevada, Utah and Arizona.[5] Colorado law is said to allow it.[6] After decades of uncertainty, Wyoming finally held "that water rights may not be acquired by adverse possession or prescription * * *."[7] Texas, which once permitted water rights to be awarded solely on equitable considerations, has now held that new water rights may only be obtained by filing an application with the Texas Water Commission.[8] The issue remains unsettled in New Mexico, Turner v. Bassett, 111 P.3d 701 (2005), declining to consider the issue, and reversing on other

---

3. Smith v. Hawkins, 110 Cal. 122, 42 P. 453 (1895) is a rare case in which a downstream junior prevailed on a forfeiture claim.

4. Sears v. Berryman, 101 Idaho 843, 623 P.2d 455 (1981).

5. See, e.g., Mont. Code Ann. § 85–2–301(3). For the peculiar Arizona situation, see San Carlos Apache Tribe v. Superior Court, 972 P.2d 179, 190–91 (Ariz. 1999).

6. See Ward H. Fischer, Adverse Possession of River Flows, The Colorado Lawyer, June 1994, at 1313.

7. Lewis v. State Bd. of Control, 699 P.2d 822, 824 (Wyo. 1985).

8. In re Adjudication of the Brazos River Basin, 746 S.W.2d 207 (Tex. 1988).

grounds a Court of Appeals holding "that water rights cannot be acquired by adverse possession," 81 P.3d 564, 570 (2003).

A leading case on prescription is excerpted below:

PEOPLE v. SHIROKOW

Supreme Court of California, 1980.
26 Cal.3d 301, 162 Cal.Rptr. 30, 605 P.2d 859.

[Shirokow owned land through which Arnold Creek, an intermittent stream, ran. In 1960 his predecessor had built a dam to capture the creek's water in winter for livestock watering and fishing. A permit to appropriate had never been obtained for this water; Shirokow had applied for a permit, but withdrew it when the state insisted, as a condition, that he remove brush alongside the stream. In 1976, the State sought to enjoin Shirokow's diversion pursuant to section 1052 of the California Water Code, which makes unauthorized diversions a trespass and subject to injunction at the instance of the State Water Resources Control Board. Had Shirokow not taken the water, it would have run downstream eventually reaching the Central Valley Project. The case is unclear as to whether the project was disadvantaged by Shirokow's diversion. The legal issue in the case was whether an appropriative water right could be acquired by prescription, or whether the acquisition of a permit to appropriate was essential.]

MOSK, JUSTICE.

* * * In this case of first impression we are asked to decide the circumstances under which the state may obtain an injunction pursuant to Water Code section 1052.[1] Our key inquiry is whether defendant's use of water is subject to the appropriation procedures of the code, so that failure to comply provides grounds for injunctive relief.[2] Defendant asserts his use of water, though unauthorized by the State Water Resources Control Board (board), is pursuant to a prescriptive right. It has long been debated whether the Water Code's comprehensive scheme for the granting of appropriative rights by the board (sec. 1200 et seq.) precludes the acquisition of prescriptive rights in circumstances such as these in which a nonriparian user asserts rights in water based on adverse use initiated after the enactment of the code.[3]

---

1. Section 1052 provides: "The diversion or use of water subject to the provisions of this division (division 2) other than as authorized in this division is a trespass, and the board (State Water Resources Control Board) may institute * * * appropriate action to have such trespass enjoined." All statutory references are to the Water Code unless otherwise noted.

2. All references to "water," unless otherwise noted, are limited to surface water and to subterranean streams flowing through known and definite channels. Per-

colating ground water is specifically excluded from our consideration. (See sec. 1200.)

3. See 3 Witkin, Summary of California Law (8th ed. 1973) Real Property, section 587, page 2253 [now in § 785, pp. 965–67—eds]; Final Report, Governor's Commission to Review California Water Rights Law (Dec. 1978) pages 31–32. For an expression of the view that no right to nonriparian use of water may be acquired short of full compliance with the appropriation permit procedures of the Water Code, see Craig, Prescriptive Water Rights in California and the

As will appear, we conclude the better view requires denial of acquisition of such rights as against the state. Accordingly, defendant's diversion of water without first obtaining a permit from the board constituted a trespass within the meaning of section 1052, and the state was authorized to seek an injunction against such trespass. * * *

Whether defendant's diversion of water may be enjoined under section 1052 turns on our interpretation of the phrase "water subject to the provisions of this division (division 2)." We are not aided by the omission in division 2 of any definition of the water which is subject to its provisions. Part 2 of the division provides a comprehensive scheme for the appropriation of water. It defines water subject to appropriation (secs. 1200–1203); declares compliance with the provisions of division 2 to be the exclusive means of acquiring the right to appropriate or use water subject to appropriation (sec. 1225); authorizes the board to act upon all applications for permits to appropriate water, to grant permits to take and use water subject to the terms and conditions of the permit, and to collect fees (secs. 1250–1550); and provides for the issuance of licenses confirming the right to appropriate such amount of water as had been beneficially used by the permittees (secs. 1600–1677). Thus it is clear that if the water diverted by defendant is water subject to appropriation, then it is water subject to the provisions of division 2 and any use thereof is conditioned upon compliance with the statutory procedure. We next consider the statutory provisions defining the water subject to appropriation. Because an understanding of section 1201 is crucial to the analysis, we set forth the language in its entirety. "All water flowing in any natural channel, excepting so far as it has been or is being applied to useful and beneficial purposes upon, or in so far as it is or may be reasonably needed for useful and beneficial purposes upon lands riparian thereto, or otherwise appropriated, is hereby declared to be public water of the State and subject to appropriation in accordance with the provisions of this code."[5] * * *

Section 1050 declares division 2 to be in furtherance of the Constitution, article X, section 2 (added by amendment as art. XIV, sec. 3, in 1928), which provides in part: "It is hereby declared that because of the conditions prevailing in this State the general welfare requires that the water resources of the State be put to beneficial use to the fullest extent of which they are capable * * * and that the conservation of such waters is to be exercised with a view to the reasonable and beneficial use thereof in the interest of the people and for the public welfare." (Cf. sec. 100.)

Necessity for a Valid Statutory Appropriation (1954) 42 Cal. L. Rev. 219; Hutchins, The California Law of Water Rights (1956) pages 334–335. For the contrary view, see Kletzing, Prescriptive Water Rights in California: Is Application a Prerequisite? (1951) 39 Cal. L. Rev. 369; Trowbridge, Prescriptive Water Rights in California: An Addendum (1951) 39 Cal. L. Rev. 525; 1 Rogers and Nichols, Water for California (1966) pages 326–327. See also Hutchins, Selected Problems in the Law of Water Rights in the West (1942) pages 400–402; Wiel, Unregistered Water Appropriations at Law and in Equity (1926) 14 Cal. L. Rev. 427.

5. Section 1200 limits the term "water," as used in connection with appropriation applications, permits, and licenses, to include only surface water and subterranean streams flowing through known and definite channels.

The Water Code articulates a policy consistent with that expressed in the 1928 amendment and provides that all water within the state is the property of the people (sec. 102), the people have a paramount interest in the use of all water of the state (sec. 104), and the state shall determine the manner in which the water of the state should be developed for the greatest public benefit (sec. 105). These declarations of policy together with the comprehensive regulatory scheme set forth in section 1200 et seq. demonstrate a legislative intent to vest in the board expansive powers to safeguard the scarce water resources of the state.

These considerations lead us to conclude section 1201 should be interpreted in such a manner that the waters of the state be available for allocation in accordance with the code to the fullest extent consistent with its terms. * * * The rights not subject to the statutory appropriation procedures are narrowly circumscribed by the exception clause of the statute and include only riparian rights and those which have been otherwise appropriated prior to December 19, 1914, the effective date of the statute.[11] Any use other than those excepted is, in our view, conditioned upon compliance with the appropriation procedures of division 2.

To conclude otherwise would substantially impair the board's ability to comply with the legislative mandate that appropriations be consistent with the public interest. (sec. 1255.) For example, the salutary effects of the comprehensive system of water rights administration would be imperiled if the board were powerless to enjoin an adverse use of water which the board had previously otherwise allocated, or desired to allocate, in the public interest.

Moreover, the board is hindered in its task by any uncertainty as to the availability of water for appropriation. The problem is compounded by nonsanctioned uses which make it difficult for the board to determine whether the waters of the state are being put to beneficial use for the greatest public benefit. (Cf. sec. 105).[12]

Our holding that the state is entitled to an injunction against defendant's unauthorized diversion of water, will not result in the destruction of all beneficial uses of water originally undertaken in reliance on prescription. The board's broad discretion to act on appropri-

---

11. Section 1201 by its terms excepts from water subject to appropriation riparian rights which are being applied to, or may be reasonably needed for, useful and beneficial purposes. The status of prospective riparian rights is discussed in our recent opinion in In re Waters of Long Valley Creek Stream System, 25 Cal. 3d 339, 158 Cal. Rptr. 350, 599 P.2d 656 (1979). The opinion holds the board possesses broad authority in statutory adjudications pursuant to section 2500 et seq. to make determinations as to the scope, nature, and priority of future riparian rights, in order to foster the most reasonable and beneficial use of the scarce water resources of the state.

12. In In re Waters of Long Valley Creek Stream System, supra, 25 Cal. 3d at page 356, footnote 12, 158 Cal. Rptr. at page 360, 599 P.2d at page 667, the opinion observes the need for certainty in the administration of water rights to be "readily apparent when one examines the statutory framework governing appropriative rights in California." See Final Report, Governor's Commission to Review California Water Rights, supra, at pages 21–25, in which the consequences of uncertainty are discussed. The report states "(P)rescription exacerbates the lack-of-knowledge problem which hinders effective planning, management, and enforcement of water and water rights." (Op. cit. supra, at 32.)

ation applications is not unfettered; while it is true the issuance of permits depends on questions of policy and judgment (sec. 1255), the board may not arbitrarily and capriciously reject an application.

In this case defendant has twice filed applications to appropriate water. The board was willing to grant him the right to continue his use if he instituted a brush removal program to salvage the required amount of water, a condition the board had authority to impose for protection of the public interest. (sec. 1253.) When he discovered it would cost $8,500 to fulfill this requirement, defendant voluntarily abandoned his efforts to obtain a permit and determined to rely on his claimed prescriptive right. * * *

Even if *arguendo* we were to hold defendant was not required to comply with the statutory appropriation procedures, his claim of a prescriptive right would fail for two reasons. First, public rights cannot be lost by prescription. Defendant alleged and the trial court agreed that as against the state he had perfected a prescriptive right. Both were mistaken. What is being challenged is the state's governmental interest in regulating the use of public waters rather than any proprietary interest in the water claimed by defendant. The stipulated facts do not reveal that the state was using the water; indeed, defendant admits the state, if successful in obtaining the injunction, will not make use of the water. Thus it is undisputed that the state's interest here at stake is nonproprietary. * * *

The second reason defendant cannot prevail in his claim of a prescriptive right is that the stipulated facts do not provide the necessary elements. Defendant has not shown his diversion was hostile to the interests of any downstream user; we are told only that there was general community knowledge that the dam and reservoir existed and water was impounded. Since it is axiomatic that common law prescriptive rights are based on adverse use, such rights could not have been obtained by defendant by a taking of excess water which did not invade the interests of another. Not only did defendant fail to identify any downstream users having actual knowledge of his diversion, no downstream users were parties to this action. Accordingly, the court lacked jurisdiction to adjudicate their rights vis-a-vis those of defendant.[15] * * *

CLARK, JUSTICE, concurring and dissenting.

The Constitution's command of conservation is as applicable to the board as it is to riparians and appropriators. The board should not be permitted to require water wastage as a means to compel applications for permits to appropriate from those persons already making reasonable and beneficial use of water. Such administrative muscle flexing runs

---

15. The extensive discussion in the concurring and dissenting opinion of our purported abolition of all property rights in water acquired by prescription bears no relationship to reality. We hold here only that defendant's claim of prescriptive rights cannot lie as against the state when it seeks to enjoin unauthorized use pursuant to section 1052. It is unnecessary for us to reach the question of whether and under what circumstances prescriptive rights in water may be perfected as between private parties.

afoul not only of the constitutional provision but also of the basic statutes relating to the board's powers and duties. (See, e.g., Wat. Code, secs. 100, 101, 105, 1256–1258.) While the board may be hindered in performing its administrative function by lack of knowledge of all water claims, this does not warrant adopting rules that encourage water wastage. Because appropriation proceedings are often expensive, requiring permits of those who reasonably and beneficially use water that otherwise would be wasted may cause discontinuance of beneficial use and therefore waste. Those who use water reasonably and beneficially should not be subjected to expensive appropriation proceedings or other administratively imposed burdens.

Although the stipulated facts do not entirely settle the matter, they indicate that enjoining defendant's appropriation will result in wastage. Defendant captures the first flow of Arnold Creek. Flood control releases exist downstream at Friant Dam. Because of our annual rainfall and snowmelt patterns, it is questionable whether the waters impounded by defendant would be used for reasonable, beneficial purposes if defendant did not appropriate. * * *

The majority today decree that no property right in surface water or subterranean stream has been acquired by prescription since 1913 [the year in which Water Code sec. 1052 was first adopted.–Eds.].[3] This is both startling and disturbing. It boldly ignores what has been occurring in the California courts for 65 years. * * * The appropriation provisions of Water Code section 1225 do not require abrogation of rights acquired by prescription. The section provides: "[N]o right to appropriate or use water *subject to appropriation* shall be initiated or acquired except upon compliance with the provisions of this division." (Italics added.) Water Code section 1201 makes clear that the waters "subject to appropriation" are surplus waters which are not reasonably needed for useful and beneficial riparian purposes or previously appropriated. (See also Wat. Code, sec. 1375, subd. (d).)

The statutes have no relation to property rights acquired by prescription because prescriptive rights may not be acquired in surplus waters. "Prescriptive water rights in California are, in a sense, the parasite of water rights. The only way to obtain such rights is to take water rights away from someone else." * * *

While Water Code section 1200 et seq. relates primarily to allocation of surplus waters, whereas prescriptive rights are obtained by adverse user infringing upon riparian rights or unenforced appropriative rights, the two acquisitions are essentially unrelated. Regarding reasonable

---

3. * * * The majority state that they are not determining "whether and under what circumstances prescriptive rights in water may be perfected as between private parties." (Ante, [n. 15].) However, as a practical matter, the majority decide the issue they disclaim. We may not expect that the board will unlawfully discriminate in exercising its power to enjoin asserted post-1913 prescriptive rights to water. Thus all will be enjoined. Faced with the certainty of injunction, private parties may not be expected to seek to establish prescriptive rights against other private parties. Accordingly, the effect of today's opinion is to prevent recognition of all post–1913 prescriptive claims.

riparian uses, prior licensed appropriative uses, and claimed prescriptive uses, the board has an adjudicatory function determining rights. Regarding surplus waters, the board possesses much greater power, performing a licensing function permitting allocation among various potential users. The statutory system is comprehensive only as to surplus waters; it is not comprehensive as to riparian rights for reasonable use, prior appropriative rights for such use, or loss of rights through prescriptive reasonable use. Accordingly, the statutory system does not support this court's abolition of rights obtained through prescription reasonable and beneficial uses exercised over the past 60 years.

It is true as the majority states that recognizing prescriptive rights may hinder the board in determining what waters are now available for appropriation. But the hindrance is minor. There being no requirement to register riparian uses, the uncertainty is not alleviated by government abrogation of prescriptive rights and resurrection of lost riparian rights.

The majority's suggestion that those losing prescriptive rights for reasonable beneficial use will now be able to acquire appropriative permits and therefore such uses are not jeopardized by today's decision must be rejected. Issuance of an appropriation permit depends on availability of surplus water. As pointed out above, prescriptive rights may not be acquired when there is surplus water. Reason suggests a paucity of situations in which there have been in the past a lack of surplus water permitting a prescriptive right under traditional law, but at the present time there exist surplus waters permitting appropriation permits. Available surplus water decreases as population increases. * * *

Notes and Questions

1. The case is discussed in Teressa Lippert, People v. Shirokow: Abolishing Prescriptive Water Rights Against the State, 69 Cal. L. Rev. 1204 (1981) and in Bruce McCoy, The Role of Adverse Possession in Water Law, 10 Harv. Envtl. L. Rev. 257 (1986). For an older view of the problem by one of the great figures of water law, see Samuel Wiel, Unregistered Water Appropriations at Law and in Equity, 14 Cal. L. Rev. 427 (1926).

2. The *Shirokow* case leaves certain questions unsettled:

• May prescriptive rights still be acquired in California as between riparians? As between private appropriators, when the State is not a party ("water rights are a species of real property capable of acquisition by adverse user," Locke v. Yorba Irr. Co., 35 Cal.2d 205, 217 P.2d 425, 429 (1950)).

• How about ground water, which is not subject to the Water Code's permit system for appropriation? In City of Barstow v. Mojave Water Agency, 99 Cal.Rptr.2d 294, 5 P.3d 853, 863 (2000), though no claim of prescriptive rights was in issue, the Court unequivocally said that groundwater appropriators could acquire prescriptive rights against overlying owners by pumping non-surplus water "where the use is actual, open, and notorious, hostile and adverse to the original owner, continuous and uninterrupted for the statutory period of five years, and under claim of right."

• A State Water Resources Control Board decision says that an up-stream riparian may still acquire prescriptive rights against downstream riparians, but only if it diverted and applied to reasonable, beneficial use a quantity of natural flows in excess of its share consistent with its riparian rights for the statutory period, and that the prescriptee was on notice throughout the period that the prescriptor, and no other user, was responsible for the diminution of flows to which it was entitled. In the Matter of Water Right Permit 16584, Order WR 99–01, at 6–8 (Cal. State Water Resources Control Bd. 1999).

• Would or should Shirokow have been better off if he could have demonstrated that the water he was using would go to waste if he were enjoined, or that his use was more beneficial than downstream uses (because there would be massive evaporation or seepage before the water reached downstream appropriators or riparians)?

3. One way to deal with the administrative awkwardness of out-of-record claims is to legalize them. See Michael McIntyre, The Disparity Between State Water Rights Records and Actual Water Use Patterns: I Wonder Where the Water Went?, 5 Land & Water L.Rev. 23 (1970).

4. Does a prescriptor takes the original appropriator's priority date, or the date of the prescriptor's own first use? The issue is mentioned in the dissenting opinion in Adams v. Portage Irr., Reservoir & Power Co., 95 Utah 1, 72 P.2d 648 (1937). The writers take opposing views. Clesson Kinney, in 2 Treatise on the Law of Irrigation and Water Rights § 1058 (2d ed. 1912), says that the prescriptor takes the original owner's priority date, the prescription being akin to an implied grant of the original water right. Accord: Note, Water Rights: Prescriptive Right to the Use of Water in Montana, 1942 Mont. L. Rev. 135, 140–43. The opposite view is taken by Samuel Wiel, in 1 Water Rights in the Western States § 580 (3d ed. 1911), who says that the prescriptor would get as a priority the date of his first use. Wiel cites Alhambra Addition Water Co. v. Richardson, 72 Cal. 598, 608, 14 P. 379 (1887) which says that "where a right rests upon the statute of limitations, the disseisor acquires a new title founded on the disseisin. He does not acquire or succeed to the title and estate of the disseisee * * *." The decision of the California State Water Resources Control Board noted above states that "in contrast to the loss of an appropriative right for nonuse, where the right reverts to the public and the water is regarded as unappropriated, * * * a water right that is lost through prescription is effectively shifted from one water user to another." In the Matter of Water Right Permit 16584, supra note 2, at 9. The issue was significant in that case because all riparian rights were superior to an appropriative right, and the appropriator had apparently claimed that if certain riparian rights had been lost by prescription, that quantum of water went back to the river and was no longer superior to the appropriator. The Board rejected that view.

5. Are you persuaded that prescription of water rights is undesirable? Consider this hypothetical California case: A, reasonably and in good faith, but erroneously, believes she is a riparian owner on the Blue River. For 25 years she diverts water for irrigation of her small farm. B, a downstream

senior on the Blue River, is thereby deprived of water to which he is entitled. B also believes A is a riparian. B dies and his heirs seek to sell the water right A has been using. If B's heirs succeed, A's farm will be made virtually worthless.

E. WATER MARKETS

One of the most debated subjects in water law today is water marketing. No one has ever questioned that when land is sold, water used on the land can be sold with it. Indeed, the general rule is that an appropriation right goes with the sale of land unless otherwise specified.[4] The interesting question is the extent to which water can be severed from the land and sold or used elsewhere by the owner. If a growing city needs additional water, for example, can it buy water from a farmer who is willing to conserve water or fallow her fields?

Proponents of such sales believe that water markets produce a number of benefits. First, water markets allow the allocation of water to adjust to changing water demands, water conditions, and technologies. The comparative water needs of individual users, economic sectors, and geographic regions today are not the same as the comparative needs a century ago or even five years ago. Markets provide a voluntary mechanism for reallocating water in response to change.

Water markets similarly permit rapid reallocations of water in response to droughts and other temporary water shortages. In 1991, for example, California was in the fourth year of a severe drought. To ensure that those who needed water the most could get water, the State of California created a drought "water bank" to purchase water from users who could get by with less and then sell the water to users with important unmet needs. By ensuring that water was available for important needs, the bank saved the California economy about $100 million.[5]

One way that water markets can help satisfy unmet needs is by promoting conservation. As discussed earlier, courts, agencies, and legislatures have often proven reticent to order water users to conserve water. Yet few water users are likely to invest voluntarily in conservation if they are unable to profit from the conservation. Some water users, moreover, do not have the financial resources necessary to invest in meaningful conservation. If state law permits existing users to retain and sell conserved water (see supra pp. 189–190), markets can provide those users with both an incentive to conserve and a means of raising the funds needed for conservation.

---

4. See, e.g., Axtell v. M.S. Consulting, 288 Mont. 150, 955 P.2d 1362, 1368 (1998); Estate of Palizzi, 854 P.2d 1256, 1258 (Colo. 1993). When a piece of land is divided and sold, most states hold that a *pro rata* portion of the water right accompanies each parcel. See, e.g., Crow v. Carlson, 107 Idaho 461, 690 P.2d 916 (1984).

5. See Richard Howitt, Nancy Moore, & Rodney Smith, A Retrospective on California's 1991 Emergency Drought Water Bank (Cal. Dept. of Water Resources, March 1992).

Many environmentalists see additional benefits to water markets.[6] By freeing up water for the West's growing urban regions, markets reduce the need to divert more water from already depleted rivers or construct new storage projects with environmental side effects. Because agricultural water use constitutes a high percentage of total water consumption in the western United States, relatively small amounts of agricultural conservation can dramatically increase the amount of water available for urban use. Two Arizona economists in the late 1980s calculated that a savings of 5 percent of the water then used in Arizona agriculture could support "an additional 1.5 million people, an increase of 50 percent over Arizona's 1985 population. In Colorado, it has been suggested that if irrigators could reduce their consumptive use by 5 percent, the amount of water available for municipal and industrial use would nearly double."[7]

Water markets also might promote water quality by reducing contaminated return flow. As discussed earlier, cities might find that it is more profitable to purify and sell their sewage water than to discharge it into a local waterway. See supra pp. 201–209. By raising the value of water, markets might also decrease unnecessary agricultural runoff. Selenium, salts, and other contaminants often lace such runoff, contaminating rivers and streams.

Finally, water markets provide governments and environmental organizations with the opportunity to purchase water for instream flow. Between 1990 and 1997, government agencies and environmental non-profits leased or purchased more than 2.3 million acre-feet of water for instream use in the western United States.[8] Environmental water acquisitions, moreover, have continued to grow; since 1995, annual environmental acquisitions have averaged over 500,000 acre-feet per year.[9] The federal Bureau of Reclamation has been the major acquirer of water for instream purposes, leasing or purchasing water in the Klamath, Sacramento, San Joaquin, Snake, and Yakima river basins. At the state level, Montana, Nevada, and New Mexico all have set up active environmental acquisition programs. Traditional non-profits (such as The Nature Conservancy, Trout Unlimited, and Environmental Defense), as well as new environmental water trusts (such as the Oregon Water Trust, Washington Water Trust, and Nevada's Great Basin Land & Water), also have acquired significant instream flows through donations, leases, and purchases.[10]

6. Environmental Defense (formerly the Environmental Defense Fund) has long been a proponent of more active water markets. See Thomas J. Graff & David Yardas, Reforming Western Water Policy: Markets and Regulation, 12 Nat. Resources & Env't 165 (1998).

7. Bonnie Colby & David Bush, Water Markets in Theory and Practice 46 (1987).

8. Clay Landry, Saving Our Streams Through Water Markets (Pol. Econ. Res. Center 1998).

9. Barton H. Thompson, Jr., Markets for Nature, 25 Wm. & Mary Envtl. L. & Pol'y Rev. 261, 270 (2000).

10. For discussions of environmental water acquisitions, see Landry, supra note 8; Thompson, supra note 9; Mary Ann King, Getting Our Feet Wet: An Introduction to Water Trusts, 28 Envtl. L. Rev. 495

Water users have bought and sold prior appropriation rights for over a century. In the mid-nineteenth century, gold miners transferred their water rights as one mining site played out and another promising site was discovered. As early as 1859, moreover, the California Supreme Court held that an appropriative right was "substantive and valuable property" which could be sold or "transferred like other property."[11]

In the late nineteenth century, however, a number of people questioned the wisdom of permitting water users to market their water. Prominent among the critics was Elwood Mead, Wyoming's State Engineer, who would later go on to head the federal reclamation program. Mead observed that early appropriators often had claimed more water than they actually needed, partly in the hope that they could later sell the excess water. In Mead's opinion, such water "speculation" was less likely to occur if water could not be sold separate from land. Mead also worried that water transfers would permit individuals to profit from a free public resource and would inevitably lead to monopoly.

If water is to be so bartered and sold, then the public should not give streams away, but should auction them off to the highest bidder.

* * * The doctrine that air, water, and sunshine are gifts from God should not be lightly set aside even in arid lands. * * * The growth and danger of monopolies in oil, copper, coal, and iron afford a warning of the greater danger of permitting monopolies in water. * * *

In monarchies streams belong to the crown, and in the early history of irrigation in Italy and other parts of Europe, favorites of the rulers were rewarded with grants of streams. But in a republic they belong to the people, and ought forever to be kept as public property for the benefit of all who use them, and for them alone, such use to be under public supervision and control.[12]

Largely because of Mead's advocacy, the Wyoming legislature in 1909 effectively prohibited the transfer of appropriation rights, as well as changes in either the use or place of use of appropriation rights.[13] At one time or another, nine prior appropriation states prohibited or severely restricted an appropriator's ability to sever appropriation rights from the

(2004); Janet C. Neuman, The Good, the Bad, and the Ugly: The First Ten Years of the Oregon Water Trust, 83 Neb. L. Rev. 432 (2004); Jason S. Wells, Leasing Water Rights for Instream Flow Protection: The Opportunities and Impediments to Improved Public Interest Involvement in Colorado's Instream Flow Protection Regime, 7 U. Denv. Water L. Rev. 309 (2004). The more general question of instream flow rights was discussed supra pp. 141–148.

11. McDonald v. Bear River Co., 13 Cal. 220, 232–33 (1859). California courts were not alone in accepting early the validity of water transfers. See, e.g., Strickler v. City of Colorado Springs, 16 Colo. 61, 26 P. 313 (1891); Johnston v. Little Horse Creek Irrigating Co., 13 Wyo. 208, 79 P. 22 (1904).

12. Elwood Mead, Irrigation Institutions 264, 365–66 (1903).

13. 1909 Wyo. Sess. Laws, ch. 68, § 1. The statute technically permitted transfers, but only with total loss of priority, making transfers useless.

land upon which the water was used. Under the laws of Arizona, Kansas, Montana, Nebraska, Nevada, North Dakota, Oklahoma, South Dakota, and Wyoming, appropriative rights were "appurtenant" to that land and could not be transferred for use elsewhere.

Today all states permit water marketing. The flat bans have been repealed or riddled with exceptions, and active water markets now exist in many parts of the West. Yet a variety of legal, institutional, and other obstacles still stand in the way of active water markets in many regions of the West.

Many of the most serious obstacles still hindering water markets are institutional or technological. Irrigation districts, for example, frequently prohibit transfers of water from their farmers to users outside the district borders. Transfers of water from one watershed to another, moreover, require an aqueduct or other conveyance facility to transport the water to the user. The cost of building a new conveyance facility is often prohibitively expensive. Even if there is an existing conveyance facility with available capacity, the owner of the facility may not want to lease the capacity or may demand an exorbitant price for its use. These institutional and technological issues are discussed further in Chapter 7 at pages 731–746.

The focus in this section is on legal restrictions of water transfers. In reading these materials, ask yourself what purposes the existing legal constraints on water transfers serve. Are there other means of accomplishing the same purposes that would be less likely to deter valuable water transfers? Are the benefits of the constraints worth the cost? Looking from the other side, is the current law too lenient? Should the law regulate water transfers even more closely?

1. LEGAL OVERSIGHT OF WATER TRANSFERS

The best way to understand the traditional legal constraints on water transfers is to work through a simple hypothetical. Assume that the Eldorado River is a fully appropriated river in an appropriation state. The Clydes, who own 640 acres of farm land along the river as shown in Figure 3–5, have an 1882 appropriative right to use 20 cfs from April to September of each year. 25 percent of the water (or 5 cfs) is consumed in the irrigation process. (This is a relatively low water "efficiency" for irrigated agriculture.[14] 50 percent is more the norm in the West, and the norm is increasing over time.) The remainder of the water returns to the Eldorado River where it is diverted by junior appropriators. The Clydes' farm has been losing money recently and they are thinking of retiring most of the acreage and selling 16 cfs of their water.

---

14. Recall that water "efficiency" is defined as the percentage of water consumed.

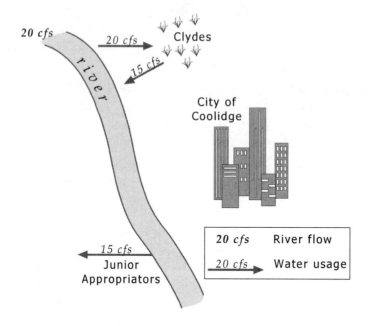

Figure 3–5

The City of Coolidge is looking for additional water to meet the needs of its growing population and has offered the Clydes a satisfactory price for their water. The city is located 15 miles downstream of the Clydes and so can take the water directly out of the river without worrying about transporting the water lengthy distances. The city would like to use the water year-round as part of its public water supply. On average, about 50 percent of the water in the city's public water system is consumed; the remainder returns to the Eldorado River through the city's sewage disposal plant and storm sewers.

How does the law restrict the proposed sale?

a.   The Application Process

Any time a water user plans to change (1) the point at which water is diverted from a river, (2) the times of the year when the water is used, (3) the place where the water is used, or (4) the nature of the use, the water user must ordinarily apply to the state for permission to make the change.[15] The City of Coolidge proposes to make all four changes and thus will definitely have to file an application. This will require Coolidge to file numerous informational reports and pay a small fee. Of greater

---

15. In Colorado, application is made to a special water court; in other states, application is generally made to the administrative agency responsible for administering water permits. Permit systems are discussed supra p. 215.

concern to Coolidge, the filing will signal the start of a potentially lengthy and litigious evaluation process.

First, notices will be published in local newspapers advising the public of the proposed change. In some states, individual notices will also be sent to neighboring water users, local water organizations, and community officials. Opponents of the proposed water transfer can then file protests with the state listing legal grounds why the change should not be allowed.[16] Most states will try to resolve protests through informal negotiations. If this does not work, the state will hold a hearing. Hearings vary in formality depending on the state and context, and last anywhere from a few hours to a number of weeks. After the hearing is completed, the state will issue a ruling on the application. The ruling is then appealable. In some states, moreover, the transfer remains open for reconsideration even after initial approval.

This process by itself may deter the Clydes and Coolidge from going forward with the proposed transfer. Objections often raise complex legal and technical issues for which lawyers and experts are necessary, increasing the cost of transfers.

> The high cost of statutory transfer proceedings almost certainly deters many transfers, particularly small or short-term trades. Small purchasers and sellers may often be able to escape high transfer costs if no one protests the transfer. But transfer proceedings can be quite expensive if anyone challenges the transfer and in states with more burdensome transfer procedures. Recent surveys of Colorado and New Mexico proceedings involving various-sized transfers, for example, revealed costs that ranged from a few hundred dollars to almost $50,000. Although large transfers can spread these costs over hundreds or even thousands of acre-feet, smaller transfers cannot. The Colorado and New Mexico surveys suggest that, on average, statutory transfer procedures impose costs of at least $300 per acre foot on transfers of twenty acre feet or less. Conservatively assuming water prices of $1500 or less per acre foot, therefore, the statutory transfer process can in a typical case add twenty percent or more onto the cost of small purchases.

> The length of the process can be equally problematic. Many transfer applications take only a month or two to resolve, but the average processing time appears to range from six months to one and one-half years (with controversial transfers occasionally taking up to several years). Such time delays are unlikely to deter many long-term transfers, which often go through considerable advance planning and negotiating. Multimonth proceedings, however, can easily deter short-term transfers, robbing

16. Most states permit any interested party to file a protest (although water users are generally given greater attention). See, e.g., Mont. Code Ann. § 85–2–308 (any interested party can file a protest); Bonham v. Morgan, 788 P.2d 497 (Utah 1989) (holding that the Utah state engineer had to consider objections of non-water users).

local regions of the ability to respond to droughts and transient changes in water needs.[17]

b. *Protection of Junior Appropriators*

The most frequent ground for objecting to a proposed change is that the change will injure other appropriators, whether senior or junior. Under the "no injury" rule followed by all western states, a proposed change will be approved only if it will not injure other appropriators or is conditioned in ways that avoid the injury.[18]

Consider the Clydes' proposed sale of 16 cfs to Coolidge, and assume for the moment that junior appropriators are withdrawing water downstream of Coolidge (as shown in Figure 3–5). The Clydes consume only 25 percent of their water. Currently, therefore, 15 cfs of the water that the Clydes divert is available as return flow to the junior appropriators. If Coolidge is permitted to use the entire 16 cfs that it proposes to buy from the Clydes, however, only 11 cfs will be available to the juniors. The Clydes will continue to use 4 cfs, of which 3 cfs will return to the river; because Coolidge consumes half of the water it withdraws, only 8 cfs of the water it withdraws will return to the river—for a total of 11 cfs. Junior appropriators will face a shortfall of 4 cfs.

The only way to protect junior appropriators is to prohibit Coolidge from withdrawing more than 8 cfs of the 16 cfs that it purchases. See Figure 3–6. Eight cfs of the purchased water will remain in the river and not be withdrawn. Of the 8 cfs that are withdrawn, 4 cfs will return to the river. 12 cfs will therefore remain available for junior appropriators which, when added to the 3 cfs of return flow from the Clydes, equals the 15 cfs of return flow available before the transfer.

---

17. Barton H. Thompson, Jr., Institutional Perspectives on Water Policy and Markets, 81 Cal. L. Rev. 673, 704–05 (1993). For an interesting but dated review of how states actually handle water transfers, see Lawrence MacDonnell, The Water Transfer Process as a Management Option for Meeting Changing Water Needs (1990).

18. See, e.g., Farmers High Line Canal & Reservoir Co. v. City of Golden, 975 P.2d 189 (Colo. 1999); W.S. Ranch Co. v. Kaiser Steel Corp., 79 N.M. 65, 439 P.2d 714 (1968).

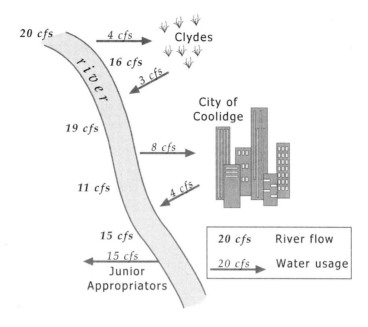

Figure 3–6

This, however, does not end the inquiry. Coolidge wants to use the water year-round while the Clydes have been appropriating water only from April through September. If Coolidge is permitted to expand the season of use, this would injure junior appropriators who currently divert the water from October through March. Coolidge thus will be allowed to take 8 cfs only from April through September.[19] If Coolidge needs water the remainder of the year, it will have to store some water for later use or find some other solution.

Differences in the timing of return flows may further complicate the proposed transfer. If Coolidge stores some water for use later in the year, this will shift some return flow to later in the year and injure junior appropriators who currently rely on the return flow from the Clydes' April through September operations. Even if Coolidge does not store water, there can be timing problems. It may currently take days or weeks for the Clydes' return flow to work its way to the river; the Clydes' use of water in September may therefore support a junior appropriation in October. If Coolidge returns water to the river faster than the Clydes, there may not be enough water in October to satisfy that junior appropriation. Thus, the shift in the timing of return flows might violate the no harm rule.

---

19. See Kelly Ranch v. Southeastern Colorado Water Conservancy Dist., 550 P.2d 297 (Colo. 1976); City of Westminster v. Church, 167 Colo. 1, 445 P.2d 52, 58 (1968).

Junior appropriators may also complain if Coolidge's sewage system does not produce the same quality of return flow as the Clydes currently provide. Although there are few cases on point, junior appropriators are protected in quality as well as quantity.[20]

To change the hypothetical slightly, assume that the junior appropriators are downstream from the Clydes but upstream from Coolidge (as shown in Figure 3–7). The junior appropriators withdraw all of the Clyde's current return flow (15 cfs) and take it to another watershed; none of the water returns to the Eldorado River. To avoid injury, the junior appropriators must be permitted to continue to take 15 cfs after the proposed sale. This, however, will leave only 5 cfs for sale to Coolidge—assuming that the Clydes are willing to sell their entire water right—and even less if they wish to continue to use some water.

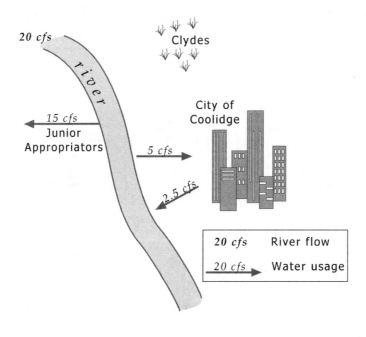

Figure 3–7

Notes and Questions

1. Even a relatively simple transfer, in short, can produce complications. The hypotheticals discussed above, moreover, assume a constant streamflow. As Willis Ellis has pointed out, any attempt to protect junior appropriators when water is being transferred becomes even more complex when one considers the possibility of diminished streamflow in times of

20. See City of Florence v. Board of Waterworks, 793 P.2d 148 (Colo. 1990); *Kelly Ranch,* supra note 19, 550 P.2d at 307; Heine v. Reynolds, 69 N.M. 398, 367 P.2d 708 (1962).

drought. See Willis Ellis, Water Transfer Problems: Law in Water Research (A. Kneese & S. Smith, eds., 1966).

Return to our original hypothetical, shown in Figure 3–5, in which the Clydes wish to sell 16 cfs of water to Coolidge. Assuming that 20 cfs of water is available, we noted above that Coolidge would be permitted to withdraw only 8 cfs in order to protect the juniors. What, however, if only 10 cfs is available in the Eldorado River? One is tempted to say that Coolidge could still withdraw 8 cfs because it would be senior after the transfer. But if the transfer did not take place, the Clydes would withdraw 10 cfs—of which 75 percent, or 7.5 cfs, would return to the river and be available to the juniors.

To make sure the juniors are not worse off after the transfer, Coolidge must be limited to 3 cfs when only 10 cfs is available in the river. See Figure 3–8. The Clydes would withdraw the 4 cfs that they are not selling and consume 1 cfs of it, leaving 9 cfs for downstream users. Coolidge would withdraw 3 cfs, of which 1.5 cfs would return to the river—leaving a total of 7.5 cfs for the juniors.

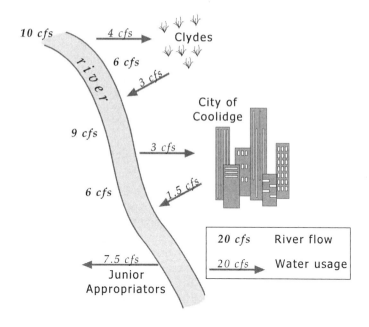

Figure 3–8

Perhaps not surprisingly, we have not found any published opinion discussing how to treat transfers during periods of below-normal streamflow. Must courts, or administrative agencies, go through new calculations for each new setting? Can the law tolerate some harm to juniors in return for administrative simplicity?

2.   Why should junior appropriators be protected against the side consequences of water transfers? A principal justification is economic. If a particu-

lar quantity of water is being used over and over, the value of that water is its worth not just to the first user but to all users. If a city is able to acquire the right to all the water for a price that merely exceeds its value to the first user, the transfer may be inefficient. The injury to junior appropriators who are now without water may exceed the marginal benefit of the water to the city. By protecting junior appropriators, the law "internalizes" that injury and forces the city to take it into account.

Equitable considerations also underlie the no injury rule. Historically, many junior appropriators did not know, and had no reason to suspect, that they were diverting the return flow of an upstream appropriator. Whatever their initial understanding, moreover, over the years junior appropriators have made investments and built farms and other businesses based on their diversions. In this setting, the law does not allow transfers to divest junior appropriators of the water they have been using.

3. By parity of reasoning, if a transfer would create new return flow (e.g., the 2.5 cfs return flow shown in Figure 3–7), the purchaser ought to be able to charge any downstream beneficiaries. Otherwise, a potential purchaser might choose to forego a transaction because the cost of the water exceeds the purchaser's private benefit—even though the total benefit to all water users would exceed the cost. See Charles Meyers & Richard Posner, Market Transfers of Water Rights: Toward An Improved Market in Water Resources 27 (1971). The law, however, does not require downstream beneficiaries of new return flow to pay the purchaser for their windfall. Should it? If so, how should the payment be calculated? Absent a legal mandate, is there any practical way that a potential purchaser could force downstream appropriators to pay for the increased return flow? If the purchaser later wished to sell the increased return flow to a third party, could the purchaser do so? See the earlier discussion of rights of recapture supra pp. 197–215.

4. As discussed in the section on rights of recapture, the law permits water users to recapture runoff before it reaches a natural stream even over the objections of a neighbor who has been using the seepage water (see supra pp. 197–201). Water importers can recapture their return flow even if that reduces the amount of water used by downstream juniors (see supra pp. 211–215). And in at least some settings, the law permits cities to sell or reuse their sewage effluent without worrying about downstream juniors who have grown reliant on that effluent (see supra pp. 201–209). Why should the law suddenly care about "downstream" users when a water right holder wishes to transfer the entire right? Are there any policy reasons to differentiate among these various situations?

5. Procedurally, a water right holder who wishes to change the point of diversion or the nature, place, or time of use has the burden of presenting at least a *prima facie* case that the change will not injure junior appropriators. See, e.g., Danielson v. Kerbs Ag., Inc., 646 P.2d 363 (Colo. 1982). In most states, the burden of proof then shifts to any protesters to refute the evidence and demonstrate that the proposed change would injure them. See, e.g., Farmer's Reservoir & Irrigation Co. v. Consolidated Mutual Water Co., 33 P.3d 799 (Colo. 2001); CF & I Steel Corp. v. Rooks, 178 Colo. 110, 495 P.2d 1134, 1136 (1972).

Presenting even a *prima facie* case of no injury can be an extremely complex task. See, e.g., Mark Squillace, Water Marketing in Wyoming, 31 Ariz. L. Rev. 865, 893–96 (1989). Because return flows are typically not a matter of record, experts must try to estimate the flows. One need only imagine a river with dozens or even hundreds of diversions, all producing and using return flow, to appreciate how difficult it can be to determine the impact of changing any given water right and having to assure that no appropriator will be worse off after a transfer.

6. Advocates of water markets have sought a way to protect junior appropriators without the difficulty, time, and expense of the current process. Which, if any, of the following approaches would improve on the current process?

• Shift the entire burden of proof to protesters to show that they *will* be injured. Supporters of this approach argue that proving a negative is inherently difficult and that protesters are likely to have better access to the information necessary to determine whether there will be an injury.

• Delay an evaluation of injury until a transfer has actually been made and there is some experience to tell us how, if at all, junior appropriators are injured. According to supporters of such "trial transfers," actual experience can avoid interminable speculation about the effects of changing the place of diversion or the time, place, or nature of use. California provided for trial transfers of one year or less beginning in 1980[21]—only to eliminate them in 1988.[22] Only three California water users, moreover, opted to use trial transfers. Is California's experience surprising? See also Colo. Rev. Stat. § 37–92–304(6) (permitting water judges to condition transfers on reconsideration of injury after a trial period).

• Use simple formulas to determine the amount of water that can be transferred. Many states, for example, have or could develop agricultural consumption tables that show the typical per acreage consumption of water for various crops and geographic regions. Where agricultural users propose retiring acreage or switching to lower consumption crops, states could use such tables to determine the amount of water that could be transferred without reducing return flow.

• Relegate junior appropriators to damages. Junior appropriators would not be able to block a change, but if they could prove injury from the transfer, they could collect damages from the transferor.

• Create a "compensation fund" by imposing a tax on all water transfers, and then use that fund to compensate junior appropriators for any injury that they suffer from the transfers.

7. Assume that the Clydes actually use their water in another watershed. Although the Clydes consume only 5 cfs of water, the remaining 15 cfs seeps into an underground aquifer where it is unavailable for further use. If the Clydes sell 16 cfs of their water to Coolidge, is there any reason why Coolidge should not be able to divert the entire amount? No junior appropriators would be injured. In a similar case, however, the Wyoming Supreme Court held that a purchaser could not consume more water than the seller

21. 1980 Cal. Stat. ch. 933, § 12.   **22.** 1988 Cal. Stat. ch. 1145, §§ 2 & 3.

consumed—even though increased consumption would not injure any junior appropriator. Basin Electric Power Coop. v. State Bd. of Control, 578 P.2d 557 (Wyo. 1978). The problem lay in the terms of the Wyoming transfer statute, which the court chose to interpret literally:

> The change in use, or change in place of use, may be allowed, provided that the quantity of water transferred by the granting of the petition shall not exceed the amount of water historically diverted under the existing use, *nor increase the historic amount consumptively used under the existing use,* nor decrease the historic amount of return flow, nor in any manner injure other existing lawful appropriators.

Wyo. Stat. § 41–3–104(a) (emphasis added). Is there any room for interpreting this statute to permit an increase in consumptive use?

8. Assume that some of the water that is not consumed by the Clydes seeps into an underground aquifer from which other farmers have been appropriating water for years. Can those farmers complain about the proposed sale? The answer may depend on the degree to which the state has integrated its surface water and groundwater allocation systems, discussed infra pp. 454–468. In many states, the farmers may not have a basis for complaint. Is there any legitimate justification for protecting junior surface water appropriators but not groundwater users?

HIGH PLAINS A & M, LLC v. SOUTHEASTERN COLORADO WATER CONSERVANCY DISTRICT

Supreme Court of Colorado, 2005.
120 P.3d 710.

JUSTICE HOBBS delivered the Opinion of the Court.

Applicants High Plains A & M, LLC and Wollert Enterprises, Inc. (collectively, "High Plains") appeal the water court's dismissal of their applications for change of water rights. High Plains applied to change water rights historically used for irrigation to any one of over fifty proposed uses in any of twenty-eight Colorado counties. The water court found the change application "so expansive and nebulous" that there was no way to determine whether vested water rights would be injured by the change or to determine if there would actually be a new beneficial use made of the water. The court found that the proposed changes were "such a deviation from the original right" that they effectively requested a new water right. As such, the court found that the applications violated Colorado's anti-speculation doctrine, and granted the objectors' motion for summary judgment.

The water court decision and the briefs and arguments of the parties focused on the application of the anti-speculation doctrine to change applications. Reviewing our cases and the applicable statutes, we determine that the anti-speculation doctrine is rooted in the requirement that an appropriation of Colorado's water resource must be for an actual beneficial use.

We hold that, in defining "change of water right" to include "a change in the type, *place*, or time *of use*" and "a change in the point of diversion" in section 37–92–103(5), C.R.S. (2005)(emphasis added), and in defining "appropriation" in section 37–92–103(3)(a)(I) and (II), Colorado's Water Right Determination and Administration Act ("the 1969 Act") anticipates, as a basic predicate of an application for a decree changing the type and place of use, that the applicant will sufficiently demonstrate an actual beneficial use to be made at an identified location or locations under the change decree, if issued.

Accordingly, we affirm the water court's judgment dismissing High Plains's change of water right applications, without prejudice to re-filing when a definite location or locations for beneficial use of the water can be identified in the applications and confirmed in the water court's proceedings.

I.

The Fort Lyon Canal Company (FLCC), a mutual ditch company in southeastern Colorado since 1897, operates an extensive system of canals and reservoirs with decreed Arkansas River direct flow and storage water rights for the benefit of its shareholders. FLCC's canals total approximately 150 miles irrigating nearly 93,000 acres of agricultural land located between La Junta and Lamar; aside from the Fort Lyon Canal, the longest in Colorado, the company has also developed an extensive reservoir system. FLCC is the largest ditch company in the Arkansas River Basin, with 93,989.41 outstanding shares.

High Plains is a private water investment company. It has purchased approximately 115 farms served by the Fort Lyon system, along with 20,000 FLCC shares. High Plains also owns options to purchase over 8,000 additional shares, for a total ownership and control of almost 29,000 shares, or approximately thirty percent of all the outstanding FLCC shares.

On December 31, 2002 and March 28, 2003, High Plains filed two essentially identical change applications for different blocks of shares it has acquired. An independent shareholders group ("ISG") filed a third, virtually identical application. ISG consists of forty-five ranchers and farmers holding almost ten percent of FLCC shares. The water court consolidated the three applications. * * *

The FLCC water rights sought to be changed have priority dates ranging from 1884 to 1969. The decreed points of diversion and storage include several reservoirs, supply ditches, and pipelines along the eastern stretches of the Arkansas River and its tributaries * * *

The applications propose several new points of diversion, including at headgates on the Holbrook and Colorado canals and "one or more alternate points of diversion" along the Arkansas River between its confluences with Adobe Creek and the Purgatoire River. The applications propose that water diverted at these new points may be stored in Holbrook, Dye, Lake Meredith, Lake Henry, and Pueblo Reservoirs. The applications do not identify structures owned or slated for construction by High Plains that would transport the water from these diversion and storage points to particular new places of use.

The applications propose to change the place of use to any of twenty-eight counties where the water might be used:

> in addition to lands currently under the Fort Lyon Canal, the subject water rights, both for the previously decreed uses and for the proposed new uses, may be used on any lands that can be served by the subject water rights from the existing and decreed points of diversion and/or places of storage and/or from the proposed alternate points of diversion and/or places of storage listed hereinabove within the following Colorado counties * * *: Otero, Bent, Prowers, Pueblo, Crowley, Kiowa, Custer, Fremont, Chaffee, Park, Teller, El Paso, Lincoln, Elbert, Douglas, Jefferson, Lake, Clear Creek, Gilpin, Denver, Arapahoe, Adams, Washington, Boulder, Broomfield, Larimer, Weld, and Morgan.

The change applications list an array of changed uses High Plains wants decreed:

> from irrigation and other presently decreed uses to: all beneficial uses, including but not limited to irrigation, municipal, domestic and household purposes, drinking, cooking, cleaning, showers, toilets, irrigation of yards, lawns, shrubbery, trees, pools, fountains, and landscapes, watering domestic animals; mechanical, manufacturing, and industrial, military, and governmental purposes; bottled water; generation of electric power and power generally; fire suppression and protection; sewage treatment; street sprinkling; irrigation of parks, grounds, golf courses, and open spaces; recreation, golf course hazards, ponds, fishing, and fish propagation; agricultural uses, livestock watering and aquiculture; land and reservoir evaporation; maintenance, preservation and conservation of wildlife, wildlife habitat, wildlife propagation, and wetlands; creating, maintaining and enhancing aesthetic values; in-stream flow; erosion control, siltation control, and flood control; maintaining storage reserves; adjustment and regulation; augmentation; replacement; groundwater recharge; exchange. * * *

The applications state that "after the change, the subject water rights will still be able to be utilized for agricultural and irrigation purposes * * * on lands under the Fort Lyon Canal."

The applications seek a decree for one-hundred percent consumptive use of the water derived from exercise of the changed water rights:

> applicants seek a decree from the Court that they have the right to use, reuse, and successively use to extinction, and dispose of, by sale, exchange or otherwise, all water lawfully diverted and/or stored pursuant to any decree entered in this case.

In compliance with FLCC bylaws, High Plains and ISG made a single, lengthy presentation to the FLCC board of directors regarding their proposed changes to their shares. After considering the evidence presented, the FLCC board found that the changes could be implemented without injury to other shareholders, if specific terms and conditions were imposed. Specifically, the board rejected the applicants' formulae for determining historic consumptive use and their characterization of certain water as non-tributary, thereby increasing the amount of return flow that they would have to pay back to the system under the change plan. Further, the board required the applicants to submit written agreements with all shareholders on lateral ditches affected by the change or used for return flow, imposed particular requirements for revegetation and management of dry-up land, and required specific survey and accounting procedures for the applicants' planned use of FLCC reservoirs for storage. The board approved the proposal to continue taking the decreed shares in rotation with other users and to continue to pay annual assessments. * * *

Objectors Southeastern Colorado Water Conservancy District, Lower Arkansas Valley Water Conservancy District, District 70 Irrigating Canals Association, Amity Mutual Irrigation Company, Carl M. Shinn, Mary Jane Shinn, and Wendy S. Shinn filed a motion for summary judgment, arguing the applications violated the anti-speculation doctrine and presented no specific plan which could be assessed for injury to other water users.

At the time it filed its applications and the water court ruled on the opposers' summary judgment motion, High Plains had no agreements with any persons or entities to place the changed water rights to beneficial use under a change decree in any of the listed twenty-eight counties.

In dismissing the applications, the water court reviewed basic principles relating to water appropriations and change applications, including the necessity for the applicant to identify an actual beneficial use to be made under the sought-for change decree. The water court made the following findings:

> Here, the Applicants seek the change for virtually any use where water may be necessary without identifying the specific use and/or end user. Applicants' plan is so expansive and nebulous that it is impossible for other holders of water rights to determine whether they will be injured. Furthermore, there is no discernible method to determine whether the water will be put to a beneficial use.

The water court found that such an application could "easily circumvent the anti-speculation doctrine" and concluded that the doctrine must be applied to the change applications. The court found the applications to be speculative in nature and granted the opposers' summary judgment motion. We affirm dismissal of the applications, for the reasons stated in this opinion.

Reviewing our cases and the applicable statutes, we determine that the anti-speculation doctrine is rooted in the requirement that an appropriation of the public's water resource must be for an actual beneficial use. To implement this requirement, adjudication of water right and change of water right applications includes identification of the structures through which the appropriated water will be diverted and delivered for identified beneficial uses at identified locations.

II.

* * *

Because they are perfected only by actual use, appropriations of surface water and tributary ground water—whether adjudicated by a conditional, absolute, or change of water right decree—have a situs that includes the point of diversion and the place where the actual beneficial use occurs. * * *

Encapsulating this long-standing principle of Colorado water law, the 1969 Act provides that " 'water right' means a right to use in accordance with its priority a certain portion of the waters of the state by reason of the appropriation of the same." § 37–92–103(12), C.R.S. (2005). "Appropriation" is the "application of a specified portion of the waters of the state to a beneficial use pursuant to the procedures prescribed by law." § 37–92–103(3)(a), C.R.S. (2005); see also Combs v. Agric. Ditch Co., 17 Colo. 146, 150–52, 28 P. 966, 967–68 (1892).[2] * * *

From the earliest days of its water law, Colorado has recognized that water users have the right to make changes to the terms of their decrees through the adjudication process the General Assembly sets forth. Strickler v. Colorado Springs, 16 Colo. 61, 70, 26 P. 313, 316 (1891) (holding that water rights, as property, may be sold and transferred to another type and place of use, so long as the rights of others are not injuriously affected); An Act in Relation to Irrigation, ch. 105, sec. 1, 1899 Colo. Sess. Laws 235 (providing for petition procedure to make changes to decreed water rights).

A change of water right decree recognizes that the priority of the existing right can be operated for new uses at different locations under conditions necessary to maintain the appropriation without injury to other decreed appropriations. Our seminal change of water rights decision, *Strickler*, involved a city's purchase of agricultural water rights for change to municipal uses. In that case, we established the following points of Colorado water law applicable to changes of water rights: (1) the water resource is the property of the public; (2) the priority of a use right obtained by irrigating a particular parcel of land is a property right

---

2. In *Combs* we considered the operations of a carrier ditch company and were particularly concerned about the possibility of carrier companies tying up large amounts of water for "speculation and monopoly;" accordingly, we held that "the privilege of diversion is granted only for uses truly ben- eficial, and not for purposes of speculation." 17 Colo. at 152, 28 P. at 968. A carrier ditch company owns title to the decreed appropriation, but it must have contract users who place the water to actual beneficial use in order for the appropriation to be obtained and maintained.

that can be separated from the land; (3) the owner of the use right may sell it to another person or governmental entity; and (4) the courts may decree a change in the point of diversion, type, time, and/or place of beneficial use, subject to no injury of other water rights. * * *[3]

The essential function of the change proceeding is to confirm that a valid appropriation continues in effect under decree provisions that differ from those contained in the prior decree. When we examine the 1969 Act, we find that the appropriator's interest in the appropriation for an actual beneficial use is a prerequisite for maintaining the application and obtaining a decree.

Section 37–92–103(3)(a)(I), C.R.S. (2005), provides that a purported appropriator must have a "legally vested interest or a reasonable expectation of procuring such interest in the land or facilities to be served by such appropriation, unless such appropriator is a governmental agency or an agent in fact for the persons proposed to be benefited by such appropriation." * * * Section 37–92–103(3)(a)(II) provides that the purported appropriator of record must have "a specific plan and intent to * * * capture, possess and control a specific quantity of water for specific beneficial uses." * * *

Section 37–92–103(3)(a)(I) and (II) apply in a change in type and place of use proceeding * * *. Accordingly, the change applicant must show a legally vested interest in the land to be served by the change of use and a specific plan and intent to use the water for specific purposes. This statutory requirement can be satisfied by a showing that the appropriator of record for purposes of the change decree is a governmental agency, or a person who will use the changed water right for his or her own lands or business or has an agreement to provide water to a public entity and/or private lands or businesses to be served by the changed water right.

Our cases concerning the anti-speculation doctrine do not disapprove of water development or private investment in water projects; rather, they re-emphasize our traditional requirement that appropriated water is applied to actual beneficial use. * * *

As our cases repeatedly demonstrate, each water right has a situs identified by the point of the diversion and the place to which the water is delivered for actual beneficial use. A water right requires both an

3. The roots of Colorado water law reside in the agrarian, populist efforts of miners and farmers to resist speculative investment that would corner the water resource to the exclusion of actual users settling into the territory and state. In this context, Colorado's adoption of the principle that the public owns the water, its abolition of riparianism (the ownership of water rights by reason of land ownership along the banks of streams), its constitutional limitations on maximum rates that individuals or corporate suppliers can charge for water, the actual beneficial use limitation restricting the amount of water that can be appropriated from the public's water resource, and the right to obtain a right-of-way to construct water facilities across the private lands of another with payment of just compensation, all reflect the anti-monopolistic undergirding of this state's water law. See David B. Schorr, Appropriation as Agrarianism: Distributive Justice in the Creation of Property Rights, 32 Ecol. L. Q. 3, 33, 41, 55–56 (2005).

appropriator and a place where the appropriation is put to actual beneficial use. Accordingly, a change decree recognizes a new situs for the appropriation. In defining "change of water right" to include "a change in the type, place, or time of use" and "a change in the point of diversion," section 37–92–103(5), C.R.S. (2005), and in defining "appropriation" in section 37–92–103(3)(a)(I) and (II), the 1969 Act anticipates, as a basic predicate of an application for a decree changing the place of use, that there is a sufficiently described actual beneficial use to be made at an identified location or locations under the change decree.

High Plains has applied for a change of water right so that it can make use of various different points of diversion and storage and can put the water to use in any number of Front Range locations for any number of purposes. The specifically-listed types of uses all appear to be components of municipal use, yet the application does not identify any particular municipal or quasi-municipal entity with which High Plains has an agreement for actual beneficial use of the water sought to be transferred. Nor does High Plains identify any parcels of private land, businesses, or a service area for specific consumers of the water to be served under the change decree.

There is a critical difference between High Plains's change application and the changes approved by water courts addressed in our prior decisions involving type and place of use changes from agricultural to municipal. In *Strickler*, where we first approved a change of farm water rights to a city, the party requesting the change was the municipality itself, Colorado Springs. Likewise, in Farmers Highline Canal & Reservoir Co. v. Southworth, 13 Colo. 111, 21 P. 1028 (1889), the City of Golden applied to change agricultural water rights that it had purchased to municipal uses. In City of Thornton v. Bijou Irrigation Co., 926 P.2d 1 (Colo. 1996), the City of Thornton applied to change water rights it purchased.

In this case, High Plains asserts that it has had some "discussions" with "water users" in fourteen of the twenty-eight counties listed in the applications, but admits that it has "not entered any contracts for use, other than irrigation" of the water rights it owns or controls. Although counsel opined on oral argument that the water might be used in El Paso and Douglas counties due to population growth and waning aquifers there, no water user or potential water user in those or any other counties stepped forward by the time of the change applications to subscribe for raw or retail water supply service from High Plains, should it obtain the change decree.

The purpose of a change of water right is to obtain a revised decree that recognizes continuation of the right to divert the water at different points, for different uses, and/or different places of actual beneficial use. A guess that a transferred priority might eventually be put to beneficial use is not what the Colorado Constitution or the General Assembly envisioned as the triggering predicate for continuing an appropriation under a change of water right decree. The change application process is intended to facilitate transfers that are calculated to result in a continued application of the appropriated water to specified beneficial uses at different identified locations from the current decree under conditions to prevent injury to other water rights.

The transfer of senior priorities to other uses and locations is a very important feature of Colorado water law.[6] In view of the over appropriated status of three of its four major rivers, this state's future well-being likely depends on continued transfers of appropriated agricultural water to other uses at other places. Colorado has grown from two million residents in 1970 to 4.6 million today, with an additional 2.5 million expected by 2030. Much of this growth has been made possible by a steady change of water rights from agriculture to municipal use that started one-hundred-fifteen years ago with *Strickler*.

Nevertheless, the General Assembly did not intend that courts and potential opposers be burdened with change applications premised on conjecture. Change proceedings can be extremely expensive to participants and consume many days of trial and appeal time—taking away from the courts' attention to other needs of the citizens of Colorado. * * *

High Plains argues that it is prejudiced by dismissal of its applications because of risk to its investment and because it cannot enter into contracts with end users until it has court approval to change the water rights. This argument reverses the well-established methodology for change of type and place of use proceedings. * * *

Applicants for a change of water right must expect full scrutiny of their applications by opposers and compliance with applicable procedures and substantive laws. * * *

It is possible that High Plains harbored unrealistic expectations when it purchased such a large interest in FLCC. The water court's concern about the "nebulous and expansive" nature and scope of the High Plains application undoubtedly stems from ambiguity about whom the requested change decree is going to serve, when, how, and in what capacity—ranging from simple resale of some or all of the shares over time to providing raw or retail water service to others. In any event, High Plains's applications for a change in the type and place of use are

---

6. Despite the importance of marketability of water rights, water use rights are not traditionally treated as if they were simply a commodity. "The situation involving water is very unusual, and it applies to virtually nothing else. For purposes of interstate commerce, for example, all other state resources may be privatized fully, and freely shipped away from the area of origin as ordinary commodities—even though states have often tried to keep such resources within their own boundaries to benefit their own residents. Such efforts have routinely and repeatedly been held unconstitutional by the courts. The only other common example where things are treated like water—that is, as community resources and not as ordinary salable commodities—arises with cultural properties, antiquities for example, where the nation of origin often asserts a national claim on the property in order to prevent exports." Joseph L. Sax, Understanding Transfers: Community Rights and the Privatization of Water, 1 West–N.W. 13, 14 (1994)(internal citations omitted).

premature in the absence of identified places of actual beneficial use for operation of the change decree. As we said in *Combs*, a stockholder in an irrigating company "can only transfer his priority to some one who will continue to use the water." 17 Colo. at 152, 28 P. at 968. Without prejudice to consideration of future applications for change of water rights associated with shares of FLCC High Plains now owns, we uphold the trial court's order dismissing the applications in this case.

III.

Accordingly, we affirm the water court's judgment.

Notes and Questions

1. Is there any way that a court can ensure that a transfer will not injure other appropriators without knowing how or where water will be used after the transfer? What if a water transferor like High Plains agrees not to divert more than has been consumptively used in the past and not to divert the water upstream of the current diversion point?

2. Why shouldn't someone be able to buy a water right without knowing for sure how it will be used? Are speculative acquisitions of water rights bad? Why? For defenses of speculation in water rights, see The Good Speculator, Rocky Mtn. News, July 18, 2004, at 7E; Stephen Williams, The Requirement of Beneficial Use as a Cause of Waste in Water Resource Development, 23 Nat. Resources J. 7 (1983). Judge Williams' article is excerpted infra p. 302, along with a longer discussion of the anti-speculation doctrine.

3. Cities often acquire water rights for their residents and businesses without knowing exactly who will be using the water, for what purposes, or where. Cities indeed often acquire water for only unspecified future needs. Yet the court in *High Plains* suggests that acquisitions of water by municipalities do not raise speculation concerns. See the court's discussion at pages 281–282. Do you agree that acquisitions by cities for future uses are different from what High Plains sought to do? If High Plains submitted a change application in which it specified that it would be selling water to industry, subdivisions, and others within a single metropolitan area, should Colorado law authorize the transfer?

4. As the court notes, High Plains argued that it needed to get court approval before it could get end users to negotiate contracts. According to one of the attorneys in the case, "That's pretty significant. A big buyer would be far more reluctant to buy, knowing the courts still had to approve the change of use. That would involve a lot of time and uncertainty." Karl Licis, Impact of Colorado Water Rights Ruling May Be Felt in Several Other Cases, The Pueblo Chieftain, July 7, 2004. Is this convincing? Couldn't High Plains and interested buyers sign contracts contingent on court approval? Assuming that the need to return to court for approval of each individual sale would make it more difficult to transfer water, should the law be changed? How?

c. Historical Use

Another frequent ground for objecting to water transfers is that the seller has not historically used his full water right or has been wasting water. Consider again the Clydes hypothetical. The facts strongly suggest that the Clydes have not been using all of their water. In most western regions, the Clydes would probably need only a small fraction of their 20 cfs to irrigate their 640–acre farm—even using relatively inefficient irrigation techniques. Early appropriations, moreover, were frequently in excess of actual need because there was no administrative system to police the amounts claimed.

Assume that, in fact, the Clydes have been diverting and using only 5 cfs. As discussed earlier at pages 247–256, a court might hold that the Clydes have either *abandoned* or *forfeited* the remainder.[7] Even if there has been no abandonment or forfeiture, most states provide that water sellers can transfer only the water that they have historically been using, whether or not they have a permit or judicial decree giving them a larger right.[8] See, e.g., Santa Fe Trail Ranches Property Owners Ass'n v. Simpson, 990 P.2d 46 (Colo. 1999); Weibert v. Rothe Brothers, Inc., 200 Colo. 310, 618 P.2d 1367 (1980). But see W.S. Ranch Co. v. Kaiser Steel Corp., 439 P.2d 714 (N.M. 1968) (decree, not historic use, determines amount of water that can be transferred).

The Clydes' abnormally low "efficiency" also suggests that the Clydes have been wasting water. If waste can be shown, junior appropriators may also object that the Clydes should not be permitted to sell water that they have been wasting. As discussed earlier at pages 189–190, some states have adopted statutes permitting water users who conserve water to use or sell the amount conserved. See, e.g., Cal. Water Code § 1011; Or. Rev. Stat. §§ 537.455 et seq. Some states, however, would not permit the Clydes to transfer conserved water.

The possibility that the Clydes' water right will be challenged for waste or lack of use further reduces the chances of a transfer. Neither the Clydes nor Coolidge may wish to bear the risk that the state will cut back on the water right. The Clydes will worry that by proposing to sell their water, they will invite attacks on their current water rights— perhaps leaving them in the unenviable position of having no sale and a reduced water right. Coolidge could agree to pay for the water no matter what the outcome of the application process, but is unlikely to want to buy a pig in a poke. To the extent that use and waste issues are raised, moreover, the parties may face considerable trial expense. Because of inadequate records, historical use questions typically devolve into complex debates between opposing experts.

---

7. See, e.g., Dovel v. Dobson, 122 Idaho 59, 831 P.2d 527 (1992).

8. Although historical use is defined differently from state to state, it is typically an average of recent years' use. See, e.g., City of Westminster v. Church, 167 Colo. 1, 445 P.2d 52, 56–57 (1968) (10–year moving average).

d. Streamlined Procedures and Exemptions

Should all transfers be subject to the same procedures? A handful of states have reduced the procedural hurdles for short-term transfers, particularly during droughts, on the dual grounds that lengthy evaluation processes can pose insurmountable barriers to such transfers and that the need for regulatory protection often is minimal. Under the typical procedure, someone wishing to make a short-term transfer notifies the state agency which then must decide whether to approve the transfer within a specified short period of time. There typically is no requirement of a general notice to the public, and the state agency must approve the transfer unless information shows that the transfer will injure other water users. See, e.g., Idaho Code § 42–222A (authorizing expedited review of short-term transfers during periods of drought emergency); Ore. Rev. Stat. § 540.523 (authorizing expedited review of transfers of 5 years or less; approval of transfer can be revoked at any time if evidence arises showing injury to other water users). See also Colo. Rev. Stat. § 37–92–309 (exempting "interruptible water supply agreements" lasting ten years or less from full judicial change procedure).

A Model Water Transfer Act, drafted by a committee of California legal and economic experts, also proposes distinguishing between short-term and long-term transfers. Under the Model Act, short-term transfers could take advantage of an expedited review process that would use agricultural consumption tables, where possible, to determine the amount of water that could be transferred. Any downstream juniors who nonetheless were injured could file claims against a compensation fund financed by a tax on water transfers. For long-term transfers, agricultural consumption tables, where usable, would establish only a rebuttable presumption of the amount that could be transferred. Protestors could overcome this presumption by proving injury. See Brian E. Gray, The Shape of Transfers to Come: A Model Water Transfer Act for California, 4 West–Northwest 23 (1996).

Water users might be able to structure some water transfers to avoid state review entirely. Assume that a junior appropriator wishes to acquire water rights from a senior on the same river. If the junior engaged in a straight-forward purchase or lease of the water rights, the junior would normally need to apply for a change in the rights. An alternative, however, might be for the junior to purchase a "consent-not-to-sue" agreement (also sometimes known as a "subordination" or "stand aside" agreement) in which the senior would agree not to object if the junior took additional water. Because no rights have exchanged hands, the latter might not require state approval. Should the two transactions be treated differently? Would that be elevating form over substance? This option only works, of course, where there is no "intervening junior" with an unmet water right who could claim a superior right to any water that the senior fails to use.

2. TRANSFERS OF PERMITS

IN RE APPLICATIONS OF THE CATHERLAND RECLAMATION DISTRICT

Supreme Court of Nebraska, 1988.
230 Neb. 580, 433 N.W.2d 161.

FAHRNBRUCH, J.

[The Little Blue Natural Resources District (Little Blue) filed four appropriation applications to divert and impound water from the Little Blue River, initiating a lengthy review proceeding that made its way up and back to the Nebraska Supreme Court several times. While the applications were still pending, Little Blue assigned its four applications to the Catherland Reclamation District (Catherland). The Nebraska Director of Water Resources approved the assignment and granted the applications. The matter then wound its way again to the Nebraska Supreme Court where a central issue was the power of Little Blue to assign its applications.]

The Director was clearly wrong in holding the assignment to be valid. The assignment is clearly invalid as a matter of law.

As the objectors point out, there is no statutory authority permitting Little Blue to assign an application for water diversion. * * *

At all relevant times herein, Neb. Rev. Stat. § 2–3233 gave natural resources districts the power to acquire and dispose of water rights in accordance with Neb. Rev. Stat. ch. 46, art. 2, and to acquire and dispose of personal property. Little Blue did not assign or transfer a "water right" to Catherland; it attempted to assign only pending applications to divert water. As hereinafter determined, applications for water rights are not personal property and are not assignable. Further, we find no provision within chapter 46, article 2, for the assignment of a water right application from one entity or individual to another.

An application to divert water is simply a request for permission to appropriate public waters of the state. Approval of an application merely authorizes the successful applicant to begin construction and to take other measures necessary to perfect the application into an appropriation. After an application is approved, § 46–237 requires that the applicant file a map or plat with the department detailing the proposed irrigation project. That section further provides that "no rights shall be deemed to have been acquired until the provisions of this section shall have been complied with * * *."

By simply filing its applications to divert water, Little Blue received no "water right" which could be "disposed of" pursuant to § 2–3233. * * * This court has made it clear that a water right applicant has no transferable property right in a mere application to divert water.

The initial step for procuring an appropriation right for irrigation purposes is the filing of an application for such permit. The granting of the application, in full or in part, is an adjudication which fixes the maximum volume of the appropriation, the rate of diversion, and the priority date. If an applicant is dissatisfied with the terms of the appropriation allowed, he must appeal, or the order becomes a final and binding adjudication. Its grant by the department is notice to senior and junior appropriators, as well as new applicants, of the extent of the appropriation. The grant of the appropriation by the department, however, is a conditional right which becomes a perfected and completed application only when the works are completed and the waters put to a beneficial use in compliance with the conditions and limitations of the grant. It confers upon the applicant the prior right to the water against all subsequent applicants during the progress of the work if, and only if, he finally complies with the conditions and limitations of the appropriation as adjudicated by the department.

Catherland sought the assignment of Little Blue's applications to take advantage of Little Blue's priority date. Permitting the assignment of applications could lead to collusion, thereby defeating the rights of other parties along a river. This would occur where, as here, an applicant no longer wished to pursue its application, but, instead of abandoning it, transfers it to someone who desires an early priority date. By such a procedure, parties having filed applications in the intervening period could be effectively deprived of their priority rights. Clearly, the effect of allowing such assignments is against the public interest.

That an assignment of a water diversion application is invalid is supported by United States v. Fallbrook Public Utility District, 165 F. Supp. 806, 855 (S.D. Cal. 1958), which held:

> Until the application to appropriate is acted upon by the State Water Rights Board favorably to the applicant, and the issuance of a permit is directed, the applicant has no property right of any kinds as against the state. [The applicant has only] an inchoate, incipient, conditional right of procedural priority over later applicants. * * *

Thus, if Little Blue could assign anything, it would only be its inchoate, incipient, conditional right of procedural priority over later applicants, not its application. Carried to its logical conclusion, allowing assignments of procedural priority over later applicants would result in unfair advantage to the highest bidder. It has been held, and we so hold, that assignments of procedural rights are void. * * *

Notes and Questions

1. What result if Little Blue had waited until its applications had been approved and then, before completing its proposed irrigation project, had tried to assign its rights under the approved applications? In Green River Development Co. v. FMC Corp., 660 P.2d 339 (Wyo. 1983), the Wyoming Supreme Court held that unperfected water permits could not be transferred. According to the court, an appropriator gains "a transferable water right only to the extent that he has put his appropriation to beneficial use."

Id. at 344. Accord Hanson v. Turney, 94 P.3d 1 (N.M. Ct. App. 2004) (agreeing that permits cannot be transferred where water has not yet been put to beneficial use). But see Nev. Rev. Stat. § 533.324 (providing that appropriated water includes water for which a permit has been issued even if the water has not been applied yet to the intended use).

2. As a matter of policy, why allow transfers of completed appropriations but not applications or unperfected permits? The value of the water that Little Blue sought to appropriate presumably was more valuable to Catherland than to Little Blue, or Little Blue would not have been willing to assign its applications. Prohibited from transferring their applications, applicants such as Little Blue might abandon their applications, but they might also decide to proceed with their water projects. Would that be a good result?

3. Should the law discourage people from selling one water right and then turning around and acquiring another? South Dakota has enacted legislation that prohibits a landowner who transfers an irrigation right to a domestic or municipal use from acquiring another irrigation right for the same land. S.D. Codified Laws § 46–5–34.1.

3. PROTECTING THIRD PARTY INTERESTS

As the number of water transfers has grown, rural communities have expressed increasing concern about the potential impact of water transfers on their economies and environment. Where a farmer conserves the water he sells, there may be little, if any, negative impact on the community or environment. In many cases, however, farmers fallow their fields and sell their water to urban areas miles away. Should the law ensure that such transfers do not damage local communities and their environment? If so, how?

The question here obviously is similar to the issue of area-of-origin protection discussed supra at pages 234–243. Water markets, however, raise concerns not only about reductions in native water supplies but about changes to existing economies and community structures. Indeed, transfers from agricultural to urban use can threaten economic and community change even where the urban use will be in the same watershed. In many cases, moreover, the community from which the water will be sold is not the area-of-origin, but an agricultural region that itself has imported the water from another watershed.

NATIONAL ACADEMY OF SCIENCES, WATER TRANSFERS IN THE WEST: EFFICIENCY, EQUITY, AND THE ENVIRONMENT

45–54 (1992).

Rural Communities

Economic and Fiscal Impacts

* * * No issue gave the committee more trouble than the question of how to characterize and evaluate the effects of water transfers on small communities. The reason is obvious: no consensus exists within

our society about the value of these communities. The communities generally have no legal right because we view them as inferior units of central state governments, and we generally allow the market to dictate their fate. Nonetheless, we do value many rural communities, and we are sometimes willing to buffer them against market pressures. The widespread use of historic preservation controls is one example of such a buffer. As the nation becomes more urbanized and homogenized in the twentieth century, the virtues of rural communities are being extolled with a Jeffersonian fervor. However, many of the justifications for the preservation of rural communities simply reflect an elegiac view of the past that cannot serve as the basis for contemporary public policy. * * *

Retiring irrigated land can lead to losses of farm jobs, crop production, and farm income. These direct effects can be measured with a fair degree of accuracy. However, indirect impacts of water transfers, such as losses of off-farm jobs, income, and production in non-farm businesses and households, are more difficult to estimate. Another type of economic impact, "induced impacts," includes changes in population, employment, and income in local businesses and activities not linked to agriculture but dependent on the vitality of the local economy in general. Retail stores, restaurants, and local services may be affected by a decline in agriculturally linked jobs and income.

Some economists have argued that water transfers will not impose large and sudden shocks on rural economies because only the marginal lands, those least suitable for crop production and least profitable to irrigate, will be sold and farmers will simply concentrate their efforts on their remaining high-quality lands and most profitable crops. However, there is growing evidence that it is not only the marginal agricultural acreage that is being purchased. Potential water buyers are willing and able to buy out the properties with the most secure and senior water rights to high-quality water sources, in the most convenient locations, regardless of the crop being grown or farm profitability. * * *

Although the impacts caused by transferring water formerly used in farming to other areas and uses are difficult to quantify, and may be small in relation to a state's entire economy, they are significant to area-of-origin residents. Although each individual water farm purchase may involve only a small fraction of the area of origin's total land and water resources, it is important to consider the cumulative effects of such purchases. Factors that make property attractive for water farms in La Paz County, Arizona, have led purchasers to concentrate in a few areas adjacent to aqueducts that can convey water to new uses. This clustering effect also is apparent in the Arkansas River Valley in Colorado. The result is that local economic impacts of transfers are borne by specific towns and counties. * * *

Environmental Effects of Retiring Irrigated Farmland

When land is retired from irrigated agriculture, the natural process of revegetation produces a secondary succession of plant species. Succession continues until the plant community has stabilized. Russian thistle (tumbleweed) is the characteristic species in the first phase of secondary succession on abandoned farmland in much of the Southwest. Tumbleweeds are effective in dispersing their seed, and they quickly dominate the land to the virtual exclusion of all other species.

The natural succession process varies with the climate and soil type. Farmland in relatively high rainfall areas and with coarse soils may move past the tumbleweed phase in a few years. But secondary succession is slow on fine-textured soil with low rainfall. In parts of Arizona, for example, little revegetation has occurred on farmland abandoned 20 years ago. Instead, the soil has crusted over in large barren areas where no vegetation can be established, generating nuisances of blowing dust and tumbleweeds. Some rural residents have noted that the value of nearby farmland decreases when adjacent land succumbs to disuse. The negative effects of farmland retirement on wildlife, especially small game, also have been noted. * * *

Social impacts caused by water transfers, which are even more difficult to quantify, but no less genuine, include effects on community cohesion, local traditions and cultural values, and the political viability of local governments and irrigation districts in the area of origin. One pervasive effect of water transfers on areas of origin is loss of local self-determination as the future of an area moves beyond the control of its residents. It is this sense of uncertainty, frustration, and vulnerability, as much as the visible, tangible damages, that is fueling the demands for regulation of water transfers from rural areas of the West.

A Cautionary Note on Area-of-Origin Protection

Several factors are relevant to evaluation of the indirect effects transfers can have on rural economics, and these need to be considered before a policy of area-of-origin protection is adopted. * * * A transfer can appear negative from a county-of-origin perspective but result in positive net benefits when viewed from a statewide perspective. For instance, one study of the Arkansas River Valley in Colorado found that recent transfers resulted in a net income loss of $53 per acre-foot, but that the market value of water in the urban areas exceeded $1,000 per acre-foot.

Although water transfers can bring negative effects, it is important to recognize that a dynamic, growing economy depends on processes that allow declining industries and firms to be displaced by growing firms and industries. Recent U.S. experience with the decline of several primary industries in the rust belt is an example. Government does not typically move to protect declining industries or to provide full indemnification to people displaced by industrial decline. * * * If the economy of the West is to remain vibrant and if national and world demands for food and fiber produced in the West do not grow substantially in coming decades, then some disinvestment in irrigated agriculture is probably inevitable and desirable. Efforts to forestall rather than to effect an orderly transition are likely to be counterproductive in the long run. * * *

ECOSYSTEMS

The integrity of ecosystems depends on healthy wetlands, riparian areas, estuaries, and associated fish, wildlife, and vegetation. Transfers of surface or ground water can have significant impacts on water-dependent flora and fauna within western riverine, riparian, and wetland ecosystems. In the arid West, these ecosystems typically occur in narrow bands along river corridors. Water development over the last century destroyed many of the large wetland complexes located at the terminus of closed-basin river systems. Entire species of plants and animals in the arid West are now threatened with extinction because of the reduction of critical river corridor habitat. At the same time, some irrigation activity actually created small wetlands that rely on the numerous leaks and seeps along earthen conveyance systems. Large riparian trees such as cottonwood and willow also came to grow along some regulated river corridors and conveyance canals. Over time, birds and mammals have become dependent on the wetlands maintained by irrigation return flow. As water is transferred, both the quantity and the quality of the water delivered to these wetlands are likely to diminish. * * *

INSTREAM FLOWS AND RELATED BENEFITS

In most states, impacts on streamflows are not routinely considered when a water transfer proposal is evaluated. Thus foregone instream benefits can be a significant third party impact caused by water transfers. As noted earlier, instream flows are vital in preserving fish and wildlife habitat in arid regions. But instream flows are also critical to water-dependent recreation, and these leisure activities draw visitors and tourism dollars to the region.

Notes and Questions

1.   As the National Academy of Sciences notes in its report, the closing of a major factory can have a severe impact on the local community, but we do not give the community or state officials the right to prevent such closings. Is there any reason to treat water transfers differently? See Joseph Sax, Understanding Transfers: Community Rights and the Privatization of Water, 1 West–Northwest 13 (1994); Barton Thompson, Water Law as a Pragmatic Exercise: Professor Joseph Sax's Water Scholarship, 25 Ecology L.Q. 363, 379–83 (1998). For an argument that communities should have veto power over plant closings, see Joseph Singer, The Reliance Interest in Property, 40 Stan. L. Rev. 611 (1988).

2.   Should it matter whether the local community from which water will be exported is the area of origin for the water or itself imported the water from another watershed. If County A imported water from County B, what grounds does it have to complain if someone now wishes to purchase the water and transfer it to County C? One of the co-authors of this book has

suggested that the important issue is not whether County A is the area of origin but whether a community has been built around its water use. "Once such uses are established, the removal of water constitutes a disruption in that community, even if the community is only a few decades old, and thus also constitutes wealth redistribution." Sax, supra note 1, at 16. Do you agree?

3. If the law should protect local communities from the potential impact of water transfers, should the law also protect them from the potential impact of regulatory changes? For example, should local communities receive compensation if the Endangered Species Act requires reductions in local water use? See Thompson, supra note 1, at 382 (arguing that the situations are very similar).

4. Not all transfers have a negative impact on the environment. As noted earlier, some transfers reduce the pressure to appropriate additional water or to construct new, environmentally damaging water projects.

> The promise of more wild rivers preserved is just one of the environmental benefits of water marketing. Fallow agricultural lands can revert to native grasslands or wetlands, letting natural flora and fauna repropagate. Whether farmers sell all their water rights or just the rights to water they manage to conserve, irrigation return flows are reduced and problems with pesticides, salts, toxic materials, and waterlogging are alleviated. * * * Since cities consumptively use less water, per acre-foot withdrawn, than irrigated agriculture, major transfers of water to urban users could create more reliable flows for fish, wildlife, and recreation—even for downstream agriculture. Moreover, urban water is often returned to a river in a less contaminated state than if it has percolated through chemically farmed croplands—especially if they overlie thick alkaline deposits, as many western farms do.

Marc Reisner & Sarah Bates, Overtapped Oasis: Reform or Revolution for Western Water 58–59 (1990).

5. As discussed supra pp. 220–234, most western states now require that new appropriations of water meet a "public interest" standard. A growing number of states also have extended the public interest standard to changes in water rights, including water transfers.

CHARLES DUMARS & MICHELE MINNIS, NEW MEXICO WATER LAW: DETERMINING PUBLIC WELFARE VALUES IN WATER RIGHTS ALLOCATION

31 Ariz. L. Rev. 817, 824–826 (1989).*

The requirement that transfers be consistent with the public welfare became [New Mexico] law in 1985.[a] Because few transfer applications

* Copyright © 1989 by the Arizona Board of Regents. Reprinted by permission.

a. As amended in 1985, N.M. Stat. Ann. § 72–5–23 provides: "All water used in this state for irrigation purposes * * * shall be considered appurtenant to the land upon which it is used, and the right to use it upon the land shall never be severed from

have been challenged on this ground, the full ramifications of the requirement are not known. The likelihood the ramifications will be prolix is perhaps best illustrated by the case of Sleeper v. Ensenada Land and Water Ass'n. This case directly pitted the economic values associated with a new ski development against the cultural values of a northern New Mexico community.

Events leading up to the *Sleeper* suit date to the late 1970's, when Tierra Grande Corporation began developing a subdivision in conjunction with a large ski resort development near Ensenada, New Mexico, a small farming community in the north central part of the state. While building roads for the new subdivision, Tierra Grande dug a gravel pit then, later, transformed the pit into a recreational lake by damming the Nutrias Creek. The Nutrias, a tributary of the Rio Brazos, empties into the Ensenada irrigation ditch before it joins the Rio Brazos. Fed mainly from snowmelt, the Nutrias runs heavily during the spring and is dry by late May or early June. The Ensenada Land and Water Association uses the creek's waters, drawn off the Ensenada ditch, to fill irrigation reservoirs and "fertilize" the soil with its rich silt. Association members use the Rio Brazos water when the Nutrias run dry.

Tierra Grande's actions in damming the creek violated laws regarding the building of dams and the diversion of water. When the state engineer discovered the lake, he ordered Tierra Grande to breach the dam. After complying with the order, Tierra Grande contracted with two local property owners to purchase their lands and appurtenant water rights. The parties conditioned the purchase upon the state engineer's approval of the property owners' application for change of use, place of use, and point of diversion of their surface water rights.

The Applicants requested a one-time diversion of 61.32 acre feet of water from Nutrias Creek to create the lake, and, thereafter, annual diversions of 13.32 acre feet to compensate for evaporative loss. These diversions necessarily would result in the retirement of agricultural land, because when water rights used to irrigate land are transferred to a nonagricultural use, the previously irrigated land must be retired from agriculture. To offset loss of water from the creek, the Applicants proposed to temporarily retire 64.55 acres of irrigated land during the year the lake was filled, then, the next year, permanently retire 14.02 acres of irrigated land.

In 1982, the Applicants applied for transfer of the surface water rights. The Ensenada Association protested, alleging that the transfer would impair existing rights and would be contrary to the public inter-

the land without the consent of the owner of the land, but, by and with the consent of the owner of the land, all or any part of the right may be severed from the land, simultaneously transferred and become appurtenant to other land, or may be transferred for other purposes, without losing priority of right theretofore established, if such changes can be made without detriment to existing water rights and are not contrary to conservation of water within the state *and not detrimental to the public welfare of the state*, on the approval of an application of the owner by the state engineer." (emphasis added).—Eds.

est. Relying upon hydrologic studies and a finding that the transfer would not impair existing rights, the hearing officer recommended that the state engineer approve the transfer application. When the state engineer acted on this recommendation, the Ensenada Association appealed his decision, and the state district court reversed in a *de novo* hearing.

At the district court hearing, Ensenada Association argued that the transfer would be contrary to the public interest because it would result in the permanent loss of agricultural land and, inasmuch as ditch maintenance expenses after the transfer would be borne by fewer people than before, would increase the financial obligations of individual Association members.

Applicants contended that economic development resulting from the proposed resort project would be in the public interest because it would stimulate the local economy. The resort would generate construction jobs, such as the building of second homes, in the Ensenada area. Eventually, the Applicants claimed, the tourist industry associated with the project would provide more local jobs shifting the populace from an agricultural subsistence economy to an economy based on tourism.

An expert for Ensenada Association countered that the development of tourism/recreation facilities would not improve the financial outlook of people currently residing in the area. The resort project would provide only menial jobs, such as those for waiters and maids. Overall, he said, most local residents would never realize any benefits from the resort economy.

Presiding at the hearing, Judge Art Encinias addressed the conflict between economic and cultural values inherent in the dispute. Although Encinias used the "public interest" rather than "public welfare," it is clear he considered the terms synonymous. * * *

IN THE MATTER OF HOWARD SLEEPER

District Court of New Mexico, First Judicial District, 1985.
No. RA 84–53(C).

ART ENCINIAS, DISTRICT JUDGE:

* * *

The evidence plainly suggests that such development creates few jobs for local inhabitants, except at menial levels. Over the long run, the local inhabitants lose management level jobs to outsiders and are relegated to service jobs, such as waiters and maids. Other locals survive on the fringe of the tourist industry by becoming professional "natives." Most other locals never realize any particular benefit from the resort economy. * * *

Northern New Mexicans possess a fierce pride over their history, traditions, and culture. * * * The deep-felt and tradition-bound ties of northern New Mexico families to the land and water are central to the maintenance of that culture. * * * [T]he evidence discloses a distinct pattern of destruction of the local culture by development which begins with small, seemingly insignificant steps.

[The judge further found that economic development, by way of a ski resort and subdivisions, would erode the community's agricultural subsistence economy through the retirement of land and would create additional community burden as members opt out of the ditch system].

I am persuaded that to transfer water rights, devoted for more than a century to agricultural purposes, in order to construct a playground for those who can pay is a poor trade, indeed. I find that the proposed transfer of water rights is clearly contrary to the public interest. * * *

Notes and Questions

1. The Court of Appeals reversed Judge Encinias' decision in Ensenada Land & Water Ass'n v. Sleeper, 107 N.M. 494, 760 P.2d 787 (Ct. App. 1988), on the ground that the public interest standard applied only to original permit applications for unappropriated water and not to applications for transfers of existing rights. Though the New Mexico law had been expressly amended in 1985 to make conservation and public welfare criteria applicable to transfer proceedings, the court held that those statutes were not in force at the time of the requested transfer in this case. The County Commission then enacted an ordinance effectively prohibiting the use of irrigation water rights for subdivision development and requiring subdividers to seek other sources of water. The "Purposes" section of Article III of the ordinance stated in part:

> Spanish settlements in the County date from the year 1598. The Spanish acequias, or ditch systems, formed the basis for social organization and community life. A distinctive way of life, based on a fusion of Spanish and Indian traditions, has been maintained in communities throughout the County based on agriculture. It is the purpose of these regulations to protect the unique culture * * * by ensuring that all subdivisions are created in harmony with this culture, and contribute positively to it, rather than detract from it.

> The County finds * * * that the transfer of water rights from traditional uses, such as irrigation by the acequias, to residential subdivision or commercial uses, will generally not promote the public welfare. * * *

Land Subdivision Regulations 1 (Rio Arriba County, N.M.). Reportedly, the developer went bankrupt, and the transfer never occurred.

2. In addition to requiring water officials to consider the general "public interest" in deciding whether to approve a transfer or other change in use, a few states also mandate specific consideration of any adverse impacts on the local community, the environment, or both. California, for example, provides that its board may approve a transfer involving a public agency

> only if it finds that the change may be made * * * without unreasonably affecting fish, wildlife, or other instream beneficial uses and

does not unreasonably affect the overall economy of the area from which the water is being transferred.

Cal. Water Code § 386. See also id. § 1736; Wyo. Stat. § 41–3–104(A) (requiring consideration of the "economic loss to the community").

Do state-level reviews of local community impacts run the risk that local concerns will be swamped by broader state interests? If so, would that be bad or good? Do broad state-level reviews of local impacts also run the risk of deterring useful transfers by unnecessarily adding to the expense and time involved in getting state approval?

3. Should states adopt any of the following approaches as either a replacement for or supplement to general state reviews of local community impacts?

• Prohibit any water transfer that would export water out of a local community or to a different use. See Neb. Rev. Stat. §§ 46–290 to 46–294 (authorizing transfers only if within the same river basin and, in the case of permanent transfers, between uses in the same preference class).

• Give local communities veto power over transfers of water to users outside their borders. If this approach were adopted, how should the local community be defined, and who should wield the veto power on behalf of the community? The Arizona legislature considered but rejected legislation that would have prohibited the export of groundwater from small rural counties without the unanimous approval of the county board of supervisors. In Nevada, county commissions make recommendations to the state engineer concerning proposed exports of water from the county, but the recommendations are not binding on the state engineer.

• Prohibit those categories of transfers that are most likely to injure the local community, such as transfers involving the fallowing of land. Alternatively, a state could give special preference to transfers that minimize local harm, such as transfers of conserved water where the current water user plans to continue the same level of economic activity.

• Restrict the total amount of water that can be transferred out of a geographical region.

• Permit water transfers only where the seller can no longer make beneficial or economic use of the water. See Nev. Rev. Stat. § 533.040; 82 Okl. Stat. § 105.22 (restriction applicable only to irrigation water); S.D. Codified Laws §§ 46–5–34 to 46–5–36 (same, with exception for transfers to municipal water system).

• Pay compensation to local communities that are injured by water transfers. Nevada provides for a tax on all inter-county transfers of groundwater that is deposited in a trust fund to help pay for economic development, health care, and education. A transferor can avoid the tax by entering into an agreement with the county of origin to mitigate any adverse economic impacts of the transfer. See Nev. Rev. Stat. §§ 533.438–533.4385. The Model California Water Transfer Act also proposes using a tax on transfers to fund compensation to local communities. See Brian Gray, The Shape of Transfers to Come: A Model Water Transfer Act for California, 4 West–Northwest 23 (1996).

4. For an entertaining fictional account of a situation with striking similarities to *Sleeper,* see John Nichols, The Milagro Beanfield War (1974). See also Shannon Parden, The Millagro Beanfield War Revisited in Ensenada Land and Water Association v. Sleeper: Public Welfare Defies Transfer of Water Rights, 29 Nat. Resources J. 861 (1989); Diane K. Brownlee, The Public Vote in the Game of Water Wars: An Unquenchable Thirst to Define and Implement "Public Values" in Western Water Laws, 70 U.M.K.C. L. Rev. 647 (2002).

4. CRITICISM OF WATER MARKETS

Recall the concerns about water markets raised by Elwood Mead in the late 19th century. See supra p. 266. Mead, in particular, argued that water was a public resource that should be regulated by the government rather than allocated by the market. Some legal scholars still question the wisdom and ethics of water markets, even if the law effectively addresses third party impacts. The following excerpt, which focuses on water markets in Hawaii, is typical of the criticisms.

WILLIAMSON CHANG, WATER: CONSUMER COMMODITY OR GOVERNMENT SUBSIDY

Water Values and Markets: Emerging Management Tools.
18, 18–20 (1986).

To many mainstream economists, the answer to all resource allocation problems is reliance on the free market. Mainstream economists believe that the most efficient allocation of water resources will take place under the notions of the "general equilibrium" and the "clearing of the market." The crux of such thinking is the view that water is a commodity like anything else and that experience and econometric equations prove the superiority of the invisible hand of the free market.

The issue of whether or not water should be treated as a commodity is presently the focus of a statewide debate in Hawaii on water policy. * * * The Advisory Study Commission on Water Resources, appointed by the Governor, recommended against the sale of water and drafted a bill which prohibited such sales.

On the other hand, the sugar industry, the largest user of freshwater on the island of Oahu, strongly favors a system allowing the purchase and sale of water rights. * * *

Many people in the state of Hawaii, however, are intuitively opposed to the purchase and sale of water. In the case of Hawaii, as in other chronically watershort areas, their intuitions appear to be correct. Their arguments against treatment of water as a commodity would apply to many other regions of the United States.

The first reason why a neoclassical market system would not work in the case of water rights in Hawaii is that there is a strong sentiment that the largest user of water in Hawaii, the sugar industry, does not have a justifiable political and moral right to profit from the sale of water.

Secondly, in Hawaii there is a strong feeling among many people that, given the significance of water to life on an island, freshwater is simply too important to be given over to free market forces. On Oahu, which has a population of 800,000, there are two large institutions which pump groundwater: the city water system and the sugar industry. If supply and demand were the only forces which governed the allocation of water, these two major institutions could easily eliminate diversified agriculture and drive out small farmers in the competition for scarce water. If such a situation developed, Hawaii would become less self-reliant in terms of food production and more dependent upon food importation. * * *

A third reason why a free market system is politically unacceptable in Hawaii is that it is difficult to justify why present users should have the right to initiate sales of such water. In other words, why should present users be granted ownership with the attendant right to sell?

Granting the power to sell to the present large users would result in unjust enrichment. The legal claims of large users to sell water is in doubt. In short, there is no reason to justify giving present users, as opposed to any other group, the windfall profits which would be theirs by the adoption of a free market system. Rather, water should be viewed as a public resource which would be granted to those who would use it in the most beneficial manner.

Finally, as water becomes more and more scarce and thus more and more important to the livelihood and future of Hawaii, water policy is too critical to be left to market forces, by which one hopes that individual greed will eventually result in policy that serves the community as a whole.

Hawaii and its water system can be analogized to a spaceship going through space on a journey which will take many generations to reach its destination. On board is a limited amount of such goods as clothing and a finite quantity of such renewable resources as food and water. Which system of allocation would work best in such a self-contained fragile environment: a system where resources were collectively pooled and distributed according to need, or a free market system where those who brought the most money on board would be allowed to hoard resources to the deprivation of others?

The grant by government permit to use water should be viewed as a policy of government subsidization of desired outcomes. Thus, water policy would be molded by limited-duration permits much as national economic policy is molded by tax deductions and credits—not unlike the creation of solar energy tax credits designed to encourage a desirable policy of self-sufficiency in energy. The water permit, like the tax credit, may go out of existence when government planning deems that a more efficient, more important use has arisen. * * *

Water should not be viewed as a commodity, because water policy should not be viewed as a commodity. Government regulation has a legitimate role in any policy-making that requires a communal outlook. This is the case for land use planning, national defense, the maintenance of a police force, and environmental concerns—including water policy.

Notes and Questions

1. Professor Eric Freyfogle has argued that water markets also send the wrong ethical signal to water users:

> The dominant message of water rights is that water is a commodity, an object that exists for humans to move and manipulate, a thing that exists primarily to serve human needs. As a commodity, water is like other commodities, like bricks or teacups or paper bags or pianos. It is something we can use and consume and throw away, all as we like. This message is not entirely false, but it is not true by more than half. Water-as-commodity misses the ecological values, the spiritual values, the aesthetic values. It erroneously and dangerously suggests that water is valuable primarily as a tool for one person—the owner—to use to gain economic advantage over other persons. The far different reality, it ought to be clear, is that water is much more than a commodity: It is something else as well, something more that the law of water needs to recognize. A sound water law would embody and transmit sensitive, ethical messages about the multiple values of water. * * *

Eric Freyfogle, Water Rights and the Common Wealth, 26 Envtl. L. 27, 35 (1996). Are markets truly antithetical to a broad ethical view of water? See also Harrison Dunning, Reflections on the Transfer of Water Rights, 4 J. Contemp. L. 109 (1977).

2. Should a water user be permitted to profit from a water right that the state originally gave away for free or for a small permit fee? California provides that, where a public entity is the buyer or seller, an appropriative right held under permit or license cannot be sold at a price exceeding the amount paid the state for the permit or license. Cal. Water Code §§ 1392 & 1629. The provision, however, is universally ignored.

3. As Professor Chang notes, a draft Hawaiian water code would have prohibited sales of water rights. The Hawaiian legislature deleted the prohibition from the final version of the code, but noted that the deletion did not imply that the legislature was affirmatively sanctioning water sales. The circumstances, if any, under which water rights can be sold in Hawaii, therefore, is somewhat uncertain. See Douglas MacDougal, Testing the Current: The Water Code and the Regulation of Hawaii's Water Resources, 10 U. Haw. L. Rev. 205, 244–46 n. 224 (1988). Section 174C–59 of Hawaii's water code permits water transfers only if they involve no change in place, quantity, or purpose of use. Section 174C–57, however, permits a permittee to apply to change the use or place of use of a permit—apparently allowing someone to transfer a water permit, without change, to a second party who then can apply for a change in use or place of use. See In re Water Use Permit Applications, 105 Haw. 1, 93 P.3d 643 (2004) (approving such a two-step process).

F. ALTERNATIVES TO CONVENTIONAL WATER RIGHTS

1. THE BENEFICIAL USE REQUIREMENT CHALLENGED

One precept of prior appropriation law, examined earlier in connection with High Plains A & M, LLC v. Southeastern Colorado Water Conservancy Dist., supra p. 276, is that water may only be acquired for use, and not as an investment or, as it is routinely put, as a "speculation." The reason for the restriction, according to the Supreme Court of Colorado, is that

> Our constitution guarantees a right to appropriate, not a right to speculate. The right to appropriate is for *use,* not merely for profit. * * * To recognize [water rights] grounded on no interest beyond a desire to obtain water for sale would as a practical matter discourage those who have need and use for the water from developing it. Moreover, such a rule would encourage those with vast monetary resources to monopolize, for personal profit rather than for beneficial use, whatever unappropriated water remains.

Colorado River Water Conservation Dist. v. Vidler Tunnel Water Co., 197 Colo. 413, 417, 594 P.2d 566, 568 (1979).

The prohibition on speculative holding of water rights is usually implemented at the permitting stage. Permit laws typically require that there is a "physically and economically feasible" plan and that "the application was filed in good faith and not for purposes of speculation or monopoly." Utah Code Ann. § 73–3–8(1)(e) (1989). If a speculative scheme is not caught at the initial permitting stage, it is likely to run afoul of the additional permit requirement that a project be completed within a specified time (due diligence). See e.g., Idaho Code § 42–204. Colorado, which has no permit system, provides a parallel requirement. The court to which application for a water right is made will grant a conditional decree for an uncompleted project, subject to a sexennial court finding of "reasonable diligence" in bringing the project to completion. Colo. Rev. Stat. §§ 37–92–301(4), 302(1)(a), 601; Colorado River Water Conservation Dist. v. Denver, 640 P.2d 1139, 1142 (Colo. 1982). Where there is no evidence of an actual project the court may refuse even to grant a conditional decree. Jaeger v. Colorado Ground Water Comm'n, 746 P.2d 515 (Colo. 1987).

The author of the excerpt that follows, now a federal judge, argues that requiring water to be put to a beneficial use as a prerequisite to acquisition of an appropriative right is not only unnecessary, but positively undesirable. Far from treating speculation in water rights as an evil, he urges that speculation in water should be embraced as a positive good.

STEPHEN F. WILLIAMS,
THE REQUIREMENT OF BENEFICIAL
USE AS A CAUSE OF WASTE IN
WATER RESOURCE DEVELOPMENT

23 Nat. Resources J. 7, 11–15, 20 (1983).

The doctrine of prior appropriation is a rule of capture. Under the doctrine, one may acquire a property right in water only by applying it to a "beneficial use," and in no state does reservation of water for future use qualify as a beneficial use. * * * As a result, anyone anticipating a surge of future demand and higher prices for water rights can exploit that insight only by investing in diversion works. Such projects are likely to be premature or economically unjustifiable regardless of their timing. To the extent that premature or otherwise uneconomic investment occurs, the beneficial use requirement—ironically—causes waste. * * *

Similar waste would result from unmitigated application of the rule of capture to oil and gas reserves—the other great resources to which it nominally applies. All the major oil and gas states, however, have adopted conservation legislation aimed at curing the problem. It is thus curious that neither legislative action nor even scholarly discussion has focused on this defect of prior appropriation law. * * *

The proposal of anticipatory rights raises a series of practical problems and possible objections. Some problems relate to (a) the initial allocation of such anticipatory rights, others to (b) the effects of such a change after initial allocation.

INITIAL ALLOCATION

If anticipatory rights were allocated without charge, as current-use rights are, obviously the amount sought would vastly exceed the available supply. Moreover, those to whom such rights were allocated would enjoy a windfall. The solution * * * is an auction of some sort, perhaps modelled on government auctions for oil and gas leases. Presumably bidders would be willing to offer roughly their estimate of the present discounted value of the proceeds of sale of the water for the uses which they anticipated.

The auction solution would give some concrete meaning to the vague proposition, so much a part of current water law, that the unappropriated waters of the state belong to "the public." An auction would enable the public to realize on that purported ownership—now a matter of rhetoric—in the form of receipts flowing into the state treasury.

Not only does an auction solve the twin goals of (a) avoiding windfalls and (b) equating supply with demand, such a method also averts problems that arise when government allocates rights on the basis of vague notions of merit or public interest. The Federal Communication Commission's allocation of valuable radio and TV channels exemplifies such a method. The result is that applicants invest enormous resources in hiring high-priced lawyers to put on a largely meaningless show—meaningless because the criteria for the public interest are necessarily so elusive. Interminable and unmanageable procedures, inconsistent results, and corruption are also likely.

Identifying the "public interest" in connection with anticipatory water rights would be no easier. An auction decentralizes and objectifies the process of identifying anticipated projects with the greatest value. Bidders who win through excessive optimism will bear the loss. As a consequence, individuals unskilled at estimating future values will tend to be driven from the field and individuals with the necessary skills will tend to prevail.

The uses that will generate the highest returns for the owners of the water rights are not *ipso facto* the uses with the highest value when all other interests are also taken into account. Uses will vary in the extent to which they generate external costs or benefits, i.e., costs or benefits external to the calculation of the owner. But the problem of varying externalities is completely independent of the ownership of anticipatory rights. If it is appropriate for government to constrain actual water uses in the light of those externalities—whether by prohibiting or taxing disfavored uses, by subsidizing favored ones, or by administrative review of such effects as part of the process of change in water use—government may do so whether or not people are able to hold anticipatory rights.

Effects of Ownership of Anticipatory Rights

The primary objection to ownership of anticipatory rights is likely to be expressed as a fear of "speculation" and "hoarding." "The big oil companies will grab up all the rights." "Money means nothing to those companies." The fear deserves a very close look.

The first answer to such opposition is that prohibition of anticipatory rights does not prevent speculation. Rules proscribing reservations for future use merely force the would-be speculator to disguise his activity by wasting resources in the construction of diversion works that are either economically unjustifiable regardless of their timing * * *, or are premature. * * *

While fear of speculation and hoarding constitutes a primary objection to ownership of anticipatory rights, a related fear is that such rights will cause waste. This objection assumes that water will not be put to use between the time of acquisition of the right and ultimate application of the water to the long term use for which it was acquired. But anticipatory water rights need not prevent other uses in the interim. Suppose X is holding anticipatory water rights based on his expectation of an application to oil shale in the year 2010. Y comes along with a project that could use the water from 1982 through 2009, and the benefits from use in that period exceed the costs of the project. Clearly this creates an opportunity for a mutually favorable transaction between X and Y. And, assuming that there are many Xs and Ys (that is, many people holding anticipatory water rights and many people interested in renting them for the intermediate or short-term), there would be a competitive market for such rentals. * * *

Of course lessees of such rights would have to pay the owners rent, an expense that would be unnecessary if the water had remained unowned. But in a competitive market the rent would be no more than what was economically sound—the value of the most valuable alternative use precluded by the lessee's use of the water. No lessee should get the water unless his use is sufficiently productive to enable him to pay such a rental.

Even in markets with only one owner of anticipatory rights, that owner would still want to maximize his returns by making rentals. Such a monopoly position might cause fewer anticipatory rights to be leased than in a competitive market. The solution to such a problem would be a prohibition on any one entity's holding an excessive fraction of the total anticipatory rights outstanding.

A parallel fear expressed in the speculation and hoarding epithets is that owners of anticipatory rights will fail to sell them to water developers even when the time is ripe. But a properly functioning market provides incentives to discourage speculators from holding on to their properties for longer than is in the public interest. For example, what prevents an owner of undeveloped land from refusing to allow its development after the time for such action is ripe? If people with ideas for alternative uses can readily make bids for undeveloped land, the owner who persists in holding his land undeveloped incurs opportunity costs. He must forego not only the money offered by bidders but also the income that he could earn by investing that money. A speculator in coffee (or any other commodity in which definite property rights exist) incurs similar opportunity costs: if he fails to sell a bag of coffee today, he must forego the income that he could enjoy from the proceeds of the rejected opportunity to sell. The holder of a bag of coffee is constantly trading off the present value of a future sale against the present value of a current one. If the price bid by current consumers were to exceed the present value of the proceeds of a future sale, some holders would sell off (thereby bringing the price relationships back into equilibrium, so that the present value of a future sale just equals the current price).

To describe the incentive mechanisms which encourage speculators to sell at the right time is not, of course, to say that the right number of speculators will necessarily do so at the right time. But the market provides great rewards for those who decide correctly. Denial of those rewards to speculators who decide incorrectly constitutes a substantial penalty for them. Natural selection is likely to eliminate (or at least confine to a small portion of the market) all would-be speculators except those who are, on the average, good at choosing their timing.

In a properly functioning water market, similar incentives would operate on the owners of anticipatory water rights. Suppose, for example, that X has acquired water rights in anticipation of sale for oil shale purposes in the year 2010, at a price that he calculates will yield returns with a present value of $2 million. If entrepreneur Y conceives of a project that will start immediately and that will yield net returns with a present value higher than those of X's project, he should be able to offer X a sum large enough to induce him to sell. If the present value of the net returns from Y's project are, for example, $3 million, both parties can gain by a sale from X to Y at any price between $2 million and $3 million. * * *

MONOPOLY

Monopolistic control of anticipatory rights might also impede sale for long-term uses. Under some conditions a monopolist might profit by selling off, in any given time period, less than the quantity of anticipatory rights that would be sold off in a competitive market.[29] But solutions are available. The statute enabling creation of anticipatory rights could provide that no single entity would hold more than some specific percent of the anticipatory rights. The prohibition would have to operate so as to avoid evasion by the use of affiliates. Further, because water transportation costs are high, markets are to some degree local; thus it might be wise to place some additional ceiling on the fraction of anticipatory rights held by any one entity in each watershed.

The problem of monopolistic control seems, therefore, reasonably susceptible of solution. * * *

Question

Does Judge Williams persuade you that speculation isn't a problem, and that all the states have got it wrong? Would he claim that due diligence and forfeiture requirements should be abolished?

2. STATE LEASING AS A SUBSTITUTE FOR APPROPRIATION: THE MONTANA LEASING LAW

When Montana revised its water law in 1985 it added several novel elements. One feature of the modified code is a requirement that water for all major consumptive uses (more than 4,000 acre-feet per year and 5.5. cubic feet per second) and most trans-basin diversions can only be acquired by leasing from the state.[1] Lessees are to pay for the water leased. The total amount of water presently available for leasing under the statute is 50,000 acre feet.[2] Leases may not exceed 50 years, with a

---

29. The monopolist typically chooses a level of output lower than would prevail under competitive conditions. In the case of sale of a resource over time, however, he will tend to move sales away from the time periods where demand is inelastic and into periods where it is relatively elastic. This tendency might work to accelerate sales. * * *

1. Mont. Code Ann. § 85–2–301.

2. Leases may include a provision requiring "that up to 25% of the water to be leased be made available to a potential user for any beneficial use upon payment by such user of the costs of tapping into and removing water from the applicant's project." Mont. Code Ann. § 85–2–141(8). This latter provision would allow smaller users to take advantage of the major *infrastruc-*

possibility of renewal for a second 50 years. Leases are to be made by the Department of Natural Resources and Conservation if it determines "it is desirable * * * to lease water to the applicant * * * [up]on the following considerations: (a) the content of [an] environmental impact statement * * *; (b) whether there is sufficient water available under the water leasing program; and (c) whether the [public interest criteria, set out supra p. 231] have been satisfied."[3] The same statutory provision states that a lease "does not constitute a permit * * * and does not establish a right to appropriate water. * * * "For purposes of the water leasing program established in this section, it is the intent of the legislature that the state act as a proprietor.[4]

What is the goal of the Montana leasing law? Consider the following excerpt.

JOHN E. THORSON, WATER MARKETING IN BIG SKY COUNTRY: AN INTERIM ASSESSMENT

29 Nat. Resources J. 479, 480, 482–484 (1989).

The fear of water marketing was, ironically, the basis for Montana accepting marketing as an important means for protecting the state's water resources. During the energy boom of the 1970's and early 1980's, Montanans worried that portions of their state would become Owens Valley to massive coal plants and thirsty new cities. One symbol embodied these fears of devastation and ruin: coal slurry pipelines. A ban on coal slurry pipelines using water was enacted 1979.[2] The state also had a ban on the exportation of water out-of-state.[3]

By 1985, Montana decision makers began to appreciate three facts that ultimately led them to acquiesce in, if not embrace water marketing: (1) many water marketing opportunities already existed under law; (2) water marketing might increase the state's ability to profit from, as well as control and condition large water uses; and (3) water marketing as a concession to a tribe was useful in negotiating Indian water rights. * * *

A. LOCAL MARKETING

The fewest changes made in water marketing law were in local marketing, as Montana law already provided for the transfer and severance of water rights through the administrative system. The legislature did, however, adopt increasingly stringent public interest criteria to govern new appropriations and transfer of or changes in existing rights.

ture investments of water lessees (for example, canals or pipelines) without sharing their cost.
   3. Mont. Code Ann. § 85–2–141(7).
   4. Mont. Code Ann. § 85–2–141(9)-(10).

2. 1979 Mont. Laws 552, § 2, repealed by 1985 Mont. Laws 573, § 24.

3. 1921 Mont. Laws 220, § 1, repealed by 1985 Mont. Laws 573, § 23.

B. REGIONAL MARKETING

In the area of subregional marketing, the legislature was much more ambitious. It established a limited state water-leasing program that involved a maximum of 50,000 acre-feet (ac-ft) of impounded water. A lease from the state is now required to obtain water in any amount for transport outside any one of five specified river basins or for uses of water in excess of 4000 acre-feet/year (ac-ft/yr) and 5.5 cubic feet per second (cfs). Lesser amount of water can also be leased.

As water is leased, it is appropriated in the name of the state, and a certificate is issued to the state department of natural resources and conservation. If lease applications exceed 50,000 ac-ft/yr of water, the department must return to the legislature for additional leasing authority. Leases are limited to 50 years but can be renewed for up to an additional 50 years. Lease must be approved by the board of natural resources and conservation.

The source of water for the leasing program is impounded water from any reservoir within Montana. * * *

Water is leased through bilateral negotiations. On receipt of an application to lease water, the department evaluates the proposal with reference to statutory public interest criteria. The department can require that 25 percent of the capacity of a proposed project be set aside for municipal and rural purposes (upon payment by the municipal or rural government of the costs of the tie-in). All other terms and conditions are determined through negotiations.

The legislature was concerned about the impacts of water marketing on agriculture. For this reason, the legislation gives specific authority to the department to use differential pricing, and the explicit legislative intent is that agriculture leasing is to be preferred. The proceeds of the leasing program go to the state general fund. * * *

Notes and Questions

1. According to the Montana Department of Natural Resources, as of 1999, the leasing provision had only been invoked twice, once for a coal slurry pipeline, and once for a coal gasification project, neither of which actually went forward. Few projects involve such large water uses. Notably agricultural use is triggered only if at least 4,000 acre-feet are consumed, not merely diverted.

2. Leasing will produce revenues for the state, but why should the state charge for water? Is there some principle involved? The government does not charge for the use of books in the public library. Where it charges for the use of public beaches it usually does so only to recover its operating costs. Is water different? Are charges a means to prevent waste, and if so can we anticipate that the waste and beneficial use doctrines will wither away as the new leasing system comes into full operation?

3. What is the expected benefit of imposing terms on leases? Is the idea that the state will have an opportunity to reconsider beneficial use from time to time, and to take water away from those who—by then-current stan-

dards—are not using it beneficially? What will this do to conventional ideas of expectations? What sort of world would it be if the government periodically reconsidered whether land in private use (such as irrigated farm land) was being beneficially used? Is water different? Does it make either economic or policy sense to distinguish the treatment of land and water on an irrigated farm? What happens when the holder of a 50 year permit wants to sell her irrigated farm in the 49th year? Moreover, if the purposes of charging money for the use of water is to discourage non-beneficial uses, why not let market transactions do the necessary sorting out? Does the market keep land from being "wasted" in places where it is scarce and valuable?

4.   The literature on term broadcast licenses says that "once obtained the right is transferable [and] * * * for all practical purposes perpetual," even though the law specifically says "no such license shall be construed to create any * * * right beyond the terms, conditions and periods of the license." (47 U.S.C. § 301). See Howard Shelanski & Peter Huber, Administrative Creation of Property Rights to Radio Spectrum, 41 J. Law & Econ. 581, 584 (1998). The basic claim is that if something is functionally like property it will, in practice, take on the characteristics of a property right (e.g., become perpetual).

5.   The idea of term permits is not new. The Model Water Use Act, Water Resources and the Law (1958), proposed the following provision:

Section 406. [Duration of Permits.]

Each permit shall be issued for a specified period, not exceeding [fifty] years, as determined by rule, regulation, or order of the Commission, depending upon the manner and nature of the water use involved.

Comment: Each permit granted by the Commission is limited in duration. This limitation insures reevaluation at periodic intervals of the beneficial characteristic of the permitted use. The duration of the permit will be determined by the Commission in the public interest. The period of the permit should be sufficiently long to permit recovery of investments and to afford sufficient time for repayment of bond issues of municipalities. * * *

Another proposal for term permits, the Regulated Riparian Model Water Code, was adopted in 1996 by the American Society of Civil Engineers. The draftsman is Professor Joseph Dellapenna of Villanova University:

§ 7R–1–02 Duration of Permits

(1) The State Agency shall issue permits for a period of time representing the economic life of any necessary investments not to exceed 20 years, except that permits may be issued for a period reasonable for the retirement of debt associated with the construction of related facilities by a governmental or other public body or public service corporation not to exceed 50 years.

(2) Not more than six (6) months prior to the expiration of any permit, a water right holder may apply for a renewal of the permit; such an application is entitled to the renewal preference provided in section 6R–3–04(3) only if received by the State Agency before the permit expires.

Commentary: Time-limited permits maximize State control by enabling the State Agency to reallocate the waters of the State to more reasonable uses as the earlier permits expire. This approach reflects a conclusion that sales of water rights will remain relatively rare under a regulated riparian system just as they have under the more strictly private property regime of appropriative rights. * * *

The language in this section is modeled after Fla. Stat. Ann. § 373.236. * * * Following this model, if the conclusion that private sales will remain relatively rare is accurate, the Agency will be able to use the expiration of permits to facilitate the application of water to more socially valuable uses. Perhaps even more important than the outright denial of renewal of a permit is the power this gives to the Agency to revise the terms and conditions of the permits in light of changing circumstances. This power is likely to lead to ever more stringent requirements of conservation measures as well as other means of furthering the public interest in the waters of the State. Somewhat more favorable renewal terms and conditions might result if the renewal applicant has been successful in applying conservation measures or in following through on a plan of conservation. The alternative to this approach is to make market transfers significantly easier than is the case in any State today, something that could only be achieved by largely ignoring the "spill-over" effects of a market transfer.

Setting the proper duration of permits requires a delicate balancing of the need of investors for the security of right necessary to assure recovery of their investments and the need of the State to continue to manage actively an important public resource. The need for security of right would nearly always be less than the duration of economic life of the assets invested in the project, so that sets the upper limit to permit life. To simply provide that the permit shall run for the period necessary to retire any related debt would enable an applicant to extend the life of a permit by arranging ever longer periods of debt service. The normal term provided here is 20 years, which the Agency can adjust through its regulations to set a situation where 5% of the total permits will expire annually, allowing a more even and predictable workload. Depending on staffing and budget, the Agency might be able to handle some higher percentage annually, and can shorten the duration by regulation appropriately.

A legislature might prefer to set the duration directly and leave little or no discretion in the Agency on the matter. Should it do so, the legislature should allow a means for staggering expiration dates to assure an even and predictable workload. The most common duration found in actual regulated riparian statutes is 10 years, with a longer period of 50 years being provided for public investments on the theory that 50 years is the common period for bond issues used to finance public investments. This provides marginally better security for such investments (would any State Agency actually terminate a permit supplying water to thousands or millions of homes and their related economic bases?) and thus enables them to

obtain slightly better interest rates from the capital market. * * *
Several regulated riparian States have found it acceptable to provide
for shorter durations than that provided in this section, apparently
without significant adverse effects on investment in water within
the state. Perhaps this reflects the reality that permits will seldom
be completely denied renewal when they expire, although new terms
and conditions will often be attached to a permit upon its renewal.
* * *

G. PRACTICAL ISSUES IN WATER ADMINISTRATION

One way to think about the administration of water rights is to
imagine a comparison with the administration of rights in land. Since
rights in land are described and recorded in a title system, there is
usually no particular difficulty in determining who owns the right to use
a given tract. And—since each parcel of land is separate from all
others—once that right is ascertained, the right-to-use problem is effectively solved. The owner of an appropriative water right may also have a
right that is described and recorded. He may, for example, have a right
to divert 1 cfs from a given river at a given location every day from May
1 to October 1, with a priority date of 1895. It is May 15 and 1 cfs is
flowing past his point of diversion? May he divert it? We know the
answer is only maybe, since that water may be needed by a prior
appropriator downstream, be subject to instream flow requirements,
obligated to a downstream state under an interstate compact or apportionment, etc. The question in this section is how, in practice, the water
law system is administered.

If some authority (such as the state water agency) is administering
the river, and if there is a comprehensive record of rights, the administrator should know when to restrict a given user in order to meet prior
obligations. If no such entity exists, each user is on his own, and takes
water subject to the risk of a demand or lawsuit by an unfulfilled senior.
These are the two extremes in administration. They do not, however,
even begin to exhaust the administrative complexity that exists in fact.
First, rivers are often long, with many tributaries, and sometimes cross
state lines. There is often no single administrator with authority over an
entire hydrologically related area. In addition, often no comprehensive
record of rights exists. Some rights (the most senior) may precede a
state's permit system. Even if there are permits, or if rights have been
adjudicated in past litigation, they may not describe water that ever was,
has recently been, or is presently, being put to beneficial use. A right
may have been abandoned or forfeited, or water may be wasted. Prior
adjudications may not have included all users on a river. So existing
rights of record (in permits or in adjudication decrees) may not be
currently valid, and courts often do not treat them as binding. In
addition, there may be off-record claims or rights, such as the rights of
Indian tribes (federal reserved rights) which were not subject to state
laws. A state may have any of a variety of instream use claims. Professor

Albert Stone described a small Montana stream that had been adjudicated in 14 lawsuits over 75 years, with the same rights relitigated repeatedly, and reaching the state supreme court eight times.[1]

There are basically four ways to deal with these problems: (1) allow people to act, and leave it to objectors to litigate (note, however, that decrees in private lawsuits only bind those who were parties, which on a river rarely means everyone who could be affected); (2) a state agency can administer a river according to rights of record, such as permits and court decrees, and await litigation by those who feel their rights are infringed; (3) a state can administer a river more proactively, taking initiatives in challenging waste or non-use, and demanding that new users put their rights on record, thus seeking to assure that the rights of record are pretty much in accord with actual, current rights; (4) states can undertake a statutory class action, known as a general adjudication, and by litigation or some administrative process serve every claimant on each river system, determine their rights, allow some process for challenges to claims, and end up with a comprehensive decree that incorporates all rights in a (hopefully) hydrologically coherent way. Montana, for example, enacted such a law, designed to avoid the problems Professor Stone had documented.[2]

Each of these methods, in one form or another, exists in the various states. They are not mutually exclusive. Nor are any of the systems fully satisfactory. Method (3), which is followed by Colorado, is generally viewed as the most successful. Method (4), the general adjudication, as we shall see, might seem ideal, but it has proven more complex, expensive, and protracted than anyone would like.

Let us first look at the difficulties presented by simply relying on rights of record, as described by Michael McIntyre, and then turn to the problems encountered by the ongoing general adjudications in a number of states. As you read the following materials, ask yourself how a truly enlightened state ought to administer its water rights, and whether there is some way out of the difficulties most states have encountered.

1. INADEQUACY OF RECORDS

MICHAEL McINTYRE,
THE DISPARITY BETWEEN STATE WATER
RIGHTS RECORDS AND ACTUAL WATER
USE PATTERNS: "I WONDER WHERE THE
WATER WENT?"

5 Land & Water L. Rev. 23 (1970).

Rights to use surface waters within the State of Wyoming are granted and supervised by the Board of Control, an administrative

---

1. See Albert Stone, Are There Any Adjudicated Streams in Montana?, 19 Mont. L. Rev. 19 (1957); Albert Stone, The Long Count on Dempsy: No Final Decision on Water Right Adjudication, 31 Mont. L. Rev. 1 (1969); Albert Stone, Montana Water Rights: A New Opportunity, 34 Mont. L. Rev. 57 (1973).

2. Mont. Code Ann. §§ 85–2–212 et seq.

agency created by the state Constitution. Shortly after the Constitution was ratified, the Board was directed to undertake a complete adjudication of all direct flow surface water rights in the state. Water rights were granted upon "proofs" submitted by the water users, which were statements and maps containing information as to the nature and extent of the water use, the date when the first use commenced, the place of diversion, the place of use and type of use, which data was collected and retained in the office of the State Engineer.

There is much doubt that these records were ever an accurate reflection of actual water uses existing in the state at any given time. Reports of the State Engineer from the early days of statehood to the present refer to substantial inaccuracies in the filings and statements initially submitted. The discrepancies have apparently compounded with the passage of time, due to increased competition for the water and changes in water uses which have gone unrecorded in the State Engineer's records. * * *

One of the main advantages of the prior appropriation system of water rights is supposed to be the relatively high degree of certainty of water use which a water right vests in its owner, by freeing him from the fear that he will be deprived of the use of available water by subsequent changes in the water use patterns affecting his source of supply. But, in fact, such changes can occur to the detriment of other appropriators. An early priority water right, long unused but not declared abandoned, may be resurrected at a subsequent date and is entitled to the protection that its early priority demands. Changes in the place of use of water without approval of the State Engineer may substantially reduce the return flow to the stream, thereby reducing the water supply available to downstream appropriators. Points of diversion could be changed as a matter of right prior to 1965, provided only that other appropriators were not injured thereby. This latter qualification meant, in practice, that the burden was upon protesting appropriators to prove injury, a burden which may be heavy indeed.

Without records which accurately show the nature and extent of actual water uses, neither the water users themselves nor the state water commissioners can readily detect deviations or identify the cause of a depleted water supply in the source. The result is that in some water-poor areas of the state, the uncertainty of the holder of a water right may be at least as great as it is alleged to be under a riparian system. * * *

Most of the western states experience significant deviations between the actual practices of water users in the field and the information recorded in the office of the water administration officials. The extent of the problem, and the seriousness of the deviations in the other states is not known, but the magnitude of the problem in Wyoming is enormous and is apparently statewide. In 1955, the records of the State Engineer showed that the adjudicated, direct flow water rights from the Little Laramie River totaled 417,00 acres, but the acreage actually irrigated by direct flow from the Little Laramie was only 200,000 acres, which is only 48% of the adjudicated acreage. In the North Platte River Basin in central and eastern Wyoming, direct flow surface water rights are adjudicated to 890,554 acres, but only 569,131 acres, 64% of the adjudicated acreage, were actually irrigated as of 1967. In one reach of a river in the water-right highlands of west central Wyoming, direct flow surface water rights are adjudicated to 10,839 acres, but only 6,600 acres are actually irrigated, 61% of the acreage shown to be irrigated by the State Engineer's records.

Many factors have been mentioned as explaining the difference between the number of acres adjudicated water rights and the substantially lesser number of acres actually being irrigated, but the two most plausible are (1) lack of water in the source sufficient to irrigate all of the lands adjudicated, and (2) the practice of concentrating the water diverted onto fewer acres than the water right shows. * * *

To compound the problem, there is no indication in the records as to what extent the lands upon which water is applied correspond to the lands to which water rights are adjudicated. Incomplete, uncertain or inaccurate descriptions of land in old water right applications, the tendency of appropriators to overstate their water use, unscientific methods of irrigation rendering land unproductive, the difficulty of detecting changes in place of use, unauthorized changes in regulated headgates, and other factors preclude the assumption that all appropriators are necessarily applying their water to lands described in their water rights.

Another source of inaccuracy may arise from the description of the point of diversion of water. Wyoming statutes have long required an applicant for a surface water right to describe in his application the location and description of the proposed ditch and diversion works, among other things. But for an almost equal length of time, Wyoming courts have held that an appropriator has the right to change his place of diversion as a matter of right, provided only that no other appropriators on the stream are injured. It was not until 1965 that the legislature enacted a statute prohibiting changes in the point of diversion without the prior approval of and subject to conditions imposed by the State Engineer. Prior to 1965, unrecorded changes of an appropriator's point of diversion were not uncommon.

There may also be errors in the State Engineer's records regarding the nature of the use which is being made of the water, but because of the general terms by which type of use is described in the water right (i.e., "municipal," "irrigation") it is not expected that such errors, if they exist, would be sufficiently widespread to create a serious problem. * * *

Notes and Questions

1. A discussion of the parallel problem in California can be found in Chapter 2 of the Final Report of the Governor's Commission to Review California Water Rights Law (Dec. 1978).

2. How should a conflict between record rights and actual practice be dealt with? McIntyre suggests ratification of existing water uses on the condition that the use terminate at a specified date, at which time the user could apply for a renewal

> subject to all laws existing on the renewal date and such other conditions as then-existing policies of resource development dictate. This conditional confirmation approach allows records to be updated in a manner consistent with present water uses, without the need for an instantaneous, state wide readjudication, while introducing flexibility. * * * [A] number of non-perpetual water rights are created to which subsequent changes in the water laws or policy can apply. * * * When the water policy for the twenty-first century is finally adopted, it can be to some degree implemented, at least as to those water rights not perpetually vested. The pressing problem of inaccurate state water use records * * * is corrected expeditiously, while the major policy questions are deferred until facts and debate allow an intelligent choice.

Michael McIntyre, The Disparity Between State Water Rights Records and Actual Water Use Patterns: "I Wonder Where the Water Went?", 5 Land & Water L. Rev. 45–46 (1970).

3. Colorado has perhaps made the fullest effort to assure that records and reality do not diverge. The division engineer in each of Colorado's seven water divisions makes and keeps up to date a tabulation of decreed water which is filed in court and subject to protest. The Engineer is also periodically to determine both partial and total abandonments. New rights are incorporated into the tabulations, as are changes in use, and there is periodic adjudication of conditional appropriations to assure that they reflect due diligence. Colo. Rev. Stat. §§ 37–92–101 to 602.

4. Some old rights have never been adjudicated and were acquired before a permit system was established. To obtain a record of actual uses, some states instituted compulsory registration requirements. See Douglas Grant, Registration of Constitutional Method Water Rights, 17 Idaho L. Rev. 7 (1980). On the constitutionality of laws requiring registration within a given time or loss of the right, see Texaco, Inc. v. Short, 454 U.S. 516 (1982).

2. ADJUDICATING WATER RIGHTS

In the introduction to this Chapter we noted some of the reasons why general adjudication decrees did less to settle competing claims than one might have expected (they were incomplete, inaccurate, subject to collateral attack, etc.). Traditional general adjudications, though they varied in quality from state to state, were often unsatisfactory to a degree that is difficult to imagine. In Colorado, for example, the state was divided up into numerous water districts that bore no hydrological relationship to actual river basins. The resulting decrees were at best uncoordinated and unintegrated. Montana's difficulties have been adverted to above. As Professor Stone observed, "experience has shown that after the rights of all the parties * * * had been adjudicated, a subsequent appropriator would appear upon the scene, * * * and ruthlessly take the water, disregarding the decreed rights. * * * The only remedy the prior appropriators had was to commence a suit against the new appropriator, the result being that all of the rights of the stream had again to be adjudicated * * * and after that decree was entered if another subsequent appropriator took the water the same process had to be gone over again."[3] The historic development of stream adjudications has been detailed in an article by John Thorson, who served as Special Master for the modern General Stream Adjudication in Arizona.[4]

Under modernized laws, a number of western states—notably Idaho, Arizona, Wyoming, Montana, and Washington—initiated general adjudications in the 1970's and 1980's.[5] The primary reason these proceedings were undertaken was to adjudicate federal water rights claims (particularly the claims of Indian tribes) that had never been determined under state law because of federal sovereign immunity; to confirm valid existing rights in states that had unrecorded or unpermitted existing uses; and to complete a centralized water use data base to improve water management.[6] After Congress enacted a law subjecting the United States to state adjudications, and the Supreme Court sustained the law (see infra p. 943, the states were eager to get federal rights settled, as they created a cloud on the title of state law appropriators since these federal reserved rights are often effectively senior to even the oldest state rights, and, unlike ordinary appropriative rights, are not lost by non-use. As of late 2005 Wyoming was the only state to have completed litigation of Indian and other federal reserved rights.

In any event, the general adjudications have now been ongoing for years, and have proven extraordinary protracted and expensive. Some are far along; the Yakima River adjudication in Washington was over 90% complete at the time of this writing, and a final decree was expected to be entered by the end of 2006, according to John Thorson's study. The size and complexity of such proceedings is almost unimaginable.[7] In Arizona, summons were sent to some 980,000 landowners and water users, and nearly 100,000 claims had been filed in the Gila and Little Colorado River adjudications. Interlocutory appeals to the Supreme Court are permitted, and the Court has had to adjudicate questions such as whether non-appropriable groundwater is subject to federal reserved rights, and whether federal reserved rights holders enjoy greater protection from groundwater pumping than holders of state water rights. In

3. 19 Mont. L. Rev. at 31 n. 63.

4. John E. Thorson, et al., Dividing Western Waters: A Century of Adjudicating Rivers and Streams, 8 U. Denv. Water L.Rev. 355 (2005).

5. For a comparison of state systems, see A. Lynne Krogh, Water Right Adjudications in the Western States, 30 Land and Water L. Rev. 9 (1995).

6. John E. Thorson, et al., Dividing Western Waters: A Century of Adjudicating Rivers and Streams, Part II, 9 U. Denv. Water L. Rev. (2006) (forthcoming).

7. As to who must constitutionally be served process in a general adjudication, where there may be tens of thousands of users, see In re Yakima River Drainage Basin, 100 Wash.2d 651, 674 P.2d 160 (1983) (due process requirement satisfied by service on water distributing agencies. Personal service on all individual water users who get water under contract from distributing agencies is not required). See also Schroeder v. City of New York, 371 U.S. 208 (1962) (notice required when New York condemned riparian rights on the Delaware River).

1997 it was reported that the Arizona adjudication had already cost $50 million, and it was still ongoing in late 2005. While the adjudication was proceeding, several tribal settlements of Indian reserved water rights were negotiated and resolved by congressional legislation.[8]

The Snake River Basin adjudication in Idaho had nearly 180,000 claims to resolve, 50,000 filed by the United States. The state was reported to be making good progress, with 114,000 water rights partially decreed. The Department of Water Resources was reportedly ready to file its final report by the end of 2005. The total cost of the adjudication from 1985 to 2005 is estimated at $67,818,000, exclusive of the cost to the United States, the Tribes and private parties.

Montana's statewide adjudication of all pre–1973[9] groundwater and surface water rights began in 1982. 219,417 claims of water rights were filed, asserted by an estimated 80,000 persons. Following numerous proceedings, legislation and rulings, including no less than 8 by the Montana Supreme Court, as of May 1, 2004, final decrees had been issued in 16,354 claims, preliminary decrees in 23,262 more, and temporary preliminary decrees in another 89,809 claims. About another 89,000 were still in examination or waiting to be examined.[10]

When asked whether these adjudications are worth the time, trouble, and expense they involve—particularly as to claims other than federal reserved rights—the participating attorneys, almost without exception, look glassy-eyed and shrug their shoulders.[11] The following is taken from the summary of a 1997 ABA water law conference on general stream adjudications, with attorneys who had been involved in adjudications in Nevada, Oregon, Colorado, Utah, Montana, Idaho, and New Mexico:

> Each panelist expressed frustration with laborious, lengthy, and costly western stream adjudications. Progress has been elusive in many states, and the simple goal of quantifying and prioritizing water rights has proved difficult to achieve. After twenty or more years of litigation in many western states, the panelists pointed out that few adjudications are complete. [Two panelists] questioned the judicial system's ability to "integrate federal and tribal rights with state-based rights." * * * The panel discussed other frustrations: lack of finality and certainty in water rights, high costs of litigation, re-examination of the basic tenets of water law, and the inability or unwillingness to ratchet down

8. 117 Stat. 782 (2003) (Zuni Indian Tribe); 118 Stat. 3478 (2004) (Gila River Indian Community).

9. Montana instituted a permit system in 1973. See Mont. Code Ann. § 3–7–101 et seq.; Mont. Code Ann. §§ 85–2–212 et seq.

10. Legislative Environmental Quality Council, Montana's Water—Where is it? Who can use it? Who decides?, House Joint Resolution No. 4, Report to the 59th Legislature of the State of Montana, at 19–34 (December 2004).

11. A number of groundwater basin adjudications in Southern California have proven successful in generating effective management systems. See discussion at Chapter 5, infra pp. 506–520. See also the discussion of the recent Santa Maria Basin adjudication in 15 California Water Law & Policy 303 (August/September 2005).

overstated state water rights. Frustrations with legislation which changed adjudication statutes midstream were seen as political solutions for only some of the players. Both Idaho and Arizona struggled with the repercussions of legislative attempts to change the rules in the midst of the adjudications.[12]

Montana's process is illustrative of a modern adjudication system. The litigants include individual ranchers and farmers, irrigation entities, municipal governments, utilities, mines and other commercial enterprises, state agencies, federal agencies and seven Indian tribes. Only small water uses (instream stockwater, stockwater wells, instream domestic, and domestic wells) are exempt from the adjudication process, but claimants may submit these rights for adjudication if they desire. The law creates a specialized water court with a chief judge and four district judges who act as water judges for water divisions corresponding to major river systems. The Department of Natural Resources and Conservation (DNRC) examines water users' claims and reports to the court. The water court issues temporary preliminary decrees for each of the 85 basins into which the state is divided. Objections to these preliminary decrees are heard by the water court, which then issues final decrees. The Montana law also created a Reserved Water Rights Compact Commission to negotiate water rights settlements with federal agencies and Indian tribes, and suspended litigation over federal and tribal rights while negotiations continue. This separation avoids one element that has made other state general adjudications especially time-consuming and complicated.

The costs of the adjudications are supported by filing fees[13] and appropriations to the water court, to the DNRC for technical work, and to the compact commission for its negotiation activity. The Compact Commission had concluded compacts with several tribes and with a number of federal agencies, such as Glacier and Yellowstone National Parks. Montana's process has gone more smoothly than some others, probably because it has severed federal water rights issues, and focused on dealing with them through negotiation rather than litigation. A sense of how difficult the process can be is suggested by the following observations from a lawyer involved in Idaho's Snake River Basin Adjudication (SRBA):[14]

12. Arizona Gen. Stream Adjudication Bull., Office of the Special Master, March 1997, at 3. The decision on the constitutional validity of Arizona's mid-stream legislative changes—some designed to protect water users from the consequences of having their long-standing uses (or non-uses) adjudicated according to standard water law rules and principles—is San Carlos Apache Tribe v. Superior Court, 193 Ariz. 195, 972 P.2d 179 (1999). The Idaho Supreme Court sustained most of the procedural changes the legislature made. State ex rel. Higginson v. United States, 128 Idaho 246, 912 P.2d 614 (1995).

13. Idaho's efforts to impose fees on the United States was litigated in United States v. Idaho, 508 U.S. 1 (1993).

14. Jeffrey Fereday, Idaho's Snake River Basin Adjudication: Private Party Perspective, in Proceedings of the American Bar Association's 15th Annual Water Law Conference (Feb. 20–21, 1997). Fereday's clients are mostly junior appropriators.

General water rights adjudications pose a simple question to the claimant: What is your water right? With the exception of the legal issues raised by some of the federal and Indian reserved water rights claims * * * the answer to this question usually is not difficult to answer, and is tied as much to physics as to law: how many acres have actually been irrigated? what is the capacity of your diversion facility? what is the actual volume of water used in your manufacturing plant?

The question may be simple, but in the SRBA achieving the answer is proving difficult. With respect to the state-law-based claims, most of the problems in adjudications, and most of the costs to the parties, can be traced to one or more of the following:

a. The difficulty and contentiousness that arise when one claims a larger water right than one has, "mistakes paper for water," disputes the usufructuary nature of water rights, or does not know (or neglects to tell) the truth about one's water right and its use. Coupled with this is the fact that there is no incentive for claimants not to overstate their water rights.

b. A failure of the fact-finder to cut through the hail of legal arguments and procedural wrangling that litigants marshal in defense of what they believe their water rights to be—in other words, a failure to zero in on the essential simplicity of the proceeding as to most disputes.

c. The problems inherent in determining or implementing the judicial procedures for carrying out a general water rights adjudication. These actions are *sui generis;* in large measure, they have to be invented especially for this purpose and often adjusted as they go along. And they are of such a large size that they are bound to be slow and unwieldy in the best of circumstances. There are strong arguments that an adjudication based on initial administrative fact-finding would be more efficient than the formal judicial model, and Idaho's statute actually allows the Department to conduct hearings as necessary. I.C. § 42–1410(1). * * *

d. The legislature attempting to override or shade the appropriation doctrine in favor of certain groups, practices, or types of use. Such efforts often lead to more litigation. An example in Idaho is the passage of the so-called "amnesty" statutes, whereby the Legislature retroactively waived the mandatory permit requirement for enlargements of use under existing water rights. I.C. § 42–1426. It took a trip to the Idaho Supreme Court for junior water right holders to show that they could not have additional water rights created now with priorities ahead of them.

————

Even if all administrative problems could be managed, the question remains, what exactly is accomplished by these adjudications? Certainly, if all the claims could be accurately ascertained, and if those determinations could then be binding, that would be an important administrative achievement. But there is little reason to anticipate either of those results. First, as might be expected in such a proceeding, there is often little real adversariness; nor (at least in some adjudications) is the state agency operating as a party in order to challenge excessive claims. Second, there has been a reluctance to make rigorous determinations about matters like historic beneficial use or forfeiture, so the adjudications have proven disappointing in getting rid of paper rights. Third, there is little reason to be confident that the determinations in the adjudications will be binding. The Idaho lawyer quoted above remarked that if too generous an interpretation was made of what constituted beneficial use so as to advantage senior rights claimants, he would just challenge those rights at a later date when the seniors tried to market them, and he would have another crack at them in a proceeding seeking a right to transfer the place of diversion or use. In addition, adjudicated rights are always vulnerable to collateral attack in the future if it is claimed that a right has been abandoned or forfeited; or that a use previously non-wasteful has become wasteful.[15] Nor do adjudications determine how much water (of a total diversion) may be transferred to another user for another purpose in another place.

For all these reasons, one may ask whether we really need general adjudications, or whether they are the best way to go about the task. Of course we need to know what rights various parties hold, and this becomes increasingly important as water rights are increasingly put on the market, or systems are stressed by new demands, instream or diversionary. You might wish to consider whether our needs could be better met by some other approaches (putting aside the generally agreed-on need to quantify federal reserved rights). Some of the things we need to know are: (1) what uses are currently being made; (2) whether they are beneficial; (3) priority dates; (4) whether current uses all date back to the claimed, or decreed, priority a claimant holds. We do have some data. For users since permit laws came into effect, we have permit records. Where there were, or are, conditional decrees, we may have due

15. Adjudicated rights have been subject to collateral attack in transfer proceedings where it was claimed that the decreed amount was never actually put to beneficial use. See, e.g., Farmers Highline Canal & Reservoir Co. v. Golden, 129 Colo. 575, 272 P.2d 629 (1954). Why shouldn't the previous adjudication be binding as against such attack? For a strong statement emphasizing the importance of finality of general adjudications, see Nevada v. United States, 463 U.S. 110 (1983). See A. Dan Tarlock, The Illusion of Finality in General Water Rights Adjudications, 25 Idaho L. Rev. 271 (1988–1989).

diligence data. We have the information from older decrees (though recognizing that they reflect a great deal of inflated "paper" water rights). For pre-permit appropriations, and for riparian and most groundwater rights, we often have no records at all. In almost all cases, we have no information about the quantum of water consumed, versus the amount of water diverted.

Can you think of some alternative system that would meet our needs to administer water rights effectively, but avoid the cumbersome and imperfect nature of the general adjudication? Some suggest that the judicial mode is central to the problem, and note that Texas and Nebraska completed statewide adjudications—at least for surface rights—through an administrative process. However, both Colorado and New Mexico, have had success with judicial adjudications.

Could a modern, well-run administrative agency make and keep up to date all the records we need? Is the problem essentially how to determine the priority dates of pre-permit-statute appropriators? Is it a question of getting rid of paper rights in old, inaccurate adjudications? Is there also a problem of improper enlargements (that is, appropriators with known pre-permit dates of appropriation, but who have increased their use in later years, and seek to cover all their uses under their early priority)? Alternatively, is the general adjudication, for all its limitations, the best we can do—necessary, albeit imperfect? For example, once a stream has been adjudicated, won't almost all users, for almost all purposes, be bound by the decree for the indefinite future?

By the way, what happens to needs for instream flows, and restoration of de-watered rivers, in an adjudication? Does anyone represent the fish? See San Carlos Apache Tribe v. Superior Court, 193 Ariz. 195, 972 P.2d 179, 199 (1999); Idaho Conservation League v. State, 128 Idaho 155, 911 P.2d 748, 749 (1995); Idaho Code § 58–1201.

3. CREATING A WORKING SYSTEM: THE EBMUD AS AN EXAMPLE

A study of all the complex and uncertain doctrines of water law makes the system seem a tangle of endless uncertainty. Is this the way it appears to those who work within it day to day? Not necessarily. The goal of those who manage water agencies is to settle conflicts and to assure a supply sufficient to create abundance, or at least adequacy, rather than chronic shortage. The following brief history shows how one municipal supplier (though it is not without problems of its own) found a way to clarify and secure its rights.

The East Bay Municipal Utility District (EBMUD), which appears at several places in this casebook, is a public agency responsible for urban and industrial water supply in Oakland, Berkeley and neighboring East Bay cities in California. Its system is a relatively simple one. It took its original supply by capturing in small reservoirs stream water from nearby hills, and by pumping local groundwater. Those sources were soon overtaxed, especially the wells, which suffered salt water incursion.

The pumps were closed down; the local reservoirs were maintained as holding facilities and for meeting short term emergencies. In the 1920's the agency went seventy miles away to the Mokelumne River on the western slope of the Sierra Nevada Mountains to build a dam, reservoir and aqueduct to carry water by gravity flow to its service area (see Figure 3–9).

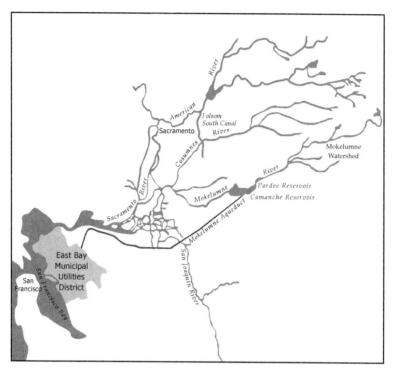

Figure 3–9

Mokelumne Aqueduct

EBMUD's rights have been secured by litigation and negotiation, one by one, with each of the other claimants on the river. This process substituted for a general adjudication. First a downstream city sued to enjoin the construction of the reservoir, claiming that EBMUD's diversion would take water needed to replenish the underground supply on which its wells depended. After lengthy litigation, a court-approved settlement required water to be provided when groundwater levels fall below a fixed measure. The settlement also resolved the rights of several small communities served by an electric company's (PG&E) existing upstream hydropower reservoirs. Then EBMUD itself went to court to establish that proposed additions to the PG&E facilities were junior to its permits. That case was settled and set operating criteria for the power company reservoirs based on storage and precipitation. EBMUD also negotiated an agreement with an irrigation district holding substantial senior rights downstream on the Mokelumne, confirming their claims, which under the agreement varies according to the inflow to the EBMUD reservoir each season.

Following the population boom and suburban growth at the end of World War II, EBMUD sought an additional appropriation on the Mokelumne to be taken through a new aqueduct. This water was to be provided through storage from diversions only during a part of the year. One problem was that in the interim a significant amount of the river's water had been appropriated by others. The State, in anticipation of a (still unbuilt) public water development project, had a permit for a great deal of water. The irrigation district had also made a large additional appropriation. PG&E was expanding its facilities and the counties of origin had also filed applications in competition with EBMUD's filing.

The State was willing to release its claims, but as a condition EBMUD had to settle with the areas of origin. It did so by letting a modest portion of the state's filing go to the area of origin counties, paying several million dollars to help them develop water projects from a watershed other than the Mokelumne and (most importantly) agreeing that it would seek no further appropriations for its own future growth from the Mokelumne. EBMUD also agreed to provide for flood control in one of its reservoirs in order to satisfy a downstream county.

As to the additional claim of the irrigation district, an agreement was worked out to let the district take additional water on an interruptible basis until EBMUD completed a new facility on another river which was to enlarge its supply. At that time the irrigation district's right to a supplemental supply is to become permanent. In 1961, in response to newer concerns about instream values, EBMUD agreed with the State Department of Fish and Game to build a fish hatchery and to make designated releases annually for the protection of fish in the lower Mokelumne River.

A chart illustrating the various rights on the Mokelumne River is set out in Figure 3–10. EBMUD is not yet using all the water from its second permit.

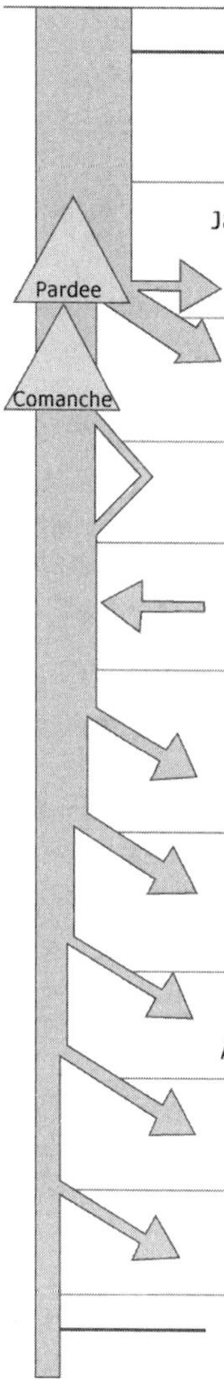

Mokelumne River flow		Water Year 1979 (typical)	Average	Range	Maximum Entitlement
	Mokelumne Hill Gage	678,300	735,500	150,300-1,788,090	———
	Jackson Valley Irrigation District	3,000	1,500	0-3,800	5,000
	EBMUD Aqueduct Draft	187,100 (=167MGD)	196,500 (175MGD) (20 years)	130,600-245,700 (117MGD-219MGD) (Last 20 years)	364,000 (=325MGD)
	Fish Releases	16,200	18,300	5,800-23,300	13,000
	Intermediate Inflow	7,100	6,600	80-13,900	———
	North San Joaquin Water Conservation District	7,400	7,400 (w/o 1976 and 1977)	4,600-9,500 (0 in 1976 & 1977)	20,000
	Woodbridge Irrigation District	76,200	95,100	51,400-121,700	116,700 (=60,000 Perm. Regulated +56,700 Interim)
	Riparians and Senior Appropriations	14,600	13,700	10,100-18,200	20,618
	Channel Losses	56,700	80,000	32,700-108,700	———
	City of Lodi	0	0	0	3,600 (if triggered by Lodi decree)
	Woodbridge Gage	341,700	453,800	15,800-1,559,600	———

(Diagram labels: Pardee, Comanche)

Figure 3–10
Mokelumne River Flow

Source: Bay-Delta Hearings Before the State Water Resources Control Board, East Bay Municipal Utilities District, Exh. No. 1, July 1987.

While controversy still exists (for example, the Department of Fish and Game called for increased downstream releases during the non-irrigation season and the American River was long mired in dispute), the central fact is that EBMUD has been able to produce a "law of the river," a set of operating principles so that everyone knows what its entitlement is. Note too that the various settlements are tailored to the specifics of a particular river, and that the various agreements and settlements are more flexible than strict water law doctrine would dictate. Both the irrigation district and PG&E's senior rights vary somewhat according to the wetness of the year; and the downstream city's rights have been made to depend on annual showings of need. Some arrangements have been made contingent on the fulfillment of other sources of supply. The negotiation process has provided a means for the various parties to make adaptations both to physical circumstances and to each others' needs. All the various constituencies have gotten their "piece of the action" and a degree of security adequate to their respective needs. A similar story of rational resolution could be told about other areas, including settlements that have been negotiated for a number of ground water basins in Southern California. See William Blomquist, Dividing the Waters (1992). Groundwater is discussed at length in chapter 5.

Chapter 4

THE EVOLUTION OF WESTERN WATER LAW

The law changes over time. Water law is no exception. Earlier chapters already have illustrated many important changes underway in water law. In response to increasing water demands, many eastern states have adopted permit systems to better track and control water allocation. Western states have adopted legislation to encourage conservation and promote water marketing. Future chapters will discuss other significant changes—new limitations on groundwater overdrafting and environmental restrictions on water diversions. Historically, the greatest change in water law accompanied the development of the western United States where climatic conditions did not fit well with the traditional riparian schemes of water allocation.

Changes in water law raise a variety of important and often difficult policy, constitutional, and institutional issues. Under what circumstances should governments abandon or modify legal principles upon which people have planned and relied? To what degree do the "takings" protections of the fifth and fourteenth amendments to the United States Constitution and of the various state constitutions limit our ability to change the law? What branch of the government—legislature, judiciary, or executive branch—is best equipped to evaluate and change various aspects of the law? This Chapter considers these questions in connection with the historical development of water law in the western United States.

The first portion of the Chapter studies the birth and evolution of the appropriation doctrine in the 17 western conterminous states and Alaska. Until the advent of modern environmental restrictions, the development of the appropriation doctrine constituted the greatest change that water law had undergone in United States history, and the change was neither linear nor unchallenged. Nine of the western states ultimately adopted a "pure" appropriation system. Other states such as California, however, ended up with hybrid or "mixed" systems in which appropriative and riparian rights coexisted uncomfortably for at least a temporary period.

The second part of the Chapter examines the legacy of Mexican and Spanish rule of the Southwest United States. Although the United States promised to honor existing water rights when it took control of the Southwest, American courts have taken advantage of uncertainties over the contours of Mexican and Spanish law to support whatever result they have wanted to reach. Indeed, judicial interpretations of Mexican and Spanish law continue to change in response to evolving needs and interests.

The final section of the Chapter considers the degree to which federal and state constitutional provisions, including takings protections, limit changes in water law by either legislatures or courts. Although courts for years have rejected constitutional challenges to such changes, a small handful of recent decisions have held both legislative and judicial changes to be unconstitutional absent compensation.

A. THE EVOLUTION OF PRIOR APPROPRIATION SYSTEMS

Given the scarcity of water in the western United States, it is possible (but far from clear) that the western states were destined to adopt the appropriation system. According to some legal and economic scholars,

> legal rules tend to converge when the issues at stake concern "self-interested behavior that threatens the general welfare." They diverge when the rules either "do not much matter" or "raise issues about which reasonable people * * * could disagree." The implicit logic behind [such an] argument is that societies will develop relatively efficient legal rules over issues that matter dearly. Whatever the rules over insignificant matters, most legal regimes will develop efficient legal rules to govern important issues, and those rules will tend to resemble each other.[1]

Supporting the argument that water-scarce regions tend to converge on the appropriation doctrine is the intriguing fact that not only the 17 conterminous American states and Alaska, but also the four western provinces of Canada and a large number of other arid and semi-arid countries have adopted the appropriation system.[2]

The early history of water allocation in what is now the western United States, however, gave little indication that the appropriation

1. Mark Ramseyer, Water Law in Imperial Japan: Public Goods, Private Claims, and Legal Convergence, 18 J. Legal Stud. 51, 73–74 (1989) (quoting Saul Levmore, Variety and Uniformity in the Treatment of the Good–Faith Purchaser, 16 J. Legal Stud. 43, 44 (1987)). For an interesting argument supporting legal convergence, see Robert Sugden, The Economics of Rights, Co-operation and Welfare (1986). For a more skeptical view, see Ramseyer, supra.

2. See, e.g., Frank Trelease, New Water Legislation: Drafting for Development, Efficient Allocation and Environmental Protection, 12 Land & Water L. Rev. 385, 415 (1977). See also Ramseyer, supra note 1 (discussing Japan's adoption of appropriation law).

doctrine would ultimately predominate. Because of the importance of irrigation, early allocation systems permitted water to be taken from a stream and consumed—often miles from the waterway. But in allocating scarce water resources, early legal systems tended to focus not on temporal priority of use but on equity and community needs. Prior appropriation did not begin its ascendancy until goldminers began flooding into California's Sierra Nevada Mountains in the middle of the nineteenth century. And as you shall see, the transition to an appropriation system posed thorny legal issues with which several western states are still wrestling.

To understand the roots and history of western water law (as well as its current variations, peculiarities, and nuances), it is necessary to start long before that almost mythical day in January 1848 when Joseph Marshall discovered gold in the tailrace of John Sutter's mill near Sacramento, California. Irrigation began in the Southwest over a millennium ago. Starting as early as 700 A.D., pre-Colombian Indians diverted water from rivers in central and southern Arizona and carried the water through more than 125 miles of canals to irrigate over 100,000 acres of corn, beans, and squash. The pre-Colombian Indians of southwestern Colorado and northern New Mexico (and their descendants, the Pueblo Indians) also constructed vast networks of dams, headgates, and canals in order to irrigate their crops of maize, squash, beans, melons, cotton, and chile. We know nothing directly about the means by which they resolved the disputes that almost certainly arose over the region's scarce water resources, but judging from the governmental systems of later American Indians, water was almost certainly considered a communal, rather than private resource.[3]

In the middle of the seventeenth century, Spanish settlement in portions of what are today Arizona, California, Colorado, New Mexico, and Texas brought European legal doctrines to the American West for the first time. Although historians today heatedly debate many of the details of the Spanish system (and the Mexican system that succeeded it), the broad contours are relatively clear.[4] Water was considered an important public asset, to be carefully controlled and regulated by governmental officials for the benefit of the entire community. Together, the central government and the local towns (or *pueblos*) held much of the water for the general use of the community. Any member of the public could use this water for drinking, bathing, recreation, and watering domesticated animals.

This did not mean that water could not be privately owned. Some grants (or *mercedes*) of riparian and non-riparian lands included water

---

3. For general discussion of early Indian irrigation, see Emil Haury, The Hohokam: First Masters of the American Desert, 131 Nat'l Geographic 670 (1967).

4. The discussion of Spanish and Mexican water law that follows relies heavily on two excellent studies—Michael Meyer, Water in The Hispanic Southwest: A Social and Legal History 1550–1850 (1984) and Hans Baade, The Historical Background of Texas Water Law—A Tribute to Jack Pope, 18 St. Mary's L.J. 1 (1986). See also Peter L. Reich, Mission Revival Jurisprudence: State Courts and Hispanic Water Law Since 1850, 69 Wash. L. Rev. 869 (1994).

rights—particularly where the land was to be used for irrigated agriculture. And individuals could obtain direct grants of water (or *mercedes de agua*) from the government if they could show the need. But most land grants did not include water rights and, where included, the water rights typically covered only a portion of the *merced*. Before placing water in private ownership (either directly or in conjunction with a land grant), moreover, governmental officials were instructed to carefully evaluate whether granting the water was in the public interest.

When disputes arose over surface water, the disagreeing parties were encouraged to try mediation through the local clergy or other neutral bystanders. If mediation did not work, the parties could turn to the Spanish courts for a *repartimiento de aguas*. In resolving the dispute, the courts were to try to find an equitable solution "such as to offend no one."[5] Recognizing some of the equitable and practical considerations that would ultimately lead western states to adopt appropriation systems, the courts considered temporal priority of use in determining the appropriate *repartimiento*. But prior appropriation was only one of several factors that the courts considered, and the courts never used it to award disputed water entirely to one litigant. In addition to temporal priority, the courts also considered any legal title that the parties claimed to the water, the need of the parties, the degree to which the parties' planned use of the water was consistent with governmental policies, and the "common good" of the community. When circumstances changed, moreover, courts were always willing to revisit earlier *repartimientos;* water rights were never considered permanent.

The first mass colonization of the West by United States citizens came in July 1847 when the Mormons entered the Great Salt Lake Valley. Within two days of the arrival of the Mormon's vanguard, the Mormons were diverting water from a local creek and irrigating freshly planted crops of potatoes and corn. The Mormons, like the Indian and Hispanic irrigators that preceded them, stressed community rights and interests. Practicing egalitarian Christianity, the Mormons emphasized the sharing of all worldly goods including water. As Brigham Young, the leader of the Mormon church, emphasized on September 30, 1848, "There shall be no private ownership of the streams that come out of the canyons. * * * These belong to the people: all the people."[6] Every settler was expected to contribute labor in the construction of dams and ditches, and church leaders allocated the water on an equitable basis.

When the Utah Territory was created in 1851 (consisting not only of what is today Utah but also portions of what are today Colorado, Idaho, Nevada, and Wyoming), the emphasis on community control and equity remained. The territorial legislature occasionally granted private individuals the right to make specific use of water. But the territory placed principal control of water resources in the hands of the local counties:

5. IV Recopilación de leyes de los reynos de las Indias, Titulo 17, Ley 5 (quoted in Michael Meyer, supra note 4, at 135).

6. See Robert Dunbar, Forging New Rights in Western Waters 13 (1983).

"The County Court has the control of all * * * water privileges, or any water course or creek; to * * * subserve the interest of the settlements, in the distribution of water for irrigation, or other purposes."[7]

Most of the early irrigation colonies in the West also shared the Mormons' communal perception of water. When in 1857 a group of German immigrants to California started the Anaheim colony in present-day Orange County to grow grapes and produce wine, they organized a cooperative irrigation company to operate the ditches. Each colonist received one share of stock in the cooperative, entitling the owner to the water necessary to irrigate the colonist's land. The Union Colony which, with the encouragement and advice of Horace Greeley, founded Greeley, Colorado, adopted a similar approach. Such communal systems were the forebears of today's mutual water companies which you will study in Chapter 7.

The appropriation system arrived with the California gold rush of the later 1840s and early 1850s:

The discovery of gold in the tailrace of Sutter's mill triggered an avalanche of gold seekers. Arriving by land and by sea, they established mining camps in an area that only recently had been acquired from Mexico by the Treaty of Guadalupe Hidalgo. As yet there were no land offices and little local government; the miners were trespassers on the public domain. Nonetheless, they had need of government, of some form of association, to protect their mining claims. So in camp after camp they met and organized mining districts, adopting rules for the definition of their property rights in the gulches. These rules limited the size of claims, restricting one to each miner. They required miners to post notices of their claims and to record them with district recorders, following the pattern of the claims clubs in the Middle West. To retain their claims, miners had to work them with diligence; otherwise they were forfeited. When questions of right arose, they were settled by reference to priority. Since the miners were squatters on the public domain, they applied the law of the public domain, first in time, first in right. He who filed first on a quarter section of land in the land office had the better right to it. Similarly, the miners ruled that he who recorded a claim first had a prior right to that claim.

After the days of the pan and shovel gave way to ditches and sluiceboxes, questions of right to use the streams arose. When they did, the miners applied the same rules to water as they had to the land—first in time, first in right. He who diverted water first had the prior right to it to the extent of his diversion for use on both riparian and nonriparian lands. To perfect the right, ditches had to be dug with diligence and the water applied to beneficial use. It was not to be wasted. As with

---

7. 1852 Utah Terr. Laws 38, § 39.

the claims, when the use ceased, the right ceased. Here was the genesis of a new property right.[8]

The miners had to reject riparian rights. For one thing, the miners did not own the land that they mined, virtually all of which belonged to the United States government under Mexican cessions. And in the beginning there were no programs under which the miners could acquire land title from the United States. As trespassers on the public domain, riparian rights would have done the miners little good. In addition, the places in which the miners needed to use water were often located quite a distance away from the rivers.

So long as settlement was sparse, non-miners did not share the miners' concerns over water allocation. The first farmers and ranchers to arrive in an area almost always located in the choicest spots near to waterways and could often gain title to their lands through various federal land statutes. Irrigation was necessary, but so long as farmers were located along waterways this required merely disavowing the English rule of natural flow, not awarding water rights on a first come, first served basis.

For over a decade, therefore, the appropriation system remained largely an oddity of mining law. The California Supreme Court used the appropriation doctrine to decide water disputes between miners as early as 1855.[9] But when confronted in 1857 by a dispute between a riparian landholder and a water company that was diverting water for the use of a neighboring community, the court sided with the riparian.[10] Where a dispute was solely between miners, the "[p]eculiar circumstances of the country, and the immense importance of [California's] mining interest," justified allocating water on the basis of prior appropriation.[11] Otherwise, however, the court—comprised necessarily of eastern trained lawyers— saw no need to abandon the traditional common-law riparian system with which they were familiar.[12]

Most early western legislatures also saw no need to provide for appropriative rights outside the mining context. Several years after the gold rush began, the California legislature provided that mining customs and usages should govern the resolution of "actions respecting 'Mining Claims.' "[13] But at a more general level, California and virtually every other western state and territory adopted statutes providing that courts should use the "common law" (sometimes the "common law of England") to resolve disputes, except where the common law was inconsis-

8. Dunbar, supra note 6, at 61.

9. See Irwin v. Phillips, 5 Cal. 140 (1855). The California Supreme Court appeared to accept the prior appropriation doctrine two years earlier in Eddy v. Simpson, 3 Cal. 249 (1853), but *Irwin* was the first case in which the court used prior appropriation principles to resolve a water dispute.

10. See Crandall v. Woods, 8 Cal. 136 (1857).

11. Id. at 142.

12. For a slightly different explanation of the split affection for appropriative and riparian rights in the early California cases, see Eric Freyfogle, *Lux v. Haggin* and the Common Law Burdens of Modern Water Law, 57 U. Colo. L. Rev. 485, 497–507 (1986).

13. 1851 Cal. Stats. ch. 5, § 621.

tent with federal or local laws.[14] Where early legislatures were more specific, they typically adopted either variants of the riparian doctrine or more general equitable allocation schemes. In 1866, indeed, the Dakota Territory adopted verbatim the New York riparian code provisions.[15]

In 1861, Colorado became the first western state or territory to adopt a general statutory scheme for allocating its surface water. Although the Colorado legislation permitted non-riparians to use water from a stream, the legislation drew heavily on riparian and equitable themes. All landholders "on the bank, margin or neighborhood" of a stream could use the water for irrigation, but where there was not sufficient water for all, water commissioners were to apportion the water "in a just and equitable proportion."[16] In 1862, moreover, the legislature proscribed diversions that would injure anyone "along the line" of a stream and directed that "there shall be at all times left sufficient water in said stream for the use of miners and farmers along said stream."[17] The Colorado legislation set a modest precedent, with similar legislation being adopted by the Montana Territory in 1865,[18] the Wyoming Territory in 1875,[19] and the Idaho Territory in 1881.[20]

As the western population grew, however, riparian and "equitable" systems of allocation came under intense pressure. Settlers who came into an area only to find the choice riparian property already taken urged that they should also have a right to water. To non-riparians, moreover, it seemed wasteful to require streams to flow unused through riparian lands when the water could be put to valuable use through appropriation. As parties to disputes multiplied, moreover, equitable schemes for allocation became more and more difficult to administer and far more difficult for entrepreneurial pioneers to predict. Starting in the 1860s, and especially by the 1870s, courts and legislatures increasingly saw the attractions of the appropriation system. The legal difficulties generated by the transition from riparian to appropriative rights are the subject of the remainder of this section.

1. PURE APPROPRIATION STATES: THE COLORADO DOCTRINE

By the time Colorado was finally admitted to the union in 1876, its policymakers saw clear advantages in the blossoming appropriation doctrine. As a result, the Colorado Constitution expressly adopted the appropriation system in Article sixteen, section six:

14. California's law, passed several months before California was admitted to the Union, was typical: "The Common Law of England, so far as it is not repugnant to or inconsistent with the Constitution of the United States, or the Constitution or laws of the State of California, shall be the rule of decision in all the Courts of this State." 1850 Cal. Stat. 219.

15. 1866 Dakota Terr. Laws, Civil Code, § 256.

16. 1861 Colo. Session Laws 67, § 1.

17. 1862 Colo. Session Laws 48, § 13.

18. Bannack's Statutes, p. 367.

19. See Farm Inv. Co. v. Carpenter, 9 Wyo. 110, 61 P. 258, 259–60 (1900).

20. 1880–81 Idaho Sess. Laws 267. Unlike the statutes of the other territories, the Idaho statute also included a provision sounding in prior appropriation—thoroughly clouding the law. Id. at 271.

The right to divert the unappropriated waters of any natural stream to beneficial uses shall never be denied. Priority of appropriation shall give the better right as between those using the water for the same purpose * * *.

Section five also declared that the "water of every natural stream, not heretofore appropriated, within the State of Colorado, is hereby declared to be the property of the public, and the same is dedicated to the use of the State, subject to appropriation as hereinafter provided."

Legally, however, it was far from clear that these constitutional provisions effectively eliminated riparian rights. First, there was the matter of the early 1861 and 1862 territorial statutes. As discussed on page 331, these appeared to provide for something akin to riparian rights. The 1862 statute in particular seemed to guarantee riparian miners and farmers that no water would be taken out of a stream to their detriment. Was the Colorado Constitution meant to abrogate such rights? Could it do so constitutionally?[21]

There was also the possibility that riparian rights existed as a matter of federal law. The federal government initially owned virtually all of the land in the western territories and states. By natural extension, one could also conclude that the federal government owned most of the water. Although territorial and state governments had the power to enact water laws, they could not constitutionally deprive the federal government of any rights that it had to water resources—absent the United States' permission. More importantly, when private individuals later acquired title to portions of the public domain under the Homestead Act of 1862 and other federal land laws, the argument was open that they acquired from the federal government riparian rights to the water on their property. Riparian rights, after all, traditionally came with the purchase of land.

The possibility that the federal government might have overriding rights to the water on the federal domain was of considerable concern to the mining community. As a result, Congress in the Mining Act of 1866 explicitly acknowledged and agreed to protect the customary appropriative rights of miners and other water users. Section 9 of that Act would go on to become one of the central focuses of debate over western water rights:

> [W]henever, by priority of possession, rights to the use of water for mining, agricultural, manufacturing, or other purposes, have vested and accrued, and the same are recognized and acknowledged by the local customs, laws, and the decisions of courts, the possessors and owners of such vested rights shall be maintained and protected in the same; and the right of way for the con-

21. In 1876, the Supreme Court had not yet held that the fourteenth amendment to the federal Constitution prevented states from taking property without the payment of just compensation. The fifth amendment, however, proscribed uncompensated takings by the federal government, and the United States approved the Colorado Constitution as part of Colorado's admission to the union.

struction of ditches and canals for the purposes aforesaid is hereby acknowledged and confirmed. * * *[22]

Because of concerns that this provision might not protect miners from homesteaders and others who later received private title to portions of the public domain, Congress in 1870 amended the Mining Act to provide that:

> all patents granted, or preemption or homesteads allowed, shall be subject to any vested and accrued water rights, or rights to ditches and reservoirs used in connection with such water rights, as may have been acquired under or recognized by the ninth section of the [1866 Act].[23]

These provisions unfortunately raised as many questions as they answered. Looking at section 9 of the 1866 Act, for example, under what circumstances does water use "vest and accrue" into a protected right? Is it sufficient that the water use be "recognized and acknowledged by the local customs, laws, and the decisions of courts" or does "vesting" require something more? Given that Colorado's 1861 and 1862 territorial legislation appeared to protect riparian rights, were Colorado appropriators protected under the 1866 and 1870 federal Mining Act provisions?

The Mining Act provisions raised even more difficult timing questions. Consider first someone who received a patent to a portion of the public domain before the Mining Act of 1866. Assume that the land is riparian to a small stream from which a miner had previously begun diverting and appropriating water for use several miles away. Is the miner's use protected under either the 1866 Mining Act or the 1870 amendments? If the Mining Act provisions are interpreted to eliminate any riparian rights that a pre–1866 patentee enjoyed, serious takings issues are raised.

Proponents of appropriative rights took considerable heart in the United States Supreme Court's opinion in Broder v. Natoma Water & Mining Co., 101 U.S. (11 Otto) 274 (1879), although it technically dealt with the right to a canal rather than the water in it. In *Broder,* the Natoma Water and Mining Company had completed a 15–mile canal across the public domain and begun appropriating water for mining, agricultural, and other uses in 1853. In 1862 and 1864, the United States conveyed part of the land across which the canal ran to the Central Pacific Railroad Company, which later conveyed the land to Jacob Broder. Broder sued to have the canal removed. The Court acknowledged that "it might be a question of some difficulty" whether the 1866 Mining Act protected Natoma's canal, but concluded that Natoma did not have to rely on the 1866 act.

> It is the established doctrine of this court that rights of miners, who had taken possession of mines and worked and developed them, and the rights of persons who had constructed

---

22. Act of July 26, 1866, 14 Stat. 253, § 9.

23. Act of July 9, 1870, 16 Stat. 218, § 17.

canals and ditches to be used in mining operations and for purposes of agricultural irrigation, in the region where such artificial use of the water was an absolute necessity, are rights which the government had, by its conduct, recognized and encouraged and was bound to protect before the passage of the act of 1866. We are of opinion that [section 9 of the 1866 Mining Act] was rather a voluntary *recognition of a pre-existing right of possession,* constituting a valid claim to its continued use, than the establishment of a new one. * * *

We turn now to the act of July 2, 1864 * * *, which makes the final grant to the Pacific railroad companies, the acceptance of which by the companies bound them to its terms, and we find in section 4, * * * this clause of reservation from the general terms of the grant: "Any lands granted by this act, or the act to which this is an amendment, shall not defeat or impair any preemption, homestead, swamp-land, *or other lawful claim,* nor include any government reservation or mineral lands, or the improvements of any *bona fide* settler on any lands returned or denominated as mineral lands, and the timber necessary to support his said improvements as a miner or agriculturist." * * *

We have had occasion to construe a very common clause of reservation in grants to other railroad companies, and in aid of other works of internal improvements, and in all of them we have done so in the light of the general principles that Congress, in the act of making these donations, could not be supposed to exercise its liberality at the expense of pre-existing rights, which, though imperfect, were still meritorious, and had just claims to legislative protection.[24]

The Court therefore concluded that the language of the railroad grant protected Natoma's canal. Because *Broder* relied on the explicit reservation in the railroad grant, the opinion did not resolve the question whether regular patentees or homesteaders of the public domain (who did not take title subject to the same type of provision) also took title subject to preexisting canals or appropriations.

Broder, moreover, did not address another important timing question. Under the Mining Act provisions, someone who took private title to a portion of the public domain after 1870 took title subject to previously vested appropriations. The possibility remained, however, that a patent to federal land might include riparian rights that were superior to *future* appropriators. Because riparian rights are not lost by nonuse, appropriators thus had to fear that at some future point a riparian property holder whose title predated the appropriations might be able to assert a superior water right.

---

24. 101 U.S. at 276–77 (emphasis added).

In the face of these conundrums, the Colorado Supreme Court was asked to decide in 1882 whether riparian rights existed in Colorado. The court's simple answer was "no"—making Colorado the first pure appropriation state. When reading the following opinion, ask yourself how convincingly the court defends its position. Although the facts are not clear from the opinion, the appropriation began prior to the date when the riparian acquired title from the federal government. Both the appropriation and title, however, came prior to the Mining Act of 1866.

COFFIN v. LEFT HAND DITCH CO.

Supreme Court of Colorado, 1882.
6 Colo. 443.

HELM, J.

Appellee, who was plaintiff below, claimed to be the owner of certain water by virtue of an appropriation thereof from the south fork of the St. Vrain creek. It appears that such water, after its diversion, is carried by means of a ditch to the James creek, and thence along the bed of the same to Left Hand creek, where it is again diverted by lateral ditches and used to irrigate lands adjacent to the last named stream. Appellants are the owners of lands lying on the margin and in the neighborhood of the St. Vrain below the mouth of said south fork thereof, and naturally irrigated therefrom.

In 1879 there was not a sufficient quantity of water in the St. Vrain to supply the ditch of appellee and also irrigate the said lands of appellant. A portion of appellee's dam was torn out, and its diversion of water thereby seriously interfered with by appellants. The action is brought for damages arising from the trespass, and for injunctive relief to prevent repetitions thereof in the future.

* * * It is contended by counsel for appellants that the common law principles of riparian proprietorship prevailed in Colorado until 1876, and that the doctrine of priority of right to water by priority of appropriation thereof was first recognized and adopted in the constitution. But we think the latter doctrine has existed from the date of the earliest appropriations of water within the boundaries of the state. The climate is dry, and the soil, when moistened only by the usual rainfall, is arid and unproductive; except in a few favored sections, artificial irrigation for agriculture is an absolute necessity. Water in the various streams thus acquires a value unknown in moister climates. Instead of being a mere incident to the soil, it rises when appropriated, to the dignity of a distinct usufructuary estate, or right of property. It has always been the policy of the national, as well as the territorial and state governments, to encourage the diversion and use of water in this country for agriculture; and vast expenditures of time and money have been made in reclaiming and fertilizing by irrigation portions of our unproductive territory. Houses have been built, and permanent improvements made; the soil has been cultivated, and thousands of acres have been rendered immensely valuable, with the understanding that appropria-

tions of water would be protected. Deny the doctrine of priority or superiority of right by priority of appropriation, and a great part of the value of all this property is at once destroyed.

The right to water in this country, by priority of appropriation thereof, we think it is, and has always been the duty of the national and state governments to protect. The right itself, and the obligation to protect it, existed prior to legislation on the subject of irrigation. It is entitled to protection as well after patent to a third party of the land over which the natural stream flows, as when such land is a part of the public domain; and it is immaterial whether or not it be mentioned in the patent and expressly excluded from the grant.

The [1866 Mining Act, which protects] in patents such right in water appropriated, when recognized by local customs and laws, "was rather a voluntary recognition of a pre-existing right of possession, constituting a valid claim to its continued use, than the establishment of new one." Broder v. Natoma W. & M. Co., 11 Otto 274.

We conclude, then, that the common law doctrine giving the riparian owner a right to the flow of water in its natural channel upon and over his lands, even though he makes no beneficial use thereof, is inapplicable to Colorado. Imperative necessity, unknown to the countries which gave it birth, compels the recognition of another doctrine in conflict therewith. And we hold that, in the absence of express statutes to the contrary, the first appropriator of water from a natural stream for a beneficial purpose has, with the qualifications contained in the constitution, a prior right thereto, to the extent of such appropriation. See Schilling v. Rominger, 4 Colo. 103.

The territorial legislature in 1864 expressly recognizes the doctrine. It says:

"Nor shall the water of any stream be diverted from its original channel to the detriment of any miner, millmen or others along the line of said stream, *who may have a priority of right,* and there shall be at all times left sufficient water in said stream for the use of miners and agriculturists along said stream." Session Laws of 1864, p. 68, sec. 32.

The priority of right mentioned in this section is acquired by priority of appropriation, and the provision declares that appropriations of water shall be subordinate to the use thereof by prior appropriators. This provision remained in force until the adoption of the constitution; it was repealed in 1868, but the repealing act re-enacted it *verbatim.*

But the rights of appellee were acquired, in the first instance, under the acts of 1861 and 1862, and counsel for appellants urge, with no little skill and plausibility, that these statutes are in conflict with our conclusion that priority of right is acquired by priority of appropriation. The only provision, however, which can be construed as referring to this subject is sec. 4 on page 68, Session Laws of 1861. This section provides for the appointment of commissioners, in times of scarcity, to apportion the stream "in a just and equitable proportion," to the best interests of all parties, *"with a due regard to the legal rights of all."* What is meant by the concluding phrases of the foregoing statute? What are the legal rights for which the commissioners are enjoined to have a "due regard"? Why this additional limitation upon the powers of such commissioners?

It seems to us a reasonable inference that these phrases had reference to the rights acquired by priority of appropriation. This view is sustained by the universal respect shown at the time said statute was adopted, and subsequently by each person, for the prior appropriations of others, and corresponding customs existing among settlers with reference thereto. This construction does not, in our judgment, detract from the force or effect of the statute. It was the duty of the commissioners under it to guard against extravagance and waste, and to so divide and distribute the water as most economically to supply all of the earlier appropriators thereof according to their respective appropriations and necessities, to the extent of the amount remaining in the stream.

It appears from the record that the patent under which appellant George W. Coffin holds title was issued prior to the act of congress of 1866, hereinbefore mentioned. That it contained no reservation or exception of vested water rights, and conveyed to Coffin through his grantor the absolute title in fee simple to his land, together with all incidents and appurtenances thereunto belonging; and it is claimed that therefore the doctrine of priority of right by appropriation cannot, at least, apply to him. We have already declared that water appropriated and diverted for a beneficial purpose is, in this country, not necessarily an appurtenance to the soil through which the stream supplying the same naturally flows. If appropriated by one prior to the patenting of such soil by another, it is a vested right entitled to protection, though not mentioned in the patent. But we are relieved from any extended consideration of this subject by the decision in Broder v. Natoma W. & M. Co., supra.

It is urged, however, that even if the doctrine of priority or superiority of right by priority of appropriation be conceded, appellee in this case is not benefited thereby. Appellants claim that they have a better right to the water because their lands lie along the margin and in the neighborhood of the St. Vrain. They assert that, as against them, appellee's diversion of said water to irrigate lands adjacent to Left Hand creek, though prior in time, is unlawful.

In the absence of legislation to the contrary, we think that the right to water acquired by priority of appropriation thereof is not in any way dependent upon the *locus* of its application to the beneficial use designed. And the disastrous consequences of our adoption of the rule contended for, forbid our giving such a construction to the statutes as will concede the same, if they will properly bear a more reasonable and equitable one.

The doctrine of priority of right by priority of appropriation for agriculture is evoked, as we have seen, by the imperative necessity for artificial irrigation of the soil. And it would be an ungenerous and inequitable rule that would deprive one of its benefit simply because he has, by large expenditure of time and money, carried the water from one stream over an intervening watershed and cultivated land in the valley of another. It might be utterly impossible, owing to the topography of the country, to get water upon his farm from the adjacent stream; or if possible, it might be impracticable on account of the distance from the point where the diversion must take place and the attendant expense; or the quantity of water in such stream might be entirely insufficient to supply his wants. It sometimes happens that the most fertile soil is found along the margin or in the neighborhood of the small rivulet, and sandy and barren land beside the larger stream. To apply the rule contended for would prevent the useful and profitable cultivation of the productive soil, and sanction the waste of water upon the more sterile lands. It would have enabled a party to locate upon a stream in 1875, and destroy the value of thousands of acres, and the improvements thereon, in adjoining valleys, possessed and cultivated for the preceding decade. Under the principle contended for, a party owning land ten miles from the stream, but in the valley thereof, might deprive a prior appropriator of the water diverted therefrom whose lands are within a thousand yards, but just beyond an intervening divide.

We cannot believe that any legislative body within the territory or state of Colorado ever intended these consequences to flow from a statute enacted. Yet two sections are relied upon by counsel as practically producing them. These sections are as follows:

"All persons who claim, own or hold a possessory right or title to any land or parcel of land within the boundary of Colorado territory, * * * when those claims are on the bank, margin or neighborhood of any stream of water, creek or river, shall be entitled to the use of the water of said stream, creek or river for the purposes of irrigation and making said claims available to the full extent of the soil, for agricultural purposes." Session Laws 1861, p. 67, sec. 1.

"Nor shall the water of any stream be diverted from its original channel to the detriment of any miner, millmen or others along the line of said stream, and there shall be at all times left sufficient water in said stream for the use of miners and farmers along said stream." Latter part of sec. 13, p. 48, Session Laws 1862.

The two statutory provisions above quoted must, for the purpose of this discussion, be construed together. The phrase "along said stream," in the latter, is equally comprehensive, as to the extent of territory, with the expression "on the bank, margin or neighborhood," used in the former, and both include all lands in the immediate valley of the stream. The latter provision sanctions the diversion of water from one stream to irrigate lands adjacent to another, provided such diversion is not to the "detriment" of parties along the line of the stream from which the water is taken. If there is any conflict between the statutes in this respect, the latter, of course, must prevail. We think that the "use" and "detriment" spoken of are a use existing at the time of the diversion, and a detriment immediately resulting therefrom. We do not believe that the legislature intended to prohibit the diversion of water to the "detriment" of parties who might at some future period conclude to settle upon the stream; nor do we think that they were legislating with a view to preserving in such stream sufficient water for the "use" of settlers who might never come, and consequently never have the use thereof.

But "detriment" at the time of diversion could only exist where the water diverted had been previously appropriated or used; if there had been no previous appropriation or use thereof, there could be no present injury or *"detriment."*

Our conclusion above as to the intent of the legislature is supported by the fact that the succeeding assembly, in 1864, hastened to insert into the latter statute, without other change or amendment, the clause, *"who have a priority of right,"* in connection with the ideal of *"detriment"* to adjacent owners. This amendment of the statute was simply the acknowledgment by the legislature of a doctrine already existing, under which rights had accrued that were entitled to protection. In the language of Mr. Justice Miller, above quoted, upon a different branch of the same subject, it "was rather a voluntary recognition of a pre-existing right constituting a valid claim, than the creation of a new one." * * *

Notes and Questions

1. Under *Coffin,* any notion of riparian rights in Colorado is banished forever. As noted in prior chapters, eight other states ultimately followed Colorado in recognizing the appropriation system to the total exclusion of riparian rights—Alaska, Arizona, Idaho, Montana, Nevada, New Mexico, Utah, and Wyoming. Collectively these states are often referred to as the "Colorado doctrine states."

2. Is it fair to say that the Colorado Supreme Court abolished riparian rights by judicial fiat? Is the court's interpretation of the 1861 and 1862 territorial acts a reasonable one? Does the court successfully rebut the argument that Coffin had riparian rights as a matter of federal law?

3. Just beneath the surface of the court's decision lies the argument that, no matter what the niceties of territorial and federal law, the appropriation doctrine must apply as a matter of "imperative necessity." Would this have been a more honest approach? Would it have been a legitimate ground on which to reject Coffin's claim to riparian rights? California and several other states survived and prospered without abolishing riparian rights. See infra pages 340–351.

4. In adopting a pure appropriation system, most Colorado doctrine states had to overcome legal obstacles similar to those posed in *Coffin*—and generally did no more a convincing job than the Colorado Supreme Court. Some states overcame even greater obstacles. In 1872, the Nevada Supreme Court had unanimously ruled in a lengthy opinion that the English rule of natural flow prevailed in Nevada. Vansickle v. Haines, 7 Nev. 249 (1872). Wishing to impose a pure appropriation system 13 years later, the Nevada

Supreme Court simply overruled its prior decision on the ground that appropriation had always been the "universal custom" in the West. Jones v. Adams, 19 Nev. 78, 6 P. 442 (1885). See also Mettler v. Ames Realty Co., 61 Mont. 152, 201 P. 702 (1921) (disavowing as dictum earlier language recognizing riparian rights).

Did the *Jones* decision "take" the property of those who had acquired riparian rights pursuant to the earlier *Vansickle* decision? Can a court constitutionally destroy a property right that it has previously recognized? See infra pages 384–392.

2. MIXED APPROPRIATION–RIPARIAN STATES: THE CALIFORNIA DOCTRINE

No matter the legal failings of the *Coffin* opinion, the Colorado Supreme Court succeeded in bestowing upon the state a relatively clean and simple system of water law. So as a general matter did the courts of the other Colorado doctrine states. Not every western state was as lucky. Consider California, which is the most frequently discussed example of a state that chose to follow both the riparian and appropriation doctrines.

Although the first California legislature adopted the "common law of England" as the law of the state, the California Supreme Court recognized appropriative rights in Irwin v. Phillips, 5 Cal. 140 (1855). In the years following *Irwin,* the California Supreme Court repeatedly applied the law of prior appropriation to water disputes between miners on the public domain. In the first case involving a non-mining riparian, however, the court unanimously held that the property holder was entitled to riparian water rights.[25] In 1872, the California legislature adopted the nation's first detailed appropriation code, but included a provision expressly protecting the "rights of riparian proprietors."

The choice of appropriative versus riparian rights finally came to a head in a late nineteenth century dispute between two of California's more famous citizens—Henry Miller and James Ben–Ali Haggin.[26] Described in an early biography as "selfish, grasping, indomitable, thrifty, with a wondrous brain that schemed and twisted and generally routed his opponent," Miller migrated from Germany to California during the gold rush and took up trade as a butcher. An inspired monopolist, Miller vertically integrated into cattle raising and formed a pact with his chief rival Charles Lux. Together, Miller and Lux acquired over a million acres of land during the 1870s, often illegally, including vast amounts of grazing land riparian to the lower sloughs of the Kern River. See Figure 4–1.

Haggin, a Kentucky lawyer who acquired his middle name from a Turkish ancestor, made his money through investments in various entrepreneurial activities including banks, utilities, mines, and railroads. Together with two others, Haggin in the 1870s put together a land

25. See Crandall v. Woods, 8 Cal. 136 (1857).

26. The legal dispute between Miller and Haggin is told in loving detail by Don- ald Pisani in From the Family Farm to Agribusiness (1984).

empire, again not always legally, that exceeded even that of Miller and Lux and ultimately became the Kern County Land & Water Company. As shown in Figure 4–1, Haggin's acreage included sizable amounts of land in the vicinity of the Kern River, much of which land was serviced by irrigation canals branching off from the Kern. Known as the "Grand Khan of the Kern," Haggin was a hero to many California farmers for his pioneering development of large-scale irrigation.

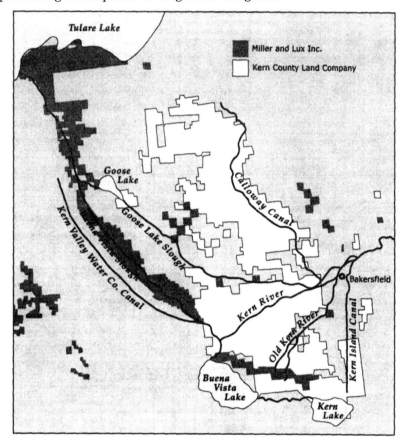

Figure 4-1

1890 Landholdings Near Kern River

After: Donald Pisani, *From the Family to Agribusiness* (1984).

Miller and Haggin peacefully coexisited in the Kern River area for several years until a major drought hit in 1877–1879 and new diversions from Haggin's Calloway canal coincided with the death of thousands of cattle owned by Miller and Lux. When attempts at a voluntary compromise failed, Miller and Lux sued Haggin—alleging that as riparians, they had superior rights. The battle was off and raging with farmers generally siding with Haggin and most ranchers siding with Miller and Lux. After a long and boring trial, the trial judge ruled for Haggin in 1881 (only to be turned out of office in the next judicial election).[27] In 1884, the California Supreme Court reversed by a vote of 4 to 3 and reaffirmed the existence of riparian rights in California.

The court's decision set off a political fire storm. An Anti–Riparian Irrigation Organization was promptly formed, which warned that "attempts * * * being made to resurrect the English common law doctrine of riparian rights from the grave to which the will of the people long since consigned it" threatened to topple "the pillars of civilization" and bring silence to California's "once busy colonies."[28] Legislators introduced bills to prohibit or at least limit riparian rights. Although nothing came of these actions, the California Supreme Court decided to vacate its decision and rehear the dispute, perhaps wisely given the electoral fate of the trial judge.

In 1886, the California Supreme Court issued its decision on rehearing. Again the court ruled in favor of Miller and Lux by a 4 to 3 vote. The excerpts that follow are just a small portion of the total opinion which, running almost 200 pages, is the longest in California history. Like *Coffin, Lux* is a complex and often exasperatingly opaque opinion that demands very careful reading. As you read *Lux,* ask yourself if it is important (1) whether an appropriation began before or after the 1866 Mining Act, and (2) whether the appropriation began before the riparian's land was patented by the federal government. Miller and Lux had acquired their riparian land from the state (which in turn had acquired the land from the federal government) in 1872; Haggin did not begin appropriating water from the Kern until 1875.

LUX v. HAGGIN

Supreme Court of California, 1886.
69 Cal. 255, 10 P. 674.

McKinstry, J.

* * *

III. *While the argument ab inconvenienti should have its proper weight in ascertaining what the law is, there is no "public policy" which can empower the courts to disregard the law; or because of an asserted benefit to many persons (in itself doubtful) to overthrow the settled law. This court has no power to legislate,—especially none to legislate in such manner as to deprive citizens of their vested rights.*

* * * It may be suggested that judges in this state should rise to the appreciation of the fact that the physical conditions here existing require

---

27. One should not feel too sorry for the judge because he was promptly hired onto Haggin's legal staff.

28. S.T. Harding, Water in California 39 (1960). Riparians were equally vociferous in their support of the Supreme Court's opinion.

an "appropriator" to be authorized to deprive, without indemnification, all the lower riparian proprietors, however numerous, on the course of an innavigable stream, of every natural advantage conferred on their land by the running water. A "public policy" has been appealed to, which has not found its expression in the statutes of the state, but rests apparently on the political maxim, "The greatest good to the greatest number"; on the claim that, by permitting such deprivation of the enjoyment of the stream by the riparian proprietors, more persons or a larger extent of territory will be benefited by the waters. The proposition is simply that, by imperative necessity, the right to take or appropriate water should be held paramount to every other right with which it may come in conflict.

But the policy of the state is not *created* by the judicial department, although the judicial department may be called upon at times to declare it; it can be ascertained only by reference to the constitution and laws passed under it, or, which is the same thing, to the principles underlying and recognized by the constitution and laws.

* * * If, in accordance with the law, [riparian] lands may be deprived of the natural irrigation without compensation to the owners, we must so hold; but we fail to discover the principles of "public policy" which are of themselves of paramount authority and demand that the law shall be so declared. * * * [And] surely it is not requiring too much to demand that the owners of lands shall be compensated for the natural advantages of which they are to be deprived. * * *

VI. *Since if not before the admission of California into the Union, the United States has been the owner of all innavigable streams on the public lands of the United States, within our borders, and of their banks and beds.*

A grant of public land of the United States carries with it the common-law rights to an innavigable stream thereon, unless the waters are expressly or impliedly reserved by the terms of the patent, or of the statute granting the land, or unless they are reserved by the congressional legislation authorizing the patent or other muniment of title.

* * * [O]n the 13th of April 1850, the legislature of California had passed an act "adopting the common law," which reads: "The common law of England, so far as it is not repugnant to or inconsistent with the constitution of the United States, or the constitution or laws of the state of California, shall be the rule of decision in all the courts of this state." * * *

* * * [F]rom a very early day the courts of this state have considered the United States government as the owner of * * * running waters on the public lands of the United States, and of their beds. Recognizing the United States as the owner of the lands and waters, and as therefore authorized to permit the occupation or diversion of the waters as distinct from the lands, the state courts have treated the prior appropriator of water on the public lands of the United States as having a better right than a subsequent appropriator, on the theory that the appropriation was allowed or licensed by the United States. It has never been held that the right to appropriate waters on the public lands of the United States was derived directly from the state of California * * *; such rights have always been claimed to be deraigned by private persons under the [Mining Act of 1866], from the recognition accorded by [that] act, or from the acquiescence of the general government in previous appropriations made with its presumed sanction and approval.

If the United States since the treaty with Mexico has been the owner of the innavigable streams and their beds, * * * the same is true as to other riparian proprietors, at least since [the 1850 act]. They have been recognized as such owners by our courts. Prior and subsequent to the [adoption of the 1872 appropriation code], the rights to the use of water by private riparian proprietors, as between themselves, have repeatedly been judicially determined by reference to the common-law rules on the subject * * *

And if the United States since the date of the admission of the state has been the owner of the innavigable streams on its lands, and of the subjacent soils, grants of its lands must be held to carry with them the appropriate common-law use of the waters of the innavigable streams thereon, except where the flowing waters have been *reserved* from the grant. To hold otherwise would be to hold * * * that the United States, as a riparian owner within the state, has other and different rights than other riparian owners, including its own grantees.

The government of the United States has the absolute and perfect title to its lands. * * * Unless, therefore, running waters are reserved, they pass by grant or patent of the United States. * * *

VIII. *It has never been held by the Supreme Court of the United States, or by the Supreme Court of this state, that an appropriation of the water on the public lands of the United States (made after the [1866 Mining Act], or the Amendatory Act of 1870) gave to the appropriator the right to the water appropriated, as against a grantee of riparian lands under a grant made or issued prior to the act of 1866; except in a case where the water so subsequently appropriated was reserved by the terms of such grant.*

* * * In Broder v. Water Company, [supra p. 333], the claim of the appropriator was recognized in the grant to the railroad company * * * In the case at bar, the grant of the lands to the state [that were later acquired by Miller & Lux] * * * was made nearly thirty years before the first appropriation of water by [Haggin] * * *

In Osgood v. Water Company, 56 Cal. 571, it was held that where a person acquired a right by appropriation to water upon the public lands of the United States, *before* the issuance of a patent [in 1868] to another for lands through which the stream ran, the patentee's rights were, "by express statutory enactment, subject to the rights of the appropriator." * * * There is nothing in that case which precludes us from [giving] the pre-emptor the better right as against an appropriator of water made after the certificate [of title] is given to the pre-emptor. * * *

Both *Broder v. Water Company* and *Osgood v. Water Company* are (by strongest implication) authority for the statement that one who acquired a title to riparian lands from the United States prior to the act of July 26, 1866, could not (in the absence of reservation in his grant) be deprived of his common-law rights to the flow of the stream by one who appropriated its waters after the passage of that act.

Much stress is laid by counsel on the language used in *Broder v. Water Co.*, supra, with reference to the clause in the act of 1866, that water-rights recognized or acknowledged by the local customs, etc., "shall be maintained and protected," "was rather a recognition of a pre-existing right of possession, constituting a valid claim to its continued use, than the establishment of a new one." But this language is to be interpreted in view of the context. The language cannot be construed as a recognition by the court of vested rights in appropriators of water, created by mere appropriation and independent of statute. The case proceeds on the assumption that neither the plaintiff nor the defendant had any rights except such as were granted or recognized by acts of congress. It holds that appropriators of water from streams on (or flowing to) the lands granted by the act of 1864 [which had provided for land grants to the railroads] were "recognized" or admitted to have rights which were protected by that act, because the act by its terms reserved from the grant to the railroad company every "lawful claim," that one who had been permitted to divert water from those lands had a claim which was not in itself unlawful; and that the reservation included "*every honest claim* evidenced by acts of possession." * * *

[In a later section of its opinion, the court also concluded that California's 1872 appropriation code, which explicitly provided that "The rights of riparian proprietors are not affected by the provisions of this title," did not abrogate the riparian rights of those who acquired their title "before an appropriation of water in accordance with the code provisions."]

MYRICK, J., dissenting.

* * * I do not think that the adoption of the common law of England * * * was intended to or did establish a rule of decision as to the right of appropriation of water for irrigation. The land of the birth of the common law of England had no occasion to consider or act upon the necessity for irrigation, and appropriation was not within the scheme of its laws. The rights of riparian owners (whatever they were) had reference to the country and its needs, of which irrigation was not an essential part. * * *

ROSS, J., dissenting.

* * * The question here is between a purchaser of a part of the public land of the state, derived from the United States, and an appropriator of water upon the public lands of the United States. From the foundation of the state, waters pertaining to the public lands of both the federal and state governments have been appropriated and used for mining, agriculture, and other useful purposes. Such appropriation and

use was first sanctioned by custom, next by the decisions of the courts, and finally by legislative action on the part of the United States as well as the states. It thus became a part of the law of the land, of which every citizen was entitled to avail himself, and of which every purchaser from the United States, as well as the state, was bound to take notice. * * *

MORRISON, C.J., dissented for the same reasons.

Notes and Questions

1. In the aftermath of the California Supreme Court's 1886 decision in *Lux,* antiriparian clubs blossomed. Various members of the California legislature introduced bills to repeal or limit riparian rights. The governor proposed a bill to reduce the size of the California court from seven to five justices, retiring two of the justices who had voted with the majority (both of whom, antiriparian politicians claimed, were mentally incompetent). Nothing came of these efforts and the *Lux* decision stood. In the meantime, Miller and Lux agreed to settle their dispute with Haggin and other appropriators from the Kern River:

> The pact was not formally ratified until July 28, 1888, when thirty-one ditch companies and fifty-eight individuals agreed to guarantee Henry Miller and his riparian neighbors exclusive use of the Kern River from September to February, and also from March through August when the stream carried less than 300 cubic feet per second. The remaining water was divided in the ratio of two-thirds to the Haggin interests, one-third to the riparian owners. To augment the existing supply, the two sides also agreed to share the cost of damming Buena Vista Lake and building new canals and levees.

Donald Pisani, From the Family Farm to Agribusiness 243 (1984).

2. The *Lux* majority appear to take a much more "conservative" view of their judicial role than the Colorado Supreme Court did in *Coffin.* To what degree should early state courts have considered general public policy, rather than just prior opinions, statutes, and constitutional provisions, in deciding whether to recognize riparian rights? See Eric Freyfogle, *Lux v. Haggin* and the Common Law Burdens of Modern Water Law, 57 U. Colo. L. Rev. 485 (1986) (criticizing *Lux*'s legal conservatism).

3. Although the California court disavows an activist role, is its opinion any less an exercise in judicial fiat than the Colorado court's decision in *Coffin*? California, unlike Colorado, had never enacted any statute that arguably created riparian rights other than the 1850 law adopting the "common law of England."

Did the 1850 statute require the California Supreme Court to recognize riparian rights? The answer depends on whether the legislature intended to adopt the specific common law doctrines applied by English courts or merely an elastic system of judge-made law. Courts of other states split on whether similar statutes in their states created riparian rights. Compare Van Dyke v. Midnight Sun Mining & Ditch Co., 177 Fed. 85 (9th Cir. 1910) and Drake v. Earhart, 2 Idaho 716, 23 P. 541 (1890) (no riparian rights) with Vansickle v. Haines, 7 Nev. 249 (1872) and Motl v. Boyd, 116 Tex. 82, 286 S.W. 458 (1926) (riparian rights). In Boquillas Land & Cattle Co. v. Curtis, 213 U.S.

339 (1909), the United States Supreme Court per Justice Holmes rejected the argument that such provisions strait-jacketed water law. According to Justice Holmes, such statutes constituted merely the "adoption of a general system" of law and were "far from saying that patentees of a ranch on the San Pedro are to have the same [water] rights as owners of an estate on the Thames."

In a passage from *Lux* omitted above, the California Supreme Court held that California's common-law adoption statute did not require the court to follow the English rule of natural flow. The court went on to hold that, in disputes between riparians, it would follow the reasonable use doctrine— thus allowing riparians to irrigate their lands. If the court was free to reject the English rule of natural flow, why was it not free also to reject riparian rights entirely?

4.   Under *Lux,* how should courts resolve water disputes involving two riparians? Two appropriators? A riparian and an appropriator? A clear set of rules is difficult to glean from the excerpts reprinted above (and even from reading the entire opinion). As clarified by other California cases, however, the basic rules are deceptively simple:

>   (1) If both the users are riparians, resolve the dispute according to the American rule of reasonable use.

>   (2) If both the users are appropriators, resolve the dispute according to the appropriation doctrine.

>   (3) If one user is riparian and the other an appropriator, the resolution becomes slightly more complex but still straightforward. First you need to know when the appropriation began—call this the "appropriation date." Second you need to know when the riparian, *or the riparian's earliest predecessor in interest,* first acquired private title to the land (or settled on the land with an intent to acquire title)—call this the "title date." If the appropriation date is prior to the title date, the appropriator wins. If the title date is prior to the appropriation date, the riparian wins.

Simple when applied to two-party disputes, these rules unfortunately can lead to a circular impasse when applied to more than two water users. Consider, for example, the hypothetical illustrated in Figure 4–2. Three farmers vie for the waters of the Loredo River. Ernest Hurst's grandfather began appropriating 100 cfs of water in 1890 for use on the farm which Ernest now owns and runs. Both Ellen Smith and Rick Kemp are riparians and also need 100 cfs each for use on their farms. The Smith land was homesteaded in 1880 (although no water was used on the land until this century). The Kemp land was homesteaded in 1900. Assume, moreover, there is no return flow from any of the farms. In a year when there is only 200 cfs of water available in the Loredo River, how much water is each of the farmers entitled to take under *Lux?*

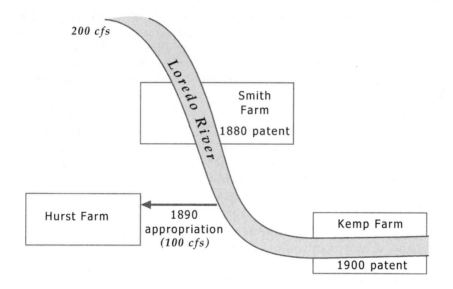

Figure 4–2

If you cannot find a solution, do not worry. Neither can we. To our knowledge, moreover, no court has ever confronted this Gordian knot in a published opinion. The issue typically does not arise because most private land in California was homesteaded or otherwise acquired before rival appropriative rights. Indeed, many treatises, articles, and even judicial opinions discussing California law simply assume that riparian rights are superior to prior appropriative rights, ignoring the complexities created by *Lux*. See, e.g., Arthur Littleworth & Eric Garner, California Water 37–38 (1995).

For a comprehensive study of California riparian rights and their interplay with appropriative rights, see David Anderson, Riparian Water Rights in California: Background and Issues (1977).

5.   The problems of recognizing both riparian and appropriative rights do not end with the difficult task of devising internally consistent rules for resolving disputes between riparians and appropriators. Because riparian rights are generally not transferable, the existence of substantial quantities of riparian rights threatens to deny water to nonriparian users who might be able to put the water to greater beneficial use. The existence of riparian rights also jeopardizes the security of appropriative rights. Riparian rights are not lost by non-use. As a result, an appropriator who has diverted water from a stream for years might suddenly need to stop diverting water because a riparian who previously has never taken any water from the stream wishes to begin exercising her superior rights.

6.   In Herminghaus v. Southern California Edison Co., 200 Cal. 81, 252 P. 607 (1926), Amelia Herminghaus owned 18,000 acres of grazing lands along the lower stretches of California's San Joaquin River. Rather than

artificially irrigating her grazing land, Herminghaus relied upon the overflow of the river during the spring and early summer to water her pasturage—even though this required 100 times more water to flow down the San Joaquin River than artificial irrigation would have required.[29] When Southern California Edison announced plans to store water upstream from Herminghaus in connection with a hydroelectric project, Herminghaus objected that the storage would deny her the benefit of the river overflow. The California Supreme Court agreed, holding that a riparian could demand the entire flow of a river against a later appropriator even when the riparian could get by with far less water.

Herminghaus raised tremendous and immediate concern. According to the state engineer, no hydroelectric or storage projects could proceed in the face of *Herminghaus*. Less than two years after the *Herminghaus* decision, therefore, California voters overwhelmingly approved a state constitutional amendment limiting all water rights, including riparian rights, to "reasonable and beneficial uses." The amendment, which is embodied today in Article X, section 2 of the California Constitution, is quoted supra p. 192 note b.

A Note on Other Hybrid Doctrine States

Seven western states (Kansas, Nebraska, North Dakota, Oklahoma, Oregon, South Dakota, and Washington) took the California Supreme Court's lead in *Lux* and held that an individual who acquired title to governmental land also received riparian rights, subject only to previous appropriators. Texas took a slightly more extreme position, ruling that persons who acquired public lands bordering on a waterway acquired riparian rights superior even to previous appropriations (so long as the land was first acquired before an 1895 statute cutting off riparian rights from future grants of public land).[30] Together, these states are often called the "California doctrine" states.

Because of the problems inherent in dual riparian-appropriative systems, courts in most of these states have slowly whittled away at riparian rights. Most California doctrine states, for example, have adopted the "source of title" rule under which, as described supra p. 30, a non-waterfront piece of riparian land that is sold off loses forever its riparian status—even if it is later recombined with the waterfront portion of the land. As riparian property is subdivided over time, the "source of title" rule shrinks potentially exercisable riparian rights.

The courts of some California doctrine states also have limited the waters in which riparians can claim rights. In Texas, for example, riparian rights extend only to the "ordinary flow and underflow" of a stream; when the waters "rise above the line of highest ordinary flow," they become "flood waters * * * to which riparian rights do not attach" and which appropriators can impound and use. Motl v. Boyd, 116 Tex. 82, 286 S.W. 458 (1926). See also Chow v. City of Santa Barbara, 217 Cal. 673, 22 P.2d 5 (1933)

---

29. The maximum flow of the river during the spring and early summer was 20,000 cfs; testimony indicated traditional irrigation would have required just 180 cfs.

30. See Motl v. Boyd, 116 Tex. 82, 286 S.W. 458 (1926); Tex. Water Code Ann. § 11.001(b).

(establishing a similar rule); State ex rel. Ham, Yearsley & Ryrie v. Superior Court, 70 Wash. 442, 126 P. 945 (1912) (no riparian rights in navigable waters).

Legislatures have adopted even more drastic measures to restrict riparian rights. In particular, the legislatures of the two Dakotas, Kansas, Oregon, and Texas have passed statutes abolishing *unexercised* riparian rights.[31] These statutes effectively cap riparian rights in these states. Riparians continue to enjoy a riparian right to any water that they were diverting and using at the time that the legislation was passed (or, in some cases, during a short grace period thereafter). But riparians cannot divert more than that amount except by appropriating the water. Riparians who were not using water when the legislation was passed, or during any grace period, enjoy no riparian right.

Washington accomplished essentially the same result with some interpretive help from its supreme court. In 1891 and again in 1917, the Washington legislature adopted detailed appropriation codes that explicitly protected riparian rights.[32] In a series of subsequent decisions, however, the state supreme court ruled that the legislature had not meant to protect riparian rights that were not used within a "reasonable time" after the appropriation codes' passage. According to the court, the legislature could not have intended to protect the right of riparians to start using water "at some distant, indefinite time in the future" to the detriment of prior appropriators.[33]

As a result, riparian rights remain a major legal issue today only in California, Nebraska, and Oklahoma. Both California and Oklahoma have tried to abolish unexercised riparian rights by statute, only to have their state supreme courts hold the statutes unconstitutional. See Tulare Irrigation Dist. v. Lindsay–Strathmore Irrigation Dist., 3 Cal.2d 489, 45 P.2d 972 (1935); Franco–American Charolaise, Ltd. v. Oklahoma Water Resources Bd., 855 P.2d 568 (Okla. 1990). The *Franco–American* decision is excerpted and discussed infra pp. 366–374.

Although California, Nebraska, and Oklahoma all retain active riparian rights, Nebraska and Oklahoma part company from California in the rules they follow to resolve disputes between riparians and appropriators. Rather than looking at the relative "seniority" of the competing rights, Nebraska and Oklahoma focus on their "relative reasonableness." As the Nebraska Supreme Court has explained:

> We cannot synthesize [appropriative and riparian rights] in one decision. Facts are so important that in the absence of legislation a viable system ought to be evolved by the process of inclusion and exclusion, case by case. * * *

31. See Kan. Stat. §§ 82a–701 & 703; Ore. Laws, 1909, ch. 216; 1955 S.D. Sess. Laws, ch. 430; Tex. Water Code § 11.303(b).

32. See 1891 Wash. Laws 327–28, § 7; 1917 Wash. Laws 447, § 1.

33. See State ex rel. Liberty Lake Irr. Co. v. Superior Court, 47 Wash. 310, 91 P. 968, 969 (1907). See also Brown v. Chase, 125 Wash. 542, 217 P. 23 (1923); In the Matter of Deadman Creek Drainage Basin, 103 Wash.2d 686, 694 P.2d 1071 (1985) (water not used by 1932 was extinguished).

An appropriator who, in using water pursuant to a statutory permit, intentionally causes substantial harm to a riparian proprietor, through invasion of the proprietor's interest in the use of the waters, is liable to the proprietor in an action for damages if, but only if, the harmful appropriation is unreasonable in respect to the proprietor. The appropriation is unreasonable unless its utility outweighs the gravity of the harm. * * *

In evaluation of the utility of the appropriation * * *, the following factors are to be considered: (1) The social value which the law attaches to the use for which the appropriation is made; (2) the priority date of the appropriation; and (3) the impracticability of preventing or avoiding the harm. * * *

In evaluation of the gravity of * * * harm * * *, the following factors are important: (1) The extent of harm involved; (2) the social value which the law attaches to the riparian use; (3) the time of initiation of the riparian use; (4) the suitability of the riparian use to the watercourse; and (5) the burden on the riparian proprietor of avoiding the harm. * * *

Wasserburger v. Coffee, 180 Neb. 149, 141 N.W.2d 738 (1966). See also Franco–American Charolaise, Ltd. v. Oklahoma Water Resources Bd., 855 P.2d 568, 578 (Okla. 1990). Is this a better approach for coordinating appropriative and riparian rights than the approach taken by California?

For a summary of the evolution of riparian rights in the California doctrine states, see Joseph Dellapenna, Riparian Rights in the West, 43 Okla. L. Rev. 51 (1990).

3. FEDERALISM ISSUES

An underlying issue in both *Coffin* and *Lux* was the power of state governments, relative to the federal government, over water resources. The issue arose again in the efforts by some California Doctrine states to rid themselves of riparian rights. In the early 20th century, the supreme courts of Oregon and South Dakota argued that Congress, in the federal Desert Land Act of 1877, had abolished riparian rights as a matter of federal law for all land settled after passage of the act—thereby overriding state decisions recognizing riparian rights.[34]

The Desert Land Act permitted settlers to claim 640–acre tracts of arid land at 25 cents an acre, with a patent to follow upon proof that the settler had irrigated the land. One section of the Desert Land Act provided that claimants were entitled only to as much water as was actually appropriated and necessarily used for irrigation on the land. The act then went on to provide that

> all surplus water over and above such actual appropriation and use, together with the water of all lakes, rivers and other sources of water supply upon the public lands and not naviga-

34. See Hough v. Porter, 51 Or. 318, 98 P. 1083 (1909); Haaser v. Englebrecht, 45 S.D. 143, 186 N.W. 572, 573 (1922); Cook v. Evans, 45 S.D. 31, 185 N.W. 262, 263–64 (1921).

ble, shall remain and be held free for the appropriation and use of the public for irrigation, mining and manufacturing purposes subject to existing rights.[35]

Although there was no suggestion in the legislative history that Congress had intended to impose the appropriative system on western states subject to the Act, this was not an unreasonable reading of the language. The United States Supreme Court finally addressed the issue in 1935.

CALIFORNIA OREGON POWER CO. v. BEAVER PORTLAND CEMENT CO.

Supreme Court of the United States, 1935.
295 U.S. 142.

[This was a suit by the owner of a hydroelectric site on Oregon's Rogue River seeking to enjoin upstream activities that lessened the flow of the river. Plaintiff claimed that it had a riparian right to the natural flow of the river stemming from an 1885 federal patent to the land; the defendants argued that the Desert Land Act put an end to all riparian claims. The federal trial court concluded that the patent did carry federal riparian rights, but that "while this was a substantial property right which could not be arbitrarily destroyed, it nevertheless was subject to the police power of the state and might be modified by legislation passed in the interest of the general welfare." This was important because, in 1909, Oregon had passed legislation effectively abolishing all riparian rights not put to a beneficial use before the legislation was passed.]

MR. JUSTICE SUTHERLAND delivered the opinion of the Court.

[After discussing the 1866 and 1870 Mining Act provisions and the history of appropriation in the western United States, the Court turned its attention to the 1877 Desert Land Act.] By its terms, not only all surplus water over and above such as might be appropriated and used by the desert land entrymen, but "the water of all lakes, rivers and other sources of water supply upon the public lands and not navigable" were to remain "free for the appropriation and use of the public for irrigation, mining and manufacturing purposes." If this language is to be given its natural meaning, and we see no reason why it should not, it effected a severance of all waters upon the public domain, not theretofore appropriated, from the land itself. From that premise, it follows that a patent issued thereafter for lands in a desert-land state or territory, under any of the land laws of the United States, carried with it, of its own force, no common law right to the water flowing through or bordering upon the lands conveyed. * * *

In United States v. Rio Grande Dam & Irrigation Co., 174 U.S. 690, * * * [the Court] said that it was within the power of any state to change the common-law rule and permit the appropriation of the flowing waters for any purposes it deemed wise. Whether a territory had the

---

35. Act of March 3, 1877, 19 Stat. 377, § 1.

same power the court did not then decide. Two limitations of state power were suggested: first, in the absence of any specific authority from Congress, that a state could not by its legislation destroy the right of the United States as the owner of lands bordering on a stream to the continued flow—so far, at least, as might be necessary for the beneficial use of the government property; and second, that its power was limited by that of the general government to secure the uninterrupted navigability of all navigable streams within the limits of the United States. With these exceptions, the court, however, thought (p. 706) that by the acts of 1866 and 1877 "Congress recognized and assented to the appropriation of water in contravention of the common law rule as to continuous flow," and that "the obvious purpose of congress was to give its assent, so far as the public lands were concerned, to any system, although in contravention to the common law rule, which permitted the appropriation of those waters for legitimate industries." * * *

As the owner of public domain, the government possessed the power to dispose of land and water thereon together, or to dispose of them separately. * * * The fair construction of the provision now under review is that Congress intended to establish the rule that for the future the land should be patented separately; and that all non-navigable waters thereon should be reserved for the use of the public under the laws of the states and territories named. The words that the water of all sources of water supply upon the public lands and not navigable "shall remain and be held free for the appropriation and use of the public" are not susceptible of any other construction. The only exception made is that in favor of *existing* rights; and the only rule spoken of is that of *appropriation.* * * *

* * * Nothing we have said is meant to suggest that the act as we construe it, has the effect of curtailing the power of the states affected to legislate in respect of waters and water rights as they deem wise in the public interest. What we hold is that following the act of 1877, if not before, all non-navigable waters then a part of the public domain became *publici juris,* subject to the plenary control of the designated states, including those since created out of the territories named, with the right in each to determine for itself to what extent the rule of appropriation or the common-law rule in respect of riparian rights should obtain. For since "Congress cannot enforce either rule upon any state," Kansas v. Colorado, 206 U.S. 46, 94, the full power of choice must remain with the state. The Desert Land Act does not bind or purport to bind the states to any policy. It simply recognized and gives sanction, in so far as the United States and its future grantees are concerned, to the state and local doctrine of appropriation, and seeks to remove what otherwise might be an impediment to the full and successful operation. * * *

For the foregoing reasons, we affirm the decree of the court below, passing without consideration [the question of whether riparian rights can be modified by legislation without paying compensation], as to which we express no opinion.

Notes and Questions

1. *California Oregon Power Co.* is typically cited today for the proposition that whether land along the border of a river carries riparian rights is a question entirely of state law. How does the Court avoid the conclusion that the Desert Land Act imposed the appropriation doctrine?

2. Does the opinion totally foreclose the possibility that a federal patentee could claim a riparian right as a matter of federal law? What of federal patentees who were granted land before enactment of the Desert Land Act? Note also that the Desert Land Act, as well as the Court's opinion, speaks only of nonnavigable waters. Could a federal patentee claim a riparian right to navigable waters? Finally, the Desert Land Act applies to all the westernmost states except Alaska, Hawaii, Kansas, Nebraska, Oklahoma and Texas. Did riparian rights survive in those states to which the Desert Land Act did not apply?

3. *California Oregon Power Co.* is a key opinion on relative state-federal powers over water. Does the opinion hold that the federal government does not have the power to impose any particular water rights doctrine on the states? Or simply that the federal government has not chosen to do so?

4. What rights does *California Oregon Power Co.* suggest the federal government has over western water? What is the source of those rights? What is the impact of the Desert Land Act on those rights? Can the federal government bar appropriations of water from a stream that flows into a national forest? We will return to these and related questions in Chapter 9.

B.　THE DOUBTFUL PROGENY OF SPANISH AND MEXICAN WATER LAW

Southwestern states have had to worry about the transition not only from riparian rights but also from Spanish and Mexican law. In the 1848 Treaty of Guadalupe Hidalgo, under which Mexico ceded to the United States much of the territory of the Southwest, the United States promised to honor pre-existing titles to property. 9 Stat. 922 (1848). This has led to serious debate in both California and New Mexico (as well as Texas which utilized Mexican laws until 1840 and honors Mexican property titles) over what, if any, water rights were created by Mexican and Spanish law.

Mexican and Spanish water law has proven exceptionally malleable in the hands of American courts. This is partly because of our dearth of knowledge concerning the subject. As noted by Michael Meyer, a leading scholar on the subject, most commentary to date has been "little more than extrapolations from general treatises on Spanish colonial law or adaptations from what we know of land usage and land ownership."[1] In this connection, it is worth noting that the "law" was not compiled and retained in one place. Indeed, the law of New Spain was exceptionally

---

1. Michael Meyer, Water in the Hispanic Southwest: A Social and Legal History 1550–1850, at 105 (1984).

diverse and varied from setting to setting. The inevitable ambiguity in Mexican and Spanish water law has allowed courts to read their own cultural and normative views into the existing fragments of history. As Meyer has again noted, there "is a strong and almost natural tendency to view the relationship of the individual and the state through the cultural prism of a later age."[2]

One major question has been what, if any, water right accompanied grants of land by the Mexican or Spanish governments. Arizona, California, New Mexico, and Texas have each concluded that Mexican and Spanish law was consistent with the state's current system of water allocation—even though the states vary widely among themselves. In Lux v. Haggin, 69 Cal. 255, 10 P. 674 (1886), supra p. 342, the California Supreme Court concluded that Mexican land grants were entitled to riparian rights. Within a decade, however, the supreme courts of both Arizona and New Mexico (both devoted Colorado Doctrine states) held that Mexico had followed the appropriation doctrine.[3] At a time when Texas was firmly in the camp of mixed doctrine states, its court decided that Spanish and Mexican land grants carried riparian rights.[4] As Texas began to move toward a primarily appropriative system, however, the state supreme court changed its mind and held land grants did not come with riparian rights.[5]

In a provocative series of articles based on original research into the records of early cases, Professor Peter Reich has suggested that some of these early courts intentionally distorted Spanish and Mexican law to reach the result they wished. As discussed earlier in this Chapter, Spanish and Mexican water rights were highly communal. Although water could be privately owned, Spanish and Mexican law viewed water as an important public asset that should be managed to the benefit of the entire community. No water right was permanent, and temporal priority of use was only one of several factors used to resolve water disputes. According to Reich, courts ignored strong evidence of the communal character of Spanish and Mexican law in order to justify the prior appropriation doctrine. In Reich's view, this was a missed opportunity:

> Spanish and Mexican communal water sharing, by which the needs of the various users were apportioned, was a system well-suited to the arid frontier. Judicial hijacking of this tradition appeared to place the authority of history behind monopolization of a scarce resource by a few cities and landowners. Had the more accurate historical arguments presented to the courts prevailed, southwestern water law would not have been left a legacy of exclusive water rights that continues to trump fair

2. Id. at 159.

3. Clough v. Wing, 2 Ariz. 371, 17 P. 453 (1888); United States v. Rio Grande Dam & Irr. Co., 9 N.M. 292, 51 P. 674 (1898), rev'd on other grounds, 174 U.S. 690 (1899).

4. Motl v. Boyd, 116 Tex. 82, 286 S.W. 458 (1926).

5. Valmont Plantations v. State, 163 Tex. 381, 355 S.W.2d 502 (1962).

distribution * * *. If judges had taken history more seriously, they would have been able to implement the lessons a previous civilization learned about environmental adaptation rather than indulging unlimited urban and agricultural expansion.

Peter Reich, Mission Revival Jurisprudence: State Courts and Hispanic Water Law Since 1850, 69 Wash. L. Rev. 869, 925 (1994). See also Peter Reich, The "Hispanic" Roots of Prior Appropriation in Arizona, 27 Ariz. St. L.J. 649 (1995).

An equally important question has been whether "pueblos" received any special water right. Many towns in the southwestern United States, including major cities such as Los Angeles, were originally organized as a form of settlement called a "pueblo" during the days of Spanish and Mexican dominion. In Lux v. Haggin, supra p. 342, the California Supreme Court suggested that pueblos were entitled to special and exclusive rights to waters within their borders. Less than a decade later, the California Supreme Court squarely held that Los Angeles, as a former pueblo, was entitled to as much of the water from the Los Angeles River as it needed for its residents and other municipal purposes.[6] And in 1958, the New Mexico Supreme Court also adopted the pueblo rights doctrine.[7] Texas, by contrast, has flatly rejected the doctrine.[8]

Pueblo rights are superior to all other riparian and appropriative rights and cannot be lost by nonuse. In San Diego v. Cuyamaca Water Co., 209 Cal. 105, 287 Pac. 475 (1930), for example, the court permitted San Diego to claim all the waters to the San Diego River even though San Diego had not used the waters for over a century and the defendant had invested over a million dollars to use the waters for irrigation. The amount of water which a pueblo can claim, moreover, expands with the needs of the city and may even be used to supply the needs of areas that are added to the city through annexation. The pueblo right extends to all streams and rivers flowing through the city and also to groundwater aquifers underlying the city.[9]

The existence of pueblo rights has come under a great deal of criticism. The decisions adopting the doctrine cite virtually no Spanish or Mexican authorities; what support is presented is questionable.[10] Despite doubts concerning the modern pueblo rights doctrine, the California Supreme Court has refused to reconsider its decision, noting that reconsideration at this late date might "unjustly impair legitimate interests built up over the years in reliance on our former decision."[11] In 2004, however, the New Mexico Supreme Court had a change of mind.

6. Vernon Irr. Co. v. City of Los Angeles, 106 Cal. 237, 39 P. 762 (1895).

7. Cartwright v. Public Service Co., 66 N.M. 64, 343 P.2d 654 (1958).

8. See In re Contests of Laredo, 675 S.W.2d 257 (Tex. App. 1984).

9. See City of Los Angeles v. City of San Fernando, 14 Cal.3d 199, 123 Cal.Rptr. 1, 537 P.2d 1250 (1975).

10. See, e.g., Wells Hutchins, Pueblo Water Rights in the West, 38 Tex. L. Rev. 748 (1960).

11. City of Los Angeles v. City of San Fernando, 14 Cal.3d 199, 123 Cal.Rptr. 1, 25, 537 P.2d 1250, 1274 (1975).

STATE OF NEW MEXICO v. CITY OF LAS VEGAS

Supreme Court of New Mexico, 2004.
135 N.M. 375, 89 P.3d 47.

SERNA, Justice.

In Cartwright v. Public Service Co. of New Mexico, 66 N.M. 64, 79–85, 343 P.2d 654, 664–69 (1958), this Court adopted the pueblo rights doctrine. Under this doctrine, municipalities that are the successors-in-interest to colonization pueblos established by antecedent sovereigns possess a pueblo water right. This water right entitles a municipality to take as much water from an adjacent water course as necessary for municipal purposes and permits expansion of the right to accommodate increased municipal needs due to population increases. Upon reexamination, we conclude that the pueblo rights doctrine is inconsistent with New Mexico's system of prior appropriation. As a result, we overrule *Cartwright*. We conclude that municipal water rights must be determined by prior appropriation based on beneficial use regardless of a colonization grant from preceding sovereigns. * * *

III. THE VALIDITY OF THE PUEBLO RIGHTS DOCTRINE IN NEW MEXICO

The State Engineer urges us to overrule *Cartwright* and reject the pueblo rights doctrine in New Mexico for two primary reasons. First, contrary to the analysis in *Cartwright*, the State Engineer contends that there is no historical basis for the pueblo rights doctrine in Spanish and Mexican law. Second, the State Engineer argues that the pueblo rights doctrine is inconsistent with fundamental precepts of New Mexico water law. We do not believe that the State Engineer's first reason provides adequate grounds to overrule *Cartwright*, but we need not take a definitive position on the historical validity of the pueblo rights doctrine because we agree with the State Engineer that *Cartwright* is based on a flawed analysis of New Mexico water law. We more fully address each of these points below. We begin, however, by reiterating the importance of stare decisis.

> Very weighty considerations underlie the principle that courts should not lightly overrule past decisions. Among these are the desirability that the law furnish a clear guide for the conduct of individuals, to enable them to plan their affairs with assurance against untoward surprise; the importance of furthering fair and expeditious adjudication by eliminating the need to relitigate every relevant proposition in every case; and the necessity of maintaining public faith in the judiciary as a source of impersonal and reasoned judgments.

Moragne v. States Marine Lines, Inc., 398 U.S. 375, 403 (1970). Based on the importance of stare decisis, "we require a compelling reason to overrule one of our prior cases." Padilla v. State Farm Mut. Auto. Ins.

Co., 133 N.M. 661, 68 P.3d 901 (2003). We consider the State Engineer's arguments with these principles in mind.

A.   Historical Basis for the Pueblo Rights Doctrine

In the district court, the State Engineer tendered the expert opinion of several witnesses discussing the question of whether the pueblo rights doctrine is supported by historical evidence: Professor G. Emlen Hall, a legal historian, Dr. Iris Engstrand, a historian, Professor Guillermo F. Margadant, an expert in Spanish and Mexican legal history, Professor Hans W. Baade, a legal historian, and Professor Daniel Tyler, a historian. Each of these experts concluded that the pueblo rights doctrine lacks a historical foundation in the law of either of the two antecedent sovereigns in New Mexico, Spain and Mexico. The State Engineer's experts provided examples of other towns established by colonization grants in New Mexico and Texas for which there is no evidence of a prior and paramount right to water. See, e.g., Daniel Tyler, The Mythical Pueblo Rights Doctrine 35–44 (1990). In response to these expert opinions, the City devoted its tender on the validity of the pueblo rights doctrine to *Cartwright* and its authorities, which primarily consisted of the California cases recognizing the pueblo rights doctrine. * * *

The State Engineer contends that the pueblo rights doctrine is historically invalid. However, because this Court adopted the pueblo rights doctrine in *Cartwright*, we do not treat the issue of the historical validity of the doctrine as we would if it were an issue of first impression. Thus, the question is not whether we agree with the State Engineer's historical view of the law of antecedent sovereigns but, instead, whether this Court's historical analysis in *Cartwright* is so clearly erroneous as to create a compelling reason for overruling *Cartwright*. Having reviewed the State Engineer's tender and the authorities upon which *Cartwright* relied, we do not believe that the historical evidence is sufficiently clear to justify overruling *Cartwright* on this basis. * * *

Moreover, we are wary of undue reliance on scholarly opinions in re-evaluating a position previously adopted by this Court. As the record in this case demonstrates, historical opinion can fluctuate based on newly found historical evidence or novel interpretations of extant sources. Unlike history as a matter of theory, however, the law, as reflected by the doctrine of stare decisis, requires a greater degree of certainty and predictability. For example, if we were to adopt the State Engineer's historical analysis, the discovery of new evidence supporting the existence of the pueblo rights doctrine in Spanish and Mexican law would remain a possibility, which would undoubtedly lead to another dispute over the historical validity of this doctrine. For property rights in general and water rights in particular, we believe that defining these rights based on prevailing scholarship would create an intolerable degree of uncertainty. Thus, while we concede that, in light of presently available historical evidence, the pueblo rights doctrine "rests * * * on a very narrow foundation," Wells A. Hutchins, Pueblo Water Rights in the West, 38 Tex. L. Rev. 748, 757 (1960), we are not convinced that this

Court's adoption of the pueblo rights doctrine in *Cartwright* represents an entirely untenable view of Spanish and Mexican law. See Hans W. Baade, The Historical Background of Texas Water Law–A Tribute to Jack Pope, 18 St. Mary's L.J. 1, 82 (1986) ("Given the high priority of [domestic and municipal] purposes, [the pueblo water right] claim seems neither implausible nor inequitable."). * * *

B.   The Pueblo Rights Doctrine's Relationship to General Principles of Water Law

The State Engineer raises what we believe to be more vital concerns with the pueblo rights doctrine than its historical validity in the law of antecedent sovereigns. The State Engineer argues that the perpetually expanding nature of the pueblo right conflicts with the fundamental principle of beneficial use that lies at the heart of New Mexico water law. As a result, the State Engineer contends that the doctrine is incompatible with water law in New Mexico and violates public policy. We agree. * * *

In New Mexico, "beneficial use shall be the basis, the measure and the limit of the right to the use of water." N.M. Const. art. XVI, § 3. * * * The principle of beneficial use is based on "imperative necessity," Hagerman Irrigation Co. v. McMurry, 16 N.M. 172, 181, 113 P. 823, 825 (1911), and "aims fundamentally at definiteness and certainty." State ex rel. State Eng'r v. Crider, 78 N.M. 312, 315, 431 P.2d 45, 48 (1967).

In applying these principles, we have recognized that water users have a reasonable time after an initial appropriation to put water to beneficial use, known as the doctrine of relation. "If the application to beneficial use is made in proper time, it relates back and completes the appropriation as of the time when it was initiated." Hagerman Irrigation Co., 16 N.M. at 180, 113 P. at 825. We have applied this principle to municipalities in order to allow for "normal increase in population within a reasonable period of time." Crider, 78 N.M. at 316, 431 P.2d at 49. In addition, a municipality may be given a more substantial "reasonable time" for its population growth than a typical water user would have to complete an appropriation. However, even for municipalities, if the water is not applied to beneficial use within a reasonable time, "such right may be lost." Id.

The pueblo rights doctrine is inconsistent with these principles. Under the doctrine, pueblos are not limited by the reasonable time requirement for applying water to beneficial use. Instead, the pueblo right contemplates an indefinite expansion to meet the growing demands of an increased population, regardless of how small the population of the initial pueblo and how long it takes the pueblo to expand. This aspect of the pueblo water right intolerably interferes with the goals of definiteness and certainty contemplated by prior appropriation; it envisions either the total loss of use of any amount of water the pueblo might potentially use in the future or temporary appropriations by other users subject indefinitely to elimination of their rights by possible population growth or increased needs of the pueblo. This level of uncertainty could potentially paralyze others from legitimately making beneficial use of unappropriated waters on the same stream as a pueblo out of fear of potential future interference with the pueblo's expansion. Whereas, with the doctrine of relation, other water users "are on notice that the law is granting them water rights that are temporary only" pending a reasonable time for the senior appropriator to complete the initial appropriation, there is no reasonable notice to other water users of a pueblo's potential water needs in the future because the pueblo right neither limits the quantity of water available to the municipality nor the amount of time available to complete its initial appropriation. Our water laws, however, are designed "to encourage use and discourage nonuse or waste." State ex rel. Reynolds v. S. Springs Co., 80 N.M. 144, 148, 452 P.2d 478, 482 (1969). The pueblo rights doctrine interferes with the necessity of utilizing water for the maximum benefits.

Additionally, unlike typical water rights, the pueblo right is not subject to forfeiture for nonuse. Forfeiture, however, is an essential punitive tool by which "the policy of our constitution and statutes is fostered, and the waters made to do the greatest good to the greatest number." S. Springs Co., 80 N.M. at 147, 452 P.2d at 481 (citations omitted). Forfeiture "prevents the waste of water—our greatest natural resource." State ex rel. Erickson v. McLean, 62 N.M. 264, 272, 308 P.2d 983, 988 (1957). The pueblo right subverts these critical policies.

By facilitating the underutilization of essential public waters, the pueblo right prevents the efficient, economic use of water that is necessary for survival in this arid region and upon which our entire system of water law is based. We therefore agree with the dissent in *Cartwright* that the ever-expanding quality of the pueblo water right "is as antithetical to the doctrine of prior appropriation as day is to night." Cartwright, 66 N.M. at 110, 343 P.2d at 686 (Federici, D.J., dissenting). We conclude that the pueblo rights doctrine is incompatible with New Mexico water law.

Moreover, we disagree with the determination in *Cartwright* that pueblo water rights are protected by the Treaty of Guadalupe Hidalgo, at least with regard to the expanding nature of the right. As pointed out by the dissent in *Cartwright*, the Treaty did not protect inchoate rights. 66 N.M. at 113–17, 343 P.2d at 687–91 (Federici, D.J., dissenting). See generally United States v. City of Santa Fe, 165 U.S. 675, 713–16 (1897). To the extent that Spanish and Mexican law recognized a pueblo water right, the nature of the right that allowed increased water usage in response to growing needs of the pueblo would have been a matter of grace, not a matter of right; future expansion of water rights subsequent to the colonization grant would have been subject to the sovereign's power of reallocation according to a change in circumstances. * * *

The water right acquired by a municipality under a colonization grant from antecedent sovereigns is recognized in New Mexico in the same manner as other municipal water rights. The colonization grant establishes the date of priority, but the priority date applies only to the quantity of water put to beneficial use within a reasonable time of the initial appropriation. Thus, the City's 1835 colonization grant created a vested right only to the amount of water put to beneficial use within a reasonable time. Any water not put to beneficial use within a reasonable time cannot be reserved by a municipality for future expansion; the unappropriated waters remaining after a reasonable time has elapsed from the initial appropriation "belong to the public and [are] subject to appropriation for beneficial use." N.M. Const. art. XVI, § 2.

Because the expanding water right recognized by this Court in *Cartwright* directly conflicts with the doctrine of prior appropriation, we conclude that the pueblo water right is a "doctrinal anachronism," Planned Parenthood of Se. Pa. v. Casey, 505 U.S. 833, 855 (1992), and that it represents a "positive detriment to coherence and consistency in the law." Patterson v. McLean Credit Union, 491 U.S. 164, 173 (1989). "The decision poses a direct obstacle to the realization of important objectives embodied" in New Mexico water law. Id. As a result, we believe that there is a compelling reason to overrule *Cartwright*.

C.   The Rule of Property and Stare Decisis

Despite the existence of adequate grounds to overrule *Cartwright*, the City contends that we should nonetheless adhere to stare decisis because *Cartwright* established a rule of property that induced substantial detrimental reliance. We have said that precedent establishing property rights "should not be disturbed or departed from except for the most cogent reasons, certainly not because of doubts as to their soundness." Duncan v. Brown, 18 N.M. 579, 585, 139 P. 140, 141 (1914). We have applied this principle in the context of judicial pronouncements relating to water rights. See State ex rel. Bliss v. Dority, 55 N.M. 12, 31, 225 P.2d 1007, 1019 (1950).

> The especial importance of stare decisis in cases involving a rule of property is twofold. First, and more generally, the anti-majoritarian nature of the judicial system makes adherence to precedent essential to promote public confidence in the law and its administration. Second, and more specific to rules affecting property or commercial transactions, adherence to precedent is necessary to the stability of land titles and commercial transactions entered into in reliance on the settled nature of the law.

Bogle Farms, Inc. v. Baca, 122 N.M. 422, 925 P.2d 1184 (1996) (citation omitted). In determining whether to defer to a rule of property, we assess the extent to which the rule announced in prior cases has become fixed or settled and the extent to which it has "induced persons to enter into transactions in actual or demonstrable reliance thereon." Id.

We reject the City's argument that *Cartwright* should be upheld as a rule of property. Regardless of whether the pueblo rights doctrine could be viewed as a settled, fixed, and stable principle, we conclude, based on the doctrine's inconsistency with the goals of prior appropriation, that "the evils of the principle laid down will be more injurious to the community than can possibly result from a change." Id. This conclusion is influenced by the fact that *Cartwright* was not a general stream adjudication and the State Engineer, who exercises "general supervision of waters of the state and of the measurement, appropriation, [and] distribution thereof," NMSA 1978, § 72–2–1 (1982), was not a party. Cf. Bogle Farms, supra (noting that "there is a public-interest aspect to rejection of *stare decisis*").

In addition, we are not convinced that *Cartwright* induced the type of reliance that is contemplated by the rule of property. *Cartwright* concerned the nature of a water right that had been granted by antecedent sovereigns. Necessarily, then, all pueblo water rights implicated by *Cartwright* had to be in existence at the time it was decided, and there could be no issuance of new pueblo water rights based on *Cartwright*. Because, under *Cartwright*, pueblo water rights could not be sold or transferred by the municipalities possessing them, New Mexico's recognition of the pueblo rights doctrine could not have induced new water rights transactions, by either municipalities or other water users. * * *

IV. PROSPECTIVITY, RELIANCE INTERESTS OF THE CITY, AND THE PROPER ADMINISTRATION OF JUSTICE

The City argues that we should apply our overruling of *Cartwright* only prospectively. While we disagree that our rejection of the pueblo rights doctrine should be given prospective application as a general matter, we agree with the City that its reliance interests are substantial. Therefore, as discussed further below, we hold that our overruling of *Cartwright* shall be given a limited prospective application with respect to the City. We hold that the City does not possess a pueblo water right, but we remand to the district court to determine the most appropriate equitable remedy that will balance the City's reliance on *Cartwright* with other water users' reliance on New Mexico's system of prior appropriation.

We begin our prospectivity analysis by restating that there is "a presumption that a new rule adopted by a judicial decision in a civil case will operate retroactively." Beavers v. Johnson Controls World Servs, Inc., 118 N.M. 391, 398, 881 P.2d 1376, 1383 (1994). * * * In the present case, a retroactive application of our rejection of the pueblo water rights doctrine would mean that no municipality in New Mexico would be entitled to claim a pueblo water right, and it would invalidate municipal appropriations of water premised on the expanding nature of the pueblo right rather than on rights properly acquired through prior appropriation. As applied to the City, its water rights from the 1835 colonization grant would be limited to the amount of water put to beneficial use within a reasonable time of its first appropriation, which has been determined in a separate proceeding. * * *

We consider three factors in determining whether a ruling should receive prospective application: (1) whether the ruling announces a new principle of law; (2) whether retroactive application will advance or hinder the purposes of the new rule; and (3) whether prospective application of the new rule is necessary to avoid an injustice or hardship due to the substantial inequity that would result from retroactive application. Beavers, 118 N.M. at 398, 881 P.2d at 1383. The presumption of retroactivity "may be overcome by a sufficiently weighty combination of one or more" of these factors. Id.

Our decision in this case clearly announces a new rule of law because we are overruling our clear past precedent adopting the pueblo rights doctrine. * * *

However, we believe the second factor weighs, at least slightly, in favor of retroactivity. The pueblo rights doctrine is inconsistent with the doctrine of prior appropriation in a number of ways. A prospective application of our ruling would not necessarily conflict with some aspects of prior appropriation, such as certainty and beneficial use, because the current beneficial use of water can be determined for municipalities that would have had pueblo water rights under *Cartwright*. Other aspects of New Mexico water law, however, would be frustrated by prospective application of our ruling. In particular, the State has continually placed considerable reliance on the doctrine of prior appropriation, both in the State Engineer's regulation of water and in the State's various obligations under interstate compacts. This reliance preceded *Cartwright* and was necessarily based on priorities in existence at the time, without reference to possible future expansion by successors to colonization pueblos. Similarly, numerous water users have expended considerable resources in reliance on the doctrine of prior appropriation by making beneficial use of what had appeared to be unappropriated water prior to our ruling in *Cartwright*. Thus, if we were to acquiesce in the current water usage by successors to colonization pueblos through a prospective ruling, we would be causing considerable harm to those who, as we have determined, properly and reasonably relied on prior appropriation. As a result, we believe that the purposes of our rejection of the pueblo rights doctrine would be hindered by a prospective ruling.

For similar reasons, we believe that the third factor, the inequity of retroactivity, is either neutral or only slightly in favor of prospectivity. The City argues that it "has relied on its Pueblo water right in planning, constructing, and operating its water system for decades." We do not doubt that successors to colonization pueblo grants may have relied on *Cartwright* to a certain extent in appropriations made since 1958, when this Court decided *Cartwright*. However, we believe that the potential inequity that retroactive application would cause from this reliance is no greater than the inequity that a prospective ruling would cause to those who relied on the doctrine of prior appropriation for an even longer period of time before our decision in *Cartwright*. * * *

Nevertheless, this case presents a rather unique circumstance. We recognize, as did the dissent in the Court of Appeals, that "Las Vegas is the one community in the state to have the benefit of a Supreme Court pronouncement that it possesses a pueblo right." State ex rel. Martinez, 118 N.M. at 265, 880 P.2d at 876 (Hartz, J., concurring in part, dissenting in part). We have also held explicitly that the plaintiffs in *Cartwright* are precluded by res judicata from relitigating their claims of trespass against the City. Cartwright, 68 N.M. at 419–21, 362 P.2d at 796–98. In addition, applying our holding in the present case to invalidate appropriations by the City of the same amount of water used before *Cartwright* would result in inconsistent judgments, which the judiciary strives to prevent. * * *

To resolve this predicament, we believe that it is appropriate to exercise our discretion to apply our overruling of *Cartwright* on a limited prospective basis with respect to the City. * * *

In *Cartwright*, we declared that the City had a senior right to appropriate all the water of the Gallinas reasonably necessary to meet its growing needs. We now overrule the aspect of this holding that recognizes an expandable water right, but we do not decide whether the narrower holding that the City has a senior right to the amount of water it was applying to beneficial use in 1955 remains viable. Under a balancing of interests, it may be just to recognize an equitable right on the part of the City to this amount. This remedy would avoid inconsistent judgments and protect the City's reliance interests while still negating the expandable right recognized in *Cartwright*. Alternatively, a more appropriate remedy might be to require the City to exercise its right of condemnation for necessary amounts of water exceeding its adjudicated rights, but to allow the City to pay less than present-day market value for those rights, either based on the value of the water rights at the time we decided *Cartwright* or the time of initial appropriation by the City or based on some other equitable calculation. This more restricted equitable remedy would ensure that the City not be placed in a worse position than it would have been in had this Court ruled in favor of the trespass claimants in *Cartwright*. However, we do not believe that it would be appropriate for this Court to resolve the issue of an equitable remedy on the present record.

The record before us is not sufficiently developed to allow us to fully consider all of the factors, and multiple points of view, relevant to an equitable remedy. These factors include the reliance interests of the City, the interests of other appropriators, and the effect of the remedy on the State Engineer's regulatory responsibilities. We believe the district court is better situated to consider these matters in the first instance. As a result, we order a remand to determine the appropriate equitable remedy following a balancing of these interests. * * *

V. CONCLUSION

We overrule *Cartwright* and hold that New Mexico does not recognize the pueblo rights doctrine. Water rights contained in colonization grants from antecedent sovereigns are limited by the principle of beneficial use and are to be quantified by the amount of water put to beneficial use by the pueblo within a reasonable time of the first appropriation. This holding is to be applied retroactively. However, in the interests of the proper administration of justice, we apply a limited prospective application of our overruling of *Cartwright* to the City. We remand this case to the district court to determine the specific aspects of the equitable remedy that would strike an appropriate balance between the reliance interests of the City, the reliance interests of other water users, and the regulatory interests of the State Engineer.

Notes and Questions

1. *Martinez* leaves California as the only state to currently recognize pueblo rights.

2. Are there any policy arguments in favor of pueblo rights? As a matter of policy, should cities have a superior claim to the waters of any rivers that flow through their borders?

3. The New Mexico Supreme Court concludes that *Cartwright* did not induce the type of reliance interest that would justify adhering to the decision as a "rule of property" but then decides to give its new decision only "limited prospective application." Are these two results consistent?

C. CONSTITUTIONAL PROTECTION OF EXISTING WATER RIGHTS

To what degree do the federal and state constitutions constrain governments from changing water law for policy or other reasons? Holders of water rights who feel threatened by the change are likely to argue that the government cannot reduce their rights under the takings clauses of the United States and state constitutions without compensating them for the reduction. See, e.g., U.S. Const. amend. V ("nor shall private property be taken for public use, without just compensation"). Decisions of the United States Supreme Court holding that various regulations of land constitute unconstitutional takings have emboldened water users in these claims. See, e.g., Lucas v. South Carolina Coastal Council, 505 U.S. 1003 (1992) (a regulation that denies a landowner all "economically viable use of his land" constitutes a per se taking); Loretto v. Teleprompter Manhattan CATV Corp., 458 U.S. 419 (1982) (a regulation that licenses a "permanent physical occupation" of land is a per se taking).

Takings cases involving water, however, raise a number of unique issues. First, to what degree are water rights constitutionally protected property? Recall that many state constitutions provide that water is the property of the public, although the water can be appropriated for private use. Water rights are also subject to various limitations, such as "reasonableness" of use, that might reduce the "investment backed expectations" that are constitutionally protected. Second, are the standards for determining when property has been "taken" the same for water as for land? The Supreme Court has developed takings doctrine largely in the context of land, and as you no doubt now realize, water is a quite different resource.

1. STATUTORY ABOLITION OF UNEXERCISED RIPARIAN RIGHTS

a. Takings Challenges

As discussed in section A of this Chapter, most California doctrine states have tried by statute to abolish unexercised riparian rights. In 1909, Oregon became the first state to do so. Oregon abolished riparian rights except for water then in use by appropriators (and water put to use within a reasonable time if construction needed to use the water was already underway). Although owners of unexercised riparian rights were not compensated, both the Oregon Supreme Court and the Ninth Circuit upheld the constitutionality of the legislation.[12] Similar legislation was later adopted and upheld against constitutional challenge in Kansas, South Dakota, and Texas.[13]

In 1963, Oklahoma became one of the most recent states to try to terminate unused riparian rights. Under a statute passed that year, riparians were limited in their water use to (1) water used for domestic purposes (defined as household uses, limited watering of livestock, and the irrigation of up to three acres) and (2) any pre-existing beneficial uses that the riparian properly validated.[14] A constitutional challenge did not make its way to the Oklahoma Supreme Court for over two decades.

FRANCO–AMERICAN CHAROLAISE LTD. v. OKLAHOMA WATER RESOURCES BOARD

Supreme Court of Oklahoma, 1990.
855 P.2d 568.

[In August 1980, the City of Ada, Oklahoma, applied to the Oklahoma Water Resources Board (OWRB) to increase its appropriation from Byrd's Mill Spring by 7,842 acre feet per year. The Water Resources Board granted the City an additional 5,340 acre feet, which was all that the board found currently available after taking into account prior appropriations and the domestic needs of riparians. Various riparians appealed, claiming that the city's increased diversions would interfere with riparian rights that the 1963 amendments had attempted to extinguish.]

OPALA, J.

This appeal challenges the constitutionality of the 1963 amendments to Oklahoma's water law insofar as the amendments regulate riparian

[handwritten margin note: RIPARIANS LIMITED TO DOMESTIC USE]

---

12. See In re Hood River, 114 Or. 112, 227 P. 1065 (1924), appeal dismissed, 273 U.S. 647 (1926); California–Oregon Power Co. v. Beaver Portland Cement Co., 73 F.2d 555 (9th Cir. 1934), aff'd on other grounds, 295 U.S. 142 (1935).

13. See Baumann v. Smrha, 145 F.Supp. 617 (D. Kan. 1956), aff'd, 352 U.S. 863 (1956); Williams v. City of Wichita, 190 Kan. 317, 374 P.2d 578 (1962); State ex rel. Emery v. Knapp, 167 Kan. 546, 207 P.2d 440 (1949); Belle Fourche Irr. Dist. v. Smiley, 84 S.D. 701, 176 N.W.2d 239 (1970); In re Water Rights of Guadalupe River Basin, 642 S.W.2d 438 (Tex. 1982).

14. 60 Okl. Stat. 1981, § 60.

rights. * * * We hold that the Oklahoma riparian owner enjoys a vested common-law right to the reasonable use of the stream. This right is a valuable part of the property owner's "bundle of sticks" and may not be taken for public use without compensation. We further hold that, inasmuch as [the 1963 water law amendments] limit the riparian owner to domestic use and declare that all other water in the stream becomes public water subject to appropriation without any provision for compensating the riparian owner, the statute violates Art. 2, § 24, Okl. Const. * * *

The issue here is whether the legislature can validly abrogate the riparian owner's right to initiate non-domestic reasonable uses in stream water without affording compensation. Art. 2, § 24, Okl. Const. provides in part:

> Private property shall not be taken or damaged for public use without just compensation. * * *

Private property protected by Art. 2, § 24 includes "easements, personal property, and every valuable interest which can be enjoyed and recognized as property."[42] In Oklahoma Water Resources Board v. Central Oklahoma Master Conservancy District,[43] we held:

> A "vested right" is the power to *do certain actions* or possess certain things lawfully, and is substantially a property right. It may be created by common law, by statute or by contract. Once created, it becomes absolute, and is protected from legislative invasion * * *

Therefore, the common-law riparian right to use stream water, as long as that use is reasonable, has been long recognized in Oklahoma law as a private property right.

The general rule is that the legislature may restrict the use of private property by exercise of its police power for the preservation of the public, health, morals, safety and general welfare without compensating the property owner. In Phillips Petroleum Co. v. Corporation Comm'n,[46] this court defined the permissible exercise of police power:

> [T]he police power is usually exerted merely to regulate the use and enjoyment of property by the owner, or, if he is deprived of his property outright, it is not taken for public use, but rather destroyed in order to promote the general welfare. * * *

Therefore, in C.C. Julian Oil & Royalties Co. v. Capshaw,[47] we declared that the legislature could regulate a landowner's use and enjoyment of natural resources to prevent waste and infringement on the rights of others. Thus, a statutory regulation of the methods to be used in

42. Graham v. City of Duncan, 354 P.2d 458, 461 (Okl. 1960).

43. 464 P.2d 748, 755 (Okl. 1968) (emphasis added).

46. 312 P.2d 916, 921 (Okl. 1956).

47. 292 P. 841, 847 (Okl. 1930).

extracting hydrocarbons was a constitutional exercise of police power where none of the hydrocarbons was taken for public use. Then, in Frost v. Ponca City,[48] we held that in the interest of health and safety, the city could exercise its police power to restrict the plaintiff's right to capture hydrocarbons underlying his property, but the city could not remove the hydrocarbons and sell them without compensating the plaintiff.

We, therefore, hold that the 1963 water law amendments are fraught with a constitutional infirmity in that they abolish the right of the riparian owner to assert his (or her) vested interest in the prospective reasonable use of the stream. The riparian owner stands on equal footing with the appropriator. His ownership of riparian land affords him *no right* to the stream water except for limited domestic use.

The case must be remanded for the trial court's determination of the issue whether the appellee-riparian owners' claim to the use of the stream flow for the enhancement of the value of the riparian land, for recreation, for the preservation of wildlife, for fighting grass fires, and for lowering the body temperature of their cattle on hot summer days is reasonable.

The OWRB argues the 1963 amendments are a permissible exercise of the police power just as a zoning ordinance would be. That contention is inapposite when, as here, the use of stream water is *not just restricted but is taken for public use.*

Although the 1963 water law amendments provided a mechanism for a riparian owner to "perfect" all beneficial uses initiated prior to the legislation, that mechanism falls short of protecting the riparian owner's common-law appurtenant right. The mechanism is constitutionally inadequate first of all because the full sweep of the riparian right is much broader than the validation mechanism could ever shield. The heart of the riparian right is the right to assert a use at *any time* as long as it does not harm another riparian who has a corresponding right. Further, yesterday's reasonable use by one riparian owner may become unreasonable tomorrow when a fellow riparian owner asserts a new or expanded use. After the 1963 amendments, the riparian owner who wants to expand a use or assert a new use may do so *only as an appropriator*. His use is not judged by its reasonableness but only by its priority in time.

Furthermore, the validation mechanism attempted to forever set in stone the maximum amount of stream water the landowner, as a riparian owner, can use. Any use asserted by the landowner, as an appropriator, is either denied because no water is available or is given a lower priority than all other uses, including those of appropriators who are non-riparian to the stream. It matters not that the riparian owner's use is reasonable when compared with prior uses. This result is antithetical to the very nature of the common-law riparian right, which places no stock in the fact of past use, present use, or even non-use. * * *

---

48.   541 P.2d 1321, 1324 (Okl. 1975).

The asserted riparian use must, of course, be reasonable. * * * Upon remand, should the trial court find that the plaintiffs' uses of the stream for their claimed purposes is unreasonable, such uses do not fall under the mantle of constitutionally protected property rights. On the other hand, should the trial court find that an asserted riparian use of the stream is reasonable, the right to a flow sufficient to supply the riparian owners' reasonable use must be preserved in the owner.

HODGES, WILSON, KAUGER and SUMMERS, JJ., concur.

REIF, S.J., concurring in part and dissenting in part.

* * * [T]he hallmark of riparian law has been the settling of controversies caused by new uses conflicting with established uses. The courts were called upon to weight the competing interests (and others that may be affected) and determine or define what constituted a reasonable use at a given point in time. Established uses had to accommodate and sometimes yield to new ones, because the law treated "the right" of riparians to the use of the waters of a stream as a qualified and not an absolute right of property. * * *

In my analysis, the legislature did nothing more in 1963 than the courts have been doing for decades: define the scope of reasonable use by a riparian. In doing so, it is not beyond the exercise of power to circumscribe uses as of a particular point in time. * * *

Prospective or future uses by riparians have not been recognized or treated as "vested" any more than the riparian right itself has been treated as an absolute right of property. Accordingly, I cannot agree that such future or prospective uses were untouchable by the 1963 legislation or that the legislature impaired or abrogated a protected right in limiting such future/prospective uses to domestic uses.

LAVENDER, J., concurring in part and dissenting in part.

I must respectfully dissent from that part of the majority opinion holding the 1963 legislative amendments to our State's stream water law unconstitutional under the guise the amendments effected a taking of property without just compensation in violation of Okla. Const. art. 2, § 24. In reaching this result the majority makes several errors.

Initially, it misperceives that future, unquantified use of stream water by a riparian is a vested property right that can only be limited or modified pursuant to judicially mandated common law factors that were generally used to decide piecemeal litigation between competing riparians in water use disputes. Secondly, it * * * fails to recognize that even assuming a vested property right is at issue, such rights in natural resources like water, may be subject to reasonable limitations or even forfeiture for failure to put the resource to beneficial use. Thirdly, its analysis of the law as to what constitutes a taking of private property requiring just compensation is flawed. In my view the majority errs in such regard by failing to view the legislation as akin to zoning regulation, which although may limit a riparian's open-ended common law right to make use of the water to benefit his land and thereby effect the value of his land, does not deprive him of all economic use of his land or absolutely deprive him of water. The lack of water to a riparian, if it occurs, is caused by his own neglect or inaction by years of failure either to put the water to beneficial use or failure to gain an appropriation permit from the Oklahoma Water Resources Board (OWRB) for uses being made prior to passage of the 1963 amendments or uses made or sought to be made between passage of the amendments and the City of Ada's appropriation at issue here. This mistake of the majority is particularly egregious because it wholly ignores the virtually admitted fact that neither riparians or appropriators own the water they are being allowed to use. All of the people in this State own the water and that ownership interest by the legislation before us is merely being channeled by the Legislature, for the benefit of those owners (i.e. the people), to those uses deemed wise.

* * * In my view only preexisting uses (i.e. uses initiated prior to passage of the amendments and subject to validation hereunder) can be said to be property in any real or actual sense. Such uses the majority admits were subject to validation under the 1963 amendments. As to any common law claim to use an unquantified amount of water in the future such open-ended claim was lost or forfeited because it was determined to be wasteful by the Legislature and was properly limited to domestic use. Furthermore, riparians, just as other potential future water users, may obtain their future needs of water in addition to domestic use by applying for an appropriation under our water laws. * * * In effect, all the legislation at issue did was to put water users in this State on an equal footing (except for a statutory preference in favor of riparian domestic use) and provide a statewide unitary system for the acquisition of water rights. * * *

The central theme of the reasonable use doctrine was that a riparian could make a reasonable use of the water for other than domestic purposes as long as the use did not injure another riparian owner. *Neither under this theory or the natural flow doctrine was the landowner considered to own the water.* His rights in it were at most a usufructuary interest, in other words he had the right to use the water while it was passing over or next to his land. * * *

[In Texaco, Inc. v. Short, 454 U.S. 516 (1982)], the United States Supreme Court upheld the Indiana Dormant Mineral Act which provided that severed mineral interests not used for a period of twenty years automatically lapsed and reverted to the current surface owner, unless certain procedural steps were taken. In said case the Supreme Court stated:

> We have concluded that the State may treat a mineral interest that has not been used for twenty years and for which no statement of claim has been filed as abandoned; it follows that, after abandonment, the former owner retains no interest for which he may claim compensation. It is the owner's failure to make any use of the property—and not action of the State—that

causes the lapse of the property right; there is no "taking" that requires compensation. The requirement that an owner of a property interest that has not been used for twenty years must come forward and file a current statement of claim is not itself a "taking."

Thus, even if it be assumed the majority is correct that the riparian had a protectible property interest to some unquantified right to make use of the water at some unspecified time in the future, this common law right could be lost or forfeited by nonuse or, at least, limited to domestic use and appropriative uses granted by the OWRB as sought to be accomplished by the legislation under review. To rule otherwise simply places a common law doctrine as an impenetrable barrier to efficient management of a natural resource never deemed to be owned by private landowners. * * *

The United States Supreme Court has long recognized that land use regulations normally do not effect a taking of property as long as the regulations at issue substantially advance legitimate state interests and do not deny a landowner economically viable use of his land. No one argues here, including the majority, that the statutory scheme under review does not substantially advance legitimate state interests. The State interests advanced are numerous. Among them are direct promotion of the efficient management of our State's water resources by preventing waste. It provides a semblance of certainty in the area of water rights and distributes this valuable resource which is owned by all the public in response to demonstrated need. Therefore, the only real question in the taking context is whether the legislation has deprived riparians of the economically viable use of their land. I do not think it has nor from my review of the record herein do I read Appellees' submissions to assert otherwise. * * *

HARGRAVE, C.J. and REIF, S.J., have joined in the views herein expressed.

[The separate dissenting opinions of HARGRAVE, C.J., and DOOLIN, J., are omitted.]

Notes and Questions

1. What can the Oklahoma legislature do now? Does *Franco–American* leave the legislature any room to limit future riparian rights other than by condemning them?

2. *Franco–American* was not well received. Acting as if the Oklahoma Supreme Court had never issued its decision, the City of Ada refiled its original appropriation application. And the legislature, hoping that it simply had not been explicit enough the first time, enacted a new statute restating that the legislature had abolished all riparian uses of water arising subsequent to 1963 except for domestic uses. See 82 Okl. St. §§ 105.1–105.32.

For a fascinating history of the *Franco–American* case and a discussion of its aftermath, see Gary Allison, Franco–American Charolaise: The Never Ending Story, 30 Tulsa L.J. 1 (1994). See also Christopher L. Len, Synthesis—A Brand New Water Law, 8 U. Denv. Water L. Rev. 55 (2004) (discussing the benefits of Oklahoma's dual system).

3. Is there any doubt that water is a constitutionally protected property right? In his dissent in *Franco–American*, Justice Lavender emphasizes that riparians do not own the water in a stream, but hold "at most a usufructuary interest." In an earlier Oregon case, one justice similarly argued that it was "difficult exactly to define in what a vested right in the use of water exists. Practically, there is no such a thing as property in the water of a flowing stream." In re Hood River, 114 Or. 112, 227 P. 1065, 1089 (1924) (McBride, C.J., concurring), appeal dismissed, 273 U.S. 647 (1926).

Should a "usufructuary" right in water be entitled to any less protection than an easement or tenancy interest in real property (both of which are clearly protected under the takings clause)? Responding to the argument that water is a "limited, usufructuary right" entitled to minimal protection, the Chief Judge of the Court of Federal Claims has written:

> *Amici* provide no reason within our constitutional tradition why water rights, which are as vital as land rights, should receive less protection [than land rights]. This is particularly true in the West where water means the difference between farm and desert, ranch and wilderness, and even life and death. This court holds that water rights are not "lesser or diminished" property rights unprotected by the Fifth Amendment. Water rights, like other property rights, are entitled to the full protection of the Constitution.

Hage v. United States, 35 Fed. Cl. 147 (1996).

4. Some forms of water rights, however, might be entitled to less protection than others. Like Justice Lavender, for example, a number of courts have argued that the Constitution does not protect water rights that are currently unused. See, e.g., State v. Knapp, 167 Kan. 546, 207 P.2d 440, 447 (1949); In re Hood River, 114 Or. 112, 227 P. 1065, 1094 (1924) (McBride, C.J. concurring), appeal dismissed 273 U.S. 647 (1926). Why should it matter whether the right is being used? A similar distinction is found in zoning cases where courts readily compensate if a zoning ordinance forces an existing use to stop immediately, but seldom compensate if a zoning ordinance simply forecloses a new future use. Perhaps the argument is that people have a far greater reliance expectation, and thus compensation claim, in rights that they are using.

Background principles of water law may also undermine a claim that a water right has been taken. Justice Lavender, for example, argues that any constitutional claim that plaintiffs might have had in *Franco–American* was lost when the legislature found that open-ended riparian claims were wasteful. For a similar argument, see In re Water Rights of Guadalupe River Basin, 642 S.W.2d 438, 444–45 (Tex. 1982).

5. Assuming that unexercised riparian rights are protected property, was the 1963 Oklahoma legislation a taking? Under current takings jurisprudence, the first question is whether the 1963 legislation was a physical taking of the riparians' water (in which case the legislation would be per se unconstitutional) or merely a regulation of the riparians' use of water (in which case the legislation would be subjected to the more deferential tests

for regulatory takings). How does the majority categorize the legislation? How do the dissenters?

In the case of land, the distinction between physical and regulatory takings is relatively clear. If the government prohibits someone from developing part of their property but leaves them with title, the prohibition is not a physical taking because the landowner still exercises a variety of potentially valuable powers, including the right to prevent others from using or developing the property. Is the distinction as clear in the case of water? If the government prohibits water withdrawals, is that a regulatory or physical taking? The Federal Court of Claims has concluded that it is a physical taking when the federal government orders reductions in water withdrawals under the Endangered Species Act. Tulare Lake Basin Water Storage Dist. v. United States, 49 Fed. Cl. 313 (2001), excerpted infra p. 653. But see Klamath Irrigation Dist. v. United States, 67 Fed. Cl. 504 (2005) (criticizing the logic and result in *Tulare Lake*), excerpted infra p. 660.

6. Property regulations that stop short of a physical taking still are unconstitutional if they deprive the property owner of all economically beneficial use of the property. See Lucas v. South Carolina Coastal Council, 505 U.S. 1003 (1992). Could the riparians in *Franco–American* argue that the 1963 legislation is an unconstitutional taking because it deprives them of all the economically beneficial use of their *unexercised* riparian rights? The question boils down to how one defines the property interest at stake. If you define the relevant interest as the riparians' entire property (as Justice Lavender does), there has been no taking because the riparian can still make valuable use of her land. If you define the relevant interest as the riparian's right to make new uses of water in the future, the legislation is arguably a taking because it totally abolishes that right (although the riparian can still appropriate unused water). For a useful discussion of the so-called "denominator" problem, see Carol Rose, *Mahon* Reconstructed: Why the Takings Issue Is Still a Muddle, 57 S. Cal. L. Rev. 561, 566–69 (1984).

7. Is imperative necessity a legitimate response to the argument that the 1963 legislation was an unconstitutional taking? Several decisions upholding the constitutionality of similar legislation have emphasized the importance to state welfare of limiting riparian rights. See, e.g., Baumann v. Smrha, 145 F.Supp. 617, 625 (D. Kan. 1956), aff'd, 352 U.S. 863 (1956); In re Hood River, 114 Or. 112, 227 P. 1065, 1092–93 (1924) (McBride, C.J., concurring), appeal dismissed, 273 U.S. 647 (1926). See also Keystone Bituminous Coal Ass'n v. DeBenedictis, 480 U.S. 470, 492 (1987) (suggesting that courts must consider the benefit of a government action in deciding whether the action is a taking). Does this argument ignore Justice Holmes' oft quoted warning that "a strong public desire to improve the public condition is not enough to warrant achieving the desire by a shorter cut than the constitutional way of paying for the change"? Pennsylvania Coal Co. v. Mahon, 260 U.S. 393, 416 (1922).

8. Does the majority's protection of unexercised riparian rights help preserve an ecological balance in Oklahoma's waterways? Should the rush to limit riparian rights be rethought in light of the need to protect instream flows? In an intriguing article, Professor Drew Kershen argues that environmental considerations may have influenced the majority opinion in *Franco–*

American. See Drew Kershen, An Oklahoma Slant to Environmental Protection and the Politics of Property Rights, 50 Okla. L. Rev. 391 (1997). Is the reinvigoration and protection of private riparian rights the best way of protecting public interests in the environment?

b. Avoiding the Constitutional Issue

Of all the California doctrine states, California has had the most difficulty trying to limit riparian rights. In the 1913 Water Commission Act, the California legislature declared that all surface water must be appropriated except where "waters are or may be reasonably needed for useful and beneficial purposes upon lands riparian thereto." The act further provided that non-use of water by a riparian "for any continuous period of ten consecutive years after the passage of this act * * * shall be deemed to be conclusive presumption that the use of such portions * * * is not needed upon said riparian lands for any useful or beneficial purpose" and thus abandoned.[1] The act, in short, tried to eliminate any riparian rights that were not used for any ten-year period after 1913.

In Tulare Irrigation Dist. v. Lindsay–Strathmore Irrigation Dist., 3 Cal.2d 489, 45 P.2d 972 (1935), however, the California Supreme Court held this provision unconstitutional. The court began by noting that a previous case had suggested that the abandonment provision unconstitutionally deprived riparians of vested water rights. See Herminghaus v. Southern Cal. Edison Co., 200 Cal. 81, 252 P. 607, 622 (1926). The court, however, held that the abandonment provision was invalid in any case under Article X, section 2 of the California Constitution which, while limiting riparians to the use of "such water as shall be reasonably required for the beneficial use to be served," also reaffirmed the right of riparians to such a reasonable use.

Article X, section 2 continues to both thwart and aid attempts to limit riparian rights in California today—as the following case involving a general adjudication of water rights reveals.

IN RE WATERS OF LONG VALLEY CREEK STREAM SYSTEM

Supreme Court of California, 1979.
25 Cal.3d 339, 158 Cal.Rptr. 350, 599 P.2d 656.

Mosk, Justice.

The significant problem in this case is the extent to which the State Water Resources Control Board (Board) has the power to define and otherwise limit prospective riparian rights when, pursuant to the statutory adjudication procedure set forth in Water Code section 2500 et seq., it determines all claimed rights to the use of water in a stream system. * * *

The action arises out of a statutory proceeding to adjudicate the rights of all claimants to the waters of the Long Valley Creek Stream

---

1.   1913 Cal. Stat., ch. 586, § 11.

System (stream system) * * *. [After a lengthy and extensive investigation, the Board entered an order determining and establishing relative rights to water in the stream system.]

Donald Ramelli (Ramelli), as a party aggrieved or dissatisfied with the order of determination, filed a notice of exceptions in the superior court pursuant to Water Code section 2757. Ramelli owns land upon which [one of the main tributaries of the stream system] originates. For the past approximately 60 years he and his predecessors have irrigated 89 acres of this land, but before the Board he claimed prospective riparian rights in the creek for an additional 2,884 acres. The order of determination nevertheless awarded him various amounts of water for only the 89 acres as to which he was currently exercising his riparian rights; it extinguished entirely his claim as a riparian landowner to the future use of water with respect to the remaining 2,884 acres.[2] * * *

A

Article X, section 2, acknowledges that in California a riparian landowner has historically possessed a common law right to the future use of water in a stream system. * * * [It also provides, however, that] riparian rights are limited by the concept of reasonable and beneficial use. * * * Moreover, the provision explicitly authorizes the Legislature to "enact laws in the furtherance of the policy in this section contained." This authorization discloses that the framers of article X, section 2, recognized that the promotion of its salutory policies would require granting the Legislature broad flexibility in determining the appropriate means for protecting scarce state water resources. * * *

* * * Ramelli argues that a riparian's prospective right cannot be defined or otherwise limited in a statutory proceeding because of our holding in [Tulare Irr. Dist. v. Lindsay–Strathmore Irr. Dist., 3 Cal. 2d 489, 45 P.2d 972 (1935)] that section 11 of the Water Commission Act which declared that 10 years' nonuse, without an intervening use, constituted an abandonment of a riparian right was "incongruous and in violation of the spirit of the constitutional provision * * *." (Id., at p. 531, 45 P.2d at p. 989.) * * * *Tulare* is distinguishable from the issue before us in that the statute therein treated the right as automatically abandoned as a result of 10 years' nonuse, without consideration of other needs and uses of the water in the stream system. The statute therefore was inconsistent with the mandate of the amendment to promote the reasonable beneficial use of state waters. * * * In light of these considerations, it is clear that Ramelli's extravagant reading of our decision in *Tulare* * * * would unduly restrict the Legislature's authority to promote the reasonable and beneficial use of state waters and thereby would contravene article X, section 2.

2. Presently only an estimated 4,130 acres are irrigated in the entire Long Valley Creek watershed area. * * * Thus, the trial court found that under the circumstances "To allow dormant riparian owners to cast a shadow over uses of water by established developments would not only be unequitable but would create chaos."

This conclusion is supported by compelling policy considerations. * * * The statutory adjudication procedure involves a complex balancing of both public and private interests, with the final decree assuring certainty to the existing economy and reasonable predictability to the uses of water in a stream system. In so doing, it falls within [article X, section 2's] specific grant of authority to the Legislature. That the statutory adjudication procedure promotes the policies of the amendment is reflected in a recent report of the Governor's Commission To Review California Water Rights Law. (Final Rep. (Dec. 1978).) This document identifies uncertainty as one of the major problems in contemporary California water rights law (id., at pp. 16–49), and it discloses that riparian rights are a principal source of this uncertainty. (Id., at pp. 18–21.)

Uncertainty concerning the rights of water users has pernicious effects. Initially, it inhibits long range planning and investment for the development and use of waters in a stream system. * * * Thus with respect to dormant riparian rights, one authority has observed: "These rights constitute the main threat to nonriparian and out-of-watershed development, they are the principal cause of insecurity of existing riparian uses * * *. They are unrecorded, their quantity is unknown, their administration in the courts provides very little opportunity for control in the public interest. To the extent that they may deter others from using the water for fear of their ultimate exercise, they are wasteful, in the sense of costing the economy the benefits lost from the deterred uses." (Trelease, A Model State Water Code for River Basin Development (1957) 22 Law & Contemp. Prob. 302, 318; see also Milliman, Water Law and Private Decision-making: A Critique (1959) 2 J. Law & Econ. 41, 47.)

RIPARIAN RIGHTS ARE WASTEFUL

Uncertainty also fosters recurrent, costly and piecemeal litigation. * * *

Finally, uncertainty impairs the state's administration of water rights. "Lack of knowledge of water use by non-statutory right holders affects decisions to grant permits, because the availability of water for appropriation and the existence and extent of other beneficial uses of water are uncertain. It also affects the ability of the Board to set meaningful terms and conditions to provide effective enforcement and protection of statutory water rights." [Governor's Com. To Review Cal. Water Rights Law, Final Rep. (Dec. 1978), supra, at p. 22.] * * *

B

A more difficult question is whether the Board may constitutionally extinguish a riparian landowner's unexercised claim to the use of water. * * *

* * * It is true that *Tulare* is distinguishable from this case. * * * In light of *Tulare'* s holding that section 11 of the Water Commission Act was unconstitutional, however, we are reluctant to conclude that the Board may altogether extinguish a riparian's future claim when it has

not been established that the imposition of other less drastic limitations on the claim would be less effective in promoting the most reasonable and beneficial use of the stream system. Because no such showing has been made in this case, it is clear that the Board's decision to extinguish Ramelli's future riparian claim raises a serious constitutional issue. Thus, since the Legislature has not clearly expressed an intention that the statute should be construed otherwise, we interpret it as not authorizing the Board in these circumstances to extinguish altogether Ramelli's claim to the future use of waters in the Long Valley stream system.

[margin note: MAY NOT EXTINGUISH WHEN LESS DRASTIC ALTS AVAILABLE]

[margin note: NOT AUTHORIZED IN THESE CIRCUMSTANCES TO COMPLETELY EXTINGUISH RIGHT]

For the future guidance of the Board, however, we undertake to identify the limitations on unexercised riparian claims that are constitutionally permissible and thus authorized by the statute in light of our analysis herein. As previously discussed, when the Board determines all rights to the use of the water in a stream system, an important interest of the state is the promotion of clarity and certainty in the definition of those rights; such clarity and certainty foster more beneficial and efficient uses of state waters as called for by the mandate of article X, section 2. Thus, the Board is authorized to decide that an unexercised riparian claim loses its priority with respect to all rights currently being exercised. Moreover, to the extent that an unexercised riparian right may also create uncertainty with respect to permits of appropriation that the Board may grant after the statutory adjudication procedure is final, and may thereby continue to conflict with the public interest in reasonable and beneficial use of state waters, the Board may also determine that the future riparian right shall have a lower priority than any uses of water it authorizes before the riparian in fact attempts to exercise his right. In other words, while we interpret the Water Code as not authorizing the Board to extinguish altogether a future riparian right, the Board may make determinations as to the scope, nature and priority of the right that it deems reasonably necessary to the promotion of the state's interest in fostering the most reasonable and beneficial use of its scarce water resources. * * *

BIRD, C. J., and TOBRINER and NEWMAN, JJ., concurred.

RICHARDSON, JUSTICE, Concurring and Dissenting.

* * * Given the clear constitutional basis for the protection and preservation of prospective riparian rights, as outlined in *Tulare* and its successors, I am unable to agree with the majority conclusion that "article X, section 2 enables the Legislature to exercise broad authority in defining *and otherwise limiting* future riparian rights, and to delegate this authority to the Board." (Ante, italics added.) * * *

The majority at length deplores the uncertainty necessarily inherent in protecting unexercised, prospective riparian uses. Yet I strongly suggest that the constitutional rights which we have repeatedly acknowledged and defined may not be compromised, limited or ignored for reasons either of convenience or expediency. * * *

CLARK, J., concurred.

MANUEL, JUSTICE, Concurring and Dissenting.

* * * I share the majority's concern—and that of the Board—over the severe problems of uncertainty caused by "dormant" riparian rights.

* * * Clearly one means of avoiding this uncertainty is through the unified statutory adjudication procedure * * *. Insofar as this procedure contemplates a present quantification of *all* such rights, I perceive no constitutional impediment to it. * * * Insofar as any particular *riparian* right is concerned, however, the Board may not in my opinion undertake such a present quantification unless it is able to determine, on the basis of an adequate record, the amount of water that "may be required or used * * * for the [reasonable and beneficial] purposes for which such lands are, or may be adaptable. * * * " (Cal. Const., art. X, § 2.) * * * In many cases it may well be possible, in light of evidence of historical and reasonably foreseeable future uses, to arrive at a reasonably accurate estimate of this amount. * * *

It is clear that present quantification of water rights, to the extent that it may be achieved with respect to any particular stream system, will operate to foster that certainty necessary to the efficient administration and use of the waters within that system. To the extent that riparian as well as other rights can be quantified, the riparian owner and other interested parties will be made aware of the total amount of water comprehended within his right. The amount of any particular right that remains "dormant" under present use will become a sum certain, subject to negotiation and disposal by the owner to appropriators and other nonriparian users. There may of course be cases where a riparian owner of a quantified right may choose to retain the whole or a significant part of his entitlement, allowing the unused and untransferred portion to remain "dormant," but such cases will become rarer as such owners, assessing the present and projected uses of their lands, come to view their water right as a disposable asset of certain scope.

* * * The Constitution, as I read it, offers no obstacle to such a procedure, and the relevant statutes clearly contemplate it. What the Constitution does not permit, in my view, is the actual or virtual extinguishment of the future aspect of riparian rights either through outright extinction or through the device, adopted by the majority, of consigning that aspect of the right to some lesser status, to be administered by the Board on the same basis as all other rights in the stream when the riparian proposes to use it. Under our Constitution the riparian right, in both its present and future aspects, is *primary* in priority. * * *

Notes and Questions

1. Is there any real difference between extinguishing Ramelli's prospective riparian rights (as the Board wanted to do) and placing them at the bottom of the priority list (as the court suggests)? Of what value is a right to future riparian use of water that is of "lower priority" than other uses that are perfected before the riparian has a need for the water? Is the California

Supreme Court's decision consistent with the Oklahoma Supreme Court's decision in *Franco–American*, supra p. 366?

2. Can an appropriator who is concerned about unexercised riparian rights simply "buy off" the rights? Do you see any problems with this solution from the standpoint of the appropriator? Would Justice Manuel's proposal to quantify unused riparian rights help promote such a solution?

3. Does the court's decision encourage riparians to use water as quickly as possible? Is that wise?

2. TAKINGS CHALLENGES TO OTHER LEGISLATIVE CHANGES

JOSEPH L. SAX, THE CONSTITUTION, PROPERTY RIGHTS, AND THE FUTURE OF WATER LAW

61 U. Colo. L. Rev. 257 (1990).

Nearly twenty-five years ago the economist Kenneth Boulding wrote a brilliant article called "The Economics of the Coming Spaceship Earth."[1] Boulding said that we were moving from what he called a cowboy economy, in which achievement was measured by "throughput," growth in production and consumption, to a spaceship economy, where achievement would be measured by our ability to maintain the stock of resources we had and to put them to effective and sustaining use. Boulding has proven to be uncannily foresighted, and nowhere is his vision more pertinent than in western water law. * * *

The goals of a spaceship economy are, by definition, sharply different. It is not by accident that we are turning toward control of waste and water marketing as ways to reallocate existing supplies and meet new demand. There is also increasing interest in re-use of existing water supplies and in technical means to achieve equal output with smaller inputs of water. Rising concern for maintenance and augmentation of instream flows is entirely congruent with these developments. It is a clear example of stock maintenance. As we move toward a fundamentally different water strategy a primary question is whether, and to what extent, claims of vested property rights constrain opportunities for change.

What exactly is the problem? At its crudest the claim would be that whatever uses an appropriator has been making, and that have been recognized as lawful in the past, must as a matter of property right be permitted to continue or be compensated as a taking. If successful, such demands would deny a state effective authority to mandate more efficient use of existing supplies. The notion seems to be that to declare an

---

1. Boulding, The Economics of the Coming Spaceship Earth, in Environmental   Quality in a Growing Economy (H. Jarrett ed., 1966).

existing use wasteful, or non-beneficial, is a sort of prohibited *ex post facto* law that impairs a vested right. * * *

The question then is under what circumstances compensation is due even for a valid exercise of the police power? There are essentially only two grounds on which it is possible to win a takings case today. The first is where there is a "physical invasion," that is, where government physically appropriates to itself some part of an owner's property, as in the recent *Nollan*,[15] *Loretto*,[16] and *Kaiser Aetna*[17] cases. The second is where the effect of the regulation, though its purpose is valid under the police power, is so greatly to diminish the value of the property that it is no longer economically viable. As to this latter test—the so-called diminution of value standard—the Supreme Court has been extremely deferential to regulators. Even diminutions approaching 90% of value have been sustained without compensation. That has been the Court's unvarying position for many decades.

Under these standards, the only new water law regulation that would *prima facie* raise a taking problem is a release requirement: requiring existing appropriators to make releases in order to augment instream flows for public purposes such as ecosystem protection and public recreation. If the appropriator's property right were an unqualified one, such a requirement might well be viewed as a "physical invasion," and would thus be compensable. But * * * original limitations on the property that can be acquired in water undermines this facially appealing claim for compensation.

Otherwise, the regulations most likely to be challenged are those that require existing uses to be cut back as wasteful. There is no property right to waste water, and that would seem to end the matter. But several claims may nonetheless be anticipated against such regulation. First, that it would be retroactive; conduct previously considered legal would be made illegal. Second, insofar as such regulation is sought to be justified under the preexisting waste doctrine, it may be urged that the doctrine has been unused or loosely construed for a long time and should not be tightened up now. Or it may be urged that definitions of waste should not change over time.

The first of these issues is easily answered. There is no constitutional bar to retroactive regulatory legislation. * * * Nonetheless, a notion seems to have been advanced in some circles that what might be called

15. Nollan v. California Coastal Comm'n, 483 U.S. 825 (1987) (state's demand for dedication of right-of-way to allow public to walk across homeowner's oceanfront land as a condition for grant of building permit to enlarge beachfront home held an unconstitutional taking because no causal nexus was found between the public harm created by the home enlargement and the public benefit of walking across beach).

16. Loretto v. Teleprompter Manhattan CATV Corp., 458 U.S. 419 (1982) (govern-

mentally required, virtually uncompensated installation of cable television wiring by landlords to benefit tenants held an unconstitutional taking of landlord's property).

17. Kaiser Aetna v. United States, 444 U.S. 164 (1979) (governmentally required public boating access to privately created marina excavated from non-navigable pond, now (but not formerly) connected to ocean, held an unconstitutional taking of marina developer's property).

the "non-conforming use" rule in land zoning states a constitutional proposition. The claim is that a use that is already being made and that was lawful when initiated cannot be regulated away without compensation. The short answer is that there has never been a non-conforming use rule in federal constitutional property law. Valid preexisting uses have been subject to rezoning and owners have been required to change their use to conform to the new law.

Although the non-conforming use rule may be a prudent one for certain relatively low priority public purposes (such as removing highway billboards or clearing commercial uses out of residential neighborhoods), it would fundamentally subvert the regulatory process if it were implemented as a constitutional principle. New fire and safety laws could hardly await a whole new generation of buildings, and for that reason required retrofitting of devices like fire sprinkles, or removal of hazards like asbestos, raise no constitutional taking problem.

The notion that a standard once set (such as a waste rule in water law) cannot be subsequently revised is just another version of the "non-conforming use" argument. Indeed, if the argument were correct that standards cannot be upgraded, all of our environmental statutes would be unconstitutional. We could not require industries to retrofit new air and water pollution control equipment to meet new, tighter standards so long as they had been in compliance with the standards that were in effect when their facility was built. Although the Supreme Court has never in so many words sustained the constitutionality of new pollution standards applied to existing facilities, betting on the constitutionality of such laws as against taking claims is as safe a wager as the law has to offer. * * *

A recent Oregon statute exemplifies the likely future direction of water law throughout the West. The law encourages conservation by permitting appropriators to sell or lease water they save. They must subtract from the saleable amount a portion of the conserved water (usually 25%) that is to be allocated to the state and held for instream flow maintenance.

As will no doubt be the case in other states, Oregon has taken a positive rather than a negative approach to the waste problem. Instead of setting out to find waste and demanding that the appropriator yield it to the state, the state gives the user an incentive to cut back existing diversions voluntarily by permitting her to profit by selling the conserved water. * * *

How does such a plan—likely to be followed in its general outlines elsewhere—stand up against potential constitutional challenges? Oregon permits an appropriator to keep water it has conserved. Obviously this presents no harm to the conserving appropriator, who will actually be better off. Moreover, since the statute protects other appropriators who might have been using the water to be conserved (as return flow, for example), they will not be harmed. The losers are junior appropriators who have not been getting water in most years, but who would get the conserved water if it were simply returned to the river and made available, rather than being held for instream flow maintenance.

Although these juniors would get the water under traditional doctrine, they do not have a strong constitutional claim to it. If the water is viewed as not being wasted, then the savings engendered by innovative conservation methods can be treated as "developed" water to which juniors are not entitled. If the water is being wasted, then in theory it should be returned to the river where the next junior in line would be entitled to it. The state can, however, deny the juniors such water. A determination could be made that beneficial use is maximized by encouraging voluntary savings rather than by seeking to identify and regulate waste. Though no case so holds, it seems likely that a legislative judgment as how best to promote efficient use would be sustained as a rational anti-waste policy. The juniors are unlikely to prevail in insisting they have a vested right to any particular form or degree of anti-waste enforcement. Any such claims by the juniors would be weakened by the fact that they had not been using the water in question previously. No existing use is being cut off. The courts have been quite willing to permit the abolition of unused water rights.

Finally, and most importantly, there is the problem presented by the state demanding that a percentage of the water conserved be allocated to it. On its face, this arrangement may seem to present the flaw the U.S. Supreme Court found in *Nollan*: the state is using its regulatory power (to permit construction in *Nollan*, to permit a sale of conserved water in the Oregon case) to exact a benefit that has no obvious nexus with its asserted regulatory intervention. * * * The claim would be that the state is simply using its position of power to extort for its own account water it should buy.

The first response is that an owner of a water right has a lesser property right than the landowner in *Nollan*. * * *

The state need not rest only on its proprietary type claims, however. It can also justify the statute as a legitimate exercise of the police power. Perhaps the best answer to a taking claim is to turn the demand around and see how much the state is giving to, rather than how much it is taking from, the appropriator. The state while staying well within the confines of the police power, might have imposed new and restrictive beneficial use requirements on all appropriators, mandating that they use water much more efficiently. For reasons explained previously in this article, no compensation would constitutionally be required for such regulation. * * *

Had the state enacted such an efficient-use regulation, the appropriators would have been required to return all the saved water to the river. The regulated appropriators would have had no right to keep or to profit from, any of the conserved water. Under the statute as enacted, the state permits sale of 75% of the water simply as an administrative device to encourage rapid and effective compliance with its conservation goals. Thus, rather than taking 25% of the appropriator's water, it has actually given the appropriator 75% of its (the public's) water. Although the percentages do not correlate directly to public needs, they presumably represent the legislature's "ballpark" estimate of the incentive necessary to get the job of conservation and reallocation done as rapidly as feasible.

Notes and Questions

1. To date the vast majority of takings cases involving water rights have involved state legislation restricting either unexercised riparian rights (such as in *Franco–American*) or groundwater withdrawals (discussed infra pp. 450–454). With the exception of *Franco–American*, all such cases have upheld the challenged legislation. Courts have also heard, and rejected, takings challenges to state statutes

   • requiring holders of water rights that are not part of a state's administrative system to register their rights with the state, at the cost of otherwise forfeiting their rights. See, e.g., Matter of Yellowstone River, 253 Mont. 167, 832 P.2d 1210 (1992); Department of Ecology v. Adsit, 103 Wash.2d 698, 694 P.2d 1065, 1069–70 (1985).

   • retroactively applying forfeiture statutes to invalidate water rights. See, e.g., Town of Eureka v. Office of State Engineer, 108 Nev. 163, 826 P.2d 948, 950–52 (1992).

   • requantifying water rights in different units of measurement than were previously used. See, e.g., McDonald v. State, 220 Mont. 519, 722 P.2d 598 (1986) (quantifying a water right in terms of both diversion rate and total annual volume that previously had been quantified only by rate).

2. Courts, in short, have been very deferential to governmental water regulation. In what situations, if any, should courts require the government to pay compensation to water right holders?

Assume that a state government is concerned by the low flow of water in a stream that cuts through a state park. If the state passes legislation requiring upstream users to reduce their diversions, would this be a taking? Should it make a difference why the state wants to increase instream flows in the park (e.g., to protect fish and wildlife, for aesthetic reasons, or to improve recreational opportunities)? If a state wishes to acquire land for a state park, the state presumably would need to condemn the land and pay compensation. Should the rule be any different where the state wishes to increase the flow of water through the park? If so, why?

3. Why should the government ever be required to pay compensation when it restricts water use in the public interest? Another co-author of this casebook has argued that

   current shifts in water policy arguably * * * demand greater security in water rights and thus stronger constitutional protections. In seeking ways to address current water problems, for example, legislatures and agencies might well find that water users are willing to trade off some of their rights in return for more secure rights—to agree, for example, to reduced diversions in return for a more certain and secure diversion right. But the government cannot effectively commit to secure water rights unless those rights are constitutionally protected from future uncompensated change.

The West also is seeing a shift in paradigms within water law— from a "public resources" paradigm, which views water as a carefully managed and regulated public resource, to a "market" paradigm, which promotes reallocation of rights through private transfers. Under the public resource paradigm, the takings protections are troublesome because they impede necessary regulatory reallocations of resources; those who strongly oppose greater constitutional protection of water are still wedded to this paradigm. However, the market paradigm only works with secure and definite water rights. Markets will not form if there is uncertainty about whether the government will honor the traded rights.

Barton Thompson, Takings and Water Rights, in Water Law: Trends, Policies, and Practice 43, 43–44 (Kathleen Carr & James Crammond, eds., 1995). Are these legitimate concerns? If so, how should courts balance the needs for both certainty and evolution?

4. In recent years, governmental efforts to protect fish under the Endangered Species Act and other environmental statutes by restricting water withdrawals have generated a number of takings challenges. Many of the water users who have brought takings challenges do not hold appropriative water rights themselves, but instead receive water pursuant to contract with the federal Bureau of Reclamation or other governmental water contracts—complicating the takings analysis. In reclamation cases, courts to date have held that reclamation water contracts do not limit Congress' ability to reduce water deliveries for regulatory reasons. See, e.g., O'Neill v. United States, 50 F.3d 677 (9th Cir. 1995); Klamath Irrigation Dist. v. United States, 67 Fed. Cl. 504 (2005). In Tulare Lake Basin Water Storage Dist. v. United States, 49 Fed. Cl. 313 (2001), the Court of Federal Claims held that the government in implementing the Endangered Species Act had taken the rights of farmers to receive water under contracts with the California State Water Project. The *Tulare* case is excerpted and discussed in Chapter 6 at page 653. *Klamath Irrigation Dist.* is excerpted later at pages 660 and 788.

5. For other interesting discussions of takings and water rights, see James Burling, Protecting Property Rights in Aquatic Resources After *Lucas*, in Water Law: Trends, Policies, and Practice, supra note 3, at 56; Gregory Hobbs, Ecological Integrity and Water Rights Takings in the Post– *Lucas* Era, in id. at 74; John D. Leshy, A Conversation about Takings and Water Rights, 83 Tex. L. Rev. 1985 (2005); Brian E. Gray, The Property Right in Water, 9 Hastings W.-N.W. J. Envtl. L. & Pol'y 1 (2002); Renay Leone & George Shark, The Stumble of Sticks: Instream Flow Legislation and Rights to Property After *Lucas v. South Carolina Coastal Council*, 4 Vil. Envtl. L.J. 267 (1993); Joseph Sax, Rights That "Inhere in the Title Itself": The Impact of the *Lucas* Case on Western Water Law, 26 Lot. L.A. L. Rev. 943 (1993).

3. JUDICIAL TAKINGS?

Do *courts* have a greater degree of freedom to change water rights than legislatures enjoy? As this Chapter highlights, courts have frequently modified water law in response to changing needs and policies. The changes continue today as some courts look for ways to protect environmental and recreational interests in water resources. Do the constitutional takings protections limit the degree to which courts can change the common law or reinterpret statutory and constitutional provisions?

One of the most recent cases to raise this issue dealt with Hawaiian water law. To understand the case, it is necessary to go back over 150 years in time. Hawaii then was a monarchy and the king owned all the lands and allocated use of the lands among his subjects in an essentially feudal fashion. In reward for service, the king granted each of his chiefs (or *konohikis*) large segments of land known as *ahupuaas*. The *ahupuaas* were typically wedge-shaped tracts running from the top of an island to its shore and thus including a share of mountain, forest, arable land, and beach. Occasionally, the king would reserve or carve out an area of land from an *ahupuaa;* these smaller tracts, or *ilis kopono*, were also frequently granted by the king to his chiefs. Grants of *ahupuaas* and *ilis* carried all natural resources, including water, not explicitly reserved by the king.

Tenants of the *konohikis* received small fertile tracts of land known as *kuleanas* upon which to cultivate taro (the root crop of *poi*, the traditional staple of the Hawaiian diet) and other native crops. Because some taro required massive amounts of water to grow, the tenants (or *hoaainas*) were entitled to divert water from natural streams and convey it by artificial ditches (or *auwais*) to their land. Tenants had a customary right to the water and the right was superior to the rights of the *konohikis*.

The mid–1800s saw both the rise of a civil government and the break up of the feudal system, under pressure from missionaries and the United States. In what is known as the "Great Mahele," the king divided all of the lands between himself, the new civil government, the tenants (who got the *kuleanas* that they had been cultivating), and the *konohikis* (who received the remainder of their *ahupuaas* or *ilis*). The *konohikis* actually received the bulk of the lands under this division (approximately 2.5 million acres), with the tenants receiving only about 30,000, albeit fertile, acres.

This division ultimately led to a fairly complicated water rights system which prevailed until 1973. Under this system, Hawaiian water law consisted of three different rights—appurtenant, surplus, and prescriptive.

Appurtenant Water Rights. Each of the tenants received an "appurtenant water right" to use on their *kuleanas*, entitling them to the amount of water that would have been necessary to grow taro on the *kuleana* at the time of the Great Mahele. Appurtenant water rights were superior to all other water rights (although they could be lost by prescription as explained below). Although the name suggests that appurtenant water rights were attached to the *kuleana*, water experts assumed (and the courts appeared to agree) that the rights could be severed from the land and either used elsewhere or sold. In practice, tremendous quantities of appurtenant rights were leased, sold, and transferred in the century or so following the Mahele.

Surplus Water Rights. To the extent that there was water remaining in a stream after all appurtenant water rights were met, the remaining or "surplus water" went to the *konohikis.* This was a simple enough rule where a river went through only one *ahupuaa* or *ili,* but required slightly more creativity when two or more *ahupuaas* or *ilis* were involved. As the law ultimately developed, "normal surplus water" went entirely to the *ahupuaa* or *ili* upon which the stream originated. "Storm and freshet" water was then divided by a relatively complex set of rules among all the various *ahupuaas* and *ilis* through which the stream ran. Surplus water rights could be diverted and used on other land and also could be leased or sold.

Prescriptive Water Rights. As in most of the conterminous United States at the time, a water user could also gain a prescriptive right—good against both appurtenant and surplus water rights.

This was the law (or at least seemed to be the law) prior to 1973. In that year, the Hawaii Supreme Court issued its decision in McBryde Sugar Co. v. Robinson, 54 Hawaii 174, 504 P.2d 1330 (1973), and radically changed the face of Hawaiian water law. The case itself involved a dispute between two large sugar growers—the McBryde Sugar Company and Gay & Robinson—over the waters of the Hanapepe River on the "Garden Island" of Kauai. As the owners of the *ili* upon which the river arose, Gay & Robinson claimed all the normal surplus waters, as well as a sizable quantity of appurtenant water rights that it had purchased over the years. Beginning in 1891, Gay & Robinson had constructed an elaborate water transportation system to carry the water to its sugar fields, many of which were outside the watershed. McBryde also had purchased large quantities of appurtenant water rights and claimed additional prescriptive water rights by adverse use. Like Gay & Robinson, McBryde also transported much of its water outside the watershed.

In a suit brought by McBryde to determine the parties' relative water rights, the trial court followed the traditional water law set out above. The court began by determining the amount of "appurtenant water rights"—awarding 4,915,400 gallons per day to McBryde, 1,533,-050 gallons per day to Gay & Robinson, and about 5,500,000 gallons per day to other appurtenant right holders (including the State of Hawaii). The court next determined that McBryde had acquired prescriptive rights to another 2,084,600 gallons per day through adverse use. The remaining "normal surplus" water was then awarded to Gay & Robinson. McBryde, Gay & Robinson, and the State all appealed—each raising slightly different issues, but none questioning the basic structure of Hawaiian water law.

In its appellate opinion, however, the Hawaii Supreme Court rewrote the state's water law—at least in the eyes of most observers.

Citing a section of the "principles" that were used to implement the Great Mahele, the court began by holding that

> the right to water was specifically and definitely reserved for the people of Hawaii for their common good in all of the land grants [of the Great Mahele]. Thus by the Mahele * * * right to water was not intended to be, could not be, and was not transferred to the awardee, and the ownership of water in natural watercourses, streams, and rivers remained in the people of Hawaii for their common good.

This holding, by itself, would probably not have provoked much concern among Hawaiian water users, although it required the court to overrule several prior cases. As the court noted, its holding was very similar to the common law rule that flowing water is *publici juris*. But the court then went on to radically rework each of the previously recognized water rights.

Appurtenant Water Rights. The court reaffirmed the existence and size of appurtenant water rights. But emphasizing that the rights are called "appurtenant," the court held that the rights attach to the land and "may only be used in connection with that particular parcel of land to which the right is appurtenant." Appurtenant rights, in short, could not be used off the land to which they attached and could not be transferred, leased, or sold apart from the land.

Surplus Water Rights. The court next ruled that surplus water is subject to the English rule of natural flow. According to the Court, earlier decisions had ignored a key 1850 statute which, as translated from the original native Hawaiian, read:

> The people [meaning owners of land] shall have a right to drinking water, and running water, and the right of way. The springs of water and running water shall be free to all, should they need them, on all lands granted in fee simple: Provided, that this shall not be applicable to wells and water courses which individuals have made for their own use.

The question, in the court's view, was what was meant by "running water":

> As the right to "drinking water and running water" in artificial watercourses constructed by individuals for their own use is excepted by the statute, the term "running water" must mean water flowing in natural water courses, such as streams and rivers. We also believe that the right to "running water" as contained therein guarantees a land owner the same flow of water in a stream or river as at the time of the Mahele, without substantial diminution, or the right to flow of a stream in the form and size given it by nature.

Noting that missionaries, "many of whom came from Massachusetts," brought with them the common law of their native state and "had tremendous influence among the leaders of the Hawaiian Kingdom," the court suggested that the 1850 provision was a "codification or statutory enactment" of the English rule of natural flow. The court therefore held that all holders of land adjoining a stream have "the right to the natural flow of the stream without substantial diminution and in the shape and size given it by nature."[1]

Prescriptive Rights. Returning to its original holding that the state owns all the waters of Hawaii, the court also ruled that McBryde had no prescriptive rights. As the court noted, the "general law is that one may not claim title to or interest in state-owned property by adverse use."

The bottom line of the decision, as the court noted in its final paragraph, was that "Neither McBryde nor Gay & Robinson has any right to divert water from the * * * Hanapepe River out of the Hanapepe Valley into other watersheds."

Justice Marumoto dissented. In his view, it was "more important that a rule of law be settled than that it be settled right." That was particularly true here where the court's ban on inter-watershed diversions was almost certain to have a tremendous financial impact on both the parties to the case and on Hawaii's agricultural industry more generally:

> The record in this case shows that the water diverted [is used in irrigating cane fields] beyond the Hanapepe valley. There is also evidence in the case that * * * [Gay & Robinson] spent approximately $119,000 and $788,000, respectively, on the system for the diversion of the water * * *, and that McBryde spent $558,000 for pumping equipment in the Hanapepe valley, $226,000 for ditches and siphons to transport the water to its cane fields beyond the valley, and $60,000 for the construction of [a] reservoir to store the water.

> Although I do not have specific information at hand, I presume, that besides the parties in this case, there are other segments in the agricultural economy of Hawaii which depend upon irrigation for the cultivation of their crops, have expended substantial sums in constructing irrigation facilities in reliance upon prior court decisions, and will be adversely affected by the decision announced today.

All of the water users petitioned for rehearing. In addition to arguing that the earlier decision had been wrong, Gay & Robinson also argued that the decision was an unconstitutional taking of its property. Gay & Robinson noted that in 1931 the Hawaii Territorial Court had explicitly confirmed Gay & Robinson's right to the "normal surplus" waters of the Hanapepe River and its right to divert that water for use outside the watershed.[2]

---

1. In a subsequent opinion, the court suggested that, due to "changing needs and circumstances," Hawaii would follow the reasonable use rule. See Reppun v. Board of Water Supply, 65 Hawaii 531, 656 P.2d 57 (1982).

2. See Territory v. Gay, 31 Hawaii 376, 387–88 (1930), aff'd, 52 F.2d 356 (9th Cir. 1931).

By a three to two vote, however, the Hawaii Supreme Court adhered to its original decision.

McBRYDE SUGAR CO. v. ROBINSON

Supreme Court of Hawaii, 1973.
55 Hawaii 260, 517 P.2d 26.

PER CURIAM

* * * After careful consideration of the briefs and arguments presented at the rehearing, we find no reason to change the decision filed herein.

LEVINSON, JUSTICE (dissenting).

Although I voted with the majority of this court in McBryde Sugar Co. v. Robinson * * * [hereinafter referred to as *McBryde I*], I am constrained to recant that position in view of my current understanding of the problems of this case. In light of the arguments adduced on rehearing, historical evidence discovered upon further research subsequent to the court's previous decision in this case, and a reappraisal of the reasoning supporting that decision, it is my opinion that the court committed error in holding that all surplus water belongs to the State and that private water rights, however acquired, may not be transferred to nonappurtenant land. * * * *McBryde I* is not in keeping with long established and unique principles of Hawaiian water law. Precisely because *McBryde I* is such a radical departure from these principles as they have been heretofore understood, moreover, I have concluded that *McBryde I* effectuates an unconstitutional taking of the [water users'] property without just compensation and should be reversed on this ground as well.

[Justice Levinson first explained in detail the historical and legal errors that he believed undercut the court's earlier decision. His principal argument was that the court's decision was inconsistent with extensive precedent, including the Territorial Court's explicit confirmation of Gay & Robinson's water rights. He also urged that the 1850 statute upon which the earlier opinion so heavily relied was mistranslated from the native Hawaiian and, correctly translated, provided no support for the result that the majority had reached.[a] Justice Levinson then turned to the constitutional issue.]

The due process clause of the fourteenth amendment to the Federal Constitution and article I, sections 4 and 18 of the State Constitution forbid the State from taking private property without just compensation. This prohibition speaks to all instrumentalities of state government equally, restraining the courts from engineering unconstitutional takings

---

a. According to Justice Levinson, the 1850 statute actually provided: "When a konohiki acquires Allodial Title to his land or lands, the native tenants * * * shall * * * have the right to drinking water, *to bring about the flowage of water* and a path-

way. The wells and water *already flowing* * * * shall be free to all native tenants from one end of the Allodial lands to the other. * * * " (Emphasis added by Justice Levinson.)—Eds.

no less than the legislature. See Chicago, Burlington & Quincy R.R. v. Chicago, 166 U.S. 226, 241 (1897). * * *

Although as a general rule judges are free to overrule prior cases which changed circumstances and perceptions reveal to have been unwisely decided, there are constitutional limits on their power to do so. * * * In particular, when prior judicial precedent has established unequivocally a certain property right, a court may not subsequently declare that the right never existed when the consequence of such a holding is to frustrate the expectations of parties who justifiably relied on prior law in the management of their affairs. * * *

* * * Gay and Robinson has expended large sums of money in the development and transportation of the surplus water which prior decisions of this court indicated that it owned, and the other private parties to this action have purchased their land, invested in irrigation systems, and entered into contractual relationships with buyers of water, all in reliance on the principle of free transferability of water rights espoused by a long line of Hawaii cases. In the circumstances, the decision of *McBryde I* that surplus water is owned by the State and that private water rights are appurtenant exclusively to the parcels of land on which they originate must be viewed as a retroactive "taking" of property theretofore recognized as privately owned. * * *

McBryde I may or may not establish a better system for the regulation of water rights than the system that heretofore has evolved in this State. Perhaps government ownership and control of Hawaii's water resources would more effectively serve the public interest than private ownership. If this is so, then it is within the power of the State to appropriate these resources after the payment of reasonable compensation for their value. I cannot agree that it is constitutionally permissible for this court to perform the task without compensating the appellants, based exclusively on the court's perception of what is best as a policy matter for the people of Hawaii.[39] * * *

[The dissenting opinion of JUSTICE MARUMOTO is omitted.]

Notes and Questions

1. The dispute over the future of Hawaiian water law that *McBryde* set off raged actively for almost two decades. After the United States Supreme Court declined to hear the *McBryde* case, the landholders sued in federal district court to enjoin state officials from enforcing the *McBryde* decision on the ground that the decision, if enforced, would unconstitutionally take their property. The district court agreed and issued the injunction. Robinson v.

---

39. As stated in Miller & Lux v. Madera Canal & Irr. Co., 155 Cal. 59, 65, 99 P. 502, 512 (1907):

Neither a court nor the Legislature has the right to say that because such water may be more beneficially used by others it may be freely taken by them. Public policy is at best a vague and uncertain guide, and no consideration of policy can justify the taking of private property without compen-

sation. If the higher interests of the public should be thought to require that the water usually flowing in streams of this state should be subject to appropriation in ways that will deprive the riparian proprietor of its benefit, the change sought must be accomplished by the use of the power of eminent domain.

* * *

Ariyoshi, 441 F.Supp. 559 (D. Haw. 1977). The Ninth Circuit affirmed. Robinson v. Ariyoshi, 753 F.2d 1468 (9th Cir. 1985).

The United States Supreme Court vacated the decision and remanded the case for further consideration of whether the takings issue was ripe for review. Ariyoshi v. Robinson, 477 U.S. 902 (1986). On remand, the State of Hawaii argued that the *McBryde* decision had not yet prevented the land-holders from using any water and might never, because the Hawaii courts might use equitable doctrines to temper the impact of *McBryde* on long-standing water users. The Ninth Circuit agreed that the constitutional challenge was premature and ordered the complaints dismissed. Robinson v. Ariyoshi, 887 F.2d 215 (9th Cir. 1989).

Where does this leave Hawaiian law? With the federal complaints dismissed, *McBryde* remains the law. Given the earlier federal opinions holding *McBryde* unconstitutional, however, any effort to enforce *McBryde* against a private water user likely could generate a new lawsuit and probably a new decision holding *McBryde* to be a taking.

2.   Can a court take property? The history of the issue is recounted in Barton Thompson, Judicial Takings, 76 Va. L. Rev. 1449, 1463–72 (1990). In the 1930s, the United States Supreme Court strongly suggested that the takings protections do not limit a court's ability to modify property rights. See Great Northern Ry. Co. v. Sunburst Oil & Refining Co., 287 U.S. 358 (1932); Brinkerhoff–Faris Trust & Sav. Co. v. Hill, 281 U.S. 673 (1930). In a 1967 concurring opinion, however, Justice Potter Stewart concluded that a "sudden change in the law, unpredictable in terms of the relevant precedents," would be an unconstitutional taking. Hughes v. Washington, 389 U.S. 290, 296–97 (1967). Since then, a number of lower federal and state courts have adopted Justice Stewart's view. See, e.g., Sotomura v. County of Hawaii, 460 F.Supp. 473 (D. Haw. 1978).

Legal scholars have split on the issue. For arguments in favor of subjecting the courts to the takings protections, see Thompson, supra; John Martinez, Taking Time Seriously: The Federal Constitutional Right to Be Free From "Startling" State Court Overrulings, 11 Harv. J. L. & Soc. Pol'y 297 (1988). For opposing arguments, see Bradford Lamb, *Robinson v. Ariyoshi:* A Federal Intrusion Upon State Water Law, 17 Envtl. L. 325 (1987); Williamson Chang, Unraveling Robinson v. Ariyoshi: Can Courts "Take" Property?, 2 U. Haw. L. Rev. 57 (1979). See also W. David Sarratt, Judicial Takings and the Course Pursued, 90 Va. L. Rev. 1487 (2004); Roderick Walston, The Constitution and Property: Due Process, Regulatory Takings, and Judicial Takings, 2001 Utah L. Rev. 379 (2001).

3.   Why would state courts be exempt from the takings limitations imposed by the fourteenth amendment? The language of the fourteenth amendment is quite inclusive, and its provisions have been applied frequently to judicial actions in other contexts. See, e.g., Shelley v. Kraemer, 334 U.S. 1 (1948) (racial discrimination); Bridges v. California, 314 U.S. 252 (1941) (freedom of speech); Cantwell v. Connecticut, 310 U.S. 296 (1940) (freedom of religion). The impact on property holders, moreover, would appear to be the same whether it is the legislature, an administrative agency, or a court that interferes with the protected property interest.

Do we trust courts more than legislatures to decide whether the public advantage in changing the law outweighs the property holder's interest in a previously recognized property right? If so, is that fact relevant to the issue of whether the property holder is entitled to compensation?

4. Assuming that courts are subject to the takings limitations, what is the remedy if a decision unconstitutionally interferes with property? As the *McBryde* dispute suggests, one possible remedy is an injunction against enforcement of the offending decision or a declaration that the decision is unconstitutional. Could the property holder sue the state for compensation in an inverse-condemnation type action? Cf. First English Evangelical Lutheran Church v. County of Los Angeles, 482 U.S. 304 (1987) (permitting an inverse condemnation action for a temporary regulatory taking).

5. If courts are subject to the takings limitations, was *McBryde* a taking? According to *McBryde,* statements in prior cases suggesting that *konohikis* owned "normal surplus" waters and could transfer the waters to other watersheds was dictum. Can one have a protected right based on mere dictum? Although you may be tempted to answer this question "no," keep in mind that what is "dictum" often depends on the eye of the beholder. For a discussion of the indeterminacy involved in separating holding from dictum, see Ken Kress, Legal Indeterminacy, 77 Calif. L. Rev. 283, 297–301 (1989).

The Hawaii Supreme Court in *McBryde* also argued that the earlier decisions had ignored statutes from the period of the Great Mahele. If the court was right in this claim, can it possibly be a taking for the court to correct its earlier rulings? Weren't the statutes the "law" no matter what the state courts previously said? On the other hand, the water users who had relied upon the earlier rulings were totally unaware of the statutes.

6. As discussed in Section A, the history of water law in most of the western United States is, in part, a history of trying to free water law from the confines of the common-law riparian doctrine. In *McBryde,* the Hawaii Supreme Court seemed intent on moving in the opposite direction. Why? There are at least two possible explanations. One is environmental. As a result of the many diversions from the Hanapepe River, by the time *McBryde* went to trial the mouth of the river was practically dry year-round. And the Hanapepe River was not unique. Riparian rights are far more solicitous of instream flows. The other, related explanation is that the Hawaii Supreme Court hoped to restore the traditional role of water in Hawaiian society. According to the Hawaii Supreme Court, earlier water decisions had ignored the "tradition of the native Hawaiians in their zeal to convert these islands into a manageable western society"—converting a communal good into a private resource. Reppun v. Board of Water Supply, 65 Hawaii 531, 656 P.2d 57, 67 (1982).

7. In 1987, the Hawaii legislature finally adopted a detailed water code for the state. The code provides for the grandfathering of at least some existing uses (Haw. Rev. Stat. § 174C–50) and authorizes the Commission on Water Resource Management to issue permits under certain conditions for out-of-watershed diversions, "[t]he common law of the State to the contrary notwithstanding" (id. § 174C–49(c)). See Douglas MacDougal, Testing the Current: The Water Code and the Regulation of Hawaii's Water Resources, 10 U. Haw. L. Rev. 205 (1988). Could a riparian property holder who wants to protect the natural flow of the stream running by her property successful argue that the issuance of a diversion permit under the water code would be a taking of her property?

Chapter 5

GROUNDWATER[1]

A. INTRODUCTION

Water law traditionally has treated groundwater and surface water separately, with independent rules for allocation. A primary historical reason for the duality was lack of knowledge about, or the inability to predict, the movement of water beneath the earth's surface. In the most famous early case on groundwater law, Acton v. Blundell, 152 Eng. Rep. 1223 (Ex. Chamb. 1843), the English court said:

> But in the case of a well, sunk by a proprietor in his own land, the water which feeds it from a neighboring soil, does not flow openly in the sight of the neighboring proprietor, but through the hidden veins of the earth beneath its surface: no man can tell what changes these under-ground sources have undergone in the progress of time: it may well be, that it is only of yesterday's date, that they first took the course and direction which enabled them to supply the well: again, no proprietor knows what portion of water is taken from beneath his own soil: how much he gives originally, or how much he transmits only, or how much he receives: on the contrary, until the well is sunk, and the water collected by draining into it, there cannot properly be said, with reference to the well, to be any flow of water at all.

Professor Morton Horwitz offered another explanation, attributing the development of a separate groundwater law to the fact that the first groundwater cases in the United States came along not only some time after surface water doctrine was worked out, but also "after laissez-faire assumptions firmly took hold of the American judges." The Transformation of American Law, 1780–1860, at 105 (1977). Changing the common law into a consciously exercised instrument of economic development meant adopting a rule of capture, giving landowners unlimited opportu-

---

1. Groundwater seems to be spelled as one word or two words (ground water) with about equal frequency. (An engineer's joke goes, "ground water" is what you get when you put ice in a blender.) We use a single word, unless we give a title or quotation where two words are used.

nity to seize groundwater that sharply contrasted with the sharing principles the courts had earlier fashioned for surface water.

Whatever its cause, the separate development of the law of groundwater has had a profound effect on the law's course ever since. Early in the twentieth century some basic knowledge of the scientific principles of groundwater hydrogeology began to be available to the legal profession.[2] It is now possible (though expensive) to map underground aquifers, to trace subterranean water movement, and to show connections between groundwater and surface streams. Groundwater is now known to be a major component of many streams and rivers (usually called, in that form, base flow). Yet the law in many jurisdictions is only haltingly adjusting to these advances. While the dichotomy between the legal regimes applicable to groundwater and surface water is breaking down, some degree of separation continues to be the rule in a majority of American states.

From a utilitarian perspective, groundwater has a number of advantages over surface water. There's much more of it; of all unfrozen freshwater found in the Earth's "hydrosphere" (all water and water vapor occurring beneath, on, or above the Earth's surface), about 95% is groundwater.[3] It is also more widely available, in both the humid East and the arid West. Because it is usually available at or near its place of use, groundwater often can be used more efficiently than surface water. No or comparatively few surface storage and transmission facilities need be built. There are no evaporation or seepage losses as with surface reservoirs.[4] Not as reliant as surface flows upon precipitation, with its seasonal and annual variations, groundwater tends to be more dependably available. With the seeming end of decades of relatively wet climatic conditions in most of the country (not to mention the possible impacts of greenhouse gas accumulations), groundwater will likely become ever more important.

There are some offsetting disadvantages; most prominently, the cost of drilling wells and of electricity to drive pumps. Water is, after all, quite heavy: about 240 gallons weighs a short ton; an acre-foot, about 1359 short tons. In some areas, physically available groundwater is so far below the surface that it is not cost-effective to pay for the pump "lift"

---

2. For a thumbnail sketch, see Joseph W. Dellapenna, Physical and Social Bases of Quantitative Groundwater Law, in 3 Waters and Water Rights § 18.01, at 18–3 to 18–4 (Robert Beck ed., repl.vol. 2003).

3. Ralph Heath, Basic Ground–Water Hydrology 1 (U.S. Geological Survey Water–Supply Paper No. 2220, 1998). California has about 425 million acre-feet of available groundwater. All of its surface water reservoirs combined can store only about one-tenth this amount. Lester Snow & Anthony Saracino, The CALFED Ground Water Program, in Proceedings of the 21st Biennial Ground Water Conference 5 (Water Resources Center Report No. 95, 1998).

4. Lake Mead, with its large surface area in the hot desert southwest, can lose one million acre-feet of water (5 to 7 feet off the surface) that way in a year. That's more than three times what the city of Phoenix, serving well over one million people, uses in the same time period. For a discussion of comparable evaporation at Lake Powell, see Scott Miller, Undamming Glen Canyon: Lunacy, Rationality, or Prophecy, 19 Stan. Envtl.L.J. 121, 176 (2000).

to the surface. Moreover, some aquifers are "recharged," or replenished, very slowly or not at all. Pumping water from these aquifers may amount to mining a non-renewable resource, much as petroleum or gold is mined. Some groundwater is of poor quality, and generally speaking, the deeper one goes the poorer the quality, because at the higher temperatures at depth, the more chemicals dissolve out of the surrounding rock into the water. In some situations groundwater withdrawals may cause the surface of the earth to subside. Land subsidence can damage or destroy surface structures such as homes or highways.[5]

For most of our nation's history, groundwater was extracted in small quantities by crude devices such as dug wells and hand pumps or pumps driven by windmills. This changed in 1937, with the invention of the high-speed centrifugal pump, which permits the extraction of large quantities of water from the ground in relatively short order.[6] At almost exactly the same time, the federal government embarked on a program of rural electrification, subsidizing the delivery of electricity to sparsely populated regions. Without these developments, groundwater use patterns might have been much different.

The result has been a steady increase in the amount of groundwater extraction nationwide. The dramatic gains came in the first three decades after World War II, from about 38 million acre-feet (MAF) of groundwater extracted in 1950 to a peak of 93 MAF in 1980. It then declined somewhat to about 86 MAF in 1995, but then increased to a new high of 93.4 MAF in 2000, probably influenced by regional droughts in the late 1990s.[7] More than two-thirds of the groundwater extracted in 2000 was used for agricultural irrigation. In fact, groundwater accounts for more than 40% of all water used in irrigated agriculture.[8] About 40% of the water the U.S. uses for domestic purposes is also supplied from groundwater. Almost all of the people in the U.S. not serviced by a public water provider (about 15% of the total population) obtain their water from groundwater withdrawals.[9] The enormous growth of groundwater extraction in the last half century has created problems throughout the country. Professor Robert Glennon has documented some of these in his Water Follies (Island Press, 2002).

5. "Land fissures are an increasing problem in growth areas [often, former irrigated farmland] throughout Arizona." Fissure Problem Runs Deep in Arizona, Arizona Republic, Sept. 26, 2005.

6. See Leslie Sheffield, Technology, in Flat Water: A History of Nebraska and its Water 87 (1993). See also Leslie Schafer, Economics and Finance, in id. at 113.

7. Susan S. Hutson, Nancy L. Barber, Joan F. Kenny, Kristin S. Linsey, Deborah S. Lumia, & Molly A. Maupin, Estimated Use of Water in the United States in 2000 (U.S. Geological Survey Circular 1268, 2004), available at http://pubs.usgs.gov/ circ/ 2004/circ1268/.

8. Id. at 4, 39, 40. Groundwater accounted for about 40% of the total water withdrawals in California in 2000. Id. at Tables 2, 4. Not surprisingly, greater volumes of groundwater use tend to be used in the West. California accounts for nearly one-fifth of the national total, followed by Texas, Nebraska, Arkansas, Florida, Idaho, Kansas, and Arizona. More than two-thirds the total national volume of groundwater withdrawal is in these eight states. Id.

9. Id. at 16–19.

Many jurisdictions adopted a law for groundwater well before they experienced much groundwater development. As reliance on groundwater became more widespread, emerging problems have led a number of jurisdictions to reexamine the assumptions on which their groundwater doctrines rested, and to modify or even abandon earlier adopted doctrines in favor of new ones. Sometimes this has been done by the courts; sometimes by state legislatures.

As with surface water, groundwater law is primarily state law, but several factors complicate its study. First, whereas there are two primary surface water doctrines (riparianism and prior appropriation), five different doctrines of groundwater law have some acceptance. Moreover, especially in recent years, statutes have altered common law doctrines, either statewide or in particular geographic areas. Increasingly, states are authorizing the creation of special governmental districts, with jurisdiction over groundwater in a particular geographic area, to manage the resource according to principles at variance from the common law. The net effect is that today few jurisdictions simply apply one of the basic doctrines of groundwater law in a pure or comprehensive manner. A final complication is that a full understanding of groundwater issues requires knowledge of how water is recharged to and discharged from aquifers, and how groundwater relates to surface water. The scientific field is known as hydrogeology, and some of its concepts and terminology are sophisticated. Increasingly the science relies on computer modeling of aquifers and groundwater movement.

The chapter opens with an overview of hydrogeology, aquifer characteristics and behavior, hydrologic connections between groundwater and surface water, and informational limits that plague groundwater law and regulation. The second section introduces legal definitions and classifications of groundwater and then covers the five distinct groundwater law doctrines, initially through a hypothetical problem, and then through a short sequence of cases and other materials that examine each of the five doctrines in a more detailed and traditional way.

The third section starts with a note on adjudicating groundwater rights, followed by cases exploring the significance and constitutionality of emergent legislation changing common law doctrines. The bulk of the section, which comprises most of the chapter, is organized around certain groundwater issues and problems that recur with increasing frequency. Each issue is examined in some detail, comparing how the different groundwater common law doctrines, and legislatures in various jurisdictions, deal with them. These are (1) groundwater-surface water interconnections; (2) well interference (a localized user conflict where one user's operations impair those of another groundwater user); (3) regional aquifer declines (a generalized condition in which more water is being removed from an aquifer than is being replaced, requiring increasing amounts of energy to remove the water from the aquifer); and (4) deliberate groundwater recharge for storing water, a technique on the cutting edge today.

B. HYDROGEOLOGY AND INFORMATIONAL LIMITS

1. BASIC PRINCIPLES OF HYDROGEOLOGY[10]

Surprisingly, for a resource that is so widely used and so important to the health and to the economy of the country, the occurrence of ground water is not only poorly understood but is also, in fact, the subject of many widespread misconceptions. * * * Because ground-water hydrology deals with the occurrence and movement of water in an almost infinitely complex subsurface environment, it is, in its most advanced state, one of the most complex of the sciences.[11]

Despite the lay perception of a "solid" Earth, myriad openings exist among grains of sand and silt, particles of clay, or even along fractures in hard rock. The total volume of these subsurface openings (which are occupied mainly by water, gas, and petroleum) is very large; it has been calculated that if these openings formed a continuous cavern beneath the entire surface of the United States, its height would be about 186 feet. Water reaches these interstices for the most part by percolating downward by gravity after being deposited on the surface of the earth as precipitation. Infiltration rates vary widely, depending upon the intensity and duration of precipitation, land use and vegetative cover, slope, and the character and moisture content of the soil.

An important fact about groundwater is that its movement under the surface can be exceedingly slow. Surface water may move tens of kilometers per day, but water below the land surface may move at *meters* per *year* or even less. The time required to replace the water in the ground (to replenish or recharge aquifers) is often measured in decades or centuries.

Water will infiltrate downward until its course is checked by a relatively impermeable stratum of rock such as a layer of shale or clay, sometimes called a confining bed. See Figure 5–1. The water fills up the spaces between the particles of the porous material found in the stratum just above this layer. The zone in which all interconnected openings are full of water is called the zone of saturation. The line marking the top of the zone of saturation is called the water table. The area above the water table is called the unsaturated zone. Water in the saturated zone is the only underground water that is available in sufficient quantity to supply wells and springs and is, strictly speaking, the only water to which the name groundwater is correctly applied. Geological formations in which groundwater is stored, and which will yield that water in a usable quantity to a well or spring, are called aquifers.

---

10. Much of the following description is derived from Heath, supra note 3. Another useful volume for the lay reader is R. Allan Freeze & John Cherry, Groundwater (1979).

11. Heath, supra note 3, at 1. The final report of the congressionally-chartered National Water Commission aptly observed that "misinformation, misunderstanding, and mysticism" plague the subject. Water Policies for the Future 230 (1973).

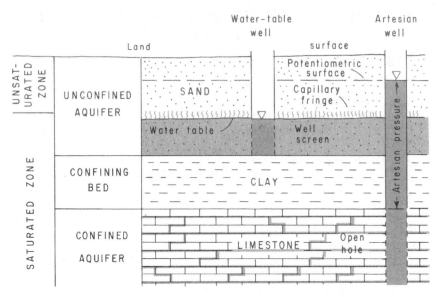

Figure 5–1
Groundwater Schematic

A crude model of one kind of aquifer is a bowl filled with sand. Most water sprinkled on the surface of the sand will percolate downward under the force of gravity. When it reaches the impermeable bowl, it forms a pool that fills all the pore spaces among the grains of sand—the zone of saturation. This is an unconfined or water-table aquifer. Because it has no layer of impermeable material above it, the upper surface of the saturated zone is free to rise and fall.[12]

But not all aquifers are unconfined. The earth's crust is often stratified; that is, composed of layers of rock of varying porosity and permeability. For example, a water-bearing sandstone formation may be located beneath a layer of relatively impermeable clay or rock. (Less permeable strata are sometimes called "aquitards.") This traps or confines groundwater below that relatively impermeable layer—think of it as a saucer embedded in the bowl of sand. Water can be extracted from such an aquifer by drilling through the clay. See again Figure 5–1.

A confined aquifer may not recharge readily. If the relatively impermeable layer covers the entire aquifer (if the saucer covers the entire layer of sand in the bowl), water sprinkled on the surface would not

---

12. Sometimes the water level may rise to or near the surface, causing waterlogging or drainage problems. On the west side of California's Central Valley, a clay layer below the surface stops the downward percolation of salty irrigation water (made worse by selenium in the soil), which pooled at the surface and evaporation concentrated the contaminants, which led to a serious problem in the 1980s at Kesterson Reservoir, described in Chapter 6 infra p. 651.

percolate down below the layer (saucer) to the aquifer. Pumping from the zone of saturation below that layer would eventually drain the aquifer. This would be an example of groundwater mining, or using up a non-renewable resource. Many aquifers are only partly confined (e.g., the saucer is smaller than the bowl), which allows some of the water sprinkled on the surface eventually to reach the zone of saturation.

By definition there is no water table in a confined aquifer; instead, there is something called a "potentiometric surface." This is a measure of the energy of the water–the water is under pressure—and indicates the height to which water will rise in a well drilled into the aquifer. The potentiometric surface always lies above the top of a confined aquifer. Wells that are drilled into confined aquifers and tightly cased (lined with an impermeable material such as metal pipe) are referred to as artesian wells. If the water level in an artesian well stands above the land surface, the well is a flowing artesian well. At one time the elevators of the Brown Palace Hotel in Denver were operated using the pressure of the artesian aquifer under the City.

The Interaction of Groundwater and Surface Water

As explained in the following excerpt, groundwater and surface water are hydrologically interconnected.

> Streams interact with ground water in all types of landscapes. The interaction takes place in three basic ways: streams gain water from inflow of ground water through the streambed (gaining stream) [see Figure 5–2], they lose water to ground water by outflow through the streambed (losing stream) [see Figure 5–3], or they do both, gaining in some reaches and losing in other reaches. * * *

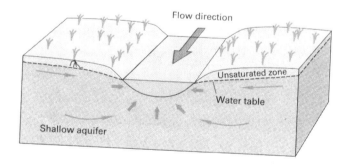

Figure 5–2
Gaining Stream

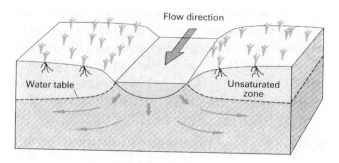

Figure 5–3
Losing Stream

Losing streams can be connected to the ground-water system by a continuous saturated zone [see Figure 5–3] or can be disconnected from the ground-water system by an unsaturated zone. Where the stream is disconnected from the ground-water system by an unsaturated zone, the water table may have a discernible mound below the stream [Figure 5–4] if the rate of recharge through the streambed and unsaturated zone is greater than the rate of lateral ground-water flow away from the water-table mound. * * *

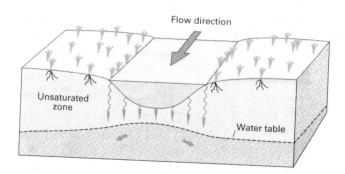

Figure 5–4
Disconnected Stream

Ground water contributes to streams in most physiographic and climatic settings. Even in settings where streams are primarily losing water to ground water, certain reaches may receive ground-water inflow during some seasons. * * * The amount of water that ground water contributes to streams can be estimated by analyzing streamflow hydrographs to determine the ground-water component, which is termed base flow. * * *

Withdrawing water from shallow aquifers that are directly connected to surface-water bodies can have a significant effect on the movement of water between these two water bodies. The effects of pumping a single well or a small group of wells on the hydrologic regime are local in scale. However, the effects of many wells withdrawing water from an aquifer over large areas may be regional in scale. * * * Withdrawing water from shallow aquifers near surface-water bodies can diminish the available surface-water supply by capturing some of the ground-water flow that otherwise would have discharged to surface water or by inducing flow from surface water into the surrounding aquifer system. [See Figure 5–5][13]

13. Thomas Winter et al., Ground Water and Surface Water: A Single Resource 9–14 (U.S. Geological Survey Circular 1139, 1998).

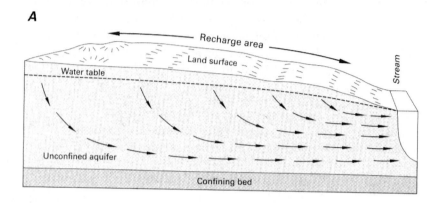

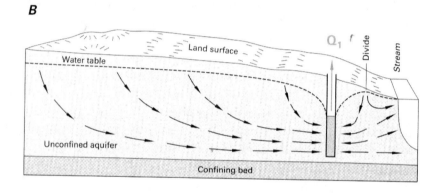

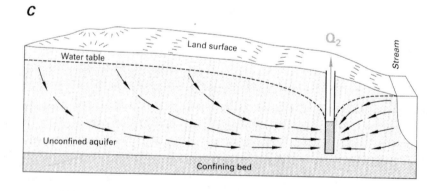

**Figure 5–5
Effect of Water Withdrawals on Surface Stream**

Well Interference

A typical well from which groundwater is extracted by pumping is like a straw stuck in the bowl of wet sand. For the well to operate, it must be drilled from the surface into the zone of saturation. When groundwater is withdrawn through a well, the water level in the well declines, and water begins to move from the surrounding aquifer into the well. The movement of water from the aquifer into the well results in the formation of what is called a cone of depression. Important differences exist between cones of depression in unconfined and confined aquifers. In unconfined aquifers, the cone of depression tends to expand slowly; in confined aquifers, it may expand very rapidly. This is because confined aquifers have a very small "storage coefficient" (volume of water an aquifer may store per unit of surface area per unit of change in head).[14] See Figure 5-6.

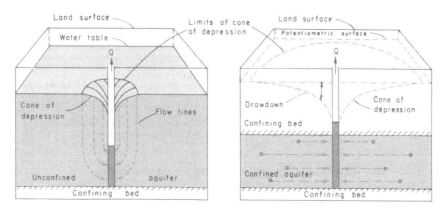

Figure 5–6
Illustration of Well Interference

As a cone of depression from a well expands, it may intercept nearby wells, and adversely affect their capacity to withdraw water. These are sometimes characterized as "well interference" situations, especially when they are drawing from abundant supplies and do not indicate a regional lowering of the water level in an aquifer. As we shall see, the legal principles applied to well interference cases may not apply to a regional or aquifer-wide decline in water levels. But there is no sharp demarcation between the two situations. Cones of depression may be caused by groups of wells (sometimes called a well field) as well as individual wells. A cone of depression may extend for many miles from the pumping center, particularly after years of pumping. The extent and shape of the cone depend upon the rate and duration of pumping, the

14.   Heath, supra note 3, at 30.

amount and location of recharge, and upon properties of the aquifer—specifically, its transmissivity, permeability and storage capacity. Major cones of depression, sometimes coalescing with others to effect a regional decline, are found throughout the United States.

General Regional Declines of Groundwater

Disputes involving a relatively widespread regional decline of groundwater levels may start the same as well interference cases, but a region-wide decline involves more than just a cone of depression of a single well or group of wells. It tends to raise larger social and economic questions as well as ones of water allocation. Geologic and climatic conditions, as well as the pattern of groundwater withdrawals, play a major role in determining where problems of widespread declines in water levels occur. Although regional declines in aquifer levels may be found across the country, arid regions are, not surprisingly, more likely to suffer serious general declines. Aridity tends both to limit groundwater supply (by limiting recharge) and to stimulate groundwater demand.

A caution needs to be introduced here regarding nomenclature. A number of potentially misleading terms are used to describe groundwater conditions by courts and others. It is frequently said, for example, that an aquifer is in an "overdraft" condition if its water level is declining. Because the decline may be temporary or permanent, care must be taken in using the term. Similarly, groundwater "mining" suggests that the withdrawal is unlikely to be replenished within a reasonable period of time, but judgments about what is a reasonable period may vary widely.

Perhaps the most slippery concept is "safe yield." The typically stated goal in dealing with an "overdraft" or "mining" situation is to limit pumping to the "safe yield" of an aquifer. Despite the reassuring word "safe," this term does not have a generally accepted definition. "Safe yield" is conventionally understood to mean the amount of water that can be withdrawn from an aquifer in perpetuity, where the rate of extraction just equals the rate of recharge. The rate of recharge is, however, a complex calculation. Some confined aquifers may have no source of natural recharge; more typically, they have a relatively small recharge zone and/or a low rate of infiltration. Because an aquifer's rate of recharge may vary with a number of factors, "[g]roundwater recharge is very difficult to estimate accurately."[15]

"Safe yield" is sometimes defined as the amount of water that can be withdrawn from an aquifer annually without producing an "undesired" result.[16] Thus it includes social and economic judgments in addition to hydrology and engineering. "[W]hat constitutes an undesirable

15. M. Anderson, Hydrogeologic Framework for Groundwater Protection, in Planning for Groundwater Protection 22–23 (G. William Page ed., 1987); see also W.P. Balleau, Water Appropriation and Transfer in a General Hydrogeological System, 28 Nat. Resources J. 269, 280 (1988); Edgar Bagley, Water Rights Law and Public Policies Relating to Ground Water Mining in the Southwestern States, 4 J.L. & Econ. 144, 166 n.78 (1961).

16. See Freeze & Cherry, supra note 10, at 364.

result * * * of course, will vary with the respondent."[17] In other words, it might be said that the "safe yield" of an aquifer is not being exceeded even when the water table in the aquifer is declining.[18] The U.S. Geological Survey no longer includes "safe yield" among its selected groundwater terms.[19]

Perhaps a better expression is "optimal yield"—"optimal" suggesting a more forthright balancing of the benefits produced by the water withdrawn from the aquifer compared to the adverse effects of continued withdrawals and water level declines. In some situations optimal yield may conceivably involve mining the aquifer to depletion; in others it may involve complete conservation. Most of the time, it will involve something in between.[20] State statutes and rules may use different nomenclature; for example, an Oregon statute calls for "reasonably stable ground water levels [to] be determined and maintained," Ore. Rev. Stat. § 537.525(7), and the Oregon Water Resources Commission adopted a rule defining that standard in certain groundwater basins to mean an average water table decline over a large area of no more than a foot a year, and no decline in the five-year average. See Waterwatch of Oregon v. Oregon Water Resources Dept., 120 Or.App. 366, 852 P.2d 902 (1993).

The causes for concern (or "undesired" results) from regional declines in groundwater levels may vary depending on the uses and characteristics of the aquifer. For example, in areas like the High Plains, underlain by the giant regional Ogallala Aquifer, an "undesired" result is higher energy costs for additional pump lifts, costs which can make crop production or other relatively marginal uses uneconomic. In coastal regions, overdraft can cause saline intrusion. As noted above, quality problems may also be encountered more frequently anywhere in the country when deeper aquifers are tapped.[21]

Subsidence

Another cause for concern from regional declines in aquifer levels is subsidence, or a decline in the elevation of the land surface. In Califor-

17. Anderson & Berkebile, Hydrogeology of the South Fork of Long Island, New York: Discussion and Reply, 88 Geological Soc'y of Am. Bull. 895 (1977); Fetter, Reply, 88 Geological Soc'y of Am. Bull. 896 (1977) (safe yield is "a subjective phenomena based upon human values").

18. H.E. Thomas, The Conservation of Groundwater 261–64 (1951) (" 'Safe Yield' is an Alice-in-Wonderland term which means whatever its user chooses").

19. Water Supply Paper No. 1988, Definitions of Selected Groundwater Terms—Revisions and Conceptual Refinements 11 (1972).

20. See Freeze & Cherry, supra note 10, at 364–65; see also Gregory Weber, Twenty Years of Local Groundwater Export Legislation in California: Lessons from a Patchwork Quilt, 34 Nat. Resources J. 657, 672–77 (1994) (documenting disputes among hy-

drologists as to definitions of safe yield and related concepts).

21. Approximately two-thirds of the United States is underlain by aquifers that yield water containing more than 1,000 mg/L of total dissolved solids. That figure is the upper limit of what the U.S. Geological Survey classifies as "fresh" water; water containing less than 500 mg/L is preferred for domestic use and for many industrial processes. See Heath, supra note 3, at 64, 69. Poorer quality at depth may have to do with the length of time groundwater is exposed to potential contaminants in the surrounding rock, which tends to be longer at greater depth. See Thomas Winter et al., Ground Water and Surface Water: A Single Resource 9–14 (U.S. Geological Survey Circular 1139, 1998).

nia's Central Valley and south-central Arizona, subsidence of land over heavily used aquifers damages buildings, pipelines, canals, highways, and other facilities.[22] Central Florida and the Texas Gulf Coast have also experienced subsidence problems. Nationally, the cost is many millions of dollars of damage each year. Not all of this is caused by groundwater withdrawals (oil and gas extraction may have similar effects), although much of it is. California, Texas, and Arizona have the most land area affected by subsidence, and they are among the heaviest users of groundwater.

Subsidence generally results from the force of gravity operating with the lowering of the water level or the potentiometric surface of water in a confined aquifer. Think of the difference in resistance between pressing down on a slightly damp sponge and one saturated with water. The land usually subsides relatively slowly in concert with the pumping, as the aquifer and adjacent aquitards (the relatively impermeable layers, which contain some water which leaks into adjacent aquifers) are compacted by the inexorable force of gravity. Subsidence may deprive the aquifer of the ability to recharge, even when water is forcibly injected into wells, and thus may permanently limit the capacity of the ground to store water for future use. By depriving future generations of the availability of groundwater, withdrawing groundwater that leads to this result is, all might agree, genuine groundwater "mining."[23]

Groundwater Storage—Aquifer Recharge and Recovery

Most aquifers recharge under natural conditions, at varying rates. Surface land uses; e.g., how much is paved with impervious materials, obviously can affect recharge rates. Enhancing the process of natural recharge has long been practiced, but there is increasing interest in artificially recharging aquifers on a broader scale, to use the aquifer to store introduced water for future use. The storage capacity of an aquifer is a function both of the porosity of the rock in the aquifer and of the elastic properties of both rock and water. Unconfined aquifers are recharged simply by refilling the pore spaces. Confined aquifers can take enormous amounts of water into storage and release it from storage through expansion and compression of the water and aquifer. The ease with which an aquifer will artificially recharge depends upon many

---

22. Parts of the Central Valley saw a decline in the elevation of the land surface of one foot a year between 1935 and 1970 as a result of groundwater pumping. See Robert Glennon, Water Follies 33 (2002); see also id. at 34, 47, 79–81.

23. For more detail on the nature and causes of subsidence, see D.L. Galloway, D.R. Jones, & S.E. Ingebritsen, Land Subsidence in the United States (USGS Circular 1182, 1999); W.M. Alley, T.E.Reilly, & O.L. Franke, Sustainability of Groundwater Resources 55–58 (USGS Circular 1186, 1999); see also see Christopher B. Amandes, Con-

trolling Land Surface Subsidence: A Proposal for a Market–Based Regulatory Scheme, 31 UCLA L.Rev. 1208, 1210–15 (1984). Occasionally, groundwater pumping may facilitate the collapse of the land surface through the sudden formation of sinkholes. This can happen when the lowering of the water table in cavernous terrain erodes fine-grained sediment that formerly filled the subterranean openings. The landscape where this can occur is called a karst landscape, after the characteristic Karst Region of Slovenia (former Yugoslavia). See Freeze & Cherry, supra note 10, at 513–14.

factors. Water may be recharged by spreading it on the surface in locations conducive to prompt percolation into the aquifer (often called "recharge basins"—streambeds may be one such place), or it may be recharged by injection through a well. Recharge basins usually require regular maintenance, because the settling of the suspended sediment in the introduced water reduces the basin's ability to conduct the water to the aquifer. Recharge can also raise aquifer contamination and water quality issues. Injection wells have been used for some time, but the technology of injection and recovery (sometimes called aquifer storage and recovery, or ASR) has significantly advanced in the last couple of decades.

2. INFORMATIONAL LIMITS

A major problem in groundwater management, regulation, and dispute resolution is the absence of detailed information about (a) hydrogeologic conditions and (b) historical and current groundwater extractions. On the former, Professor William Blomquist has observed:

> [T]he difficulties encountered by groundwater users in any given location will depend in large measure on the properties of the basin on which they rely. If users hope to cope with and overcome these difficulties, they will have to know not only the general principles of "how a groundwater basin works" but also learn about the particular characteristics of the basin they are using. The solutions they devise (if they do) will relate to the particular characteristics of that basin and may not resemble the solutions arrived at in another place (even an adjacent basin) despite the fact that users in both places are drawing their supplies from groundwater basins and applying some general knowledge of groundwater in the process.

William Blomquist, Dividing the Waters 24 (1992). "The information requirements are enormous." Id. at 25.

There are at least three methods of determining the behavior of water in aquifers. One is to inject a fluorescent dye or other tracer into the groundwater and observe its occurrence through observation wells. Another is to pump groundwater from a centrally located well at a constant rate and measure the level in other observation wells. A third method is to examine samples of water taken from individual wells and use surface and geological observations to draw inferences of aquifer characteristics. Each of these can be expensive (the third tends to be the cheapest); they may be used in various combinations.[24]

Particularly when litigation arises over groundwater, or it becomes necessary to manage extractions, it is usually important to know who is using, or has historically used, how much water from a particular

---

24. See generally Peter Davis, Wells and Streams: Relationship at Law, 37 Mo. L. Rev. 189, 235 n.4 (1972); David Todd, Groundwater, in Handbook of Applied Hy-

drology 13:12 to 13:27 (Ven Te Chow ed., 1964); Raphael Kazmann, Modern Hydrology 153–58 (1965); R.C. Ward, Principles of Hydrology 276–84 (1967).

aquifer. A basic information-gathering technique is to require that wells be registered with the government. The registration requirement may or may not be implemented by a permit system. That is, the law may either merely require a well to be recorded with the state (with or without a periodic report on withdrawals); or it may prohibit construction of new (or operating existing) wells without a permit. Most jurisdictions were relatively slow to adopt such requirements. It was not until 1955, after several decades of booming population growth, that California adopted a law requiring large capacity wells (pumping 25 acre-feet or more a year) to be registered in four southern California counties.[25] Nebraska, another heavy groundwater using state, did something similar in 1957.[26] The pace of adoption of well registration requirements has picked up considerably in recent years, as many states have adopted well registration laws for larger wells—e.g., Missouri in 1983 (Mo. Rev. Stat. §§ 256.400(4), 256.410), Wisconsin in 1986 (Wis. Stat. § 281.35(3)), Ohio in 1988 (Ohio Rev. Code Ann. § 1521.16), and Virginia in 1992 (Va. Code Ann. §§ 62.1–260 to 62.1–264). See Joseph W. Dellapenna, The Regulated Riparian Approach to Groundwater, in 3 Waters and Water Rights, § 23.02(a) (Robert Beck ed., repl. vol. 2003).

Most jurisdictions with well registration requirements usually exempt wells they consider "small" and not worth the time and trouble (including the political heat) to gather information about, much less regulate. Typically these are wells for domestic use by individual residences—a rough rule of thumb is that an average family of four or five uses one acre-foot of water (326,000 gallons) per year. But the size cutoff in these statutes may be much larger than that; e.g., Missouri exempts wells pumping under 100,000 gallons *per day*, which if pumped continuously would yield more than 100 acre-feet per year. Mo. Rev. Stat. §§ 256.400(4), 256.410. Louisiana exempts wells pumping 50,000 gallons per day. La. Rev. Stat. Ann. § 38:3094(A)(1). Exempt wells are typically found in rural areas (nearly all rural residents across the country depend upon groundwater for domestic use), because local water utilities usually serve domestic users in urban and suburban areas.[27] In Department of Ecology v. Campbell & Gwinn, 146 Wash.2d 1, 43 P.3d 4 (2002), the Washington Supreme Court upheld a state crackdown on the cumulative use of twenty exempt wells by the developer of "Rambling Brooks Estates," a twenty unit subdivision. The court read the statutory exemp-

25. Cal. Water Code §§ 4999, 5001. See Zachary Smith, Rewriting California Groundwater Law: Past Attempts and Prerequisites to Reform, 20 Cal. West. L. Rev. 223, 239 (1984).

26. See Neb. Rev. Stat. § 46–602A; see also Richard Harnsberger, Nebraska Ground Water Problems, 42 Neb. L. Rev. 721, 733 (1963); J. David Aiken, Nebraska Ground Water Law and Administration, 59 Neb. L. Rev. 917, 949 (1980).

27. According to the National Ground Water Association, about 800,000 boreholes are drilled annually, and approximately for-

ty million Americans are served from over fifteen million private wells. The average household well is drilled to a depth of 217 feet and costs about $3000. Presumably many of these wells are drilled near surface streams where aquifers are likely to be found at shallow depths. Therefore they can pose a direct threat to streamflows. See Robert Glennon & Thomas Maddock, The Concept of Capture: The Hydrology and Law of Stream/Aquifer Interactions, 43 Rocky Mt. Min. L. Inst. 22–1, 22–47 to 22–57 (1997).

tion for wells withdrawing not more than 5000 gallons per day "for single or group domestic uses" to prohibit such cumulation, and rejected arguments by numerous *amici curiae* developers that the result would hobble housing development in the state because the state Department of Ecology, the permitting agency, had insufficient staff to handle the volume of permits required. The court explained that was for the legislature to address.

Well capacity does not necessarily translate into actual use. When actual measurement of groundwater withdrawals becomes important, regulatory bodies or courts adjudicating groundwater disputes may need more information. In some adjudications, power company records have been used to estimate groundwater pumping, even going back decades, because rather accurate calculations of the amount of water pumped can be made based on the depth to groundwater and the amount of electricity consumed. For examples, see Briggs v. Golden Valley Land & Cattle Co., 546 P.2d 382, 386–87 (Idaho 1976); May v. United States, 756 P.2d 362, 366 (Colo. 1988).

Groundwater Modeling

Even if information is available on aquifer size and other characteristics, and on historic and current rates of pumping, it may be difficult to establish the kind of causal relationships between pumping and aquifer water levels necessary to manage the resource intelligently, at least without evidence that may be costly and time-consuming to gather. "[G]round water systems are difficult to observe and describe, not only because they are hidden from view, but also because they are three-dimensional and often very heterogeneous." National Research Council, Groundwater Models: Scientific and Regulatory Applications 219 (1990) (NRC Report). For this reason, groundwater models have been developed as tools to "understand ground water systems and simulate and predict their behavior." Id. at 22. "Modeling can be defined as the art and science of collecting a set of discrete observations (our incomplete knowledge of the real world) and producing predictions of the behavior of a system. Such predictions will be necessarily uncertain, as will be our knowledge of the true behavior of the system." Id. at 216. It could be very difficult to begin to understand very complex hydrogeologic situations without the use of models.

The basic input to the model is whatever information is available about soils, aquifer properties, precipitation and other data relevant to hydrologic system. The subsurface is divided into layers and units which are assigned characteristics reflecting their assumed ability to store and transmit water. Such "inputs are often highly variable in time and/or space. Some may be inherently uncertain." Id. Inputs are usually based on some sort of sampling, which introduces uncertainty because of "(1) its inherent randomness, (2) measurement error, and perhaps most important, (3) limited sampling of the highly variable physical, chemical, and biological properties of ground water systems." NRC Report at 218. Processes at work in the real world, "including those induced by proposed management actions, act on these inputs to yield the true, or real, outputs that characterize the behavior of the system." Id. at 217. "These true outputs are, of course, themselves often variable and uncertain." Id. Despite the variability and uncertainty, information is "critical to the successful use of computerized systems in managing groundwater." Joseph W. Dellapenna, Physical and Social Bases of Quantitative Groundwater Law, 3 Waters and Water Rights § 18.04 (Robert Beck ed., repl. vol. 2003). With all this complexity, one can begin to see why the NRC report called modeling an "art" as well as a "science."

The preface to the NRC report observed that hydrogeologists are "being caught in the middle between some major advances in science and increasing pressure from legal and regulatory bodies to use models to provide answers to specific questions." Id. at vii. It pointed out that the "physical processes controlling the flow of water through fully saturated porous rock or soil are well understood, both theoretically and experimentally," id. at 81, and with the vast increases in affordable computational power made possible by modern computers, significant progress has been made in three-dimensional models. Still, because comprehensive data are lacking, "successful application of ground water flow models rests on the skill and art of the hydrogeologist in understanding when, where, and how to simplify and respond to a lack of information." Id. at 85.[28] In short, while models can be very useful, indeed essential to regulating groundwater use, they are complex and not as transparent as lay people would like. See Michael Sklash, Matthew Schroeder & James Dragun, Groundwater Models: Can You Believe What They Are Saying?, 13 Nat. Res. & Envt. 542 (1999).

As groundwater models are used more and more for regulatory decisions, we may expect more judicial probing of their bases and utility. For an example of competing models involving a controversial proposal to withdraw and export 200,000 acre-feet of groundwater from Colorado's San Luis Valley, see American Water Dev., Inc. v. City of Alamosa, 874 P.2d 352, 367–68 (Colo. 1994); see also Robert Schween & Steven Larson, Groundwater Modeling: Capabilities and Limitations, Use and Abuse, 32 Rocky Mt. Min. L. Inst. 22–1 (1986); Allen Kezsbom & Alan Goldman, The Boundaries of Groundwater Modeling Under the Law: Standards for Excluding Speculative Expert Testimony, 4 Envtl. Claims J. 1 (1991). Modeling played a crucial role in proceedings before special masters to the U.S. Supreme Court to gauge the effect of groundwater pumping on streamflow in two recent disputes involving interstate water compacts. See Kansas v. Nebraska, 538 U.S. 720 (2003), where the Court approved a settlement that, among other things, requires use of a water model to track the interaction between ground and surface water. See Final Report of the Special Master with Certification of the Adoption of

28. See also A.D. Das Gupta, J. Premchitt & S.A. Hussain, Groundwater Basin Response: Simulation with Mathematical Model, 16 Water Int'l 17 (1991); T.E. Reilly & A.W. Harbaugh, Guidelines for Evaluating Ground–Water Flow Models (USGS Scientific Investigations Report #2004–5038, 2004). The American Society for Testing and Materials (ASTM) issued several "Standard Guides" for using groundwater models between 1993 and 1996.

RRCA Groundwater Model (Sept. 17, 2003); see also several reports of the Special Master in Kansas v. Colorado, 533 U.S. 1 (2001). Both cases are briefly discussed in chapter 8, infra p. 851. Admitting evidence of modeling can involve application of the Supreme Court's teaching on the admissibility of scientific evidence in Daubert v. Merrell Dow Pharmaceutical, Inc., 509 U.S. 579 (1993). See Itzchak E. Kornfeld, A Postscript on Groundwater Modelling: Daubert, "Good Grounds," and the Central Role of Cross–Examination, 29 Tort & Ins. L.J. 646 (1994).

C. THE PRINCIPAL DOCTRINES OF GROUNDWATER LAW

1. WHAT IS "LEGAL" GROUNDWATER?

Seemingly to confuse law students, the common law has not only historically distinguished between groundwater and surface water, but early on, it also distinguished between two types of groundwater: (a) that found flowing in" underground streams," and (b) so-called "percolating" groundwater, or that which did not "flow" but rather "oozed" through small interstices like water through coffee grounds. Although common law courts first developed the distinction between underground streams and percolating groundwater (see, e.g., Hale v. McLea, 53 Cal. 578 (1879); Commonwealth v. Sebastian, 345 S.W.2d 46 (Ky. 1961)), a number of legislatures codified it. See generally Joseph W. Dellapenna, Legal Classifications, in 3 Waters and Water Rights § 19.05(a)(3) (Robert Beck ed., repl. vol. 2003).

Some courts have identified a third legal category of underground water—that considered to be the "subflow" of a surface stream. In a refreshing bow to hydrogeological reality, the California Supreme Court took the concept of subflow quite far in Hudson v. Dailey, 156 Cal. 617, 105 P. 748, 753 (1909):

> There will always be great difficulty in fixing a line, beyond which the water in the sands and gravels over which a stream flows, and which supply or uphold the stream, ceases to be a part thereof and becomes what is called "percolating [ground-]water." * * * [In] the case of percolating waters feeding the stream and necessary to its continued flow * * * [t]here is no rational ground for any distinction between such percolating waters and the waters in the gravels immediately beneath and directly supporting the surface flow, and no reason for applying a different rule to the two classes * * * if, indeed, the two classes can be distinguished at all.

The subflow of surface streams and water flowing in underground streams were both generally made subject to the same law that applied to surface water,[29] while a separate groundwater law was developed for

---

29. Some courts held that, "in order to be subject to the law of surface water, the existence, location, and flow of the water must be known to the owner of the land through which it flows, or it must be discoverable from the surface of the earth."

the rest, or "percolating" groundwater. Most states recognized a presumption that groundwater was not in an underground stream. See Joseph W. Dellapenna, Legal Classifications, in 3 Waters and Water Rights, supra. The definitions of subflow and underground stream were not always strictly applied. Either could be regarded as elastic enough to embrace a rather large category of underground water. Where this was the case, drawing a line between the kind of underground water to which surface water law applied (subflow of surface streams and underground streams) and the kind of underground water to which groundwater law applied (percolating groundwater) was not easy. See, e.g., Pima Farms v. Proctor, 30 Ariz. 96, 245 P. 369 (1926), where the groundwater in question was deemed an underground stream to which surface water law applied, even though it splayed to more than a mile in width. See generally John Leshy & James Belanger, Arizona Law Where Ground and Surface Water Meet, 20 Ariz. St. L.J. 657, 674–76 (1988).

For those looking to narrow the division between surface and groundwater law, expanding the concept of subflow of a surface stream is a good way to do it. See Joseph L. Sax, We Don't Do Groundwater: A Morsel of California Legal History, 6 U. Denv.Water L.Rev. 270 (2003). Arizona has had a particularly colorful history of grappling with this issue.[30] But some states define the categories to ignore physical reality; e.g., an Oklahoma statute defines groundwater as water under the surface that is outside the "cut bank of any definite stream," Okla. Stat. T. 82, § 1020.1(1), and treats it as separate from surface water, even if the two are hydrologically connected. See generally Okla Stat. T. 82, ch. 11; see also Kevin Patrick & Kelly Arch, A Comparison of State Groundwater Laws, 30 Tulsa L.J. 123, 125–30 (1994).

A related concept used in some states is that of "tributary groundwater," defined as that which is tributary to a surface stream. As developed in some Western states, it led to a rebuttable presumption that groundwater is tributary, and subject to the same legal management as surface water. See Joseph W. Dellapenna, Legal Classifications, in 3 Waters and Water Rights, § 19.05(a)(4) (Robert Beck ed., repl. vol. 2003). Colorado has refined this concept the most. While the Colorado Supreme Court has held that groundwater taking more than a century to reach a surface stream is *not* tributary, Kuiper v. Lundvall, 187 Colo. 40, 529 P.2d 1328 (1974), groundwater which, if extracted, could affect a stream within forty years *is* tributary. District 10 Water Users Ass'n v. Barnett, 599 P.2d 894 (Colo. 1979). The Colorado legislature followed up these decisions with a 1985 statute that defined nontributary groundwater in much of the state as water, "the withdrawal of which will not, within one hundred years, deplete the flow of a natural stream * * * at an annual rate greater than one-tenth of one percent of the annual rate

Clinchfield Coal Corp. v. Compton, 148 Va. 437, 139 S.E. 308 (1927); see also Jones v. Home Bldg. & Loan, 252 N.C. 626, 114 S.E.2d 638 (1960).

30. See John Leshy & James Belanger, Arizona Law Where Ground and Surface Water Meet, 20 Ariz. St. L.J. 657 (1988); see also infra pp. 463–465.

of withdrawal." Colo. Rev. Stat. § 37–90–103(10.5).[31] For an application of the statute in a hotly contested case, see American Water Dev., Inc. v. City of Alamosa, 874 P.2d 352, 366–70 (Colo. 1994).

Finally, statutes in a number of jurisdictions exempt certain kinds of groundwater from ordinary groundwater law. For example, groundwater pumped from a mine to allow mineral extraction may be exempt from groundwater regulatory schemes—an ironic result considering that the seminal common law groundwater case, *Acton v. Blundell* (supra p. 393), involved mine dewatering. See Albert Utton, The Challenge of Mine Dewatering to Western Water Law and the New Mexico Response, 15 Land & Water L. Rev. 445 (1980). In some modern open-pit mining, staggering amounts of groundwater are extracted; e.g., in the Carlin trend in northern Nevada, several hundred thousand acre-feet of groundwater are pumped each year from mine pits to keep large gold mines in operation. The largest mine, American Barrick's Betze Pit, is being dewatered at a rate of about an acre-foot every eight minutes. Excavation of more than a billion tons of rock in this mining operation will produce a pit nearly 2000 feet deep; once mining ceases, the pit will fill to form the largest lake wholly within Nevada, two-thirds as deep as Lake Tahoe (which is one of the ten deepest in the world). The Nevada State Engineer issues permits for mine dewatering, and requires mines to recharge the groundwater where feasible, but apparently recharge is often considered infeasible. Some of the water pumped out is consumptively used in the mining operations, but much of it is simply discharged to surface water. Thus mine dewatering essentially converts groundwater in the Humboldt Basin to surface water, and leads to evaporative losses from the pit lake surfaces that would not otherwise occur, as well as potential quality problems. Moreover, once the mining ceases, some experts think the Humboldt River is likely to go mostly dry for decades as the aquifer recovers and the pit fills, because the deficit in the aquifer equals up to a quarter of a century's flow in the Humboldt.[32]

A new mineral rush is on in the intermountain west, this time for coalbed methane (CBM), which is natural gas trapped in coal deposits. The first step in its extraction is to pump out water trapped in the

31. Colorado easily wins the prize for the most complex classifications of underground water. Besides tributary groundwater and nontributary groundwater, in 1985 Colorado adopted, for four named aquifers in the populated Front Range area that the legislature found to be of "great economic importance," a separate classification labeled, to the chagrin of English teachers everywhere, "not nontributary groundwater." Colo. Rev. Stat. Ann. § 37–90–103 (10.7). The Colorado Supreme Court has recently explored the complexities of the state's groundwater law in Chatfield East Well Co. v. Chatfield East Property Owners Ass'n, 956 P.2d 1260 (Colo. 1998), and Park County Sportsmen's Ranch LLP v. Bargas,

986 P.2d 262 (Colo. 1999). See also Gregory Hobbs, Colorado Water Law: An Historical Overview, 1 U. Denv. Water L. Rev. 1, 20 (1997).

32. See Robert Glennon, Water Follies, 169–81 (2002); G.C. Miller, W.B. Lyons, & A. Davis, Understanding the Water Quality of Pit Lakes, 30 Envtl. Sci. & Technology News 118 (1996). For more on mining and groundwater, see two reports by the National Research Council, Surface Coal Mining Effects on Ground Water Recharge (1990); and Hardrock Mining on Federal Lands (1999). See also Kirk Johnson, "Drier, Tainted Nevada May Be Legacy of Gold Rush," New York Times, Dec. 30, 2005.

coalbeds. Large quantities of water may be involved; about 75,000 acre-feet per year in Wyoming alone, according to one estimate. Disposing of this groundwater once brought to the surface has become a controversial issue in several parts of the region, especially in Wyoming, Montana, Colorado and New Mexico. Depending on state law, there may be a question whether this water should be legally classified as water subject to state water authorities, or instead as "exploration and production waste" subject to control by state oil and gas regulatory authorities. A recently filed lawsuit in Colorado argues that groundwater production in CBM extraction should be regulated under state water law. Ranchers: Gas Drilling, Water Don't Mix, Durango Herald, Dec. 2, 2005. Another question now being argued in Wyoming state courts is whether water removed in the extraction process can be added to surface streams over the objection of downstream landowners; that is, whether it enjoys the same public easement as "waters of the state" when it is discharged into a natural watercourse. Billings Gazette, Sept. 21, 2005. One major CBM producer is spending $50 million to reinject the water back into the ground. Casper Star–Tribune, Oct. 2, 2005. See generally Thomas F. Darin, Waste or Wasted?—Rethinking the Regulation of Coalbed Methane Byproduct Water in the Rocky Mountains: A Comparative Analysis of Approaches, 17 J. Envtl. L. & Litig. 281 (2002).[33]

2. A HYPOTHETICAL GROUNDWATER DISPUTE

The Very Small Basin Aquifer (VSBA) is an imaginary unconfined aquifer with unrealistically tidy characteristics lying under 100 acres of land. It has the capacity to store 1000 acre-feet of water. It receives annual recharge (infiltration of "new" water) from a distant source at the rate of 200 acre-feet per year (assume any excess water drains away and is lost in the bowels of the earth). The bottom of the aquifer lies 1000 feet below the earth's surface, and the top of the aquifer is just below the root zone of the plants. The aquifer is uniform in all of its characteristics and water moves freely within it. Thus, if a single well was dug to the bottom of the aquifer, it could withdraw all 1000 acre-feet of water stored there; if that single well was dug to a depth of 500 feet, it could withdraw only 500 acre-feet of water because the rest of the water stored in the aquifer would be below the bottom of the well.

The VSBA is the only source of water to the three people who own land over the aquifer: Patricia Prior Pumper (P) owns 50 acres, and Owen Overlying Owner (O) and Erwin Enterprising Exporter (E) each own 25 acres. P has been irrigating her parcel for the last three years. She has dug a well to a depth of 400 feet and withdraws 400 acre-feet of water per year for growing cotton on her land, of which 200 acre-feet are consumed and the other 200 acre-feet seeps back into the ground and recharges the aquifer. P's use maintains the water stored in the aquifer

---

33. Yet another category of groundwater often exempted from regulation as groundwater is water so hot in the ground that it has value as a geothermal resource. See, e.g., Laura MacGregor Bettis, In Hot Water: Can Idaho's Ground Water Laws Adequately Govern Low Temperature Geothermal Resources?, 30 Idaho L.Rev. 113 (2002) (discussing the law in the western states).

in equilibrium: her withdrawals of 400 acre-feet per year are exactly balanced by the additions to the aquifer (200 acre-feet of seepage from P's use and 200 acre-feet of annual recharge from a distant source).

Historically, neither O nor E have withdrawn any water from the VSBA. In the current year O begins operation of a dude ranch and aquatic park on his 25 acres that will require 200 acre-feet per year in groundwater withdrawals from the VSBA, all of which will be consumed by evaporation. Also in the current year, E enters into a long term contract with Electricity Producers, Inc.(EPI), to supply water to cool EPI's power plant a few miles away, to be supplied through a pipeline from the well on E's land. The amount of water to be supplied depends on EPI's needs, which could be as little as 200 or as much as 500 acre-feet in any given year. Both O and E dig their wells to a depth of 1000 feet and begin pumping.

Soon after O and E begin operations, the water level in the aquifer drops below P's well and it fails. She brings suit against O and E. The outcome will depend on the legal rule that applies to such cases. The following summarizes the possibilities in American jurisdictions.

Rule of Capture. This doctrine—sometimes called the "English rule," "absolute dominion" or, misleadingly, "absolute ownership"—is more of a rule of non-liability in tort than a rule of property ownership. In the hypothetical it gives no legal protection to anyone. P has no legal remedy under this rule even though the withdrawals of O and E have caused the water level in the aquifer to fall below the bottom of P's well. Her only practical remedy is to deepen her well to pump from the bottom of the aquifer. Even then, within approximately two years (depending upon the amount of E's withdrawal), the combined withdrawals of the three competing pumpers (P=400, O=200, E=200–500) will totally exhaust the water stored in the aquifer. This would leave the three to compete for the 200 acre-feet of water being recharged into the aquifer each year, plus whatever seeps back from P's use on her land.

American Reasonable Use. This is a modified rule of capture, adding two wrinkles: The water must be (a) put to a reasonable use, (b) on the overlying tract. Applying the "appurtenancy" or on-tract limitation, P may obtain an injunction against E's pumping of groundwater for export. Assuming O's end use qualifies as reasonable, however, it is fully protected by the law. Thus, P (400) and O (200) will compete to pump the available water. On the facts as given, 600 is pumped and 400 recharges (200 from a distant source and 200 from P's irrigation), so the water level in the aquifer declines by 200 acre-feet per year. The water table will quickly fall below the bottom hole of P's well. Unless P deepens her well, she will get no water; if that happens, O will pump 200 acre-feet per year and the water level in the aquifer will remain constant because the amount of recharge equals O's withdrawals. Should P deepen her well, she and O will deplete the remaining water in the aquifer at the rate of 200 acre-feet per year, and end up in a two-way competition for the 200 acre-feet per year of recharge plus whatever seeps back from P's use on her land.

Correlative Rights. This doctrine can be described as "riparianism on its side." It generally requires a sharing of the available water on an equitable basis among overlying landowners who are using (or seek to use) water on their overlying tracts. (This doctrine can overlap to a substantial extent with the previous doctrine, depending on how "reasonable use" is determined under it.) Off-tract uses are subordinate and are legally protected only in the event "surplus" water is available; that is, if recharge is in excess of current withdrawals. (If surplus water is available, prior appropriation is applied to allocate water among off-tract users.) In this problem, the on-tract uses of P (400) and O (200) exceed the amount of recharge (400) and if not limited will deplete the aquifer. Because there is no "surplus" water available, E's off-tract uses will be enjoined. P and O will share the available water (the safe annual yield of 200 acre-feet of water plus whatever seeps into the aquifer from P's use) so that each receives "a fair and just proportion."[34] To the extent the apportionment is on the basis of overlying land ownership, P would receive 2/3's and O 1/3 of the available water. The court might give P 200 (100 of which would recharge) and O 100. Although E could not export water on these facts, he is not barred from commencing an on-tract use in the future. If E could, for example, persuade EPI to locate its power plant on E's land and serve it with groundwater, a new apportionment of the available supply among P, O, and E would be required.

Restatement (Second) of Torts Reasonable Use. The Restatement (Second) of Torts contains a section on groundwater which operates as a rule of allocation, even though it is stated as a liability rule. Section 858 (see infra p. 435) holds a groundwater extractor liable for unreasonable harm to others that occurs by lowering the water table or withdrawing water in excess of a reasonable share of the annual supply or total store of groundwater. It identifies several factors (the same ones that apply to reasonable use riparianism in surface water) to be considered to evaluate the reasonableness of uses in competition with one another. The Restatement approach is not purely "riparianism turned on its side," because it does not draw a strong distinction between use on and off the overlying land. On the facts here, all of the uses appear to be of value, with none of a more essential character than the others. (A domestic or municipal water supply use might be favored.) All three of the users are seeking rights to a disproportionate share and should expect to be scaled back. As a matter of proportion, P, as owner of 50% of the overlying land, has a plausible basis for claiming that she should be awarded half of the available water, with O and E having claims on that basis to share the other half equally. While a court might be influenced by the highly consumptive nature (and seeming profligacy) of O's use, or by the high water duty (8 acre-feet per acre) of P's farm, a

34. The quoted phrase appears in the seminal California case of Katz v. Walkinshaw, 141 Cal. 116, 74 P. 766 (1903), infra p. 429.

decree awarding 100 acre-feet to P, and 50 each to O and E would not be surprising.

Prior Appropriation. P is first in time and therefore first in right. She has the right to pump 400 acre-feet of water per year for use on her farm before either O or E receive any water from the aquifer on a continuing basis. Under a strict application of the priority system, O and E will be enjoined from any pumping at all, because it would interfere with P's right to obtain her full senior appropriative right. This would mean P effectively controls all the water in the aquifer, including the 600 acre-feet she is not using, because any additional withdrawals will interfere with her ability to obtain her full water right. Under a less strict application, O and/or E might be given an appropriation, with P being held to a duty to deepen her well to the bottom of the aquifer. This would make the remaining 600 acre-feet available for use by O and/or E, at least temporarily, until the aquifer is exhausted.

3. THE FIVE DOCTRINES OF GROUNDWATER LAW REVISIT-ED IN DETAIL

For a number of reasons, it is difficult to compile an accurate list identifying which states adhere to which particular groundwater doctrine. Some state courts have revisited groundwater law so rarely, and so haphazardly, that it is not easy to predict exactly what doctrine or variant thereof will be followed in the next case. Some courts have blurred the distinction between the American reasonable use and correlative rights doctrines. More important, legislative and administrative overlays in many states now make it hard to ascertain how much of the common law has survived and how much of it has been superseded. Furthermore, some states have adopted different rules in different geographic locations in the state, either directly or through the creation of local or regional special governmental districts with authority over groundwater. California, for example, has some of the most progressive groundwater management in the country in its southern coastal plain, but almost a complete lack of regulation in its vast Central Valley.

With that strong caveat, here's an attempt at generalizing: The rule of capture survives in very few jurisdictions. Most of the more humid states have moved to some variation of the American reasonable use rule. A number of states have adopted some variation of the correlative rights doctrine invented in California. Most western states apply prior appropriation to groundwater. The Restatement approach has made little headway, being adopted in only a handful of jurisdictions. Regardless of what common law doctrine they follow, states are increasingly adopting management devices, such as permit systems, that may modify the common law. Many of these may apply only in specific geographic areas rather than state-wide.

a. *Capture*

Remarkably, this doctrine has not yet been consigned to the dustbin of history. Most notably, the Texas Supreme Court not long ago reaffirmed its continued viability in the Lone Star State. See Sipriano v. Great Spring Waters of America, 1 S.W.3d 75 (Tex. 1999). The case arose when the defendant began pumping large amounts of groundwater in 1996 and dried up neighboring wells, whose owners sued. The court in *Sipriano* noted that it first adopted the rule of capture in 1904, when it

> faced a choice between the rule of capture and its counterpart, the rule of reasonable use. No constitutional or statutory considerations guided or constrained our selection at that time. Articulating two public-policy reasons, we chose the rule of capture. First, we noted that the movement of groundwater is "so secret, occult, and concealed that an attempt to administer any set of legal rules in respect to [it] would be involved in hopeless uncertainty, and would, therefore, be practically impossible." And second, we determined that "any * * * recognition of correlative rights would interfere, to the material detriment of the commonwealth, with drainage and agriculture, mining, the construction of highways and railroads, with sanitary regulations, building, and the general progress of improvement in works of embellishment and utility."

In the wake of droughts the Texas Constitution was amended in 1917 to make the "conservation," "development," and "preservation" of all of the State's natural resources, including water, the responsibility of the legislature. Subsequent Texas Supreme Court decisions generally adhered to the rule of capture, while observing that some aspects of it were "harsh and outmoded." On one occasion the court upheld legislative modification of the common law rule for a single important aquifer. In adhering to capture as the common law standard, the *Sipriano* court emphasized that the Texas legislature in 1997 had enacted Senate Bill 1, which, among other things, sought to "streamline the process" for creating "locally-controlled" groundwater conservation districts and giving them authority for "establishing requirements for groundwater withdrawal permits and for regulating water transferred outside the district." The legislation also required the Texas Natural Resource Conservation Commission (TNRCC) and the Texas Water Development Board to "identify areas anticipated to experience critical groundwater problems, and streamlined the process by which the TNRCC or the Legislature can create a district in these areas." Even though it acknowledged that the plaintiffs had presented "compelling reasons for groundwater use to be regulated," the court found that the Legislature had

> chosen a process that permits the people most affected by groundwater regulation in particular areas to participate in democratic solutions to their groundwater issues. It would be improper for courts to intercede at this time by changing the common-law framework within which the Legislature has attempted to craft regulations to meet this state's groundwater-conservation needs. Given the Legislature's recent actions to improve Texas's groundwater management, we are reluctant to make so drastic a change as abandoning our rule of capture and

moving into the arena of water-use regulation by judicial fiat. It is more prudent to wait and see if Senate Bill 1 will have its desired effect, and to save for another day the determination of whether further revising the common law is an appropriate prerequisite to preserve Texas's natural resources and protect property owners' interests.

Two Justices concurred in the result, but provided a harsher assessment of groundwater management in Texas. They noted that a half-century after the Legislature first authorized the creation of groundwater conservation districts, only a small fraction of the state was covered by such districts. As they tersely put it, "[n]ot much groundwater management is going on," even though more than half of all water used in the state (include more than two-thirds of farm use and 41% of municipal use) was groundwater. The concurring Justices also noted that for decades there had been calls for comprehensive regulation amidst warnings of "severe, impending problems" with groundwater use, "which predicted problems have in fact occurred." Resistance to regulation was fueled, in their view, by the common law rule of capture, even though the reasons for "[t]he extensive regulation of oil and gas production proves that effective regulation of migrant substances far below the surface is not only possible but necessary and effective. In the past several decades it has become clear, if it was not before, that it is not regulation that threatens progress, but the lack of it." The concurring Justices found the approach of section 858 of the Restatement (Second) of Torts, infra p. 435, preferable to the rule of capture, but rather reluctantly concluded, "for now," that "it would be inappropriate to disrupt the processes created and encouraged by the 1997 legislation before they have had a chance to work."

Notes and Questions

1. Suppose General Utilities Corp. pumps 10,000 acre-feet of water from a quarter-acre parcel of land it owns and pipes it to cool a nuclear power plant several miles away, and its pumping dries up all the domestic wells in the neighborhood. Does it have any liability under Texas common law? Suppose Hatfield sinks a well on her land and starts to extract groundwater simply to dry up her neighbor McCoy's well. Is she liable in Texas? There is authority protecting even spiteful pumping, Huber v. Merkel, 94 N.W. 354 (Wis. 1903), but the following year the Indiana Supreme Court refused to take the English rule that far, and enjoined malicious pumping. Gagnon v. French Lick Springs Hotel Co., 72 N.E. 849 (1904).

2. Note the two reasons the Texas Supreme Court gave in its 1904 decision for adopting the rule of capture. Regarding the first reason, a Pennsylvania court said in an early decision that users of groundwater should not be held responsible for some effect of which they "cannot by any possibility have notice." Wheatley v. Baugh, 25 Pa. 528, 534 (1855). Some courts drew the analogy to capturing a wild animal under the doctrine of *ferae naturae*. Westmoreland & Cambria Natural Gas Co. v. De Witt, 130 Pa. 235, 18 A. 724 (1889).

3. The second reason is that economic development would be hampered by any notion of "correlative rights," which could arguably increase costs to new users of groundwater. But what effect does a rule of capture have on investment in activities dependent upon groundwater extraction? Great Spring Waters, the defendant and later investor, is protected here, but is he protected against a still later investor (such as General Utilities in Note 1) who may sink a deeper well or install a more powerful pump?

4. Is it consistent for jurisdictions that apply the riparian doctrine to surface waters (based on the notion that the waters are a common pool resource) to apply a rule of capture to groundwater?

5. Though some call this doctrine "absolute ownership," is it really about ownership? Does it vest landowners with any legally protected property interest in groundwater? Does it give a groundwater pumper any right to exclude any other landowner from use of the aquifer? The Massachusetts Supreme Judicial Court put it this way in Greenleaf v. Francis, 35 Mass. (18 Pick.) 117, 121 (1836) (seven years before the English court handed down the more famous Acton v. Blundell): "Every one has the liberty of doing in his own ground whatsoever he pleases, even although it should occasion his neighbor some other sort of inconvenience." Compare Thomas W. Merrill, Property and the Right to Exclude, 77 Neb. L.Rev. 730, 730 (1998) ("Give someone the right to exclude others from a valued resource * * * and you give them property. Deny someone the exclusion right and they do not have property."); Corwin W. Johnson, The Continuing Voids in Texas Groundwater Law: Are Concepts and Terminology to Blame?, 17 St. Mary's Law J. 1281, 1288–89 (1986) (pointing out that while the term "absolute ownership" may "conjure up * * * the notion that groundwater ownership in Texas is a super-right subject to no limitations whatever, even legislative control," in Texas the term has been used to mean basically that a "landowner is entitled to no judicial protection from harmful pumping by others" and thus his "ownership" "lacks one of the most significant aspects of ownership"). Thus one might say the label "absolute ownership" resembles the Holy Roman Empire in Voltaire's quip—being neither holy, nor Roman, nor an empire. Columbia World of Quotations #630003 (1996). Still, the claim of property rights is a huge political obstacle to sound management of groundwater because, as Professor Thompson has noted, property claims "reinforce a sense of entitlement to an unlimited harvest" and allow those with such claims to "convert property rights from practical tools into absolute moral rights that prevent them from thinking carefully about the potential benefits of averting the tragedy [of the commons]." Barton H. Thompson, Jr., Tragically Difficult: The Obstacles to Governing the Commons, 30 Envtl. L. 241, 257 (2000).

6. Another way to think about "ownership" under this doctrine is that it does not connote ownership of groundwater in place, but rather attaches ownership only to the molecules of water brought to the surface. Thus, extracting groundwater does not establish any right in the groundwater *in situ*, in the same way that capture of one wild deer does not give the capturer any right in the remaining wild deer in the herd. See Note 6 p. 453 infra. This means that any "ownership" involved in a rule of capture is not an application of the idea that the owner of the soil owns everything above it to the heavens and below it to the center of the earth (the Latin maxim is

"cujus est solum, ejus est usque ad coelum et ad inferos"). Looked at in this way, do considerations of property rights limit the Texas legislature in enacting new laws that may restrict or even prohibit the ability of Texas landowners to pump groundwater? Limit the right of Texas groundwater conservation districts in deciding whether to grant landowners permits for new wells? See John D. Leshy, A Conversation About Takings and Water Rights, 83 Tex.L.Rev. 1985, 1986–91 (2005).

7. The Texas General Land Office has been considering selling groundwater underneath its millions of acres of state lands, creating consternation among nearby landowners. See Ralph Blumenthal, West Texans Sizzle Over a Plan to Sell Their Water, New York Times, Dec. 11, 2003, at A22. For a description of recent legislative activity in Texas, see Joseph W. Dellapenna, The Absolute Dominion Rule, in 3 Waters and Water Rights § 20.07(a)(2)(B) (Robert Beck ed., repl. vol. 2003). The Maine Supreme Court reaffirmed its capture rule the same year as Texas. Maddocks v. Giles, 728 A.2d 150 (Me. 1999). Prof. Dellapenna reports that Indiana also still follows the rule, and perhaps Massachusetts and Rhode Island. 3 Waters and Water Rights, supra, at § 20.07.

8. *Sipriano* rehearses the age-old debate about when courts should defer to the legislatures in modifying or abolishing common law rules that are admittedly no longer suited to the times. Why does the Texas Supreme Court cling to this doctrine while admitting there are "compelling reasons for groundwater use to be regulated"? What is wrong with changing a common law rule, which is created by judicial fiat, by judicial fiat? As the court acknowledged, advances in the science of hydrogeology and a reluctance to immunize actions that cause serious injury to others have combined to send the absolute ownership doctrine toward extinction. See, e.g., Earl Murphy, The Recurring State Judicial Task of Choosing Rules for Groundwater: How Occult Still?, 66 Neb. L. Rev. 120, 124–31 (1987).

A Digression on Oil and Water

As we saw in the discussion of hydrogeology near the beginning of this Chapter, the interstices of the sand, gravel, and other solid materials that make up the earth are filled with water, oil or gas. This commonality between groundwater and the other mobile subterranean natural resources suggests, as noted by the concurring justices in *Sipriano*, that the legal systems applied to oil and gas might hold useful comparisons for groundwater. Admittedly, the analogy between oil and gas on the one hand and water on the other is not perfect. Groundwater supplies may be replenished on a time scale useful for human planning, while oil and gas cannot. Furthermore, unlike petroleum, groundwater is often connected to surface water, and thus groundwater extractions can have relatively direct impact on surface water uses and flows, and associated environmental impacts. But there are enough common features, in physical occurrence and character and in treatment in the law, to warrant a brief examination.[35]

35. An interesting comparison is between the volume of oil and groundwater used. In 2004 the United States consumed somewhat more than 20 million barrels of

Oil and gas were extracted in large quantities before groundwater extraction became well-established, and the legal system that applied to oil and gas development preceded, for the most part, the development of significant groundwater extraction law. In California's pioneering correlative rights case, Katz v. Walkinshaw, infra p. 429, Justice Shaw rejected the argument that groundwater law had to be consistent with oil and gas law because, he said, petroleum "is not extracted for use in agriculture, or upon the land from which it is taken, but solely for sale as an article of merchandise, and for use in commerce and manufactures." 74 P. at 772–73. Is this persuasive? Can't it be argued that water is or can be just a marketable commodity like oil?

Originally, a capture rule was generally applied to petroleum. See 1 Williams & Meyers, Oil and Gas Law § 204.4, at 54–59 (Patrick Martin & Bruce Kramer eds., 1997). Not long after the petroleum age dawned, this doctrine, by vesting rights to extract common pool subsurface oil in a multiplicity of landowners, began to collide with sound management principles. Among other things, it led to proliferating numbers of wells, each producing full tilt, a situation which could rapidly deplete underground pressure and lead to premature exhaustion of a field. The solution was to "unitize" oil and gas fields, to bring the resource under unitary management. In order to do this, an oil field had to be apportioned among the multiple owners of the resource, under judicial or administrative supervision. This idea initially encountered much resistance in the free-wheeling industry, and its advocates were "widely attacked, and indeed, savagely abused." See Daniel Yergin, The Prize 221 (1991). With the Great Depression, the development of the giant East Texas oil field in 1930, and a collapse of oil prices, systems of "forced-pooling" or compulsory unitization arrangements were adopted in most states. After much litigation, the industry eventually acquiesced. Id. at 223–28, 248–59; see generally Jacqueline Weaver, Unitization of Oil and Gas Fields in Texas (1986). The courts generally upheld these restrictions. The rationale of the U.S. Supreme Court in one of the earliest cases was that the regulation of oil and gas extraction provided better protection for all of the overlying land owners than a simple rule of capture. See, e.g., Ohio Oil Co. v. Indiana, 177 U.S. 190 (1900); cf. Euclid v. Ambler Realty Co., 272 U.S. 365 (1926) (using a similar rationale that zoning restrictions on land use benefits all property owners in a community).

Judge Richard Posner, in Law, Pragmatism and Democracy 246–47 (2003), used the oil and gas context to explore what a judge should do in deciding whether to apply the common law capture rule to a common pool resource like oil and gas (or groundwater). A "legal positivist," he suggested, "would be likely to start with the cases on property rights in wild animals and ask whether oil and gas are enough like wild animals to

oil per day, or about 7.3 billion barrels over the year. At 42 gallons per barrel, that is approximately 307 billion gallons, or about 940,000 acre-feet of oil. Currently, about 93 million acre-feet of groundwater, or about one hundred times the volume of oil consumed, is extracted annually in the United States.

justify the same legal treatment." The "pragmatic judge,"on the other hand, would be more inclined to use the "teachings of natural-resources economists and oil and gas engineers," which would show that the capture rule will usually "lead to too rapid exploitation" because "each landowner will have an incentive to pump as much and as fast as he can, whereas optimal exploitation of the field as a whole might dictate fewer wells and more gradual extraction." Posner concedes that the "plodding positivist" would "promote stability in law, a genuine public good," and the legislature is available to correct mistakes. But he suggests that "American legislatures, in contrast to European parliaments, are so sluggish when it comes to correcting judicial mistakes that a heavy burden of legal creativity falls inescapably on the shoulders of judges[, who cannot] bear the burden unless they are pragmatists."

Groundwater conservation measures "often were borrowed from the law of oil and gas." Joseph W. Dellapenna, Legal Classifications, in 3 Waters and Water Rights § 19.05(b)(3) (Robert Beck ed., repl. vol. 2003). Well spacing is a common regulatory technique developed in oil and gas fields and increasingly common in groundwater, to prevent or mitigate problems of well interference discussed further below. Id. See also Robert McClesney, Maybe Oil and Water Should Mix—At Least in Texas Law: An Analysis of Current Problems with Texas Ground Water Law and How Established Oil and Gas Law Could Provide Appropriate Solutions, 1 Tex. Wesleyan L. Rev. 207 (1994); see also Judge Stephen Williams' article criticizing the beneficial use requirement, supra p. 302.

b.   *The American Reasonable Use Rule*

MARTIN v. CITY OF LINDEN

Supreme Court of Alabama, 1995.
667 So.2d 732.

MADDOX, JUSTICE

[This is] * * * a dispute between a municipality and a landowner over the reasonable use of a common aquifer, or bed of groundwater, that lies beneath the property of both. The specific question is whether the City of Linden can drill a permanent well on a one-acre tract of land it owns outside its municipal limits, and pump the water by pipeline at an estimated rate of 700 gallons per minute or 500,000 gallons [eds. about 1.6 acre-feet] per day to the City. * * *

The City of Linden's water supply is contaminated with saltwater and is unfit for consumption. The City presently purchases the water it furnishes to its citizens from the City of Uniontown. In 1983, the City purchased a one-acre tract of land next to Judy Martin's farm. The City's sole purpose in purchasing the land was to drill a deep-water well from which it would extract water for use by its residents; the water would be carried 15 miles by pipeline to the city and would be used for any and all purposes, including resale. * * *

Judy Martin contends that the City's withdrawal of water from the proposed well will deplete or irreparably damage the water table beneath her farm. She sought to enjoin the drilling of the well, and she appeals from a summary judgment in favor of the City that denied her relief.

* * * We must now turn our attention to the trial court's holding that Mrs. Martin's action was premature, and that she must wait until the permanent well has been drilled and she can show that she has suffered actual damage before requesting injunctive relief. * * * Mrs. Martin asserts, and we agree, that she has the right to bring this action under Ala. Code 1975, § 6–5–210, which reads: "The owner of realty having title downwards and upwards indefinitely, any unlawful interference with his rights, below or above the surface alike, gives him a right of action." Also, Mrs. Martin contends, and we agree, that waiting until a permanent well has been drilled and a pipeline constructed at great expense to the City could substantially affect her chances of prevailing in a later action. The law states that where a public use of water has been developed at great expense, landowners whose rights are adversely affected are not entitled to an injunction if, with knowledge of the development, they stood by without objection. See Barton v. Riverside Water Co., 155 Cal. 509, 101 P. 790 (1909).

Several other reasons justify bringing the action at the present time. The proposed permanent well and pipeline will be an expensive undertaking, and this matter should be addressed before citizens' money is expended. This Court has noted the contentions of the parties regarding the potential "drawdown effect" to Mrs. Martin's well as a result of the City's well, i.e., a potential lowering of the water table, forcing Mrs. Martin to drill a deeper well than the one she now has. We agree with the City that this potential harm is not sufficient to warrant the issuance of an injunction, because the appellant has an adequate remedy at law, and the City has offered to pay for any damage or new equipment and drilling needed by the plaintiff.

However, more significantly, Mrs. Martin offered expert testimony concerning more serious potential damage to both her land and her water supply if the City is allowed to continue to drill its well. * * * This testimony concerns the prevalence of saltwater contamination throughout much of the aquifers in Marengo County, which is one of the reasons the City needs a supply of freshwater. Very little is known about the location of the saltwater contamination front and its proximity to Mrs. Martin's well in the freshwater aquifer at issue here. A hydrologist * * * testified that the large amount of freshwater drawn daily by this proposed well could cause the saltwater contamination front to move further into the freshwater of the aquifer; if this happened, it would be irreversible and would cause the freshwater aquifer to become more mineralized and eventually to be ruined for human consumption. This in turn could leave Mrs. Martin with no freshwater for either domestic or agricultural use upon her farmlands, effectively destroying much of the value of the land. Taken one step further, if the City continued to use the well, eventually the water supply could be ruined for the City as well, and one of the few sources for freshwater in the area would be destroyed. The City argues that the possibility of saltwater contamination of the freshwater aquifers in the area of Mrs. Martin's well is simply that, a possibility, and that it has offered expert testimony that any potential drawdown effect on the aquifers would be so small as to preclude saltwater contamination.

Viewed in a light most favorable to Mrs. Martin, the evidence shows that the potential contamination to Mrs. Martin's water supply would constitute an irreparable injury for which there would be no adequate remedy at law. * * *

* * * Both Mrs. Martin and the City concede that the rule of reasonable use applies in this case. * * * [In] Henderson v. Wade Sand & Gravel Co., 388 So. 2d 900 (Ala. 1980), * * * this Court overruled [earlier decisions and replaced] the "English Rule" of capture, pursuant to which a landowner could take as much water as the landowner wanted from the land with no thought of the consequences to others, * * * [with] the "American Rule" of "reasonable use." This Court stated:

> "[R]easonable" was used in a very special or restricted sense. A waste of water or a wasteful use of water was unreasonable only if it caused harm, and any nonwasteful use of water that caused harm was nevertheless reasonable if it was made on or in connection with the overlying land. * * * The American rule came into being with the invention of the high capacity pump, when cities bought land or easements for well fields in the county and lowered the water table beyond the reach of the domestic wells of neighboring farmers. The rule forced the cities to pay damages to the farmers or provide them with better wells and pumps and was an application of the common tort policies of distributing losses and of requiring those who receive the benefits of a harmful activity to pay its costs.

Henderson, 388 So. 2d 900, 902 (1980). This Court in *Henderson* found that the quarry owner's diversion of the groundwater, incidental to the use of the owner's land, interfered with the plaintiff's use to such an extent that a balance needed to be struck and that the rules of liability under the laws of nuisance applied. This ruling changed the controlling legal theory in land subsidence cases from a traditional negligence theory to a nuisance theory in the context of property damage caused by a continuing activity involving the use of underground water. See Harper v. Regency Development Co., 399 So. 2d 248, 253 (Ala. 1981).

The American "reasonable use" rule was formally adopted by this Court in Adams v. Lang, 553 So. 2d 89 (Ala. 1989), as controlling in cases involving disputes over underground water. In *Adams*, this Court affirmed a summary judgment in favor of the defendant, whose use of the water under his land (to fill his commercial catfish ponds) was held to be reasonable, even though this use periodically caused his neighbor's wells to run dry. This Court distinguished *Adams* from *Henderson*, noting that *Henderson* concerned the interference with a plaintiff's use (for consumption or subterranean support) of groundwater by a defendant's diversion of that water incidental to use of his own land, whereas *Adams* concerned itself with a beneficial use of the water to the land from which it was withdrawn.

Adams dealt with the use of water beneficial to the land from which it was taken, and did not address the issue presented in this case— whether one landowner, here a municipality, can pump water from a common bed of groundwater beneath its property for use off that property if the adjoining landowners are injured or damaged.

Because the precise issue presented in this case is one of first impression in Alabama, we have reviewed the case law of other jurisdictions. Other states faced with this particular fact situation agree with this Court's conclusion. As the Supreme Court of Pennsylvania stated in the case of Rothrauff v. Sinking Spring Water Co., 339 Pa. 129, 14 A.2d 87 (1940):

> [T]he marked tendency in American jurisdictions in later years has been away from the doctrine that the owner's right to sub-surface waters is unqualified; on the contrary there has been an ever-increasing acceptance of the viewpoint that their use must be limited to purposes incident to the beneficial enjoyment of the land from which they are obtained, and if their diversion or sale to others away from the land impairs the supply of a spring or well on the property of another, such use is not for a "lawful purpose" within the general rule concerning percolating waters, but constitutes an actionable wrong for which damages are recoverable. While there is some difference of opinion as to what should be regarded as reasonable use of such waters, the modern decisions are fairly harmonious in holding that a property may not concentrate such waters and convey them off his land if the springs or wells of another are impaired.

* * * We also note that there are cases in other jurisdictions that hold to the contrary. However, these cases differ materially from the instant case in the facts and the applicable laws. In some cases, the land containing the water at issue was being condemned or annexed by the municipality or district, or the water was upon land previously owned by the city or corporation, making it first in time and right as to possession of the land. Still others dealt with disputes over water rights granted by statute and administered by state agencies. * * *

The City contends that it is seeking a safe water supply for its citizens, that it has complied with all the statutory requirements for the drilling of the permanent well, and that the injury to Mrs. Martin if the well is drilled must be weighed against any injury to the public if it is not. This Court is very aware that the City is attempting to find a permanent source of freshwater, but we do not believe that, in supplying their subscribers with water, municipalities enjoy greater rights than do private individuals or corporations, and in such instances municipalities stand upon the same footing as do private corporations. * * * Therefore, the reasonable use rule must apply. As the Supreme Court of Oklahoma stated in Canada v. City of Shawnee, 179 Okla. 53, 64 P.2d 694 (1936):

> There is no apparent reason for saying that, because the defendant is a municipal corporation, seeking water for the inhabitants of the city, it may do what a private owner of the land may not do. The city is a private owner of this land; and the furnishing of water to its inhabitants is a private business. It is imperative that the people of the city have water; it is not imperative that they secure it at the expense of those owning lands adjoining lands owned by the city * * *. The inhabitants of a city must have water, but by our statutes and our Constitution the city is afforded a means of obtaining it without pauperizing those innocent private citizens who have devoted their lifetimes to improving, developing, and maintaining their homesteads.

City of Shawnee, 64 P.2d at 695, 698–700.

In regard to the City's assertion that the plaintiff is asking this Court to usurp the rights of the legislature, we note that Alabama does not have an agency devoted to the conservation and management of its water resources. In the absence of statutory authority, disputes like this one must be decided by the courts, applying common law and equitable principles. The City asserts that it has statutory authority under Ala. Code 1975, § 11–50–5 and § 11–50–235(a)(4), to purchase this property outside its corporate limits for the purposes stated, but that statutory authority in no way exempts the City from the rule of reasonable use.

We also note that the City of Linden is currently purchasing an adequate and healthy supply of water from the City of Uniontown, and that the equities of this case do not compel us to uphold the summary judgment in its favor.

Based on the foregoing, we reverse the judgment of the trial court and remand the cause to that court for further proceedings consistent with this opinion.

Notes and Questions

1. The reasonable use rule was apparently first adopted in New Hampshire in 1862. Around the turn of the century several other jurisdictions followed suit, including Iowa (1894), West Virginia (1905), Kentucky (1908), and Michigan (1915). By the 1930s, the reasonable use rule had become the plurality rule and was often called the "American" rule. Some western states which had embraced it (e.g., Washington in 1892 and Idaho in 1915) later changed to prior appropriation. See Joseph W. Dellapenna, The Reasonable Use Rule, in 3 Waters and Water Rights § 22.03, at 22–12 n.54 (Robert Beck ed., repl. vol. 2003).

2. Is the adjective "reasonable" an accurate description of how the rule operated in *Martin*? What kind of "reasonableness" did the court examine? The respective kinds of uses of the parties? Or something else? Would the

residents of Linden concede that the result in this case is reasonable? Note that the City has "offered to pay [Mrs. Martin] for any damage or new equipment and drilling needed" if the City's pumping draws down the water table. Why isn't this enough to make its proposed use reasonable under the American reasonable use doctrine? Is the doctrine simply one of appurtenancy of use, or does it involve some weighing of relative reasonableness of uses like surface water riparian rights? To the extent the main feature of the doctrine is appurtenancy of use, does it operate the same as the rule of capture as applied to competing on-land uses from the same aquifer? In Brady v. Abbott Laboratories, 433 F.3d 679 (9th Cir. 2005), the 9th Circuit, applying Arizona law in a diversity case, reversed a trial court award of $618,000 in compensatory and a like amount in punitive damages to the Bradys, pecan farmers. Abbott Labs had pumped 122 AF of groundwater to dewater the site where it was constructing a large underground storage structure under its manufacturing plant. The pumping reduced the groundwater table under plaintiffs' nearby land, killing their pecan trees. Plaintiff relied exclusively on Arizona's common law doctrine of reasonable use. The court found that Abbott was withdrawing the water in connection with improving its own land, and Arizona law does not require the withdrawn water actually to be "used" on the land. Abbott had a dewatering permit under Arizona's groundwater management act to withdraw only 2.07 AF, and admitted it had failed to report the excessive pumping and agreed to pay a fine of $6508.50 to the State Department of Water Resources.

3. The fact situation in *Martin*—an urban area seeking water for its expanding population by seeking to pump and transport water (whether surface or groundwater) from rural areas—is a common one. How may the City of Linden meet its water needs in light of this decision? Could it purchase Martin's land and then pump groundwater back to the City? Could neighboring landowners still enjoin the transport of groundwater? Must the City purchase all the land over the aquifer in order to pump and transport with impunity? (Compare the situation of the non-riparian and municipality seeking to use streamflow in a riparian rights jurisdiction, as described in Chapter 2, supra p. 79.

4. What is the rationale for the on-tract limitation (appurtenancy) as part of the common law reasonable use doctrine? Here the explanation offered is to protect farmers against high capacity wells sunk by growing cities looking for water. Another rationale is that requiring on-tract usage effectively requires sharing a common pool resource in a rough justice sort of way. In an era where there was no feasible means for determining how much water was available for use from an aquifer, limiting usage to overlying tracts provided a readily enforced method of sharing. The doctrine tended to allocate groundwater in rough proportion to ownership of overlying land, because a larger overlying tract in most instances could be expected to require more groundwater than a smaller tract. (This is not always true, of course: a power plant sited on a few acres could withdraw much more water than a farm of comparable size.) Another rationale for the on-tract limitation is that it promotes recharge of the aquifer (from seepage) and thus encourages recycling of the water in the community dependent upon the aquifer. This is similar to a rationale that could be offered for requiring use of

surface waters on riparian land, to promote return flow to the stream for further use downstream.

5. Suppose both the City's well site and Martin's farm were within the city limits. Could the City pump groundwater and deliver water all over the city through a distribution system? Should the land within the city distribution system be regarded as "overlying land" or an "on-tract" use for purposes of the doctrine? If not, does that mean the doctrine effectively prohibits a municipality from ever using groundwater if any landowners in the city have their own wells and might be injured by a city's pumping? Does that make sense?

6. Some states have relaxed the seemingly strict appurtenancy limitation in certain circumstances. For example, in Jarvis v. State Land Dept. (II), 106 Ariz. 506, 479 P.2d 169 (1970), the Arizona Supreme Court invoked its equitable powers to allow the City of Tucson to pump and transport groundwater off overlying land to the city distribution system several miles away, so long as it purchased title to irrigated farmland in the area, stopped the irrigation, and transported no more than "an amount equal to the annual historical maximum use [made] upon the lands so acquired." The court later clarified that Tucson was limited to the consumptive use (the amount pumped minus the amount which seeped back to recharge the groundwater after use). Jarvis v. State Land Dept. (III), 113 Ariz. 230, 550 P.2d 227 (1976). The Arizona experience is discussed further infra pp. 486–487. Note that even though the City's pumping under such limitations will not affect other pumpers in the area any more than continued pumping by the farmer who sells the land to Tucson would, the rural area may still be harmed. The loss of farm production in the area could adversely affect local farm-dependent businesses (such as farm equipment dealers). See pp. 289–298 supra (protecting third party interests).

7. Note that in its decision in *Adams* (discussed in the principal case), the Alabama Supreme Court had upheld the use of groundwater on overlying land even though it harmed the neighbors' use of groundwater. This is in line with most cases applying the American reasonable use doctrine: "As the doctrine has developed, it has generally been held that all uses of water upon the land from which it is extracted are 'reasonable,' even if they more or less deplete the supply to the harm of neighbors, unless the purpose is malicious or the water simply wasted." William B. Stoebuck & Dale A.Whitman, Hornbook of the Law of Property § 7.4, at 428–29 (3d ed. 2000). The more that courts applying the reasonable use rule look to relative reasonableness of uses in sorting out conflicts among those who are using on the overlying land, the more this doctrine looks like correlative rights. See Note 5 after the next case, infra p. 432.

c. Correlative Rights

KATZ v. WALKINSHAW

Supreme Court of California, 1903.
141 Cal. 116, 74 P. 766.

SHAW, J.

[Plaintiff landowners alleged that their wells, which extracted groundwater for irrigation and domestic use on their own land, were dried up by the wells of the defendant, who extracted groundwater and conveyed it "to a distant tract, and there using it." Among other things, defendant argued that an 1850 statute adopting the common law in California incorporated the rule of capture which "has become a rule of property in this state, upon the faith of which enormous investments have been made, and that it should not now be departed from, even if erroneous."]

[The court concluded that the rule of capture would leave groundwater users] constantly threatened with danger of utter destruction of the valuable enterprises and systems of waterworks which they control, and that all new enterprises of the same sort will be subject to the same peril. They will have absolutely no protection in law against others having stronger pumps, deeper wells, or a more favorable situation, who can thereby take from them unlimited quantities of the water, reaching to the entire supply, and without regard to the place of use. We cannot perceive how a doctrine offering so little protection to the investments in and product of such enterprises, and offering so much temptation to others to capture the water on which they depend, can tend to promote developments in the future or preserve those already made, and therefore we do not believe that public policy or a regard for the general welfare demands the doctrine. * * *

The doctrine of reasonable use, on the other hand, affords some measure of protection to property now existing, and greater justification for the attempt to make new developments. It limits the right of others to such amount of water as may be necessary for some useful purpose in connection with the land from which it is taken. * * *

[The court went on in an extended dictum—provided "in view of the * * * scope of argument"—to describe how its version of reasonable use would work.] The controversies arising will naturally divide into classes.

[a] There will be disputes between persons or corporations claiming rights to take such waters from the same strata or source for use on distant lands. There is no statute on this subject, as there now is concerning appropriations of surface streams; but the case is not without precedent. When the pioneers of 1849 reached this state, they found no laws in force governing rights to take waters from surface streams for use on nonriparian lands. Yet it was found that the principles of the common law, although not previously applied to such cases, could be adapted thereto, and were sufficient to define and protect such rights under the conditions. * * * The principles which * * * were applied to protect appropriations and possessory rights in visible streams, will, in general, be found applicable to such appropriations of percolating waters, either for public or private use, and will suffice for their protection as against other appropriators. Such rights are usufructuary only, and the first taker who with diligence puts the water in use will have the better right. * * *

[b] In controversies between an appropriator for use on distant land and those who own land overlying the water-bearing strata, there

may be two classes of such landowners—those who have used the water on their land before the attempt to appropriate, and those who have not previously used it, but who claim the right afterwards to do so. Under the decision in this case the rights of the first class of landowners are paramount to that of one who takes the water to distant land, but the landowner's right extends only to the quantity of water that is necessary for use on his land, and the appropriator may take the surplus. As to those landowners who begin the use after the appropriation, and who, in order to obtain the water, must restrict or restrain the diversion to distant lands or places, it is perhaps best not state a positive rule. Such rights are limited at most to the quantity necessary for use, and the disputes will not be so serious as those between rival appropriators.

[c] Disputes between overlying landowners, concerning water for use on the land, to which they have an equal right, in cases where the supply is insufficient for all, are to be settled by giving to each a fair and just proportion. And here again we leave for future settlement the question as to the priority of rights between such owners who begin the use of the waters at different times. * * *

Notes and Questions

1. Note the court's rationale for *rejecting* the absolute ownership rule. Did the Texas Supreme Court, in its 1904 decision (discussed supra p. 418), use the same rationale to justify *adopting* the absolute ownership rule and rejecting correlative rights? Which is more persuasive?

2. Justice Shaw soon had occasion to answer the two questions he avoided answering in *Katz*, by holding that earlier appropriators of groundwater for use on distant tracts are subordinate to newly-initiated extraction of groundwater for use on the overlying land (see Burr v. Maclay Rancho Water Co., 154 Cal. 428, 98 P. 260 (1908)), and by holding that priority was irrelevant among users on overlying lands (see Hudson v. Dailey, 156 Cal. 617, 105 P. 748 (1909)). In the latter, the court said that, among overlying landowners, groundwater

> should be considered a common supply, in which all who by their natural situation have access to it have a common right, and of which they may each make a reasonable use upon the land so situated * * *. The natural rights * * * in this common supply of water would therefore be coequal, except as to quantity, and correlative.

105 P. at 753. See also Lucien Shaw, The Development of the Law of Waters in the West, 10 Cal. L. Rev. 443 (1922).

3. Taken together, these cases provide the framework of what has come to be known as the correlative rights doctrine. As noted earlier, it can be thought of as riparianism tilted vertically. Where there is a conflict among overlying landowners over an insufficient supply, both seeking to use the groundwater on the overlying land, how are rights to be apportioned? In the riparian surface water situation, the inquiry is into the reasonableness of the respective uses (see supra pp. 47–61. In the correlative rights groundwa-

ter situation, the instruction in *Katz* was to give each landowner "a fair and just proportion." Is that the same standard?

4. In Tehachapi–Cummings County Water District v. Armstrong, 49 Cal.App.3d 992, 1001, 122 Cal.Rptr. 918 (1975), the court of appeals said:

> As between overlying owners, [groundwater] rights, like those of [surface] riparians, are correlative, i.e., they are mutual and reciprocal. This means that each has a common right to take all that he can beneficially use on his land if the quantity is sufficient; if the quantity is insufficient, each is limited to his proportionate fair share of the total amount available based upon his reasonable need. The proportionate share of each owner is predicated not on his past use over a specified period of time, nor on the time he commenced pumping, but solely on his current reasonable and beneficial need for water.

How much predictability and security of investment does that provide to landowners over an aquifer? You are a lawyer for a manufacturing company that is considering building a new, water-use-intensive factory on land it owns, and to install and operate wells to supply it with groundwater. The land is over a large aquifer, over which there are thousands of landowners, some of whom have irrigation wells, in a jurisdiction that follows correlative rights. What do you advise the company as to the security of its ability to pump?

5. How much of a difference is there between the American reasonable use doctrine and the correlative rights doctrine, insofar as uses on overlying land are concerned? Do landowners using groundwater on their own land under either doctrine face the possibility of having to reduce their pumping in order to share the groundwater resource with later-initiated pumping for use on other overlying tracts? While situations are hard to find where the American reasonable use doctrine has been applied to fashion some apportionment of groundwater uses among overlying landowners, courts that purport to apply the doctrine sometimes interject a notion of sharing among overlying landowners. This can make it difficult to differentiate between jurisdictions that purport to apply one or the other doctrine. See Joseph W. Dellapenna, Correlative Rights Today, in 3 Waters and Water Rights § 21.01, at 21–2 (Robert Beck ed., repl. vol. 2003). Professor Dellapenna adopts the view that *correlative rights* requires "strict proportional sharing," *reasonable use* requires "sharing on the basis of the reasonableness of the competing uses," and *capture* (or what he calls "absolute dominion") allows "unlimited pumping, even as limited by appurtenance rules." Id. at 21–4 to 21–5. Under that classification scheme, a state that ostensibly followed the American reasonable use doctrine, but had never applied it to limit or apportion water among users of groundwater on overlying land (see Note 7, p. 429, supra), would be considered as following the rule of capture.

6. Under the California version of correlative rights, groundwater can be exported off the land from which it is pumped if there is no injury to others. Nebraska follows a version of correlative rights for groundwater, but muddies the waters by generally prohibiting the use of water off the overlying land unless the legislature has specifically provided for it. A statute adopted in 1995 allows groundwater to be transported off the land from

which it is pumped for agricultural purposes, or for any purpose related to pollution remediation, so long as the transport and use (a) will not significantly adversely affect any other water user, (b) is consistent with all applicable statutes and rules and regulations, and (c) is in the public interest. Neb. Rev. Stat. § 46–691. In Springer v. Kuhns, 571 N.W.2d 323, 330 (1997), the court deemed the statute to have a retroactive effect, even though the legislative history was "rather scant," and legislative changes in the common law are usually deemed prospective. This was to avoid "disruptive economic and legal consequences" because it found the Legislature "acted with the knowledge that such transfers had occurred and were occurring." See also In re Lower Platte S. Nat. Res. Dist., 621 N.W.2d 299 (Neb. 2001).

7.   Suppose that the recharge of an aquifer is 100 acre-feet per year and that in year 1 the only groundwater being used is 50 acre-feet per year by overlying owner O, on her overlying tract. Suppose that in year 2 Senior (S) initiates an off-tract use that requires 25 acre-feet per year. In year 3 Junior (J) initiates an off-tract use also requiring 25 acre-feet annually. In year 4, O decides to increase by 10 acre-feet her reasonable on-tract use of water. Can O do that? What is the effect on S and J? Same result if, instead of O, another overlying owner (X) who had previously made no use of water, initiates an on-tract use of 10 acre-feet?

8.   Under the correlative rights doctrine, is a municipality pumping within its service area, but from a well-site on a small parcel of land, considered an overlying landowner for correlative rights purposes? The question is rarely discussed but the answer seems to be no. See City of San Bernardino v. City of Riverside, 186 Cal. 7, 198 P. 784, 791–92 (1921) (Shaw, J.); see also Orange County Water Dist. v. City of Colton, 226 Cal.App.2d 642, 38 Cal.Rptr. 286, 290 (1964) (if a city acquires the right to store and extract groundwater by deed from overlying landowners, those grantors may be estopped from objecting to the city's pumping, but the deed "does not authorize such use over objection by other overlying land owners"). See also supra p. 51, discussing non-riparians seeking to use streamwater in riparian jurisdictions.

9.   The application of the correlative rights doctrine in connection with groundwater mining is discussed further below at p. 488.

d. Restatement (Second) of Torts Reasonable Use

McNAMARA v. CITY OF RITTMAN

Supreme Court of Ohio, 2005.
838 N.E.2d 640.

PFEIFER, J.

The Sixth Circuit Court of Appeals has certified a single question to this court arising from two cases. The question is a general one, so we need not delve deeply into the facts of the cases at issue.

Both cases involve the effect of construction by governmental entities on the water supplies of individual homeowners. In *McNamara*, the petitioners are homeowners who reside in Sterling, Ohio. In 1973, respondent, the city of Rittman, purchased a tract of land near Sterling for the purpose of drilling three wells on the land to serve Rittman's water needs. Petitioners allege that Rittman's operation lowered their aquifer, causing water shortages and poor quality water. [In 2000, petitioners filed a takings lawsuit in federal court and lost in the district court on statute of limitations grounds.] * * *

Hensley evolved in much the same way. In *Hensley,* the city of Columbus and others, in order to extend sewer lines, dug a trench up to 60 feet deep near petitioners' property. To keep water out of the trench during construction, groundwater was pumped out from under the petitioners' property. That "dewatering" caused petitioners' wells to go dry. * * * [The *Hensley* plaintiffs filed a takings case in federal district court and lost on the ground that] Ohio does not recognize a property interest in groundwater, thus negating any claim of a governmental taking of property.

Both cases were appealed to the Sixth Circuit Court of Appeals. Finding that the issue of whether petitioners have a property right in groundwater is dispositive and noting that this court has yet to address the issue, the court posed an identical certified question in both cases:

"Does an Ohio homeowner have a property interest in so much of the groundwater located beneath the land owner's property as is necessary to the use and enjoyment of the owner's home?"

We agreed to answer the certified question in both cases.

LAW AND ANALYSIS

We are asked in this case to answer a general question of law, not to resolve the underlying cases. Whether there were takings in these two cases is not for us to decide; corrective measures taken by the cities are likewise irrelevant to our discussion. We are asked a question in the abstract: Whether Ohio recognizes a property right in that amount of groundwater beneath a landowner's property that is necessary to the use and enjoyment of the owner's home. Our response is that Ohio recognizes that landowners have a property interest in the groundwater underlying their land and that governmental interference with that right can constitute an unconstitutional taking.

In *Frazier v. Brown* (1861), 12 Ohio St. 294, this court established an absolute ownership standard for groundwater in Ohio. According to that doctrine, "such water is to be regarded as part of the land itself, to be enjoyed absolutely by the proprietor within whose territory it lies." Id. at 308. The court refused to recognize any rule requiring the sharing of water among landowners overlying a common aquifer. Thus, any owner of property was entitled to use all the groundwater he could, without regard to how that use affected neighboring landowners. The *Frazier* court set forth two reasons for its holding, which resulted "mainly from considerations of public policy":

"1. Because the existence, origin, movement and course of such waters, and the causes which govern and direct their movements, are so secret, occult and concealed, that an attempt to administer any set of legal rules in respect to them would be involved in hopeless uncertainty, and would be, therefore, practically impossible. 2. Because any such recognition of correlative rights, would interfere, to the material detriment of the common wealth, with drainage and agriculture, mining, the construction of highways and railroads, with sanitary regulations, building and the general progress of improvement in works of embellishment and utility."

Frazier's absolute dominion standard stood for over 100 years, until this court adjusted the course of Ohio groundwater law in the watershed case, *Cline v. Am. Aggregates Corp.,* 15 Ohio St.3d 384, 474 N.E.2d 324 [1984]. *Cline* established that each landowner has property rights with respect to groundwater.

In *Cline,* this court set out to create a workable standard for the resolution of groundwater disputes in Ohio. To that end, the court adopted the "reasonable use" doctrine applicable to groundwater set forth in 4 Restatement of the Law 2d (1979), Torts, Section 858, which states:

"A proprietor of land or his grantee who withdraws ground water from the land and uses it for a beneficial purpose is not subject to liability for interference with the use of water by another, unless

"(a) the withdrawal of ground water unreasonably causes harm to a proprietor of neighboring land through lowering the water table or reducing artesian pressure,

"(b) the withdrawal of ground water exceeds the proprietor's reasonable share of the annual supply or total store of ground water, or

"(c) the withdrawal of the ground water has a direct and substantial effect upon a watercourse or lake and unreasonably causes harm to a person entitled to the use of its water."

The *Cline* standard assumes nonliability—a landowner is able to withdraw as much groundwater as he can put to beneficial use. *Cline* breaks from *Frazier*'s absolute rule as soon as a common user is harmed. Both *Frazier* and *Cline* recognize that aquifers are not neatly contained within property lines and that one landowner's use of water can have a detrimental effect on an adjoining landowner's groundwater supply. However, the *Frazier* court held that what happens below the surface of the land is so unknowable that we cannot determine with any certainty whether one person's use affects another person's use. *Cline* rejects that notion. In *Cline,* this court concluded that the 100 years of science since *Frazier* have enabled us to reliably determine the effect of one landowner's water use on another landowner's property. The court was persuaded by "[o]ther American decisions [that] have recognized that the advancement of scientific knowledge can insure the protection of a landowner's property rights in ground water to the same degree that the riparian doctrine protects the interests of land owners adjacent to a stream." We note that the *Cline* court speaks of protecting a landowner's groundwater "property rights."

Cline should thus be read as protecting landowners' property rights in groundwater, rather than limiting them. Through *Cline,* a property owner has a remedy against another property owner with land overlying a common aquifer, if the other landowner's use of the water unreasonably diminishes his water supply. Under *Cline,* a property owner's right to use the water underlying his property is not subject to a neighboring property owner's superior pumping system, as it would have been under *Frazier.* Instead, a landowner's right to the water underlying his property is protected by law. A property owner has a potential cause of action against anyone who unreasonably interferes with his property right in groundwater. That cause of action arises only from the effect on the landowner's water rights—no other effect on the overlying property is necessary for the cause of action to proceed.

Respondents argue that although *Cline* established that property owners have the right to the reasonable use of the groundwater beneath their property, they have no right of title, no ownership right, in the water itself. Thus, they argue, the government has not taken anything that the petitioners own.

We disagree. The title to property *includes* the right to use the groundwater beneath that property. The "reasonable use" standard set forth in *Cline* greatly expanded water rights protection, reflecting the importance of water rights to every piece of property. *Cline* recognizes the essential relationship between water and property and confirms that groundwater rights are a separate right in property. The Restatement section cited in *Cline* "recognizes that the right to withdraw ground water is a property right that may be granted and sold to others." 4 Restatement of Law 2d, Torts, Section 858, Comment *b.* That right is one of the fundamental attributes of property ownership and an essential stick in the bundle of rights that is part of title to property.

Although a cause of action for unreasonable use of water sounds in tort, it is based upon the property right of the landowner making the claim, much like a claim for trespass. The cause of action "retains the property basis of the common law rules pertaining to ground water." 4 Restatement of Torts, Section 858, Comment *b.* * * *

The dark arts theory of *Frazier*—that the movements of groundwater are so mysterious that we should not even try to determine who has rights to the water—has been abandoned. *Cline* held that landowners do have rights to groundwater and that those rights are not so murky that they should be unprotected. They are entitled to protection, as riparian rights are. * * *

Ohio has its own unique water resources and water needs. More than 700,000 Ohioans have their own wells to meet their entire water needs; industry uses more than 240 million gallons of groundwater per day, and Ohio's farmers use approximately two billion gallons of groundwater per year.

Groundwater rights are knowable and protectible. This court in *Cline* established the nature of the right, and Ohio has statutorily defined what constitutes reasonable use. R.C. 1521.17. The well-being of Ohio homeowners, the stability of Ohio's economy, and the reliability of real estate transfers require the protection of groundwater rights. We therefore hold that Ohio landowners have a property interest in the groundwater underlying their land and that governmental interference with that right can constitute an unconstitutional taking.

MOYER, C.J., concurring in judgment only.

I concur in the response of the majority to the extent that it holds that an Ohio landowner has a constitutionally protected property interest in groundwater that regularly occupies an aquifer underlying his land. The majority concludes that a property interest in groundwater originates from the reasonable-use component set forth in 4 Restatement of the Law 2d, Torts (1979), Section 858, specifically, subsection (1)(a). Though I agree with the determination that a property interest exists, I write separately because I do not believe that it originates from the reasonable-use rule. Instead, I believe that a property interest in groundwater originates from the correlative-rights component of Section 858 found in subsection (1)(b). Section 858(1)(b) provides that a landowner whose withdrawal of groundwater interferes with the use of water by another is not subject to liability unless the withdrawal "exceeds the proprietor's reasonable share of the annual supply or total store of ground water." It was the recognition of correlative rights in respect to groundwater that created a property interest in groundwater.

LUNDBERG STRATTON, J., concurs in the foregoing opinion.

Notes and Questions

1. The Court quotes from § 858(1) of the Restatement. Section 858(2), not quoted, provides: "The determination of liability under clauses (a), (b) and (c) of Subsection (1) is governed by the principles stated in sections 850 to 857." The principles of §§ 850–857 are the principles of reasonable use applied in surface water riparianism. See supra pp. 57–61. The Ohio statute (R.C. 1521.17) quoted in the last paragraph of the majority opinion basically incorporates these factors in defining whether a particular use of water is reasonable.

2. The introduction to these Restatement provisions explains that although "the interests protected * * * are property rights arising out of the ownership and possession of land," an "interference with a right to the use of water logically and analytically belongs in the field of tort liability. * * * [L]ike a trespass or nuisance, it is a tort directed at an interest in property." Did landowners have a legally protected property right in groundwater when

Ohio followed the capture rule? Do they now, as a result of adopting the Restatement?

3.   Given the facts stated in the court's opinion, has there been a taking of plaintiffs' water right in groundwater? What further inquiry need be made? Into the reasonableness of both the plaintiffs' and defendants' use of water in each case, as measured by the "reasonableness factors" laid out in the Restatement §§ 850–57 (incorporated into the Ohio statute)? What is defendant's "use" of water in the *Hensley* case? How predictable is the outcome? Does it make a difference that in each of the two consolidated cases here, the plaintiff is a governmental entity, and is withdrawing groundwater for its own purposes (municipal needs in the first case, dewatering a sewer construction project in the second), rather than generally regulating the use of groundwater by others?

4.   Section 858 of the Restatement discards the preference for on-tract uses which is found in both the American reasonable use and the correlative rights doctrines. Comment b to § 858 notes that it "permits the sale of ground water and the grant of the right to extract it to persons who need water but do not want the land overlying it. Placing ground water on the market in this fashion also tends to promote its development and use by those who can make the most valuable use of it." Does that comment suggest that the City of Rittman, which is transporting the water off the land from which it is pumped, is not liable for a taking here?

5.   Despite § 858's recognition that off-tract uses may be desirable, moving groundwater away from the land where it is extracted can still give rise to liability if it "unreasonably causes harm" to neighboring landowners (subsection (a)), if it exceeds the "proprietor's reasonable share" (subsection (b)), or if hydrologically connected surface water uses are "unreasonably cause[d] harm" (subsection (c)). Comment e emphasizes that a "salient factor [in determining reasonableness of a use] is not the place of the use but the withdrawal of water in unprecedented quantities for purposes not common to the locality."

6.   How much certainty or predictability does the Restatement doctrine provide to groundwater users, compared to the other doctrines we've covered? For example, would the Restatement's application have changed the result of *Martin v. Linden*, supra p. 423? To the extent § 858 encourages courts to resolve disputes on a case-by-case basis, does it undermine the predictability of results that may be important to investment?

7.   Does the Restatement doctrine function best under conditions of relative abundance of groundwater, where few hard cases of water allocation demand resolution? Suppose an aquifer is being tapped by many wells for agricultural irrigation, and withdrawal rates exceed recharge by 10%. Farmer A, who has been pumping 1000 acre-feet for use on his 500 acres; quits farming and leases his land to City B, which commences withdrawing 2000 acre-feet for transportation to the City. C, an overlying landowner who had not used groundwater in the past, now proposes to start pumping to irrigate his land. The remaining irrigators bring suit against A, B, C, and all other overlying landowners. Under § 858 what should the court do? For the Restatement's own answer, see Restatement (Second) of Torts § 858, illustration 4.

8. As of this writing, the Restatement doctrine is batting .500 among states which have expressly considered it, being adopted in Michigan and Wisconsin as well as Ohio, and rejected in Indiana, Maine and Texas. See Joseph W. Dellapenna, Legal Classifications, in 3 Waters and Water Rights § 19.05(b)(2) (Robert Beck ed., repl. vol. 2003).

e. Prior Appropriation

Like surface water law, there is a marked contrast in groundwater law between geographic regions. Several of the Western states that early on embraced the prior appropriation doctrine for surface streams adopted some version of that doctrine for groundwater. The first clear adoption of the doctrine was by statute in New Mexico in the late 1920s and by the Supreme Court of Idaho shortly afterward (Hinton v. Little, 50 Idaho 371, 296 P. 582 (1931)). Utah followed by statute and court decision in 1935, and Washington by statute in 1945. Kansas, the Dakotas, Nevada, Oregon, Wyoming, and Montana are also credited with following the doctrine now. Colorado is a somewhat special case. Much but not all of its groundwater is governed by the prior appropriation doctrine. See supra p. 413 n.31, and infra pp. 459–461 & 485.

The prior appropriation doctrine that is applied to groundwater shares many features with its surface water sibling. Water rights are obtained by putting the water to a beneficial use; they have a specified point of diversion and are quantified as to amount; they can be lost for non-use; and they can be transferred so long as no harm is suffered by other water rights holders. Most conspicuously, temporal priority is a determining factor in allocating water between claimants in the event of a conflict.

Despite the overall congruity of the groundwater and surface water prior appropriation doctrines, there are some common situations—such as simple well interference—where the treatment of senior groundwater appropriators may diverge somewhat from the treatment of their surface water counterparts. A classic example pits a senior domestic water user having a small, shallow well against a junior with a large well for agricultural irrigation, where the cone of depression from the big junior well causes the water table to fall below the bottom of the senior's well. The senior will argue that this case is indistinguishable from a surface water case in which the unsatisfied senior can "call the river" from the interfering junior; that is, the senior can compel upstream juniors to close their headgates to insure that sufficient water arrives at the senior's is point of diversion. The senior may enjoy this right even if the result is inefficient; that is, if the stream loses water (by evaporation or seepage) in transit from the point of the upstream junior's diversion to the point of the senior's diversion.

The junior will argue that the surface water case is quite different, because it involves an absolute shortage of water; that is, not enough is water available for both the senior and junior. In contrast, in the groundwater situation there is often water in the aquifer to satisfy both users. All the senior well owner has to do is deepen her well (presumably at her expense) to reach the water. If the rule were otherwise, the junior will argue, the shallowness of the senior's well in effect allows the senior effectively to "lock up" from effective use all the water in the aquifer below the bottom of her well, thwarting its widespread use and the benefits it could provide.

In many situations, the junior's position seems more reasonable, because there is usually groundwater available at greater depths. Unless there is some overriding environmental issue, it arguably makes little policy sense to allow a shallow senior to "call" a huge aquifer, rather than insisting that the senior's water be obtained in a manner that allows fuller exploitation of the aquifer, such as by deepening her well.

That policy does not, however, answer the question of who, in a prior appropriation system, ought to bear the cost of that change. Strict protection of seniority argues for a "junior pays" rule; that is, the junior should pay the cost of deepening senior's well or, if feasible, the junior could supply the senior with water from the junior's deeper well at the cost senior had been paying. The junior might be charged with notice that the senior was there with a shallow well when the junior invested in the deeper well and the more powerful pump. (The notice rationale is, however, arguably more attenuated than in the surface water context, because groundwater pumping may be less obvious than a surface diversion.)

But applying a rule that obligates the junior to compensate the senior with water or cash is more complicated in the groundwater situation. As we have seen, a basic difference between groundwater and surface water is that, given the relative slowness of movement of groundwater compared to surface water, the effects of the junior's pumping may sometimes not be felt for some time. It may take years, in fact, for the cone of depression from junior's well to expand enough to intercept the bottom of senior's well. Can the junior be made liable before the injury is manifest? What if junior's property has changed hands in the meantime?

Other principles of surface water prior appropriation law could be invoked to put the cost of deepening the senior's shallow well on the senior. The senior's well could be deemed a waste of the remaining waters of the aquifer. Or it could be deemed an unreasonable means of diversion, much like a senior surface water user's diversion by inefficient means (a water wheel or a wing dam) that requires the stream water level to be maintained. We will examine below how the courts, legislatures, and administrative agencies have all tried their hand at shaping rules to govern such cases.

Sometimes prior appropriation must be applied in situations of groundwater mining, when the amount of water being withdrawn from the aquifer regularly exceeds the amount of water being recharged. There it is only a matter of time before the aquifer runs dry, the quality declines below usable levels, or whatever water remains is at such a depth as to be beyond the economic reach of potential users. A senior appropriator under those conditions sees existing or proposed new junior appropriators as depleting the stock of water that would otherwise be available to satisfy the senior's superior right in future years. As you might guess, the prior appropriation doctrine's application there varies with particular circumstances and jurisdictions. In theory, the most straightforward approach would seem to be for an administrative agency to make a determination of how much water will be allowed to be withdrawn from the aquifer each year. This could be the rate of recharge (so that equilibrium is maintained), or it could be the rate of "safe" or "optimal" yield—the amount that can be withdrawn without unacceptable adverse effects (however those are defined—see the discussion of these terms at supra pp. 404–405). If the aquifer has little or no recharge, the initial determination of how much water to pump is based on a decision about how fast to exhaust the aquifer. The rights to withdraw the allowable amount would then be allocated on the basis of seniority. Note that new appropriations might be allowed even where an aquifer is currently being mined, if the "optimal" yield is not being exceeded by existing appropriators (see Mathers v. Texaco, infra p. 479). The general idea is that public policy on resource management will determine how much water will be pumped, and seniority of appropriation determines who gets that water.

This approach presumes a pro-active government without political constraints and with sufficient knowledge of aquifer conditions to engage in such a rational exercise. The real world is usually considerably less tidy. The state may have granted appropriations (or appropriators may have drilled wells before any state administrative system was established) long before aquifer characteristics were known. Often, in other words, aquifers may be "over-appropriated" just like surface waters are. But there is one big difference—in an overappropriated surface stream the most junior appropriators hold "paper rights," unable to be satisfied by the existing supply in a normal flow year. In an overappropriated aquifer, on the other hand, the water usually exists to supply all appropriators, and can be extracted by even the most junior appropriator. The consequence is mining or depleting the aquifer, steadily dropping its water level. Put another way, the consequence of granting an appropriation to surface water in excess of the normal supply does not strain the supply; the opposite is usually true for excess groundwater appropriations. If a government imposed the kind of rational management described in the preceding paragraph on a situation where existing users are already using in excess of the amount determined to be "safe" or "optimal" yield, the government will have to shut down altogether the pumps of some existing users. This is a step government at any level does not easily take.

Finally, some jurisdictions that apply prior appropriation to groundwater are beginning to wrestle with proposals to pump large amounts of groundwater for export. (Similar proposals may be made in jurisdictions that apply other groundwater doctrines, but their teachings may make the issues easier to resolve; e.g., in capture jurisdictions there are no limits.) Nevada presents the most visible current proposal. Demand for water in Las Vegas, the fastest growing metropolitan area in the country, now on the order of 500,000 acre-feet, is expected to nearly double in the next three decades. Its local dependable water supply (almost wholly groundwater) is limited, as is the State's share of the Colorado River, as explained in Chapter 8, Section A. The Southern Nevada Water Authority has a multi-faceted plan for dealing with the population growth, which includes conservation and securing new supplies. A prime target for the latter is groundwater underlying valleys in the Basin and Range country to the north and east of the City. The Authority has filed applications to appropriate groundwater in the region, and expects that perhaps 200,000 acre-feet can be extracted and exported on a long-term sustainable basis without affecting existing appropriations. The targeted area is relatively sparsely populated with relatively little groundwater pumping occurring now. The federal Bureau of Land Management is currently preparing an environmental impact statement on proposed grants of rights of way across federal lands for the project, and the Nevada State Engineer is beginning to consider how much unappropriated water is available, the effect on existing rights, and whether the application is in the public interest. National Wildlife Refuges and endangered species might be affected, and there is also a potential interstate issue (see chapter 8), as some of the targeted basins may extend hydrologically into Utah. More information can be found at the Southern Nevada Water Authority's web site; see also Matt Jenkins, Squeezing Water from a Stone, High Country News (September 19, 2005).

Review Questions to Compare the Five Doctrines

1.   To what extent is ownership of land relevant to one's right to pump groundwater under each of these doctrines?

2.   To what extent is priority of use relevant under each of these doctrines in defining the rights of competing, neighboring pumpers of groundwater from the same source?

3.   Consider the practical effect of each of these doctrines on groundwater use by (a) farmers, (b) domestic users, (c) municipal suppliers, (d) industries like power plants using substantial amounts of water for cooling, and (e) the environment (instream flows). To what extent, if any, does each doctrine tend to favor or protect each of these uses at the expense of others?

4.   For a survey of the range of potential legislative options for groundwater management, see Earl Murphy, The Potential for Legislative Choice Concerning Groundwater and Aquifers, 4 J. Land Use & Envtl. L. 23 (1988) (contrasting regulatory management of groundwater with reliance on property rules and private decisionmaking); see also Earl Murphy, Some Legal Solutions for Contemporary Problems Concerning Groundwater and Aquifers, 4 J. Min. L. & Pol'y 49 (1988); Ronald Kaiser, Deep Trouble: Options for Managing the Hidden Threat of Aquifer Depletion in Texas, 32 Tex. Tech L.Rev. 249 (2001).

5.   For a free-market approach to groundwater allocation that nevertheless acknowledges, grudgingly, some role for government in establishing and

policing the system, see David Fractor, Property Rights and Groundwater Management, in Natural Resources: Bureaucratic Myths and Environmental Management 69–71, 78–83 (Richard Stroup & John Baden, eds., 1983). Fractor would assign "well-defined, fully transferable property rights" to groundwater, leaving it to unregulated market forces to "ensure that the resource is put to its most highly valued uses." The property right would have two parts: one part would be comprised of a fixed percentage of the long-run average annual recharge (which the author calls its "flow component"), and the second part a fixed absolute quantity (to be used just once) of the amount of water in storage in the aquifer (the "stock component"). The government would have to determine how much of the stock component could be removed from the aquifer without causing environmental problems, for only what it determined was the "safe" amount of "surplus stock" would be allocated. Courts would initially allocate these property rights based on "historical, equitable, or other considerations," but the initial allocation is irrelevant to the economic efficiency of the system. Despite its seeming elegance and simplicity, apparently such a system has never been adopted anywhere. Why? How daunting are the political problems of making the initial allocation of rights?

D. MODERN GROUNDWATER MANAGEMENT DISPUTES AND CRISES—TOOLS AND TECHNIQUES

Although it is often said that water law is all about shortages, disputes that give rise to modern groundwater law development and reform usually do not stem simply from raw shortage of supply. There may be a large new extraction of groundwater that threatens or dries up existing wells when there is still plenty of water in the aquifer. There may be an emerging problem of increasing pump lifts (well deepening and associated increases in electricity costs) that can result from long-term "mining" of limited supplies. There may be a collision between groundwater pumping and surface water rights or environmental imperatives (e.g., endangered species), where groundwater and surface water are linked. There may be quality problems such as salinity intrusion or industrial contamination of aquifers; indeed, such tort cases have been described as "today the most common form of private litigation regarding groundwater." Joseph W. Dellapenna, Physical & Social Bases of Quantitative Groundwater Law, in 3 Waters and Water Rights § 18.03(b) (Robert Beck ed., repl.vol. 2003). There may be a growing problem of surface land subsidence, or there may be some combination of these factors.

General Adjudications of Groundwater Rights

Almost all groundwater litigation is between a limited number of parties—that is, historically, there have been very few basin-wide groundwater adjudications, seeking to quantify and correlate all rights in a particular area. This may be contrasted with surface waters, where such adjudications are not uncommon, particularly in the West. One reason for the difference is that many jurisdictions have not provided a clear statutory basis for such adjudications.[36] Another reason is that, especially if the area has not had well registration or record-keeping requirements, gathering the basic facts on water use may be expensive and time-consuming. Also, perhaps more than surface waters, users and uses appear and disappear, and physical conditions may change as both the quality and quantity of water in the aquifer are modified by continued pumping. Finally, under some groundwater doctrines (American reasonable use and correlative rights), all owners of land overlying the aquifer in question may have to be joined, since each has a potential interest. The net result: It is very rare–even if an aquifer is being overdrafted—for pumpers to undertake the time and expense of a general adjudication.

California is a partial exception. There any groundwater user can initiate an adjudication in court, which can refer it to the State Water Resources Control Board to act essentially as a special master. See Cal. Water Code §§ 2000–2001. The Board itself can initiate court action to "restrict pumping, or to impose physical solutions, or both, to the extent necessary to prevent destruction of or irreparable injury to the quality of such water." Id. § 2100. Nevertheless, only about fifteen of California's 500 groundwater basins have completed adjudications. See Department of Water Resources, Adjudicated Ground Water Basins in California 2–3 (Jan. 1996). Commentators have attributed the paucity to "the time and cost of the adjudicative process." Joseph W. Dellapenna, Correlative Rights Today, in 3 Waters and Water Rights, § 21.05 (Robert Beck ed., repl.vol. 2003) (citing Russell Kletzing, Imported Groundwater Banking: The Kern Water Bank—A Case Study, 19 Pac. L.J. 1225, 1235, 1295 (1988)). A few very large groundwater adjudications have been conducted in southern California. See, e.g., City of Pasadena v. City of Alhambra, 33 Cal.2d 908, 207 P.2d 17 (1949); City of Los Angeles v. City of San Fernando, 14 Cal.3d 199, 123 Cal.Rptr. 1, 537 P.2d 1250 (1975). The former took sixteen years from the filing of the original complaint to a decision in the state supreme court; the latter took twenty-four years. California groundwater management is considered in more detail infra pp. 506–520.

1. THE EMERGENCE OF GROUNDWATER MANAGEMENT LEGISLATION

The trend in groundwater management is toward legislative reform, though on a basis that has been described as "highly fragmentary" and "piecemeal." Joseph W. Dellapenna, Legal Classifications, in 3 Waters and Water Rights, supra, at § 19.05. Because groundwater tends to be more a more complex resource than surface water, groundwater statutes

---

36. Some general adjudication statutes could be applied to groundwater—Arizona's statute, for example, authorizes adjudications of the water rights "in any river system and source," Ariz. Rev. Stat. § 45–251—but this has rarely if ever been attempted.

usually differ somewhat from each other, as well as from their surface water counterparts.

HARLOFF v. CITY OF SARASOTA

District Court of Appeal of Florida, 1991.
575 So.2d 1324.

ALTENBERND, JUDGE.

Roger Harloff appeals a final order of the Southwest Florida Water Management District granting him a consumptive use permit for water allowances which are substantially less than the amounts he had requested. * * * The District's final order will undoubtedly force Mr. Harloff to substantially alter his agricultural activities in Manatee County in order to protect a wellfield supplying water to the City of Sarasota. We write this opinion, in part, because we fear that the facts of this case may become a common theme in Florida as urban and agricultural demands on groundwater reach the capacity of this resource. Whether our current statutory and regulatory structure provides the optimum method to fairly allocate water between competing neighbors is not the issue in this appeal. The facts of this case, however, may be helpful to those in the legislature who are responsible for establishing our state's water policy.

The City of Sarasota owns the Verna Wellfield in the northeast corner of Sarasota County, Florida. This wellfield is located near the southern boundary of Manatee County, Florida, and is very close to Mr. Harloff's farmland. The Verna Wellfield was constructed in 1966. Along with a reverse osmosis plant [eds: used for purifying salty water], it supplies water for approximately 75,000 residents of the City.

The Verna Wellfield contains thirty-nine wells. They obtain water primarily from the Intermediate Aquifer at a depth of 140 feet. When the state first required consumptive use permits for water in 1977, this wellfield had a production rate of 6.9 million gallons per day (mgd). At that time, the City obtained a permit to continue its use of these wells. In January 1985, the District permitted the City to withdraw 6 mgd average with a 7 mgd maximum. Slightly greater consumptive water uses are permitted when the reverse osmosis plant is not in operation. This permit expired in January 1991, during the pendency of this appeal.

Since 1966, there has been a substantial lowering of the water table at the Verna Wellfield. The static water level has declined 40 feet, and the average pumping levels in the field have declined 25 feet. In the spring of 1989, the wellfield was unable to meet its peak demands for the first time. This area is now part of a water use caution area due to a lack of rainfall and a shortage of groundwater. The hearing officer found that the condition of the wellfield is serious and indicative of more serious future problems unless the supply of groundwater is carefully managed.

Mr. Harloff farms approximately 8,500 acres in Manatee County. He grows tomatoes and other fruits and vegetables. He has 200 full-time employees and over 800 additional part-time workers. No one questions the economic importance and significance of his farming operations in Manatee County.

Although in theory Mr. Harloff could implement a more efficient, more expensive, drip irrigation system, he currently uses a semi-closed ditch irrigation system. His current irrigation system is a common system and is extensively used by many good farmers in Florida. This record does not establish whether a drip system would be economically feasible for Mr. Harloff's operation.

In September 1988, Mr. Harloff applied to the District for a consumptive use permit. Agricultural use of groundwater has grown rapidly in this region of Florida, and the City decided to challenge this permit on the ground that the extent of Mr. Harloff's requested water use would interfere with the City's existing water use. The City requested a formal administrative hearing. Mr. Harloff amended his application in August 1989, requesting a permit for approximately 26 mgd as a seasonal average, 32 mgd as a seasonal daily maximum, and 15 mgd as an annual average. The District's staff studied this request and recommended a permit with limits of 15.6 mgd seasonal average, 20.1 mgd seasonal daily maximum, and 11.1 mgd annual average.

It should be noted that Mr. Harloff intends to withdraw water from a deeper aquifer that provides water of lower quality than the aquifer used by the City. Although these aquifers are at different levels, they are geologically interrelated. Unfortunately, aquifers do not respect county lines. Thus, the withdrawal of water at Mr. Harloff's farmland in Manatee County will impact on the amount of water available at the City's wellfield in Sarasota County. Accordingly, the mixed question of fact and law presented to the hearing officer and the District was the extent to which Mr. Harloff should be permitted to withdraw water that could interfere with the permit previously issued to the City.

To obtain a permit pursuant to the provisions of chapter 373, an applicant must establish that the proposed use of water:

> (a) Is a reasonable-beneficial use as defined in section 373.019(4);

> (b) Will not interfere with any presently existing legal use of water; and

> (c) Is consistent with the public interest.

§ 373.223, Fla. Stat. (1989). A "reasonable-beneficial use" means "the use of water in such quantity as is necessary for economic and efficient utilization for a purpose and in a manner which is both reasonable and consistent with the public interest." § 373.019(4), Fla. Stat. (1989).

In this case, it is clear that Mr. Harloff's intentions to grow produce and his methods to do so would establish a reasonable-beneficial use in the absence of a competing demand for water. In order to obtain a permit, however, Mr. Harloff was required to prove that his use would not interfere with the City's existing legal use of water and that it would be consistent with the public interest under the environmental conditions which existed in the region at the time of the application.

After a lengthy hearing, the hearing officer approved an extensive set of factual findings. Based on the testimony of Mr. Harloff's expert, these findings state that Mr. Harloff's water consumption would result in an additional 1.7 foot drawdown in the Upper Floridan Aquifer underlying a portion of the Verna Wellfield. Other expert testimony, accepted in the findings of fact, provides that this amount of drawdown "would seriously degrade the productive capacity" of twelve wells in the Verna Wellfield. Mr. Harloff's own proposed and accepted findings of fact state that no party had provided the hearing officer with an analysis of "how much additional impact the Verna Wellfield can withstand."

Despite this evidence, the hearing officer recommended that Mr. Harloff receive a consumptive use permit for the entire allowance of water that he had requested. The City filed an exception to the hearing officer's recommendation. Following a public hearing, the District accepted the hearing officer's findings of fact, but concluded that he had made an error of law. The District concluded that, as a matter of law, Mr. Harloff had not proven the three factors which he was required to establish for his requested permit. It authorized a permit which allocated to Mr. Harloff the amount of water recommended by its staff.

On appeal, Mr. Harloff contends that the District improperly substituted its own decision for that of the hearing officer. He believes that he is the victim of a political decision rather than the recipient of a rational, scientific determination. His suspicions are perhaps heightened by the District's failure to explain with any particularity the legal errors which were made by the hearing officer. On full review of the record, however, we are convinced that the District correctly found errors of law in the hearing officer's proposal and that the District's final order is supported by competent, substantial evidence.

The District has broad powers to reject conclusions of law which have been proposed by the hearing officer. * * * Although this broad power could easily be abused, there is merit in placing the power to interpret this narrow area of the law in the hands of the District's board. The District is responsible for implementation of the state water use plan in southwest Florida. If that plan is to be fairly, consistently, and uniformly applied while interpreting such complex concepts as "reasonable-beneficial use" and "interference," permits must be carefully reviewed by a single, experienced governmental body that is responsible for that function and responsive to the electorate. If the legal interpretation of these policies were left to various hearing officers, the concepts would inevitably receive different meanings before different hearing officers. Because agency boards are charged with the responsibility of enforcing the statutes which govern their area of regulation, courts give great weight to their interpretations of those statutes. * * *

The factors described in section 373.223 and in the definition of "reasonable-beneficial use" create mixed questions of law and fact. An agency's decision on such a mixed question is entitled to "increased weight when it is infused by policy considerations for which the agency has special responsibility." Santaniello v. Dept. of Prof. Reg., 432 So. 2d 84, 85 (Fla. 2d DCA 1983). We defer to the District's legal interpretation of this section. Although the District was not free to reject the hearing officer's findings of fact related to these mixed issues in this case, it was free to substitute its judgment concerning the legal question of whether those facts established a permit which would "not interfere" with the City's water use under its existing permit and would be a "reasonable-beneficial use."

From a review of this record, it is apparent that the hearing officer made at least two errors of law which tainted his legal conclusions. First, the hearing officer's recommended order appears to place the burden of proof on the City or the District staff to establish that Mr. Harloff's requested permit would interfere with the water supply at the Verna Wellfield. The statute, however, clearly places the burden on Mr. Harloff to prove that his request would not interfere. Since Mr. Harloff had the burden of proof, his own proposed finding that no party had prepared an analysis demonstrating the extent of the drawdown that his requested water use would create in the Verna Wellfield was quite damaging to his case.

Second, the hearing officer's decision was based, in part, on steps which the City could take to improve the condition of the Verna Wellfield. The hearing officer assumed that there would be no significant interference of the wellfield by Mr. Harloff's activities because the City could deepen its wells and expend funds to upgrade those wells from their current condition. While it would certainly make sense for the City to take those steps, this hearing was not a hearing on the City's permit. One might question whether adjacent properties with large water consumptions should be compelled to file competing applications. § 373.233, Fla. Stat. (1989). If the City seeks additional water in 1991, for example, Mr. Harloff's permit will presumably be a legal existing use entitled to superiority in the City's hearing. Nevertheless, the statutes do not compel such a pairing process. Legally, the City's permit was an existing permit entitled to superiority. The District's final order correctly recognized the superior status of the City's permit.

Affirmed.

Notes and Questions

1. Florida used to be generally classified as following the groundwater doctrine of correlative rights. See, e.g., Cason v. Florida Power Co., 74 Fla. 1, 7, 76 So. 535 (1917) ("property rights relative to [percolating groundwater that underlies several landowners] are correlative; and each land owner is restricted to a reasonable use of his property as it affects subsurface waters passing to or from the land of another"). What role did common law groundwater allocation doctrine play in *Harloff*? Note Harloff is an overlying landowner. And note that the City is exporting water from the land it owns to distribute to private landowners in the City. Wouldn't that make the city

an "appropriator" and subordinate to Harloff under the correlative rights doctrine? If that fact has no relevance to the decision here, does that mean water law in Florida is now wholly statutory, administered through executive branch decisionmaking (here, regional water management districts), and governed by principles of administrative law? Is the effect of the permit statute and the *Harloff* decision to create the functional equivalent of a prior appropriation system for Florida groundwater administered through a permit system? Suppose a global-warming-triggered rise in the ocean level increases the threat of salt water intrusion contaminating the aquifer. Does the Florida statute empower the District to tell landowners over the aquifer no new groundwater permits will be issued?

2. Does the statute (§ 373.223) mandate aquifer management in accordance with "safe yield" principles; that is, does it forbid groundwater mining? Would the statute have allowed the District to grant the permit to Harloff to pump over Sarasota's objection? On what rationale(s)? Might Harloff have won if he had done more extensive hydrologic studies; that is, was his failure one of proof? Does the court give the District a relatively free hand, even a blank check, to interpret and apply the statute? Put a little differently, Harloff alleged he was the "victim of a political decision" by the District. Does the statute in fact call for exactly that; i.e., are the statutory criteria so larded with policy judgments as to call for a "political" decision?

3. Note that permits issued under the Florida statute are of limited duration. The City's initial permit for its wellfield was issued in 1977 (the wellfield was constructed in 1966; the Florida permit statute was enacted in 1972). The permit expired in 1991 while *Harloff* was on appeal. Could the Southwest Florida Water Management District deny Sarasota a renewal of its permit, and issue a permit to Harloff instead, consistent with the statute? Is it relevant that the City pumps about 7 mgd to serve 75,000 residents, while Harloff proposes to pump more than twice as much (15 mgd on average) to operate a single (albeit large) farm?

4. The Florida statute was modeled on the 1972 Model Water Code, which was developed by law professors Frank Maloney, Richard Ausness and James Morris. The code's emphasis on administrative discretion and management through government plans and permits of limited duration was severely criticized by another member of the academy, Frank Trelease, in The Model Water Code, the Wise Administrator and the Goddam Bureaucrat, 14 Nat. Resources J. 207 (1974). Much of the discussion of surface water permit systems in riparian jurisdictions found in Chapter 2 (see supra pp. 101–118) is relevant to this model groundwater code.

5. Although some groundwater statutes date back more than a century (see generally Robert Clark, Ground Water Legislation in the Light of Experience in the Western States, 22 Mont. L. Rev. 42 (1960)), general statutory regulatory schemes for groundwater withdrawals would not begin to emerge until the second half of the twentieth century. The pace picked up considerably toward the end of the millennium, as a number of states have adopted permit systems that govern at least larger groundwater withdrawals, though they may apply only to portions of a state rather than statewide. For a partial survey, see Joseph W. Dellapenna, The Absolute Dominion

Rule, § 20.06, and The Regulated Riparian Approach to Groundwater, § 23.03(b)(1) in 3 Waters and Water Rights (Robert Beck ed., repl.vol. 2003).

6. It is difficult to generalize about groundwater statutes. They may be local or statewide. They may merely modify or entirely replace common law. They may be informational or regulatory. They may act through state administrative agencies, local districts, or courts. They may adopt incentives and market approaches or be more traditional command-and-control. They may carry out social policies that don't directly involve water—e.g., an Oklahoma law prohibits issuing a permit for groundwater if it is to be used in a swine feeding operation within three miles of a camp or recreational site owned or operated by a nonprofit organization. See Okla. Stat. tit. 82, § 1020.11a. We will encounter a variety of statutes in the remainder of the Chapter. A question that overarches all this material is, what kinds of legal rules and regimes (whether adopted by the courts or the legislatures) best facilitate fair and effective management of the complex groundwater resource?

2. LEGISLATIVE REGULATION AND PROPERTY RIGHTS IN GROUNDWATER

Professor Dellapenna notes that the common law of groundwater, like the common law of torts, can be summed up in the word "individualism," or "permitting freedom of action where the effects of individual action cannot be demonstrated with specific proof." Legal Classifications, in 3 Waters and Water Rights § 19.05(b)(3), at 19–48 (Robert Beck ed., repl. vol. 2003) (citing 1 Fowler Harper and Fleming James, The Law of Torts xxvii (1956)). As we have seen, common law groundwater doctrines have expressed this individualism by conferring on overlying landowners (and to some extent other users) what they frequently call a kind of property right in groundwater. This section examines groundwater litigation where those who claim property rights in groundwater challenge governmental rules aimed at controlling groundwater extraction, on the ground these rules unconstitutionally "take" their property interests.

BAMFORD v. UPPER REPUBLICAN NATURAL RESOURCES DISTRICT

Supreme Court of Nebraska, 1994.
245 Neb. 299, 512 N.W.2d 642.

BOSLAUGH, JUSTICE

[In 1977, the State Director of Water Resources designated the area involved in this litigation a groundwater "control area" under state law. The next year the defendant District adopted rules governing withdrawals of groundwater in the control area, and in 1988 issued an order setting a maximum use of 75 acre-inches of groundwater per irrigated acre for the five calendar years 1988–92 [i.e., an average of 15 inches per year]. Plaintiff groundwater pumpers exceeded their allocations by the end of 1991. In March 1992 the defendant District ordered plaintiffs to cease withdrawing groundwater from nine wells for irrigation use. The court rejected plaintiffs' claim that the order was an uncompensated taking. It first noted that the 1977 designation of the groundwater control area by the Director of Water Resources "established that the underground water supply was insufficient for all owners using that supply." Because plaintiffs did not seek judicial review of that order within thirty days of its issuance, as allowed by state law, the question whether the underground water supply was insufficient for all water users was not an issue properly before either the defendant District in the 1992 proceeding nor the courts.]

The appellants attempt to lay a foundation for their takings claim by citing language from Sorensen v. Lower Niobrara Nat. Resources Dist., 221 Neb. 180, 376 N.W.2d 539 (1985). In *Sorensen*, this court stated that "the right of an owner of overlying land to use ground water is an appurtenance constituting property protected by Neb. Const. Art. I, section 21: 'The property of no person shall be taken or damaged for public use without just compensation therefor.'" However, groundwater, as defined in [Neb.Rev. Stat. §] 46–657, is owned by the public, and the only right held by an overlying landowner is in the use of the groundwater. Furthermore, placing limitations upon withdrawals of groundwater in times of shortage is a proper exercise of the State's police power. See Sporhase v. Nebraska ex rel. Douglas, 458 U.S. 941 (1982).

[Prior Nebraska Supreme Court decisions set out] Nebraska's common law of groundwater:

> The * * * rule is that the owner of land is entitled to appropriate subterranean waters found under his land, but he cannot extract and appropriate them in excess of a reasonable and beneficial use upon the land which he owns, especially if such use is injurious to others who have substantial rights to the waters, and if the natural underground supply is insufficient for all owners, each is entitled to a reasonable proportion of the whole. * * *

Under this rule, when the underground water supply is sufficient for all users, a landowner is entitled to reasonable and beneficial use of that supply. Apparently with that in mind, the appellants point to language in Prather v. Eisenmann, 200 Neb. 1, 7, 261 N.W.2d 766, 770 (1978), stating: "Under the reasonable use doctrine, two neighboring landowners * * * can withdraw all the supply he [sic] can put to beneficial and reasonable use. What is reasonable is judged solely in relationship to the purpose of such use on the overlying land." The appellants then conclude that they were entitled to withdraw as much water as was required to use their land as they chose—in this case, to grow a corn crop.

The appellants' reliance on *Prather* is improvident, for the court specifically found that under the circumstances of that case, the water supply was sufficient for all users. Contrarily, as discussed previously, the designation of a control area which included appellants' irrigated land established that in this instance the available supply of water was insufficient for all users.

In addition, while the common-law rule for ground water was adopted in [Olson v. City of Wahoo, 124 Neb. 802, 248 N.W. 304 (1933)], the Legislature has the power to determine public policy with regard to ground water and can alter the common law governing the use of ground water.

Finally, the appellants state that they were deprived of all economic use of their land during 1992 and argue that under Lucas v. South Carolina Coastal Council, 505 U.S. 1003 (1992), they were therefore entitled to compensation. In *Lucas*, the Court found that a landowner was entitled to compensation because South Carolina's Coastal Zone Management Act prohibited all economically beneficial use of his land. However, the appellants' assertions in this instance are little more than a claim that because they could not withdraw enough water to grow a corn crop, they were therefore deprived of all economic use of their land. The record here fails to show that the appellants were, in fact, deprived of all economic use of their land in 1992, and, if only for that reason, Lucas in inapplicable under the circumstances presented here.

Notes and Questions

1.   Is the groundwater control district here simply carrying out Nebraska's common law rule that overlying landowners are entitled only to a "reasonable proportion" of the groundwater supply in circumstances where it is insufficient to meet all needs of overlying landowners? Would the result be the same if Nebraska had followed the prior appropriation doctrine? The rule of capture, the American reasonable use rule, or the Restatement? What more facts about the situation here might you need to know before answering those questions?

2.   Did the plaintiffs' defeat here rest on the notion that they were wasting water? Compare Lindsley v. Natural Carbonic Gas Co., 220 U.S. 61, 77 (1911), where the Supreme Court upheld a New York statute that prohibited pumping mineral waters simply for the purpose of extracting gas therefrom. The "evil" the statute was designed to correct was that the gas extractor pumpers used an "undue proportion of the comingled waters," and a large portion of the waters pumped for that purpose was "permitted to run to waste." This led to an "unreasonable and wasteful depletion of the common supply and in a corresponding injury to others equally entitled to resort to it." The statute preserved the right of landowners to extract the water but merely "so regulates its exercise as reasonably to conserve the interests of all who possess it."

3.   Is plaintiffs' claim of a water right merely a feature of owning land or is it separable from land ownership? If plaintiffs can still dry farm, or build a baseball diamond, or make some other economically advantageous use of the land surface that may not require groundwater, can a takings claim based on being deprived of the right to pump groundwater ever succeed in Nebraska? Is the groundwater merely one stick in the bundle of sticks of landownership, so that the relevant analysis is of the "parcel as a whole," or is the relevant property just the groundwater, without any regard for possible other uses of the surface estate? Cf. Tahoe–Sierra Pres. Council v. Tahoe Reg'l Planning Agency, 535 U.S. 302, 327 (2002) (the focus in

regulatory takings cases must be on "the parcel as a whole"); and supra pp. 365–374.

4. The Florida statute applied in *Harloff*, supra p. 445, sparked a takings challenge by Jupiter, an overlying landowner which applied for a permit to pump groundwater from a shallow aquifer for a 120 unit condominium project. The state denied Jupiter's application because the local village of Tequesta's nearby well field was already pumping the aquifer to its safe capacity, and further pumping could threaten the aquifer with salinity intrusion from the nearby Atlantic Ocean. The Florida Supreme Court rejected Jupiter's inverse condemnation suit against the village in Village of Tequesta v. Jupiter Inlet Corp., 371 So.2d 663 (Fla. 1979). It overruled previous cases and concluded that "the term 'ownership' as applied to [ground]water never meant that the overlying owner had a property or proprietary interest in the corpus of the water itself." Noting that groundwater is "migratory in nature," the Court said that groundwater which is "reduced to [the landowner's] possession and control * * * becomes [the landowner's] personal property," but that "ownership of the land does not carry with it any ownership of vested rights to underlying ground water not actually diverted and applied to beneficial use. The Florida permit legislation (the Water Resources Act of 1972, Fla. Stat. § 373.226(3)) gave holders of common law rights to pump groundwater two years to convert to statutory permits. The Florida Supreme Court noted tersely:

> Tequesta had acquired the permit and Jupiter was merely a proposed user. The Florida Water Resources Act makes no provision for the continuation of an *unexercised* common-law right to use water. Jupiter had perfected no legal interest to the use of the water beneath its land which would support an action in inverse condemnation.

371 So.2d at 671 (emphasis in original).

5. On the other hand, might conversion to a permit system such as Florida has done actually firm up or enlarge the claim of a landowner (who obtains a permit) to a property right in groundwater, compared to whatever claim she may have had as a landowner under common law? That is, might the landowner/permit holder seek relief for invasion of her property right in the permit against newer permit holders, or the state for granting new permits, where interference with her pumping results? The answer would seem to depend largely on the terms of the permit statute, and of the permit itself. (In Florida, as noted above, the permits are for a specific term.)

6. The opinion in *Bamford* does not reveal whether the plaintiff landowners were already pumping groundwater in 1975 when the statute was enacted, or in 1977 when the Director of Water Resources had declared the area a groundwater control area. Would it make any difference if they had been pumping at either of these two points in time? In *Jupiter*, the overlying landowner was not extracting groundwater when the legislature enacted the permit statute, and thus was not exercising whatever latent or potential rights it might have in the groundwater underlying the land. Other courts have agreed with *Jupiter* that overlying landowners do not have a constitutionally protected right in groundwater beneath their property *in situ*; instead, property rights attach to the water only when it is brought to

the surface. See, e.g., Town of Chino Valley v. City of Prescott, 131 Ariz. 78, 638 P.2d 1324 (1981), appeal dismissed, 457 U.S. 1101 (1982) ("there can be no ownership in [ground] waters until they are reduced to actual possession and control by the person claiming them because of their migratory character. Like wild animals free to roam as they please, they are the property of no one"); Knight v. Grimes, 127 N.W.2d 708, 711 (S.D. 1964) (the "notion" that an overlying landowner has "actual ownership of the water prior to withdrawal has been demonstrated to be legally fallacious"); Williams v. City of Wichita, 374 P.2d 578, 588 (Kan. 1962) ("the use of the term 'ownership' as applied to [ground] water has never meant that the overlying owner had a property or proprietary interest in the corpus of the water itself").

7. Some courts have given short shrift to takings claims even from those currently pumping groundwater. In Peterson v. Dept. of Ecology, 596 P.2d 285, 290–91 (1979), a landowner with an active well challenged an order of the state Department of Ecology that he limit his withdrawal of groundwater, pending further study of the available groundwater resources in the area. The Washington Supreme Court had little patience with his argument that the state's action constituted an unconstitutional taking of his property right:

> The relevant inquiry in such a challenge is whether the regulatory scheme is an exercise of police power rather than one of condemnation. The question is one of social policy which requires the balancing of the public interest in regulating the use of private property against the interests of the private landowners not to be encumbered by restrictions on the use of their property. The court must decide each case on its own facts. We find the permit requirement to be a reasonable exercise of the State's police power.

8. The constitutional questions raised by substituting statutory regulation for common law uses of groundwater by overlying landowners are the same as those raised in the surface water context and discussed supra pp. 365–374, "if not easier," according to Professor Dan Tarlock, Law of Water Rights and Resources § 4.29 (2005). Under the absolute ownership and American reasonable use doctrines, for example, the overlying landowner's right to use water is "subject to complete destruction by a more powerful overlying pumper," making a landowner's "expectation of exclusive use of groundwater * * * close to illusory." Id. See also note 5, p. 420 supra.

9. Claims of property rights in groundwater are frequently asserted in non-judicial fora by landowners and groundwater pumpers. No matter how flimsy these claims are in court, one should not underestimate their political appeal in legislatures, or before administrative agencies devising regulatory restrictions under legislative delegation. They make it much more difficult to overcome inertia against change in order to manage groundwater use for the long term, and are a primary reason why the law has not caught up with the massive increase in groundwater use over the past half century.

3. GROUNDWATER–SURFACE WATER INTERCONNECTIONS

A generation ago the National Water Commission called the need to integrate the management of surface water and groundwater one of the three principal problems in groundwater law, management and administration (the others were groundwater mining and quality problems). Water Policies for the Future 232 (1973). It is emerging as an important issue in many jurisdictions, not surprising because groundwater is the source of almost 40% of the streamflow in the entire country, according to the U.S. Geological Survey.[37] The matter involves hydrogeological complexity, is plagued by information gaps, and reveals practical limitations on crafting a regulatory scheme. Finally, it illustrates the difficulties of assigning water rights to groundwater and surface water separately without taking adequate account of the fact that the water involved is often part of a single, hydrologically integrated source. As a long-time Colorado water rights lawyer once put it, the law in many jurisdictions creates a "hydrologic bicycle" out of the hydrologic cycle. Raphael Moses, Basic Groundwater Problems, 14 Rocky Mtn. Min. L. Inst. 501, 503 (1968).

It has been known for a long time that some groundwater had a relatively direct connection to surface water.[38] Much slower to emerge, however, has been an understanding of the nature of these connections sufficient to allow disputes to be fairly resolved, and to allow for genuinely integrated management of groundwater and surface water. So long as there was little or no scientifically adduced information available about the connections, little willingness on the part of government to spend the money to get the information, and, until the advent of high-speed computers, no way to systematically model the movement of water in aquifers in relation to streamflow, it was both easy and in some sense necessary to ignore them. Further, until the emergence of large-scale groundwater extraction near the middle of the twentieth century, there were relatively few situations in which groundwater extraction was significant enough to threaten surface streams.

Professor Sax has ruminated over why California has to this day failed to "bring its water law into line with contemporary knowledge, and with scientific reality," because that state (and it is scarcely alone) extensively regulates surface water and does not regulate groundwater at all, except in some local areas, even when groundwater withdrawals threaten holders of surface water rights. Joseph L. Sax, We Don't Do Groundwater: A Morsel of California Legal History, 6 U. Denv. Water L. Rev. 269, 270 (2003). Part of the answer, he suggests, is that a "great many surface water users are also groundwater pumpers," and probably "the most plausible answer is that water users of all stripes dislike the existing regulatory system, and feel the less regulation, the better." Id. at 271.

37. David W. Moody, Jerry Carr, Edith B. Chase & Richard W. Paulson, National Water Summary, 1986, at 3 (USGS, Water Survey Paper 2325, 1988).

38. Early twentieth century water law treatise writers like Samuel Wiel were quite aware of it. His article, Need for Unified Law for Surface and Underground Water, 2 S. Cal. L. Rev. 358, 369 (1929), argued that the law "cannot prosper" in "ignorance or disregard" of the connection between ground and surface water. See also John Leshy & James Belanger, Arizona Law Where Ground and Surface Water Meet, 20 Ariz. St. L.J. 657, 658–59, 682–84 (1988).

Like in California, the common law nearly everywhere created different legal doctrines for groundwater and surface water. But the problem is considerably more complicated than that. To get at those complications, we begin our examination with groundwater-surface water interconnection problems in jurisdictions that ostensibly apply the same legal principles—the prior appropriation doctrine—to both surface water and hydrologically related groundwater.

CITY OF ALBUQUERQUE v. REYNOLDS

Supreme Court of New Mexico, 1962.
71 N.M. 428, 379 P.2d 73.

GEO. L. REESE, JR., DISTRICT JUDGE.

The City of Albuquerque filed with the state engineer four separate applications for permits to appropriate underground waters from the Rio Grande Underground Water Basin. Under each application it was proposed that a well be drilled to a depth of 1200 feet at a described location on the mesa, some six or seven miles east of the Rio Grande River within the exterior boundaries of the basin, and that 1500 acre feet of water per annum be pumped and used for municipal water supply. * * *

The applications in question were filed pursuant to [state statutes that] provide for application by one desiring to appropriate public unappropriated water for beneficial use * * *. [Following notice, an opportunity for protest, and a hearing, the statute] provided in pertinent part:

> * * * the state engineer shall, if he finds that there are in such underground * * * reservoir * * * unappropriated waters, or that the proposed appropriation would not impair existing water *rights from such source,* grant the said application and issue a permit to the applicant to appropriate all or a part of the waters applied for subject to the rights of all prior appropriators from said source. (Emphasis added)

It is apparent that under this statute there are only two questions to be determined: (1) whether there are unappropriated waters; and (2) whether the taking of such waters will impair existing water rights from such source. * * *

It is an admitted fact that the surface waters of the Rio Grande are fully appropriated. It is also an admitted fact that the underground waters, in the area where the city proposed to drill its wells, contribute substantially to the flow of the Rio Grande, thus constituting a part of the source of the stream flow. The state engineer and the district court each found that the granting of the applications would impair existing rights to the use of the surface waters of the Rio Grande.

In his memorandum decision, which is referred to and made a part of his findings on which he denied the city's applications, the state engineer made further findings and conclusions as follows:

* * * The scientific considerations discussed hereinabove show clearly that accretions from the underground reservoir constitute a major source of the fully appropriated surface water supply of the Rio Grande. These considerations also show that over a 75–year period about one-half of the water proposed to be taken would be extracted from surface flows and about one-half would be taken from underground storage. Much of the water in storage in the Rio Grande underground reservoir is unappropriated and may be taken for beneficial use under an application properly formed to insure against the impairment of existing surface water rights.

Under proper application the appropriator may take advantage of ground water that can be removed from storage without impairment of existing rights, and can take advantage of an accounting of the return flow from his appropriation. The permits applied for could be granted without danger of any impairment of existing surface water rights under the following conditions: 1) That the amount of water pumped be measured. 2) That the amount of return flow be measured. 3) That existing rights to the consumptive use of surface water would be retired to the extent necessary to offset the effects of the appropriation on the Rio Grande. * * *

* * * [T]he city argues, first, that the statutes, from which the state engineer derives his authority to act, do not interrelate and do not authorize the state engineer to interrelate surface and underground waters so as to require the retirement of one as a prerequisite to the appropriation of the other. * * *

The mere fact that the territorial legislature in the water code, Chapter 49, Laws 1907, dealt only with surface waters and therein gave the territorial engineer certain jurisdiction over these waters does not, as argued by the city, imply a legislative intention that subsequent statutes dealing with underground waters are to be looked upon and treated entirely separate and apart as though dealing with two entirely different subjects. The jurisdiction and duties of the state engineer with reference to streams and underground waters are the same. They each relate to public waters subject to use by prior appropriators. There does not exist one body of substantive law relating to appropriation of stream water and another body of law relating to appropriation of underground water. The legislature has provided somewhat different administrative procedure whereby appropriators' rights may be secured from the two sources but the substantive rights, when obtained, are identical. * * *

Having found legislative authority in the state engineer to deny the city's applications on the ground that their granting would result in impairment of the rights of Rio Grande River appropriators, we next consider the argument that the state engineer exceeded his power and jurisdiction by establishing and promulgating rules and regulations requiring the retirement of surface water rights as a condition to new appropriations of underground water from the Rio Grande Underground Water Basin. * * * [If] the underground waters in question cannot be taken without impairment to the rights of the river appropriators, even though there are unappropriated underground waters in the basin, then it would seem to follow that some method should be devised, if possible, whereby the available unappropriated water can be put to beneficial use. * * *

We feel constrained to hold that the state engineer adopted the only known plan to avoid impairment to existing rights and that his requirement, that surface rights be retired to the extent necessary to protect prior stream appropriators as a condition of the granting of an application to appropriate from the basin, is within the lawful power and authority of the state engineer.

Notes and Questions

1. The defendant State Engineer here, Steve Reynolds, was a somewhat legendary figure in western water law—a crusty and independent public official who managed to alienate practically every important water interest in the region at one time or another over his long career from 1955 until his death in 1990. See G. Emlen Hall, Steve Reynolds—Portrait of a State Engineer as a Young Artist, 38 Nat. Resources J. 537 (1998).

2. Although the court's opinion doesn't make it completely clear, the statutes that the court cites (N.M. Stat. §§ 75–12–1 et seq.) apply only to underground waters, defined as the water of "underground streams, channels, artesian basins, reservoirs or lakes, having reasonably ascertainable boundaries * * *." A separate water code article governs surface water appropriations. See N.M. Stat. §§ 72–5–1 et seq. The state administers groundwater not hydrologically connected to surface water on the basis of priorities that are completely independent of the surface water priorities, just like two different unconnected surface streams would have their own independent priority systems. Was the State Engineer here in effect completely merging the two priority systems where the two water sources—the aquifer and the Rio Grande River—were connected? Or was he maintaining a separate priority system for the aquifer, to the extent it could be pumped without an effect on surface water supplies? (He did say that "much of the water in storage in the Rio Grande underground reservoir is unappropriated.") Does the answer make any difference to the outcome?

3. Could the State Engineer have reached the opposite result? That is, could he have ruled for the City, holding that all the groundwater it wanted to pump was unappropriated and thus available to it, even though there was some hydrologic connection between the aquifer and the river, and therefore the groundwater extraction would have some impact on the exercise of senior surface water rights in the Rio Grande?

4. Suppose (although this order of development rarely occurs) that the City commenced pumping groundwater *before* there were any surface water appropriations in the Rio Grande. Farmer Jones then applies for a surface water appropriation upstream from the City's wells. The City objects, arguing that the Jones' proposed depletion of streamflow will, over time, draw water away from the aquifer and impair its groundwater pumping. Same result? Does the principle of merging the groundwater and surface

water priority systems work to protect prior appropriators, regardless of whether they are taking surface water or groundwater?

5. Here State Engineer Reynolds found that, over a 75–year period, one-half of the water the City would pump from its proposed wells will come from aquifer storage, and one-half will be drawn from Rio Grande River flows. This illustrates an important complexity in managing groundwater and surface water on an integrated basis; namely, that the rate of groundwater movement through subsurface materials is much slower than a flowing stream. Pumping from an aquifer may not affect hydrologically connected surface streams for years or even decades. See the earlier discussion of tributary groundwater supra pp. 412–413. This can pose substantial difficulties for courts and regulators, because if they limit or prohibit pumping from junior wells in order to protect senior surface rights, it may be a long time before improvement in surface streamflow can be discerned.

6. In most Western states, farmers typically made the senior surface water appropriations. As urban areas burgeoned after World War II, municipal water providers embarked on a search for new sources of water, both surface and underground. The Albuquerque experience described in this case (assuming the senior appropriators in the Rio Grande are farmers) is typical, in other words. Note that in the end Albuquerque got all the water it wanted to pump from its proposed wells. What price did it have to pay? Is that a fair result overall? But what if the demand for surface water were not to satisfy senior surface appropriators, but instead the needs of the endangered silvery minnow, whose only habitat is the Rio Grande? In fact, in recent years water management in the Rio Grande basin has been significantly influenced by the dictates of the Endangered Species Act; see, e.g., Rio Grande Silvery Minnow v. Keys, 355 F.3d 1215 (10th Cir. 2004).

7. Another jurisdiction that applies prior appropriation to both surface water and hydrologically related groundwater is Colorado, which defines "tributary" groundwater very broadly. See supra p. 412. Here too most surface water rights are senior to most uses of tributary groundwater. Is the effect of a broad definition of tributary groundwater in Colorado to lock up most groundwater supplies in order to support and protect surface water appropriations? If so, is that sound social policy—to deny the use of an otherwise available natural resource because, several decades from now, there will be a slight impact on streamflow that supports senior water rights? Or does the expansive definition simply require that senior surface appropriators be made whole or otherwise properly compensated by new junior groundwater pumpers (assuming efforts to protect the environment don't dictate a different result)?

These issues have been explored in a case growing out of the modern phenomenon of subdividing mountain property for recreational homesites. The new arrivals to "Glacier View Meadows" need water but the surface streams in the area are overappropriated. Groundwater is available in fact, but is it available in law? In Cache LaPoudre Water Users Ass'n v. Glacier View Meadows, 191 Colo. 53, 550 P.2d 288 (1976), the court upheld a "plan of augmentation" under Colorado law by which the subdivider purchased and retired surface water rights to prevent any adverse effect on downstream appropriators of surface water from the groundwater pumping through the wells the developer was installing to serve the new homes as they were built. The plan was quite precise in its estimates of water depleted from surface streams by groundwater withdrawals. Downstream senior appropriators objected that the depletion of the surface stream from the groundwater pumping "cannot be determined with sufficient accuracy" to guarantee the plan would work. The court responded by quoting with approval the water court's discussion:

> Inherent in the hydrological and geological analysis upon which the plan for augmentation herein is founded, is a degree of uncertainty, but the uncertainty is no greater than that inherent in the administration of water rights generally and is not of great significance. The assumptions upon which the plan is based allow more than adequate latitude. If the plan for augmentation is operated in accordance with the detailed conditions herein, it will have the effect of replacing water in the stream at the times and places and in the amounts of the depletions caused by the development's use of water. As a result, the underground water to be diverted by the development wells, which would otherwise be considered as appropriated and unavailable for use, will now be available for appropriation without adversely affecting vested water rights or decreed conditional water rights on the * * * River or its tributaries.

550 P.2d at 296. The uncertainty "inherent in the administrations of water rights" is likely to increase substantially as result of alterations in the hydrologic regime occasioned by moving into a long-term dry cycle, possibly exacerbated by global warming.

8. Most of the cases discussed so far in this section involved applications for a new appropriation of groundwater that was found to tap some water upon which some senior surface appropriations depended. Because most jurisdictions came relatively late to recognize hydrologic connections between groundwater and surface water, and because the effect of groundwater pumping on stream flow may not be felt for years, it may often be the case that already-granted rights to appropriate in both sources turn out to conflict with each other. A number of jurisdictions are now beginning to untangle that situation, with attendant controversy as groundwater pumpers, some of whom have been pumping for years, now face curtailment to protect surface water rights. Colorado has led the way here. For many years what might be characterized as lax administration by the Colorado State Engineer had allowed well owners along major rivers like the South Platte and the Arkansas to pump and take groundwater out of priority. Eventually, when drought made the problem intolerable to senior surface water right appropriators, they sought relief in the courts, and the Colorado Supreme Court ordered their senior priorities be protected. Empire Lodge Homeowners' Ass'n v. Moyer, 39 P.3d 1139 (Colo. 2002) ("The security and reliability of water rights turn on the enforceability of priorities when natural supply is not adequate * * * and administration of decreed rights is necessary to ensure the property value of water rights"). As a result, some 1500 wells were shut down across northeastern Colorado. The complexities of the situation in the South Platte, which has required legislative intervention, are discussed in Lain Strawn, The Last GASP: The Conflict Over Management of Replacement Water in the South Platte River Basin, 75

U.Colo.L.Rev. 597 (2004). Similar situations are cropping up elsewhere. In Idaho where holders of senior water rights along the Snake River have demanded that the state enforce priority and shut down hundreds of wells. See David Olinger & Chuck Plunkett, Law Makes, Breaks Men, Denver Post, Nov. 23, 2005.

9. The Colorado Supreme Court provided a reverse twist on the groundwater-surface water interconnection issue in Alamosa–La Jara Water Users Protection Ass'n v. Gould, 674 P.2d 914 (Colo. 1983). The court was reviewing the State Engineer's rules designed to limit the use of water in the San Luis Valley in order to meet the State's legal obligation, under an interstate compact, to deliver a certain amount of water in the Rio Grande River at the New Mexico border. A vast amount of groundwater supported surface streams in the San Luis Valley. Junior well owners and others argued that the "reasonable means of diversion" doctrine ought to require the senior appropriators to switch to groundwater. This would "eliminate the need for supporting the surface stream, thereby freeing the underground water for maximum beneficial use." The court agreed:

> The water court held that, under certain circumstances, surface stream appropriators may be required to withdraw underground water tributary to the stream in order to satisfy their surface appropriations. We affirm this legal conclusion and return the proposed well rules to the state engineer for consideration of whether the reasonable-means-of-diversion doctrine provides, in this case, a method of achieving maximum utilization of water * * *. We note that the policy of maximum utilization does not require a single-minded endeavor to squeeze every drop of water from the valley's aquifers. [A state statute] makes clear that the objective of "maximum use" administration is "optimum use." Optimum use can only be achieved with proper regard for all significant factors, including environmental and economic concerns. * * * The [state engineer might consider] requiring senior appropriators to drill new wells before requiring curtailment of junior rights * * *. Similarly, the state engineer's reconsideration might result in assessment to junior appropriators of the cost of making those improvements to seniors' diversions which are necessitated by junior withdrawals. Selection among these and other possibilities * * * is a policy decision to be made by the state engineer, after consideration of all relevant factors.

674 P.2d at 935. The evidence showed that the enormous aquifer under the valley can sustain a modest amount of groundwater mining for a long time, and also suggested that a switch to groundwater will not only permit groundwater juniors to receive water, but also probably result in a net water savings because it would dry up some surface vegetation and limit evapotranspiration losses. But what about the environment, including any riparian areas found along the surface streams? Would the approach endorsed by the court be possible or desirable if endangered fish were found in the surface waters of the San Luis Valley streams, or if the riparian vegetation watered by the surface water and its subflow provided essential habitat for endangered birds? Compare County of Inyo v. City of Los Angeles, 61 Cal.App.3d 91, 132 Cal.Rptr. 167 (1976), which did not involve water law,

but rather the requirements of the California Environmental Quality Act as it applied to the City of Los Angeles' pumping of groundwater in a rural county as part of an export project, with the court limiting its pumping pending full compliance with the Act.

———

Colorado and New Mexico manage most hydrologically connected groundwater together with surface water. The end result seems salutary, although it must be noted that both states have a history of active water rights administration. The two states are very different, however, in that Colorado has special water courts that are nearly continuously involved in adjudicating water rights disputes, while New Mexico relies much more heavily on the State Engineer, with relatively little judicial involvement and a history of deferential judicial review.

Other Western states that apply the prior appropriation doctrine to both groundwater and surface water have not gone so far as Colorado or New Mexico. But most have some mechanism for considering the relative effects of a surface water appropriation on a groundwater appropriation and vice versa. Wyoming, for example, allows a senior appropriator, whether of ground or surface water, to complain to the State Engineer of interference by a junior appropriator, regardless of whether either is using ground or surface water. Wyo. Stat. § 410–3–911; see also Wyoming State Engineer v. Willadsen, 792 P.2d 1376 (Wyo. 1990) (evidence did not support the allegation by the senior surface appropriator of interference by a junior appropriator of groundwater). In Montana Trout Unlimited v. Montana Dept. of Nat. Res. and Conservation, 331 Mont. 483, 133 P.3d 224 (2006), the court followed hydrogeologic reality in interpreting a Montana statute which forbade the state agency from processing new applications for groundwater in over-appropriated basins when the groundwater is "immediately or directly connected to surface water." The state agency had adopted regulations effectively interpreting the prohibition to apply only when the groundwater, if extracted, would have pulled surface water from a stream (the court called this "induced infiltration"), and not to apply when the groundwater pumping intercepted groundwater that otherwise would have entered the stream (the court called this "prestream capture of tributary groundwater"). The court overturned the regulations, noting that the agency possesses "a wealth of information" that contradicted its approach, and that it made "no difference to senior appropriators whether groundwater pumping reduces surface flows because of induced infiltration or from the prestream capture of tributary groundwater."

It was not until 1993 that the Washington Supreme Court construed a 1945 statute confirming that groundwater was subject to appropriation as a legislative recognition of "the potential connections between ground water and surface water * * * [making] evident the Legislature's intent that ground water rights be considered a part of the overall water appropriation scheme, subject to the paramount rule 'first in time, first in right.' " Rettkowski v. Dept. of Ecology, 858 P.2d 232, 236 n. 1 (1993). Four years later, the state court of appeals upheld the Department of Ecology's authority to condition new groundwater permits on the maintenance of minimum streamflows in circumstances where, according to the Department's regulations, there was a "significant hydraulic continuity" between the groundwater proposed to be tapped and a surface stream in which the state set a minimum instream flow. Hubbard v. State, 86 Wash.App. 119, 936 P.2d 27 (1997). The Hubbards objected to a condition on a well permit they had received in the early 1990s that required them to cease pumping whenever the river fell below the minimum flow the Department had established for the river in 1976. The court found the Department had not abused its discretion even though there was evidence that the well pumping would have a relatively small effect on streamflow—the Hubbards' hydrogeologist thought the effect was minuscule, amounting to a .004 percent reduction during low flows. See Jeffrie Minier, Conjunctive Management of Stream–Aquifer Water Rights: the *Hubbard* Decision, 38 Nat. Resources J. 651 (1998); see generally Douglas Grant, The Complexities of Managing Hydrologically Connected Surface Water and Groundwater Under the Appropriation Doctrine, 22 Land & Water L. Rev. 63 (1987).

On management of hydrologically related groundwater to protect surface streams in an interstate context, see chapter 8, infra p. 873.

Groundwater–Surface Water Interactions Under Other Groundwater Doctrines

Professor Frank Trelease argued strongly for applying the same legal doctrine to surface water and hydrologically related groundwater: "Regardless of [the difficulty of administration], if we are to correlate the rights in interconnected waters, the essential starting point is to put all rights to both types of water within the same framework; the rights in one source must be relative to the rights in the other." Frank J. Trelease, Conjunctive Use of Groundwater and Surface Water, 27 Rocky Mtn. Min.L.Inst. 1853, 1857 (1982). As sensible as that advice seems, it is not often followed.

Arizona follows prior appropriation for surface water, and the American reasonable use doctrine for groundwater (except in areas where a detailed statutory regulatory scheme, the 1980 Arizona Groundwater Management Act, is in force). In Collier v. Arizona Dept. of Water Resources, 150 Ariz. 195, 722 P.2d 363 (Ct. App. 1986), Collier applied for a surface water appropriation in a spring in a dry creekbed on his land, which was opposed by ranchers with senior appropriations of surface water in the creek further downstream. The court ruled for the ranchers, but noted "it was conceded [at oral argument] that if the Colliers wanted to pump from beneath their own land the same amount of percolating water that flows naturally [the spring], they would be free to do so notwithstanding that this pumping would reduce the flow of [the creek]." This is because Arizona water law has is a "bifurcated system in which percolating groundwater is regulated under a set of laws completely distinct from the laws regulating surface water. While this bifurcation provides a workable legal system, it often ignores the scientific reality that groundwater and surface water are often connected."

Notes and Questions

1. Note that it is the same water whether Collier waits till it emerges in the spring, or pumps it from the ground before it emerges. And the effect on the downstream ranchers is the same. Can the line the court draws, admittedly arbitrary from a hydrologic standpoint, be defended on the ground it leads to predictable results? The line does put surface water users on notice that their water rights are fragile, susceptible of being nullified by groundwater pumpers.

2. Could the underground water feeding the spring be categorized either as an the subflow of the surface stream (though the streambed was dry here), or an underground stream, and in either case appropriable under Arizona law? (The pertinent statute, Ariz. Rev. Stat. § 45–131, defines appropriable water as water flowing in streams or in definite underground channels.) For an argument along these lines, that Arizona law should be construed to take hydrologic realities into account by applying the appropriation doctrine to groundwater hydrologically connected to surface streams, see John Leshy & James Belanger, Arizona Law Where Ground and Surface Water Meet, 20 Ariz. St. L.J. 657, 678 (1988). In Spear T Ranch v. Knaub, 691 N.W.2d 116, 126 (Neb. 2005) (discussed in more detail in ¶¶ 6–7 below), the Nebraska Supreme Court refused to apply the prior appropriation doctrine to tributary groundwater, even though it applied prior appropriation to surface water, because it feared it would "have the effect of shutting down all wells in any area where surface water appropriations are hydrologically connected to ground water." Does such a well shutdown necessarily follow? Could the court instead require the junior groundwater users to pay damages to senior surface water appropriators, or supply the seniors with substitute water? Such techniques have been used elsewhere, see Lawrence J. MacDonnell, Colorado's Law of 'Underground Water': A Look at the South Platte Basin and Beyond, 59 U. Colo. L. Rev. 579 (1988). In fact the plaintiff in *Spear T* had requested damages. See 691 N.W.2d at 124.

3. A massive general stream adjudication has been underway in Arizona since the late 1970s to determine and correlate all surface water rights in the Gila River system, whose watershed covers most of the land area in the state. If the *Collier* view of Arizona's bifurcated system is followed, will that lengthy, expensive effort yield useful results? Will owners of senior surface water rights decreed in that adjudication have any recourse if junior surface appropriators, or persons who had not previously used water at all, sink wells near streams subject to those decreed rights and begin pumping groundwater, with the effect that the surface streams dry up? After *Collier*, the Arizona Supreme Court first took a narrow view of the appropriable subflow of surface streams, and thus in effect acknowledged this as a likely outcome. See In re General Adjudication of Gila River System, 857 P.2d 1236 (1993). On remand, the trial court, in a rather cheeky move, implicitly acknowledged that ignoring hydrologic reality would not work, and adopted a more expansive test for defining subflow in the San Pedro River basin (applying it to the "saturated floodplain Holocene alluvium") than the

Supreme Court had seemingly contemplated, but grounded its approach on rather extensive findings of fact regarding the occurrence of groundwater in that basin, discussed in the next paragraph. On appeal, the Arizona Supreme Court affirmed, saying it was not arbitrary for the trial court, on the facts before it, to adopt this more expansive legal test, especially because it "comports with hydrological reality, as it is currently understood." In re General Adjudication of Gila River System, 9 P.3d 1069 (2000).

4. What are the consequences for use of groundwater if the concept of subflow is broadly construed? The San Pedro River, a small tributary of the Gila, originates in Mexico and flows northward across the border into southeastern Arizona. A large aquifer north of the border helps supply the stream's base flow, and contains perhaps 50 million acre feet of water. The San Pedro River and the aquifer are tapped by farmers, ranchers, an Army base, and urban dwellers (the area is a rapidly growing retirement community). The watershed is also home to one of the largest surviving expanses of southwestern cottonwood-willow riparian forest, and serves as an important corridor for millions of migratory birds. (Birder's Digest named the area the premier birdwatching site in the country.) Congress in 1988 designated the federal lands along the riparian area as the nation's first Riparian National Conservation Area. See 16 U.S.C. §§ 460xx et seq. There is growing concern that increased groundwater pumping will eventually wholly deplete the streamflow during dry periods. Should the 50 million acre-feet in the aquifer go untapped in order to sustain a stream that flows a total of a few thousand acre-feet in a year? Is that an efficient use of water? An international commission established by side agreement to the North American Free Trade Agreement (NAFTA), explored ways to protect the streamflow, discussing water conservation, purchase and retirement of irrigated farmland, importation of water from other basins, and recharging groundwater to create a barrier or curtain between the river and cones of depression from nearby pumping. See Commission on Environmental Cooperation, Sustaining and Enhancing Riparian Migratory Bird Habitat on the Upper San Pedro River (1999); see also Robert Glennon, Water Follies, 541–66 (2002). In the face of continuing inaction, Congress in 2003 required the Secretary of the Interior to prepare a report on the "management and conservation measures * * * needed to restore and maintain the sustainable yield of the regional aquifer by and after September 30, 2011." See 117 Stat. 1392, 1437–39 (2003). Meanwhile, in July 2005, a stretch of the River near the Basin's largest city went dry for eight days for the first time since gauges were installed seventy years ago. Local developers and municipalities blamed a drought; defenders of the River blamed groundwater pumping. The war of words, and the groundwater pumping, continue.

5. The federal legislation creating the San Pedro Riparian National Conservation Area expressly reserved water under federal law to sustain the riparian area. 16 U.S.C. § 460xx–1(d). A leading case on federal water rights (Cappaert v. United States, 426 U.S. 128 (1976)) acknowledges that federal-law-based surface water rights require curtailment of groundwater pumping that is lawful under state law. These issues are explored in Chapter 9 at pp. 912–917; see also infra pp. 502–506. The ongoing saga of the Edwards Aquifer in Texas illustrates how another federal law, the Endangered

Species Act, 16 U.S.C. §§ 1531–43, can direct groundwater management to protect surface water; see infra pp. 661–668.

6.   Nebraska applies a form of correlative rights to groundwater and prior appropriation to surface water. In 2005 in Spear T Ranch v. Knaub, supra Note 2, it became the first state to adopt the doctrine found in § 858 of the Restatement (Second) of Torts for resolving conflicts between groundwater users and those with rights to hydrologically connected surface water. This doctrine makes the groundwater user liable if her withdrawal "has a direct and substantial effect upon a watercourse or lake and unreasonably causes harm to a person entitled to the use of its water." See supra p. 435. How predictable are outcomes of groundwater-surface water disputes resolved by that standard? See John S. Lowe, Lon C. Ruedisili, & Bruce N. Graham, Beyond Section 858: A Proposed Ground–Water Liability and Management System for the Eastern United States, 8 Ecology L.Q. 131, 140–47 (1979). The Nebraska Supreme Court emphasized "the test is flexible and * * * a trial court should consider any factors it deems relevant." 691 N.W.2d at 132. For an illuminating discussion of the Restatement rule, see J. David Aiken, Hydrologically–Connected Ground Water, Section 858 and the Spear T Ranch Decision, 84 Neb. L. Rev. 962 (2006).

7.   The *Spear T* litigation was triggered by the advent of large-scale groundwater pumping in the Pumpkin Creek watershed, which reduced the creek's flow by two thirds in the last three decades, and allegedly injured plaintiff's 1954–1956 surface appropriation. Professor Aiken concedes that considering hydrologically related groundwater as tributary water subject to the same prior appropriation system as surface water "more closely mirrors hydrologic reality," but he argues that, because groundwater users in Nebraska "historically have faced few development constraints, it seems fairer to put surface water appropriators and ground water users on a more or less equal footing legally, which the Section 858 approach of balancing the equities essentially does." Aiken, supra Note 6, at 984 n.118. Aiken points out that "[s]treams can go dry but irrigation wells can almost always be deepened," and this "gives the ground water pumper an inevitable advantage over surface appropriators." His recommendation: "If the law wants to treat the parties equitably, it should not penalize the surface appropriator for her inherent disadvantages. The broad approach to section 858 adopted by the *Spear T* court will doubtless take these factors into account." Otherwise, he says, there would be no accounting for the fact that ground water pumping often will turn "perennially flowing streams into essentially drainage ditches." Id. at 995. Thus, he says: "If ground water users are not financially liable for the harm resulting from dried up streams, the larger message is that protecting streamflows has no value, a message that could well doom future administrative efforts to protect [them]." Id. at 996.

8.   In Collens v. New Canaan Water Co., 155 Conn. 477, 234 A.2d 825 (1967), plaintiff riparian owners complained that a public utility had unlawfully "diverted waters of the Noroton river by means of wells," depleting the natural flow and interfering with their riparian water rights. The court held for plaintiffs, finding it "immaterial in what manner the diversion of the stream by the defendants is effected." It thus chose to follow hydrologic reality to protect surface water rights, even though prior decisions of the court had applied the rule of capture to groundwater. As this dispute

period in which the high capacity well is being pumped. It is generally a *temporary* hydraulic phenomenon, as distinguished from long term over-all lowering of the water level in an aquifer caused by pumping which exceeds recharge.

States such as Iowa, Minnesota, and South Dakota, which border on humid and arid regions, have experienced dramatically increased ground-water irrigation in the last decade. Although the actual number of well interference cases in these states has been relatively small, and aggregate economic damages thus far appear to have been minor, the political impact has been significant. The problem has thus become a major factor in shaping the future course of groundwater policy in these states. * * *

Well interference is a classic example of an economic externality of production, that is, an activity of one economic unit that unintentionally affects the utility or well-being of another. When the pumping of a high capacity well, such as an irrigation well, causes interference with neighboring wells, the owners of the neighboring wells incur costs that they would not have incurred if the high capacity well had not been used. These costs may include higher energy expenditures as the result of pumping from a greater depth, the cost of installing a new pump or constructing a new and deeper well, or health and production losses of livestock.

Well interference as an externality has both equity and efficiency effects. An efficiency gain to society results insofar as the value of the marginal product exceeds the marginal social cost of pumping the water. However, beyond a certain point efficiency loss results because the irrigator using the high capacity well does not bear all the costs to society of pumping. The irrigator has incentive to pump more than is optimal from a resource efficiency standpoint. The supra-optimal or excess use of resources results in a dead weight loss to society.[41]

The equity effect is that the irrigator gains the value of the marginal product of the water. A portion of that gain is at the expense of the owner of the neighboring well who bears the higher pumping costs and perhaps experiences temporary water shortages.

The efficiency and equity effects can be illustrated with a simple graphic model as set forth in Figure [5–7]. In this model the producer faces two economic parameters. One such parameter is his marginal cost of pumping water, MC_p, which is determined by fuels and other variable costs and is nearly horizontal within the relevant range. The producer also faces a value of marginal product curve, VMP. For many activities which use water, particularly agricultural irrigation, the value of marginal product is a decreasing function which may decline to zero or even become negative as more water is applied to a fixed area of land.[42]

41. A dead weight loss is one for which there is a loss to one or more parties, but for which there are no offsetting gains to others in the economy.

42. The VMP Curve declines because of the law of diminishing returns. That is, as more variable input (water in this case) is added, marginal physical product declines.

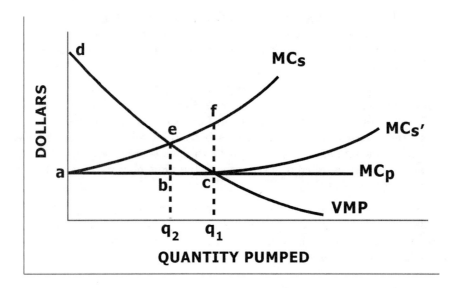

Figure 5-7

Economic Transfers and Losses

Caused by Well Interference

As a rational profit maximizer, the producer pumps until the value produced by the last unit of water he uses is equal to the cost of pumping that water. In Figure [5-7] that quantity of water is q_1. The producer realizes a surplus of value produced over costs equal to the triangular area *acd*. Unfortunately, costs to society are not limited to those incurred by the producer by pumping. The external costs of well interference, when added to producers' pumping costs, form the cost to society as a whole which rise rapidly at higher levels of pumping. The marginal costs to society at each level of water use are represented by the curve MC_s. The marginal cost of well interference at any point is the vertical distance between MC_p and MC_s.

The model reveals that part of the producers' surplus *acd* is in fact an income transfer from persons affected by well interference. The amount of the transfer is equal to the area of the triangle *ace*, which is made up of triangles *abe* and *bce*. Triangle *abe* represents the pure equity effect of well interference.

It is efficient to pump to at least point q_2 because VMP > MC_s. However, the difference between MC_s and MC_p represents a transfer from the neighbor to the irrigator.

The remaining portion of the transfer, *bce,* has both equity and efficiency implications. From the point of view of society as a whole, the optimal level of water use does not occur at q_1, but rather at q_2, where the VMP is equal to the marginal cost to society rather than the marginal cost to the producer. Producing at a level q_1 rather than at q_2 has two effects—a transfer from society (or in this case from neighbors) to the producer equal to triangle *bce,* and a dead weight loss equal to triangle *cfe.* Triangles *bce* and *cfe* represent the efficiency effect of well interference.

In this model the difference between the producer's marginal cost, MC_p, and the marginal cost to society, MC_s, consists of the additional cost of pumping water in affected wells and the damages caused by temporary water shortages during one pumping season. In the long run, owners of the neighboring domestic wells may reduce or eliminate these costs by constructing new and/or deeper wells. Such action might shift the seasonal marginal costs to society downward to MC_s, and would allow the producer to continue to pump q_1 units of water without causing the appreciable transfers or losses. This solution would be preferable for society if the cost of new wells were less than the present value of the external costs represented by area *ace,* assuming that pumping in the absence of new wells were restricted by rules or administrative procedures to q_2. Under this condition, triangle *abe* represents external costs which no longer occur because of the new wells which relieve interference problems. Triangle *bce* represents additional product enabled by increasing pumping from q_2 to q_1.

In the absence of regulations designed to restrict pumping to level q_2, pumping would normally occur to point q_1. New investment, which would shift MC_s to MC_s, would be efficient if the costs of the new wells were less than the present value of area *acf* in future years. Area *ace* represents the value of the additional product, and *cef* represents the dead weight loss which no longer occurs.

Based on these equity and efficiency characteristics of well interference, one can derive several criteria by which to evaluate specific well interference policies. With respect to efficient resource allocation, laws and administrative regulations should minimize dead weight losses to society while enabling real income gains that may result from high capacity pumping. With respect to equitable considerations, laws, rules and regulations, in our view, should recognize the income transfers which may occur under high capacity pumping and depending on the value judgment of society, should reduce or compensate for such income transfers.

In his classic article, Coase argues that externalities can be efficiently handled through the marketplace.[43] However, we take a less sanguine view, more in line with Mishan's theory that the "structure" of the market and resulting high transaction costs more often than not preclude efficient handling of externalities in the marketplace.[44] As pointed out later in this article, public policy may facilitate or provide means for

43. Coase, The Problem of Social Cost, 3 J.L. & Econ. 1 (Oct. 1960).

44. Mishan, The Postwar Literature on Externalities: An Interpretive Essay, 9 (No. 1) J. Econ. Literature 1–27 (March 1971).

encouraging the private negotiation of externalities. In most situations, however, this facilitation will require affirmative public policy action rather than a policy of benign neglect.

Equity considerations have implications for efficiency concerns since failure to provide for compensation may prevent irrigation benefits from accruing.[45] Finally, policies and procedures which are adopted should not result in equity or efficiency effects that are as or more costly to society than the problems which they are intended to alleviate. For example, cumbersome administrative procedures and/or litigation are real costs to society. Furthermore, procedures which involve litigation tend to favor high income individuals who already enjoy favored status in society.

PRATHER v. EISENMANN

Supreme Court of Nebraska, 1978.
200 Neb. 1, 261 N.W.2d 766.

SPENCER, JUSTICE.

This is an action brought by domestic well owners to enjoin the pumping of ground water from an irrigation well owned by defendants, and for damages. The District Court found defendants' withdrawal caused a loss of artesian pressure in plaintiffs' wells, interfering with their domestic appropriation.

The court found the water was sufficient for all users if plaintiffs lowered their pumps to below the aquifer and defendants did not lower their pump. It permanently enjoined defendants from lowering their pump and from pumping for the period of time reasonably required by plaintiffs to lower their pumps. The court awarded plaintiffs the necessary costs of providing an assured alternative method of water supply, or a total recovery of $5,346.58. We affirm.

Plaintiffs Prather are the owners of a 9–acre tract upon which they maintain their residence. The residence is supplied with water by an artesian well located on the premises. The artesian pressure was normally sufficient to force water in the well to a level 5 to 6 feet above the ground. The well was 121 feet 10 inches deep and 2 inches in diameter.

Two other landowners, Furleys and Zessins, assigned their claims to Prathers. * * *

Defendants Eisenmanns purchased a 90–acre tract of land in the area in March of 1976. On July 9, 1976, they completed an irrigation well on the premises. The well was 179 feet deep and had a capacity of 1,250 gallons per minute on a 2–hour test.

On July 9, 1976, Eisenmanns commenced pumping from the well at an estimated rate of 650 gallons per minute. Prathers and Furleys lost the use of their wells on July 10, 1976. Zessins lost the use of their well between the evening of July 12 and the morning of July 13 when the

45. Potential benefits from irrigation would be precluded, for example, if a mora- torium were placed on new irrigation per- mits.

water level dropped below the level of the submersible pump. Because of the loss of water, the Zessins' pump overheated and welded itself to the casing. Zessins were unable to dislodge the pump and were forced to drill a new well to a depth of 164 feet.

Following a stipulation by the parties, a temporary injunction was issued on July 20, 1976, to permit the University of Nebraska Conservation and Survey Division to conduct certain tests on the wells. The tests consisted of pumping the irrigation well at a rate of 375 gallons per minute for 3 days, then measuring the draw down of the Eisenmanns' well and a number of other observation wells which included the three domestic wells. At the end of the pumping period the measured draw down on the Prathers' well was 61.91 feet; the Furleys' well, 65.45 feet; and the Zessins' well, 65.6 feet. The draw down of the Eisenmanns' well was 97.92 feet. All the wells recovered to the prepumping level within 11 days after cessation of pumping from the irrigation well.

The two hydrologists who conducted the tests made certain findings: (1) The irrigation well and the domestic wells were drawing from the same aquifer. (2) The aquifer could be defined with reasonable scientific certainty. (3) The pumping by Eisenmanns depressed the artesian head of the domestic wells. (4) The cone of influence caused by Eisenmanns' pumping intercepted or affected the plaintiffs' wells. (5) The common aquifer from which the domestic and irrigation wells draw water is sufficient to supply both domestic and irrigation needs. (6) For plaintiffs to obtain water from their wells during periods when Eisenmanns were pumping, they would have to pump water from the top of the shale. [The court did not explain what this meant; presumably the shale was an impermeable layer that formed the floor of the aquifer from which all were pumping.—Eds.] * * *

Nebraska has had few decisions dealing with underground water problems. In Olson v. City of Wahoo, 124 Neb. 802, 248 N.W. 304, our court, in 1933, enunciated a modified reasonable use rule. It said: "The American rule is that the owner of land is entitled to appropriate subterranean waters found under his land, but he cannot extract and appropriate them in excess of a reasonable and beneficial use upon the land which he owns, especially if such use is injurious to others who have substantial rights to the waters, *and if the natural underground supply is insufficient for all owners, each is entitled to a reasonable proportion of the whole,* and while a lesser number of states have adopted this rule, it is, in our opinion, supported by the better reasoning." (Italics supplied.) The portion emphasized was not a part of the American rule as enunciated in a majority of the states. Nebraska, in *Olson,* adopted the rule of reasonable use with the addition of the California doctrine of apportionment [Eds: among overlying landowners; i.e., correlative rights] in time of shortage. * * *

Under the reasonable use doctrine, two neighboring landowners, each of whom is using the water on his own property overlying the common supply, can withdraw all the supply he can put to beneficial and reasonable use. What is reasonable is judged solely in relationship to the purpose of such use on the overlying land. It is not judged in relation to the needs of others. Harnsberger, Oeltjen, & Fischer, Groundwater: From Windmills to Comprehensive Public Management, 52 Neb. L. Rev. 179 at p. 205 (1973). * * *

The Nebraska rule * * * must be construed, however, in the light of our preference statute, section 46–613, R.R.S.1943. This statute provides as follows:

> Preference in the use of underground water shall be given to those using the water for domestic purposes. They shall have preference over those claiming it for any other purpose. Those using the water for agricultural purposes shall have the preference over those using the same for manufacturing or industrial purposes.

> As used in this section, domestic use of ground water shall mean all uses of ground water required for human needs as it relates to health, fire control, and sanitation and shall include the use of ground water for domestic livestock as related to normal farm and ranch operations.

It is our statute which distinguishes the Nebraska rule from other rules. Under the statute, the use of underground water for domestic purposes has first preference. It takes priority over all other uses. As between domestic users, however, there is no preference or priority. Every overlying owner has an equal right to a fair share of the underground water for domestic purposes. If the artesian head in the present situation had been lowered by other domestic users, plaintiffs would be entitled to no relief so long as they still could obtain water by deepening their wells. If the water became insufficient for the use of all domestic users, each domestic user would be entitled to a proportionate share of the water. All domestic users, regardless of priority in time, are entitled to a fair share of the water in the aquifer.

That, however, is not the present problem. We are dealing with plaintiffs who have preferential rights. * * *

Plaintiffs can still obtain sufficient water for domestic purposes by drilling wells to the shale. It would not have been necessary for them to incur the necessary expense to do so except for the action of defendants. Without question, plaintiffs have been damaged by the operation of defendants' well. As the trial court found, defendants' withdrawal of water caused unreasonable harm to plaintiffs by lowering the water table or reducing the artesian pressure. Plaintiffs had obtained a property right in that use so they should have a remedy for their damage.

The remedy devised by the trial court presents a very equitable solution. It reimburses the plaintiffs only for the expense they were forced to incur because of the action of the defendants. Plaintiffs' wells were very adequate for their own purposes. Their use of water for domestic purposes took precedence over the appropriation for agricultural purposes by the defendants. Plaintiffs had a valuable property right in the extraction of water for domestic purposes. It was solely defendants' action which deprived them of their right. Defendants, by pumping large quantities of water from the same aquifer, destroyed the artesian pressure for two of the wells. For the other well, which was deeper and used a pump, defendants' action lowered the water below the reach of the pump and the resultant heat froze the pump to the pipe. The only way plaintiffs could be assured of water for domestic purposes was to drill wells to the shale. This expense was thrust upon plaintiffs solely as a consequence of defendants' action in destroying plaintiffs' artesian pressure and lowering the water below the reach of their domestic wells. Plaintiffs' right to the extraction of water from their existing wells was appropriated or destroyed by the action of defendants. What should be the extent of plaintiffs' damage? Certainly it should be the cost of restoring or obtaining what plaintiffs had before it was appropriated by defendants' action. * * *

The solution devised by the District Court is the correct one. The judgment is affirmed.

Notes and Questions

1.   The Nebraska preference statute (and the interpretation given to it by the court) made the outcome here easy. The shallow well domestic user receives compensation from the deep well agricultural user who caused the domestic wells to fail. The amount of compensation is based on the cost of deepening the adversely affected wells so that all of the parties can receive water in the future. Is that full compensation? Two of plaintiffs, Prather and Furley, apparently had no pumps, because the artesian pressure brought the water to the surface in their wells. Thus it might be said that the impact of Eisenmann's well on plaintiffs included the cost of (1) deepening their wells (and drilling a new well for Zessin); (2) purchasing and installing a pump for Prather and Furley, and replacing Zessin's burned-out pump; and (3) electricity to operate the pumps. The court's opinion does not make completely clear how much of these costs Eisenmann should bear. Should plaintiffs bear any of these costs? May Eisenmann simply choose to supply plaintiffs with water from his own well, or may the court order that relief?

2.   The same basic result was reached on similar facts in a jurisdiction applying prior appropriation to groundwater. Parker v. Wallentine, 650 P.2d 648 (Idaho 1982). The court held that Parker, the senior domestic well owner, could obtain an injunction against Wallentine, the owner of a junior irrigation well. Although an Idaho statute required wells to be dug to a reasonable depth, and protected prior appropriators "only in the maintenance of reasonable groundwater pumping levels as may be established by" the state engineer, Idaho Code § 42–226, the court held the statute did not apply to domestic wells because such wells had been generally exempted from the requirements of the Ground Water Act. See Idaho Code § 42–227. The court went on to say that if Wallentine paid Parker's expense in changing his method or means of diversion, the court could lift the injunction.

3. What might be the rationale for establishing a different rule for domestic wells—i.e., giving them more protection than would be provided by applying a "reasonable pumping level" standard? Because domestic water is necessary for survival and settlement? Does it rest on an unspoken premise about cost-bearing ability? The cost of a domestic well would likely only be recaptured through the subsequent sale of the homestead, rather than through the sale of water itself, or any commodity produced with the water. Furthermore, the ability of domestic users to pay for well-deepening may vary greatly, and a reasonable pumping level requirement could lead to *de facto* eviction of poorer users. If this social equity concern is at the base of the domestic well exemption, is the exemption the proper means of solving the problem? See generally Douglas Grant, Reasonable Groundwater Pumping Levels Under the Prior Appropriation Doctrine: The Law and Underlying Economic Goals, 21 Nat. Resources J. 1 (1981).

4. What if Eisenmann's well was located some distance from Prather's property, and the hydrogeology of the aquifer were such that the effect of Eisenmann's well on Prather's is delayed (and therefore perhaps not so obvious)? What if there were numerous other fairly new irrigation wells in the vicinity, making it difficult to establish causation and fix responsibility among possible defendants? Are the courts institutionally equipped to address such problems (say, through defendant class actions) or is this kind of problem better addressed through governmental regulation, such as administrative rules for well spacing? Note that the Idaho statute discussed in Note 2 points in that direction, for competing non-domestic pumpers, by authorizing the director of the state department of water resources to establish reasonable groundwater pumping levels. Or should all wells tapping an aquifer be taxed to create a domestic well-deepening fund?

5. Most prior appropriation states now limit the protection given to senior well owners in their means of diversion in accordance with a standard such as reasonable pumping levels. See, e.g., Grant, supra Note 3, at 35; Wayman v. Murray City Corp., 23 Utah 2d 97, 458 P.2d 861 (1969) ("all users are required where necessary to employ reasonable and efficient means in taking their own waters in relation to others * * * "). What might be critical determinants in measuring the reasonableness of a method of diversion of groundwater? As in other areas of the law, a reasonableness standard requires line drawing. A very senior but very shallow well drawing from a vast aquifer appears unreasonable. When it was dug, however, it was almost assuredly a reasonable method of obtaining water. Cf. Tulare Irr. Dist. v. Lindsay–Strathmore Irr. Dist., supra p. 165 (customary irrigation practices deemed reasonable/beneficial use). The cost of deepening the well might render the owner's existing use uneconomic. Is the owner of a senior shallow well properly charged with having foresight that the aquifer would be developed more extensively at a later date? Should uses that are only marginally profitable and whose profitability rests on avoiding the expense of digging a new well be forced out of business by a highly capitalized water company with a new deep well? The vagueness and discretionary determination of "reasonableness" of pumping levels is criticized as an obstacle to market transfers of water in Jacque Emel, Groundwater Rights: Definition and Transfer, 27 Nat. Resources J. 653 (1987).

6. Is the issue here the same as sometimes occurs in surface water, where a senior appropriator may be using a highly inefficient means of diversion, such as a water wheel or brush dam? In 1995, the South Dakota Water Management Board issued a groundwater withdrawal permit to a Coca–Cola bottling facility despite Rapid City's claim that it would have an adverse effect on an artesian well the City developed for municipal use. The Board noted there was ample water in the aquifer for both uses, and that Rapid City had decided to drill its well only 320 feet below the surface even though the aquifer extended another 1000 feet downward. The Board said it would not allow Rapid City to "reserve one thousand feet of head pressure [in the aquifer] for itself," because that would be inconsistent with state law that water resources are not to be wasted but used to the fullest extent. In the Matter of Water Permit Application No. 2313–2 (S.D. Water Mgmt. Bd., June 7, 1995).

7. What outcome in *Prather* or *Parker* if the plaintiff and defendant were both engaged in uses of water of equal statutory rank; e.g., both using groundwater for irrigation? What outcome on the facts (earlier domestic user versus later irrigation user) would have been reached in jurisdictions following the rule of capture? The Restatement (Second) of Torts? Under the latter, is lowering of the water table and/or artesian pressure deemed to be unreasonable in every case?

8. In MacArtor v. Graylyn Crest III Swim Club, 187 A.2d 417, 420 (Del.Chancery Ct. 1963), MacArtor complained that the new high volume well of a nearby swim club interfered with his domestic well. The court purported to apply the American reasonable use rule, and cast doubt on the reasonableness of the swim club's pumping. It noted, among other things, that the club's recreational use was "not entitled to quite the same consideration as a household use," and that it was withdrawing a large amount of water in concentrated time periods and in relation to the land area it was occupying, even though it may have been "reasonably entitled to believe that the well it sank would not interfere with wells such as plaintiffs'." The court left the question of possible remedies to subsequent proceedings (unreported). Was the chancellor applying the American reasonable use rule, or some version of the correlative rights doctrine? It may be hard to tell. See supra pp. 429–432.

9. One strategy for dealing with well interference is well spacing requirements, which Professor Aiken reports have reduced seasonal disputes between high-capacity wells in Nebraska. J. David Aiken, Nebraska Ground Water Law & Administration, 59 Neb. L. Rev. 917, 948–50, 978–80 (1980). South Dakota has an administrative rule that mandates controlling the spacing of larger wells (those with a capacity of 18 gallons per minute) "to assure domestic use and other prior water right water supplies in adequate wells," and also makes spacing a criterion applied "in determining the availability of unappropriated water when considering individual applications for permits to appropriate groundwater." ARSD 74.02.05.02 (2005); see also S.D. Codified Laws §§ 46–1–6(13), 46–6–6.1. The simplicity of such an approach brings with it relatively low administrative costs. It remains a relatively crude technique; i.e., a uniform spacing requirement applied to a variety of hydrogeologic conditions may be sometimes too protective and sometimes not protective enough.

10.   In Minnesota, if it appears likely that a proposed irrigation well may interfere with existing domestic wells, the state agency will not issue a permit until the applicant reaches an agreement with those well owners detailing the abatement procedures or compensation which the applicant will offer to the potentially damaged party, or, if no agreement is reached, the proposed irrigator "shall be responsible for all costs necessary to provide an adequate supply with the same quality and quantity as prior to the applicant's or permittee's interference." Minn. R. 6115.0730(4)(A)(1). The rule immunizes holders of groundwater permits from liability for any interference their pumping causes new domestic wells (which are exempt from permit requirements) if the area has adequate groundwater, because it makes it the responsibility of the prospective new domestic well owner to drill the well to an adequate depth to account for the permitted appropriation. Id. 6115.0730(3). Commentators have extolled this approach, finding that the bargaining process, relatively equal bargaining power, and the incentive "to negotiate prior to irrigation minimize the chances of costly and wasteful litigation." See Edward Lotterman & John Waelti, Efficiency and Equity Implications of Alternative Well Interference Policies in Semi–Arid Regions, 23 Nat. Resources J. 323, 333 (1983).

5.   INADEQUATE SUPPLIES OF GROUNDWATER (GROUND-WATER MINING)

This section examines issues created when there is not enough water in an aquifer to supply the demands of its users for a sustained period of time. This was one of the three principal problems in groundwater law, management and administration identified by the National Water Commission. Water Policies for the Future 232 (1973). The law here must guide not only allocations of water among users, but also determinations of how much of the limited supply of groundwater will be made available for use over time.

Regional declines may occur for two reasons. First, water may be withdrawn from an aquifer having little or no recharge—usually this is what may be called "fossil water," deposited very slowly over time or in an earlier geologic era. Second, even if an aquifer has substantial recharge, water may be extracted from it in excess of the recharge rate. In either situation, as the water level in the aquifer declines, pumpers face increasing pump lifts, and shallower wells may lose their water supply altogether. If water-bearing strata undergo compaction, the land surface may subside; if so, the aquifer will lose its ability to be recharged. See supra pp. 405–406.

Sometimes the limits on further groundwater extraction may be physical; that is, it may no longer be possible to extract groundwater from storage. More often, the limits are economic—the level in the aquifer declines to a depth from which it is not economical to pump (usually determined by the cost of electricity to drive the pumps), or the quality is lowered beyond the user's economic ability to purify. Other considerations are relevant. Groundwater left in place will not be used to help satisfy contemporary human needs other than subjacent support of land and, where the water table is near the surface, to support surface streams and vegetation. On the other hand, one might make a case for leaving groundwater in place to benefit future generations.

Pondering what social policy should govern groundwater mining naturally invites comparison to another mined natural resource on which the U.S. is so heavily dependent; viz., petroleum. From time to time the United States government makes an effort to guide or otherwise mitigate the operation of the free market of supply and demand that is a primary determinant of oil production and consumption rates. The success of these efforts is a matter of vigorous debate. How much, if at all, ought policies toward groundwater mining be influenced by experiences with petroleum? See pp. 421–423 supra. The National Water Commission's conclusion about groundwater mining policy was succinctly stated: "Mining ground water is not inherently wrong. It is wrong, however, when the water is mined out without taking account of the future value of the water and the storage capacity of the reservoir." Water Policies for the Future 239 (1973).

Many but by no means all of the sophisticated attempts to deal with groundwater mining have come in prior appropriation jurisdictions. This should not be surprising, for most jurisdictions applying the prior appropriation doctrine to groundwater are relatively arid and in some, groundwater is heavily used. Favoring earlier over later users, the prior appropriation doctrine seems to offer a more straightforward and predictable way to allocate limited supplies of groundwater than other doctrines. The following case shows, however, that these jurisdictions tend not to woodenly enforce priority in situations of regional aquifer decline.

MATHERS v. TEXACO, INC.

Supreme Court of New Mexico, 1966.
77 N.M. 239, 421 P.2d 771.

LaFel E. Oman, Judge.

The applicant-appellant, Texaco, Inc. * * * filed applications with the State Engineer for permits to appropriate 700–acre feet of water per year from the Lea County Underground Water Basin. Upon the hearing of the applications and the protests thereto, the respondent-appellant, the State Engineer * * * made and entered findings and an order that the applications should be granted for the appropriation by Texaco of 350–acre feet per year for the purpose of water flooding 1,360 acres of oil-bearing formation in a producing oil field. By this water flooding operation, which has been approved by the New Mexico Oil Conservation Commission, it is contemplated that slightly in excess of one million barrels of oil will be recovered.

The protestants-appellees * * * who had acquired prior rights to appropriate waters from the Lea County Underground Water Basin, appealed to the district court of Lea County from the findings and order of the State Engineer. The trial judge * * * concluded that the findings and order of the State Engineer were contrary to the evidence, and therefore, arbitrary, unreasonable and unlawful. Judgment was entered accordingly, and from this judgment Texaco and the State Engineer have taken this appeal.

There is no question concerning the following facts:

(1) The use of the water for the proposed flooding of the oil field is a reasonable and beneficial use;

(2) The fresh water in the Lea County Underground Water Basin is found in the Ogallala formation which varies in thickness from a thin edge to something over 200 feet;

(3) The waters in the basin are replenished only by surface precipitation, which is very limited, and which is just about equaled by a natural discharge from the basin. Thus, for all practical purposes, no recharge takes place, and the pumping of any water from the basin depletes the stock or supply to that extent, and in effect amounts to a mining operation;

(4) In 1952 the State Engineer made a determination of the amount of water in each township in the basin, the amount of water that had been appropriated in each township, and the amount of water that would be drawn from the stock or supply in each township into the surrounding townships, when the waters in the surrounding townships were fully appropriated.

In determining what constitutes full appropriation in each township, and thus in the basin as a whole, he calculated the amount of water that could be withdrawn from each township and still leave one-third of the water in storage at the end of forty years. At that time it was contemplated that some of the remaining water could be economically withdrawn for domestic, and perhaps some other uses, but that it would no longer be economically feasible to withdraw the water for agricultural and most other purposes.

On the basis of this method of administration and operation established in 1952, there remains and is available for appropriation by Texaco the 350–acre feet per year which the State Engineer granted;

(5) The appropriation of the water by Texaco will unquestionably lower the water table in the wells of the protestants, and will result in an increase in pumping costs and in shortening the time during which the protestants can economically pump water from their wells. * * *

The administration of a non-rechargeable basin, if the waters therein are to be applied to a beneficial use, requires giving to the stock or supply of water a time dimension, or, to state it otherwise, requires the fixing of a rate of withdrawal which will result in a determination of the economic life of the basin at a selected time.

The very nature of the finite stock of water in a non-rechargeable basin compels a modification of the traditional concept of appropriable supply under the appropriation doctrine. Each appropriation from a limited supply of nonreplaceable water of necessity reduces the supply in quantity and shortens the time of use to something less than perpetuity. Each appropriator, subsequent to the initial appropriation, reduces in amount, and in time of use, the supply of water available to all prior appropriators, with the consequent decline of the water table, higher pumping costs, and lower yields.

This leads us directly to the main issue on this appeal, and that is whether or not the rights of prior appropriators are impaired, because a subsequent appropriator, by withdrawing waters from a non-rechargeable basin, causes a decline in the water level, higher pumping costs, and lower pumping yields. * * *

Protestants take the position that an application for a permit to withdraw waters from an underground basin must be denied if the evidence establishes that such withdrawal will cause a decline in the water table, because prior appropriators will, of necessity:

> * * * be damaged and their rights impaired by the lowering of the water table through the shortening of the useful life of the wells, the additional lift costs and the decline in the ability to produce in proportion to a square, making it necessary to drill more wells to produce the same amount of water. * * *

If the position of protestants be correct, then Texaco, as stated in its brief in chief,

> * * * shot itself out of the saddle with its own undisputed evidence that the Lea County basin is a *non-rechargeable* basin, that the taking of any water from it constitutes a *mining* operation, and that its appropriation for what the court found was a reasonable and beneficial use could "never be replaced."

In fact, if the position of protestants be correct, then each and all of the many permits to withdraw waters from this basin issued by the State Engineer, subsequent to the initial permit, have been issued wrongfully and unlawfully, because each withdrawal, to some degree, has caused a lowering of the water level, and thus an impairment of the rights of the initial appropriator. * * *

The only premise upon which the position of protestants can be logically supported is that "existing rights" embraces the element of perpetuity. As above stated, the beneficial use by the public of the waters in a closed or non-rechargeable basin requires giving to the use of such waters a time limitation. In the case of the Lea County Underground Water Basin, that time limitation was fixed by the State Engineer in 1952 at forty years, after having first made extensive studies and calculations. There is nothing before us to prompt a feeling that this method of administration and operation does not secure to the public the maximum beneficial use of the waters in this basin.

The rights of the protestants to appropriate water from this basin are subject to this time limitation, just as are the rights of all other appropriators. A lowering of the water level in the wells of protestants, together with the resulting increase in pumping costs and the lowering of pumping yields, does not constitute an impairment of the rights of protestants as a matter of law. These are inevitable results of the beneficial use by the public of these waters.

Section 75–11–3, N.M.S.A.1953, provides in part that:

> the state engineer shall, if he finds that there are in such * * * [groundwater], unappropriated waters, or that the proposed appropriation would not impair existing water rights from such source, grant the said application and issue a permit to the applicant to appropriate all or a part of the waters applied for subject to the rights of all prior appropriators from said source.

The State Engineer found that there were unappropriated waters, and that the appropriation granted would not impair existing rights. As above stated, on the basis of the method of administration and operation established in 1952, there were available for appropriation by Texaco the 350 acre feet of water per year. * * *

The judgment of the trial court overruling and reversing the findings and order of the State Engineer is hereby reversed.

Notes and Questions

1. Neither Texaco nor the State Engineer alleged that senior groundwater appropriators like Mathers were making non-beneficial uses, or were using unreasonable means of extracting the water; e.g., from a shallow well. Thus a straightforward (some might say wooden) application of the priority principle that is the bedrock of the prior appropriation doctrine means that Mathers wins. That would be the result if this were a dispute involving surface water in New Mexico. Why should the fact that there is no recharge of the aquifer here limit the nature of the prior appropriation right to groundwater?

2. This is widely regarded as the pioneering case on groundwater mining in a prior appropriation jurisdiction. What guidance had the state legislature provided in N.M. Stat. Ann. § 75–11–3, quoted in the opinion, to the State Engineer or to the courts to deal with this circumstance? If the policy crafted by the State Engineer for managing a non-recharging aquifer not dictated by the statute, should the State Engineer have waited for the legislature (or the courts) to make clear rules here? Where should a state's policy on groundwater mining be made—in the legislature, in a state executive branch water resources agency (like the State Engineer here), or by local communities that are dependent on the aquifer for their livelihood? Some states have chosen the third option (see, e.g., Texas, discussed supra pp. 417–421).

3. Lacking guidance from the legislature, the State Engineer here either had to grant or to deny Texaco's application to appropriate 350 acrefeet of groundwater from this essentially non-recharging aquifer. If the State Engineer decided to *deny* Texaco's application on the ground the aquifer was already fully, or over-appropriated, must the State Engineer also, upon the request of the most senior pumper in the aquifer, order all other pumpers of

the aquifer to stop pumping as well? Is it rational to distinguish new from existing pumpers when mining is already occurring? Should the State Engineer have provoked a crisis here (by, for example, shutting down all but the most senior of the existing pumpers) to force the legislature to act–to require elected representatives (rather than an unelected executive branch official) to decide on the economic future of this area? As we will see infra p. 487, that's what the Arizona Supreme Court effectively did in analogous circumstances.

4.   Did the State Engineer fashion a sensible policy? Note the decisions he made:

• This large, non-recharging aquifer should be subdivided into administrative units corresponding to surface townships and then made available for use by more than the first appropriator, even if this converts what is conventionally understood as a perpetual water right into something more limited.

• The overall management objective is to perpetuate an irrigation farming economy in this region of eastern New Mexico for another forty years.[46] At the end of that time, absent the development and importation of new supplies, there would presumably be only dry land farming or no farming, because presumably the depth to groundwater will be beyond the range of economical pumping for all but the highest valued uses (such as domestic).

• The aim is to leave the aquifer about one-third full at the end of the forty year period, so residents still have groundwater available for domestic uses.

This might be regarded, in our democratic system, as a breathtaking bit of social and economic planning for an unelected state official to engage in, and for the courts to uphold without much if any direction from the state legislature. How, if at all, would you improve on the State Engineer's approach? See generally Douglas Grant, Reasonable Groundwater Pumping Levels Under The Appropriation Doctrine: The Law and Underlying Economic Goals, 21 Nat. Resources J. 1 (1981); see also Edgar Bagley, Water Rights and Public Policies Relating to Groundwater "Mining" in the Southwestern States, 4 J.L. & Econ. 144 (1961); Michael Kelly, Management of Groundwater Through Mandatory Conservation, 61 Denver L. J. 1 (1983).

5.   *Mathers* involved water *quantity*, not quality. Does its holding apply to a proposed change in groundwater use that introduces poorer quality groundwater into an aquifer? In Stokes v. Morgan, 680 P.2d 335, 339 (1984) the New Mexico Supreme Court suggested an impairment of quality is more serious because it affects everyone and may be more difficult or impossible to remedy. Nevertheless, the Court went on to defer to the "special knowledge and experience" of the state water administrator in finding that the objectors had not produced evidence to show that the quality of groundwater

---

46. State Engineer Steve Reynolds reported that the forty year term was chosen to reflect the passing of two generations, and also because it coincided with the payback period established by federal law for federal reclamation projects. Charles Corker, Groundwater Law, Management and Administration 176 (Nat'l Water Comm'n Legal Study No. 6, 1971).

would be sufficiently reduced to justify disapproving the proposed change in groundwater well location and use.

6.   There is an irony in *Mathers*: An oil company applies for permission to mine 350 acre-feet of groundwater in order to reinject it deeper into the ground to maximize the mining of petroleum. (The one million barrels the company estimated it could recover is, at 42 gallons per barrel, about 126 acre-feet of oil.) Market forces dictate this outcome—the company can pay the electricity and other costs involved in pumping and reinjecting, and still make a profit from the additional oil brought to the surface. But should Texaco get the right to extract groundwater for free? Should it be required to pay some farmer or other pumper in the vicinity not to pump 350 acre-feet of groundwater during the years Texaco is operating here? Texaco's operation is by definition limited in tenure; it ceases once the petroleum has been recovered. The farmers and others dependent upon groundwater may have a longer planning horizon; for example, Mathers may desire to bequeath the family farm to the children to operate. Should Mathers (who is, after all, a senior appropriator) be compensated when the demise of its farm enterprise is hastened by a later appropriator with a temporary, albeit more financially lucrative, use?

7.   The State Engineer's approach depends quite heavily upon the quality of information available about the amount of recoverable water in the aquifer and existing pumping patterns. The approach also requires some big (and fragile) assumptions about a variety of things, including the course of farm commodity prices and electricity costs (perhaps the most important variables in determining groundwater demand in this region) over the next forty years. If farm prices rise and/or electricity costs decline dramatically during that time, the aquifer might be mined to exhaustion well before forty years had gone by. Conversely, if farm prices fall and/or electricity costs rise, aquifer depletion might be much less than forecast, which could mean applicants for new wells might have been turned away unnecessarily.

8.   The Lea County underground basin contained an estimated 26.4 million acre-feet of water; estimated annual average recharge was about 29,000 acre-feet. Charles Harris, Water Allocation under the Appropriation Doctrine in the Lea County Underground Basin of New Mexico, in The Law of Water Allocation in the Eastern United States 155 (David Haber & Stephen Bergen eds., 1958). The aquifer here is part of the giant Ogallala formation, which stretches across several plains states—eastern New Mexico and Colorado, western Texas, Oklahoma, Kansas, and Nebraska—and has an average recharge rate of about a half-inch a year, with withdrawals averaging one to five feet per year. Depending on the distance from the site of this case to the Texas border, and the rate at which groundwater in this giant aquifer moves laterally in response to pumping, it may be that the more water saved by judicious management in New Mexico, the more water is saved for rapacious pumping in Texas under its capture doctrine.[47] Should

47.   Pumping in the West Texas portion of the aquifer averaged 5 million acre-feet in the 1950s, compared to estimates of annual recharge of 100,000–350,000 acre-feet. See National Water Commission, Water Policies for the Future 239 (1973). For a general discussion of water management issues in the Ogallala Aquifer, see National Research Council, A New Era for Irrigation 128–39 (1996); V.L. McGuire, et al., Water in Storage and Approaches to Ground–Water Management, High Plains Aquifer, 2000 (USGS Circular 1243, 2003).

the New Mexico State Engineer take this into account in crafting a management policy for this aquifer? Interstate groundwater management is considered further in Chapter 8, infra pp. 851 & 872–873.

A Sampling of Groundwater Mining Policies in Other Appropriation States

Colorado: The Colorado Supreme Court affirmed the denial of an application to drill a new well in Colorado's portion of the Ogallala Aquifer in Fundingsland v. Colorado Ground Water Comm'n, 468 P.2d 835 (1970). The applicable Colorado statute provided somewhat more direction than its New Mexico counterpart. It required the state agency to consider yield, recharge rates, the priority and quantity of existing claims, and the proposed method of use, and then to determine whether the proposed use would involve, among other things, an "unreasonable lowering of the water level * * * beyond reasonable economic limits of withdrawal or use." Colo. Rev. Stat. § 37–107(5). The state agency had fleshed out the statutory command by developing a "three mile test," which involved drawing a circle with a three mile radius around the proposed well site, and determining what level of pumping would result in a 40% depletion of the available groundwater in that area over a period of 25 years. If existing wells within the circle already exceed that rate of pumping, no new wells may be permitted. Similar to *Mathers*, the Colorado agency assumed that a 40% depletion of the aquifer would lower the aquifer level "beyond reasonable economic limits of withdrawal or use for irrigation." The 25 year period was deemed a "reasonable, average period in which a loan for the construction of well facilities would have to be repaid."

The court held that the statute foreclosed Fundingsland's argument that economics alone should control whether he should be able to pump, because the statutory "policies of protecting senior appropriators and maintaining reasonable ground water pumping levels * * * require management which takes into account the long range effects of intermittent pumping in the aquifer." See also Upper Black Squirrel Creek Ground Water Mgmt. Dist. v. Goss, 993 P.2d 1177 (Colo. 2000) (noting that the designated ground water aquifer involved there "is being mined and is regulated for a reasonable rate of depletion").

Idaho: The leading case is Baker v. Ore–Ida Foods, Inc., 513 P.2d 627 (Idaho 1973). The aquifer at issue was determined to have an average recharge rate of 5,500 acre-feet per year, but had recently been pumped far in excess of that rate, dropping the water level in the aquifer twenty feet per year. The pertinent statutory guidance (Idaho Code § 42–237a(g)) was that groundwater pumping should not result in the "withdrawing of the ground water supply at a rate beyond the reasonably anticipated average rate of future natural recharge." The court construed the statute to prohibit mining altogether, and enjoined pumping from all but the four most senior wells. In 1994 the Idaho legislature relaxed the strict no-mining policy applied in *Baker*, by giving the Director of Water Resources authority to allow groundwater mining upon finding that (a) it is "in the public interest," (b) a "program exists or likely will exist" to bring withdrawals into balance with recharge "within a time period acceptable to the Director," and (c) senior right holders will not thereby have to pump water from below "established reasonable pumping * * * levels." Idaho Code § 42–237a(g).

Oregon: An Oregon statute applicable to a particular "Critical Ground Water Area" somewhat loosely called for groundwater depletion to be prevented or controlled "within practicable limits." Or. Rev. Stat. 537.525(8). The Oregon Supreme Court firmly rejected farmers' argument that the statute gave them license to pump groundwater so long as they could afford it and still raise a profitable crop. Doherty v. Oregon Water Resources Dir., 783 P.2d 519 (Or. 1989).

Groundwater Mining under Capture and the American Reasonable Use Doctrine

The common law rule of capture makes no attempt to prevent or control mining of aquifers—the winners are the biggest pumps, deepest wells, and deepest pockets (to cover increased pumping costs).

Arizona's application of the American reasonable use doctrine to groundwater mining has proved most colorful. Ending decades of uncertainty, the Arizona Supreme Court decided in Bristor v. Cheatham, 255 P.2d 173 (1953), that the state would follow the American doctrine of reasonable use, and allow the "extraction of ground water subjacent to the soil so long as it is taken in connection with a beneficial enjoyment of the land from which it is taken." Subsequent cases applied this doctrine to place no limits on groundwater mining at all, so long as the water was used on the overlying land. That is, the court refused to distinguish among types of uses on the overlying land, and to inquire as how efficiently overlying landowners are using water. See, e.g., Farmers Investment Co. (FICO) v. Bettwy, 558 P.2d 14 (1976). The net effect was to apply a capture rule among landowners who were withdrawing groundwater for use on their overlying land. In dissent, Justice Cameron pointed out the problem this posed (558 P.2d at 25):

> [T]he time has come to consider again the doctrine of correlative rights under which the owners of land overlying a common supply of water are each limited to taking a proportionate share of the available water * * *. Under existing law, two adjacent landowners may pump each other dry to the detriment of themselves and others nearby. The result is all too frequently that the access to water * * * is determined by a race for consumption controlled not by reasonable use but the physical ability to extract water from the common supply. This encourages wasteful over-consumption and proclaims a right that cannot be protected. * * * To the small or family farmer the

right to water then becomes a cruel illusion, proclaimed by law, but unobtainable in practice. * * *

As between pumpers using water on the overlying land, and pumpers using water off the overlying land, the latter are prohibited from pumping and transporting water in a groundwater mining situation. See Jarvis v. State Land Dept., 479 P.2d 169, 170, 171 (1970) (groundwater "may not be used off the lands from which [it is] pumped if thereby others whose lands overlie the common supply are injured. * * * Such waters can only be used in connection with the land from which they are taken"). Once again no distinction is made among types or efficiencies of use; the only criterion is where the water is used.

The principal issue in *FICO* was how broadly or narrowly to construe the concept of overlying land—whether it included only the parcel of land containing the well site, or any land owned or used by the well owner anywhere over the aquifer. The court took the narrow view, and thus set in motion a chain of events that culminated, four years later, in adoption of the landmark Arizona Groundwater Management Act of 1980. Earlier court decisions had allowed the state's fast-growing urban jurisdictions to tap aquifers with limited recharge if they purchased farmland and retired it from irrigation—so that their pumping and export caused no net increase in withdrawals from the aquifer. See Jarvis v. State Land Dept., 456 P.2d 385 (1969) (Jarvis I); 479 P.2d 169 (1970) (Jarvis II); 550 P.2d 227 (1976) (Jarvis III). But *FICO* closed this escape valve for the burgeoning cities, and to boot it essentially shut down the big copper mines, then important economic engines in southern Arizona, because they were also transporting groundwater off the land from which it was pumped. In giving a relative handful of farmers command of the state's limited groundwater supplies, and a consequent stranglehold on the state's economy, *FICO* could not stand. Under firm prodding by the State's activist governor, Bruce Babbitt, the state's major water interests went far beyond a simple cure of the immediate problem to craft a unique and complex combination of rules that thoroughly overhauled Arizona water law in the principal water-using areas of the state. In this effort Babbitt was aided by Secretary of the Interior Cecil Andrus, who used the leverage afforded him by Congress in authorizing the federal Central Arizona Project (see infra p. 504). After many months of negotiations produced a finely balanced, detailed, sweeping regulatory code, the landmark legislation breezed through the state legislature in a few hours with little debate and no amendments. See generally Desmond Connall, A History of the Arizona Groundwater Management Act, 1982 Ariz. St. L.J. 313. The Act has been repeatedly tinkered with by the legislature, but its basic framework has survived. It revolutionized groundwater management in Arizona, was generally sustained in the courts, and spawned several related pieces of water management legislation. The Arizona saga is *sui generis* and much too complicated for even limited treatment here. For an overview, see A. Dan Tarlock, Law of Waters and Water Rights §§ 6.21–6.30 (2005).

Groundwater Mining in the East

Aquifer-wide overdraft and declining water tables are not unknown in the East, but they remain relatively infrequent subjects of analysis and litigation. Principal areas of concern include New Jersey, where large-scale pumping to support urban populations has drawn down regional aquifer water levels; Long Island, New York; and in the booming coastal region from Virginia to Florida. See, e.g., Robert Abrams, Charting the Course of Riparianism: An Instrumentalist Theory of Change, 35 Wayne L. Rev. 1381, 1424 (1989). In coastal areas the threat of saline intrusion from excessive pumping creates the same management incentives as does conventional overdraft. See, e.g., *Harloff* and the *Village of Tequesta* cases from Florida, supra pp. 445, 453; and Robert Glennon, Groundwater Follies 71–86 (2002) (Tampa Bay).

As noted earlier, in the humid parts of the country the capture rule has for the most part been replaced either by the American reasonable use doctrine, or, even more commonly, by state-run permit systems. These systems vary widely in their reach and characteristics; the majority do not have provisions specifically tailored to prevent or remedy overdraft situations. But see *Harloff*, supra p. 445. Their regulatory machinery nevertheless offers the possibility of eventual managerial control of overdraft. See Robert Abrams, Water Allocation by Comprehensive Permit Systems in the East: Considering a Move Away From Orthodoxy, 9 Va. Envtl. L. Rev. 255, 270–80 (1990); Joseph W. Dellapenna, The Law of Water Allocation in the Southeastern States at the Opening of the Twenty–First Century, 25 U.Ark.Little Rock L.Rev. 9 (2002). Some eastern states offer tax credits for the construction of surface water facilities that reduce dependence on groundwater. See Ark. Stat. Ann. §§ 26–51–1005 to 26–51–1009; Ga. Code Ann. § 48–7–40.11.

Groundwater Mining in Correlative Rights Jurisdictions

Katz v. Walkinshaw (supra p. 429) and its progeny establish the general principle that when there is not enough groundwater to meet all demands, overdraft shall be curtailed first by stopping all "appropriators" (those using the water off the land from which it is pumped) in order of priority, and thereafter by "giving to each [overlying landowner] a fair and just proportion" of the aquifer's safe yield. Despite the relative clarity of the doctrine, enforcement of the principle favoring overlying users has not always occurred, nor has a strict priority system always been applied when there is enough groundwater to supply some but not all exporters. This is amply illustrated by the saga of bringing groundwater mining under control in populous basins of southern California, the most prominent correlative rights jurisdiction, an experience recounted in some detail at the end of this Chapter (infra pp. 506–520) which seeks to illuminate some general issues about groundwater management systems.

Groundwater Mining and the Internal Revenue Code

Groundwater pumpers in the Ogallala formation have enjoyed favorable tax treatment. The Internal Revenue Code allows a cost depletion deduction for mines, oil and gas wells, "and other natural deposits." 26 U.S.C. § 611(a). An irrigator in Texas who pumped from the aquifer was allowed to claim the deduction because the court thought under Texas law the irrigator "owns the soil and the percolating water which is part of the soil." United States v. Shurbet, 347 F.2d 103 (5th Cir. 1965). The Internal Revenue Service quickly extended the allowance to New Mexico even though the prior appropriation doctrine applies there (see Rev. Rul. 65–296, 1965–2 C.B. 181), and it later extended it to the rest of the aquifer, where the pumper could show that the groundwater is being depleted and recharge is negligible. See Rev. Rul. 82–214, 1982–2 C.B. 115. But the extension of the deduction to recharging aquifers has been denied. Linebery v. Comm'r, 64 T.C. 108, 117 n.4 (1975). What is the policy underlying this use of the tax code to subsidize a landowner's pumping of a finite and vital natural resource like groundwater? See generally Raphael J. Moses and M. Wray Witten, Taxation of Water Rights, 25 S.D.L.Rev. 475, 494–95 (1980).

Groundwater Mining and Liability for Land Subsidence

As we saw early in this Chapter (supra p. 405), one consequence of groundwater mining is land subsidence. Those who suffer injury from subsidence (typically in the form of damage to surface structures) may seek to hold groundwater pumpers legally responsible. Courts have split on the threshold question whether to analyze the issues in terms of tort law (negligence or nuisance) or water law (rights of overlying landowners in groundwater). In Henderson v. Wade Sand & Gravel Co., 388 So.2d 900 (Ala. 1980) (discussed in *Martin v. Linden*, supra p. 423), homeowners sued a nearby quarry, alleging its dewatering had caused land subsidence that damaged their homes. The Alabama Supreme Court reversed the trial court's ruling for the quarry owner which had relied on the American reasonable use groundwater doctrine, and held instead that the issue should be analyzed under the tort law of nuisance. In a later case, the court explained *Henderson*'s decision not to apply groundwater law on the basis that the quarry owner was pumping groundwater not to use it, but merely to facilitate another use of the land—quarrying. Adams v. Lang, 553 So.2d 89 (Ala. 1989).

By contrast, in Finley v. Teeter Stone, Inc., 251 Md. 428, 248 A.2d 106 (1968), the Maryland Supreme Court applied the American reasonable use groundwater doctrine to deny relief to plaintiff farmers whose land was damaged by sinkholes as a result of dewatering by a nearby quarry. The court expressed sympathy because it found "little question" the plaintiffs "have been gravely injured by the sink holes," but held that any remedy must be provided by the state legislature. Friendswood Development Co. v. Smith–Southwest Industries, Inc., 576 S.W.2d 21 (Tex. 1978) presented a more confused message. Relying on the capture rule, the Texas Supreme Court refused to hold an industrial, high-volume groundwater pumper liable for severe and predictable subsidence of neighboring lands, but said that "if the landowner's manner of withdrawing ground water from his land is negligent," and if "such conduct is the proximate cause of the subsidence of the land of others," the landowner is liable for the consequences "caused by future withdrawals of ground water from wells either produced or drilled in a negligent manner." Two years earlier, the Texas legislature had authorized the creation of a Coastal Subsidence District in the Harris County–Galveston region where *Friendswood* originated, and empowered it to limit groundwater withdrawals through a permit system, and to collect fees for groundwater withdrawals. The legislation was sustained in Beckendorff v. Harris–Galveston Coastal Subsidence Dist., 558 S.W.2d 75 (Tex. Civ. App. 1977).

Reversing the position of the first Restatement, the Restatement (Second) of Torts recognizes liability for subsidence if groundwater pumping "unreasonably causes harm to a proprietor of neighboring land." See § 858(1)(a), supra p. 435. See also Christopher Amandes, Controlling Land Surface Subsidence: A Proposal for a Market–Based Regulatory Scheme, 31 U.C.L.A. L. Rev. 1208 (1984); Susan Kincaid, Cities Supported by Sticks in the Mud: A Variation on the Settlement of Land and Structures Caused by Ground Water Removal, 15 B.C. Envtl. Aff. L. Rev. 349 (1988). The practical difficulties of bringing subsidence litigation seem daunting. An aquifer may extend over many square miles. Hundreds or thousands of wells may be withdrawing water from it. By the time subsidence occurs or damage on the surface manifests itself, pumping may have gone on for many years. Basic information concerning the number of wells and rate of pumping, both historical and current, may be lacking. If a negligence theory is used, it may be difficult to show which wells are the primary cause of subsidence, and that they were, in the language of *Friendswood*, "either produced or drilled in a negligent manner."

6. RECHARGE RIGHTS TO STORE WATER IN AQUIFERS

Americans have long been accustomed to thinking of water storage for future use mostly in terms of dams and surface reservoirs,[48] even though deliberate recharge of groundwater dates back many decades.[49] Evolving knowledge and values have, however, finally led to new appreciation of the advantages of groundwater storage (described in the second page of this Chapter), moving the idea from the fringes to the mainstream of water management:

48. Reaching its apotheosis with Hoover Dam, built under budget and ahead of schedule in the depths of the Great Depression to tame the Colorado River, the construction of large dams captured the imagination of generations of Americans. See, e.g., Joseph Stevens, Hoover Dam (1988); Russell Martin, A Story Stands That Like a Dam (1989) (Glen Canyon Dam). The allure of these engineering feats is fading somewhat, as the environmental and other costs of converting free-flowing rivers to slackwa-ter reservoirs have become more apparent to a more environmentally sensitive public.

49. See, e.g., Alameda County Water Dist. v. Niles Sand & Gravel Co., 37 Cal. App.3d 924, 112 Cal.Rptr. 846 (1974), where the District—formed in 1914 to conserve groundwater and prevent saline intrusion on the east side of San Francisco Bay, and which had engaged in a "water replenishment" program since 1935—was protected against pumping being carried out to dewater sand and gravel pits.

Groundwater storage is clearly a significant supply augmentation strategy. The legal and administrative problems often are more complex than surface reservoir construction and management, but the existing constraints on new reservoir construction increase the financial and administrative feasibility of subsurface storage of excess surface water. Further, well-managed recharge projects tend to be lower in cost than surface storage alternatives and often avoid negative environmental impacts. Also, recharge projects can be designed to enhance the environment by including artificial wetland components.

Western Water Policy Review Advisory Commission, Water in the West: The Challenge for the Next Century 3–10 (1998). See also Ronald Robie & Patricia Donovan, Water Management of the Future: A Ground Water Storage Program for the California State Water Project, 11 Pac. L.J. 41, 46–47 (1979). The hydrogeology of groundwater storage was briefly discussed supra pp. 406–407. This section discusses some of the legal issues posed by groundwater storage and recovery.

Land over most aquifers is usually divided among many owners. As a result, water stored in an aquifer by infiltration or injection from a single surface parcel will typically not respect ownership boundaries; some of it will be stored beneath lands belonging to others. This raises the question of whether the party engaging in the storage of water is somehow overstepping the rights of other overlying owners by placing the water under their land. Groundwater law's early roots in the real property concept of absolute dominion over everything above and below one's land might be construed to give landowners overlying an aquifer an ownership interest in that portion of the aquifer's storage capacity found underneath their land. If so, they would be in a position to prevent groundwater storage absent their consent, either on a trespass theory or, if the storage is pursuant to state authorization, for the uncompensated taking of their private property for public use.

IN RE APPLICATION U–2
Supreme Court of Nebraska, 1987.
226 Neb. 594, 413 N.W.2d 290.

GRANT, J.

On November 2, 1984, the Central Nebraska Public Power and Irrigation District (hereinafter Tri–County) filed an application (Application U–2) with the Department of Water Resources (DWR), seeking recognition of incidental water storage in the three-county area of Gosper, Phelps, and Kearney Counties. The application alleged that a large mound of underground water had formed in this area as a result of seepage from Tri–County's 600–mile surface canal irrigation system. * * * Application U–2 was objected to by numerous owners of lands overlying the water mound * * *.

The order [of the DWR approving most aspects of the application found] sufficient evidence * * * to support the belief that Tri–County's irrigation project had resulted in the formation of the underground water mound * * *. Hydrologists, qualified as expert witnesses testifying for Tri–County, established the level of the ground water underlying the three-county area in the predevelopment period (using data from between 1931 and 1952) before Tri–County began its irrigation services in 1941. The level of the ground water in 1983 was also established. The difference between the two levels was determined to be water incidentally stored underground as a result of Tri–County's irrigation operation and the seepage therefrom. The perimeters of the underground storage area were also established by expert witnesses, using data from wells drilled in the area between 1941 and 1983. The quantity of such incidentally stored water was determined to be between 6.5 million and 7 million acre-feet of water, in natural underground storage, beneath approximately 684,000 acres of land located in the three-county area.

This amount of land includes the 138,000 acres already identified as being irrigated by Tri–County's 12 existing water appropriations. In addition to this land, the water mound lies beneath approximately 546,000 acres of land which were not being served by any of Tri–County's existing appropriations. In this area, 257,300 acres are currently being irrigated by well, and 288,700 acres are not being irrigated in any manner. * * *

Appellants * * * contend § 46–226.01 is unconstitutional because it allows for the taking of storage space beneath overlying property owners' land without just compensation, citing Neb. Const. art. I, § 21, which provides, "The property of no person shall be taken or damaged for public use without just compensation therefor." Appellants urge that landowners have a constitutionally protected property right in the storage space beneath their property, derived from their right to use the water.

In this connection, the manner in which water is treated in the Nebraska Constitution and the statutes enacted thereunder becomes of critical importance. Neb. Const. art. XV, § 4, provides: "The necessity of water for domestic use and for irrigation purposes in the State of Nebraska is hereby declared to be a natural want."

In Metropolitan Utilities Dist. v. Merritt Beach Co., 179 Neb. 783, 140 N.W.2d 626 (1966) [this Court said] * * *

> Underground waters, whether they be percolating waters or underground stream, are a part of the waters referred to in the Constitution as a natural want. * * * Because of the ever-increasing demands for water control of underground waters as well as the flow of rivers and streams, it is becoming more important and extremely necessary that regulation and control of all sources of water supply be attained. * * *

[The court then quoted from two Nebraska statutes. The first, Neb. Rev. Stat. § 46–657(2), states: "Ground water shall mean that water which occurs, moves, seeps, filters, or percolates through ground under the surface of the land." The second, Neb. Rev. Stat. § 46–296(4), states:

"Underground water storage shall mean the act of storing or recharging water in underground strata. Such water shall be known as water stored underground, but the term shall not include ground water, as defined in section 46–657, which occurs naturally."]

This court has held that an overlying property owner has a protected right in the use of ground water, as defined in § 46–657, arising from his ownership of the surface above the ground water. [In] Sorensen v. Lower Niobrara Nat. Resources Dist., 221 Neb. 180, 376 N.W.2d 539 (1985), * * * we held the right of an owner of overlying land to use ground water is an appurtenance constituting property protected by the Constitution. That right to use water beneath one's land, however, is clearly not unfettered. Nebraska has developed a rule for ground water based on reasonable use and correlative rights. * * *

In their brief at 17, appellants state, "The right to use groundwater establishes the right to use underground storage for groundwater." The protected right of landowners is the right to the use of the ground water, and does not reach the ownership of the water itself. Nebraska's ground water is itself publicly owned. State ex rel. Douglas v. Sporhase, 208 Neb. 703, 305 N.W.2d 614 (1981), rev'd on other grounds 458 U.S. 941 (1982). Ground water is owned by the public, and the only right held by an overlying landowner is in the use of the ground water. The right is recognized by statute. Section 46–656 provided in part, at the time of the hearing in this case, "Every landowner shall be entitled to a reasonable and beneficial use of the ground water underlying his or her land subject to the provisions of Chapter 46, article 6, and the correlative rights of other landowners when the ground water supply is insufficient for all users." Appellants urge that the right to use the ground water gives rise to the exclusive right to use the storage space, that the storage space is theirs, and that "the recognition of incidental underground storage" constitutes an unconstitutional taking of their property. We disagree. We are here concerned with two general classifications of water existing beneath the ground: (1) ground water, as defined in § 46–657, which occurs naturally, and (2) water which has accumulated incidentally underground as a result of seepage from manmade facilities. * * *

[Neb.Rev.Stat.]   Section 46–226.01 provides:

> Any person having an approved perfected appropriation may file with the department an application for recognition of incidental underground water storage associated with such appropriation, and for recovery of such water, on a form prescribed and furnished by the department without cost. Upon receipt of an application, the department shall proceed in accordance with rules and regulations adopted and promulgated by the department.

That legislative enactment does not purport to have the director of DWR authorize any taking of an interest in land, but only sets out a procedure for recognizing an appropriator's interest in water incidentally stored underground, if authorized.

There was no evidence before the director as to any harm resulting to appellants' lands from that recognition. Appellants have not shown that § 46–226.01 amounts to an unconstitutional taking without just compensation. A statute cannot deprive a person of property unless it prevents him from doing an act which he desires to do or diminishes the enjoyment or profit which he would otherwise derive from his property. 16A C.J.S. Constitutional Law § 506 (1984). Appellants in this case have presented no evidence which indicates that § 46–226.01 interferes with the use of their property. Absent such a showing, appellants have no standing to assert the unconstitutionality of the statute as taking their property. * * *

Appellants' rights in the use of the "ground water" (within the meaning of § 46–657) under their lands are not affected. The calculation of the amount of that water is now more difficult, but clearly can be made. Indeed, as set out above, the calculation of the amount of water incidentally stored in this case was based on establishing the level of § 46–657 ground water before incidental storage began after the construction of appellee's facilities, which eventually resulted in the § 46–226.01 "underground water storage." * * *

We determine that the director has not erred as alleged by appellants. The order of the director of DWR approving Application U–2 is affirmed.

Notes and Questions

1. Some of the water this decision vested in the District physically occupies space under the objecting landowners' land. Why isn't that a trespass or a compensable taking? Compare Loretto v. Teleprompter Manhattan CATV Corp., 458 U.S. 419, 434–35 (1982) (government-authorized placement of a cable TV wire on private property requires compensation because "our cases uniformly have found a taking" where governmental action accomplishes a "permanent physical occupation of property," and this is "without regard to whether the action achieves an important public benefit or has only minimal economic impact on the owner"); see also Lucas v. South Carolina Coastal Council, 505 U.S. 1003, 1015 (1992) ("regulations that compel the property owner to suffer a physical 'invasion' of his property" require compensation "no matter how minute the intrusion, and no matter how weighty the public purpose behind it"); Hendler v. United States, 952 F.2d 1364, 1375–78 (Fed. Cir. 1991) (groundwater monitoring wells installed on private land by government regulators to monitor groundwater pollution from a nearby hazardous waste site constitute a taking requiring compensation to the landowner); but see Chance v. BP Chemicals, Inc., 670 N.E.2d 985 (Ohio, 1996) (rejecting a landowner's claim of ownership and trespass against one who injected brine into a very deep aquifer underlying its property). Does it have to do with the fugitive nature of water? With its character as a public good? With the notion that the landowners are not made worse off, and may benefit by the recharge? Is the court here creating a public servitude in groundwater aquifers? Is that what it means by citing the state constitutional provision declaring the necessity of water for domestic and irrigation uses to be a "natural want"?

2. Is storage of water underground different from underground storage of other fugacious natural resources like natural gas? In Anderson v. Beech Aircraft Corp., 699 P.2d 1023 (Kan. 1985), the Kansas Supreme Court held that natural gas injected underground for storage becomes subject to the law of capture. There does not seem to be a general rule on the subject of natural gas; the decided cases "are few in number and are not in harmony." 1 Eugene Kuntz, The Law of Oil and Gas § 2.6(c), at 75 (1962 & Supp. 1998). A number of states resolve the issue by statute, and many states provide for condemnation of subsurface structures for gas storage. Id. at 77–78. If the Tri–County District had to acquire underground storage space by eminent domain, how would a court go about determining fair market value?

3. Same result if the plaintiff landowners had been able to show an injury from the District's action in storing groundwater under their land? Cf. United States v. Causby, 328 U.S. 256, 260–61, 266 (1946) (rejecting the common law doctrine that ownership of the land extends to the heavens and bowels of the earth—*cujus est solum ejus est usque ad coelum*—as having "no place in the modern world," but holding that airplane overflights may cause a taking if they are "so low and so frequent as to be a direct and immediate interference with the enjoyment and use of the land"). Would plaintiffs here have a remedy if the District's recharge raised the water table so much as to make their land swampy, rendering it unsuitable for farming or other uses?

4. Suppose the protesting landowners here wanted to start their own venture to store groundwater under their lands for future use or sale. Would this be the kind of diminishment of the landowner's "enjoyment or profit which he would otherwise derive from his property" that the court speaks of as an unconstitutional taking?

5. *U–2* seems to say that it is the state's function to allocate groundwater storage capacity among competitors, through its statutory power to approve applications for incidental storage. The statute merely authorizes the Nebraska DWR to promulgate rules, however, and DWR's rule provides no clue as to an allocation policy. Instead, it merely requires that each application be "accompanied by sufficient hydrologic information to identify the extent and scope of the underground water storage and naturally occurring ground water." Neb. Admin. R. & Regs. tit. 457, ch. 16, art. 002. How should a state allocate aquifer storage capacity? By priority of application for storage projects? By proposed end use of the water, or whether for fixed use or for speculation to meet market demand for water? By proportion of land ownership overlying the aquifer? By other factors?

6. Note that Nebraska law views groundwater as "owned by the public," but it follows the correlative rights doctrine and recognizes that "an overlying property owner has a protected right in the use of groundwater" found beneath the land. Is that right interfered with by the district's activities here? Under the court's decision, do the landowners here retain whatever rights they previously had to use the naturally occurring groundwater underneath their lands? Would the court have come out the same way on the groundwater storage issue if Nebraska had followed some other groundwater doctrine?

7. In Board of Commissioners v. Park County Sportsmen's Ranch, LLP, 45 P.3d 693 (Colo. 2002), the Colorado Supreme Court, per Justice Hobbs—quoting an early decision that "rules respecting the tenure of private property must yield to the physical laws of nature, whenever such laws exert a controlling influence" (Yunker v. Nichols, 1 Colo. 551, 553 (1872))—held that the "water-bearing capacity of natural formations [does not] belong to a landowner as a stick in the property rights bundle." The result was expressed in sweeping terms; that is, a landowner has no "right to prevent access to the water source or require compensation for the water use right holder's employment of the natural water bearing surface and subsurface formations on or within the landowners' properties for the movement of its appropriated water." Justice Kourlis, writing separately, criticized the majority for going too far, and suggested that the result might be different if the landowners "could demonstrate injury, invasion of use, or even ... that the applicant intended to use a natural, self-contained cavern [on their land] that was not part of an underground aquifer for storage purposes."

8. One of the first court decisions to deal with groundwater replenishment grew out of Los Angeles' storied "raid" on the surface water of the Owens Valley east of the Sierra Nevada escarpment early in the twentieth century. (See supra pp. 240–241.) Some of the water imported to the Southland was stored in the aquifer underlying the San Fernando Valley, north of the City proper, and eventually the City sued the City of Glendale to enjoin the latter's pumping of this imported, stored groundwater. See City of Los Angeles v. City of Glendale, 23 Cal.2d 68, 142 P.2d 289 (1943). The court ruled for Los Angeles. The City's "availing itself of these natural [underground] reservoirs" was to be applauded, the court said, because it was cheaper than surface storage. It relied by analogy on the fact that the courts and the California legislature had long "permitt[ed] the use of natural surface facilities, stream beds, dry canyons and the like, for the transportation of water," to avoid a "harsh rule * * * [that would] require those engaged in these enterprises to construct an actual ditch * * * and to refuse them the economy that nature occasionally afforded in the shape of a dry ravine, gulch, or cañon." It also found that the City had not, by storing the imported water underground, abandoned its right to it.

Twelve years later, in 1955, Los Angeles brought a case claiming rights to groundwater derived from imported water, whether deliberately or incidentally recharged, in the Upper Los Angeles River area. After twenty years of litigation, the California Supreme Court agreed, finding that Los Angeles was entitled to all of the estimated 40% of annual groundwater recharge in the area that was derived from imported water. City of Los Angeles v. City of San Fernando, 14 Cal.3d 199, 537 P.2d 1250 (1975). The court said the use to which the imported water was put before it found its way to the aquifer made no difference: "The referee's report shows that *some* portion of the water delivered in the basin for practically *any* type of purpose reaches the ground supply. * * * [A]n alteration in the type of use from which imported water is returned to the ground does not impair the importer's claim to it as return water." A number of commentators have addressed the issue of groundwater storage in the wake of this decision.[50]

In Central and West Basin Water Replenishment Dist. v. S. Cal. Water Co., 109 Cal.App.4th 891, 135 Cal.Rptr.2d 486 (2003), the Court rejected an argument by holders of about 50% of the decreed pumping rights in LA's Central Basin that their right to pump carried with it a concomitant and proportional right to use (with imported water) what they estimated was about 645,000 acre-feet of storage capacity in the aquifer. Among other things, the Court said that "[e]xtraction and storage are different physical processes; establishing a hydrologic link between them is not sufficient to show that a legal interest in one creates an interest in the other." The Court concluded that under California law, "unused storage space [in an aquifer] is a public resource," and that by statute the legislature has vested authority to manage it in the water replenishment district. See Tara L. Taguchi, Whose Space Is It, Anyway? Protecting the Public Interest in Allocating Storage Space in California's Groundwater Basins, 32 S.W.U. L.Rev. 117 (2003).

JENSEN v. DEPARTMENT OF ECOLOGY

Supreme Court of Washington, 1984.
102 Wash.2d 109, 685 P.2d 1068.

WILLIAM H. WILLIAMS, CHIEF JUSTICE.

Appellant Jensen's application for a permit to withdraw public groundwaters was denied by the Department of Ecology (DOE) on March 20, 1981 * * * based on the determination that no public groundwater was available for appropriation * * *.

In 1968, appellant purchased property in the Quincy basin, an area in Eastern Washington. Since 1952, large portions of that area have been irrigated with waters made available by the Grand Coulee Dam as part of the Columbia Basin Project [a federal reclamation project]. As a result of percolation of imported irrigation water, the naturally occurring groundwater table has been substantially augmented. Appellant's property did not receive project irrigation water, but is located in an area where the groundwater table has been increased. On February 28, 1974, he filed an application with the DOE for a permit to withdraw public groundwater. At that time, the DOE had tentatively determined that all public groundwater had been fully appropriated. He was told that his application would be held for priority purposes only. There were 186 other applicants who preceded him in priority. In 1975, appellant filed

50. See, e.g., Ronald Robie & Patricia Donovan, Water Management of the Future: A Ground Water Storage Program for the California State Water Project, 11 Pac. L.J. 41 (1979); Victor Gleason, Los Angeles v. San Fernando: Ground Water Management in the Grand Tradition, 4 Hastings Const. L.Q. 703 (1977); Norman Thorson, Storing Water Underground: What's the Aqui–Fer?, 57 Neb. L. Rev. 581 (1978). See also Russell Kletzing, Imported Groundwater Banking: The Kern Water Bank—A Case Study, 19 Pac. L.J. 1225 (1988); Ella Foley–Gannon, Institutional Arrangements for Conjunctive Water Management in California and Analysis of Legal Reform Alternatives, 6 Hastings W.–N.W. J. Env. L. & Pol'y 273 (2000).

an application to withdraw artificially stored groundwater. The permit, issued soon afterwards, requires applicants to enter into an agreement with the United States Bureau of Reclamation (Bureau) to pay for withdrawn water. While Jensen noted on his application that he did not recognize the Bureau's claim of ownership of the water, he did enter into the required agreement. Appellant then requested the DOE to process his 1974 application for public groundwater. The DOE denied his application on April 3, 1980, basing the denial on its determination that all public groundwater had been fully appropriated, and that further withdrawal would impair existing rights. * * *

Appellant argues * * * that the Bureau's water was either abandoned, or else that it lost its identity by virtue of its commingling with naturally occurring groundwater. In either case, appellant concludes, the water has become public groundwater available for appropriation.

In 1923, the United States Supreme Court was confronted with arguments similar to Jensen's, specifically whether the United States had a right to recapture and utilize seepage from irrigation waters in the Shoshone [Bureau of Reclamation] Project in Wyoming. Quoting United States v. Haga, 276 F. 41 (D. Idaho 1921), the Court said:

> One who by the expenditure of money and labor diverts appropriable water from a stream, and thus makes it available for fruitful purposes, is entitled to its exclusive control so long as he is able and willing to apply it to beneficial uses, and such right extends to what is commonly known as wastage from surface run-off and deep percolation, necessarily incident to practical irrigation. Considerations of both public policy and natural justice strongly support such a rule. Nor is it essential to his control that the appropriator maintain continuous actual possession of such water. So long as he does not abandon it or forfeit it by failure to use, he may assert his rights. It is not necessary that he confine it upon his own land or convey it in an artificial conduit. It is requisite, of course, that he be able to identify it; but, subject to that limitation, he may conduct it through natural channels and may even commingle it or suffer it to commingle with other waters. In short, the rights of an appropriator in these respects are not affected by the fact that the water has once been used.

Ide v. United States, 263 U.S. 497, 506 (1924).

The test for determining whether water has been abandoned was enunciated in Miller v. Wheeler, 54 Wash. 429, 103 P. 641 (1909). There the court said:

> [A]bandonment like appropriation is a question of intent, and to be determined with reference to the conduct of the parties. The intent to abandon and an actual relinquishment must concur, for courts will not lightly decree an abandonment of a property so valuable as that of water in an irrigated region.

Appellant offered no evidence that the Bureau intended or in fact relinquished control of its water. In contrast, the [state board that first reviewed DOE's finding of fact in this case] found that the Bureau intended from the inception of the Columbia Basin Project to recapture waters from the northern portions of the project for use in the southern portions. * * *

Appellant's argument that the artificially stored groundwater has commingled with naturally occurring groundwater, and has thus lost its identity and become public groundwater is without support in either case law or statute. The court in *Miller* found that the mingling of waters from separate sources did not cause a loss of identity, as water is distinguishable and measurable by quantity. Later, this court said that foreign waters which increased the volume of natural streams do not become part of the natural stream by virtue of entry therein. Elgin v. Weatherstone, 123 Wash. 429, 212 P. 562 (1923). Also, the natural waterways of the state may be used for the conveyance of stored water. Pleasant Valley Irrigation & Power Co. v. Barker, 98 Wash. 459, 167 P. 1092 (1917); RCW 90.03.030. Nothing in the statutory scheme suggests that commingling causes artificially stored water to lose its identity. * * *

The [reviewing board] found by clear and persuasive evidence that public groundwater in the Quincy subarea was fully appropriated before appellant applied for a permit to appropriate public groundwater. A division by volume of artificially stored and naturally occurring groundwater is supported by law and statute. * * * The findings and conclusions * * * are therefore affirmed.

Notes and Questions

1. Consider the issue here in comparison to surface water cases in Chapter 3 involving appropriation of seepage waters and the recapture of sewage effluent—e.g., Bower v. Big Horn Canal Ass'n, supra p. 197; Stevens v. Oakdale Irrig. Dist., supra p. 211; and Arizona Public Service Co. v. Long, supra p. 201. Was the Washington Supreme Court correct in relying on surface water cases, or should the fact that here the new supply is groundwater rather than surface water make any difference?

2. Suppose there was no evidence that the Bureau of Reclamation intended, at the time it planned and constructed the Columbia Basin Project, to recapture the groundwater replenished by the application of project water in surface irrigation. Is it sufficient that the importer simply knew (or believed) the groundwater would be improved by the project? Or should the importer win regardless of its knowledge, belief or intent? Because the imported, incidentally recharged water would not be there but for the risk-taking and investment of the importer, are there any equities favoring a local incidental beneficiary like Jensen? That is, in order to encourage investment in such projects, shouldn't the importer be allowed to charge the local user for the improvement brought about by the project, regardless of the importer's intent or knowledge in constructing the project? Does it make any difference whether the importer is a governmental or a private entity?

Historically, this would have been mostly a moot point, as nearly all significant importation schemes have been undertaken by federal or state agencies or special governmental entities such as irrigation districts.

3. The facts behind *Jensen* are these: Congress authorized the Columbia Basin Project in 1937, and project water was first delivered in 1952. A five year study completed by the state of Washington in 1972 showed that, as a result of percolation from project irrigation between 1952 and 1968, a shallow aquifer had been filled with nearly 3 million acre-feet of water. The land over this aquifer could not be irrigated due to the nature of the terrain and soil until center-pivot irrigation was introduced in the mid–1960s. The State closed the aquifer to new appropriation in 1973 and took the steps that led to the decision in *Jensen*. The Bureau of Reclamation did not file a claim to the groundwater until after local landowners had begun to sink wells and pump the water. See Flint v. United States, 906 F.2d 471 (9th Cir. 1990) (federal law authorizes the Bureau of Reclamation to contract with landowners to recover costs associated with furnishing this water, and the fixing of the costs was committed by law to agency discretion).

4. Should an importer have an indefinite claim on all "proceeds" of the importation? For example, once Jensen pumps and irrigates with the project-improved groundwater, presumably some portion will again seep to the aquifer, where it could again be brought to the surface by Jensen or another farmer and used again. Should that second pumper also be required to pay the importer for that portion of the groundwater resulting from the importation? (Note that the calculations involved here may become complex.) Should the outcome be controlled by the State of Washington as a matter of water rights administration, or should it be controlled by the importer's (here, the Bureau of Reclamation's) contracting policies? That is, could the State decide that the Bureau is entitled to be paid only for the first reuse of imported water withdrawn from the ground, even if the Bureau wants to be paid for subsequent uses as well? On what basis?

5. If the policy objective is to allow the replenisher of groundwater to charge all those who may benefit from the replenishment, the beneficiaries may extend beyond direct pumpers of groundwater to include, for example, coastal property owners who are aided by the replenishment's prevention of saltwater intrusion, or overlying landowners who do not use water, but benefit from reduced subsidence risk. How might the water replenisher charge this more diffuse class of beneficiaries? Through property taxes or assessments?

6. Note that groundwater may be replenished by "native" as well as imported water. Most agricultural irrigation results in some groundwater recharge. Groundwater levels around large surface reservoirs may dramatically increase as a result of seepage from the impoundment. Lake Powell behind Glen Canyon Dam on the Colorado has been estimated to lose from between 350,000 to 600,000 acre feet every year into the surrounding Navajo sandstone formations. See Scott Miller, Undamming Glen Canyon: Lunacy, Rationality, or Prophecy, 19 Stan. Envtl. L.J. 121, 176 (2000). In these situations of incidental replenishment with "native" water, are the answers to the above questions different from the answers when the groundwater replenishment comes from imported water?

7. In recent years a number of states have adopted statutes to govern groundwater recharge and recovery operations. Typically they direct state water administrators to control these activities through issuing permits for both recharge and recovery activities. See, e.g., Utah Code Ann. §§ 73–3–2(vi), 73–3b–101 to–402. Texas charts its own path; see Texas Rivers Protection Ass'n v. Texas Natural Resource Conservation Comm'n, 910 S.W.2d 147 (Tex. App. 1995), which upheld a state permit to divert surface water for storage in an aquifer, with the court noting that once it was in the aquifer, the water might be subject to capture by anyone. See Joseph W. Dellapenna, Physical and Social Bases of Quantitative Groundwater Law, in 3 Waters and Water Rights § 18.03(b), at 18–33. Arizona's legislation is the most complex and comprehensive:

> Starting in 1986 and continuing through 1996, Arizona has adopted a series of laws dealing with artificial groundwater recharge. * * * Arizona Department of Water Resources oversees the permitting of recharge projects and keeps track of the amount of water stored for permit holders. * * * The legal character of the water remains what it was when the water was stored. For example, if a party stores excess Central Arizona Project water in 1996 and recovers that water in 2006, the water will still be considered to legally be Central Arizona Project water and not groundwater. * * * Recharge statutes allow the groundwater aquifers to be used in a manner analogous to a large reservoir by providing for the issuance of long-term storage credits if the stored water can be demonstrated to be surplus to direct use needs. The statutes also allow * * * water to be recharged in one location and then recovered in another location in the same year. This technique, called annual storage and recovery, allows a water user to use a recharge project as an alternative to treating surface water and piping it long distances to the place of use. For accounting purposes, the water recovered from a well again retains its legal character as if the water were used directly. * * * Over the past few years, nearly 1 million acre-feet have been stored in Arizona aquifers taking advantage of these statutes.

> More recent statutes have focused on the creation of institutions for the purpose of recharging water. The Central Arizona Groundwater Replenishment District was created as a mechanism to help meet the [requirement of state law that new residential subdivisions in the state's major urban areas have a one hundred year "assured" supply of water]. If a subdivision or a municipal provider lacks access to adequate amounts of renewable water resources, but did have available an adequate supply of groundwater, then it might want to use the service of the Replenishment District. The District * * * is responsible to purchase and recharge an amount of water equivalent to the amount of water mined by the subdivision. This mechanism allows the District to act as a broker in finding municipal water supplies, which saves both time and money for individual water users. A second water recharging entity was created in 1996 with the formation of the Arizona Water Banking Authority * * * [whose] mission is to purchase excess

Central Arizona Project water while it is currently available and store that water in Arizona's aquifers for recovery in times of shortage. Funding for the Authority comes from property taxes, groundwater withdrawal fees, and general tax funds. The Authority is also authorized to enter into interstate agreements with entities in California or Nevada to bank water on their behalf when extra water is available.

Western Water Policy Review Advisory Commission, Water in the West: The Challenge for the Next Century 3–18 (1998); Ariz. Rev. Stat. §§ 45–801.01 to–898.01, 48–3771 to–3783, 48–4401 to–4575.

8. Although aquifer recharge may seem as beneficent as motherhood and apple pie, not all recharge projects may benefit the environment. In Central Platte Natural Resources Dist. v. City of Fremont, 549 N.W.2d 112 (Neb. 1996), the Nebraska Supreme Court affirmed a governmental denial of a water right for a proposal to divert up to 129,000 acre-feet from the Platte River to store in the ground for eventual withdrawal for agricultural irrigation, on the basis of a state law protecting endangered species, because of concern about the project's effect on whooping crane habitat. See J. David Aiken, Balancing Endangered Species Protection and Irrigation Water Rights: The Platte River Cooperative Agreement, 3 Great Plains Nat. Res. J. 119 (1999).

Notes on the Role of the Federal Government in Groundwater Use, Storage and Replenishment

1. *The Bureau of Reclamation. Jensen* provides the opportunity for a brief segue into the federal role on some of the issues discussed in this Chapter. First, note the interplay between federal and state law in *Jensen*. The United States Bureau of Reclamation is the importer through its construction and operation of the Columbia Basin federal reclamation project and, according to the Washington Supreme Court, controls the recapture of the groundwater improved by the importation. Is the court applying federal law, or state law, or do both point to the same result? In Ide v. United States, 263 U.S. 497 (1924), quoted and followed by *Jensen*, the U.S. Supreme Court said that "state law and [federal reclamation law] both contemplate" a reuse of water once used under an appropriation for the "reclamation and cultivation of all the lands within the project." 263 U.S. at 505. Could the Washington Supreme Court have reached the opposite result under state law, and held that the Bureau of Reclamation did not retain any authority over the imported water once it seeped into the aquifer, so that the state Department of Ecology could issue a permit to Jensen to appropriate it, even over the objection of the Bureau of Reclamation? Cf. California v. United States, infra p. 753 (holding that a federal reclamation project must comply with various aspects of state water law). (*Ide* also quoted with approval a federal district court case, United States v. Haga, 276 Fed. 41, 43 (D. Idaho 1921), to the effect that commingling the water with other waters before reuse does not change the result.)

Westwide, the federal Bureau of Reclamation has not taken a consistent approach to groundwater improved as a result of its surface water irrigation projects. Many reclamation contracts contain a term like the following (the exact language varies):

> The United States does not abandon or relinquish any of the waste, seepage or return flow waters attributable to the irrigation of the lands to which water is supplied under this contract. All such waters are reserved and intended to be retained for the use and benefit of the United States as a source of supply for the project.

This provision may have been originally drafted without groundwater much in mind (*Ide* was a surface water case), but it easily covers incidental recharge of groundwater from project irrigation. (A few reclamation contracts modify the quoted language expressly to exclude incidentally recharged groundwater; for example, the contract with the Solano County Water Agency in California adds "provided, that this shall not be construed as claiming for the United States any right to groundwater recharge within the boundaries" of the entity receiving the water.)

Although its contracts frequently give the Bureau a credible claim to incidentally recharged groundwater, the agency has not often asserted one. The Columbia Basin Project situation litigated in *Jensen*—where the Bureau worked with the state water administration and issued contracts authorizing individual landowners to pump groundwater incidentally recharged by the federal reclamation project—is the exception, not the rule.

Some Bureau contracts reflect other approaches. The contract with the San Benito County Water Conservation and Flood Control District in California specifically authorizes the local entity to use the project water for groundwater recharge. Other more recent contracts not only acknowledge groundwater recharge as a use of project water, but walk a tightrope between state and federal law. For example, a contract with the Bella Vista Irrigation District in California's Central Valley Project provides that use of project water

> in a groundwater recharge program shall be permitted under this contract to the extent that it is recognized as a reasonable and beneficial use of water under California law and is otherwise carried out in accordance with California law; provided, however, that such a groundwater recharge program cannot be undertaken until the Contractor submits a groundwater management plan that is consistent with and in compliance with any Central Valley Project-wide groundwater recharge policies that may hereafter be adopted by the Bureau of Reclamation and that demonstrates to the [Bureau's] satisfaction that groundwater recharge will enhance the Contractor's use and management of its overall water supply.

Finally, many reclamation contracts specifically provide that the local water district

> shall not be deemed to have furnished irrigation water to excess or ineligible lands [those that exceed the acreage limitations Congress placed on those receiving federal reclamation project subsidized water—see infra pp. 747–750] if such lands are irrigated with ground water that reaches the underground strata as an unavoidable result of the furnishing of irrigation water to eligible lands.

2. *More Generally.* Almost all the law studied so far in this Chapter is state law, and that is with good reason. Although national policies have promoted groundwater use in various ways (rural electrification; federally subsidized hydropower to operate pumps; federal crop subsidies; the tax depletion allowance in the Ogallala Aquifer), the national government has rarely played more than an indirect role in groundwater management. Even in the New Deal, when the national government assumed new responsibilities in many areas of American life, groundwater management remained beyond the federal pale, for several reasons: There wasn't much groundwater pumping going on. Federal "hands off" respected the powerful strain of localism over land and water use in national culture. Local variations in the extent and character of groundwater cut against the notion of national rules and policies. Groundwater had less of an interstate dimension that had led to such large federal multipurpose surface water projects as Hoover Dam. Finally, groundwater management lacks political appeal compared to the romance and glamour of taming a wild river through some colossal engineering achievement.

For most of the twentieth century, federal policy with respect to groundwater focused primarily on building new water projects to "rescue" states whose laissez-faire approach to groundwater pumping had led to troubling overdrafts. In 1968, however, Congress did something remarkable in authorizing the Central Arizona Project (CAP) to bring water from the lower Colorado River several hundred miles (and several hundred feet higher in elevation) to central Arizona. (The story of the CAP is told in Chapter 8 at p. 807.) The authorizing legislation specifically forbade the Secretary of the Interior from delivering CAP water to any area in Arizona that did not have "adequate" groundwater control measures in place (43 U.S.C. § 1524(c)). The rationale was simple: Spurred on by Californians who were in competition with Arizona for limited Colorado River supplies, and by out-of-basin interests who did not want their local rivers eventually tapped to pay the price for Arizona's profligate mining of native groundwater, Congress wanted to deter Arizona from coming back for another expensive federal rescue project. The federal prod eventually helped lead to Arizona's enactment of its landmark 1980 Groundwater Management Act (see p. 487 supra). This federal "carrot" to promote more hands-on state management of limited groundwater supplies helped open a new chapter in state-federal relations over groundwater. The Western Water Policy Review Advisory Commission called on Congress to apply the CAP precedent across the board, by "requir[ing] state management of groundwater and regulation of withdrawals as a condition of federal financial assistance for construction of new water storage projects," while urging federal agencies and the Congress to raise their awareness of rates of depletion and the "presence or absence of groundwater regulation and management." Western Water Policy Review Advisory Commission, Water in the West: The Challenge for the Next Century 6–23 (1998).[51]

51. See Arkansas Rice Farmers Run Dry, and U.S. Remedy Sets Off Debate, New York Times, Nov. 11, 2002, recounting how rice farmers are draining one of Arkansas' biggest aquifers dry (despite the fact the state averages almost 50" of rain a year) and are now seeking a $319 million federal project (with two-thirds of the cost paid by the federal taxpayer) to import replacement water from the White River. See

The courts also helped carve out a federal role in groundwater. There are substantial federal reserved rights claims to surface water that may be threatened by groundwater pumping lawful under state law, and the Supreme Court's 1976 decision in Cappaert v. United States (infra p. 912) held that these federal rights can be protected against interference by such pumping. There are, furthermore, substantial federal-law-based claims (especially on behalf of Indian tribes) to groundwater itself. All these federal water rights claims, discussed in Chapter 9, have also helped stimulate efforts to improve management of groundwater and related surface water. Federal law developed in the context of interstate streams also has sometimes addressed groundwater issues. For example, the Supreme Court's decree in Arizona v. California, infra p. 831, covers water in the mainstream of the lower Colorado River, "including water drawn from the mainstream by underground pumping." Arizona v. California, 376 U.S. 340 (1964) (art. I(C)).[52]

The federal government has also played a larger role in groundwater management in recent years through its efforts to protect surface water from groundwater pumping being carried out under state law, in order to preserve important aquatic and riparian habitats that support imperilled species. Texas finally was moved to limit its rule of capture in the vital Edwards Aquifer in part because federal courts had required pumping restrictions in order to preserve endangered species that live only in the springs fed by the aquifer's discharge. See infra pp. 661–668; see also the discussion of the San Pedro Riparian National Conservation Area supra p. 465. A massive, multibillion dollar plan to restore the Florida Everglades enacted by the U.S. Congress and the Florida legislature in 2000 involves, among other things, the installation of several hundred wells around Lake Okeechobee to inject and store hundreds of thousands of acre-feet of water into an underground aquifer, to be withdrawn and used during drought. See 114 Stat. 2572, 2680–93 (2000). The aquifer storage and recovery project, with a price tag of $1 billion, raises a number of questions about contamination and pollution that a pilot program is designed to answer. The well sites for the project require much smaller acreage than would be required for surface reservoirs offering equivalent storage in the flat topography of south Florida.

The last two paragraphs show some ways how federally owned lands, which comprise nearly one-third of the real estate in the country, are a hook for federal involvement in groundwater. In addition, federal land managers could condition federal permits to use federal land on measures that would protect groundwater. See chapter 9, infra pp. 1004–1007. They could also make federal land available for storage of underground water. Should the

G. Alan Perkins, Arkansas Water Rights: Review and Considerations for Reform, 25 U.Ark.Little Rock L.Rev. 1223; (2002) http://www.mvm.usace.army.mil/grandprairie/ contains a project description.

52. A 1994 U.S. Geological Survey report recommended that wells in the River's 100–year floodplain be presumed to be pumping mainstream water, as should wells outside the floodplain if the static elevation of the well is equal to or lower than the river elevation. U.S. Geological Survey Rep. No. 94–4005, Method to Identify Wells That Yield Water That Will Be Replaced by Colorado River Water in Arizona, California, Nevada, and Utah (1994). The Bureau of Reclamation has tried to address this situation in various ways, but unregulated pumping of mainstream water through wells remains a continuing problem along the lower River.

federal government seek to charge "rent" for the storage space? Does it make any difference what state law says on this subject, or can an independent federal law rule be crafted? Finally, a number of modern federal statutes dealing with groundwater pollution prevention and mitigation have sometimes had significant effects on state and local management of groundwater. These are discussed briefly in Chapter 10 at pp. 1070–1075.

More than three decades ago, the National Water Commission made several recommendations that the federal government become more involved in promoting needed reforms in groundwater management. Its report was remarkably able and prescient, and noteworthy because westerners with substantial experience in state-level water management dominated its membership. See generally John D. Leshy, The Federal Role in Managing the Nation's Groundwater, 11 Hastings W.-N.W. J. Envt'l L. & Pol'y, 1, 10–13 (2004). Its recommendations have, however, mostly gone unimplemented. Id. at 13. Still:

> Arizona is managing its groundwater much better than it was before the federal government helped engineer its reform. The Arizona experience suggests the right path for federal policy—to use a mixture of information-gathering, carrots (federal dollars), sticks (federal claims of water rights and enforcement of federal regulatory laws like the Endangered Species Act), and persuasion (conditions in federal reclamation contracts and federal land use permits), to move the states toward more active management of groundwater.
> * * *

> As Aldous Huxley said, facts do not cease to exist simply because they are ignored. The nation and its constituent states have not fully faced up to serous groundwater problems. Robert Glennon's stories of depletion of groundwater and associated surface water are grim reminders of a resource in trouble. Droughts of recent years—possibly long-term, possibly exacerbated by humanly-induced climate change—[are] leading to more groundwater extraction, more depletion, and more adverse effects on surface water rights and ecosystems.

> Grappling with these questions is not easy. * * * While the scientific, technical and legal challenges are daunting, there is room for optimism, if the federal government is willing to assume a more active role. There is much at stake.

Id. at 15, 18–19.

7. THE CUTTING EDGE: GROUNDWATER MANAGEMENT IN SOUTHERN CALIFORNIA

The populous valleys of Southern California contain a series of underground aquifers. By the middle of the twentieth century, the region's enormous population growth had long ago outstripped relatively scarce surface supplies, and importation projects from the Owens Valley and the Colorado River had not been enough to head off declines in the region's aquifers. This had become a serious problem, especially in coastal areas, where saline intrusion was advancing. The water table in parts of Orange County, for example, had dropped below sea level, and several hundred thousand acre-feet of overdraft led to saline contamination up to four miles inland.

Over the next several decades, in a major if relatively little-heralded success story, groundwater use in many of southern California's groundwater basins was brought under management control and major crises averted, at least so far. Exactly how this was done is not a simple story, and the techniques and processes have varied considerably from basin to basin.[53] The saga is best and most comprehensively told in William Blomquist, Dividing the Waters: Governing Groundwater in Southern California (1992).[54] This book examines eight different basins from Orange County through the San Fernando Valley to the Mojave Desert.

To explore how this happened, we start with the applicable legal principles. Recall that California follows the doctrine of correlative rights, which teaches that when there is not enough groundwater to meet all demands, pumping restrictions should be visited first on all "appropriators" (those using the water off the land from which it is pumped) in priority order. If further restrictions are necessary, each overlying landowner is allowed "a fair and just proportion" of the aquifer's supply for use on the overlying land. These legal principles are well understood; applying them in practice has been another story indeed. A major development came in City of Pasadena v. City of Alhambra, 33 Cal.2d 908, 207 P.2d 17 (1949), where Pasadena brought suit against many pumpers in the forty-square-mile Raymond Basin to adjudicate groundwater rights and alleviate an annual overdraft that threatened to deplete the aquifer. The evidence showed the recharge rate was 18,000 acre-feet annually, while withdrawals averaged 24,000 acre-feet. Eventually all the parties but one (the California–Michigan Land and Water Company) stipulated to a decree that reduced each party's pumping proportionally by the amount necessary to eliminate the overdraft. The reduction was applied to all users, regardless of whether they were using on the overlying land or appropriating for use elsewhere, and among the latter, regardless of when they began appropriating for export. The holdout (which was one of the early exporters of water from the basin, and exported about 3/4 of the groundwater it extracted) appealed.

53. In the seven basins that have had success in managing groundwater, total annual water use in the mid–1980s averaged about 2.5 million acre-feet annually, with about 40% of that furnished by local groundwater, and the rest from imported and reclaimed water. Most of the territory in these seven basins is within the jurisdiction of the giant Metropolitan Water District of Southern California (MWD, or MET), the umbrella regional water agency that imports Colorado River supplies and some State Water Project water to the Southland (although some local districts have signed separate contracts with the State for delivery of State Water Project water).

54. Another interesting treatment is found in Elinor Ostrom, Governing the Commons: The Evolution of Institutions for Collective Action (1990), esp. at pp. 104–139. See also William Blomquist, Edella Schlager, & Tanya Keikkila, Common Waters, Diverging Streams: Linking Institutions and Water Management in Arizona, California, and Colorado (Resources for the Future, 2004).

The California Supreme Court upheld the settlement, and applied it to the holdout. The court noted that the rights of overlying users are "paramount, and the right of an appropriator [exporter], being limited to the amount of the surplus, must yield to that of the overlying owner in the event of a shortage, unless the appropriator has gained prescriptive rights through the taking of non-surplus waters." This last clause was key to the outcome, because the court went on to hold that the appropriators' exports had ripened into a prescriptive right, because they were open and notorious for many years after increased pump lifts had signaled to all users that water levels in the aquifer were declining. Because all were pumping and using groundwater in excess of the rate of recharge, the court fashioned and applied a doctrine of "mutual prescription" to hold that all parties, including the appellant, had an obligation to proportionally reduce their pumping to so-called safe-yield levels, regardless of whether they were exporting or using the water on overlying land.

Notes and Questions

1. Ordering pro rata reductions in existing uses to combat overdraft has obvious equitable attractions for courts (and legislatures and administrative agencies, for that matter). If the reductions are not pro rata, it is likely some court or other body may—if overdraft is to be effectively controlled—have to require some current users to go completely without water (e.g., off-tract users in favor of on-tract users, present or future). Protecting existing uses through some notion of sharing is not foreign to water law. It is an explicit factor of reasonableness under the Restatement (Second) of Torts approach to riparian water rights (see supra p. 57) and also plays a role in equitable apportionment of interstate water resources among states (see infra pp. 858–873). One question asked after the *Pasadena* decision was whether the court simply crafted a doctrine of mutual prescription as a way to uphold a settlement that seemed equitable and had been embraced by all parties except the single holdout, or whether it signaled a broader shift toward more equitable sharing of limited groundwater resources and a rejection of the artificiality of the "on-tract"/"off-tract" distinction that is fundamental to the American reasonable use and correlative rights groundwater doctrines. For an argument that the decision was a prototype of a major shift in the western states toward a greater sharing of water resources, see Harrison Dunning, State Equitable Apportionment of Western Water Resources, 66 Neb. L. Rev. 76, 98–105 (1987).

2. You are counsel to a city in another part of California which pumps groundwater and exports it for distribution through the city's water system to municipal users. The aquifer is being tapped by many users, some for export and some for use on the overlying land. Its water level is declining steadily, signaling pumping in excess of the rate of recharge. What advice do you give to your client immediately after the *Pasadena* decision? Increase pumping to maximum, so that when the courts come to apply mutual prescription and reduce all pumpers proportionately, your client will come out better? What advice do you give to a client landowner who is not now pumping groundwater, but is considering installing pumps and sending

water off the land to some consumer? Hurry up? A quarter-century after *Pasadena*, the California Supreme Court, in City of Los Angeles v. City of San Fernando, 14 Cal.3d 199, 123 Cal.Rptr. 1, 537 P.2d 1250 (1975) (briefly discussed supra p. 496 in connection with recharge issues), noted:

> A possible undesirable side effect of the so-called mutual prescription doctrine is that it may encourage a "race to the pumphouse" after overdraft commences, each party endeavoring to increase the volume of continuous use on which his prescriptive right will be based. Of course only reasonably beneficial uses will qualify for this purpose, and deliberate increases in qualified extractions from the ground basin are likely to be possible only for those parties who have multiple sources of supply and can manipulate the proportions of the amounts they draw from each source. Plaintiff points out that if it had anticipated that its rights in the San Fernando basin would be limited to a prescriptive right based on ground water usage after 1941–1942, the year found by the trial court as the commencement of overdraft, plaintiff "could easily have engineered its pumping to maximize the amount of prescriptive rights to which it would be entitled under the *Pasadena* formula."

537 P.2d at 1299.

3. While *Pasadena*'s doctrine of mutual prescription had the ironic effect of providing an incentive to increase pumping where aquifer water levels were declining, it was seemingly hobbled by subsequent decisions. In *Los Angeles v. San Fernando*, the California Supreme Court construed a California Civil Code provision immunizing cities from claims of adverse possession or prescription to apply to water rights as well as land. The statute had not come into play in the *Pasadena* case because the holdout party was not a city but a public utility, which was not at the time subject to the statute. Because the statute was subsequently broadened to protect water utilities as well as cities, commentators have tended to consider the mutual prescription doctrine a virtual dead letter, applicable only upon consent of all the affected municipalities and water companies. See California Governor's Comm'n To Review Cal. Water Rights Law, Final Report 143 (1978); Ronald Robie & Patricia Donovan, Water Management of the Future: A Ground Water Storage Program for the California State Water Project, 11 Pac. L.J. 41, 54 (1979). The doctrine would presumably still have application to overdrafts involving only private users of groundwater, but such situations are very rare. In practice, however, the doctrine has showed some staying power, through negotiation, as shown further below.

4. Suppose Paragon Pictures owns land in the Raymond Basin adjudicated in the *Pasadena* case, has never pumped groundwater, and was not a party to the case, but five years after the decree decides to construct a giant water park on its property as a tourist attraction, and to pump groundwater to supply it. Can it do so, even if that means drawing down the water level in the aquifer? What would you argue as attorney for Paragon? For one of the parties to the *Pasadena* decree? If Paragon can commence a major new withdrawal of groundwater for use on its overlying land, must the court administering the *Pasadena* decree adjust the entitlements under the decree downward to keep the basin from going into overdraft? If so, which parties

ought to be reduced? All proportionately, regardless of whether they are using water on or off the land?

5. The disruptive potential of unexercised correlative rights to groundwater, like those of unexercised riparian rights in surface water, is significant. Not surprisingly, groundwater users in California have sought to adjudicate such rights, arguing that the courts should follow the approach of the California Supreme Court in the *Long Valley* case, supra p. 374, which had confirmed the possibility of quantifying unexercised riparian rights to surface water, or subordinating them to appropriative rights, as part of a comprehensive statutory stream adjudication proceeding. In Wright v. Goleta Water Dist., 174 Cal.App.3d 74, 219 Cal.Rptr. 740 (1985), the defendant district, which had appropriated groundwater for export, was sued by a group of overlying owners to determine rights to the waters of the aquifer. The district sought to have the lawsuit determine with finality all rights to the aquifer's water, including the correlative rights of overlying owners who were making no present use of the aquifer. The California court of appeals was sympathetic, but ultimately said no:

> In *Long Valley,* the Supreme Court held that the Legislature had enacted a *comprehensive administrative scheme* for the final determination of *all* rights in a stream system and had granted the [State Water Resources Control] Board the power to define and otherwise limit prospective riparian rights, when pursuant to Water Code section 2500 et seq., it determines all claimed rights to use of water in the stream system. * * *

> *Long Valley* in a riparian setting, recognized the pernicious effects of uncertainty concerning the rights of water users, including the inhibition it causes on long-range planning and investment for development and use of water, and the fostering of costly and piecemeal litigation. Those same factors *should* apply with equal vigor to groundwater rights * * * [because l]ike the unexercised riparian right, the unexercised groundwater right of an overlying landowner is unrecorded, of unknown quantity, with little opportunity for control in the public interest, and wasteful to the extent it deters others from using water for fear of its ultimate exercise. * * * Even though it may appear a logical extension of *Long Valley* to allow a trial court adjudicating competing claims to groundwater to subordinate an unexercised right to a present appropriative use, we must hold such extension inappropriate. Philosophically, we agree with District's position but stare decisis and due process considerations, not a concern under the current riparian statutory scheme, compel us to reach the opposite conclusion in this case. * * *

> [In particular,] absent a statutory scheme for *comprehensive determination* of all ground water rights, the application of *Long Valley* to a private adjudication would allow prospective rights of overlying landowners to be * * * subject to the vagaries of an individual plaintiff's pleading without adequate due process protections.

219 Cal.Rptr. at 748–49, 750 (emphasis in original). In City of Barstow v. Mojave Water Agency, 23 Cal.4th 1224, 99 Cal.Rptr.2d 294 (2000), the California Supreme Court declined to disturb this holding, but noted that *Wright* did "suggest that, in theory at least, a trial court could apply the *Long Valley* riparian right principles to reduce a landowner's future overlying water right use below a current but unreasonable or wasteful usage," so long as notice adequate to satisfy procedural due process was provided to those whose claims were limited. The Court also warned: "If Californians expect to harmonize water shortages with a fair allocation of future use, courts should have some discretion to limit the future groundwater use of an overlying owner who has exercised the water right and to reduce to a reasonable level the amount the overlying user takes from an overdrafted basin." 23 Cal.4th at 1249, n.13.

———

Professor Blomquist, supra p. 507, observed that water users in the seven southern California basins which have achieved some success in managing groundwater originally undertook collective action not to promote efficiency, but simply to prevent catastrophic loss of local groundwater through depletion and/or salinity intrusion. That risk was reduced by a combination of importing water from elsewhere (augmenting and replenishing local aquifers) and restricting demand on local supplies. See Blomquist, supra, at 303–05. The following material offers some examples and lessons from this diverse experience.

The Central Basin

This area, roughly between downtown Los Angeles and Long Beach, underwent thorough urbanization in the 1930s. Total water use declined slightly as agriculture gave way to urban uses, but groundwater extractions increased to almost 300,000 acre-feet annually by 1960. Some of this increase was attributed to a response to the mutual prescription doctrine adopted by the California Supreme Court in the nearby Raymond Basin adjudication, *Pasadena v. Alhambra*. A groundwater replenishment program was begun in the 1950s, with some success, but by 1960, the overdraft was regarded as critical, with saltwater intrusion threatening the basin's main water-bearing aquifers. See generally Blomquist, supra p. 507, at 129–35.

Basin interests collectively and reluctantly concluded, after much discussion, that merely increasing supplies was not enough; instead, some "enforceable reduction in pumping would be necessary" to reduce the overdraft. Id. at 146. In 1962 the local replenishment district instituted a general adjudication against 750 well owners in the basin. A 1955 statute had required groundwater producers to record and report their groundwater production, so a data base was available for use in negotiations, which began even before the suit was filed. Three years later, a stipulated judgment was filed, which required a 20% reduction in each pumper's "assumed relative right." That right was based on actual pumping and on imported water which was, under the California Water

Code, counted as a preserved groundwater pumping right if the imported water substituted for groundwater pumping. A 50% reduction would have been required to reach equilibrium by this method alone, but the parties decided to rely on the artificial replenishment program and surface water inflows into the basin to avoid such a sharp reduction. Id. at 148–50.

The program has worked well; groundwater pumping has stayed within the limits of the judgment. The number of active pumpers has declined from the 508 that originally joined the judgment to about 175, as many smaller pumpers sold their rights to cities, with the 33 largest pumpers accounting for 93% of the total amount pumped.

Three other basins—the Main San Gabriel Basin, the Chino Basin, and the Upper Los Angeles River Area (ULARA)—also limit pumping in accordance with some sort of court-decreed standard reached, as in the Central Basin, through a negotiated settlement. The pumping limit is made through an annual operating "safe yield" determination set in accordance with that year's water supply conditions. As a result, groundwater pumping in those basins shows more variability from year to year. The Raymond Basin was settled through the *Pasadena v. Alhambra* litigation discussed earlier. The West Basin was also brought under control by settlement of an adjudication. In all six basins, as Blomquist noted, "[demand] limitations negotiated by the water users * * * forced them to rely on more expensive imported water supplies rather than deplete the local groundwater sources." Id. at 304.

Orange County

Orange County is the only one of these basins not to have undergone some sort of process to determine rights to pump groundwater. It has, however, used a technique we have seen employed in several other instances in this Chapter—the creation, under state law, of a special water district with substantial powers to manage water use. The Orange County Water District (OCWD), created by state legislation enacted in 1933, is sometimes cited as a model for effective groundwater management. As in other Southland basins, the population of the area covered by the OCWD grew dramatically from the 1930s through the 1990s, at the same time the dominant water use shifted from agricultural irrigation to urban uses.

The District has "chosen to manage the basin from the supply side," Blomquist, supra, at 250. It engaged in a major program of importation and replenishment beginning in the 1950s. Over the next couple of decades the OCWD essentially eliminated groundwater overdraft by importing more than 2.2 million acre-feet from the Colorado River, and about 250,000 acre-feet from the State Water Project. See Paula Smith, Coercion and Groundwater Management: Three Case Studies and a "Market" Approach, 16 Envtl. L. 797, 823 (1986).

With groundwater levels stabilized, the District moved to a conjunctive management program designed to "alter use patterns in order minimize reliance on [local groundwater] as a source of supply for daily needs and preserve it for * * * emergency and peaking periods." Blomquist, supra, at 261. The District acquired substantial capacity to recharge the local aquifers, and undertook projects to effectively wall off the freshwater aquifers from the saline seawater, including injection wells to create a mound of fresh water against the sea, and a series of wells to extract brackish water heading inland and send it back to the sea through surface channels. Id. at 265–66. In short, Orange County uses a combination of imported surface supplies (for immediate use and for recharge) and local groundwater and limited local surface supplies to meet demand.

The management techniques used by the OCWD do not directly limit pumping or attempt to prevent waste. In fact, OCWD is forbidden from directly limiting the amount of groundwater an individual user may withdraw, although it may levy a "basin equity assessment" against pumpers who withdraw groundwater above some level set by the district. The OCWD does not attempt to manage groundwater withdrawals to prevent or minimize well interference. See generally Smith, supra, at 824–38.

Notes and Questions

1.   The availability of supplemental water supplies (usually local surface water supplies plus water imported from elsewhere, e.g., the Colorado River or from northern California via the State Water Project) was a key factor in making it possible to forge an agreement among local groundwater users. These supplemental supplies provide a cushion against shortage when groundwater pumping is restricted, and a source of water in wet years to replenish local groundwater supplies for use in drier years.

2.   The institutional arrangements that govern groundwater in these basins are very complex. Water allocation and use are "governed by rules that were fashioned by the water users and their representatives and formalized in court judgments." Blomquist, supra, at 339. The water managers are usually special governmental districts, but county governments and the Metropolitan Water District also play some role in water management. The state legislature has enacted laws, drafted by local water users, to create the districts, and has also supported information-gathering and other such efforts. Other than in Orange County the courts have, in Blomquist's words, "made the basin-and watershed-level constitutions that water users wrote enforceable and adaptable through their continuing jurisdiction and the appointment of watermasters to administer the judgments." Id. at 339–40. A variety of federal and state agencies have also provided information and physical facilities to make these arrangements work.

3.   The six basins that have determined rights to pump groundwater have done so through a process of negotiation rather than through a contested trial in court. In general, the basis for negotiated rights to pump was some percentage of the actual historical pumping, apparently without regard for whether the pumper was using water on or off the land, even though California correlative rights law favored giving preference to those using on the land. What factors do you suppose led all parties to a negotiated

solution, especially one that appeared not to conform strictly to the applicable legal principles? For example, why would a pumper using water on the overlying land agree to give a pumper for export an equal priority, when that seems inconsistent with the correlative rights doctrine—and mutual prescription seems now to have such limited application? Does it represent altruism, stemming from appreciation of the common threat of continued aquifer decline? A perception that across-the-board pumping reductions were fair, regardless of whether they were consistent with applicable legal principles? A clear-eyed appraisal of the expense of litigation? Overall, are these cases of a collective agreement to ignore the legal principles because they don't seem to help resolve the situation actually facing the parties? In assessing the failure of water users in the inland Mojave Basin (discussed further below) to negotiate a settlement of groundwater rights to bring overdraft under control, Blomquist says that Mojave Basin users have "not had a shared picture of their water supplies and water use," and this "disagreement over the nature and boundaries of the resource" has prevented water users from "construct[ing] a governance structure or devis[ing] a strategy to treat the area's water problems" successfully. Blomquist, supra, at 240–41. Does this suggest that the necessary first step toward addressing groundwater problems is to develop information and educate users and community leaders about the supply and demand for groundwater? How is that best done?

4. Blomquist observes that in some of these "adjudicated" basins, "the adjudication process itself eliminated many of the small producers. They abandoned pumping rather than pay the costs of defending their right to a few acre-feet or less of groundwater." Blomquist, supra, at 314. In some adjudications, smaller pumpers with minimal overall impact on the aquifer were "specifically identified and exempted." Id. (Smaller pumpers continue to exist in Orange County as well, where there has been no adjudication of rights.) Which is the better approach? Exempting smaller pumpers means they don't have to pay the higher costs for imported water. Is there social value in keeping the opportunity to pump groundwater available for smaller producers? Blomquist also points out that the decline in smaller pumpers is not solely attributable to the adjudication process. Urbanization leads small farmers to become or sell out to developers, who usually prefer to rely on municipal water supply systems. Thus Orange County has seen a steady decline in smaller pumpers (the number pumping 25 acre-feet or less declined from 780 in 1970 to 250 in 1985), even though it has never been adjudicated. Blomquist, supra, at 315. When smaller pumpers stop pumping in Orange County, other groundwater users are benefitted, but they don't have to compensate the smaller pumpers.

5. What if any role should basin residents who do not pump groundwater ("nonproducers," Blomquist calls them) play in groundwater management governance? In several of the basins studied, the governing boards of the managing agencies are elected by all residents. In some of them, however, only groundwater pumpers participate in the governing process. Blomquist, supra, at 357.

6. In 1953, with the support of Orange County basin water users, the state legislature changed the OCWD statute to authorize it to levy a tax on groundwater pumping. Such a tax might have at least two goals: (1) to limit

demand for groundwater pumping; and (2) to raise sufficient funds to buy imported water to replenish local aquifers. Are these goals fully consistent with each other? For example, the more inelastic the demand for water, the higher the tax will need to be in order to reduce groundwater pumping, even though a lower tax may raise ample revenue for replenishment purposes. Note also that the more successful the replenishment program, the higher the water level in the aquifer, and thus the lower the cost of extracting groundwater. In practice, the OCWD has generally set the pump tax rate to raise revenue for replenishment, rather than to limit demand, in keeping with its general philosophy of focusing on the supply side rather than the demand side. See generally Blomquist, supra, at 253–55.

7. Across the nation, and especially in this era where a sizeable part of the population seems to equate any form of taxation with theft, the political will to impose pump taxes rarely exists, so they are not a common tool of groundwater management. Like surface water supplies, groundwater is generally regarded as a nearly free good. Economic theory would promote optimal use of groundwater by taxing groundwater users at a rate that reflects the marginal social value of the groundwater they use, plus any costs the user imposes on others through lowering aquifer levels (increasing pump lifts for others and subsidence damages). See, e.g., Bruce Wetzel, Efficient Water Use in California: Economic Modeling of Groundwater Development with Applications to Groundwater Management (1978). How difficult might it be to calibrate the pump tax rate to achieve this end? Although Orange County came eventually to embrace a pump tax to reduce the threat of saltwater intrusion and catastrophic aquifer contamination, pumping there is not taxed to the extent economic theory would suggest. Although some economists criticize politicians for failing to understand economics, does this suggest that the problem might be the other way round—that economic theorists don't understand politics?

8. Blomquist spends some time comparing the Orange County approach (not to worry about who is pumping how much, but rather using a tax to raise sufficient money to pay for imports in wet years to replenish groundwater basins depleted in dry years) with the approach in the other basins, which have used an adjudication to determine, and ratchet down from historic levels, rights to pump groundwater. He concludes that Orange County's

> decision not to assign and limit pumping rights * * * has resulted in some loss of efficiency and some increase in risk. Without defined and transferable pumping rights, basin users have no means of moving groundwater production from lesser-to higher-valued uses. Users who stop pumping from the basin benefit other users but receive nothing in return.
>
> Without a limitation of pumping rights, the Orange County basin management program has had to accommodate unlimited groundwater production. The OCWD has responded by expending considerable sums on acquiring and operating extensive replenishment facilities, which in an ordinary year have substantial excess capacity. The decision not to limit pumping has also left basin users heavily dependent on the availability of imported replenishment

water to maintain basin conditions, and more exposed to importers' decisions to curtail water deliveries in dry periods. The Orange County management program therefore may exhibit some vulnerability in an extended drought.

Blomquist, supra, at 270. He also concludes that Orange County water users have not "saved themselves much money by forgoing an adjudication and limitation of pumping rights," because they have had to invest more heavily in replenishment facilities and to purchase more imported replenishment water. Id. at 308.

9. Blomquist also performs some economic calculations to compare the cost of replacing the groundwater in these seven basins entirely with surface storage and imported water, which would be the result if the aquifers had been drained or destroyed by salinity intrusion. He concludes that "basin preservation has been an extraordinarily good bargain." Water costs are one-third to one-quarter as much as water users in these areas "would be facing by now if the basins had been destroyed," and the area made totally dependent upon imported water and surface storage. Blomquist, supra, at 311. As he points out (id. at 309):

Groundwater basins have value not only a sources of water supply, however, but also as water storage and distribution facilities, regulating the variability of surface water supplies and providing water for peak and emergency use while base supply needs are met from surface and imported supplies. There is strong reason to believe that these uses of groundwater basins are their more valuable uses.

10. Who pays for this management? In most of the six adjudicated basins, according to Blomquist, "management costs, including the costs of replenishment and injection water purchases, are paid by water users through assessments on pumping." Blomquist, supra, at 312, 355. In one of the six basins, appropriators (those using the water off the land from which it is pumped) pay most of the costs, and overlying agricultural users get a nearly free ride. Id. at 312–13. In Orange County, much of OCWD's revenue comes from ad valorem property taxes rather than pump taxes. Therefore groundwater users do not pay the full cost of replacement water, and property owners in effect subsidize groundwater pumping. Id. at 308. Blomquist estimates that Orange County pumpers pay about $166 per acre-foot, compared to a total cost of basin management of about $286 per acre-foot. Id. Is it unfair to require property owners to shoulder some of the costs of groundwater management, even if they are not pumping groundwater? Do they (and their property values) benefit from groundwater management? How? By avoidance of subsidence, or of indirect injuries from groundwater contamination?

11. Concern about protecting the environmental resources of the Sacramento–San Joaquin Delta and San Francisco Bay has led to an intensive focus on the possibilities of a systematic recharge program, concentrated in the Central Valley, to free up some surface water supplies, particularly in drought years, for environmental purposes. One study reports that groundwater banking "has the potential to provide approximately 1 million acre-feet of additional annual yield, with the greatest benefit coming in new opportunities to supply consumptive demands and to enhance stream flows."

David Purkey et al., Feasibility Study of a Maximal Program of Groundwater Banking in California 1 (Natural Heritage Institute, 2d ed. 1998).

The Mojave Basin

The glaring failure in groundwater management in southern California basins has been the inland Mojave River Basin. In 1990, amidst declining groundwater levels, litigation was brought to determine the rights of many groundwater pumpers (it was not a true general adjudication, because certain small well owners and overlying landowners not now withdrawing groundwater were not joined). The trial court, concluding that the "constitutional mandate of reasonable and beneficial use dictates an equitable apportionment of all rights when a [ground]water basin is in overdraft," adopted a "physical solution," negotiated among most of the parties, that gave each pumper an allocation of water, required each to pay a fee for pumping water in excess of the amount allocated, and used the fee to purchase supplementary water supplies. As with similar settlements described earlier, this approach drew no distinctions between overlying pumpers and appropriators, although the court did not purport to adjudicate any individual water rights. In its unanimous decision in City of Barstow v. Mojave Water Agency, 23 Cal.4th 1224, 99 Cal.Rptr.2d 294 (2000), the California Supreme Court set the trial court decision aside on the ground it had no power to short-change the superior rights of overlying landowners who were pumping groundwater, as against those pumping for export. "Respondents simply fail to produce compelling authority for their argument that courts can avoid prioritizing water rights and instead allocate water based entirely on equitable principles." 23 Cal.4th at 1241. Mutual prescription under the doctrine of *Pasadena v. Alhambra* was not available for the reasons discussed on p. 509 supra. Thus the courts continue to cling to the basic distinction the correlative rights doctrine draws between pumpers for use on the overlying land and exporters.

Notes and Questions

1. What should the parties to the *City of Barstow* case do now? Should the parties using groundwater for export offer to buy out the rights of pumpers using on the overlying land?

2. Was the court correct in upholding the formal water law doctrine it had worked out over the past century, as compared to the more informal equitable apportionment most of the parties had worked out? Which approach is likely more efficient?

3. The executive and legislative branches of the California government had very little to do with this process, and with the solutions worked out. Why? What factors prevent these more democratic institutions from operating to address groundwater overdraft, even in the fact of serious environmental threat from salinity intrusion? See, e.g., Peter Menell, Institutional Fantasylands: From Scientific Management to Free Market Environmentalism, 15 Harv. J.L. & Pub Pol'y 489 (1992).

Concluding Thoughts: Whither Groundwater Management and Regulation?

It seems clear more active management and regulation of groundwater uses is in the offing throughout the country, and California's experience is useful to ponder. A fundamental issue is whether to favor local, state, or judicial management. (As many examples in this chapter show, local management is generally done by special governmental district, an institution discussed in Chapter 7.) In 1978, the Governor's Commission to Review California Water Rights Law concluded that "local management, if it is properly undertaken, offers the best opportunity for workable and effective control." Gov. Comm'n to Review Cal. Water Rights Law, Final Report 166–67 (1978). The U.S. Advisory Commission on Intergovernmental Relations issued a report in 1991 that praised the conjunctive use management practiced under the aegis of local water districts in southern California. U.S. Advisory Comm'n on Intergovernmental Relations, Coordinating Water Resources in the Federal System: The Groundwater–Surface Water Connection 37 (1991). See also David A. Sandino, California's Groundwater Management Since the Governor's Commission Review: The Consolidation of Local Control, 36 McGeorge L. Rev. 471 (2005).

California remains utterly schizophrenic in its approach, however. Despite the cutting-edge sophistication of southern California efforts, there has historically been almost no groundwater management in California's intensively agricultural (but increasingly urbanizing) Central Valley, and not much along the Central Coast, with a booming population, intensive agriculture, and salinity intrusion problems. A 1980 Department of Water Resources publication found that eleven groundwater basins, mostly in the San Joaquin Valley, were critically overdrafted, that is, in such a condition that "continuation of present water management practices would probably result in significant adverse overdraft-related environmental, social, or economic impacts." Ground Water Basins in California 3, 13–58 (Cal. Dept. Water Resources Bull. 118–80, 1980). The attitude of most groundwater users in these areas is to "pump until you are sued," and for various reasons litigation in these areas has been a little-used tool. See Eric Garner, Michelle Ouellette, & Richard Sharff, Institutional Reforms in California Groundwater Law, 25 Pac. L.J. 1021, 1022 (1994); Barton H. Thompson, Jr., Tragically Difficult: The Obstacles to Governing the Commons, 30 Envtl. L.241, 250–53 (2000).

Across the state can be found a dizzying array of non-management, management in adjudicated basins, management by special management districts, and management by county ordinance. See Gregory Weber, Twenty Years of Local Groundwater Export Legislation in California: Lessons From a Patchwork Quilt, 34 Nat. Resources J. 657 (1994); California Dept. of Water Resources, Groundwater Management in California (1998). In 1991 and 1992, "[a]t the expense of adding one more type of patch to the patchwork quilt, the legislature (through a law commonly known as AB 3030) created incentives for the quilt to become more uniform statewide and for establishment of management regimes where they were most needed—in overdrafted groundwater basins." Andy Christensen, AB 3030 and Groundwater Management in California 22 (unpublished manuscript, 1998). These laws authorize any local agency that provided water service to establish, in its service area, groundwater management programs. An agency may limit or prohibit pumping only if it "has determined through study and investigation that groundwater replenishment programs or other alternative sources of water supply have proved insufficient or infeasible to lessen the demand for groundwater," Cal. Water Code § 10753.8(c), and it may not "make a binding determination of water rights of any person or entity," Cal. Water Code § 10753.8(b). The local agency may assess pump taxes for various management activities, but must first gain majority approval from the voters in the area subject to such taxes. Cal. Water Code § 10754.

As of 2003, more than 200 local districts and agencies had adopted such plans, although they varied widely in scope and detail. Many "have had little or no implementation, and many counties focus primarily on limiting exports rather than on a comprehensive management program." Department of Water Resources, California's Groundwater, Bulletin 118, Update 2003, at 54. Not only have local agencies moved to institute export controls over local groundwater,[55] but they have also acted to ensure that no other agency obtain authority over their respective service areas (because the law provides that once an agency adopts a groundwater management plan, no other agency may overlap it), and to head off pressure for more top-down, state-level regulation. Christensen, supra, at 32–33.

While a step in the right direction, AB 3030 has notable flaws. Among other things, the plans are done by local agencies within their service areas, which may not bear any correlation to aquifer boundaries, with the result that a single aquifer may be subject to several different plans and managing agencies. The law provides some encouragement, but only that, to coordinate plans among agencies overlying the same aquifer. Cal. Water Code § 10755.2. In 2002, the California legislature beefed up the groundwater management planning process by requiring the plans to include management objectives and monitoring in order to qualify for state funding. See generally Department of Water Resources, California's Groundwater, Bulletin 118, Update 2003, which discusses groundwater management in California over the past decade. See also, Eric L. Garner & Jill N. Willis, Right Back Where We Started From: The Last Twenty–Five Years of Groundwater Law in California, 36 McGeorge L.Rev. 413 (2005); Ella Foley–Gannon, Institutional Arrangements for

---

55. For example, Fresno County prohibits extraction of groundwater for transfer out of the county without a permit (subject to some exceptions). Fresno Cty. Ordinances, Ch. 14.03. See Antonio Rossmann, County Groundwater Regulation: Half a Governor's Commission Legacy Is Better than None, 36 McGeorge L. Rev. 456, 468–69 (2005).

Conjunctive Water Management in California and Analysis of Legal Reform Alternatives, 6 Hastings W.-N.W. Envtl. L. & Pol'y 273 (2000).

The jury is still out on whether California will ever effectively manage groundwater in the Central Valley and Central Coast regions. Professor Rodney Smith has advocated groundwater management through basin adjudications, arguing they are superior to either local or state regulation. Rodney Smith, The Case for Groundwater Adjudication, in Proceedings of the 18th Biennial Conference on Ground Water 47 (Cal. Water Resources Ctr. Rep. No. 77, 1992). Others argue for comprehensive, centralized groundwater management. Garner, Ouellette, & Sharff, supra, at 1043. Others favor management through special governmental districts, with or without adjudications. William Blomquist, Political or Hydrologic Management?, in Proceedings of the 21st Biennial Ground Water Conference 187–93 (Cal. Water Resources Ctr. Rep. No. 95, 1998). The debate, and the experiments, continue.

Chapter 6

PUBLIC RIGHTS IN WATER: FROM NAVIGABILITY TO THE PUBLIC TRUST

Thus far we have focused almost exclusively on private property rights in water. Yet the most distinctive legal feature of water is its status as a public resource that cannot be privatized in the ordinary way. At one level this is a familiar matter. Everyone knows there is a public right of navigation and that no one can own the Mississippi River in the exclusive way one owns a tract of land. Until recently the private and public elements in water coexisted with little friction. Public rights were primarily rights of navigation, and such rights were principally exercised on rivers that still had substantial flows, rather than on those that had been largely dewatered by irrigation or municipal diversions. Occasionally a private dock would have to be removed to facilitate navigation, there would be a dispute over oyster farming in shallow waters,[1] or a shoreline filling and building project would be rejected. Such cases pretty much described the arena of private-public conflict.

In recent years dramatic change has occurred. It began with the modern growth of water-based recreation and the appearance of canoeists and kayakers on small streams that had traditionally experienced little or no public use. Even more recently public claims have begun to be recognized in the ecological values of rivers and lakes, and those claims are asserted in the very places where major diversions occur. These changes have generated a fundamental clash between public and private interests in water. The very thing that constitutes a private water right—entitlement to divert water out of a river—is now often said to violate the public right to maintain instream flows in order to protect fish and wildlife, riparian ecosystems, or recreational use.

At the end of this Chapter we shall encounter these public claims at the current cutting edge of water law, where established appropriators

---

1. Bonnie McCay, Oyster Wars and the Public Trust: Property, Law, and Ecology in New Jersey History (1998).

are asked to release some part of their diversion rights to maintain or restore downstream ecological values; or where new diversions are denied in order to assure the protection of species or of recreational opportunities downstream. It hardly needs to be emphasized that these new demands are a source of considerable anxiety to water users, and that they are sometimes condemned as radical revisions of established water law. In one respect modern environmental claims *are* radically new; for such constraints were not previously imposed on appropriators. But the claims are also part of a tradition of public rights with a long and interesting history. Most of this Chapter is devoted to an exploration of the tradition, setting out the backdrop to such modern cutting-edge controversies as the 1983 Mono Lake decision (infra p. 610).

A. NAVIGABILITY OR TIDALITY FOR TITLE

In Roman law, the sea and the seashore were not capable of private ownership but were held as commons for public use. In England too there was a public right of navigation and fishery in navigable tidal waters, and it was understood that such water and the land beneath it was held in trust by the Crown for common use.[2] Similarly 17th Century New England ordinances recognized a public right of fishing, fowling and navigation in what were called Great Ponds.[3] Out of this unmistakable, though imprecise, tradition,[4] nineteenth century American law established the proposition that navigable waters, and the lands beneath them seaward of the high-water mark, were held in public ownership to secure public uses.[5] Though dispositions were not prohibited, grants were not interpreted as absolute (despite the absence of limiting language), but were subject to a servitude in behalf of the public. Indeed a celebrated early case held that the public servitude was inalienable, and that a contrary position "never could be borne by a free people."[6] Several decades later, in an 1851 Massachusetts case, Commonwealth v. Alger, 61 Mass. 53, 94, Chief Justice Shaw, speaking of tideland development, said:

> [The colonial government] must have well understood that all estate granted by the government to individuals is subject, by reasonable implication, to such restraints in its use, as shall make the enjoyment of it by the grantee consistent with the equal enjoyment by others, of their several and common rights.

2. See William Drayton, The Public Trust in Tidal Areas: A Sometime Submerged Traditional Doctrine, 79 Yale L.J. 762 (1970); Arnold v. Mundy, 6 N.J.L. 1 (1821); Shively v. Bowlby, 152 U.S. 1 (1894); Illinois Cent. R. Co. v. Illinois, 146 U.S. 387 (1892).

3. Lincoln Smith, The Great Pond Ordinance, Collectivism in Northern New England, 30 B.U. L. Rev. 178 (1950); John Whittlesey, Law of the Seashore, Tidewaters and Great Ponds in Massachusetts and Maine (1932).

4. The implementation of public rights in practice has been a subject of considerable controversy. See, e.g., Patrick Deveney, Title, Jus Publicum, and the Public Trust: An Historical Analysis, 1 Sea Grant L.J. 13 (1976).

5. See Molly Selvin, The Public Trust Doctrine in American Law and Economic Policy, 1789–1920, 1980 Wis. L. Rev. 1403.

6. Arnold v. Mundy, 6 N.J.L. 1, 13 (1821).

Legally, the new American states were deemed successors to the English king, so that the navigable waters and submerged lands passed to them in the same sort of trust ownership in which they had been held by the Crown. In the leading case, Illinois Central Railroad Co. v. Illinois, 146 U.S. 387, 452 (1892), the Supreme Court put it this way:

> [T]he State holds the title to the lands under the navigable waters. * * * But it is a title different in character from that which the State holds in lands intended for sale. It is different from the title which the United States holds in the public lands which are open to preemption and sale. It is a title held in trust for the people of the State that they may enjoy the navigation of the waters, carry on commerce over them, and have liberty of fishing therein freed from the obstruction or interference of private parties. * * *

The original thirteen states took on such ownership at the time of establishment of the Union. As to the later-admitted states, the theory is that the federal government held these lands and waters in trust until the date of the state's admission to the Union, at which time the new state—being on an equal footing with the original states—took on the trust ownership of lands beneath navigable waters. Pollard's Lessee v. Hagan, 44 U.S. (3 How.) 212 (1845). The authoritative statement of the situation is set out in Shively v. Bowlby, 152 U.S. 1, 49–50 (1894):

> The Congress of the United States, in disposing of the public lands, has constantly acted upon the theory that those lands, whether in the interior, or on the coast, above the high water mark, may be taken up by actual occupants, in order to encourage the settlement of the country; but that the navigable waters and the soils under them, whether within or above the ebb and flow of the tide, shall be and remain public highways; and, being chiefly valuable for the public purposes of commerce, navigation and fishery, and for the improvements necessary to secure and promote those purposes, shall not be granted away during the period of territorial government; but, unless in case of some international duty or public exigency, shall be held by the United States in trust for the future States, and shall vest in the several States, when organized and admitted into the Union, with all the powers and prerogatives appertaining to the older States in regard to such waters and soils within their respective jurisdictions; in short, shall not be disposed of piecemeal to individuals as private property, but shall be held as a whole for the purpose of being ultimately administered and dealt with for the public benefit by the State, after it shall have become a completely organized community.

Shively set the tone for the future of navigable waters and the submerged lands beneath them: that being especially valuable for public purposes, they should not be treated as ordinary property nor be routinely disposed of into private ownership. The Supreme Court has even rejected Indian tribal claims to the submerged lands beneath navigable waters on reservations, holding that such land passed, upon statehood, to the State in which the reservation was located,[7] though in its most recent decision, a sharply divided Court held against the State of Idaho and in favor of a retention for the Coeur d'Alene tribe.[8] Even more recently, the Court held that the United States retained submerged lands under Glacier Bay National Monument in Alaska prior to statehood, but noting that such intention to retain must be "definitely declared or otherwise made very plain.".[9] One question you might keep in mind is what sort of responsibilities the states bear for the properties that came into their trust ownership. Is the fate of these lands entirely a matter of state law, or is it subject to ultimate oversight by the Supreme Court as common obligations of each sovereign member of the national union?

Note: The Territorial Sea

In 1947 the Supreme Court held that the United States owned title to submerged lands constituting the nation's coastline. See United States v. California, 332 U.S. 19 (1947). Congress then returned title to lands beneath coastal waters, up to three miles offshore (three marine leagues along the Gulf of Mexico) to the states. See Submerged Lands Act of 1953, 43 U.S.C. §§ 1301–1315. In Alaska v. United States, 545 U.S. 75 (2005), the question was who owned the submerged lands in the Alexander Archipelago, consisting of many islands off Alaska's southeastern panhandle area. The lands in question are more than three nautical miles from any of the islands, and also more than three miles from the coast of the continental shoreline. If they were lands beneath inland navigable waters, then they would belong to Alaska under the equal footing doctrine described above. Or, even if not inland (that is, landward of the Alaska state boundary), they would belong to Alaska under the Submerged Lands Act if they were submerged lands within three miles of its coastline constituting its state boundary. Thus (and you would be well-advised to look at a map of Alaska while reading this), if the islands of the Archipeligo are within a bay of Alaska, then all the waters would be inland waters and belong to Alaska; but if the islands are outside a bay, then the coastline is drawn along the continental coast, and the islands are separate parts of Alaska (and ownership would be determined by whether the lands are either less than three miles from the continental coast or less than three miles from any island). As noted, the submerged lands in question were both more than three miles from the continental coast or from any of the islands. The Supreme Court, applying the standard for determining what is a bay from the Convention on the Territorial Sea and the

7. There is a strong presumption against pre-statehood grants of submerged land. See Montana v. United States, 450 U.S. 544, 552 (1981); Utah Div. of State Lands v. United States, 482 U.S. 193 (1987).

8. Idaho v. United States, 533 U.S. 262 (2001). See also Choctaw Nation v. Okla-homa, 397 U.S. 620 (1970) ("very peculiar circumstances"); United States v. Cherokee Nation of Okla., 480 U.S. 700, 704 (1987).

9. Alaska v. United States, 545 U.S. 75, ___, 125 S.Ct. 2137, 2157 (2005) (Glacier Bay National Monument).

Contiguous Zone, and historical treatment of the area as international waters, held that the submerged lands did not belong to Alaska.

Since a critical determinant of ownership of submerged lands within a state is the "navigability" of the overlying waters, the first question is, what determines navigability? The test of navigability for title[10] is set out in the excerpt from Utah v. United States that follows.

UTAH v. UNITED STATES

Supreme Court of the United States, 1971.
403 U.S. 9.

MR. JUSTICE DOUGLAS delivered the opinion of the Court.

This suit was initiated by Utah to resolve a dispute between it and the United States as to shorelands around the Great Salt Lake. Utah's claim to the lands is premised on the navigability of the lake at the date of statehood, viz., January 4, 1896. If indeed the lake were navigable at that time, the claim of Utah would override any claim of the United States, with the possible exception of a claim based on the doctrine of reliction, not now before us.

The operation of the "equal footing" principle has accorded a newly admitted State the same property interests in submerged lands as was enjoyed by the Thirteen Original States as successors to the British Crown. Pollard's Lessee v. Hagan, 3 How. 212, 222–223, 228–230. That means that Utah's claim to the original bed of the Great Salt Lake— whether now submerged or exposed—ultimately rests on whether the lake was navigable (Martin v. Waddell, 16 Pet. 367, 410, 416–417) at the time of Utah's admission. Shively v. Bowlby, 152 U.S. 1, 26–28. It was to that issue that we directed the Special Master, Hon. J. Cullen Ganey, to address himself. See Utah v. United States, 394 U.S. 89. In the present report the Special Master found that at the time in question the Great Salt Lake was navigable. We approve that finding.

The question of navigability is a federal question. The Daniel Ball, 10 Wall. 557, 563. Moreover, the fact that the Great Salt Lake is not part of a navigable interstate or international commercial highway in no way interferes with the principle of public ownership of its bed. United States v. Utah, 283 U.S. 64, 75; United States v. Oregon, 295 U.S. 1, 14. The

---

10. There are other definitions of navigability for other purposes: e.g., under the Federal Power Act, for purposes of federal regulatory jurisdiction (United States v. Appalachian Elec. Power Co., 311 U.S. 377, 407 (1940) ("waters * * * which either in their natural or improved condition are used or suitable for use")), for admiralty jurisdiction (The Propeller Genesee Chief v. Fitzhugh, 53 U.S. (12 How.) 443, 457 (1852); The Montello, 87 U.S. (20 Wall.) 430 (1874) ("The capability of use by the public, for purposes of transportation and commerce affords the true criterion of the navigability of a river. Rather than the extent and manner of that use.")), or under the Clean Water Act, 33 U.S.C. § 1362(7). For the definition of navigability under state law, see infra p. 554 infra.

test of navigability of waters was stated in The Daniel Ball, supra, at 563:

> Those rivers must be regarded as public navigable rivers in law which are navigable in fact. And they are navigable in fact when they are used, or are susceptible of being used, in their ordinary condition, as highways for commerce, over which trade and travel are or may be conducted in the customary modes of trade and travel on water. * * *

While that statement was addressed to the navigability of "rivers" it applies to all water courses. United States v. Oregon, supra, 295 U.S. at 14.

The United States strongly contests the finding of the Special Master that the Great Salt Lake was navigable. Although the evidence is not extensive, we think it is sufficient to sustain the findings. There were, for example, nine boats used from time to time to haul cattle and sheep from the mainland to one of the islands or from one of the islands to the mainland. The hauling apparently was done by the owners of the livestock, not by a carrier for the purpose of making money. Hence it is suggested that this was not the use of the lake as a navigable highway in the customary sense of the word. That is to say, the business of the boats was ranching and not carrying water-borne freight. We think that is an irrelevant detail. The lake was used as a highway and that is the gist of the federal test.

It is suggested that the carriage was also limited in the sense of serving only the few people who performed ranching operations along the shores of the lake. But that again does not detract from the basic finding that the lake served as a highway and it is that feature that distinguishes between navigability and non-navigability.

There was, in addition to the boats used by ranchers, one boat used by an outsider who carried sheep to an island for the owners of the sheep. It is said that one sheep boat for hire does not make an artery for commerce; but one sheep boat for hire is in keeping with the theme of actual navigability of the waters of the lake in earlier years.

There was, in addition, a boat known as the *City of Corinne* which was launched in May 1871 for the purpose of carrying passengers and freight; but its life in that capacity apparently lasted less than a year. In 1872 it was converted into an excursion boat which apparently plied the waters of the lake until 1881. There are other boats that hauled sheep to and from an island in the lake and also hauled ore, and salt, and cedar posts. Still another boat was used to carry salt from various salt works around the lake to a railroad connection.

The United States says the trade conducted by these various vessels was sporadic and their careers were short. It is true that most of the traffic which we have mentioned took place in the 1880's, while Utah became a State in 1896. Moreover, it is said that the level of the lake had so changed by 1896 that navigation was not practical. The Master's

Report effectively refutes that contention. It says that on January 4, 1896, the lake was 30.2 feet deep. He finds that on that date "the Lake was physically capable of being used in its ordinary condition as a highway for floating and affording passage to water craft in the manner over which trade and travel was or might be conducted in the customary modes of travel on water at that time." He found that the lake on January 4, 1896, "could have floated and afforded passage to large boats, barges and similar craft currently in general use on inland navigable bodies of water in the United States." He found that the areas of the lake that had a depth sufficient for navigation "were several miles wide, extending substantially through the length and width of the Lake."

Most of the history of actual water transportation, to be sure, took place on the lake in the 1880's, yet the findings of the Master are that the water conditions which obtained on January 4, 1896, still permitted navigation at that time.

In sum, it is clear that Utah is entitled to the decree for which it asks. * * *

Notes and Questions

1.   To be navigable for title under the Daniel Ball, the water must be suitable to be used as a highway for commerce. Is recreation commerce? On Alaska's Gulkana River, at the date of statehood, "guided fishing and sightseeing trips began to be conducted with watercraft customary for that time period. A substantial industry of such transportation for profit emerged* * * " Is this river navigable for title? See State of Alaska v. Ahtna, Inc., 891 F.2d 1401, 1405 (9th Cir. 1989), cert. denied, 495 U.S. 919 (1990).

2.   Note that the navigability-for-title standard has never required an interstate body of water, despite the language in *Kaiser Aetna*, infra p. 546.

In 1988 the Supreme Court held for the first time that upon admission to the Union the States also took ownership of the land beneath their tidal, non-navigable waters.

PHILLIPS PETROLEUM CO. v. MISSISSIPPI

Supreme Court of the United States, 1988.
484 U.S. 469.

JUSTICE WHITE delivered the opinion of the Court.

The issue here is whether the State of Mississippi, when it entered the Union in 1817, took title to lands lying under waters that were influenced by the tide running in the Gulf of Mexico, but were not navigable-in-fact.

As the Mississippi Supreme Court eloquently put it: "Though great public interests and neither insignificant nor illegitimate private interests are present and in conflict, this in the end is a title suit." Cinque

Bambini Partnership v. State, 491 So.2d 508, 510 (1986). More specifically, in question here is ownership of 42 acres of land underlying the north branch of Bayou LaCroix and 11 small drainage streams in southwestern Mississippi; the disputed tracts range from under one-half acre to almost 10 acres in size. Although the waters over these lands lie several miles north of the Mississippi Gulf Coast and are not navigable, they are nonetheless influenced by the tide, because they are adjacent and tributary to the Jourdan River, a navigable stream flowing into the Gulf. The Jourdan, in the area involved here, is affected by the ebb and flow of the tide. Record title to these tracts of land is held by petitioners, who trace their claims back to prestatehood Spanish land grants.

> The State of Mississippi, however, claiming that by virtue of the "equal-footing doctrine" it acquired at the time of statehood and held in public trust all land lying under any waters influenced by the tide, whether navigable or not, issued oil and gas leases that included the property at issue. This quiet title suit, brought by petitioners, ensued.

* * *

II

As petitioners recognize, the "seminal case in American public trust jurisprudence is Shively v. Bowlby, 152 U.S. 1 (1894)." The issue in *Shively v. Bowlby* was whether the state of Oregon or a pre-statehood grantee from the United States of riparian lands near the mouth of the Columbia River at Astoria, Oregon, owned the soil below the highwater mark. Following an extensive survey of this Court's prior cases, the English common law, and various cases from the state courts, the Court concluded:

> "At common law, the title and dominion in lands flowed by the tide water were in the King for the benefit of the nation. * * * Upon the American Revolution, these rights, charged with a like trust, were vested in the original States within their respective borders, subject to the rights surrendered by the Constitution of the United States.
>
> " * * *
>
> "The new States admitted into the Union since the adoption of the Constitution have the same rights as the original States in the tide waters, and in the lands under them, within their respective jurisdictions." Ibid. at 57.

Shively rested on prior decisions of this Court, which had included similar, sweeping statements of States' dominion over lands beneath tidal waters. Knight v. United States Land Association, 142 U.S. 161, 183 (1891), for example, had stated that, "It is the settled rule of law in this court that absolute property in, and dominion and sovereignty over, the soils under the tide waters in the original States were reserved to the several States, and that the new States since admitted have the same rights, sovereignty and jurisdiction in that behalf as the original States possess within their respective borders." On many occasions, before and since, this Court has restated and reaffirmed these words from *Knight* and *Shively*.

Against this array of cases, it is not surprising that Mississippi claims ownership of all of the tidelands in the State. Other States have done as much. The 13 original States, joined by the Coastal States Organization (representing all coastal States), have filed a brief in support of Mississippi, insisting that ownership of thousands of acres of tidelands under non-navigable waters would not be disturbed if the judgment below were affirmed, as it would be if petitioners' navigability-in-fact test were adopted. * * *

Petitioners rely on early state cases to indicate that the original States did not claim title to non-navigable tidal waters. * * * But it has been long-established that the individual States have the authority to define the limits of the lands held in public trust and to recognize private rights in such lands as they see fit. Shively v. Bowlby, 152 U.S., at 26. Some of the original States, for example, did recognize more private interests in tidelands than did others of the 13—more private interests than were recognized at common law, or in the dictates of our public trusts cases. * * * Because some of the cases which petitioners cite come from such States (i.e., from States which abandoned the common law with respect to tidelands), they are of only limited value in understanding the public trust doctrine and its scope in those States which have not relinquished their claims to all lands beneath tidal waters.

Finally, we note that several of our prior decisions have recognized that the States have interests in lands beneath tidal waters which have nothing to do with navigation. For example, this Court has previously observed that public trust lands may be used for fishing—for both "shell-fish [and] floating fish." See, e.g., Smith v. Maryland, 18 How. 71, 75 (1855). On several occasions the Court has recognized that lands beneath tidal waters may be reclaimed to create land for urban expansion. E.g., Hardin v. Jordan, 140 U.S. 371, 381–382 (1891); Den v. Jersey Co., 15 How. 426, 432 (1854). Because of the State's ownership of tidelands, restrictions on the planting and harvesting of oysters there have been upheld. McCready v. Virginia, 94 U.S. (4 Otto) 391, 395–397 (1877). It would be odd to acknowledge such diverse uses of public trust tidelands, and then suggest that the sole measure of the expanse of such lands is the navigability of the waters over them.

Consequently, we reaffirm our long-standing precedents which hold that the States, upon entry into the Union, received ownership of all lands under waters subject to the ebb and flow of the tide. Under the well-established principles of our cases, the decision of the Mississippi Supreme Court is clearly correct: the lands at issue here are "under tide waters," and therefore passed to the State of Mississippi upon its entrance into the Union.

III

Petitioners do not deny that broad statements of public trust dominion over tidelands have been included in this Court's opinions since the early 19th century. Rather, they advance two reasons why these previous statements of the public trust doctrine should not be given their apparent application in this case.

A

First, petitioners contend that these sweeping statements of State dominion over tidelands arise from an oddity of the common law, or more specifically, of English geography. Petitioners submit that in England practically all navigable rivers are influenced by the tide. * * * Thus, "tidewater" and "navigability" were synonyms at common law. See Illinois Central R. Co. v. Illinois, 146 U.S. 387, 436 (1892). Consequently, in petitioners' view, the Crown's ownership of lands beneath tidewaters actually rested on the navigability of those waters rather than the ebb and flow of the tide. * * *

The cases relied on by petitioner, however, did not deal with tidal, non-navigable waters. And we will not now enter the debate on what the English law was with respect to the land under such waters, for it is perfectly clear how this Court understood the common law of royal ownership, and what the Court considered the rights of the original and the later-entering States to be. * * *

B

Petitioners, in a related argument, contend that even if the common law does not support their position, subsequent cases from this Court developing the *American* public trust doctrine make it clear that navigability—and not tidal influence—has become the *sine qua non* of the public trust interest in tidelands in this country.

It is true that The Genesee Chief, 12 How., at 456–457, overruled prior cases of this Court which had limited admiralty jurisdiction to waters subject to tidal influence. Cf. The Thomas Jefferson, 10 Wheat. 428, 429 (1825). The Court did sharply criticize the "ebb and flow" measure of admiralty inherited from England in The Genesee Chief, and instead insisted quite emphatically that the different topography of America—in particular, our "thousands of miles of public navigable water[s] * * * in which there is no tide"—required that "jurisdiction [be] made to depend upon the navigable character of the water, and not upon the ebb and flow of the tide." 12 How., at 457. Later, it came to be recognized as the "settled law of this country" that the lands under navigable freshwater lakes and rivers were within the public trust given the new States upon their entry into the Union, subject to the federal navigation easement and the power of Congress to control navigation on those streams under the Commerce Clause. Barney v. Keokuk, 94 U.S. (4 Otto) 324, 338 (1877). See also Illinois Central R. Co. v. Illinois, supra, 146 U.S., at 435–436. * * *

But we do not read those cases as simultaneously withdrawing from public trust coverage those lands which had been consistently recognized in this Court's cases as being within that doctrine's scope: all lands beneath waters influenced by the ebb and flow of the tide. See Mann v. Tacoma Land Co., 153 U.S. 273 (1894). * * *

IV

Petitioners in passing, and amici in somewhat greater detail, complain that the Mississippi Supreme Court's decision is "inequitable" and would upset "various * * * kinds of property expectations and interests [which] have matured since Mississippi joined the Union in 1817." They claim that they have developed reasonable expectations based on their record title for these lands, and that they (and their predecessors-in-interest) have paid taxes on these lands for more than a century.

We have recognized the importance of honoring reasonable expectations in property interests. Cf. Kaiser Aetna v. United States, 444 U.S., at 175. But such expectations can only be of consequence where they are "reasonable" ones. Here, Mississippi law appears to have consistently held that the public trust in lands under water includes "title to all the land under tidewater." Rouse v. Saucier's Heirs, 166 Miss. 704, 713, 146 So. 291, 291–292 (1933). Although the Mississippi Supreme Court acknowledged that this case may be the first where it faced the question of the public trust interest in non-navigable tidelands, 491 So. 2d, at 516, the clear and unequivocal statements in its earlier opinions should have been ample indication of the State's claim to tidelands. Moreover, cases which have discussed the State's public trust interest in these lands have described uses of them not related to navigability, such as bathing, swimming, recreation, fishing, and mineral development. See, e.g., Treuting v. Bridge and Park Comm'n of City of Biloxi, 199 So. 2d 627, 632–633 (Miss. 1967). These statements, too, should have made clear that the State's claims were not limited to lands under navigable waterways. Any contrary expectations cannot be considered reasonable.

* * * And as for the effect of our decision today in other States, we are doubtful that this ruling will do more than confirm the prevailing understanding—which in some States is the same as Mississippi's, and in others, is quite different. As this Court wrote in Shively v. Bowlby, 152 U.S., at 26, "there is no universal and uniform law upon the subject; but * * * each State has dealt with the lands under the tide waters within its borders according to its own views of justice and policy."

V

Because we believe that our cases firmly establish that the States, upon entering the Union, were given ownership over all lands beneath waters subject to the tide's influence, we affirm the Mississippi Supreme Court's determination that the lands at issue here became property of the State upon its admission to the Union in 1817. Furthermore, because we find no reason to set aside that court's state-law determination that subsequent developments did not divest the State of its ownership of these public trust lands, the judgment below is

Affirmed.

JUSTICE KENNEDY took no part in the consideration or decision of this case.

JUSTICE O'CONNOR, with whom JUSTICE STEVENS and JUSTICE SCALIA join, dissenting.

Breaking a chain of title that reaches back more than 150 years, the Court today announces a rule that will disrupt the settled expectations of landowners not only in Mississippi but in every coastal State. Neither our precedents nor equitable principles require this result, and I respectfully dissent from this undoing of settled history.

As the Court acknowledges * * * this case presents an issue that we never have decided: whether a State holds in public trust all land underlying tidally influenced waters that are neither navigable themselves nor part of any navigable body of water. * * *

In my view, the public trust properly extends only to land underlying navigable bodies of water and their borders, bays, and inlets. * * *

Navigability, not tidal influence, ought to be acknowledged as the universal hallmark of the public trust. * * *

"It is, indeed, the susceptibility to use as highways of commerce which gives sanction to the public right of control over navigation upon [navigable waterways], and consequently to the exclusion of private ownership, either of the waters or the soils under them." Packer v. Bird, 137 U.S. 661, 667 (1891).

* * * Although the States may commit public trust waterways to uses other than transportation, such as fishing or land reclamation, this exercise of sovereign discretion does not enlarge the scope of the public trust. Even the majority does not claim that the public trust extends to every waterway that can be used for fishing or for land reclamation. Nor does the majority explain why its * * * tidal test is superior to a navigability test for the purpose of identifying waterways that are suited to these other uses. * * *

For public trust purposes, navigable bodies of water include the non-navigable areas at their boundaries. The question of whether a body of water is navigable is answered waterway by waterway, not inch by inch. The borders of the ocean, which certainly is navigable, extend to the mean high tide line as a matter of federal common law. * * * Hence the States' public trusts include the ocean shore over which the tide ebbs and flows. This explains why there is language in our cases describing the public trust in terms of tidewaters: each of those cases concerned the shores of a navigable body of water. * * *

Notes and Questions

1. As the majority indicates, some states have granted into private ownership some of the submerged lands that came to them upon admission

to the Union. In the past, states sometimes granted away the land between the high and low tide lines in order to promote filling and development. State public trust law may impose limits on the permissible extent of such grants. In Arizona, the courts have twice rejected legislative efforts to disclaim wholesale title to stream beds as nonnavigable as violative of the public trust and the gift clause of the Arizona Constitution. See Arizona Ctr. for Law in the Pub. Int. v. Hassell, 172 Ariz. 356, 364–66, 837 P.2d 158, 166–68 (Ct. App. 1991); Defenders of Wildlife v. Hull, 199 Ariz. 411, 18 P.3d 722 (Ct. App. 2001). The legislature tried again following the Defenders decision, see Arizona Laws 2001, ch. 166, §§ 1 et seq. See San Carlos Apache Tribe v. Superior Court, 193 Ariz. 195, 215, 972 P.2d 179, 199 (1999).

2. The majority opinion suggests that there is no federal law constraint on state disposition of its submerged lands. Does this imply that there is no federal public trust doctrine? Does it seem odd that the states obtain these lands upon statehood as a matter of federal law, yet there is no federal law policy meant to be implemented through state ownership and control? Did the states originally get these lands in order to promote a national interest in promoting navigation and commerce, or only to put the new states on an equal footing with the original thirteen states which already owned such lands before the Union was formed? If, as the *Coeur d'Alene* case (supra p. 524, n. 8) indicates, ownership of submerged trust lands is an element of the states' sovereignty, might there be a federal interest in assuring maintenance of that sovereign ownership and control?

3. If, as Justice O'Connor's opinion says, the public trust doctrine was founded on a concern for protecting public use for navigation, shouldn't navigability alone be the test of state ownership? Isn't there force to her historically based argument that the public goals for the use of submerged lands at the time the Union was formed must determine what lands were reserved to the states? Isn't it clear that navigation was the essential public goal at that time? What is the argument on the other side?

B. BOUNDARIES, BED OWNERSHIP, AND SHIFTING SHORELINES

1. FEDERALLY NAVIGABLE OR TIDAL–FOR–TITLE WATERS

Where state ownership obtains under the federal rules of title discussed in the preceding section, the state owns the land below the mean (or ordinary) high water mark both on tidal and inland navigable waters.[1] On shores affected by the tides, the ordinary high water mark or

---

1. Some states have granted ownership down to the low-water mark to the riparian upland owner (see, e.g., Michaelson v. Silver Beach Improvement Ass'n, 342 Mass. 251, 173 N.E.2d 273 (1961)), but the grantee usually takes subject to a public trust easement. See People v. California Fish Co., 166 Cal. 576, 589, 138 P. 79, 84 (1913) (states are free to grant private ownership down to the low water mark of tidal lands, however, such ownership is subject to an "easement and servitude of the public for purposes of navigation and for commerce by means of navigation, and to the public right of free access to the navigable waters over the frontage, whenever it is necessary for such public purpose."). For a state-by-state list of the positions adopted, see A. Dan Tarlock, Law of Water Rights and Resources § 3.69 (2000). The ordinary high water mark may also be set by statute. See, e.g., 1955 Mich. Pub. Acts 247; but see Purdie v. Attorney General, 732 A.2d 442 (N.H. 1999)

mean high tide line is "the average height of all the high waters" over the lunar cycle of 18.6 years that governs tides.[2] This simple statement generates a variety of complicated and technical questions which we can touch on only briefly here.

First, the line of mean high water on tidelands is not a fixed place that one can identify visually. While a surveyor can fix that line as a matter of altitude at any given moment in time, its location on the earth (the place where that horizontal line intersects the beach) can and often does change significantly over the years. Identifying the location of the line can be problematic, as the following excerpt reveals:

> This dispute arose as defendants were engaged in a beach-clean-up operation in Westerly. As defendants traveled along the beach, they were stopped by Wilfred Kay, a littoral owner, and Patrolman Byron Brown of the Westerly police department. Kay, believing his private property extended to the mean-high-water line, had staked out that line previously. He informed defendants that they were not permitted to cross the landward side of it. The defendants, on the other hand, believed that their right to traverse the shore extended to the high-water mark. This line was defined by defendants in the Superior Court as a visible line on the shore indicated by the reach of an average high tide and further indicated by drifts and seaweed along the shore. It has been stipulated by the parties that defendants had crossed the mean-high-tide line but were below the high-water mark at the time of their arrest. Also, at the time of the arrest, the mean-high-tide line was under water. We have referred to the term "high water mark" as used by defendants and accepted by the Superior Court. We shall now discuss the term "mean high tide line." This line is relied upon by the state as the proper boundary, and it is the line accepted by the District Court. The mean high tide is the arithmetic average of high-water heights observed over an 18.6 year Metonic cycle. It is the line that is formed by the intersection of the tidal plane of mean high tide with the shore.[3]

The situation on inland navigable lakes is a little different than along the coasts. The physical phenomena that account for the fluctua-

(a common law question for courts; legislative redefinition further up the beach a taking of property).

2. See Borax Consolidated, Ltd. v. Los Angeles, 296 U.S. 10, 22–23, 26–27 (1935). This cycle begins and ends when a new moon occurs on the same day of the year as it did at the beginning of the last cycle; that is, at the end of a metonic cycle the phases of the moon recur in the same order and on the same days as in the preceding cycle.

3. State v. Ibbison, 448 A.2d 728, 729–730 (R.I. 1982). For a more thorough analy-

sis of the issues raised in this subsection, see generally Frank Maloney & Richard Ausness, The Use and Legal Significance of the Mean High Water Line in Coastal Boundary Mapping, 53 N.C. L. Rev. 185 (1974); Kathryn Beaumont & Louisa Libby-Nelson, The Need for a Uniform Public-Private Boundary: Application of the High Water Boundary to Inland Navigable Lakes, 12 U.C. Davis L. Rev. 125 (1979); Richard Hamman & Jeff Wade, Ordinary High Water Line Determination: Legal Issues, 42 Fla. L. Rev. 323 (1990).

tions (precipitation, runoff, filtration, evaporation, human consumption and outflow through natural river outlets) are less regular than the tides and offer no obviously relevant long-term period for measurement from which a mean can be calculated. As a result, approaches to defining the ordinary high water mark have been more varied, with the most common choice being to define ordinary high water in terms of readily observable physical characteristics of the watercourse involved. This might be the point on the shore where there is no longer evidence of the water's action, such as a vegetation line.[4]

The impermanent location of the line between public and private ownership can create very troublesome practical problems. For example, on an oceanfront tract where the mean high tide line is at a certain place, X, in 1890 when the tract is patented to a private owner, that line might have moved significantly a century later, either seaward as a result of accretion to the beach, or landward as a result of erosion.

The general common law rule that governs such matters is this: If the shore moves gradually and imperceptibly, either by erosion (the gradual process of material being scoured away from the bank or shore, causing it to recede) so that the water invades the area of former upland; by reliction (exposure of uplands through the gradual recession of water), or by accretion (gradual buildup of the shore through the deposit of material by the water) so that the dry land area moves into what was formerly a submerged area), then the boundary moves with that gradual and imperceptible change. Conversely if the change is avulsive (usually the sudden change in the course of a river or stream from one channel into another, or the sudden scouring of shore material, as in a hurricane), then the boundaries do not change. These rules apply whether the boundary is a public/private one, or the boundary is between two private owners.

Some special considerations apply where a river is the boundary between two states, a matter of federal common law. Where the boundary is an active river, the location of the boundaries can be continually changing. The solution adopted by many states is to fix their boundaries by compact. Boundary disputes raising the question whether a change is accretion or avulsion continue to arise.[5]

In Strom v. Sheldon, 12 Wash.App. 66, 527 P.2d 1382 (1974), the reason for the rules was explained this way:

4. On non-tidal rivers and lakes, one court described the measure as "the line of ordinary high water * * * the highest level reached by the stream each year, including the annual spring flood, averaged over a period of years." United States v. Pend Oreille Pub. Util. Dist., 926 F.2d 1502 (9th Cir. 1991). See also California v. Superior Court, 29 Cal.3d 240, 172 Cal.Rptr. 713, 625 P.2d 256, 260–261 (1981); California v. Su-

perior Court, 29 Cal.3d 210, 232, 172 Cal. Rptr. 696, 625 P.2d 239, 252 (1981).

5. Georgia v. South Carolina, 259 U.S. 572 (1922) & 497 U.S. 376 (1990); Louisiana v. Mississippi, 466 U.S. 96, 100 (1984) & 510 U.S. 941 (1993) (allowing commencement of original suit). New Jersey v. New York, 523 U.S. 767 (1998) (fill added to Ellis Island).

The fact that riverbank, lake, and tidewater boundaries rarely remain static for an extended period of time has produced a body of law which seeks on the one hand to preserve the interests of riparian ownership, and on the other hand to maintain some stability in established boundaries. Thus, as a general proposition, when there is a gradual and imperceptible deposit of sediment along the shore (an accretion) the upland owner acquires title to the newly formed land, to the detriment of the owner of the bed. The boundaries may likewise be adjusted when dry land is exposed by a gradual recession of the water (a reliction). But when there is an avulsion—a sudden change in the course of the stream—boundaries are unaffected. Courts frequently do not distinguish between natural and artificial causes; rather, the criterion is the speed of the change. Note, Lundquist, Artificial Additions to Riparian Land: Extending the Doctrine of Accretion, 14 Ariz. L. Rev. 315, 327 (1972).

These rules may perhaps best be explained by saying that the accretion-reliction doctrines preserve riparian interests and usually do not significantly harm other property interests, while the avulsion doctrine encourages boundary stability by maintaining the status quo in the face of the frequently wild fluctuation of watercourses undergoing a nature-induced avulsive change.

It has also been suggested that in applying these doctrines as rules of construction, it should be presumed that the parties fixing the boundaries with reference to the water "had in mind the probability of its gradual change with the passage of years, but did not have in mind the possibility of a sudden and perceptible change." 4 B. Jones, Tiffany, Real Property ¶ 1222 at 623 (3d ed. 1939).[3]

There are some special exceptions to these rules. Understandably, a landowner cannot create his own accretion, and thus increase the size of his tract at the expense of the public or a neighbor, by simply dumping fill (however gradually) at his shoreline boundary.[4] Sometimes it is very

---

3. Several other explanations for these rules have been offered. One is a de minimis rationale, based on the maxim "de minimis non curat lex." Another explanation is that a riparian owner is compensated for losses due to erosion by allowing gains due to accretion. The Roman theory of accession provides yet another reason, e.g., one acquires title to the apples on his tree, and the offspring of his female livestock. Finally, it has been explained that productivity is favored by allowing a riparian owner to use accreted land, rather than the state or a stranger. The most popular explanation for the accretion doctrine is found in a statement made by the Minnesota court in Lamprey v. Metcalf, 52 Minn. 181, 53 N.W.

1139, 1142 (1893): "The incalculable mischiefs that would follow if a riparian owner is liable to be cut off from access to the water, and another owner sandwiched in between him and it, whenever the water line had been changed by accretions or relictions, are self-evident * * *."

4. A Massachusetts case held that a shoreline owner, who had granted an easement of beach use measured by a fixed distance upland from the high water line, and that came closer to his house than he wanted, could not move the easement seaward by putting in fill and shifting the location of the high water mark away from his house. The owner's effort was charac-

difficult factually to untangle the sources of shoreline movement. On the Mississippi Gulf Coast, near Biloxi, for example, periodic hurricanes take away beachland, then the Army Corps of Engineers restores the beaches; there is also natural accretion and erosion, and shoreline owners of fishing operations have generated artificial accretion by disposing of unwanted seashells over the years. Historic maps, if available, plus coring of the shoreland, can help to untangle the historic story.

California's distinctive rule is that "[a]s between the state and private upland owners, land along tidelands and navigable rivers that accretes by artificial means, such as local dredging and construction of wing dams and levees, remains in state ownership, and does not go to the upland owner. * * * Accretion is artificial if directly caused by human activities in the immediate vicinity of the accreted land. But accretion is not artificial merely because human activities far away and, in the case of hydraulic mining, long ago contributed to it." California ex rel. State Lands Comm'n v. Superior Court, 11 Cal.4th 50, 44 Cal. Rptr.2d 399, 900 P.2d 648, 650 (1995). Likewise, some states have developed legislated rules. See, e.g., N.D. Cent. Code §§ 47–06–06 to 47–06–08 (1989). For the most part, state law rules govern these boundary changes, Oregon ex rel. State Land Bd. v. Corvallis Sand & Gravel Co., 429 U.S. 363 (1977), except where oceanfront land is involved. See Hughes v. Washington, 389 U.S. 290 (1967); California ex rel. State Lands Comm'n v. United States, 457 U.S. 273 (1982). The boundaries of Indian Reservations are governed by federal law, which in that setting adopts state law as the federal rule. See Wilson v. Omaha Indian Tribe, 442 U.S. 653 (1979).[1]

Problems

1. An individual owns a tract of land in California on the Pacific Ocean coast that runs down to the mean high tide line as its seaward boundary. With that line at its present location, his tract is large enough to build a house consistent with the zoning. But he fears future erosion from natural causes may diminish the size of his tract over time. He would like to bring a quiet title suit to permanently settle his property boundary at the present high tide line. He then intends to build a house, and to construct a seawall to protect his land against erosive forces from the ocean. (1) Can he quiet title against the state? (2) Should he be allowed to protect his land against rising sea levels or erosion that will make the public/private line permanent as against natural changes? See generally Lechuza Villas West v. California Coastal Comm'n, 60 Cal.App.4th 218, 70 Cal.Rptr.2d 399 (1997). California has a statute that permits the State Lands Commission to establish the ordinary high water mark by agreement or in a quiet title action. Cal. Pub.

terized by the court as "accretion by steam shovel." Bergh v. Hines, 44 Mass.App.Ct. 590, 692 N.E.2d 980 (1998), review denied, 427 Mass. 1106, 699 N.E.2d 850 (1998).

1. For an excellent discussion of the policies underlying the decisions in this area, see John Cabaniss, Federal Common Law and Its Application to Disputes Involving Accretive and Avulsive Changes in the Bounds of Navigable Waters, 17 Land & Water L. Rev. 329 (1982). See also Sanford Landress, After the Flood, Who Owns the Bed of the River? State Ownership Overwhelmed by the Avulsion Rule, 60 Ore. L. Rev. 273 (1981).

Res. Code § 6357; see also id. § 6332. Do such determinations effectively terminate the impact of accretion and erosion on boundaries? See Sotomura v. Hawaii County, 460 F.Supp. 473 (D. Haw. 1978). Does the answer likely depend on whether the land has been developed or not? Does a determination simply authorize the upland owner to build structures to prevent the movement of the ordinary high water mark, but not to change the common law rules if the line in fact moves?

2. Assume that global warming will cause rising sea levels along the Pacific coast, with the result that coastal properties, such as that described in the problem above, will eventually be inundated. The owners want to build seawalls to protect their properties, but the state opposes such efforts because it fears a loss of coastal wetlands if the rising sea is blocked from its natural course. Is there a constitutional property right to protect one's land against loss from the destructive forces of nature? What sort of public policies are appropriate in such a situation? See Joseph Sax, The Fate of Wetlands in the Face of Rising Sea Levels: A Strategic Proposal, 9 U.C.L.A. J. Envtl. L. & Pol'y 143 (1991); James Titus, Rising Seas, Coastal Erosion, and the Takings Clause: How to Save Wetlands and Beaches Without Hurting Property Owners, 57 Md. L. Rev. 1279 (1998).

3. Imagine a navigable-for title river, with a bend in it known as an oxbow. The submerged land belongs to the state, pursuant to the equal footing doctrine. A massive flood forces the water in the river to bypass the oxbow and creates a new channel straight down the course of the river. The old oxbow's submerged land is now dry land. Does it still belong to the state? The new submerged land channel was private land. Does it now become state land? Or, following the usual rule of avulsion, does it remain private land, while the rest of the river's submerged land is owned by the state? Can the newly submerged land be impressed with a public trust without regard to its ownership? See United States v. Keenan, 753 F.2d 681 (8th Cir. 1985); Rutledge v. State, 94 Idaho 121, 482 P.2d 515 (1971); In re Ownership of the Bed of Devils Lake, 423 N.W.2d 141 (N.D. 1988) (reliction of a navigable-for-title lake).

4. The level of a very large, federally navigable-for-title lake, is permanently raised by a dam installed at its outlet. The result is that privately-owned shoreland (previously above the mean high water mark) is submerged. Does the public now have a right to navigate on the water above that submerged land, as it can on the rest of the lake surface? Can the owner of the submerged land fill and build on it, thus excluding the public? See Wilbour v. Gallagher, 77 Wash.2d 306, 462 P.2d 232 (1969); State v. Superior Court (Fogerty), 29 Cal.3d 240, 172 Cal.Rptr. 713, 625 P.2d 256 (1981).

2. NON–NAVIGABLE OR TIDAL–FOR–TITLE WATERS (PRIVATELY OWNED BEDS)

Rivers and Streams

When a single parcel straddles the water course, the beds of the stream belong to the owner whose lands surround them. When a river or stream forms the boundary between the parcels of two riparians, the usual rule is that each owns the bed adjacent to her parcel to the center of the stream. The center of the stream is usually defined as either the mid-point between the banks, or the thread of the main channel.[2] Deeds to the property can deviate from this general rule, but the intent to do so must be evident. For example, a deed that merely described the waterward boundary as the bank of the river would be construed to have granted the beds to the center of the stream unless there was some other indication of an intent on the part of the grantor to sever the tract from the adjacent beds.

Where the shoreline is of irregular shape, the simple rules stated above don't quite do the job.[3] In Joyce v. Templeton, 57 Md.App. 101, 468 A.2d 1369 (1984), the Maryland Court of Special Appeals, summarizing a number of previous cases, succinctly described the principal ways courts respond to irregularly-shaped waterbodies:

If the shore line is straight, the riparian lines are to be extended from the divisional lines on shore into the water, perpendicular to the shore line. If, on the other hand, the shore line is concave, converging lines shall be run from the divisional shore lines to the line of navigability. If the shore lines are convex, the lines will be divergent to the line of navigability. However, it is self-evident that each of these rules cannot be strictly applied where irregular shore lines are involved, if all affected property owners are to be treated equitably. * * * [T]he most equitable rule to fit the given situation was the one which must be adopted, to afford each property owner "the fullest utilization of the respective properties."

* * * [N]o rule can be laid down which will be applicable to all cases. We have no doubt, however, that in all cases, it was intended, if practicable, to give to every proprietor the flats in front of his upland of equal width with his lot at high-water mark.

But this in many cases has been found impracticable. So was the fact in the leading case of Rust v. Boston Mill Corporation, 6 Pick. 158. In that case the flats to be divided were within a deep cove, the mouth of which was narrow, so that it was impossible to make the division among the several proprietors by parallel lines; and from necessity the division was made by running converging divisional lines from high-water mark to the mouth of the cove. And this rule of necessity has been followed in many other cases. * * *

Lakes and Ponds

When the deeds to the parcels surrounding a lake or a pond include the beds and describe the underwater boundaries, the deeds control the

2. In state and international boundary cases, the dividing line is along the "live thalweg," defined as the middle or deepest or most navigable channel. Louisiana v. Mississippi, 466 U.S. 96, 100 (1984).

3. The standard authority, containing detailed illustrations, is Aaron Shalowitz, Shore and Sea Boundaries (1962–64).

location of the subaqueous boundaries. When the deeds are silent the usual method of determining boundaries is to extend lines from the landward property lines to the center point of the lake and award bed ownership in pie-shaped wedges to each respective upland owner. The configuration of some lakes makes this method problematic. For example, the boundary lines for the subaqueous portions of a long narrow lake (perhaps a lake formed in a former stream valley where geologic events have sealed the downstream end) would form tracts of varied shape, a number of which would have narrow slivers extending from the ends of the lake toward the center. For those lakes a more sensible method is to treat each end of the lake as a half-circle and use the wedge method; and then to treat the middle portion of the lake like a stream and assign boundaries in rectangular shapes from the shore to the midline of the lake. Bays and coves will require the more intricate treatment described above in the excerpt from Joyce v. Templeton.[4]

C. THE FEDERAL NAVIGATION SERVITUDE

The federal navigation servitude (called navigation easement in *Phillips Petroleum*, supra p. 527) is another right held for the public in navigable-for-title waters. In practical effect, it is an interest which permits the federal government to displace or destroy state-recognized property rights which would ordinarily be compensable as takings of property. To take the simplest example, a riparian owner commonly has a right under state law to wharf out into the river on which he is a riparian, thereby gaining access directly from shore to the deeper water capable of permitting docking for a boat. Wharfing out is a property right in most states which may be asserted against other riparians.[5] If the river is navigable under the federal navigability-for-title test, however, and if the wharf is deemed by the federal government to be an obstruction to navigation, the government can require it to be removed, and no compensation as for a taking of property will be required.

When used in the clear pursuit of public navigation, the exercise of the navigation servitude is uncontroversial. The governmental actions at issue in navigation servitude cases often involve physical alterations of the watercourse to promote navigation. The federal government may place structures on the bottomlands of navigable rivers (even when those bottomlands have passed into private ownership), or it may build a levee to increase water flows for navigation and cut off access to the river by a riparian without having to compensate.[6] In addition, it can diminish the flow of a navigable river, or raise the river permanently to the high

---

4. A more extensive set of examples illustrative of the rules used to determine private bed ownership can be found in two ALR notations: 65 A.L.R.2d 143 (rivers) and 14 A.L.R.4th 1028 (lakes).

5. See, e.g., Shorehaven Golf Club v. Water Resources Comm'n, 146 Conn. 619, 624, 153 A.2d 444, 446 (1959). In some states it is only permissive. See, e.g., Woods v. Johnson, 241 Cal.App.2d 278, 50 Cal.

Rptr. 515, 517 (1966) ("The state, acting by the State Lands Commission, may allow a littoral owner to wharf out on payment of fees, or may proceed in ejectment against one who trespasses on submerged lands without permit").

6. See Gibson v. United States, 166 U.S. 269 (1897).

water mark and not have to pay compensation, even though such actions damage the uses of the riparian owners, and even though the private uses impaired are otherwise recognized as enforceable property rights.

In a few settings controversy surrounds the use of the navigation servitude. Some of the hard cases are readily conjured up by asking whether compensation is due to the adversely affected riparians in the following instances:

• To promote navigation on a navigable river, the government permanently maintains the river's level at the high water mark, with the effect that the level of a non-navigable tributary is also permanently raised above its natural level, damaging a riparian on that tributary.[7]

• As part of a navigation project, the government condemns riparian land above the high water mark that is owned by a power company. Admittedly compensation is due for the land, but how is its value measured? By its (high) value because its proximity to the navigable water will support hydroelectric generation activities, or by the much lower value if proximity to the water is excluded.[8]

In the case that follows, the Supreme Court explains the nature of the servitude, and applies it to one troublesome situation.

UNITED STATES v. WILLOW RIVER POWER CO.

Supreme Court of the United States, 1945.
324 U.S. 499.

[The Power Company owned a dam on the Willow River, a non-navigable tributary of the navigable St. Croix River, to which it ran parallel and from which it was separated above the confluence by a narrow neck of land. The Power Company had built a canal from its dam on the Willow to the St. Croix, and profited from the difference in elevation (power head) between the Willow, and the St. Croix, which was about 17 feet lower at its high water mark, 672 feet above sea level. As part of a navigation project, the government raised the level of the St. Croix, which reduced the Power Company's head. Had the government done no more than maintain the St. Croix permanently at the high water mark level of 672 feet, it was agreed that no compensation would be due, though that would have damaged the Power Company. But in fact the government maintained the St. Croix at 675 feet, three feet *above* the high water mark. The Power Company sought compensation solely for the damage done by that additional three foot loss of head. By raising the water above the high-water mark, the government no doubt flooded some of the Power Company's riparian land on the St. Croix, but in this

---

7. See United States v. Kansas City Life Ins. Co., 339 U.S. 799 (1950) (the Court required compensation, by a 5–4 vote).

8. The owner may not recover for value that inheres in the land because of its prox-

imity to navigable waters. See United States v. Chandler–Dunbar Water Power Co., 229 U.S. 53 (1913); United States v. Twin City Power Co., 350 U.S. 222 (1956).

case there was no dispute over compensation for land. The Power Company claimed only that it had a state-created property right in the flow of the St. Croix as a power head, and that the government's servitude extended only to the high water mark, and no higher. For all losses of power head above that level, the Company said, it was entitled to compensation.]

MR. JUSTICE JACKSON delivered the opinion of the Court.

The court [of claims] held that the Government "had a right to raise the level of the river to ordinary high-water mark with impunity, but it is liable for the taking or deprivation of such property rights as may have resulted from raising the level beyond that point." * * *

It is clear, of course, that a head of water has value and that the Company has an economic interest in keeping the St. Croix at the lower level. But not all economic interests are "property rights"; only those economic advantages are "rights" which have the law back of them, and only when they are so recognized may courts compel others to forbear from interfering with them or to compensate for their invasion. * * * We cannot start the process of decision by calling such a claim as we have here a "property right"; whether it is a property right is really the question to be answered. * * * The claimant's assertion that its interest in a power head amounts to a "property right" is made under circumstances not present in any case before considered by this Court.

While riparian owners on navigable streams usually were held to have the same rights to be free from interferences of other riparian owners as on non-navigable streams, it was recognized from the beginning that all riparian interests were subject to a dominant public interest in navigation. The consequences of the latter upon the former have been the subject of frequent litigation.

Without detailing the long struggle between such conflicting interests on navigable streams, it may be pointed out that by 1909 the lines had become sharply drawn and were then summarized by a leading author:[4] "The older authorities hold that [a riparian] owner has no private rights in the stream or body of water which are appurtenant to his land, and, in short, no rights beyond that of any other member of the public, and that the only difference is that he is more conveniently situated to enjoy the privileges which all the public have in common, and that he has access to the waters over his own land, which the public does not." "Access to and use of the stream by the riparian owner is regarded as merely permissive on the part of the public and liable to be cut off absolutely if the public sees fit to do so. * * * But this [access and use] is a mere convenience, arising from his ownership of the lands adjacent to the ordinary high water mark, and does not prevent the State from depriving him entirely of this convenience, by itself making erections on the shore, or authorizing the use of the shore by others, in such a way as to deprive him of this convenience altogether, and the injury resulting to

4.   1 Lewis on Eminent Domain 116, 119
(3d ed. 1909).

him therefrom, although greater than that sustained by the rest of the public, is *damnum absque injuria.*" On the other hand, the author pointed out, there were cases holding that the riparian owners on navigable streams "have valuable rights appurtenant to their estates, of which they cannot be deprived without compensation." He considered this the better rule, and suggested that the courts indicated some tendency to adopt it.

However, in 1913 this Court decided United States v. Chandler–Dunbar Co., 229 U.S. 53. It involved the claim that water power inherent in a navigable stream due to its fall in passing riparian lands belongs to the shore owner as an appurtenant to his lands. The Court set aside questions as to the right of riparian owners on non-navigable streams and all questions as to the rights of riparian owners on either navigable or non-navigable streams as between each other. And it laid aside as irrelevant whether the shore owner did or did not have a technical title to the bed of the river which would pass with it "as a shadow follows a substance." It declared that "In neither event can there be said to arise any ownership of the river. Ownership of a private stream wholly upon the lands of an individual is conceivable; but that the running water in a great navigable stream is capable of private ownership is inconceivable." 229 U.S. at pages 62, 69. This Court then took a view quite in line with the trend of former decisions then reviewed, that a strategic position for the development of power does not give rise to a right to maintain it as against interference by the United States in aid of navigation. We have adhered to that position. United States v. Appalachian Electric Power Co., 311 U.S. 377, 424. The *Chandler–Dunbar* case held that the shore owner had no appurtenant property right in two natural levels of water in front of its lands or to the use of the natural difference between as a head for power production. In this case the claimant asserts a similar right to one natural level in front of his lands and a right of ownership in the difference between that and the artificial level of the impounded water of the Willow River. It constituted a privilege or a convenience, enjoyed for many years, permissible so long as compatible with navigation interests, but it is not an interest protected by law when it becomes inconsistent with plans authorized by Congress for improvement of navigation.

It is conceded that the riparian owner has no right as against improvements of navigation to maintenance of a level below high-water mark, but it is claimed that there is a riparian right to use the stream for run-off of water at this level. High-water mark bounds the bed of the river. Lands above it are fast lands and to flood them is a taking for which compensation must be paid. But the award here does not purport to compensate a flooding of fast lands or impairment of their value. Lands below that level are subject always to a dominant servitude in the interests of navigation and its exercise calls for no compensation. United States v. Chicago, M., St. P. & P.R. Co., 312 U.S. 592, 313 U.S. 543; Willink v. United States, 240 U.S. 572. The damage here is that the water claimant continues to bring onto its lands through an artificial canal from the Willow River has to leave its lands at an elevation of 675 instead of an elevation of 672 feet. No case is cited and we find none which holds a riparian owner on navigable waters to have such a legal right. * * *

Rights, property or otherwise, which are absolute against all the world are certainly rare, and water rights are not among them. Whatever rights may be as between equals such as riparian owners, they are not the measure of riparian rights on a navigable stream relative to the function of the Government in improving navigation. Where these interests conflict they are not to be reconciled as between equals, but the private interest must give way to a superior right, or perhaps it would be more accurate to say that as against the Government such private interest is not a right at all.

Operations of the Government in aid of navigation ofttimes inflict serious damage or inconvenience or interfere with advantages formerly enjoyed by riparian owners, but damage alone gives courts no power to require compensation where there is not an actual taking of property. Such losses may be compensated by legislative authority, not by force of the Constitution alone. * * *

We hold that claimant's interest or advantage in the high-water level of the St. Croix River as a run-off for tail waters to maintain its power head is not a right protected by law and that the award below based exclusively on the loss in value thereof must be reversed.

[The dissenting opinion of MR. JUSTICE ROBERTS, in which the CHIEF JUSTICE concurred, is omitted].

Notes and Questions

1. Another important question, not raised in *Willow River,* is whether the no-compensation rule applies only to government projects to promote navigation, or applies whenever the government takes an action within its constitutional power that affects navigable waters: if, for example, it demanded removal of a dam in order to promote recovery of a species listed under the Endangered Species Act. A related question was raised, but not decided, in United States v. Gerlach Live Stock Co., 339 U.S. 725 (1950). There, in building the Central Valley Project in California to provide irrigation water to farmers in the region, the federal government diverted water from the navigable San Joaquin River, depriving riparians along the River of the use of the water. The riparian owners sought compensation, claiming that since there was no navigation purpose, the navigation servitude did not apply. The Court finessed the issue, holding that Congress, by statute, had intended to compensate, whether or not it was constitutionally required to do so. The Court said, "we need not ponder whether, by virtue of a highly fictional navigation purpose, the Government could destroy the flow of a navigable stream and carry away its waters for sale to private interests without compensation to those deprived of them. We have never held that or anything like it, and we need not here pass on any question of constitutional power; for we do not find that Congress has attempted to take or authorized the taking, without compensation, of any right valid under state law." Id. at

737. See United States v. Cherokee Nation, 480 U.S. 700, 705 (1987) (dictum: "every purpose which is in aid of navigation"). Does the decision in *Phillips Petroleum,* supra p. 527, cast new light on this issue, insofar as it recognizes a governmental interest that goes beyond "mere" navigation?

2.   The unanswered question in *Gerlach Live Stock* raises the question of the source of the navigation servitude. If it arises from the right of the public to navigation, it would seem to be limited to navigation purposes. On the other hand, if it arises from the existence of the Commerce Clause, of which navigation is simply one element, then it would seem to be applicable to all exercises of commerce clause power. Alternatively, why should there be no private rights in navigable rivers when the commerce power is exercised, and a different result if the war power, or the treaty power, is exercised? Or does *Willow River* state an even broader rule, which is that there are no private rights in navigable waters as against the federal government, period. The Supreme Court has never very clearly explained the source of the navigation servitude. Perhaps the closest it has come is the following statement from Gilman v. Philadelphia, 70 U.S. (3 Wall.) 713, 724–25 (1866): "The power to regulate commerce comprehends the control for that purpose, and to the extent necessary, of all the navigable waters of the United States * * *. For this purpose they are public property of the nation, and subject to all the requisite legislation by Congress." Does this "explanation" tell you how the Court would have resolved the question in the *Gerlach Live Stock* case, if it had been obliged to do so? A contemporary effort to describe the servitude can be found in Katie John v. United States, 1994 WL 487830 (D. Alaska 1994), rev'd, State of Alaska v. Babbitt, 54 F.3d 549, 553 (9th Cir. 1995), reaffirmed in John v. United States, 247 F.3d 1032 (9th Cir. 2001).

3.   In United States v. Rands, 389 U.S. 121 (1967), Rands owned land riparian to the navigable Columbia River in Oregon. Rands leased its land to the State of Oregon, giving the State an option to buy at a rather high price, the land being valuable as a port site. Before the option could be exercised, the United States condemned Rands' land pursuant to a navigation project on the Columbia River. The question was whether Rands was entitled to be compensated for the port site value of the land, or for its much lesser value if its proximity to the river was excluded. Not surprisingly, in light of the cases described above, the court held that Rands was only entitled to the dry-land value (value excluding proximity to the river). What made the case interesting was that the United States, instead of using the land for its own project, then sold it to the State of Oregon at a price much below the option price at which Rands could have sold it. The practical result was to enrich the State of Oregon at the expense of Rands by means of the exercise of the federal navigation servitude. Congress then effectively overruled *Rands* by enacting a statute that provides:

> In all cases where real property shall be taken by the United States for the public use in connection with any improvement of rivers, harbors, canals, or waterways of the United States, * * * compensation to be paid for real property taken by the United States above the normal high water mark of navigable waters of the United States shall be the fair market value of such real property based upon all uses to which such real property may reasonably be put,

including its highest and best use, any of which uses may be dependent upon access to or utilization of such navigable waters.

Rivers and Harbors Act of 1970, § 111, 33 U.S.C. § 595a. See United States v. 30.54 Acres of Land, 90 F.3d 790, 793 (3d Cir. 1996).

4. The no-compensation rule of the navigation servitude has had an impact in other areas of law. Perhaps the most interesting case is United States v. Fuller, 409 U.S. 488 (1973). An individual owned a tract of land, and had a federal permit to graze his cattle on adjacent federal land. Such permits are common in the West, and in practical effect greatly increase the value of the private tract. Though the grazing permits are revocable, and though the statute expressly provides that "issuance of a permit * * * shall not create any right, title, interest, or estate in or to the lands" for which the permit is issued (43 U.S.C. § 315b), private land benefitted by a grazing permit is routinely sold for prices that include the value of the permit. (Permits are rarely revoked.) In the *Fuller* case, the United States condemned the private tract, and the question was whether the amount due as compensation should reflect the market value (which included the value of the grazing permit). The Court, citing *Rands* and other navigation servitude cases, held that since there was no property in the grazing permit, the landowner was not entitled to be compensated for its value. Four Justices dissented.

5. A state navigation servitude has been recognized in California. In Colberg, Inc. v. State ex rel. Dept. of Pub. Works, 67 Cal.2d 408, 62 Cal.Rptr. 401, 432 P.2d 3 (1967), compensation was denied when construction of freeways over a navigable channel denied shipyard owners access to a deep water channel. Contrast Wernberg v. State, 516 P.2d 1191 (Alaska 1973), where a right to compensation was recognized when the state cut off a riparian's access to deep water by building a road across the access creek.

6. For a discussion of the servitude that cites many earlier articles, see Martha Haber, The Navigation Servitude and the Fifth Amendment, 26 Wayne L. Rev. 1505 (1980).

D.　PUBLIC RIGHTS OF RECREATIONAL ACCESS AND USE

1.　FEDERAL COMMERCE CLAUSE NAVIGABILITY VERSUS NAVIGABILITY–FOR–TITLE

KAISER AETNA v. UNITED STATES

Supreme Court of the United States, 1979.
444 U.S. 164.

MR. JUSTICE REHNQUIST delivered the opinion of the Court.

The Hawaii Kai Marina was developed by the dredging and filling of Kuapa Pond, which was a shallow lagoon separated from Maunalua Bay and the Pacific Ocean by a barrier beach. Although under Hawaii law Kuapa Pond was private property, the Court of Appeals for the Ninth Circuit held that when petitioners converted the pond into a marina and thereby connected it to the bay, it became subject to the "navigational servitude" of the Federal Government. Thus, the public acquired a right of access to what was once petitioners' private pond.

* * * The pond was contiguous to the bay, which is a navigable waterway of the United States, but was separated from it by the barrier beach.

Early Hawaiians used the lagoon as a fishpond and reinforced the natural sandbar with stone walls. Prior to the annexation of Hawaii, there were two openings from the pond to Maunalua Bay. The fishpond's managers placed removable sluice gates in the stone walls across these openings. Water from the bay and ocean entered the pond through the gates during high tide, and during low tide the current flow reversed toward the ocean. The Hawaiians used the tidal action to raise and catch fish such as mullet.

Kuapa Pond, and other Hawaiian fishponds, have always been considered to be private property by landowners and by the Hawaiian government. Such ponds were once an integral part of the Hawaiian feudal system. And in 1848 they were allotted as parts of large land units, known as "ahupuaas," by King Kamehameha III during the Great Mahele or royal land division. Titles to the fishponds were recognized to the same extent and in the same manner as rights in more orthodox fast land. Kuapa Pond was part of an ahupuaa that eventually vested in Bernice Pauahi Bishop and on her death formed a part of the trust corpus of petitioner Bishop Estate, the present owner.

In 1961, Bishop Estate leased a 6,000–acre area, which included Kuapa Pond, to petitioner Kaiser Aetna for subdivision development. The development is now known as "Hawaii Kai." Kaiser Aetna dredged and filled parts of Kuapa Pond, erected retaining walls and built bridges within the development to create the Hawaii Kai Marina. Kaiser Aetna increased the average depth of the channel from two to six feet. It also created accommodations for pleasure boats and eliminated the sluice gates.

When petitioners notified the Army Corps of Engineers of their plans in 1961, the Corps advised them they were not required to obtain permits for the development of and operations in Kuapa Pond. Kaiser Aetna subsequently informed the Corps that it planned to dredge an 8–foot–deep channel connecting Kuapa Pond to Maunalua Bay and the Pacific Ocean, and to increase the clearance of a bridge of the Kalanianaole Highway—which had been constructed during the early 1900's along the barrier beach separating Kuapa Pond from the bay and ocean—to a maximum of 13.5 feet over the mean sea level. These improvements were made in order to allow boats from the marina to enter into and return from the bay, as well as to provide better waters. The Corps acquiesced in the proposals, its chief of construction commenting only that the "deepening of the channel may cause erosion of the beach."

At the time of trial, a marina-style community of approximately 22,000 persons surrounded Kuapa Pond. It included approximately 1,500 marina waterfront lot lessees. The waterfront lot lessees, along with at least 86 nonmarina lot lessees from Hawaii Kai and 56 boat owners who are not residents of Hawaii Kai, pay fees for maintenance of the pond and for patrol boats that remove floating debris, enforce boating regulations, and maintain the privacy and security of the pond. Kaiser Aetna controls access to and use of the marina. It has generally not permitted commercial use, except for a small vessel, the *Marina Queen*, which could carry 25 passengers and was used for about five years to promote sales of marina lots and for a brief period by marina shopping center merchants to attract people to their shopping facilities.

In 1972, a dispute arose between petitioners and the Corps concerning whether (1) petitioners were required to obtain authorization from the Corps, in accordance with section 10 of the Rivers and Harbors Appropriation Act of 1899, 33 U.S.C. section 403,[2] for future construction, excavation, or filling in the marina, and (2) petitioners were precluded from denying the public access to the pond because, as a result of the improvements, it had become a navigable water of the United States. The dispute foreseeably ripened into a lawsuit by the United States Government against petitioners in the United States District Court for the District of Hawaii. In examining the scope of Congress' regulatory authority under the Commerce Clause, the District Court held that the pond was "navigable water of the United States" and thus subject to regulation by the Corps under section 10 of the Rivers and Harbors Appropriation Act. 408 F. Supp. 42, 53 (D.Haw.1976). It further held, however, that the Government lacked the authority to open the now dredged pond to the public without payment of compensation to the owner. Ibid., at 54. In reaching this holding, the District Court reasoned that although the pond was navigable for the purpose of delimiting Congress' regulatory power, it was not navigable for the purpose of defining the scope of the federal "navigational servitude" imposed by the Commerce Clause. * * *

The question before us is whether * * * petitioners' improvements to Kuapa Pond caused its original character to be so altered that it became subject to an overriding federal navigational servitude, thus converting into a public aquatic park that which petitioners had invested

---

2. Title 33 U.S.C. § 403 provides: "The creation of any obstruction not affirmatively authorized by Congress, to the navigable capacity of any of the waters of the United States is prohibited; and it shall not be lawful to build or commence the building of any wharf, pier, dolphin, boom, weir, breakwater, bulkhead, jetty, or other structures in any port, roadstead, haven, harbor, canal, navigable river, or other water of the United States, outside established harbor lines, or where no harbor lines have been established, except on plans recommended by the Chief of Engineers and authorized by the Secretary of the Army; and it shall not be lawful to excavate or fill, or in any manner to alter or modify the course, location, condition, or capacity of, any port, roadstead, haven, harbor, canal, lake, harbor of refuge, or inclosure within the limits of any breakwater, or of the channel of any navigable water of the United States, unless the work has been recommended by the Chief of Engineers and authorized by the Secretary of the Army prior to beginning the same."

millions of dollars in improving on the assumption that it was a privately owned pond leased to Kaiser Aetna.[3]

* * * The position advanced by the Government, * * * presumes that the concept of "navigable waters of the United States" has a fixed meaning that remains unchanged in whatever context it is being applied. * * * [A]ll of this Court's cases dealing with the authority of Congress to regulate navigation and the so-called "navigational servitude" cannot simply be lumped into one basket. * * * "[A]ny reliance upon judicial precedent must be predicated upon careful appraisal of the purpose for which the concept of 'navigability' was invoked in a particular case."

It is true that Kuapa Pond may fit within definitions of "navigability" articulated in past decisions of this Court. But it must be recognized that the concept of navigability in these decisions was used for purposes other than to delimit the boundaries of the navigational servitude: for example, to define the scope of Congress' regulatory authority under the Interstate Commerce Clause, to determine the extent of the authority of the Corps of Engineers under the Rivers and Harbors Appropriation Act of 1899, and to establish the limits of the jurisdiction of federal courts conferred by Art. III, section 2, of the United States Constitution over admiralty and maritime cases. Although the Government is clearly correct in maintaining that the now dredged Kuapa Pond falls within the definition of "navigable waters" as this Court has used that term in delimiting the boundaries of Congress' regulatory authority under the Commerce Clause, this Court has never held that the navigational servitude creates a blanket exception to the Takings Clause whenever Congress exercises its Commerce Clause authority to promote navigation. Thus, while Kuapa Pond may be subject to regulation by the Corps of Engineers, acting under the authority delegated it by Congress in the Rivers and Harbors Appropriation Act, it does not follow that the pond is also subject to a public right of access.

A

Reference to the navigability of a waterway adds little if anything to the breadth of Congress' regulatory power over interstate commerce. It has long been settled that Congress has extensive authority over this Nation's waters under the Commerce Clause. Early in our history this Court held that the power to regulate commerce necessarily includes power over navigation. Gibbons v. Ogden, 9 Wheat. 1, 189 (1824). As stated in Gilman v. Philadelphia, 3 Wall. 713, 724–725 (1866):

> "Commerce includes navigation. The power to regulate commerce comprehends the control for that purpose, and to the extent necessary, of all the navigable waters of the United States which are accessible from a State other than those in which they lie. For this purpose they are the public property of

---

3. Petitioners do not challenge the Court of Appeals' holding that the Hawaii Kai Marina is within the scope of Congress' regulatory power and subject to regulation by the Army Corps of Engineers pursuant to its authority under section 10 of the Rivers and Harbors Appropriation Act, 33 U.S.C. § 403.

the nation, and subject to all the requisite legislation by Congress."

The pervasive nature of Congress' regulatory authority over national waters was more fully described in United States v. Appalachian Power Co., 311 U.S. [377], at 426–427:

> "[I]t cannot properly be said that the constitutional power of the United States over its waters is limited to control for navigation. * * * In truth the authority of the United States is the regulation of commerce on its waters. Navigability * * * is but a part of this whole. Flood protection, watershed development, recovery of the cost of improvements through utilization of power are likewise parts of commerce control. * * * [The] authority is as broad as the needs of commerce. * * * The point is that navigable waters are subject to national planning and control in the broad regulation of commerce granted the Federal Government."

Appalachian Power Co. indicates that congressional authority over the waters of this Nation does not depend on a stream's "navigability." * * * [A] wide spectrum of economic activities "affect" interstate commerce and thus are susceptible of congressional regulation under the Commerce Clause irrespective of whether navigation, or, indeed, water, is involved. The cases that discuss Congress' paramount authority to regulate waters used in interstate commerce are consequently best understood when viewed in terms of more traditional Commerce Clause analysis than by reference to whether the stream in fact is capable of supporting navigation or may be characterized as "navigable water of the United States." With respect to the Hawaii Kai Marina, for example, there is no doubt that Congress may prescribe the rules of the road, define the conditions under which running lights shall be displayed, require the removal of obstructions to navigation, and exercise its authority for such other reason as may seem to it in the interest of furthering navigation or commerce.

B

In light of its expansive authority under the Commerce Clause, there is no question but that Congress could assure the public a free right of access to the Hawaii Kai Marina if it so chose. Whether a statute or regulation that went so far amounted to a "taking," however, is an entirely separate question. * * * When the "taking" question has involved the exercise of the public right of navigation over interstate waters that constitute highways for commerce, however, this Court has held in many cases that compensation may not be required as a result of the federal navigational servitude. See, e.g., United States v. Chandler–Dunbar Co., 229 U.S. 53 (1913).

C

The navigational servitude is an expression of the notion that the determination whether a taking has occurred must take into consideration the important public interest in the flow of interstate waters that in their natural condition are in fact capable of supporting public navigation. See United States v. Cress, 243 U.S. 316 (1917). Thus, in United States v. Chandler–Dunbar Co., *supra*, 229 U.S., at 69, this Court stated that "the running water in a great navigable stream is [incapable] of private ownership * * *." And, in holding that a riparian landowner was not entitled to compensation when the construction of a pier cut off his access to navigable water, this Court observed:

> "The primary use of the waters and the lands under them is for purposes of navigation, and the erection of piers in them to improve navigation for the public is entirely consistent with such use, and infringes no right of the riparian owner. Whatever the nature of the interest of a riparian owner in the submerged lands in front of his upland bordering on a public navigable water, his title is not as full and complete as his title to fast land which has no direct connection with the navigation of such water. It is a qualified title, a bare technical title, not at his absolute disposal, as is his upland, but to be held at all times subordinate to such use of the submerged lands and of the waters flowing over them as may be consistent with or demanded by the public right of navigation." Scranton v. Wheeler, 179 U.S. 141, 163 (1900).

For over a century, a long line of cases decided by this Court involving Government condemnation of "fast lands" delineated the elements of compensable damages that the Government was required to pay because the lands were riparian to navigable streams. The Court was often deeply divided, and the results frequently turned on what could fairly be described as quite narrow distinctions.

* * * But none of these cases ever doubted that when the Government wished to acquire fast lands, it was required by the Eminent Domain Clause of the Fifth Amendment to condemn and pay fair value for that interest. * * *

Here, the Government's attempt to create a public right of access to the improved pond goes so far beyond ordinary regulation or improvement for navigation as to amount to a taking. * * * More than one factor contributes to this result.[9] It is clear that prior to its improvement, Kuapa Pond was incapable of being used as a continuous highway for the purpose of navigation in interstate commerce. Its maximum depth at high tide was a mere two feet, it was separated from the adjacent bay and ocean by a natural barrier beach, and its principal commercial value was limited to fishing.[10] It consequently is not the sort

---

9. We do not decide, however, whether in some circumstances one of these factors by itself may be dispositive.

10. While it was still a fishpond, a few flat-bottomed shallow draft boats were operated by the fishermen in their work. There is no evidence, however, that even

these boats could acquire access to the adjacent bay and ocean from the pond.

Although Kuapa Pond clearly was not navigable in fact in its natural state, the dissent argue that the pond nevertheless was "navigable water of the United States"

of "great navigable stream" that this Court has previously recognized as being "[incapable] of private ownership." And, as previously noted, Kuapa Pond has always been considered to be private property under Hawaiian law. Thus, the interest of petitioners in the now dredged marina is strikingly similar to that of owners of fast land adjacent to navigable water.

We have not the slightest doubt that the Government could have refused to allow such dredging on the ground that it would have impaired navigation in the bay, or could have conditioned its approval of the dredging on petitioners' agreement to comply with various measures that it deemed appropriate for the promotion of navigation. But what petitioners now have is a body of water that was private property under Hawaiian law, linked to navigable water by a channel dredged by them with the consent of the Government. While the consent of individual officials representing the United States cannot "estop" the United States, it can lead to the fruition of a number of expectancies embodied in the concept of "property"—expectancies that, if sufficiently important, the Government must condemn and pay for before it takes over the management of the landowner's property. In this case, we hold that the "right to exclude," so universally held to be a fundamental element of the property right, falls within this category of interests that the Government cannot take without compensation. This is not a case in which the Government is exercising its regulatory power in a manner that will cause an insubstantial devaluation of petitioners' private property; rather, the imposition of the navigational servitude in this context will result in an actual physical invasion of the privately owned marina. * * * Thus, if the Government wishes to make what was formerly Kuapa Pond into a public aquatic park after petitioners have proceeded as far as they have here, it may not, without invoking its eminent domain power and paying just compensation, require them to allow free access to the dredged pond while petitioners' agreement with their customers calls for an annual $72 regular fee. * * *

Mr. Justice Blackmun, with whom Mr. Justice Brennan and Mr. Justice Marshall join, dissenting. [Opinion omitted.]

Notes and Questions

1. In a companion case to *Kaiser Aetna,* Vaughn v. Vermilion Corp., 444 U.S. 206 (1979), the court suggested that under some circumstances the public right of navigation in navigable waters might extend to adjacent non-navigable waters. That case involved dredging in non-navigable coastal waters off of Louisiana that resulted in a lowering of the water level in the previously navigable public channels. The various private channels created in this manner were used primarily in oil production operations. The party seeking to assert the public navigation interest was engaged in commercial

prior to its development because it was subject to the ebb and flow of the tide. This Court has never held, however, that whenever a body of water satisfies this mechani- cal test, the Government may invoke the "navigational servitude" to avoid payment of just compensation irrespective of the pri- vate interests at stake.

shrimping operations in the area. The actual disposition of the case was a remand to consider whether the facts supported a finding that the dredging activities had impaired public navigation.

2. Is *Kaiser Aetna* to be interpreted as meaning that a right of public use applies only to waters that meet the navigability-for-title test, and that permitting public use on any other waters constitutes a taking? Such a reading of *Kaiser Aetna* would mean that natural rivers meeting the federal test of navigability for regulation, but not meeting the navigability-for-title test, are not, based on federal law alone, open to public use. It has been assumed that a river need not meet the federal navigable-for-title test in order to be open to public use under state law, but the Supreme Court has never addressed that question.

3. The Court in *Kaiser Aetna,* citing United States v. Appalachian Elec. Power Co., says the constitutional *regulatory* authority of Congress over waters is as broad as the scope of the commerce power, which is very broad indeed. When Congress employs the term "navigable waters of the United States" in legislation, the matter is largely one of statutory interpretation which requires the judiciary first to determine what waters Congress intended to regulate under the particular statute. Thereafter, a much narrower constitutional issue remains which consists in determining whether regulation of that set of waters is beyond the ambit of the commerce power. As an example of a very broad use of the phrase "navigable waters of the United States" consider modern federal water pollution legislation. As interpreted, the Clean Water Act, 33 U.S.C. § 1362(7), applies even to nonnavigable tributaries that do not reach a navigable river. See United States v. Ashland Oil & Transp. Co., 504 F.2d 1317 (6th Cir. 1974); Buttrey v. United States, 573 F.Supp. 283, 294 (E.D. La. 1983). But see United States v. Wilson, 133 F.3d 251 (4th Cir. 1997) (narrower interpretation), and see Justice Thomas' dissent to the denial of certiorari in Cargill, Inc. v. United States, 516 U.S. 955 (1995) (scope of commerce power). However, see the most recent interpretations of the law in the SWANCC case, and others in which the Supreme Court has recently granted review, infra p. 639.

4. Another source of federal regulatory authority over waters is the Property Clause of the Constitution: "The Congress shall have Power to dispose of and make all needful Rules and Regulations respecting the Territory or other Property belonging to the United States * * * ." U.S. Const., art. IV, § 3. In Federal Power Comm'n v. Oregon, 349 U.S. 435 (1955), Oregon objected to the granting of a power license for the Pelton Dam on the Deschutes River on the ground (among others) that the dam would interfere with fisheries. The Supreme Court said:

> Here the jurisdiction [of the Federal Power Commission] turns upon the ownership or control by the United States of the reserved lands on which the licensed project is to be located. The authority to issue licenses in relation to navigable waters of the United States springs from the Commerce Clause of the Constitution. The authority to do so in relation to public lands and reservations of the United States springs from the Property Clause.

At one time the Pelton Dam decision was widely feared to be an open sesame for the United States to create water rights for itself simply by acquiring land. Those fears seem now to have been put to rest. See Sho Sato, Water Resources—Comments Upon the Federal–State Relationship, 48 Calif. L. Rev. 43 (1960). See p. 903 infra discussing federal property and federal reservations.

5.   Footnote 10 in the principal case was written nearly ten years before *Phillips Petroleum*, supra p. 527. Would the result in *Kaiser Aetna* have been different if it had arisen after *Phillips Petroleum*, with the pond qualifying as tideland?

Problem

Imagine a lagoon similar to that in Kaiser–Aetna, except that it was directly connected to the ocean in its natural state, with no barrier beach separating it. The lagoon was about three feet deep in its natural state, and though there is no evidence of such use, clearly it could have been navigated from the ocean by small boats. In 1829, to create a fish pond, a barrier wall was built across the lagoon entrance to the ocean, thus blocking boat access. The pond was held and used as private property under Native Hawaiian law. In 1946 a tidal wave destroyed the wall, which was rebuilt in the mid 1970's. Some boats surely went in and out of the lagoon during the modern period when the wall was down. Recently, the lagoon has been sold to a developer who needs a permit for various development activities from the Corps of Engineers. The Corps insists, as a condition of the permit, that the lagoon be open to public navigational use from the ocean, saying it was navigable in its natural condition and is thus subject to the federal navigational servitude. The Corps further says that both Hawaiian Native law, and later Hawaiian state law, is irrelevant to the case, since the navigation servitude is a federal property interest that cannot be divested by others. See Boone v. United States, 944 F.2d 1489 (9th Cir. 1991).

2. STATE LAW NAVIGABILITY

A third issue raised under the label of navigability—in addition to bottomland ownership and the servitude—is navigation itself. It is uniformly agreed that the public may float on and use for either commercial or recreational purposes any water that meets the federal navigability-for-title test. The more interesting question with which this section deals is whether the public may also use some waters that do *not* meet that test. The answer in many states is "yes." These jurisdictions have their own state test of navigability, less demanding than the federal navigability-for-title test. In such states, even though the bottomlands are privately owned, the public is entitled to float above them.[1] We include several cases, all from riparian jurisdictions, reflecting contrasting views of state law navigability.

ARKANSAS v. McILROY
Supreme Court of Arkansas, 1980.
268 Ark. 227, 595 S.W.2d 659.

HICKMAN, JUSTICE.

W. L. McIlroy and his late brother's estate, owners of 230 acres in Franklin County, sought a chancery court declaration that their rights

1. Note that this could occur on naviga-ble-for-title waters as well in those situa-tions where the state has divested itself of bottomland ownership.

as riparian landowners on the Mulberry River were, because the stream was not a navigable river, superior to the rights of the public.

McIlroy joined as defendants the Ozark Society, a conservationist group, and two companies that rent canoes for use on the Mulberry and other Ozark Mountain streams. The State of Arkansas, intervening, claimed the Mulberry was a navigable stream and the stream bed the property of the state, not the McIlroys.

The Ozark Society and the other defendants generally claimed that the Mulberry was a navigable stream but that even if the court found otherwise, a public easement in the Mulberry should be recognized. The defendants also argued that the public had acquired a prescriptive easement in the river and that the act admitting Arkansas into the Union placed the Mulberry in the public domain.

The chancellor declared the Mulberry was not a navigable stream. He found the McIlroys owned it as riparian property owners with the incidental right to prevent the public from using the stream (the McIlroys owned land on both sides of the Mulberry). He declined to enjoin the Ozark Society from the publication of "The Mighty Mulberry," a brochure proclaiming the Mulberry as an excellent stream for canoeing.

The State, the Ozark Society and one of the canoe suppliers appealed. Their essential allegations of error are that the chancellor was wrong in his determination that the Mulberry was not navigable and in failing to find the existence of a public or prescriptive easement. * * *

As we define the term "navigable" we find the Mulberry River, as it passes through McIlroy's property, to be navigable. Consequently, we reverse the chancellor's decree in that regard. Our decision precludes the necessity to discuss any of the other issues raised on appeal.

The Mulberry River, located in northwest Arkansas, heads up in the Ozark Mountains and flows in a westerly direction for about 70 miles until it joins the Arkansas River. It could best be described as an intermediate stream, smaller than the Arkansas River, the lower White and Little Red Rivers and other deep, wide rivers that have been used commercially since their discovery. But neither is it like the many small creeks and branches in Arkansas that cannot be regularly floated with canoes or flatbottomed boats for any substantial period of time during the year. The Mulberry is somewhere in between. It is a stream that for about 50 or 55 miles of its length can be floated by canoe or flatbottomed boat for at least six months of the year. Parts of it are floatable for longer periods of time. The Mulberry is a typical rock-bottomed Ozark Mountain stream, flowing with relatively clear water and populated by a variety of fish. Smallmouth bass favor such a stream and populate the Mulberry.

For most of its distance it is a series of long flat holes of water interrupted by narrower shoals. These shoals attract the canoeists. McIlroy describes the stream as following a tortuous course; canoeists find it an exciting stream testing the skill of an experienced canoeist. Watergaps, affairs of wire or boards erected across the stream to hold cattle, have at times been erected but, according to W. L. McIlroy, they go down with the first rise of water. It is not a stream easily possessed. In recent years, the Mulberry has claimed the lives of several canoeists.

Annually, since 1967, the Ozark Society has sponsored for its members one or more float trips on the Mulberry River. These trips take them through McIlroy's property, which is located about 23 miles up the river from where the Mulberry enters the Arkansas. McIlroy said he had a confrontation with Ozark Society members in 1975 when about 600 people put in at a low water bridge on his property. The bridge, near Cass, serves a county road, and is indisputably a public bridge. Canoeists and fishermen have regularly used it as an access place to the river.

Although we are aware of the general characteristics of the river, we must here only determine the navigability of the Mulberry as it flows through the appellees' property. The chancellor faced this issue and ruled the river non-navigable. We reverse his decision and hold that the Mulberry River is navigable. While our decision will be a precedent for this river and should be used by the public and landowners as such, of necessity the judgment is directed only to the parties to this lawsuit.

This is essentially a lawsuit about the river as it passes through McIlroy's property. W.L. McIlroy testified that just below the bridge is a long hole of water, perhaps the longest on that stretch of the river, which is about 100 feet wide; it narrows to a shoal. He said a man could wade the water almost any time of the year. He claimed the river could sometimes not be canoed for an entire year. He said dry spots usually existed for six to eight months of the year. He denied seeing a canoe before 1974. However, from 1947 to 1971, McIlroy was in California. During that time he would spend only a week or so a year in Arkansas.

The great preponderance of the evidence conflicts with McIlroy's estimate of the river. It is floatable for at least six months of the year. According to a pamphlet, "The Float Streams of Arkansas," published by an Arkansas state agency, the floating season is October through June. This is for a course from a point considerably upstream from McIlroy's property to the river's mouth, a distance of about 50 miles. Numerous canoeists testified they had floated the Mulberry through the Cass area, mostly in the spring of the year. It was not disputed, however, that at times, usually in the summer months, the Mulberry could not be floated.

The evidence by testimony and exhibits demonstrates conclusively that the Mulberry had been used by the public for recreational purposes for many years. It has long been used for fishing and swimming and is today also popular among canoeists. * * *

[A substantial recitation of the testimony regarding the use of the Mulberry is omitted.]

The original government plat made of this area in 1838 was introduced and shows the "Mulberry Creek" was "meandered" by the surveyors. Meander lines are those representing the border line of a stream and such lines are considered prima facie evidence of navigability.

The facts presented prove that the Mulberry River at the point in question is capable of recreational use and has been used extensively for recreational purposes. We must now decide whether such a stream is navigable.

Determining the navigability of a stream is essentially a matter of deciding if it is public or private property. Navigation in fact is the standard modern test of navigability, and, as embroidered by the federal courts, controls when navigation must be defined for federal purposes—maritime jurisdiction, regulation under the Commerce Clause, and title disputes between the state and federal governments. See Hitchings v. Del Rio Woods Recreation & Park District, 55 Cal. App. 3d 560, 127 Cal. Rptr. 830 (1976); Day v. Armstrong, 362 P.2d 137 (Wyo. 1961). Otherwise, the states may adopt their own definitions of navigability. Donnelly v. United States, 228 U.S. 243 (1913).

While navigation in fact is widely regarded as the proper test of navigability, it is a test which should not be applied too literally. For example, it has been said a stream need not be navigable at all its points or for the entire year to be navigable. The real issue in these cases is the definition of navigation in fact.

Arkansas has adopted the standard definition of navigability. That test, which was similar to the general test used by the federal courts, defines navigability in terms of a river's potential for commercial usefulness; that is, whether the water could be used to remove the products of the surrounding land to another place. That definition reads:

> * * * Nor is it necessary that the stream should be capable of floating boats or rafts the whole, or even the greater part of the year. Upon the other hand, it is not sufficient to impress navigable character that there may be extraordinary times of transient freshets, when boats might be floated out. For, if this were so, almost all insignificant streams would be navigable. The true criterion is the dictate of sound business common sense, and depends on the usefulness of the stream to the population of its banks, as a means of carrying off the products of their fields and forests, or bringing to them articles of merchandise. If, in its natural state, without artificial improvements, it may be prudently relied upon and used for that purpose at some seasons of the year, recurring with tolerable regularity, then in the American sense, it is navigable, although the annual time may not be very long. Products may be ready and boats prepared, and it may thus become a very great convenience and materially promote the comfort and advance the prosperity of the community. But it is evident that sudden freshets at uncertain times cannot be made available for such

purposes. No prudent man could afford the expense of preparation for such events, or could trust to such uncertainty in getting to market. The result of the authorities is this, that usefulness for purposes of transportation, for rafts, boats or barges, gives navigable character, reference being had to its natural state, rather than to its average depth the year round. (citing authorities). [Lutesville Sand & Gravel Co. v. McLaughlin, 181 Ark. 574, 576–77, 26 S.W.2d 892, 893 (1930).]

Therefore, a river is legally navigable if actually navigable and actually navigable if commercially valuable. However, in the case of Barboro v. Boyle, 119 Ark. 377, 178 S.W. 378 (1915), this Court foresaw, no doubt, that things would change in the future and that recreation would become an important interest of the people of Arkansas. The language in the Barboro case is almost prophetic. While adhering to the standard definition of navigability, with its dependence upon a commercial criterion, the Court went on to say:

It is the policy of this state to encourage the use of its water courses for any useful or beneficial purpose. There may be other public uses than the carrying on of commerce of pecuniary value. The culture of rice is being developed in this state and the waters of the lake could be used for the purpose of flooding the rice fields and for other agricultural purposes. As the population of the state increases, the banks of the lake may become more thickly populated, and the water could be used for domestic purposes. Pleasure resorts might even be built upon the banks of the lake and the water might be needed for municipal purposes. *Moreover, the waters of the lake might be used to a much greater extent for boating, for pleasure, for bathing, fishing and hunting than they are now used.* (Emphasis added.) Id. at 382–383, 178 S.W. at 380.

Since that time no case presented to us has involved the public's right to use a stream which has a recreational value, but lacks commercial adaptability in the traditional sense. Our definition of navigability is, therefore, a remnant of the steamboat era.

However, many other states have been presented with this same problem. Back in 1870, the Massachusetts Supreme Court found a stream navigable that could only be used for pleasure. The stream was about two feet deep at low water. The court stated:

If water is navigable for pleasure boating, it must be regarded as navigable water though no craft has ever been upon it for the purpose of trade or agriculture. Attorney General v. Woods, 108 Mass. 436, 440 (1870).

In Ohio, the court recently was faced with this problem and decided to change its definition of navigation. The Ohio court said:

We hold that the modern utilization of our water by our citizens requires that our courts, in their judicial interpretation of the navigability of such waters, consider their recreational use as well as the more traditional criteria of commercial use. State ex rel. [Brown] v. Newport Concrete Co., 44 Ohio App. 2d 121, 127, 336 N.E.2d 453, 457, 73 Ohio Ops. 2d 124 (1975).

Applying a "public trust" to the Little Miami River, the Ohio court found that the State of Ohio " * * * holds these waters in trust for those Ohioans who wish to use the stream for all legitimate uses, be they commercial, transportational, or recreational." State ex rel. v. Newport Concrete Co., supra.

Michigan reached a similar conclusion in 1974. Navigability in Michigan was significantly affected by whether logs had been, or could be, floated down a stream. That "floatable test" had been used by the Michigan court until it was confronted with the same problem that we have. Michigan readily admitted that its definition needed to be changed:

> We therefore hold that members of the public have the right to navigate and to exercise the incidents of navigation in a lawful manner at any point below high water mark on waters of this state which are capable of being navigated by oar or motor propelled small craft. Kelley, ex rel. MacMullen v. Hallden, 51 Mich. App. 176, 214 N.W.2d 856, 864 (1974).

For examples of other states that have adopted similar definitions of navigation, see: People v. Mack, 19 Cal. App. 3d 1040, 97 Cal. Rptr. 448 (1971); Lamprey v. State, 52 Minn. 181, 53 N.W. 1139 (1893); Luscher v. Reynolds, 153 Or. 625, 56 P.2d 1158 (1936).

Arkansas, as most states in their infancy, was mostly concerned with river traffic by steamboats or barges when cases like *Lutesville*, supra, were decided. We have had no case regarding recreational use of waters such as the Mulberry. It may be that our decisions did or did not anticipate such use of streams which are suitable, as the Mulberry is, for recreational use. Such use would include flatbottomed boats for fishing and canoes for floating or both. There is no doubt that the segment of the Mulberry River that is involved in this lawsuit can be used for a substantial portion of the year for recreational purposes. Consequently, we hold that it is navigable at that place with all the incidental rights of that determination.

McIlroy and others testified that the reason they brought the lawsuit was because their privacy was being interrupted by the people who trespassed on their property, littered the stream and generally destroyed their property. We are equally disturbed with that small percentage of the public that abuses public privileges and has no respect for the property of others. Their conduct is a shame on us all. It is not disputed that riparian landowners on a navigable stream have a right to prohibit the public from crossing their property to reach such a stream. The McIlroys' rights in this regard are not affected by our decision. While there are laws prohibiting such misconduct, every branch of Arkansas' government should be more aware of its duty to keep Arkansas, which is a beautiful state, a good place to live. No doubt the state cannot alone solve such a problem, it requires some individual effort of the people. Nonetheless, we can no more close a public waterway because some of those who use it annoy nearby property owners, than we could close a public highway for similar reasons.

In any event, the state sought a decision that would protect its right to this stream. With that right, which we now recognize, goes a responsibility to keep it as God made it.

Reversed.

FOGLEMAN, CHIEF JUSTICE, concurring in part and dissenting in part.

I cannot join in the court's new definition of navigability, even though I concur in the reversal of the decree in this case. My disagreement is based upon the court's departure from two overriding and interrelated legal principles, i.e., the effect of a rule of property and the vesting of property rights.

Never before in Arkansas, has determining the navigability of a stream been essentially a matter of deciding if the water is public or private property. Quite the reverse the rights of riparian owners have depended upon the test of navigability. * * *

The test of navigability is the means of determining the property rights of riparian owners. As such it is a rule of property. To repudiate this rule of property by judicial decision will have the effect of invalidating titles that were acquired in reliance upon the rule and such a change, if desirable, should be brought about by legislation, which operates only prospectively and cannot upset titles already vested. * * *

The adoption of a so-called modern test changes a rule of property and apparently divests titles that have been vested under the prior test. In Arkansas, unlike communist states, it is the right of private property, not the rights of the public, that rises above constitutional sanction. * * *

Less than four months ago, the Supreme Court of the United States held that the government could not give the public a right of access or prevent the owners from denying public access, to waters which had been private property under state law, without paying just compensation to the owners, even though the character of the waters had been changed from non-navigable to navigable. Kaiser Aetna v. United States, 444 U.S. 164 (1979). * * *

[The opinion went on to find that the public had acquired rights to use the stream by prescription, thereby providing an alternate ground that did not violate the property rights of McIlroy.]

Notes and Questions

1. What is the driving force in defining state law navigability in terms of recreational value? Is it a changing concept of what the common good requires? See Joseph Sax, Some Thoughts on the Decline of Private Property, 58 Wash. L. Rev. 481 (1983); Robert Abrams, Governmental Expansion of Recreational Water Use Opportunities, 59 Or. L. Rev. 159, 169–71 (1980).

2.   Consider the period in United States history when many states first developed their own state law definitions of navigability. The prominence of logging as an important economic activity led to adoption in many forested states of log floating as the test for allowing public use of river. See, e.g., Gaston v. Mace, 33 W.Va. 14, 10 S.E. 60 (1889). See generally James Willard Hurst, Law and Economic Growth: The Legal History of the Lumber Industry in Wisconsin, 1836–1915 (1964). Does recreation hold a parallel position in modern times? Although its claim of necessity to the common good may not be as strong as that of logging in eras past, the economic value of the recreation industry (tourism, boating and fishing equipment, etc.) is important.

3.   Does reference in *Kaiser Aetna,* supra p. 546, to the importance of exclusivity among the bundle of rights that make up private property offer any insight into the proper resolution of constitutional challenges such as those raised by the private riparians in *McIlroy*? Are the state law navigability cases distinguishable on the ground that unlike *Kaiser Aetna,* no single riparian owned the entire bed and all surrounding lands? Does that fact suggest that no riparian had an investment backed expectation in exclusivity of use? If so, does that mean there was no expectation of a right to exclude the general public?

4.   Could the decision in *McIlroy* be said to constitute a judicial taking? See the discussion supra pp. 384–392.

5.   New York, like Arkansas, has adopted a recreational boating test for state navigability, Adirondack League Club v. Sierra Club, 92 N.Y.2d 591, 706 N.E.2d 1192, 684 N.Y.S.2d 168 (1998), but the public right it supports is surprisingly, and uncharacteristically, narrow, as the following case reveals.

DOUGLASTON MANOR, INC. v. BAHRAKIS

Court of Appeals of New York, 1997.
89 N.Y.2d 472, 678 N.E.2d 201, 655 N.Y.S.2d 745.

BELLACOSA, J.

Plaintiff-appellant, Douglaston Manor, Inc., owns approximately one-mile-long sections of both shorelines of the Salmon River in Oswego County and the riverbed in between. * * * The issue is whether Douglaston's ownership entitles it to exclude the public from fishing in, though not from navigating through, its portion of the river. * * * It operates the Douglaston Salmon Run within its section of the river. Salmon Run is an exclusively managed private sport fishery from which the general public is excluded and for which users pay Douglaston a fee. * * *

This lawsuit stems from Douglaston's desire to * * * prevent (by injunction) defendants, commercial fishing guides, from future anchoring upon and fishing in Douglaston's privately owned section of the Salmon River. The complaint alleges that defendants entered upon the river at a point upstream of Douglaston's property, navigated into and within the Salmon Run, and anchored, waded and fished within Douglaston's protected enclave. Douglaston asserts that it possesses exclusive fishing

rights by virtue of its ownership of the bed and both banks of the river.
* * *

Though the court found a public right of navigation because the Salmon River is a navigable-in-fact river, it held that navigation did not include a public right to fish and anchor.

* * * The Appellate Division held that the public has the right to fish, ferry and transport on the navigable waters of the Salmon River, including Douglaston's Salmon Run section.

We granted Douglaston leave to appeal. * * * We now reverse and reinstate the ruling rendered by Supreme Court, because the settled law of New York continues to recognize the common-law distinction concerning the rights which a private owner may acquire and retain in nontidal, navigable-in-fact rivers and streams. These rights are distinguishable from public trust protections generally associated with waters deemed navigable-in-law or tidal navigable-in-fact waters, neither of which classification is before us in this case.

Douglaston rests its claim of exclusive fishing rights solely on its record ownership of the bed and the banks of the Salmon River. * * * The defendants counter that because the Salmon River is navigable, the State irrevocably holds a public trust easement that protects anyone's navigation of the river, which includes a right of public fishery. We must decide, therefore, whether New York State * * * has the power to transfer exclusive fishing rights to private parties in a nontidal, navigable-in-fact river, as part of a conveyance of property ownership, and whether the State in fact did so in the 205–year-old Macomb Patent, derivatively at issue here.

On this appeal, the parties do not dispute that the Salmon River is navigable. * * *

A river is defined as "navigable in its natural or unimproved condition, affording a channel for useful commerce of a substantial and permanent character conducted in the customary mode of trade and travel on water * * * hav[ing] practical usefulness to the public as a highway for transportation" (Navigation Law § 2 [5] [emphasis added]). The common law more particularly distinguishes and "considers a river, in which the tide ebbs and flows, an arm of the sea, and as navigable, and devoted to the public use, for all purposes, as well for navigation as for fishing. It, also, considers other rivers, in which the tide does not ebb and flow, as navigable, but not so far belonging to the public as to divest the owners of the adjacent banks of their exclusive rights to the fisheries therein" (Hooker v. Cummings, 20 Johns. 90, 100 (Sup. Ct. 1822) (emphasis added)).

The *Hooker* case acknowledged the key distinction by presuming the Salmon River was nonnavigable at common law because the tide did not ebb and flow in it. The court then held that the plaintiff could maintain an action in trespass against a defendant where plaintiff alleged that defendant fished in that portion of the river in which the plaintiff possessed riparian ownership rights including the exclusive right of fishery (Hooker v. Cummings, supra, 20 Johns, at 100). As to the discrete public right of navigation, the court noted that "in the case of a private river, * * * he who owns the soil has, prima facie, the right of fishing; * * * that the river was liable and subject to the public servitude, for the passage of boats; the private rights of the owners of the adjacent soil were no[t] otherwise affected." * * * While *Hooker* is not dispositive of the only issue we resolve as to this controversy, it nevertheless provides important guidance.

* * * [T]his Court has long held that grants by the State to private owners of land under navigable-in-fact rivers remain subject to an implied, reserved public easement of navigation. * * *

"[T]here is no necessary conflict between the reservation to the public of the right of navigation and the recognition of the exclusive privilege expressly granted to the owner. The public right, whatever it might otherwise be, must be held limited in such a situation to the right to use the waters for the purposes of a public highway. * * * [T]he easement of passage over navigable waters does not involve a surrender of other privileges which are capable of enjoyment without interference with the navigator."

* * * Defendants, instead, urge a definitive landmark ruling from this Court, through the instrumentality of this case, that New York State has abandoned the common-law property distinction between rivers navigable-in-fact and those navigable-in-law. As a result, they claim a public right of fishery in all "navigable" waters. This is not so and is too simplistic an approach, which would precipitate serious destabilizing effects on property ownership principles and precedents.

* * * Importantly, New York State, as the original grantor of the Macomb Patent directly descending to the title involved in this case, has long respected private fishing rights in navigable-in-fact rivers and has even been engaged in purchasing precisely such rights for public benefit. * * * We see no reason * * * to countenance the view that the State has been expending public moneys unnecessarily on rights, according to defendants' theory, the State already irrevocably holds in public trust. * * *

* * * The Macomb Patent describes the transfer of certain real property from the State to Douglaston's predecessor in interest. It encompasses the disputed portion of the Salmon River bank and bed "[t]ogether with all and singular Rights, Hereditaments and Appurtenances to the same belonging or in anywise appertaining; Excerpting and Reserving to ourselves, all Gold and Silver Mines, and five acres of every Hundred Acres of the said Tract of Land for Highways." This Court has previously held that when land under rivers is included within the boundaries of a grant, the general language of conveyance is sufficient to transfer to the grantee the bed of the river and associated exclusive right of fishery (Trustees of Brookhaven v. Strong, 60 N.Y., at 71–72 * * *). Moreover, the State's reservation of designated mineral

rights and specific public rights of way, without reserving to the public a right of fishery, additionally supports our analysis and conclusion that Douglaston enjoys a duly surveyed exclusive right of fishery.

In sum, the desirable definiteness attendant upon discrete property rights and principles, along with reliable, predictable expectations built upon centuries of precedent, ought not to be sacrificed to the vicissitudes of unsupportable legal theories.

Accordingly, the order of the Appellate Division * * * should be reversed, with costs, and the order of Supreme Court reinstated.

Notes and Questions

1. Is the Court's view that only tidal waters are "navigable-in-law" (title of bottomlands standard)? This view was rejected in Barney v. Keokuk, 94 U.S. 324, 337–38 (1877), though it was apparently understood to be the law in New York in 1822, when the *Hooker* case was decided. If the Salmon River is navigable-in-fact under the standard described in the case, quoting from New York's Navigation Law, wouldn't ownership of the bottomland be in the State? Isn't this a question of federal law, and not of New York law?

2. If waters are navigable under the federal title rule, doesn't the public have rights to navigate and fish as a matter of federal law, a right that the state cannot take away? Or is this a question of state public trust law? In the original 13 states there may be royal grants that preceded the Revolution; the scope of those grants is said to be measured by the King's intent, according to Kraft v. Burr, 476 S.E.2d 715 (Va. 1996).

3. Does the result in the Douglaston case turn on an interpretation of the rights understood to go to a grantee at the time of the 1792 Macomb patent? If so, how could the Court justify subjecting Douglaston to recreational boaters?

4. Do you think patents to riparian owners in other states, such as Arkansas, reserved fishing rights to the public? Should the presence of fishing rights be a matter of deed interpretation, or—as is apparently the case in Arkansas—a product of the judicially fashioned common law of state navigability?

BOTT v. MICHIGAN DEPARTMENT OF NATURAL RESOURCES

Supreme Court of Michigan, 1982.
415 Mich. 45, 327 N.W.2d 838.

[The statement of facts is taken from the dissenting opinion.]

FACTS

Bott

John Bott is the owner in fee of 800 acres of land located in Otsego County, Michigan, which he maintains as a vacation place. Entirely within his property is a body of water known as Linton Lake which is approximately 35 acres in size. Linton Lake has no inlet, being spring-fed, but has an outlet connecting it to Big Chub Lake. Big Chub Lake is approximately 75 acres in size and has numerous riparian owners and a public access site. As well as encompassing Linton Lake, Mr. Bott's property surrounds both sides of the outlet. His property line extends beyond the outlet into Big Chub Lake making him a riparian owner on Big Chub Lake.

The present controversy arose shortly after Mr. Bott purchased the property and was informed by local authorities that the public's access to Linton Lake could not be blocked. Thereafter, Bott filed suit seeking a declaratory judgment that Linton Lake and its outlet connecting it to Big Chub Lake were non-navigable, private bodies of water from which the public could be excluded.

Bott filed a motion seeking summary judgment. An affidavit filed in response to Bott's motion indicated that the outlet is a natural channel 240 feet in length varying in width from 100 feet at its widest point to 15 feet at its narrowest point. The depth of the water is approximately 2 feet except for one point where it is 8 inches deep. Another affidavit indicated that the outlet is boatable by small oar and motor-propelled craft without making contact with the banks or bed of the channel. Partial summary judgment was granted in favor of appellee Bott * * *. The order of the trial court declared Linton Lake to be a private, non-navigable body of water from which the public could be excluded. Further, the judgment expressed no opinion as to the navigability of Linton Lake's outlet.

Nicholas

William and Caroline Nicholas are owners in fee of approximately 120 acres of land located in Montcalm County, Michigan, which they maintain as a vacation place. The Nicholas property surrounds both sides of Burgess Creek, the navigability of which is disputed. Burgess Creek lies upon a watercourse involving several bodies of water.

At one end of the watercourse lies Burgess Lake, a body of water approximately 60 acres in size which has 50 riparian owners and no public access site. The lake has no inlet, being spring-fed, but has an outlet which is Burgess Creek. The creek is a natural watercourse approximately 800 feet long. From bank to bank, the creek varies in width from 12 ½ feet at its narrowest point to over 80 feet at its widest point. Located at the creek's widest point is a bog which borders an open channel of water 7 ½ feet in width. The creek has a silty or soft bed and its depth varies from a maximum of 15 inches to a minimum depth at one point of 6 inches. The average depth of the stream appears to be from 8 to 10 inches.

Burgess Creek empties into a 35–acre body of water known as Dogfish or Pine Lake. Dogfish Lake has an outlet, referred to as Dogfish Creek, which flows into a 3–to–5–acre pond called Salt Springs or Mill Pond. The outlet from this pond eventually flows past a waterwheel, through a culvert under Baker Road and into Wabash Creek and Morgan Lake.

The Nicholas property includes land fronting on Burgess Lake and the land through which Burgess Creek flows. Their land also includes 7/8 of the property surrounding Dogfish Lake and the land on both sides of Dogfish Creek to a point approximately halfway between Dogfish Lake and Mill Pond.

Mr. and Mrs. Nicholas purchased the property in 1959 or 1960 and built a cottage on Burgess Lake. In the fall of 1970, Mr. Nicholas constructed a footbridge spanning Burgess Creek at a point close to where Burgess Lake flows into Burgess Creek. The bridge lies 6 inches above the water and effectively obstructs passage on the stream by small craft, although evidence was introduced which showed that some people continued to use the stream by pulling a boat over the bridge.

On August 1, 1975, Mr. and Mrs. Nicholas filed suit against appellees McDaniel and Rademacher alleging trespass by appellees' children. Mr. and Mrs. Nicholas sought a declaratory judgment that the creek was private and non-navigable and requested a restraining order preventing further passage on the stream.

On October 14, 1975, the State of Michigan, through its Department of Natural Resources (DNR), filed suit against Mr. and Mrs. Nicholas. DNR sought a declaratory judgment that Burgess Creek was navigable and thus open for passage by the public, including riparians on Burgess Lake. DNR requested removal of the bridge and an injunction restraining further obstructions of the stream by Nicholas.

A trial was conducted and testimony was heard from numerous witnesses concerning the dimensions and navigability of Burgess Creek. The testimony of all witnesses indicated that one could traverse Burgess Creek from Burgess Lake to Dogfish Lake by small boat—either in a rowboat propelled by motor or oars, or in a canoe propelled by paddles.

The testimony indicated that small boats had traversed Burgess Creek since the early 1950's up to the time of trial. Most of the witnesses testified to having traversed the creek only as far as Dogfish Lake. Others stated they traveled as far as the culvert located under Baker Road. One witness testified to making a trip to Morgan Lake. Most witnesses testified to making an average of one to three trips per summer through the creek.

The point which divided the witnesses was the ease or difficulty with which the creek could be navigated by small craft. Appellant Nicholas and his witnesses testified that boaters had to push and pole their way through the stream. Other witnesses testified that a boat could be freely floated on the creek except for a point close to the entrance of the creek where navigation around a log and under low-lying branches was necessary. Some witnesses stated that at another point halfway down the stream they had to push or pull their boats over a large log submerged in the water. Others testified to floating, paddling, and motoring parts of the stream without making contact with the banks or bed of the stream.

The trial court weighed the conflicting evidence and found that the creek could be traversed freely by boats and canoes propelled by oar or paddles and in some portions by motors. The judge found the creek to be navigable based on its being boatable. The court also found the entire watercourse extending from Burgess Lake to the culvert under Baker Road to be navigable by small craft. The bridge was ordered removed and further obstructions enjoined. * * *

LEVIN, JUSTICE.

The established law of this state is that the title of a riparian or littoral owner includes the bed to the thread or midpoint of the water, subject to a servitude for commercial navigation of ships and logs, and, where the waters are so navigable, for fishing.

In the instant cases, it appears that the creeks connecting the smaller with the larger lakes are too shallow to permit the flotation of logs. The creeks are, therefore, not navigable under the law as it has heretofore been stated, and only the littoral owners have a right to use the lakes.

Prior case law also provides that although there is a navigable means of access, the littoral owner of all the land surrounding a small inland dead-end lake has the sole right to use it. Winans v. Willetts, 197 Mich. 512, 163 N.W. 993 (1917).

The only recreational use heretofore recognized by this Court as an incident of the navigational servitude is fishing.

The dissenting opinion would change established rules of property law in the following respects:

(1) It would substitute a recreational-boating test for the log-flotation test of determining navigability stated in Moore v. Sanborne, 2 Mich. 519, 59 Am. Dec. 209 (1853).

(2) It would overrule the dead-end lake rule stated in Winans v. Willetts.

(3) It would enlarge the recreational use permitted in navigable waters beyond fishing to include "the right to make reasonable use of the lake's surface" for "navigation, fishing, and recreational use". * * *

I

The recreational-boating test is characterized in the dissenting opinion as a natural outgrowth of the rationale of Moore v. Sanborne, where this Court expanded the common-law rule that waterways usable by ships in commerce are navigable, to include waterways capable of floating logs or timber.

Moore does not support the claim that public needs other than for commercial use justify expansion of the servitude. In adopting the log-flotation test, *Moore* advanced the same interests—encouragement of commerce and industry—as had been encouraged when England expanded the concept of navigability to include inland waters capable of serving as public highways. *Moore* is replete with references to "valuable floatage" and the "necessities of trade and commerce", and of the need to use the rivers and streams to develop forest and mineral wealth.

The navigable-in-fact commercial shipping test antedating *Moore* rested on the concept that commercial needs justified public use of inland waters. *Moore,* drawing on that concept, recognized that Michigan's waterways could be put to commercial uses other than ferrying goods by ship. The log-flotation test reflected this differing commercial reality and a commonly accepted public need. The rationale remained unchanged; navigability turned on commercial use. * * *

II

Prior to *Winans,* this Court had held in Giddings v. Rogalewski, 192 Mich. 319, 158 N.W. 951 (1916), that a lake entirely surrounded by private property was not navigable. *Giddings* reasoned, on the basis of the rationale of Moore v. Sanborne, that a lake unconnected to other waterways could not form part of an aquatic highway for "commerce, trade, and travel * * * by the usual and ordinary modes of navigation" and that thus there was no justification for a navigational servitude.

III

It is said that the log-flotation test is an anachronism and is difficult to administer. When this Court examines the need for a change of law, it focuses on whether the proposed change is consonant with widely shared societal values, fairly treats those who have relied on past law, and is appropriate for judicial implementation.

A

It is asserted that the recreational-boating test will meet a public need for access to recreational waters. Even if one accepts the premise that public need justifies such a change in the law, the public's need for expanded recreational uses stands before this Court as a bare, undocumented claim without support in the record or in any materials to which our attention has been directed.

It has yet to be shown that the lakes, rivers, and streams heretofore opened to the public are not adequate to meet public needs. Nor is there evidence that a recreational-boating test would significantly increase the recreational opportunities of those who are unable to use the present waterways. The number of private waters which the recreational-boating test would make available, and whether those waters would become accessible to many persons now inadequately served, is unknown.

The argument based on public need assumes that recreational values should be given paramount consideration and makes no attempt to consider competing public values. Recreational use has a cost. The inland waters aid the nesting of wildfowl and the propagation of aquatic life. An expansion of public use would also affect the communities where the waters are located. * * *

B

Our attention has been directed to "growing numbers of states" that have reportedly adopted a recreational-boating test. * * *

Six states have adopted the recreational-boating test directly or de facto. In three, the recreational-boating test is not so much an outgrowth of common-law method as it is of either a constitutional or statutory commitment to public access to inland waters.

Turning to the three states that have adopted a recreational-boating test as a matter of judicial decision,[37] we note that the test has not been applied to provide the public with access to narrow, shallow streams, themselves unfit for meaningful recreation. The stated purpose of the recreational-boating test is to identify waterways fit for recreational use.

The creeks connecting Linton and Big Chub Lakes and Dogfish and Burgess Lakes are narrow and shallow. At many spots, less water is to be found than in a bathtub. They are narrow, and pleasure boats can be steered through them only with difficulty. While there are those who would like to use these creeks to reach Linton or Dogfish Lakes, the creeks are not themselves suitable for recreational canoeing or boating.

C

Even were it granted that a need for expanded public recreational uses is a value that has hardened into social consensus, we cannot ignore the conflict with another well-recognized norm, the unfairness of eliminating a property right without compensation.

This Court has previously declared that stare decisis is to be strictly observed where past decisions establish "rules of property" that induce extensive reliance.

The justification for this rule is not to be found in rigid fidelity to precedent, but conscience. The judiciary must accept responsibility for its actions. Judicial "rules of property" create value, and the passage of time induces a belief in their stability that generates commitments of human energy and capital.

The proposed changes in law would not have a purely theoretical effect. It is said that adoption of the recreational-boating test will respond to the asserted increase in the public's need for access to recreational waters and yet not produce quantitatively different results than the log-flotation test. These two propositions are irreconcilable. If the new test is adopted to meet a need which the former test is not able

---

37. See Southern Idaho Fish & Game Ass'n v. Picabo Livestock, Inc., 96 Idaho 360, 528 P.2d 1295 (1974); Mentor Harbor Yachting Club v. Mentor Lagoons, Inc., 170 Ohio St. 193, 163 N.E.2d 373 (1959); Coleman v. Schaeffer, 163 Ohio St. 202, 126 N.E.2d 444 (1955); People v. Sweetser, 72 Cal. App. 3d 278, 140 Cal. Rptr. 82 (1977); Hitchings v. Del Rio Woods Recreation & Park Dist., 55 Cal. App. 3d 560, 127 Cal. Rptr. 830 (1976); People v. Mack, 19 Cal. App. 3d 1040, 97 Cal. Rptr. 448 (1971).

to satisfy, there necessarily must be some quantitative difference when the two tests are actually applied or there is no need for a new test.

Recreational boats, such as kayaks and canoes, displace far less water than logs, are highly maneuverable, and can travel through waterways unfit for floating logs to market. Michigan is a state of numerous inland waters, many of which are likely to have physical characteristics similar to those of the creeks connecting the lakes in the instant cases. Adoption of a recreational-boating test would subject many formerly private inland waters to what are in essence recreational easements.

Public access to these previously non-navigable waters will diminish enjoyment of surrounding property. Many of those who own such property are vacationers who acquired the property for peaceful retreat. A rule which opens these waters to curious boaters and enterprising fishermen may render the property unfit as a refuge or retreat. Even if these interests are thought to be too intangible to warrant protection, it cannot be denied that some landowners have invested their savings or wealth in reliance on a long-established definition of navigability. It also cannot be denied that the heretofore private character of the waters adjacent to their property significantly adds to its market value.

Vacationers are not manufacturers who can pass on their losses to a large class of consumers. Techniques to safeguard past reliance on prior law such as prospective overruling are unavailable where property rights are extinguished. Prevention of this hardship could be avoided through compensation, but this Court has no thought of providing compensation to riparian or littoral owners for the enlarged servitude and the resulting reduction in amenities and economic loss.

D

Adjudication without an evidentiary record provides no assurance that the information needed for a wise decision will surface or that the relative strength of competing societal values can be accurately measured. The Legislature has the resources to make a comprehensive inquiry into the public's need for increased water recreation and the effect of a change in the law on existing property rights. As a majoritarian body, the Legislature can provide a forum that will attract those affected and, without fearing a loss of legitimacy, proceed to take the measure of their convictions.

The obligation to pay compensation to owners for a governmental taking will discipline legislative inquiry by assuring that the loss inflicted on private parties will be considered, and that recreational access will be granted only if indeed highly prized. That obligation will further assure that those whose property is seized will receive fair treatment. Providing compensation will also vindicate riparian or littoral owner reliance on this Court's past decisions.

Finally, legislative consideration allows a solution capable of responding to a broader range of public needs and one far more sensitive to the dislocation of private interests. A recreational-boating test would operate indiscriminately in waters both fit and unfit for recreational use. The Legislature can exercise its powers selectively, it can identify those waters most suited for recreational use, including lakes that do not have inlets or outlets, and avoid unnecessary seizures. This will not only increase the likelihood of successfully meeting the public need, but prevent gratuitous economic loss.

A judicial recreational-boating test would increase the utilization of the inland waters and do nothing to protect them. Many of Michigan's lakes are in wilderness areas, and enlarged public access might destroy their scenic beauty. Other lakes might be so attractive that they would be overutilized.

IV

Faced with an uncertain societal consensus, an inability to compensate riparian owners for the loss of a valuable right, and the need for a comprehensive legislative solution, we believe that this Court is not an appropriate forum for resolving the competing societal values which underlie this controversy.

We affirm in *Bott* and reverse in *Nicholas*.

FITZGERALD, C.J., and KAVANAGH and COLEMAN, JJ., concurred with LEVIN, J.

WILLIAMS and RYAN, JUSTICES.

This opinion was written by JUSTICE BLAIR MOODY, JR., prior to his death on November 26, 1982. We concur in this opinion and adopt it as our own. * * *

The courts in Michigan have utilized the common-law "navigable in fact" test, similar to the federal test, in determining the navigability of some Michigan waters. Under this test, waters navigable in fact by large vessels engaged in commerce are navigable in law. * * *

However, early in the jurisprudence of the state, this Court rejected the English common-law or federal tests as the sole bases for determining navigability and public uses of our inland lakes and streams. Moore v. Sanborne, 2 Mich. 519, 59 Am. Dec. 209 (1853). In *Moore,* the Court held that inland waterways capable of floating logs or timber were navigable even when the water's capacity to float logs was not continuous. Waters of the state capable of supporting such public uses came to be known as "qualifiedly navigable." * * *

In the 1853 seminal case of *Moore, supra,* this Court not only rejected the common-law rule restricting navigability to those waters capable of supporting large vessels engaged in commerce as the sole test, but it also rejected rigid application of precedent which was non-responsive to the public's need for use of the waterways at that time. In adopting the rule that waterways capable of floating logs to market fell within the category of navigable streams, the Court stated its rationale as follows:

"The servitude of the public interest depends rather upon the purpose for which the public requires the use of its streams, than upon any particular mode of use—and hence, in a region where the principal business is lumbering, or the pursuit of any particular branch of manufacturing or trade, the public claim to a right of passage along its streams must depend upon their capacity for the use to which they can be made subservient." *Moore,* 2 Mich. 525.

The concept of navigability announced in *Moore* represented a pragmatic judicial response in recognition of the public need for use of inland waters as it existed at that time. The public need for certain uses and not the narrow manner or mode of use was the animating principle of the Court's decision.

For many years the log flotation test served as a practical and fair measure of whether our inland lakes and streams should be considered navigable and open for public use. During years when Michigan waters were actually used for floating logs to market, utilization of this test made sense.

The log flotation test remained the standard for adjudicating navigability of inland lakes and streams long after most waterways had ceased to be used for transporting lumber. However, application of the test changed as the public's required uses of these waters evolved from commercial to recreational in nature.

The log flotation test has long outlived its usefulness. Continued application of this test ignores the *Moore* Court's rationale that concepts of navigability must be fashioned in response to the public's required uses of waterways. Over time the public's required use of inland waters has changed from logging and commercial travel to recreational activities. The log flotation test constitutes no meaningful measure of whether a waterway is navigable and thus open to the public for recreational as well as commercial uses.

A test which fairly balances the rights of the public and of those persons owning property adjacent to water is the recreational boating test. Under this test if waters are capable of being navigated by small craft propelled by oar, paddle, or motor, the water is navigable and open to the public for navigation, fishing, and recreational use. * * *

In accordance with the principle first set forth in *Moore* that concepts of navigability and public access should be fashioned in response to current public needs for use of our waterways and motivated by pragmatic concerns, we join the growing numbers of states that have adopted the recreational boating test. We therefore hold that waters capable of being navigated by oar-, paddle-, or motor-propelled small craft are navigable. So long as access to such waters may be obtained without trespassing upon private property, the public may boat, fish, and exercise other lawful incidents of navigation on these waters up to the high water mark. * * *

The most recent case decided by this Court, in which riparian owners on an inland lake challenged the right of the public to use the lake, was Pigorsh v. Fahner, 386 Mich. 508, 194 N.W.2d 343 (1972). The body of water involved in *Pigorsh* was Wood Lake, approximately 74 acres in size, with no inlet or outlet. All the land surrounding the lake was owned by two families. These families erected a fence at the water's edge to prevent the public from entering the water from a private road which terminated at or near the water's edge. The lake, which was presumably boatable, was held to be a private body of water:

> "Decisions establishing the 'rule of property' which of right control disposition of this case were gathered in Putnam v. Kinney, 248 Mich. 410 [227 N.W. 741] (1929). *Putnam* is 'on all fours' here. These decisions go back to the simple proposition *that one who is owner in fee of all of the upland surrounding one of our wholly private inland lakes, a lake having no navigable inlet and no navigable outlet, (a) really owns the subaqueous land of the lake and the water over the latter as well as the upland, and (b) that his property right is such that he may exclude all others from the lake, the general public included.*"
> (Emphasis changed.) *Pigorsh*, 513–514, 194 N.W.2d 343.

Therefore, as developed in *Pigorsh,* the "wholly private lake" category included only those lakes having no navigable inlets or outlets, completely surrounded by the land of "one who is owner in fee." * * *

Upon a review of case law, we are convinced that for purposes of deciding whether the public has the right to use a lake for recreation or transportation, wholly private lakes are limited to those having no navigable inlet or outlet which are completely surrounded by the land of one who is owner in fee. *Pigorsh*, supra. This conclusion is compelled for a number of reasons.

First, cases which do not address the issue of navigability, but which deal with whether members of the public have access to a lake, reveal there are very few "wholly" private lakes in the sense that a landowner on a lake may exclude all other persons, including the general public, from using the surface of the lake overlying his land. It is now well settled that on a lake having more than one riparian owner, each riparian holds title to different portions of the lake bed, but must share the right to use the entire surface of the lake with all other riparians. Burt v. Munger, 314 Mich. 659, 23 N.W.2d 117 (1946); Bauman v. Barendregt, 251 Mich. 67, 71, 231 N.W. 70 (1930). * * *

Second, in cases primarily concerned with determining the navigability of inland lakes, whether the public has had lawful access to a lake by land or by water has been an important consideration in deciding whether the lake is wholly private or navigable and available for use by the public. * * *

Public access by water has been a key consideration in litigation concerning whether a lake is navigable. In framing the rule defining private inland lakes, the Court in *Pigorsh* emphasized that private lakes

are limited to those having no navigable inlet and no navigable outlet.
* * *

The presence of a navigable inlet or outlet to a lake is most
important because it indicates that the public has a lawful means of
access to the lake. * * *

Finally, construing the "wholly private lake" exception to include
only those lakes with no navigable inlet and no navigable outlet is
consonant with the recreational boating test as the general test of
navigability. If a lake has an inlet or outlet which is capable of supporting navigation by small recreational craft, and if the lake itself is
boatable, the public has lawful access to the lake and the right to make
reasonable use of the lake's surface. * * *

Notes and Questions

1. Among the leading decisions adopting the recreational boating test
of navigability are the following: Adirondack League Club, Inc. v. Sierra
Club, 92 N.Y.2d 591, 706 N.E.2d 1192, 684 N.Y.S.2d 168 (1998); Hitchings v.
Del Rio Woods Recreation & Park Dist., 55 Cal.App.3d 560, 127 Cal.Rptr.
830 (1976); Lamprey v. Metcalf, 52 Minn. 181, 53 N.W. 1139, 1143–44
(1893); Muench v. Pub. Serv. Comm'n, 261 Wis. 492, 53 N.W.2d 514 & 55
N.W.2d 40 (1952); Day v. Armstrong, 362 P.2d 137, 146–47 (Wyo. 1961);
Elder v. Delcour, 364 Mo. 835, 269 S.W.2d 17 (1954).

2. Since *Bott* was decided Montana has joined the list of states adopting
the recreational boating test, but with some statutory restrictions. See Galt
v. State Dept. of Fish, Wildlife & Parks, 225 Mont. 142, 731 P.2d 912 (1987),
interpreting Mont. Code Ann. § 23–2–302(1). Prior appropriation states are
more likely to rely on state constitutional provisions such as the section
claiming all waters as "the property of the state for the use of its people."
Southern Idaho Fish & Game Ass'n v. Picabo Livestock, Inc., 96 Idaho 360,
528 P.2d 1295 (1974); Montana Coalition for Stream Access, Inc. v. Curran,
210 Mont. 38, 682 P.2d 163 (1984). The Montana court reasoned as follows:

> In essence, the question is whether the waters owned by the State
> under the Constitution are susceptible to recreational use by the
> public. The capability of use of the waters for recreational purposes
> determines their availability for recreational use by the public.
> Streambed ownership by a private party is irrelevant. If the waters
> are owned by the State and held in trust for the people by the State,
> no private party may bar the use of those waters by the people. The
> Constitution and the public trust doctrine do not permit a private
> party to interfere with the public's right to recreational use of the
> surface of the State's waters. * * * In sum, we hold that, under the
> public trust doctrine and the 1972 Montana Constitution, any
> surface waters that are capable of recreational use may be so used
> by the public without regard to streambed ownership or navigability
> for nonrecreational purposes.

Id. at 52–53.

3. On the other side, Colorado says the state ownership provision in its
Constitution that declares water public property "subject to appropriation"

was intended to protect diversions for mining and irrigation and not to grant a right of public recreation and thereby "subvert a riparian bed owner's common law right to the exclusive surface use of waters bounded by his lands," though the court noted "it is within the competence of the General Assembly to modify rules of common law within constitutional parameters." People v. Emmert, 198 Colo. 137, 597 P.2d 1025, 1027 (1979). The legislature enacted a law limiting criminal trespass so as to suggest that floating without touching the banks or bottom was lawful, notwithstanding Emmert (Colo. Rev. Stat. 18–4–504.5), and that was the interpretation given in an Attorney General opinion in 1983, and a letter from a subsequent Attorney General in June, 2001 said the matter "remains legally unclear." Floating by recreational users has remained a hot, and unresolved, issue in Colorado. In 2001, four prominent kayakers were arrested and cited with criminal trespass as they floated down a stretch of the South Platte River bordered by private property. No subsequent test case has reached the Colorado Supreme Court, though the Court has cited Emmert's strong ownership language in more recent cases, e.g. Bijou Irr. Dist. v. Empire Club, 804 P.2d 175 (Colo. 1991).

The public trust theory has also been rejected in Kansas, apparently on the ground that in order to recognize public rights of use in waters not navigable for title there must be a legislative declaration of a public trust. State ex rel. Meek v. Hays, 246 Kan. 99, 785 P.2d 1356 (1990).

4. Who wins the debate, the *McIlroy* court, or the *Bott* court? If you are impressed with Justice Levin's reluctance to impose a new property rule upon riparians in Michigan, you may want to note the following statement from the Supreme Court decision in Rushton ex rel. Hoffmaster v. Taggart, 306 Mich. 432, 11 N.W.2d 193, 196 (1943):

> While the *Sanborne* case only disposed of the right of floatage and did not decide that a floatable stream has the status of waters navigable for all purposes, *the public character of water was held to be determined by reference to the public necessity for its use. It is this broad underlying principle rather than the narrow rule of the Sanborne case which* was in effect adopted by the court in Collins v. Gerhardt [237 Mich. 38, 211 N.W. 115, 116 (1926)] when it held that floatability determined the public character of a stream and affixed therein the public right of fishing.

The *Collins* case, in turn, had relied upon the leading Minnesota case of Lamprey v. Metcalf, 52 Minn. 181, 53 N.W. 1139 (1893). Has Justice Levin taken liberties with the interpretation of the Michigan precedents?

In many jurisdictions navigability matters not only for the existence of public use rights, but also to determine the rights of co-riparians to use the entire surface of the shared watercourse. The law is far from uniform. Some jurisdictions grant exclusive use of the overlying water surface to owners of the subaqueous beds while others, including Michigan, Illinois, and Minnesota, hold that riparian status on a non-navigable natural lake includes the right reasonably to use the entire surface. See, Chapter 2, supra p. 34.

5. Should it matter that Michigan is blessed with abundant recreational water resources that are open to extensive public water recreation? Is the factual showing of public need a necessary (or sensible) precondition for the

public use claim to succeed in *Bott,* or is it simply a convenient rationalization?

6. Courts usually permit the public to portage onto private land to avoid barriers. Elder v. Delcour, 364 Mo. 835, 269 S.W.2d 17 (1954), is the leading case and is one of many allowing an incidental use of private bottom lands and fast lands in effectuating the public recreational right. See also Buffalo River Conservation & Recreation Council v. National Park Serv., 558 F.2d 1342 (8th Cir. 1977) (fisherman may carry his boat onto riparian owner's upland to get around obstacles in the river and tie up the boat to the bank while fishing in the river). Is there a meaningful distinction between allowing the public to use fast lands to portage around an obstacle, allowing the public to tie their craft to the bank while resting or fishing, and allowing the public to picnic on those same banks?

3. PUBLIC, PRIVATE, AND COMMON RIGHTS IN WATERS FOR RECREATIONAL USE

a. *Common Rights: Riparian Access to Waters*

As you have just seen, opportunities for public recreational use of the surface of rivers and lakes depends on whether the water is navigable under state law. Even where lakes are not navigable, all riparian owners ordinarily have the right to use the entire surface in common. Also only riparians have a right to wharf out (to build a dock and keep a boat). So the question arises, who is a riparian? This is an especially important issue on inland lakes, where direct water access can greatly increase the value of property. Where land is adjacent to the water in its natural state, there is usually no problem. So long one owns enough shoreline to keep or launch a boat, he or she can use the entire surface of the lake, and can wharf out.[1]

Since natural riparian shoreland is limited in quantity, owners and developers have devised a variety of schemes to increase the effective extent of the lakeshore.[2] The most familiar such effort, illustrated in the case that follows, involves dredging canals through upland, creating additional "waterfront" lots. You can easily imagine some of the other devices. One buys a tract of riparian waterfront land, denominates it a yacht club, and sells memberships to all the owners of non-waterfront lots he has sold near (but not on) the lake. Or one buys a waterfront lot, tears down the old single-family house on it, and builds a large hotel resort, thus providing direct water access to every guest. A variant of the

---

1. Most courts have adopted the so-called "civil law" rule that all riparians have a shared interest in the surface of a lake. See, e.g., Beacham v. Lake Zurich Property Owners Ass'n, 123 Ill.2d 227, 526 N.E.2d 154 (1988); Snively v. Jaber, 48 Wash.2d 815, 296 P.2d 1015 (1956); Johnson v. Seifert, 257 Minn. 159, 100 N.W.2d 689 (1960). A few courts, however, still follow the "common law" rule that grants recreational exclusivity in non-public waters to the owner of the beds underlying the waters. Lanier v. Ocean Pond Fishing Club, Inc., 253 Ga. 549, 322 S.E.2d 494 (1984); People v. Emmert, 198 Colo. 137, 597 P.2d 1025 (1979). Even in states that deny use of the entire surface, it is possible to obtain a prescriptive easement to use of the entire surface. See Carnahan v. Moriah Property Owners Ass'n, Inc., 716 N.E.2d 437 (Ind. 1999).

2. Artificially created waters are discussed in Chapter 2, supra, p. at 61.

latter plan is to tear down the house and build a condominium apartment house, with every unit owner actually having an ownership interest in the waterfront land, which is part of the condominium's common area.

The question presented in these cases is how the law is going to define or redefine the conventional definition of riparian. The smaller the lake, the bigger the problem.

THOMPSON v. ENZ

Supreme Court of Michigan, 1967.
379 Mich. 667, 154 N.W.2d 473.

[A developer purchased a piece of land fronting on Gun Lake for a large subdivision, to be called Sunrise Shores, which would significantly expand the number of people with direct and easy access to the lake. Several of the current riparian homeowners on Gun Lake sued alleging that the proposed development would dramatically increase the use of Gun Lake and thereby infringe on their rights as riparian owners. Both sides moved for summary judgment, and the trial court ruled in favor of the plaintiffs.]

KAVANAGH, JUSTICE.

* * *

This case concerns certain property rights in and around Gun Lake, which is situated partly in Barry county and partly in Allegan county. The parties agree that this lake has approximately 2,680 acres of surface area and approximately 30 miles of shore line.

The defendant corporation is a contract purchaser of a riparian parcel of land having approximately 1,415 feet of frontage on said lake, and the individual defendants are the sole stockholders of the corporation. * * *

Defendants are in the process of developing and subdividing their parcel of land into from 144 to 153 lots. Of these lots, approximately 16 will abut on the natural shore line of the lake. The remainder of the lots will front on canals. To give the back lot purchasers access to the lake the defendants' plan calls for excavating across riparian lots Nos. 13 and 76. [See Figure 6–1.] The defendants purport to grant to the purchasers of those lots fronting on the canals riparian rights to the lake and rights of access through the excavation to the lake. The back lots would have frontage on the canals of approximately 11,000 feet.

[The court began by rejecting defendants' argument that, because the entire parcel of land was currently riparian to Gun Lake, all of the lots would retain their riparian status even after being subdivided:]

As it was stated in Harvey Realty Co. v. Borough of Wallingford, 111 Conn. 352, 358, 150 A. 60, 63:

"A riparian proprietor is an owner of land bounded by a water course or lake or through which a stream flows, and riparian rights can be claimed only by such an owner. * * * "

In the case of Schofield v. Dingman, 261 Mich. 611, 247 N.W. 67, the Court was considering a situation similar to the case at bar. One Turner owned land bordering on Lake Michigan and had prepared a plat of a part of it. There was a bluff about 50 feet above the water at this point along the lake and at times the water washed the foot of the bluff. Most of the time, however, there was a sand beach between the bluff and the water. The plat was laid out along the top of the bluff. Turner planned to sell those lots for resort purposes and to promote sales attempted to convey riparian rights with the lots. Turner died, and the defendants acquired his rights to the land between the bluff and the water and claimed exclusive right to possession and control thereof. Of the granting of the riparian rights to the back lot purchasers, the Court said (p. 613, 247 N.W. p. 68):

" 'Riparian rights,' accorded lot owners separated from the beach by intervening lots, can be given no greater meaning than right of access to the beach and enjoyment thereof for the purposes of recreation."

In the case of Hilt v. Weber, 252 Mich. 198, 233 N.W. 159, at p. 165, 71 A.L.R. 1238, the Court said:

Figure 6–1

All Lots Front on the Channel or the Lake

"It is settled law both in this state and elsewhere, so settled that no contrary authority has been cited, that the interposition of a fee title between upland and water destroys riparian rights, or rather transfers them to the interposing owner. *The basis of the riparian doctrine, and an indispensable requisite to it, is actual contact of the land with the water.*" (Emphasis supplied.)

[The court also rejected defendants' argument that the back lots in the subdivision would carry riparian rights because they would front on the canals. The court noted that prior cases in both Michigan and other states clearly established that land "abutting on an artificial watercourse has no riparian rights."]

[The next question is] whether or not riparian rights may be conveyed to a grantee or reserved by the grantor in a conveyance which divides a tract of land with riparian rights into more than one parcel, of which parcels only one would remain bounded by the watercourse.

In the case of Harvey Realty Co. v. Borough of Wallingford, supra, Justice Hinman, writing for the Court, stated (150 A. p. 63):

> "It is clear that the grantees or contractees, from the plaintiff, of lots separated from and not bordering on Pine Lake can have, of their own right, no riparian privileges in its waters. *And any attempted transfer of the right made by a riparian to a non-riparian proprietor is invalid.*" (Citing cases.) (Emphasis supplied.)

* * *

We hold that riparian rights are not alienable, severable, divisible or assignable apart from the land which includes therein or is bounded by a natural watercourse.

While riparian rights may not be conveyed or reserved—nor do they exist by virtue of being bounded by an artificial watercourse—easements, licenses and the like for a right of way for access to a watercourse do exist and ofttimes are granted to non-riparian owners.

We will, therefore, treat the proposal here as though easements for rights of way for access are given to the back lot purchasers. We must then consider what right, if any, the owners of the back lots have to use these rights of way. In so doing, attention must be given to the use of riparian rights by the defendants and the remaining proprietors on Gun Lake.

Riparian uses are divided generally into two classes. The first of these is for natural purposes. These uses encompass all those absolutely necessary for the existence of the riparian proprietor and his family, such as to quench thirst and for household purposes. Without these uses both man and beast would perish. Users for natural purposes enjoy a preferred non-proratable position with respect to all other users rather than a correlative one.

The second of these is a use for artificial purposes. Artificial uses are those which merely increase one's comfort and prosperity and do not rank as essential to his existence, such as commercial profit and recreation. Users for artificial purposes occupy a correlative status with the other riparians in exercise of their riparian rights for artificial purposes. Use for an artificial purpose must be (a) only for the benefit of the riparian land and (b) reasonable in light of the correlative rights of the other proprietors. * * * It is clear in the case before us that the use made of the property by the defendants is for a strictly artificial purpose and must meet the test of reasonableness. * * *

The trial court made no finding of fact as to the reasonableness of the use. This record is insufficient for us to make a determination as to reasonableness. Therefore, we remand to the trial court for such determination. The trial court should keep in mind the following factors in determining whether the use would be reasonable:

First, attention should be given to the watercourse and its attributes, including its size, character and natural state. In determining the reasonableness of the use in the case at bar, it should be considered that Gun Lake is not a large lake, that it is used primarily for recreational purposes, and that the defendants are changing its natural state by expanding the lake frontage of their property from an actual 1,415 feet to a total inclusive of the canals, of 12,415 feet, being an increase in frontage of approximately 800 per cent.

Second, the trial court should examine the use itself as to its type, extent, necessity, effect on the quantity, quality and level of the water, and the purposes of the users. Factors in this particular case that should be considered include: (a) that this use would permanently add approximately one family without riparian rights to each 18 acres of surface area (or 137 families); (b) the possibility that the level of the lake may be reduced by withdrawing trust waters into over 2 miles of the proposed canals, as is alleged by the Attorney General in his motion to intervene; (c) the possibility that pollution may result; (d) that there is nothing in the record showing any necessity for this use; and (e) the fact that it appears that the purpose of the defendants herein is merely commercial exploitation.

Third, it is necessary to examine the proposed artificial use in relation to the consequential effects, including the benefits obtained and the detriment suffered, on the correlative rights and interests of other riparian proprietors and also on the interests of the State, including fishing, navigation, and conservation. An additional fact to be considered by the trial court in this litigation is whether the benefit to the defendant subdividers would amount merely to a rich financial harvest, while the remaining proprietors who now possess a tranquil retreat from everyday living would be forced to endure the annoyances which would come from an enormous increase in lake users. * * *

BLACK, SOURIS and ADAMS, JJ., concurred with KAVANAGH, J.

BRENNAN, JUSTICE [dissenting].

    * * *

[After agreeing with the majority that the back lots were not riparian to Gun Lake, the opinion continued.] Here, the developer wishes to subdivide his property and convey back lots by deeds which will expressly grant easements for rights of way, permitting access to the lake through the canal. There is no doubt that a riparian owner can grant an easement over his land to permit a non-riparian owner to have access to the water.

A great many inland lakes in Michigan have been developed in this fashion, where cottages or homes do not have actual lake frontage, but do enjoy, in common with other property owners, the use of a granted or reserved easement providing for access to the water for recreational purposes. If the easement proposed in this case were a road, rather than a canal, no serious issue would be raised concerning the defendants' right to convey back lots with such an easement included in the grant.

* * * The real issue in this case, then, is: Can this defendant lawfully dig this proposed canal on his property?

Absent statutory regulations to the contrary, mere alteration of the natural shore line does not *per se* adversely affect the riparian rights of other owners of lake front property. Seawalls, boatwells, and permanent docks are all examples of alterations of the natural shore line. No one contends that such improvements infringe upon the riparian rights of other owners in the absence of specific allegations of harm flowing therefrom, as for example, if a dock were to be of such length as to interfere with traffic upon the lake. Generally, riparian rights comprise such uses of the waters as do not deprive other riparian owners of the same uses.

Whether the dredging of any given canal by a riparian owner constitutes an infringement upon the riparian rights of the other riparian owners is a question of fact.

Will the lake level be lowered?

Will the lake be polluted?

Will the fish die, or the birds fly away, or the lake bottom become rocky or mucky or weedy?

In short, these riparian plaintiffs have the burden of alleging and proving some actual damage to themselves that will flow from the dredging of the canal.

Such factual questions could have been raised in this case, but they were not.[a]

To remand this cause to circuit court for trial upon factual issues never alleged by the parties or framed by the pleadings is to impose upon

a. Plaintiffs in their complaint did not allege that Sunrise Shores would pollute Gun Lake, lower the lake level, or otherwise injure the environment, but rested their case solely on allegations of overcrowding. The first suggestion that Sunrise Shores might lower the lake level came in an *amicus* brief that the State of Michigan filed in support of plaintiffs' summary judgment motion.—Eds.

b. *Providing Public Use Through Land Acquisition*

Is it fair to the riparian owners to saddle them with the burdens of a foreseeable series of trespassory invasions of the fast land portions of their property that will necessarily occur if the public is permitted to use the water surface? If enforcement of trespass laws seems an inadequate remedy for littering of fast lands and the like, can a governmental authority step in and legislate away the public recreational right as a means of protecting the riparian owners? One case that considered such protection is People ex rel. Younger v. El Dorado County, 96 Cal.App.3d 403, 157 Cal.Rptr. 815 (1979). The court of appeals found that the legislation was an impermissible restriction of the public right which it claimed amounted to a constitutional guarantee on the basis of Marks v. Whitney, infra p. 597. The following case provides another solution to the problem.

BOTTON v. STATE

Supreme Court of Washington, 1966.
69 Wash.2d 751, 420 P.2d 352.

HILL, JUDGE.

The State of Washington, through its Department of Game, acquired by purchase a waterfront lot on Phantom Lake (nonnavigable) which it has developed to be used as a public fishing access area. Its use or abuse, for that purpose, has resulted in the present action by other owners of waterfront property on the lake, asking that the state be enjoined from maintaining its public access area.

The trial court made very comprehensive findings of fact:

Since the defendant, through its Game Department, put in the public access area, the plaintiffs have suffered the following as a result of it:

1. The fair market value of plaintiffs' property has been decreased.

2. Thievery on the lake has greatly increased, particularly the stealing of boats, oars, outdoor furniture, tools and miscellaneous items of personal property of all kinds. In many of the cases it was definitely ascertained that the thieves gained access to the lake from the public access area.

3. Persons relieving themselves in the lake as well as on the property and front yards of various of the plaintiffs, to the considerable embarrassment and annoyance of the plaintiffs, their families and guests.

4. Beer cans, worm cans, sandwich bags, pop bottles, rafts, and other assorted trash has been deposited in the lake and on the plaintiffs' beaches in considerable quantity.

5. Repeated and frequent trespasses on the plaintiffs' front yards, docks, beaches and property. In addition to the

trespasses by persons coming in by the access area, numerous other trespassers have crossed the plaintiffs' yards, docks, beaches and property from other adjoining residential areas, and which trespassers, when confronted by the plaintiffs, have justified their actions by saying to the effect that, "Well, now, it's a public lake, isn't it."

6. Numerous of the plaintiffs, their children and grand-children, have severely and frequently been cut by broken beer bottles left on the beaches.

7. Fishermen using plaintiffs' docks, and fishing immediately adjacent to their beaches and front yards, would refuse to leave when requested and would stare and make remarks when plaintiffs, their wives and daughters would try to use their beaches for sun bathing, swimming or the entertainment of guests. The plaintiffs, as a result of this, cut down very considerably in their use of their front yards and beaches.

8. Although hunting and shooting on the lake are illegal, hunters come in and hunt and shoot on the lake. Persons also come in and shoot at ducks with air rifles.

9. Speed boating on the lake has greatly increased. In some cases it has increased to the extent that it has become a danger to the plaintiffs' children.

10. The public use of the lake has interfered with the plaintiffs' use of the lake for boating, swimming, fishing and recreational purposes.

11. The noise on the lake has substantially increased.

From these findings, the trial court drew the legal conclusions that the state's opening up of the lake to public use through its access area, without resorting to eminent domain, constituted a taking and damaging of private property without compensation to the owners thereof; and that the state's opening up of the lake to public use constituted an unreasonable interference with the rights of the plaintiffs.

Based on these conclusions, the trial court entered an injunction enjoining the state

from maintaining its public access area on Phantom Lake as a public access area and from admitting the public to Phantom Lake and across the access area until such time as it condemns the plaintiffs' property and property rights in the manner provided by law.

The state appeals, urging that as a riparian owner on a nonnavigable lake it can permit the public to enjoy the right to fish from boats over every portion of the lake so long as this does not constitute an unreasonable interference with the rights of the other riparian owners. This implies an obligation to police and control the use of the nonnavigable lake by the public to prevent such use becoming an unreasonable interference with the rights of the other riparian owners thereon. * * *

The lake is small and shallow, covering 63.2 acres, and with depths running from extremely shallow to a maximum of 47 feet near the middle. The shore of the lake is partly surrounded with nice homes (most of the homeowners reside on the lake the year-round) and partly by as yet undeveloped properties. It lies between Lake Washington and Lake Sammamish (within only a few hundred feet of the latter), both of which are large, navigable lakes with many public access areas, parks, and beaches. There are no commercial establishments, resorts or public beaches on Phantom Lake. Nor were there any public streets, roads, or street ends which would give the public an access to the lake, until the state, acting through its Department of Game, acquired approximately a hundred feet of lake frontage, extending back some 800 feet to a public thoroughfare, and developed it to provide an access for fishermen and their boats.

There has been no serious attempt by the state to limit access to the lake to fishermen; and the trial court found that this access area had been open to any member of the public. We do not question the right of the state, as a riparian owner, to ignore the county's zoning regulations and to permit the public, as its licensees, access to the lake over its property. There is, however, a limitation, and that is that it cannot permit such use of its property as constitutes an unreasonable interference with the rights of the other riparian owners.

We have stated the law applicable in the present case quite succinctly in Snively v. Jaber, 48 Wash. 2d 815, 821, 296 P.2d 1015, 1019, 57 A.L.R.2d 560 (1956):

> We hold that with respect to the boating, swimming, fishing, and other similar rights of riparian proprietors upon a nonnavigable lake, these rights or privileges are owned in common, and that any proprietor or his licensee may use the entire surface of a lake so long as he does not unreasonably interfere with the exercise of similar rights by the other owners. This rule does not have the effect of making the nonnavigable lake public, since a stranger has no right to enter upon the lake without the permission of an abutting owner. The rule we have announced affords equal protection to the interest of all riparian owners in the use of the water and seeks to promote the greatest beneficial use by each with a minimum of harm to other owners.

In that case, the defendant Jaber had a dance hall, picnic grounds, and a swimming area on Angle Lake (nonnavigable) and rented some 30 rowboats to the public. The conduct of the licensees in rented rowboats was such that the trial court found it necessary to enjoin that operation for a 2–year period, and this we affirmed.

The depredations and conduct of Jaber's licensees, which warranted an injunction in that case, could be characterized as a Sunday-school picnic as compared with the indecencies and obscenities to which the other riparian owners on Phantom Lake have been subjected. Added to this is the physical danger to other riparian owners, their children and grandchildren from broken beer bottles left on the beaches and from the operation of speed boats dangerously close to bathers and swimmers near the shore. While the trial court's injunction was justified at the time of trial, it was too extensive in time and was not properly conditioned as to termination.

The dedicated people who make up the great fishing fraternity in this state should not be deprived of the opportunity and pleasure of fishing for perch, crappie, and the like (the water is too warm for trout) because of the conduct of a relatively few hooligans.

The state, as a riparian owner, does not have to acquire by condemnation the rights of the other riparian owners before it permits fishermen in reasonable numbers access to the waters of Phantom Lake; but it does have the obligation, and counsel for the state so concede, to so regulate the number and conduct of its licensees as to prevent any undue interference with the rights of other riparian owners.

The injunction should be continued only until the state, through its Department of Game, presents a plan for the controlled operation of its property that satisfies the trial court that the rights of other riparian owners will be adequately safeguarded. The state is entitled to all the rights of a riparian owner, but it should also accept the responsibility of a riparian owner for the conduct of its licensees. We are in accord with the trial court's conclusion, from the facts in this case, that there has been an unreasonable interference by the state's licensees with the rights of other riparian owners and that an injunction was properly granted, but it should be modified and limited as indicated herein; and the cause is remanded for that purpose.

Each party will bear his own costs on this appeal.

DONWORTH, WEAVER, and HAMILTON, JJ., concur.

[Separate opinions of FINLEY, JUDGE (concurring specially in the majority opinion) and OTT, JUDGE (concurring in part and dissenting in part) are omitted.]

Notes and Questions

1. Professor Ralph Johnson of the University of Washington Law School reported that subsequent to the decision of the Washington Supreme Court, the Department of Game was unable to reach an agreement with the riparian owners, and public access to Phantom Lake was closed. The Department determined that it could not afford to station a full-time employee at the site to regulate the public use. Then, in 1993, an application by the City of Bellevue for a viewing dock and boat launch for small boats in a public park on Phantom Lake was approved, subject to caveats about how the area was to be regulated, with the consent of the Phantom Lake Homeowners Association. Washington officials reported that temporary access closings were an occasional response to complaints by neighbors about water recreation abuses by the public. In more remote areas of the state, a

program of selective road closures in co-operation with federal agencies is also employed to prevent misuse of public access points, but the road closure program is intended primarily to prevent illegal hunting activities.

2. *Botton* is roughly analogous to Snively v. Jaber, discussed in the principal opinion, the major difference being that the access provider is governmental rather than private. Should this difference in identity alter the responsibility of the access provider? In some areas of tort law, the duty of care owed by government is different than that owed by private proprietors engaged in the same activity. For example, in the repair and maintenance of streets and sidewalks, government is often held to have no duty of inspection or discovery of defects, whereas private landowners must reasonably inspect their streets and walks to discharge their duty to motorists and pedestrians. Is government as riparian equally entitled to a lower duty in controlling its licensees? One rationale that is proffered to justify a lower governmental standard of care is that government maintains many more streets and walks than does any private entity and therefore can't be expected to exercise the same care. A second rationale is that government is providing a free benefit and cannot be expected to have the same resources available to inspect and repair its premises as would a for-profit entity. Do either of these rationales have a place in the recreational provider situation?

3. A Minnesota statute authorizes the Department of Natural Resources to acquire public access sites if:

> (1) The body of water to which access is being provided and surrounding lands can withstand additional recreational use without undue damage to the environment or undue risks to the health and safety of water users;

> (2) Public access to the body of water is either nonexistent or inadequate.

Minn. Stat. Ann. § 86A.05(9)(b). An action taken by the Minnesota Commissioner of Natural Resources pursuant to this statute was reviewed and upheld over the objection of private riparians in Stony Ridge & Carlos View Terrace Ass'n v. Alexander, 353 N.W.2d 700 (Minn. App. 1984).

4. In Branch v. Oconto County, 13 Wis.2d 595, 109 N.W.2d 105 (1961), the county condemned a 50 foot wide strip across private land to provide public access to a shallow lake valuable for duck hunting. The tract had considerable value for development as a private hunting club. The question was the measurement of compensation to the condemnee, who previously had been able to exclude the public because of his ownership of the land surrounding the lake. The court said the question was "whether a land owner who enjoys virtually private use of navigable waters because of his ability to exclude the public is entitled to damages for the loss of his monopoly when a parcel of his land is taken by the public to provide access." The answer it gave was that "the benefit he is able to derive from exclusion of the public from the waters is not a right of property for which he is entitled to compensation. * * * The very purpose of reserving in the people the power of eminent domain is to prevent an owner of a site especially available for a public work, but not of great value for other purposes, from trading upon the necessities of the public when it is sought to acquire his land for public use. * * * A somewhat similar problem was considered by the

United States Supreme Court in United States v. Twin City Power Co., 350 U.S. 222 (1956). In that case, the United States condemned land adjoining a navigable river, and the court held that the just compensation which the Fifth Amendment requires to be paid does not include the value of the water power in the flow of the stream." *Branch*, 109 N.W.2d at 109–10. Does this ruling mean the condemnee will only get the trivial value of the strip itself, considered as an isolated tract of land, even though the value of his remaining hundreds of acres of lake and surrounding land has now dropped very sharply?

E. THE HISTORIC PUBLIC TRUST

In the material on the navigability-for-title doctrine, you will recall the Supreme Court's statement in *Illinois Central* that "the state holds the title to the lands under the navigable waters * * * in trust for the people * * *." Up to this point we have considered public rights as against private claims. Now we turn to the question of government responsibility in its status as a trustee. The issue is not whether government may permit public use of navigable waters, but the extent of state authority to *limit* public use. The public trust doctrine addresses the *responsibilities* of the state in regulating the use of navigable waters and the lands beneath them.

The scope of the public trust has been dynamic. In its original form, the trust was founded in the proprietary interest the states took in tidal and navigable-for-title waters and the lands beneath them. It was applied only to navigation, commerce and fishing in the early cases, but more recently it has been expanded to protect the ecological values of the waters and submerged lands. There has been much modern debate about the physical scope of the trust. Some states base state navigability on a public trust where the waters do not meet the federal title test for navigability. The trust has been applied to non-navigable tributaries of navigable lakes, and also to beach lands above the high water mark that give access to trust lands and waters. There have also been efforts, unsuccessful thus far, to apply the trust to the federal public lands.

The classic context in which the question of trust responsibility has been litigated is where the state transfers title to land beneath navigable waters to a private grantee, and the new private owner seeks to exclude the public (as by filling in and building on tidelands). Alternatively, government itself may obstruct traditional public uses, by filling in navigable waters to build an airport, or by leasing submerged lands into private use for a yacht club or a high rise apartment development. In the most recent cases, as you will see in the next section, the question is whether the state violates its public trust responsibility when it permits appropriators to divert from a water body and thereby diminish the public (public trust) claim to protection of it as a habitat for fish and wildlife, or for public recreation.

JOSEPH L. SAX,
THE PUBLIC TRUST DOCTRINE IN NATURAL
RESOURCE LAW: EFFECTIVE JUDICIAL
INTERVENTION

68 Mich. L. Rev. 471, 489–90 (1970).

D.   The Lodestar in American Public Trust Law:
Illinois Central Railroad Company v. Illinois

The most celebrated public trust case in American law is the decision of the United States Supreme Court in Illinois Central Railroad Company v. Illinois.[59] In 1869 the Illinois legislature made an extensive grant of submerged lands, in fee simple, to the Illinois Central Railroad. That grant included all the land underlying Lake Michigan for one mile out from the shoreline and extending one mile in length along the central business district of Chicago—more than one thousand acres of incalculable value, comprising virtually the whole commercial waterfront of the city. By 1873 the legislature had repented of its excessive generosity, and it repealed the 1869 grant; it then brought an action to have the original grant declared invalid.

The Supreme Court upheld the state's claim and wrote one of the very few opinions in which an express conveyance of trust lands has been held to be beyond the power of a state legislature. It is that result which has made the decision such a favorite of litigants.[60] But the Court did not actually prohibit the disposition of trust lands to private parties; its holding was much more limited. What a state may not do, the Court said, is to divest itself of authority to govern the whole of an area in which it has responsibility to exercise its police power; to grant almost the entire waterfront of a major city to a private company is, in effect, to abdicate legislative authority over navigation.

But the mere granting of property to a private owner does not *ipso facto* prevent the exercise of the police power, for states routinely exercise a great deal of regulatory authority over privately owned land. The Court's decision makes sense only because the Court determined that the states have special regulatory obligations over shorelands, obligations which are inconsistent with large-scale private ownership. The Court stated that the title under which Illinois held the navigable waters of Lake Michigan is

different in character from that which the state holds in lands intended for sale * * *. It is a title held in trust for the people of the state that they may enjoy the navigation of the waters, carry on

59.   146 U.S. 387 (1892).   **60.**   E.g., Town of Ashwaubenon v. Public Service Comn., 22 Wis. 2d 38, 125 N.W.2d 647 (1963).

commerce over them, and have liberty of fishing therein freed from the obstruction or interferences of private parties.[61]

With this language, the Court articulated a principle that has become the central substantive thought in public trust litigation. When a state holds a resource which is available for the free use of the general public, a court will look with considerable skepticism upon *any* government conduct which is calculated *either* to reallocate that resource to more restricted uses *or* to subject public uses to the self-interest of private parties.

Note

For recent discussions of the Illinois Central case see Douglas L. Grant, Underpinnings of the Public Trust Doctrine: Lessons from Illinois Central Railroad, 33 Ariz. St. L.J. 849 (2001); Joseph D. Kearney & Thomas W. Merrill, The Origins of the American Public Trust Doctrine: What Really Happened in *Illinois Central*, 71 U. Chicago L.Rev.799 (2004).

GLASS v. GOECKEL

Supreme Court of Michigan, 2005.
473 Mich. 667, 703 N.W.2d 58.

CORRIGAN, J.

The issue presented in this case is whether the public has a right to walk along the shores of the Great Lakes where a private landowner ostensibly holds title to the water's edge. To resolve this issue we must consider two component questions: (1) how the public trust doctrine affects private littoral title; and (2) whether the public trust encompasses walking among the public rights protected by the public trust doctrine. * * *

* * * [W]e conclude that the public trust doctrine does protect her right to walk along the shores of the Great Lakes. American law has long recognized that large bodies of navigable water, such as the oceans, are natural resources and thoroughfares that belong to the public. In our common-law tradition, the state, as sovereign, acts as trustee of public rights in these natural resources. Consequently, the state lacks the power to diminish those rights when conveying littoral property to private parties. This "public trust doctrine," as the United States Supreme Court stated in Illinois Central R. Co. v. Illinois, 146 U.S. 387, 435 (1892), and as recognized by our Court in Nedtweg v. Wallace, 237 Mich. 14, 16–23 (1926), applies not only to the oceans, but also to the Great Lakes.

Defendants own property on the shore of Lake Huron, and their deed defines one boundary as "the meander line of Lake."[5] * * * This present appeal concerns * * * plaintiff's right *as a member of the public* to walk along the shoreline of Lake Huron, irrespective of defendants'

---

61.   46 U.S. at 452.

5.   We note that the parties do not contest the terms of the deed by which defendants own their property. We take as given that defendants hold title to their property according to the terms of their deed. The

record does not reflect any argument over the meaning of the term "meander line" in this context. The issue before us is not how far defendants' private littoral title extends, but how the public trust affects that title.

private title. During the proceedings below, plaintiff sought to enjoin defendants from interfering with her walking along the shoreline. Defendants sought summary disposition * * * for failure to state a claim upon which relief may be granted and for failure to state a defense. Defendants argued that, as a matter of law, plaintiff could not walk on defendants' property between the ordinary high water mark and the lake without defendants' permission.

The Court of Appeals [held] "[t]hat the state of Michigan holds in trust the *submerged lands* beneath the Great Lakes within its borders for the free and uninterrupted navigation of the public * * *." The Court [of Appeals] held that, apart from navigational issues, the state holds title to previously submerged land, subject to the exclusive use of the riparian owner up to the water's edge. Thus, under the Court of Appeals analysis, neither plaintiff nor any other member of the public has a right to traverse the land between the statutory ordinary high water mark and the literal water's edge. * * *

Throughout the history of American law as descended from English common law, our courts have recognized that the sovereign must preserve and protect navigable waters for its people. This obligation traces back to the Roman Emperor Justinian, whose Institutes provided, "Now the things which are, by natural law, common to all are these: the air, running water, the sea, and therefore the seashores. Thus, no one is barred access to the seashore * * * ." Justinian, Institutes, book II, title I, § 1. The law of the sea, as developed through English common law, incorporated the understanding that both the title and the dominion of the sea, and of rivers and arms of the sea, where the tide ebbs and flows, and of all the lands below high water mark, within the jurisdiction of the Crown of England, are in the King. Such waters, and the lands which they cover, either at all times, or at least when the tide is in, are incapable of ordinary and private occupation, cultivation and improvement; and their natural and primary uses are public in their nature, for highways of navigation and commerce, domestic and foreign, and for the purpose of fishing by all the King's subjects. Therefore the title, *jus privatum,* in such lands ... belongs to the King as the sovereign; and the dominion thereof, *jus publicum,* is vested in him as the representative of the nation and for the public benefit.

This rule—that the sovereign must sedulously guard the public's interest in the seas for navigation and fishing—passed from English courts to the American colonies, to the Northwest Territory, and, ultimately, to Michigan. Michigan's courts recognized that the principles that guaranteed public rights in the seas apply with equal force to the Great Lakes. Thus, we have held that the common law of the sea applies to the Great Lakes. In particular, we have held that the public trust doctrine from the common law of the sea applies to the Great Lakes. In this decision, we consider the public trust doctrine only as it has applied to the Great Lakes and do not consider how it has applied to inland bodies of water.

Accordingly, under longstanding principles of Michigan's common law, the state, as sovereign, has an obligation to protect and preserve the waters of the Great Lakes and the lands beneath them for the public. The state serves, in effect, as the trustee of public rights in the Great Lakes for fishing, hunting, and boating for commerce or pleasure. Although not implicated in this case, we note that the Great Lakes and the lands beneath them remain subject to the federal navigational servitude. * * * Apart from this servitude, the federal government has relinquished to the state any remaining ownership rights in the Great Lakes.

The state, as sovereign, cannot relinquish this duty to preserve public rights in the Great Lakes and their natural resources. As we stated in *Nedtweg*:

> The State may not, by grant, surrender such public rights any more than it can abdicate the police power or other essential power of government. But this does not mean that the State must, at all times, remain the proprietor of, as well as the sovereign over, the soil underlying navigable waters.... The State of Michigan has an undoubted right to make use of its proprietary ownership of the land in question, [subject only to the paramount right of] the public [to] enjoy the benefit of the trust. [237 Mich. at 17]

Therefore, although the state retains the authority to convey lakefront property to private parties, it necessarily conveys such property *subject to the public trust*.

At common law, our courts articulated a distinction between *jus privatum* and *jus publicum* to capture this principle: the alienation of littoral property to private parties leaves intact public rights in the lake and its submerged land. Indeed, other states also recognize the distinction between private title and public rights. *Jus publicum* refers to public rights in navigable waters and the land covered by those waters; *jus privatum,* in contrast, refers to private property rights held subject to the public trust. As the United States Supreme Court explained in Shively v. Bowlby, 152 U.S. 1, 14:

> In England, from the time of Lord Hale, it has been treated as settled that the title in the soil of the sea, or of arms of the sea, below the ordinary high water mark, is in the King, except so far as an individual or a corporation has acquired rights in it by express grant or by prescription or usage; and that this title, *jus privatum,* whether in the King or in a subject, is held subject to the public right, *jus publicum,* of navigation and fishing. [Citations omitted.]

Thus, when a private party acquires littoral property from the sovereign, it acquires only the *jus privatum.* Our courts have continued to recognize this distinction between private title and public rights when they have applied the public trust doctrine. Public rights in certain types of access to the waters and lands beneath them remain under the protection of the state. Under the public trust doctrine, the sovereign never had the power to eliminate those rights, so any subsequent conveyances of littoral property remain subject to those public rights. Consequently, littoral landowners have always taken title subject to the limitation of public rights preserved under the public trust doctrine.

Having established that the public trust doctrine is alive and well in Michigan, we are required in this appeal to examine the *scope* of the doctrine in Michigan: whether it extends up to the ordinary high water mark or whether, as defendants argue, it applies only to land that is *actually* below the waters of the Great Lakes at any particular moment. * * *

In applying the public trust doctrine to the oceans, courts have traditionally held that rights protected by this doctrine extend from the waters themselves and the lands beneath them to a point on the shore called the "ordinary high water mark." * * * An "ordinary high water mark" therefore has an intuitive meaning when applied to tidal waters. Because of lunar influence, ocean waves ebb and flow, thus reaching one point on the shore at low tide and reaching a more landward point at high tide. The latter constitutes the high water mark on a tidal shore. The land between this mark and the low water mark is submerged on a regular basis, and so remains subject to the public trust doctrine as "submerged land." Michigan's courts have adopted the ordinary high water mark as the landward boundary of the public trust. * * *

Our Court has previously suggested that Michigan law leaves some ambiguity regarding whether the high or low water mark serves as the boundary of the public trust. But the established distinction in public trust jurisprudence between public rights (*jus publicum*) and private title (*jus privatum*) resolves this apparent ambiguity. Cases that seem to suggest, at first blush, that the public trust ends at the low water mark actually considered the boundary of the littoral owner's private property (*jus privatum*) rather than the boundary of the public trust (*jus publicum*). Because the public trust doctrine preserves public rights separate from a landowner's fee title, the boundary of the public trust need not equate with the boundary of a landowner's littoral title. Rather, a landowner's littoral title might extend past the boundary of the public trust. Our case law nowhere suggests that private title necessarily ends where public rights begin. To the contrary, the distinction we have drawn between private title and public rights demonstrates that the *jus privatum* and the *jus publicum* may overlap. * * *

We have established thus far that the private title of littoral landowners remains subject to the public trust beneath the ordinary high water mark. But plaintiff, as a member of the public, may walk below the ordinary high water mark only if that practice receives the protection of the public trust doctrine. We hold that walking along the shore, subject to regulation (as is any exercise of public rights in the public trust) falls within the scope of the public trust.

We first note that neither party contests that walking falls within public rights traditionally protected under our public trust doctrine. Rather, they dispute where, not whether, plaintiff may walk: below the literal water's edge or below the ordinary high water mark. While the parties' agreement on this point cannot determine the scope of public rights, this agreement does indicate the existence of a common sense assumption: walking along the lakeshore is inherent in the exercise of traditionally protected public rights.

Our courts have traditionally articulated rights protected by the public trust doctrine as fishing, hunting, and navigation for commerce or pleasure. Indeed, we have even noted that the public might cut ice or, in the context of inland waters, might float logs downriver. In order to engage in these activities specifically protected by the public trust doctrine, the public must have a right of passage over land below the ordinary high water mark. Indeed, other courts have recognized a "right of passage" as protected with their public trust. We can protect traditional public rights under our public trust doctrine only by simultaneously safeguarding activities inherent in the exercise of those rights. Walking the lakeshore below the ordinary high water mark is just such an activity, because gaining access to the Great Lakes to hunt, fish, or boat required walking to reach the water. Consequently, the public has always held a right of passage in and along the lakes.

We must conclude with two caveats. By no means does our public trust doctrine permit *every* use of the trust lands and waters. Rather, this doctrine protects only limited public rights, and it does not create an unlimited public right to access private land below the ordinary high water mark. The public trust doctrine cannot serve to justify trespass on private property. Finally, any exercise of these traditional public rights remains subject to criminal or civil regulation by the Legislature.

Notes and Questions

1. Which branch of government is being charged with a surrender of public trust rights in the *Glass* case? Here, prior to the reversal of its decision, the court of appeals defined property rights in a way that subjected 3,200 miles of Michigan's Great Lakes shoreline to the exclusive possession of the littoral owners up to the literal, moment-to-moment water's edge. This makes the legislative giveaway in *Illinois Central* seem small by comparison. How persuasive is it to say that the court of appeals was only doing what courts always do, interpreting the law, in this case an aspect of property law? That same argument usually carries sway when court decisions interpreting and curtailing property rights are assailed as unconstitutional takings of property. See, the discussion of the radical judicial revision of Hawaiian law, supra p. 384. When used to instantiate public rights, the public trust doctrine has a special position that makes acts validly taken in its furtherance virtually immune to takings claims. Almost all littoral or riparian land titles adjacent to the nation's major waterbodies are impressed with the trust, obviating any possibility of claiming a diminution of property rights.

2. What other uses of the foreshore, in addition to walking, are incidents of the public trust doctrine as announced by *Glass*? Fishing? Sunbathing? Beach volleyball and cookouts? The test that the Michigan Supreme Court majority applies to uphold the public's right to walk the beach links use of the foreshore to effectuation of the primary trust purposes of navigation, fishing, and bathing, all of which, to a degree, require pedestrian access.

3. Some of the details addressed by the *Glass* court, such as locating the ordinary high water mark, are clearly matters left to each state. Is some part of the trust obligation obligatory on the states as a matter of federal law? See Charles F. Wilkinson, The Headwaters of the Public Trust Doctrine: Some of the Traditional Doctrine, 19 Envt'l Law 425, 453–64 (1989).

MARKS v. WHITNEY

Supreme Court of California, 1971.
6 Cal.3d 251, 98 Cal.Rptr. 790, 491 P.2d 374.

McComb, Justice.

This is a quiet title action to settle a boundary line dispute caused by overlapping and defective surveys and to enjoin defendants (herein "Whitney") from asserting any claim or right in or to the property of plaintiff Marks. The unique feature here is that a part of Marks' property is tidelands acquired under an 1874 patent issued pursuant to the Act of March 28, 1868 (Stats.1867–1868, c. 415, p. 507); a small portion of these tidelands adjoins almost the entire shoreline of Whitney's upland property. Marks asserted complete ownership of the tidelands and the right to fill and develop them. Whitney opposed on the ground that this would cut off his rights as a littoral owner and as a member of the public in these tidelands and the navigable waters covering them. He requested a declaration in the decree that Marks' title was burdened with a public trust easement; also that it was burdened with certain prescriptive rights claimed by Whitney.

The trial court settled the common boundary line to the satisfaction of the parties. However, it held that Whitney had no "standing" to raise the public trust issue and it refused to make a finding as to whether the tidelands are so burdened. It did find in Whitney's favor as to a prescriptive easement across the tidelands to maintain and use an existing seven-foot wide wharf but with the limitation that "Such rights shall be subject to the right of Marks to use, to fill and to develop" the tidelands and the seven-foot wide easement area so long as the Whitney "rights of access and ingress and egress to and from the deep waters of the Bay shall be preserved" over this strip.

The appeal is on a limited record, namely, the Clerk's Transcript and designated exhibits, including certified copies of official recorded patent, maps, surveys, surveyor's notes, etc. This court may take judicial notice of these official documents. Only questions of law are presented.

[Figure 6–2 illustrates the general location of the parcels in relation to the bay shore.–Eds.] * * *

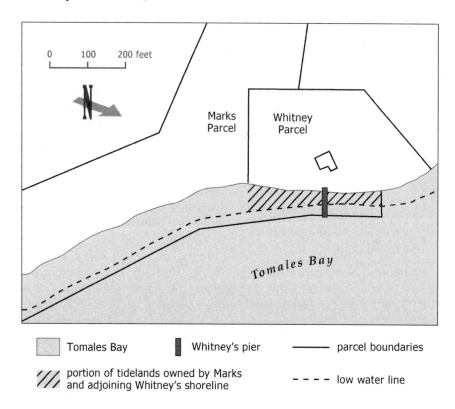

Figure 6–2

Appearing as amici curiae on the appeal are: the Attorney General, on behalf of the State Lands Commission, the Bay Area Conservation and Development Commission (BCDC) and as chief law enforcement officer of the state;[1] Sierra Club;[2] and Westbay Community Associates.[3]

1. California holds the state-wide public easement in tidelands and owns the submerged lands abutting the tidelands. The Legislature has vested in the State Lands Commission "All jurisdiction and authority remaining in the State as to tidelands and submerged lands as to which grants have been or may be made" and has given the commission exclusive administration and control of such lands. (Pub. Resources Code, section 6301.) BCDC is charged with specific duties concerning dredging and filling in San Francisco Bay (Gov. Code, sections 66600–66610). The Attorney General is presently involved in litigation involving lands in San Francisco Bay which were patented under the Act of March 28, 1868 and other statutes. The Attorney General

asks this court to declare the existence of the public easement and to recognize the right of Whitney as a member of the public and as a littoral owner to have the existence of the easement in these tidelands declared in this action.

2. Sierra Club expresses the concern of its 60,000 members in public questions raised herein. It asks this court not only to declare that these lands are subject to the public easement and that Whitney has standing to raise this issue but asks this court to declare the scope and extent of the public servitude in areas of navigable waters over tidelands.

3. Westbay Community Associates is also involved in San Francisco Bay Area

Questions: First. Are these tidelands subject to the public trust; if so, should the judgment so declare?

Yes. Regardless of the issue of Whitney's standing to raise this issue the court may take judicial notice of public trust burdens in quieting title to tidelands. This matter is of great public importance, particularly in view of population pressures, demands for recreational property, and the increasing development of seashore and waterfront property. A present declaration that the title of Marks in these tidelands is burdened with a public easement may avoid needless future litigation.[4]

Tidelands are properly those lands lying between the lines of mean high and low tide * * * covered and uncovered successively by the ebb and flow thereof. * * * The trial court found that the portion of Marks' lands here under consideration constitutes a part of the Tidelands of Tomales Bay, that at all times it has been, and now is, subject to the daily ebb and flow of the tides in Tomales Bay, that the ordinary high tides in the bay overflow and submerge this portion of his lands, and that Tomales Bay is a navigable body of water and an arm of the Pacific Ocean.

This land was patented as *tidelands* to Marks' predecessor in title. The patent of May 15, 1874, recites that it was issued by the Governor of California "by virtue of authority in me vested" pursuant to "statutes enacted from time to time" for the "Sale and Conveyance of the *Tide Lands belonging to the State by virtue of her sovereignty.*"[5] (Emphasis added.)

The governing statute was the act of March 28, 1868,[6] entitled "An Act to provide for the management and sale of the lands belonging to the

litigation. It asks this court to limit its consideration of early patents of land situated on Tomales Bay and, because of the pending litigation, not to consider patents to lands situated on San Francisco Bay.

4. There has been sufficient confusion already engendered in this lawsuit. After the first Court of Appeal opinion, 11 Cal. App.3d 1089, 90 Cal.Rptr. 220, herein the Los Angeles Metropolitan News, Sept. 16, 1969, headlined its news release thereon "Patent Title to Tidelands Unrestricted." See also, critique by Professor Joseph L. Sax, The Public Trust Doctrine in Natural Resource Law: Effective Judicial Intervention (1970) 68 Mich. L. Rev. 473, 530–531.

5. California acquired title to the navigable waterways and tidelands by virtue of her sovereignty when admitted to the Union in 1850. (Borax Consolidated Ltd. v. Los Angeles, 296 U.S. 10, 15–16 (1935).) This title is different in character from that which the state holds in lands intended for sale. (Illinois Cent. R.R. v. Illinois (1892)

146 U.S. 387, 452; Oakland v. Oakland Water–Front Co. (1897) 118 Cal. 160, 208–209, 50 P. 277.) The state holds tidelands in trust for public purposes, traditionally delineated in terms of navigation, commerce and fisheries. (City of Long Beach v. Mansell (supra) 3 Cal.3d 462, 482, 91 Cal.Rptr. 23, 476 P.2d 423.)

6. (Stats.1867–1868, p. 507.) The Act of March 28, 1868 is distinguishable from the Act of March 30, 1868 and the amendatory Act of April 1, 1870 (Stats.1867–1868, p. 716; Stats.1869–1870, p. 541.) The latter were enacted in aid of navigation and for the purpose of providing for the improvement of designated parts of San Francisco Bay and they operated to free such tidelands from the public trust. (Knudson v. Kearney (1915) 171 Cal. 250, 252–253, 152 P. 541; Alameda Conservation Ass'n v. City of Alameda (1968) 264 Cal.App.2d 284, 287, 70 Cal.Rptr. 264.) Some of the cases upholding the authority of the state to make an absolute disposition of tidelands consistent

State." By its terms it repealed all other laws relating to the sale of swamp and overflowed, salt-marsh and tidelands. These laws, including the Act of March 28, 1868, were * * * explicitly and expansively considered by this court entirely separate from the restrictions contained in Article 15, sections two and three, of the State Constitution (enacted in 1879). * * * Prior to the issuance of this patent it was held that a patent to tidelands conveyed no title * * * or a voidable title. * * * It was not until 1913 that this court decided in People v. California Fish Co., *supra,* 166 Cal. 576, 596, 138 P. 79, 87, that "The only practicable theory is to hold that all tideland is included, but that the public right was not intended to be divested or affected by a sale of tidelands under these general laws relating alike both to swamp land and tidelands. Our opinion is that * * * the buyer of land under these statutes receives the title to the soil, the *jus privatum,* subject to the public right of navigation, and in subordination to the right of the state to take possession and use and improve it for that purpose, as it may deem necessary. In this way the public right will be preserved, and the private right of the purchaser will be given as full effect as the public interests will permit."

The tidelands embraced in these statutes extend from the Oregon line to Mexico and include the shores of bays and navigable streams as far up as tide water goes and until it meets the lands made swampy by the overflow and seepage of fresh water streams. * * * No issue is here presented of swamp or overflowed lands. These are true tidelands within the meaning of these statutes, the patent of May 15, 1874, and the public trust doctrine. They are, therefore, subject to a reserved easement in the state for trust purposes.

Public trust easements are traditionally defined in terms of navigation, commerce and fisheries. They have been held to include the right to fish, hunt, bathe, swim, to use for boating and general recreation purposes the navigable waters of the state, and to use the bottom of the navigable waters for anchoring, standing, or other purposes. * * * The public has the same rights in and to tidelands.

The public uses to which tidelands are subject are sufficiently flexible to encompass changing public needs. In administering the trust the state is not burdened with an outmoded classification favoring one mode of utilization over another. * * * There is a growing public recognition that one of the most important public uses of the tidelands— a use encompassed within the tidelands trust—is the preservation of those lands in their natural state, so that they may serve as ecological units for scientific study, as open space, and as environments which provide food and habitat for birds and marine life, and which favorably affect the scenery and climate of the area. It is not necessary to here define precisely all the public uses which encumber tidelands.

with the public trust are reviewed in People v. California Fish Co. (1913) 166 Cal. 576, 585–586, 138 P. 79, and City of Long Beach v. Mansell, supra, 3 Cal.3d 462, 483–486, 91 Cal.Rptr. 23, 476 P.2d 423.

"[T]he state in its proper administration of the trust may find it necessary or advisable to cut off certain tidelands from water access and render them useless for trust purposes. In such a case the state through the Legislature may find and determine that such lands are no longer useful for trust purposes and free them from the trust. When tidelands have been so freed from the trust—and if they are not subject to the constitutional prohibition forbidding alienation—they may be irrevocably conveyed into absolute private ownership." (City of Long Beach v. Mansell, supra, 3 Cal.3d 462, 482, 91 Cal.Rptr. 23, 37, 476 P.2d 423, 437.)

The power of the state to control, regulate and utilize its navigable waterways and the lands lying beneath them, when acting within the terms of the trust, is absolute * * * except as limited by the paramount supervisory power of the federal government over navigable waters. * * * We are not here presented with any action by the state or the federal government modifying, terminating, altering or relinquishing the *jus publicum* in these tidelands or in the navigable waters covering them. Neither sovereignty is a party to this action. This court takes judicial notice, however, that there has been no official act of either sovereignty to modify or extinguish the public trust servitude upon Marks' tidelands. The State Attorney General, as *amicus curiae,* has advised this court that no such action or determination has been made by the state.

We are confronted with the issue, however, whether the trial court may restrain or bar a private party, namely, Whitney, "from claiming or asserting any estate, right, title, interest in or claim or lien upon" the tidelands quieted in Marks. The injunction so made, without any limitation expressing the public servitude, is broad enough to prohibit Whitney from asserting or in any way exercising public trust uses in these tidelands and the navigable waters covering them in his capacity as a member of the public. This is beyond the jurisdiction of the court. It is within the province of the trier of fact to determine whether any particular use made or asserted by Whitney in or over these tidelands would constitute an infringement either upon the *jus privatum* of Marks or upon the *jus publicum* of the people. It is also within the province of the trier of fact to determine whether any particular use to which Marks wishes to devote his tidelands constitutes an unlawful infringement upon the *jus publicum* therein. It is a political question, within the wisdom and power of the Legislature, acting within the scope of its duties as trustee, to determine whether public trust uses should be modified or extinguished * * * and to take the necessary steps to free them from such burden. In the absence of state or federal action the court may not bar members of the public from lawfully asserting or exercising public trust rights on this privately owned tidelands.

There is absolutely no merit in Marks' contention that as the owner of the *jus privatum* under this patent he may fill and develop his property, whether for navigational purposes or not; nor in his contention that his past and present plan for development of these tidelands as a marina have caused the extinguishment of the public easement. Reclamation with or without prior authorization from the state does not *ipso facto* terminate the public trust nor render the issue moot. * * *

A proper judgment for a patentee of tidelands was determined by this court in People v. California Fish Co., supra, 166 Cal. at pp. 598–599, 138 P. at p. 88, to be that he owns "the soil, subject to the easement of the public for the public uses of navigation and commerce, and to the right of the state, as administrator and controller of these public uses and the public trust therefor, to enter upon and possess the same for the preservation and advancement of the public uses, and to make such changes and improvements as may be deemed advisable for those purposes."

Second: Does Whitney have "standing" to request the court to recognize and declare the public trust easement on Marks' tidelands?

Yes. The relief sought by Marks resulted in taking away from Whitney rights to which he is entitled as a member of the general public. It is immaterial that Marks asserted he was not seeking to enjoin the public. The decree as rendered does enjoin a member of the public.

Members of the public have been permitted *to bring* an action to enforce a public right to use a beach access route * * * *to bring* an action to quiet title to private and public easements in a public beach * * * and *to bring* an action to restrain improper filling of a bay and secure a general declaration of the rights of the people to the waterways and wildlife areas of the bay * * *. Members of the public have been allowed *to defend* a quiet title action by asserting the right to use a public right of way through private property * * *. They have been allowed to assert the public trust easement for hunting, fishing and navigation in privately owned tidelands *as a defense* in an action to enjoin such use * * * and to navigate on shallow navigable waters in small boats * * *.

Whitney had standing to raise this issue. The court could have raised this issue on its own. "It is now well settled that the court may finally determine as between the parties in a quiet title action all of the conflicting claims regarding any estate or interest in the property." (Hendershott v. Shipman (1951) 37 Cal.2d 190, 194, 231 P.2d 481, 483.) Where the interest concerned is one that, as here, constitutes a public burden upon land to which title is quieted, and affects the defendant as a member of the public, that servitude should be explicitly declared.

Notes and Questions

1. Marks v. Whitney is most notable for its expansion of the public trust "to encompass changing public needs," a position that is commending itself to other states. E.g., Orion Corp. v. State, 109 Wash.2d 621, 747 P.2d 1062, 1073 (1987); State Dept. of Envtl. Protection v. Jersey Central Power & Light Co., 125 N.J.Super. 97, 101–02, 308 A.2d 671, 673 (1973), rev'd on other grounds, 69 N.J. 102, 351 A.2d 337 (1976). At the opposite end of the spectrum is the Supreme Judicial Court of Maine which has held that the public trust easement in tidelands does not extend beyond the uses reserved

in the Colonial Ordinance of 1641–7, that is, fishing, fowling and navigation. Bell v. Town of Wells, 557 A.2d 168 (Me. 1989). The decision is sharply criticized for failing to understand the Colonial Ordinance. See Orlando Delogu, Intellectual Indifference—Intellectual Dishonesty: The Colonial Ordinance, The Equal Footing Doctrine and the Maine Law Court, 42 Maine L. Rev. 43 (1990).

2. There is a considerable literature on the public trust doctrine. An exhaustive article, citing many other studies, is Richard Lazarus, Changing Conceptions of Property and Sovereignty in Natural Resources: Questioning the Public Trust Doctrine, 71 Iowa L. Rev. 631 (1986). A useful historic study is Molly Selvin, The Public Trust Doctrine in American Law and Economic Policy, 1789–1920, at 1980 Wis. L. Rev. 1403.

3. California is a major source of public trust litigation. Among the important cases following *Marks* and preceding the crucial *National Audubon* case, infra p. 610, are:

- State v. Superior Court (Lyon), 29 Cal.3d 210, 172 Cal.Rptr. 696, 625 P.2d 239 (1981), and State v. Superior Court (Fogerty), 29 Cal.3d 240, 172 Cal.Rptr. 713, 625 P.2d 256 (1981) (trust extends to non-tidal navigable lakes including portions of lake maintained artificially by a federal dam).

- City of Berkeley v. Superior Court, 26 Cal.3d 515, 162 Cal.Rptr. 327, 606 P.2d 362 (1980) (19th century tideland grant in San Francisco Bay did not convey title free of the trust, but filled lands under that specific grant are now free of the trust if they are not subject to tidal action). See City of Alameda v. Todd Shipyards Corp., 632 F.Supp. 333 (N.D. Cal. 1986) (filling does not automatically free lands of the trust).

4. A variant of the issue raised in the *City of Berkeley* case has been much litigated in the East. Submerged lands were granted many years ago for commerce-related uses, such as wharves. Now the wharves are no longer needed, and the owners want to redevelop the land for ordinary private uses, such as residential high-rise apartments. The question is whether the wharf grantees obtained a fee title, or a title burdened by some public trust obligation. See Boston Waterfront Dev. Corp. v. Commonwealth, 378 Mass. 629, 393 N.E.2d 356 (1979); Opinion of the Justices, 383 Mass. 895, 424 N.E.2d 1092 (1981); State v. Central Vermont Ry., 153 Vt. 337, 571 A.2d 1128 (1989); Opinion of the Justices, 437 A.2d 597 (Me. 1981).

5. As to whether the public trust implies a continuing duty of state supervision, the California Supreme Court held that while trust lands could be leased for oil and gas development, "[t]he state may at any time remove structures from the ocean erected by its citizens, even though they have been erected with its license or consent, if it subsequently determines them to be purprestures or finds that they substantially interfere with navigation or commerce." Boone v. Kingsbury, 206 Cal. 148, 192–93, 273 P. 797, 816 (1928), appeal dismissed, 280 U.S. 517 (1929).

6. The public trust generally allows members of the public to use the shore up to the ordinary high water mark, which is usually thought of as the wet beach. This is true even on non-tidal waters such as the Great Lakes

shoreline, where the measure is "the point on the bank or shore up to which the presence and action of the water is so continuous as to leave a distinct mark." Glass v. Goeckel (supra p. 592).

7. In New Jersey, the reach of the public trust for recreational use of the beach has been broadly interpreted. In Borough of Neptune City v. Borough of Avon–By–The–Sea, 61 N.J. 296, 294 A.2d 47 (1972), the court held that the trust applied to a municipally-owned dry sand beach immediately landward of the high water mark. In Matthews v. Bay Head Improvement Ass'n, 95 N.J. 306, 471 A.2d 355 (1984), it extended this holding to a dry sand beach owned by a non-profit corporation whose primary functions were municipal ones such as cleaning, policing and making bathing beaches safe in the borough. Then in Raleigh Ave. Beach Assn. v. Atlantis Beach Club, Inc., 185 N.J. 40, 879 A.2d 112 (2005) the Court held that the upland sands of a private beach club must be made available to the public for access, at a reasonable fee, where there was access allowed prior to the establishment of the club, there was a lack of publicly owned beaches in the area, and there was demand for access.This is the farthest any state has gone to date.

Conversely, a New Hampshire court has prohibited legislative redefinition of the location of the high water mark (higher up on the beach) as a taking of private property. Purdie v. Attorney General, 732 A.2d 442 (N.H. 1999); see also Bell v. Town of Wells, 557 A.2d 168 (Me. 1989); Opinion of the Justices, 365 Mass. 681, 313 N.E.2d 561 (1974).

8. For other ways in which public rights in beaches landward of the high water mark have been attained see, e.g., Gion v. Santa Cruz (Gion–Dietz), 2 Cal.3d 29, 84 Cal.Rptr. 162, 465 P.2d 50 (1970) (involuntary dedication to the public)[7]; State ex rel. Thornton v. Hay, 254 Or. 584, 462 P.2d 671 (1969) (customary use). Under Hawaiian customary law, the seaward boundary of an upland private parcel ends at the vegetation line, so there is public ownership of the dry sand beach. Application of Ashford, 50 Hawaii 314, 440 P.2d 76 (1968). Cf. Sotomura v. Hawaii County, supra p. 391. Whatever the public's right along the shorefront of the beach, the state may not demand the grant of a public easement across the beach in exchange for permitting the owners of such land to develop their property unless there is some nexus between the impact of the development and the easement sought to be exacted. Nollan v. California Coastal Comm'n, 483 U.S. 825 (1987); Dolan v. City of Tigard, 512 U.S. 374 (1994).

9. Among the crucial questions in public trust cases is whether a facility on trust lands is for a public rather than a private purpose, whether it substantially interferes with public use of the remaining lands and waters, and whether it needs to be sited at the water's edge. All these issues were posed in Kootenai Environmental Alliance v. Panhandle Yacht Club, 105 Idaho 622, 671 P.2d 1085 (1983), where the Court permitted trust land to be leased to a private yacht club for docking facilities on a very small part of the very large Lake Coeur d'Alene. For cases holding invalid a state statute

---

7. Gion was largely abrogated for the future by the amendment of Civil Code §§ 1009, 813.

expressly granting trust land to a private company because it was for a private, rather than a public, purpose, see People ex rel. Scott v. Chicago Park Dist., 66 Ill.2d 65, 4 Ill.Dec. 660, 360 N.E.2d 773 (1976); Lake Michigan Federation v. U.S. Army Corps of Engineers, 742 F.Supp. 441 (N.D. Ill. 1990).

10.   Is there a federal public trust? Imagine a situation where there are offshore oil rigs in federal ocean waters beyond state boundaries. State trust law does not apply. If there is no federal public trust, presumably there would be nothing extending the duty of continuing supervision described in Boone v. Kingsbury, Note 5 supra, to federal waters. This question seems never to have been considered by the federal courts. Compare with *Boone* the decision in Union Oil Co. v. Morton, 512 F.2d 743 (9th Cir. 1975), holding that shutting down an existing offshore oil operation was an uncompensated taking of property. In District of Columbia v. Air Florida, Inc., 750 F.2d 1077 (D.C. Cir. 1984), the court said: "In this country the public trust doctrine has developed almost exclusively as a matter of state law. * * * Neither the Supreme Court nor the federal courts of appeals have expressly decided whether public trust duties apply to the United States. There appear to be only two district court cases which explicitly hold that this common-law rule applies to the federal government. * * * In Re Steuart Transportation Co., [495 F.Supp. 38 (E.D. Va. 1980).] * * * In United States v. 1.58 Acres of Land, [523 F.Supp. 120 (D. Mass. 1981)], the court held that the United States could condemn state public trust property and hold such property in fee simple, but noted in dictum that the federal government is as restricted as are states in its ability to abdicate its sovereign responsibilities for public trust land to private individuals." The court declined to determine whether there was a federal public trust in the Potomac River.

Problem

Consider this twist on claims of public access to the beach. Plaintiffs are owners of oceanfront property in the town of Oak Island, North Carolina. They have previously had access to the ocean from their homes along the entire length of their shoreline. But recently the U.S. Corps of Engineers completed a beach renourishment project in order to restore sea turtle nesting areas that had been damaged by erosion. The project added sand at the water's edge, and thereby moved the high water mark seaward of the plaintiffs' properties. Under North Carolina law such additions vest the new land in the state. The town then placed a fence along the beach paralleling the landward terminus of the new sand area (where the high water mark had previously been located), and—to protect the turtles—access was allowed only at certain designated public access points. Plaintiffs claimed their property right of access to the ocean had been violated. Do they prevail? Slavin v. Town of Oak Island, 160 N.C.App. 57, 584 S.E.2d 100 (2003), appeal dismissed, 357 N.C. 659, 590 S.E.2d 271 (2003). Incidentally, according to a July 23, 2003 AP press report of another case from the oceanfront town of Manteo in the same state, " * * *the dry sand beach traditionally has been public domain in North Carolina and accessible to anyone."

F.   THE NEW PUBLIC RIGHTS AND THE OLD PRIVATE RIGHTS: ON THE CUTTING EDGE

JOSEPH L. SAX, THE LIMITS OF PRIVATE RIGHTS IN PUBLIC WATERS

19 Envtl. L. 473, 479–87 (1989).

In *Georgia v. Tennessee Copper Co.,*[14] Justice Holmes said, "[T]he State has an interest independent of and behind the titles of its citizens, in all the earth and air within its domain. It has the last word as to whether its mountains shall be stripped of their forests and its inhabitants shall breathe pure air."[15] In that 1907 case, which involved land, Justice Holmes left open the question whether the exercise of such interest would require compensation.[16] A year later, however, Justice Holmes sustained the right of New Jersey to prohibit the diversion of water for export from the Passaic River against a water company's claimed property right. This time the Justice faced the property question directly. The language he used in that case, *Hudson County Water Co. v. McCarter,*[17] seems almost eerily prescient of the issues posed by * * * contemporary demands for renewed and retained in-stream flows:

> [F]ew public interests are more obvious, indisputable and independent of particular theory than the interest of the public of a State to maintain rivers that are wholly within it substantially undiminished, except by such drafts upon them as the guardian of the public welfare may permit for the purpose of turning them to a more perfect use. This public interest is omnipresent wherever there is a State, and grows more pressing as population grows. It is fundamental, and we are of opinion that the private property of riparian proprietors cannot be supposed to have deeper roots.
>
> * * * The private right to appropriate is subject not only to the rights of lower owners but to the initial limitation that it may not substantially diminish one of the great foundations of public welfare and health.[18]

This may be the most important statement the Court has ever made about the constitutional status of water rights. The Court has rarely addressed in explicit terms the limits on the acquisition of private

---

14.   206 U.S. 230 (1907).

15.   Id. at 237.

16.   For a contemporary example, see Hodel v. Virginia Surface Mining & Reclamation Ass'n, 452 U.S. 264 (1981).

17.   209 U.S. 349 (1908).

18.   Id. at 356.

property rights in state water resources. Justice Holmes was not only a great jurist, but one who took property rights very seriously. * * * [I]t was * * * he who spoke of "the petty larceny of the police power."[20] Thus, coming from him, the statement that "the private property of riparian proprietors cannot be supposed to have deeper roots" than the right of the state to protect its rivers undiminished for public use, stands as a fundamental building block of property jurisprudence.[21]

By 1931, in *New Jersey v. New York,*[22] Justice Holmes again encountered the property question in a water rights case. New York's demands on the Delaware River, it was asserted, would violate the riparian rights of landowners in New Jersey. By ordinary standards of water law, the claim of interference with property rights was potent, but Justice Holmes brushed it aside with language reminiscent of what he had said in the *Georgia* case: "A river is * * * a necessity of life that must be rationed among those who have power over it. * * * [Notwithstanding riparian law] New Jersey [could not] be permitted to require New York to give up its power altogether in order that the River might come down to it undiminished."[23] These cases are entirely congruent with what the Court said in the now well-known language of *Illinois Central*[24] when it observed as matter of trust obligation that "the general control of the State over lands under the navigable waters of an entire harbor or bay, or of a sea or lake" cannot be abdicated, and "cannot be relinquished by a transfer of the property."[25] * * *

20. 1 Holmes–Laski Letters 457 (M. Howe ed. 1953).

21. Is this principle undermined by the Supreme Court's decision in Summa Corp. v. California ex rel. State Lands Comm'n, 466 U.S. 198 (1984), which suggests that a property right *can* be acquired against the state, at least in the land beneath navigable waters? I think not. The case need not be read as asserting more than a process-fairness principle, requiring the state to come in and assert its public trust claim when there is what amounts to a general adjudication of a property right.

Limits on the possibilities of private ownership were reaffirmed by the Supreme Court recently in United States v. Cherokee Nation, 480 U.S. 700 (1987). Though under "very peculiar circumstances * * * the Indians were promised virtually complete sovereignty over their * * * lands," and were held—despite the strong contrary presumption—to have obtained title to the land beneath the navigable waters of their reservation. Nonetheless, the Court held, that did not turn the river into a "private stream" or "a private waterway belonging exclusively" to the Cherokees. The United States was held not to have surrendered its public navigation servitude in the waters—a waiv-

er of sovereign authority, the surrender of which, the Court held, will never be implied in recognition of the "unique position [of] the Government in connection with navigable waters." Id. at 704.

A rather different view, though expressed only as dictum, appears in Justice Stone's opinion in Fox River Paper Co. v. Railroad Comm'n, 274 U.S. 651 (1927): "If the state chooses to resign to the riparian proprietor sovereign rights over navigable rivers which it acquired upon assuming statehood, it is not for others to raise objections." Id. at 655 (citing Barney v. Keokuk, 94 U.S. 324, 338 (1876)). The *Fox River* Court found that the state had not surrendered to the riparian owner the rights the riparian claimed, and it made the above statement in the context of observing that state law controlled the question of what property the owner had, and therefore what property could be taken. Nonetheless, the tone of Justice Stone's statement is at odds with the views expressed by Justice Holmes.

22. 283 U.S. 336 (1931).

23. Id. at 342.

24. Illinois Cent. R.R. v. Illinois, 146 U.S. 387 (1892).

25. Id. at 452–53.

Questions

Does Justice Holmes answer the concerns expressed by the dissent in *McIlroy,* supra p. 554, and by Justice Levin in *Bott,* supra p. 564? Can Holmes' language be dismissed as a mere rhetorical flourish?

1. THE PUBLIC TRUST LIMIT ON APPROPRIATION

We have already seen several illustrations of changing values: the *East Bay M.U.D.* case, supra p. 191, and the emergent law of instream appropriations for ecosystem protection, supra p. 141. You are now about to encounter this perspective in its newest, and most dramatic form. The Supreme Court of California has held that the public trust limits appropriations where diversions would impair public rights in navigable waters.

a. *The Mono Lake Case*

Sometimes competing and incompatible uses of water must be accommodated. Homeowners around a lake want the level to be maintained for recreational use, while one littoral owner may wish to extract water for irrigation. The problem of incompatible instream and off-stream uses is presented in a modern environmental context in the case excerpted below, where for the first time the public trust doctrine is posed against demands of appropriators who want to remove water from the tributaries that feed the lake in order to meet municipal water supply needs.

Mark Twain described Mono Lake, the subject of the next case, in his 1871 journal Roughing It.

> Mono Lake lies in a lifeless, treeless, hideous desert, eight thousand feet above the level of the sea. * * * This solemn, silent, sailless sea—this lonely tenant of the loneliest spot on earth—is little graced with the picturesque. It is an unpretending expanse of grayish water, about a hundred miles in circumference, with two islands in its center, mere upheavals of rent and scorched and blistered lava. * * * There are no fish in Mono Lake—no frogs, no snakes, no polliwogs—nothing, in fact, that goes to make life desirable. * * * Mono Lake is a hundred miles in a straight line from the ocean—and between it and the ocean are one or two ranges of mountains—yet thousands of sea-gulls go there every season to lay their eggs and rear their young. One would as soon expect to find sea-gulls in Kansas. * * * Half a dozen little mountain brooks flow into Mono Lake, but *not a stream of any kind flows out of it.* It neither rises nor falls, apparently, and what it does with its surplus water is a dark and bloody mystery.

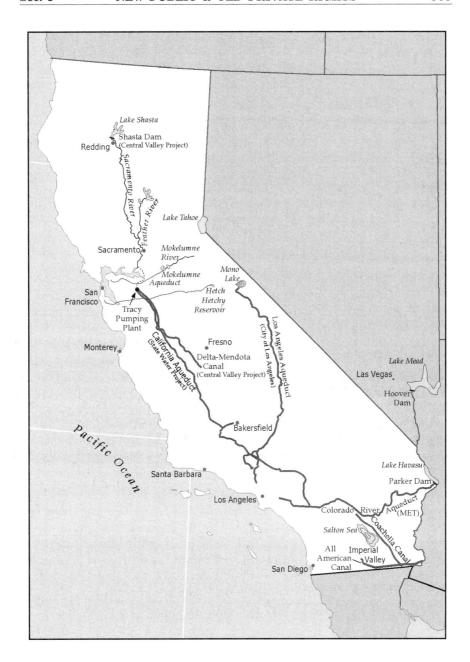

Figure 6–3

Los Angeles Aqueduct & Other Importing Systems

NATIONAL AUDUBON SOCIETY
v. SUPERIOR COURT

Supreme Court of California, 1983.
33 Cal.3d 419, 189 Cal.Rptr. 346, 658 P.2d 709.

BROUSSARD, JUSTICE.

Mono Lake, the second largest lake in California, sits at the base of the Sierra Nevada escarpment near the eastern entrance to Yosemite National Park. The lake is saline; it contains no fish but supports a large population of brine shrimp which feed vast numbers of nesting and migratory birds. Islands in the lake protect a large breeding colony of California gulls, and the lake itself serves as a haven on the migration route for thousands of Northern Phalarope, Wilson's Phalarope, and Eared Grebe. Towers and spires of tufa on the north and south shores are matters of geological interest and a tourist attraction.

Although Mono Lake receives some water from rain and snow on the lake surface, historically most of its supply came from snowmelt in the Sierra Nevada. Five freshwater streams—Mill, Lee Vining, Walker, Parker and Rush Creeks—arise near the crest of the range and carry the annual runoff to the west shore of the lake. In 1940, however, the Division of Water Resources, the predecessor to the present California Water Resources Board, granted the Department of Water and Power of the City of Los Angeles (hereafter DWP) a permit to appropriate virtually the entire flow of four of the five streams flowing into the lake. DWP promptly constructed facilities to divert about half the flow of these streams into DWP's Owens Valley aqueduct. In 1970 DWP completed a second diversion tunnel, and since that time has taken virtually the entire flow of these streams.

As a result of these diversions, the level of the lake has dropped; the surface area has diminished by one-third; one of the two principal islands in the lake has become a peninsula, exposing the gull rookery there to coyotes and other predators and causing the gulls to abandon the former island. The ultimate effect of continued diversions is a matter of intense dispute, but there seems little doubt that both the scenic beauty and the ecological values of Mono Lake are imperiled.

Plaintiffs filed suit in superior court to enjoin the DWP diversions on the theory that the shores, bed and waters of Mono Lake are protected by a public trust. Plaintiffs' suit was transferred to the federal district court, which requested that the state courts determine the relationship between the public trust doctrine and the water rights system. * * *

This case brings together for the first time two systems of legal thought: the appropriative water rights system which since the days of the gold rush has dominated California water law, and the public trust doctrine which, after evolving as a shield for the protection of tidelands, now extends its protective scope to navigable lakes. Ever since we first recognized that the public trust protects environmental and recreational values (Marks v. Whitney (1971) 6 Cal. 3d 251, 98 Cal. Rptr. 790, 491 P.2d 374), the two systems of legal thought have been on a collision course. (Johnson, Public Trust Protection for Stream Flows and Lake Levels (1980) 14 U.C. Davis L. Rev. 233.) They meet in a unique and dramatic setting which highlights the clash of values. Mono Lake is a scenic and ecological treasure of national significance, imperiled by continued diversions of water; yet, the need of Los Angeles for water is apparent, its reliance on rights granted by the board evident, the cost of curtailing diversions substantial.

Attempting to integrate the teachings and values of both the public trust and the appropriative water rights system, we have arrived at certain conclusions which we briefly summarize here. In our opinion, the core of the public trust doctrine is the state's authority as sovereign to exercise a continuous supervision and control over the navigable waters of the state and the lands underlying those waters. This authority applies to the waters tributary to Mono Lake and bars DWP or any other party from claiming a vested right to divert waters once it becomes clear that such diversions harm the interests protected by the public trust. The corollary rule which evolved in tideland and lakeshore cases barring conveyance of rights free of the trust except to serve trust purposes cannot, however, apply without modification to flowing waters. The prosperity and habitability of much of this state requires the diversion of great quantities of water from its streams for purposes unconnected to any navigation, commerce, fishing, recreation, or ecological use relating to the source stream. The state must have the power to grant nonvested usufructuary rights to appropriate water even if diversions harm public trust uses. Approval of such diversion without considering public trust values, however, may result in needless destruction of those values. Accordingly, we believe that before state courts and agencies approve water diversions they should consider the effect of such diversions upon interests protected by the public trust, and attempt, so far as feasible, to avoid or minimize any harm to those interests.

The water rights enjoyed by DWP were granted, the diversion was commenced, and has continued to the present without any consideration of the impact upon the public trust. An objective study and reconsideration of the water rights in the Mono Basin is long overdue. The water law of California—which we conceive to be an integration including both the public trust doctrine and the board-administered appropriative rights system—permits such a reconsideration; the values underlying that integration require it. * * *

1. BACKGROUND AND HISTORY OF THE MONO LAKE LITIGATION

DWP supplies water to the City of Los Angeles. Early in this century, it became clear that the city's anticipated needs would exceed the water available from local sources, and so in 1913 the city constructed an aqueduct to carry water from the Owens River 233 miles over the Antelope–Mojave plateau into the coastal plain and thirsty city.

The city's attempt to acquire rights to water needed by local farmers met with fierce, and at times violent, opposition. (See generally County of Inyo v. Public Utilities Com. (1980) 26 Cal. 3d 154, 156–157, 161 Cal. Rptr. 172, 604 P.2d 566; Kahrl, Water and Power: The Conflict Over Los Angeles' Water Supply in the Owens Valley (1982).) But when the "Owens Valley War" was over, virtually all the waters of the Owens River and its tributaries flowed south to Los Angeles. Owens Lake was transformed into an alkali flat.

The city's rapid expansion soon strained this new supply, too, and prompted a search for water from other regions. The Mono Basin was a predictable object of this extension, since it lay within 50 miles of the natural origin of Owens River, and thus could easily be integrated into the existing aqueduct system.

After purchasing the riparian rights incident to Lee Vining, Walker, Parker and Rush Creeks, as well as the riparian rights pertaining to Mono Lake,[4] the city applied to the Water Board in 1940 for permits to appropriate the waters of the four tributaries. At hearings before the board, various interested individuals protested that the city's proposed appropriations would lower the surface level of Mono Lake and thereby impair its commercial, recreational and scenic uses.

The board's primary authority to reject that application lay in a 1921 amendment to the Water Commission Act of 1913, which authorized the board to reject an application "when in its judgment the proposed appropriation would not best conserve the public interest." (Stats. 1921, ch. 329, § 1, p. 443, now codified as Wat. Code, § 1255.)[5] The 1921 enactment, however, also "declared to be the established policy of this state that the use of water for domestic purposes is the highest use of water" (id., now codified as Wat. Code, § 1254), and directed the Water Board to be guided by this declaration of policy. Since DWP sought water for domestic use, the board concluded that it had to grant the application notwithstanding the harm to public trust uses of Mono Lake.

The board's decision states that "[i]t is indeed unfortunate that the City's proposed development will result in decreasing the aesthetic advantages of Mono Basin but there is apparently nothing that this office can do to prevent it. The use to which the City proposes to put the water under its Applications * * * is defined by the Water Commission Act as the highest to which water may be applied and to make available unappropriated water for this use the City has, by the condemnation proceedings described above, acquired the littoral and riparian rights on

---

4. Between 1920 and 1934, the city purchased lands riparian to creeks feeding Mono Lake and riparian rights incident to such lands. In 1934, the city brought an eminent domain proceeding for condemnation of the rights of Mono Lake landowners. (City of Los Angeles v. Aitken (1935) 10 Cal. App. 2d 460, 52 P.2d 585.)

5. In theory, the board could have rejected the city's application on the ground that the waters of the streams were already being put to beneficial use or that the DWP proposed an unreasonable use of water in violation of article X, section 2 of the California Constitution. It does not appear that the board considered either proposition.

Mono Lake and its tributaries south of Mill Creek. This office therefore has no alternative but to dismiss all protests based upon the possible lowering of the water level in Mono Lake and the effect that the diversion of water from these streams may have upon the aesthetic and recreational value of the Basin." * * *

The Scope of the Public Trust

Early English decisions generally assumed the public trust was limited to tidal waters and the lands exposed and covered by the daily tides; many American decisions, including the leading California cases, also concern tidelands. It is, however, well settled in the United States generally and in California that the public trust is not limited by the reach of the tides, but encompasses all navigable lakes and streams.

* * * Mono Lake is, as we have said, a navigable waterway. The beds, shores and waters of the lake are without question protected by the public trust. The streams diverted by DWP, however, are not themselves navigable. Accordingly, we must address in this case a question not discussed in any recent public trust case—whether the public trust limits conduct affecting nonnavigable tributaries to navigable waterways. * * * [Eds—The Court's discussion of this issue is omitted] * * * We conclude that the public trust doctrine, as recognized and developed in California decisions, protects navigable waters from harm caused by diversion of nonnavigable tributaries.[19]

Duties and Powers of the State as Trustee

* * * [P]arties acquiring rights in trust property generally hold those rights subject to the trust, and can assert no vested right to use those rights in a manner harmful to the trust. * * *

[I]n our recent decision in City of Berkeley v. Superior Court, 26 Cal. 3d 515, 162 Cal. Rptr. 327, 606 P.2d 362, we considered whether deeds executed by the Board of Tidelands Commissioners pursuant to an 1870 act conferred title free of the trust. Applying the principles of earlier decisions, we held that the grantees' title was subject to the trust, both because the Legislature had not made clear its intention to authorize a conveyance free of the trust and because the 1870 act and the conveyances under it were not intended to further trust purposes.

Once again we rejected the claim that establishment of the public trust constituted a taking of property for which compensation was required: "We do not divest anyone of title to property; the consequence of our decision will be only that some landowners whose predecessors in interest acquired property under the 1870 act will * * * hold it subject to the public trust."[22]

---

19. In view of the conclusion stated in the text, we need not consider the question whether the public trust extends for some purposes—such as protection of fishing, environmental values, and recreation interests—to nonnavigable streams. For discus-

sion of this subject, see Walston, The Public Trust Doctrine in the Water Rights Context: The Wrong Environmental Remedy (1982) 22 Santa Clara L. Rev. 63, 85.

22. We noted, however, that "any improvements made on such lands could not

In summary, the foregoing cases amply demonstrate the continuing power of the state as administrator of the public trust, a power which extends to the revocation of previously granted rights or to the enforcement of the trust against lands long thought free of the trust. Except for those rare instances in which a grantee may acquire a right to use former trust property free of trust restrictions, the grantee holds subject to the trust, and while he may assert a vested right to the servient estate (the right of use subject to the trust) and to any improvements he erects, he can claim no vested right to bar recognition of the trust or state action to carry out its purposes. Since the public trust doctrine does not prevent the state from choosing between trust uses, the Attorney General of California, seeking to maximize state power under the trust, argues for a broad concept of trust uses. In his view, "trust uses" encompass all public uses, so that in practical effect the doctrine would impose no restrictions on the state's ability to allocate trust property. We know of no authority which supports this view of the public trust. * * * Most decisions and commentators assume that "trust uses" relate to uses and activities in the vicinity of the lake, stream, or tidal reach at issue. The tideland cases make this point clear; after City of Berkeley v. Superior Court, no one could contend that the state could grant tidelands free of the trust merely because the grant served some public purpose, such as increasing tax revenues, or because the grantee might put the property to a commercial use.

Thus, the public trust is more than an affirmation of state power to use public property for public purposes. It is an affirmation of the duty of the state to protect the people's common heritage of streams, lakes, marshlands and tidelands, surrendering that right of protection only in rare cases when the abandonment of that right is consistent with the purposes of the trust. * * *

4. THE RELATIONSHIP BETWEEN THE PUBLIC TRUST DOCTRINE AND THE CALIFORNIA WATER RIGHTS SYSTEM

As we have seen, the public trust doctrine and the appropriate water rights system administered by the Water Board developed independently of each other. Each developed comprehensive rules and principles which, if applied to the full extent of their scope, would occupy the field of allocation of stream waters to the exclusion of any competing system of legal thought. Plaintiffs, for example, argue that the public trust is antecedent to and thus limits all appropriative water rights, an argument which implies that most appropriative water rights in California were acquired and are presently being used unlawfully. Defendant DWP,

be appropriated by the state without compensation." (Pp. 533–534, 162 Cal. Rptr. 327, 606 P.2d 362, citing Illinois Central R. Co. v. Illinois, supra, 146 U.S. 387, 455.) In State of California v. Superior Court (Fogerty), supra, 29 Cal. 3d 240, 249, 172 Cal. Rptr. 713, 625 P.2d 256, we stated that owners of shoreline property in Lake Tahoe would be entitled to compensation if enforcement of the public trust required them to remove improvements. By implication, however, the determination that the property was subject to the trust, despite its implication as to future uses and improvements, was not considered a taking requiring compensation.

on the other hand, argues that the public trust doctrine as to stream waters has been "subsumed" into the appropriative water rights system and, absorbed by that body of law, quietly disappeared; according to DWP, the recipient of a board license enjoys a vested right in perpetuity to take water without concern for the consequences to the trust.

We are unable to accept either position. In our opinion, both the public trust doctrine and the water rights system embody important precepts which make the law more responsive to the diverse needs and interests involved in the planning and allocation of water resources. To embrace one system of thought and reject the other would lead to an unbalanced structure, one which would either decry as a breach of trust appropriations essential to the economic development of this state, or deny any duty to protect or even consider the values promoted by the public trust. Therefore, seeking an accommodation which will make use of the pertinent principles of both the public trust doctrine and the appropriative water rights system, and drawing upon the history of the public trust and the water rights system, the body of judicial precedent, and the views of expert commentators, we reach the following conclusions:

a. The state as sovereign retains continuing supervisory control over its navigable waters and the lands beneath those waters. This principle, fundamental to the concept of the public trust, applies to rights in flowing waters as well as to rights in tidelands and lakeshores; it prevents any party from acquiring a vested right to appropriate water in a manner harmful to the interests protected by the public trust.

b. As a matter of current and historical necessity, the Legislature, acting directly or through an authorized agency such as the Water Board, has the power to grant usufructuary licenses that will permit an appropriator to take water from flowing streams and use that water in a distant part of the state, even though this taking does not promote, and may unavoidably harm, the trust uses at the source stream. The population and economy of this state depend upon the appropriation of vast quantities of water for uses unrelated to in-stream trust values.[26] California's Constitution, its statutes, decisions, and commentators all emphasize the need to make efficient use of California's limited water resources: all recognize, at least implicitly, that efficient use requires diverting water from in-stream uses. Now that the economy and population centers of this state have developed in reliance upon appropriated water, it would be disingenuous to hold that such appropriations are and have always been improper to the extent that they harm public trust uses, and can be justified only upon theories of reliance or estoppel.

26. In contrast, the population and economy of this state does *not* depend on the conveyance of vast expanses of tidelands or other property underlying navigable waters. (See Comment, The Public Trust Doctrine and California Water Law: National Audubon Society v. Dept. of Water and Power (1982) 33 Hastings L.J. 653, 668.) Our opinion does not affect the restrictions imposed by the public trust doctrine upon transfer of such properties free of the trust.

c. The state has an affirmative duty to take the public trust into account in the planning and allocation of water resources, and to protect public trust uses whenever feasible.[27] Just as the history of this state shows that appropriation may be necessary for efficient use of water despite unavoidable harm to public trust values, it demonstrates that an appropriative water rights system administered without consideration of the public trust may cause unnecessary and unjustified harm to trust interests. As a matter of practical necessity the state may have to approve appropriations despite foreseeable harm to public trust uses. In so doing, however, the state must bear in mind its duty as trustee to consider the effect of the taking on the public trust, and to preserve, so far as consistent with the public interest, the uses protected by the trust.

Once the state has approved an appropriation, the public trust imposes a duty of continuing supervision over the taking and use of the appropriated water. In exercising its sovereign power to allocate water resources in the public interest, the state is not confined by past allocation decisions which may be incorrect in light of current knowledge or inconsistent with current needs.

The state accordingly has the power to reconsider allocation decisions even though those decisions were made after due consideration of their effect on the public trust.[28] The case for reconsidering a particular decision, however, is even stronger when that decision failed to weigh and consider public trust uses. In the case before us, the salient fact is that no responsible body has ever determined the impact of diverting the entire flow of the Mono Lake tributaries into the Los Angeles Aqueduct. This is not a case in which the Legislature, the Water Board, or any judicial body has determined that the needs of Los Angeles outweigh the needs of the Mono Basin, that the benefit gained is worth the price. Neither has any responsible body determined whether some lesser taking would better balance the diverse interests. Instead, DWP acquired rights

27. Amendments to the Water Code enacted in 1955 and subsequent years codify in part the duty of the Water Board to consider public trust uses of stream water. (See, p. 363 of 189 Cal.Rptr., p. 726 of 658 P.2d).) The requirements of the California Environmental Quality Act (Pub. Resources Code, § 21000 et seq.) impose a similar obligation. (See Robie, *Some Reflections on Environmental Considerations in Water Rights Administration*, 2 Ecology L.Q. 695,(1972).

These enactments do not render the judicially fashioned public trust doctrine superfluous. Aside from the possibility that statutory protections can be repealed, the noncodified public trust doctrine remains important both to confirm the state's sovereign supervision and to require consideration of public trust uses in cases filed directly in the courts without prior proceedings before the board.

28. The state Attorney General asserts that the Water Board could also reconsider the DWP water rights under the doctrine of unreasonable use under article X, section 2. DWP maintains, however, that its use of the water for domestic consumption is prima facie reasonable. The dispute centers on the test of unreasonable use—does it refer only to inordinate and wasteful use of water, as in Peabody v. City of Vallejo, supra, 2 Cal. 2d 351, 40 P.2d 486, or to any use less than the optimum allocation of water? On this question, see generally Joslin v. Marin Mun. Water Dist., supra, 67 Cal. 2d 132, 138–141, 60 Cal. Rptr. 377, 429 P.2d 889. In view of our reliance on the public trust doctrine as a basis for reconsideration of DWP's usufructuary rights, we need not resolve that controversy.

to the entire flow in 1940 from a water board which believed it lacked both the power and the duty to protect the Mono Lake environment, and continues to exercise those rights in apparent disregard for the resulting damage to the scenery, ecology, and human uses of Mono Lake.

It is clear that some responsible body ought to reconsider the allocation of the waters of the Mono Basin. No vested rights bar such reconsideration. We recognize the substantial concerns voiced by Los Angeles—the city's need for water, its reliance upon the 1940 board decision, the cost both in terms of money and environmental impact of obtaining water elsewhere. Such concerns must enter into any allocation decision. We hold only that they do not preclude a reconsideration and reallocation which also takes into account the impact of water diversion on the Mono Lake environment. * * *

[The court next went on to consider whether the plaintiffs needed to exhaust administrative remedies before raising their public trust claims in court.]

On the one hand, we have the board with experience and expert knowledge, not only in the intricacies of water law but in the economic and engineering problems involved in implementing water policy. The board, moreover, is charged with a duty of comprehensive planning, a function difficult to perform if some cases bypass board jurisdiction. On the other hand, we have an established line of authority declaring the concurrent jurisdiction of the courts, and reliance upon that authority by the plaintiffs.

We have seriously considered whether, in light of the broad powers and duties which the Legislature has conferred on the Water Board, we should * * * declare that henceforth the board has exclusive primary jurisdiction in matters falling within its purview. We perceive, however, that the Legislature has chosen an alternative means of reconciling board expertise and judicial precedent. Instead of granting the board exclusive primary jurisdiction, it has enacted a series of statutes designed to permit state courts, and even federal courts, to make use of the experience and expert knowledge of the board.

Water Code section 2000 provides that "[i]n any suit brought in any court of competent jurisdiction in this State for determination of rights to water, the court may order a reference to the board, as referee, of any or all issues involved in the suit." Section 2001 provides alternatively that the court "may refer the suit to the board for investigation of and report upon any or all of the physical facts involved." Finally, recognizing that some water cases will be filed in or transferred to federal courts, section 2075 provides that "[i]n case suit is brought in a federal court for determination of the rights to water within, or partially within, this State, the board may accept a reference of such suit as master or referee for the court."

These statutes necessarily imply that the superior court has concurrent original jurisdiction in suits to determine water rights, for a reference to the board as referee or master would rarely if ever be appropriate in a case filed originally with the board. The court, however, need not proceed in ignorance, nor need it invest the time required to acquire the skills and knowledge the board already possesses. When the case raises issues which should be considered by the board, the court may refer the case to the board. Thus the courts, through the exercise of sound discretion and the use of their reference powers, can substantially eliminate the danger that litigation will bypass the board's expert knowledge and frustrate its duty of comprehensive planning.[33]

CONCLUSION

This has been a long and involved answer to the two questions posed by the federal district court. In summarizing our opinion, we will essay a shorter version of our response.

The federal court inquired first of the interrelationship between the public trust doctrine and the California water rights system, asking whether the "public trust doctrine in this context [is] subsumed in the California water rights system, or * * * function[s] independently of that system?" Our answer is "neither." The public trust doctrine and the appropriative water rights system are parts of an integrated system of water law. The public trust doctrine serves the function in that integrated system of preserving the continuing sovereign power of the state to protect public trust uses, a power which precludes anyone from acquiring a vested right to harm the public trust, and imposes a continuing duty on the state to take such uses into account in allocating water resources.

Restating its question, the federal court asked: "[C]an the plaintiffs challenge the Department's permits and licenses by arguing that those permits and licenses are limited by the public trust doctrine, or must the plaintiffs * * * [argue] that the water diversions and uses authorized thereunder are not 'reasonable or beneficial' as required under the California water rights system?" We reply that plaintiffs can rely on the public trust doctrine in seeking reconsideration of the allocation of the waters of the Mono Basin. * * *

This opinion is but one step in the eventual resolution of the Mono Lake controversy. We do not dictate any particular allocation of water. Our objective is to resolve a legal conundrum in which two competing systems of thought—the public trust doctrine and the appropriative water rights system—existed independently of each other, espousing principles which seemingly suggested opposite results. We hope by

---

33. The state Attorney General argues that even though the courts generally possess concurrent jurisdiction in water cases, the board should have exclusive jurisdiction over actions attacking a board-granted water right. In view of the reference power of the courts, we think this exception unnecessary. The court presently has the power to refer such cases to the board whenever reference is appropriate; a rule of exclusive jurisdiction, requiring all such cases to be initiated before the board, would not significantly improve the fairness or efficiency of the process. In some cases, including the present one, it would lead to unproductive controversy over whether the plaintiff is challenging a right granted by the board or merely asserting an alleged right of higher priority.

integrating these two doctrines to clear away the legal barriers which have so far prevented either the Water Board or the courts from taking a new and objective look at the water resources of the Mono Basin. The human and environmental uses of Mono Lake—uses protected by the public trust doctrine—deserve to be taken into account. Such uses should not be destroyed because the state mistakenly thought itself powerless to protect them. * * *

[The concurring opinion of KAUS, J., and the concurring and dissenting opinion of RICHARDSON, J., are omitted.]

Notes and Questions

1. For discussion of the public trust doctrine see Michael Blumm & Thea Schwartz, Mono Lake and the Evolving Public Trust in Western Water, 37 Ariz. L. Rev. 701 (1995); Cynthia Koehler, Water Rights and the Public Trust Doctrine: Resolution of the Mono Lake Controversy, 22 Ecology L.Q. 541 (1995); Ralph Johnson, Public Trust Protection for Stream Flows and Lake Levels, 14 U.C.D. L. Rev. 233 (1980); Harrison Dunning, The Significance of California's Public Trust Easement for California's Water Rights Law, 14 U.C.D. L. Rev. 357 (1980); Joseph Sax, The Public Trust Doctrine in Natural Resource Law: Effective Judicial Intervention, 68 Mich. L. Rev. 471 (1970); Joseph Sax, The Constitution, Property Rights and the Future of Water Law, 61 U. Colo. L. Rev. 401 (1990); Patrick Deveney, Title, Jus Publicum, and the Public Trust: An Historical Analysis, 2 Sea Grant L.J. 13 (1976).

2. Other than in Hawaii (infra p. 621), the *Mono Lake* decision has not been widely cited outside California. After the Idaho Supreme Court followed the California approach (Selkirk–Priest Basin Ass'n v. State, 127 Idaho 239, 899 P.2d 949 (1995); Idaho Conservation League v. State, 128 Idaho 155, 911 P.2d 748 (1995)), the legislature enacted a statute providing that the public trust doctrine shall not apply to the appropriation or use of water, or to any other procedure or law applicable to water rights in the State of Idaho. See Idaho Code §§ 58–1201 to 58–1203. See Michael Blumm, Harrison Dunning, & Scott Reed, Renouncing the Public Trust Doctrine: An Assessment of the Validity of Idaho House Bill 794, 24 Ecology L.Q. 461 (1997). Cf. Department of State Lands v. Pettibone, 216 Mont. 361, 702 P.2d 948 (1985); United Plainsmen Ass'n v. North Dakota State Water Conservation Com'n, 247 N.W.2d 457 (N.D. 1976).

3. On the question the *Audubon* court deferred, whether the public trust applies to purely non-navigable waters, see People v. Truckee Lumber Co., 116 Cal. 397, 400–01 (1897) ("the dominion of the state for * * * protecting * * * fish * * * is not restricted * * * only when found within * * * navigable or otherwise public waters. * * * It extends to all waters within the state * * * ").

4. In Golden Feather Community Ass'n v. Thermalito Irrig. Dist., 199 Cal.App.3d 402, 244 Cal.Rptr. 830 (1988), aff'd on reh'g, 209 Cal.App.3d 1276, 257 Cal.Rptr. 836 (1989), a dam and reservoir had been constructed in 1924 on a non-navigable river. In the ensuing years fishing and recreational use of the reservoir had developed. The owner later wanted to use the water for irrigation and began releasing water, thus lowering the level of water

behind the dam. Suit was brought to prohibit lowering the level of the reservoir, asserting a public trust in the artificial lake. In rejecting the public trust claim and distinguishing the Mono Lake decision, the *Golden Feather* court noted both that the water body was non-navigable and that the lake was artificial. Elsewhere the California Supreme Court has recognized a public trust in artificially created waters. See State of California v. Superior Court (Fogerty), 29 Cal.3d 240, 172 Cal.Rptr. 713, 625 P.2d 256 (1981) (lands submerged by damming Lake Tahoe are impressed with a public trust). See also Wilbour v. Gallagher, 77 Wash.2d 306, 462 P.2d 232 (1969) and Kray v. Muggli, 84 Minn. 90, 86 N.W. 882 (1901). Is *Golden Feather* properly distinguishable from these other "artificial water" cases?

5. In 1996, in order to protect fish, a trial court ordered an irrigation district to increase the amount of its previously mandated releases from storage, pursuant to the public trust and § 5937 of the California Fish and Game Code, though that diminished the safe yield of the reservoir by 7%. Brief of State of California, Amicus Curiae, Putah Creek Council v. Solana Irrig. Dist., No. 3–CIVIL–CO–25527 (Cal. Ct. App., May 21, 1998).

6. City of Los Angeles v. Aitken, 10 Cal.App.2d 460, 52 P.2d 585 (1935) was the original Mono Lake case. The City of Los Angeles condemned whatever rights to lake level maintenance private littoral owners held. The Forest Service is a principal proprietor of land riparian to the Lake. The federal government did not object to the project at the time. In 1984 Congress established a Mono Basin National Forest Scenic Area in order to protect the geologic, ecologic and cultural resources of Mono Basin. The Scenic Area statute provides, however, that "nothing in [this law] shall be construed to * * * affect the present (or prospective) water rights of any person * * * including the City of Los Angeles." 16 U.S.C. § 543c(h).

7. For an analogous case, involving efforts to obtain restoration of fish populations on the San Joaquin River, but involving the Endangered Species Act and Bureau of Reclamation irrigation water contracts, see NRDC v. Rodgers, 381 F.Supp.2d 1212 (E.D. CA 2005).

b. *The Aftermath of the Mono Lake Decision*

The first few years following the California Supreme Court decision were unusually wet and the level of Mono Lake actually rose, despite continuing diversions to Los Angeles. Then there was an extended drought which brought the lake down near its historic low level. Meanwhile, the court sent the case back to the Water Board to determine how best to balance municipal water needs and the protection of trust values at Mono Lake. While awaiting the Water Board studies, the case was returned to the trial court where a preliminary injunction was issued requiring that the Lake be maintained at 6377 feet above sea level, some two feet above its then current level, but still more than forty feet below the level it attained prior to L.A.'s diversion project. Following extensive studies of the ecosystem of the lake and of available alternatives for Los Angeles, the Water Board finally issued its decision (D. 1631) in 1994, eleven years after the court opinion. That decision calls for a lake level of 6392 feet above sea level, 20 feet higher than the Lake's historic low, but 25 feet lower than its level when Los Angeles' diversions began. Estimates are that it will take about 20 years to achieve the mandated level, during which time some diversions will be allowed. Once the lake reaches 6392 feet, Los Angeles will be allowed to divert an average of 31,000 acre-feet per year, about one-third of its previous diversions. Los Angeles was also ordered to prepare a plan to restore damage it caused to the tributary streams and associated waterfowl habitat (Water Board Order No. 98–05 (1998)). Restoration work at Mono Lake is mandated to continue well into the 21st Century.

While this resolution was being developed, things were not idle in the Mono Basin. There was a remarkable amount of collateral action, only the major outlines of which are described here. First, an entirely new series of suits were brought under two obscure provisions of the California Fish and Game Code (§§ 5937, 5946) requiring releases from dams sufficient to re-establish and maintain fisheries which had developed during the wet years following the Supreme Court decision. The court finessed L.A.'s claim that it had vested water rights that preceded the crucial Fish and Game Code provision, which was enacted in 1953: the court found that at least 50,000 a.f./year of water (about one-half the total Mono basin diversion) had not actually been diverted until the 1970's and that no earlier vested right attached to that water. California Trout, Inc. v. Superior Court, 218 Cal.App.3d 187, 266 Cal.Rptr. 788 (1990). The court ordered that historic fisheries on all four diverted streams be restored.

On the legislative front, California enacted a statute that established a $60 million fund to help Los Angeles build water reclamation and conservation facilities.[1] In 1992, Congress passed legislation authorizing federal expenditures to develop 120,000 acre-feet of reclaimed water in Southern California intended to offset diminished Mono Lake Diversions.[2] These funds have produced reclamation facilities producing 50,-000 acre-feet of water per year, with a goal of 135,000 acre-feet. The State and the federal government have also helped fund Los Angeles' water conservation programs, such as the Ultra–Low–Flow Toilet program, which have helped the City reduce its per capita water use by 20%.

For a detailed account of the law and politics of the *Mono Lake* case and its aftermath, see Craig Anthony (Tony) Arnold, Working Out An Environmental Ethic: Anniversary Lessons From *Mono Lake*, 4 Wyoming L. Rev. 1 (2004).

c. Hawai'i: The Waiāhole Ditch Case

In 2000, the Hawai'i Supreme Court decided a very important, and very far-reaching, public trust case. In its essentials the facts were quite straightforward. Nearly a century ago, in order to provide irrigation water for sugar plantations on the dry (leeward) side of the island of Oahu, a complex set of tunnels were built on the wet (windward) side of

---

1. Environmental Water Act of 1989, Cal. Water Code §§ 12929 et seq.

2. 43 U.S.C. § 390h–11; H.R. Conf. Rep. No. 102–1016, at 183, 1992 U.S.C.C.A.N. 4041.

the island, in order to capture streams and groundwater that flowed into the ocean on that side. From 1915 until 1995, when sugar cultivation was terminated, much of the water in that area on the windward side that had previously served small farms growing traditional crops such as taro, and had supported the marine ecosystem there, was diverted to leeward side agriculture. By the 1990's, though the water was no longer needed for sugar irrigation, the Waiāhole Irrigation Company (WIC) which had been diverting it, sought new water right applications, the idea being to keep it available for future urban development on the leeward side (where Honolulu is located). But in the interim, the Water Commission ordered WIC to leave now-surplus water in its native streams. Having done so, it appeared that the long-dormant indigenous ecosystem could be restored. The Commission determined that the public trust required it to establish instream flow standards for the windward side streams, and it did so, setting interim instream standards. There followed much dispute about how much water should be allocated to the windward streams, and how that amount should be calculated. That matter had still not been finally decided as of late 2005. The Commission's original allocation was challenged in court, and that litigation led to the Hawai'i Supreme Court decision which is excerpted below, spelling out the basic principles of the public trust doctrine in that State.

IN RE WATER USE PERMIT APPLICATIONS FOR THE WAIĀHOLE DITCH

Supreme Court of Hawai'i, 2000.
94 Haw. 97, 9 P.3d 409.

NAKAYAMA, Justice.

* * *

1. *History and Development*

* * *

This court endorsed the public trust doctrine in King v. Oahu Railway & Land Co., 11 Haw. 717 (1899). Quoting extensively from *Illinois Central,* we agreed that "[t]he people of Hawaii hold the absolute rights to all its navigable waters and the soils under them for their own common use. The lands under the navigable waters in and around the territory of the Hawaiian Government are held in trust for the public uses of navigation." Id. at 725 (citation omitted). Later decisions confirmed our embrace of the public trust doctrine. * * *

In McBryde Sugar Co. v. Robinson, 54 Haw. 174, 504 P.2d 1330, aff'd on reh'g, 55 Haw. 260, 517 P.2d 26 (1973), appeal dismissed and cert. denied, 417 U.S. 962 (1974), we contemplated the public interest in water resources. Consulting the prior laws and practices of this jurisdiction, we observed that, in granting land ownership interests in the Mahele,[27] the Hawaiian Kingdom expressly reserved its sovereign prerog-

---

27. The Mahele and the subsequent Kuleana Act instituted the concept of private property in the Hawaiian Kingdom. For an overview of its operation, see *McBryde Sug-*

atives "[t]o encourage and even to enforce the usufruct of lands for the common good. * * * "The right to water," we explained, is one of the most important usufruct of lands, and it appears clear to us that by the foregoing limitation the right to water was specifically and definitely reserved for the people of Hawaii for their common good in all of the land grants. Thus by the Mahele and subsequent Land Commission Award and issuance of Royal Patent right to water was not intended to be, could not be, and was not transferred to the awardee, and the ownership of water in natural watercourses and rivers remained in the people of Hawaii for their common good. * * *

In Robinson v. Ariyoshi, 65 Haw. 641, 658 P.2d 287 (1982), we elaborated on our *McBryde* decision, comparing the retained sovereign "prerogatives, powers and duties" concerning water to a "public trust":

> [W]e believe that by [the sovereign reservation], a public trust was imposed upon all the waters of the kingdom. That is, we find the public interest in the waters of the kingdom was understood to necessitate a retention of authority and the imposition of a concomitant duty to maintain the purity and flow of our waters for future generations and to assure that the waters of our land are put to reasonable and beneficial uses. This is not ownership in the corporeal sense where the State may do with the property as it pleases; rather, we comprehend the nature of the State's ownership as a retention of such authority to assure the continued existence and beneficial application of the resource for the common good.

* * *

2. *Relationship to the State Water Code*

Several parties [claim that] the Code "subsumes and supplants whatever common law doctrine of public trust may previously have existed in Hawai'i." * * * The Code does not evince any legislative intent to abolish the common law public trust doctrine. * * * To the contrary, the legislature appears to have engrafted the doctrine wholesale in the Code. * * *

* * * Most importantly, the people of this state have elevated the public trust doctrine to the level of a constitutional mandate. * * *

Article XI, section 1 of the Hawai'i Constitution mandates that, "[f]or the benefit of present and future generations, the State and its political subdivisions shall protect and conserve * * * all natural resources, including * * * water * * * and shall promote the development and utilization of these resources * * * in a manner consistent with their conservation" and further declares that "[a]ll public natural resources are held in trust for the benefit of the people." Article XI, section 7 reiterates the State's "obligation to protect, control and regulate the

ar Co., 504 P.2d at 1337–38; Jon J. Chinen,   Kame'eleihiwa, Native Lands and Foreign
The   Great   Mahele   (1958);   Lilikala   Desires (1992).

use of Hawaii's water resources for the benefit of its people." The plain reading of these provisions manifests the framers' intent to incorporate the notion of the public trust into our constitution. * * * "There can be no question that the [constitution] declares and creates a public trust of public natural resources for the benefit of all people (including future generations as yet unborn) * * * "; *State v. Bleck,* 114 Wis.2d 454, 338 N.W.2d 492, 497 (1983) (grounding the public trust doctrine in the state constitution). * * *

3. *The State Water Resources Trust*

Having established the public trust doctrine's independent validity, we must define its basic parameters with respect to the water resources of this state. In so doing, we address: a) the "scope" of the trust, or the resources it encompasses; and b) the "substance" of the trust, including the purposes or uses it upholds and the powers and duties it confers on the state.

a. *Scope of the Trust*

* * * [U]nder article XI, sections 1 and 7 and the sovereign reservation, the public trust doctrine applies to all water resources without exception or distinction. KSBE and Castle advocate for the exclusion of ground waters from the public trust. Their arguments, first, contradict the clear import of the constitutional provisions, which do not differentiate between categories of water in mandating the protection and regulation of water resources for the common good.[31] The convention's records confirm that the framers understood "water resources" as "includ[ing] ground water, surface water and all other water." Debates, in 2 Proceedings, at 861 (statement by Delegate Fukunaga).

* * * [T]he landscape of law and custom at the time of the Mahele compellingly demonstrates that, despite the transition to a private property regime, water remained a resource reserved to the community. * * * All lands granted in the Mahele, even the King's retained private estate, passed into individual hands burdened with the reservation of this usufruct for the common good. * * *

* * * Moreover, assuming that the ancient Hawaiians had no custom with respect to "ground water," at least in terms of water actually drawn from under the surface by artificial wells or tunnels, it does not follow that the sovereign reservation must exclude such water. Indeed, if the precise extent of ancient usage always determined the effect of the reservation, diversions impairing the "natural flow" of surface streams and transfers of water outside watershed boundaries would still be largely prohibited. * * *

---

31. With respect to article XI, section 1, [one party] contends that the provision's reference to "public natural resources" indicates an intent to exclude "privately owned" waters from the public trust. This argument misses the point; at least in the water resources context, we have maintained that, apart from any private rights that may exist in water, "there is, as there always has been, a superior public interest in this natural bounty."

Even more fundamentally, just as ancient Hawaiian usage reflected the perspectives of that era, the common law distinctions between ground and surface water developed without regard to the manner in which "both categories represent no more than a single integrated source of water with each element dependent upon the other for its existence." *Id.* at 555, 656 P.2d at 73. Modern science and technology have discredited the surface-ground dichotomy. * * *

In sum, given the vital importance of all waters to the public welfare, we decline to carve out a ground water exception to the water resources trust. Based on the plain language of our constitution and a reasoned modern view of the sovereign reservation, we confirm that the public trust doctrine applies to all water resources, unlimited by any surface-ground distinction.

b. *Substance of the Trust*

The public trust is a dual concept of sovereign right and responsibility. See *Robinson*, 65 Haw. at 674, 658 P.2d at 310 (describing the trust as "a retention of authority and the imposition of a concomitant duty"(emphases added)); see also *Reppun*, 65 Haw. at 547–48 & n. 14, 656 P.2d at 68–69 & n. 14 (explaining the correlation of "right" and "duty" underlying the ancient Hawaiian system). Previous decisions have thoroughly reviewed the sovereign authority of the state under the trust. * * * The arguments in the present appeal focus on the state's trust duties. In its decision, the Commission stated that, under the public trust doctrine, "the State's first duty is to protect the fresh water resources (surface and ground) which are part of the public trust res," a duty which it further described as "a categorical imperative and the precondition to all subsequent considerations." The public trust, the Commission also ruled, subjects offstream water uses to a "heightened level of scrutiny." * * *

i. *Purposes of the Trust*

In other states, the "purposes" or "uses" of the public trust have evolved with changing public values and needs. * * *

Whether under riparian or prior appropriation systems, common law or statute, states have uniformly recognized domestic uses, particularly drinking, as among the highest uses of water resources. * * * Accordingly, we recognize domestic water use as a purpose of the state water resources trust. * * *

In acknowledging the general public's need for water, however, we do not lose sight of the trust's "original intent." As noted above, review of the early law of the kingdom reveals the specific objective of preserving the rights of native tenants during the transition to a western system of private property. Before the Mahele, the law "Respecting Water for Irrigation" assured native tenants "their equal proportion" of water. See Laws of 1842, reprinted in Fundamental Laws of Hawaii 29 (1904). Subsequently, the aforementioned Kuleana Act provision ensured tenants' rights to essential incidents of land beyond their own kuleana, including water, in recognition that "a little bit of land even with allodial title, if they be cut off from all other privileges would be of very little value," * * * [W]e continue to uphold the exercise of Native Hawaiian and traditional and customary rights as a public trust purpose. * * *

[One party] asserts that the public trust in Hawai'i encompasses private use of resources for "economic development," * * * [T]he public trust may allow grants of private interests in trust resources under certain circumstances, they in no way establish private commercial use as among the public purposes protected by the trust.

Although its purpose has evolved over time, the public trust has never been understood to safeguard rights of exclusive use for private commercial gain. Such an interpretation, indeed, eviscerates the trust's basic purpose of reserving the resource for use and access by the general public without preference or restriction. * * *

We hold that, while the state water resources trust acknowledges that private use for "economic development" may produce important public benefits and that such benefits must figure into any balancing of competing interests in water, it stops short of embracing private commercial use as a protected "trust purpose." We thus eschew LURF's view of the trust, in which the " 'public interest' advanced by the trust is the sum of competing private interests" and the "rhetorical distinction between 'public trust' and 'private gain' is a false dichotomy." To the contrary, if the public trust is to retain any meaning and effect, it must recognize enduring public rights in trust resources separate from, and superior to, the prevailing private interests in the resources at any given time. See *Robinson*, 65 Haw. at 677, 658 P.2d at 312 ("[U]nderlying every private diversion and application there is, as there always has been, a superior public interest in this natural bounty.").

ii.   *Powers and Duties of the State under the Trust*

We have indicated a preference for accommodating both instream and offstream uses where feasible. See *Reppun*, 65 Haw. at 552–54, 556–63 & n. 20, 656 P.2d at 71–72, 73–78 & n. 20 (allowing ground water diversions short of "actual harm" to surface uses); *Robinson*, 65 Haw. at 674, 658 P.2d at 310 (describing the trust as "authority to assure the continued existence *and* beneficial application of the resource for the common good" (emphasis added)). In times of greater scarcity, however, the state will confront difficult choices that may not lend themselves to formulaic solutions. Given the diverse and not necessarily complementary range of water uses, even among public trust uses alone, we consider it neither feasible nor prudent to designate absolute priorities between broad categories of uses under the water resources trust. Contrary to the Commission's conclusion that the trust establishes resource protection as "a categorical imperative and the precondition to all subsequent considerations," we hold that the Commission inevitably must weigh competing public and private water uses on a case-by-case basis, according to any appropriate standards provided by law. See *Robinson*, 65 Haw. at 677, 658 P.2d at 312; see also *Save Ourselves*, 452 So.2d at 1152 (reading the constitution to establish a "rule of reasonableness" requiring the balancing of environmental costs and benefits against economic, social, and other factors).

Having recognized the necessity of a balancing process, we do not suggest that the state's public trust duties amount to nothing more than a restatement of its prerogatives, see *Robinson*, 65 Haw. at 674 n. 31, 658 P.2d at 310 n. 31, nor do we ascribe to the constitutional framers the intent to enact laws devoid of any real substance and effect, see *supra* notes 29, 36 & 40. Rather, we observe that the constitutional requirements of "protection" and "conservation," the historical and continuing understanding of the trust as a guarantee of public rights, and the common reality of the "zero-sum" game between competing water uses demand that any balancing between public and private purposes begin with a presumption in favor of public use, access, and enjoyment. See, e.g., *Zimring*, 58 Haw. at 121, 566 P.2d at 735 ("[T]he State as trustee has the duty to protect and maintain the trust [resource] and regulate its use. Presumptively, this duty is to be implemented by devoting the [resource] to actual public uses, e.g., recreation."). Thus, insofar as the public trust, by nature and definition, establishes use consistent with trust purposes as the norm or "default" condition, we affirm the Commission's conclusion that it effectively prescribes a "higher level of scrutiny" for private commercial uses such as those proposed in this case.[43] In practical terms, this means that the burden ultimately lies with those seeking or approving such uses to justify them in light of the purposes protected by the trust. * * *

c. *Standard of Review under the Trust*

Finally, the special public interests in trust resources demand that this court observe certain qualifications of its standard of review. As in other cases, agency decisions affecting public trust resources carry a presumption of validity. The presumption is particularly significant where the appellant challenges a substantive decision within the agency's expertise as "clearly erroneous," "arbitrary," "capricious," or an "abuse of discretion." * * *

The public trust, however, is a state constitutional doctrine. As with other state constitutional guarantees, the ultimate authority to interpret and defend the public trust in Hawai'i rests with the courts of this state. * * *

Judicial review of public trust dispensations complements the concept of a public trust. [The Arizona Supreme Court] said * * *, "The

---

43. It is widely understood that the public trust assigns no priorities or presumptions in the balancing of public trust purposes. See *National Audubon*, 189 Cal. Rptr. 346, 658 P.2d at 723; Jan S. Stevens, The Public Trust: A Sovereign's Ancient Prerogative Becomes the People's Environmental Right, 14 U.C. Davis L.Rev. 195, 223–225 (1980). Such balancing, nevertheless, must be reasonable, see, e.g., *State v.* *Public Serv. Comm'n*, 81 N.W.2d at 73–74 (noting that no one public use would be destroyed or greatly impaired and that the benefit to public use outweighed the harm), and must conform to article XI, section 1's mandate of "conservation." The Commission, in other words, must still ensure that all trust purposes are protected to the extent feasible.

duties imposed upon the state are the duties of a trustee and not simply the duties of a good business manager. * * * Just as private trustees are judicially accountable to their beneficiaries for dispositions of the res, so the legislative and executive branches are judicially accountable for the dispositions of the public trust. The beneficiaries of the public trust are not just present generations but those to come. The check and balance of judicial review provides a level of protection against improvident dissipation of an irreplaceable res. * * *

* * * This is not to say that this court will supplant its judgment for that of the legislature or agency. However, it does mean that this court will take a "close look" at the action to determine if it complies with the public trust doctrine and it will not act merely as a rubber stamp for agency or legislative action. * * *

Notes

1. The Supreme Court's decision following its remand in the above matter is found at 105 Haw. 1, 93 P.3d 643 (2004).

2. For a more detailed consideration of Native Hawaiian rights and water see In re Waiola O Molokai, Inc., 103 Haw. 401, 83 P.3d 664 (2004).

2. SAN FRANCISCO BAY DELTA: THE MERGER OF QUANTITY AND QUALITY

The tangled history of the Bay–Delta deserves a book, rather than a few paragraphs. For our purposes, however, the relevant facts can be briefly sketched. Diversions on the Sacramento and San Joaquin Rivers upstream of the Delta, together with the pumps that suck water back from the Delta for export to the Central Valley and Southern California, generate both mortalities and degradation of habitat for fish, and salt water intrusion resulting from diminished downstream flows into the estuary. Salinity intrusion is also harmful to water users in the downstream reaches of the system. The Delta has for decades been a water battleground, plagued by pollution from growing urban areas, unstable levees supporting agricultural lands, loss of wetlands, pesticide infiltration, as well as salinity and losses of spawning grounds for anadromous fish and refuge for wintering wildfowl.

The Delta is perhaps the key focal point in the nation where water quantity claims (by agricultural and municipal appropriators and riparians) meet water quality demands. For many years California interests struggled unsuccessfully to find a resolution. Instream flow demands threatened certainty of supply for existing users. Efforts to redirect water and limit the impact of pumping on fish ignited or re-ignited traditional North–South anxieties about increasing exports to Southern California. The newer mandates of the Federal Water Pollution Control Act, and the Endangered Species Act (ESA), intensified pressures on the Delta. State administrative standards were litigated and overturned. New standards were proposed in a draft decision by the State Water Board and then withdrawn by the Governor following indications from the federal Environmental Protection Agency that it would reject Bay–Delta standards similar to those in the draft decision, and that they were already inadequate as to species listed under the federal ESA. Stalemate and crisis bumped elbows.

One response was the enactment in 1992 of the Central Valley Project Improvement Act (CVPIA).[1] That law was designed to help meet California's water problems in several ways, including provision for marketing of water by individual farmers within the Central Valley Project (CVP), mandating doubling of anadromous fish from Central Valley Streams, permitting purchase of supplemental water for the environment, creating a restoration fund from user fees for mitigation of past environmental damage, and—most controversially—by requiring the government to dedicate 800,000 acre-feet of CVP yield for environmental purposes.[2] The CVPIA is unusual in several ways: a flat goal of doubling fish populations is a rather "unbiological" approach; and the 800,000 acre-foot set-aside is an unusual departure from congressional deference to state governance of water allocation (traditionally the Bureau of Reclamation obtains a state water permit with purposes stated in broad, generic terms).

Finally, in 1994, with strong federal participation and support, a so-called CALFED process was put into place, with a commitment to bring forward a plan to address four problem areas: ecosystem quality, levee system integrity, water supply reliability, and water quality. A central feature of the plan seeks to ensure the availability of substantially increased outflows through the Delta, and limitations upon exports from the federal and state water projects during crucial spring months. Not surprisingly, the main issue that has divided the participants is the demand to assure supply reliability by building additional storage (supported by water users), versus a focus on control of use and demand by non-structural means. In June of 1999, the federal government issued its long-awaited preferred alternative.[3] It does not fully satisfy any of the stakeholder groups, but it essentially proposes an incremental plan with elements of storage, conveyance, water transfers, water quality, ecosystem restoration, water use efficiency, levee integrity, and watershed management. The idea essentially is to move forward on various fronts, deferring the most controversial projects, and leaving it open to the participants to opt out; but with the hope that the

---

1. Pub. L. 102–575, 106 Stat. 4706, § 3406.

2. Both water users and environmental groups challenged the Interior Department's implementation of section 3406(b)(2). See San Luis & Delta Mendota Water Users Ass'n v. United States, CV–F–97–6140 (E.D. Cal. 1999). "Strictly speaking, all Congress did was to dedicate the uncontracted-for portion of the CVP yield to environmental uses. In fact, however, existing project users benefitted from the availability of this * * * capacity. * * * Wa-

ter stored * * * in high-runoff years had been available to project water users in drought years." Lawrence MacDonnell, Managing Reclamation Facilities for Ecosystem Benefits, 67 U. Colo. L. Rev. 197, 226 (1996).

3. CALFED Bay–Delta Program, Draft Programmatic EIS/EIR Technical Appendix, Revised Phase II Report (June 1999). The Report is a concise explanation of the CALFED Bay–Delta Program, its purpose and proposed processes.

stakeholders will (1) become invested in finding mutually agreeable solutions, and (2) acknowledge that the alternatives—such as protracted litigation and ecosystem management by court injunctions—are likely to be less attractive. Needless to say, one significant incentive is the presence of substantial sums of public money, both state and federal, to lighten the economic burden on the direct beneficiaries of the Bay–Delta system.

The excerpt that follows is one of the decisions that helped bring the crisis in the Delta to a head, and encouraged stakeholders to come to the table to seek a negotiated solution. If all goes well with the CALFED process, the legal issues it raised will not have to be finally adjudicated. They are, however, the very issues that created the backdrop for negotiations. What follows are brief extracts from a very long and complex opinion. The key issues raised are these: (1) What legal obligation, if any, do water users with vested state law water rights bear to resolve water quality problems such as salt water intrusion and decline in fish populations generated by upstream diversions? Are diverters of water legally responsible for these harms in the same way that industrial users are responsible for harm from effluents they discharge into streams? (2) If diverters are responsible, and diversions must be limited, must the remedy be in accord with water law priorities (that is, all the burden must be borne by the most junior rights-holders), or is some sort of equal-sharing-of-pain permissible in this situation? (3) What laws and doctrines govern these questions: common law water rights, statutory provisions, permit terms, the public trust?

In reading the following excerpt, keep in mind that the two biggest diverters on the system are the federal Central Valley Project (CVP) and the State Water Project (SWP), that the Water Board had issued an order imposing all the burden on them equally (and not on other diverters from the system), and that the CVP held more senior rights than the SWP.

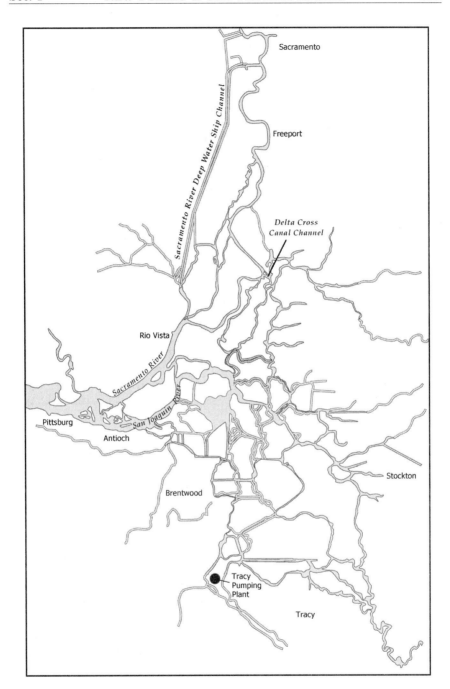

Figure 6–4
Sacramento–San Joaquin Delta

UNITED STATES v. STATE WATER RESOURCES
CONTROL BOARD

California Court of Appeal, 1986.
182 Cal.App.3d 82, 227 Cal.Rptr. 161.

RACANELLI, P.J.

[A] constitutional amendment was enacted in 1928 subjecting all water users—riparians and appropriators alike—to the universal limitation that water use must be reasonable and for a beneficial purpose. (Cal. Const., art. X, § 2.) This "rule of reasonable use" is now the cardinal principle of California's water law. [Cal. Water Code § 100.] * * * The courts have construed this rule as a valid exercise of the police power of the state to regulate the use and enjoyment of water rights for the public benefit. * * * [T]his paramount limitation applies "to all water rights enjoyed or asserted in this state, whether the same be grounded on the riparian right or * * * the appropriative right." Thus, no water rights are inviolable; all water rights are subject to governmental regulation. More recently, in National Audubon Society v. Superior Court, * * * the California Supreme Court underscored a further significant limitation on water rights: the "public trust" doctrine. The court there held that the state's navigable waters are subject to a public trust and that the state, as trustee, has a duty to preserve this trust property from harmful diversions by water rights holders. Thus, the court determined that no one has a vested right to use water in a manner harmful to the state's waters. * * *

The primary purpose underlying the revised water quality standards contained in the Sacramento–San Joaquin Delta Plan was salinity control in order to protect consumptive uses (agricultural, industrial and municipal) of the Delta waters. * * * In its water quality role of setting the level of water quality protection, the Board's task is not to protect water rights, but to protect "beneficial uses." The Board is obligated to adopt a water quality control plan consistent with the overall statewide interest in water quality ([Cal. Water Code] § 13240) which will ensure "the reasonable protection of beneficial uses" (§ 13241). Its legislated mission is to protect the "quality of all the waters of the state * * * for use and enjoyment by the people of the state." (§ 13000, 1st par.) * * *

The Board's attachment to the concept of protecting "rights" rather than "beneficial uses" apparently stems from the assumption that protection of beneficial uses will require maintenance of constant flow levels in the Delta even during water shortages, whereas protection of water rights will permit some variations in water flow depending upon availability since riparians are entitled only to the natural flow. But such a view overlooks the Board's statutory commitment to establish objectives assuring the "reasonable protection of beneficial uses." (§ 13241.) We think this statutory charge grants the Board broad discretion to establish reasonable standards consistent with overall statewide interest. The Board's obligation is to attain the highest reasonable water quality "considering all demands being made and to be made on those waters and the total values involved, beneficial and detrimental, economic and social, tangible and intangible." (§ 13000) * * * At common law, holders of water rights were entitled to the natural flow of the water undiminished in quality. * * * Accordingly, such holders could always maintain a nuisance action against upstream polluters. * * * But while common law clearly affords water rights holders relief from pollution, it is debatable whether such protection included the right to require upstream subsequent appropriators to curtail their use of water solely to permit a sufficient flow to resist natural saltwater intrusion. In the early case of Antioch v. Williams Irr. Dist. (1922) 188 Cal. 451, the court confronted the issue of saltwater intrusion in the context of appropriators' rights. In that case, the City of Antioch sought to enjoin upstream diversions of the Sacramento River which depleted the fresh water barrier and allowed Bay salt water to flow into the San Joaquin River, rendering Antioch's water supply unfit for domestic use. While recognizing the right of appropriators to water in its natural state free of pollution, the court distinguished the case before it from those granting relief from upstream polluters because "[nothing] has been placed in the stream above by the defendants that in the least affects the purity of the water flowing therein." * * *

The pollution of the water complained of is caused by the fact that the depleted volume of the stream does not hold back the rising tide of salt water from the bay below as effectually as the natural volume might do. To allow the freshwater appropriator below to enjoin upstream diversions to maintain a sufficient supply for a hydraulic barrier, the court continued, would be "extremely unreasonable and unjust [to upstream beneficial users] and highly detrimental to the public interests besides." The court ultimately concluded that the city's appropriation rights did not include the right to insist that junior appropriators curtail their upstream use so that a sufficient flow remains to hold back tidal intrusion. Whatever final conclusion is to be drawn from Antioch regarding the nature and extent of common law riparian rights to salinity control, existing constitutional and legislative authorities encompass the Board's obligation to protect the quality of the Delta waters from saltwater intrusion. As mentioned above, the water quality legislation unmistakably requires the Board to formulate water quality standards to provide salinity control to "ensure the reasonable protection of beneficial uses" (§ 13241), a statutory classification earlier noted as wide-ranging (§ 13050, subd. (f)). Though there can be no doubt concerning the Board's authority to take action necessary to protect the consumptive uses (agricultural, industrial and municipal) in the Delta, its approach to that task was seriously flawed by equating its water quality planning function with protection of existing water rights. * * * Once the Board establishes water quality objectives which ensure reasonable protection of beneficial uses (§ 13241), the Board has the added responsibility to complete the water quality control plan by preparing an implementation program to achieve the water quality objectives. * * * [O]ne of the major uncertainties in the water quality legislation concerns the scope of the Board's power to take actions necessary to implement the water quality standards. * * *

[T]he Board's enforcement powers are far from clear. Though the Board has been given express statutory authority to regulate waste discharges (§§ 13320–13389), excess salinity due to tidal water intrusion certainly does not qualify as "waste." Apart from regulating waste discharge, the Board's express authority to implement water quality standards seems limited to recommending actions by other entities. * * * Enforcement authority—in the form of clear and direct orders, injunctive relief and civil penalties—is provided only for unauthorized discharge of pollutants. (§§ 13320, 13331,13340, 13350, 13386.)

In the absence of explicit legislative authority to regulate water users, the principal enforcement mechanism available to the Board is its regulation of water rights to control diversions which cause degradation of water quality. * * * [T]he major responsibility for regulating water quality has been left to the states to permit water quality and water rights decisions to be coordinated. * * * California, of course, has already combined both water resource functions within the exclusive jurisdiction of the Board. The stated purpose of this merger was to ensure that "consideration of water pollution and water quality" would become an integral part of the appropriative rights process. (§ 174.)

In the 1978 proceedings the Board * * * exercised its water rights authority as a means to implement the water quality standards for the Delta. * * * [T]he Board modified the appropriation permits held by the projects [CVP and SWP] to require them to reduce their exports or release more water into the Delta to maintain the water quality standards contained in the Plan. * * *

Authority of Board to Modify Permits to Enforce Water Quality Control Standards

The U.S. Bureau and federal contractors argue strongly that the Board had no authority to modify or interfere with the appropriative rights held by the U.S. Bureau for operation of the CVP.[21] They contend that once an appropriation permit is issued, it is final and non-modifiable. We disagree and will conclude that the Board's actions are supported on two independent grounds.

Reserved Jurisdiction

In the present proceedings the Board explicitly grounded its authority to impose water quality standards on the CVP on its reserved jurisdiction. The trial court agreed. The trial court confirmed the Board's authority to modify the appropriation permits of the U.S.

---

21. The [State] Department of Water Resources does not challenge the authority of the Board to modify its permits. Each of DWR's permits for the SWP contains a clause expressly reserving jurisdiction of the Board to modify the terms for purposes of salinity control and protection of fish and wildlife.

Bureau because the Board expressly reserved jurisdiction in * * * decisions affecting the CVP [in order to] to coordinate the terms and conditions with the SWP. The record of the Board's decisions in issuing permits for each unit of the CVP * * * supports the court's determination that jurisdiction to coordinate the terms of project units was expressly reserved. The Board's authority to reserve jurisdiction to amend permits and to "coordinate" the terms of the permits with those of other units of the projects was expressly conferred by the Legislature in 1959. During that banner year of water resources legislation, section 1394 was enacted granting authority to the Board to reserve jurisdiction in order to impose new terms and conditions as necessary. * * *

Unreasonable Use

Independent of its reserved powers, we think the Board was authorized to modify the permit terms under its power to prevent waste or unreasonable use or methods of diversion of water. All water rights, including appropriative, are subject to the overriding constitutional limitation that water use must be reasonable. (Cal. Const., art. X, sec. 2; sec. 100). * * * The Board is expressly commissioned to carry out that policy. (sec. 1050.) To that end, the Board is empowered to institute necessary judicial, legislative or administrative proceedings to prevent waste or unreasonable use * * * including imposition of new permit terms. * * * Moreover, all permits of the projects are subject to the continuing authority of the Board to prevent unreasonable use. (See generally, People ex rel. State Water Resources Control Bd. v. Forni, supra, 54 Cal. App. 3d 743, 753.)

Determination of reasonable use depends upon the totality of the circumstances presented: " 'The scope and technical complexity of issues concerning water resource management are unequalled by virtually any other type of activity presented to the courts. What constitutes reasonable water use is dependent upon not only the entire circumstances presented but varies as the current situation changes.' * * * '[What] is a reasonable use of water depends on the circumstances of each case, such an inquiry cannot be resolved in vacuo from statewide considerations of transcendent importance.' " (Environmental Defense Fund, Inc. v. East Bay Mun. Utility Dist., supra, 26 Cal. 3d 183, 194.)

Here, the Board determined that changed circumstances revealed in new information about the adverse effects of the projects upon the Delta necessitated revised water quality standards. Accordingly, the Board had the authority to modify the projects' permits to curtail their use of water on the ground that the projects' use and diversion of the water had become unreasonable. * * * Curtailment of project activities through reduced storage and export was eminently reasonable and proper to maintain the required level of water quality in the Delta. We perceive no legal obstacle to the Board's determination that particular methods of use have become unreasonable by their deleterious effects upon water, quality. Obviously, some accommodation must be reached concerning the major public interests at stake: the quality of valuable water resources and transport of adequate supplies for needs southward. The decision is essentially a policy judgment requiring a balancing of the competing public interests, one the Board is uniquely qualified to make in view of its special knowledge and expertise and its combined statewide responsibility to allocate the rights to, and to control the quality of, state water resources.

Joint Responsibility to Maintain and Monitor Water Quality

In 1960 the U.S. Bureau and the DWR entered into a preliminary agreement for the coordinated operation of the two projects. That agreement provides for a sharing of water in the Delta in times of shortage "after the consumptive use requirements of the Delta Lowlands are met." * * *

In its Plan the Board determined that project operations were to be"coordinated"; thus, in its Decision implementing the Plan involving modification of some 34 permits held by the projects, the Board made the projects equally responsible for maintaining water quality and for monitoring water quality in the Delta. * * * The U.S. Bureau has challenged the Board's authority to impose joint responsibility, contending that the Board's action impaired its prior vested water rights.[25]

[T]he Board disclaimed any intent to alter the relative priorities of the projects. Instead, the Board—aware of project negotiations for a new joint operating agreement committed resolution of the details of implementing the standards to the projects' cooperative efforts. The trial court's determination [was] that the Board's Decision erroneously altered the priority of the CVP permits. We think the trial court erred.

As previously discussed, the projects' permits were subject to the reserved jurisdiction of the Board to "coordinate" project operations. Those activities are inextricably interrelated: the projects use parts of the Sacramento River and Delta channels in their transfer of water. Such natural intermingling and integrated use plainly requires coordination by the Board, a function clearly contemplated by the Legislature. (§§ 12202, 12205.) Thus, in our view, the Board's power to modify the permits pursuant to its reserved jurisdiction includes the authority to impose responsibility to maintain water quality upon the projects equally.

25. The law of water rights involves a hierarchy of priorities: Riparian rights as a class have priority which must be satisfied before any appropriative rights are exercised. As among appropriators, "the first in time is the first in right." In times of water shortage, the most junior rights-holder must reduce use even to the point of discontinuance before the next senior appropriative rights-holder must cut back at all. (Hutchins, op. cit. supra, pp. 154–160.) Any impairment of the rights of the prior appropriator constitutes an invasion of private rights for which a remedy lies at law and in equity. (Joerger v. Pacific Gas & Electric Co. (1929) 207 Cal. 8, 26 [276 P. 1017].)

Under the statutory scheme, priority of the issued permit is based upon the application date. (§§ 1450, 1455.) For the most part, the CVP applications preceded those of the SWP, so that most appropriative water rights of the CVP have a higher priority than the rights of the SWP.

Our determination is supported by relevant statutory and case law. The issuance of a permit grants the right to appropriate water "only to the extent * * * allowed in the permit" (§ 1381) subject to the conditions enumerated therein (§ 1391), including reserved jurisdiction of the Board (§ 1394).

Moreover, the power of the Board to set permit terms and conditions (§ 1253) includes the power to consider the "relative benefit" to be derived. (§ 1257.) If the Board is authorized to weigh the values of competing beneficial uses, then logically it should also be authorized to alter the historic rule of "first in time, first in right" by imposing permit conditions which give a higher priority to a more preferred beneficial use even though later in time. * * *

East Bay M. U. Dist. v. Dept. of P. Wks., supra, 1 Cal. 2d 476, is instructive. In that case, involving a permit for use of the Mokelumne River for power purposes, the Board imposed the condition that such use "shall not interfere with future appropriations of said water for agricultural or municipal purposes," the two highest uses of water. (§§ 106, 1254.) Consequently, East Bay MUD's permit became subordinate to future permits, contrary to the recognized "first-in-time" priority system. The Supreme Court upheld the Board's action over the objections of East Bay MUD, reasoning as follows: "[Unless] and until the statutory requirements and conditions are met, the applicant obtains no property right or any other right against the state. If the statutory prerequisites are not present, the application may be rejected in its entirety or, as here done, a permit may be issued with qualifications as to use of the water. * * *"

Such reasoning is equally applicable here. The scope and priority of appropriative rights are properly defined by the Board acting within its powers to consider the relative benefits of competing interests and to impose such conditions as are necessary to protect the public interest. Here, the projects' permits were issued subject to the continuing jurisdiction of the Board to coordinate project operations. D 1485 was an exercise of that continuing jurisdiction. Accordingly, when the Board imposed Term 2—requiring equal responsibility for maintaining the water quality standards—it acted well within its authority and did not infringe upon or otherwise unlawfully impair the "vested" appropriative rights of the U.S. Bureau, which held its permits subject to the exercise of such authority. * * *

Enforcement of Water Quality Standards
for Nonconsumptive, Instream Uses

In addition to protecting consumptive uses of the Delta, the Board formulated revised standards of water quality to protect fish and wildlife, a function expressly authorized by state and federal law.

The Porter–Cologne Act requires the establishment of water quality objectives to "ensure the reasonable protection of beneficial uses * * *" (§ 13241), a protected category which includes "preservation and en-

hancement of fish, wildlife, and other aquatic resources * * *"
(§ 13050, subd. (f)). Similarly, the FWPCA requires the state pollution
control agency to establish and periodically revise water quality standards "taking into consideration their use and value for * * * propagation of fish and wildlife * * *." (33 U.S.C. § 1313(c)(2).) Thus, the
Board acted within its water quality authority to establish standards for
the protection of fish and wildlife. * * *

In the proceedings below, the U.S. Bureau argued the Board had no
authority to modify an appropriation permit once issued, and that the
new standards for the protection of fish and wildlife will result in
impairment of its vested appropriative rights. These arguments were,
quite properly, rejected by the trial court. * * *

The issue is now clearly controlled by National Audubon Society v.
Superior Court. * * * In that case the Supreme Court clarified the scope
of the "public trust doctrine" and held that the state as trustee of the
public trust retains supervisory control over the state's waters such that
no party has a vested right to appropriate water in a manner harmful to
the interests protected by the public trust. * * * "Once the state has
approved an appropriation, the public trust imposes a duty of continuing
supervision over the taking and use of the appropriated water. In
exercising its sovereign power to allocate water resources in the public
interest, the state is not confined by past allocation decisions which may
be incorrect in light of current knowledge or inconsistent with current
needs. The state accordingly has the power to reconsider allocation
decisions No vested rights bar such reconsideration." * * * This landmark decision directly refutes the Bureau's contentions and firmly
establishes that the state, acting through the Board, has continuing
jurisdiction over appropriation permits and is free to reexamine a previous allocation decision. * * * The objectives contained in the Plan for
the protection of fish and wildlife were determined necessary by the
Board to provide a reasonable level of protection. That determination
must be upheld absent a review of the administrative record and a
showing of arbitrary or capricious conduct. * * *

In summary, the Board's evaluation process was not only a valid
exercise of its reserved jurisdiction but also, in retrospect, a proper
exercise of its public trust authority as confirmed by our high court:
"The state has an affirmative duty to take the public trust into account
in the planning and allocation of water resources, and to protect public
trust uses whenever feasible * * *."

Notes and Questions

1. Should downstream Delta juniors be better off because the cause of
their harm was saltwater intrusion into their supply resulting from upstream diversions by seniors, rather than a cutting off of their supply
altogether as a result of upstream diversions by seniors?

2. If, in addition to the harm hypothesized in the preceding paragraph,
there is also a harm to Delta fisheries, does that permit the juniors described

above to "piggy back" on the public trust and beneficial use rights of the fish in the Delta, and in effect take water that previously belonged to upstream seniors? Might not downstream juniors frequently be able to make such a showing in a heavily appropriated river? Will these water quality considerations become a bonanza for downstream junior water users?

3.   Is the Delta water case like, or unlike, a conventional pollution case? Could one say that water quality was impaired by abstracting water rather than by adding pollutants to it (suffocating the fish rather than poisoning them)? See Joseph Sax, The Constitution Property Rights and the Future of Water Law, 61 U. Colo. L. Rev. 257, 271 (1990).

3. ENVIRONMENTAL STATUTES AS LIMITS ON APPROPRIA-TIONS

a. § 404 of the Federal Clean Water Act

Section 404 of the Federal Water Pollution Control Act, 33 U.S.C. § 1344, also known as the Clean Water Act, is a modern supplement to one of the oldest federal water laws—section 10 of the Rivers and Harbors Act of 1899, 30 Stat. 1151, 33 U.S.C. § 403. That law made it unlawful to excavate or fill in navigable waters without authorization from the U.S. Army Corps of Engineers (Secretary of the Army). Section 10 was originally intended to protect navigable capacity, but it became an anti-pollution law through judicial interpretation. United States v. Republic Steel Corp., 362 U.S. 482 (1960). The Clean Water Act, under a definition of navigable waters as "the waters of the United States," 33 U.S.C. § 1362(7), has become a major tool to regulate wetlands development.

Although section 404(a) of the Clean Water Act was very broadly interpreted in a 1985 case, United States v. Riverside Bayview Homes, Inc., 474 U.S. 121, 133 (1985), more recently the Supreme Court, in a sharply divided decision, narrowed the interpretation of § 404(a) and raised–without deciding–a question of whether navigability operates as a limit on Congress' constitutional power to regulate waters was under the Commerce Power. The case, commonly known as the SWANCC decision, is excerpted below. At the time of this writing, the Supreme Court had granted certiorari in two more cases raising related navigability questions: United States v. Rapanos, 376 F.3d 629 (6th Cir. 2004), cert. granted 126 S.Ct. 414 (2005); Carabell v. United States Army Corps of Engineers, 391 F.3d 704 (6th Cir. 2004), cert. granted 126 S.Ct. 415 (2005).

The case following SWANCC, James City County v. EPA, details the very broad authority the Clean Water Act gives to the EPA in those settings where a section 404 permit is required, and reveals what may seem a surprising federal environmental ability to veto western water projects.

SOLID WASTE AGENCY OF NORTHERN COOK COUNTY v. UNITED STATES ARMY CORPS OF ENGINEERS

Supreme Court of the United States, 2001.
531 U.S. 159.

CHIEF JUSTICE REHNQUIST delivered the opinion of the Court.

Section 404(a) of the Clean Water Act, 33 U.S.C. § 1344(a), regulates the discharge of dredged or fill material into "navigable waters." The United States Army Corps of Engineers (Corps) has interpreted § 404(a) to confer federal authority over an abandoned sand and gravel pit in northern Illinois which provides habitat for migratory birds. We are asked to decide whether the provisions of § 404(a) may be fairly extended to these waters, and, if so, whether Congress could exercise such authority consistent with the Commerce Clause, U.S. Const., Art. I, § 8, cl. 3. We answer the first question in the negative and therefore do not reach the second.

Petitioner, the Solid Waste Agency of Northern Cook County (SWANCC), is a consortium of 23 suburban Chicago cities and villages that united in an effort to locate and develop a disposal site for baled nonhazardous solid waste. The Chicago Gravel Company informed the municipalities of the availability of a 533–acre parcel. * * * [T]he old mining site eventually gave way to a successional stage forest, with its remnant excavation trenches evolving into a scattering of permanent and seasonal ponds of varying size (from under one-tenth of an acre to several acres) and depth (from several inches to several feet).

* * * [B]ecause the operation called for the filling of some of the permanent and seasonal ponds, SWANCC contacted federal respondents (hereinafter respondents), including the Corps, to determine if a federal landfill permit was required under § 404(a) of the CWA, 33 U.S.C. § 1344(a).

Section 404(a) grants the Corps authority to issue permits "for the discharge of dredged or fill material into the navigable waters at specified disposal sites." The term "navigable waters" is defined under the Act as "the waters of the United States, including the territorial seas." § 1362(7). The Corps has issued regulations defining the term "waters of the United States" to include

"waters such as intrastate lakes, rivers, streams (including intermittent streams), mudflats, sandflats, wetlands, sloughs, prairie potholes, wet meadows, playa lakes, or natural ponds, the use, degradation or destruction of which could affect interstate or foreign commerce. . . ." 33 CFR § 328.3(a)(3) (1999).

In 1986, in an attempt to "clarify" the reach of its jurisdiction, the Corps stated that § 404(a) extends to intrastate waters:

"a. Which are or would be used as habitat by birds protected by Migratory Bird Treaties; or "b. Which are or would be used as habitat by other migratory birds which cross state lines; or

"c. Which are or would be used as habitat for endangered species; or

"d. Used to irrigate crops sold in interstate commerce." 51 Fed.Reg. 41217.

This last promulgation has been dubbed the "Migratory Bird Rule."

The Corps initially concluded that it had no jurisdiction over the site because it contained no "wetlands," or areas which support "vegetation typically adapted for life in saturated soil conditions," 33 CFR § 328.3(b) (1999). However, after the Illinois Nature Preserves Commission informed the Corps that a number of migratory bird species had been observed at the site, the Corps reconsidered and ultimately asserted jurisdiction over the balefill site pursuant to subpart (b) of the "Migratory Bird Rule." The Corps found that approximately 121 bird species had been observed at the site, including several known to depend upon aquatic environments for a significant portion of their life requirements. Thus, on November 16, 1987, the Corps formally "determined that the seasonally ponded, abandoned gravel mining depressions located on the project site, while not wetlands, did qualify as 'waters of the United States' * * * based upon the following criteria: (1) the proposed site had been abandoned as a gravel mining operation; (2) the water areas and spoil piles had developed a natural character; and (3) the water areas are used as habitat by migratory bird [sic] which cross state lines. During the application process, SWANCC made several proposals to mitigate the likely displacement of the migratory birds and to preserve a great blue heron rookery located on the site. Its balefill project ultimately received the necessary local and state approval. By 1993, SWANCC had received a special use planned development permit from the Cook County Board of Appeals, a landfill development permit from the Illinois Environmental Protection Agency, and approval from the Illinois Department of Conservation.

Despite SWANCC's securing the required water quality certification from the Illinois Environmental Protection Agency, the Corps refused to issue a § 404(a) permit. The Corps found that SWANCC had not established that its proposal was the "least environmentally damaging, most practicable alternative" for disposal of nonhazardous solid waste; that SWANCC's failure to set aside sufficient funds to remediate leaks posed an "unacceptable risk to the public's drinking water supply"; and that the impact of the project upon area-sensitive species was "unmitigatable since a landfill surface cannot be redeveloped into a forested habitat." * * *

This is not the first time we have been called upon to evaluate the meaning of § 404(a). In United States v. Riverside Bayview Homes, Inc., 474 U.S. 121(1985), we held that the Corps had § 404(a) jurisdiction over wetlands that actually abutted on a navigable waterway. In so doing, we noted that the term "navigable" is of "limited import" and that Congress evidenced its intent to "regulate at least some waters that would not be deemed 'navigable' under the classical understanding of that term." Id., at 133. But our holding was based in large measure upon Congress' unequivocal acquiescence to, and approval of, the Corps' regulations interpreting the CWA to cover wetlands adjacent to navigable waters. See id., at 135–139. We found that Congress' concern for the protection of water quality and aquatic ecosystems indicated its intent to regulate wetlands "inseparably bound up with the 'waters' of the United States." Id., at 134.

It was the significant nexus between the wetlands and "navigable waters" that informed our reading of the CWA in Riverside Bayview Homes. Indeed, we did not "express any opinion" on the "question of the authority of the Corps to regulate discharges of fill material into wetlands that are not adjacent to bodies of open water...." Id., at 131–132, n. 8. In order to rule for respondents here, we would have to hold that the jurisdiction of the Corps extends to ponds that are *not* adjacent to open water. But we conclude that the text of the statute will not allow this.

Indeed, the Corps' *original* interpretation of the CWA, promulgated two years after its enactment, is inconsistent with that which it espouses here. Its 1974 regulations defined § 404(a)'s "navigable waters" to mean "those waters of the United States which are subject to the ebb and flow of the tide, and/or are presently, or have been in the past, or may be in the future susceptible for use for purposes of interstate or foreign commerce." 33 CFR § 209.120(d)(1). The Corps emphasized that "[i]t is the water body's capability of use by the public for purposes of transportation or commerce which is the determinative factor." § 209.260(e)(1). Respondents put forward no persuasive evidence that the Corps mistook Congress' intent in 1974.[3]

Respondents next contend that whatever its original aim in 1972, Congress charted a new course five years later when it approved the more expansive definition of "navigable waters" found in the Corps' 1977 regulations. In July 1977, the Corps formally adopted 33 CFR § 323.2(a)(5) (1978), which defined "waters of the United States" to include "isolated wetlands and lakes, intermittent streams, prairie potholes, and other waters that are not part of a tributary system to interstate waters or to navigable waters of the United States, the degradation or destruction of which could affect interstate commerce." Respondents argue that Congress was aware of this more expansive interpretation during its 1977 amendments to the CWA. * * * The

---

3. Respondents refer us to portions of the legislative history that they believe indicate Congress' intent to expand the definition of "navigable waters." Although the Conference Report includes the statement that the conferees "intend that the term 'navigable waters' be given the broadest possible constitutional interpretation," S. Conf. Rep. No. 92–1236, p. 144 (1972), U.S.Code Cong. & Admin.News 1972 pp. 3668, 3822, neither this, nor anything else in the legislative history to which respondents point, signifies that Congress intended to exert anything more than its commerce power over navigation. Indeed, respondents admit that the legislative history is somewhat ambiguous.

failure to pass legislation that would have overturned the Corps' 1977 regulations and the extension of jurisdiction in § 404(g) to waters "other than" traditional "navigable waters," respondents submit, indicate that Congress recognized and accepted a broad definition of "navigable waters" that includes nonnavigable, isolated, intrastate waters.

Although we have recognized congressional acquiescence to administrative interpretations of a statute in some situations, we have done so with extreme care. "[F]ailed legislative proposals are 'a particularly dangerous ground on which to rest an interpretation of a prior statute.' * * * A bill can be proposed for any number of reasons, and it can be rejected for just as many others." * * *

We conclude that respondents have failed to make the necessary showing that the failure of the 1977 House bill demonstrates Congress' acquiescence to the Corps' regulations or the "Migratory Bird Rule," which, of course, did not first appear until 1986. Although respondents cite some legislative history showing Congress' recognition of the Corps' assertion of jurisdiction over "isolated waters," as we explained in Riverside Bayview Homes, "[i]n both Chambers, debate on the proposals to narrow the definition of navigable waters centered largely on the issue of wetlands preservation." 474 U.S., at 136, 106 S.Ct. 455. Beyond Congress' desire to regulate wetlands adjacent to "navigable waters," respondents point us to no persuasive evidence that the House bill was proposed in response to the Corps' claim of jurisdiction over nonnavigable, isolated, intrastate waters or that its failure indicated congressional acquiescence to such jurisdiction. * * *

Respondents—relying upon all of the arguments addressed above—contend that, at the very least, it must be said that Congress did not address the precise question of § 404(a)'s scope with regard to nonnavigable, isolated, intrastate waters, and that, therefore, we should give deference to the "Migratory Bird Rule." See, e.g., Chevron U.S.A. Inc. v. Natural Resources Defense Council, Inc., 467 U.S. 837 (1984). We find § 404(a) to be clear, but even were we to agree with respondents, we would not extend Chevron deference here.

Where an administrative interpretation of a statute invokes the outer limits of Congress' power, we expect a clear indication that Congress intended that result. See Edward J. DeBartolo Corp. v. Florida Gulf Coast Building & Constr. Trades Council, 485 U.S. 568, 575 (1988). This requirement stems from our prudential desire not to needlessly reach constitutional issues and our assumption that Congress does not casually authorize administrative agencies to interpret a statute to push the limit of congressional authority. This concern is heightened where the administrative interpretation alters the federal-state framework by permitting federal encroachment upon a traditional state power. See United States v. Bass, 404 U.S. 336, 349,(1971) ("[U]nless Congress conveys its purpose clearly, it will not be deemed to have significantly changed the federal-state balance"). Thus, "where an otherwise acceptable construction of a statute would raise serious constitutional problems, the Court will construe the statute to avoid such problems unless such construction is plainly contrary to the intent of Congress." *DeBartolo, supra.* * * *

* * * We thus read the statute as written to avoid the significant constitutional and federalism questions raised by respondents' interpretation, and therefore reject the request for administrative deference.

We hold that 33 CFR § 328.3(a)(3) (1999), as clarified and applied to petitioner's balefill site pursuant to the "Migratory Bird Rule," 51 Fed.Reg. 41217 (1986), exceeds the authority granted to respondents under § 404(a) of the CWA. The judgment of the Court of Appeals for the Seventh Circuit is therefore

Reversed.

JUSTICE STEVENS, with whom JUSTICE SOUTER, JUSTICE GINSBERG, and JUSTICE BREYER join, dissenting.

In the CWA * * * Congress broadened the Corps' mission to include the purpose of protecting the quality of our Nation's waters for esthetic, health, recreational, and environmental uses. The scope of its jurisdiction was therefore redefined to encompass all of "the waters of the United States, including the territorial seas." That definition requires neither actual nor potential navigability.

The Court has previously held that the Corps' broadened jurisdiction under the CWA properly included an 80–acre parcel of low-lying marshy land that was not itself navigable, directly adjacent to navigable water, or even hydrologically connected to navigable water, but which was part of a larger area, characterized by poor drainage, that ultimately abutted a navigable creek. United States v. Riverside Bayview Homes, Inc., 474 U.S. 121 (1985). Our broad finding in Riverside Bayview that the 1977 Congress had acquiesced in the Corps' understanding of its jurisdiction applies equally to the 410–acre parcel at issue here. Moreover, once Congress crossed the legal watershed that separates navigable streams of commerce from marshes and inland lakes, there is no principled reason for limiting the statute's protection to those waters or wetlands that happen to lie near a navigable stream.

In its decision today, the Court draws a new jurisdictional line, one that invalidates the 1986 migratory bird regulation as well as the Corps' assertion of jurisdiction over all waters except for actually navigable waters, their tributaries, and wetlands adjacent to each. Its holding rests on two equally untenable premises: (1) that when Congress passed the 1972 CWA, it did not intend "to exert anything more than its commerce power over navigation," * * * and (2) that in 1972 Congress drew the boundary defining the Corps' jurisdiction at the odd line on which the Court today settles. * * *

The 1972 Act * * * appropriated large sums of money for research and related programs for water pollution control * * * and for the construction of water treatment works. * * * Strikingly absent from its declaration of "goals and policy" is *any* reference to avoiding or removing obstructions to navigation. Instead, the principal objective of the Act, as stated by Congress in § 101, was "to restore and maintain the chemical, physical, and biological integrity of the Nation's waters. * * *

Because of the statute's ambitious and comprehensive goals, it was, of course, necessary to expand its jurisdictional scope. Thus, although Congress opted to carry over the traditional jurisdictional term "navigable waters" from the R[ivers &] H[arbors] A[ct] and prior versions of the FWPCA, it broadened the *definition* of that term to encompass all "waters of the United States." § 1362(7). Indeed, the 1972 conferees arrived at the final formulation by specifically deleting the word "navigable" from the definition that had originally appeared in the House version of the Act. The majority today undoes that deletion. * * *

The Conference Report explained that the definition in § 502(7) was intended to "be given the broadest possible constitutional interpretation." S. Conf. Rep. No. 92–1236, p. 144 (1972), reprinted in 1 Leg. Hist. 327. The Court dismisses this clear assertion of legislative intent with the back of its hand. The statement, it claims, "signifies that Congress intended to exert [nothing] more than its commerce power over navigation."

The majority's reading drains all meaning from the conference amendment. By 1972, Congress' Commerce Clause power over "navigation" had long since been established. The Daniel Ball, 10 Wall. 557 (1871); Gilman v. Philadelphia, 3 Wall. 713 (1866); Gibbons v. Ogden, 9 Wheat. 1 (1824). Why should Congress intend that its assertion of federal jurisdiction be given the "broadest possible constitutional interpretation" if it did not intend to reach beyond the very heartland of its commerce power? The activities regulated by the CWA have nothing to do with Congress' "commerce power over navigation." Indeed, the goals of the 1972 statute have nothing to do with *navigation* at all. * * *

The majority accuses respondents of reading the term "navigable" out of the statute. But that was accomplished by Congress when it deleted the word from the § 502(7) definition. After all, it is the *definition* that is the appropriate focus of our attention. * * * Moreover, a proper understanding of the history of federal water pollution regulation makes clear that—even on respondents' broad reading—the presence of the word "navigable" in the statute is not inexplicable. The term was initially used in the various Rivers and Harbors Acts because (1) at the time those statutes were first enacted, Congress' power over the Nation's waters was viewed as extending only to "water bodies that were deemed 'navigable' and therefore suitable for moving goods to or from markets," Power 513; and (2) those statutes had the primary purpose of protecting navigation. Congress' choice to employ the term "navigable waters" in the 1972 Clean Water Act simply continued nearly a century of usage. Viewed in light of the history of federal water regulation, the broad § 502(7) definition, and Congress' unambiguous instructions in the Conference Report, it is clear that the term "navigable waters" operates in the statute as a shorthand for "waters over which federal authority may properly be asserted." * * *

JAMES CITY COUNTY v. ENVIRONMENTAL PROTECTION AGENCY

United States Court of Appeals for the Fourth Circuit, 1993.
12 F.3d 1330.

Sprouse, Senior Circuit Judge:

The United States Army Corps of Engineers in 1988 granted a permit under section 404(b) of the Clean Water Act, 33 U.S.C. §§ 1251–1387, to James City County, Virginia, to construct a dam and reservoir across Ware Creek located within the County. The Environmental Protection Agency (EPA) "vetoed" the permit under the authority granted it by section 404(c) of the Clean Water Act, 33 U.S.C. § 1344(c). After the County contested that action in the district court, the court granted it summary judgment and ordered the Corps of Engineers to issue the permit. In a previous appeal, we affirmed the district court's holding that there was not substantial evidence to support the EPA's finding in its final determination that the County had practicable alternatives to building the Ware Creek reservoir for its local water supply, but remanded to the EPA to afford it the opportunity to decide whether environmental considerations alone would justify its veto * * *. We instructed the EPA not to revisit the issue of practicable alternatives.

On remand, the EPA considered its administrative record and again vetoed the § 404 permit—basing its veto solely on environmental considerations. The County again brought an action in the district court, which again granted summary judgment and ordered issuance of the permit. The EPA now appeals that judgment to this court. We reverse.

I.

The stated objective of the Clean Water Act is "to restore and maintain the chemical, physical, and biological integrity of the Nation's waters." 33 U.S.C. § 1251(a). A review of the statute and legislative history reflects that Congress' intention in enacting the Clean Water Act * * * was to eliminate pollutant discharge, restore chemical, physical, and biological integrity of the Nation's waters, set water quality goals, prohibit toxic discharges, and develop waste treatment projects. * * *

Section 404 of the Act, 33 U.S.C. § 1344, relates narrowly to the placement of dredged or fill material into the Nation's waters. It is this section which covers the issuance of permits for the construction of reservoirs by damming streams, and it is the statutory provision upon which this appeal is centered. It provides, in relevant part:

§ 1344. Permits for dredged or fill material

(a) Discharge into navigable waters at specified disposal sites.

The Secretary [of the Army or the Corps of Engineers] may issue permits, after notice and opportunity for public hearings for the discharge of dredged or fill material into the navigable waters at specified disposal sites. * * *

(b) Specification for disposal sites.

Subject to subsection (c) of this section, each such disposal site shall be specified for each such permit by the Secretary (1) through the application of guidelines developed by the Administrator [of the EPA], in conjunction with the Secretary. * * *

(c) Denial or restriction of use of defined areas as disposal sites.

The Administrator [of the EPA] is authorized to prohibit the specification (including the withdrawal of specification) of any defined area as a disposal site, and he is authorized to deny or restrict the use of any defined area for specification (including the withdrawal of specification) as a disposal site, whenever he determines, after notice and opportunity for public hearings, that the discharge of such materials into such area will have an unacceptable adverse effect on municipal water supplies, shellfish beds and fishery areas (including spawning and breeding areas), wildlife, or recreational areas. Before making such determination, the Administrator shall consult with the Secretary. The Administrator shall set forth in writing and make public his findings and his reasons for making any determination under this subsection.

Pursuant to the mandate of section 404(b), the EPA and the Corps have jointly issued guidelines to be followed by both agencies in making their respective determinations under section 404. See 40 C.F.R. § 230. These guidelines state that a permit should not be issued if: (1) practicable, environmentally superior alternatives are available, (2) the discharge would result in a violation of various environmental laws, (3) the discharge would result in significant degradation to the waters of the United States, or (4) appropriate and practicable steps have not been taken to minimize potential adverse impacts of the proposed discharge. In addition to the guidelines issued jointly by the EPA and the Corps of Engineers, the EPA has issued regulations, which, among other things, define"unacceptable adverse effect" as "impact on an aquatic or wetland ecosystem which is likely to result in significant degradation of municipal water supplies(including surface or ground water) or significant loss of or damage to fisheries, shellfishing, or wildlife habitat or recreation areas." 40 C.F.R. § 231.2(e). These regulations also provide that "in evaluating the unacceptability of such impacts, consideration should be given to the relevant portions of the section 404(b)(1) guidelines." Id.

In JCC I, the County applied for and the Corps of Engineers granted the permit issue in this appeal. The permit would allow the construction of a water reservoir by the erection of a dam across Ware Creek, a tributary of the York River, which, in turn, flows into the Chesapeake Bay. In its final determination of whether to veto the permit the EPA discussed in detail its opinion that construction of the dam would have "unacceptable adverse effects" on municipal water supplies, fish, wildlife, and recreational areas such as are prohibited by section 404(c) of the Act, 33 U.S.C. § 1344(c). It determined, among other things, that the construction would have a damaging impact on environmental contributions to the York River and to the Chesapeake Bay. * * *

In its Final Determination After Remand, the EPA, of the view that our remand required it, deleted the discussion of a putative regional water supply and concluded that its veto was justified solely on the basis of unacceptable adverse effects on the environment. The district court, in ruling for the County, held that the EPA lacked the authority to base its veto solely on the grounds of adverse effects to the environment. It opined that the agency must consider the County's need for water. Alternatively, the district court ruled that there was not sufficient evidence to support the EPA's conclusion of unacceptable adverse environmental effects. * * *

We are presented * * * with * * * determining whether the EPA has the authority to justify its sec. 404(c) veto in this case solely on the basis that it would cause unacceptable adverse effects on the environment. Although we find no precedent and little legislative history, we are persuaded by the structure and language of the Act that it has that authority.

II

The district court, in ruling that the EPA erred in not discussing the County's need for water, cited 40 C.F.R. § 231.1(a) which defines the "purpose and scope" of Part 231 relating to procedures and directs that the EPA consider "all information available to [it]."

On appeal, the County * * * urges that the EPA is required to consider a wide range of factors in determining what is "unacceptable." It points out that the EPA's position in other litigation has been grounded on this same argument. The EPA, in reply, asserts that while it may in its sole discretion consider the need for water, the only requirement placed on it by Congress is to consider the project's potential adverse impacts on the environment. In support of its argument, the agency points to the preamble to 40 C.F.R. Part 231: Section 404(c) does not require a balancing of environmental benefits against non-environmental costs such as the benefits of the foregone project. This view is based on the language of 404(c) which refers only to environmental factors. The term "unacceptable" in EPA's view refers to the significance of the adverse effect—e.g. is it a large impact and is it one that the aquatic and wetland ecosystem cannot afford. * * * Even when there is no alternative available, and "vetoing" the site means stopping a project entirely, the loss of the 404(c) resource may still be so great as to be "unacceptable." 44 Fed. Reg. 58,076, 58,078 (Oct. 9, 1979). The County does not seriously contest the EPA's interpretation negating a cost/benefit analysis. It forcefully contends, however, that before imposing a veto some consideration must be given to a community's need for water and emphasizes that this does not require a cost/benefit analysis. * * *

Congress obviously intended the Corps of Engineers in the initial permitting process to consider the total range of factors bearing on the necessity or desirability of building a dam in the Nation's waters, including whether the project was in the public interest. For example, as stated earlier, under 40 C.F.R. § 230.10, in deciding whether to issue a permit, the Corps takes into account * * * the public and private need for the project, whether the same result could be achieved through other means, and the "extent and permanence" of the benefits and harms the proposed project is likely to produce. * * * Ultimately, however, recognizing the EPA's expertise and concentrated concern with environmental matters, Congress gave the final decision whether to permit a project to that agency. Its authority to veto to protect the environment is practically unadorned. It is simply directed to veto when it finds that the discharge "will have an unacceptable adverse effect on municipal water supplies, shellfish beds and fishery areas (including spawning and breeding areas), wildlife, or recreational areas." * * * This broad grant of power to the EPA focuses only on the agency's assigned function of assuring pure water and is consistent with the missions assigned to it throughout the Clean Water Act.

We think it significant that the only mention of responsibility for the quantities of water available to communities is contained in section 101(g) entitled "Authority of States over water" which states: "It is the policy of Congress that the authority of each State to allocate quantities of water within its jurisdiction shall not be superseded, abrogated or otherwise impaired by this chapter. It is the further policy of Congress that nothing in this chapter shall be construed to supersede or abrogate rights to quantities of water which have been established by any State. Federal agencies shall co-operate with State and local agencies to develop comprehensive solutions to prevent, reduce and eliminate pollution in concert with programs for managing water resources." 33 U.S.C. § 1251(g).

In our view, the EPA's only function relating to the quantities of available water is limited to assuring purity in whatever quantities the state and local agencies provide. For these reasons, we think its veto based solely on environmental harms was proper. * * *

Notes and Questions

1. Is the message that the EPA now has the last word on every water project, within the reach of the definition of navigability, guided by no standards but its own judgment of environmental acceptability, and without any responsibility to meet water supply needs? If so, the implications of even the newly-limited § 404 could be more far reaching than those of the *Mono Lake* decision. You might want to look ahead at California v. United States, infra p. 753, which discusses Congress' desires, in the context of the federal reclamation law, generally not to displace state water law.

2. The Court refers briefly to section 101(g) of the Clean Water Act. Professor Michael Blumm explains:

> The principal question concerning the effect of the 404 program on state water allocation systems is whether and under what conditions a 404 permit can be denied to construct diversion works where the applicant has secured a state water right. Until the passage of the 1977 Amendments it was relatively clear that 404 permits could be denied or conditioned for such diversions.[4] The 1977 Amendments complicate the 404 water allocation relationship through a new section 101(g) * * * provid[ing] that state allocation of water "shall not be superseded, abrogated, or otherwise impaired by this Act" [the Wallop Amendment]. Although this declaration might be construed as removing federal authority to deny or condition 404 permits where conflicts with state water allocations would result, the section's legislative history does not justify this interpretation* * *.[5] Thus the Conference Report sanctions intrusions on state water allocation systems where necessary to achieve Clean Water Act goals. * * * EPA has concluded that although * * * 404 * * * permits * * * may incidentally interfere with state water rights, they may do so only where clearly necessary to meet Clean Water Act requirements * * *.

Michael Blumm, The Clean Water Act's Section 404 Permit Program Enters its Adolescence: An Institutional and Programmatic Perspective, 8 Ecology L.Q. 409, 410, 466–68 (1980).

3. In his article Water Rights, Clean Water Act Section 404 Permitting and the Takings Clause, 60 U. Colo. L. Rev. 901, 912 (1989), Professor Jan Laitos points out that beyond its own force:

> the 404 permit requirement also triggers analysis under the Endangered Species Act [16 U.S.C. §§ 1531–1543] and the Fish and Wildlife Improvement Act [16 U.S.C. §§ 742(a)–754(d)]. * * * Third, a water storage or diversion structure requiring a 404 permit must also obtain section 401 certification from the relevant state agency [33 U.S.C. § 1341]. Because state 401 certification ensures that applicable water quality standards will not be violated during both construction and operation of the diversion or storage project, this certification has become an important vehicle for regulation of the non-discharge water quality impacts of diversions and dams [33 C.F.R. §§ 320.3(a), 323.2(f); 40 C.F.R. §§ 121.26, 230.10(b)]. Fourth, neither the dam nor diversion may result in impairment of

4. Section 510(2) of the Act spoke directly to this issue: "Except as expressly provided in this chapter, nothing * * * shall be construed as impairing or in any manner affecting any right or jurisdiction of the States with respect to the waters * * * of such States." 33 U.S.C. § 1370(2) (1976). Since section 404 is an express provision of the Act, the 404 program can affect state systems of water allocation where Clean Water Act requirements clearly warrant permit conditions or denials.

5. * * * Senator Wallop (the sponsor) stated: "This 'state's jurisdiction' amendment reaffirms that it is the policy of Congress that this act is to be used for water quality purposes only. * * * Legitimate water quality measures authorized by this act may at times have some effect on the method of water usage. * * * The requirements of section 402 and 404 permits may incidentally affect individual water rights. * * * It is not the purpose of this amendment to prohibit those incidental effects."

a state's anti-degradation policy, which federal law requires as part of a state water quality standards regulation [40 C.F.R. § 131.12].

Other federal statutes that come into play are the National Environmental Policy Act, 42 U.S.C. §§ 4321–4370f, and the Federal Land Policy and Management Act, 43 U.S.C. §§ 1701–1785. See also City and County of Denver v. Bergland, 695 F.2d 465, 480 (10th Cir. 1982) (rights-of-way across federal land). The Laitos article explores the claim that permit denial under section 404 may constitute a taking without compensation of a vested property right.

4. The array of laws that may be invoked in water quality matters ranges very broadly, even including statutes such as the Migratory Bird Treaty Act, 16 U.S.C. §§ 703–712. In one illustrative case, irrigation drainage water contaminated with selenium flowed from the Westlands Water District in California's Central Valley into a reservoir that was part of the Kesterson National Wildlife Refuge, poisoning migrating birds that fed on fish in the reservoir. What remedies are available? Could deliveries to irrigators be reduced in order to reduce the quantum of contaminated return flow? See Felix Smith, The Kesterson Effect: Reasonable Use of Water and the Public Trust, 6 San Joaquin Agric. L. Rev. 45 (1996); Richard Rappaport, Crisis at Kesterson: A Review of San Joaquin Valley Agricultural Drainage Problems and Possible Solutions, 5 U.C.L.A. J. Envtl. L. & Pol'y 187 (1986). See also Clean Water Act §§ 402(*l*), 502(14), 33 U.S.C. §§ 1342(*l*), 1362(14) (status of return flows from irrigated agriculture under the Clean Water Act).

5. Water projects may have to comply with local land use regulations as well. See supra p. 236.

6. For a case discussing the impact of the Endangered Species Act on the section 404 permitting process, see Riverside Irrigation District v. Andrews, 758 F.2d 508 (10th Cir. 1985).

b. *The Endangered Species Act*

The Endangered Species Act (ESA), 16 U.S.C. §§ 1531–1544, is one of the strongest federal environmental laws on the books. The Secretary of the Interior is mandated to determine species of animals and plants whose survival is endangered or threatened through all or a significant part of their range, and based on the best scientific and commercial data available, to list such species and (with some qualifications) to designate their critical habitat. Once listed, the law orders each federal agency to insure that any action authorized, funded or carried out by it is not likely to jeopardize the continued existence of any endangered species or to result in harm to critical habitat. ESA § 7, 16 U.S.C. § 1536(a). The law also prohibits any person from "tak[ing]" listed species, which includes disturbance of habitat. See ESA § 9(a)(1)(B), 16 U.S.C. § 1538(a)(1)(B); Babbitt v. Sweet Home Chapter, 515 U.S. 687 (1995). The Secretary must develop a recovery program for listed species. ESA § 4(f), 16 U.S.C. § 1533(f). Habitat protection is a primary means for implementation of the Act.[1]

1. See generally Michael Moore, Water Allocation in the American West: Endan-gered Fish Versus Irrigated Agriculture, 36 Nat. Resources J. 319 (1996); Oliver Houck,

The Act essentially provides two paths for implementation and enforcement of its requirements. Where federal agency action is involved, a consultation process must be initiated if a listed species is present and may be affected. If a so-called jeopardy opinion finds jeopardy to a species or adverse modification of its habitat from the proposed action, the Secretary proposes "reasonable and prudent alternatives" which could avoid jeopardy, and which would allow some "incidental" take of the species. ESA § 7(b)(4), 16 U.S.C. § 1536(b)(4). Compliance with such reasonable and prudent alternatives provides a means by which the Act can be implemented without simply shutting down or enjoining all conduct that contributes to putting a listed species in jeopardy. A parallel process is provided for individuals or entities whose conduct involves "take" of a listed species, even if no federal agency action is involved. The Secretary is allowed to authorize incidental take if there is an approved habitat conservation plan (HCP) that does not appreciably reduce the likelihood of survival and recovery of the species in the wild, and the applicant will minimize and mitigate impacts to the maximum extent practicable. ESA § 10(a)(2), 16 U.S.C. § 1539(a)(2). There is a provision by which an exemption from the operation of the Act may be obtained (ESA § 7(h), 16 U.S.C. § 1536(h)), but it is extremely rigorous and has been very rarely invoked.

For the most part, ESA water problems arise either because additional instream flows are required where needed water is already in use by others with state water rights, or because a desired new or enlarged project, such as a dam and reservoir, would create jeopardy; and where, for whatever reasons, the parties and the federal officials (either the Fish and Wildlife Service or the National Marine Fisheries Service) have been unable to agree on a plan of reasonable and prudent alternatives, or on an HCP. Water users may claim that demanded restrictions on diversions constitute an uncompensated taking of their property rights in water in violation of the Fifth Amendment "takings" provision of the Constitution; that diminished deliveries of water violate their contract rights, most commonly with the Bureau of Reclamation; and/or that Congress did not intend the ESA's requirements to preempt traditional state control over water (for example, state authorities may demand that a state permit for instream use be obtained before water is released to meet ESA requirements).[2]

One example of how intensely controversial such matters may be is the following hypothetical instance: Two states sharing an interstate river have, after decades of negotiation, agreed to an interstate compact, or litigated an interstate apportionment in the Supreme Court, that divides the flow of the river according to a specified formula (e.g., an average of 1 maf must be delivered at the state line each year). Now a

The Endangered Species Act and Its Implementation by the U.S. Departments of Interior and Commerce, 64 U. Colo. L. Rev. 277 (1993).

2. See Joseph Sax, Environmental Law at the Turn of the New Century, 88 Cal. L. Rev. 2375 (2000).

biological opinion determines that a minimum of 1.3 maf must be delivered each year to avoid jeopardy to a listed fish. The question is whether the ESA in effect rewrites the compact or the judicial apportionment.[3] As you can imagine, upstream states strenuously oppose any such interpretation. Some years ago, a Colorado official testifying on this matter, said:

> One result of the Act's inflexibility * * * is the *de facto* interstate apportionment and intrastate appropriation of waters which the FWS [Fish & Wildlife Service of the U.S. Department of the Interior] is effectively accomplishing by imposing substantial minimum flow releases on water storage projects. For example, in order to obtain a non-jeopardy opinion [under the Endangered Species Act] on the Colorado River squawfish from FWS on its White River Dam, the State of Utah recently had to agree to release a minimum of 250 second-feet (cfs) of water at the dam during most of the year, with higher releases in the spawning season. * * * All this has the potential to interfere with appropriative rights under State water laws as well as interstate apportionments under the Upper Colorado River Basin Compact.[4]

Such very sensitive issues have not yet been judicially resolved,[5] but a number of other similarly divisive matters have arisen in litigation. The following disputes are illustrative.

TULARE LAKE BASIN WATER STORAGE DISTRICT v. UNITED STATES

United States Court of Federal Claims, 2001.
49 Fed. Cl. 313.

WEISE, Judge.

Plaintiffs are California water users who claim that their contractually-conferred right to the use of water was taken from them when the federal government imposed water use restrictions under the Endangered Species Act. They now seek Fifth Amendment compensation for their alleged loss. The case is before the court on the parties' cross-motions for summary judgment as to liability. * * * We now rule in favor of plaintiffs, and deny the government's cross-motion for summary judgment.

FACTS

This case concerns the delta smelt and the winter-run chinook salmon—two species of fish determined by the United States Fish and

3. This issue is briefly discussed in chapter 8, infra p. 850.

4. Endangered Species Act of 1982: Hearing on S. 2309 Before the Subcommittee on Environmental Pollution of the Senate Committee on Environment and Public Works, 97th Cong., 2d Sess. 233–34 (1982)

(prepared statement of Roland C. Fischer, Sec'y.of Eng., Colorado River Water Conservation Dist., Glenwood Springs, Colo.).

5. A variant of it arose in the reopened case of Nebraska v. Wyoming, 515 U.S. 1 (1995) (evidence of harm to species in downstream state may be considered).

Wildlife Service ("USFWS") and the National Marine Fisheries Service ("NMFS") to be in jeopardy of extinction. The efforts by those agencies to protect the fish—specifically by restricting water out-flows in California's primary water distribution system—bring together, and arguably into conflict, the Endangered Species Act and California's century-old regime of private water rights. The intersection of those concerns, and the proper balance between them, lie at the heart of this litigation.

The development of California's water system has a long and detailed history well chronicled in case law. See, e.g., United States v. State Water Resources Control Bd., 182 Cal.App.3d 82, 227 Cal.Rptr. 161 (1986). That system, in brief, involves the transport of water from the water-rich areas in northern California to the more arid parts of the state. Various water projects or aqueduct systems have been built to facilitate that goal; two—the Central Valley Project ("CVP") and the State Water Project ("SWP")—are the focus of the present litigation.

Although CVP is a federal project managed by the Bureau of Reclamation ("BOR") and SWP is a state project managed by the Department of Water Resources ("DWR"), the two projects share a coordinated pumping system that requires, as a practical matter, that the systems be operated in concert. * * *

Both BOR and DWR are granted water permits by the State Water Resources Control Board ("SWRCB" or "the Board")—a state agency with the ultimate authority for controlling, appropriating, using and distributing state waters. See California v. United States, 438 U.S. 645 (1978). BOR and DWR in turn contract with county water districts, conferring on them the right to withdraw or use prescribed quantities of water. Of the present plaintiffs, two—Tulare Lake Basin Water Storage District and Kern County Water Agency—have contracts directly with the State Water Project. * * *

In fulfillment of the duties assigned to it under the ESA, the National Marine Fisheries Service initiated discussions with the federal Bureau of Reclamation and state Department of Water Resources to determine the impact of the Central Valley Project and the State Water Project on the winter-run chinook salmon. As a result of those discussions, the NMFS issued a biological opinion on February 14, 1992, concluding that the proposed operation of SWP and CVP was likely to jeopardize the continued existence of the salmon population. Included in the agency's findings was a reasonable and prudent alternative ("RPA") designed to protect the fish by restricting the time and manner of pumping water out of the Delta. As a result, water that would otherwise have been available for distribution by the water projects was made unavailable. * * *

The RPAs were thus implemented in each of the years in question, giving rise to the present claims. According to plaintiffs, the restrictions imposed by the RPAs deprived Tulare Lake Basin WSD of at least 9,770 acre-feet of water in 1992; at least 26,000 acre-feet of water in 1993, and at least 23,050 acre-feet of water in 1994. Kern County Water Agency, by contrast, is alleged to have lost a minimum of 319,420 acre-feet over that same period. * * *

In arguing against the existence of a taking, the government offers three lines of defense. First, defendant maintains that the implementation of the RPAs merely frustrated the contract's purpose and, under Omnia Commercial Co. v. United States, 261 U.S. 502 (1923), did not therefore effectuate a taking. Second, it argues that the criteria for a regulatory taking—specifically the existence of reasonable, investment-backed expectations and of a significant decrease in economic value—have not been met. Finally, defendant contends that the federal government cannot be held liable for a taking when it does no more than impose a limit on plaintiffs' title that the background principles of state law would otherwise require. We address these arguments in turn.

II.

Turning then to the merits of plaintiffs' claim, we begin by determining the nature of the taking alleged. Courts have traditionally divided their analysis of Fifth Amendment takings into two categories: physical takings and regulatory takings. A physical taking occurs when the government's action amounts to a physical occupation or invasion of the property, including the functional equivalent of a "practical ouster of [the owner's] possession. * * *

Plaintiffs urge us to consider this action as a case involving a physical taking of property. Under that theory, plaintiffs possessed contract rights entitling them to the use of a specified quantity of water. By preventing them from using that water, plaintiffs argue, the government deprived them of the entire value of their contract right.

Defendant sees the case differently. In defendant's view, the court must examine the government's conduct under the three-part test that *Penn Central* prescribes for the evaluation of regulatory action that interferes with an owner's use of his property * * *.

Of the two positions, plaintiffs', we believe, is the correct one. Case law reveals that the distinction between a physical invasion and a governmental activity that merely impairs the use of that property turns on whether the intrusion is "so immediate and direct as to subtract from the owner's full enjoyment of the property and to limit his exploitation of it." United States v. Causby, 328 U.S. 256, 265 (1946). In *Causby*, for instance, the Court ruled that frequent flights immediately above a landowner's property constituted a taking, comparing such actions to a more traditional physical taking: "If, by reason of the frequency and altitude of the flights, respondents could not use this land for any purpose, their loss would be complete. It would be as complete as if the United States had entered upon the surface of the land and taken exclusive possession of it." Id. at 261 (footnote omitted).

While water rights present an admittedly unusual situation, we think the *Causby* example is an instructive one. In the context of water rights, a mere restriction on use—the hallmark of a regulatory action—

completely eviscerates the right itself since plaintiffs' sole entitlement is to the use of the water. See Eddy v. Simpson, 3 Cal. 249, 252–253 (1853) ("the right of property in water is usufructuary, and consists not so much of the fluid itself as the advantage of its use."). Unlike other species of property where use restrictions may limit some, but not all of the incidents of ownership, the denial of a right to the use of water accomplishes a complete extinction of all value. Thus, by limiting plaintiffs' ability to use an amount of water to which they would otherwise be entitled, the government has essentially substituted itself as the beneficiary of the contract rights with regard to that water and totally displaced the contract holder. That complete occupation of property—an exclusive possession of plaintiffs' water-use rights for preservation of the fish—mirrors the invasion present in *Causby*. To the extent, then, that the federal government, by preventing plaintiffs from using the water to which they would otherwise have been entitled, have rendered the usufructuary right to that water valueless, they have thus effected a physical taking. * * *

Defendant attempts to distinguish [other physical takings] cases on the ground that each involved actual diversions of water by the government for its own consumptive use, whereas here, it is claimed, the government has merely regulated the plaintiffs' method of diverting water. Additionally, defendant argues that the government could not by law have physically appropriated plaintiffs' property right since California does not recognize a right to appropriate water for in-stream uses (citing Fullerton v. State Water Resources Control Bd., 90 Cal.App.3d 590, 153 Cal.Rptr. 518 (1979)). But as defendant readily admits, the ultimate result of those rate and timing restrictions on pumping is an aggregate decrease in the water available to the water projects. Under those circumstances, whether the government decreased the water to which plaintiffs had access by means of a dam or by means of pumping restrictions amounts to a distinction without a difference.

III.

Having concluded that a deprivation of water amounts to a physical taking, we turn now to the question of whether plaintiffs in fact owned the property for which they seek to be compensated. * * * Additionally, defendant argues that plaintiffs' contract rights are subject to the public trust doctrine, the doctrine of reasonable use, and common law principles of nuisance, all of which provide for the protection of fish and wildlife. To the extent that the reductions in the water supply that plaintiffs suffered are designed to advance those interests, defendant argues, the reductions merely reflect the limitations of title inherent in the background principles of state law. And, defendant adds, no right to compensation attends the assertion of such background principles. * * *

II. THE PUBLIC TRUST DOCTRINE, THE DOCTRINE OF REASONABLE USE AND NUISANCE LAW

* * * [D]efendant offers a number of common law justifications for limiting the scope of plaintiffs' property right: specifically, that plaintiffs

can have no vested right in a use or method of diverting water that is unreasonable or violates the public trust. In support of that position, defendant refers us to various SWRCB decisions, as well as to assorted background principles of state law for the proposition that plaintiffs' proposed use is unreasonable or in contravention of California water law. The difficulty with defendant's argument, however, is that the water allocation scheme in effect for the period 1992–1994, as set forth in D–1485, specifically allowed for the allocations of water defendant now seeks to deem unreasonable. We explain further.

There is, as an initial matter, no dispute that all California water rights are subject to the universal limitation that the use must be both reasonable and for a beneficial purpose. Cal. Const. art. XIV, § 3, amended by Cal. Const. art. X, § 2. Included in that definition of reasonable use is the preservation of fish and wildlife. Indeed, the California legislature has specifically declared that the protection of fish and wildlife is among the purposes of the state water projects. Cal. Water Code § 11900 (Deering 1977).

Whether a particular use or method of diversion is unreasonable or violative of the public trust is a question committed concurrently to the State Water Resources Control Board and to the California courts. See National Audubon Soc'y v. Superior Court of Alpine County, 33 Cal.3d 419, 451–452, 189 Cal.Rptr. 346, 658 P.2d 709 (1983). Thus, while we accept the proposition that plaintiffs have no right to use or divert water in an unreasonable manner, nor in a way that violates the public trust, the issue now before us is whether such a determination has in fact been made.

Plaintiffs argue that the State Water Resources Control Board's decision D–1485—a comprehensive water rights scheme balancing the needs of and allocating water rights among competing users—defines the full scope of their contract rights. In plaintiffs' view, D–1485 represents the state's determination of various water rights, thereby reflecting the amount of water, under state law, they reasonably can expect and to which they are reasonably entitled. Plaintiffs argue that unless and until D–1485 is modified by the State Water Resources Control Board, or the terms of D–1485 are declared by that board or a California court to be unreasonable or violative of the public trust, DWR has a right recognized and protected under California law to divert water in accordance with D–1485.

In defendant's view, D–1485 fails to encapsulate the board's approach to the endangerment of the delta smelt and salmon, both because it was promulgated before the fish were found to be in jeopardy, and because the board enacted D–95–1—a 1995 decision whose provisions adopt measures found in the RPAs—to protect the fish. Additionally, defendant argues that D–1485 should be read as an evolving document, one informed by later developments in water needs and altered by subsequent state actions. In support of that theory, defendant offers various state actions that it claims serve to limit plaintiffs' contract rights: California's listing as "endangered" under the California Endangered Species Act ("CESA") the winter-run chinook salmon in 1989 and the delta smelt in 1993; the Department of Water Resources's consultation with the National Marine Fisheries Service in formulating the biological opinions; and the California Department of Fish and Game's adoption of the 1993 NMFS biological opinion and the RPA under CESA.

We cannot accept defendant's position. As an initial matter, the responsibility for water allocation is vested in the State Water Resources Control Board. Cal. Water Code §§ 174, 179; California v. United States, 438 U.S. 645, 653, 98 S.Ct. 2985, 57 L.Ed.2d 1018 (1978). Once an allocation has been made—as was done in D–1485—that determination defines the scope of plaintiffs' property rights, pronouncements of other agencies notwithstanding. While we accept the principle that California water policy may be ever-evolving, rights based on contracts with the state are not correspondingly self-adjusting. Rather, the promissory assurances they recite remain fixed until formally changed. In the absence of a reallocation by the State Water Resources Control Board, or a determination of illegality by the California courts, the allocation scheme imposed by D–1485 defines the scope of plaintiffs' contract rights. None of the doctrines to which defendant resorts—the doctrine of reasonable use, the public trust doctrine or state nuisance law—are therefore availing.

* * * And while the administrative determinations issued by the SWRCB in 1995—the 1995 the Water Control Plan and the Water Right Decision 95–6—served to reallocate water allotments, they did so only after the period in dispute, and cannot therefore be construed as altering the scope of plaintiffs' contract rights for the 1992–1994 period.

Defendant argues against this position, urging us to anticipate how the Board or the California courts would apply the doctrine of reasonable use if the issue were before them. On that basis, defendant urges us to find that plaintiffs' proposed use of water is unreasonable—and therefore unlawful—to the extent that it endangers the fish. Defendant points to a myriad of state and federal actions as evidence that either the SWRCB or the California courts would have deemed plaintiffs' proposed use unreasonable. The issue, defendant contends, is not what limitations the state in fact imposed on plaintiffs' titles, but what limitations the state *could* have imposed under state background principles. * * *

* * * [According to d]efendant * * * the state does not have to declare a use a nuisance or unreasonable before the federal government can, without effecting a taking, exercise its own regulatory powers to abate that use. Put differently, the issue, in defendant's view, is whether the use could have been prohibited under state water or nuisance law. If so, defendant argues, the federal government is free to operate within the regulatory space carved out by the state background principles, whether or not the state has preceded it. * * *

* * * As the *Lucas* Court explained in describing those interests that, on the basis of nuisance principles, are non-compensable: "The use

of these properties for what are now expressly prohibited purposes was *always* unlawful, and (subject to other constitutional limitations) it was open to the State at any point to make the implication of those background principles of nuisance and property law explicit." *Lucas,* 505 U.S. at 1030.

That the use now being challenged was not always unlawful is evident from the fact that it was specifically authorized by the state in D–1485. Were we now to deem that use a nuisance, we would not be making explicit that which had always been implied under background principles of property law, but would instead be replacing the state's judgment with our own. That we cannot do.

* * * The public trust and reasonable use doctrines each require a complex balancing of interests—an exercise of discretion for which this court is not suited and with which it is not charged.

To the extent that water allocation in California is a policy judgment—one specifically committed to the SWRCB and the California courts—a finding of unreasonableness by this court would be tantamount to our *making* California law rather than merely applying it. This is especially true where, as here, the Board charged with such determinations has responded, and continues to respond, to the concerns about fish and wildlife that the government was seeking to address through the implementation of the ESA.[9]

While we are often asked to interpret state or federal statutes or regulations to determine the scope of a property interest under a takings claim, those determinations do not extend to matters of discretion committed to the authority of the state. Accordingly, we conclude that plaintiffs' right to divert water in the manner specified by their contracts and in conformance with D–1485 continued until a determination to the contrary was made either by the SWRCB or by the California courts. As no such determination was made during the period 1992–1994, and subsequent amendments to policy cannot, for contract purposes, be made retroactive, plaintiffs were indeed entitled to the water use provided for in D–1485 and in their contracts.

9. The California Court of Appeals has characterized D–1485 as "a policy judgment requiring a balancing of the competing public interests, one the Board is uniquely qualified to make in view of its special knowledge and expertise and its combined statewide responsibility to allocate the rights to, and to control the quality of, state water resources." United States v. State Water Resources Control Bd., 182 Cal. App.3d 82, 130, 227 Cal.Rptr. 161 (1986). The fact that fish and wildlife concerns were considered in D–1485 is evident from the decision's language that "full protection" of all fish species was not obtainable without the "virtual shutting down of the project export pumps"—an alternative the Board rejected. D–1485 at 13. The Board opted instead for what was described as "a reasonable level of protection." It is also notable that, since the 1992–1994 period that is the subject of suit, the SWRCB has indeed addressed the fish preservation issue: signing the "Principles for Agreement on Bay–Delta Standards between the State of California and the Federal Government" on December 15, 1994; adopting, after hearing and comment, WR 95–1, the 1995 Bay–Delta Plan, on May 22, 1995; and implementing various interim changes to D–1485 with regard to the responsibilities of water rights holders, including measures to ensure the preservation of fish.

CONCLUSION

There is, in the end, no dispute that DWR's permits, and in turn plaintiffs' contract rights, are subject to the doctrines of reasonable use and public trust and to the tenets of state nuisance law. Nor is there serious challenge to the premise that the SWRCB, under its reserved jurisdiction, could at any time modify the terms of those permits to reflect the changing need of the various water users. The crucial point, however, is that it had not. * * *

For the reasons stated, plaintiffs' motion for summary judgment must therefore be granted and defendant's cross-motion for summary judgment denied.

Note

For a critique of the *Tulare Lake* decision, see Brian E. Gray, The Property Right in Water, 9 Hastings W.-Nw J. Envtl. L. & Pol'y. 1 (2002).

Contra, Allegretti & Co. v. County of Imperial, 138 Cal.App. 4th 1261, 42 Cal.Rptr.3d 122 (2006). See Esplanade Properties, LLC v. City of Seattle, 307 F.3d 978, 985–86 (9th Cir. 2002).

KLAMATH IRRIGATION DISTRICT
v. UNITED STATES

United States Court of Federal Claims, 2005.
67 Fed. Cl. 504.

ALLEGRA, Judge.

* * *

In arguing * * * that the Bureau effectuated a taking of their contract rights, plaintiffs harken to this court's decision in Tulare Lake Basin Water Storage District v. United States, 49 Fed. Cl. 313 (2001). In that case, various districts in California argued that their contractually conferred water rights were taken as a result of the Bureau's restrictions on water use as required by the ESA. * * * This court ruled that a physical taking had occurred as a result of the restrictions and granted the plaintiffs summary judgment * * *. But, with all due respect, *Tulare* appears to be wrong on some counts, incomplete in others and, distinguishable, at all events.

For one thing, *Tulare* failed to consider whether the contract rights at issue were limited so as not to preclude enforcement of the ESA. Rather, the court treated the contract rights possessed by the districts essentially as absolute, without adequately considering whether they were limited in the case of water shortage, either by prior contracts, prior appropriations or some other state law principle. * * * ("[t]hose contracts confer on plaintiffs a right to the exclusive use of prescribed quantities of water"). Thus, although the court noted that there were agreements between the United States and the State of California creating a coordinated pumping system, * * * it did not examine those agreements to see whether they, like the district contracts here, limited the plaintiffs' rights derivatively * * *. Rather, it focused on the districts' contracts with state agencies as if they were free-standing. * * * Nor did the court consider whether the plaintiffs' claimed use of water violated accepted state doctrines, including those designed to protect fish and wildlife, finding that issue to be reserved exclusively to the state courts * * *. Because the state courts had not ruled on those issues, this court refused to rule on them, as well. As a result, it awarded just compensation for the taking of interests that may well not exist under state law. * * * On these counts, this court disagrees with the approach taken in *Tulare* and concludes that decision lends no support to the views espoused by plaintiffs here. * * *

Notes and Questions

1. For background on the Klamath dispute see Holly Doremus & A. Dan Tarlock, Fish, Farms, and the Clash of Cultures in the Klamath Basin, 30 Ecology L.Q. 279 (2003); Reed D. Benson, Giving Suckers (and Salmon) an Even Break: Klamath Basin Water and the Endangered Species Act, 15 Tulane Envtl. L.J. 197 (2002).

2. For what may be an earlier version of the sort of issue raised by Tulare Lake and Klamath, see Fox River Paper Co. v. Railroad Comm'n of Wisconsin, 274 U.S. 651 (1927), where the Court held it was not a taking of a dam owner's riparian property right for the state to require, as a condition of a permit to dam a navigable stream, agreement that the state could acquire the dam from the licensee riparian essentially at cost, though less than the market value. "We accept as conclusive," the Court said, "the state court's view of the rights of riparian owners."

3. The Endangered Species Act has generated a variety of different approaches, some very controversial. For example, diverters with right-of-way permits to cross national forest lands may have to yield "bypass flows" for fish downstream in order to get their permits renewed (see infra p. 1004). Similarly, ESA-needed flows have been imposed as conditions in hydropower facility (FERC) relicensing proceedings. Charles Sensiba, Who's In Charge Here? The Shrinking Role of the Federal Energy Regulatory Commission in Hydropower Relicensing, 70 U. Colo. L. Rev. 603 (1999).

———

The Edwards Aquifer Case

Probably no ESA water case has been as fiercely litigated, or as difficult to bring to resolution, as the Edwards Aquifer dispute in Texas. The number and variety of lawsuits it spawned is legion, and despite years of controversy, and the legislative establishment of an Aquifer Authority to deal with its problems, it was reported that "as of June 2002, three of the four primary tasks delegated by the legislature had not been completed * * * delays in the enforcement of the statutory limit on withdrawals; overestimation of available aquifer water for planning purposes; and inadequacy of trigger levels for the implementation of drought management rules * * *." Todd H. Votteler, Raiders of the Lost Aquifer? Or, the Beginning of the End to Fifty Years of Conflict Over the Texas Edwards Aquifer, 15 Tulane Envtl. L.J. 257, 277–78 (2002).

For our purposes, the essence of the case can be rather simply described. A groundwater aquifer in Southwest Texas, in which water moves essentially eastward is the sole water source for 2 million people, principally in the City of San Antonio. It also supplies many agricultural irrigators with traditional, rather inefficient means of distribution. Near the eastern end of the aquifer, water emerges from springs that feed the Guadalupe River, and supports a number of species listed under the ESA. The aquifer is very transmissive and therefore dependent upon the highly-variable annual rainfall for recharge. When, as happens fairly frequently, there is drought, pumping from the aquifer increases and the flow from the springs declines dramatically, jeopardizing the survival of the listed species, and causing "takes." The excerpt that follows describes the legal dispute that the Edwards Aquifer case generated.

TODD H. VOTTELER,
THE LITTLE FISH THAT ROARED: THE ENDANGERED SPECIES ACT, GROUNDWATER LAW, AND PRIVATE PROPERTY RIGHTS COLLIDE

28 Envtl. L. 845, 853–79 (1998).

The fountain darter at Comal Springs is typically the first species to be affected by declining springflow, and therefore the population of the darter serves as an early warning indicator of stress to the Edwards Aquifer system. A flow rate of 200 cubic feet per second (cfs) at Comal Springs, below which a taking can occur, is the tripwire for ESA litigation. When fountain darters are being taken, flows from the Aquifer are diminishing to the Springs as well as to downstream ecosystems and users in the Guadalupe River system. The Guadalupe River also provides freshwater inflows for San Antonio Bay, winter home of the endangered whooping crane (Grus americana). * * *

With the exception of the Gulf Coast Aquifer in the Houston and Galveston areas, and now the Edwards Aquifer, groundwater use in Texas is governed by the "rule of capture," also known as "the law of the biggest pump."[a]

The rule provides that a landowner, lessee, or assignee has the right to pump as much water as desired, provided the water is not willfully wasted, used maliciously to injure a third party, or pumped negligently.

---

a. For a discussion of Texas' adherence to the "rule of capture," see supra pp. 417–419 supra—Eds.

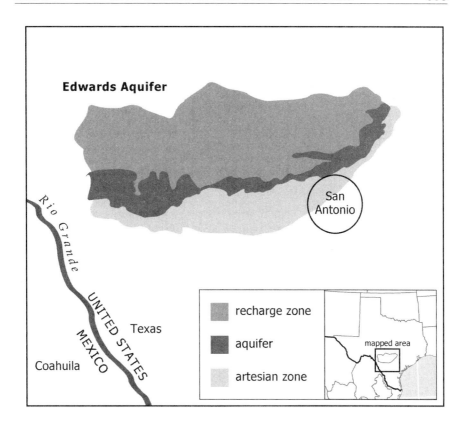

Figure 6–5

The Edwards Aquifer, San Antonio Section

In accordance with this rule, underground water is the exclusive property of the owner of the overlying land. * * * [W]ater planning legislation passed by the Texas Legislature in 1997 retained the rule of capture as the framework for regulating groundwater with a few exceptions.[b]

* * * [I]mposing state regulation of Edwards Aquifer water to protect endangered species has fueled the private property rights movement in Texas. * * *

IV. Sierra Club v. Babbitt

In 1991, the Sierra Club * * * filed a suit in the U.S. District Court in Midland, Texas against the Secretary of the Interior and the USFWS, alleging that the Secretary of the Interior had allowed takings of endangered species by not ensuring water levels in the Edwards Aquifer adequate to sustain the flow of Comal and San Marcos Springs. * * * [P]laintiffs requested that the court enjoin the defendants to restrict pumping from the Edwards Aquifer under certain conditions and to develop and implement recovery plans for certain endangered and

b. The Texas Supreme Court affirmed the rule of capture as Texas groundwater   law in Sipriano v. Great Spring Waters of America, 1 S.W.3d 75 (Tex. 1999)—Eds.

threatened species found in the Aquifer and at Comal and San Marcos Springs.

A.   *The Sierra Club and the Guadalupe–Blanco River Authority.*

On February 1, 1993, Judge Lucius Bunton ruled in favor of the plaintiffs. The court required the USFWS to determine the springflow requirements to avoid a taking or jeopardy of the listed species in both Springs. The court subsequently set a deadline for the State to prepare a plan that would protect minimum continuous springflows and Aquifer levels: "The next session of the Texas legislature offers the last chance for adoption of an adequate state plan before the 'blunt axes' of Federal intervention have to be dropped." * * *

The Sierra Club indicated that if it had to return to court, it would seek regulation of the Aquifer by the USFWS, placing the Aquifer under federal judicial control.

B.   *Senate Bill 1477, The Edwards Aquifer Authority Enabling Statute*

Senate Bill 1477[59] was adopted by the Legislature on May 30, 1993, one day before the deadline for federal action established by Judge Bunton. The bill, passed pursuant to the Conservation Amendment in the Texas Constitution,[60] established a conservation and reclamation district, the Edwards Aquifer Authority (EAA), to regulate groundwater withdrawals and manage the Aquifer. * * *

[I]n February 1996, after USFWS published a recovery plan for the threatened and endangered species at Comal and San Marcos Springs, and the appellate court concluded that all action required by Judge Bunton's 1993 amended judgment had been fulfilled. * * * [T]he litigation resulted in the end of the rule of capture for the Edwards Aquifer and the creation of a state entity specifically designed to regulate pumping. * * *

In the latter half of 1995 and most of 1996, much of Texas * * * suffered * * * a severe drought * * *. The EAA board, facing their first elections in November, was divided about taking the controversial emergency action that would reduce pumping from the Aquifer while running for reelection.

* * * After a vote by the EAA board declined on July 31, 1996 to declare a water use emergency, Judge Bunton appointed the author of this Article as Special Master on August 1, and directed him to produce a draft of a regional plan to reduce pumping from the Aquifer within ten days. A draft plan was developed within the deadline, released for public comment, then quickly revised and adopted by Judge Bunton as the 1996 Emergency Withdrawal Reduction Plan for the Edwards Aquifer (1996 EWRP). The 1996 EWRP contained a schedule of staged reductions of municipal pumping of discretionary water use from the Aquifer to be

---

59. S. 1477, 73d Leg., Reg. Sess. (Tex. 1993).   **60.** Tex. Const. art. XVI, 59.

triggered by declining flows from Comal Springs. The plan was designed to allow individual municipalities as much flexibility as possible to achieve the required reductions mandated by the court.

With none of the federal, state, or local government agencies acting to significantly reduce pumping from the Aquifer, Judge Bunton issued an order on August 23, 1996, setting a deadline of October 1, 1996 for the activation of the 1996 EWRP and directing the Special Master to monitor the 1996 EWRP's implementation as well as perform other additional duties. * * *

On April 30, 1997, after the crisis had passed, the Fifth Circuit vacated Judge Bunton's August 23, 1996 order, finding that the court should have abstained from acting on a matter that could be handled by EAA.[c]

* * * The next cycle began in 1998. This time USFWS warned pumpers that the agency was prepared to file civil lawsuits or bring criminal charges against pumpers to protect species in danger of dying from diminished springflow. In response to the drought, EAA implemented its plan, the Critical Period Management Plan, which restricted certain uses of water. * * * On August 5, 1998 a state district court in Travis County issued a temporary injunction against EAA, enjoining EAA from implementing or enforcing its rules * * * over concerns that rules adopted by EAA would treat some users of Edwards Aquifer water arbitrarily when allocating pumping. * * * A second ruling on September 11, 1998, this time by 38th State District Court Judge Mickey Pennington, also enjoined EAA from enforcing its rules and found that the Act creating EAA violated the Texas Private Real Property Rights Preservation Act by failing to conduct a takings impact assessment as required by the Act. On August 14, 1998, the Sierra Club notified EAA and USFWS of its intent to sue over violations of the ESA resulting from the "failure" of those entities to limit pumping from the Aquifer as required by Senate Bill 1477 and to enforce the recovery plan. * * * As a response to the threat of renewed ESA litigation, State Representative John Shields, whose district includes portions of San Antonio, filed suit against the Secretary of the Department of the Interior, Bruce Babbitt, the director of USFWS, Jamie Rappaport Clark, and the Sierra Club. Among other charges, Representative Shields alleges that the ESA has taken the private property rights of pumpers from the Aquifer, and that the ESA does not apply to the species listed at Comal and San Marcos Springs because they are "wholly intrastate species" residing completely within the boundaries of Texas. On September 14, 1998, the Environmental Defense Fund notified EAA of its intent to sue over violations of the ESA as a result of EAA allowing pumping from the Aquifer "in quantities great enough so as to reduce springflows at Comal and San Marcos Springs to the point that listed species are harmed and harassed." * * *

c. Sierra Club v. San Antonio, 112 F.3d
789 (5th Cir. 1997)—Eds.

The inability to regulate the Edwards Aquifer through local government placed the initiative to limit pumping from the Aquifer in the State's hands. When the State was unable to regulate the Aquifer, the federal government became the focus for managing withdrawals because of the effect of diminished springflow upon federally listed endangered species. When USFWS did not develop and implement a recovery plan for the endangered species, the authority for limiting withdrawals became the U.S. district court. With encouragement from the court, the State passed a statute designed to create a market for groundwater through a regional regulatory body. Despite numerous opportunities to do so at earlier dates, the court did not move to reduce pumping from the Aquifer until flow at Comal and San Marcos Springs declined significantly below the level at which jeopardy begins for the fountain darter. While sometimes accused of a "federal power grab," the district court consistently exercised restraint until the duty to enforce federal law was overwhelming. By refusing to accept some restrictions on pumping through local governments, those who dreaded the loss of control over their ability to pump from the Aquifer brought on the very result they professed to fear most—federal intervention. Even then, the court gave the state legislature opportunities to protect the species without imposing federal control. * * *

Notes and Questions

1. In his 2002 follow-up article, cited above, Todd Votteler further explains why the Edward Aquifer problem continued to be so troublesome for so long. While the state-created Aquifer Authority has authority to issue permits and reduce pumping to amounts that would meet environmental limits, it has shown reluctance to do so in the face of demands by existing users, and was considering seeking legislative authority to raise the authorized pumping limits (above the scientists' determined acceptable maxima). Resolution was also impaired by a Supreme Court ruling protecting existing irrigation users, finding that pumpers must receive a permit for at least the average amount of water withdrawn annually during the pre-regulation period. One result is that all the required reductions have to be imposed on municipal and industrial users. One proposed solution for them is to divert new surface water for San Antonio from the Guadalupe River downstream of its confluence with the San Antonio River, but this presents its own problems. For one, it raises issues of the ecological impact of reducing freshwater inflows to the Guadalupe Estuary and San Antonio Bay, as well as a legal problem if such a project is considered an interbasin transfer since Texas law makes all such transfers junior in priority to water rights in the basin of origin—and so such uses would be of limited reliability (see Texas Water Code Ann. § 11.085). Even if such new surface sources do become available, the cost of such water, treated and pumped uphill to San Antonio would be about $829 per acre-foot, vastly more than the value of the water in irrigation (though apparently a system of charges on urban users to finance some such system is in place). Desalted seawater has also been proposed as a source, though it is at least equally costly. To add to this mixture, there is apparently controversy about technical issues, such as the

existing estimates of the freshwater ecological needs of the bays and estuaries.

2. Does a state law that changes the rights of groundwater users in order to meet ESA requirements constitute a constitutional taking of their property without compensation? Agricultural interests thought so. But Votteler says:

> Agricultural interests contended that the regulation of Edwards water is a taking of private property. * * * [H]owever, under [the new Texas legislation] the regulation and allocation of Edwards water through annual withdrawal permits is actually creating quantifiable property rights that can be protected under law for the first time [as contrasted with the traditional rule of capture groundwater law of Texas]. Once permits issued by the Edwards Aquifer Authority to withdraw specific amounts of water from the Edwards Aquifer are final, a free-market will exist because the fundamental characteristics of a property system will be present.
>
> In the Edwards Aquifer, none of the conditions establishing a true property right were met prior to regulation. There was no universality because entitlements could not be quantified under a system where a pumper's reserve of water was vulnerable to extraction by a neighbor under the rule of capture. Exclusivity did not exist because * * * well owners did not have the option of leasing or selling the water to which they had access, since there was no * * * guarantee to assure a fixed available quantity to the purchaser. Similarly, transferability did not exist since there was no documentary evidence of a claimed right. Even if one well owner was paid not to pump water, another nearby landowner was not prevented from drilling a new well * * *. There was no effective way to prevent one pumper from encroaching on another individual's claimed right.

15 Tulane Envtl. L.J., at 314.

3. Votteler's 1998 article also noted that Texas interests had declined to develop a Habitat Conservation Plan (HCP), a statutorily authorized, federally-approved negotiated solution among federal, local government, and private interests, that can legitimate some incidental "take" of listed species so long as the plan as a whole avoids jeopardy. See ESA § 10(a), 16 U.S.C. § 1539(a). For a discussion of HCP's, and references to the literature, see Barton H. Thompson, Jr., The Endangered Species Act: A Case Study in Takings and Incentives, 49 Stan. L. Rev. 305 (1997).

4. Should what happened in the Edwards Aquifer be described as a "federal takeover" of state water law? Certainly all the activity, though done through the form of state legislation and regulation, was generated by federal law and a federal court decision. How might one expect the Congress, sensitive as it is to state water law prerogatives, to react to the series of events described in the Votteler article, all generated by the need to protect federally listed species? Or is the lesson that the feds should have taken over even more directly, since Texas has taken so long and had so much trouble

in coming to some resolution of the problem?[1] Is this just an example of the inevitable problems when new demands for a limited supply upset longstanding uses and expectations? Is the Edwards Aquifer just one example of what many other places are experiencing, or are destined to experience if we are serious about protecting water-dependent ecosystems? Is it just about endangered species, or is it part of the more pervasive problem of traditional agricultural irrigation confronting rapidly growing populations, especially in the Southwest?

c. *National Environmental Policy Act*

The National Environmental Policy Act of 1969 (NEPA),[2] although held to be essentially a procedural statute, also helps shape water development projects. Under NEPA, a federal agency must prepare an environmental impact statement (EIS) whenever it recommends legislation or undertakes "major Federal actions significantly affecting the quality of the human environment."[3] There has been extensive litigation over what is "major," "federal," "significant," and so on as to each term in this provision. Virtually any water development project undertaken by a federal agency, however, will be a major federal action.[4] At least one court has held that the issuance of a section 404 permit by the Army Corps of Engineers in connection with a private, state, or local water project is also a major federal action, and the Corps has issued regulations for complying with NEPA in issuing permits. See Beaufort–Jasper County Water Auth. v. United States Army Corps of Engineers, 22 Env't Rep. Cas. (BNA) 1410, 1416 (D.S.C. 1984); 33 C.F.R. pt. 325, app. B. To determine whether such actions have a significant effect on the environment and thus require an EIS, agencies generally prepare an initial "environmental assessment" (EA) of the proposed action.

According to NEPA, an EIS must include a detailed discussion of:

(i) the environmental impact of the proposed action,

(ii) any adverse environmental effects which cannot be avoided should the proposal be implemented,

(iii) alternatives to the proposed action,

(iv) the relationship between local short-term uses of man's environment and the maintenance and enhancement of long-term productivity, and

---

1. Note that in 1997, the Fifth Circuit ordered the district court to abstain, saying the Edwards Aquifer matter could be handled by the Edwards Aquifer Authority (Sierra Club v. San Antonio, 112 F.3d 789 (1997)): "[T]he Edwards Aquifer Act can fairly be characterized as a comprehensive regulatory scheme. It represents a sweeping effort by the Texas Legislature to regulate the aquifer, with due regard for all competing demands for the aquifer's water. The Act vests the Edwards Aquifer Authority

with 'all the powers and privileges necessary to manage, conserve, preserve, and protect the aquifer'. * * *"

2. 42 U.S.C. §§ 4331 et seq.

3. 42 U.S.C. § 4332(2)(C).

4. But see Westlands Water Dist. v. Natural Resources Defense Council, 43 F.3d 457, 460–461 (9th Cir. 1994) (CVPIA elements exempt from NEPA review).

(v) any irreversible and irretrievable commitments of resources which would be involved in the proposed action should it be implemented.[5]

Most NEPA litigation has involved the adequacy of an EIS, with one of the most frequent questions being whether an EIS has adequately considered alternatives to the proposed project. The EIS must consider all reasonable alternatives to the proposed action—although the Supreme Court has cautioned that an agency need not consider "every alternative device and thought conceivable by the mind of man."[6] In the case of a water project designed to supply water to off-stream users, alternatives might include modified project plans, reliance on alternative sources of water such as market purchases, and conservation.

Another frequently litigated issue of relevance to water projects is the proper scope of an EIS. Where a federal agency is planning to undertake a number of projects in the same water basin, for example, is it sufficient to prepare an EIS for each project or must a "programmatic" EIS be prepared covering the basinwide effects? In Kleppe v. Sierra Club, 427 U.S. 390 (1976), the Supreme Court refused to require an areawide EIS for a regional coal development plan. On occasion, Congress has explicitly exempted water projects in some basins from an obligation to prepare a programmatic EIS.[7]

It is important to emphasize that NEPA, as interpreted, is essentially procedural. Although circuits were originally split on the question whether NEPA imposed any substantive requirements, the Supreme Court in Strycker's Bay Neighborhood Council v. Karlen, 444 U.S. 223 (1980), held that "once an agency has made a decision subject to NEPA's procedural requirements, the only role for a court is to insure that the agency has considered the environmental consequences; it cannot 'interject itself within the area of discretion of the executive as to the choice of the action to be taken.'" And in Robertson v. Methow Valley Citizens Council, 490 U.S. 332 (1989), the Court reconfirmed that "NEPA itself does not mandate particular results, but simply prescribes the necessary process. * * * Other statutes may impose substantive environmental obligations on federal agencies, but NEPA merely prohibits uninformed—rather than unwise—agency action."

The details of NEPA and its EIS requirements have generated their own specialty field of law. For a comprehensive treatise, see Daniel Mandelker, NEPA Law and Litigation (2d ed. 1994). From a policy standpoint, the major question has been the impact of the EIS requirement on agency decisionmaking. A leading study, focusing on the Corps of Engineers and the Forest Service, is Serge Taylor, Making Bureaucracies Think: The Environmental Impact Statement Strategy of Administrative Reform (1984).

5. 42 U.S.C. § 4332(2)(C).

6. Vermont Yankee Nuclear Power Corp. v. Natural Resources Defense Council, 435 U.S. 519, 551 (1978).

7. See, e.g., 92 Stat. 1279, 1291.

Some 15 states have also adopted comprehensive environmental assessment legislation more or less modeled on NEPA and applying to state actions. They are detailed in Mandelker, supra, ch. 12.

d. Wild and Scenic Rivers Legislation

i. Federal Law[8]

The Wild and Scenic Rivers Act of 1968, 16 U.S.C. §§ 1271–1287, declares in section 1271 that certain selected rivers "shall be preserved in free-flowing condition * * *." It does this by prohibiting federal licensing of development that would be incompatible with protection of the river, and by controlling development along designated river corridors. Section 7(a) of the Act, 16 U.S.C. § 1278(a), forbids the Federal Energy Regulatory Agency from licensing any project "on or directly affecting" a designated river, and forbids other federal agencies from undertaking or assisting any water projects "that would have a direct and adverse effect on the values for which such river was established."

Conflict between the statute and state water law has not yet been settled in litigation, though Congress did anticipate some problems. Section 13, 16 U.S.C. § 1284, states:

(b) The jurisdiction of the States and the United States over waters of any stream included in a national wild, scenic or recreational river area shall be determined by established principles of law. Under the provisions of this chapter, any taking by the United States of a water right which is vested under either State or Federal law at the time such river is included in the * * * system shall entitle the owner thereof to just compensation. Nothing in this chapter shall constitute an express or implied claim or denial on the part of the Federal Government as to exemption from State water laws. * * *

(d) The jurisdiction of the States over waters of any stream included in a national wild * * * river area shall be unaffected by this chapter to the extent that such jurisdiction may be exercised without impairing the purposes of this chapter or its administration.

The statute reserves—in effect appropriates to the federal government as a matter of federal law—certain unappropriated water in order to assure flows needed to meet the purposes of the Act.

Section 13(c) provides:

Designation of any stream or portion thereof as a national wild, scenic or recreational river area shall not be construed as a reservation of the waters of such streams for purposes other than those specified in this [Act], or in quantities greater than necessary to accomplish these purposes.

Section 10 of the Act, § 1281(a) says:

---

8. There is additional discussion of this issue in chapter 9, infra p. 934.

Each component of the national wild and scenic rivers
system shall be administered in such a manner as to protect and
enhance the values which caused it to be included in said
system without, insofar as is consistent therewith, limiting
other uses that do not substantially interfere with public use
and enjoyment of these values.

Professor Brian Gray has made a detailed study of the law in his
article, No Holier Temples: Protecting the National Parks Through Wild
and Scenic River Designation, 58 U. Colo. L. Rev. 551 (1988). Among the
situations he considers is that of a national park through which a river
runs, but where the park is located downstream of potential private
appropriations on the river. In such a situation can park officials in
effect veto any proposed new diversions upstream of that portion of the
river which has been designated under the Wild and Scenic Rivers Act?
Does section 13 of the Act, cited above, give the state anything to say
about whether such diversions may be made, or is this entirely a
question of federal law? Professor Gray makes the following observation
at p. 579 of his article:

The most obvious application of the federal water right
would be to prevent upstream junior users from diminishing the
flow of the river below the level needed to supply the various
purposes for which the river was included in the national rivers
system. Thus, consistent with traditional prior appropriation
law, the federal water right empowers the Park Service to place
a call on the river to demand from junior users sufficient water
to supply its senior rights. Moreover, the water right grants the
Park Service the legal authority to defeat proposals for new
diversion projects upstream of the parks that threaten the
values of the wild or scenic river area.

Isn't Professor Gray obviously correct? If so, doesn't the statute
effectively destroy state jurisdiction over designated rivers despite its
denials?

ii. State Laws

Some states have their own wild and scenic river designation laws.[9]
For a discussion of the circumstances under which an appropriation is
permissible upstream of a designated river under Oregon's Scenic Waterways Act, see Diack v. City of Portland, 306 Or. 287, 759 P.2d 1070
(1988). The California statute provides:

* * * nor shall any water diversion facility be constructed
on any such river and segment unless and until the Secretary
[for Resources] determines that the facility is needed to supply
domestic water to the residents of the county * * * through
which the river and segment flows, and unless and until the
secretary determines that facility will not adversely affect the

9. See, e.g., Mich. Comp. Laws Ann. § 30.26; Me. Rev. Stat. Ann. §§ 12–403;
§§ 324.30501–324.30515; Wis. Stat. Ann. Okla. Stat. Ann., tit. 82, § 1451.

free-flowing condition and natural character of the river and segment.

Cal. Pub. Res. Code § 5093.55. "The Department of Water Resources estimates that 25% of stream runoff in California is set aside in the north coastal area under the Wild and Scenic Rivers Act and is not available for water supply development." Anne J. Schneider, Legal Aspects of Instream Water Use in California (Staff Paper No. 6, Governor's Comm'n to Review California Water Rights Law, Dec. 23, 1977). For a detailed discussion of the federal and California laws, and their role as foci for conflict between developmental and preservationist interests, see Sally Fairfax, Barbara Andrews, & Andrew Buchsbaum, Federalism and the Wild and Scenic Rivers Act: Now You See It, Now You Don't, 59 Wash. L. Rev. 417 (1984).

e. Federal Power Act: Dams in the Environmental Era

The Federal Power Act of 1920[10] required a license for all nonfederal hydropower dams on rivers defined (broadly, for that purpose)[11] as navigable. During the heyday of hydropower, the Federal Power Commission, now the Federal Energy Regulatory Commission (FERC) issued thousands of such licenses for terms extending from 30 to 50 years. One consequence of the many dams constructed under these licenses was a drastic diminution of fish populations, despite the installation of required facilities such as fish ladders. By the time many of the licenses came up for renewal, in the late 1980's and early 1990's, hydropower had become a much less important source of electricity in most of the country, and—in an environmentally conscious period—what had once seemed unthinkable became a subject of serious debate: dam removal as an element of fish-friendly river restoration. Interior Secretary Bruce Babbitt began raising the issue in public speeches. While talk began about removal of even the biggest dams, such as Glen Canyon, for the most part serious attention focused on smaller, obsolete dams, that had little economic value but were significant obstructions to fish, such as the Elwha River dams on the Olympic Peninsula in Washington. In fact several dams were removed in the 1990's, including Newport No. 11 on the Clyde River in Vermont, the Western Canal Dam on a tributary of the Sacramento River in California, and the Quaker Neck Dam on the Neuse River in North Carolina.

None of those dams had been removed because they were denied a relicensing by FERC, however. Indeed, FERC had never denied a relicensing. On November 26, 1997, however, a new precedent was set. For the first time, the Commission issued an order denying a new license and ordering a dam removed in a case where the licensee was actively seeking a new license. The facility in question was the Edwards Dam on

---

10. 16 U.S.C. §§ 791(a) et seq.

11. United States v. Appalachian Elec. Power Co., 311 U.S. 377, 426–27 (1940)

("[The] authority is as broad as the needs of commerce").

the Kennebec River in Maine.[12] Under a rather elaborate set of agreements, the license was transferred to the State of Maine, which assumed responsibility and liability for removal of the dam. Several industries on the River agreed to contribute to the costs of removal and related costs as elements of mitigation for other developments of their own on the Kennebec. Thus the Edwards Dam matter was settled without the necessity to litigate the panoply of intriguing legal questions that would be put in question where relicensing is denied and dam removal is mandated. Between 1993 and 2010, 419 FERC licenses expire. Proceedings on some of them will doubtless be controverted and raise a variety of issues, in particular the legal status of a license.[13]

For example, industry has argued that FERC cannot simply deny a license or decommission an existing project upon expiration. Instead, it claims, the Commission may either take over the project upon payment to the licensee of fair market or net investment value; relicense upon reasonable terms to the existing licensee or a new licensee (upon payment to the existing licensee); or issue a temporary non-power license when it finds that a license project should no longer be used for power purposes. Among the unanswered questions are these: (1) If FERC does deny hydropower relicensing, does it retain any other regulatory authority at the site? May it, for example, still require installation of fish ladders, or would regulatory authority then simply devolve to the state? (2) Even if FERC can deny relicensing, does it have authority to order removal of the dam, and to require the licensee the pay those costs.[14] (3) Could FERC allow relicensing on conditions designed to protect or restore environmental values if the cost of meeting those conditions made the project economically non-viable.[15]

The following is an excerpt from FERC's Policy Statement in which it addresses the questions just posed.

PROJECT DECOMMISSIONING AT RELICENSING: POLICY STATEMENT

Federal Energy Regulatory Commission, Dec. 14, 1994.
69 F.E.R.C. ¶ 61,336.

I. INTRODUCTION AND SUMMARY

The Federal Energy Regulatory Commission (Commission) is adopting a policy statement that addresses issues related to relicensing and decommissioning. * * *

---

12. Edwards Manufacturing Co., Inc., Project No. 2389–012, Order Denying New License and Requiring Dam Removal, 81 F.E.R.C. ¶ 61,255 (Nov. 25, 1997).

13. See Alabama Power Co. v. Federal Power Comm'n, 128 F.2d 280 (D.C. Cir. 1942) (grant of a license is a "privilege").

14. State of Wisconsin v. FERC, 104 F.3d 462 (D.C. Cir. 1997) (dictum: FERC

could "provide for decommissioning" of projects).

15. See Wisconsin Public Service Corp. v. FERC, 32 F.3d 1165, 1168 (7th Cir. 1994) ("there can be no guarantee of profitability of water power projects under the Federal Power Act").

In those instances where it has been determined that a project will no longer be licensed, because the licensee either decides not to seek a new license, rejects the license issued, or is denied a new license, the project must be decommissioned. The [question is] * * * the extent of the Commission's authority over decommissioning and the process to be applied when a project is to be decommissioned. The statutory language does not expressly address, in any comprehensive manner, the Commission's authority over decommissioning and the process to be applied in carrying it out. In such a situation, the Commission has the authority to fill in gaps left by the statute and to ensure that a project is decommissioned in a manner that is consistent with the public interest. The Commission will take a very flexible approach to the carrying out of this process. * * *

II. THE COMMISSION'S OPTIONS AT RELICENSING

A. The Original Legislation

When the Federal Water Power Act (FWPA)[3] was enacted in 1920 after several years of consideration and debate, sections 14 and 15 were key parts of the legislation. There was a keen interest by some members of Congress in providing the opportunity for eventual Federal takeover of Commission-licensed power projects, and that became reflected in section 14. This section was designed as a vehicle that would permit the Federal government to own, maintain, and operate valuable water-power projects under terms which could make such takeover practical when the circumstances warranted.[4]

Congress further provided in section 15 of the FWPA that if Congress did not elect the first option of taking over and operating the project when a license expired, then the Commission was authorized to issue a new license either to the original licensee or to a new licensee. * * *

The focus during this period was plainly on the three options: Federal takeover and continued operation; a new license to a new licensee and continued operation; and a new license to the old licensee, who would also continue operation. In the first two cases, the entity taking over the operation would have to pay the existing licensee for the project, according to the formula established in section 14.

This did not, however, necessarily mean continuation of business as usual. The statute provided for license terms of up to 50 years on original licenses.[7] * * * By so limiting the duration for which these licenses could be granted, Congress intended to preserve for the Nation the opportunity of reevaluating the use to which each project site should be put in light of changing conditions and national goals.

3. Pub. L. 66–280, 41 Stat. 1063 (June 10, 1920).

4. That was before the period of the large-scale construction of hydropower projects by the Federal Government that would mark future decades. At that point, proponents of Federal ownership faced considerable resistance to the concept. * * *

7. Section 6 of the FWPA.

During the license period, as reflected in sections 6 and 28 of the FWPA, licensees enjoyed considerable security. At the end of that period, the Commission would reexamine the statutory standard and make a new determination. Under section 10 of the FWPA, new licenses (except the interim annual licenses) could be issued only on the condition: "That the project adopted * * * shall be such as in the judgment of the commission will be best adapted to a comprehensive scheme of improvement and utilization for the purposes of navigation, of water-power development, and of other beneficial uses; and if necessary in order to secure such scheme the commission shall have the authority to require the modification of any project and of the plans and specifications of the project works before approval."

Any new license that the Commission issued would be pursuant to the terms of the then-prevailing laws and regulations and carry such further reasonable terms and conditions as the Commission then deemed appropriate to implement the statutory standard.[10] Each license was to be conditioned on acceptance of those terms.[11] * * * There was no mention in the legislation of the possibility of denying a license, which would put the project out of business. At the same time, there was no discussion of what was to occur if, at relicensing, the Commission could not make the requisite finding under the comprehensive development standard. * * * That is, there was no direction concerning how the Commission was to reconcile the potentially conflicting terms of sections 10 and 15.

B.   The Current Statutory Scheme

Section 14 remains on the books, although the Federal Government has never taken over a licensed project under its terms, nor has the Commission ever recommended that it do so. Section 15 likewise remains on the books. As the first licenses were about to expire, 50 years after initial passage of the FWPA, a term was added to section 15 of what was now the Federal Power Act,[13] authorizing the Commission to issue non-power licenses.[14] No such license has been issued, either. In nearly every instance, existing licensees have applied for, and received, new power licenses when their old ones expired.

All of these decisions have been made in the context of the Commission's implementation of the comprehensive development standard of section 10(a) of the Act. At the same time, section 10(a) has evolved since 1920.[15] It no longer has the almost exclusively pro-development focus of

10.   Section 15 of the FWPA.

11.   Section 6 of the FWPA.

13.   16 U.S.C. 791a, et seq.

14.   Section 3 of Pub. L. 90–451, 82 Stat. 617 (Aug. 3, 1968).

15.   Section 10(a) now reads: "That the project adopted * * * shall be such as in the judgment of the Commission will be best adapted to a comprehensive scheme for improving and developing a waterway or waterways for the use and benefit of interstate or foreign commerce, for the improvement and utilization of water power development, for the adequate protection, mitigation, and enhancement of fish and wildlife (including related spawning grounds and habitat), and for other beneficial public uses, including irrigation, flood control, water supply, and recreational and

the 1918–20 period, when the original legislation was propelled by the largely undeveloped status of the country's water-power resources and the power shortages that had existed during World War I.[16]

Environmental considerations evoked virtually no comment in the debates and reports immediately preceding adoption of the FWPA.[17] However, these considerations have become important factors since the 1950s, as experience with the effects of water-power project operation has grown. This has resulted in new license conditions that have generally increased the costs associated with running hydropower projects.

The first steps in this direction were taken by the Commission in various individual licensing orders it issued.[18] Then, as States began to challenge Commission environmental actions, and seek concurrent jurisdiction, the courts put their imprimatur on the matter. They generally upheld the Commission's preemptive authority in this area,[19] but underscored further the Commission's responsibilities for environmental protection.[20]

Finally, in 1986 changes were made to the Act which codified and extended the earlier actions.[21] This is reflected principally in sections 10(a) and 10(j). Section 10(a) was expanded to refer explicitly to fish and wildlife concerns. A new section 10(j) was added to require expressly that, in every license it issues, the Commission establish conditions for the adequate and equitable protection of, mitigation of, damages to, and enhancement of fish and wildlife.

The 1986 legislation directed the Commission, when establishing license conditions, to reach an appropriate balance between power and other developmental interests and the protection of non-development resources, such as fish and wildlife. It must consider, but need not give controlling weight to, the recommendations of various Federal and State resource agencies. There are however two long-standing provisions which authorize other federal agencies to promulgate license conditions. The Secretaries of the Interior and Commerce have their own power under section 18 to require construction, maintenance, and operation of fishways. In many instances fishways were not required at the time of initial licensing, but are being mandated at the time of relicensing.

other purposes referred to in section 4(e)." * * *

16. See, e.g., H.R. Rep. No. 715, 65th Cong., 2d Sess. 15, 29 (1918); H.R. Rep. No. 61, 66th Cong., 1st Sess. 4 (1919); 1918 House Hearings 5–15, 458–59; 56 Cong. Rec. 8929, 9120–22, 9614 (1918); 58 Cong. Rec. 1932 (1919).

17. As discussed later, there were two provisions included in the 1920 legislation, involving fishways and Federal reservations, which have environmental overtones. However, both were carry-overs from predecessor legislation (requiring permits for projects on Federal lands or in navigable waters), and were not the subject of any significant attention at that time.

18. The first time such considerations were reflected in the Commission's Standard Terms and Conditions for licenses was in 1964. See, e.g., 31 FPC 286, 530; 32 FPC 73, 841, 1116 (1964). However, such terms began to appear with increasing frequency in licenses issued during the 1950s.

19. FPC v. Oregon, 349 U.S. 435 (1955).

20. Udall v. FPC, 387 U.S. 428 (1967).

21. Pub. L. 99–495, 100 Stat. 1243 (Oct. 16, 1986).

Similarly, where the project is built in a National Forest or other Federal reservation, under section 4(e) of the Act the Secretary of the department responsible for supervision of the reservation is empowered to establish, at the time of licensing, conditions he or she believes to be necessary for the adequate protection and utilization of the reservation. These conditions may also be revisited at relicensing. * * *

C. Discussion

As the Commission interprets the terms of the Act, the statutory scheme contemplates that normally the balancing between power and environmental interests can and will be accommodated through license conditions. If the licensee's proposal does not satisfy the comprehensive development standard of section 10(a), then the Commission will add terms that will bring it into compliance.

To date, the Commission has not been confronted with any relicensing situation where its conditioning authority has been inadequate to do the job, i.e., where there was unacceptable environmental damage that proved irremediable. Nonetheless, if such a situation were to occur, the Commission does not read the Act as requiring it to issue a license. Such an approach would compel it to ignore the strictures of section 10(a), which the courts have long recognized rests at the core of the Commission's licensing responsibilities.[25]

* * * Actually by the time the first licenses began to expire, the concept of the inevitability of power operation from a particular project was eroding. In 1968, the statute was amended to provide for nonpower licenses. Section 15(f) of the Act states (emphasis added):

> In issuing any licenses under this section except an annual license, the Commission, on its own motion or upon application of any licensee, person, State, municipality, or State commission, after notice to each State commission and licensee affected, and after opportunity for hearing, *whenever it finds that in conformity with a comprehensive plan for improving or developing a waterway or waterways for beneficial public uses all or part of any licensed project should no longer be used or adapted for use for power purposes*, may license all or part of the project works for non-power use.

The underscored language shadows that of section 10(a), and recognizes that there can be situations where the standard embodied therein cannot be met and the Commission decides that a project should no longer be used for power purposes.

Later, in language added to section 4(e) of the Act in 1986, Congress further stated (emphasis added):

> In deciding *whether to issue any license under this Part for any project*, the Commission, in addition to the power and

25. FPC v. Union Electric Co., 381 U.S. 90, 98 (1965); First Iowa Hydro–Electric   Cooperative v. FPC, 328 U.S. 152, 180–81 (1946).

development purposes for which licenses are issued, shall give equal consideration to the purposes of energy conservation, the protection, mitigation of damage to, and enhancement of, fish and wildlife (including related spawning grounds and habitat), the protection of recreational opportunities, and the preservation of other aspects of environmental quality.

* * * Given this history, it is the Commission's view that, in those cases where, even with ample use of its conditioning authority, a license still cannot be fashioned that will comport with the statutory standard under section 10(a), the Commission has the power to deny a license.

The Commission rejects any suggestion that, rather than denying a new license, the United States would have to take over the property under section 14. It is abundantly clear from the legislative history of the FWPA that section 14 was designed to permit the Federal Government to take over and operate the property, not close it down. * * * There is nothing in that legislation that contemplates the prospect of requiring the Government to routinely bail out projects that can no longer pass muster under section 10(a) because of serious and irremediable adverse public impacts. * * *

To this point, the discussion has focused on license denial, which is expected to be highly unusual. The more likely scenario is one in which the Commission is required to condition a new power license with environmental mitigation measures, and the licensee is unwilling to accept the license tendered. The licensee may prefer to take the project out of business, because the costs of doing business have become too high. There is no merit to the suggestion by some industry commenters that a condition in a power license is per se unreasonable if, as a result of imposing the condition, the project is no longer economically viable. The statute calls for a balancing of various development and nondevelopment interests, and those commenters' position would elevate power and other development interests far above the environmental concerns. It would mean that severe environmental damage would have to be accepted in order to protect even a very marginal hydropower project. The Commission does not read the Federal Power Act to compel such a result. As the Court of Appeals for the Seventh Circuit recently observed:[31] "[T]here can be no guarantee of profitability of water power projects under the Federal Power Act; profitability is at risk from a number of variable factors, and values other than profitability require appropriate consideration." * * *

There may be some occasions where the obligation to pay increased environmental costs at relicensing will force a hydropower project to close down. With the increasing emphasis on competition in the electric power industry today, the prospect of shutting down certain power projects may increase. However, this is not unique to hydroelectric projects.

31. Wisconsin Public Service Corp. v. FERC, 32 F.3d 1165, 1168 (7th Cir. 1994).

The possibility that a project may have to shut down is not a legitimate basis for the Commission to ignore its obligations to impose necessary environmental conditions. However, the Commission is required to balance a number of different factors under sections 4(e) and 10(a) of the Act in its licensing decisions. Should it be demonstrated that the environmental costs would be excessive or that loss of power supplied by the project would be significant, that evidence can be considered in assessing the power and development aspects to be weighed under section 10(a)'s comprehensive development standard * * *.

III.   THE DECOMMISSIONING PROCESS

A.   *Experience with Project Retirement*

* * *

Rather late in the legislative process leading to the FWPA, Congress added to the other terms of section 6 a brief reference to surrender of licenses, without explanation or comment. * * * []The Commission issued a regulation * * * [providing that] if any project works had been constructed, the surrender had to be "upon such conditions with respect to the disposition of such works as may be determined by the Commission." * * *

B.   *The Commission's Role in Decommissioning*

Sections 6 and 15(f) deal expressly with only two situations—surrenders during a license term and situations where the Commission has issued a non-power license at the end of a license term. However, there is no evidence to suggest that Congress determined or intended that the Commission was to be left powerless to deal with other, analogous situations. As the Court of Appeals for the District of Columbia Circuit has recognized:[40] "The Act is not to be given a tight reading wherein every action of the Commission is justified only if referable to express statutory authorization. On the contrary, the Act is one that entrusts a broad subject-matter to administration by the Commission, subject to Congressional oversight, in the light of new and evolving problems and doctrines."

Likewise, the Supreme Court has observed, "The power of an administrative agency to administer a congressionally created * * * program necessarily requires the formulation of policy and the making of rules to fill any gap left, implicitly or explicitly, by Congress."

The Commission is of the opinion that implicit in the section 6 surrender provision is the view that a licensee ought not to be able simply to walk away from a Commission-licensed project without any Commission consideration of the various public interests that might be implicated by that step. Rather, the Commission should be able to take appropriate steps that will satisfactorily protect the public interests involved. * * *

---

40. Niagara Mohawk Power Corp. v. FPC, 379 F.2d 153, 158 (D.C. Cir. 1967).   See also Northern States Power Co. v. FPC, 118 F.2d 141, 143 (7th Cir. 1941).

E. *The Project After Decommissioning*

When a project will no longer be licensed, the Commission's jurisdiction is going to end. The future operation of any remaining works is then the responsibility of whoever next assumes regulatory authority. The Commission does not believe that, at that point, it has the authority to require the existing licensee to install new facilities, such as fish ladders.

Basically, the Commission issues a license for a particular period, subject to certain conditions. The licensee may have an opportunity to obtain a new license at the end of that term, subject to new conditions; but, if it elects not to do so, the Commission cannot go forward and require the same future steps to be taken anyway, as part of the decommissioning process. * * *

IV. FUNDING DECOMMISSIONING COSTS

* * * Normally, * * * the Commission anticipates that the licensee will be responsible for paying the costs (up to a reasonable level) of the steps needed to decommission the project, since the licensee created the project and benefitted from its operations. * * *

Chapter 7

WATER ORGANIZATIONS

The preceding chapters reveal how often the parties to water disputes are organizations such as a water district, mutual water company, or municipality. Such organizations control and distribute a great deal of water, particularly in the West. Most water lawyers, moreover, are concerned as much with the legal powers of such organizations as with the water rights issues you have studied up to this point. We leave to courses in local government, public utility regulation, business law, and taxation much of the law relevant to water organizations. In this Chapter, we examine some of the organizational questions of special importance to the allocation and control of water resources.

A. A BRIEF HISTORY AND OVERVIEW OF WATER ORGANIZATIONS

Water organizations are used to achieve numerous purposes. One purpose is to reduce the cost and risk of water development. The storage and delivery of water enjoys considerable economies of scale. Organizations that supply water to a group of users can dramatically reduce the cost that the users would pay if they had to develop their own separate water supplies; by tapping multiple sources, moreover, such organizations can reduce the risk that an individual with only a single supply would face. Another purpose is to improve local management of water resources. Groundwater management districts, for example, can provide effective regulation that is contoured to the local aquifer and local uses. See supra pp. 512–520. A final purpose is to take advantage of special legal powers often held by the organizations. For example, governmental water districts can condemn water rights and land, tax local property, and issue tax-exempt bonds.

Municipal Water Suppliers

Organizations have always played an important role in providing water to city residents. Prior to the American Revolution, cities generally supplied the water themselves through public wells.[1] As water demand increased in the late 18th century, private water companies responded. Ten percent of all the corporations formed during the last decade of that century were created to supply water to city users.[2] Criticism, however, soon arose that private water companies were charging exorbitant rates, favoring the more prosperous areas of towns, and failing to reinvest adequate sums in system growth. During the height of typhoid fears, many cities also worried that private suppliers would try to save money by ignoring water quality. In the words of one progressive reformer:

> We have municipal ownership of our police and fire protection because we know enough not to entrust the safety of ourselves and our family silver to seekers after profit. * * * Municipal ownership [should dominate] the water industry for the same reason. * * * We will entrust our light, heat and transportation, but not our life, to the mercies of money-making concerns.[3]

In response, many cities retook principal responsibility for domestic water delivery.

Rapid urban population increases also encouraged many cities to get back into the water business. Private businesses generally were not willing to risk their capital on the massive water projects that cities believed necessary to provide for future growth. So cities decided to build the projects themselves, importing sizable quantities of water from often distant watersheds. Philadelphia led the way in 1815 when it dammed the Schuylkill River upstream of the city and brought the water to its residents by aqueduct; New York followed when in 1842 it opened its 40–mile aqueduct from the Croton River. Over the next century, Boston, Denver, Los Angeles, San Francisco, and numerous other cities followed suit.

Today, public and private water organizations furnish water to over 80 percent of the nation's domestic and commercial users and almost 20 percent of its industrial users. Although private water companies outnumber public systems, the public systems are far bigger—supplying water to approximately 85 percent of the population serviced by water organizations.

Agricultural Water Suppliers

Organizations have also long been central to irrigated agriculture. Irrigation in early Indian communities of the American Southwest were community, not individual endeavors. In the 18th and 19th centuries,

1. For a history of urban water suppliers, see Nelson Blake, Water for the Cities (1956).

2. One of the largest was the Manhattan Company, formed by Aaron Burr to furnish water to New York City (and incidentally to engage in financial investments). Today, the Manhattan Company is no longer in the water business and is known as JPMorgan Chase. With assets of $1.2 trillion, JPMorgan Chase is one of the leading financial service firms in the world.

3. Evan Clark, Municipal Ownership in the United States, 5 Intercollegiate Socialist 1 (1916).

Spanish communities continued this tradition by constructing hundreds of community *acequias,* or irrigation canals, which were maintained and operated under the supervision of an elected *mayordomo,* or ditch boss. The *acequias* continue of importance in the Upper Rio Grande watershed of New Mexico and Colorado today—both in meeting water needs and as a central focus of many rural communities.[4]

When the Mormons began their colonization of the West, the church oversaw the development and allocation of water; by 1850, church distribution systems furnished water to over 16,000 acres of land.[5] When the federal government threatened the Mormon hegemony over Utah, the church-dominated legislature responded by passing a law in 1865 permitting a majority of citizens in a county to form an irrigation district. The district, whose officers were elected by the local citizens, could tax property and use the money to build and operate waterworks for the county. The Utah districts were modern extensions of the earlier community organizations discussed above. As Professor Donald Worster has cautioned, however, the districts also revealed that water organizations could be used for questionable political objectives. The Mormon Church often used the districts as "engines of oppression" to "exclude from power and prosperity all non-Mormon farmers [and] to maintain the power of the religious hierarchy."[6]

Carrier Ditch Companies

The growth of irrigated agriculture throughout the western United States encouraged the development of other water organizations in the late 19th century. As settlers located on land farther and farther away from adequate water sources, land promoters and others often organized companies to bring water in on a commercial contract basis. Early "carrier ditch companies" typically survived only short periods of time— victims often of financial misplanning or engineering misjudgment.

Over time, the role of private for-profit companies in providing irrigation water declined. The incidents of financial and engineering error made farmers very suspicious of for-profit companies. Farmers also feared that for-profit companies would use their "natural monopoly" over water supplies to charge excessive rates. Because building alternative waterworks would be expensive, a for-profit company might well be able to raise prices without attracting competitors. Most investors, moreover, were not anxious to invest in for-profit water supply companies. Engineering and building waterworks was often expensive and risky. Investors also feared that, once a water system was completed, customers might enjoy what is known as "monopsony power." Because

4. See Michael Meyer, Water in the Hispanic Southwest (1984); Wells Hutchins, The Community Acequia, 31 Sw. Hist. Q. 275 (1928); Gregory A. Hicks & Devon G. Pena, Community Acequias in Colorado's Rio Culebra Watershed: A Customary Commons in the Domain of Prior Appropriation, 74 U. Colo. L. Rev. 387 (2003); Jose A.

Rivera, Irrigation Communities of the Upper Rio Grande Bioregion: Sustainable Resource Use in the Global Context, 36 Nat. Resources J. 731 (1996).

5. See Donald Worster, Rivers of Empire 74–83 (1985).

6. Id. at 79.

distribution facilities would be fixed, a water company was at the mercy of customers within its service area; farmers could band together and demand an extremely low (or "monopsony") price just high enough to keep the company in business. For all of these reasons, carrier ditch companies are important today only in Texas and California. Westwide, such companies furnish water for less than one percent of the irrigated acreage.[7]

Mutual Water Companies

In much of the West, one of the most prominent forms of agricultural water suppliers has been and continues to be the mutual water company. Similar to the *acequias* and early Mormon community projects, mutual water companies are cooperative water ventures. Irrigators jointly organize a non-profit company to construct ditches and bring water to their fields; each irrigator owns stock in the company proportionate to the water she will receive. Because a secure supply of water is crucial to farmers' businesses, farmers like controlling the entity that is supplying the water. Mutuals also solve many of the problems that historically confronted carrier ditch companies. Because the irrigators own the company, the company has no incentive to charge monopoly rates, nor do the irrigators have an incentive to demand monopsony rates. By pooling resources and pledging their lands as collateral, members of a mutual water company also can raise necessary capital.[8]

In the late 19th century, farmers often did not even worry about raising capital. Each farmer contributed his labor in building the necessary waterworks, in return for shares in the mutual. By sheer strength and perseverance, mutuals often built massive waterworks. The Hardy Irrigation Canal Company, organized in 1870 by six Arizona pioneers, ultimately built a 24–mile long canal near the present site of Tempe that irrigated over 24,000 acres.[9]

Today shares of stock in a mutual reflect the value of the water that is being delivered. As noted, shareholders typically receive water in proportion to the amount of stock they own. During periods of water shortage, a mutual typically reduces everyone's deliveries proportionately. Mutuals cover their operating costs through assessments on the shareholder's stock.

Mutual water companies currently constitute about 85 percent of the organizations providing irrigation water to western farmers, and supply water to about 20 percent of the irrigated acreage. Mutuals are the dominant supplier of irrigation water in several states such as

7. See Barton H. Thompson, Jr., Institutional Perspectives on Water Policy and Markets, 81 Calif. L. Rev. 673, 690 (1993).

8. For a discussion of the economic advantages of mutual water companies, see id. at 689–694. For many of the reasons listed in the text, farmers have also organized cooperatives to furnish petroleum, feed, and other farming supplies. See Henry Hansmann, Ownership of the Firm, 4 J. L. Econ. & Org. 267, 286–91 (1988); Richard Heflebower, Cooperatives and Mutuals in the Market System (1980).

9. See Robert Dunbar, Forging New Rights in Western Waters 29–30 (1983).

Colorado and Utah—where mutuals service about 70 and 90 percent of the irrigated acreage respectively. In some communities, mutuals also provide domestic water.[10]

Water Districts

The true legacies of modern irrigated agriculture are the irrigation districts which today help irrigate a quarter of the irrigated acreage in the western United States (and over half of the irrigated acreage in California and Washington).[11] Irrigation districts are local governmental entities that supply water to farmers within specified geographical boundaries and are governed by a board of directors elected by all or some of the local residents. As water users are the owners of a mutual, water users are the electorate for the irrigation district.

Although Utah invented the irrigation district, it was California that gave irrigation districts extensive powers and encouraged their growth. The impetus was the California Supreme Court's decision in Lux v. Haggin, supra p. 342, which held that riparian rights in California were superior to all subsequent appropriations.

> [*Lux*] put the irrigator without stream frontage at a disadvantage—potentially a fatal disadvantage for his fortunes. For that reason, irrigators felt compelled to find a way to undo the court's ruling, and the best immediate chance for that, they decided, was to pass a law authorizing the formation of irrigation districts around the state. A Modesto lawyer, C.C. Wright, was elected to the legislature on a promise to do just that, and one year after his election, he delivered. The Irrigation District Act became law in late February 1887. Put briefly, the law permitted agricultural communities to organize as official governing units to construct and operate collectively the irrigation works they needed. * * * When fifty freeholders (or a majority in an area) petitioned the state to form such a district, an election was held. Two-thirds of the voters living in the designated area had to approve of the idea. The act did not measure voting power by the acreage owned, for it was feared that a few large landowners might thereby sabotage the community will. Once approved, the district elected officers, and they were given broad authority. They could take by the power of eminent domain any land they needed for an irrigation canal; they could make contracts to build works and tax property in the district or sell bonds to pay for them; and most important perhaps, they could condemn all individual water rights, including riparian, and purchase them in the name of the district. The Wright Act was, according to Thomas Malone, "California's major nineteenth century contribution to irrigation law."[12]

10. See Thompson, supra note 7, at 687–694.

11. See id.

12. Worster, supra note 5, at 108–09, quoting Thomas Malone, The California Irrigation Crisis of 1886: Origins of the

The power of irrigation districts to condemn riparian rights led to their rapid rise in California. The districts' power to condemn needed land, tax local property, and sell bonds secured by their taxing authority proved attractive throughout the West. By 1917, all seventeen conterminous western states had adopted variations on the Wright Act.

Today, the irrigation district has spawned multiple forms of local governmental water districts. These water districts are "rather like snowflakes, each with its own unique form," designed to meet the needs and interests of each region and its water users.[13] California alone has adopted approximately 40 general water district acts, authorizing the creation of various generic forms of districts, and over 100 special acts creating unique individual water districts. Water districts today furnish water not only to agricultural users but to sizable numbers of domestic, commercial, and industrial users. Some areas have multiple levels of water districts, with large "umbrella" districts, such as Southern California's Metropolitan Water District, importing and distributing water to smaller water districts or municipalities in the area. Another type of umbrella district, the "conservancy district," coordinates the water activities of a single watershed. Water districts' activities also have expanded. As discussed in Chapter 5, for example, California has organized water districts to manage groundwater withdrawals. See infra pp. 512–520.

Although today's water districts make up quite an eclectic set of organizations, some generalizations are possible.[14] To form a water district, a majority of landowners within the boundaries of the proposed district normally must petition local officials. Most states then investigate and report on the adequacy of the proposed district's water supply, although typically the report is purely advisory. A formation election finally is held, at which a majority of the proposed district's residents—in some states, two-thirds or more of the residents—must approve the idea.

Once organized, the district can appropriate water; construct reservoirs, canals, and other irrigation works; and distribute water to the district's residents. Most districts also have the authority to engage in related functions such as the production and sale of hydroelectric power. Districts moreover enjoy a number of uniquely governmental powers including the power to (1) assess (i.e., tax) property within the district, (2) condemn property (including water rights), and (3) issue bonds the interest of which, under current tax laws, is exempt from federal income

Wright Act (Ph.D. dissertation, Stanford University, 1965). For additional history on the Wright Act, see Alan Paterson, Land, Water, and Power 37–60 (1987); Donald Pisani, From the Family Farm to Agribusiness 250–82 (1984).

13. John Leshy, Special Water Districts–The Historical Background, in Spe-

cial Water Districts: Challenges for the Future (James Corbridge ed., 1983).

14. For detailed discussions of water districts, see Special Water Districts: Challenges for the Future, supra note 13; Special Project: Irrigation Districts, 1982 Ariz. St. L.J. 345.

taxes. Because water districts are technically subdivisions of the state, they also are exempt from state property tax.

Districts are governed by their boards of directors, the members of which are generally elected by the districts' landowners. Although some water districts are pure conduits for the water they distribute, most control who receives water and how much. There frequently are set rules for the distribution of water during normal times; water may be distributed in proportion to property assessments, acreage, or the amount of water that can be beneficially used. Most districts enjoy a great deal of discretion over the allocation of water during periods of shortage.

Federal Agencies

The federal government has also long been involved in water development and distribution. The Army Corps of Engineers was the first federal agency to engage in water projects, initially by enlarging and improving waterways for transportation purposes, later by constructing massive flood control projects. Western farmers, however, encouraged the federal government to also become involved in the delivery of water. Looking for additional capital to build large irrigation projects, the first National Irrigation Congress in 1891 (chaired by C.C. Wright) urged Congress to cede the public arid lands to the states in the belief that the states could then organize irrigation efforts. Congress responded three years later with the Carey Act[15] under which each arid state could apply for up to one million acres of federal land to be sold to farmers; the states were to oversee and guarantee the development of water to irrigate the land. Perhaps because the money from the land sales was to go to the federal government, the Carey Act was an utter disaster. Only Idaho ultimately applied for many acres under the act.

When western cries for aid did not subside, Congress responded with the Reclamation Act of 1902[16] under which the federal government would itself construct irrigation projects and furnish water to western farmers, who in turn would pay off the government's costs, interest free, over a period of years. According to many historians, two factors motivated the Reclamation Act—western agrarian pressure and the nationalistic Progressivism embodied by the then President, Theodore Roosevelt. As Professor Donald Worster has emphasized, the Reclamation Act was also strongly advocated by railroads and eastern merchants who wanted to develop new markets for their services and goods.[17] It was also favored by those who feared growing unrest in the underclass of eastern cities. Senator Thomas Patterson argued that the reclamation program would permit the underclass to load up their wagons and head West; it would be "better than a standing army."[18]

---

15. 43 U.S.C. §§ 641 et seq.

16. 32 Stat. 388.

17. See Worster, supra note 5, at 161–69.

18. Cong. Rec., March 1, 1902, p. 2283. Useful histories of the reclamation program can be found in Worster, supra note 5, and in Amy Kelley, Federal Reclamation Law, in 4 Water and Water Rights § 41.02, at 41–2 to 41–11 (Robert Beck ed., repl. vol. 2004).

Under the guidance of the Bureau of Reclamation, a wing of the Department of the Interior, the federal reclamation program has radically transformed the West over the last century. The Bureau has built over 600 dams, 16,000 miles of canals and aqueducts, 280 miles of tunnels, 37,000 miles of laterals, 50 hydroelectric generators, and 140 pumping stations. Through local water districts, the Bureau currently supplies water to roughly 10 million acres of cropland—about half of all the land irrigated by surface water in the West—as well as to 30 million domestic users. The federal reclamation program, however, has generated considerable criticism. Reclamation water is heavily subsidized by federal taxpayers and, in many parts of the West, goes to large farmers who often have enjoyed other federal farm subsidies. Few Bureau projects have ever paid for themselves, even if you ignore the interest that the federal government absorbs on every project. Numerous Bureau projects, moreover, have caused sizable environmental damage.

State Water Projects

The states have ended up playing a largely secondary role to the federal government in developing and distributing water supplies—although occasionally a significant role. California's State Water Project, for example, supplies approximately two and a half million acre-feet of water in a normal year to urban and agricultural water districts throughout much of the State. In total, the project delivers water to about two-thirds of California's population. The project encompasses approximately 30 storage reservoirs, five hydroelectric power facilities, 650 miles of canals and pipeline, and 20 pumping plants. State projects also supply irrigation water in Montana, Texas, and Utah. Most state projects are financed through water payments and bond sales rather than taxes and involve far lower subsidies than Bureau of Reclamation projects do. Many state projects, however, have still been criticized as unnecessary, economically unjustified, and/or environmentally damaging.

B. LEGAL ISSUES RAISED BY LOCAL WATER ORGANIZATIONS

1. FORMATION AND CONTROL OF WATER DISTRICTS

Water districts enjoy considerable power. Water districts decide how much water to appropriate and bring into a region. Where necessary, they can condemn water and other property needed to supply local users. Subject to statutory constraints, water districts then decide how to allocate the water among the local users. Water districts can require conservation and, in some cases, impose moratoria on new uses. Water districts also decide how to pay for their water and for any facilities required to store, transport, or treat the water. Districts choose what water rates to charge—e.g., whether to charge a flat rate per acre of land irrigated, a flat rate per acre-foot of water delivered, or a tiered rate that increases with the quantity of water used. Districts, moreover, choose whether to finance any costs through local property taxes and, if so, how much to assess each landowner.

These powers inevitably have generated intense political debate. Some property owners have chafed at being included in water districts. Happy with the status quo, such property owners have objected to having their water rights or property condemned, paying property taxes in support of the district, or complying with district regulations. Other water users have objected to the way in which their water district chooses its board of directors or makes policy decisions, recognizing that the allocation of political power can determine the allocation of water and costs.

a. Can Landowners Object to Being Included in a Water District?

Inclusion in a water district is not voluntary. Once the requisite number of voters in an area choose to form a water district, everyone within the district's jurisdiction is subject to its authority—including its powers of eminent domain and taxation.[1] Although the vast majority of landowners and residents are generally happy to be members of the district and to receive district water, some may decide that the costs of being in the district outweigh any benefits.

California, as noted earlier, became the first state to promote the formation of irrigation districts when it passed the 1887 Wright Act.[2] Within weeks after the formation of the first California irrigation districts under this act, property holders who did not want to be subject to the districts' eminent domain and taxation powers challenged the act's constitutionality. Opponents of the Wright Act argued that irrigation districts benefitted one group of landowners at the expense of other landowners. According to the opponents, the powers of taxation and eminent domain were reserved for public use, not the use of a select set of private irrigators. In 1888, however, the California Supreme Court upheld the Wright Act. While conceding that private irrigators benefitted from irrigation districts, the court concluded that irrigation also stimulated immigration, increased the value of property, and strengthened the economy, all "to the common advantages of all the people of the state."[3]

Opponents of the Wright Act therefore turned to federal court. In 1892, Maria King Bradley challenged the Wright Act in federal circuit court. The Fallbrook Irrigation District near San Diego included 40 acres of Bradley's property. Bradley did not irrigate nor need to irrigate her property. When the district assessed her $51.41, she refused to pay; her property was confiscated and sold. In court, Bradley argued that the Wright Act permitted the unconstitutional taking of private property for private use. She also argued that only property owners who benefit from a district should be subject to taxation by that district and that taxes

---

1. The only exception is a limited right of exclusion, discussed infra in Note 3 on p. 693.

2. 1887 Cal. Stat. 29.
3. Turlock Irr. Dist. v. Williams, 76 Cal. 360, 18 P. 379, 380 (1888).

should be proportionate to benefits received. The circuit court agreed with Bradley that the Wright Act permitted property to be taken for a private use:

> No man's property can be constitutionally taken from him without his consent, and transferred to certain other men for their use, however numerous they may be. And that is just what the legislation in question authorizes to be done. Private property is thereby authorized to be assessed and sold to provide water to supply the landowners in a certain district, more or less limited in extent, for irrigation purposes. * * * Of course, the property of those individuals would thereby be improved, and, indirectly, the public good be thereby advanced. But every improvement advances the public good. Every enterprise, no matter how strictly private it may be, if it be lawful, and adds to the wealth, comfort, and happiness of the people, is for the public good. The building of a house, or the planting of a useful or beautiful tree, is for the public good. But surely private property cannot be taken against the owner's consent, on the ground that the public interest would be thus promoted.[4]

The irrigation district appealed to the United States Supreme Court.

FALLBROOK IRRIGATION DISTRICT v. BRADLEY

Supreme Court of the United States, 1896.
164 U.S. 112.

MR. JUSTICE PECKHAM, after stating the case, delivered the opinion of the court.

* * * Referring to the [due process clause of the Fourteenth Amendment which extends to the states the proscription that property can be taken only for a public use and with just compensation,] the appellees herein urge several objections to [the Wright Act.] They say, First, that the use for which the water is to be procured is not in any sense a public one * * *.

Is this assessment, for the non-payment of which the land of the plaintiff was to be sold, levied for a public purpose? The question has, in substance, been answered in the affirmative by the people of California, and by the legislative and judicial branches of the state government. * * * The people of California and the members of her legislature must in the nature of things be more familiar with the facts and circumstances which surround the subject and with the necessities and the occasion for the irrigation of the lands then can any one be who is a stranger to her soil. * * *

Viewing the subject for ourselves and in the light of these considerations we have very little difficulty in coming to the same conclusion reached by the courts of California.

---

4. Bradley v. Fallbrook Irr. Dist., 68 Fed. 948, 957 (1895).

The use must be regarded as a public use, or else it would seem to follow that no general scheme of irrigation can be formed or carried into effect. In general, the water to be used must be carried for some distance and over or through private property which cannot be taken *in invitum* if the use to which it is to be put be not public, and if there be no power to take property by condemnation it may be impossible to acquire it at all. * * * A private company or corporation without the power to acquire the land *in invitum* would be of no real benefit, and at any rate the cost of the undertaking would be so greatly enhanced by the knowledge that the land must be acquired by purchase, that it would be practically impossible to build the works or obtain the water. * * *

While the consideration that the work of irrigation must be abandoned if the use of the water may not be held to be or constitute a public use is not to be regarded as conclusive in favor of such use, yet that fact is in this case a most important consideration. Millions of acres of land otherwise cultivable must be left in their present arid and worthless condition, and an effectual obstacle will therefore remain in the way of the advance of a large portion of the State in material wealth and prosperity. To irrigate and thus to bring into possible cultivation these large masses of otherwise worthless lands would seem to be a public purpose and a matter of public interest, not confined to the landowners, or even to any one section of the State. * * * It is not essential that the entire community or even any considerable portion thereof should directly enjoy or participate in an improvement in order to constitute a public use. * * *

Second. The second objection urged by the appellees herein is that the operations of this act need not be and are not limited to arid, unproductive lands but include within its possibilities all lands, no matter how fertile or productive * * *.

The legislature by this act has not itself named any irrigation district, and, of course, has not decided as to the nature and quality of any specific lands which have been included in any such district. It has given a general statement as to what conditions must exist in order to permit the inclusion of any land within a district. The land which can properly be so included is, as we think, sufficiently limited in its character by the provisions of the act. It must be * * * of such a character that it will be benefited by irrigation by the system to be adopted. This, as we think, means that the amount of benefit must be substantial and not limited to the creation of an opportunity to thereafter use the land for a new kind of crop, while not substantially benefiting it for the cultivation of the old kind, which it had produced in reasonable quantities and with ordinary certainty and success, without the aid of artificial irrigation. The question whether any particular land would be thus benefited is necessarily one of fact.

The legislature not having itself described the district, has not decided that any particular land would or could possibly be benefited as described, and, therefore, it would be necessary to give a hearing at some time to those interested upon the question of fact whether or not the land of any owner which was intended to be included would be benefited by the irrigation proposed. * * * Does [the act] provide for a hearing as to whether the petitioners are of the class mentioned and described in the act * * * ? Is there any opportunity provided for a hearing upon notice to the landowners interested in the question whether their lands will be benefited by the proposed irrigation? We think the right to a hearing in regard to all these facts is given by the act, and that it has been practically so construed by the Supreme Court of California * * *.

Fourth. * * * It is insisted that the basis of the assessment upon the lands benefited, for the cost of the construction of the works, is not in accordance with and in proportion to the benefits conferred by the improvement, and, therefore, there is a violation of the constitutional amendment referred to, and a taking of the property of the citizen without due process of law.

* * * Can an *ad valorem* assessment[a] * * * be legally levied in such a case as this? Assume that the only theory * * * upon which they can stand is that they are imposed on account of the benefits received, and that no land ought in justice to be assessed for a greater sum then the benefits received by it, yet it is plain that the fact of the amount of benefits is not susceptible of that accurate determination which appertains to a demonstration in geometry. * * * Some choice is to be made, and where the fact of some benefit accruing to all the lands has been legally found, can it be that the adoption of an *ad valorem* method of assessing the lands is to be held a violation of the Federal Constitution? It seems to us clearly not. It is one of those matters of detail in arriving at the proper and fair amount and proportion of the tax that is to be levied on the land with regard to the benefits it has received, which is open to the discretion of the state legislature, and with which this court ought to have nothing to do. The way of arriving at the amount may be in some instances inequitable and unequal, but that is far from rising to the level of a constitutional problem and far from a case of taking property without due process of law.

After careful scrutiny of the objections to this act we are compelled to the conclusion that none of such objections is well taken. * * *

MR. CHIEF JUSTICE FULLER and MR. JUSTICE FIELD dissented.

Notes and Questions

1. Should all property owners within a water district be forced to participate in and contribute to the district? Would water districts be unworkable if individual landowners could opt out of the district at will? Do water districts benefit landowners even if the landowners do not want any water from the district? Although supporters of governmental irrigation programs frequently argue that irrigation benefits all residents in a region,

a. An *ad valorem* assessment is a property tax apportioned according to the value of the property.—Eds.

not just those who use the irrigation water, economists are skeptical. See Dwight Lee, Political Provision of Water: An Economic/Public Choice Perspective, in Special Water Districts: Challenges for the Future 52 (James Corbridge ed., 1982).

2. *Fallbrook* implies that a water district cannot constitutionally include land that does not substantially benefit from inclusion. Is the constitutional basis for this clear?

Despite the dictum in *Fallbrook*, landowners have seldom succeeded in constitutional efforts to avoid inclusion in a water district or other public water system. In Stern v. Scillitani, 158 F.3d 729 (3d Cir. 1998), several landowners with personal wells challenged a local ordinance that required them to close their wells and connect to the local public water supply system, arguing the ordinance violated both substantive due process and the takings clause. The court upheld the ordinance as a legitimate safety measure, and therefore a constitutional exercise of the police power, even though there was no evidence that the wells were unsafe.

> Because pure water is a precondition for human health, regulating the water supply is a basic and legitimate governmental activity. A municipal water supply replaces a myriad of private water sources that may be unmonitored or, at best, difficult, expensive, and inefficient to monitor. Therefore, a legislature may rationally conclude that a public water supply is the simplest and safest solution for its citizenry as a whole without proof of danger to each and every affected person. The danger is significant, the burden of connecting to nearby waterlines is not great, and the costs and benefits of such legislation are widely shared throughout the area of service. For these reasons, the overwhelming majority of courts that have addressed the issue have found that mandatory connection to public water is a legitimate exercise of police power.

But see City of Midway v. Midway Nursing & Convalescent Center, 195 S.E.2d 452 (Ga. 1973) (holding that the city did not have the authority, as a matter of either general welfare or police power, to mandate that local residents connect to the city's water system).

3. Although public water organizations may enjoy broad constitutional authority to compel landowner participation, most states provide by statute that a property holder may petition to exclude her land from a water district if the land does not benefit by inclusion therein. See, e.g., Cal. Water Code § 32222; Idaho Code §§ 43–1101 to 43–1119; Nevada Rev. Stat. §§ 539.736–.748. See also Ariz. Rev. Stat. § 48–2945 (land can be excluded if "not susceptible of irrigation"); Mont. Code § 85–7–1822 (same).

Courts, however, have been quite lenient in upholding a district's conclusion that particular land benefits and should be included. In Atchison, Topeka & Santa Fe Ry. Co. v. Kings County Water Dist., 47 Cal.2d 140, 302 P.2d 1 (1956), for example, the court upheld a district's finding that a railway right-of-way substantially and directly benefitted because the land might be used for irrigated agriculture at some future point in time. And in DeLoreto v. Goleta County Water Dist., 234 Cal.App.2d 164, 44 Cal.Rptr. 137 (1965), the court upheld a finding that residential land substantially and directly benefitted even though the land received the little water it needed from a neighboring municipality; the district argued that the land benefitted by having two alternative water sources. See also Foster v. Sunnyside Valley Irr. Dist., 102 Wash.2d 395, 687 P.2d 841 (1984).

4. Forced inclusion in a water district can threaten not only property owners' pocketbooks but, on occasion, local cultural values. In the 1960s and 1970s, New Mexico pursued several major reclamation projects that would have required the formation of conservancy districts. As Hispanic members of community *acequias* learned about the powers of conservancy districts, they grew more opposed to the planned projects. John Nichols (author of the *Milagro Beanfield War*) wrote of the opposition to one of the projects:[1]

> [P]eople learned that the only way the government could build the Indian Camp Dam was by imposing a conservancy district on the most irrigable portions of the Taos Valley. And when they figured out that conservancy districts are one of the more powerful political subdivisions of the state, with enormous planning and taxing and foreclosure powers, and when it began to be clear who would control the Taos conservancy district, the fourteen major ditch systems in the area which would fall within the conservancy borders, and which up until then had been represented on a local council working with state and federal agencies to implement the Indian Camp Dam, * * * banded into an organization called the Tres Rios Association, and prepared to fight the dam and the conservancy district tooth and nail.

The Hispanic community had four major concerns. First, the proposed conservancy district would have held liens on everyone's land for fifty years. Although the district's assessments would not have been large, failure to pay could have resulted in foreclosure. The idea of an agency having this power was intimidating to owners of small plots of land. Second, the district's fees, though relatively small, would have been a significant stretch for owners of small plots, many of whom did not have the money to pay them. Most landowners, moreover, did not think the benefits outweighed the fees. Third, the conservancy district would have supplanted existing *acequias* that had governed the watershed for two centuries, seriously altering Hispanic traditions in dealing with water. Finally, local state judges would have appointed the district's board. Small Hispanic landowners felt this procedure was undemocratic and feared that appointed directors would represent mainly Anglo owners of large tracts. See F. Lee Brown & Helen Ingram, Water and Poverty in the Southwest 61–62 (1987); John Nichols, To Save a Dying Culture, Race Relations Rep., July 1974, at 20. The Indian Camp Dam project was ultimately abandoned.

b. *Voting Rights and the Control of Power*

Given the often immense importance of a water district's decisions to local water users, political power in the district is often a crucial issue. California's original Wright Act provided that irrigation districts would be divided into a number of precincts, each with its own director, and

---

1. Nichols is quoted in F. Lee Brown & Helen Ingram, Water and Poverty in the Southwest 61 (1987).

that directors would be elected by majority vote of all precinct residents qualified to vote in general elections. The goal was to maximize local and popular control of district operations. But the system threatened large property holders who feared placing the power of irrigation districts in the hands of the general population. As a result of pressure from large property holders, virtually every western state today provides that, at least in some water districts, only property owners can vote. In a sizable number of districts, votes are weighted by acreage owned or by the assessed value of that acreage.[2]

These voting systems have come under attack as the demographics of districts have changed and districts have expanded their services. Consider, for example, the Salt River Agricultural Improvement and Power District which furnishes water and power to large portions of Phoenix and surrounding cities.[3] When the district was formed in 1937, it furnished water to 236,000 acres of land, 94 percent of which was agricultural. Large property holders insisted, as a condition of the district being formed, that voting be limited to property owners and weighted by acreage and that tax assessments be on a per acre basis (rather than *ad valorem*). Because water deliveries were to be financed by water charges and by bonds secured by the tax assessments, the voting scheme was arguably fair at the time.

Forty years later, however, the district had changed. By 1980, only 44 percent of the district land was agricultural; the remainder formed portions of such growing towns as Phoenix, Scottsdale, and Tempe. As a result, 40 percent of the district's water went to non-agricultural users. In 1955, moreover, the district had gained the exclusive right to furnish electricity to large portions of these cities. By 1980, the district provided electricity to 313,000 customers. Although there was no evidence of rate gouging, the district used the revenues from its power operations to subsidize its water deliveries. In 1980, 98 percent of the district's revenues came from electricity sales, and 90 percent of the district's debt was secured by electricity revenues, not land or tax assessments.

Prior to the late 1970s, however, there had been virtually no change in the district's system for electing directors. The only change came in 1969 when the Arizona legislature provided that owners of a partial acre would, for the first time, be entitled to a fractional vote; previously they had not been entitled to any vote.

In the mid–1970s, the district's election system was challenged on the ground that it violated the one-person, one-vote rule announced in Reynolds v. Sims, 377 U.S. 533 (1964).

---

2. Current voting systems are summarized in Tim De Young, Governing Special Districts: The Conflict Between Voting Rights and Property Privileges, 1982 Ariz. St. L.J. 419, 424.

3. The facts here are taken from the briefs in Ball v. James, 451 U.S. 355 (1981). For a more detailed description of the district, see Comment, Voter Restrictions in Special Districts: A Case Study of the Salt River Project, 1969 L. & Soc. Ord. 636.

BALL v. JAMES

Supreme Court of the United States, 1981.
451 U.S. 355.

JUSTICE STEWART delivered the opinion of the Court.

This appeal concerns the constitutionality of the system for electing the directors of a large water reclamation district in Arizona, a system which, in essence, limits voting eligibility to landowners and apportions voting power according to the amount of land a voter owns. The case requires us to consider whether the peculiarly narrow function of this local governmental body and the special relationship of one class of citizens to that body releases it from the strict demands of the one-person, one-vote principle of the Equal Protection Clause of the Fourteenth Amendment. * * *

This lawsuit was brought by a class of registered voters who live within the geographic boundaries of the [Salt River Project Agricultural Improvement and Power] District, and who own either no land or less than an acre of land within the District. The complaint alleged that the District enjoys such governmental powers as the power to condemn land, to sell tax-exempt bonds, and to levy taxes on real property. It also alleged that because the District sells electricity to virtually half the population of Arizona, and because, through its water operations, it can exercise significant influence on flood control and environmental management within its boundaries, the District's policies and actions have a substantial effect on all people who live within the District, regardless of property ownership. * * *

[In extending the one-person, one-vote principle of *Reynolds v. Sims* to local governments that exercise "general governmental powers," the Court in Hadley v. Junior College Dist., 397 U.S. 50, 56 (1970), warned:] "It is of course possible that there might be some case in which a State elects certain functionaries whose duties are so far removed from normal governmental activities and so disproportionately affect different groups that a popular election in compliance with *Reynolds* * * * might not be required * * *."

The Court found such a case in [Salyer Land Co. v. Tulare Lake Basin Water Storage Dist., 410 U.S. 719 (1973).] The Tulare Lake Basin Water Storage District involved there encompassed 193,000 acres, 85% of which were farmed by one or another of four corporations. Under California law, public water districts could acquire, store, conserve, and distribute water, and though the Tulare Lake Basin Water Storage District had never chosen to do so, could generate and sell any form of power it saw fit to support its water operations. The costs of the project were assessed against each landowner according to the water benefits the landowner received. At issue in the case was the constitutionality of the scheme for electing the directors of the district, under which only landowners could vote, and voting power was apportioned according to the assessed valuation of the voting landowner's property. The Court recognized that the Tulare Lake Basin Water Storage District did exercise "some typical governmental powers," including the power to hire and fire workers, contract for construction of projects, condemn private property, and issue general obligation bonds. Nevertheless, the Court concluded that the district had "relatively limited authority," because "its primary purpose, indeed the reason for its existence, is to provide for the acquisition, storage, and distribution of water for farming in the Tulare Lake Basin." The *Salyer* Court thus held that the strictures of *Reynolds* did not apply to the Tulare District * * *.

As noted by the Court of Appeals, the services currently provided by the Salt River District are more diverse and affect far more people than those of the Tulare Lake Basin Water Storage District. Whereas the Tulare District included an area entirely devoted to agriculture and populated by only 77 persons, the Salt River District includes almost half the population of the State, including large parts of Phoenix and other cities. Moreover, the Salt River District, unlike the Tulare District, has exercised its statutory power to generate and sell electric power, and has become one of the largest suppliers of such power in the State. Further, whereas all the water delivered by the Tulare District went for agriculture, roughly 40% of the water delivered by the Salt River District goes to urban areas or is used for nonagricultural purposes in farming areas. Finally whereas all operating costs of the Tulare District were borne by the voting landowners through assessments apportioned according to land value, most of the capital and operating costs of the Salt River District have been met through the revenues generated by the selling of electric power. Nevertheless, * * * these distinctions do not amount to a constitutional difference.

First, the District simply does not exercise the sort of governmental powers that invoke the strict demands of *Reynolds*. The District cannot impose ad valorem property taxes or sales taxes. It cannot enact any laws governing the conduct of citizens, nor does it administer such normal functions of government as the maintenance of streets, the operation of schools, or sanitation, health, or welfare services.

Second, though they were characterized broadly by the Court of Appeals, even the District's water functions, which constitute the primary and originating purpose of the District, are relatively narrow. The District * * * [does] not own, sell, or buy water, nor [does it] control the use of any water [it has] delivered. The District simply stores water behind its dams, conserves it from loss, and delivers it through project canals. It is true, as the Court of Appeals noted, that as much as 40% of the water delivered by the District goes for nonagricultural purposes. But the distinction between agricultural and urban land is of no special constitutional significance in this context. The constitutionally relevant fact is that all water delivered by the Salt River District, like the water delivered by the Tulare Lake Basin Water Storage District, is distributed according to land ownership, and the District does not and cannot control the use to which the landowners who are entitled to the water choose to put it. As repeatedly recognized by the Arizona courts, though the state legislature has allowed water districts to become nominal public entities in order to obtain inexpensive bond financing, the districts remain essentially business enterprises, created by and chiefly benefiting a specific group of landowners. * * *

Finally, neither the existence nor size of the District's power business affects the legality of its property-based voting scheme. As this Court has noted in a different context, the provision of electricity is not a traditional element of governmental sovereignty, and so is not in itself the sort of general or important governmental function that would make the government provider subject to the doctrine of the *Reynolds* case. * * *

The appellees claim * * * that the sheer size of the power operations and the great number of people they affect serve to transform the District into an entity of general governmental power. But no matter how great the number of nonvoting residents buying electricity from the District, the relationship between them and the District's power operations is essentially that between consumers and a business enterprise from which they buy. * * *

The functions of the Salt River District are therefore of the narrow, special sort which justifies a departure from the popular-election requirement of the *Reynolds* case. And as in *Salyer,* an aspect of that limited purpose is the disproportionate relationship the District's functions bear to the specific class of people whom the system makes eligible to vote. The voting landowners are the only residents of the District whose lands are subject to liens to secure District bonds. Only these landowners are subject to the acreage-based taxing power of the District, and voting landowners are the only residents who have ever committed capital to the District through stock assessments charged by the Association. * * *

As in the *Salyer* case, we conclude that the voting scheme for the District is constitutional because it bears a reasonable relationship to its statutory objectives. Here, according to the stipulation of the parties, the subscriptions of land which made the * * * District possible might well have never occurred had not the subscribing landowners been assured a special voice in the conduct of the District's business. Therefore, as in *Salyer,* the State could rationally limit the vote to landowners. Moreover, Arizona could rationally make the weight of their vote dependent upon the number of acres they own, since that number reasonably reflects the relative risks they incurred as landowners and the distribution of benefits and the burdens of the District's water operations. * * *

JUSTICE WHITE, with whom JUSTICE BRENNAN, JUSTICE MARSHALL, and JUSTICE BLACKMUN join, dissenting.

* * * The District involved here clearly exercises substantial governmental powers. The District is a municipal corporation organized under the laws of Arizona and is not, in any sense of the word, a private corporation. Pursuant to the Arizona Constitution, such districts are "political subdivisions of the State, and vested with all the rights,

privileges and benefits, and entitled to the immunities and exemptions granted municipalities and political subdivisions under this Constitution or any law of the State or of the United States." Ariz. Const., Art. 13, § 7. * * * The District's bonds are tax exempt, and its property is not subject to state or local property taxation. * * * The District also has the power of eminent domain, a matter of some import. The District has also been given the power to enter into a wide range of contractual arrangements to secure energy sources. Inherent in this authorization is the power to control the use and source of energy generated by the District, including the possible use of nuclear energy. * * *

The District here also has authority to allocate water within its service area. It has veto power over all transfers of surface water from one place or type of use to another, and this power extends to any "watershed or drainage area which supplies or contributes water for the irrigation of lands within [the] district. * * * " Ariz. Rev. Stat. Ann. § 45–172.5 (Supp. 1980–1981).

Like most "private" utilities, which are often "natural monopolies," private utilities in Arizona are subject to regulation by public authority. The Arizona Corporation Commission is empowered to prescribe "just and reasonable rates" as well as to regulate other aspects of the business operations of private utilities. See Ariz. Rev. Stat. Ann. § 40–321 (1974). The rate structure of the District now before us, however, is not subject to control by another state agency because the District is a municipal corporation and itself purports to perform the public function of protecting the public interest that the Corporation Commission would otherwise perform. See Ariz. Const., Art. 13, § 7, Art. 15, § 2. * * * With respect to energy management and the provision of water and electricity, the District's power is immense and its authority complete. * * *

[I]t is indeed curious that the Court would attempt to characterize the District's electrical operations as "incidental" to its water operations, or would consider the power operations to be irrelevant to the legality of the voting scheme. The facts are that in *Salyer* the burdens of the Water District fell entirely on the landowners who were served by the District. Here the landowners could not themselves afford to finance their own project and turned to a public agency to help them. That agency now subsidizes the storage and delivery of irrigation water for agricultural purposes by selling electricity to the public at prices that neither the voters nor any representative public agency has any right to control. Unlike the situation in *Salyer,* the financial burden of supplying irrigation water has been shifted from the landowners to the consumers of electricity. * * *

It is apparent in this case that landowning irrigators are getting a free ride at the expense of the users of electricity. It would also seem apparent that except for the subsidy, utility rates would be lower. Of course, subsidizing agricultural operations may well be in the public interest in Arizona, but it does not follow that the amount of the subsidy and the manner in which it is provided should be totally in the hands of a select few.

Notes and Questions

1. Challenges to landowner-only electoral systems continue to be brought—and more often than not rejected. See, e.g., Johnson v. Killingsworth, 271 Mont. 1, 894 P.2d 272 (1995) (rejecting a challenge to a requirement that district commissioners must be landowners); Moores v. Edelbrock, 223 Cal.App.3d 941, 272 Cal.Rptr. 919 (1990) (rejecting a challenge to a landowner-only voting rule). But see Bjornestad v. Hulse, 223 Cal.App.3d 507, 272 Cal.Rptr. 864, vacated & remanded, 276 Cal.Rptr. 320, 801 P.2d 1071 (Cal. 1990) (rejecting argument that water district was exempt from one-person, one-vote rule). See also Wilson v. Denver, 125 N.M. 308, 961 P.2d 153 (1998) (interpreting statute to permit one-person, one-vote elections in acequias in part because of concern that allocation of votes in proportion to water rights might be unconstitutional).

2. Is it a sufficient answer to residents of the Salt River district who own little or no property that they are equal participants in the election of state legislators who in turn determine the voting scheme for the district? The Court felt the point important enough to footnote in a portion of *Ball* omitted above. 451 U.S. at 371 n. 20. And in a concurring opinion, Justice Powell wrote:

> The authority and will of the Arizona legislature to control the electoral composition of the District are decisive for me in this case. The District is large enough and the resources it manages are basic enough that the people will act through their elected legislature when further changes in the governance of the District are warranted.

Following the district court decision in *Ball,* the Arizona legislature in fact modified the election procedure. The board was enlarged from 10 to 14 members with the new members being elected at large with each landowner getting one vote. Large farmers still control the board, however, through the other 10 directors.

3. State public utility commissions regulate the rates of private companies that furnish water to a community. By contrast, public water agencies such as water districts generally are exempt from such regulation. The Advisory Committee on Intergovernmental Relations recommended four decades ago that state regulatory agencies review and approve the pricing policies of all special districts. See The Problem of Special Districts in American Government 81 (1964).

Is the Salt River district more like a public utility than a government? If the Salt River district were subject to regulation by a state public utility commission, would the challengers in *Ball* have had any significant reason to complain of the method of electing directors?

4. The Salt River district is not an isolated instance of a once agricultural district now serving an increasingly urban clientele. As long ago as 1980, almost a third of the irrigation and conservancy districts in the eleven westernmost states were located at least partially within metropolitan areas.

See Tim DeYoung, Discretion Versus Accountability: The Case of Special Water Districts, in Special Water Districts: Challenges for the Future 32, 39–41 (James Corbridge ed., 1982). With continued urbanization in the West, the number of districts serving domestic users in metropolitan areas has almost certainly expanded further since then. When the use of property qualifications in elections was last surveyed in 1982, however, a growing percentage of districts had adopted them. See Merrill Goodall & John Sullivan, Water System Entities in California: Social and Environmental Effects, in id. at 71, 96–98.

5. Under what circumstances is a water district subject to the one-person, one-vote rule? In Bjornestad v. Hulse, 223 Cal.App.3d 507, 272 Cal.Rptr. 864, vacated & remanded, 276 Cal.Rptr. 320, 801 P.2d 1071 (Cal. 1990) (*Bjornestad I*), several residents of the Sierra Lakes County Water District challenged the district's landowner-only voting scheme. The district served a mountain community consisting of approximately 1,043 residential properties, most of which were vacation homes. Less than 200 people lived year-long in the district, and many of these were renters who could not vote in the district elections.

The court found that the district did not come within the *Ball* exception for several reasons. First, the Sierra Lakes district enjoyed broader governmental powers than the Salt River district, including the right to impose *ad valorem* taxes and operate a sewage system. Second, the district exercised greater authority over water; it could buy and sell water and impose conservation measures on local users. Finally, one-third of the district's revenue came from water and sewage charges that, although billed to landowners, might well be passed on to renters. Are these distinctions convincing? See Moores v. Edelbrock, 223 Cal.App.3d 941, 272 Cal.Rptr. 919 (1990) (rejecting a constitutional challenge under similar facts).

6. If a district permits local residents to each have a vote, would it be unconstitutional to also give a vote to each non-resident landowner within the district? As the United States Supreme Court noted in Reynolds v. Sims, 377 U.S. 533, 555 (1964), "the right of suffrage can be denied by a debasement or dilution of the weight of a citizen's vote just as effectively as by wholly prohibiting the free exercise of the franchise."

After the decision in *Bjornestad I*, the California legislature modified the voting system for the Sierra Lakes County Water District so that each registered voter residing in the district and each landowner, whether residing in the district or not, received a vote. Local residents again challenged the voting scheme under the equal protection clause, arguing that the enfranchisement of nonresident landowners unconstitutionally diluted the votes of local residents. The 60–some registered voters residing in the district were far outnumbered by the almost 1000 property owners, including corporations, who qualified to vote in district elections. The court, however, upheld the voting system. See Bjornestad v. Hulse, 229 Cal.App.3d 1568, 281 Cal.Rptr. 548 (1991). Because the district was not "a governmental entity of general purpose and powers," the court concluded that no fundamental interest was at stake and that the voting system was subject not to strict scrutiny but merely a "rational basis" test. A less rigorous test was appropriate here than in challenges to landowner-only voting systems because no one was denied the right to vote; "overinclusiveness is a lesser evil than underinclusiveness." The court had no problem concluding that the new voting system was rational: landowners bore the weight of financial responsibility and, because the district was a vacation home community, most landowners did not have their voting residence in the community. See also Collins v. Town of Goshen, 635 F.2d 954 (2d Cir. 1980).

7.   What difference does a district's voting system actually make in the operation of the district? An economic study of the differences between California districts employing one-person, one-vote schemes and those with property qualifications found that one-person, one-vote districts had greater voter participation and more competitive elections. In some property qualification districts, a handful of landowners controlled a majority of votes, and elections were never contested. More importantly, the financial performance of property qualification districts was far less stable than that of one-person, one-vote districts—the result, according to the economists, of not having to consider and harmonize competing policy views. See Merrill Goodall, John Sullivan, & Tim De Young, California Water: A New Political Economy (1978); Merrill Goodall & John Sullivan, Water District Organization: Political Decision Systems, in California Water Planning and Policy: Selected Issues (Ernest Engelbert ed., 1979).

A separate economic study showed that water districts with one-person, one-vote elections tended to subsidize water rates through property assessments more than districts where votes were allocated by acreage. Can you speculate why? According to the authors, subsidization tends to favor the small farmer who has more say in the one-person, one-vote elections. Where a district has electricity operations, however, property qualification districts appear more likely to use electricity profits to subsidize water. See John McDowell & Keith Ugone, The Effect of Institutional Setting on Behavior in Public Enterprises: Irrigation Districts in the Western States, 1982 Ariz. St. L.J. 453.

8.   Is there any easy answer to what voting system is proper for a water district serving a diverse population? A study of the Middle Rio Grande Conservancy District in New Mexico highlights some of the conflicts that can arise between urban residents and irrigators. The city folks wanted the district to spend its money on flood control, which did not interest the farmers nearly as much. They also wanted the ditches that ran through urban areas fenced to prevent drownings, a concern that did not move the farmers. See M. Brian McDonald et al., Case Studies in the Development of New Mexico Water Resources Institutions: The Middle Rio Grande Conservancy District and Urban Water Pricing (N.M. Water Resources Res. Inst., Jan. 1981). Is acreage voting suitable for a district facing these and other urban-agricultural conflicts? Does a one-person, one-vote system also present problems?

9.   In the wake of Ball v. James, state courts sometimes have invoked state constitutional provisions to invalidate district voting systems that diverge from a one-person, one-vote scheme. See, e.g., Foster v. Sunnyside Valley Irr. Dist., 102 Wash.2d 395, 687 P.2d 841 (1984) (invalidating district election scheme that excluded anyone who did not own land used for horticultural or agricultural purposes); Timpanogos Planning & Water Man-

agement Agency v. Central Utah Water Conservancy Dist., 690 P.2d 562 (Utah 1984) (judicial appointment of conservancy district directors violated separation of powers). See also Choudhry v. Free, 17 Cal.3d 660, 131 Cal.Rptr. 654, 552 P.2d 438 (1976) (striking down requirement that directors be landowners).

10. Plaintiffs also may be able to bring a challenge to district voting rules under the federal Voting Rights Act, 42 U.S.C. § 1973, which prohibits any "voting qualification or prerequisite to voting or standard, practice, or procedure" that "results in a denial or abridgment of the right of any citizen of the United States to vote on account of race or color." In Smith v. Salt River Project Agric. Improvement & Power Dist., 109 F.3d 586 (9th Cir. 1997), several African–American residents of the Salt River district at issue in *Ball* challenged the land ownership voting requirement as discriminatory because only 40 percent of African–Americans in the district owned their homes, compared to 60 percent of white heads-of-household. The court held that the Voting Rights Act applies to special districts, but that the plaintiffs had not proven the land ownership requirement was discriminatory.

11. Although membership in a mutual water company is "voluntary," mutuals also can generate concerns over imbalances in political power. As suburbs encroach into rural communities, the demographics of many mutuals have changed. Large numbers of domestic consumers are now served by mutuals that once served only irrigators and, because the shares in most mutuals are allocated by water use, farmers may well be able to outvote domestic customers even if the farmers are numerically outnumbered. Although the domestic consumers are free to get their water elsewhere, that is not a viable option for most consumers.

Yet as private entities, mutuals are exempt from relevant constitutional strictures and the Voting Rights Act. Many states, moreover, exempt mutuals from rate supervision by the state public utility commission. See, e.g., Cal. Pub. Util. Code § 2705 (mutuals exempt from regulation if they deliver water to no one except stockholders, the state, or another mutual). Recognizing the possibility that some customers may not have an effective voice in a mutual, courts have narrowly interpreted such provisions. See, e.g., Yucaipa Water Co. v. Public Utilities Comm'n, 54 Cal.2d 823, 9 Cal.Rptr. 239, 357 P.2d 295 (1960) (exemption does not apply where a mutual delivers water to lessees); Corona Water Co. v. Public Utilities Comm'n, 54 Cal.2d 834, 9 Cal.Rptr. 245, 357 P.2d 301 (1960) (holding the exemption did not apply where "the largely agricultural independent stockholders * * * were in a position to subsidize their water service at the expense" of domestic customers). But see West Valley Land Co. v. Nob Hill Water Ass'n, 107 Wash.2d 359, 729 P.2d 42 (1986) (holding that a cooperative water association serving 3700 members was exempt from state price regulation, in part because all members had a "voice" in governance).

12. What are the implications of voting right cases for groundwater management districts? Local groundwater users may be unwilling to form a groundwater management district if the district will be subject to a one-person, one-vote rule where groundwater users might be readily outvoted. Could the state allocate votes according to historic groundwater usage? See R. Tim Hay, Blind Salamanders, Minority Representation, and the Edwards

Aquifer: Reconciling Use–Based Management of Natural Resources with the Voting Rights Act of 1965, 25 St. Mary's L.J. 1450, 1506 n. 144 (1994) (arguing that groundwater management districts may not be exempt from the one-person, one-vote requirement, because they involve a "substantial governmental function").

As described in Chapter 6, Texas in 1993 created the Edwards Aquifer Authority to regulate withdrawals from the Edwards Aquifer, which furnishes water to both farmers and a number of cities including San Antonio, after a court ruled that the withdrawals threatened a number of endangered species, implicating the Endangered Species Act. See pages 661–668 supra. The Texas legislature initially provided for the appointment, rather than election, of the Authority's board. The United States Department of Justice, however, refused to "preclear" the appointment process under the federal Voting Rights Act because the Edwards Aquifer Authority replaced a previous (and ineffectual) groundwater district whose board was elected; according to the federal government, the switch from an elective system to an appointment process could dilute minority influence on groundwater issues. See Hay, supra. The Texas legislature subsequently amended the law to provide for election of board members. Does it surprise you that the Edwards Aquifer Authority significantly delayed taking any aggressive action to restrain groundwater withdrawals? Which type of a board do you believe is more likely to restrain groundwater pumping despite pressure to meet local water needs—a locally elected board or a board appointed by the state government?

2. SUPPLYING MUNICIPAL WATER

Municipalities are the fastest growing users of water in the United States today. Aggregate water use in the United States peaked in 1980 and has actually shrunk about 10 percent over the last quarter of a century. Domestic water consumption, by contrast, has grown on both a total and per capita basis. "Nationally, domestic use withdrawals nearly doubled between 1960 and 1990, while population increased by only 75%. Domestic use's growth reflects the new sprawling landscape of office campuses, gated communities, and golf courses as well as continued rapid U.S. population growth."[1] Cities and their needs consequently drive much of modern water law. As a result, municipal water suppliers deserve special attention.

a. Obtaining Water Supplies

As previous chapters have described, cities have often enjoyed a variety of advantages in obtaining needed water supplies. Under the prior appropriation law of most western states, for example, cities have been able to appropriate water before they had a beneficial need for all of the water. In order to avoid "speculation," the prior appropriation system requires most water users to demonstrate a beneficial use before they appropriate water. See supra p. 301. Most states, however, have loosened this anti-speculation stricture for municipal water suppliers and

---

1. A. Dan Tarlock, We Are All Water Lawyers Now: Water Law's Potential But Limited Impact on Urban Growth Management, in Wet Growth: Should Water Law Control Land Use? 57, 67 (Craig Anthony (Tony) Arnold ed., 2005).

allowed cities to appropriate enough water to meet reasonably anticipated future needs. See, e.g., Reynolds v. City of Roswell, 99 N.M. 84, 654 P.2d 537, 540 (1982) (courts should "look to a city's planned future use of water" in evaluating the extent of a municipal water right); City & County of Denver v. Northern Colo. Water Conservancy Dist., 276 P.2d 992, 997 (Colo. 1954) (cities can appropriate water for "reasonably anticipated requirements"). Some western states similarly have permitted cities to avoid statutory forfeiture where water is being held by a municipality for such future needs. See, e.g., Utah Code Ann. § 73–1–4–3(a). In California (and, for a brief period of time, in New Mexico), some cities have also enjoyed pueblo rights that expand as the cities' needs grow. See supra pp. 356–365.

Where cities have faced legal obstacles (such as the historic riparian restriction on water use in the eastern United States) or where other water users already have perfected claims to the available water, cities have generally been able to use their eminent domain power to condemn the water. See supra pp. 80–87. Most states explicitly provide that cities can use their eminent domain power outside city borders in order to acquire needed water supplies. Where the power is not explicit, courts have held that the power to acquire water from beyond the city's boundaries is implied. See, e.g., Hall v. Mayor & Council of Calhoun, 140 Ga. 611, 79 S.E. 533 (1913).

For more extensive discussions of the advantages that cities often enjoy in obtaining new water supplies, see A. Dan Tarlock, We Are All Water Lawyers Now: Water Law's Potential But Limited Impact on Urban Growth Management, in Wet Growth: Should Water Law Control Land Use? 57, 73–93 (Craig Anthony (Tony) Arnold ed., 2005); Barton H. Thompson, Jr., Water Management and Land Use Planning: Is It Time for Closer Coordination?, in id. at 95, 97–100; Wilbert Zeigler, Acquisition and Protection of Water Supplies by Municipalities, 57 Mich. L. Rev. 349 (1959).

Notes and Questions

1. Should cities be able to appropriate, and thus tie up, water for anticipated future needs, while farmers and other water users cannot? If so, should the right to appropriate for future needs be extended to private developers and others involved in furnishing water for growing municipal areas?

In State Dept. of Ecology v. Theodoratus, 957 P.2d 1241 (Wash. 1998), the Washington Supreme Court held that a private developer could not appropriate water for future needs. Although the court noted that it was not deciding whether cities could appropriate water for future needs, it rejected the argument that permitting appropriations only for current beneficial uses would impede future housing development. Allowing a larger appropriation "would allow speculation in water rights and lead to uncertainty in management of this fixed resource at a time when availability of water is a significant concern and management of limited water resources is of utmost importance." Id. at 1247. Justice Sanders vigorously dissented, arguing that what he labeled the "growing communities doctrine" was both well established law and good policy:

> The growing communities doctrine serves important functions. It allows communities to secure a source of water to meet growing needs. It also allows a community to construct a properly scaled water system at the start rather than constantly expanding the system on a piece-meal basis to meet growing population. The realities of business life and common sense come into play as well. [The growing communities doctrine] "serves important purposes: it allows municipalities to rationally plan and provide for future requirements." B. Faller, Special Treatment of Municipal Water Suppliers Under Washington Water Law at 1–14.

As commentators explain,

> As a practical reality, it is impossible for a municipality simply to tack on infrastructure and water rights year by year as its needs grow. Instead, municipalities typically plan one or two years ahead, or more. The infrastructure required to serve a city cannot gradually be sized up. Pipes, treatment facilities and other components must be sized at the time of design to meet growing needs over time. Likewise, in order to carry out its responsibility to its citizens, the city must acquire water rights of sufficient size to meet those growing demands. Waiting until the last minute to acquire water rights for a growing community would be the height of irresponsibility.

J.E. Carpenter, Symposium on Northwest Water Law at 137. See also Frank J. Trelease, Preferences to the Use of Water, 27 Rocky Mtn. L. Rev. 133, 139 (1954) ("A city without some excess water or promise of water cannot grow, and typically municipal supplies are procured in large amounts that exceed present needs and permit expansion").

2. Should restrictions be placed on the ability of cities to condemn needed water rights? In the mid–1970s, the Colorado legislature created a three-person commission to determine whether cities needed to condemn water rights and, if a city did, the appropriate compensation. Before condemning water rights, moreover, the legislation required cities to prepare and update a community growth development plan and to submit a detailed statement to the commission evaluating the economic and environmental effects of the condemnation, as well as alternative sources of water. The legislation also provided that no city could condemn water rights "for any anticipated or future needs in excess of fifteen years." In City of Thornton v. Farmers Reservoir & Irrigation Co., 194 Colo. 526, 575 P.2d 382 (1978), however, the Colorado Supreme Court held that the legislation was an unconstitutional intrusion into the power of "home rule" municipalities to determine necessity and exercise the right of eminent domain.

3. As cities grow, their water needs can be met through new water supplies, conservation, or a combination of the two. Can city water managers be trusted to decide among these alternatives without external oversight?

Institutional managers may find expanding the water supply a more appealing growth solution than reducing per capita demand (through price increases or other means) for several reasons. First, cities and counties have traditionally rewarded managers for ensuring that water supplies stay ahead of, and thus do not choke off, growth. By turning down an opportunity to acquire a sizable new water supply, managers may well fear that they will permanently lose the supply * * *.

Second, managers have long relied on the conservation capacity within their institution to ride out droughts with minimal consumer backlash. Many cities have historically been able to manage short droughts merely by calling on their residents to save water voluntarily; even where cities have been forced to ration water, the existing conservation capacity has softened the impact. Managers may reasonably fear that, if they use up their conservation capacity to meet growth, droughts will lead to far greater political controversy—making their lives more difficult and possibly even endangering their jobs. * * *

Finally, as a political matter, managers may find water trades easier to justify to their constituents than the steps necessary to achieve significant conservation. Urban residents have seldom questioned the cost of new water supplies. * * * The various conservation options, in contrast, present managers with unwanted problems.

Barton H. Thompson, Jr., Institutional Perspectives on Water Policy and Markets, 81 Calif. L. Rev. 673, 759–60 (1993).

If oversight of new municipal acquisitions is needed, who should review whether cities need new acquisitions? And what standards should be used? See Environmental Defense Fund v. East Bay Municipal Utility Dist., 125 Cal.Rptr. 601 (Cal. App. 1975), aff'd, 20 Cal.3d 327 (1977), supra p. 191.

b. The "Duty to Serve" in an Age of Scarcity

Municipal water suppliers historically believed that they had an obligation to meet the water needs of not only their current populations but also whatever growth was approved by city planners. In the 1950s, for example, the Metropolitan Water District of Southern California, which is the largest urban water supplier in the United States, proclaimed in its so-called "Laguna Declaration" that it would provide water for any needs that arose within its massive Southern California service area.[2]

In several recent cases, however, water districts have argued that they sometimes have the right to stop supplying water for new development—at least temporarily. The issue typically arises where a growing municipality begins to strain its available water supply. Lacking a ready or economical source of additional water, the water supplier sometimes

---

2. See Steven P. Erie & Pascale Joassart–Marcelli, Unraveling Southern California's Water/Growth Nexus: Metropolitan Water District Policies and Subsidies for Suburban Development, 1928–1996, at 36 Cal. W. L. Rev. 267, 271 (2000).

fears that adding new customers will compromise its ability to meet the needs of current residents. Even if additional water is available, local voters occasionally oppose expanding the water supply system for fear that it will encourage further growth. In these cases, can the water supplier refuse to hook up additional customers? Or must the water supplier keep taking on more customers by rationing existing customers? Does the water supplier have any obligation to develop additional water supplies if doing so would be expensive or is opposed by local voters?

SWANSON v. MARIN MUNICIPAL WATER DISTRICT

Court of Appeal of California, 1976.
56 Cal.App.3d 512, 128 Cal.Rptr. 485.

ROUSE, ASSOCIATE JUSTICE.

Defendant Marin Municipal Water District (hereinafter "District") appeals from a judgment granting plaintiff Albert Swanson a peremptory writ of mandate compelling District to grant plaintiff a pipeline extension and to provide water service to his real property. * * *

[In 1973, the District concluded that, although its storage reservoir was filled to capacity, current water consumption in the District exceeded the "annual safe yield" of the water supply system. If there were below average water runoff, it would be necessary to institute mandatory rationing. Although there was no "immediate emergency," the District concluded that the District faced a water shortage emergency "due to a threatened water shortage." The District therefore amended its rules to prohibit water service to new customers. Swanson applied for a hookup for a home that he was in the process of building for himself and his family. When the District rejected the application pursuant to the moratorium, Swanson sued.]

District contends that the water moratorium enacted by it was specifically authorized by sections 350 et seq. of the California Water Code.[2] * * * The language of section 350 makes it clear that a water district is empowered to anticipate a future water shortage and to impose appropriate regulations and restrictions where, lacking such control, its water supply will become depleted and it will be unable to meet the needs of its consumers. * * *

Plaintiff Swanson has made no real attempt to meet [the Marin Municipal Water District's] arguments. His position is that, within the meaning of section 350, a water shortage emergency condition can only

---

2. Section 350 states that "The governing body of a distributor of a public water supply * * * may declare a water shortage emergency condition to prevail within the area served by such distributor whenever it finds and determines that the ordinary demands and requirements of water consumers cannot be satisfied without depleting the water supply of the distributor to the extent that there would be insufficient wa-ter for human consumption, sanitation, and fire protection." * * *

Section 355 provides that "The regulations and restrictions shall thereafter be and remain in full force and effect during the period of the emergency and until the supply of water available for distribution within such area has been replenished or augmented."

be declared when "an immediate existing water shortage" is actually present. Plaintiff contends that since District's reservoir was filled to capacity and contained 53,000 acre feet of water when the moratorium was declared, there was in no sense an immediate existing water shortage, since if District were to use the water in its reservoir to supply the needs of its consumers, it would take two years, with minimal rainfall, before there would actually be insufficient water for human consumption, sanitation and fire protection. Plaintiff argues that "The summer two years away does not present an immediate threat and is, rightfully, an administrative problem."

Plaintiff's position does not find support in the language of the applicable Water Code sections. * * * To hold that this statute, as codified in the Water Code, requires an immediate present water shortage before a water district can take steps to conserve its water supply, is an unreasonable interpretation of its provisions.

Plaintiff raises the additional arguments that sections 350 through 358 are unconstitutional because (1) they provide for a taking of property without just compensation and (2) they discriminate between individuals already receiving water service from District and those who wish to obtain water service in the future, even though all of these individuals would use the water solely for human consumption and domestic purposes.

Plaintiff's constitutional arguments must fail on their merits. His contention that his property was taken without just compensation and that he had an absolute right to be treated in the same manner as existing water consumers within the water district is not valid since it is evident that a potential water user does not possess any absolute right to be afforded water service and that the Constitution does not require that he be treated in the same manner as established users of the water system. In Butte Co. W.U. Assn. v. Railroad Com. (1921), 185 Cal. 218, 230, 196 P. 265, 269, our Supreme Court aptly stated that "a water company supplying water for irrigation has not the power to take on new consumers without limit. Its power to supply water is, of course, limited by the amount of its supply, and when the demands of its consumers upon it have reached this limit, it has no right to take on new consumers to the necessary injury of those it has. But it is not always easy to determine just when the limit of supply is reached, and the factor of safety which should be allowed against exceptional seasons may vary from locality to locality. * * * The matter is one of judgment, a judgment which it may well be should be exercised conservatively, but a matter of judgment nevertheless."

The author of a recent law review article observes that "Although the general rule applied by the courts to public utilities is that a public utility must serve on reasonable terms all those who desire the service it renders, and may not arbitrarily discriminate against members of the public, discrimination as to service may be based upon a reasonable classification. The right of inhabitants of a municipality to compel extension of service to them is not an absolute and unqualified right; it is based to a large extent on the reasonableness of the demand. Because a public utility may not discontinue service to consumers, knowing they are dependent on the service, a refusal to extend service to new customers would seem reasonably justified when the resource demanded becomes limited. When there is barely enough water to service present users, refusal to inconvenience them by adding additional burdens to the water system surely cannot be termed arbitrary and discriminatory." (Dewey, Battle of the Heavyweights: In This Corner Environmental Rights and In The Far Corner Free Travel Rights, 1 Hastings Const. L.Q. 153, 164–165 (1974).) * * *

In passing, it must be noted that, as to Mr. Swanson and others who are similarly situated, we are not unmindful of the somewhat dire consequences which flow from our decision in this matter. Politically, the power to "cut off one's water" by the simple expedient of imposing a moratorium such as the one here involved is a potent weapon in effecting a no-growth policy within a community. Since District has neither the power nor the authority to initiate or implement such a policy, the imposition of any restriction on the use of its water supply for that purpose would be invalid. We hasten to point out, however, that, as indicated by our decision, we find no evidence in the record before us of any such abuse of authority. Nevertheless, we do foresee a continuing obligation on the part of District to exert every reasonable effort to augment its available water supply in order to meet increasing demands. Clearly, the Legislature anticipated the need for such a requirement when it limited the duration of such restriction to the period of the emergency and "until the supply of water available for distribution within such area has been replenished or augmented." Cal. Water Code § 355. * * *

Notes and Questions

1. Courts consistently have upheld water moratoria against statutory and constitutional challenges. See, e.g., Kawaoka v. City of Arroyo Grande, 17 F.3d 1227 (9th Cir. 1994); Hollister Park Inv. Co. v. Goleta County Water Dist., 82 Cal.App.3d 290, 147 Cal.Rptr. 91 (1978). Only one case has given property owners who cannot get water as a result of moratoria a glimmer of hope, but perhaps not much more, that they might be able to raise a successful constitutional claim. In Lockary v. Kayfetz, 917 F.2d 1150 (9th Cir. 1990), the court held that a property holder can establish a taking if he can show that a moratorium prevents "all practical use" of his land. The court also suggested that, if a district was wasting water and had sufficient water to permit additional hookups, a moratorium might be arbitrary and thus a violation of due process or equal protection. Demonstrating the difficulty of meeting these standards, the plaintiffs chose not to pursue their action on remand. See Lockary v. Kayfetz, 974 F.2d 1166 (9th Cir. 1992).

For a comprehensive discussion of the issues raised in challenges to water moratoria, see Dennis Herman, Sometimes There's Nothing Left to Give: The Justification for Denying Water Service to New Consumers to Control Growth, 44 Stan. L. Rev. 429 (1992).

2. In the final paragraph of *Swanson,* the Court of Appeal suggests that a water district does have an obligation to make reasonable efforts to meet increasing demands. However, the apparent basis for this dictum—section 355 of the California Water Code—does not explicitly require that new water be brought in and thus provides only slender support at best for the suggestion. Assuming there is an obligation, what must a water district do to meet it? If a court concludes that a district is not making reasonable efforts to supply its residents' needs, what remedies can the court impose?

In Building Industry Ass'n v. Marin Municipal Water Dist., 235 Cal. App.3d 1641, 1 Cal.Rptr.2d 625 (1991), plaintiffs argued that the Marin Municipal Water District had failed to make reasonable efforts to obtain additional water. According to plaintiffs, the district had failed, in the six years before the lawsuit, to "take effective action to control demand or augment its available water supply"; the district estimated that it would take yet another five to ten years to authorize and construct necessary new facilities. The court nevertheless refused to order the district to take additional steps.

> The district has not refused to take action; appellants themselves have acknowledged in their petitions that the District has "commenced studies of water supply options." * * * The *Swanson* court did not attempt to outline precisely how a district might satisfy the "continuing obligation," and its admonition that a district must make every "reasonable" effort is itself a recognition that the task can only be accomplished through the measured exercise of discretion. What appellants seek here is the exercise of that discretion in a particular manner to reach a result of their choosing, but mandate is unavailable for that purpose.

1 Cal.Rptr.2d at 629–30. Is this an admission that courts will not police the efforts of water districts to meet their customer's needs so long as the districts are doing something, no matter how little?

3. Do districts have an obligation to impose moratoria on new customers if necessary to meet their current customers' demands? In Residents for Adequate Water v. Redwood Valley County Water Dist., 34 Cal.App.4th 1801, 41 Cal.Rptr.2d 123 (1995), the court ordered a moratorium on new service connections after finding that a water "district did not possess a water source capacity sufficient to supply the needs of its users under maximum demand conditions." The court concluded that the district had an obligation to halt new service connections under the California Safe Drinking Water Act.

4. Should a community be entitled to organize a water district specifically to prevent additional water from being imported into the community? In 1960, residents of Hidden Valley (a small rural community northwest of Los Angeles) formed the Hidden Valley Municipal Water District to prevent the neighboring Calleguas Municipal Water District from annexing the community and bringing in a supplemental water supply which could stimulate unwanted growth. A property holder who wanted additional water petitioned for exclusion from the new district, but the petition was denied. On appeal, the California Court of Appeal upheld the denial:

[A] district of this type is normally formed and maintained for the purpose of bettering either the water supply or the water service, or both, within its boundaries * * *. But in our view a water district may properly be formed and maintained for largely negative purposes as well as for positive purposes. * * * We see nothing wrong in the use of a water district for this purpose. The people of Hidden Valley are using this local public entity to control and determine for themselves their own water future—in this case, for the present, negatively instead of positively. By the exercise of their right of political self-determination, they thereby, as an incident thereto, regulate the kind of land use that can prevail within the Valley.

Wilson v. Hidden Valley Mun. Water Dist., 256 Cal.App.2d 271, 63 Cal.Rptr. 889, 897–98 (1967).

5.   Communities, as noted, sometimes declare water moratoria in order to block new growth. Is this an effective or wise strategy?

This strategy suffers from a number of problems. First, it is not clear that the strategy is effective. The strategy, of course, works only in those situations where there is a limited water supply. To justify a water moratorium, at least legally, a community must have used up its available water supply through prior growth. Such communities have a difficult time withstanding long-term droughts. As droughts continue, local citizens ultimately may lose their patience with water shortages and demand increased water supplies. Once the water supply is increased, however, new growth again can occur. This has been the experience of those California communities that have tried to use water to restrict growth. * * *

Even if the strategy proved effective, there would be a more serious problem: the strategy is a subterfuge. * * * The question of growth * * * should focus on the issues that are really at stake, e.g., air pollution or traffic, and be decided through the land use planning process designed for evaluating these issues.

Barton H. Thompson, Jr., Water Management and Land Use Planning: Is It Time for Closer Coordination?, in Wet Growth: Should Water Law Control Land Use? 95, 117 (Craig Anthony (Tony) Arnold ed., 2005). Do you agree?

Taking Water Supplies Into Account in Local Land Use Planning

To what degree should land use planning take into account available water supplies—and the potential environmental and economic impacts of increasing the water supply? In recent years, legislatures and courts in several states have taken steps to require developers and land use planners to consider the impact of new development on water supplies. Concerned about growing groundwater overdrafts, for example, Arizona in 1980 mandated that all new developments in areas experiencing significant overdrafting ("active management areas") establish that "sufficient ground water, surface water or effluent will be continuously available to satisfy the water needs of a proposed use for at least one hundred years." Ariz. Rev. Stat. § 45–576.07. In 1995, California passed a law that required large developers to show that they had sufficient water to supply the development.[4] Illustrating the difficulty of getting developers to take water issues seriously, however, most developers either ignored or found means to evade the legislation.[5] In 2001, therefore, the California legislature strengthened the law by banning local cities and counties from issuing construction permits for subdivisions of 500 or more residential units unless and until the local water supplier shows that it can provide the projects with water for at least 20 years. Cal. Gov't Code § 66473. Florida law also requires local officials to consider regional water supply plans in evaluating potential new growth. Fla. Stat. §§ 163.3177 & 163.3191.

On the judicial front, California courts have demanded that environmental impact reports for new subdivisions, which local governments must file under the state's version of NEPA (see pp. 668–670 supra), include evidence of reliable water supplies and discuss the steps that will be taken to mitigate any adverse environmental impacts that will be caused by meeting the subdivisions' water demands. See, e.g., Santa Clarita Org. for Planning the Env't v. County of Los Angeles, 106 Cal.App.4th 715, 131 Cal.Rptr.2d 186 (2003); Save Our Peninsula Comm. v. Monterey County Bd. of Supervisors, 87 Cal.App.4th 99, 104 Cal. Rptr.2d 326 (2001).

Notes and Questions

1. How best can water issues be incorporated into land use planning? Do laws, like those in Arizona and California, that require developers or cities to obtain water supplies that are adequate for decades or even a century risk spurring even greater water development? See, e.g., A. Dan Tarlock & Sarah B. Van de Wetering, Growth Management and Western Water Law: From Urban Oases to Archipelagos, 5 Hastings N.-Nw. J. Envtl. L. & Pol'y 163, 177 (1999) (noting that the Arizona's law "initially triggered a race to acquire water ranches and other new sources of supply"); Sue Fox, New Water Law Is Unlikely to Halt the Region's Planned Home Projects, L.A. Times, Oct. 21, 2001, pt. 2, at 3 (noting that the 2001 California law will encourage developers to "look everywhere—underground aquifers, creeks, far-flung water agencies, storage banks, and reclamation plants—for the billions of gallons needed to supply future faucets"). Do such laws merely speed up the inevitable?

2. Should developers be required to look first to conservation before new water supplies in meeting the needs of their projects? In 1991, Los Angeles's Mayor Tom Bradley proposed that builders be permitted new water hookups only where they "offset some percentage" of the new water use by conserving water elsewhere in the city. A builder, for example, could gain the right to hookup new buildings by retrofitting existing buildings with

---

4. See Norris Hundley, Jr., The Great Thirst: Californians and Water: A History 524–25 (rev. ed. 2001); A. Dan Tarlock & Lora A. Lucero, Connecting Land, Water, and Growth, Land Use L. & Zoning Dig., Spr. 2002, at 3, 5.

5. See Sue Fox, New Water Law Is Unlikely to Halt the Region's Planned Home Projects, L.A. Times, Oct. 21, 2001, pt. 2, p. 3.

water-saving devices. See Bradley Proposes a Trade–Off for Allowing New Water Hookups, L.A. Times, Feb. 23, 1991. Bradley intended his proposal to be a temporary measure to help Los Angeles cope with a water supply shrunk considerably by five years of drought. Would Bradley's idea be a good long-term method of balancing growth and water supply?

3. For interesting discussions of the issues of land use planning and water development, see Craig Anthony (Tony) Arnold, Introduction: Integrating Water Controls and Land Use Controls: New Ideas and Old Obstacles, in Wet Growth: Should Water Law Control Land Use? 1 (Craig Anthony (Tony) Arnold ed., 2005); Craig Anthony (Tony) Arnold, Polycentric Wet Growth: Policy Diversity and Local Land Use Regulation in Integrating Land and Water, in id. at 292; David L. Callies et al., Balancing Water Values and Human Needs in an Enlightened Land Use Planning Regime, in id. at 335; A. Dan Tarlock, We Are All Water Lawyers Now: Water Law's Potential But Limited Impact on Urban Growth Management, in id. at 57; Barton H. Thompson, Jr., Water Management and Land Use Planning: Is It Time for Closer Coordination, in id. at 95.

Obligations to Non–Residents

Cities and other public water suppliers generally have no obligation to provide water to non-residents even if they have water available within their system. See, e.g., Fairway Manor, Inc. v. Board of Comm'rs, 36 Ohio St.3d 85, 521 N.E.2d 818 (1988); Five Mile Prairie v. City of Spokane, 51 Wash.App. 816, 755 P.2d 836 (1988); City of Colorado Springs v. Kitty Hawk Development Co., 154 Colo. 535, 392 P.2d 467 (1964).

Courts, however, have occasionally required a city to provide water to an area outside its borders where the city has previously suggested that it would service the area and has deterred other water suppliers from servicing the area. In Robinson v. City of Boulder, 190 Colo. 357, 547 P.2d 228 (1976), for example, the Colorado city of Boulder had decided in the 1960s to be the only water supplier for an area outside its borders "in order to gain indirect control over the development of property located within the service area." Boulder entered into agreements with other local water suppliers "which had the effect of precluding these entities from servicing" residents in the area; it had even opposed one water company's application to the Colorado Public Utilities Commission to provide water to the area. Because Boulder had secured an effective monopoly over water service in the area, the Colorado Supreme Court held that Boulder had to furnish water to the area's residents:

> [W]e hold that inasmuch as Boulder is the sole and exclusive provider of water and sewer services in the area surrounding the subject property, it is a public utility. As such, it holds itself out as ready and able to serve those in the territory who require the service. There is no utility related reason, such as insufficient water, preventing it from extending these services to the

landowners. Unless such reasons exist, Boulder cannot refuse to serve the people in the subject area.

A related issue is whether, if a city or public water agency voluntarily provides water to non-residents, it can charge the nonresidents more for water than it charges non-residents. Cities and other public agencies are generally exempt from state utility regulation. See Board of County Comm'rs v. Denver Bd. of Water Comm'rs, 718 P.2d 235 (Colo. 1986). Historically, moreover, courts refused to police the water rates charged to non-residents, and some courts still refuse for all practical purposes to do so. See, e.g., Bennett Bear Creek Farm Water & Sanitation Dist. v. City & County of Denver, 928 P.2d 1254 (Colo. 1996) (differences in rates subject only to a rational basis review); Fairway Manor, Inc. v. Board of Comm'rs, 36 Ohio St.3d 85, 521 N.E.2d 818 (Ohio 1988) (refusing to review rates charged to nonresidents).

A growing number of courts, however, subject municipalities and other public water agencies to a common law duty to charge reasonable and nondiscriminatory rates for water whether to residents or nonresidents. See, e.g., Platt v. Town of Torrey, 949 P.2d 325 (Utah 1997); Hansen v. City of San Buenaventura, 42 Cal.3d 1172, 233 Cal.Rptr. 22, 729 P.2d 186 (1986); City of Pompano Beach v. Oltman, 389 So.2d 283 (Fla. Dist. Ct. App. 1980); Barr v. First Taxing Dist., 151 Conn. 53, 192 A.2d 872 (1963). In *Platt*, a number of factors convinced the court to impose a common law duty of reasonableness. First, non-residents have little political recourse to combat unreasonable rates. Second, the "most fundamental principle of water law" in the arid West is that all the waters are "the property of the public." Finally, because nonresidents' use of a city's water protects the city against forfeiture of that water, "municipalities ought to deal reasonably with those who purchase the surplus water and who might otherwise be able to appropriate it for their own use."

Most cities, however, have found it relatively easy to meet the reasonableness test. Nonresidents have the burden of proof to show that the rates are unreasonable, and courts have emphasized that rate making "is an inexact science." Platt v. Town of Torrey, 949 P.2d 325, 334 (Utah 1997). Should the burden be eased—or even reversed? One of the co-authors of this casebook has suggested that, because nonresidents often do not have access to key pricing data, cities should have a "duty of compiling and producing the cost data for each item which is utilized in determining the rates." See Joseph Sax, Municipal Water Supply for Nonresidents: Recent Developments and a Suggestion for the Future, 5 Nat. Resources J. 54 (1965).

c. *Privatization of Municipal Water Supplies*

As noted in the introduction, public agencies dominate the supply of municipal water. Although there are thousands of private water suppliers spread out throughout the United States, public agencies supply 85 percent of the delivered domestic water. That is in stark contrast to other utilities, such as electricity, natural gas, and telephone service—where investor-owned companies dominate. A growing, but still limited number of cities, have begun to consider "privatizing" their water supply systems by bringing in private companies to either run or partner with public agencies in running the systems. In one study in the late 1990s of the 100 largest metropolitan governments, almost a third reported that they were considering privatizing some or all of their water supply infrastructure and services.

Privatization is a broad term that encompasses a variety of different actions. At one end of the spectrum, a city may sell or lease its municipal water supply system to a private company, which then manages the system as a public utility or under contract. In 1996, for example, the New Jersey–American Water Company (the largest investor-owned water utility in New Jersey) purchased the entire water system of Howell Township, New Jersey, servicing 16,000 customers, for $35.1 million. At the other end of the spectrum, a city can contract to a private company for the construction, operation, and/or maintenance of one of its supply facilities. Houston, Texas, for example, contracts for the private management of its Southeast Water Purification Plant. Somewhere in between these two extremes, many cities retain ownership and control of their water supply systems, but contract out for the day-to-day operation, maintenance, and management of that system. Buffalo, New York and Evanston, Indiana are two examples of cities that have taken this latter approach.

Multiple factors are leading cities to consider privatizing their supply systems. First, many cities see some forms of privatization as a means of getting private-sector help in financing the cost of satisfying stringent new drinking water standards, upgrading or replacing aging facilities, and meeting new water demands. The Environmental Protection Agency estimates that the cost of complying with the federal Safe Drinking Water Act through 2020 all by itself will cost at least $140 billion nationally.

Another frequently mentioned reason for privatization is increased efficiency and expertise. Many smaller cities that run their own water supply systems do not enjoy the expertise or scale economies from which larger cities and private suppliers benefit. Although studies suggest that private suppliers do not enjoy an inherent cost advantage over public suppliers, a number of cities have been able to lower costs and/or reduce planned rate increases through privatization.[6]

A third major reason for privatization is reallocation of risks between the private and public sector. Albeit for a financial premium, private water contractors may be willing to assume risks such as cost overruns in the design and construction of new infrastructure; of unforeseen increases in maintenance, operating, or replacement costs; and of

---

6. See National Association of Water Companies, NAWC Privatization Study: A Survey of the Use of Private–Public Part-nerships in the Drinking Water Utility Sector 41–43 (1999).

changing regulatory standards. By transferring financial risks, cities hope to ensure stabler and more predictable water rates that are politically popular and can attract new industrial, commercial, and domestic development.

Some cities also mention other factors in deciding to privatize. Some cities, for example, have used privatization as a public form of "home equity loan." In return for a long-term management agreement or a lease or sale of the water supply system, cities often receive sizable up-front cash payments that they can use to finance other essential infrastructure or to reduce existing debt or taxes.

Privatization, however, has proven extremely controversial—both in the United States and abroad. Indeed, privatization efforts overseas have sometimes generated violent demonstrations. The following excerpt from a global study by the Pacific Institute for Studies in Development, Environment, and Security explain some of the reasons why—and highlight the connection between privatization and other issues examined in this casebook.

PETER H. GLEICK, GARY WOLFF, ELIZABETH L. CHALECKI, & RACHEL REYES, THE NEW ECONOMY OF WATER: THE RISKS AND BENEFITS OF GLOBALIZATION AND PRIVATIZATION OF FRESH WATER

iii-v (2002).

The move toward privatization of water services raises many concerns, and in some places, even violent opposition. In large part, opposition arises because of doubts about whether purely private markets can address the many different social good aspects of water, or whether some non-market mechanisms are necessary to serve social objectives.

Other concerns relate to a fundamental distrust of corporate players and worries about the transfer of profits and assets outside of a community or even a country.[a] The greatest need for water services often exists in those countries with the weakest public sectors; yet the greatest risks of failed privatization also exist where governments are weak.

The rapid pace of privatization in recent years and the inappropriate way several projects have been implemented have compounded the worries of local communities, non-governmental organizations, and policymakers. * * *

One of the leading arguments offered by proponents of privatization is that private management or ownership of water systems can reduce the water prices paid by consumers. Ironically, one of the greatest concerns of local communities is that privatization will lead to *higher* costs for water and water services. The actual record is mixed—both results have occurred. * * *

a. Many of the major private companies pushing for privatization are European, including Veolia Environnement and Ondeo, two major French multinationals.—Eds.

Privatization of water management can, under some circumstances, lead to the loss of local ownership of water systems, which in turn can lead to neglect of the public interest. Many of the concerns expressed about privatization relate to the control of water rights and changes in water allocations, rather than explicit financial or economic problems. In part, this is the result of the deep feelings people have for water. * * *

Many privatization contracts include provisions to encourage the development of new water supplies, often over a longer period of time. If privatization contracts do not also guarantee ecosystem water requirements, development of new supply options will undermine ecosystem health and well-being (for both public and private developments). Balancing ecological needs with water supply, hydroelectric power, and downstream uses of water is a complex task involving many stakeholders.

One of the greatest concerns of privatization watchdogs is that efficiency programs are typically ignored or even cancelled after authority for managing public systems is turned over to private entities. Improvements in efficiency reduce water sales, and hence may lower revenues. As a result, utilities or companies that provide utility services may have little or no financial incentive to encourage conservation. In addition, conservation is often less capital intensive and therefore creates fewer opportunities for investors. Consequently, it may be neglected in comparison with traditional, centralized water-supply projects. * * *

Public water companies are usually subject to political dispute-resolution processes involving local stakeholders. Privatized water systems are subject to legal processes that involve non-local stakeholders and perhaps non-local levels of the legal system. This change in *who* resolves disputes, and the rules for dispute resolution, is accompanied by increased potential for political conflicts over privatization agreements. * * *

When governments transfer control over their water system to private companies, the loss of internal skills and expertise may be irreversible, or nearly so. Many contracts are long term—for as much as 10 to 20 years. Management expertise, engineering knowledge, and other assets in the public domain may be lost for good. Indeed, while there is growing experience with the transfer of such assets to private hands, there is little or no recent experience with the public sector re-acquiring such assets from the private sector.

Notes and Questions

1. What steps should the law take to address the concerns expressed about privatization? Professor Tony Arnold has suggested that states in the U.S. should pass laws requiring minimum standards and processes for privatization. According to Professor Arnold, the statute should:

- Require competitive bidding.
- Establish a process for evaluating privatization proposals that ensures transparency and an opportunity for public input.

- Mandate the preparation of an "impact assessment" and the submission by the potential contractor of a "statement of water services provider qualifications and history."

- Prohibit the transfer or development of watershed or groundwater-protection lands to or by private entities.

- Require review and approval by an appropriate state agency.

Craig Anthony (Tony) Arnold, Privatization of Public Water Services: The States' Role in Ensuring Public Accountability, 32 Pepp. L. Rev. 561 (2005).

2. A number of states already have adopted laws setting out specific procedures and standards for evaluating the privatization of water and wastewater systems. See, e.g., Ky. Rev. Stat. §§ 107.700–.770; Minn. Rev. Stat. §§ 471A.01–.12; N.J. Rev. Stat. §§ 58.26–1 to –27; Utah Code § 73–10d–1.

3. For interesting articles on the privatization debate, see Jennifer Davis, Private–Sector Participation in the Water and Sanitation Sector, 30 Ann. Rev. Env't & Resources 145 (2005); Barton H. Thompson, Jr., Privatization of Municipal Water Supplies, Looking Ahead, May/June 1999, at 1.

3. WHO OWNS THE WATER—THE WATER ORGANIZATION OR ITS MEMBERS?

If a water district or mutual water company supplies water to a farm, who owns the water—the organization or the farmer? This question can be extremely important in a variety of contexts and is becoming more important over time. If the water is condemned, for example, who is entitled to compensation? Can the farmer apply directly to the state to change the type or place of use? Or is that a decision for the water organization? Who has the power to sell or lease the water to a third party? The following two cases, the first involving a water district and the second a mutual water company, illustrate some of the contexts in which the question arises.

JENISON v. REDFIELD

Supreme Court of California, 1906.
149 Cal. 500, 87 P. 62.

ANGELLOTI, JUSTICE.

This is an action for damages alleged to have been suffered by plaintiff, a landowner of Walnut Irrigation District, by reason of the failure and refusal of defendants, directors of said district, to distribute and apportion to him his proportion of the water of said district. * * *

It appears that plaintiff owned considerable land outside of said district, upon which he had planted alfalfa and walnuts, and the real question presented by this case is as to whether he was entitled to receive from defendants any portion of his share of water for use upon said land without the boundaries of the district. There is no pretence that he was ever denied water for use upon such of his land as was within the district, and unless he was entitled to have the water to the extent of his share for the sole purpose of carrying the same beyond the limits of the district and irrigating lands outside thereof, the defendants in no respect failed or refused to apportion and distribute to him any water to which he was entitled. * * *

It is apparent that to sustain the claim of plaintiff, it must be held that the effect of our statutes relative to irrigation districts, is to make each owner of land within a district the absolute owner of the proportionate share of the water of the district to which his land entitles him, to do with as he sees fit, even to the extent of diverting all thereof from the irrigation of lands within the district.

It seems very clear that such a conclusion would be opposed to the whole plan or scheme of the legislation for irrigation districts, converting a district organized, acquiring and holding water solely for a certain specified purpose—viz. the procuring and furnishing of water for the improvement by irrigation of the lands included therein, into a mere agency for the distribution of its water to individuals for use by them outside the district for any purpose whatever. Under plaintiff's theory, the use to which the water is to be appropriated is entirely immaterial, and the irrigation district is, in effect, although constituted and avowedly acquiring its water for an entirely different purpose, nothing more or less than an ordinary water company, the original absolute owners of the property of which are the landowners, each owning such proportion thereof as the value of his land entitles him to, and at liberty to deal with it as he sees fit, without regard to the improvement of the land of the district. He may retain it, and use the water for any purpose and in any place, or he may transfer it to any other person for any kind of use, and thereupon such transferee succeeds to his rights and becomes entitled to the water. Such a construction of the provisions of the Irrigation Act entirely ignores the object of its enactment.

The whole object of the legislation authorizing the organization of irrigation districts is to enable owners of lands susceptible of irrigation from a common source, and by the same system of works, to form a district composed of such lands, which district when formed is a public corporation for the sole purpose of obtaining and distributing such water as may be necessary for the irrigation thereof, thus enabling each one to have for his land in the district, the benefit of a common system of irrigation, and bringing about the reclamation of the land of the district from aridity to a condition of suitability for cultivation. * * *

The ultimate purpose of a district organized under the Irrigation Act is the improvement, by irrigation, of the lands within the district. It can, under the law, be organized and exist and acquire property only for such purpose. This we think is so clearly apparent as not to require further discussion here. Such a district holds all property acquired by it solely in trust for such ultimate purpose, and can divert it to no other use. It has to do solely with the irrigation of lands within the district, and cannot appropriate water to any other purpose. The right of a landowner of the district to the use of the water acquired by the district is a right to be exercised in consonance with and in furtherance of such ultimate purpose—viz. for the improvement by irrigation of lands within the district—and in no other way. His right is always in subordination to the ultimate purpose of the trust. So far as he proposes to use the water for the irrigation of lands within the district, he is proposing to use it in furtherance of the purpose of the trust, and is entitled to have distributed to him for that purpose such proportion as his assessment entitles him to. To this extent only can he be held to be the owner of any share or portion of the water, except that he may assign the right to the whole or any portion of the share to which he is entitled. This does not mean, however, that he may make an effectual transfer of his share, free from the trust by which it is encumbered. It still remains subject to that trust, and therefore can be used only for the irrigation of lands within the district, and the irrigation district has no authority to distribute it for any other purpose. * * *

EAST JORDAN IRRIGATION CO. v. MORGAN

Supreme Court of Utah, 1993.
860 P.2d 310.

HALL, CHIEF JUSTICE.

Plaintiff East Jordan Irrigation Company ("East Jordan") appeals from a grant of summary judgment upholding the state engineer's decision allowing defendant Payson City Corporation ("Payson"), a shareholder in East Jordan, to change the point of diversion of a portion of East Jordan's water without the company's consent. We reverse.

East Jordan is a nonprofit mutual water corporation owning legal title to certain water rights in Utah Lake and the Jordan River. The corporation diverts water from the river and the lake into a canal and delivers it to its 650 shareholders to be used primarily for irrigation in Salt Lake County. Each of the 10,000 shares entitles the shareholder to receive a pro rata share of the company's water through the canal.

Payson bought 38.5 shares of East Jordan's stock (representing 186.34 acre-feet of water) in 1987. Soon after, it filed an application with the state engineer to change the point of diversion of the water to a city-owned well that draws water from a basin flowing into Utah Lake. Payson sought to use this water for year-round municipal purposes.

East Jordan, Salt Lake City Corporation, and the Provo River Water Users' Association protested the proposed change.[2] They argued, inter alia, that (1) the change application should have been filed by East Jordan as owner of the water right, and (2) the proposed change would impair their vested rights to water in Utah Lake. The state engineer held two informal hearings and approved the change. He concluded that Payson had a vested water right by virtue of its ownership of East

2. Salt Lake City Corporation owns 2,067 shares of stock in East Jordan (20.67%). * * *

Jordan stock and therefore could file a change application in its own name. The engineer considered a number of factors, including the amount of water consumed by irrigation, the amount of water that would be returned to Utah Lake from municipal use, and the seasonal variation in water use. He then ordered that Payson be allowed to divert 144 acre-feet between April 15 and October 31 and 38 acre-feet the rest of the year and that East Jordan reduce the diversion into its canal by 186.34 acre-feet per year. Finally, the order required that Payson install a meter on its diversion well to be available for inspection by East Jordan and that Payson remain liable for assessments and "any other obligations it may incur as a shareholder in the Company."

East Jordan brought this action in the fourth district court, seeking to overturn the engineer's decision. The parties filed cross-motions for summary judgment on a stipulated statement of facts on the issues of (1) whether Payson as a shareholder in the corporation had the legal right to file a change application in its own name without consent of East Jordan, and (2) whether the state engineer had jurisdiction to consider such an application. The trial court denied East Jordan's motion, granted Payson's cross-motion, and subsequently entered judgment in favor of Payson. East Jordan appeals from that judgment. * * *

The right to change a point of diversion, place, or purpose of water is governed by Utah Code Ann. § 73–3–3(2) (1989), which provides: "(a) Any person entitled to the use of water may make [a permanent or temporary change in the place of diversion, place of use, or purpose of use of the water]."

This case ultimately turns on whether a shareholder in a mutual water corporation is "a person entitled to the use of water" under the statute. Payson narrowly focuses on the language of this section to support its position that it has the right to change its point of diversion over East Jordan's objection. However, section 73–3–3(2)(a) must be read in light of the entire statutory scheme. * * * Utah Code Ann. § 73–3–1 directs how one becomes legally "entitled" to the use of water:

> Rights to the use of unappropriated waters of this state may be acquired only as provided in this title. No appropriation of water may be made and no rights to the use thereof initiated and no notice of intent to appropriate shall be recognized except application for such appropriation first be made to the state engineer in the manner hereinafter provided, and not otherwise.

Payson has not filed an application to become an appropriator of public waters. To the contrary, title to company water rights was judicially confirmed in East Jordan under the Morse and Booth Decrees. Payson's ownership of shares in East Jordan does not afford it a right conferred by the state to "the use of water" as contemplated by section 73–3–3(2). It necessarily follows that any change in point of diversion can be initiated only by East Jordan itself since it alone owns the right as an appropriator to the use of public waters. Therefore, Payson does not have standing before the state engineer to seek a change in the point of diversion.

Payson claims to be an "equitable owner" of its shares of East Jordan's water rights. However, its equitable ownership remains subject to the general rule governing corporations that directors, rather than shareholders, control the affairs of the corporation. * * * Article VII of East Jordan's articles of incorporation provides, "The Board of Directors shall have the general supervision, management, direction & control of all the business and affairs of the company, of whatever kind." A change in point of diversion certainly implicates management of the water supply as a whole. It necessarily follows that any change in the point of diversion of water from a source other than East Jordan's canal can be initiated only by East Jordan itself since it alone is empowered with the right to manage and control the affairs of the company.

What Payson did gain by its purchase of East Jordan shares is the right to receive a proportionate share of the water distributed by East Jordan out of its system in the same manner as all other shareholders. East Jordan's articles of incorporation, as amended, set forth the objective, powers, and purposes of the water company. Article III thereof reads in pertinent part:

> The pursuit or business of this association is, and shall be the construction, operation and maintenance of a canal—said canal to extend from a point in the Jordan River * * * to * * * Salt Lake City, * * * the purpose of said canal being to direct a portion of the waters of the said Jordan River, to be appropriated, used, and disposed of, sold and distributed by said association, for agricultural, manufacturing, domestic or ornamental purposes * * * and to do and perform such work and acts, and use such mechanical or other means and appliances as may he necessary to maintain or increase the flow of water in the said Jordan River.

Payson's rights as a shareholder and its relationship with East Jordan are dependent on and limited by the scope of East Jordan's articles of incorporation, which Payson agreed to by virtue of its purchase of shares. Here, Payson is seeking a point of diversion, place of use, and nature of use that are substantially different from those of the other shareholders and those anticipated in East Jordan's articles of incorporation. Payson purports to divert its share of the water before it enters East Jordan's delivery system, to transport the water outside of East Jordan's service, and to use it for municipal purposes. * * *

Three other states have addressed this issue. Payson argues that we should follow the Colorado rule set forth in Wadsworth Ditch Co. v. Brown.[15] The court in *Wadsworth* essentially held that a shareholder has the right to change a point of diversion over the objection of the company. *Wadsworth* involved a shareholder who could no longer benefi-

15. 39 Colo. 57, 88 P. 1060 (Colo. 1907).

cially use his water at the original diversion point and therefore petitioned the water court to change the diversion point. The trial court approved the change provided that Brown's stock remained liable for assessment to maintain the company ditch. The Colorado Supreme Court concluded that the right to change the diversion point was a property right belonging to the stockholder in a mutual ditch company.[16]

* * * We are more persuaded by California authority that has established through case law what Utah has established by statute. In Consolidated People's Ditch Co. v. Foothill Ditch Co.,[18] the California court held that a shareholder does not have the right to change its point of diversion over the objection of the company. In *Consolidated People's Ditch Co.*, the defendant bought stock in a number of different mutual water corporations along a river and started to enlarge a canal upstream to divert the water represented by this stock. The trial court enjoined construction of the canal, and the supreme court affirmed. The court noted that shareholders in mutual water corporations are entitled to proportionate distribution of the water of the corporation, but no more. "Such stockholders are in that sense and to that extent, but to none other, owners of the water and water rights which the corporation possesses, and over the distribution of which it exercises under general laws and under its particular by-laws full and exclusive control."

The court also noted that the term "mutual water company" had no legal meaning that would differentiate such companies from other corporations administering property for the benefit of their stockholders. The court stated that "it would seem to be too clear for argument that neither one nor any number of such stockholders would or could possess the legal right to take or to receive the amount of water to which [they] may be entitled by another manner or means than those supplied by the corporation itself." To recognize such a right

> would necessarily be to admit the possession of similar rights in each and every stockholder in each of said corporations to go and do likewise, and it is too plain for argument that such an admission would result in a state of inextricable discord and confusion among the owners of water rights of various sorts [all over California]. The creation or threatened danger of such a consequence would of itself supply a sufficient reason for the use of the injunctive processes of the court in the way of its prevention.

* * * We are persuaded by the reasoning of the California court in *Consolidated People's Ditch Co.* that allowing the shareholder this right would ultimately lead to "a state of inextricable discord and confusion among the owners of water rights." This would certainly apply in this situation, where East Jordan has 650 shareholders. We fear the havoc

---

16. We note that Idaho followed Colorado for some time but changed its position by statute in 1943 to provide explicitly what the Utah statute provides for implicitly, namely, that a shareholder may not change its point of diversion without the consent of the corporation.

18. 205 Cal. 54, 269 P. 915 (Cal. 1928).

that would invariably ensue if every shareholder in the corporation were to attempt to govern the corporate affairs as they relate to the appropriation of waters. Indeed, water companies could well be destroyed by complete changes of use of water. In addition, some rivers in Utah, for example, the Sevier River, are extremely long. It would be impossible to manage the appropriation if each individual water user were allowed to take water from anywhere along the river.

It should be observed that our ruling today does not leave the shareholder without a remedy. * * * Payson's proper course of action in this matter was to bring its request for change application to the East Jordan board of directors. In the event that its request for change was unreasonably refused after consideration by the board, the shareholder could have sought judicial relief wherein Payson's arguments concerning the appropriateness of board policy regarding change applications and the regulation of the shareholder's rights could have been fully explored. * * *

DURHAM, JUSTICE, dissenting.

I respectfully dissent. The majority holds that a shareholder in a mutual water corporation does not have the right to change his or her point of diversion because the water rights are owned by the company rather than the shareholder. In so holding, the majority makes a number of crucial errors. First, the majority improperly treats water like an ordinary corporate asset and assumes that mutual water companies are the same as other corporations. The majority further ignores long-established Utah case law holding that mutual water corporations may not interfere with a shareholder's use of his or her share of water unless the shareholder's use harms the corporation or other shareholders. Finally, the holding is bad policy; it assumes without adequate analysis that allowing shareholders to change their points of diversion would destroy water corporations, and it ignores the need for flexibility and transferability of water rights.

The main opinion reasons that East Jordan, as the true "owner" of the water rights, has the sole right to change the point of diversion. This position ignores the fact that we have previously established that shareholders in mutual water companies do in fact have ownership interests in the water rights. * * *

> Water rights are pooled in a mutual company for convenience of operation and more efficient distribution, and perhaps for more convenient transfer. But the stock certificate is not like the stock certificate in a company operated for profit. It is really a certificate showing an undivided part ownership in a certain water supply.

Genola Town v. Santaquin City, 80 P.2d 930 (Utah 1938). * * *

The majority opinion also fails to acknowledge case law that has developed regarding the relative rights of mutual water companies and their shareholders. While this court has never faced the precise issue of whether a shareholder may change his or her point of diversion without company consent, we have considered the relationship in a number of other contexts. These cases establish that a shareholder in a mutual water corporation has a right to do whatever he or she wants with his or her share of the water, and the company may not interfere with this right. Further, the shareholder has the exclusive right to determine where and how the water will be used.

In Baird v. Upper Canal Irrigation Co., 257 P. 1060 (Utah 1927), the plaintiff shareholder brought an action in mandamus to compel the defendant mutual water corporation to connect her pipeline to the company's main line at a certain point. The plaintiff was already receiving her share of company water through three other connections, but she sought a new connection so that she could supply twelve or thirteen other houses with water. The trial court found for the plaintiff and ordered the company to make the connection as long as the plaintiff paid the expenses of doing so.

This court affirmed. On appeal, the company argued, among other things, that it could not be compelled to connect the shareholder's pipe because doing so would violate a company regulation that prohibited any future connections that would divert culinary water outside the company's service area. The court rejected this argument:

> Nor do we see upon what theory the stockholders of the defendant company claim the right to limit the use of the culinary and domestic water to the homes and premises within the area irrigated by water controlled and regulated by the defendant company. When a stockholder has the water to which he is entitled delivered into his private pipe line, it becomes his personal property. One of the incidents of the ownership of property is the right to use, lease, or otherwise dispose of the same as the owner may desire so long as the rights of others are not interfered with. In this case it is difficult to see how the rights of the other stockholders would be affected by the mere fact that the water flows out of a private pipe line beyond the limits of the land irrigated by water controlled by the defendant company rather than within such boundary lines. A regulation made solely upon such a basis is an unwarranted interference with the rights of stockholders not consenting thereto.

> * * *

A shareholder's rights are not unlimited, of course. This court has decided several shareholder-company disputes in favor of the corporations, but only where the shareholder's claim would have increased the company's costs or interfered with the management and distribution of the water supply. For example, we have held that a mutual water corporation is not required to extend a company ditch to reach a shareholder's lands. Swasey v. Rocky Point Ditch Co., 617 P.2d 375 (Utah 1980). * * * The majority asserts that mutual water corporations cannot manage their affairs if shareholders are allowed to make these changes but fails to specify how this is so. Instead, like the California Supreme Court sixty-five years ago, the majority simply assumes that affirming the engineer's order would be the downfall of such corporations. As the majority acknowledges, however, shareholders in Colorado have been able to make changes in their points of diversion since at least 1907, and nothing suggests that disaster has resulted. Indeed, a recent study reveals that mutual water companies still "dominate the water market in Colorado." Timothy D. Tregarthen, Water in Colorado: Fear and Loathing of the Marketplace, in Water Rights: Scarce Resource Allocation, Bureaucracy, and the Environment 119, 131 (Terry L. Anderson ed., 1983); see also Barton H. Thompson, Jr., Institutional Perspectives on Water Policy and Markets, 81 Cal. L. Rev. 671, 688 table 2 (1993). * * *

Not only is the majority's holding contrary to Utah case law, but it is also bad policy. First, it will not actually increase East Jordan's control over its water supply. Payson will still be free to use its share of company water for municipal purposes. As discussed above, under *Baird*, the corporation must connect the shareholder to the company canal at any point the shareholder chooses, as long as it does not injure the corporation or the other shareholders. *Baird* also established that a shareholder may do whatever he or she wants with water once it is delivered. Thus, there is nothing East Jordan can do to prevent Payson from taking its water from the East Jordan canal and pumping it to the city. In my view, the majority's approach will increase the costs for everyone involved without providing any benefits.

Further, preventing shareholders from changing their points of diversion interferes with the ability of water users to respond to new needs for water. Utah's population has been and is expected to continue growing at a substantial rate, and there is not enough water available to meet the increasing demands in many parts of the state. While in the past these concerns have been addressed by the construction of dams and large-scale water diversions, such projects are no longer as economically or politically feasible as they once were. As the demand for water approaches the supply, the natural solution will be to seek transfers of water rights. Commentators agree that agricultural users are the most likely sources of water rights for transfer.

This case presents a classic example. The person who sold the stock to Payson apparently decided that he or she could receive a higher return by selling the water rights than by using them for farming. Presumably, Payson likewise concluded that the returns from the new water exceeded the purchase and transfer costs and that purchase of East Jordan stock was more economically attractive than any other option. But by refusing to allow shareholders to change their points of diversion, the majority increases the cost of these transactions, perhaps to the point of making them prohibitive.

I do not mean to imply that economic efficiency is the sole consideration in water law or that transfers must be allowed without restrictions.

One commentator has noted: "It must be emphasized that policies which restrict market activities and make transactions more costly are not necessarily wasteful or inefficient. They are an expression of the concerns that members of society and policy makers have about reallocating water through market processes and they provide protection for third-parties who may be impacted by water transfers." Bonnie G. Colby, Economic Impacts of Water Law—State Law and Water Market Development in the Southwest, 28 Nat. Res. J. 721, 722 (Fall 1988). There can be little doubt that social and environmental concerns should override economic efficiency in some situations. I also believe that some protection should be provided for third parties affected by large-scale water transfers. However, the only interest served by the holding in this case is East Jordan's desire to have the water flow through its canal. Further, area-of-origin protections and other concerns implicated by large-scale water transfers should be handled by some sort of governmental entity rather than by a private corporation pursuing its own goals.[15] * * *

Notes and Questions

1. Courts have given varying answers to the abstract question of who "owns" the water that is distributed by a water organization. In the case of mutual water companies, most courts have held that the shareholders are the "real owners" of the water rights (even though the mutual might hold "naked title" to the rights). See, e.g., Avery v. Johnson, 59 Wash. 332, 109 P. 1028 (1910); Slosser v. Salt River Valley Canal Co., 7 Ariz. 376, 65 P. 332 (1901). The Utah Supreme Court, however, is not alone in holding that the mutual owns the water right in trust for its shareholders. See, e.g., Consolidated People's Ditch Co. v. Foothill Ditch Co., 205 Cal. 54, 269 P. 915 (1928).

In the case of water districts, most courts have held that the district owns the water rights in trust for its landowners and to fulfill its statutory purposes. The courts often speak of district landowners as the "beneficial and equitable owners" of the water rights. See, e.g., Bradshaw v. Milner Low Lift Irr. Dist., 85 Idaho 528, 381 P.2d 440 (1963); Madera Irr. Dist. v. All Persons, 47 Cal.2d 681, 306 P.2d 886 (1957), rev'd on other grounds sub nom. Ivanhoe Irr. Dist. v. McCracken, 357 U.S. 275 (1958); Colo. Rev. Stat. §§ 37–41–115 & 37–42–113(1) (water rights vested in district in trust for district purposes). A few courts, however, have stated that landowners actually own the water rights. See, e.g., State Dept. of Ecology v. Acquavella, 100 Wash.2d 651, 674 P.2d 160 (1983).

Abstract pronouncements on "ownership" of water, however, can be highly misleading when applied to specific questions. As most property books emphasize, "ownership" consists of a bundle of different rights. A court's conclusion that a member of a mutual or district "owns" water rights for one purpose, therefore, does not necessarily mean that the member "owns" the water for a different purpose. Indeed, some state supreme courts have reached different conclusions regarding "ownership" depending on the issue

---

15. The record reveals that East Jordan has allowed the Salt Lake County Water Conservancy District, which owns 2000 shares (20 percent) of company stock, to change the diversion of its 10,000 acre-feet of company water for delivery outside of East Jordan's service area.

being addressed. The best answer to the question "Who owns the water?" is thus "Why do you want to know?"

2. *Jenison* is the only case yet to address whether landowners in water districts can transfer their water to uses outside the district. Most commentators, however, have assumed that, absent express statutory authority, landowners cannot engage unilaterally in external transfers. See, e.g., Barton H. Thompson, Jr., Institutional Perspectives on Water Policy and Markets, 81 Calif. L. Rev. 673, 726 (1993).

3. Under *Jenison*, could a California irrigation district permit one of its members to lease unneeded water to someone outside the district? Could the district do so itself? Would either of these actions violate the "trust" responsibility identified by the California Supreme Court? Today, a number of California statutes explicitly authorize districts to engage in external transfers or to permit their members to do so. See, e.g., Cal. Water Code §§ 382–383, 1022, 1745.02–1745.11, 22259, 35425.

4. Courts have split on the question whether mutual shareholders can transfer their water to external uses. As noted in *East Jordan*, Colorado courts have long permitted such transfers. Even in Colorado, however, mutuals can impose reasonable restrictions on external transfers. In Fort Lyon Canal Co. v. Catlin Canal Co., 642 P.2d 501 (Colo. 1982), the Colorado Supreme Court approved a mutual by-law requiring board approval of any external transfer. In a followup case, the Colorado Supreme Court held that the board's refusal to approve a particular transfer was subject to judicial review, but only under an "arbitrary, capricious, or abuse of discretion" standard. See Fort Lyon Canal Co. v. Catlin Canal Co., 762 P.2d 1375 (Colo. 1988).

5. What is the ultimate holding of *East Jordan*? Can Payson still ask the East Jordan board of directions for permission to transfer its water? If the board refuses permission, can Payson challenge that decision in court? On what grounds? If the board agrees to the transfer, must Payson still get the approval of the Utah state engineer? If so, who must apply for that approval—Payson or East Jordan?

6. While exports of water from water districts or mutuals typically require the organization's permission, most courts have held that members unilaterally can engage in internal transfers so long as the transfers do not injure other members. See, e.g., Great Western Sugar Co. v. Jackson Lake Reservoir & Irrig. Co., 681 P.2d 484 (Colo. 1984) (mutual); Cline v. McDowell, 132 Colo. 37, 284 P.2d 1056 (1955) (water district); Hard v. Boise City Irrig. & Land Co., 9 Idaho 589, 76 P. 331 (1904) (mutual).

Large water organizations often foster active internal markets. Indeed, "institutional transfers" of water among members of water organizations appear to far outnumber the limited number of "statutory transfers" that occur under the state transfer laws discussed in Chapter 3 at pp. 264–300:

> Only three states currently average more than 100 statutory transfers per year; Utah enjoys the most with almost 400. Some major states such as California and Arizona see only a few statutory transfers each year. By comparison, a study of water rentals in Colorado during 1959 found 645 institutional transfers within just

five mutuals in the South Platte Basin and another 376 institutional transfers within the Northern Colorado Water Conservancy District. A similar study of institutional transfers among four large Utah mutuals between 1951 and 1964 revealed between 290 to 629 transfers per irrigation season. More recently, members of California's Westlands Water District negotiated roughly 4500 institutional transfers during the 1990–1991 water year alone. The limited data available on transfer volumes as a percent of total water supply also indicate that institutional transfers are far more significant than statutory transfers.

Thompson, supra note 2, at 713–14.

7. How *should* the "ownership" of water for transfer purposes be allocated between a water organization and its members? Should "ownership" of water for transfer purposes be separated from the right to use the water? Recall that one argument for water markets is that the opportunity to sell water provides water users with an incentive to conserve. How might the separation of "ownership" from the right to use affect the incentive to conserve?

8. Other questions that have arisen concerning ownership of water include:

a. If some members of a water district separate and form their own district, can they take their share of the original district's water with them? See Madera Irrigation Dist. v. All Persons, 306 P.2d 886 (Cal. 1957), rev'd on other grounds sub nom. Ivanhoe Irrig. Dist. v. McCracken, 357 U.S. 275 (1958) (answer: no).

b. Can the members of water organizations claim compensation under the constitution if the water is "taken" by the government? See State Dept. of Ecology v. Acquavella, 100 Wash.2d 651, 674 P.2d 160 (1983) (answer: yes). See also Jacobucci v. District Court, 189 Colo. 380, 541 P.2d 667 (1975) (mutual shareholders are indispensable parties for purposes of a condemnation proceeding).

c. Can a water organization claim the right to recapture and allocate the return flow from the water that it imports and distributes to its members? Most courts have held that organizations have a sufficient interest in the water (even if inferior or subservient to the interests of its members) to recapture imported water. See, e.g., Jensen v. Dept. of Ecology, supra p. 497; Stevens v. Oakdale Irr. Dist., supra p. 211. But see Strawberry Water Users Ass'n v. Bureau of Reclamation, 133 P.3d 410 (Utah 2006) (concluding that the question remains open in Utah).

d. If a water organization ceases to exist, is its water right abandoned or can its members continue to use the water? In St. George City v. Kirkland, 17 Utah 2d 292, 409 P.2d 970 (1966), the court held that the shareholders of a mutual are the "real owners" of the water and therefore can continue to use the water.

9. Can these various holdings be rationalized into any general rules on how to resolve "ownership" disputes? Do the holdings suggest that the organization "owns" the water vis-a-vis the water user, but that the water user "owns" the water vis-a-vis the rest of the world? Would this be a

sensible rule? For general discussions of the ownership issue, see Jeffrey Fereday, Ownership of Water Rights in Irrigation Water Delivery Organizations: An Outline of the Major Issues, in Water Organizations in a Changing West (Nat. Resources L. Ctr., U. Colo. Sch. of L., June 14–16, 1993); Barton H. Thompson, Jr., The Relevance of Water "Ownership" to Water Markets and Other Issues, in id.

4. WATER ORGANIZATIONS IN AN ERA OF MARKETS

Institutional issues are of increasing importance to water markets in the western United States. Most major water transfers involve large water organizations. Cities and other large public water suppliers are the largest purchasers of water in the West. Large agricultural water districts and mutuals, moreover, typically provide the greatest opportunities for water sales. Such organizations supply about half of the irrigation water in the 17 western states. Purchasing water from a large agricultural water organizations is also generally easier than purchasing water from a large number of individual farmers.

The involvement of water organizations in water transfers raises key legal issues that are as important to the future of water markets as are the state legal constraints on water transfers discussed in Chapter 3 at pp. 264–300. Who, if anyone, has the power to sell water distributed by a public water district or private mutual—the organization, the individual users, or both? If the organization sells water that it holds, how should the proceeds of the sale be distributed among the members of the organization? To what degree can one water organization use the facilities of another water organization to transport the water?

Water transfers involving the Imperial Irrigation District (IID) in Southeastern California illustrate some of the issues involved in water marketing among large public organizations. IID holds one the largest water entitlements in the United States. For years, IID has received approximately 3 million acre-feet of water per year from the Colorado River, about a quarter of the river's average annual flow. In 1983, the Environmental Defense Fund (now known simply as "Environmental Defense") published a report advocating the transfer of conserved water from IID to the coastal cities of Southern California.[1] The Environmental Defense Fund believed that such water transfers would benefit IID while also relieving pressure on Northern California water supplies, which Southern California hoped to export to meet the needs of its growing population.

1. Robert Stavins & Zach Willey, Trading Conservation Investments for Water (1983).

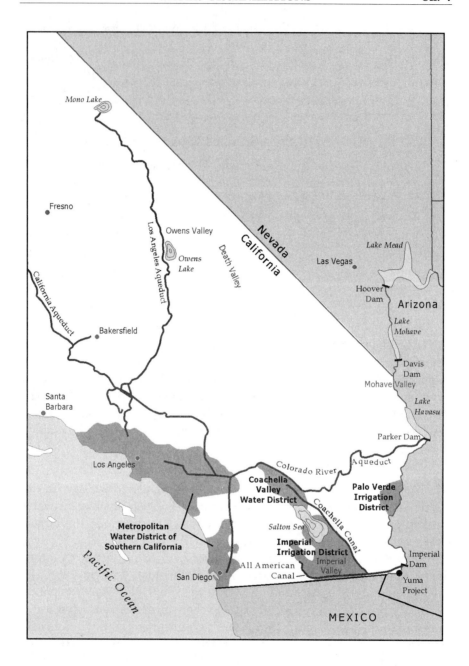

Figure 7–1

Southern California and Its Water Facilities

IID did not voluntarily pursue a transfer, despite the potential financial advantages. After the California State Water Resources Control Board in 1984 found that IID was wasting water and ordered IID to conserve 100,000 acre-feet of water,[2] however, IID began discussions with the Metropolitan Water District of Southern California (MWD), which supplies water to 27 member agencies in the coastal basin of Southern California, about a potential sale of the conserved water. In 1985, IID and MWD reached a preliminary memorandum of understanding providing for the transfer of 100,000 acre-feet of conserved water to MWD in return for an annual payment of $10 million. Even in the face of the regulatory pressure to conserve water, however, IID's board of directors refused to ratify the proposed agreement. A final agreement between IID and MWD took almost a decade more of on-again, off-again negotiations to complete. The IID board signed off on the final agreement only after the state board issued its order specifying the exact amount that IID would have to conserve.

In the mid–1990s, IID approached the San Diego County Water Authority about leasing water to San Diego for a limited period of time. IID and San Diego agreed to the transfer of up to 200,000 acre-feet of water, approximately seven percent of the district's water supply from the Colorado River, for up to 75 years. IID would receive approximately $250 an acre-foot for the water, far more than the $16 an acre-foot that the water costs IID's farmers. The proposed deal, however, ran into a variety of problems, including:

- Who owned the water that IID was using? As discussed in Chapter 8 at pp. 808–811, entitlements among California agencies to Colorado River water were not entirely clear.

- How would the water be transported to San Diego? Building a new pipeline to San Diego was economically infeasible. The most logical approach was to transport the water through the Colorado River Aqueduct, which already linked Southern California to the Colorado River. See Figure 7–1. MWD, however, owned the aqueduct and balked at allowing San Diego to use the aqueduct. If San Diego did use the aqueduct, moreover, MWD insisted that San Diego pay a rate that would have made the water deal with IID prohibitively expensive.

- How would the revenues from the proposed deal be used? The original concept was to use the money primarily to support more efficient irrigation on the district's approximately 400 farms, with a small amount of the money going to the larger community. Many of the farmers, however, believed that the funds should go directly to them to use as they wanted. Members of the community, by contrast, felt that more should go to the community to compensate for potentially adverse economic impacts.

In 2002, yet another issue arose and temporarily derailed the agreement: the potential impact of the water transfer on the Salton Sea. Runoff from IID provides the major source of water for the 15–by–35 mile sea, which was formed when flood waters from the Colorado River

2. California Water Resources Control Board, Imperial Irrigation District: Alleged Waste and Unreasonable Use of Water (1984), supra p. 176.

in 1905 broke through an early diversion system used by farmers in the Imperial Valley. Conserving and transferring 200,000 acre-feet of water out of the valley could speed up the demise of the sea, which is already shrinking, threatening birds and other species that rely on the sea. One alternative would be to take farmland out of production, transferring part of the freed-up water and letting the remainder continue to flow into the Salton Sea, but this could potentially harm the local economy.

When IID refused to move forward with the deal, the Department of the Interior (which supplies IID with its Colorado River water by contract) cut IID's allocation of water by 10 percent on the ground that the district's farmers were wasting water. IID sued to enjoin the cutback, but in late 2003, IID's board finally relented and voted 3–2 to approve the transfer. In the next board election, an anti-transfer farmer defeated the board member who had been the swing vote for the transfer.

Although some water has finally begun to flow under the agreement, the parties are still working out some of the implications of the agreement. Several lawsuits, moreover, have been filed challenging the transfer. In one lawsuit, a group of farmers in the district argues that the IID board does not have the authority to make water deals without the approval of its farmers.

The materials that follow examine some of the institutional issues raised by the IID–MWD and IID–San Diego transfers. Chapter 3 discusses the original waste proceeding before the California State Water Resources Control Board at pp. 176–182. Chapter 8 covers Colorado River issues raised by the proposed San Diego transfer at pp. 808–811.

a. Water Organization Authority Over Transfers

One fundamental issue raised by the IID transfers is who, if anyone, has the authority to transfer water used by an agricultural water organization. IID, as noted, has never enthusiastically pursued water transfers. If an individual farmer in the Imperial Valley wanted to transfer water, could she? Would she need IID's approval? Would the answer be different if IID was a mutual water company rather than an irrigation district? Both East Jordan Irrigation Co. v. Morgan, supra p. 721, and Jenison v. Redfield, supra p. 719, provide insights into this issue.

Although there has been no comprehensive empirical study, mutuals in a number of states appear to have facilitated the movement of large quantities of water from agriculture to both domestic and industrial uses in recent decades.[3] Indeed, according to two knowledgeable students of water markets, mutuals provide a "well-tried mechanism" for water transfers.[4] The articles of incorporation and bylaws of most mutuals

---

3. See Barton H. Thompson, Jr., Institutional Perspectives on Water Policy and Markets, 81 Calif. L. Rev. 673, 724–25 (1993).

4. Rodney Smith & Roger Vaughan, Irrigation Districts: Obstacles to Water Marketing, Am. Water Works Ass'n J., Mar. 1988, at 10, 10.

permit shareholders to sell their stock (and thus their water) to anyone, including water users outside the mutuals' service area. Although shareholders in most states must obtain the approval of the mutual's board before changing the location of their water use, boards appear to be receptive to such requests where the change would not injure other shareholders—*East Jordan* notwithstanding.

Transfers from water districts have been more problematic. Two situations need to be examined. In the first, the water district itself wishes to market some of the water that it holds. Such a water district faces numerous legal issues. One is who owns the water for purposes of transferring it—the district or its members. Assuming that the district owns the water, a second question is whether the district has the legal authority to market water to outsiders. Although states generally permit districts to lease their water to outsiders, some states directly or implicitly ban sales, and a number also limit the length of leases. States that permit sales or leases, moreover, typically permit them only where the water is not "needed" by district users. Several states also have erected procedural hurdles to external transfers by requiring a special district election, written permission of district landowners, or court approval.[5]

The second situation is where a farmer in the water district is interested in marketing the water that she has been using. The farmer will face even more hurdles than the district. First, the question again will arise whether any transfers of water out of the district are legally permitted. Second, the farmer almost certainly will need to gain the approval of her water district and perhaps of a number of other public agencies. To appreciate the multiple levels of approval that may be needed, assume that a farmer in the Wheeler Ridge Water Storage District of Kern County, California, has the ability to conserve some water and would be interested in marketing the conserved water to a city elsewhere in California. The farmer receives water through the tiered distribution system shown in Figure 7–2. To transfer the water, the farmer must first request her local water district to transfer the water under Cal. Water Code §§ 382–383, because California law does not permit individual farmers to directly transfer water that they receive from a water district.[6] If the district approves the transfer (and the district is under no statutory obligation to do so), approval next must be obtained from the Kern County Water Agency which supplies the water to the district. Historically, the Kern County Water Agency has required districts to make every effort to find a purchaser within the agency before the agency will consider a transfer to a city outside Kern County. The district must also obtain the approval of the California Department of Water Resources (DWR) which runs the State Water Project from

5. The various state rules are catalogued in Thompson, supra note 3, at 726–28.

6. Section 383(c) permits a water district to transfer water "where the water user and the [district] agree, upon mutually satisfactory terms, that the water user will forego use for the period of time specified in the agreement and that the [district] shall act as agent for the water user to effect the transfer."

which the Kern County Water Agency receives its water. Assuming that the potential purchaser is outside the boundaries of the service area set out in the DWR's appropriation permit, the California State Water Resources Control Board also must approve a change in the appropriation permit as discussed in Chapter 3 at pp. 264–286.

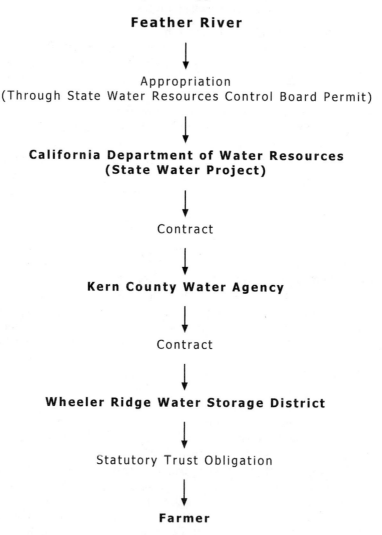

Feather River

↓

Appropriation
(Through State Water Resources Control Board Permit)

↓

**California Department of Water Resources
(State Water Project)**

↓

Contract

↓

Kern County Water Agency

↓

Contract

↓

Wheeler Ridge Water Storage District

↓

Statutory Trust Obligation

↓

Farmer

Figure 7–2
Example of Tiered Water Distribution,
Kern County, California

Source: Barton Thompson, "Water Markets and the Problem of Shifting Paradigms" in *Water Marketing – The Next Generation 1*, 12. Terry Anderson & Peter Hill, eds., 1997.

Most agricultural water districts, moreover, like IID, have been relatively hostile to external water transfers. Few districts have expressed any interest in marketing water themselves, and virtually all have opposed efforts by their farmers to transfer water to outsiders.[7] The next excerpt considers the possible reasons why.

BARTON H. THOMPSON, JR., INSTITUTIONAL PERSPECTIVES ON WATER POLICIES AND MARKETS

81 Calif. L. Rev. 673, 731–39 (1993).

The reticence of many water districts to engage in external transfers partially stems from problems in current incentive structures that make it difficult to pass transfer profits through to the districts' members. In many states, either districts do not have the authority to distribute profits directly to their members, or their authority is unclear. * * * Because virtually all districts were formed before the recent upsurge of interest in transfers, district rules and governing statutes give no guidance on how profits should be divided [assuming they can be divided at all]. Where, as is typically the case, a district's water supply is viewed as common property, no one can claim a legal or even expectational right to a specific share of the proceeds. A proposed external district transfer, therefore, may generate considerable political debate over who should benefit. * * *

The reasons for institutional opposition to external transfers go beyond structural incentive problems. Some degree of institutional control over external transfers is justified by legitimate member concerns. For example, if external transfers were entirely unfettered, many transfers would impose physical externalities on other users.[258] Although most external transfers must undergo statutory review to ensure that other appropriators are not injured, state law may not protect against some externalities like lost groundwater or against externalities that are purely internal to the institution. Districts also have a proper interest in ensuring that external transfers do not reduce the revenue available to the district to cover fixed costs. * * *

Worries about community impacts also motivate institutional opposition to external transfers * * *. With growing frequency and intensity, local farming communities have considered external transfers to be threats to their economy and vitality [see the discussion in this casebook supra pp. 289–298]. * * *

---

7. See Thompson, supra note 3, at 725, 728–30; Barton H. Thompson, Jr., Water Markets and the Problem of Shifting Paradigms, in Water Marketing—The Next Generation, 1, 11–13 (Terry Anderson & Peter Hill eds., 1997).

258. Some transfers, for example, would reduce return flow into either the institution's water system or underlying aquifers. * * * By decreasing the flow in distribution canals, moreover, transfers could also increase seepage and evaporative losses.

External [transfers by individual members of a district] can also conflict with the ethic of many agricultural districts. District members often view the district's water supply as a common resource that should be equitably shared among members and used to promote local agriculture. Public subsidization of the water supply, either by the district itself or by another governmental agency, reinforces this community ethic. External entitlement transfers directly violate the ethic: rather than return unneeded water to the community, users convert the water and any public subsidy into a purely personal monetary profit. * * *

Underneath the veneer of community and ethical concerns may often lie the entirely self-interested desire by many members to maintain the currently restricted market for any surplus water within their institution. [If district water cannot be transferred to outsiders,] users who need additional water can generally obtain it from others within their institution at relatively inexpensive prices. If institutional water supplies were opened to outside users (particularly to urban areas which are willing to pay far more than most farmers for their water), the price of internal institutional transfers would almost certainly rise. * * *

Managers of institutions also often oppose external transfers [by individual members]. Managers often publicly justify this opposition on administrative grounds. To protect against the potential negative effects of external transfers, managers claim that they would need to engage in expensive and time-consuming case-by-case reviews of transfer proposals if external transfers were widely allowed. Furthermore, many districts still have only rudimentary systems for recording and monitoring water transfers. Finally, districts often complain that unfettered external transfers would make long-range planning far more difficult. In deciding whether to construct new pipelines or storage reservoirs and in determining needed water supplies, most districts rely on existing crop patterns and expected future growth in their service areas. The possibility that water might be traded to users outside the service area threatens to complicate this planning task. * * *

Managerial self-interest might be a far more powerful source of managers' opposition to external transfers. Economic studies of bureaucracies suggest that district managers and boards may find it in their self-interest to oppose * * * external transfers. Drawing on such studies, Micha Gisser and Ronald Johnson have argued that the power and esteem enjoyed by managers and institutional boards depend on the size and budgets of their institutions.[287] * * * By reducing the institution's water supply and perhaps its customer base, external transfers directly threaten managers and boards.

Like most political officials, managers and board members also have strong incentives to avoid controversial issues. Most agricultural districts

287. See Micha Gisser & Ronald Johnson, Institutional Restrictions on the Transfer of Water Rights and the Survival of an Agency, in Water Rights: Scarce Resource Allocation, Bureaucracy, and the Environment 137, 157–60 (Terry Anderson, ed., 1983) (discussing New Mexico's Rio Grande Conservancy District).

are politically sleepy; policy stability, and thus consensus decisionmaking, are prized. Board elections are rarely contested, and managers are seldom fired. Inaction is safe. External transfers create controversy. When external transfers have been forced on districts, boards have found themselves facing an uncontrollable political maelstrom and, in some cases, have been defeated for reelection. Few managers and boards are likely to brave such a maelstrom voluntarily.

Notes and Questions

1. Should states enact legislation authorizing members of water districts to engage in member-initiated external transfers over the opposition of the district? Alternatively, should states strictly limit the grounds on which districts can prohibit a member-initiated transfer? In 1991, the California legislature considered a bill that would have given anyone receiving water from a public water organization the right to sell his or her individual "allocation" to outside users even over the opposition of the organization. Assembly Bill 97, 1993–1994 Reg. Sess. (Cal.). The legislative sponsor extolled the bill as "breaking the backs of water districts who are blocking water trades." See Barton H. Thompson, Jr., Water Markets and the Problem of Shifting Paradigms, in Water Marketing—The Next Generation 1, 15 (Terry Anderson & Peter Hill eds., 1997). The bill, however, did not pass.

> Such bills suggest that it will be politically difficult, at least under current circumstances, to pass legislation that effectively prevents districts from vetoing external transfers that they do not like. Recognizing that districts can have legitimate concerns about external transfers for a diversity of reasons (including adverse effects on contractual obligations, flow head, and groundwater recharge), all bills have given districts at least circumscribed veto power over transfers. Because of the difficulty in defining the precise grounds on which a district can object, even the most radical proposals have left districts with considerable discretion. Districts and market opponents, moreover, have [argued successfully] for less radical changes. After several rounds of agriculture-inspired amendments, for example, Assembly Bill 97 would have permitted districts to veto transfers based on any "relevant factors that may create an adverse financial, operations, or water supply impact on the water supplier or its water users." Agricultural interests still opposed the bill as insufficiently [protective of] the local public interest in water resources.

Id. at 15–16.

The Central Valley Project Improvement Act, discussed in more detail at pages 777–779, limits the authority of water districts in the Central Valley Project of California to preclude member-initiated transfers of federal reclamation water to water users outside the districts.

See also Brian Gray, The Shape of Transfers to Come: A Model Water Transfer Act for California, 4 West–Northwest 23, 42–44 (1996) (discussing a draft provision in the California Model Water Transfer Act authorizing member-initiated transfers, which was removed because of agricultural opposition).

2. As noted in the Thompson excerpt, one reason for district opposition to external transfers is the fear of adverse impacts on the local community. Are water districts the best entities to decide whether exports should go forward in the face of community concerns? Is that role better played by a state agency or by the local county? If the state or county has the authority to block transfers that it believes would be unduly damaging to the local community, is there any downside to also giving that authority to water districts?

3. Professor Rodney Smith has proposed that districts treat transfer offers from outsiders like a corporate tender offer. Under one version of this approach, a city interested in acquiring conserved water from a water district would go to the district with a proposal to purchase or lease a set quantity of water. The manager and board of the district would meet with the potential purchaser/lessee and negotiate the best deal that they could for the district's water users. The offer would then be presented to water users along with the board's and manager's views on the offer; a public meeting also might be held to discuss the offer. Each water user could then decide how much, if any, of her water to tender. If an offer for a fixed amount was undersubscribed, the prospective purchaser/lessee could improve the offer, go elsewhere, or accept the offered quantity; if the offer was oversubscribed, subscribing water users would be entitled to participate in the transfer on a pro rata basis. See Rodney Smith, Water Transfers, Irrigation Districts, and the Compensation Problem, 8 J. Pol'y Analysis & Mgmt. 446, 452–59 (1989); Barton H. Thompson, Jr., Institutional Perspectives on Water Policy and Markets, 81 Calif. L. Rev. 671, 751–52 (1993).

Would this be a good way of dealing with the issue of district transfers? See Thompson, supra note 1, at 17 (suggesting that the tender offer model would increase the bargaining leverage and information available to district members interested in conserving and transferring water).

b. Dividing the Proceeds

Uncertainty and conflict over how the proceeds from a water transfer will be distributed among the members of a water district often pose major obstacles to water transfers. Consider how IID might divide the proceeds of its deal with San Diego. As an irrigation district, IID is governed by a board that is elected on a one-person, one-vote basis by all local residents. Historically, moreover, farmers within IID did not hold entitlements to fixed amounts of IID's water supply; IID instead allocated water to farmers on an on-demand basis. Should the proceeds of the San Diego sale go to water users or to the community more broadly? If both, how should the proceeds be divided among the two groups? If the proceeds should go to water users, how should the proceeds be divided among the users? Should it go to those farmers who invest in water conservation? Should it be divided among all farmers based on historic use? Irrigated acreage? Should IID instead use the proceeds to lower the water rates for all users? If some of the proceeds should go to the community, who should receive those proceeds, and for what purposes? How would you divide the proceeds, and why?

Apportionment of the proceeds from the sale or lease of a district's water is easiest where the district historically has allocated fixed shares of water to individual users (e.g., based on each user's acreage). In these cases, the district is likely to allocate most or all of the proceeds to those water users who are willing to reduce their deliveries to free up water for the transfer. Not only are those users making the transfer possible, but such a division gives water users an incentive to free up the water needed for the transfer. The district, however, will still face the question of whether to apportion any of the proceeds to the community at large. By allocating proceeds to the community at large, the district risks undermining conservation and support of the transfer by the water users. If the district's board is elected by the community at large, however, the board might decide that a wider distribution of the proceeds is politically necessary. The board also might decide that a broader distribution is appropriate either because the water transfer might have an adverse economic impact on the community or because the district believes that the water belongs to the district as a whole and not to individual users.

Apportionment of the proceeds becomes more complex where a water district, like IID, historically has not created individual water entitlements but has allocated water within the district on demand. Here, there is no internal water allocation method on which to base a division of profits. One approach in these cases is to switch the district to a system of individual entitlements, after which the district can divide the proceeds based on the willingness of individual farmers to give up portions of their entitlement. How though should the district determine the entitlements? Should the district, for example, base the entitlements on historic use? On acreage? On some other measurement? Alternatively, the district can divide the proceeds among water users (and perhaps the wider community) without creating fixed entitlements to water within the district. Here again, however, the district faces the difficult choice of an apportionment method.

For further consideration of these issues, see Barton H. Thompson, Jr., Institutional Perspectives on Water Policy and Markets, 81 Calif. L. Rev. 671, 741–44 (1993).

c. Water Wheeling

Another controversial water marketing issue raised by the IID transfer is "water wheeling"—or the use of a water organization's transportation facilities by a third party to convey marketed water to a purchaser or lessee. Except where a natural waterway can be used, transporting water any distance requires a conveyance facility. And conveyance facilities today can be expensive to build. In the 1980s, for example, the city of Phoenix, Arizona estimated that, if it had to build a new aqueduct to import water that it had recently purchased in a distant

WATER ORGANIZATIONS Ch. 7

county for $30 million, the canal would cost over $250 million. Phoenix decided that it thankfully could use the Central Arizona Project aqueduct to transport the water, but the city estimated that just building a canal to get the water to the aqueduct would cost $50 million.

Because new facilities are expensive, access to any available capacity in existing facilities will be critical to the future of water marketing. To date, most urban water purchasers have successfully negotiated access to needed conveyance facilities. As time passes, however, conveyance capacity will grow scarcer, and access is likely to become more difficult and contentious. Some policymakers have already expressed concern that the owners of conveyance facilities may try to use their natural monopoly over the facilities to control water market activity or garner high rents for the use of the facilities.

The IID–San Diego transfer illustrates the issue. As noted, the most economic means of getting the water to San Diego is through the Colorado River Aqueduct owned by the Metropolitan Water District of Southern California (MWD). See Figure 7–1, supra p. 732. MWD supplies water to 27 member agencies on the coast of Southern California, including San Diego. These agencies, in turn, serve 16 million residents. MWD historically has not entered into delivery contracts with its members for any set quantity of water, but instead has stood ready to supply water on an as-needed basis. MWD receives water from two main sources—the Colorado River (via the Colorado River Aqueduct) and the State Water Project (which imports water from Northern California through the California Aqueduct). As Southern California grows, MWD continually is looking for additional water supplies and has shown an active interest in water markets.

By law, MWD charges all of its customers a uniform rate for each class of water delivery. Thus, San Diego pays the same rate for any given class of water delivery as Los Angeles and all of MWD's 25 other member agencies pay. MWD's water rates cover 75 percent of MWD's fixed and variable costs. The balance of costs are covered through property taxes and miscellaneous service charges.

In early 1997, MWD adopted a "wheeling rate" of $141 per acre-foot for use of any available capacity in its conveyance facilities. MWD announced that, like its water charges, its wheeling rate would apply uniformly to all conveyances of water, no matter how far water is being transported. In calculating its wheeling rate, MWD included not only the costs of operating its conveyance facilities, but also various "fixed and unavoidable" costs of MWD's operations including payments under its water contract with the State Water Project (SWP), various system-wide operating and maintenance costs, and subsidies paid by MWD to member agencies for conservation and recycling. If MWD charged a wheeling rate for use of the Colorado River Aqueduct that consisted only of the actual costs of physically transporting water through the aqueduct, the wheeling rate would be only about $10.

In justification of its higher wheeling rate, MWD noted that all member agencies who purchase water from MWD pay a share of the "fixed and unavoidable" costs included in the wheeling rate. In MWD's view, permitting someone to use MWD's conveyance facilities without paying a share of these costs would be unfair to those purchasing water from MWD. MWD also expressed concern that, if a member agency could purchase water from a third party and use MWD's conveyance facilities without paying for these "fixed and unavoidable" costs, third parties could unfairly undercut MWD's water rates and attract away customers. According to MWD, moreover, if a member agency could turn to a third party for its water and avoid paying these "fixed and unavoidable" costs, MWD would be forced to shift the costs to its other customers by raising its water rates.

San Diego and other water users, by contrast, argued that MWD's wheeling rate unfairly charged transferors for costs unrelated to the use of MWD's conveyance facilities. MWD's wheeling rate, moreover, threatened to make some water transfers unprofitable.

In anticipation of wheeling disputes, California adopted wheeling legislation in 1986. Relevant provisions of the legislation are as follows:

§ 1810. *Unused capacity*

Notwithstanding any other provision of law, neither the state, nor any regional or local public agency may deny a bona fide transferor of water the use of a water conveyance facility which has unused capacity, for the period of time for which that capacity is available, if fair compensation is paid for that use, subject to the following: * * *

(c) Any person or public agency that has a water service contract with or the right to receive water from the owner of the conveyance facility who has an emergency need may utilize the unused capacity that was made available pursuant to this section for the duration of the emergency.

(d) This use of a water conveyance facility is to be made without injuring any legal user of water and without unreasonably affecting fish, wildlife, or other instream beneficial uses and without unreasonably affecting the overall economy or the environment of the county from which the water is being transferred.

§ 1811. *Definitions*

As used in this article, the following terms shall have the following meanings: * * *

(c) "Fair compensation" means the reasonable charges incurred by the owner of the conveyance system, including capital, operation, maintenance, and replacement costs, increased costs from any necessitated purchase of supplemental power, and including reasonable credit for any offsetting benefits for the use of the conveyance system.

(d) "Replacement costs" mean the reasonable portion of costs associated with material acquisition for the correction of unrepairable wear or other deterioration of conveyance facility parts which have an anticipated life which is less than the conveyance facility repayment period and which costs are attributable to the proposed use.

(e) "Unused capacity" means space that is available within the operational limits of the conveyance system and which the owner is not using during the period for which the transfer is proposed and which space is sufficient to convey the quantity of water proposed to be transferred.

§ 1812. *Determination of amount and availability of unused capacity; terms and conditions for use*

The state, regional, or local public agency owning the water conveyance facility shall in a timely manner determine the following:

(a) The amount and availability of unused capacity.

(b) The terms and conditions, including operation and maintenance requirements and scheduling, quality requirements, term of use, priorities, and fair compensation.

§ 1813. *Findings by public agency*

In making the determinations required by this article, the respective public agency shall act in a reasonable manner consistent with the requirements of law to facilitate the voluntary sale, lease, or exchange of water and shall support its determinations by written findings. * * *

§ 1814. *Application of article*

This article shall apply to only 70 percent of the unused capacity.

———

1. Assume that San Diego approaches MWD under this statute and seeks permission to use the Colorado River Aqueduct for 35 years to transport the Colorado River water that it will lease from IID. How should MWD determine the "unused capacity" of the Colorado River Aqueduct? If MWD currently has "unused capacity" in the aqueduct but anticipates that it might need more of the aqueduct's capacity in future years, can it grant San Diego the right to use the capacity only until such time as MWD needs it—viz., can it give San Diego capacity only on an "as available" basis? If so, what are the purposes of sections 1810(c) and 1814? If you were San Diego, would you go forward with a transfer without knowing whether you have firm conveyance capacity for the length of the transfer?

Alternatively, must MWD try to predict the unused capacity of its aqueduct for the entire 35 years? Could MWD legally decide that it will not have any unused capacity after the fifth year because it plans to acquire additional Colorado River water of its own in that year—even if MWD currently does not have any firm contract for that water?

2. Can MWD set a uniform wheeling rate for all transfers no matter how many miles of conveyance facilities the transferor wishes to use? Must someone who wishes to use five miles of an MWD facility pay the same wheeling rate as San Diego pays to use the entire length of the Colorado River Aqueduct? Should MWD be forced to set wheeling rates on an individualized basis even though it sells water at a uniform price to all its member agencies (some of which are farther from the water source than others)?

3. Can MWD include in the wheeling rate that it charges San Diego costs that are not directly related to the expense of physically transporting IID water to San Diego through MWD facilities? MWD argues that its $141 wheeling rate is justified under the California wheeling legislation for at least two reasons:

(a) Section 1811(c) defines "fair compensation" as "reasonable charges incurred by the owner of the conveyance *system* * * * for the use of the conveyance *system*." Emphasizing that the statute uses the term "system" rather than "facility," MWD argues that the legislature's intent was to permit the owner of a conveyance facility to recover any costs in its entire system that are reasonably related to the wheeling.

(b) To the degree that a member agency such as San Diego purchases water from a third party rather than from MWD, the costs that MWD otherwise would have covered through its water sale must be shifted to other member agencies. But section 1810(d) provides that "use of a water conveyance facility is to be made without injuring any legal user of water." To avoid cost shifting, the costs thus must be included in the wheeling rates.

How strong are these arguments? What responses would you make if you were San Diego? How would you resolve the issues if you were a court? See San Luis Coastal Unified School Dist. v. City of Morro Bay, 97 Cal. Rptr. 2d 323 (Ct. App. 2000) (lost sales do not constitute an "injury" for purposes of section 1810(d)).

4. In early 1998, a California trial court judge held that MWD's wheeling rate violated the California wheeling legislation. The California Court of Appeal subsequently reversed and upheld MWD's wheeling rate. See Metropolitan Water Dist. v. Imperial Irrigation Dist., 96 Cal. Rptr. 2d 314 (Ct. App. 2000) (holding that owners of conveyance facilities can, in setting wheeling rates, recover for lost sales, and that rates need not be set on a case-by-case basis). San Diego, in the meantime, had reached a separate agreement with MWD on a wheeling rate for the IID–San Diego transfer that all sides found acceptable.

5. How effective is California's wheeling legislation in addressing the issues that are likely to arise in wheeling disputes? Could the statute be improved? If so, how? Are there better ways of dealing with the wheeling issue? Consider the following options:

Borrowing from the rules governing natural gas pipelines, facilities could be governed by traditional utility regulation. Open access would be mandated and rates would be regulated [e.g., by the state public utility commission]. Shortages of capacity would be resolved either through a preference system (e.g., preferences to domestic uses) or through queuing of conveyance requests.

A more sophisticated approach, although one not used in similar transportation contexts today, would create a market in conveyance capacity paralleling the market in water rights. Current transportation systems would be divided into units of conveyance capacity and then traded through spot markets (for immediate conveyance), future markets (to ensure future capacity), and options markets (to guarantee capacity during critical periods).

Barton H. Thompson, Jr., Water Markets and the Problem of Shifting Paradigms, in Water Marketing—The Next Generation 1, 18–19 (Terry Anderson & Peter Hill eds., 1997).

For more on the wheeling issue, see Scott S. Slater, A Prescription for Fulfilling the Promise of a Robust Water Market, 36 McGeorge L. Rev. 253, 269–288 (2005); Timothy Quinn, Wheeling Provisions of the Model Water Transfer Act, 4 West–Northwest 83 (1996); Brian Gray, The Shape of Transfers to Come: A Model Water Transfer Act for California, 4 West–Northwest 23, 44 (1996).

6. Beyond the wheeling issue, do water markets present a danger to water purveyors such as MWD that offer water at a uniform charge to all customers? If a particular customer can buy water less expensively from a third party such as IID, the customer might reduce its purchases from the water purveyor. To cover fixed costs, the water purveyor might then need to shift costs that the first customer would have paid to its other customers. But faced with higher rates, other customers might then be tempted to purchase water from other sellers—leading to what MWD has labeled a "death spiral." Is the concern legitimate? Should water purveyors such as MWD have the authority to prevent their customers from buying water from a third party? Could MWD solve the problem simply by entering into long-term supply contracts with its customers?

C. THE FEDERAL RECLAMATION PROGRAM

Of water organizations, none has been more important to the West than the federal Bureau of Reclamation. The Reclamation Act of 1902[1]

1. 32 Stat. 388.

authorized the federal government to build storage facilities in places it considered promising, deliver the water to irrigators, and recover its costs through payments that the irrigators would make over time from the profits of their newly irrigated land. The desert would bloom and, in a phrase once popular, reclamation would pay its own way.

The reclamation program has indeed helped the desert bloom. Today the Bureau supplies water for over 20 percent of the irrigated land in the western seventeen states—over 50 percent of the land irrigated by surface water. Although the reclamation program initially supplied water only to agriculture users, today it also supplies drinking water to approximately 30 million domestic residents of the West, and the percentage of reclamation water going to cities is growing.

The reclamation program, however, has never paid its own way and has been controversial since birth. From the outset, Congress subsidized reclamation projects out of general tax revenues, and the size of the subsidy expanded over time until, by the early 1980s, some irrigators were paying back less than 5 percent of their projects' total cost. This subsidy has raised equity issues, particularly to the degree that large corporate farms have enjoyed the benefit of the subsidy. City residents have wondered why they are paying several hundred dollars per acre foot for their water, while most farmers are paying water rates in the single or double digits. The subsidy also has undercut incentives to conserve. Reclamation projects, moreover, often have caused substantial environmental harm through reduced instream flow, dams, and pumping operations. Finally, some reclamation projects have generated conflicts with Native American tribes dependent on, and with rights to, the water being siphoned off.

Reclamation Subsidies

Farmers and other users of federal reclamation water repay some of the cost of constructing federal reclamation projects.[2] The Bureau of Reclamation contracts with local water districts to provide the districts with reclamation water; in return, the districts agree to pay a charge meant to cover operating and maintenance (O & M costs) and at least part of the project's capital costs.[3] The districts in turn pass these costs on to their members in the form of water charges, *ad valorem* taxes, or other payments.

Farmers, however, have never paid the full cost to the government of supplying them with reclamation water. The 1902 Act provided that irrigators would have ten years to repay the costs of a project *interest*

---

2. For an excellent discussion of reclamation pricing policies, see Duane Mecham & Benjamin Simon, Forging a New Federal Reclamation Water Pricing Policy: Legal and Policy Considerations, 27 Ariz. St. L.J. 507 (1995).

3. Originally the Bureau of Reclamation contracted directly with water users for the delivery of water. To avoid forcing the Bureau to distribute water to end users and monitor use of the water, however, Congress in 1926 instructed the Secretary of the Interior to contract instead with irrigation districts which would take on the responsibility for distribution and monitoring.

free. At the prevailing federal borrowing rate of the time, this interest subsidy constituted about 15 percent of the total cost of a project. Farmers, however, wanted greater subsidies and, in many cases, needed them to make their farms financially viable. The Bureau of Reclamation also supported a larger subsidy; the Bureau wanted to build more projects, which Congress would authorize only if farmers requested the projects and if prior projects were not plagued by embarrassing defaults.[4]

Congress responded by increasing the subsidy in several ways. First, Congress extended the interest-free repayment period for standard reclamation contracts to up to 50 years—an 81 percent subsidy at a 7 percent interest rate.[5] Second, in the Reclamation Project Act of 1939, Congress directed that for multipurpose projects—i.e., projects providing not only irrigation water but flood control, hydropower, recreation, and other benefits—the cost of the project should be divided among the various purposes in proportion to the benefits provided for each purpose by the project. Even where farmers receive and enjoy virtually all of the water from a multipurpose project, much of the cost has been allocated to other purposes. And the temptation has been to allocate as large a share of the costs to the other purposes as can be credibly defended. Although power users pay the share of costs attributed to hydropower, the federal treasury picks up much of the share attributed to recreation, fish and wildlife, and flood control.

The 1939 Act also authorized the Bureau to shift any costs exceeding an irrigator's "ability to pay" to other project beneficiaries such as power consumers.[6] About 75 percent of all reclamation projects involve such "irrigation assistance."[7] According to a 1996 study by the United States General Accounting Office, irrigation assistance has reduced the costs that irrigators must repay by almost 50 percent.[8] Finally, the 1939 Act authorized the Bureau, if it wishes, to enter into "water service contracts" of up to 40 years duration providing for the delivery of water at a rate that the Bureau considers "appropriate." Under a water service contract, water users do not necessarily need to repay the capital costs of their project within the initial contract period; at the end of the initial contract term, the Bureau negotiates a new water service contract.

The Bureau has further increased the size of the subsidy through its implementation of the reclamation program. For example, although

4. For a good analysis of the political economy of federal reclamation subsidies, see Daniel McCool, Command of the Waters (1987); Randall Rucker & Price Fishback, The Federal Reclamation Program: An Analysis of Rent–Seeking Behavior, in Water Rights: Scarce Resource Allocation, Bureaucracy, and the Environment (Terry Anderson ed., 1983).

5. The 50 years consists of a 10–year "development period" followed by a 40–year payback term. See Reclamation Project Act of 1939, 53 Stat. 1187, § 9(d).

6. Id. § 9. In determining a farmer's ability to pay, the Bureau looks at the increased income that the farmer receives from irrigated, rather than dry, farming.

7. Western Water Policy Review Advisory Commission, Water in the West: Challenge for the Next Century 3–20 (1998).

8. See U.S. General Accounting Office, Bureau of Reclamation: Information on Allocation and Repayment of Costs of Constructing Water Projects (1996). See also U.S. General Accounting Office, Federal Charges for Irrigation Projects Reviewed Do Not Cover Costs (1981).

reclamation law is quite clear that contract rates must cover O & M costs in addition to capital repayment, many reclamation contracts negotiated prior to 1982 set fixed rates that failed to provide for inflation. Early reclamation contracts in the California Central Valley Project set fixed or maximum rates, ranging from as little as $2 to $8 per acre-foot, for the entire length of a contract. As O & M costs rose rapidly during the late 1960s and 1970s, an increasing share of these rates went toward covering O & M costs, leaving little to repay construction costs. By the 1980s, O & M costs exceeded most district's contract rates—and the debt that the districts "owed" the federal government began to grow rather than shrink. By 1985 (only a few years short of the expiration of many of the contracts), water users in the CVP had repaid only 4 percent of the project's capital costs.

As summarized by a 1997 report of the Congressional Budget Office, the combined subsidies have been substantial.

> The present value of federal outlays made between 1902 and 1986 for [reclamation projects] was $22 billion to $23 billion (in 1986 dollars). The present value of the money repaid by irrigators over that same period was $2 billion. The repayment figure may ultimately increase by another $1 billion, based on existing contracts. Thus, the federal government's contribution to the cost of constructing and financing irrigation projects amounts to about 85 percent to 90 percent of the total cost allocated to irrigation.[9]

The subsidies have raised significant equity concerns. Should Congress be using federal tax dollars to subsidize agricultural operations in selected regions of the West? Why should farmers pay so much less for their water than domestic users?

But the subsidies also have led to serious resource misallocations. First, the subsidies have created pressure to construct economically dubious projects. One egregious example is the Garrison diversion project in North Dakota which at one point was slated to cost about $1.7 million for each farm that it would have served while producing benefits of slightly less than $25,000 per farm.[10] If Congress wished to subsidize North Dakota farmers, a cheaper means of doing so would have been to pay each farmer $100,000—quadrupling the benefit to the farmer while decreasing the government's cost by $1.6 million dollars. In 1999, Congress reauthorized the Garrison diversion project, but in a vastly slimmed down form.

---

9. U.S. Congressional Budget Office, Water Use Conflicts in the West: Implications of Reforming the Bureau of Reclamation's Water Supply Policies 13 (Aug. 1997). See also National Research Council, Irrigation–Induced Water Quality Problems 55 (1989) (estimating that, from 1902 to 1986, reclamation subsidies summed to roughly $10 billion); E. Phillip LeVeen & Laura King, Turning Off the Tap on Federal Water Subsidies 122–23 (Nat. Resources Def. Council, Aug. 1985).

10. See William Sander, Shooting the Political Rapids of Western Water, Wall St. J., April 13, 1987, at 22.

Second, the subsidies have lessened water users' fiscal incentive to conserve. There is far less reason to invest in expensive irrigation control or to line canals when you are receiving water for only a fraction of its true cost. Local water districts have further undermined conservation by charging farmers water fees based on the number of acres each farmer owns in the district or on the value of that acreage rather than on the volume of water used. Farmers who engage in conservation thus do not reduce their water costs.

Finally, the subsidies have encouraged western farmers to grow crops that often could be more efficiently grown elsewhere. For years, the subsidies operated at cross-purposes with agricultural programs designed to limit national production of certain crops. Before reforms in the mid–1990s, the United States Department of Agriculture paid out millions of dollars each year to reduce production of various "surplus crops" such as wheat, grain, cotton, and rice. At the same time, the federal government was providing subsidized reclamation water to western farms growing these identical surplus crops. In the early 1980s, almost half of the lands irrigated by Bureau water grew surplus crops. For land in the Central Valley Project, the figure was 59 percent.[11]

Populist Provisions

For populist and anti-speculative reasons, the authors of the 1902 Reclamation Act wanted to benefit family farms, not large farms owned by absentee investors. The 1902 Act therefore provided that water could be supplied only to people who lived on or in the "neighborhood" of their land—which regulations ultimately defined as living within 50 miles of the farm.[12] More importantly, the Act provided that "[n]o right to the use of water for land in private ownership shall be sold for a tract exceeding one hundred and sixty acres to any one landowner."[13] This 160–acre limitation paralleled the federal Homestead Act, which limited homestead claims to 160 acres, and reflected Congress' view that 160 acres was a reasonable size family farm.

The 1902 Act, however, did not forbid a water recipient from owning more than 160 acres; reclamation water simply could not be furnished for more than 160 acres of a farmer's holdings. In the 1926 Omnibus Adjustment Act,[14] Congress provided that reclamation water could be furnished even for "excess lands" over 160 acres if the landowners first entered into "recordable contracts" with the Secretary of the Interior agreeing to sell the land within a fixed period of time (historically ten years) at a price that did not reflect the availability of subsidized reclamation water.

Large farmers, however, wanted reclamation water for all their acreage. Once again the Bureau of Reclamation was an ally. The Bureau

11. See LeVeen & King, supra note 9, at 17–18.

12. 32 Stat. 388, § 5; 43 C.F.R. § 230.65 (1980).

13. 32 Stat. 388, § 5.

14. 44 Stat. 636.

wanted to minimize defaults, and large farmers were more likely to make their payments; large farmers were also major supporters of reclamation projects. By the 1930s, the Bureau was ignoring the residency requirement (which it argued had been abolished by the 1926 Omnibus Adjustment Act) and not objecting when farmers found ingenious ways to circumvent the acreage limitation.[15] Because the 1902 Act did not say whether *leased* acreage counted toward the 160–acre limit, the most typical way large farmers got around the acreage limitation was to own 160 acres and lease the rest. Farmers who wanted to own their land resorted to trusts and multi-party ownership devices to circumvent the limitation. In a few cases, Congress exempted projects from the acreage and residency limitations. See Bryant v. Yellen, 447 U.S. 352 (1980) (concluding that Congress had implicitly exempted the Imperial Irrigation District from the populist limitations).

By 1979, almost 10 percent of the farmers in Bureau projects received water for more than 160 acres of land they *owned;* these farmers held 27 percent of all the land receiving federal reclamation water. Over 25 percent of the recipients of federal reclamation water owned *or leased* more than 160 acres, and these farms constituted over 75 percent of the total acreage furnished with water.[16]

Environmental Concerns

Over the decades, the federal reclamation program has compounded the ecological problems facing the watersheds of the West. A few examples illustrate the changes that the reclamation program has brought.[17] Construction of the very first reclamation project, the Newlands Project in the Great Basin of Nevada, siphoned water from the few natural waterbodies found in the region, dramatically reducing the water level of Pyramid Lake and totally drying up Lake Winnemuca. Changes to Pyramid Lake have led to the extinction of the native stock of Lahontan cutthroat trout and to the listing as an endangered species of the only other migratory fish native to the lake, the Cui-ui. The project also has reduced flows into Stillwater Marsh, which was described by one observer at the turn of the 20th century as a "half shallow lake, half tule swamp which extends for twenty miles along the valley bottom and furnishes enough salt grass, sedges, and tules to winter many thousand head of stock, and a breeding ground for great numbers of water and

15. For a discussion of the numerous ways in which the acreage limitation was circumvented, see Amy Kelley, Federal Reclamation Law, in 4 Water and Water Rights §§ 41.03–41.03(b), at 41–11 to 41–23 (Robert Beck ed., repl. vol. 2004).

16. These figures come from a draft environmental impact statement prepared by the Bureau of Reclamation. See Acreage Limitation: Draft Environmental Impact Statement, Westwide Report Appendix (1981).

17. Several of these examples are drawn from Lawrence MacDonnell, Managing Reclamation Facilities for Ecosystem Benefits, 67 U. Colo. L. Rev. 197 (1996), which provides both an excellent overview of the ecological problems created by the reclamation program and some of the steps being taken to correct them. See also University of Colorado, Natural Resources Law Center, Restoring the West's Waters: Opportunities for the Bureau of Reclamation (1996) (summarizing a multi-year study of 15 reclamation projects).

shore birds.''[18] Contaminants in the waters entering the marsh, some of which come from the irrigation that the Newlands Project has made possible, have had deleterious effects on local fish and waterfowl.

While hydroelectric facilities pose perhaps the greatest danger to salmon in the Pacific Northwest, federal reclamation projects in the Yakima River Basin also have contributed to the problem. Each year, irrigation users draw almost 2.5 million acre-feet of water from the Yakima River and its tributaries, seriously reducing the natural flow of water in some stretches critical to salmon and steelhead. Irrigation also has reduced the quality of river flows.

The Central Valley Project (CVP) in California has been the subject of some of the most intense environmental criticism. As Professor Harrison Dunning has noted, the CVP initially contemplated practically the complete diversion of the San Joaquin River to irrigate land on the east side of the San Joaquin Valley. "Thus, a major river in the West was entirely and deliberately dewatered, except in flood years."[19] After World War II,

> a second round of projects expanded the CVP [to assist farmers on the west side of the San Joaquin Valley]. * * * The Trinity River in Northern California was dammed * * *. While the Trinity was not entirely dewatered, most of its water was diverted to assist westside irrigation, causing enormous damage to fisheries. Despite a growing consciousness about damage to fisheries, those of the Trinity River were basically sacrificed, with the salmon runs cut by about ninety percent. * * *

> One of the most recent aspects of the CVP has been the construction of canals on the west side of the Sacramento Valley. * * * When building the Red Bluff Diversion Dam, the federal government vowed it would take care of the fish by installing state-of-the-art fish protection facilities. However, the fish facilities in these units simply have not worked. Even worse, much of the agricultural drainage elsewhere in the Central Valley has been discovered to be toxic, with absolutely disastrous environmental consequences.[20]

For a discussion of the impacts of the CVP and other water diversions on the Sacramento–San Joaquin Delta, see supra pp. 628–639.

1. FEDERAL VERSUS STATE AUTHORITY

From the time the federal reclamation program was first conceived, a central question has been the degree to which state water law should

---

18. See Steven Thompson & Kenneth Merrit, Western Nevada Wetlands: History and Current Status, 1 Nev. Pub. Aff. Rev. 42 (1988).

19. Harrison Dunning, Confronting the Environmental Legacy of Irrigated Agriculture in the West: The Case of the Central Valley Project, 23 Envtl. L. 943, 951 (1993).

20. Id. at 951–52. The agricultural drainage problems referenced by Professor Dunning led to significant loss of waterfowl in the Kesterson National Wildlife Refuge. See supra p. 651, Note 4.

control the operation of reclamation projects and the distribution and use of reclamation water. Can the Bureau of Reclamation, for example, demand greater conservation measures than state law requires? Conversely, can the Bureau insulate reclamation water users from strict state conservation requirements? Must the Bureau comply with state environmental laws and regulations?

CALIFORNIA v. UNITED STATES

Supreme Court of the United States, 1978.
438 U.S. 645.

MR. JUSTICE REHNQUIST delivered the opinion of the Court.

The United States seeks to impound 2.4 million acre-feet of water from California's Stanislaus River as part of its Central Valley Project. The California State Water Resources Control Board ruled that the water could not be allocated to the Government under state law unless it agreed to and complied with various conditions dealing with the water's use. The Government then sought a declaratory judgment in the District Court for the Eastern District of California to the effect that the United States can impound whatever unappropriated water is necessary for a federal reclamation project without complying with state law. * * *

I

* * *

If the term "cooperative federalism" had been in vogue in 1902, the Reclamation Act of that year would surely have qualified as a leading example of it. * * * Reflective of the "cooperative federalism" which the Act embodied is section 8, whose exact meaning and scope are the critical inquiries in this case.

> [N]othing in this Act shall be construed as affecting or intended to affect or to in any way interfere with the laws of any State or Territory relating to the control, appropriation, use, or distribution of water used in irrigation, or any vested right acquired thereunder, and the Secretary of the Interior, in carrying out the provisions of this Act, shall proceed in conformity with such laws, and nothing herein shall in any way affect any right of any State or of the Federal Government or of any landowner, appropriator, or user of water in, to, or from any interstate stream or the waters thereof: Provided, That the right to use of water acquired under the provisions of this Act shall be appurtenant to the land irrigated, and beneficial use shall be the basis, the measure, and the limit of the right. [43 U.S.C. § 383 (emphasis added).]

* * *

The New Melones Dam, which this litigation concerns, is part of the California Central Valley Project, the largest reclamation project yet authorized under the 1902 Act. The Dam, which will impound 2.4

million acre-feet of water of California's Stanislaus River, has the multiple purposes of flood control, irrigation, municipal use, industrial use, power, recreation, water quality control and the protection of fish and wildlife. The waters of the Stanislaus River that will be impounded behind the New Melones Dam arise and flow solely in California.

The United States Bureau of Reclamation, as it has with every other federal reclamation project, applied for a permit from the appropriate state agency, here the California State Water Resources Control Board, to appropriate the water that would be impounded by the Dam and later used for reclamation. After lengthy hearings, the State Board found that unappropriated water was available for the New Melones Dam during certain times of the year. Although it therefore approved the Bureau's applications, the State Board attached 25 conditions to the permit. California State Water Resources Control Board, Decision 1422 (Apr. 14, 1973). The most important conditions prohibit full impoundment until the Bureau is able to show firm commitments, or at least a specific plan, for the use of the water.[8] The State Board concluded that without such a specific plan of beneficial use the Bureau had failed to meet the California statutory requirements for appropriation. * * *

II

The history of the relationship between the Federal Government and the States in the reclamation of the arid lands of the Western States is both long and involved, but through it runs the consistent thread of purposeful and continued deference to state water law by Congress. * * *

[The court recounted the early history of state-national relations in the water field, discussed in this casebook at pp. 332–334, & 351–354, to demonstrate a tradition of Congressional deference to state water law.]

* * * One school of legal commentators held the view that, under the equal-footing doctrine, the Western States, upon their admission to the Union, acquired exclusive sovereignty over the unappropriated waters in their streams. In 1903, for example, one leading expert on reclamation and water law observed that "[it] has heretofore been assumed that the authority of each State in the disposal of the water-supply within its borders was unquestioned and supreme, and two of the States have constitutional provisions asserting absolute ownership of all water supplies within their bounds." E. Mead, Irrigation Institutions 372

---

8. Other conditions prohibit collection of water during periods of the year when unappropriated water is unavailable; require that a preference be given to water users in the water basin in which the New Melones Dam is located; require storage releases to be made so as to maintain maximum and minimum chemical concentrations in the San Joaquin River and protect fish and wildlife; require the United States to provide means for the release of excess waters and to clear vegetation and structures from the reservoir sites; require the filing of additional reports and studies; and provide for access to the project site by the State Board and the public. Still other conditions reserve jurisdiction to the Board to impose further conditions on the appropriations if necessary to protect the "beneficial use" of the water involved. The United States did not challenge any of the conditions under state law, but instead filed the federal declaratory action that is now before us.

(1903). * * * It was clearly the opinion of a majority of the Congressmen who spoke on the [1902 Reclamation Act that section 8] was unnecessary except out of an excess of caution. According to Congressman Lacey, Chairman of the House Committee on Public Lands and a principal sponsor of the 1897 Act, the water through which the reclamation would be accomplished:

> does not belong to the [Federal] government. The reservoirs in which the water is stored belong to the Government, but the water belongs to the States and will be controlled by them. The amendment proposed by the gentleman from Illinois relieves this measure from all possible doubt upon that subject. I think there could be no doubt anyhow, but this amendment takes away the possibility of any question being raised as to the right of the States and Territories to regulate and control the management and the price of the water.

Congressman Lacey's statement found reflection in contemporaneous decisions of this Court holding that, with limited exceptions not relevant to reclamation, authority over intrastate waterways lies with the States. In United States v. Rio Grande Dam & Irrig. Co., 174 U.S. 690 (1899), for example, New Mexico's authority to adopt a prior appropriation system of water rights for the Rio Grande River was challenged. The Court unhesitatingly held that "as to every stream within its dominion a State may change [the] common law rule and permit the appropriation of the flowing waters for such purposes as it deems wise." * * * The Court * * * was careful to emphasize * * * that, except where the reserved rights or navigation servitude of the United States are invoked, the State has total authority over its internal water. * * *

Similarly, in Kansas v. Colorado, 206 U.S. 46 (1907), the United States claimed that it had a right in the Arkansas River superior to that of Kansas and Colorado stemming from its power "to control the whole system of the reclamation of arid lands." The Court disagreed and held that state reclamation law must prevail. The United States, of course, could appropriate water and build projects to reclaim its own public lands. * * * But federal legislation could not "override state laws in respect to the general subject of reclamation. * * * [E]ach State has full jurisdiction over the lands within its borders, including the beds of streams and other waters." * * *

III

It is against this background that Congress passed the Reclamation Act of 1902. * * *

From the legislative history of the Reclamation Act of 1902, it is clear that state law was expected to control in two important respects. First, and of controlling importance to this case, the Secretary would have to appropriate, purchase, or condemn necessary water rights in strict conformity with state law. * * * The Secretary of the Interior could not take any action in appropriating the waters of the state streams "which could not be undertaken by an individual or corporation if it were in the position of the Government as regards the ownership of its lands." H. R. Rep. No. 794, 57th Cong., 1st Sess., 7–8 (1902). * * *

Second, once the waters were released from the Dam, their distribution to individual landowners would again be controlled by state law. As explained by Senator Clark of Wyoming, one of the principal supporters of the reclamation bill in the Senate, "the control of waters after leaving the reservoirs shall be vested in the States and Territories through which such waters flow." 35 Cong. Rec. 2222. As Senator Clark went on to explain:

> [I]t is right and proper that the various States and Territories should control in the distribution. The conditions in each and every State and Territory are different. What would be applicable in one locality is totally and absolutely inapplicable in another. * * *

Ibid. As Representative Sutherland, later to be a Justice of this Court, succinctly put it, "if the appropriation and use were not under the provisions of the State law the utmost confusion would prevail." 35 Cong. Rec. 6770. Different water rights in the same State would be governed by different laws and would frequently conflict.[21] * * *

Both sponsors and opponents of the Reclamation Act also expressed constitutional doubts as to Congress' power to override the States' regulation of waters within their borders. Congress was fully aware that the Supreme Court had "in several decisions recognized the right of the State to regulate and control the use of water within its borders." 35 Cong. Rec. 6697 (1902) (Cong. Mondell). According to the House Report, "Section 8 *recognizes State control over waters of nonnavigable streams* such as are used in irrigation." H. R. Rep. No. 794, 57th Cong., 1st Sess., 6 (1902) (emphasis added).

IV

For almost half a century, this congressionally mandated division between federal and state authority worked smoothly. No project was constructed without the approval of the Secretary of the Interior, and the United States through this official preserved its authority to deter-

---

21. Congress did not intend to relinquish total control of the actual distribution of the reclamation water to the States. Congress provided in section 8 itself that the water right must be appurtenant to the land irrigated and governed by beneficial use, and in section 5 Congress forbade the sale of reclamation water to tracts of land of more than 160 acres. It is conceivable, of course, that Congress may not have intended to actually override state law when inconsistent with these other provisions but instead only intended to exercise a veto power over any reclamation project that, because of state law, could not be operated in compliance with these provisions. * * *

In previous cases interpreting section 8 of the 1902 Reclamation Act, however, this Court has held that state water law does not control in the distribution of reclamation water if inconsistent with other congressional directives to the Secretary. We believe that this reading of the Act is also consistent with the legislative history and indeed is the preferable reading of the Act. * * *

mine how federal funds should be expended. But state laws relating to water rights were observed in accordance with the congressional directive contained in section 8 of the Act of 1902. In 1958, however, the first of two cases was decided by this Court in which private landowners or municipal corporations contended that state water law had the effect of overriding specific congressional directives to the Secretary of the Interior as to the operation of federal reclamation projects. In Ivanhoe Irrigation District v. McCracken, 357 U.S. 275 (1958), the Supreme Court of California decided that California law forbade the 160–acre limitation on irrigation water deliveries expressly written into section 5 of the Reclamation Act of 1902, and that therefore, under section 8 of the Reclamation Act, the Secretary was required to deliver reclamation water without regard to the acreage limitation. Both the State of California and the United States appealed from this judgment, and this Court reversed it, saying:

> Section 5 is a specific and mandatory prerequisite laid down by the Congress as binding in the operation of reclamation projects, providing that "[n]o right to the use of water * * * shall be sold for a tract exceeding one hundred and sixty acres to any one landowner". * * * Without passing generally on the coverage of section 8 in the delicate area of federal-state relations in the irrigation field, we do not believe that the Congress intended section 8 to override the repeatedly reaffirmed national policy of section 5.

Five years later, in City of Fresno v. California, 372 U.S. 627 (1963), this Court affirmed a decision of the United States Court of Appeals for the Ninth Circuit holding that section 8 did not require the Secretary of the Interior to ignore explicit congressional provisions preferring irrigation use over domestic and municipal use.

Petitioners do not ask us to overrule these holdings, nor are we presently inclined to do so. Petitioners instead ask us to hold that a State may impose any condition on the "control, appropriation, use, or distribution of water" through a federal reclamation project that is not inconsistent with clear congressional directives respecting the project. Petitioners concede, and the Government relies upon, dicta in our cases that may point to a contrary conclusion. Thus, in *Ivanhoe*, the Court went beyond the actual facts of that case and stated:

> As we read section 8, it merely requires the United States to comply with state law when, in the construction and operation of a reclamation project, it becomes necessary for it to acquire water rights or vested interests therein. * * * We read nothing in section 8 that compels the United States to deliver water on conditions imposed by the State.

Like dictum was repeated in *City of Fresno*, supra, at 630, and in this Court's opinion in Arizona v. California, 373 U.S. 546 (1963) * * *

While we are not convinced that the above language is diametrically inconsistent with the position of petitioners, or that it squarely supports the United States, it undoubtedly goes further than was necessary to decide the cases presented to the Court. *Ivanhoe* and *City of Fresno* involved conflicts between section 8, requiring the Secretary to follow state law as to water rights, and other provisions of Reclamation Acts that placed specific limitations on how the water was to be distributed. Here the United States contends that it may ignore state law even if no explicit congressional directive conflicts with the conditions imposed by the California State Water Resources Control Board.

In Arizona v. California, the States had asked the Court to rule that state law would control in the distribution of water from the Boulder Canyon Project, a massive multistate reclamation project on the Colorado River. After reviewing the legislative history of the Boulder Canyon Project Act, 43 U.S.C. § 617 et seq., the Court concluded that because of the unique size and multistate scope of the Project, Congress did not intend the States to interfere with the Secretary's power to determine with whom and on what terms water contracts would be made. While the Court in rejecting the States' claim repeated the language from *Ivanhoe* and *City of Fresno* as to the scope of section 8, there was no need for it to reaffirm such language except as it related to the singular legislative history of the Boulder Canyon Project Act.

But because there is at least tension between the above-quoted dictum and what we conceive to be the correct reading of section 8 of the Reclamation Act of 1902, we disavow the dictum to the extent that it would prevent petitioners from imposing conditions on the permit granted to the United States which are not inconsistent with congressional provisions authorizing the project in question. * * *

V

Because the District Court and the Court of Appeals both held that California could not impose any conditions whatever on the United States' appropriation permit, those courts did not reach the United States' alternative contention that the conditions actually imposed are inconsistent with congressional directives as to the New Melones Dam. Nor did they reach California's contention that the United States is barred by principles of collateral estoppel from challenging the consistency of the permit conditions. Assuming, *arguendo,* that the United States is still free to challenge the consistency of the conditions, resolution of their consistency may well require additional factfinding. We therefore reverse the judgment of the Court of Appeals and remand for further proceedings consistent with this opinion.

Reversed and remanded.

MR. JUSTICE WHITE, with whom MR. JUSTICE BRENNAN and MR. JUSTICE MARSHALL join, dissenting.

* * *

The short of the matter is that no case in this Court, until this one, has construed section 8 as the present majority insists that it be construed. All of the relevant cases are to the contrary.

Our cases that the Court now discards are relatively recent decisions dealing with an issue of statutory construction and with a subject matter that is under constant audit by Congress. As the majority suggests, reclamation project authorizations are normally accompanied by declarations that the provisions of the reclamation laws shall be applicable. Here, the New Melones Dam, which was and is a part of the Central Valley Project, was first authorized in 1944, and again in 1962. The latter legislation provided for construction of the Dam by the Army Corps of Engineers but for operation and maintenance by the Secretary of the Interior "pursuant to the Federal reclamation laws * * *." Those laws included section 8, which by that time had been construed in *Ivanhoe* as set out above. There were no amendments to section 8, which is now codified in 43 U.S.C. §§ 372 and 383, when the project was reauthorized in 1962.

Furthermore, in amending the reclamation laws in 1972, Congress provided that except as otherwise indicated in the amendments, "the provisions of the Federal reclamation laws, and Acts amendatory thereto, are continued in full force and effect." 43 U.S.C. § 421d. * * * There is no hint of disagreement with the construction placed on these sections in *Ivanhoe,* Dugan v. Rank, 372 U.S. 609 (1963), *Fresno,* and *Arizona.*

Only the revisionary zeal of the present majority can explain its misreading of our cases and its evident willingness to disregard them. Congress has not disturbed these cases, and until it does, I would respect them. * * *

Although I do not join the Court in reconstructing the controlling statutes as it does, the Court's work today is a precedent for "setting things right" in the area of statutory water law so as to satisfy the views of a current Court majority. And surely the dicta with which the Court's opinion is laced today deserve no more or no less respect than what it has chosen to label dicta in past Court decisions. Of course, the matter is purely statutory and Congress could easily put an end to our feuding if it chose to make it clear that local authorities are to control the spending of federal funds for reclamation projects and to control the priorities for the use of water developed by federal projects.

Notes and Questions

1. The aftermath of the legal dispute in California v. United States is described in Barbara Andrews & Marie Sansone, Who Runs the Rivers? Dams and Decisions in the New West (Stan. Envtl. L. Soc'y 1983). On remand, the Court of Appeals upheld the conditions imposed by the California State Water Resources Control Board. See United States v. California, 694 F.2d 1171 (9th Cir. 1982). The following year, however, a less environmentally sympathetic governor took office in California, the California Energy Commission proclaimed the benefits of inexpensive hydroelectric

power, and the Bureau came forward with evidence that water from the project was needed to alleviate water deficiencies in the San Joaquin Valley. As a result, on March 8, 1983, the State Water Resources Control Board voted to permit the United States to fill the reservoir.

> But the Board did not back down entirely. The Board required the Bureau to develop and implement a water conservation program * * *. It also reasserted its ongoing authority to "reserve jurisdiction" to review future Bureau water deliveries—an authority recently reinforced by the California Supreme Court['s decision in National Audubon Soc'y v. Superior Court, supra page 610] that the Board must protect the "public trust" in the granting and administering of water rights. The Board strongly hinted that just as current conditions justified filling the reservoir, future conditions could lead to imposition of new requirements for releases from the reservoir to maintain water quality and protect fish and wildlife.

Andrews & Sansone, supra, at 431–32.

2. The majority in California v. United States goes out of its way to emphasize early Supreme Court cases holding that the states have exclusive power over water allocation except to the extent the federal government needs water for federal lands or wishes to promote navigation. Is there any constitutional limitation on the federal government's ability to override state water law? Most commentators today assume that the answer is "no"—that the commerce clause and the federal government's power to tax and spend for the general welfare would support virtually any action Congress wished to take to promote reclamation, and the supremacy clause would invalidate any state law inconsistent with Congress' actions.

3. As to the statutory preemption question, Justice White in dissent accuses the majority of "revisionary zeal." Is that a fair accusation? Both the language and history of section 8 would seem to support the majority's position. For an argument that the majority's recounting of the legislative history is selective, however, see Amy Kelley, Staging a Comeback—Section 8 of the Reclamation Act, 18 U.C. Davis L. Rev. 97 (1984). Even assuming that the majority's interpretation of section 8 is consistent with the original intent, was the court too cavalier in rejecting Ivanhoe, Fresno, and Arizona?

Justice White also suggests that Congress could put an end to the dispute over how to read section 8 by statutorily clarifying its intent. Neither before or after California v. United States, however, has Congress revisited the issue. Why? Is the role of state law such an unimportant question that Congress does not care? Or is the issue so politically sensitive that Congress is happy not to address it? By not clarifying its intent, Congress has left the issue to shifting alignments of Supreme Court justices.

4. What are the policy considerations in deciding on the states' role in the federal reclamation program? Roderick Walston, who argued California v. United States for the State, urges that deference to state law is necessary to avoid "potentially inconsistent regulation of water rights within one river. * * * Water rights, more than most other forms of property rights, are 'highly interdependent' * * *." Roderick Walston, State Regulation of Federally-Licensed Hydropower Projects: The Conflict Between California and First Iowa, 43 Okla. L. Rev. 87, 100 (1990). In a more general context,

Professor Richard Stewart has suggested that local autonomy on environmental issues carries several benefits, including "the greater sensitivity of local officials to the preferences of citizens * * *; the diffusion of governmental power and the promotion of cultural and societal diversity; and the enhancement of individual participation in and identification with governmental decisionmaking." Richard Stewart, Pyramids of Sacrifice? Problems of Federalism in Mandating State Implementation of National Policy, 86 Yale L.J. 1196 (1977). What are the countervailing federal interests? How should they be balanced?

5. What exactly is the test in California v. United States for determining if state law controls? Consider the following problems:

a. In California v. United States, Congress had authorized a dam of specific capacity. Several of the conditions imposed by the State Water Resources Control Board were designed to prevent the United States from filling the reservoir until the United States could show that the water was needed for irrigation purposes. Were these conditions consistent with Congress' specification of a particular capacity? The Ninth Circuit, in its decision on remand, finessed the issue by asserting that the California conditions merely deferred filling the dam to capacity rather than forbidding it. 694 F.2d at 1178–79.

b. Section 7(a)(1) of the Endangered Species Act, 16 U.S.C. § 1536(a)(1), provides that the Secretary of the Interior "shall review * * * programs administered by him and utilize such programs in furtherance of the purposes of this chapter." This section appears to authorize the Secretary to go beyond the mandatory requirements of the Endangered Species Act to help the recovery of endangered species. If the Bureau of Reclamation decides to reduce its deliveries of water pursuant to this section beyond any reductions otherwise required by the Endangered Species Act, could the state override the reduction under California v. United States?

c. For environmental reasons, Congress passes legislation requiring a specified reduction in the amount of water being delivered to a reclamation project. If the state in which the project is located believes that the reduction is inadequate to address the environmental problem, can the state require a greater reduction?

In Natural Resources Defense Council v. Houston, 146 F.3d 1118, 1131–32 (9th Cir. 1998), Congress ordered the Bureau of Reclamation to restore fish habitat below Friant Dam, but explicitly provided that water from the dam was not to be released "as a measure to implement this title." The court concluded that this directive did not preclude application to Friant Dam of a California law that required releases of sufficient water "to keep in good condition any fish that may be planted or exist below the dam." Cal. Fish & Game Code § 5937. Congress had barred releases only in the implementation of the *federal* fish plan, not across the board. 146 F.3d at 1132. The court reserved the question whether the California law was consistent with other Congressional provisions.

d. Section 8 of the Reclamation Act of 1902 also provides that "beneficial use shall be the basis, the measure, and the limit of the right" to reclamation water. Who determines whether an irrigation district receiving

reclamation water is wasting water? If a state agency determines that the
district is making reasonable and beneficial use of reclamation water, can
the Bureau nonetheless reduce deliveries based on its own finding that the
district is wasting water? Or is the Bureau bound by the state agency's
findings? See United States v. Alpine Land & Reservoir Co., 503 F.Supp. 877
(D. Nev. 1980), aff'd, 697 F.2d 851 (9th Cir. 1983) ("beneficial use itself was
intended to be governed by state law").

6.   Outside the reclamation context, the Supreme Court has held that a
federal statute can preempt state law both explicitly and implicitly. By
referring only to "explicit congressional directives" at page 758, did the
Court in California v. United States mean to hold that section 8 precludes
implicit preemption under the reclamation laws? On remand, the Court of
Appeals concluded that this was not the Supreme Court's intent and that
state law is preempted if it "clashes with an express or clearly implied
Congressional intent or works at cross-purposes with an important federal
interest served by the Congressional scheme." 694 F.2d at 1177.

7.   Federal agencies also have disagreed with states over the regulation
of hydroelectric projects. Section 27 of the Federal Power Act (FPA), under
which the Federal Energy Regulatory Commission regulates hydroelectric
dams, was modeled after section 8 of the Reclamation Act and provides that
nothing in the FPA "shall be construed as affecting or intending to affect or
in any way to interfere with the laws of the respective States relating to the
control, appropriation, use, or distribution of water used in irrigation or for
municipal or other uses, or any vested right acquired therein." In California
v. Federal Energy Reg. Comm'n, 495 U.S. 490 (1990), California argued that
this language permitted it to impose a greater minimum streamflow on a
hydroelectric project than the Federal Energy Regulatory Commission had
set.

The Supreme Court unanimously held that the FPA preempted California's authority to set higher instream flow requirements. In First Iowa
Hydro–Electric Co–op. v. Federal Power Comm'n, 328 U.S. 152 (1946), the
Court had held that section 27 required compliance only with state laws
concerning "the control, appropriation, use or distribution of water in
irrigation or for municipal or other uses of the same nature." And although
this might have been an overly stingy reading of section 27, the Court was
unwilling to revisit the issue. Any suggestion that it should, according to the
Court, misconceived "the deference this Court must accord to long-standing
and well-entrenched decisions, especially those interpreting statutes that
underlie complex regulatory regimes."

Is California v. Federal Energy Reg. Comm'n consistent with California
v. United States? Which decision controls when a state attempts to regulate
the hydroelectric aspects of federal reclamation projects? See United States
v. California, 694 F.2d 1171, 1179–80 (9th Cir. 1982) (California can refuse
to permit water to be appropriated for hydroelectric purposes); Amy Kelley,
supra note 3, at 174–79.

STRAWBERRY WATER USERS ASS'N
v. BUREAU OF RECLAMATION

Supreme Court of Utah, 2006.
133 P.3d 410.

McIFFF, District Judge.

[The Strawberry Valley Project was one of the first reclamation projects authorized in the United States. The project diverts water from the upper Deshesne River watershed in Utah and transports it for use by farmers in southern Utah County. In 1922, the farmers formed the Strawberry Water Users Association (Strawberry) to contract with the United States to repay the Project's construction costs, operate and maintain the Project, and deliver water to the users. The United States and Strawberry entered into contracts in 1926, 1928, and 1940. In 1974, Strawberry paid the United States the final installment on the Project's original construction costs. In 1985, however, the federal government as part of the Central Utah Project built a new dam (the Soldier Creek Dam) to replace the original Project dam and expanded the size of the Strawberry Reservoir. Strawberry and the United States subsequently entered into a new agreement, known as the 1991 Operating Agreement, which guarantees Strawberry annual deliveries of 61,000 acre-feet from the enlarged reservoir.]

The current dispute first arose in August 1997, when Strawberry filed three change applications seeking to update and correctly reflect current points of diversion and place of use of Project water and to provide for municipal and industrial use. More specifically, Strawberry sought the right to use Project water for the irrigation of small lots, including lawns and gardens, as opposed to larger agricultural tracts. In its protest before the State Engineer, the United States claimed that it was the owner of the water and urged the State Engineer to dismiss the Strawberry applications until the ownership issue could be resolved, presumably in Utah courts. After the lawsuits were filed, the United States advanced the further claim that Strawberry is contractually prohibited from changing use without consent of the Secretary of the Interior. In due course, the United States sought to have all matters adjudicated in the federal district court.

Separate and apart from these initial change applications filed by Strawberry are competing applications filed by each of the parties in December 1997 seeking to recapture Project water after it has been fully utilized and passed beyond the control of either party. These applications are extremely ambitious and far-reaching. The application of the United States, filed December 4, 1997, seeks to appropriate 49,200 acre-feet of return flow of Project water for storage in Utah Lake and delivery in Salt Lake County. Strawberry's "exchange application," filed eight days later, seeks to recover the return flow from 64,400 acre-feet by pumping or diverting from existing wells, springs, and streams in southern Utah County. * * *

Waiver of Sovereign Immunity—the McCarran Amendment

We now consider whether and for what purposes the United States is subject to joinder in either the federal or the state court suits that have been filed. We begin with the proposition that the United States is immune from suit unless Congress has waived that immunity. Lehman v. Nakshian, 453 U.S. 156, 160 (1981).

Congress has waived the United States' sovereign immunity for joinder in both federal and state court actions arising out of federal water reclamation projects. It has consented to joinder in federal district court "to adjudicate, confirm, validate, or decree the *contractual rights* of a contracting entity and the United States regarding any contract executed pursuant to federal reclamation law." 43 U.S.C. § 390uu (2005) (emphasis added). It has consented to joinder in state court

> (1) for the adjudication of *rights to the use of water of a river system or other source*, or (2) for the administration of such rights, where it appears that the United States is the owner of or is in the process of acquiring water rights by appropriation under state law * * * and the United States is a necessary party to such suit.

43 U.S.C. § 666 (emphasis added).

The consent to joinder in state court came in the McCarran Amendment to the 1902 Reclamation Act. Section 8 of the Act had decreed noninterference with state law "relating to the control, appropriation, use, or distribution of water," and further, that "the Secretary of the Interior, in carrying out the provisions of this Act, shall proceed in conformity with [state] laws." 43 U.S.C. § 383. These mandates had limited meaning unless the United States could be compelled to join in state court proceedings. The 82nd Congress came to grips with this problem in 1952 with the adoption of the McCarran Amendment. * * *

STRAWBERRY'S PETITIONS AND THE UNITED STATES' RESPONSE

Strawberry advanced three claims for relief in the petitions filed in the general adjudications in the Third and Eighth District Courts. First, it sought a declaration that Strawberry, for the use and benefit of its shareholders, holds equitable title to Project water which the shareholders have applied to beneficial use over approximately the last ninety years. It claims this ownership extends to the right to recapture return flows. Second, Strawberry sought a declaration that the Association and the individual water users have the right to use the water for purposes of irrigation regardless of the size of the tract. Finally, Strawberry sought a declaration that it has the right to file change applications with the State Engineer without the consent or approval of the United States. * * *

The fact that two parties contract with each other to cooperatively pursue a certificated right to the use of water belonging to the people of the State of Utah does not lead to the conclusion that the water rights "derive from contracts" or that the rights of one derive from its contract with the other. That is a simplistic surface analysis that disregards the source of the water rights. The rights of both parties derive from the State of Utah through their joint effort in following the appropriation procedure outlined by statute. Simply stated, the foundation of these water rights is an approved application to appropriate followed by actual beneficial use on the ground. As stated in Robinson v. Schoenfeld, 62 Utah 233, 218 P. 1041, 1043 (Utah 1923), "The sine qua non of making a valid appropriation is and was to apply the water attempted to be appropriated to some beneficial use." The contracts between these parties were designed to facilitate this process, but they are not the source of the right to use the water.

* * * The 1991 Operating Agreement is not before us, nor are the earlier agreements of 1926, 1928, and 1940. Under 43 U.S.C. § 390uu (2005), it is the prerogative of the federal district court to examine the contractual relationship and "to adjudicate, confirm, validate, or decree the *contractual rights* * * * regarding any contract executed pursuant to Federal reclamation law." (Emphasis added.) Separate and apart from this prerogative is the prerogative of Utah courts to determine how the contractual relationship plays out under Utah water law. That law cannot be changed by contract. We reiterate that the Secretary of the Interior in carrying out the provisions of the Reclamation Act is obliged to "proceed in conformity with [state] laws * * * relating to the *control, appropriation, use, or distribution of water.*" 43 U.S.C. § 383 (emphasis added). Further, we note and underscore that the United States presumes more than it should when it undertakes to articulate Utah law regarding return flows from a transbasin diversion. * * *

WATER OWNERSHIP IN UTAH

In navigating a course through Utah water law, it is easy to be misled by the word "ownership." In some respects it is a misnomer. It is only the right to use water that is subject to ownership. The first and over-arching principle of Utah water law is this: "All waters in this state, whether above or under the ground, are hereby declared to be the property of the public, subject to all existing rights to the use thereof." Utah Code Ann. § 73–1–1 (2004). Of equal importance is the second fundamental principle: "Beneficial use shall be the basis, the measure and the limit of all rights to the use of the water in this state." Id. § 73–1–3. * * *

The State Engineer draws this court's attention to two decisions where entitlement to file change applications was tied to the holder of the certificate of appropriation. The two decisions are East Jordan Irrigation Co. v. Morgan, 860 P.2d 310 (Utah 1993), and Badger v. Brooklyn Canal Co., 922 P.2d 745 (Utah 1996). Each case illustrates the importance of asking not only the "title" or "ownership" question, but also the second question, which probes roots, purposes, and entitlements. *East Jordan* and *Brooklyn Canal* support the concept that a mutual water company as the owner of record of the collective rights of its shareholders is alone empowered to file change applications. But ownership for this purpose is not in derogation of the rights and entitlements of the shareholders who are the ultimate users, it is rather for their benefit. "The agreement between East Jordan and its shareholders imposes the duty on the association to manage its affairs *in the interest of its shareholders as a whole.*" 860 P.2d at 314 (emphasis added). It is a form of ownership akin to that of a trustee. * * *

Our holdings in *East Jordan* and *Brooklyn Canal* cannot be read as empowering the United States to emasculate rather than protect the rights of the ultimate beneficial users. Nothing in either decision will support an ownership status other than a protective role on behalf of the rank-and-file persons who have applied the water to beneficial use. In the final analysis, the principal thrust of *East Jordan* and *Brooklyn Canal* is not to undermine the importance of beneficial use, but rather to shift the protective focus from the individual shareholder to the shareholders as a collective whole. The effort to use these decisions as a sword against, rather than as a shield in protection of, the collective whole of the individual users is completely untenable. The only way the United States (or the State Engineer in behalf of the United States) could rely upon these cases would be to acknowledge that the United States stands in the same shoes worn by the mutual irrigation companies and that it holds title for the benefit of the ultimate users, and for no other purpose, a role it must share with the Strawberry Water Companies.

Casting the United States in a protective role for the benefit of the ultimate users is the approach embraced by the United States Supreme Court in Nevada v. United States, 463 U.S. 110 (1983). In that case, the Bureau of Reclamation sought to reduce the entitlement of irrigators to project water in order to provide additional water to an Indian tribe to whom the Department of the Interior owed a fiduciary duty. The Bureau claimed that as the title holder of the water rights it could alter the allocation of project water. In rejecting this position, the Supreme Court stated:

> The Government is completely mistaken if it believes the water rights confirmed to it * * * were like so many bushels of wheat, to be bartered, sold, or shifted about as the Government might see fit. Once * * * lands were acquired by settlers in the Project, *the Government's "ownership" of the water rights was at most nominal*; the beneficial interest in the rights confirmed to the Government resided in the owners of the land * * * to which these rights became appurtenant upon application of the Project water to the land.

463 U.S. at 126 (emphasis added). The Court chided the government for wholly ignoring "the [protective] obligations that necessarily devolve upon it from having *mere title to water rights* * * * when the beneficial ownership of these water rights resides elsewhere." Id. at 127 (emphasis added). * * *

Permanent or temporary changes in the point of diversion or purpose of use is governed by Utah law. Utah Code section 73–3–3 outlines a careful procedure for the filing and approval process. The qualification for filing relevant to our inquiry is stated as follows:

>   (2)(a) any *person entitled to the use* of water may make permanent or temporary changes in the:
>
>   (i) place of diversion;
>
>   (ii) place of use; or
>
>   (iii) purpose of use for which the water was originally appropriated.

Utah Code Ann. § 73–3–3(2)(a)(i)-(iii) (1989 & Supp. 2005) (emphasis added).

As heretofore noted, *East Jordan* and *Brooklyn Canal* have construed this statutory provision in favor of a mutual irrigation company as opposed to an individual shareholder. Here the relationship is three-layered: the United States, the Strawberry companies, and the shareholders. The Strawberry companies represent the collective use of all their shareholders. They owe these shareholders a fiduciary duty and have a responsibility to manage for the common good. The concern in *East Jordan* and *Brooklyn Canal* that one shareholder would pursue a course at variance with the interests of the other shareholders is nonexistent in this case. The risk here is that the United States as holder of the certificate would seek to pursue a course at variance with the Strawberry companies and their shareholders, whose interests are aligned. Such a course would be contrary to the cited decisions and to the protective role recognized in *Nevada*, 463 U.S. at 126–27.

The considerations in *East Jordan* and *Brooklyn Canal* which led to the decisions favoring the mutual irrigation companies do not favor the United States. These same considerations favor continued recognition of the right of the mutual irrigation companies to make change application decisions for the benefit of the collective whole of the shareholders whom they represent and who, through their votes, control the boards of directors. The United States, on the other hand, is a stranger to the day-by-day beneficial use and lacks a direct equation with the actual users. Moreover, even if the United States were entitled to file the applications, it could not do so in derogation of the rights and entitlements of the ultimate users in whose interest it is obliged to act. Failure to protect this interest would violate the principles established in *Nevada*.[11] * * *

Deferral to Federal District Court

In its federal court counterclaim, the United States advances the position that "the federal government retains the ultimate approval

---

11. We do not foreclose the possibility that in the proper circumstance the United States should be allowed to file the change application. In addition to "entitlement to the use of water" as a qualifying basis, Utah's statute empowers the holder of an "approved application for the appropriation of water" to file. Utah Code Ann. § 73–3–3(8)(a). Here the "approved application" matured into a "certificate of appropria-tion," but the right of use became separated from the holder of the certificate. The statute does not have a separate provision for the holder of the certificate. We need not determine how these provisions should be applied to the United States in its role in this case since it is only the right to file belonging to the actual users (Strawberry) that has been challenged.

authority with respect to both the distribution of project water and any change of place or purpose of use that might be contemplated." It claims that this is mandated both by the contract between the parties and by federal statutes. It further claims that as the "title owner of record" it alone has the authority to file a change application with the State Engineer.

We have addressed the latter argument, but must now defer to the federal court for construction of the federal statutes as well as the contracts between the parties. We note, however, that the position advanced by the United States seriously calls into question the primacy of state water law guaranteed by Section 8 of the Reclamation Act. Notwithstanding the over-arching importance of this issue, any further response by Utah courts must await the federal court review. * * *

The Claims to Return Flow from Imported Water

We come at last to the competing claims to return flow water. This does not appear to be a change application issue, but a dispute about which party, if either, can extend control beyond the initial use made by Strawberry. It ventures into uncharted territory. * * *

By some yet unarticulated theory, the United States seeks to recapture the return flow from water beneficially used by the Strawberry Water Users on their lands, the United States being a complete stranger to both the lands and the water since delivery of the latter to these users at a far distant point high in the watershed. Presumably, the United States places complete reliance upon the assumption that imported water should be afforded special treatment unlike all other water belonging to the public and that it, as opposed to the Strawberry Water Users, should be the beneficiary of that special treatment. Quite clearly, this involves major policy issues "relating to the control, appropriation, use or distribution of water" and is therefore governed by state water law under the express language of Section 8 of the Reclamation Act. 43 U.S.C. § 383 (2005). Utah courts will have to grapple with these issues. * * *

Conclusion

Jurisdiction rests in the federal district court to "adjudicate, confirm, validate or decree * * * contractual rights." 43 U.S.C. § 390uu. Jurisdiction rests in state district court as to issues dealing with the "control, appropriation, use or distribution of water," 43 U.S.C. § 383, and "adjudication of the right to use of water of a river system." 43 U.S.C. § 666. The United States has consented to joinder in both courts. In Utah, "ownership" of water rights is equated with "right of use," and title can be held in a protective capacity for those who have that right. The water rights dispute of these parties is appropriate for resolution under Utah's general adjudication statute * * *. It has been properly invoked by the Strawberry Water Users. * * *

Notes and Questions

1. Can the Strawberry Water Users Association now seek guidance from a federal district court under 43 U.S.C. § 390uu regarding its contractual rights? In Orff v. United States, 125 S.Ct. 2606 (2005), farmers in

California's Westlands Water District sued the Bureau of Reclamation in federal district court for allegedly breaching its water delivery contract by reducing deliveries in compliance with the Endangered Species Act and environmental provisions of the Central Valley Project Improvement Act. The United States Supreme Court held that 43 U.S.C. § 390uu does not give water users the right to sue the United States directly for relief:

> Section 390uu grants consent "to *join* the United States *as a necessary party defendant* in any suit to adjudicate" certain rights under a federal reclamation contract. (Emphasis added.) This language is best interpreted to grant consent to join the United States in an action between other parties—for example, two water districts, or a water district and its members—when the action requires construction of a reclamation contract and joinder of the United States is necessary. It does not permit a plaintiff to sue the United States alone.

125 S.Ct. at 2610. The Court emphasized that, by contrast, the Tucker Act, 28 U.S.C. § 1491, authorizes suits directly against the United States for damages stemming from breaches of contract. 125 S.Ct. at 2611.

In light of *Orff*, how can the Strawberry Water Users Association challenge the Bureau of Reclamation's position that any change in use, whether or not approved by the state engineer, requires the permission of the Secretary of the Interior?

2.   The Supreme Court has addressed the "ownership" of reclamation water in several contexts. In Ickes v. Fox, 300 U.S. 82 (1937), the question was whether the United States was an indispensable party to a lawsuit against the Bureau of Reclamation seeking to enforce the terms of a reclamation contract. The contract provided that the bureau would store and deliver water to be appropriated by the Sunnyside Water Users Association under state law. When the bureau unilaterally demanded a higher price than set in the contract for some of the water, the association sued. The United States argued that it was the owner of the water rights and thus an indispensable party to the lawsuit. The Supreme Court disagreed:

> * * * So far as these [landowners] are concerned, the government did not become the owner of the water-rights, because those rights by [the Reclamation Act of 1902] were made "appurtenant to the land irrigated"; and by a Washington statute, in force at least since 1917, were "to be and remain appurtenant to the land." Moreover, by the contract with the government, it was the land owners who were "to initiate rights to the use of water," which rights were to be and "continue to be forever appurtenant to designated lands owned by such shareholders."

> Respondents had made all stipulated payments and complied with all obligations by which they were bound to the government, and, long prior to the issue of the notices and orders here assailed, had acquired a vested right to the perpetual use of the waters as appurtenant to their lands. * * * Although the government diverted, stored and distributed the water, the contention of the [government] that thereby ownership of the water or water-rights became vested in the United States is not well founded. Appropriation was

made not for the use of the government, but, under the Reclamation Act, for the use of the land owners; and by the terms of the law and of the contract already referred to, the water-rights became the property of the land owners, wholly distinct from the property right of the government in the irrigation works. The government was and remained simply a carrier and distributor of the water, with the right to receive the sums stipulated in the contracts as reimbursement for the cost of construction and annual charges for operation and maintenance of the works.

Id. at 93–95.

3. In Nebraska v. Wyoming, 325 U.S. 589 (1945), the United States argued that it owned the water being used by two reclamation projects in Nebraska and Wyoming and thus should be apportioned the water in an interstate apportionment case involving the Platte River. The Supreme Court again disagreed. Although the Bureau of Reclamation had filed the appropriation applications, the state

issued decrees and certificates in favor of the individual water users. The certificates named as appropriators the individual landowners. * * * All of these steps make plain that those projects were designed, constructed and completed according to the pattern of state law as provided in the Reclamation Act. We say here what was said in *Ickes v. Fox*: "Although the government diverted, stored and distributed the water, the contention of petitioner that thereby ownership of the water or water-rights became vested in the United States is not well founded. * * * "

Id. at 613–614.

4. In the Supreme Court's most recent consideration of who "owns" reclamation water, the United States reallocated water from a reclamation project to an Indian reservation. The reclamation users argued that a 1944 federal court decree had confirmed the reclamation project's water rights and was res judicata. In response, the United States argued that the case involved simply a "reallocation of the water decreed * * * to a single party— the United States—from reclamation uses to a Reservation use with an earlier priority." The Court once again disagreed and ruled for the reclamation users. After quoting from both *Ickes* and *Nebraska v. Wyoming*, the Court concluded that the United States held "mere title" to the water, with "beneficial ownership" residing in the reclamation users. Nevada v. United States, 463 U.S. 110, 127 (1983).

5. In applying *Ickes*, *Nebraska v. Wyoming*, and *Nevada v. United States* to other settings, two cautions should be kept in mind. First, all of the cases relied to at least some degree on the local state law providing that appropriations are appurtenant to the land where the water is put to beneficial use. Other states may employ different legal principles. Second, as the Utah Supreme Court emphasizes in *Strawberry*, the concept of "ownership" can be misleading without a context. "Ownership" by itself seldom resolves the legal question.

6. The question of "ownership" recently has arisen in connection with claims by reclamation users that the federal government has taken their

"property rights" by reducing deliveries under the Endangered Species Act or other federal laws. As covered in more detail at pp. 788–796, reclamation contracts often provide that the federal government is not liable for reductions in deliveries. Lacking a contract right to full deliveries, reclamation users have attempted—so far without success—to argue that they "own" the reclamation water and thus have a separate takings claim based on state water rights.

2. REFORMING THE RECLAMATION PROGRAM

As the Western Water Policy Review Advisory Commission observed in 1998, the mission of the federal reclamation program is changing:

> Viewed in budgetary terms, Reclamation still remains primarily a construction agency. In the 1980s, construction funds accounted for about 75 percent of its appropriations, but there has been a marked decline in the number of congressionally authorized Reclamation water projects since the 1970s. The last * * * traditional irrigation project approved by the Congress and constructed by Reclamation (North Loup Project in Nebraska) was authorized in 1972. By fiscal year 1997, construction accounted for only about 40 percent of total Reclamation appropriations, which began to decline in the 1990s and which, by 2002, are projected to be 33 percent less (in constant dollars) than 1997 levels. The number of employees has declined as well.

> The nature of new Reclamation projects is changing. More than a third of the Reclamation projects authorized since 1979 are demonstration projects for wastewater recycling or water reuse, while only a quarter involve traditional multipurpose projects.[1]

As the traditional construction program has wound down, attention has turned to reform of the reclamation program. A 1997 report of the Congressional Budget Office ("CBO") identifies at least three reform objectives that members of Congress have pursued in one piece of legislation or another.[2] All three objectives reflect a belief that "farmers use too much water and pay too little for it as a consequence of the Bureau of Reclamation's policies." The first objective has been to ensure that farmers pay their fair share of the costs of reclamation projects. A second objective has been to "allocate water more efficiently." Many experts believe that, because farmers have received subsidized reclamation water, these farmers use too much water compared to other sectors. Reallocating some of the water from agriculture to cities and other sectors could improve overall social welfare. The final objective has been to "increase the amount of water allocated to public purposes, such as

---

1. Western Water Policy Review Advisory Commission, Water in the West: Challenge for the Next Century 5–23 (1998).

2. See Congressional Budget Office, Water Use Conflicts in the West: Implications of Reforming the Bureau of Reclamation's Water Supply Policies 15 (Aug. 1997). For other useful discussion of potential reform measures, see Duane Mecham & Benjamin Simon, Forging a New Federal Reclamation Water Pricing Policy: Legal and Policy Considerations, 27 Ariz. St. L.J. 507 (1995).

meeting environmental needs (improving water quality and providing habitat for fish and wildlife) and satisfying the claims of Native Americans." A central element of this final objective has been to increase instream flows depleted by reclamation projects.

a. Reform Options

As the CBO report discusses, Congress has considered a number of different reform policies to try to achieve these goals. The first reform is to increase the price that the Bureau of Reclamation charges water districts for federal water. This obviously is the most direct way of achieving the first objective of ensuring that farmers pay their fair share of reclamation costs. If the price increase is passed onto individual farmers, it also might encourage the farmers to engage in greater conservation, saving water that could be returned to rivers and streams or used by other sectors. Unfortunately, as the CBO report notes, "the bureau has no control over how districts pass the costs on to farmers. Some districts may not even have the capability to charge per-unit water prices. To do so, districts must have or install devices for measuring water use and a system of accounting for it. Without information about the exact level of water use, farmers would be unable to respond to price signals."

A related reform therefore is to require water districts to adopt new pricing policies that send stronger price signals to their individual farmers. Traditionally, many water districts financed their costs through a per-acre charge that was independent of the quantity of water used. As the CBO report notes, the "marginal price" under this type of system is zero. As a result, such "charges can never motivate an efficient decision about water use." Interest therefore has grown in "uniform" and, to an even greater degree, "tiered" pricing systems.

> Uniform price structures charge the same per-unit price no matter how much water is used. Tiered, or block-rate, prices rise or fall in discrete jumps as the total quantity purchased rises. For example, the price might be $10 per unit for the first 10 units, $15 each for the next 10 units, $20 per unit for the next 10 units, and so on. An individual purchasing 13 units would pay $145 ($10 x 10 units plus $15 each for the next three). The marginal price—the price for the last unit—would be $15. By comparison, the average price would be $11.15.

> Uniform prices can motivate farmers to use water efficiently if the price is set correctly. Tiered price structures can motivate the same decisions as uniform prices, but tiered prices have a smaller impact on farmers' income. According to economic theory, farmers decide whether to apply an additional unit of water based on the relative benefits and costs of using that unit. That decision is independent of the price of earlier units. Therefore, raising the price for all units or only for applications

that exceed a specified number of units can encourage farmers to reduce their water use.

From a farmer's perspective, the advantage of a tiered price structure over a uniform price increase is that the higher price has to be paid on a smaller quantity of water. In addition, tiered water prices may seem fairer to farmers because they penalize the least efficient farmers most. Farmers who conserve water may pay the higher price on very few units, or on none at all. As with any policy-motivated price increase, the effectiveness of tiered water prices depends on the price levels and quantities in each tier.

Another related reform, which can both increase the share of costs paid for by farmers and provide for environmental improvement, is an environmental surcharge. Such surcharges "can be applied generally or targeted toward certain user groups. They can be designed to discourage water use that is particularly damaging locally, or they can be intended simply to raise funds for environmental restoration projects."

An alternative approach to reform is to mandate changes in water use. Congress, for example, can require farmers to conserve or mandate that water districts adopt water conservation programs. Congress also can reduce the amount of federal water being delivered to water districts and order that the undelivered water be left in-stream. As the CBO study discusses, mandatory reallocations of water to the environment can be economically inefficient and more costly to current water users than price reforms:

> Farmers would respond to economic incentives to reduce water use [e.g., higher prices] by eliminating the lowest-valued uses (for example, less profitable crops, such as wheat, or fields with low yields), and farmers with lower-valued uses would cut back more than farmers with higher-valued production (for example, more profitable specialty crops such as fruits and vegetables). In contrast, a mandatory reduction in water supply could affect high-and low-valued farming operations equally.

A final reform approach that Congress has considered is the creation of active water markets for reclamation water.

> Water markets can create a win/win situation for participants. Farmers will be better off because they will transfer water only if the benefit from doing so is greater than the cost (or foregone profits) of not using the water. Water users with insufficient supplies—primarily urban customers—will also be better off because purchasing water from farmers can cost significantly less than buying water from the next-cheapest source. The total benefit of using the bureau's water will increase because the transfers allow water to be put to higher-valued uses.

Water markets are most effective for * * * improving the efficiency of water allocations among private economic uses. In the southwest regions such as California and the lower Colorado River basin, where excess demand by cities is great, water markets can be particularly effective in moving water from agricultural uses to urban uses. In the Pacific Northwest, the value of water used in producing hydropower may be higher than its value in agriculture in drought years. A water market can, in theory, reduce inefficiencies in allocations between those uses, although state laws * * * may create a greater impediment to water markets in the region than do the Bureau of Reclamation's policies.

Water markets also can increase the amount of water devoted to the environment. As discussed in Chapter 3, both governments and environmental groups have purchased water in recent years for environmental purposes. See supra pp. 142–148 & 265. As the CBO report warns, however, "environmental uses may have great difficulty competing in a water market with uses that carry a high economic value, such as municipal and industrial uses. * * * In an era of declining agency budgets and financially strapped environmental organizations, water markets may provide water for public purposes only when combined with a tool, such as an environmental surcharge, that provides funds for that purpose."

Water markets by themselves do not eliminate subsidies. Indeed, by allowing farmers to profit from the sale of subsidized water, water markets can increase the perceived inequities of the federal reclamation program.

Notes and Questions

1. What do you see as the pros and cons of the various reform measures available to Congress? If you were a member of Congress, what would you do? Are there other reform steps that you believe Congress should consider?

2. Should Congress hesitate before raising the rates that farmers must pay for reclamation water? What of farmers who relied on the subsidy in making longterm investment decisions—e.g., expanding their planted acreage or buying farm equipment?

It is also important to distinguish the farmer who owned land prior to a reclamation project and the farmer who purchased later. To the original farmer, the reclamation subsidy is a windfall and it may not seem unfair to eliminate or reduce it. Later purchasers, however, buy their property at a price that generally reflects the subsidy and will suffer a loss if the subsidy is eliminated or reduced. Should rate reforms distinguish between these two sets of water users? Is there any effective way of going after those who sold land prior to rate reform at prices that reflected the prior subsidy?

3. Does Congress need to authorize the marketing of federal reclamation water, or can water districts simply sell or lease federal water pursuant to state law? Section 8 of the 1902 Reclamation Act, 43 U.S.C. § 372, not

only speaks to the relevance of state law to the operation of federal reclamation projects (see supra pp. 752–762) but also provides that "the right to the use of water acquired under the provisions of this Act shall be appurtenant to the land irrigated." The only legislative history on the appurtenancy requirement is the following statement by Representative Mondell, one of the sponsors of the 1902 act:

> These most important provisions of the law prevent all the evils which come from recognizing a property right in water with power to sell and dispose of the same elsewhere and for other purposes than originally intended. This is an advance over the water usage of most of the States, and it is not denied that making water rights appurtenant to the tract irrigated will in some cases work hardship, but it is believed that it is much better to risk the individual hardships which will inevitably occur under a provision of appurtenance than to risk the evils certain to result from unlimited authority to transfer water rights.

35 Cong. Rec. 6679 (June 2, 1902). Although the Bureau has assumed for some time that later acts implicitly repealed the appurtenancy requirement, courts do not favor repeals by implication and thus uncertainty remains.

4. Assuming that reclamation water can be transferred without explicit Congressional authorization, must a contractor obtain Bureau permission to transfer its water? *Should* federal approval be required? Most reclamation contracts provide that no transfer is valid until approved by the Secretary of the Interior. Proponents of water transfers, however, fear that federal permission, which typically will require an environmental review of the proposed transfer under the National Environmental Policy Act (see supra pp. 668–670), could delay and complicate transfers. Proponents also express concern that federal authority over transfers might be abused or otherwise deter worthwhile transfers. Given California v. United States, supra p. 753, can the Secretary of the Interior refuse to approve a transfer that is permissible under state law? See United States v. Alpine Land & Reservoir Co., 697 F.2d 851, 858 (9th Cir. 1983) ("Congress intended transfers to be subject to state water law"); United States v. Alpine Land & Reservoir Co., 878 F.2d 1217 (9th Cir. 1989) (same). See also Strawberry Water Users Ass'n v. Bureau of Reclamation, supra p. 763.

In 1989, Wyoming's Casper–Alcova Irrigation District (CAID) proposed to loan federal reclamation water to the Goshin Irrigation District (GID) which was hard hit by drought. The Bureau insisted that CAID obtain the Bureau's approval and that GID sign a contract with the Bureau. Rather than complying with the Bureau's requests, the two districts and the State of Wyoming sued for declaratory relief in federal district court. The case was ultimately settled out of court without a decision on the central legal issue.

5. Should current users of reclamation water be permitted to profit from the transfer of the water? Should transferors be required to repay the federal government for current subsidies? For past subsidies? People, not surprisingly, have strongly disagreed on the answer. Compare Joseph Sax, Selling Reclamation Water Rights: A Case Study in Federal Subsidy Policy, 64 Mich. L. Rev. 13 (1965) with Raymond Anderson, Windfall Gains From Transfer of Water Allotments Within the Colorado–Big Thompson Project,

43 Land Econ. 265 (1967). The major argument for letting people profit is that it's necessary in order to encourage transfers. Unless current water users can profit to at least some degree from a transfer, they typically will have little incentive to engage in a transfer. Is it necessary, however, to let people charge the *full* market price in order to encourage transfers? Could the government on a transfer-by-transfer basis determine how much profit the seller needs to make the transfer worthwhile and either cap the selling price at that level or require any additional profit to be paid to the government? Is such a proposal workable?

b. *Reclamation Reform Act of 1982*

Congress took its first major reform step with the Reclamation Reform Act of 1982, 96 Stat. 1261. Farmers provided the initial impetus for reform. Several lawsuits had been filed challenging the Bureau of Reclamation's failure to enforce the populist limitations of the 1902 Reclamation Act—the 160–acre limitation and the residency requirement (see supra pp. 750–751)—and farmers sought legislative relief. Congress agreed to abolish the residency requirement and raise the acreage limitation, but the price for weakening the populist limitations was price reform.

Under the Reclamation Reform Act, farmers can obtain water for up to 960 acres of land they own and for an unlimited number of leased acres. Water for the first 960 acres is priced largely as before, but the price has to be "at least sufficient to recover all operations and mainte-nance charges." (As discussed at pp. 748–749, the price under many of the older, fixed price contracts was no longer sufficient to cover the O & M charges by the early 1980s.) The price for any water going to "excess acreage" beyond 960 acres has to cover O & M charges and include interest on any unpaid capital and accumulated O & M deficit. Although the Reform Act calls this price a "full cost" rate, the price is still less than the actual cost of the water to the government: the designated interest rate is less than the real interest rate, and various non-interest subsidies remain untouched. Nonetheless, the "full cost" price repre-sents a dramatic increase over preexisting prices.

These provisions apply to new or amended contracts. To encourage districts to amend their contracts and incorporate these provisions, the Reform Act also included a "hammer clause": If a district did not elect to amend its contract by April 12, 1987, its farmers had to pay the "full cost" price for any land held in excess of 160 acres. If a district did not elect to come under the new provisions, in short, they had to live with even more draconian pricing rules.

In the 1982 Reform Act, Congress also directed the Bureau of Reclamation to encourage water conservation and required water dis-tricts to develop water conservation plans. The Bureau has chosen to take an incentives-based approach to this provision rather than mandat-ing that districts take particular steps. Since 1997, the Bureau of Reclamation has provided guidance and assistance to water districts in four areas: (1) water management planning, (2) conservation education,

(3) demonstration of innovative conservation technologies, and (4) implementation of effective conservation measures.

Notes and Questions

1. Reforming the federal reclamation program is easier legislated than accomplished. As Professor Amy Kelley has detailed, water users quickly found a variety of ways to avoid or delay implementation of the pricing provisions of the Reclamation Reform Act of 1982:

> Resistance to both the leasing/full-cost provisions and the hammer clause was predictably stiff, vigorous, and innovative. Two approaches were taken. The first way was simply to find other ways of controlling massive quantities of land than through either ownership (subject to recordable contract rules) or leasing (subject to full cost rules for excess acres). One of the most egregious evasions, the revocable trust, was limited statutorily by a 1987 amendment, but various sophisticated approaches continue to flourish.[143] * * * Another avoidance mechanism of choice has been the farm management arrangement.[145] Regulations promulgated in 1996 and 2000 were intended to corral some of the abuses; it remains to be seen how effective they are. The second approach was head-on confrontation: litigation to declare various reform laws unconstitutional.

Amy Kelly, Federal Reclamation Law, in 4 Waters and Water Rights § 41.03, at 41–11 (Robert Beck ed., repl. vol. 2004). Several of the cases that water users have brought challenging the Reclamation Reform Act and other reform efforts are excerpted or discussed starting at page 779.

2. Does the use of trusts and farm management arrangements to evade the Reclamation Reform Act suggest that any effort to limit the reclamation subsidy to a given class of water users (e.g., farmers of 960 acres or less) will be doomed to failure? That the only way to reform the reclamation price system is to reduce or eliminate the subsidy across the board?

c. Central Valley Project Improvement Act

Congress continued its reform efforts with the Central Valley Project Improvement Act of 1992, 106 Stat. 4600, 4706 (CVPIA), which addresses problems identified in the Central Valley Project (CVP) in California, the largest single water project in the United States. The CVPIA starts out by shortening the length of new reclamation contracts. As CVP contracts come up for renewal, the Bureau can renew them for only 25 years (compared to 40 years under prior law), with an option for

143. * * * [The General Accounting Office] gives one particularly striking example: "One 12,345–acre cotton farm (roughly 20 square miles, operating under a single partnership), was reorganized into 15 separate landholdings through 18 partnerships, 24 corporations, and 11 trusts * * *."

145. [Hal Candee, The Broken Promise of Reclamation Reform, 40 Hastings L.J. 657, 673 (1989)] summarizes a typical scenario: "For example, a 7,000–acre operation in Westlands previously operated under a lease would simply 'restructure' the leased lands into separate 960–acre parcels, each owned by a different business partner or investor, who then collectively 'manage' the entire operation via a separate company that is owned or controlled by the same partners or investors." * * *

future 25–year renewals. Congress' goal is to provide for more frequent review of contract terms to ensure that they meet changing conditions.

The CVPIA uses a variety of the tools identified in the Congressional Budget Office report to try to reform CVP operations. First, as existing CVP contracts come up for renewal, the CVPIA provides for further price reform. The CVPIA imposes a tiered pricing system on both agricultural and urban water districts. The first 80 percent of a district's water allotment is paid for at the contract price specified by the Reclamation Reform Act, the next 10 percent at a price that averages the contract price and the "full cost" price, and the final 10 percent at the "full cost" price. The CVPIA also assesses a number of surcharges on water users, including $6 per acre-foot on all agricultural water users and $12 on all urban water users, to increase with inflation. The surcharges go to a Central Valley Project Restoration Fund to finance restoration, improvement, and acquisition of habitats for fish and wildlife.

Second, the CVPIA also reallocates project water directly to the environment. The CVPIA takes 800,000 acre-feet (600,000 acre-feet in dry years) "off the top" of project water and dedicates it to meeting the needs of fish and wildlife in the Sacramento River and the Sacramento/San Joaquin River delta. The CVPIA mandates that another 400,000 acre-feet of water be used for wildlife reserves in the Central Valley. Much of this latter amount again comes off the top of current deliveries; the remainder is to come from voluntary purchases. Finally, the CVPIA provides for the protection of instream flows in the Trinity River that could result in a further 100,000–200,000 acre-feet reduction in yearly CVP deliveries.

Third, the CVPIA authorizes water transfers from CVP contractors to "any other California water user or water agency, State or Federal agency, Indian Tribe, or private non-profit organization." The CVPIA leaves the price of water transfers to the market. Contractors must pay the Bureau of Reclamation for transferred water at rates that include interest charges and a $25 per acre-foot surcharge on transfers to non-CVP entities, but otherwise the CVPIA does not attempt to recapture existing subsidies on transferred water. The Secretary of the Interior must approve all transfers after ensuring that the transfer does not injure the area of origin, the district from which the water is being transferred, fish and wildlife habitat, or groundwater; the transfer also must be "consistent with state law."

In a particularly controversial move, the CVPIA also authorizes water transfers by individual farmers rather than just by districts. If proposed transfers involve less than twenty percent of the CVP water received by the district, the district has no authority to prohibit transfers by their members. Districts can veto transfers involving more than this amount, but only on circumscribed grounds.

Notes and Questions

1.   California state law does not explicitly authorize members of a water district to transfer water without the approval of the district. If a farmer tries to use the provisions of the CVPIA to transfer water without the approval of his district, can the Secretary of the Interior approve the transfer as "consistent with state law"? Can the state refuse to approve the transfer under California v. United States, supra p. 753? For an overview and critique of the CVPIA transfer provisions, see Barton H. Thompson, Jr., Institutional Perspectives on Water Policy and Markets, 81 Calif. L. Rev. 673, 728, 745–52 (1993).

2.   For general discussions of the CVPIA and proposals to amend the CVPIA, see Harrison Dunning, Confronting the Environmental Legacy of Irrigated Agriculture in the West: The Case of the Central Valley Project, 23 Envtl. L. 943 (1993); Ernest Conant, The Central Valley Project Improvement Act Proposed Reforms, 6 S.J. Agri. L. Rev. 27 (1996).

d. *Legal Challenges to Reform*

MADERA IRRIGATION DISTRICT v. HANCOCK

United States Court of Appeals for the Ninth Circuit, 1993.
985 F.2d 1397.

KLEINFELD, CIRCUIT JUDGE.

Madera Irrigation District sued for a declaratory judgment and injunction, to prevent the United States from changing the terms of its water purchases when Madera renewed its contract. The district court dismissed for failure to state a claim. We conclude that the government has the power to impose the particular requirements at issue, and affirm.

I. FACTS

In 1939, Madera Irrigation District sold land and San Joaquin River water rights to the United States. As part of the consideration, the United States promised to build the Friant Dam and the Madera Canal and enter into contracts, when the project was completed, to sell Madera a permanent supply of 270,000 acre feet of water annually. The parties agreed that "it is not possible at this time to fix a price to be paid by the District for said water, but the United States agrees that the cost of said water to the District shall not exceed charges made to others than the District for the same class of water and service from the said Friant Dam and Reservoir." Contract for Purchase of Property and Water Rights at 13 (May 24, 1939) [hereinafter the "1939 Contract"].

In 1951, when construction was done, Madera and the government entered into a forty year contract for purchase and sale of water. They agreed upon a "permanent" supply, but a contract term of forty years. Prices were limited to no more than $3.50 per acre-foot for "class one water," a dependable supply out of the first 800,000 acre feet from the project, and $1.50 for "class two water," a residue to be supplied if available but which was not expected to be as dependable. Under the 1951 contract and "under succeeding contracts the rates to be charged the District for water service shall not exceed charges made to others than the District for the same class of water and service from Friant Dam and Reservoir." Contract Between the United States and the Madera Irrigation District for Water Service and Construction of a Distribution System at 9 (May 14, 1951) [hereinafter the "1951 Contract"].

As the end of the forty year term approached, the parties began negotiation of the renewals. The irrigation district claims that two provisions in the proposed new contract violate its rights under the previous contracts. First, the government insists upon an addition to the rate in the renewal contract of an amount which would recoup the excess of operation and maintenance costs under the 1951 contract over the rates charged during that forty year term. Second, the government insists upon a term in the renewal contract which might require an environmental impact statement and Endangered Species Act consultation, with possible subsequent modifications to the contract. * * *

Congress can change federal policy, but it cannot write on a blank slate. The old policies deposit a moraine of contracts, conveyances, expectations and investments. Lives, families, businesses, and towns are built on the basis of the old policies. When Congress changes course, its flexibility is limited by those interests created under the old policies which enjoy legal protection. Fairness toward those who relied on continuation of past policies cuts toward protection. Flexibility, so that government can adapt to changing conditions and changing majority preferences, cuts against. Expectations reasonably based upon constitutionally protected property rights are protected against policy changes by the Fifth Amendment. Those based only on economic and political predictions, not property rights, are not protected. Our task is to determine whether the renewal provisions insisted upon by the government violated Madera's Fifth Amendment property rights. * * *

II. OPERATION AND MAINTENANCE COSTS

The irrigation districts claim that the change in the price term, to recover maintenance and operation costs which were not charged in the 1951–1991 period, is improperly retroactive. The government insists upon a provision in the renewal contract which would recover with interest the subsidy in operations and maintenance costs accumulated during the old forty year contract. In so doing, the executive branch is carrying out a policy enunciated by Congress. Congress passed a statute requiring the recoupment for Central Valley Project irrigation districts such as Madera:

> The Secretary of the Interior shall include in each new or amended contract for the delivery of water from the Central Valley project provisions ensuring that any annual deficit (outstanding or hereafter arising) incurred by a Central Valley

project water contractor in the payment of operation and maintenance costs of the Central Valley project is repaid by such contractor under the terms of such new or amended contract, together with interest on any such deficit which arises on or after October 1, 1985 * * *.

Water Resource and Small Reclamation Projects Act, Pub. L. No. 99–546, § 106, 100 Stat. 3050, 3052 (1986).

Madera was entitled to buy water for a maximum of $3.50 and $1.50 per acre-foot under its 1951 contract. The government conditions renewal on payment during the renewal contract of millions of dollars for operation and maintenance costs incurred during the 1951 contract term. The effect, as Madera sees it, is that it will be paying more than the $3.50 and $1.50 price ceilings for its water purchased under the 1951 contract.

Madera argues that the charges cannot be imposed, for two reasons. First, it had and has a contractual right to pay no more than $3.50 and $1.50 per acre-foot for water under the 1951 contract, and the charges retroactively require it to pay more. Second, it has a contractual right to pay no more for water than other districts, and the charges would cause its price to be higher than that charged to other districts. * * *

We accept Madera's general proposition that a valid contract right of an irrigation district against the United States is property protected by the Fifth Amendment. Lynch v. United States, 292 U.S. 571, 579 (1934). Rights against the United States arising out of a contract are property rights protected from deprivation or impairment by the Fifth Amendment. Barcellos & Wolfsen, Inc. v. Westlands Water District, 899 F.2d 814, 821 (9th Cir. 1990). The Due Process Clause limits the exercise of sovereign power which would impair obligations under government contracts. To demonstrate a wrongful taking or impairment, Madera must establish that it has cognizable property rights arising out of its contracts with the government, and that the government has abrogated its contractual rights.

Two general principles constrain our interpretation. First, we must "construe legislation in a constitutional manner 'if fairly possible.'" Knapp v. Cardwell, 667 F.2d 1253, 1260 (9th Cir. 1982) (quoting Crowell v. Benson, 285 U.S. 22, 62 (1932)). Second, we must construe a contract with the government to avoid, if possible, foreclosing the exercise of sovereign authority. Sovereign power " 'will remain intact unless surrendered in unmistakable terms.'" Bowen v. Public Agencies Opposed to Social Security Entrapment, 477 U.S. 41, 52 (1986) (quoting Merrion v. Jicarilla Apache Tribe, 455 U.S. 130, 148 (1982)); Peterson v. U.S. Dep't of Interior, 899 F.2d 799, 807 (9th Cir. 1990). These two principles compel a construction somewhat more liberal toward the government than might be appropriate were the contract a purely private transaction. They enable it to change, not just execute past policies. But too liberal an interpretation of the residual sovereign power of the government to override its contractual commitments would eviscerate the government's power to bind itself to contracts. In addition to the moral offensiveness of allowing the government to break its promises, too liberal a construction would have the paradoxical consequence of weakening the sovereign power to implement policy. If the government's commitments need not be honored, then it can induce responses to policies only by cash or coercion.

A. Right to Renewal

The government offers a broad justification for the operation and maintenance charges and all the other changes at issue which we cannot accept. It urges that Madera had no renewal right under the 1951 contract, so the government was free to offer renewal on any terms. We cannot reconcile that with the terms of the 1939 and 1951 contracts. Madera did not exchange its land and its water rights for a forty year supply of water. It exchanged them, as its 1951 contract recites, for a "permanent" supply of water. Section 4 of the 1951 contract expressly provided for renewal at the expiration of the forty year term and terms for the "succeeding contracts" * * *.

B. Retroactivity

The government and amici argue that Madera's contract and the Reclamation Act always contemplated that Madera would pay the cost of the water, and the subsidy was accidental, so the purpose of the contract is served by the recoupment of the operating and maintenance deficits. We cannot reconcile this argument with the ceiling price in the 1951 contract. When parties contract for a price not to exceed a certain dollar figure, that necessarily carries the implication that the seller bears the risk that its costs will exceed that ceiling. A government contract supported by consideration to pay a subsidy is legitimate and enforceable. The promise to subsidize if necessary may be an instrument of policy designed to induce people to do things they otherwise would not do, such as transfer water rights and land to the United States, settle in the West and start a farm, or invest in an existing farm and equipment. We will not construe away the unmistakable term establishing a ceiling price in the 1951 contract on the ground that it granted an unintended subsidy.

Nevertheless, we conclude that the recoupment of the operations and maintenance expense does not violate Madera's rights under the 1951 contract. Madera got its water during the forty year term, and need pay no more for the old water than the price to which it agreed. Were it to buy no more water, it would owe no more money for the operations and maintenance expense. The recoupment will be a factor in the price of water under the renewal contract. The price of the new water will be calculated in such a way as to recoup a subsidy previously granted, as though the subsidy were a debt, but the subsidy is not owed like a debt. Madera has no obligation to repay it. The means by which the price of new water will be established looks retroactively at the costs of supplying the old water, but Madera could not be forced to pay the money in the absence of a renewal contract, so it is a charge for new water calculated on the basis of the old water, rather than an additional charge for the old water.

The difference between a retroactive means of calculating the price of new water, and a retroactive charge for the old water, becomes clearer when one thinks about the people to whom Madera will pass on the charges. Most of the farmers who used the more heavily subsidized water during the first two decades of the 1951 contract have probably sold out and retired by now, and some of them have probably died. They are not going to get billed for their share of the operations and maintenance costs deficit. Instead, many of the people to whom they sold their farms will pay more than they expected in the future for water. In practical effect, the recoupment of the operations and maintenance charge is entirely a burden on future rather than past purchasers of water, and largely on those who expected the subsidy rather than those who received it. The people who got the subsidy can keep the profits they earned from their crops based on the cheaper water, and they can also probably keep, unless their contracts provide otherwise, the money they received from the buyers of their farms attributable to the expected water subsidy. The burden of what the statute calls recovery of a deficit will fall largely on people other than the beneficiaries. The practical effect is a sharp policy shift, arguably disruptive of well-founded expectations, but it is not retroactive.

* * * Reasonable expectations arising out of past policy but without a basis in cognizable property rights may be honored by prudent politicians, because to do otherwise might be unfair, or because volatility in government policy will reduce its effectiveness in inducing long term changes in behavior. But violation of such expectations cannot give rise to a Fifth Amendment claim. Although Congress cannot take back a subsidy for which it has bound itself by contract, it may nevertheless quit subsidizing, and even tax the previously subsidized activity, once its contractual obligation to subsidize ends. The additional charge for new water does no more than that.

C. *Higher rates than others*

Madera also pleads that as a result of the government's calculation of the operation and maintenance deficit, it will be required to pay more for water than other Friant Dam districts. The practical effect of a higher maintenance and operations charge against Madera will be that an acre-foot of new water will cost more in the Madera Irrigation District than in some other Central Valley Project districts.

We find this the most troubling issue in the case. * * * Madera purchasers will pay more per acre-foot for new water under the renewal contract than purchasers in other districts, assuming that Madera's operation and maintenance cost recoupment is higher.

The two general principles of avoiding unconstitutionality and construing contracts to preserve sovereign authority nevertheless compel us to reject Madera's argument. The contractual words, "for the same * * * service," preserve Congressional authority to require a different charge for different service. Service requiring more expensive operation and maintenance is different from service requiring less expensive operation and maintenance. The equality promised applies to "rates," and the 1951 contract puts rates in section 7, and operation and maintenance cost in a separate section 15, evidently contemplating in section 16 that the irrigation district would take over operation and maintenance. This suggests that the parties did not intend that Madera's operation and maintenance cost could not exceed that of other districts.

Congress decided in the plainest terms to change its policy, so that instead of buying subsidized water, purchasers of the new water will have to pay its full operation and maintenance costs, plus an increment measured by the subsidy furnished to purchasers of the old water. We are unable to say that by the words, "shall not exceed charges made to others than the District for the same class of water and service," the government's sovereign authority to charge more for water service with a higher operation and maintenance cost was "surrendered in unmistakable terms." Peterson v. United States Dep't of Interior, 899 F.2d 799, 807 (9th Cir. 1990). * * *

III. THE ENVIRONMENTAL REQUIREMENTS

The United States has also required a term in Article 14 of the new contract that provides:

> * * * (C)(2) The United States and the Contractor [Madera] agree that the Secretary will also complete a programmatic Environmental Impact Statement (EIS) in accordance with the National Environmental Policy Act (NEPA) and a consultation in accordance with Section 7 of the Endangered Species Act (ESA) studying the environmental impacts associated with the execution and renewal of this and other water service contracts in the Friant Unit of the Central Valley Project and with the continued diversion and delivery of water thereunder. The United States and the Contractor further agree that the provisions of this contract are subject to modification by the United States, after public meetings and discussions with the Contractor, in accordance with the results of the final EIS and ESA consultation referenced in the immediately preceding sentence and ESA and NEPA: Provided, That the Contractor reserves and does not waive any right it may have to challenge the legality and validity of any such modifications made to this contract pursuant to this subarticle 14(c). Notwithstanding any other provision of this contract (including the preceding sentences of this subarticle), the provisions of this contract covering the right to long-term renewal and quantity of water are non-discretionary and not subject to change except as required by applicable law.

Madera argues that the language, "that the provisions of this contract are subject to modification by the United States, after public meetings and discussions with the Contractor," makes the contract offered to them a nullity, and so deprives Madera of its right to a renewal contract. We agree with Madera's legal proposition, that the government cannot reserve to itself an unlimited right to escape its contractual obligations "without rendering its promises illusory and the contract void." Torncello v. United States, 231 Ct. Cl. 20, 681 F.2d 756, 760 (Cl. Ct. 1982). Here, though, the reserved power to modify is limited. * * * The government, like any contracting party, can enter into a binding agreement subject to a qualified right of modification or other avoidance of obligations.

Both of the laws pursuant to which the government reserves rights under the proposed language are new. The National Environmental Policy Act and the Endangered Species Act were promulgated after the 1951 contract was executed, and represent policies subsequently adopted. Madera claims that its renewal rights cannot be burdened with these new policies. That proposition goes too far. The constitutionally permissible burden will depend on what the general policies may turn out to mean in application. * * *

HALL, CIRCUIT JUDGE, concurring.

I concur in parts I and III of the majority's opinion. As to the issues raised in part II, I concur in the result, but on the ground very ably set forth by the district court: The Appellants' right to purchase water from the government is subject to subsequent legislation affecting the exercise of that right.

" 'Sovereign power, even when unexercised, is an enduring presence that governs all contracts subject to the sovereign's jurisdiction, and will remain intact unless surrendered in unmistakable terms.' Therefore, contractual arrangements, including those to which a sovereign itself is party, 'remain subject to subsequent legislation' by the sovereign." Bowen v. Public Agencies Opposed to Social Security Entrapment, 477 U.S. 41, 52 (1986) (quoting Merrion v. Jicarilla Apache Tribe, 455 U.S. 130, 148, 147 (1982)). "Contracts should be construed, if possible, to avoid foreclosing exercise of sovereign authority." Id. at 52–53.

Appellants' asserted property right in the rates set in the 1951 Contract ultimately rests on the argument that by virtue of the 1939 and 1951 Contracts, Congress has surrendered its right to exercise its sovereign power to legislate and the executive's obligation to act in conformance with legislation. Examination of Appellants' contracts fails to disclose the requisite unequivocal surrender of sovereignty. Rather, the language of the contracts appears to reserve Congress' right to exercise its sovereign power. Both provide that they are executed pursuant to the 1902 Federal Reclamation Act and all acts amendatory or supplementary thereto. The 1939 Contract explicitly recognizes that the Appellants' right to purchase water is subject to both congressional action and implementation by regulation.

Appellants point to language in the 1951 Contract providing that the Secretary may set the water rates annually "but *in no event* shall the rates so announced be in excess" of $3.50 and $1.50 per acre-foot for Class One and Class Two water, respectively. This language is insufficient to unmistakably surrender Congress' right to legislate. It is doubtful that the Secretary of the Interior could, by contract, waive the right of Congress to pass laws; but in any case, it does not appear that such a waiver was even contemplated. As stated above, the contracts were made pursuant to the Reclamation Act and statutes amending or supplementing the Act by their own terms. * * * Assuming for the moment that the reference to water rates in the 1951 Contract is even applicable to the imposition of operation and maintenance costs, in this context, the words "in no event" may be interpreted to mean "in no event under the current legislative regime" or "in no event unless Congress legislates otherwise" would the Secretary adjust cost-sharing arrangements. * * * Even if the contracts did not explicitly acknowledge that they were subordinate to statute, the doctrine of reserved sovereign power would compel the same conclusion. The language of the contracts does not unequivocally surrender congressional power to charge the district for the actual cost of operating and maintaining the Madera Canal.

Notes and Questions

1. If the Bureau of Reclamation had been a private water company, how do you believe the court would have ruled in *Madera Irrigation District*? Should the federal government be held to a different standard of contractual compliance than private parties?

2. Does Judge Hall suggest a different legal standard than the majority? How do the standards differ? Which standard would you adopt?

3. Federal courts to date have consistently upheld efforts by the federal government to reform the federal reclamation program, employing both a liberal interpretation of the contracts at issue and the rule that sovereign authority must be surrendered "in unmistakable terms." In Peterson v. United States Dept. of Interior, 899 F.2d 799 (9th Cir. 1990), for example, the Ninth Circuit upheld the "hammer clause" of the Reclamation Reform Act of 1982 requiring farmers in districts that do not amend their contracts to pay "full cost" for water delivered to all acres, owned or leased, in excess of 160 acres. See p. 776 supra. The Ninth Circuit concluded that the plaintiffs did not have a constitutionally protected right to delivery of water at the subsidized contract price for lands leased in excess of 160 acres. The contracts did not "expressly authorize the delivery of water to leased tracts" and prohibited deliveries to more than 160 acres of owned land. According to the court, moreover, "governmental contracts should be interpreted against the backdrop of the legislative scheme that authorized them":

> [T]he implied right asserted here clearly violates the spirit, if not the letter, of the reclamation laws which authorized such contracts. The reclamation projects were funded by the federal government with the express intent that the subsidized water be used to promote the development of family farms. * * * The fact that the Department of the Interior * * * turned a blind eye to the practice

of large-scale leasing does not lessen the importance of these restrictions to the congressional scheme. * * * To find a vested contract right with these facts, we believe, would seriously impair Congress's sovereign power to pass laws for the public welfare.

Id. at 810–11. The Court also emphasized that the contracts contained no language "that can be construed as a 'surrender in unmistakable terms' of the sovereign's ability to regulate the quantity of subsidized water that may be provided to leased farm lands." Id. at 812 (quoting Bowen v. Public Agencies Opposed to Social Security Entrapment, 477 U.S. 41, 52 (1986)). See also Barcellos & Wolfsen, Inc. v. Westlands Water Dist., 899 F.2d 814 (9th Cir. 1990) (upholding a separate pricing provision of the Reclamation Reform Act).

4. *Peterson* was a relatively easy case because the farmers arguably had never been entitled to receive subsidized reclamation water for their excess acreage. Could the federal government insist on a higher price for the water legitimately delivered to the first 160 acres of land? Does a contract setting a particular water rate "surrender in unmistakable terms" the federal government's ability to decide later that reclamation subsidies are problematic and should be eliminated? How would the majority in *Madera Irrigation District* resolve the question? The concurrence? If changing the price itself would be unconstitutional, could the government impose an "environmental surcharge" on each acre-foot of water delivered, to be used to pay for restoration of habitat damaged by the reclamation project?

5. Can reclamation water users complain if the government retroactively changes a policy set out in a federal regulation? No, according to the federal Court of Appeals in Barcellos & Wolfsen, Inc. v. Westlands Water Dist., 899 F.2d 814 (9th Cir. 1990). "A legislature may repeal a statute that created non-contractual expectations as long as there is a rational basis for repeal. It follows *a fortiori* that a repeal of regulations under that statute is subject to no greater judicial scrutiny." Id. at 825 (emphasis in original).

6. Can states and local governments constitutionally restrict water deliveries for which water districts have contracted? In 1978, the California Water Resources Control Board ordered the CVP to reduce its diversions in order to protect the water quality of California's Sacramento–San Joaquin Delta. In United States v. State Water Resources Control Board, 182 Cal.App.3d 82, 227 Cal.Rptr. 161 (1986), supra p. 632, water districts that had contracted with the CVP for water argued that the Board's order was an unconstitutional impairment of the districts' contracts with the Bureau of Reclamation because it would result in a cutback in water deliveries. See U.S. Const. art. I, § 10 ("No State shall * * * pass any * * * Law impairing the Obligation of Contracts"). The California Court of Appeal disagreed:

> Our threshold inquiry is whether a substantial impairment of contractual rights is factually demonstrated. * * * In determining the extent of impairment, the court may consider a variety of factors, including whether the industry has been so regulated in the past that the contractor has notice that further state restrictions apply. * * * Nor is every impairment constitutionally proscribed. Contract rights, like other property rights, may be altered by the

exercise of the state's inherent police power to safeguard the public welfare. * * *

Here * * * no substantial impairment appears. * * * The CVP's appropriated water rights are, by definition, conditional— subject to the continuing supervisory authority of the Board, the constitutional limitation of reasonable use, and the priorities of senior right holders. * * * Even were we, arguendo, to find the impairment substantial, we think the Board's action was justified as a valid exercise of the state police power. * * * [T]he Board unques- tionably was performing a legitimate public purpose.

227 Cal.Rptr. at 198–200.

7. The plaintiffs in *Madera* argued that the federal government had violated their "Fifth Amendment property rights" by modifying the contract terms. Why was *Madera* decided as a takings case rather than a straight- forward contract dispute? The following case addresses that question, as well as examines the degree to which the federal government, without violating the rights of reclamation users, can reduce water deliveries pursuant to the Endangered Species Act or other efforts to increase instream flows for environmental purposes. You encountered the case previously in Chapter 6 at p. 660, where the court expressly disagreed with the *Tulare Lake* decision. In the excerpts that follow, the court considers both what legal rights reclamation users hold and how they affect the government's ability to reduce water deliveries for environmental purposes.

KLAMATH IRRIGATION DISTRICT
v. UNITED STATES

United States Court of Federal Claims, 2005.
67 Fed. Cl. 504.

ALLEGRA, Judge.

What is property? The derivation of the word is simple enough, arising from the Latin *proprietas* or "ownership," in turn stemming from *proprius*, meaning "own" or "proper." But, this etymology reveals little. Philosophers such as Aristotle, Cicero, Seneca, Grotius, Pufendorf and Locke each, in turn, have debated the meaning of this term, as later did legal luminaries such as Blackstone, Madison and Holmes, and even economists such as Coase.

Here, the court must give practical meaning to the term "property" as used in a specific legal context, a constitutional one, *to wit*, the Fifth Amendment's mandate "nor shall private property be taken for public use, without just compensation." In the case *sub judice*, a group of water districts and individual farmers seek just compensation under the Fifth Amendment, as well as damages for breach of contract, owing to tempo- rary reductions made in 2001 by the Department of Interior's Bureau of Reclamation (the Bureau) on the use, for irrigation purposes, of the water resources of the Klamath Basin of southern Oregon and northern California. At issue in the pending cross-motions for partial summary judgment is whether plaintiffs' various interests in the use of Klamath

River Basin water constitute cognizable property interests for purposes of the Takings Clause. Relatedly, the court must consider the limitations, if any, inherent in such interests, particularly regarding various forms of contract rights possessed by the plaintiffs to receive water from the Klamath Basin reclamation project. As will be seen, it is ultimately these contract rights, and not any independent interests in the relevant waters, that dominate the analysis here.

Plaintiffs—13 agricultural landowners and 14 water, drainage or irrigation districts in the Klamath River Basin area of Oregon and northern California—all receive, directly or indirectly, water from irrigation works constructed or operated by the Bureau. They trace their alleged interests in that water to a variety of sources, including federal reclamation law, general state water law principles, water-delivery contracts between the irrigation districts and the United States, deeds to real property purporting to convey a right to receive water, and a federal-state water law compact. The landowning plaintiffs seek just compensation both as beneficiaries of the district plaintiffs' contracts with the United States and as owners of what they describe as "Klamath Project water rights" that exist independently of the district contracts. The districts, in turn, seek breach of contract damages, as well as just compensation on behalf of their members, who are the beneficiaries of the district contracts and the persons ultimately harmed by the Bureau's reduction in water deliveries in 2001.

* * * Of the 13 districts that have water delivery contracts with the Bureau, eight include provisions holding the United States harmless for "any damage, direct or indirect," resulting "on account of drought or other causes" of "a shortage in the quantity of water available" from Project sources. Some of those provisions also require the United States to "use all reasonable means to guard against such shortages." Four other districts' contracts include a similar provision stating that "the United States shall not be liable for failure to supply water under this contract caused by . . . unusual drought." The contract for plaintiff Van Brimmer Ditch Company includes no such shortage provision.

* * * [T]he issues whether and, if so, to what extent, the plaintiff-irrigators possess property rights in the waters of the Klamath Basin require the court to look at three possible sources for such rights: Federal law, apart from the Constitution; Oregon, and to the extent relevant, California, law; and, potentially, contract law, looking at whether the farmers acquired rights from a third party. The court will consider these potential sources, and the parties' conflicting arguments with respect thereto, *seriatim*.

Federal Reclamation Law

Plaintiffs' banner assertion is that their property interests in the Klamath water spring from the Reclamation Act of 1902. Their view is bottomed on section 8 of that Act, which provides, in pertinent part:

Nothing in this Act shall be construed as affecting or intended to affect or to in any way interfere with the laws of any State or Territory relating to the control, appropriation, use, or distribution of water used in irrigation * * * and the Secretary of the Interior, in carrying out the provisions of this Act, shall proceed in conformity with such laws * * *; Provided, *That the right to use of water acquired under the provisions of this Act shall be appurtenant to the land irrigated, and beneficial use shall be the basis, the measure, and the limit of the right.*

43 U.S.C. §§ 372, 383 (2000) (emphasis added). Focusing on the highlighted language, the irrigators asseverate that because they own the irrigated land that is appurtenant to the water in question, the statute confers upon them a property interest in that water. Thus, they contend, their interests in the water derive directly from Federal law, rather than the law of Oregon or California. There are sundry reasons, however, why this contention is rootless.

To begin with, there is the statutory language. On its face, section 8 requires the Secretary, in carrying out his responsibilities under the Reclamation Act, to "proceed in conformity with" state laws relating to the "control, appropriation, use, or distribution of water." * * * Nothing in this language suggests that third parties, including irrigators, could obtain title to appropriative water rights at Bureau projects other than through state law. Indeed, while the Reclamation Act indicates that the right to the use of certain water "shall be appurtenant to the land irrigated," this language refers only to water "acquired under the provisions of this Act," which "provisions" require the claimant to obtain those rights in accordance with state law. Accordingly, the Reclamation Act does not, as plaintiffs intimate, independently define who owns interests in the water of Bureau projects, including the Klamath Basin. To the contrary, that question is controlled by state law, in this case, that of Oregon, or perhaps, California.

This reading of the statute is confirmed by extensive legislative history. * * * Opponents of what would become the Reclamation Act espoused the view that, if the Federal government was to build and operate the projects, it should control the appropriation and distribution of the water. Supporters, however, retorted that this control should reside in the Western States, each of which, by this time, had regimes for dealing with water rights. They noted that the creation of a Federal regime for establishing water rights would inevitably compete with the preexisting state regimes, threatening a life-blood issue for the arid states and leading potentially to unintended results. * * *

State Law

[In 1905, Oregon passed legislation permitting an appropriate federal official to file with the State Engineer "a written notice that the United States intends to utilize certain specified waters * * * unappropriated at the time of the filing." The filing of such a notice would result in those waters being "deemed to have been appropriated by the United States" and "not * * * subject to further appropriation" under state law.] * * *

In February of 1905, the Congress authorized the development of the Klamath Irrigation Project. Pursuant to that legislation, on May 17, 1905, the United States filed a notice of intention to appropriate Klamath River water. * * * Every indication is that the May 1905 notice triggered the provisions of the 1905 Oregon legislation, thereby vesting in the United States, as of that time, the appropriative water rights associated with the Klamath project that were unappropriated as of the date of the filing. This conclusion is confirmed by In re Waters of the Umatilla River, 88 Ore. 376, 168 P. 922, 925 (Or. 1917), in which the Oregon Supreme Court held that, under the 1905 legislation, a similar notice by the United States "vested the United States with title to all the then unappropriated water of the Umatilla River." * * *

The 1909 Oregon Water Rights Act established a procedure under which persons could obtain a certificate to divert and use water for specified purposes. The water rights created under this law were generally characterized by a priority date, an authorized point of diversion, an authorized rate of diversion, a place of use, purpose of use, season of use and a "duty" expressed in acre-feet per acre. But, these provisions did not apply to the Klamath Project water, given the 1905 Oregon law's admonition that "no adverse claim to the use of the water required in connection with such plans shall be acquired under the laws of this state except as for such amount of said waters described in such notice as may be formally released in writing by an officer of the United States thereunto duly authorized which release shall also be filed in the office of the state engineer." Instead, it appears that whatever interests were obtained by the plaintiffs after 1905 were obtained—necessarily so— directly from the United States, as the Klamath Project was constructed. * * *

Interests Based on Contracts

* * * It is, of course, well-established that "rights against the United States arising out of a contract with it are protected by the Fifth Amendment." Lynch v. United States, 292 U.S. 571, 579 (1934). Nonetheless, the Federal Circuit "has cautioned against commingling takings compensation and contract damages." Hughes Communications Galaxy, Inc. v. United States, 271 F.3d 1060, 1070 (Fed. Cir. 2001). In *Hughes*, the plaintiff asserted that NASA's breach of a contract to launch its satellites amounted to a takings, entitling it to prejudgment interest. The Federal Circuit rejected this claim, reasoning—

> If, as Hughes, asserts, the Government's breach of the [contract] was a taking under the Fifth Amendment, then nearly all Government contract breaches would give rise to compensation under the Fifth Amendment. * * * Indeed, "the concept of taking as a compensable claim theory has limited application to

the relative rights of party litigants when those rights have been voluntarily created by contract. In such instances, interference with such contractual rights generally gives rise to a breach claim not a taking claim." * * * Taking claims rarely arise under government contracts because the Government acts in its commercial or proprietary capacity in entering contracts, rather than in its sovereign capacity. * * * Accordingly, remedies arise from the contracts themselves, rather than from the constitutional protection of private property rights. * * *

Hughes, 271 F.3d at 1070 (quoting Sun Oil Co. v. United States, 572 F.2d 786, 818, 215 Ct. Cl. 716 (Ct. Cl. 1978)). These principles have been applied by the Federal Circuit and this court in rejecting a wide range of Fifth Amendment takings claims deriving from the alleged interference with contract rights. See J.J. Henry Co. v. United States, 411 F.2d 1246, 1249, 188 Ct. Cl. 39 (Ct. Cl. 1969); Detroit Edison Co. v. United States, 56 Fed. Cl. 299, 303 (2003) (noting that it is inappropriate to permit a plaintiff "to pursue a takings remedy in order to circumvent the limitations inherent in its contractual relationship with the Government"); Home Sav. of Am., F.S.B. v. United States, 51 Fed. Cl. 487, 494 (2002) (same).

In the *Winstar* context, the refusal to invoke takings principles has been explained as directly resulting from the availability of contract remedies. As Justice Scalia wrote in his concurrence in *Winstar*, "virtually *every* contract operates, not as a guarantee of particular future conduct, but as an assumption of liability in the event of nonperformance: 'The duty to keep a contract at common law means a prediction that you must pay damages if you do not keep it—and nothing else.'" United States v. Winstar Corp., 518 U.S. 839, 919 (1996) (Scalia, J., concurring) (citations omitted) (emphasis in original). More recently, in Castle v. United States, 301 F.3d 1328 (Fed. Cir. 2002), the Federal Circuit opined that "despite breaching the contract, the government did not take the plaintiffs' property because they retained 'the range of remedies associated with the vindication of a contract.'" Id. at 1342 (quoting Castle v. United States, 48 Fed. Cl. 187, 219 (2000)). * * * Under this approach, the availability of contract remedies is sufficient to vitiate a takings claim, even if it ultimately is determined that no breach occurred.

Both of the rationales favoring the use of contractual remedies over takings remedies apply here—that is, the United States may be viewed as acting in its proprietary capacity in entering into the water contracts in question, and it appears that the affected plaintiffs retain the full range of remedies with which to vindicate their contract rights. It follows that while the contracts between the districts and the United States, as well as that between Van Brimmer and the United States, gave rise to private property rights within the meaning of the Fifth Amendment, the proper remedy for the alleged infringement lies in a contract claim, not one for a takings. * * *

The foregoing analysis, of course, applies to the individual irrigators only to the extent that they actually have contract claims against the United States. For that to be true, "there must be privity of contract between the plaintiff and the United States." Chancellor Manor v. United States, 331 F.3d 891, 899 (Fed. Cir. 2003). Such privity would exist if the irrigators are properly viewed as third-party beneficiaries to the district contracts. * * * A review of the relevant district contracts reveals that they each express the intent of the relevant district and the United States to benefit the irrigators directly by having the district assume the primary responsibility for providing water within the district in exchange for collecting amounts owed by the irrigator in payment for their water. * * *

Accordingly, the court must conclude that the individual irrigators here are third-party beneficiaries of the district contracts. Because of this, their claims against the United States also sound in contract, not in takings. This result makes particular sense in the context of this case, in which, from a contracts perspective, the irrigators claiming interests based upon their contracts with the districts cannot possibly have rights to water that exceed the limitations found in the contracts between those districts and the United States. Simply put, plaintiffs could not obtain an interest from the districts better than what the districts themselves possessed or once possessed—"*nemo dat qui non habet*," the venerable maxim provides, "one who does not have cannot give." Indeed, while "rights that arise independently from the contract may be brought through a takings action," Allegre Villa v. United States, 60 Fed. Cl. 11, 18 (2004), such is not the case as to the third-party beneficiaries here. Rather, even to the extent that they may claim that there was a taking of their contract rights *vis a vis* the districts, it remains that those rights are entirely subsumed within the contract claim based on the alleged breach, by the United States, of the district contracts. * * * As such, the irrigators qualifying as third-party beneficiaries must proceed in contract.

So where does this leave us? Before this case was reassigned, briefing was stayed on the ultimate issue whether the Bureau breached the district contracts in question in 2001. Accordingly, that issue must await another day. But, based upon arguments fully briefed by the parties, several observations regarding the nature of the contract rights at issue are appropriate.

First, for most of the district contracts *sub judice*, plaintiffs' "beneficial interest" in the Klamath Project water is not, as they claim, an absolute right, limited only by appurtenancy and beneficial use. This is particularly true as to those contracts which provide, either in exact or similar terms, that the government shall not be liable for "water shortages" resulting from "drought or other causes." The plain language of these provisions expressly absolves the United States from liability for all types of water shortages—not only the hydrologic causes, as claimed by plaintiffs, but also any other cause that impacts the availability of water through the system. See Barcellos & Wolfsen v. Westlands Water

Dist., 849 F. Supp. 717, 723–24 (E.D. Cal. 1993) ("The express language of [the shortage clause] negates any absolute contract right in Movants to the unqualified delivery of irrigation water."); Brian Gray, "The Property Right in Water," 9 Hastings W.—Nw. J. Envtl. L. & Pol'y 1, 26 (2002) ("The Klamath Project water contracts * * * expressly absolve the United States of liability for all types of water shortages—hydrologic, regulatory, or hybrid—that may occur within the system."). From a contractual standpoint, the shortage clauses thus limit plaintiffs contractual rights and thus become the focus of whether a breach occurred when water deliveries were strictly limited in 2001.

Notably, various courts have construed similar water shortage clauses as protecting the United States from damages based upon the enforcement of the ESA. In O'Neill v. United States, 50 F.3d 677, 682–84 (9th Cir. 1995), for example, the Ninth Circuit held that the terms of the water delivery contract did not obligate the Bureau to deliver the full contractual amount of water if such delivery would not be consistent with the ESA and a second statute, the Central Valley Project Improvement Act. In terms reminiscent of several of the district contracts here, Article 11(a) of the water service contract at issue provided that the government would not be held liable for "any damage, direct or indirect, arising from a shortage on account of errors in operation, drought, or any other causes." The Ninth Circuit concluded that this language absolved the Bureau of any liability for complying with the Congressional mandates, observing that—

> The terms of Article 11(a) admit of one meaning and are internally consistent. On its face, Article 11 (a) unambiguously disclaims any liability for damages in the event the United States is unable to supply water in times of shortage. Clearly captioned "United States Not Liable for Water Shortage," Article 11 explicitly recognizes that "there may occur at times during any year a shortage in the quantity of water available for furnishing to the District" and provides that "in no event shall any liability accrue against the United States * * * for any damages * * * arising from a shortage on account of errors in operation, drought, *or any other causes*." * * * As the district court duly noted, there are no enumerated exceptions to this provision * * *

Id. at 683 (emphasis in original). The court concluded that "the contract's liability limitation is unambiguous and that an unavailability of water resulting from the mandates of valid legislation constitutes a shortage by reason of 'any other causes.' " Id. at 684. * * *

Second, even as to the contracts that do not contain broad water shortage clauses, it is at least arguable that any reductions ordered by the Bureau here did not result in a breach under the so-called sovereign acts doctrine. This doctrine recognizes that "the Government-as-sovereign must remain free to exercise its powers," Yankee Atomic Elec. Co.

v. United States, 112 F.3d 1569, 1575 (Fed. Cir. 1997), and shields the United States from contract liability based upon its "public and general acts as a sovereign," Horowitz v. United States, 267 U.S. 458, 461 (1925). The Federal Circuit has indicated that determining whether the government, in passing legislation, is acting as a contractor or a sovereign, requires "a case-specific inquiry that focuses on the scope of the legislation in an effort to determine whether, on balance, that legislation was designed to target prior governmental contracts." *Yankee Atomic*, 112 F.3d at 1575. An act of government will be considered to be sovereign so long as its impact on a contract is "merely incidental to the accomplishment of a broader governmental objective." *Winstar*, 518 U.S. at 898. But, such an act will not be held to be "public and general if it has the substantial effect of releasing the Government from its contractual obligations." *Id*. at 899.

Several courts have concluded that the enactment and subsequent enforcement of the ESA should be viewed as sovereign acts that override the Bureau's obligations to provide water under various contracts. See, e.g., Klamath Water Users Protective Ass'n v. Patterson, 204 F.3d 1206, 1213 (2000) (noting "it is well settled that contractual arrangements can be altered by subsequent Congressional legislation"); see also Madera Irr. Dist. v. Hancock, 985 F.2d 1397, 1406–07 (9th Cir. 1993) (Hall, J., concurring). Other cases in this court have likewise held that the suspensions of contracts under the ESA qualify as "public and general acts." See, e.g., Precision Pine & Timber, Inc. v. United States, 50 Fed. Cl. 35, 72–73 (2001) (suspension of timber sales contracts under the ESA); Croman Corp. v. United States, 44 Fed. Cl. 796, 806–07 (1999) (same), withdrawn in part, 49 Fed. Cl. 776, 782–84 (2001). While these cases suggest that plaintiffs face an uphill battle in showing that the ESA was designed to abrogate their various contracts, that issue, as well as other aspects of the applicability of the sovereign acts doctrine, have not been adequately briefed and, in the court's view, should be decided only in the context of determining whether, in fact, a breach of the various water contracts here occurred in 2001. * * *

Conclusion

Concluding this *tour d'horizon*, the court is mindful that, despite the potential for contractual recovery here, this ruling may disappoint a number of individuals who have long invested effort and expense in developing their lands based upon the expectation that the waters of the Klamath Basin would continue to flow, uninterrupted, for irrigation. But, those expectations, no matter how understandable, do not give those landowners any more property rights as against the United States, and the application of the Endangered Species Act, than they actually obtained and possess. Like it or not, water rights, though undeniably precious, are subject to the same rules that govern all forms of property—they enjoy no elevated or more protected status. In the case *sub judice*, those rights, such as they exist, take the form of contract claims and will be resolved as such.

Notes and Questions

1. Is *Klamath Irrigation Dist.* consistent with *Strawberry Water Users Ass'n* (supra p. 763), *Ickes v. Fox* (supra p. 769), *Nebraska v. Wyoming* (supra p. 770), and *Nevada v. United States* (supra p. 770), all of which suggested that the United States held at best naked title to the water rights at issue in those cases and that the reclamation users were the beneficial owners of the water? Does the 1905 Oregon water legislation described in *Klamath Irrigation Dist.* distinguish those cases?

2. The question of whether the Bureau of Reclamation has the discretion to deliver less than the contractually agreed quantity of water has also arisen in cases challenging the ESA's applicability to the federal reclamation program. Natural Resources Defense Council v. Houston, 146 F.3d 1118 (9th Cir. 1998), for example, considered whether the bureau must consult with the federal Fish & Wildlife Service under the ESA before renewing reclamation contracts. Fourteen contracts in the CVP had expired, and the government renewed them without engaging in an ESA consultation. Several of the districts defended the renewals on the ground that "the Bureau had no discretion to alter the terms of the renewal contracts, particularly the quantity of water delivered," and thus did not need to consult. The Ninth Circuit Court of Appeals agreed that "[w]here there is no agency discretion to act, the ESA does not apply." Id. at 1125–26, citing Sierra Club v. Babbitt, 65 F.3d 1502, 1509 (9th Cir. 1995). But the court concluded that the Bureau enjoyed some discretion to reduce the amount of water available for delivery, as well as "alter other key terms in the contract," and therefore voided the contract. Id. at 1126. See also Rio Grande Silvery Minnow v. Keys, 333 F.3d 1109, 1133–34 (10th Cir. 2003).

D. WATER ORGANIZATIONS AND SOCIETY

Two social historians have considered the societal implications of water organizations. In the 1950s, Karl Wittfogel studied the large irrigation organizations of pre-industrial China and saw in them both a severe danger to individualism and the precursors of twentieth-century totalitarian governments. Karl Wittfogel, Oriental Despotism (1957). Wittfogel warned that "hydraulic societies" can evolve into two classes of citizens—decisionmakers and those affected by the decisions—with the latter stripped of an effective voice in societal management. To Wittfogel, redemption lay only in a strong system of private property.

More recently, Donald Worster, a history professor at the University of Kansas, has studied the history of irrigation in the western United States and come to a similar, but less libertarian and ethnocentric conclusion.

DONALD WORSTER,
RIVERS OF EMPIRE: WATER, ARIDITY,
AND THE GROWTH OF THE AMERICAN WEST

332–34 (1985).

One of the most compelling intuitions of the last few decades has been that the unprecedented environmental destructiveness of our time is largely the result of * * * big organizations * * *. Whatever they may accomplish in the manufacture of wealth, they are innately anti-ecological. Immense centralized institutions, with complicated hierarchies, they tend to impose their outlook and their demands on nature, as they do on the individual and the small human community, and they do so with great destructiveness. They are too insulated from the results of their actions to learn, to adjust, to harmonize. That is another way of saying that a social condition of diffused power is more likely to be ecologically sensitive and preserving. In contrast to the big organization, whether it be a state or corporation, the small community simply cannot afford massive intervention in the environment. Moreover, it lacks the technical hubris common to concentrated power. When it does undertake to make use of an entity like a river, that effort is more easily undone if it goes awry, and the damage is more readily perceived and repaired. * * *

In the years to come, practical men and women looking to create a new West along these lines might reexamine the social and environmental ideals of John Wesley Powell, distilling out of them their democratic essence. He proposed * * * a West divided into hundreds of watershed-defined communities. Each of them was to be left responsible for its own development and for the conservation of its own lands and waters, reaching from streambeds to the natural divides separating one community from another. Much of that territory was to be owned in common and managed for the public good. Power was to be seated within and limited to the boundaries of the communities. They would have to generate much of their own capital, through their own labor, just as the Mormons initially did in Utah. They would have to use their own heads instead of those of outside experts, though science and technology might, if carefully controlled and kept open to popular participation, be put to their service. * * * The resulting communities, relying on their own capital and their own knowledge, could free themselves from the distant, impersonal structures of power that have made democracy little more than a ritual of ratifying choices already made by others—of acquiescing in what has been done to us. * * *

Redesigning the West as a network of more or less discrete, self-contained watershed settlements would have another environmental benefit. It would train the widest possible number of people in the daily task of understanding and adapting to their ecological conditions. They would not be able to turn the job over to a federal agency. They would be forced to restrain their lives more closely within the limits of their immediate world, and those limits would be starkly before them, impossible to ignore or evade. * * * By and large, [this] has not been a road taken by Americans. Instead, we have tried constantly to evade the discipline of nature * * * by drawing on distant sources of commodities when we exhausted local supplies, and by calling on a federal agency for help when we got in trouble. A West organized more along Powell's lines would make all those options less available, leading to a more ecologically conscious people.

Notes and Questions

1.   From your short study of water organizations, do either Wittfogel's or Worster's image of large-scale water organizations ring true? If so, what should be done? At this late date, can the West do much other than tinker with the structure that it has created? Is Worster's proposal of hundreds of watershed-defined communities, along the lines first proposed by John Wesley Powell, at all realistic? For a practical consideration of how the West might move today toward Powell's vision for a "dryland democracy," see Janet C. Neuman, Dusting Off the Blueprint for a Dryland Democracy: Incorporating Watershed Integrity and Water Availability Into Land Use Decisions, in Wet Growth: Should Water Law Control Land Use? 171 (Craig Anthony (Tony) Arnold ed., 2005).

2.   To the extent that organizations have led to the overdevelopment and overuse of water, are the governmental powers and subsidies enjoyed by many public water agencies the major cause? What might the West look like today if public water districts and the federal Bureau of Reclamation had never existed?

Chapter 8

WATER AS A REGIONAL AND SHARED RESOURCE

A. THE COLORADO RIVER

The story of the Colorado River is *the* great epic of water law and politics in America.[1] It implicates virtually every aspect of western water law in one way or another: not only the division of the river among the Colorado basin states, but Indian water rights, water marketing in California, pollution control, groundwater legislation in Arizona, Denver's water supply, the federal reclamation program, dam operation and dealing with drought. Though an interstate compact divided the river more than 80 years ago, and a monumental Supreme Court opinion determined the relative rights of the states of the lower basin in 1963, in addition to much other legislation and litigation, intense controversy over the river continues.[2]

Legal issues involving the Colorado are numerous and enormously complex, partly because something called "The Law of the River", rather than (or in addition to) ordinary water law, governs it. This "Law" consists of an intricate melange of interstate compacts, federal statutes, regulations, court decisions, contracts, and state law.[3] Mastering these matters is virtually a lifetime commitment, and it is not your responsibil-

---

1. Much of the historical description that follows is based on Norris Hundley, The West Against Itself: The Colorado River—An Institutional History, in New Courses for the Colorado River: Major Issues for the Next Century 9 (Gary Weatherford & F. Lee Brown eds., 1986). Professor Hundley is the leading historian of the Colorado River. He is the author of Water and the West: The Colorado River Compact and the Politics of Water in the American West (1975) [hereinafter Water and the West]. The story is also told in Philip Fradkin, A River No More (1981).

2. For a play-by-play discussion of many contemporary issues, by the players themselves, see Water Education Foundation,

75th Anniversary Colorado River Compact Symposium Proceedings (1997).

3. A list of the major components of the law of the river (as well as a detailed bibliography of literature on the Colorado) appears in Dale Pontius, Colorado River Basin Study, reprinted in Report to the Western Water Policy Review Advisory Commission app. B (1998). Texts through 1978 are printed in two federal publications, Ray Lyman Wilbur & Northcutt Ely, The Hoover Dam Documents (1948) and Milton Nathanson, Updating the Hoover Dam Documents (1978). Unfortunately, there is no more recent updating volume.

ity here. But there are a few large issues with which you should be familiar, and with which you can usefully grapple based on the materials presented below. An effort to engage with these matters will give you at least a broad sense of Colorado River issues, and thereby of water law and politics on its grandest scale. Here are some of the major contemporary legal questions on the Colorado:

1.   Interbasin transfers. The River is divided into two basins, each of which has been allotted a share of the water. The Upper Division States (Wyoming, Colorado, Utah, and New Mexico) have developed more slowly than those of the Lower Division (Arizona, Nevada, and California), and still are not using their total allotment, while the Lower Division is fully using allotment, and could use much more. Can water be marketed from the Upper Basin to the Lower, and if so by whom (users, the states, Indian tribes)?[4]

2.   Intrabasin interstate transfers. Can water be marketed among the three lower division states? A Supreme Court decree (among other things) determines the allocation of water among those states and makes marketing or other voluntary redistribution arrangements complicated. The states–always worried about shortages and future needs–are reluctant to see water move beyond their borders, though there has been some Arizona-to-Nevada marketing.

3.   Intrastate transfers, essentially from agricultural irrigation to growing urban areas. Some such transfers have been consummated within California—most recently from the Imperial Irrigation District to San Diego—but they have presented extremely difficult problems (e.g. impact on endangered species in the transferor area, adverse impacts on the transferor community and whether its general public is entitled to some of the economic benefits from the sale). The transaction has also involved dispute over the price of carriage through the aqueduct (owned by the Met, which was not sympathetic to the transfer), and whether such transfers are governed by state law or federal law, or both.

4.   Managing the River. The Colorado is a very "managed" river, with some 60 million acre-feet of storage, primarily in the two largest federal reservoirs, Lake Mead and Lake Powell. How these facilities are operated affects how the risk of shortage is allocated between the basins. The more water that is held in Lake Powell, the more the risk of a shortage in the Lower Basin during periods of drought. Releases from Glen Canyon Dam are governed by the complex provision in § 602(a) of the 1968 Colorado River Basin Project Act (43 U.S.C. § 1552). Operation of the dams also involves trade-offs between water supply and power production (note the priorities in Article IV of the 1922 Compact and § 6 of the Boulder

4. The Upper Basin view (no interbasin marketing) has been extensively argued in James S. Lochhead, An Upper Basin Perspective on California's Claims to Water from the Colorado River Part I: The Law of the River, 4 U. Denv. Water L.Rev. 290 (2001).

Canyon Project Act), and how one decides whether (under the 1964 Supreme Court Decree) there is a normal amount to distribute (as set out in the allotments), a shortage, or a surplus in the Lower Basin. That determination each year specifies the amounts to which users are entitled. Different Lower Basin states may have very different views of the criteria that should be applied to determine surplus and shortage (e.g. Arizona's Central Arizona Project [CAP] would bear the brunt of a lower basin shortage under the statutory CAP-subordination law that made the CAP politically acceptable to California[5], while pre-Hoover–Dam agricultural users would be the last to feel the effects of a shortage).

5. The Mexican Treaty issue. Under a 1944 Treaty, the United States is obliged to provide Mexico specified amounts of water (Article 10(a)), with certain guarantees of quality under a subsequent international agreement known as Minute 242. One question that has spawned intense controversy is how responsibility for meeting the Mexican Treaty obligation is to be divided between the two basins under Article III(c) of the 1922 Compact. Since the Lower Basin is using more than 8.5 maf between its allotments from the mainstem and Arizona's diversions from the Yuma River, the Upper Basin has claimed there is "surplus" under Article III(c). Another unresolved question is how Mexico would be impacted by a shortage declaration in the Lower Basin (Treaty Art. 10(b)).

6. Environmental problems. All the allotments on the River were made in the pre-environmental era. Like the rest of the country, the Colorado River is affected by laws like the Endangered Species Act. The interplay among these matters and the "Law of the River", when combined with international U.S./Mexico overtones, is extraordinarily delicate. The United States takes no responsibility for protection of the environmentally important Mexican Delta at the mouth of the River, which gets significant flows only during years of great abundance when the United States spills excess water into Mexico. The amount delivered under the Treaty is effectively all consumed by users, primarily agriculture, in Mexico.

7. The status of lower basin tributaries (not included in the original allocations to the states between the basins or within them) has recently become a matter of intense controversy. Note the Supreme Court's observations about tributaries in its 1963 decision. One current controversy is whether water-short Southern Nevada can increase its use of the Colorado by taking some water from the tributary Virgin River that runs through Utah and Nevada. Would it make a difference whether it diverts the Virgin before it enters the Colorado mainstream; or could it wait and take the water from its Las Vegas intake in Lake Mead, still treating it as tributary water

---

5. The subordination provision appears in § 301(b) of the 1968 Colorado River Basin Project Act (43 U.S.C. § 1521(b)) which authorized construction of the Central Arizona Project.

and thus not counting against Nevada's mainstream allotment? The latter option, if lawful, would be much more economical than building infrastructure to carry water from the Virgin River overland to Las Vegas. Is this a question of federal law (The Law of the River), or simply a matter of Nevada law, assuming the State Engineer grants a permit to divert the Virgin out of Lake Mead?

8. Would California be entitled to an apportionment from the Virgin River if and when it is equitably apportioned, on the ground that it is a part of the Colorado River to which California is riparian?

There are numerous other unsettled issues that have been around for decades, including a variety of questions of Compact interpretation, still not settled after more than 80 years. For example, does the Compact divide the river between the two basins, or does the obligation in Article III(d) of the Compact give a superior position to the lower division states, so that in time of shortage the Upper Basin must continue to deliver its 75 maf per decade to the Lower Basin even if that means shutting down uses in the Upper Basin? Is the maximum obligation of the upper basin for the Mexican Treaty obligation .75 maf, or must it provide an additional amount to compensate for evaporation losses between the basin dividing line at Lee Ferry and the international border? Debate and disagreement goes on and on.

1. HISTORICAL BACKGROUND

The Colorado River rises in Western Colorado and wends its way for more than a thousand miles through the Southwest and Mexico until it empties into the Sea of Cortez. See Figure 8–1. It cuts through one of the least populated areas of the country and its flow is only a tiny fraction of the Mississippi's or the Columbia's; yet it is the sole dependable supply for more than 25 million people in nearly a quarter of a million square miles. The River has been a bloody battleground of states' rights feuding, but every major user—cities on the eastern slope of the Continental Divide in Colorado, urban Southern California, Las Vegas, Albuquerque, Phoenix and Tucson, and California's Imperial Valley—gets water as a result of major dam, reservoir and aqueduct projects built by the federal government.

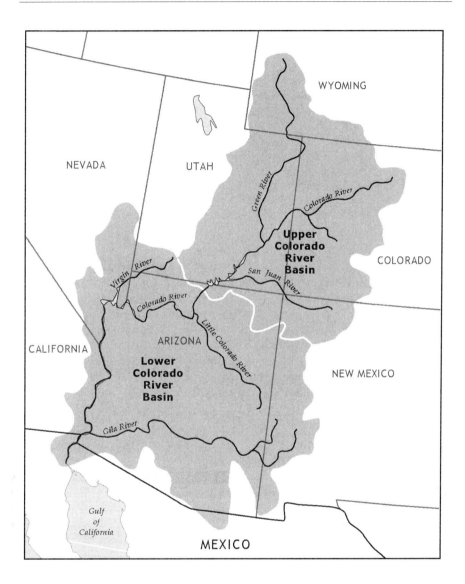

Figure 8–1
Colorado River Basin

The story begins around the turn of the twentieth century. Farmers in the 600,000 acre fertile but arid Imperial Valley of California and in Mexico just across the boundary began taking Colorado River water for irrigation through an old overflow channel located entirely in Mexico known as the Alamo Canal. Though the farmers were diverting the entire river, in the absence of dams and reservoirs to regulate flows there was often insufficient water in summertime even as early as 1914.

The Imperial Valley settlers were the first to go to the federal government for help in exploiting the Colorado River. They wanted an "All–American" canal located north of the border so that they wouldn't have to share the water with Mexican farmers. In addition, serious flooding problems—a 1905 flood had broken into the Valley and created the Salton Sea—meant that no canal would be sufficient without a dam on the mainstream to control flows. The prospect of a dam brought Los Angeles into the picture, which was at first interested in the River for its electricity-generating potential. A prolonged drought induced it to look to the Colorado for water as well, and it organized other Southern California communities into what is now the Metropolitan Water District ("MWD" or "Met") in order to lobby in Washington for a Colorado River dam and aqueduct. MWD interests were then compatible with those of the Imperial Valley, and together they comprised the first constituency for development of the lower basin.

At about the same time, the growing City of Denver was looking to trans-mountain diversion of the Colorado River for its future supply. It and others in the upper reaches of the river viewed California's interest in the Colorado with alarm, since California was the fastest-growing state. The assumption, fortified by the 1922 Supreme Court decision in Wyoming v. Colorado apportioning the Laramie River,[6] was that prior appropriation would determine rights in western interstate rivers. Colorado and the other mountain states in the upper basin were not ready to respond with equally large development projects of their own, so they proposed an interstate compact to allocate an entitlement in the River to each of the basin states.[7]

Compact negotiators were unable to devise a satisfactory formula for settling each state's claims, but they were able to divide the River between the upper and lower states. The dividing line was Lee Ferry in northern Arizona near the Utah boundary. Though New Mexico, Utah and Arizona are partly (to a small extent) in both basins, essentially the Compact divided the waters between a so-called Upper Division (Colorado, Utah, Wyoming and New Mexico) and a Lower Division (Arizona, California and Nevada). The River was to be divided by requiring the Upper Division states to assure a designated flow at Lee Ferry. We shall look at the (often confusing) provisions of the Compact presently. Based on records going back to 1899, it was assumed that the river would not on average produce less than 15 million acre feet (maf) per year at Lee Ferry,[8] and they seem to have thought the reliable flow was closer to 20 maf. Therefore the compact commission proposed to divide 15 maf between the two basins. Since yearly flows were variable, the Compact provided that the Upper Basin would deliver 75 maf over every ten year

6. 259 U.S. 419 (1922).

7. See Daniel Tyler, Delphus Emory Carpenter and the Colorado River Compact of 1922, 1 U. Den. Water L. Rev. 228 (1998).

8. Hundley, Water and the West, supra note 1, at 192. The Bureau of Reclamation had estimated an average flow of 16.4 maf/year. Even 15 maf has turned out to be too optimistic. The reliable flow is closer to 14 maf/year. See discussion of the Water Budget infra p. 811.

period. A question then arose about the relation of this allocation to tributaries below Lee Ferry. The Gila River produced nearly 3 maf/year. Arizona's representative said that if 7.5 maf/year was a total allocation of Colorado River system water to the Lower Basin, the Lower Basin might only be able to acquire a right to 4.5 maf of the River at Lee Ferry. The question whether Arizona would be able to keep all her own tributary water, and 7.5 maf/year was to be allocated in addition to the Lower Basin, was not clearly settled in the Compact. In order to assuage Arizona's concerns, a compromise was effected to give an additional 1 maf (clearly only a portion of the Gila River flow) to the Lower Basin.[9] That is the source of Article III(b) of the Compact.

The Compact addressed several matters in addition to quantitative allocation. Anticipating a possible treaty with Mexico, the compact provided that any allotment to Mexico should first come from surplus water and if that wasn't sufficient, then the two basins would share the burden equally. No specific provision was made for Indian tribes on the River. Article VII simply provided that "nothing in this compact shall be construed as affecting the obligations of the United States of America to Indian tribes."[10]

Every basin state but Arizona soon ratified the 1922 Colorado River Compact (Arizona ratified in 1944, following adoption of a Treaty with Mexico guaranteeing that nation 1.5 maf annually).[11] Arizona saw the Compact providing benefits to everyone but her: The Upper Basin allotment safeguarded those states from the prior appropriation rule, but—since the Compact made no intra-basin allotments—it did not protect Arizona from fast-growing California. Moreover, the Compact opened the way to federal legislation to build the Boulder Canyon dam that would permit urban southern California to construct an aqueduct and begin using Colorado River water. The All–American Canal would secure existing agricultural appropriations in California; and regulation of the River would make it possible for Mexico to take additional water, which Arizona feared would come from her Colorado River tributaries. Meanwhile bringing water from the River to central Arizona (the Phoenix–Tucson area) was seen as economically unfeasible since it would involve pumping water some 1,800 feet uphill.

Rather than accept a stand-off, the other six states decided to go forward with a compact that would bind them, assuming (correctly, as it turned out) that Arizona was in no position to take water out of the Colorado on her own without federal help. California was willing to go ahead so long as Congress promised to build the Boulder Canyon dam and the All–American Canal. The Upper Division states agreed to go along if California would limit her total appropriation, the idea being

9. Hundley, Water and the West, supra note 1, at 197–98.

10. See generally Reuel Olson, The Colorado River Compact (1926).

11. The Mexico–U.S. Water Treaty, 59 Stat. 1219 (1944). All the states except California—which feared that the Mexican share would come out of its existing uses, which were already in excess of 5 maf—favored the treaty. Apparently the other states felt that it was better to limit Mexico to existing uses, and an agreed-on amount, than to see its demands increase at the possible expense of the basin states.

that if a sufficient share of the Lower Basin allocation was left available for Arizona, she would not eventually come after the Upper Basin share. Southern Nevada was still largely unpopulated; Las Vegas' explosive growth would not begin until decades later, and there was nothing back then to suggest that anything like today's reality (population about 1.8 million) would ever come to pass.

The deal that was finally made in the Boulder Canyon Project Act of 1928[12] limited California to 4.4 maf plus one-half of any unallocated surplus. It then authorized the Boulder Canyon (Hoover) dam and the All–American Canal. By 1936 the dam provided electricity for southern California and by 1941 water was flowing toward the coast through the Colorado River Aqueduct. The Act also included a provision in which Congress gave its advance approval to a Lower Basin Compact that would allocate its 7.5 maf share as follows: 4.4 maf to California, 2.8 maf to Arizona and .3 maf to Nevada.[13] No such compact was ever made by the Lower Basin states. A major question the Supreme Court would have to settle was whether Arizona could keep all the water in her tributaries or whether that water would count toward the presence of a surplus. California counted on the tributaries to provide a surplus out of which she could take water additional to her basic 4.4 maf allotment.

Arizona was effectively left out in the cold, standing by to watch California grow. Neither state was satisfied with the allocation suggested in the Boulder Canyon Project Act, and so they were unable to agree on a compact. In 1930 Arizona decided, in the first of four original jurisdiction suits it was to bring against California,[14] to seek relief in the United States Supreme Court. For years, the Court declined to decide the case because, without an active project to bring Colorado River water to central Arizona, it had no controversy ripe for judicial solution. That was to remain the situation for nearly thirty more years as both California and Arizona grew, and Arizona pumped more and more of its groundwater. Finally, the Court took and decided the case in 1963. The ultimate decision was a stunning victory for Arizona. It got 2.8 maf, the amount Congress had "suggested" in the Boulder Canyon Project Act of 1928, and in addition it got all the water in the Gila River. The decision was also a great victory for the five tribes of the Colorado River Indian

---

12.   45 Stat. 1057, 43 U.S.C. § 617.

13.   Where did these numbers come from? Of the 7.5 maf supposedly available, first 300,000 was allocated to Nevada on the ground that there were only 100,000 acres of practicably irrigable acreage in the state. That (pre-Las Vegas) aspect of the division was not controversial. The question then was division of the remaining 7.2 maf between California and Arizona. Arizona demanded half the remainder (3.6 maf), but the upper basin governors at meetings in 1925 and 1927 determined that California already had perfected rights to use 600,000 af more than Arizona. Consequently, they subtracted 600,000 from Ari-

zona's claim of 3.6 maf, and recommended 3 maf to Arizona and 4.2 maf to California. Nonetheless, California held out for 4.6 maf, a measure of its anticipated needs. This was 400,000 af more than the governors had recommended. The Senate compromised, giving California one-half of the additional 400,000 af it sought over and above the original recommendation. So California got 4.2 maf plus 200,000 af, or 4.4 maf. See 70 Cong. Rec. 172, 175–76 (Dec. 6, 1928).

14.   Arizona v. California, 283 U.S. 423 (1931), 292 U.S. 341 (1934), 298 U.S. 558 (1936), 373 U.S. 546 (1963).

Reservations who were awarded nearly 1 maf (these were not all the tribes with claims on the Colorado River by any means) and for the federal government's reservations such as wildlife refuges. Those amounts came out of the allocations of the state in which the reservations were located.

The Court's decision finally opened the way for a project to bring water from the Colorado up to central Arizona, and in 1968 Congress authorized the Colorado River Basin Project Act to construct the Central Arizona Project (CAP).[15] To get California's acquiescence, the CAP was made subordinate to its 4.4 maf uses, and the Upper Basin was given a number of new reclamation projects (only some of which have been built). Now in place, and capable of delivering about 1.5 maf annually, the CAP—a $4.7 billion, highly subsidized public works project—is essentially a vast canal that takes water out of the Colorado at Lake Havasu, pumps it up a total of about 1800 feet to serve Phoenix, central Arizona towns, Indian Reservations and Tucson. Agricultural irrigators, for whose benefit CAP was originally proposed and promoted, have turned out to be unable to afford CAP water (which is more expensive than pumped groundwater). Arizona, eager to fully use its allotment, supplied CAP water to farmers at state-subsidized rates,[16] and takes some Colorado River water which it stores underground for future use. In recent years, through litigation and arrangements with the federal government to resolve tribal claims of Arizona Indians, the state has been successful in cutting back its economic costs for the CAP.

The Upper Basin had nothing like the conflict that divided Arizona and California. An Upper Colorado River Compact was rather easily negotiated in 1948. It allocated the basin's share among the states on a percentage basis, 51.75% to Colorado, 23% to Utah, 14% to Wyoming, 11.25% to New Mexico, and 50,000 acre-feet (the only specific amount) to Arizona for its Upper Basin share.[17] The allocations were based primarily on a calculation of present and potential needs, including Indian water needs.[18] Though Denver already had the federal Big Thompson transbasin diversion project, a compact was a practical prerequisite to congressional approval of additional Upper Basin projects. The major feature of the anticipated Upper Basin facilities was the Glen Canyon dam, a facility much-lamented by conservationists,[19] but which secured supplies in storage so the Upper Basin could meet its release obligations to the Lower Basin. Glen Canyon dam also serves as a hydropower revenue producer for the various Upper Basin dams that were authorized, such as Flaming Gorge on the Green River, Blue Mesa on the Gunnison and Navajo on the San Juan River.

15. 82 Stat. 885, 43 U.S.C. §§ 1501 et seq. See Pontius, supra note 3, at 33.

16. Any so-called unused apportionment is allocated by the Secretary of the Interior under § II(B)(6) of the Supreme Court's 1964 Decree, see infra p. 833.

17. 63 Stat. 31 (1949).

18. Hearings on the Upper Colorado River Basin Compact Before the House Comm. on Public Lands, Subcomm. on Irrigation & Reclamation, 81st Cong. 85–87, 113 (1949).

19. Eliot Porter, The Place No One Knew: Glen Canyon on the Colorado (David Brower ed., 1963).

Relations between the United States and Mexico present a distinct and fascinating saga that can only be briefly described here. The United States/Mexico boundary is almost 2,000 miles long, and mostly arid. The two nations share two major rivers, the Rio Grande and the Colorado, each of which is the subject of the same treaty that made possible cooperative dam building and river management that brought valuable benefits to both sides.[20] Unlike the upper Rio Grande and the Colorado, both of which are comprised almost exclusively of precipitation that falls on U.S. territory, about 70% of the flow of the lower Rio Grande comes from Mexican tributaries.

The 1944 treaty regarding the Colorado (59 Stat. 1219) guaranteed Mexico an annual quantity of 1.5 million acre-feet, although in the event of "extraordinary drought or serious accident to the irrigation system in the United States, thereby making it difficult" to deliver that amount, water allotted to Mexico "will be reduced in the same proportion as consumptive uses in the United States are reduced." The treaty also provides that in any year in which "as determined by the United States" * * * there exists a surplus of waters * * * in excess of the amount necessary to supply uses in the United States and the * * * 1,500,000 acre-feet * * * to Mexico, the United States undertakes to deliver to Mexico * * * additional waters of the Colorado River system to provide a total quantity not to exceed 1,700,000 acre-feet.[21] As noted above, Article III (c) of the 1922 Compact sets out the obligation of the two basins in meeting the (then anticipated) Mexican Treaty obligation. The treaty did not expressly address water quality, but serious quality problems came to the fore in the 1960's with a formal protest by the Mexican government. Those problems were caused by a federally built drain that funneled hypersaline waste from the Wellton Mohawk Irrigation District to the Colorado River just above the border. The problem eventually resulted in the negotiation of a "Minute" to the 1944 treaty that committed the United States to take various measures to protect the quality of the water delivered to Mexico, essentially keeping it within a percentage of the quality delivered in the lower reach of the river in the United States. Despite the heavy use of groundwater on both sides of the border, no general agreement between the two nations on the subject has been seriously attempted, but scholarly interest in the matter has produced a draft treaty.

2. RECENT DEVELOPMENTS: THE CALIFORNIA 4.4 PLAN AND THE QSA

For many years, relying on unused parts of Arizona's and Nevada's allocations, and a period of unusually high river flows, California had

20. The details of the Rio Grande Treaty of 1906 (dealing with waters of the River above Fort Quitman, Texas) and the Rio Grande (lower River), Colorado and Tijuana Treaty of 1944 are chronicled in Albert Utton, Mexican International Waters, in 5 Waters and Water Rights 99 (Robert Beck ed., repl. vol. 1998).

21. See Charles Meyers & Richard Noble, The Colorado River: The Treaty with Mexico, 19 Stan. L. Rev. 367, 415 (1967).

(lawfully, as surplus or unused apportionment) been taking about 5.2 maf, 800,000 af over its 4.4. maf allocation. As the CAP neared completion in the 1990's, and both Arizona and Nevada began taking nearly their entire allocations, pressures mounted to get California to reduce its Colorado River usage to its allocation. In the mid–90's, with the encouragement of the other basin states, Interior Secretary Bruce Babbitt proposed a multi-faceted California 4.4 Plan, designed simultaneously to resolve a number of California problems. The basic idea was to get the California agricultural agencies, which jointly held the great bulk of California's allocation (3.85 maf out of 4.4 maf), to market some of its Colorado River entitlement to urban southern California, which had been relying on the excess water California had been using. In effect urban users would pay farmers to improve the efficiency of their irrigation operations, plus an incentive bonus, and get the saved water, thus reducing the state's total demand on the Colorado.

The plan had numerous elements, and it seemed like a win-win for everyone involved. San Diego, which did not like being so reliant on the Met which supplied it, and in which it had junior rights, wanted its own water supply, and was eager to buy water from agriculture. As discussed in Chapter 7, supra pp. 731–734, San Diego therefore signed an agreement with the Imperial Irrigation District (IID) in 1998 to get up to 200,000 af/year for up to 75 years. The four California agricultural district users had priorities among themselves, but did not have fixed amounts or shares of the 3.85 maf. The Coachella Valley Water District, junior to IID, was vulnerable to be cut off if IID used too much water, and for years had accused IID of waste (see supra p. 176). IID was eager to avoid litigation over claims it was wasting water, and also needed to have its rights quantified so it knew what it had to sell. That would also resolve its continuing conflicts with Coachella, and some additional water would come to Coachella to deal with its groundwater overdraft problem. Babbitt's plan also insisted that a longstanding demand for water by the San Luis Rey California Indians be settled by the deal. Some additional water would also be obtained by lining the leaky All–American Canal. To give California time to get the transfers in place, the other basin states were agreeable to the Secretary declaring regular surpluses to be available for about 15 years (under what are known Interim Surplus Guidelines)[22], allowing delivery of more than 4.4 maf, so that California could gradually step down to a total usage of 4.4 maf, which was what all the other basin states eagerly desired.[23] A document known as the Quantification Settlement Agreement (QSA) was the basic instrument to put all these deals in place. One might have thought it would all happen without a hitch.

However, it turned out that the water IID was assertedly wasting, indicated by its huge drainage into the Salton Sea, and that it would

22. 66 Fed.Reg. 7772–82 (Jan. 25, 2001).

23. The IID/San Diego deal accounted for only a fraction of the substitution California will ultimately have to make to get down to 4.4 maf.

save—and thus be able to sell—by efficiency fixes, was nourishing endangered species listed under both state and federal law,[24] and that some of the drainage water would have to continue to flow into the Sea to keep it from becoming hypersaline. IID began to hesitate for several reasons. It was concerned about its potential endangered species liability (state legislation ultimately was enacted to establish a Salton Sea Restoration Fund);[25] and there was reluctance to generate the water for marketing by taking land out of production (fallowing), which was seen as potentially diminishing the agricultural economy. After much controversy, and threats by the federal government to challenge IID's uses as wasteful[26], the QSA was finally signed.[27] But that didn't end the problems either, and they are still being fought out as this is written.

Among the issues remaining are these: (1) Some IID farmers are unhappy with the way the District is dealing with issues arising out of the marketing of IID water, and see themselves as the real owners of the water. In the past no specific allocation of water was made to individual farmers; they just got delivery of whatever they needed, and apparently there was always ample water to meet all demands; (2) The larger community (Imperial County) claims that it is entitled to some of the benefits obtained from marketing IID's water, to compensate for adverse impacts on the community (so called third party effects of water marketing); (3) Mexico filed suit claiming that lining the All–American Canal is depriving it of seepage water that has come across the border for many years, and created valuable and productive wetlands.[28]

A San Diego County newspaper report of November 12, 2005 brings the story more or less up to date:

> Two years after agreeing to sell billions of gallons of water to San Diego County residents for the next 45 years, Imperial Valley leaders continue to be angry over the deal ... Recognizing that taking farmland out of production in cash-poor Imperi-

24. There have been a variety of proposals to save the Salton Sea, including diking off part of it as freshwater and leaving the rest as a salt sink; or building a desalination plant on the Sea's shores, generating freshwater and potentially creating a market for residential communities adjacent to the Sea. All the ideas for saving the Sea seem to be extremely expensive, in the billions, and none has so far gained sufficient support to be adopted. Some even wonder whether the Salton Sea is worth saving, as compared (for example) with trying to save the ecologically much richer Mexican Delta. Whatever the outcome, the Salton Sea dilemma may be a lesson about the disruption that major water transfers can engender, however desirable they may be from an economic and water supply perspective. See Pacific Institute, Haven or Hazard: The Ecology and Future of the Salton Sea (1999) (which includes an extensive bibliog-

raphy). See also Cal. Water Code § 1013; City of Los Angeles v. Aitken, 10 Cal.App.2d 460, 52 P.2d 585 (1935) (dealing with lake level maintenance).

25. The complex of arrangements were enacted in 2003 in Senate Bills 277, 317 and 654.

26. The irony that IID was accused of waste if it did dump water into the Salton Sea, and of ESA violations if it stopped dumping the water, was not lost on anyone.

27. The detailed story of the evolution of the QSA is told (by San Diego's lawyer) in two parts in the April and December, 2003, issues of the California Water Law and Policy Reporter.

28. Consejo de Desarrollo Economico de Mexicali v. United States, U.S. District Court, D. Nevada, CV–S–05–0870–KJD–PAL.

al County could cause economic damage, the [San Diego] Water Authority also agreed to pay extra millions … if economic studies showed financial harm in the valley. In December 2004, an independent panel of economists said the economic harm created in the Valley had been more than offset by the money the Water Authority had paid for the water. The report has been a sore spot in Imperial Valley ever since, with everyone from farmworkers to county supervisors to irrigation board members disputing it.[29]

People in the IID area get a rather different perspective on the situation. The following is an excerpt from the Imperial Valley Press, dated November 22, 2005:

> Negotiations between the Imperial Irrigation District and the San Diego County Water Authority over the amount of money needed to mitigate the socioeconomic impacts of fallowing in the Imperial Valley have reached a critical stage. The water transfer agreement between the two agencies has been in effect since 2003, but the fundamental dispute over fallowing persists and the mitigation plan that was supposed to make the local economy whole has never gotten off the ground. This is * * * a direct result of San Diego's continuing intransigence and IID's chronic inability to do anything about it. * * *

> The only thing that turned out to be true about this water transfer agreement is that it appears to be as "bulletproof" as advertised. The trouble is that all the safety features built in to the deal protect San Diego, not the IID.

> There was a time when we thought of this as merely ironical, but now we have come to regard it, and the agreement that spawned it, as shameful.

> Some weeks ago, the IID board resolved not to enter into any more water transfers in the future, a good idea, but one that arrived one transfer agreement too late to be of any use to the people or economy of the Imperial Valley.

3. THE WATER BUDGET ON THE COLORADO

There is no official number for the annual dependable virgin flow at Lee Ferry (the River exclusive of Lower Basin tributaries). The most recent study estimates long-term mean annual flow at Lee Ferry as 14.3 maf.[30] At the present time, consumptive use is about 4 maf in the upper basin states, 8 maf in the Lower Basin states (2.8 maf in Arizona, .3 maf in Nevada, 5 maf in California, including a temporary arrangement to provide some surplus to California, while it diminishes its use down to its 4.4 maf allotment), and 1.5 delivered to Mexico, for a total of about

---

29. Gig Conaughton, "Imperial Still Unhappy Over Water Transfer," North County Times, Nov. 12, 2005.

30. Connie A Woodhouse et al., Updated Streamflow [etc.], 42 Water Resources Research WO5415 (2006).

13.5 maf. In addition there is around 2 maf of evaporation loss, but it is compensated by some 1.5 maf of lower basin tributary inflow, bringing the consumptive use to about 14 maf. So average actual use has been about in balance with the supply in normal years, though the system was under considerable strain during the first years of this century which experienced 5 years of severe drought. Though no shortage was declared, levels in Lakes Mead and Powell sharply declined, and had the drought not abated by 2005, it was clear that the stage was set for a shortage declaration. During normal conditions, assuming that California reduces its ordinary use to 4.4 maf, the River will be about in equilibrium. That, of course, assumes no growth in use in the Upper Basin, no increased use of Lower Basin tributaries, no adverse impacts from global warming, and no increased allocations of water to environmental uses in the Mexican Delta or elsewhere. It also assumes no interbasin marketing of agricultural water to urban or environmental use,[31] and no augmentation such as trades with coastal desalination plants, weather modification, or importation of foreign water. With a storage capacity of some 60 maf, of which perhaps 50 maf is usable, there is considerable capacity to accommodate periods of excess demand and to withstand fairly protracted dry periods (though with some hydropower losses). Assuming a series of years with Colorado River flows as low as 7 maf/year, all current use could still be met through eight years of such extreme drought by fully drawing down the reservoirs (an unlikely scenario). At the present time, there are no criteria for declaration of a shortage, though the basin states–at Secretarial urging—have been meeting to try to find an agreed-upon formula that could be presented to the Secretary for adoption.

While the River is considerably over-allocated in terms of entitlements (as opposed to actual current use), at present–and absent a protracted drought–it is essentially in equilibrium. The problem is that there is no room for growth, or for dealing with drought, and the Law of the River makes it extremely difficult to consummate voluntary transfers–both interstate and interbasin—despite the economic benefits to be reaped from selling low-value ag water to well-endowed urban users. One might reasonably conclude that there is not so much a water crisis on the River as there is a water *law* or water *politics* crisis. Moreover, there is definitely a shortage mentality within the various basin states. The states of the upper basin tenaciously hold to the view that the 1922 Compact protected their long term right of future development (as against the more rapidly growing lower basin), and they are reluctant to see anything happen that would diminish their right ultimately to use up to their 7.5 maf allotment, even if such use is very distant in time. Ideas about stretching supplies through various innovative transfer schemes receive intense and often hostile scrutiny. Along the same line, the states tend to take a worst-case view of possible futures, so each is inclined to

---

31. Arizona, which is taking virtually its entire 2.8 maf entitlement, does not really have a present need for that much water, has effectively marketed some water for a period of time to Nevada, and may want to market some to California as well. A federal regulation authorizing such marketing is now in place. See 64 Fed. Reg. 58,986 (Nov. 1, 1999), 43 C.F.R. pt. 414 (2000).

secure as much water or water-entitlement as possible, and to prepare for the worst possible scenario of drought-induced shortages combined with maximum projections of growth and demand. The River is basically managed by people whose goal is to acquire as much water as they can, rather than to try to benefit through minimizing their needs (and, e.g., turning whatever excess they could produce into money through market-ing). To be sure, urban water suppliers are basically utilities, and they don't want people to turn on the tap and find no water comes out, so they are–not surprisingly–suspicious of change that has any element of risk. The least risky approach usually appears to be a sort of water mercantilism, storing up as much aqueous wealth as possible and squir-reling it away somewhere.

Notes and Question

1. You now know essentially how the River was divided among the basins and the states within each basin. What general principle governed those allocations? What alternative principles or rules might have been employed? Prior Appropriation? Riparianism? Ecological integrity? Equitable apportionment among states? Economic efficiency? In an article entitled The Untried Market Approach to Water Allocation, an economist named B. Delworth Gardner said: "[A] well-functioning water market would obviate the need for any political allocation such as the Colorado River Compact. This is its great virtue. So much for a half century of political wrangling!" New Courses for the Colorado River 166 (Gary Weatherford & F. Lee Brown eds., 1986). What would the distribution of water in the Colorado River system be today if the market approach had been tried beginning back in 1922? Considering the relative population/wealth distribution of California, Nevada, and Arizona at that time, would a "well-functioning water market" have produced a different result than the prior appropriation system?

2. In terms of outcome, what is the lesson that Colorado River users should have learned from the half-century of wrangling that occurred? The widespread assumption in the arid west is that the operative law of water is "use it or lose it." Does the history of the Colorado support that view? Indeed, as you might conclude from reading about recent developments, below, hasn't California's fate been "use it *and* lose it."

3. Does equity suggest that Mexico is entitled to one-half the River, so that the dividing line should be the international border rather than Lee Ferry? When the river was divided, Mexico was using about 10% of the flow, and it got what was thought to be about 10% of the average annual flow of 15 maf. Do newly recognized environmental demands in the Mexican Delta call for a revision of the Law of the River? If not, what is the appropriate international rule? Does the 1944 treaty bar Mexico from making additional claims now? Should anything depend on how efficiently Mexico uses its existing allocation for agriculture and urban supply by comparison with users in the United States?

4. Note that the treaty allots Mexico additional water from surplus in excess of that required to supply users in the United States. If the United States declares a surplus in the United States, would Mexico have any stake in how the surplus is administered here? E.g., what if American users are

allowed to take surplus water and store it underground for future use, and as a result the entire available surplus is utilized in this country? Could Mexico claim it had been cheated of its additional 200,000 acre-foot treaty right?

5. Water is being taken in the United States and stored underground for future use, primarily by Arizona. While that is obviously a beneficial use under ordinary water law principles, is that a permissible use under the allocations set out in the Law of the River, which speak of surplus and of unused apportionment? It certainly wasn't the sort of "use" that was in mind when the Law of the River was developed either at the time of the 1922 Compact, the 1928 Boulder Canyon Project Act, or when the Supreme Court made its decision in 1963. On the other hand, isn't husbanding of entitlements for future use much better than just taking one's maximum and using it extravagantly?

6. Interbasin transfers. Assume that fast-growing Las Vegas would like to increase its assured supply of water and that Utah, which sees little prospect in the foreseeable future of using all its apportionment, would like to reap some economic benefit from its unused entitlement. Has it got something to market? Consider the following colloquy:

> GETCHES [Dean, University of Colorado Law School]: * * * [W]hy in the world would a Lower Basin state or interest want to buy what it already had a right to receive [under] Article III(e) of the Compact. * * *

> LINDGREN [Attorney for Southern Nevada Water Authority]: * * * If you take one approach to Article III(e), and that is there is simply a Lower Basin call on Upper Basin water made generally on behalf of the Lower Basin, does the water arrive as surplus for purposes of the Lower Basin? If it does, then for example, Nevada has only 4 percent of it. And so to assure Nevada of * * * 30,000 acre-feet, * * * the Secretary would have to declare a surplus of 750,000 acre-feet. * * * The question would be, can you have yellow water, green water, blue water, and purple water? * * * My answer * * * is, "Absolutely, yes." That is, water * * * in a stream may be of two entirely different legal characters. * * *[32]

7. Some other unresolved questions are whether only the state could market water out of the state, or whether an individual with a water right could do so. Could a state constitutionally prohibit export sales, consistent with dormant commerce clause principles (see infra p.

32. 75th Anniversary Colorado River Compact Symposium Proceedings, supra note 2, at 79–81. See Sharon Gross, The Galloway Project and the Colorado River Compacts: Will the Compacts Bar Transbasin Water Diversions?, 25 Nat. Resources J. 935 (1985); Stephanie Landry, The Galloway Proposal and Colorado Water Law: The Limits of the Doctrine of Prior Appropriation, 25 Nat. Resources J. 961 (1985); Richard Simms & Jennifer Davis, Water Transfers Across State Systems, 31 Rocky Mtn. Min. L. Inst. 22–21, 22–25 (1985).

Another issue may be presented by the operating criteria for the upper basin reservoirs, found in Milton Nathanson, Updating the Hoover Dam Documents viii–5 (1978), pursuant to section 602(a) of the Colorado River Basin Project Act, 43 U.S.C. § 1552. Criteria for Coordinated Long–Range Operation of the Colorado River Reservoirs Pursuant to the Colorado River Basin Project Act, sec. III, are printed at 35 Fed. Reg. 112, 8951 (1970). See also Grand Canyon Protection Act, Pub. L. 102–575, 106 Stat. 4600, 4669 (1992).

880), or are those principles not applicable to water that has been allocated by compact? Could an Indian tribe that has federal reserved water rights within a state, either used or unused, market its water rights interstate without state permission?

8. *Intrabasin interstate transfers.* Is there any water legally available for marketing in the lower basin? Section II(B)(6) of the Supreme Court decree (infra p. 833) provides that if water apportioned to one state is not consumed in that state in a given year, the Secretary is authorized to release "such apportioned but unused water during such year for consumptive use in the other states [of the lower basin]." Isn't this literally a 'use it or lose it' rule? This is the provision under which, in the past, the Secretary had released unused Arizona apportionment to California, for the benefit of the Metropolitan Water District. Nonetheless, Arizona and Nevada have found a way around this seeming problem. Arizona enacted an offstream banking law.[33] Under a decree-structured-rubric called "intentionally created unused apportionment" Arizona takes some of its allotment and puts it in storage underground for future use. Nevada pays Arizona for the right to have Arizona in future years take less than its full allotment out of the River, using the stored water in place of the amount of its apportionment it leaves in the River that year. That leaves "intentionally created unused apportionment" that by agreement can be taken by Nevada and added to its allocation. The Bureau of Reclamation has issued regulations that permit implementation of this arrangement,[34] which was seen as one essential element of Southern Nevada's need to meet the needs of its rapidly growing population, in light of its very small Colorado River apportionment, and its limited instate resources. Look at the 1964 Decree, and ask yourself how this arrangement can be squared with Article II(B)(6). What if California asks the Secretary to release the assertedly unused Arizona entitlement to it? And what of § II(B)(4)? Why wouldn't Nevada be charged with getting water in excess of its apportionment?[35]

9. *Environmental Issues.* When the "Law of the River" was put in place, environmental issues were not on anyone's mind. Indeed, it has been suggested that Articles I and III of the Colorado River Compact exclude environmental uses as authorized beneficial uses.[36] (If that is the law, how can Colorado River water be required to be discharged into the Salton Sea to save endangered species?) Can such demands now somehow be incorporated into management of the Colorado? Can an interstate compact or a Supreme Court decree be unilaterally reopened by Congress without the consent of the signatory states?[37] Has Congress done so through the Endangered Species Act, Clean Water Act and other environmental laws? Cf. Southwest

---

33. See Ariz. Rev. Stat. 45–2471.

34. See supra note 31.

35. Section 204(f) of The Fallon Paiute Shoshone Indian Tribes Water Rights Settlement Act of 1990, 104 Stat. 3289, 3303, expressly provides for interstate, intrabasin transfers, and provides that "use of water so transferred shall be charged to the allocation of the state wherein use of water was being made prior to the transfer."

36. For a consideration of that claim see Robert Glennon & Peter Culp, The Last Green Lagoon: How and Why the Bush Administration Should Save the Colorado River Delta, 28 Ecol. L.Q. 903 (2002).

37. Regarding congressional changes in a compact, compare article IV(a) of the Compact with section 6 of the Boulder Canyon Project Act, and see Laughlin River Tours, Inc. v. Bureau of Reclamation, 730 F.Supp. 1522, 1523 (D. Nev. 1990).

Ctr. for Biological Diversity v. U.S. Bureau of Reclamation, 143 F.3d 515 (9th Cir. 1998) (does the Secretary of the Interior have the authority to lower the water level of Lake Mead to avoid jeopardy to species listed under ESA, or would that violate the "Law of the River"?). A Multiple Species Conservation Plan was recently adopted on the Lower Colorado River, with the goal of improving habitat for riparian species, but without diverting any water from other uses; the environmental community considered it insufficient and pulled out of participation in it.

10. Compact Interpretation. As the River is currently operated, the Upper Basin delivers 8.25 maf (8.23 maf at Lee Ferry, plus 20,000 af from the Paria River, a tributary below Glen Canyon) into the Lower Basin; 7.5 maf pursuant to Article III(d), plus one-half the Mexican Treaty obligation, under Article III(c). However, the Upper Basin takes the position that since the Lower Division States are using in excess of the 8.5 maf apportioned to them under the Compact, counting both mainstream and Lower Basin tributary use (primarily Arizona's diversions from the Gila), the Upper Basin is relieved of any obligation to contribute to the Mexican Treaty delivery to the extent that the excess over 8.5 maf used in the Lower Basin suffices to meet the Treaty obligation to Mexico. The legal argument rests on the "surplus" language in Article III(c) of the Compact. The Lower Basin response would likely invoke Herbert Hoover's contemporaneous explanation of the provision when he was questioned about it at the time. The claim would be that the term "surplus" refers only to *unutilized* water remaining above the allocated quantities. Hoover, then Secretary of Commerce and the Chairman of the Compact Commission, was explicitly asked in 1923 whether there was any possibility that water stored in dams on Arizona's tributaries could be released for use in Mexico "to the injury of the water users" on those tributaries.[38] Hoover replied, "I cannot conceive of the making or the ratification of a treaty which would have such an effect." He had just been told that more than 1 maf was already being used on Lower Basin tributaries.

4. SELECTED LAW OF THE RIVER DOCUMENTS

Colorado River Compact[39]

* * *

Article I

The major purposes of this compact are to provide for the equitable division and apportionment of the use of the waters of the Colorado

38. A Colloquy between Hoover and Carl Hayden, Arizona's Member of Congress, titled Analysis of the Colorado River Compact, was reported in the Congressional Record of January 30, 1923, at p. 2710, in Congressman's Hayden's Extension of Remarks.

39. The text of the Compact was not printed in the Statutes at Large or the U.S.

Code. It appears in several sources, including in 70 Cong. Rec. 324 (1928) and U.S. Dept. of the Interior, Documents on the Use and Control of the Waters of Interstate and International Streams 39 (1956). The President's proclamation declaring the Compact in effect appears at 46 Stat. 3000. See H. Doc. No. 67–605, at 8–12 (1923).

River System; to establish the relative importance of different beneficial uses of water; to promote interstate comity; to remove causes of present and future controversies; and to secure the expeditious agricultural and industrial development of the Colorado River Basin, the storage of its waters, and the protection of life and property from floods. To these ends the Colorado River Basin is divided into two Basins, and an apportionment of the use of part of the water of the Colorado River System is made to each of them with the provision that further equitable apportionments may be made.

ARTICLE II

As used in this compact:

(a) The term "Colorado River System" means that portion of the Colorado River and its tributaries within the United States of America.

(b) The term "Colorado River Basin" means all of the drainage area of the Colorado River System and all other territory within the United States of America to which the waters of the Colorado River System shall be beneficially applied.

(c) The term "States of the Upper Division" means the States of Colorado, New Mexico, Utah, and Wyoming.

(d) The term "States of the Lower Division" means the States of Arizona, California, and Nevada.

(e) The term "Lee Ferry" means a point in the main stream of the Colorado River one mile below the mouth of the Paria River.

(f) The term "Upper Basin" means those part of the States of Arizona, Colorado, New Mexico, Utah, and Wyoming within and from which waters naturally drain into the Colorado River System above Lee Ferry, and also all parts of said States located without the drainage area of the Colorado River System which are now or shall hereafter be beneficially served by waters diverted from the system above Lee Ferry.

(g) The term "Lower Basin" means those parts of the States of Arizona, California, Nevada, New Mexico, and Utah within and from which waters naturally drain into the Colorado River System below Lee Ferry, and also all parts of said States located without the drainage area of the Colorado River System which are now or shall hereafter be beneficially served by waters diverted from the system below Lee Ferry.

(h) The term "domestic use" shall include the use of water for household, stock, municipal, mining, milling, industrial, and other like purposes, but shall exclude the generation of electrical power.

ARTICLE III

(a) There is hereby apportioned from the Colorado River system in perpetuity to the Upper Basin and to the Lower Basin, respectively, the exclusive beneficial consumptive use of 7,500,000 acre-feet of water per annum, which shall include all water necessary for the supply of any rights which may now exist.

(b) In addition to the apportionment in paragraph (a), the Lower Basin is hereby given the right to increase its beneficial consumptive use of such waters by one million acre-feet per annum.

(c) If, as a matter of international comity, the United States of America shall hereafter recognize in the United States of Mexico any right to the use of any waters of the Colorado River System, such waters shall be supplied first from the waters which are surplus over and above the aggregate of the quantities specified in paragraphs (a) and (b); and if such surplus shall prove insufficient for this purpose, then the burden of such deficiency shall be equally borne by the Upper Basin and the Lower Basin, and whenever necessary the States of the Upper Division shall deliver at Lee Ferry water to supply one-half of the deficiency so recognized in addition to that provided in paragraph (d).

(d) The States of the Upper Division will not cause the flow of the river at Lee Ferry to be depleted below an aggregate of 75,000,000 acre-feet for any period of ten consecutive years reckoned in continuing progressive series beginning with the first day of October next succeeding the ratification of this compact.

(e) The States of the Upper Division shall not withhold water, and the States of the Lower Division shall not require the delivery of water which can not reasonably be applied to domestic and agricultural uses.

* * *

Article IV

(a) Inasmuch as the Colorado River has ceased to be navigable for commerce and the reservation of its waters for navigation would seriously limit the development of its Basin, the use of its waters for purposes of navigation shall be subservient to the uses of such waters for domestic, agricultural, and power purposes. If the Congress shall not consent to this paragraph, the other provisions of this compact shall nevertheless remain binding.

(b) Subject to the provisions of this compact, water of the Colorado River System may be impounded and used for the generation of electrical power, but such impounding and use shall be subservient to the use and consumption of such water for agricultural and domestic purposes and shall not interfere with or prevent use for such dominant purposes.

(c) The provisions of this article shall not apply to or interfere with the regulation and control by any State within its boundaries of the appropriation, use, and distribution of water.

* * *

Article VII

Nothing in this compact shall be construed as affecting the obligations of the United States of America to Indian tribes.

ARTICLE VIII

Present perfected rights to the beneficial use of waters of the Colorado River System are unimpaired by this compact. Whenever storage capacity of 5,000,000 acre-feet shall have been provided on the main Colorado River within or for the benefit of the Lower Basin, then claims of such rights, if any, by appropriators or users of water in the Lower Basin against appropriators or users of water in the Upper Basin shall attach to be satisfied from water that may be stored not in conflict with Article III.

All other rights to the beneficial use of waters of the Colorado River System shall be satisfied solely from the water apportioned to that basin in which they are situate. * * *

THE BOULDER CANYON PROJECT ACT

43 U.S.C. §§ 617 et seq. (1928).

* * *

SECTION 4(a). 43 U.S.C. § 617c(a).

This Act shall not take effect and no authority shall be exercised hereunder and no work shall be begun and no moneys expended on or in connection with the works or structures provided for in this Act, and no water rights shall be claimed or initiated hereunder, and no steps shall be taken by the United States or by others to initiate or perfect any claims to the use of water pertinent to such works or structures unless and until (1) the States of Arizona, California, Colorado, Nevada, New Mexico, Utah, and Wyoming shall have ratified the Colorado River compact, * * * and the President by public proclamation shall have so declared, or (2) if said States fail to ratify the said compact within six months from the date of the passage of this Act then, until six of said States, including the State of California, shall ratify said compact and shall consent to waive the provisions of the first paragraph of Article XI of said compact, which makes the same binding and obligatory only when approved by each of the seven States signatory thereto, and shall have approved said compact without conditions, save that of such six-State approval, and the President by public proclamation shall have so declared, and, further, until the State of California, by act of its legislature, shall agree irrevocably and unconditionally with the United States and for the benefit of the States of Arizona, Colorado, Nevada, New Mexico, Utah, and Wyoming, as an express covenant and in consideration of the passage of this Act, that the aggregate annual consumptive use (diversions less returns to the river) of water of and from the Colorado River for use in the State of California, including all uses under contracts made under the provisions of the Act and all water necessary for the supply of any rights which may now exist, shall not exceed four million four hundred thousand acre-feet of the waters apportioned to the lower basin States by paragraph (a) of Article III of the Colorado River compact, plus not more than one-half of any excess or surplus waters unapportioned by said compact, such uses always to be subject to the terms of said compact.

The States of Arizona, California, and Nevada are authorized to enter into an agreement which shall provide (1) that of the 7,500,000 acre-feet annually apportioned to the lower basin by paragraph (a) of Article III of the Colorado River compact, there shall be apportioned to the State of Nevada 300,000 acre-feet and to the State of Arizona 2,800,000 acre-feet for exclusive beneficial consumptive use in perpetuity, and (2) that the State of Arizona may annually use one-half of the excess or surplus waters unapportioned by the Colorado River compact, and (3) that the State of Arizona shall have the exclusive beneficial consumptive use of the Gila River and its tributaries within the boundaries of said State, and (4) that the waters of the Gila River and its tributaries, except return flow after the same enters the Colorado River, shall never be subject to any diminution whatever by any allowance of water which may be made by treaty or otherwise to the United States of Mexico but if, as provided in paragraph (c) of Article III of the Colorado River Compact, it shall become necessary to supply water to the United States of Mexico from waters over and above the quantities which are surplus as defined by said compact, then the State of California shall and will mutually agree with the State of Arizona to supply, out of the main stream of the Colorado River, one-half of any deficiency which must be supplied to Mexico by the lower basin, and (5) that the State of California shall and will further mutually agree with the States of Arizona and Nevada that none of said three States shall withhold water and none shall require the delivery of water, which cannot reasonably be applied to domestic and agricultural uses, and (6) that all of the provisions of said tri-State agreement shall be subject in all particulars to the provisions of the Colorado River compact, and (7) said agreement to take effect upon the ratification of the Colorado River compact by Arizona, California, and Nevada.

SECTION 5. 43 U.S.C. § 617d.

That the Secretary of the Interior is hereby authorized, under such general regulations as he may prescribe, to contract for the storage of water in said reservoir and for delivery thereof at such points on the river and on said canal as may be agreed upon, for irrigation and domestic uses, and generation of electrical energy and delivery at the switchboard to States, municipal corporations, political subdivisions, and private corporations of electrical energy generated at said dam, upon charges that will provide revenue which, in addition to other revenue accruing under the reclamation law and under this Act, will in his judgment cover all expenses of operation and maintenance incurred by the United States on account of works constructed under this Act and the payments to the United States under subdivision (b) of section 4. Contracts respecting water for irrigation and domestic uses shall be for permanent service and shall conform to paragraph (a) of section 4 of this Act. No person shall have or be entitled to have the use for any purpose of the water stored as aforesaid except by contract made as herein stated.

* * *

SECTION 6. 43 U.S.C. § 617e.

The dam and reservoir provided for by section 1 hereof shall be used first, for river regulation, improvement of navigation, and flood control; second, for irrigation and domestic uses and satisfaction of present perfected rights * * *; and third, for power. * * *

ARIZONA v. CALIFORNIA

Supreme Court of the United States, 1963.
373 U.S. 546.

MR. JUSTICE BLACK delivered the opinion of the Court.

In 1952 the State of Arizona invoked the original jurisdiction of this Court by filing a complaint against the State of California and seven of its public agencies. Later, Nevada, New Mexico, Utah, and the United States were added as parties either voluntarily or on motion. The basic controversy in the case is over how much water each State has a legal right to use out of the waters of the Colorado River and its tributaries. * * * As we see this case, the question of each State's share of the waters of the Colorado and its tributaries turns on the meaning and the scope of the Boulder Canyon Project Act passed by Congress in 1928.[6] That meaning and scope can be better understood when the Act is set against its background—the gravity of the Southwest's water problems; the inability of local groups or individual States to deal with these enormous problems; the continued failure of the States to agree on how to conserve and divide the waters; and the ultimate action by Congress at the request of the States creating a great system of dams and public works nationally built, controlled, and operated for the purpose of conserving and distributing the water. * * *

Seeking means which would permit ratification by all seven basin States, the Governors* * *met at Denver in 1925 and again in 1927. As a result of these meetings the Governors of the upper basin States suggested* * *that out of the average annual delivery of water at Lee Ferry required by the Compact—7,500,000 acre-feet—Nevada be given 300,000 acre-feet, Arizona 3,000,000 and California 4,200,000, and that unapportioned waters, subject to reapportionment after 1963, be shared equally by Arizona and California. Each Lower Basin State would have "the exclusive beneficial consumptive use of such tributaries within its boundaries before the same empty into the main stream," except that Arizona tributary waters in excess of 1,000,000 acre-feet could under some circumstances be subject to diminution by reason of a United States treaty with Mexico. This proposal foundered because California held out for 4,600,000 acre-feet instead of 4,200,000 and because Arizona

---

6. Boulder Canyon Project Act, 45 Stat. 1057 (1928), 43 U.S.C. §§ 617–617t.

held out for complete exemption of its tributaries from the Mexican burden.

Finally, the fourth Swing–Johnson bill passed both Houses and became the Boulder Canyon Project Act.* * * The earlier bills had offered no method whatever of apportioning the waters among the States of the Lower Basin. The Act as finally passed did provide such a method, and, as we view it, the method chosen was a complete statutory apportionment intended to put an end to the long-standing dispute over Colorado River waters.* * *

The Special Master appointed by this Court found that the Colorado River Compact, the law of prior appropriation, and the doctrine of equitable apportionment—by which doctrine this Court in the absence of statute resolves interstate claims according to the equities—do not control the issues in this case. The Master concluded that, since the Lower Basin States had failed to make a compact to allocate the waters among themselves as authorized by sections 4(a) and 8(b), the Secretary's contracts with the States had within the statutory scheme of sections 4(a), 5, and 8(b) effected an apportionment of the waters of the mainstream which, according to the Master, were the only waters to be apportioned under the Act. The Master further held that, in the event of a shortage of water making it impossible for the Secretary to supply all the water due California, Arizona, and Nevada under their contracts, the burden of the shortage must be borne by each State in proportion to her share of the first 7,500,000 acre-feet allocated to the Lower Basin, that is, 4.4/7.5 by California, 2.8/7.5 by Arizona, and .3/7.5 by Nevada, without regard to the law of prior appropriation.

Arizona, Nevada, and the United States support with few exceptions the analysis, conclusions, and recommendations of the Special Master's report. * * *

California is in basic disagreement with almost all of the Master's Report. She argues that the Project Act, like the Colorado River Compact, deals with the entire Colorado River System, not just the mainstream. This would mean that diversions within Arizona and Nevada of tributary waters flowing in those States would be charged against their apportionments and that, because tributary water would be charged against their apportionments and that, because tributary water would be added to the mainstream water in computing the first 7,500,000 acre-feet available to the States, there would be a greater likelihood of a surplus, of which California gets one-half. The result of California's argument would be much more water for California and much less for Arizona. California also argues that the Act neither allocates the Colorado River waters nor gives the Secretary authority to make an allocation. Rather she takes the position that the judicial doctrine of equitable apportionment giving full interstate effect to the traditional western water law of prior appropriation should determine the rights of the parties to the water. Finally, California claims that in any event the Act does not control in time of shortage. Under such circumstances, she says, this Court should divide the waters according to the doctrine of equitable apportionment or the law of prior appropriation, either of which, she argues, should result in protecting her prior uses. * * *

ALLOCATION OF WATER AMONG THE STATES AND DISTRIBUTION TO USERS

We have concluded, for reasons to be stated, that Congress in passing the Project Act intended to and did create its own comprehensive scheme for the apportionment among California, Arizona, and Nevada of the Lower Basin's share of the mainstream waters of the Colorado River, leaving each State its tributaries. Congress decided that a fair division of the first 7,500,000 acre-feet of such mainstream waters would give 4,400,000 acre-feet to California, 2,800,000 to Arizona, and 300,000 to Nevada; Arizona and California would each get one-half of any surplus. Prior approval was therefore given in the Act for a tri-state compact to incorporate these terms. The States, subject to subsequent congressional approval, were also permitted to agree on a compact with different terms. Division of the water did not, however, depend on the States' agreeing to a compact, for Congress gave the Secretary of the Interior adequate authority to accomplish the division. Congress did this by giving the Secretary power to make contracts for the delivery of water and by providing that no person could have water without a contract.

A. Relevancy of Judicial Apportionment and Colorado River Compact

We agree with the Master that apportionment of the Lower Basin waters of the Colorado River is not controlled by the doctrine of equitable apportionment or by the Colorado River Compact. It is true that the Court has used the doctrine of "equitable apportionment" to decide river controversies between States. But in those cases Congress had not made any statutory apportionment. In this case, we have decided that Congress has provided its own method for allocating among the Lower Basin States the mainstream water to which they are entitled under the Compact. Where Congress has so exercised its constitutional power over waters, courts have no power to substitute their own notions of an "equitable apportionment" for the apportionment chosen by Congress. Nor does the Colorado River Compact control this case. Nothing in that Compact purports to divide water among the Lower Basin States nor in any way to affect or control any future apportionment among those States or any distribution of water within a State. * * * Therefore, we * * * would * * * look to [the Compact] to resolve disputes between the Upper and Lower Basins, were any involved in this case. But no such questions are here. We must determine what apportionment and delivery scheme in the Lower Basin has been effected through the Secretary's contracts. For that determination, we look to the Project Act alone.

B. Mainstream Apportionment

The Congressional scheme of apportionment cannot be understood without knowing what water Congress wanted apportioned. Under California's view, which we reject, the first 7,500,000 acre-feet of Lower

Basin water, of which California has agreed to use only 4,400,000, is made up of both mainstream and tributary water, not just mainstream water. Under the view of Arizona, Nevada, and the United States, with which we agree, the tributaries are not included in the waters to be divided but remain for the exclusive use of each State. Assuming 7,500,000 acre-feet or more in the mainstream and 2,000,000 in the tributaries, California would get 1,000,000 acre-feet more if the tributaries are included and Arizona, 1,000,000 less.

California's argument that the Project Act, like the Colorado River Compact, deals with the main river and all its tributaries rests on § 4(a) of the Act, which limits California to 4,400,000 acre-feet "of the waters apportioned to the lower basin States by paragraph (a) of Article III of the Colorado River Compact, plus not more than one-half of any excess or surplus waters unapportioned by said compact * * *." And Article III(a), referred to by § 4(a), apportioned in perpetuity to the Lower Basin the use of 7,500,000 acre-feet of water per annum "from the Colorado River System," which was defined in the Compact as "that portion of the Colorado River and its tributaries within the United States of America."

Arizona argues that the Compact apportions between basins only the waters of the mainstream, not the mainstream and the tributaries. We need not reach that question, however, for we have concluded that whatever waters the Compact apportioned the Project Act itself dealt only with water of the mainstream. In the first place, the Act, in § 4(a), states that the California limitation, which is in reality her share of the first 7,500,000 acre-feet of Lower Basin water, is on "water of and from the Colorado River," not of and from the "Colorado River System." But more importantly, the negotiations among the States and the congressional debates leading to the passage of the Project Act clearly show that the language used by Congress in the Act was meant to refer to mainstream waters only. Inclusion of the tributaries in the Compact was natural in view of the upper States' strong feeling that the Lower Basin tributaries should be made to share the burden of any obligation to deliver water to Mexico which a future treaty might impose. But when it came to an apportionment among the Lower Basin States, the Gila, by far the most important Lower Basin tributary, would not logically be included, since Arizona alone of the States could effectively use that river. Therefore, with minor exceptions, the proposals and counterproposals over the years, culminating in the Project Act, consistently provided for division of the mainstream only, reserving the tributaries to each State's exclusive use. * * *

Statements made throughout the debates make it quite clear that Congress intended the 7,500,000 acre-feet it was allocating, and out of which California was limited to 4,400,000, to be mainstream water only. * * *

Finally, in considering California's claim to share in the of other States, it is important that from the beginning of the discussions and negotiations which led to the Project Act, Arizona consistently claimed that she must have sole use of the Gila, upon which her existing economy depended. * * *

C. The Project Act's Apportionment and Distribution Scheme

The legislative history, the language of the Act, and the scheme established by the Act for the storage and delivery of water convince us also that Congress intended to provide its own method for a complete apportionment of the mainstream water among Arizona, California, and Nevada.

Not only do the closing days of the debate show that Congress intended an apportionment among the States but also provisions of the Act create machinery plainly adequate to accomplish this purpose, whatever contingencies might occur. As one alternative of the congressional scheme, section 4(a) of the Act invited Arizona, California, and Nevada to adopt a compact dividing the waters along the identical lines that had formed the basis for the congressional discussions of the Act: 4,400,000 acre-feet to California, 300,000 to Nevada, and 2,800,000 to Arizona. Section 8(b) gave the States power to agree upon some other division, which would have to be approved by Congress. Congress made sure, however, that if the States did not agree on any compact the objects of the Act would be carried out, for the Secretary would then proceed, by making contracts, to apportion water among the States and to allocate the water among users within each State.

In the first section of the Act, the Secretary was authorized to "construct, operate, and maintain a dam and incidental works * * * adequate to create a storage reservoir of a capacity of not less than twenty million acre-feet of water" * * * for the stated purpose of "controlling the floods, improving navigation and regulating the flow of the Colorado River, providing for storage and for the delivery of the stored waters thereof for reclamation of public lands and other beneficial uses * * *," and generating electrical power. The whole point of the Act was to replace the erratic, undependable, often destructive natural flow of the Colorado with the regular, dependable release of waters conserved and stored by the project. Having undertaken this beneficial project, Congress, in several provisions of the Act, made it clear that no one should use mainstream waters save in strict compliance with the scheme set up by the Act. Section 5 authorized the Secretary "under such general regulations as he may prescribe, to contract for the storage of water in said reservoir and for the delivery thereof at such points on the river * * * as may be agreed upon, for irrigation and domestic uses * * *." To emphasize that water could be obtained from the Secretary alone, section 5 further declared, "No person shall have or be entitled to have the use for any purpose of the water stored as aforesaid except by contract made as herein stated." The supremacy given the Secretary's contracts was made clear in section 8(b) of the Act, which provided that, while the Lower Basin States were free to negotiate a compact dividing the waters, such a compact if made and approved after January 1, 1929, was to be "subject to all contracts, if any, made by the Secretary of the Interior under section 5" before Congress approved the compact.

These several provisions, even without legislative history, are persuasive that Congress intended the Secretary of the Interior, through his section 5 contracts, both to carry out the allocation of the waters of the main Colorado River among the Lower Basin States and to decide which users within each State would get water. The general authority to make contracts normally includes the power to choose with whom and upon what terms the contracts will be made. When Congress in an Act grants authority to contract, that authority is no less than the general authority, unless Congress has placed some limit on it. * * *

The argument that Congress would not have delegated to the Secretary so much power to apportion and distribute the water overlooks the ways in which his power is limited and channeled by standards in the Project Act. In particular, the Secretary is bound to observe the Act's limitation of 4,400,000 acre-feet on California's consumptive uses out of the first 7,500,000 acre-feet of mainstream water. This necessarily leaves the remaining 3,100,000 acre-feet for the use of Arizona and Nevada, since they are the only other States with access to the main Colorado River. Nevada consistently took the position, accepted by the other States throughout the debates, that her conceivable needs would not exceed 300,000 acre-feet, which of course, left 2,800,000 acre-feet for Arizona's use. Moreover, Congress indicated that it thought this a proper division of the waters when in the second paragraph of section 4(a) it gave advance consent to a tri-state compact adopting such division. While no such compact was ever entered into, the Secretary by his contracts has apportioned the water in the approved amounts and thereby followed the guidelines set down by Congress. * * *

Notwithstanding the Government's construction, ownership, operation, and maintenance of the vast Colorado River works that conserve and store the river's waters and the broad power given by Congress to the Secretary of the Interior to make contracts for the distribution of the water, it is argued that Congress in §§ 14 and 18 of the Act took away practically all the Secretary's power by permitting the States to determine with whom and on what terms the Secretary would make water contracts.

Section 14 provides that the reclamation law, to which the Act is made a supplement, shall govern the management of the works except as otherwise provided, and § 8 of the Reclamation Act, much like § 18 of the Project Act, provides that it is not to be construed as affecting or interfering with state laws "relating to the control, appropriation, use, or distribution of water used in irrigation * * *."[87] In our view, nothing in

---

87. "Nothing in (this Act) shall be construed as affecting or intended to affect or to in any way interfere with the laws of any State or Territory relating to the control, appropriation, use, or distribution of water used in irrigation, or any vested right acquired thereunder, and the Secretary of the Interior, in carrying out the provisions of such sections, shall proceed in conformity with such laws, and nothing (herein) shall

any of these provisions affects our decision, stated earlier, that it is the Act and the Secretary's contracts, not the law of prior appropriation, that control the apportionment of water among the States. Moreover, contrary to the Master's conclusion, we hold that the Secretary in choosing between users within each State and in settling the terms of his contracts is not bound by these sections to follow state law.

The argument that § 8 of the Reclamation Act requires the United States in the delivery of water to follow priorities laid down by state law has already been disposed of by this Court in Ivanhoe Irr. Dist. v. McCracken, 357 U.S. 275 (1958), and reaffirmed in City of Fresno v. California, 372 U.S. 627 (1963). In *Ivanhoe* we held that, even though § 8 of the Reclamation Act preserved state law, that general provision could not override a specific provision of the same Act prohibiting a single landowner from getting water for more than 160 acres. We said:

"As we read § 8, it merely requires the United States to comply with state law when, in the construction and operation of a reclamation project, it becomes necessary for it to acquire water rights or vested interests therein. But the acquisition of water rights must not be confused with the operation of federal projects. As the Court said in State of Nebraska v. State of Wyoming, supra, 325 U.S. at page 615, 65 S.Ct. at page 1349: 'We do not suggest that where Congress has provided a system of regulation for federal projects it must give way before an inconsistent state system.' * * * We read nothing in § 8 that compels the United States to deliver water on conditions imposed by the State." Id., 357 U.S. at 291—292.

Since § 8 of the Reclamation Act did not subject the Secretary to state law in disposing of water in that case, we cannot, consistently with Ivanhoe, hold that the Secretary must be bound by state law in disposing of water under the Project Act.[a]

Section 18 states:

Nothing herein shall be construed as interfering with such rights as the States now have either to the waters within their borders or to adopt such policies and enact such laws as they may deem necessary with respect to the appropriation, control, and use of waters within their borders * * *.

Nor does § 18 of the Project Act require the Secretary to contract according to state law. That Act was passed in the exercise of congressional power to control navigable water for purposes of flood control, navigation, power generation, and other objects, and is equally sustained by the power of Congress to promote the general welfare through

in any way affect any right of any State or of the Federal Government or of any landowner, appropriator, or user of water in, to, or from any interstate stream or the waters thereof." 43 U.S.C. § 383.

a. For the Court's most recent interpretation of § 8, see California v. United States, supra p. 753, which is quite different from the view expressed in this case. § 18, however, is specific to the Boulder Canyon Project Act.—Eds.

projects for reclamation, irrigation, or other internal improvements. Section 18 merely preserves such rights as the States "now" have, that is, such rights as they had at the time the Act was passed. While the States were generally free to exercise some jurisdiction over these waters before the Act was passed, this right was subject to the Federal Government's right to regulate and develop the river. Where the Government, as here, has exercised this power and undertaken a comprehensive project for the improvement of a great river and for the orderly and beneficial distribution of water, there is no room for inconsistent state laws. As in *Ivanhoe*, where the general provision preserving state law was held not to override a specific provision stating the terms for disposition of the water, here we hold that the general saving language of § 18 cannot bind the Secretary by state law and thereby nullify the contract power expressly conferred upon him by § 5. Section 18 plainly allows the States to do things not inconsistent with the Project Act or with federal control of the river, for example, regulation of the use of tributary water and protection of present perfected rights. What other things the States are free to do can be decided when the occasion arises. But where the Secretary's contracts, as here, carry out a congressional plan for the complete distribution of waters to users, state law has no place.

Before the Project Act was passed, the waters of the Colorado River, though numbered by the millions of acre-feet, flowed too haltingly or to freely, resulting in droughts and floods. The problems caused by these conditions proved too immense and the solutions too costly for any one State or all the States together. In addition, the States, despite repeated efforts at a settlement, were unable to agree on how much water each State should get. With the health and growth of the Lower Basin at stake, Congress responded to the pleas of the States to come to their aid. The result was the Project Act and the harnessing of the bountiful waters of the Colorado to sustain growing cities, to support expanding industries, and to transform dry and barren deserts into lands that are livable and productive.

In undertaking this ambitious and expensive project for the welfare of the people of the Lower Basin States and of the Nation, the United States assumed the responsibility for the construction, operation, and supervision of Boulder Dam and a great complex of other dams and works. Behind the dam were stored virtually all the waters of the main river, thus impounding not only the natural flow but also the great quantities of water previously allowed to run waste or to wreak destruction. The impounding of these waters, along with their regulated and systematic release to those with contracts, has promoted the spectacular development of the Lower Basin. Today, the United States operates a whole network of useful projects up and down the river, including the Hoover Dam, Davis Dam, Parker Dam, Headgate Rock Dam, Palo Verde Dam, Imperial Dam, Laguna Dam, Morelos Dam, and the All–American Canal System, and many lesser works. It was only natural that the United States, which was to make the benefits available and which had accepted the responsibility for the project's operation, would want to make certain that the waters were effectively used. All this vast, interlocking machinery—a dozen major works delivering water according to congressionally fixed priorities for home, agricultural, and industrial uses to people spread over thousands of square miles—could function efficiently only under unitary management, able to formulate and supervise a coordinated plan that could take account of the diverse, often conflicting interests of the people and communities of the Lower Basin States. Recognizing this, Congress put the Secretary of the Interior in charge of these works and entrusted him with sufficient power, principally the s 5 contract power, to direct, manage, and coordinate their operation. Subjecting the Secretary to the varying, possibly inconsistent, commands of the different state legislatures could frustrate efficient operation of the project and thwart full realization of the benefits Congress intended this national project to bestow. We are satisfied that the Secretary's power must be construed to permit him, within the boundaries set down in the Act, to allocate and distribute the waters of the mainstream of the Colorado River. * * *

III

APPORTIONMENT AND CONTRACTS IN TIME OF SHORTAGE

We have agreed with the Master that the Secretary's contracts with Arizona for 2,800,000 acre-feet of water and with Nevada for 300,000, together with the limitation of California to 4,400,000 acre-feet, effect a valid apportionment of the first 7,500,000 acre-feet of mainstream water in the Lower Basin. There remains the question of what shall be done in time of shortage. The Master, while declining to make any findings as to what future supply might be expected, nevertheless decided that the Project Act and the Secretary's contracts require the Secretary in case of shortage to divide the burden among the three States in this proportion: California 4.4/7.5; Arizona 2.8/7.5; Nevada .3/7.5. While pro rata sharing of water shortages seems equitable on its face, more considered judgment may demonstrate quite the contrary. Certainly we should not bind the Secretary to this formula. We have held that the Secretary is vested with considerable control over the apportionment of Colorado River waters. And neither the Project Act nor the water contracts require the use of any particular formula for apportioning shortages. While the Secretary must follow the standards set out in the Act, he nevertheless is free to choose among the recognized methods of apportionment or to devise reasonable methods of his own. This choice, as we see it, is primarily his, not the Master's or even ours. And the Secretary may or may not conclude that a pro rata division is the best solution. * * *

MR. JUSTICE HARLAN, whom MR. JUSTICE DOUGLAS and MR. JUSTICE STEWART join, dissenting in part.

I dissent from so much of the Court's opinion as holds that the Secretary of the Interior has been given authority by Congress to apportion, among and within the States of California, Arizona, and

Nevada, the waters of the mainstream of the Colorado River below Lee Ferry. I also dissent from the holding that in times of shortage the Secretary has discretion to select or devise any "reasonable method" he wishes for determining which users within these States are to bear the burden of that shortage. * * *

In my view, it is the equitable principles established by the Court in interstate water-rights cases, as modified by the Colorado River Compact and the California limitation, that were intended by Congress to govern the apportionment of mainstream waters among the Lower Basin States, whether in surplus or in shortage. A *fortiori*, state law was intended to control apportionment among users within a single State.

The Court's conclusions respecting the Secretary's apportionment powers, particularly those in times of shortage, result in a single appointed federal official being vested with absolute control, unrestrained by adequate standards, over the fate of a substantial segment of the life and economy of three States. Such restraint upon his actions as may follow from judicial review are, as will be shown, at best illusory. Today's result, I venture to say, would have dumbfounded those responsible for the legislation the Court construes, for nothing could have been farther from their minds or more inconsistent with their deeply felt convictions. * * *

It is inconceivable that such a Congress intended that the sweeping federal power which it declined to exercise—a power even the most avid partisans of national authority might hesitate to grant to a single administrator—be exercised at the unbridled discretion of an administrative officer, especially in the light of complaints registered about "bureaucratic" and "oppressive" interference of the Department which that very officer headed. It is utterly incredible that a Congress unwilling because of concern for States' rights even to limit California's maximum consumption to 4,400,000 acre-feet without the consent of her legislature intended to give the Secretary of the Interior authority without California's consent to reduce her share even below that quantity in a shortage. * * *

The delegation of such unrestrained authority to an executive official raises, to say the least, the gravest constitutional doubts. See Schechter Poultry Corp. v. United States, 295 U.S. 495; Panama Refining Co. v. Ryan, 293 U.S. 388; cf. Youngstown Sheet & Tube Co. v. Sawyer, 343 U.S. 579, 587–589. * * *

Notes and Questions

1. Even after the historic 1963 ruling, various issues concerning the decision returned to the Supreme Court for additional review. The 1963 rulings were cast into a final decree, Arizona v. California, 376 U.S. 340 (1964); a supplemental decree listing present perfected rights was entered, 439 U.S. 419 (1979); and water rights of several Indian tribes were fixed with reference to newly established reservation boundaries, 460 U.S. 605 (1983), 466 U.S. 144 (1984); consolidated decree, 126 S.Ct. 1543 (2006).

2. The case itself is a historic one and has produced a number of valuable scholarly writings. Among the most prominent works are Charles Meyers, The Colorado River, 19 Stan. L. Rev. 1 (1966) and Frank Trelease, Arizona v. California: Allocation of Water Resources to People, States and Nation, 1963 Sup. Ct. Rev. 158.

3. The dissent of Justice Harlan turned on the lack of congressional intent to apportion the River. Norris Hundley, Water and the West: The Colorado River Compact and the Politics of Water in the American West 270 (1975) has the following to say about the legislative history:

> While some congressmen thought that Congress was infringing upon states' rights by even suggesting a lower-basin pact, Pittman [U.S. Senator from Nevada] strenuously disagreed. "If California and Nevada and Arizona do not like this agreement," he explained, "they do not have to approve it." "All I have in mind," he protested, is "trying to save six or seven months' time." If the lower-basin states were to enter into an agreement that already had congressional approval, he observed, then they would not have to return later to Congress for approval. "I may not be accomplishing anything; but Arizona seems to be wedded to a certain plan. If the California Legislature does not like it, it does not put us in any worse fix than we are in if we do not adopt it."

> Congress agreed, and Pittman's proposal was incorporated into section 4(a) of the bill. Thirty-five years later the U.S. Supreme Court would misconstrue this action and decide that the Boulder Canyon Act provided a statutory apportionment of the waters of the lower Colorado. In 1928, however, Congress appeared confident that it was merely suggesting a way in which the lower states *might* settle their problem themselves.

ARIZONA v. CALIFORNIA (DECREE)

Supreme Court of the United States, 1964.
376 U.S. 340.

It is ORDERED, ADJUDGED AND DECREED that

I. For purposes of this decree:

(A) "Consumptive use" means diversions from the stream less such return flow thereto as is available for consumptive use in the United States or in satisfaction of the Mexican treaty obligation;

(B) "Mainstream" means the mainstream of the Colorado River downstream from Lee Ferry within the United States, including the reservoirs thereon;

(C) Consumptive use from the mainstream within a state shall include all consumptive uses of water of the mainstream, including water drawn from the mainstream by underground pumping, and including but not limited to, consumptive uses made by persons, by agencies of that state, and by the United States for the benefit of Indian reservations and other federal establishments within the state; * * *

(E) "Water controlled by the United States" refers to the water in Lake Mead, Lake Mojave, Lake Havasu and all other water in the mainstream below Lee Ferry and within the United States;

(F) "Tributaries" means all stream systems the water of which naturally drain into the mainstream of the Colorado River below Lee Ferry; * * *

(H) "Present perfected rights" means perfected rights * * * existing as of June 25, 1929, the effective date of the Boulder Canyon Project Act; * * *

II.   The United States, its officers, attorneys, agents and employees be and they are hereby severally enjoined:

(A) From operating regulatory structures controlled by the United States and from releasing water controlled by the United States other than in accordance with the following order of priority:

(1) For river regulation, improvement of navigation, and flood control;

(2) For irrigation and domestic uses, including the satisfaction of present perfected rights; and

(3) For power;

Provided, however, that the United States may release water in satisfaction of its obligations to the United States of Mexico under the treaty dated February 3, 1944, without regard to the priorities specified in this subdivision (A);

(B) From releasing water controlled by the United States for irrigation and domestic use in the States of Arizona, California and Nevada, except as follows:

(1) If sufficient mainstream water is available for release, as determined by the Secretary of the Interior, to satisfy 7,500,000 acre-feet of annual consumptive use in the aforesaid three states, then of such 7,500,000 acre-feet of consumptive use, there shall be apportioned 2,800,000 acre-feet for use in Arizona, 4,400,000 acre-feet for use in California, and 300,000 acre-feet for use in Nevada;

(2) If sufficient mainstream water is available for release, as determined by the Secretary of the Interior, to satisfy annual consumptive use in the aforesaid states in excess of 7,500,000 acre feet, such excess consumption use is surplus, and 50% there of shall be apportioned for use in Arizona and 50% for use in California; provided, however, that if the United States so contracts with Nevada, then 46% of such surplus shall be apportioned for use in Arizona and 4% for use in Nevada;

(3) If insufficient water is available for release, as determined by the Secretary of the Interior to satisfy annual consumptive use of 7,500,000 acre feet in the aforesaid three states, then the Secretary of the Interior, after providing for satisfaction of present perfected rights in the order of their priority dates without regard to state

lines and after consultation with the parties to major delivery contracts and such representatives as the respective states may designate, may apportion the amount remaining available for consumptive use in such manner as is consistent with the Boulder Canyon Project Act as interpreted by the opinion of this Court herein, and with other applicable federal statutes, but in no event shall more than 4,400,000 acre feet be apportioned for use in California including all present perfected rights;

(4) Any mainstream water consumptively used within a state shall be charged to its apportionment, regardless of the purpose for which it was released;

(5) Notwithstanding the provisions of Paragraphs (1) through (4) of this subdivision (B), mainstream water shall be released or delivered to water users * * * only pursuant to valid contracts made with such users by the Secretary of the Interior, pursuant to Section 5 of the Boulder Canyon Project Act or any other applicable federal statute.

(6) If, in any one year, water apportioned for consumptive use in a state will not be consumed in that state, whether for the reason that delivery contracts for the full amount of the state's apportionment are not in effect or that users cannot apply all of such water to beneficial uses, or for any other reason, nothing in this decree shall be construed as prohibiting the Secretary of the Interior from releasing such apportioned but unused water during such year for consumptive use in the other states. No rights to the recurrent use of such water shall accrue by reason of the use thereof. * * *

COLORADO RIVER BASIN PROJECT ACT

43 U.S.C. §§ 1501 et seq. (1968).

SECTION 301(b) [43 U.S.C. § 1521(b)]. Limitation on water diversions in years of insufficient main stream Colorado River water.

Article II(B)(3) of the decree of the Supreme Court of the United States in Arizona against California (376 U.S. 340) shall be so administered that in any year in which, as determined by the Secretary, there is insufficient main stream Colorado River water available for release to satisfy annual consumptive use of seven million five hundred thousand acre-feet in Arizona, California, and Nevada, diversions from the main stream for the Central Arizona Project shall be so limited as to assure the availability of water in quantities sufficient to provide for the aggregate annual consumptive use by holders of present perfected rights, by other users in the State of California served under existing contracts with the United States by diversion works heretofore constructed, and by other existing Federal reservations in that State, of four million four hundred thousand acre-feet of mainstream water, and by users of the same character in Arizona and Nevada. Water users in the State of Nevada shall not be required to bear shortages in any proportion greater than would have been imposed in the absence of this subsection. This subsection shall not affect the relative priorities, among themselves, of water users in Arizona, Nevada, and California which are senior to diversions for the Central Arizona Project, or amend any provisions of said decree.

* * *

SECTION 602(a) [(43 U.S.C. § 1552)]. Criteria for long-range operation of reservoirs

(a) Promulgation by Secretary; order of priorities

In order to comply with and carry out the provisions of the Colorado River Compact, the Upper Colorado River Basin Compact, and the Mexican Water Treaty, the Secretary shall propose criteria for the coordinated long-range operation of the reservoirs constructed and operated under the authority of the Colorado River Storage Project Act [43 U.S.C.A. §§ 620 et seq.], the Boulder Canyon Project Act [43 U.S.C.A. §§ 617 et seq.], and the Boulder Canyon Project Adjustment Act [43 U.S.C.A. §§ 618 et seq.]. To effect in part the purposes expressed in this paragraph, the criteria shall make provision for the storage of water in storage units of the Colorado River storage project and releases of water from Lake Powell in the following listed order of priority:

(1) releases to supply one-half the deficiency described in article III(c) of the Colorado River Compact, if any such deficiency exists and is chargeable to the States of the Upper Division, but in any event such releases, if any, shall not be required in any year that the Secretary makes the determination and issues the proclamation specified in section 1512 of this title;

(2) releases to comply with article III(d) of the Colorado River Compact, less such quantities of water delivered into the Colorado River below Lee Ferry to the credit of the States of the Upper Division from other sources; and

(3) storage of water not required for the releases specified in clauses (1) and (2) of this subsection to the extent that the Secretary, after consultation with the Upper Colorado River Commission and representatives of the three Lower Division States and taking into consideration all relevant factors (including, but not limited to, historic stream-flows, the most critical period of record, and probabilities of water supply), shall find this to be reasonably necessary to assure deliveries under clauses (1) and (2) without impairment of annual consumptive uses in the upper basin pursuant to the Colorado River Compact: *Provided*, That water not so required to be stored shall be released from Lake Powell: (i) to the extent it can be reasonably applied in the States of the Lower Division to the uses specified in article III(e) of the Colorado River Compact, but no such releases shall be made when the active storage in Lake Powell is less than the active storage in Lake Mead, (ii) to maintain, as nearly as practicable, active storage in Lake Mead equal to the active storage

in Lake Powell, and (iii) to avoid anticipated spills from Lake Powell.

* * *

B. INTERSTATE ALLOCATION OF WATER

The continuing saga of the Colorado River is perhaps the quintessential example of water that must be shared by competing users with conflicting interests. The legal instruments apportioning the Colorado, congressional apportionment and interstate compacts, do not exhaust the possibilities. Other devices—equitable apportionment litigation between or among states in the United States Supreme Court, and more ordinary litigation in federal courts between or among water users, with or without state or federal governmental involvement—have been used to allocate interstate waters for uses in different states. There are also situations where states (whether humid or arid) have tried to retain their "native" water and thwart interstate sharing by resisting its use in other states.[1] In recent decades, such hoarding efforts have been fended off by applying the principle of free interstate trade embodied in the so-called dormant commerce clause of the U.S. Constitution.

The materials that follow consider in detail the working of these five legal devices—apportionment by congressional statute, by interstate compact, or by the Supreme Court in original jurisdiction equitable apportionment litigation; ordinary litigation involving interstate waters, and the dormant commerce clause—that govern interstate sharing of water.

1. CONGRESSIONAL APPORTIONMENT

The authority of Congress to apportion the waters of interstate rivers is an aspect of its power to regulate commerce among the several states. See U.S. Const. art. I, § 8. The supremacy clause (art. VI, cl. 2), making congressional action the supreme law of the land, binds states to the terms of congressional acts. Although congressional apportionment is an effective way to allocate the beneficial use of an interstate watercourse, it has been done only twice in the Nation's history. The first time, in the 1928 Boulder Canyon Project Act, went unnoticed for thirty-five years, until the United States Supreme Court strained to find that result in its decision in Arizona v. California, supra p. 821.

An explanation for the rarity of congressional apportionment is found in the nature of the political process in the legislative branch. The states' equal representation in the U.S. Senate makes congressional action favoring one state and disadvantaging others difficult. Legislators from non-participant states do not relish voting to impose an unpopular allocation on a disputant state, for fear their own states could suffer the same fate at some point in the future. Overcoming the normal burden of

---

1. Recall from Section A, above, that Arizona persuaded the Supreme Court in effect to segregate Gila River water from the basin-wide allocation of the Colorado River. See p. 805 supra.

inertia against legislative action is even more difficult in the context of water, with its high cultural value, where political demagoguery comes easily and effectively.

The second and, as of this writing, the only other congressional apportionment came in 1990, dividing the waters of the Truckee and Carson Rivers and Lake Tahoe between California and Nevada.[2] See Pub. L. 101–618, § 204, 104 Stat. 3289, 3295–3304 (1990). The apportionment had actually been negotiated in the form of an interstate compact between California and Nevada between 1955 and 1968, but had never been approved by Congress largely because of opposition by the Pyramid Lake Paiute Tribe and the Interior Department as trustee for the Tribe. In the meantime, the two states had generally complied with the compact terms while waiting for Congress to act, and the Supreme Court had refused to find a justiciable controversy between California and Nevada over interstate apportionment while the compact was awaiting ratification by Congress.[3]

The Tribe and the Interior Department had been concerned that the apportionment the two states had negotiated would threaten tribal interests in its fishery in Pyramid Lake (at the terminus of the Truckee River), but they eventually withdrew their opposition when the apportionment was augmented by several other features that brought benefits to the Tribe and the Lake. Besides the interstate apportionment, the overall settlement involved special problems raised by the presence of tribal reserved water rights, endangered and threatened species, federal reclamation projects, national wildlife refuges, and several separate lawsuits and court judgments, some of which had already effectively allocated much of the available water.

Although its complicating factors limit its value as a model for future congressional apportionments, some of its features are of more general interest. Anticipating that future disputes are inevitable, the settlement provides that each state, "by accepting the allocations under this section, shall be deemed to have waived any immunity from the jurisdiction of" the federal courts in Nevada and the Eastern District of California to hear claims alleging failure to comply with the allocations or any other provision of the apportionment. Id. § 204(d)(2). The settlement expressly contemplates "the interstate transfer of water * * * for use within the Truckee River basin," but also provides, among other things, that such transfers "shall comply with all State laws" governing

---

2. The apportionment does not officially take effect until Nevada and California negotiate and execute an operating agreement and complete an assessment of environmental impacts. This has still not been done more than a decade later. See 69 Fed. Reg. 65213 (2004) (comment period on draft EIS). For more background, see Barbara Cosens, Farmers, Fish, Tribal Power and Poker: Reallocating Water in the Truckee River Basin, Nevada and California, Hastings W–NW J. Envtl. L. & Pol'y 89 (2003);

A. Dan Tarlock, The Creation of New Risk Sharing Water Entitlement Regimes: The Case of the Truckee–Carson Settlement, 25 Ecology L.Q. 674, 685–88 (1999).

3. See John Kramer, Lake Tahoe, the Truckee River, and Pyramid Lake: The Past, Present, and Future of Interstate Water Issues, 19 Pac. L.J. 1339, 1367–69 (1988); see also United States v. Nevada, 412 U.S. 534, 537 (1973).

the transfer of water rights (including state laws designed to protect the environment or the "overall economy of the [exporting] area"), so long as such laws "apply equally to interstate and intrastate transfers." Id. § 204 (f). States may not deny or condition a transfer application made by the United States if it would be "inconsistent with any clear congressional directive," id. § 204(f)(3). Federal or Indian uses shall generally be charged to the allocation of the state "wherein the use is made," id. § 204(g). See generally E. Leif Reid, Ripples from the Truckee: The Case for Congressional Apportionment of Disputed Interstate Water Rights, 14 Stan. Envtl. L.J. 145, 166–73 (1995).

Notes and Questions

1. Considering California's vast population superiority (and its greater representation in the U.S. House of Representatives—during the 1990's, fifty-two members to Nevada's two), should it have greater influence than Nevada on how the waters of these Rivers are apportioned?

2. Note that Congress refused to approve the compact the two states negotiated because of federal concerns related to Indians. Compacts will be covered in the next section. Consider, as you go through those materials, the suggestion in the Truckee–Carson experience of an advantage of congressional apportionment over interstate compacts and especially over judicial apportionment; namely, Congress can lard a statutory interstate allocation with "sweeteners" to make it more palatable to the disputants and interested parties.

3. As with most congressional powers, Congress can delegate the power to apportion water among the states to the Executive Branch, see Arizona v. California, supra p. 821, and according to Justice Harlan's dissent in that case, can do so virtually without intelligible standards, pp. 829–830.

4. Congress can and often does take actions that indirectly affect the allocation of interstate waters, or even operate effectively to make such an allocation. In 1986, for example, Congress gave the governors of Great Lakes states veto power over new out-of-basin diversions from any portion of the Great Lakes, or any tributary thereof, within the United States. See 42 U.S.C. § 1962d–20; infra pp. pp. 900–901; Charles F. Glass, Jr., Enforcing Great Lakes Water Export Restrictions Under the Water Resources Development Act of 1986, 103 Colum. L. Rev. 1503 (2003). Congress may authorize and fund storage and diversion projects on interstate rivers that have the effect of underwriting water use in a particular state.

5. Sometimes the process works the other way round; that is, Congress's contemplation of a major project on an unallocated interstate stream spurs the interested states to apportion its waters, either through compact or litigation. Recall (from supra pp. 802–808) that the Colorado River Compact was linked closely to congressional consideration and eventual enactment of legislation authorizing Hoover Dam and the All–American Canal to benefit California's Imperial Valley; and that Arizona could not persuade Congress to authorize the Central Arizona Project until its dispute with California over allocation of the lower Colorado was settled by the Supreme Court.

6. Federal regulatory programs, such as the Clean Water Act and Endangered Species Act, may also affect the pattern of water uses interstate. The same is true of federal land and river corridor management policies (such as under the Wild & Scenic Rivers Act and the Wilderness Act), especially in the federal-land-rich and arid western states. And the same is true of federal licensing of hydroelectric dams under the Federal Power Act. Recall North Carolina's efforts to use the federal Clean Water Act to thwart Virginia Beach, Virginia's quest for water, supra pp. 87–101. The Endangered Species Act may sometimes create demand for instream flows across state lines that might exceed the downstream state's allocation under compact, court decree or statute. Other illustrations can be found supra pp. 660–661 and infra pp. 840, 849–851, 1004–1006.

Managing the Waters of the Mighty Missouri River

It may seem as if every major river basin in the United States has its own epic "story" that captures some particular facet of interstate water management. The Missouri River basin—the scene of much of Lewis & Clark's exploration—is no exception. Although a few of its tributaries have been the subject of compact or equitable apportionment, the waters of the main stem of the Missouri have never been formally allocated by Congress, compact or the courts. How its waters are managed amid competing state demands (as with the Colorado, primarily between upper and lower basin states) is worth a brief look.

Nearly twenty-five hundred miles long, the Missouri rises near the continental divide in western Montana, flows east into the Dakotas, then south forming parts of the border of Nebraska, Iowa and Kansas, before turning east again to flow through Missouri to its terminus where it joins the Mississippi. Its basin embraces ten U.S. states, several Canadian provinces and twenty-five Indian tribes.[4] In its natural state the Missouri could be a destructive river. Occasional extensive floods in the lower basin would batter low-lying towns and cities along its banks and take vast tracts out of production. In the mid-twentieth century heyday of public works, Congress appropriated substantial funds for the building of several dams and other water works that would tame the river, make its lower reaches navigable and, as an added benefit, support irrigation and generate electric power in the upper basin. The Army Corps of Engineers was given control over the timing and amount of releases from the dams to promote navigation and flood control. Several of those same reservoirs also supply water for irrigation through distribution facilities built and managed by the Bureau of Reclamation. Uses in the upper basin are mostly for irrigation, municipal supply and, more recently, recreation and fishery. In the lower basin, the last 735 miles of the river (from Sioux City, Iowa to St. Louis, Missouri) are maintained for navigation by the Army Corps of Engineers.[5]

4. See generally John Davidson, Missouri River Basin, in 6 Waters and Water Rights 151 (Robert Beck ed., repl. vol. 1994).

5. The conflict between the Corps and Bureau for supremacy on the Missouri has been told in Marc Reisner, Cadillac Desert. 191–202 (1986); John Ferrell, The Big Dam

The process of subjecting the Missouri to federal control through public works projects funded largely by the nation's taxpayers gave the lower basin, most observers agree, the best of the bargain. The flood control and navigation benefits of these projects to the lower basin were substantial, while much of the inexpensive electric power produced had no ready users in the upper basin and found its way downstream. The upper basin was able to develop some irrigation projects, but Congress was far less generous in doling out reclamation largess to this region compared with other parts of the West. Worse still, the upper basin (and particularly Indian Tribes in the basin) paid a heavy price for these projects. The massive reservoirs along the Missouri mainstem flooded hundreds of thousands of acres of the prime bottom lands, the very best farmland in an area not blessed with an abundant supply. Lake Oahe, for example, flooded more than three-quarters of a million acres in South and North Dakota, inundating lands from Pierre, South Dakota northward for more than one hundred miles into North Dakota.

Although proposals have been made from time to time to apportion the waters of the Missouri among the basin states,[6] differences between upper and lower basin states have prevented attainment of that objective. In the wake of the 1973 oil embargo and enactment of the Clean Air Act, water demand associated with the development of the large (and largely low sulfur) coal resources of the northern Great Plains provoked much discussion. Control of the water stored behind the Oahe Dam became the focus of an intense legal battle when South Dakota approved the sale of 20,000 acre feet per year of Oahe Reservoir water[7] to ETSI, Inc., a consortium of energy companies, for diversion to Wyoming for use in a slurry pipeline to transport Wyoming coal to Arkansas for electricity generation. The federal Bureau of Reclamation issued a contract for diversion of water out of Lake Oahe.

The downstream states sued and ultimately the U.S. Supreme Court held that because the reservoirs are under the control of the Corps of Engineers, that agency must approve marketing water out of them. See ETSI Pipeline Project v. Missouri, 484 U.S. 495 (1988). Although the issue of whether Corps approval is necessary might seem bureaucratically mundane, it points to the heart of the struggle between the upper and lower basins. The Corps' emphasis on navigation and flood control primarily serves lower basin interests, while the Bureau's historic fealty

Era: A Legislative and Institutional History of the Pick–Sloan Missouri Basin Program (1993); John Ferrell, Soundings: One Hundred Years of the Missouri River Navigation Project (1996). (Ferrell is a historian with the United States Army Corps of Engineers). See also the collection of articles on the Missouri in 2 Great Plains Nat. Resources J. (1997); John Thorson, River of Promise, River of Peril: The Politics of Managing the Missouri River (1994). For a masterful treatment of early Corps of Engi-

neers navigation and flood control activities, focusing on the Mississippi River, see John M. Barry, Rising Tide (1997).

6. See Davidson, supra note 4, at 179.

7. This quantity is a pittance compared to the flow of the Missouri; indeed, it is but a small fraction of the annual evaporation off the surface of Oahe Reservoir, which can store considerably more than 20 million acre-feet.

to state law is regarded by the upper basin as giving them more control in the allocation of mainstem water.

The demise of the ETSI project and the dampening of interest in massive development of the coal resources of the Northern Great Plains did not end the dispute between the upper and lower basin states. The upper basin states now want Missouri River water held back to support a burgeoning water recreation and fishery-based tourism industry, while the lower basin states want sufficient water releases to maintain navigation. The State of South Dakota attempted to institute an original action in the Supreme Court to contend that Congress had effectively apportioned Missouri River waters in the so-called O'Mahoney–Milliken amendment, 33 U.S.C. § 701–1(b). This statute, part of the 1944 Flood Control Act, says navigation uses "of waters arising in States lying wholly or partly west of the ninety-eighth meridian shall be only such use as does not conflict with any beneficial consumptive use, present or future" in those upstream states. South Dakota's objective and line of reasoning was the same as in the *ETSI* case—that Congress wanted the upstream storage projects to be managed by the Bureau of Reclamation and therefore state law in the upper basin states was to be given primacy in management of this water. Ultimately the Supreme Court denied leave to file the complaint,[8] leaving, as Professor Davidson has put it, "the underlying issues simmer[ing]."[9]

In the late 1980s, drought sparked controversy over management of the mainstream reservoirs, leading to a direct confrontation between the upper basin states and the Corps of Engineers. Again the focus of the upper basin was to preserve water in the upper basin reservoirs for a burgeoning recreation industry, which conflicted with the Corps' desire for releases to serve navigation interests downstream. In 1990 South Dakota, North Dakota and Montana sued the Corps to limit releases in order to protect gamefish spawning. The Corps said such limits were inconsistent with its Master Manual, which contains its rules for river management. The district court issued a preliminary injunction in favor of the plaintiffs, but eventually the Court of Appeals dismissed the case as moot due to the passage of the spawning season, though not before expressing skepticism about the wisdom of the district court's action.[10]

Continuing drought led the upper basin states to pursue new litigation to protect recreation interests in the upper basin. In this suit they attacked the primacy of navigation directly, and argued, among other things, that fish, wildlife and recreation interests in the upper basin were much more valuable than the faltering navigation industry down-

8. South Dakota v. Nebraska, 485 U.S. 902 (1988) & 475 U.S. 1093 (1986). See Gene Olson, The O'Mahoney–Milliken Amendment: The West Sinks the Navigation Power, 65 N.D. L. Rev. 91 (1989); for an explication of South Dakota's argument, see John Guhin, The Law of the Missouri, 30 S.D. L. Rev. 347 (1985).

9. Davidson, supra note 4, at 180.

10. South Dakota v. Hazen, 914 F.2d 147 (8th Cir. 1990). The issues underlying the litigation are discussed in Brian Morris, Unanswered Prayers: The Upper Missouri River Basin States Take on the U.S. Army Corps of Engineers, 68 N.D. L. Rev. 897, 924–30 (1992).

stream.[11] The suit was settled when the Corps agreed to draft a new Master Manual to address this conflict. Also making their presence felt at this point were three endangered species of wildlife—the least tern, the pallid sturgeon, and the piping plover—that were at risk from river operations. The U.S. Fish and Wildlife Service issued a series of biological opinions that called for more natural river flows to avoid jeopardy, and the National Academy of Sciences essentially confirmed the Service's conclusions in a January 2002 report, The Missouri River Ecosystem: Exploring the Prospects for Recovery. As drought gripped the region, upper and lower basin states obtained conflicting injunctions from "home-town" federal district courts regarding river management. On appeal, the Eighth Circuit held that the upper basin injunctions requiring maintenance of reservoir levels were improperly entered, and affirmed the lower basin injunctions requiring release of water for navigation. South Dakota v. Ubbelohde, 330 F.3d 1014 (8th Cir. 2003). Environmentalists meanwhile filed suit in the District of Columbia federal court to reduce navigation flows to protect endangered species. A monumental litigation battle ensued, involving six different courts in six states, and for a while species-protective flow limitations were enforced. In March 2004 the Corps finally released its updated Master Manual and accompanying final environmental impact statement.[12]

In the meantime, in the Congress, navigation interests led by downstream Senator Kit Bond of Missouri, prevailed over upstream Senators, led by Byron Dorgan of North Dakota. A change in the White House also helped. President Clinton had vetoed a prior attempt by Senator Bond to protect navigational flows through a rider on appropriations legislation. President Bush has generally supported navigational interests, which some observers think helped him carry the key battleground state of Missouri in the 2000 election.

The worst of the drought appeared to abate in 2005, easing the likelihood that total storage in the River system would fall to 31 million acre-feet (compared to a total capacity of around 58 MAF), at which point the Master Manual calls for releases for navigation to cease. Nevertheless, the barge industry has shriveled with shorter seasons. Meanwhile, to protect endangered species, the Corps was constructing new shallow water habitat for the pallid sturgeon and manipulating releases to protect the piping plover and least tern during their nesting seasons.[13] The latest judicial guidance gave the Corps great deference in sorting these matters out. In re Operation of Missouri River System Litig., 421 Fed. 3d 618 (8th Cir. 2005). See generally Sandra B. Zellmer,

11. The recreation benefits have been calculated as high as $114 million per annum, compared to navigation benefits at less than $10 million. See American Rivers, Voyage of Recovery: The Missouri River (1999); Davidson, supra note 4, at 181. (The Missouri River in recent years has carried little more than 1 million tons of barge cargo annually. By comparison the Missis-sippi and Ohio Rivers carry 300 and 100 million tons, respectively.). Upstream interests have lately favored a straight federal buyout of the barge industry.

12. Available at http://www.nwd-mr. usace. army.mil/mmanual/mast-man.htm.

13. Details are available at http://mis-souririver.ecr.gov/.

A New Corps of Discovery for Missouri River Management, 83 Nebraska L. Rev. 305–61 (2004); Ross K. Den Herder, The Battle for the Basin: The Struggle for Priority Among Competing Interests in the Management of the Missouri River Reservoir System, 9 Great Plains Nat. Res. J. 34 (2005).

2. INTERSTATE COMPACTS

The compact clause of the United States Constitution states: "No State shall, without the Consent of Congress, * * * enter into any Agreement or Compact with another State * * *." Art. I, § 10, cl. 3. Although the text seems to require congressional ratification for all agreements among states, the Supreme Court has said that the clause requires Congress to consent to "the formation of any combination [of States] tending to increase political power in the States" at the expense of the federal government.[14] Besides protecting the national interest, the Framers may have also been concerned that combinations of some states might work to the detriment of other states, although this rationale is less prominent in the history of the clause and in subsequent judicial opinions. Congressional consent can be given either before or after the states sign a compact, and may be implied. See Jerome Muys, Interstate Water Compacts: The Interstate Compact and Federal–Interstate Compact 241–55 (Nat'l Water Comm'n Legal Study No. 14, 1971).

We have already seen one illustration of what the framers were concerned about, in the refusal of Congress to ratify the proposed California–Nevada Compact on the Truckee and Carson Rivers because of misgivings about its effect on Indians. See supra p. 836. Another illustration is provided by the Republican River, where a tri-state compact negotiated by Nebraska, Kansas, and Colorado was approved by the Congress, but vetoed by President Franklin Roosevelt because it contained language declaring the River to be "non-navigable" in an apparent attempt to curtail federal authority over the River. See H.R. Doc. No. 77–690 (1942) (veto message).[15] The offending language was removed and the President then signed legislation approving the compact. 57 Stat. 86 (1943). See also infra p. 900, discussing Congress's 1968 ratification of only part of the Great Lakes Basin Compact, deleting a provision that allowed the Provinces of Ontario and Quebec to participate in compact governance.

Modern interstate compacts involving the allocation of the waters of interstate streams usually are negotiated by states (with or without close

14. Virginia v. Tennessee, 148 U.S. 503, 518–21 (1893); see also Intake Water Co. v. Yellowstone River Compact Commission, 590 F.Supp. 293, 297 (D. Mont. 1983) (congressional consent required for any state-state agreements that "encroach on the supremacy of the United States."). Two states agreeing on the precise location of an ancient boundary between them is an example of a kind of interstate agreement that may not require congressional consent. See, e.g., New Hampshire v. Maine, 426 U.S. 363, 369–70 (1976).

15. As this shows, although the Constitution requires only "Congress" to consent to compacts, it has generally been understood that congressional consent requires legislation to be presented to the President for concurrence or veto.

federal participation), and then folded into legislation adopted by each of the compacting states, and only then taken to Congress for ratification in federal legislation. The Colorado River was an exceptional case, where congressional approval of the compact preceded Arizona's assent to its terms. See supra p. 805. As that example shows, usually the most challenging task is to reach agreement among the affected states on how the waters of the shared basin should be utilized. As of this writing, little more than two dozen interstate water compacts that apportion water or contain a mechanism for apportioning water are in force. See Douglas L. Grant, Water Apportionment Compacts Between States, in 4 Water and Water Rights § 46.01 (Robert Beck ed., 2004).

Compacts offer benefits that cannot be provided by ordinary state regulation. Once ratified, they become federal law, a fact that has two important consequences. First, via the supremacy clause, the compact takes precedence over inconsistent state laws. This means that a state's compact obligations can be enforced under federal authority, and a compacting state may not withdraw from a compact on any terms other than those set forth in the compact itself. The materials that follow regarding the Pecos River Compact between Texas and New Mexico illustrate this. Second, because Congress's approval of an interstate compact takes the so-called "dormant" commerce clause out of play, compacts are not vulnerable to scrutiny under that doctrine, which avoids issues such as those raised in the *Sporhase* case, infra p. 880. Finally, interstate water compacts sometimes establish a commission or other interstate administrative body and give it authority to manage the shared water resource in accordance with the standards laid out in the compact.[16] The leading example of such a governance structure for basin-wide interstate water resource management is the Delaware River Basin Commission formed by the Delaware River Basin Compact, addressed at some length in subsection b, below.

a. The Special Status and Coercive Power of Compacts

The case that follows is complicated and somewhat hard to follow. At bottom, it involves an ill-fashioned compact that led to a deadlock of the compact commission, which rendered the commission and the compact ineffective. The difficulties created by the non-functioning compact commission led the United States Supreme Court to probe institutional issues regarding its own power to apportion the water, once Congress had exercised its power by ratifying the compact.

TEXAS v. NEW MEXICO

Supreme Court of the United States, 1983.
462 U.S. 554.

JUSTICE BRENNAN delivered the opinion of the Court.

* * * The Pecos River rises in north-central New Mexico and flows in a southerly direction into Texas until it joins the Rio Grande near

---

16. See Douglas Grant, Water Apportionment Compacts Between States, in 4 Water and Water Rights § 46.03 (Robert Beck ed., 2004); Joseph W. Dellapenna, Interstate Struggles Over Rivers: The Southeastern States and the Struggle over the 'Hooch, 12 N.Y.U.Envtl.L.J. 828, 839–50 (2005).

Langtry, Texas. It is the principal river in eastern New Mexico, draining roughly one-fifth of the State, and it is a major tributary of the Rio Grande.

Due in large part to many natural difficulties, the Pecos barely supports a level of development reached in the first third of this century. If development in New Mexico were not restricted, especially the ground-water pumping near Roswell, no water at all might reach Texas in many years. As things stand, the amount of water Texas receives in any year varies with a number of factors besides beneficial consumption in New Mexico. These factors include, primarily, precipitation in the Pecos Basin over the preceding several years, evaporation in the McMillan and Alamogordo Reservoirs, and nonbeneficial consumption of water by salt cedars and other riverbed vegetation. * * *

[The Pecos River Compact, 63 Stat. 159, ratified by Congress in 1949, was intended to resolve recurring squabbles between Texas and New Mexico. But it did not actually quantify a division of the waters between the states; instead, it provided a method by which the amount was to be quantified.] The crucial substantive provision of the Pecos River Compact is found at Art. III(a): "New Mexico shall not deplete by man's activities the flow of the Pecos River at the New Mexico–Texas state line below an amount which will give to Texas a quantity of water equivalent to that available to Texas under the 1947 condition." The term "1947 condition" was expressly defined as "that situation in the Pecos River Basin as described and defined in the Report of the Engineering Advisory Committee." Art. II(g). In turn, the Report was defined to include "basic data, processes, and analyses utilized in preparing that report," Art. II(f), and "deplete by man's activities" was defined to include any "beneficial consumptive uses of water within the Pecos River Basin," but to exclude diminutions of flow due to "encroachment of salt cedars" or "deterioration of the channel of the stream," Art. II(e). * * *

[The measuring apparatus incorporated in the Compact was complicated and murky. One important part was an "Inflow–Outflow Manual" which was supposed to be used to predict how much water should be delivered at the state line, but which in practice turned out to be woefully inaccurate. In almost every year following 1947, the flows in the River failed to reach the 1947 baseline level, even though there had been no significant changes in water use or natural hydrologic conditions.[1] Thus, every year Texas, the downstream state, received less water at the state line than the Inflow–Outflow Manual would have required. Texas was aggrieved by the under-delivery of water; New Mexico was of the

---

1. [For the technical explanation why the compact did not work out as planned, see R. Bruce Frederick, Salvaged Water: The Failed Critical Assumption Underlying the Pecos River Compact, 33 Nat. Resources J. 217 (1993)—Eds.]

view that the amount of water due was being calculated by reference to a mistaken standard. The compact provided that it was to be administered by a three-member Pecos River Commission, comprised of representatives of each state and the United States. Only the two state commissioners were given a vote, however. Predictably, efforts to forge a new, more accurate model for evaluating New Mexico's compact obligations failed when the two states' voting commissioners could not agree. This impasse lasted for years until Texas ran out of patience.]

In June 1974, Texas invoked the original jurisdiction of this Court under Art. III, section 2, cl. 2 of the United States Constitution and 28 U.S.C. § 1251. Its bill of complaint alleged that New Mexico had breached its obligations under Art. III(a) of the Compact "by countenancing and permitting depletions by man's activities within New Mexico to the extent that from 1950 through 1972 there has occurred a cumulative departure of the quantity of water available from the flow of the Pecos River at the Texas–New Mexico State Line in excess of 1,200,000 acre-feet from the equivalent available under the 1947 condition * * *." Texas sought a decree commanding New Mexico to deliver water in accordance with the Compact. The United States intervened to protect its own claims on the waters of the Pecos River, which had been preserved in Arts. XI–XII of the Compact. * * *

Recognizing that the Commission would be unlikely to act by unanimous vote of both State Commissioners, and that continued impasse favored the upstream State, the Special Master recommended:

[T]he equity powers of the Court are adequate to provide a remedy. If within a reasonable time * * * the States do not agree on a tie-breaking procedure, the Court would be justified in ordering * * * that either the representative of the United States, or some other third-party, be designated and empowered to participate in all the Commission's deliberations and act decisively when the States are not in agreement. The order should provide that the decision of the tie-breaker is final, subject only to appropriate review by the Court. Upon the selection of a tie-breaker, the States should be ordered to return to the Commission for determination of this long-standing controversy.

At the same time, the Special Master rejected two pending motions, one by New Mexico for dismissal of the case altogether, and one by Texas to adopt a simpler method than the Inflow–Outflow Manual provides for determining the extent of shortfalls in state-line water deliveries.

Both the United States and New Mexico have filed exceptions to the Special Master's key recommendation—that either the United States Commissioner or some other third party be given a vote on the Pecos River Commission and empowered to participate in all Commission deliberations. We sustain their exceptions.

Under the Compact Clause, two States may not conclude an agreement such as the Pecos River Compact without the consent of the

United States Congress. However, once given, "congressional consent transforms an interstate compact within this Clause into a law of the United States." Cuyler v. Adams, 449 U.S. 433, 438 (1981); see Pennsylvania v. Wheeling & Belmont Bridge Co., 13 How. 518, 566 (1852). One consequence of this metamorphosis is that, unless the compact to which Congress has consented is somehow unconstitutional, no court may order relief inconsistent with its express terms. Yet that is precisely what the Special Master has recommended. The Pecos River Compact clearly delimits the role of the United States Commissioner. * * * To provide a third, tiebreaking vote on regular Commission business would be to alter fundamentally the structure of the Commission.

Congress may vest a federal official with the responsibility to administer the division of interstate streams. See Arizona v. California, 373 U.S. 546, 564–567 (1963). Other interstate compacts, approved by Congress contemporaneously with the Pecos River Compact, allow federal representatives a vote on compact-created commissions, or expressly provide for arbitration by federal officials of commission disputes. E.g., Upper Colorado Basin Compact, 63 Stat. 31, 35–37 (1949); Arkansas River Compact, 63 Stat. 145, 149–151 (1949); Yellowstone River Compact, 65 Stat. 663, 665–666 (1951). The Pecos River Compact clearly lacks the features of these other compacts, and we are not free to rewrite it.

Without doubt, the structural likelihood of impasse on the Pecos River Commission is a serious matter. In light of other States' experience, Texas and New Mexico might well consider amending their Compact to provide for some mutually acceptable method for resolving paralyzing impasses such as the one that gave rise to this suit. Nevertheless, the States' failure to agree on one issue, however important, does not render the Compact void, nor does it provide a justification for altering its structure by judicial decree. The Commission *has* acted on many matters by unanimous vote. We cannot say whether unanimity would have been achieved had a tie-breaker stood ready to endorse one State's position over the other's. Under the Compact as it now stands, the solution for impasse is judicial resolution of such disputes as are amenable to judicial resolution, and further negotiation for those disputes that are not. * * *

The question for decision, therefore, is what role the Pecos River Compact leaves to this Court. The Compact itself does not expressly address the rights of the States to seek relief in the Supreme Court, although it clearly contemplates some independent exercise of judicial authority. Fundamental structural considerations, however, militate against New Mexico's theory [that the case should be dismissed]. First, if all questions under the Compact had to be decided by the Commission in the first instance, New Mexico could indefinitely prevent authoritative Commission action solely by exercising its veto on the Commission. As New Mexico is the upstream State, with effective power to deny water altogether to Texas except under extreme flood conditions, the Commission's failure to take action to enforce New Mexico's obligations under

Art. III(a) would invariably work to New Mexico's benefit. Under New Mexico's interpretation, this Court would be powerless to grant Texas relief on its claim under the Compact.

If it were clear that the Pecos River Commission was intended to be the exclusive forum for disputes between the States, then we would withdraw. But the express terms of the Pecos River Compact do not constitute the Commission as the sole arbiter of disputes between the States over New Mexico's Art. III obligations. Our equitable power to apportion interstate streams and the power of the States and Congress acting in concert to accomplish the same result are to a large extent complementary. See Frankfurter & Landis, The Compact Clause of the Constitution—A Study in Interstate Adjustments, 34 Yale L.J. 685, 705–708 (1925). Texas' right to invoke the original jurisdiction of this Court was an important part of the context in which the Compact was framed; indeed, the threat of such litigation undoubtedly contributed to New Mexico's willingness to enter into a compact. It is difficult to conceive that Texas would trade away its right to seek an equitable apportionment of the river in return for a promise that New Mexico could, for all practical purposes, avoid at will. In the absence of an explicit provision or other clear indications that a bargain to that effect was made, we shall not construe a compact to preclude a State from seeking judicial relief when the compact does not provide an equivalent method of vindicating the State's rights. * * *

* * * The crucial question that remains to be decided is the fourth: "[H]as New Mexico fulfilled her obligations under Article III(a) of the Pecos River Compact?" That question necessarily involves two subsidiary questions. First, under the proper definition of the "1947 condition," what is the difference between the quantity of water Texas could have expected to receive in each year and the quantity it actually received? For the 1950–1961 period, that difference has been determined by unanimous vote of the Commission; for 1962 to the present, determining the extent of the shortfall will require adjudicating disputes between the States as to specific issues raised by the 1947 Study, the Review of Basic Data, and the Inflow–Outflow Manual. The States have fully briefed their positions, however, and the Special Master has already heard extensive evidence on these questions. Second, to what extent were the shortfalls due to "man's activities in New Mexico"?

Time and again we have counselled States engaged in litigation with one another before this Court that their dispute "is one more likely to be wisely solved by co-operative study and by conference and mutual concession on the part of the representatives of the States which are vitally interested than by proceedings in any court however constituted." New York v. New Jersey, 256 U.S. 296, 313 (1921). It is within this Court's power to determine whether New Mexico is in compliance with Article III(a) of the Pecos River Compact, but it is difficult to believe that the bona fide differences in the two States' views of how much water Texas is entitled to receive justify the expense and time necessary to obtain a judicial resolution of this controversy. With that observation, we return this case to the Special Master for determination of the unresolved issues framed in his Pre–Trial Order, in a manner consistent with this opinion.

It is so ordered.

Notes and Questions[1]

1. After a remand and the filing of a new report by the Special Master, the case once again came before the Supreme Court. Texas v. New Mexico, 482 U.S. 124 (1987). The shortfall to Texas was calculated at 340,100 acre-feet for the period 1950–1983, and the Special Master recommended that New Mexico be required to repay it in kind by delivering an average of 34,010 acre-feet beyond its compact obligations in each of the next ten years. He also recommended charging "water interest" in the event that New Mexico lagged behind in making the payments. New Mexico preferred paying in cash, not water. The Supreme Court discussed the question of remedy this way:

> The Special Master's report also states that both sides would probably be better off with monetary repayment but * * * observes that the Compact contains no explicit provision for monetary relief. The Master concluded that the Compact contemplated delivery of water and that the Court could not order relief inconsistent with the Compact terms. The State of Texas supports the Master's view. * * * [T]he lack of a specific provision for a remedy in case of breach does not, in our view, mandate repayment in water and preclude damages. * * * [W]e are quite sure that the Compact itself does not prevent our ordering a suitable remedy, whether in water or money.

482 U.S. at 130. The opinion likened the grant of a water remedy to a grant of specific performance in equity, which "requires some attention to the relative benefits and burdens that the parties may enjoy or suffer as compared with a legal remedy in damages." The case was once again remanded to the Special Master for his "recommendation as to whether New Mexico should be allowed to elect a monetary remedy and, if so, to suggest the size of the payment and other terms New Mexico must meet." Two years later the two states settled on a cash payment of $14,000,000.

2. The settlement of the claim for past damages did not end New Mexico's troubles in meeting its compact obligations. In the 1990s the state spent $50 million for one-time purchases of water from agricultural irrigators to send downstream to Texas. Eventually it adopted legislation authorizing the New Mexico Interstate Stream Commission to purchase several thousand acres of land and water rights (and retire the latter permanently) to satisfy its compact obligations. Part of the acquisitions are of senior water rights, in order to avoid cutting off some rich farms and dairies with junior

---

1. For an interesting meditation on the "scientific failure of the brightest and best of the West's engineers and hydrologists" on the Pecos, see G. Emlen Hall, The Mismeasure of the Pecos River: Royce Tipton and the 1948 Pecos River Compact, 9 Western Legal History 55 (1996); see also G. Emlen Hall, Steve Reynolds—Portrait of a State Engineer as a Young Artist, 38 Nat. Resources J. 537, 551–61 (1998) (critically examining Reynolds' role in the Pecos River situation).

water rights. About $40 million has been spent so far, with at least that much more needed. In the meantime, the Commission is leasing water from the farmers (paying $100 per acre-foot for 34,000 acre-feet in 2005). The program has remained controversial, but a state district court in November 2004 dismissed an attempt by some water rights holders to enjoin the purchases on the ground it violated the New Mexico constitution and other laws. Field v. Interstate Stream Comm'n, No. CIV–98–193 (N.M. 5th Judicial Dist., Lea County).

3.   Should the Supreme Court encourage the formation of compacts, so as to lessen the need for the courts to engage in the difficult task of apportioning interstate waters themselves, by equitable apportionment (discussed in the next section)? If that is the goal, was it served by the Supreme Court's decision here? How will this decision influence states as they contemplate whether to enter into compacts with their neighbors?

4.   One lesson of the Pecos River Compact litigation is the importance of avoiding, where possible, a structure likely to result in compact commission gridlock, especially where key issues remain open for post-enactment resolution. Another lesson is to avoid ambiguity where possible (although it is often not possible). A compact is simultaneously both a statute and a contract. See Oklahoma v. New Mexico, 501 U.S. 221, 235 n. 5 (1991). Should its ambiguities be resolved by principles of interpretation applied to ambiguities in statutes, or by those applied to ambiguities in contracts? In Oklahoma v. New Mexico, a bare majority, over a vigorous dissent, applied principles of statutory interpretation, rather than the contracts-based parol evidence rule, to a dispute over the proper interpretation of the Canadian River Compact. See also Joseph Robertson, Oklahoma and Texas v. New Mexico: A Hastily Negotiated River Compact Leads to Problems in Equitable Apportionment of the Canadian River, 32 Nat. Resources J. 705 (1992).

5.   Drought in the Northern Great Plains has led Montana and Wyoming to squabble over interpretation of the Yellowstone River Compact of 1950, apportioning the waters of the longest undammed river in the Nation. The Compact provides that "[a]ppropriative rights to the beneficial uses of the water of the Yellowstone River System existing in each signatory State as of January 1, 1950, shall continue to be enjoyed in accordance with the laws governing the acquisition and use of water under the doctrine of appropriation," and goes on to proscribe a percentage-based allocation of "unused and unappropriated waters" of the Yellowstone River system. 65 Stat. 653. Wyoming contends the quoted language means the compact addresses only post–1950 water rights, and thus it has no duty to shut off its pre–1950 junior water rights in order to satisfy senior rights downstream in Montana. See Casper Star Tribune, Feb. 23, 2005.

6.   Should the Supreme Court have refused to resolve the Pecos River dispute? As discussed in the next section of this chapter, the Supreme Court has long exercised authority to apportion interstate waters where no compact exist. Should it exercise such authority where there is a compact, but it is not working? Whether a compact exists or not, any decision by the Court is subject to revision by Congress, exercising its interstate commerce power.

7.   As pointed out in the introductory note to this section, the compact itself is federal law, on a par with other federal law and trumping inconsis-

tent state laws. This means, among other things, that a compact controls over state water law and defeats any water right granted by a state in an interstate stream that exceeds that state's entitlement under the compact. See Hinderlider v. La Plata River & Cherry Creek Ditch Co., 304 U.S. 92 (1938). Suppose there are two rivers, the Black and the Blue, which both flow from State X to State Y. Suppose state X has sound reasons for seeking, in compact negotiations with downstream state Y, the right to divert more water from the Black River. In exchange for State Y's agreement to give it more water on the Black, could State X agree to a compact with State Y on the Blue River that apportions to State Y some water Farmer Jones currently diverts from the Blue in state X under state X's appropriation permit, without compensating Farmer Jones? The political dynamic linking the two rivers is not fanciful; some observers believe something similar happened in the simultaneous treaty negotiations between the United States and Mexico over the Rio Grande and Colorado Rivers; see infra pp. 893–894.

8. The Tenth Circuit has held that the Upper Colorado River Basin Compact does not establish a private right of action to enforce its provisions. Three Forks Ranch v. City of Cheyenne, 96 Fed. Appx. 567 (10th Cir. 2004) (unpublished).

9. Actions to implement a compact which are taken by federal land or water management agencies, or by a compact commission or other body set up to administer the compact, are subject to regulatory and procedural laws that apply to federal actions, such as the National Environmental Policy Act and the Endangered Species Act. Environmental advocates may seek to use these statutes as a way to inject fish, wildlife and water quality concerns into the administration of compacts which were, for the most part, negotiated and executed before the modern environmental movement brought such concerns to the fore. Suppose a compact allocates a certain portion of river flow for use in upstream state A, which is stored and diverted for use from a federal Bureau of Reclamation reservoir on the river. In an ESA consultation with the Bureau on its dam operation, the U.S. Fish and Wildlife Service officials determine that endangered whooping cranes in downstream state B need more water than the compact apportions to state B. The operation of the ESA here may effectively modify the compact's apportionment by limiting the Bureau of Reclamation's diversion in order to protect the species.[2]

10. Even if there is no direct federal nexus, regulatory provisions like the ESA's section 9, 16 U.S.C. § 1538 (see supra pp. 651–652), which prohibits anyone from "taking" a listed species, might operate to limit diversions that are otherwise called for or permitted by compacts. Similarly, the federal Clean Water Act allows states to set water quality standards that, once approved by the federal Environmental Protection Agency, may be enforced against activities in other states, see Arkansas v. Oklahoma, 503 U.S. 91 (1992), which might in some circumstances affect compact allocations. Cf. PUD No. 1 v. Washington Dep't of Ecology, 511 U.S. 700 (1994) (Clean Water Act allows state to impose instream flow requirements for fish protection on certain federally-licensed projects). How should an apparent

---

2. Note, however, that some state or federal legal doctrines may not apply to actions taken under compacts. See Joseph W. Dellapenna, Interstate Struggles Over Rivers: The Southeastern States and the Struggle over the 'Hooch, 12 N.Y.U.Envtl. L.J. 828, 832–35 (2005).

conflict between a compact and another federal law be resolved? The same way other conflicts among federal laws are resolved; that is, are compacts and laws like the ESA of equal stature? An unpublished district court opinion, Rio Grande Silvery Minnow v. Keys, 2002 WL 32813602, addressed whether water used for endangered species protection in the Rio Grande was to be considered a "beneficial consumptive use" within the meaning of a pertinent compacts, and concluded "[t]here is no direct conflict between the ESA and the Compacts, and the Compacts do not limit BOR's discretion under the ESA." See also Klamath Irr. Dist. v. United States, 67 Fed. Cl. 504, 539–40 (2005) (nothing in the Klamath River Basin Compact "enhances the rights of any [beneficiaries of a federal reclamation project in the basin] as against the United States" even though the Compact provided that the U.S. "shall not, without payment of just compensation, impair any rights to the use of water" within the basin, because the Compact also provided that nothing in it "shall be deemed: [t]o impair or affect any rights [or] powers * * * of the United States * * * over and to the waters of the Klamath River Basin"); and see United States v. Adair, 723 F.2d 1394, 1419 (9th Cir. 1983) (Klamath River Basin Compact did not "control the government's acquisition of" water rights for the benefit of Indians in the basin).

11. What law governs a claim that a state, by entering into an interstate compact delegating management powers to a compact commission, violated its own state law? See State ex rel. Dyer v. Sims, 341 U.S. 22 (1951) (U.S. Supreme Court can review and override a state supreme court's application of state's constitution to an interstate compact where it implicates "the rights of other states and the United States"). See also People ex rel. Simpson v. Highland Irrig. Co., 917 P.2d 1242, 1249 (Colo. 1996) (state courts should not "usurp mechanisms for operation and dispute resolution" included in interstate compacts).

12. According to Professor Douglas Grant, only a small minority of the compacts in force make any explicit reference to groundwater. See Douglas Grant, Water Apportionment Compacts Between States, in 4 Waters and Water Rights § 46.03 (Robert Beck ed., 2004). Two recent cases brought by Kansas effectively extended compacts to hydrologically related groundwater. In Kansas v. Colorado, 514 U.S. 673 (1995), the Court upheld Kansas' argument that pumping in Colorado of groundwater associated with the Arkansas River violated a requirement of the 1949 Arkansas River Compact (which did not expressly mention groundwater) that the waters of the River "shall not be materially depleted in usable quantity or availability" by development of "works for the purposes of water utilization and control." Six years later the Court approved a damages award to Kansas for Colorado's post-Compact increases in groundwater pumping. Kansas v. Colorado, 533 U.S. 1 (2001). In Kansas v. Nebraska, 538 U.S. 720 (2003), the Court approved a settlement of Kansas's claim that upstream Nebraska was stealing Republican River water Kansas was entitled to under a 1943 Compact by allowing the pumping of hydrologically related groundwater; Nebraska's defense was that the compact did not address groundwater. The settlement requires use of a water model to track the interaction between ground and surface water, establishes a moratorium on new wells in certain locations, and creates a dispute resolution mechanism. (On groundwater modeling, see chapter 5, supra pp. 409–411.) Given the fact that hydrologic

connections often exist between groundwater and surface water, and that sound policy suggests attention be paid to these connections (see supra pp. pp. 454–456), should the Supreme Court adopt a presumption that silence or ambiguity in a compact apportioning streamflow be construed as incorporating hydrologically related groundwater?

13.   Professor Grant challenges the conventional wisdom that compacts are permanent arrangements in Interstate Water Allocation Compacts: When the Virtue of Permanence Becomes the Vice of Inflexibility, 74 U. Colo. L. Rev. 105–80 (2003). That notion stems from the Supreme Court's decision in Green v. Biddle, 21 U.S. (8 Wheat.) 1 (1823), which held that the U.S. Constitution's Contract Clause (U.S. Const. art. I, § 10, cl. 1, forbidding states from passing any law impairing the Obligation of Contracts") extends to compacts between states, subject to some exceptions based on a state's inalienable sovereignty. Grant argues that the principal exception—that a state cannot bargain away its sovereign responsibility to protect things like public health—gives a state severely disadvantaged by an old compact a credible claim to withdraw from it in some circumstances. He points out that while western states are, unsurprisingly, the main participants in water compacts, most of the agreements were forged several decades ago, in the heyday of (non-Indian) irrigation, before massive urban population growth and the rise of environmental concern and vigorous assertion of Indian water rights. One example Grant uses to illustrate his argument involves the Pecos River. Around the time Texas and New Mexico reached agreement on a cash settlement for past losses on remand from the Supreme Court, the U.S. Fish and Wildlife Service listed the Pecos bluntnose shiner as a threatened species and required alterations in river flows to protect it. This has impaired supplies to some farmers in New Mexico, and also reduced (because of evaporative losses) flows at the state line. The U.S. government has been making cash payments for the loss, but if the U.S. were to stop doing so, New Mexico would have to curtail diversions to meet its compact obligations. Professor Grant points out that New Mexico has a reasonable policy argument that both states should share the burden of protecting endangered species, and suggests there might be enough uncertainty about the permanence of the compact to persuade Texas, if circumstances in New Mexico were dire enough, to consider renegotiating it.

14.   The most recently approved interstate water compacts, as of this writing, were nothing more than compacts to negotiate compacts, and have proved to be an abysmal failure. They involved two parallel river systems flowing through Georgia, Alabama and Florida. Both the Apalachicola–Chattahoochee–Flint (ACF) and the Alabama–Coosa–Tallapoosa (ACT) Compacts, 111 Stat. 2219, 2233 (1997) created compact commissions charged with the responsibility to "develop an allocation formula for equitably apportioning the surface waters" of the river basins involved, while protecting water quality and the environment. The compacts were negotiated with considerable dispatch after rapid population growth in the Atlanta metropolitan area (8–fold in the last half-century) and a five-fold increase in irrigated acres in southern Georgia in the last quarter century combined with droughts in the late 1980s and again in the late 1990s to spur the Corps of Engineers to take steps to reallocate water from its reservoirs in the two basins, and led the downstream states to challenge the Corps in federal

court. A basic part of the dispute pits upstream Georgia's desire for more diversions (the Atlanta area is the headwaters of five stream systems, four of which flow out of state) against downstream Florida's desire to maintain a viable shellfishing industry and ecological amenities. Each compact gave each of the three basin states one vote and required unanimity. A Federal Commissioner, appointed by the President, was given no vote but the power to veto the allocation plan on the basis of federal law. The compacts expired by a date certain if no allocation formula was agreed to, and after numerous extensions, the ACF compact was allowed to expire in August 2003 and the ACT Compact in July 2004. In the wreckage numerous pieces of litigation relating to basin water management remain on file in various courts involving various entities, including the states (see pp. 96–97 supra), and the possibility looms of an equitable apportionment suit in the U.S. Supreme Court. Joseph W. Dellapenna, Interstate Struggles Over Rivers: The Southeastern States and the Struggle Over the 'Hooch, 12 N.Y.U. Envtl. L.J. 828 (2005); Benjamin L. Snowden, Bargaining in the Shadow of Uncertainty: Understanding the Failure of the ACT and ACT Compacts, 13 N.Y.U. Envtl. L.J. 134 (2005).

15. Materials on interstate and international issues involving the Great Lakes are found at pp. 899–902 below, including a brief discussion of a proposed new interstate water compact now before the eight basin states.

b. Compact Management Capabilities: The Delaware River Basin Compact

Just as the story of the Colorado River looms large in the water history of the West, so does the Delaware River's story in the East. The watershed includes areas in Delaware, New Jersey, New York and Pennsylvania. Although a geographically small basin, draining only about 13,500 square miles (less than 1% of the United States), it is the principal water source for more than 20 million people, including residents of New York City and Philadelphia. The upper River to the Trenton Falls is free-flowing, clean and contains some of the finest championship trout streams in the country. The lower river is heavily industrial, with oil refineries, nuclear power and chemical plants lining its banks. It is the only undammed river of any size in the east.

Commensurate with its importance as a source of supply to so many people, increasing demands for its water led to a pitched battle for control of the river. Compacts were negotiated in 1925 and 1927 but were defeated in the New Jersey legislature. See Richard Albert, Damming the Delaware: The Rise and Fall of Tocks Island Dam 17–20 (1987). Lawsuits were then filed in the United States Supreme Court seeking an apportionment of the river (a topic studied in detail in the next section). The Court made an initial apportionment in 1931,[3] and the decree was modified in 1954.[4] State and local officials, dissatisfied with judicial solutions, pushed for both a comprehensive basin plan and a

---

3. New Jersey v. New York, 283 U.S. 336 (1931).

4. New Jersey v. New York, 347 U.S. 995 (1954).

commission to implement it.[5] This led, in 1961, to approval of an interstate compact which sought to manage the Delaware as a regional resource, rather than as the property of the individual states in accordance with their apportioned shares.[6] At the core of the compact was the Delaware River Basin Commission (DRBC), one of the most powerful regional agencies ever created. Under the compact, the commission is granted broad powers to control all water uses in the basin.[7]

The DRBC is constructed along straightforward lines, with one representative from each of the four basin states and a United States commissioner appointed by the President. All are voting members— giving the U.S. a vote was an innovation. A simple majority vote controls on most issues, but a unanimous vote is required in matters affecting water allocation. See generally Delaware River Basin Compact §§ 2.1– 2.7. A primary purpose of the DRBC was to formulate a comprehensive plan for present uses and the long-term development of the basin. Id. § 3.2. Although it took many years to develop, such a plan was eventually adopted, and now serves as a central point of reference.

Besides its planning function, the Commission is empowered to control every important aspect of river management: water quality, water allocation, hydroelectric power generation, recreational use, flood control and watershed preservation. The leverage of the Commission over the basin states and private parties lies in the requirement that the Commission must approve all projects in the basin having substantial effect on the water resources of the basin. Approval is refused to projects not in conformity with the comprehensive plan. Id. § 3.8. The Commission manages the supply of water throughout the basin for all uses, including domestic, municipal, industrial and agricultural. Id. § 4. The DRBC can acquire, operate, and maintain dams, reservoirs and other facilities for the utilization of surface and groundwater supplies. Id. § 4.2. The Commission's discretion in water allocation is, however, limited by the 1954 equitable apportionment Supreme Court decree, which can be altered only in times of emergency, declared so by a unanimous vote of the Commission. An important feature of the compact is that it makes all new federal water projects in the basin subject to Commission authority.

A key motivation for the compact was to provide a mechanism for allocating basin waters in times of shortage, which is exactly what

---

5. For a comprehensive discussion of the pre-compact years see Jerome Muys, Interstate Water Compacts: The Interstate Compact and Federal–Interstate Compact (Nat'l Water Comm'n Legal Study No. 14, 1971).

6. Pub. L. 87–328, 75 Stat. 688.

7. For a dated but still useful discussion of the problems of shared use of the Delaware River, see Joseph Sax, Water Law, Planning and Policy 151–85 (1968). The Delaware River Basin Compact was the model for the Susquehanna River Compact signed by the United States, Maryland, New York, and Pennsylvania. 84 Stat. 1509 (1970). These two compacts are "notable exceptions" among interstate water compacts, with managerial regimes that "go beyond anything found elsewhere." Joseph W. Dellapenna, Interstate Struggles Over Rivers: The Southeastern States and the Struggle over the 'Hooch, 12 N.Y.U. Envtl. L.J. 828, 840 (2005).

confronted the Commission almost as soon as it was created, quickly putting its array of management powers to a severe test. A severe drought in the mid–1960s led New York City to defy the Court's decree to maintain releases into the Delaware. In June 1965, but a summit meeting of basin governors and federal officials three weeks later led to the declaration of a basin-wide emergency, temporary adjustment of decree-mandated diversion and release rates, and the Basin muddled through.[8] The drought led the DRBC to undertake a program of basin water supply development. Its centerpiece was a dam at Tocks Island in the Delaware mainstem which Congress had authorized in 1962. The dam became controversial because of concern over its adverse environmental consequences. After fifteen years of debate, it was abandoned and in 1978 the relevant stretch of the Delaware River was instead protected by designation under the Wild & Scenic Rivers Act.[9] Up to that point, some smaller dam and reservoir projects had been completed on tributaries in the upper basin, but abandonment of the Tocks Island dam project left downstream Pennsylvania cities, including Philadelphia, vulnerable to the upstream encroachment of salinity in time of drought, absent potentially devastating reductions in New York City's withdrawals from the river system near its headwaters.

A new drought in 1980–82 led Pennsylvania to threaten to go back to the U.S. Supreme Court, and eventually the basin states and New York City entered into the "Good Faith Agreement"[10] that combined several elements, including (a) setting salinity standards protective of the estuary and downstream cities; (b) providing a coordinated plan of reservoir releases and giving DRBC control of all state, federal and private utility reservoir releases in low flow emergency situations; (c) authorizing DRBC to establish a water use budget and to insist that initiation of new uses be linked to availability of actual storage capacity; and (d) committing the parties to support (politically and financially) several additional storage and flow control projects. See Joseph Dellapenna, The Delaware and Susquehanna River Basins, in 6 Waters and Water Rights 137 (Robert Beck ed., repl. vol. 1994).

The Good Faith Agreement appeared to succeed where litigation and uneasy cooperation had failed. The DRBC exercises control over in-basin projects and insists that all water users abide by water budgeting requirements. New storage and flow control facilities have been completed, and in drought conditions of the late 1990s the system generally met water supply needs, although there are increasing concerns about species threatened by low flows. Joseph W. Dellapenna, Interstate Struggles Over Rivers: The Southeastern States and the Struggle Over the 'Hooch,

---

8. R. Timothy Weston, The Delaware River Basin: Courts, Compacts and Commissions, in Boundaries and Water: Allocation and Use of a Shared Resource (U. Colo. Nat. Res. L. Ctr. 1989).

9. 16 U.S.C. § 1274(20).

10. See Interstate Water Management Recommendation of the Parties to the United States Supreme Court Decree to the DRBC Pursuant to Commission Resolution 78–20 (Nov. 1982). Final signing occurred in February 1983 and included as a signatory the Mayor of New York.

12 N.Y.U. Envtl. L.J. 828, 839–49 (2005). One knowledgeable observer has summed up the Commission's performance this way:

> Faced with serious challenges and changing conditions, the DRBC has proven a relatively effective water management tool. The DRBC takes credit for key achievements in (1) developing a unified drought management plan; (2) adopting a joint reservoir operations program; (3) resolving interstate conflicts over water allocations and transfers; (4) implementing comprehensive water quality standards; (5) promulgating water conservation standards; and (6) providing a vehicle for joint investment in new water management facilities.[11]

Notes and Questions

1.   The Delaware basin is usually cited as an example of successful basin management. What might be the DRBC's advantages over a compact that simply allocates water among states; e.g., a simple agreement that obligates upstream states to deliver a specific quantity or flow to downstream states, and otherwise leaves each state to manage the water within its jurisdiction? Professor Dellapenna has observed that none of the states involved in the ACT–ATF compact negotiations (see supra p. 852) "seriously considered the model of the Delaware Compact * * * that would cooperatively manage the waters of the shared rivers rather than attempt to allocate the waters according to some formula, leaving each state largely free to do as it wishes with its share of the waters." Joseph W. Dellapenna, Interstate Struggles Over Rivers: The Southeastern States and the Struggle over the 'Hooch, 12 N.Y.U.Envtl.L.J. 828, 878 (2005). Why has the Delaware Basin model not proved attractive?

2.   The late Dean Charles Meyers argued that congressional apportionment is superior to the compact process:

> First, a congressional division is likely to be more expeditious than compact or Supreme Court apportionment. A division by compact may never take place; a Court division is unlikely to be completed in less than ten years. Such delays can be very costly. Second, a congressional apportionment is in fact a form of compact, negotiated by the states' water officials through their congressional delegation rather than through appointed commissioners.

Charles Meyers, The Colorado River, 19 Stan. L. Rev. 1, 47–48 (1966). Although less critical of the compact process, Professor John Carver some years later expressed the view that, "the interstate water compact has had its day in the sun; the compact approach to the resolution of problems of apportionment of interstate streams will survive, if it does, as a gesture of goodwill by a dominating federal government." John Carver, Interstate Water Compacts 566–67 (unpublished paper, June 1982). For a generally more favorable view of the compact process, see David Ladd, Federal and Interstate Conflicts in Montana Water Law: Support For A State Water

---

11. Weston, supra note 8, at 1. The Commission's web site is at <http://www.state.nj.us/drbc>.

Plan, 42 Mont. L. Rev. 267 (1981); Jerome Muys, Interstate Water Compacts: The Interstate Compact and Federal–Interstate Compact (Nat'l Water Comm'n Legal Study No. 14, 1971).

3.   The Delaware River Compact embodies a waiver by all parties of their rights to go back to the Supreme Court to modify the 1954 decree. It also provides that water allocation orders (including the declaration of water emergencies) require a unanimous vote of the commissioners. What remedy do other parties to the compact have if New York unilaterally diverts water in excess of compact limits? Does the United States Supreme Court's construction of the Pecos River Compact in a way that protected Texas against New Mexico's unilateral action signal that the Court would protect the downstream parties in this setting as well?

4.   For many years the DRBC has played an important role in controlling water pollution, especially in the cleanup of the heavily polluted lower reaches of the river. To control pollution the commission uses a variety of tools ranging from surveys and investigations to construction and operation of pollution abatement facilities. As with state pollution control agencies operating under the federal Clean Water Act, the DRBC issues permits to dischargers regulating their effluent. The DRBC enforces those permits by issuing pollution abatement orders which then can be the basis for litigation if compliance is not obtained. In more recent years the DRBC has begun monitoring the levels of toxic substances in the surface and groundwater of the basin, trying to avoid serious problems before they develop. For a dated but still interesting study of the DRBC's efforts to clean up the Delaware, see Bruce Ackerman et al., The Uncertain Search for Environmental Quality (1974). The cleanup has had measurable success—the lower Delaware has been cleaned up enough that fish have returned, though there is a ban on eating them.

5.   Another problem facing the DRBC is the depletion of groundwater aquifers within the basin. Certain areas in Pennsylvania have been declared "groundwater protected areas" and any person wishing to make withdrawals from that source must obtain a permit from the DRBC. Permits limit quantities and impose conservation requirements as conditions to be met by the water user. Another problem groundwater area is south central New Jersey where long-term regional aquifer declines have led to the threat of salt water intrusion into the aquifer. To solve these problems and avoid similar future ones, the DRBC and the Army Corps of Engineers have considered development of a groundwater augmentation system that would capture and store excess surface water that would otherwise run to the sea unused.

6.   A key to the continued success of the DRBC is adequate funding. The compact calls for equitable apportionment of costs among the signatory states and the federal government. Can a compacting state legally refuse to pay its share if the assessment is adopted by a majority vote of the commissioners? West Virginia ex rel. Dyer v. Sims, 341 U.S. 22 (1951) suggests a negative answer. Section 3.7 of the Compact appears to give the DRBC the right to impose user fees, but the Commission has not exercised the authority. A major contemporary problem is that New York state and the

federal government have fallen millions of dollars behind in payments owed to the Commission. N. Y. Times, Dec. 6, 2004, at A21.

3. EQUITABLE APPORTIONMENT

In the absence of mutual agreement or congressional action, disputant states making conflicting claims to a common pool natural resource like the water of an interstate river turn to the United States Supreme Court to serve as arbiter of the dispute. The Court, as Justice Holmes once put it, is "competent to deal with [a dispute between states] which, if it arose between independent sovereignties, might lead to war."[12] One source of the Court's authority is the Constitution's grant of original jurisdiction to it in cases "in which a State shall be a Party" (art. III, § 2, cl. 2). These adjudications, or "equitable apportionments" as they are called, have become the principal instrument other than negotiation for resolving interstate water disputes. As with other disputes within its original jurisdiction (see, e.g., Texas v. New Mexico, supra p. 843), the Court typically appoints a Special Master to hear the evidence and make a recommended decision.

The first equitable apportionment case the Court resolved involved the Arkansas River. Kansas v. Colorado, 206 U.S. 46 (1907). Kansas, the downstream state, claimed harm from upstream diversions in Colorado. At the time Kansas followed the riparian rights doctrine, and it claimed a right to the "continual flow of the stream" and, in the alternative, that if a rule of priority were applied, uses in Kansas were senior in time to the uses in Colorado. Colorado claimed the right to keep any water from flowing into Kansas. Justice Brewer, writing for the Court, set the tone for all future equitable apportionment cases:

> One cardinal rule, underlying all the relations of the States to each other, is that of equality of right. Each State stands on the same level with all the rest. It can impose its own legislation on no one of the others, and is bound to yield its own views to none. Yet, whenever * * * the action of one State reaches through the agency of natural laws, into the territory of another State, the question of the extent and the limitations of the rights of the two States becomes a matter of justiciable dispute between them, and this court is called upon to settle that dispute in such a way as will recognize the equal rights of both and at the same time establish justice between them. In other words, through these successive disputes and decisions this court is practically building up what may not improperly be called interstate common law.[13]

Applying those broad precepts of equality and justice, the Court concluded that, though Colorado had made heavy use of Arkansas River water, irrigating thousands of acres and diminishing the River's flow to

---

12. Missouri v. Illinois, 200 U.S. 496, 518 (1906). See also Richard B. Stewart, Interstate Resource Conflicts: The Role of the Federal Courts, 6 Harv. Envtl.L.Rev. 241 (1982).

13. 206 U.S. at 97–98.

the "perceptible injury" of Kansas, yet Kansas has not shown enough injury to warrant the intervention of the Court. The Court did warn that the time might come when "Kansas may justly say that there is no longer an equitable division of benefits, and may rightfully call for relief * * *."[14]

This is an important limitation, which in practice has made it hard to pry open the doors of the Supreme Court, for in many subsequent cases the Court has rejected invitations to issue equitable apportionment decrees by finding disputes not of such "serious magnitude" as to require it to exercise what it has described as its "extraordinary power * * * to control the conduct of one state at the suit of another." New York v. New Jersey, 256 U.S. 296, 309 (1921). It has also dismissed suits when the United States government had such an important interest at stake that it was regarded as an indispensable party, and it refused to waive its sovereign immunity to join the litigation. See, e.g., Texas v. New Mexico, 352 U.S. 991 (1957); Arizona v. California, 298 U.S. 558 (1936); but see Idaho v. Oregon, 444 U.S. 380 (1980) (United States not an indispensable party to a suit to equitably apportion anadromous fish in the Columbia–Snake River System). Sometimes the United States chooses to participate voluntarily, as in the litigation that resulted in the landmark Arizona v. California 1963 decision set out supra p. 821.

The following dispute is the most recent equitable apportionment case to be litigated to a conclusion in the Supreme Court. The facts resemble a classic law school hypothetical—all the water of an interstate stream is being used in the downstream state and the upstream state now wants a share, and both states apply the prior appropriation doctrine. In some respects the case is atypical (a small river with a limited number of fairly simple uses), but it required the Court to wrestle with some broad principles.

COLORADO v. NEW MEXICO (I)

Supreme Court of the United States, 1982.
459 U.S. 176.

JUSTICE MARSHALL delivered the opinion of the Court.

* * * The Vermejo River is a small, nonnavigable river that originates in the snowbelt of the Rocky Mountains in southern Colorado and flows southeasterly into New Mexico for a distance of roughly 55 miles before it joins the Canadian River. The major portion of the river is located in New Mexico. The Colorado portion consists of three main

14. 206 U.S. at 117. Nearly forty years later Kansas, claiming changed conditions, again sought apportionment and again was denied. Although Colorado appropriations added up to more than the dependable flow of the river, the evidence also showed that, due to return flows from Colorado diversions, more water was reaching Kansas than in the past. Colorado v. Kansas, 320 U.S. 383 (1943). Eventually, in 1949, the two states entered into a compact (see 63 Stat. 145 (1949)), and in 1985 Kansas brought yet another lawsuit, this one based on Colorado's alleged compact violations. See supra p. 851.

tributaries that combine to form the Vermejo River proper approximately one mile below the Colorado–New Mexico border. At present there are no uses of the water of the Vermejo River in Colorado, and no use or diversion has ever been made in Colorado. In New Mexico, by contrast, farmers and industrial users have diverted water from the Vermejo for many years. In 1941 a New Mexico state court issued a decree apportioning the water of the Vermejo River among the various New Mexico users.

In 1975, a Colorado corporation, Colorado Fuel and Iron Steel Corporation (C.F. & I.), obtained in Colorado state court a conditional right to divert 75 cubic feet per second from the headwaters of the Vermejo River. C.F. & I. proposed a transmountain diversion of the water to a tributary of the Purgatoire River in Colorado to be used for industrial development and other purposes. * * * [Thereafter, upon the request of private appropriators in New Mexico, a New Mexico federal district court enjoined the exercise of this right. Kaiser Steel Corp. v. C.F. & I. Steel Corp., Civil No. 76–224 (D.N.M. 1976). The State of Colorado then brought an original jurisdiction action in the Supreme Court to gain recognition of a share of the Vermejo's waters. Following discovery and a trial on the merits, the Special Master recommended that Colorado be permitted a diversion of 4,000 acre-feet per year, and New Mexico objected.]

Equitable apportionment * * * is a flexible doctrine which calls for "the exercise of an informed judgment on a consideration of many factors" to secure a "just and equitable" allocation. Nebraska v. Wyoming, 325 U.S. 589, 618 (1945). We have stressed that in arriving at "the delicate adjustment of interests which must be made," ibid., we must consider all relevant factors, including:

> physical and climatic conditions, the consumptive use of water in the several sections of the river, the character and rate of return flows, the extent of established uses, the availability of storage water, the practical effect of wasteful uses on downstream areas, [and] the damage to upstream areas as compared to the benefits to downstream areas if a limitation is imposed on the former. [Ibid.]

Our aim is always to secure a just and equitable apportionment "without quibbling over formulas." New Jersey v. New York, 283 U.S. 336, 343 (1931).

The laws of the contending states concerning intrastate water disputes are an important consideration governing equitable apportionment. When, as in this case, both states recognize the doctrine of prior appropriation, priority becomes the "guiding principle" in an allocation between competing States. Nebraska v. Wyoming, 325 U.S. at 618. But state law is not controlling. Rather, the just apportionment of interstate waters is a question of federal law that depends "upon a consideration of the pertinent laws of the contending States and *all other relevant facts*." Connecticut v. Massachusetts, 282 U.S. [660,] 670–671 [(1931)] (emphasis added).

In reaching his recommendation the Special Master did not focus exclusively on the rule of priority, but considered other factors such as the efficiency of current uses in New Mexico and the balance of benefits to Colorado and harm to New Mexico. New Mexico contends that it is improper to consider these other factors. * * * We disagree * * *.

In addition, we have held that in an equitable apportionment of interstate waters it is proper to weigh the harms and benefits to competing States. * * * We noted that the rule of priority should not be strictly applied where it "would work more hardship" on the junior user "than it would bestow benefits" on the senior user. [Nebraska v. Wyoming, 325 U.S.] at 619. The same principle is applicable in balancing the benefits of a diversion for *proposed* uses against the possible harms to existing uses. See, e.g., Wyoming v. Colorado, supra.

We recognize that the equities supporting the protection of existing economies will usually be compelling. The harm that may result from disrupting established uses is typically certain and immediate, whereas the potential benefits from a proposed diversion may be speculative and remote. Under some circumstances, however, the countervailing equities supporting a diversion for future use in one state may justify the detriment to existing users in another state. This may be the case, for example, where the state seeking a diversion demonstrates by clear and convincing evidence that the benefits of the diversion substantially outweigh the harm that might result.[13] In the determination of whether the state proposing the diversion has carried this burden, an important consideration is whether the existing users could offset the diversion by reasonable conservation measures to prevent waste. This approach com-

13. Our cases establish that a state seeking to prevent or enjoin a diversion by another state bears the burden of proving that the diversion will cause it "real or substantial injury or damage." Connecticut v. Massachusetts, supra, 282 U.S. at 672. See also New Jersey v. New York, 283 U.S. at 344–345; Kansas v. Colorado, 206 U.S. at 480; Colorado v. Kansas, 320 U.S. at 393–394. This rule applies even if the state seeking to prevent or enjoin a diversion is the nominal defendant in a lawsuit. In Colorado v. Kansas, for instance, Colorado sued Kansas seeking to enjoin further lawsuits by Kansas water users against Colorado users. Although Kansas was the defendant, we granted Colorado an injunction based on Kansas' failure to sustain the burden of showing that the Colorado diversions had "worked a serious detriment to the substantial interests of Kansas." Id. at 400.

New Mexico must therefore bear the initial burden of showing that a diversion by Colorado will cause substantial injury to the interests of New Mexico. In this case New Mexico has met its burden since *any* diver-sion by Colorado, unless offset by New Mexico at its own expense, will necessarily reduce the amount of water available to New Mexico users.

The burden has therefore shifted to Colorado to establish that a diversion should nevertheless be permitted under the principle of equitable apportionment. Thus, with respect to whether reasonable conservation measures by New Mexico will offset the loss of water due to Colorado's diversion, or whether the benefit to Colorado from the diversion will substantially outweigh the possible harm to New Mexico, Colorado will bear the burden of proof. It must show, in effect, that without such a diversion New Mexico would be using "more than its equitable share of the benefits of a stream." Id. at 394. Moreover, Colorado must establish not only that its claim is of a "serious magnitude," but also that its position is supported by "clear and convincing evidence." Connecticut v. Massachusetts, 282 U.S. at 669. See also Colorado v. Kansas, 320 U.S. at 393; Washington v. Oregon, 297 U.S. at 522.

ports with our emphasis on flexibility in equitable apportionment and also accords sufficient protection to existing uses.

We conclude, therefore, that in the determination of an equitable apportionment of the water of the Vermejo River the rule of priority is not the sole criterion. While the equities supporting the protection of established, senior uses are substantial, it is also appropriate to consider additional factors relevant to a just apportionment, such as the conservation measures available to both states and the balance of harm and benefit that might result from the diversion sought by Colorado. * * * We remand for specific factual findings relevant to determining a just and equitable apportionment of the water of the Vermejo River between Colorado and New Mexico.

It is so ordered.

CHIEF JUSTICE BURGER, with whom JUSTICE STEVENS joins, concurring in the opinion and the judgment.

* * * I emphasize that under our prior holdings these two states come to the Court on equal footing. Neither is entitled to any special priority over the other with respect to use of the water. Colorado cannot divert all of the water it may need or can use simply because the river's headwaters lie within its borders. Nor is New Mexico entitled to any particular priority of allocation or undiminished flow simply because of first use. Each state through which rivers pass has a right to the benefit of the water but it is for the Court, as a matter of discretion, to measure their relative rights and obligations and to apportion the available water equitably. As the Court's opinion states, in the process of apportioning the water, prior dependence and inefficient uses may be considered in balancing the equities. But no state has any priority over any other state. It is on this understanding of the Court's holding that I join the opinion and the judgment.

[JUSTICE O'CONNOR, joined by JUSTICE POWELL, concurred separately, expressing the view that the Court should be extremely hesitant to apportion the water of a fully appropriated stream to would-be future users absent "*compelling* evidence of waste." (Emphasis in original)]

COLORADO v. NEW MEXICO (II)

Supreme Court of the United States, 1984.
467 U.S. 310.

JUSTICE O'CONNOR delivered the opinion of the Court.

Last Term, we remanded for additional factual findings on five specific issues. The case is before us again on New Mexico's exceptions to these additional findings. We now conclude that Colorado has not demonstrated by clear and convincing evidence that a diversion should be permitted. Accordingly, we sustain New Mexico's exceptions and dismiss the case. * * *

Last Term, the Court made clear that Colorado's proof would be judged by a clear-and-convincing-evidence standard. * * * [This standard is] necessary to appropriately balance the unique interests involved in water rights disputes between sovereigns * * * [and it] accommodates society's competing interests in increasing the stability of property rights and in putting resources to their most efficient uses * * *.

To establish whether Colorado's proposed diversion could be offset by eliminating New Mexico's nonuse or inefficiency, we asked the Master to make specific findings concerning existing uses, supplies of water, and reasonable conservation measures available to the two States. After assessing the evidence both States offered about existing uses and available supplies, the Master concluded that * * * more careful water administration in New Mexico would * * * ensure that users fully devote themselves to development of available resources. * * *

We share the Master's concern that New Mexico may be overstating the amount of harm its users would suffer from [the proposed diversion upstream in Colorado]. Water use by appropriators along the Vermejo River has remained relatively stable for the past 30 years, and this historic use falls substantially below the decreed rights of those users. Unreliable supplies satisfactorily explain some of this difference, but New Mexico's attempt to excuse three decades of nonuse in this way is, at the very least, suspect. Nevertheless, whatever the merit of New Mexico's explanation, we cannot agree that Colorado has met its burden of identifying, by clear and convincing evidence, conservation efforts that would preserve any of the Vermejo River water supply.

For example, * * * [Colorado] did not actually point to specific measures New Mexico could take to conserve water. * * * [T]he administrative improvements Colorado suggests are either too general to be meaningful or involve redistribution, as opposed to preservation, of water supplies. * * * Our cases require only conservation measures that are "financially and physically feasible" and "within practicable limits." New Mexico submitted substantial evidence that the District * * * has taken considerable independent steps—including, the construction, at its own expense and on its own initiative, of a closed stockwater delivery system—to improve the efficiency of its future water use. The Master did not find to the contrary; indeed, he commended New Mexico for the substantial efforts it had taken. Nevertheless, he accepted Colorado's general assertion that the District was not as efficient as other reclamation projects and concluded that New Mexico's inefficient use should not be charged to Colorado. But Colorado has not identified any "financially and physically feasible" means by which the District can further eliminate or reduce inefficiency and, contrary to the Master's suggestion, we believe that the burden is on Colorado to do so. A State can carry its burden of proof in an equitable apportionment action only with specific evidence about how existing uses might be improved, or with clear evidence that a project is far less efficient than most other projects. Mere assertions about the relative efficiencies of competing projects will not do.

Finally, there is no evidence in the record that "Colorado has undertaken reasonable steps to minimize the amount of the diversion that will be required." Nine years have passed since C.F. & I. first proposed diverting water from the Vermejo River. Yet Colorado has presented no evidence concerning C.F. & I.'s inability to relieve its needs through substitute sources. Furthermore, there is no evidence that C.F. & I. has settled on a definite or even tentative construction design or plan, or that it has prepared an economic analysis of its proposed diversion. * * * [I]t would be irresponsible of us to apportion water to uses that have not been, at a minimum, carefully studied and objectively evaluated, not to mention decided upon. Financially and physically feasible conservation efforts include careful study of future, as well as prudent implementation of current, water uses. Colorado has been unwilling to take any concrete steps in this direction.

Society's interest in minimizing erroneous decisions in equitable apportionment cases requires that hard facts, not suppositions or opinions, be the basis for interstate diversions. In contrast to Justice Stevens, we do not believe Colorado has produced sufficient facts to show, by clear and convincing evidence, that reasonable conservation efforts will mitigate sufficiently the injury that New Mexico successfully established last Term that it would suffer were a diversion allowed. No State can use its lax administration to establish its claim to water. But once a State successfully proves that a diversion will cause it injury, the burden shifts to the diverter to show reasonable conservation measures exist. Colorado has not carried this burden.

We also asked the Master to help us balance the benefits and harms that might result from the proposed diversion. The Master found that Colorado's proposed interim use is agricultural in nature and that more permanent applications might include use in coal mines, timbering, power generation, domestic needs, and other industrial operations. The Master admitted that "[t]his area of fact finding [was] one of the most difficult [both] because of the necessarily speculative nature of [the] benefits * * * "and because of Colorado's "natural reluctance to spend large amounts of time and money developing plans, operations, and cost schemes. * * * " Additional Factual Findings 23. Nevertheless, because the diverted water would, at a minimum, alleviate existing water shortages in Colorado, the Master concluded that the evidence showed considerable benefits would accrue from the diversion. Furthermore, the Master concluded that the injury, if any, to New Mexico would be insubstantial, if only because reasonable conservation measures could, in his opinion, offset the entire impact of the diversion. Id., at 24–28.

Again, we find ourselves without adequate evidence to approve Colorado's proposed diversion. Colorado has not committed itself to any longterm use for which future benefits can be studied and predicted. Nor has Colorado specified how long the interim agricultural use might or might not last. All Colorado has established is that a steel corporation wants to take water for some unidentified use in the future.

By contrast, New Mexico has attempted to identify the harms that would result from the proposed diversion. New Mexico commissioned some independent economists to study the economic effects, direct and indirect, that the diversion would have on persons in New Mexico. The study these economists produced was submitted at the original hearing, conducted prior to the remand, as evidence of the injury that would result from the reduction in water supplies. No doubt, this economic analysis involved prediction and forecast. But the analysis is surely no more speculative than the generalizations Colorado has offered as "evidence." New Mexico, at the very least, has taken concrete steps toward addressing the query this Court posed last Term. Colorado has made no similar effort.

Colorado objects that speculation about the benefits of future uses is inevitable and that water will not be put to its best use if the expenditures necessary to development and operation must be made without assurance of future supplies. We agree, of course, that asking for absolute precision in forecasts about the benefits and harms of a diversion would be unrealistic. But we have not asked for such precision. We have only required that a State proposing a diversion conceive and implement some type of long-range planning and analysis of the diversion it proposes. * * *

As a final consideration, the Master pointed out that approximately three-fourths of the water in the Vermejo River system is produced in Colorado. He concluded, therefore, that "the equities are with Colorado, which requests only a portion of the water which it produces." Additional Factual Findings 29. * * * [We reject] the notion that the mere fact that the Vermejo River originates in Colorado automatically entitles Colorado to a share of the river's waters. Both Colorado and New Mexico recognize the doctrine of prior appropriation, and appropriative, as opposed to riparian, rights depend on actual use, not land ownership. It follows, therefore, that the equitable apportionment of appropriated rights should turn on the benefits, harms, and efficiencies of competing uses, and that the source of the Vermejo River's waters should be essentially irrelevant to the adjudication of these sovereigns' competing claims. To the extent the Master continued to think the contrary, he was in error. * * *

Accordingly, we sustain the State of New Mexico's exceptions to the Special Master's Report and Additional Factual Findings, and dismiss the case.

It is so ordered.

JUSTICE STEVENS, dissenting.

* * * The first of the two alternative grounds supporting the Master's recommendation is "that New Mexico could compensate for some or all of the Colorado diversion through reasonable water conservation measures." [A review of Colorado's evidence on this issue is omitted.] * * * New Mexico simply continues to cling to the position that it should not be required to employ conservation measures to facilitate

Colorado's proposed uses, notwithstanding the fact that we explicitly rejected this position last term and in doing so quoted the following language from our seminal decision in this area:

> "The question here is not what one State should do for the other, but how each should exercise her relative rights in the waters of this interstate stream. * * * Both subscribe to the doctrine of appropriation, and by that doctrine rights to water are measured by what is reasonably required and applied. Both States recognize that conservation within practicable limits is essential in order that needless waste may be prevented and the largest feasible use may be secured. This comports with the all-pervading spirit of the doctrine of appropriation and takes appropriate heed of the natural necessities out of which it arose. We think that doctrine lays on each of these States a duty to exercise her right reasonably and in a manner calculated to conserve the common supply." Wyoming v. Colorado, 259 U.S. 419, 484 (1922).

[A discussion of the New Mexico State Engineer's near-total lack of monitoring of actual water use practices is omitted.]

Colorado is correct when it states that "New Mexico should not be permitted to use its own lack of administration and record keeping to establish its claim that no water can be conserved. That position, if accepted by the Court, would encourage states to obscure their water use practices and needs in order to avoid their duty to help conserve the common supply." * * * New Mexico's manifestly lax, indeed virtually non-existent, administration of the Vermejo surely substantially diminishes its rights to the waters. It invites waste, and renders the amount of that waste an unknown. * * *

Alternatively, the Master found that the benefit to Colorado from the diversion would outweigh the injury, if any, to New Mexico. The identifiable benefits to Colorado included projected permanent uses, interim uses, and the alleviation of the existing shortages in the Purgatoire River system. * * * The Master properly acknowledged that there could be no certainty that all of Colorado's proposed uses would actually materialize, but he concluded that "if even half of them are fully implemented," the diversion would be justified. * * * The Special Master's task was not to draw up blueprints for New Mexico to eliminate its waste. The Master, based on all the evidence, concluded that reasonable conservation efforts in New Mexico would offset the effects of the Colorado diversion. * * * My examination of the testimony persuades me that that conclusion is supported by the record.

Accordingly, I respectfully dissent.

Notes and Questions

1. Does Justice O'Connor's opinion in the second decision apply the tests set forth in Justice Marshall's footnote 13 in the first decision, or does it change direction?

2.   What is the relevance, if any, of the fact that most of the Vermejo's waters are "produced" in Colorado by precipitation and runoff? In the first decision Justice Marshall says "all relevant factors," including "physical and climatic conditions," must be considered. What does Justice O'Connor say on this point in the second decision? Should interstate equitable apportionment reward (or penalize) a state for its natural bounty (or lack thereof)? International law principles for determining a sovereign's right to a reasonable and equitable share of international waters take into account the geography and the hydrology of the basin, including "the contribution of water by each" State. See infra p. 891. Can a difference between interstate and international law on this point be justified? Does it have something to do with the sovereignty of nations versus the sovereignty of states?

3.   Does Justice O'Connor's opinion effectively eliminate any incentive for a senior appropriating state to engage in conservation measures on interstate waterbodies? Assuming New Mexico users are doing far less than they could to conserve the Vermejo's waters, is the Supreme Court's ruling in their favor any different from the attitude of many western states, which regard wasteful but customary irrigation practices as "beneficial"? Should it be? Should the federal common law of equitable apportionment aspire to more than the lowest common denominator of state laws? Shortly after the first decision, the Court had opined that "States have an affirmative duty under the doctrine of equitable apportionment to take reasonable steps to conserve and even to augment the natural resources within their borders for the benefit of other States." Idaho v. Oregon, 462 U.S. 1017, 1025 (1983) (involving salmon, not water). Why did the majority in the second decision pass up the opportunity to promote better water management and serve the interests of brethren sovereign states?

4.   Suppose the river was entirely within one state, and a proposed new user with a more efficient use brought a suit against existing appropriators alleging they are inefficient and wasteful. What result? Are New Mexico users any different from senior appropriators who have an unreasonable means of diversion? From shallow senior groundwater pumpers who do not want to deepen their wells so that others can tap the aquifer?

5.   In Nebraska v. Wyoming, 515 U.S. 1 (1995), the Court seemed to veer back toward Colorado v. New Mexico (I). Wyoming claimed that federal management of Bureau of Reclamation reservoirs in the basin was unlawful because, among other things, it promotes "inefficiency and waste of water contrary to federal and state law." The Court said Wyoming ought to be given an opportunity to prove that the federal government "pays no heed to federal law's beneficial use limitations" (section 8 of the Reclamation Act of 1902; see supra p. 761, Note 5d) by failing "to police consumption," with consequent injury to Wyoming. The case was later settled; see 534 U.S. 40 (2001).

6.   Does Justice O'Connor's opinion apply the idea expressed by Justice Brewer, in Kansas v. Colorado, supra p. 858, that the states come before the Court in equitable apportionment actions on an equal footing? Should New Mexico have to produce some compelling evidence of genuine need for the water it had "appropriated," but was not actually using, before Colorado's request for an apportionment of some portion of the Vermejo River is

denied? Was its showing of a mere paper appropriation enough to saddle Colorado with a heavy if not impossible evidentiary burden? (In previous cases like Nebraska v. Wyoming 325 U.S. 589 (1945), discussed further below, the Court did look behind the paper rights to real world uses of water and the impacts of possible decrees.)

7. What would you advise a state in the situation of Colorado here (seeking a share where all the water of the interstate stream is currently being used in a downstream state) to do? Spend the money on consultants to make the detailed showings the majority seems to require? Make a risky investment in a substantial water diversion project in an attempt to persuade the Court its needs are genuine?

8. Suppose Colorado had appropriated and diverted all the water out of the river, so that the Vermejo no longer flows in New Mexico. Would the concept of equitable apportionment support a claim by New Mexico for water to protect its environment, to re-establish an instream flow in the river? Suppose the dry riverbed is potentially prime habitat for an endangered species of fish, if the upstream state would release some water. Would that change the equities in an equitable apportionment? In Nebraska v. Wyoming, 515 U.S. 1 (1995), one of Nebraska's complaints was that Wyoming's upstream diversion was injuring wildlife and habitat. Wyoming countered that the claim was "purely speculative and best left to other forums." The Special Master proposed to hear Nebraska's evidence of injury "not only to downstream irrigators, but also to wildlife and wildlife habitat." The Court agreed, holding that alleged adverse environmental effects of upstream development in the downstream state are relevant in the equitable apportionment context. 515 U.S. at 11–13. Does this suggest that downstream Florida's desire to preserve its environment as well as its shellfish industry may meet with favor in an equitable apportionment action in its dispute with Georgia in the ACF river basin? See supra p. 853, and J.B. Ruhl, Equitable Apportionment of Ecosystem Services: New Water Law for a New Water Age, 19 J. Land Use 47 (2002); see also Robert Haskell Abrams, Interstate Water Allocation: A Contemporary History for Eastern States, 25 U. Ark. Little Rock L. Rev. 155 (2002).

———

A Brief Tour of Equitable Apportionment Decisions That Have Actually Apportioned Rivers

In only three equitable apportionment cases has the Court actually decreed a division of the waters of a river on an interstate basis. The first was in Wyoming v. Colorado, 259 U.S. 419 (1922), which involved a dispute between two prior appropriation states to the waters of the Laramie River, a tributary of the North Platte. In earlier decisions involving competing *private* claims in different states (both of which followed the prior appropriation doctrine) to water in an interstate stream, the Court had simply applied a single prior appropriation system to the stream and ignored the state line.[1] Wyoming v. Colorado required

---

1. Bean v. Morris, infra p. 874, and Rickey Land & Cattle Co. v. Miller & Lux, 218 U.S. 258 (1910).

the Court to resolve the tension between this approach and the broad precept of equality announced in its first equitable apportionment case, Kansas v. Colorado, 206 U.S. 46 (1907) (see supra p. 858), which seemed to signal that strict priority may not be followed when the states themselves were the disputants. The Court followed the teachings of the cases involving private appropriators, and its decree generally protected the priorities of the individual state law appropriators regardless of the state in which they were located. Thus, senior appropriators in upstream Colorado were protected even in low flow years.[2]

A couple of decades later, the Court took a somewhat different approach, departing from strict application of priority in a dispute among the prior appropriation states Colorado, Wyoming, and Nebraska over the waters of the North Platte River. Nebraska v. Wyoming, 325 U.S. 589 (1945). The Court carefully elaborated the factual underpinnings of the dispute, noting that in its central Nebraska reaches, the Platte[3] is a slow-moving, broad and shallow stream that is often described as "two miles wide and one inch deep." Because the Platte was a major migration route westward, and settled from east to west, the senior appropriations were mostly in downstream Nebraska, with the most junior uses upstream in Colorado. Nebraska naturally argued for applying the rule of priority across state lines, but the Court rejected it, explaining:

> As the Special Master points out the flowage time of water from North Park [far upstream in Colorado] to Bridgeport, Nebraska is between two and three weeks. If a canal in North Park were closed to relieve the shortage of a senior appropriator in Nebraska, it would be highly speculative whether the water would reach the Nebraska appropriator in time or whether the closing of the Colorado canal would work more hardship there than it would bestow benefits in Nebraska. Moreover, there is loss of water in transit from the upper to the downstream sections, increasing with distance. The lower appropriator thus receives less than the upper appropriator loses. And there is evidence that a river-wide priority system would disturb and disrupt long established uses.

325 U.S. at 619. Based on those perceptions of the equities, the Court fashioned a decree that protected Colorado uses even though they were out of priority on a river-wide basis. For example, Wyoming was enjoined from irrigating more than 168,000 acres with water from the main stem or tributaries above certain locations within its borders, in order to protect some junior appropriations. The Court justified this because the water was used by "hundreds of small irrigators," and the "practical

2. While the decision favored some senior appropriators in Colorado, it threatened Colorado's overall claims to water because California was developing much more rapidly and had designs on Colorado River water; thus, this decision was a major impetus to negotiation of the Colorado River compact a few months later. See supra p. 804.

3. The name changes when the North Platte is joined by the South Platte just west of the Nebraska border.

difficulties" of reducing the amount of water they use "would seem to outweigh any slight benefit which senior appropriators might obtain." In the "pivotal section of the river around which the central problems of this case turn," a heavily used section along the Wyoming–Nebraska border, there was a hodge-podge of priorities; some in Nebraska and some in Wyoming in no particular pattern. The Master recommended a division of the natural flow during irrigation season, with 25% to Wyoming and 75% to Nebraska. The Court upheld the Master. It rejected Wyoming's argument for a fixed quantity allocation to Nebraska, with Wyoming taking the rest, on the ground it was inequitable because river flow was so variable. It rejected the argument of Nebraska and the United States for a strict priority system, finding it would be administratively burdensome and deprive each State of "full freedom of intrastate administration of her share of the water."

In between these two decisions, the Court demonstrated that interstate water disputes and equitable apportionment are not confined to the West by deciding New Jersey v. New York, 283 U.S. 336 (1931). The case involved New Jersey's attempt to halt New York City's upstream diversion out of the watershed from Delaware River tributaries. New Jersey argued for a "strict application" of the common law riparian doctrine, arguing that all the basin states followed that doctrine. The Court rejected the argument with a classically terse response by Justice Holmes:

> We are met at the outset by the question what rule is to be applied. * * * [A] more liberal answer may be given than in a controversy between neighbors members of a single State. Different considerations come in when we are dealing with independent sovereigns having to regard the welfare of the whole population and when the alternative to settlement is war. In a less degree, perhaps, the same is true of the quasi-sovereignties bound together in the Union. A river is more than an amenity, it is a treasure. It offers a necessity of life that must be rationed among those who have power over it. New York has the physical power to cut off all the water within its jurisdiction. But clearly the exercise of such a power to the destruction of the interest of lower States could not be tolerated. And on the other hand equally little could New Jersey be permitted to require New York to give up its power altogether in order that the river might come down to it undiminished. Both States have real and substantial interests in the River that must be reconciled as best they may. The different traditions and practices in different parts of the country may lead to varying results but the effort always is to secure an equitable apportionment without quibbling over formulas.[4]

New Jersey complained that the proposed diversion would interfere with navigation, water power projects and other industrial uses, munici-

4. 283 U.S. at 342–43.

pal supplies, water quality, fisheries, recreation, and streamside agriculture. The Master considered all the evidence and found that a diversion of 600 million gallons daily would not materially affect the River downstream, except for recreation and possible difficulty with the oyster fishery as a result of increased salinity. Finding this damage "greater than New Jersey ought to bear," the Master recommended limiting New York's diversion to 440 million gallons daily, and reducing it when required to maintain a certain minimum flow in the River. The Master also recommended requiring New York State to treat sewage it was discharging to the River, in order to protect water quality downstream. The Court per Justice Holmes adopted the Master's recommendations. Its decree also provided:

> The diversion herein allowed shall not constitute a prior appropriation and shall not give the State of New York and City of New York any superiority of right over the State of New Jersey and Commonwealth of Pennsylvania in the enjoyment and use of the Delaware River and its tributaries.

The decree was amended in 1954 to permit New York a much larger withdrawal, again conditional on certain minimum flow requirements being satisfied. See New Jersey v. New York, 347 U.S. 995 (1954). In fact, however, serious water conservation efforts in Gotham have reduced its demand on the River in recent years. Post-decree efforts at river management by interstate compact are discussed supra pp. 853–858.

Notes and Questions

1. In Connecticut v. Massachusetts, 282 U.S. 660 (1931), the Court rejected Connecticut's request to enjoin Boston's upstream diversion of Connecticut River water, finding an insufficient demonstration of injury to Connecticut's interests. The Court in such cases has demanded a finding that the "threatened invasion" of another state's rights must be of "serious magnitude." Washington v. Oregon, 297 U.S. 517, 522 (1936). Why has the Court set the bar to get in the courtroom so high?

2. What are the contours of the doctrine of equitable apportionment? What bearing does the water law doctrine followed by each state have on the outcome? Priority of use? Comparing the costs and benefits of uses, regardless of priority?

3. Is the Court acting in these cases primarily as an arbitrator and peacemaker, rather than in the more judicial role of applying legal rules to facts? How else can you explain the seemingly ad hoc character of the decree in Nebraska v. Wyoming?

4. Does the doctrine of equitable apportionment provide sufficient guidance to allow states to structure their interstate water relations without need of lengthy and expensive Supreme Court adjudication? Does it afford investor-appropriators on interstate streams sufficient guidance and security for their investments in advance of an equitable apportionment?

5. Equitable apportionment litigation can be lengthy and costly, and the states pay the salaries and costs of the Special Master. See Joseph W.

Dellapenna, Interstate Struggles Over Rivers: The Southeastern States and the Struggle over the 'Hooch, 12 N.Y.U. Envtl. L.J. 828, 888–89 (2005).

Finality in Equitable Apportionment Decrees

Several of the apportionments described in the preceding materials have been to the Supreme Court more than once. What kind of change of circumstances would justify the State of Colorado seeking to reopen the dispute over the Vermejo River? Might a decree in an equitable apportionment case be likened to one in a riparian rights case; that is, the adjudication is unassailable only to the extent the specific conditions that prevailed at the time of its rendering continue?

The Court provided some guidance on this question in its 1993 decision in Nebraska v. Wyoming. In 1986 this long-dormant case was reopened at the behest of Nebraska, which petitioned the Supreme Court for an injunction under the decree's "reopener" provision.[5] Nebraska alleged various actual and threatened violations of the decree by Wyoming with the effect of interfering with Nebraska's entitlement to 75% of the natural flow of a particular section of the North Platte. The Court distinguished between two "markedly different" types of claims, one calling for enforcement of the prior decree, and the other seeking modification of the decree. The former mainly involves interpretation of the decree, where injury need not be shown by the complainant, whereas the latter "may well entail the same sort of balancing of equities that occurs in an initial proceeding to establish an equitable apportionment."

> When the plaintiff essentially seeks a reweighing of equities and an injunction declaring new rights and responsibilities, we think the plaintiff still must make a showing of substantial injury to be entitled to relief. This is so not only because a new injunction would work a new infringement on sovereign prerogatives, but also because the interests of certainty and stability counsel strongly against reopening an apportionment of interstate water rights absent considerable justification.

507 U.S. 584, 593 (1993).

Equitable Apportionment and Groundwater

No case has ever been brought to equitably apportion a groundwater aquifer that underlies more than one state; however, there seems to be no reason why the Court would not apply the doctrine of equitable apportionment to an interstate aquifer in an otherwise suitable case, for it has spoken of the "significant federal interest . . . in fair allocation of this diminishing [groundwater] resource," Sporhase v. Nebraska ex rel. Douglas, 458 U.S. 941, 953 (1982).[6] Recently interstate groundwater

---

5. The Court's decrees in these cases typically include a provision retaining jurisdiction and allowing the parties to apply for further relief as may be "necessary or appropriate."

6. Equitable apportionment is flexible not only in its contours but also in regard to the resources to which it may be applied. In Idaho v. Oregon, 462 U.S. 1017, 1024 (1983), the Court held it was an "appropri-

disputes have threatened to erupt. The Southern Nevada Water Authority, serving rapidly growing Las Vegas, has announced plans to pump and export groundwater from sparsely populated rural valleys many miles northeast of the City. Some of the valleys include land in Utah. Studies are now underway to determine the impact of projected pumping, but farmers and officials in Utah are expressing concern that Nevada might be stealing "its" groundwater.

Although the Court has not yet been asked to apportion interstate aquifers, as in compact litigation, groundwater hydrologically related to surface water is beginning to be swept within the ambit of prior equitable apportionment decrees. In Nebraska v. Wyoming, 515 U.S. 1 (1995), the Court agreed to hear Nebraska's complaint that increased groundwater pumping upstream within Wyoming threatened substantial depletion of the river flows to Nebraska's detriment. Wyoming alleged unclean hands because, it said, Nebraska failed to regulate groundwater pumping within its own borders. The Court responded this way:

> We fail to see how the mere fact of unregulated pumping within Nebraska can serve to bar Nebraska's claim. Nebraska is the downstream State and claims that Wyoming's pumping hurts it; Wyoming * * * has yet to make a showing that Nebraska's pumping hurts it or anyone else. If Wyoming ultimately makes such a showing, it could well affect the relief to which Nebraska is entitled, but that is a question for trial * * *.

515 U.S. at 14. In 2001, the Court approved a settlement in this case constraining Wyoming's pumping of hydrologically-connected groundwater, which the parties defined as pumped from a well "so located and constructed that if water were intentionally withdrawn continuously for 40 years, the cumulative stream depletion would be greater than or equal to 28% of the total groundwater withdrawn by that well." See Nebraska v. Wyoming, 534 U.S. 40, 53 (2001); Final Report of Special Master Owen Olpin, p. 31.

The Binding Effect of an Equitable Apportionment Decree

Unlike an order resolving private riparian rights litigation, the decree in an equitable apportionment case binds many not before the Court. State law water rights holders (like CF & I Steel in Colorado v. New Mexico) do not participate as parties; their interests are deemed to be represented by their state under the *parens patriae* doctrine and they are bound by any decree that results. See, e.g., Wyoming v. Colorado, 286 U.S. 494, 509 (1932); Badgley v. New York, 606 F.2d 358 (2d Cir. 1979), cert. denied, 447 U.S. 906 (1980). Note that Colorado v. New Mexico was triggered by private litigation in federal district court involving water users from the same watercourse in different states. The principles at work in such private interstate litigation are addressed in the next section.

ate mechanism for resolving allocative disputes" to anadromous fish that migrate through a river system traversing several states.

4. PRIVATE INTERSTATE WATER LITIGATION

The approaches to interstate water disputes addressed so far (like those used in international treaties discussed in this Chapter's final section) involve apportioning water and letting the respective sovereigns (or a special regional agency) administer it. There are, however, many waterbodies (including aquifers) that cross state boundaries but which have not been apportioned among states through congressional action, interstate compact, or equitable apportionment litigation. When conflicts develop among users of such waterbodies in different states, and the pertinent state governments do not have the interest or will to negotiate a compact or seek an equitable apportionment (and if the Congress displays its usual extreme reluctance to step in), ordinary litigation may be the only way ultimately to resolve such disputes.

As we have seen, in the United States most privately held water rights are property rights created by state law (federal law-based rights are covered in the next chapter). State-law-based water rights have a territorial aspect, because the sovereign power creating them has a territorial component. Thus Idaho (and its Department of Water Resources) has no sovereign authority over a user of Columbia River water located downstream in the State of Washington, even though much of the Columbia's flow originates in Idaho. And vice-versa—Washington has no authority over a user upstream in Idaho.

Some mechanisms do exist to enforce water rights across state lines. Under the full faith and credit clause of the United States Constitution (art. IV, § 1), for example, the laws of the several states and their judicial decisions are entitled to some extra-territorial effect. Congress itself may set ground rules for giving effect to state laws and decisions in other states. Finally, even absent compulsion, states may have good reason to recognize and extend comity to rights created by other states.

BEAN v. MORRIS

Supreme Court of the United States, 1911.
221 U.S. 485.

Mr. Justice Holmes delivered the opinion of the court.

This suit was brought [in federal court in Montana by Morris, an appropriator downstream in Wyoming, to prevent Bean, an appropriator upstream in Montana] from so diverting the waters of Sage Creek in Montana as to interfere with an alleged prior right of Morris, by appropriation, to 250 inches of such waters in Wyoming. Afterwards the other respondent, Howell, was allowed to intervene and make a similar claim. Sage Creek is a small creek, not navigable, that [arises in Montana and] joins the Stinking Water in Wyoming, the latter stream flowing into the Big Horn, which then flows back northerly into Montana again, and unites with the Yellowstone. The circuit court made a decree that Morris was entitled to 100 inches miner's measurement, of date April, 1887, and that, subject to Morris, Howell was entitled to 110 inches, of date August 1, 1890, both parties being prior in time and right to the petitioners. On appeal the findings of fact below were adopted and the decree of the circuit affirmed by the circuit court of appeals.

It was admitted at the argument that but for the fact that the prior appropriation was in one State, Wyoming, and the interference in another, Montana, the decree would be right, so far as the main and important question is concerned. * * * [W]e pass at once to the question of private water rights as between users in different States.

We know no reason to doubt, and we assume, that, subject to such rights as the lower State might be decided by this court to have, and to vested private rights, if any, protected by the Constitution, the State of Montana has full legislative power over Sage Creek while it flows within that State. Kansas v. Colorado, 206 U.S. 46, 93–95. Therefore, subject to the same qualifications, we assume that the concurrence of the laws of Montana with those of Wyoming is necessary to create easements, or such private rights and obligations as are in dispute, across their common boundary line. Missouri v. Illinois, 200 U.S. 496, 521. But with regard to such rights as came into question in the older states, we believe that it always was assumed, in the absence of legislation to the contrary, that the States were willing to ignore boundaries, and allowed the same rights to be acquired from outside the State that could be acquired from within. [citations omitted] There is even stronger reason for the same assumption here. Montana cannot be presumed to be intent on suicide, and there are as many if not more cases in which it would lose as there are in which it would gain, if it invoked a trial of strength with its neighbors. In this very instance, as has been said, the Big Horn, after it has received the waters of Sage Creek, flows back into that State. But this is the least consideration. The doctrine of appropriation has prevailed in these regions probably from the first moment that they knew of any law, and has continued since they became territory of the United States. It was recognized by the statutes of the United States, while Montana and Wyoming were such territory, Rev. Stat. §§ 2339, 2340, p. 429, Act of March 3, 1877, c. 107, 19 Stat. 377, and is recognized by both States now. Before the state lines were drawn of course the principle prevailed between the lands that were destined to be thus artificially divided. Indeed, Morris had made his appropriation before either State was admitted to the Union. The only reasonable presumption is that the States upon their incorporation continued the system that had prevailed theretofore, and made no changes other than those necessarily implied or expressed. See Willey v. Decker, 11 Wyoming, 496; Smith v. Denniff, 24 Montana, 20.

It follows from what we have said that it is unnecessary to consider what limits there may be to the powers of an upper State, if it should seek to do all that it could. The grounds upon which such limits would stand are referred to in Rickey Land & Cattle Co. v. Miller & Lux, 218 U.S. 258, 261. So it is unnecessary to consider whether Morris is not protected by the Constitution; for it seems superfluous to fall back upon the citadel until some attack drives him to that retreat. Other matters adverted to in argument, so far as not disposed of by what we have said, have been dealt with sufficiently in two courts. It is enough here to say that we are satisfied with their discussion and confine our own to the only matter that warranted a certiorari or suggested questions that might be grave.

Decree affirmed.

Notes and Questions

1. The Montana federal court's jurisdiction was based on diversity of citizenship of the parties. Presumably this would often be the case in interstate litigation over interstate waters; that is, the entity doing the act complained of and the complainant are likely to be citizens of different states. Where diversity jurisdiction is not available, the case could presumably be brought in a state court of general subject matter jurisdiction.

2. Several other technical, jurisdictional, and choice-of-law problems could arise in litigation involving state-law-based rights in interstate streams, where the combatants are in different states. Consider, for example, why the plaintiff Morris, a Wyoming citizen, chose to go to federal court in the defendant's state of residence. Probably because it may have been impossible for any Wyoming court, state or federal, to obtain extraterritorial service on the defendant at that time. The failure to obtain good service and *in personam* jurisdiction over the defendant would render the Wyoming judgment a nullity, not entitled to full faith and credit. In modern times, with long-arm statutes and much easier means for obtaining extraterritorial service of process, *in personam* jurisdiction could likely be established in a case like *Bean*. On the other hand, because plaintiff was seeking an injunction rather than damages,[7] it may have been advisable to sue in the defendant's state, because full faith and credit does not invariably require that a state aid in the enforcement of injunctive relief ordered by the courts of a sister state. See, e.g., Russell Weintraub, Commentary on the Conflict of Laws 558–68 (3d ed. 1986).

3. While here both states apply the general doctrine of prior appropriation, they might apply the doctrine differently in certain circumstances, and those differences could control the outcome. Suppose Bean claimed that Morris was wasting water, and suppose Morris was using an amount of water for his irrigation in Wyoming that would be inconsistent with how Montana applies the "beneficial use" principle, but consistent with how Wyoming would apply the principle. Which state's water law should the Montana court apply to evaluate Morris's Wyoming water right?[8]

4. Could an equitable apportionment suit in the United States Supreme Court reverse this victory for the downstream Wyoming appropriator, Morris? See the Supreme Court's 1945 decision in Nebraska v. Wyoming, discussed supra p. 869, which protected junior priority uses in Colorado at the expense of senior users in Nebraska.

---

7. This was made clear in the lower court decision. See Morris v. Bean, 146 F. 423, 426 (C.C.D. Mont. 1906).

8. The federal court in a diversity case like *Bean* faces the same choice of law ques-

tions a state court would, because the federal Rules of Decision Act requires the federal court to apply state law to the case. Erie R.R. Co. v. Tompkins, 304 U.S. 64 (1938).

5. Could Montana reverse Morris's victory through an interstate compact with Wyoming? That is, might the two states agree to apportion to Montana water that is necessary to supply Morris's appropriation in Wyoming? Cf. Hinderlider v. La Plata River & Cherry Creek Ditch Co., 304 U.S. 92 (1938), discussed supra p. 850.

6. It may seem surprising, but there are not many lawsuits of the Bean v. Morris variety. Indeed, most of the reported ones took place at the turn of the twentieth century or in its first few decades. For a thorough discussion, see Douglas Grant, Private Interstate Suits, § 44.01, in 4 Waters And Water Rights (Robert Beck ed., 2001). Part of the explanation for the modern scarcity of such cases is the rise of equitable apportionment (beginning with Kansas v. Colorado in 1907) and interstate water compacts (the first one negotiated was the Colorado River Compact in 1922, although the first one to take effect was the La Plata River Compact in 1925). Recall that in Colorado v. New Mexico, supra p. 859 (Vermejo River equitable apportionment), a *Bean*-type lawsuit initially barred development of the River's water in upstream Colorado. See also Colorado v. Kansas, 320 U.S. 383 (1943), where the Supreme Court enjoined Kansas water users from prosecuting pending private suits in federal district court against Colorado users, after finding that Colorado users were not exceeding Colorado's equitable share of the River.

7. But many interstate water bodies have still not been subject either to equitable apportionment litigation or to compact. Furthermore, previously existing legal hurdles to such interstate litigation have been steadily lowered. See, e.g., International Shoe v. Washington, 326 U.S. 310 (1945) (long-arm jurisdiction). And the Supreme Court has given states fairly wide latitude to apply their own laws to a set of facts that involve another state as well as their own; that is, a state may, consistent with the due process clause and the full faith and credit clause, apply its law if it has a "significant contact or significant aggregation of contacts, creating state interests, such that the choice of its law is neither arbitrary nor fundamentally unfair." Phillips Petroleum Co. v. Shutts, 472 U.S. 797, 818 (1985) (quoting Allstate Ins. Co. v. Hague, 449 U.S. 302, 312–13 (1981)). Thus the absence of such suits seems puzzling.

8. In Bean v. Morris, Justice Holmes presumes that states are willing to recognize the same rights in waters to be acquired from outside the state that could be acquired from within. If adjacent states apply the same water law doctrines, what principled rationale (other than naked self-interest) do they have for not doing so? While adjacent states are much more likely than not to apply the same surface water doctrines (even if, as noted in paragraph 3 above, their laws might differ in the details), that's not always true; e.g., California still recognizes riparian rights but none of its neighbors do. Furthermore, groundwater doctrines follow a much more crazy-quilt pattern, and several states have unique statutory approaches to groundwater. How should the courts handle private interstate disputes to watercourses when the state laws applicable to the common resource are considerably different from each other? Develop and apply special rules under the rubric of federal common law? For a discussion, see Grant, Private Interstate Suits, supra para. 6, § 44.05(b)(2), in 4 Waters and Water Rights (Robert Beck, ed., 2001).

9.   A ditch company was using its direct diversion surface water rights in the Carson River to irrigate lands in California. Desiring to convert these rights to storage rights in a reservoir on the same river downstream in Nevada, it applied to the Nevada State Engineer for approval, pursuant to a previous court decree in a general stream adjudication (United States v. Alpine Land & Reservoir Co., 697 F.2d 851 (9th Cir. 1983)). The State Engineer approved, but on the condition that the ditch company make no attempt to irrigate its California farmlands with groundwater that the State Engineer found was hydrologically linked to Carson River flows. The ditch company protested the condition, arguing it was beyond the authority of the Nevada State Engineer to impose. The court conceded that the Nevada State Engineer "cannot regulate groundwater development in California and does not purport to do so" by including this condition, but held that the condition was nevertheless a "proper exercise of the State Engineer's authority." United States v. Alpine Land & Reservoir Co., 919 F.Supp. 1470, 1479 (D. Nev. 1996).

10.   The City of Virginia Beach seeks to divert water from the Roanoke River in Virginia before it flows across the border into North Carolina. Both states follow the riparian rights doctrine, but the waters of the Roanoke have never been allocated between them. What can the city do (other than try to persuade Virginia to seek a compact or a federal statute or to initiate equitable apportionment litigation) in order to secure a right to divert against downstream riparians in North Carolina? Bring a defendant class action against some large riparian owners in North Carolina for a declaratory judgment? See supra pp. 97–102, and Robert H. Abrams, Secure Water Rights in Interstate Waters, in Water Law: Trend, Policies and Practice 330–36 (Kathleen Carr & James Crammond eds., 1995).

5.   STATE EFFORTS TO LOCALIZE WATER

The arid states are not the only ones which attach high cultural and political, as well as economic, value to water. As the discussion of water transfers from the Great Lakes shows (see infra pp. 898–902), competition for water among states can be a spectator sport anywhere in the country. Besides arguing for larger shares of interstate water bodies in the courts or in compact negotiations (and occasionally in the Congress), states have sometimes enacted laws that take a more direct (and often locally politically popular) approach, seeking to preserve waters diverted within their boundaries from export to other states. This section examines legal limits—most important, the so-called dormant commerce clause of the U.S. Constitution—on such efforts.

The first major case to address this issue was Hudson County Water Company v. McCarter, 209 U.S. 349 (1908), where the Supreme Court examined a 1905 New Jersey statute that—asserting the need to preserve the fresh water of the State for the health and prosperity of its citizens—made it "unlawful for any person or corporation to transport or carry, through pipes, conduits, ditches or canals, the waters of any fresh water lake, pond, brook, creek, river, or stream of this State into any other State, for use therein." The defendant water company contracted to supply water from the City of Bayonne in New Jersey to the

New York City Borough of Richmond. The lower courts upheld the statute, finding the export ban consistent with New Jersey's adherence to the riparian rights doctrine (which frowns on the use of water on non-riparian tracts); and that the State had a "residuum of public ownership" in the waters found within its borders. The Supreme Court affirmed, speaking through Justice Holmes:

> But we prefer to put the [State's] authority * * * upon a broader ground than that which was emphasized below, since in our opinion it is independent of the more or less attenuated residuum of title that the State may be said to possess. * * *

> The problems of irrigation have no place here. Leaving them on one side, it appears to us that few public interests are more obvious, indisputable and independent of particular theory than the interest of the public of a State to maintain the rivers that are wholly within it substantially undiminished, except by such drafts upon them as the guardian of the public welfare may permit for the purpose of turning them to a more perfect use. This public interest is omnipresent wherever there is a State, and grows more pressing as population grows. It is fundamental, and we are of opinion that the private property of riparian proprietors cannot be supposed to have deeper roots. * * * [W]e agree with the New Jersey courts, and think it quite beyond any rational view of riparian rights that an agreement, of no matter what private owners, could sanction the diversion of an important stream outside the boundaries of the State in which it flows. The private right to appropriate is subject not only to the rights of lower owners but to the initial limitation that it may not substantially diminish one of the great foundations of public welfare and health.

> We are of opinion, further, that the constitutional power of the State to insist that its natural advantages shall remain unimpaired by its citizens is not dependent upon any nice estimate of the extent of present use or speculation as to future needs. The legal conception of the necessary is apt to be confined to somewhat rudimentary wants, and there are benefits from a great river that might escape a lawyer's view. But the State is not required to submit even to an aesthetic analysis. Any analysis may be inadequate. It finds itself in possession of what all admit to be a great public good, and what it has it may keep and give no one a reason for its will. * * *

> The other defenses also may receive short answers. A man cannot acquire a right to property by his desire to use it in commerce among the States. Neither can he enlarge his otherwise limited and qualified right to the same end. The case is covered in this respect by Geer v. Connecticut, 161 U.S. 519 [1896], and the same decision disposes of the argument that the New Jersey law denies equal privileges to the citizens of New

York. It constantly is necessary to reconcile and to adjust different constitutional principles, each of which would be entitled to possession of the disputed ground but for the presence of the others, as we already have said that it is necessary to reconcile and to adjust different principles of the common law. The right to receive water from a river through pipes is subject to territorial limits by nature, and those limits may be fixed by the State within which the river flows, even if they are made to coincide with the state line. Within the boundary citizens of New York are as free to purchase as citizens of New Jersey. * * * There is nothing else that needs mention. We are of opinion that the decision of the Court of Errors and Appeals was right.

209 U.S. at 356–58. What did Holmes mean by his quip that "benefits from a great river * * * might escape a lawyer's view"? Were he writing today, would he have added "or an economist's"?

Despite Holmes' pro-states' rights explanation in *Hudson County*, over the next seven decades the Supreme Court rather consistently invalidated state schemes (not involving water) that discriminated in favor of state residents or state products for purposes of state economic self-interest.[9] This line of cases included decisions striking down state laws prohibiting exportation of natural resources as unconstitutional impediments to interstate commerce.[10]

The Court summarily affirmed, curiously without opinion (and therefore without attempting to distinguish *Hudson County*), a lower court decision striking down a Texas statute prohibiting export of groundwater across state lines. See City of Altus v. Carr, 255 F.Supp. 828 (W.D.Tex. 1966), aff'd per curiam, 385 U.S. 35 (1966). The Court also expressly overruled the *Geer* case, which Holmes had cited favorably in *Hudson*, and which had held that states had an ownership interest in wildlife found within their borders sufficient to withstand commerce clause scrutiny. Hughes v. Oklahoma, 441 U.S. 322 (1979). *Hudson County* was never overruled, however.

SPORHASE v. NEBRASKA EX REL. DOUGLAS

Supreme Court of the United States, 1982.
458 U.S. 941.

JUSTICE STEVENS delivered the opinion of the Court.

Appellants challenge the constitutionality of a Nebraska statutory restriction on the withdrawal of ground water from any well within Nebraska intended for use in an adjoining State. The challenge presents three questions under the Commerce Clause: (1) whether ground water

9. See, e.g., Hunt v. Washington State Apple Advertising Comm'n, 432 U.S. 333 (1977); Philadelphia v. New Jersey, 437 U.S. 617 (1978).

10. See, e.g., West v. Kansas Natural Gas Co., 221 U.S. 229 (1911) (natural gas); Pennsylvania v. West Virginia, 262 U.S. 553 (1923) (same).

is an article of commerce and therefore subject to Congressional regulation; (2) whether the Nebraska restriction on the interstate transfer of ground water imposes an impermissible burden on commerce; and (3) whether Congress has granted the States permission to engage in ground water regulation that otherwise would be impermissible.

Appellants jointly own contiguous tracts of land in Chase County, Nebraska, and Phillips County, Colorado. A well physically located on the Nebraska tract pumps ground water for irrigation of both the Nebraska tract and the Colorado tract. Previous owners of the land registered the well with the State of Nebraska in 1971, but neither they nor the present owners applied for the permit required by § 46–613.01 of the Nebraska Revised Statutes. That section provides:

> "Any person, firm, city, village, municipal corporation or any other entity intending to withdraw ground water from any well or pit located in the State of Nebraska and transport it for use in an adjoining state shall apply to the Department of Water Resources for a permit to do so. If the Director of Water Resources finds that the withdrawal of the ground water requested is reasonable, is not contrary to the conservation and use of ground water, and is not otherwise detrimental to the public welfare, he shall grant the permit if the state in which the water is to be used grants reciprocal rights to withdraw and transport ground water from that state for use in the State of Nebraska."

Appellee brought this action to enjoin appellants from transferring the water across the border without a permit.[2] The trial court rejected the defense that the statute imposed an undue burden on interstate commerce and granted the injunction. The Nebraska Supreme Court affirmed. 208 Neb. 703, 305 N.W.2d 614 (1981). It held that, under Nebraska law, ground water is not "a marketable item freely transferable for value among private parties, and therefore (is) not an article of commerce." * * *

[The Court discussed its prior decisions in *Hudson County, City of Altus*, and *Hughes v. Oklahoma* (overruling *Geer v. Connecticut*), and continued:] [Nebraska] insists, however, that Nebraska water is distinguishable from other natural resources. The surface owner who withdraws Nebraska ground water enjoys a lesser ownership interest in the water than the captor of game birds in Connecticut or minnows in Oklahoma or groundwater in Texas, for in *Geer, Hughes*, and *City of Altus* the States permitted intrastate trade in the natural resources once they were captured. Although appellee's greater ownership interest may not be irrelevant to Commerce Clause analysis, it does not absolutely

---

2. Because of the reciprocity requirement of § 46–613.01, appellants would not have been granted a permit had they applied for one. Their failure to submit an application therefore does not deprive them of standing to challenge the legality of the reciprocity requirement.

remove Nebraska ground water from such scrutiny. For appellee's argument is still based on the legal fiction of state ownership. * * *

The second asserted distinction is that water, unlike other natural resources, is essential for human survival. Appellee, and the [states filing *amici* briefs] have convincingly demonstrated the desirability of state and local management of ground water. But the States' interests clearly have an interstate dimension. Although water is indeed essential for human survival, * * * over 80% of our water supplies is used for agricultural purposes. The agricultural markets supplied by irrigated farms are worldwide. They provide the archetypical example of commerce among the several States for which the Framers of our Constitution intended to authorize federal regulation. The multistate character of the Ogallala aquifer—underlying appellants' tracts of land in Colorado and Nebraska, as well as parts of Texas, New Mexico, Oklahoma, and Kansas—confirms the view that there is a significant federal interest in conservation as well as in fair allocation of this diminishing resource.

The Western States' interests, and their asserted superior competence, in conserving and preserving scarce water resources are not irrelevant in the Commerce Clause inquiry. Nor is appellee's claim to public ownership without significance. Like Congress' deference to state water law, these factors inform the determination whether the burdens on commerce imposed by state ground water regulation are reasonable or unreasonable. But appellee's claim that Nebraska ground water is not an article of commerce goes too far: it would not only exempt Nebraska ground water regulation from burden-on-commerce analysis, it also would curtail the affirmative power of Congress to implement its own policies concerning such regulation. If Congress chooses to legislate in this area under its commerce power, its regulation need not be more limited in Nebraska than in Texas and States with similar property laws. Ground water overdraft is a national problem and Congress has the power to deal with it on that scale.

Our conclusion that water is an article of commerce raises, but does not answer, the question whether the Nebraska statute is unconstitutional. For the existence of unexercised federal regulatory power does not foreclose state regulation of its water resources, of the uses of water within the State, or indeed, of interstate commerce in water. * * * Determining the validity of state statutes affecting interstate commerce requires a more careful inquiry:

> "Where the statute regulates evenhandedly to effectuate a legitimate local public interest, and its effects on interstate commerce are only incidental, it will be upheld unless the burden imposed on such commerce is clearly excessive in relation to the putative local benefits. If a legitimate local purpose is found, then the question becomes one of degree. And the extent of the burden that will be tolerated will of course depend on the nature of the local interest involved, and on whether it could be promoted as well with a lesser impact on interstate activities."

Pike v. Bruce Church, Inc., 397 U.S. 137, 142 (1970) (citation omitted.)

The only purpose that appellee advances for § 46–613.01 is to conserve and preserve diminishing sources of ground water. The purpose is unquestionably legitimate and highly important, and the other aspects of Nebraska's groundwater regulation demonstrate that it is genuine. Appellants' land in Nebraska is located within the boundaries of the Upper Republican Ground Water Control Area, which was designated as such by the Director of the Nebraska Department of Water Resources based upon a determination "that there is an inadequate ground water supply to meet present or reasonably foreseeable needs for beneficial use of such water supply." The Upper Republican Natural Resources District has promulgated special rules and regulations governing ground water withdrawal and use. The rules and regulations define as "critical" those townships in the control area in which the annual decline of the groundwater table exceeds a fixed percentage; appellants' Nebraska tract is located within a critical township. The rules and regulations require the installation of flow meters on every well within the control area, specify the amount of water per acre that may be used for irrigation, and set the spacing that is required between wells. They also strictly limit the intrastate transfer of ground water: transfers are only permitted between lands controlled by the same groundwater user, and all transfers must be approved by the district board of directors.

The State's interest in conservation and preservation of ground water is advanced by the first three conditions in § 46–613.01 for the withdrawal of water for an interstate transfer. Those requirements are "that the withdrawal of the ground water requested is reasonable, is not contrary to the conservation and use of ground water, and is not otherwise detrimental to the public welfare." Although Commerce Clause concerns are implicated by the fact that § 46–613.01 applies to interstate transfers but not to intrastate transfers, there are legitimate reasons for the special treatment accorded requests to transport ground water across state lines. Obviously, a State that imposes severe withdrawal and use restrictions on its own citizens is not discriminating against interstate commerce when it seeks to prevent the uncontrolled transfer of water out of the State. An exemption for interstate transfers would be inconsistent with the ideal of evenhandedness in regulation. At least in the area in which appellants' Nebraska tract is located, the first three standards of § 46–613.01 may well be no more strict in application than the limitations upon intrastate transfers imposed by the Upper Republican Natural Resources District.

Moreover, in the absence of a contrary view expressed by Congress, we are reluctant to condemn as unreasonable measures taken by a State to conserve and preserve for its own citizens this vital resource in times of severe shortage. Our reluctance stems from the "confluence of (several) realities." First, a State's power to regulate the use of water in times and places of shortage for the purpose of protecting the health of its citizens—and not simply the health of its economy—is at the core of its police power. For Commerce Clause purposes, we have long recognized a difference between economic protectionism, on the one hand, and health and safety regulation, on the other. Second, the legal expectation that under certain circumstances each State may restrict water within its borders has been fostered over the years not only by our equitable apportionment decrees, but also by the negotiation and enforcement of interstate compacts. Our law therefore has recognized the relevance of state boundaries in the allocation of scarce water resources. Third, although appellee's claim to public ownership of Nebraska ground water cannot justify a total denial of federal regulatory power, it may support a limited preference for its own citizens in the utilization of the resource. In this regard, it is relevant that appellee's claim is logically more substantial than claims to public ownership of other natural resources. Finally, given appellee's conservation efforts, the continuing availability of ground water in Nebraska is not simply happenstance; the natural resource has some indicia of a good publicly produced and owned in which a State may favor its own citizens in times of shortage. A facial examination of the first three conditions set forth in § 46–613.01 does not, therefore, indicate that they impermissibly burden interstate commerce. Appellants, indeed, seem to concede their reasonableness.

Appellants, however, do challenge the requirement that "the state in which the water is to be used grants reciprocal rights to withdraw and transport ground water from that state for use in the State of Nebraska"—the reciprocity provision that troubled the Chief Justice of the Nebraska Supreme Court. Because Colorado forbids the exportation of its ground water, the reciprocity provision operates as an explicit barrier to commerce between the two States. The state therefore bears the initial burden of demonstrating a close fit between the reciprocity requirement and its asserted local purpose.

The reciprocity requirement fails to clear this initial hurdle. For there is no evidence that this restriction is narrowly tailored to the conservation and preservation rationale. Even though the supply of water in a particular well may be abundant, or perhaps even excessive, and even though the most beneficial use of water might be in another State, such water may not be shipped into a neighboring State that does not permit its water to be used in Nebraska. If it could be shown that the State as a whole suffers a water shortage, that the intrastate transportation of water from areas of abundance to areas of shortage is feasible regardless of distance, and that the importation of water from adjoining States would roughly compensate for any exportation to those States, then the conservation and preservation purpose might be credibly advanced for the reciprocity provision. A demonstrably arid state conceivably might be able to marshal evidence to establish a close means-end relationship between even a total ban on the exportation of water and a purpose to conserve and preserve water. Appellee, however, does not claim that such evidence exists. We therefore are not persuaded that the reciprocity requirement—when superimposed on the first three restrictions in the statute—significantly advances the State's legitimate conservation and preservation interest; it surely is not narrowly tailored to serve that purpose. The reciprocity requirement does not survive the "strictest scrutiny" reserved for facially discriminatory legislation. * * *

The reciprocity requirement of Neb. Rev. Stat. § 46–613.01 violates the Commerce Clause. We leave to the state courts the question whether the invalid portion is severable. The judgment of the Nebraska Supreme Court is reversed and the case is remanded for proceedings not inconsistent with this opinion.

[Justice Rehnquist, joined by Justice O'Connor, dissented, arguing that Nebraska "so regulates ground water that it cannot be said that the State permits any 'commerce,' intrastate or interstate, to exist in this natural resource." That is, because Nebraska law "recognizes only a limited right to use ground water on land owned by the appropriator, it cannot be said that 'commerce' in ground water exists as far as Nebraska is concerned," and "[t]herefore it cannot be said that the [Nebraska statute] either discriminates against, or 'burdens,' interstate commerce."]

Notes and Questions

1.   On remand the Nebraska Supreme Court held the reciprocity provision severable, leaving the remainder of the statute in force. Nebraska v. Sporhase, 213 Neb. 484, 329 N.W.2d 855 (1983). Thereafter, the Nebraska Department of Water Resources approved Sporhase's application to export Nebraska groundwater into Colorado, finding that the use would not jeopardize groundwater availability for public health and safety, and conditioning the permit on compliance with Nebraska's regulations imposed on in-state users.

2.   The Supreme Court has said that equitable apportionment and the dormant commerce clause rest in part on the same principle; namely, "a State may not preserve solely for its own inhabitants natural resources located within its borders." Idaho v. Oregon, 462 U.S. 1017, 1025 (1983).

3.   What is meant by "demonstrably arid" in Justice Stevens' opinion? If it refers simply to climatic conditions, then most of the West would qualify. Is the phrase intended to involve the court in scrutiny of how tightly the means chosen to protect state water resources fit the enunciated threat? See Maine v. Taylor, 477 U.S. 131 (1986) (a rare case upholding a state's outright discrimination against interstate commerce—its ban on imported live baitfish—because it was justified by state's strong interest in protecting its wild fish from parasites found in imported baitfish, and no alternative to the ban was available).

4.   Has *Sporhase* breathed new life into *Hudson County?* Under what circumstances may a state erect a "limited preference" to safeguard its water resources by restricting export? Does it make any difference whether the water source is wholly within the state or is itself crosses state lines? (The aquifer in *Sporhase* was, as the Court noted, part of the multi-state Ogallala aquifer.)

5.   A cottage industry for lawyers and legal commentators sprang up in the aftermath of *Sporhase*. See, e.g., Richard Harnsberger, Josephine Potuto

& Norman Thorson, Interstate Transfers of Water After *Sporhase*, 70 Neb. L. Rev. 754 (1991). How far toward protectionism may a state go to husband water supplies found within its borders? Suppose Nebraska applied the same criteria of "reasonableness" and "not detrimental to the public welfare" to permit applications for use of water in-state. (Compare the discussion of the "public interest" in appropriations supra pp. 220–226.) May it apply such criteria in a way that discriminates against appropriations for export? Might it be difficult to prove such discrimination, if the state at least purports to apply the same criteria to appropriations for in-state use? Reconsider these questions after reading the note on the El Paso litigation, below.

6.   Note that the Court in *Sporhase* laid some emphasis on the fact that Nebraska had regulations in place to regulate groundwater pumping in-state. In fact, however, there was ample reason to believe that the state did not do much regulation. See J. David Aiken, Nebraska Ground Water Law and Administration, 59 Neb.L.Rev. 917 (1980). Does regulation of water appropriations for export have to be exactly coterminous with the regulation of appropriations for in-state use in order for the state to survive dormant commerce clause scrutiny? In Ponderosa Ridge LLC v. Banner County, 250 Neb. 944, 554 N.W.2d 151 (1996), the Nebraska Supreme Court upheld the denial of a permit to export 1532 acre-feet of water a year drawn from a well fifty feet from the Wyoming state line, rejecting a commerce clause challenge. The court noted that Nebraska state law required the state agency to consider somewhat different factors in deciding whether to grant a permit for an *inter*state as opposed to an *intra*state transfer, but held that "the differences do not require interstate commerce to suffer any greater burden than that placed on intrastate commerce," and therefore the "overall regulation relevant to this litigation is evenhanded." 554 N.W.2d at 164–65. Compare Ariz. Rev. Stat. § 45–292(B)(5), enacted in 1989, which limits permits to appropriate water for export from the state to fifty years. No groundwater pumping permits for in-state use are subject to such a limit, except for two narrow categories (see Ariz. Rev. Stat. §§ 45–514(B), 45–515(B)). Is that discrimination consistent with *Sporhase*?

7.   States interested in limiting water exports have been emboldened by the "market participant" doctrine that the Supreme Court developed in Reeves, Inc. v. Stake, 447 U.S. 429 (1980). The idea is that when a state participates in the market by buying or selling goods, it is not a market-regulating sovereign to which the dormant commerce clause limitations apply. (This seems to be what Justice Stevens was referring to when he said in *Sporhase* that Nebraska's water conservation program gives the groundwater resource "some indicia of a good publicly produced and owned in which a State may favor its own citizens in times of shortage.") This raises the question of how a state can become a "participant" in the water "market." Suppose a state forbids all appropriations over a certain quantity, and instead chooses to act as lessor and lease larger blocs of state-"owned" water into a market. (Montana has actually done this for quantities over 4000 acre-feet. See supra p. 305.) Does this qualify for market-participant status? Note it allows the state to charge a price for the water (and thereby to profit from any exports) and to recapture the use of the water for in-state uses at the end of the lease period. See James Crammond, Leasing Water Rights for Instream Flow Uses: A Survey of Water Transfer Policy, Prac-

tices, and Problems in the Pacific Northwest, 26 Envtl. L. 225, 238–39 (1996); Norman Thorson, Water Marketing in Big Sky Country: An Interim Assessment, 29 Nat. Resources J. 479 (1989).

8.   For another approach to "market participant" status, consider an approach recommended by a New Mexico study written by Professor Charles DuMars and others, entitled State Appropriation of Unappropriated Groundwater: A Strategy for Insuring New Mexico's Water Future (N.M. Resources Research Inst. & U.N.M. L. Sch., 1986). It proposed, among other things, that the state appropriate unappropriated water, buy some existing water rights, and create a water market that has a temporal dimension, rather like commodities futures markets. The state could market water interstate in order to raise capital for in-state water projects. Is a state's appropriation of unappropriated water subject to dormant commerce clause analysis? Does it matter whether the state-appropriated water is being put to beneficial use, or is otherwise treated differently from other appropriations in the state? For a view that *Sporhase* does not prohibit reservation by a state of unappropriated water, see Frank Trelease, Interstate Use of Water—Sporhase v. El Paso, Pike & Vermejo, 22 Land & Water L. Rev. 315 (1987); see also Ann Rodgers, The Limits of State Activity in the Interstate Water Market, 21 Land & Water L. Rev. 357 (1986).

9.   The power of Congress over interstate commerce allows it to authorize states to act in ways that the dormant commerce clause would otherwise prohibit. In the wake of *Sporhase*, for example, Congress could (assuming it could muster the political will) enact a federal law that allowed Nebraska to prohibit export of groundwater. Or consider this: Article X of the Yellowstone River Compact executed by Montana, North Dakota, and Wyoming, and approved by the United States Congress, provides: "No water shall be diverted from the Yellowstone River Basin without unanimous consent of all the signatory states." 65 Stat. 663, 669 (1951). Intake Water Company sought to export Yellowstone River water for an out-of-basin use, and challenged this provision under the commerce clause. The court rejected the challenge, concluding:

> [T]he Compact is federal law. See Texas v. New Mexico. Federal legislation is not subject to the restrictions that the Commerce Clause imposes on state laws affecting commerce. * * * Just as Congress may itself enact a law that interferes with interstate commerce, it may also give its approval to a state law interfering with interstate commerce and thereby immunize the law from challenge under the Commerce Clause. * * * In many cases, the issue is whether Congress in fact approved the state law for which immunity from Commerce Clause attack is claimed. That is not an issue in the present case; the Compact was before Congress and Congress voted to approve it.

Intake Water Co. v. Yellowstone River Compact Comm'n, 590 F.Supp. 293 (D. Mont. 1983), aff'd, 769 F.2d 568, 570 (9th Cir. 1985), cert. denied, 476 U.S. 1163 (1986).

10.   Unlike the Yellowstone River Compact, most interstate water compacts do not *expressly* address the issue of out-of-basin or out-of-state exports. Suppose a compact simply allocates half the flow of the Blue River

to state X and the other half to state Y, and Congress approves it. State X forbids export of any of its half out of state. Does Congress's approval of the compact remove State X's action from dormant commerce clause scrutiny? For an argument yes, see Frank Trelease, Interstate Use of Water—Sporhase v. El Paso, Pike & Vermejo, 22 Land & Water L. Rev. 315, 339 (1987); for an argument no, see Douglas Grant, State Regulation of Interstate Water Export, in 4 Waters and Water Rights § 48.0(c)(6) (Robert Beck ed., repl. vol. 2004).

11.   For a study of states' authority to limit the interstate marketing of Indian water rights, see Chris Seldon, Interstate Marketing of Indian Water Rights: The Impact of the Commerce Clause, 87 Cal. L. Rev. 1545 (1999).

The El Paso Litigation

The Hueco Bolson is a large aquifer found underneath west Texas and southeastern New Mexico. El Paso obtains nearly all its water supply from the Hueco Bolson within Texas, but is concerned that its pumping on the Texas portion will eventually be impaired by increased salinity. The area's principal surface water system, the Rio Grande, has long been overappropriated. In the 1980s El Paso sought to establish groundwater pumping rights in New Mexico for export. New Mexico's resistance led to the most ardently litigated and closely watched post-*Sporhase* water export limitation case.

In the first decision, New Mexico's outright ban on export of groundwater did not survive scrutiny. In El Paso v. Reynolds, 563 F.Supp. 379 (D.N.M. 1983), the court found that New Mexico was not facing an imminent shortage, that its present policies were not designed to conserve water, and that the embargo was not a narrowly tailored means to achieve the goals the Supreme Court found acceptable in *Sporhase*. The New Mexico legislature promptly amended its law, and the matter quickly came back before the same court. See El Paso v. Reynolds, 597 F.Supp. 694 (D.N.M. 1984). The basic provision under attack required that exports be "not contrary to the conservation of water within the state" and "not otherwise detrimental to the public welfare of the citizens of New Mexico." N.M. Stat. Ann. § 72–12B–1(C). Another statute, § 72–12–3E, applied the same requirements to new appropriations of ground water from certain basins for use in New Mexico.

El Paso claimed that "this evenhandedness is only superficial because for in-state uses these criteria are meaningless." 597 F.Supp. at 699. The court agreed with El Paso that New Mexico's "general policy has been to put as much water to use within the State as soon as possible, the converse of conservation, at least as to underground waters." Nevertheless, the court rejected El Paso's facial attack on the statute, largely because it found it "unclear at this time how the conservation and public welfare criteria will be applied to in-state appropriations." Id.

The court then addressed El Paso's argument that, because New Mexico law required the state engineer to consider the "public welfare of the citizens of New Mexico" before allowing export, it was "intrinsically discriminatory" against non-citizens like El Paso. In rejecting the argument, the court elaborated on the Supreme Court's reasoning in *Sporhase* that under some circumstances a demonstrably arid state may act to protect its water from export. It noted, first, that "public welfare" is a "broad term involving health and safety, recreational, aesthetic, environmental and economic interests." Thus, almost "every aspect of the public welfare has economic overtones." Id. at 700–01. Then it said:

> A state may favor its own citizens in times and places of shortage. *Sporhase*, 458 U.S. at 956–57. Of course, this does not mean that a state may limit or bar exports simply because it anticipates that one day there will not be enough water to meet all future uses. Even some of the most water-abundant states predict shortages at some future date. The preference envisioned by the Supreme Court must be limited to times and places where its exercise would not place unreasonable burdens on interstate commerce relative to the local benefits it produces.

> On the other hand, it would be unreasonable to require a state to wait until it is in the midst of a dire shortage before it can prefer its own citizens' use of the available water over out-of-state usage. A limited preference which could not be exercised until water resources were almost depleted would be no preference at all. If the limited preference is to be meaningful the states must be permitted to prefer local usage while there is still water to conserve. The proximity in time of projected shortage, the certainty that it will occur, its predicted severity, and whether alternative measures could prevent or alleviate the shortage are all factors which must be weighed when balancing the local interests served by the exercise of a preference against the burdens it places on interstate commerce.

> New Mexico need not wait until the appropriate time and place of shortage arises to enact a statute limiting exports. The State may enact a law to provide for future contingencies. If facially valid, any constitutional attack on such a statute for violation of the Commerce Clause must await its application.

597 F.Supp. at 701. The court then addressed El Paso's argument that the New Mexico statute discriminated against interstate commerce because it applied the conservation and public welfare criteria to *all* interstate uses but only *some* in-state uses; e.g., water from domestic wells used within New Mexico was excepted. El Paso was particularly disadvantaged by this because it was seeking to drill a domestic well in New Mexico for use in Texas. Here the court handed El Paso a victory, finding that the statute discriminates on its face against interstate commerce, in much the same way as the "reciprocity clause" struck down in *Sporhase*. 597 F.Supp. at 704.

On remand, the New Mexico State Engineer reconsidered El Paso's applications and, to no one's surprise, rejected them, finding that "no water rights in New Mexico are needed by El Paso for a water development plan or to protect its water supply for reasonably projected needs within 40 years * * *." The crux of the ruling was that El Paso's safe supply exceeded its needs and, if that calculation should prove erroneous, condemnation of Rio Grande surface water rights was a preferable means of obtaining additional supply.

El Paso litigated this rejection for a time, but ultimately settled the case. The settlement resulted in the formation of the New Mexico–Texas Water Commission, which has as specific goals developing a transboundary regional water plan, promoting water conservation, and providing assurances by New Mexico entities that they will aid El Paso in acquiring surface water from the Rio Grande to meet El Paso's future needs. The Commission has expended goodly sums of money on hydrologic studies in both states aimed at procuring El Paso a reliable supply of Rio Grande surface water, in lieu of groundwater in New Mexico. El Paso has also embarked on an extensive and effective program of water conservation and has been seeking to buy rural ranches in Texas to capture and extract groundwater for export back to the City.

Notes and Questions

1. How much does the 1984 district court opinion signal a willingness to let New Mexico act in advance of an actual emergency, and thus create some flexibility for states to limit exports of water from an aquifer undergoing general decline? If the degree of threat depends upon fact-finding, should courts defer to the fact-finding of the state engineer in the source state? Or does the commerce clause properly require the courts to regard state agency findings with a certain degree of skepticism because of the obvious impulse toward protectionism?

2. Did El Paso make a strategic mistake in challenging the New Mexico statute on its face, rather than as applied to it?

3. Does the water law doctrine a state follows make a difference in the dormant commerce clause analysis? Suppose New Mexico followed the rule of capture for groundwater. Would that make it harder for New Mexico to impose restrictions on export of groundwater consistent with the dormant commerce clause? Does the fact that Texas follows the rule of capture make it harder for El Paso to claim a right to New Mexico groundwater? Did the fact that New Jersey follows the riparian rights doctrine make it easier for the Supreme Court to uphold New Jersey's export ban in Hudson County Water Co. v. McCarter?

4. Considered broadly, did El Paso—while winning some commerce clause litigation battles—effectively lose the war over export of groundwater from New Mexico? If in fact sufficient surface water rights in the Rio Grande were available to meet El Paso's needs (at least when coupled with a conservation program), would El Paso have been better off trying to negotiate with New Mexico before embarking on the bitter, lengthy, and costly litigation battle? Would it have been in New Mexico's interest to negotiate? Note that the agreement was not a formal compact between two states, and

was not approved by Congress. Does that make any difference to its enforceability?

C. INTERNATIONAL WATERS

International law has long been faced with the need to devise rules for resolving controversies over shared natural resource systems. The governing principle appears to be the traditional property law maxim, prominent in the early development of riparianism in the United States, *sic utere tuo ut alienum non laedas,* one should not use his own property as to injure that of another. What this means in terms of water has been summarized as a series of general principles by the International Law Association in a document known as the Helsinki Rules.[1] The most basic precept is that, "[E]ach basin State is entitled to a reasonable and equitable share in the beneficial uses of the waters of an international drainage basin."[2] The factors which are to give content to the formula's vague terms "reasonable and equitable" are:

(a) the geography of the basin, including in particular the extent of the drainage area in the territory of each basin State;

(b) the hydrology of the basin, including in particular the contribution of water by each basin State;

(c) the climate affecting the basin;

(d) the past utilization of the waters of the basin, including in particular existing utilization;

(e) the economic and social needs of each basin State;

(f) the population dependent on the waters of the basin in each basin State;

(g) the comparative costs of alternative means of satisfying the economic and social needs of each basin State;

(h) the availability of other resources;

(i) the avoidance of unnecessary waste in the utilization of the waters of the basin;

(j) the practicability of compensation to one or more of the co-basin States as a means of adjusting conflicts among uses; and

(k) the degree to which the needs of a basin State may be satisfied, without causing substantial injury to a co-basin State.[3]

---

1. The Helsinki Rules have no legal force of their own. In that way, the rules resemble the American Law Institute's Restatements of the Law. They were the first effort to collect the law of international watercourses, and have been widely recognized as having substantial influence on the practice of nations. See Charles Bourne, The International Law Association's Contri-bution to International Water Resources Law, 36 Nat. Resources J. 155 (1996)

2. International Law Ass'n, Report of the 52nd Conference, Helsinki Rules on the Use of the Waters of International Rivers, art. IV (1966) (hereinafter "Helsinki Rules").

3. Id. art. V(2).

These principles are reminiscent of reasonable use riparianism, especially as set out in the Restatement (Second) of Torts, supra p. 57. Some of them resemble the general tenets of equitable apportionment as elaborated in various U.S. Supreme Court opinions. One important difference is that, in stark contrast to (b) above, the U.S. Supreme Court has specifically rejected the relevance of how much water each basin state contributes to the water body at issue. See Colorado v. New Mexico, discussed supra pp. 865–867. The principles acknowledge that a degree of sharing of the resource is required, but do not offer specific guidance as to what acts by the upstream nation would overstep the bounds of fair utilization of the resource within its borders.[4]

The Helsinki Rules did not address all groundwater, but only that groundwater that is hydrologically related to interstate surface waters.[5] In 1986, the 62nd Conference of the International Law Association adopted the Seoul Rules on the Law of International Groundwater Resources, which extended the principle of equitable utilization to international aquifers that were not connected to an international surface watercourse.[6] Culminating a several-year effort, the United Nations General Assembly in 1997 approved a Convention on the Law of Non–Navigational Uses of International Watercourses.[7] Its list of factors relevant to reasonable and equitable use is shorter, but generally comparable to that in the Helsinki Rules. In 2004, the ILA adopted the Berlin Rules[8], which updated and incorporated the Helsinki and Seoul Rules. Most of the Berlin Rules (a few only apply to international drainage basins) are "applicable to all waters—meaning all surface waters and groundwater other than marine waters—regardless of whether the waters in question are found in an international drainage basin." Id. at 4.

These principles and factors help shape solutions to international conflicts over water, preferably by negotiation. If negotiation fails there are international tribunals, such as the International Court of Justice ("ICJ"), to which disputes may be submitted by consent of the parties. Nations may also agree to submit disputes to arbitration. Suits sounding in international law can also be litigated in domestic tribunals of a disputant state if its law permits it. Within the United States, state courts of general jurisdiction are generally competent to decide matters sounding in international law. There are, however, other barriers to hearing such cases on the merits; for example, sovereign immunity may be interposed as a complete defense.[9]

---

4. See Jerome Lipper, Equitable Utilization, in The Law of International Drainage Basins 15, 23–28 (Albert Garretson et al. eds., 1967); see generally Albert Utton, International Streams and Lakes Generally, in 5 Waters and Water Rights § 49.07(b) (Robert Beck ed., repl. vol. 1998 Repl. Volume).

5. Helsinki Rules, supra note 2, art. II.

6. Seoul Rules, art. II(2). See also Robert Hayton & Albert Utton, Transboundary Groundwaters: The Bellagio Draft Treaty, 29 Nat. Resources J. 663 (1989).

7. The convention is reprinted in 36 Int'l Legal Mat'ls 700 (1997).

8. See http://www.ila-hq.org/ pdf/Water-Resources/ FinalReport2004.pdf.

9. This power to claim immunity is probably unaffected by the Foreign Sovereign Immunities Act of 1976 (FSIA), 28 U.S.C. §§ 1330, 1332(a)(2)-(4), 1391(f), 1441(d), 1602–1611. That act abrogates the

Treaties are another way to address disputes over international watercourses. They can set out agreed means for the shared utilization of the water resource, and provide mechanisms for resolving future clashes over its use. Within the United States, international treaties ratified by the U.S. Senate enjoy a status equal to other federal legislation, and superior to contrary state laws. Having a domestic status on a par with other federal legislation also means that treaties can be abrogated by a simple vote of Congress to repeal the treaty or to authorize actions inconsistent with the obligations of the United States under the treaty.[10]

1. UNITED STATES–MEXICAN RELATIONS

The United States/Mexico boundary is almost 2,000 miles long, and the lands on both sides are mostly arid. Two major rivers are shared by the two nations: the Rio Grande and the Colorado. Both are the subject of bilateral treaties. The allocation provisions of the 1944 treaty regarding the Colorado were discussed in the first section of this chapter, supra pp. 801–808. Water quality issues with Mexico on the Colorado are discussed in more detail in Chapter 10, infra pp. 1064–1068. The details of the Rio Grande Treaty of 1906 (dealing with waters of the River above Fort Quitman, Texas) and the Rio Grande (lower River), Colorado and Tijuana Treaty of 1944 are chronicled in Albert Utton, Mexican International Waters, in 5 Waters and Water Rights § 51.01, at 99 (Robert Beck ed., repl. vol. 1998). Unlike the flows of the upper Rio Grande and the Colorado, both of which are comprised almost exclusively of precipitation that falls on U.S. territory, about 70% of the flow of the lower Rio Grande comes from Mexican tributaries.

The issues relating to the Rio Grande mostly involve matters of water allocation. Because of its highly variable seasonal flows, under natural conditions much of its water flowed into the Gulf of Mexico unused, while also causing substantial downstream flooding in periods of high flow. The treaties made possible cooperative dam building and river management that brought valuable benefits to both sides. But tensions have emerged in recent years. The lower Rio Grande is fed principally by the Rio Conchos, which flows out of a high desert in Mexico and feeds the Rio Grande upstream from the Big Bend in Texas. The 1944 Treaty

immunity of foreign sovereigns in American courts in certain classes of cases involving commercial and tortious behavior of foreign governments and their agencies. The FSIA is not likely to abrogate immunity in a shared basin lawsuit against the Canadian or Mexican government unless the action involved is tortious. In the event that the FSIA did apply, there would also be concurrent subject matter jurisdiction in the federal district courts. See 28 U.S.C. § 1330, as construed in Verlinden B.V. v. Central Bank of Nigeria, 461 U.S. 480 (1983).

10. For general discussions of transboundary water issues involving the United States, see The North American Experience Managing International Transboundary Water Resources: The International Joint Commission and the International Boundary and Water Commission, 33 Nat. Resources J. 1–459 (1993) (papers and commentaries prepared for a 1991 Ford Foundation sponsored conference); see also Albert Utton, Canadian International Waters, in 5 Waters and Water Rights, supra note 4, § 50.01, at 51; Albert Utton, Mexican International Waters, in id., § 51.01, at 99.

requires Mexico to deliver about 350,000 acre-feet to the Rio Grande (compared to the 1.5 million acre-feet the United States is obligated to send to Mexico down the Colorado River by the Colorado River Treaty ratified that same year). From about 1993 to 2002 Mexico fell about 1.5 million acre-feet in arrears on its obligation, and the River dried up before it reached the Gulf. American farmers and the Texas governor have protested. Drought is a factor, as is new development in the Rio Conchos basin. (The population of the Rio Grande valley has increased from 200,000 to 20 million since the 1944 Treaty was signed.) Both countries agree the irrigation systems on both sides of the border are antiquated and inefficient. In an interim arrangement negotiated in 2002, the two countries agreed that Mexico would deliver 90,000 acre feet to the River and in return the U.S. would make a multi-million dollar loan to help Mexico modernize its water infrastructure. Rains and increased deliveries from Mexico in recent years have reduced the deficit substantially,[11] but in 2004 farmers and irrigation districts in Texas filed a proceeding under Chapter 11 of the 1994 North American Free Trade Agreement (NAFTA) asking for $500 million in damages against the government of Mexico. Chapter 11 authorizes damage awards for cross-border investments expropriated without just cause, and it would appear to be a novel interpretation to apply it trump a treaty dealing with an international resource. NAFTA calls for such claims to be decided by a three-person tribunal, and decisions cannot be appealed. See generally Francisco S. Nogales, The NAFTA Environmental Framework, Chapter 11 Investment Provisions, and the Environment, 8 Ann. Surv. Int'l & Comp. L. 97 (2002).

Notes and Questions

1. International sharing of groundwater is of increasing concern throughout the world. See Robert Hayton & Albert Utton, Transboundary Groundwaters: The Bellagio Draft Treaty, 29 Nat. Resources J. 663 (1989). The United States and Mexico share numerous aquifers along their 2,000–mile border, but the 1906 and 1944 treaties are silent on groundwater. Despite the heavy use of groundwater on both sides of the border, no general agreement between the two nations on the subject has been seriously attempted, but scholarly interest in the matter has produced a draft treaty. See Ann Rodgers & Albert Utton, The Ixtapa Draft Agreement Relating to the Use of Transboundary Groundwaters, 25 Nat. Resources J. 713 (1985); see also Stephen P. Mumme, Advancing Binational Cooperation in Trans-boundary Aquifer Management on the U.S.-Mexico Border, 16 Colo. J. Int'l Envt'l. L. & Pol'y 77 (2005).

2. A few other watercourses traverse the border between Mexico and the United States, and are not subject to any treaty. One is the San Pedro, which rises in Mexico and flows into Arizona, where it eventually empties (trickles is a more apt description) into the Gila River, itself a tributary of the Colorado. The San Pedro sustains, for now at least, a biologically world-class riparian zone that Congress has designated as the nation's first

11. Up-to-date figures can be obtained at the IBWC web-site, http://www.ibwc.state.gov/html/mexico_deliveries. html.

Riparian National Conservation Area. For a description of the domestic issues raised by the San Pedro, see supra pp. 465–466. Upstream diversions of San Pedro water and hydrologically related groundwater in Mexico for agriculture and industrial purposes may be contributing to depletions of flows downstream in the United States. The Center for Environmental Cooperation (CEC), a body created by the environmental "side agreement" to the North American Free Trade Agreement, issued a report in 1999 that discussed the threats to the San Pedro. See Ribbon of Life: An Agenda for Preserving Transboundary Migratory Bird Habitat on the Upper San Pedro River (1999). Some efforts have been made to address the problem, but a treaty is not under consideration.

3. The 1906 Rio Grande Treaty created an International Water Commission which was renamed the International Boundary and Water Commission (IBWC) in the 1944 Treaty. It has broad authority to "settle all differences that may arise between the two Governments with respect to the interpretation or application of this Treaty, subject to the approval of the two Governments." 1944 Treaty, art. 24(d). The late Professor Utton said the IBWC "has gained a well-deserved reputation for resolving difficult international water problems * * * [and] has established itself as a model of international cooperation." Albert Utton, Mexican International Waters, in 5 Waters and Water Rights § 51.04(f), at 129 (Robert Beck ed., repl. vol. 1998).

2. UNITED STATES–CANADIAN RELATIONS

Many international water resource issues arise along the 3000–mile United States–Canadian border, which includes areas of great water abundance and areas of relative aridity, and jurisdictions which follow the law of prior appropriation and those which follow riparianism. In some places international waters traverse the boundary; elsewhere, as in the Great Lakes, they form the boundary for hundreds of miles. Canada contains 20% of the world's fresh water, and some have predicted it could become the Saudi Arabia of water in an era of global warming.

There has not been much serious friction over the boundary waters and their uses. The basic framework for dealing with issues that do arise is the Boundary Waters Treaty of 1909 (BWT).[12] The Treaty came about as the result of a dispute over a project the U.S. was considering to divert the waters of the St. Mary River into the Milk River in Montana at a point where both rivers were within the United States. Canada protested that the diversion would harm Canadian appropriators on the St. Mary located downstream from the proposed point of diversion. When the United States continued preparations for the project, Canada authorized a diversion from the Milk to the St. Mary at a point where both rivers were wholly in Canadian territory, which would have negated the benefits of the proposed American project downstream. As Professor Utton summarized it, the "ability of each country to threaten diversion from an upstream position" brought the two nations to the bargaining

---

12. Treaty with Great Britain Relating to Boundary Waters Between the United States and Canada, Jan. 11, 1909, 36 Stat. 2448 (1910). (At that time Great Britain officially governed Canada's external relations.) This treaty is considered below.

table to negotiate a solution not only to this dispute but more generally to shared basin water problems.[13]

The Boundary Waters Treaty is a succinct but complex agreement that purports to govern all basins shared by the United States and Canada. A central principle of the treaty, preserving to each nation the ability to benefit from the use of Great Lakes and other boundary waters, is expressed in Article VIII: "The High Contracting Parties shall have, each on its own side, equal and similar rights to use of the waters hereinbefore defined as boundary waters."

The treaty creates a distinction between waters that form the boundary between the United States and Canada, and waters that either are tributary to boundary waters or that flow across the border. The regime for boundary waters is set forth in Article III of the Treaty. The key portions of those provisions are as follows:

> It is agreed that, in addition to the uses, obstructions, and diversions heretofore permitted or hereafter provided for by special agreement of the Parties hereto, no further or other uses or obstructions or diversions, whether temporary or permanent, of boundary waters on either side of the line, affecting the natural level or flow of boundary waters on the other side of the line shall be made except by authority of the United States or the Dominion of Canada within their respective jurisdictions and with the approval, as hereinafter provided, of a joint commission, to be known as the International Joint Commission. * * *[14]

The regime for tributaries to boundary waters and waters that traverse the boundary is set forth in Article II. The pertinent treaty language is as follows:

> Each of the High Contracting Parties reserves to itself or to the several State Governments on the one side and the Dominion or Provincial Governments on the other side * * * the exclusive jurisdiction and control over the use and diversion, whether temporary or permanent, of all waters on its own side of the line which in their natural channels would flow across the boundary or into boundary waters; but it is agreed that any interference with or diversion from their natural channel of such waters on either side of the boundary, resulting in any injury on the other side of the boundary, shall give rise to the same rights and entitle the injured parties to the same legal remedies as if such injury took place in the country where such diversion or interference occurs; but this provision shall not apply to cases

13. See Utton, Canadian International Waters, supra note 10, at 53–56.

14. Article IV prescribes a similar scheme for the governance of water works that might raise water levels and cause transboundary inundation of lands.

already existing or to cases expressly covered by special agreement between the parties hereto.[15]

In addition to creating governing rules for the sharing of the water resources, the Treaty created the International Joint Commission ("IJC") to administer the treaty and assigned it jurisdiction over disputes referred by the two national governments. It is a six-member commission, with three commissioners selected by each nation. This composition would seem to create a possibility of deadlock not unlike that observed in the Pecos River Compact (see Texas v. New Mexico, supra p. 843). The treaty tends to limit that possibility, however, by the way in which some of its parts are structured. For example, an affirmative vote of the IJC is required to grant a permit for diversion of water from an article III boundary water. In the event of a tie vote, the permit would be denied and the diversion blocked. The Commission has earned a "reputation for objectivity" that has given it considerable success in mediating and settling border disputes.[16]

The treaty also gives the IJC substantive guidance in exercising its authority. Article VIII provides in part:

The following order of precedence shall be observed among the various uses enumerated hereinafter for these waters, and no use shall be permitted which tends materially to conflict with or restrain any other use which is given preference over it in this order of precedence: (1) uses for domestic and sanitary purposes; (2) uses for navigation, including the service of canals for the purpose of navigation; (3) uses for power and irrigation purposes.

The treaty has been supplemented from time to time by more specific treaties or agreements between the United States and Canada. In most regards the treaty seems to have helped limit conflict between the nations over their shared water resources.[17] Nevertheless, a couple of thorny water quality disputes have arisen recently which the treaty has so far not played much of a role in resolving. In one, Montana Governor Schweitzer has objected that an open-pit coal mine proposed just north of Glacier National Park could compromise water quality south of the border, in the Park and downstream in Flathead Lake. When an earlier, similar proposal was made in the 1980s, the two national governments referred the matter to the IJC, which formed a scientific team that ultimately recommended against the mine going forward, and the project was shelved for a time. Recently, however, British Columbia officials recently approved coal mining exploration in the region, and Schweitzer

15. The Article also disclaimed any waiver of rights regarding injury to navigation.

16. Utton, Canadian International Waters, supra note 10, § 50.02(c), at 66.

17. The Treaty contained other important provisions that are of relatively little water law interest; for example, Article I guaranteed free navigation to vessels of both nations and included Lake Michigan within the waters covered by that guarantee.

called for a similar referral to the IJC. This time the U.S. resisted. Missoulian (May 27, 2005).

A possible reason may be found a few hundred miles to the east, where the shoe is on the other foot. Canada lodged objections to a plan by North Dakota to drain water from Devils Lake, a natural waterbody that has no natural outlet, into the Red River system which flows north across the border and ultimately into Lake Winnipeg. A dozen years of wetter-than-normal weather has enlarged the Lake, flooding houses, roads and farmlands. Canada, joined by environmentalists, worry that the drainage water will contaminate the watershed with exotic biota, salt and farm chemicals. Canada sought unsuccessfully to have the IJC look at the matter, and the U.S. resisted. As North Dakota was finishing construction of a $28 million dollar drainage facility, the two countries agreed on a deal that looks like a fig leaf for Canada, calling on the U.S. to install a $50,000 crude rock-and-gravel filter at the outlet (which North Dakota had already constructed), and for the two countries to design and build a more advanced filtration system at some point in the future. A member of the Canadian Parliament appraised the situation this way: "We've played all of our cards and we've done our best and the Americans won. The Americans always win." Toronto Daily Globe and Mail (August 8, 2005).

Great Lakes Diversion Issues[18]

Of the boundary waters governed by the treaty, the Great Lakes make a particularly inviting target for diversion proposals. These lakes contain a staggering amount of fresh water (5,500 cubic miles, 95% of the total fresh water in the Nation and 20% of the total on Earth, enough to cover the lower 48 states to a depth of 9.5 feet). The average flow of the Detroit River is roughly ten times that of the Colorado River. If all the water to supply the Central Arizona Project were drawn from Lakes Michigan and Huron (the two are a single lake hydrologically), their level would be lowered by less than three inches. See Robert H. Abrams, Setting Regional Policy on Diverting Great Lakes Water to the Arid West: Scaling Down the Myths, The Wayne Lawyer (Fall 1982).

Nevertheless, a good case can be made that this water is a largely non-renewable resource because the Lakes' drainage basin is surprisingly small, less than 1% of their waters are replenished by annual precipitation, and it takes 300 years for water from Lake Superior to reach the Atlantic. See Jerome Hinkle, Troubled Waters: Policy and Action in the Great Lakes, 20 T.M. Cooley L.Rev. 281, 288 (2003). In a nutshell, depending on your point of view, large-scale diversions of Great Lakes water to other basins are laughable or inevitable. Proposals were ad-

---

18. There is an extensive literature on Great Lakes water diversion and management issues. See sources collected in Joseph W. Dellapenna, Interstate Struggles Over Rivers: The Southeastern States and the Struggle over the 'Hooch, 12 N.Y.U.Envtl.L.J. 828, 850–64 (2005). An ex-

cellent summary of the issues, periodically updated, is Stephen R. Viña and Pervaze Sheikh, Great Lakes Water Withdrawals: Legal and Policy Issues, Congressional Research Service Report # RL32956 (2005) (hereafter, CRS Report).

vanced in the 1970s and 1980s to divert Great Lakes water to recharge areas of the Ogallala aquifer, but high cost and environmental objections doomed them.[19] More recently, there have been proposals to increase the diversion from Lake Michigan at Chicago in order to provide greater flows in the Mississippi to mitigate droughts which have sometimes reduced Mississippi flows to one-quarter of normal, suspending barge traffic.

Although 500 cfs of water had been diverted at Chicago since 1848, its current form was initiated at the beginning of the twentieth century to help flush the City's sewage into the Illinois River, and thence into the Mississippi, in order to maintain Lake Michigan as the city's drinking water supply. An engineering feat of some acclaim, the project reversed the flow of the Chicago River so that it now flows away from the Great Lakes. The magnitude of the diversion has always been controversial. When the Boundary Waters Treaty came into effect, the Chicago Sanitary District (the state subdivision operating the system) was operating under a permit from the federal Corps of Engineers that allowed diversions of 4,167 cfs. When the Sanitary District unilaterally increased the diversions, the British (on behalf of Canada) protested and the United States sued successfully to enjoin the Sanitary District from increasing the diversion. Noting that this was "not a controversy between equals," and that the United States had a foreign relations as well as domestic commerce interest in the matter, Justice Holmes firmly upheld federal authority.[20] Eventually further litigation involving a number of the basin states resulted in the Chicago diversion being fixed at approximately an annual average of 3,200 cfs, with a dispensation to the Corps of Engineers to alter the amount in the event of an emergency.[21]

At its current rate, the Chicago diversion reduces Lake Michigan/Huron water levels by about 2.5 inches; Lake Erie by a little less than 2 inches; Lake Ontario by 1.2 inches; and Lake Superior by a little less than one inch.[22] About a quarter of a century ago, a study of a proposal to divert an additional 10,000 cfs from the western side of the Great Lakes projected a net average annual loss of benefits to the region at more than $100 million. B. DeCooke, J. Bulkley & S. Wright, Great Lakes Diversions: A Preliminary Assessment of Economic Impacts 19 (1984) (unpublished paper). The losses primarily related to hydropower

19. See J.W. Bulkley, S.J. Wright & D. Wright, Preliminary Study of the Diversion of 10,000 cfs from Lake Superior to the Missouri River Basin, 68 J. Hydrology 461, 469 (1983); Patrick Corbett, The Overlooked Farm Crisis: Rapidly Depleting Water Supply, 61 Notre Dame L. Rev. 454 (1986). The now-dated Bulkley study estimated the cost of building a project to deliver 10,000 cfs of Great Lakes water into the Missouri River basin at $26 billion, which did not include getting the water to the site of use.

20. See Sanitary District of Chicago v. United States, 266 U.S. 405 (1925).

21. Wisconsin v. Illinois, 278 U.S. 367 (1929), 281 U.S. 179 (1930), 388 U.S. 426 (1967), decree amended, 449 U.S. 48 (1980). The diversion has exceeded the decreed amount, and in the late 1990s the State of Illinois agreed to repay the deficit by the year 2019. See CRS Report, supra note 18, at p. 4.

22. International Joint Comm'n, Great Lakes Diversions and Consumptive Uses 15 (1985). The effect on Lake Superior can be manipulated to some degree by the operation of dams at its outlet.

production and increased dredging costs to maintain navigation. As the CRS Report discloses, currently diversions *into* the Great Lakes Basin (mainly from the Canadian side into Lake Superior) in fact exceed the diversions *out*—the Chicago Diversion being by far the largest of the latter. See CRS Report, supra note 18, at p. 4.

In 1955, all of the Great Lakes basin states enacted legislation authorizing the formation of a Great Lakes Commission as part of the Great Lakes Basin Compact.[23] Congress finally approved the compact in 1968, except for provisions which granted a role to Canadian provinces, because of its fear that allowing foreign entities a role in an interstate compact might violate congressional authority under the compact clause. The compact merely authorizes the commission to collect information and develop proposals for basin management that the states are thereafter required to consider.

In 1985, the basin's eight governors and two premiers entered into an agreement entitled "The Great Lakes Charter." The Charter pledged the states and provinces "to conserve the levels and flows of the Great Lakes and their tributary and connecting waters * * *," and enumerates five overriding principles: (1) the integrity of the basin, (2) cooperation among the jurisdictions, (3) protection of the water resources, (4) notice and consultation regarding diversions and (5) sharing of data and research efforts. The Charter launched an era of concerted political action by the states and provinces to establish a means for insuring regional control over the lakes. Mindful of the experience with the 1955 Compact, Congress was not asked to ratify the Charter as an interstate compact because of its inclusion of the Canadian provinces. See Symposium, How Do Canadian Provinces and U.S. States View the Importance of Their Relationship with Their Cross–Border Counterparts?, 27 Can.-U.S. L.J. 137 (2001). The Charter has been characterized as not legally binding but instead a "kind of gentlemen's agreement between the Governors of the Great Lakes States and the Provinces of Ontario and Quebec." Little Traverse Bay Bands of Odawa Indians v. Great Spring Waters of America, Inc., 203 F. Supp. 2d 853, 857, (W.D.Mich.2002).

Both before and after the Charter, legislation requiring permits for water use was enacted by some of the Great Lakes states and provincial governments, but the impact of these statutes on water exports was hard to discern.[24] More important in a post-*Sporhase* world, in 1986 the U.S. Congress, in response to the region's lobbying, enacted a statute giving each basin state's governor a veto over out-of-basin diversions of Great Lakes water by any private or governmental entity on the U.S. side of the lakes.[25] Exercising this authority, the Governor of Michigan has

---

23. Great Lakes Basin Compact, Pub. L. 90–419, 82 Stat. 414 (1968).

24. See, e.g., Lisa Pittman, Plugs to Pull: Proposals for Facing High Great Lakes Water Levels, 8 U.C.L.A. J. Envtl. L. & Pol'y 213, 247–249 (1989).

25. Water Resources Development Act of 1986, 42 U.S.C. § 1962d–20. The statute grandfathers all pre-existing diversions, such as the diversion at Chicago. For a mixed review of the law's wisdom and efficacy, see J. David Prince, State Control of Great Lakes Water Diversion, 16 Wm.

vetoed even minor diversions of Lake Michigan water to towns in Indiana a few miles from the lakefront across a low divide. (Michigan is wholly within the Great Lakes basin and therefore no diversion in that state is subject to veto by another Great Lakes state governor.) See George William Sherk, Resolving Interstate Water Conflicts in the Eastern United States: The Re–Emergence of the Federal–Interstate Compact, 30 Water Resources Bull. 397 (1994).

In 2000, Congress amended the statute to give the governors a veto over "exports" as well as "diversions" of Great Lakes water outside the basin, 42 U.S.C. § 1962d–20(d), giving rise to the question whether the Governor of Michigan might have a veto over shipping bottles of beer brewed with Lake Michigan water in Milwaukee out of the basin. As this is being written, Waukesha, Wisconsin (fifteen miles from Lake Michigan across a barely perceptible divide), is currently seeking to import 20 million gallons daily from the Lake to deal with unacceptably high natural radium content being encountered in its deep wells. The City argues that other sources of water are much more expensive, and that it has evidence its wells draw water from the Great Lakes already through a deep hydrologic connection, but many are opposing the plan, fearing the precedent it could create. N.Y. Times, August 12, 2005. Akron, Ohio, which sits astride the boundary of the watershed, gained approval to use Lake Erie water in 1998, but only on the condition it send back to the Lake an equivalent amount of treated wastewater.

In the late 1990s a Canadian company called the Nova Group proposed to ship Lake Superior water to Asia via tankers, and an argument was made that water should be viewed as a tradable commodity under the trade agreements like the North American Free Trade Agreement and the General Agreement on Tariffs and Trade. This spurred the basin states and provincial governors to take another look at export restrictions. After several years of discussion, on December 13, 2005, the eight basin state governors signed a Great Lakes–St. Lawrence River Basin Water Resources Compact and, along with the leaders of the Canadian provinces of Ontario and Quebec, a companion Great Lakes–St. Lawrence River Basin Sustainable Water Resources Agreement.

The detailed compact, which requires ratification by each state legislature and the U.S. Congress to be effective, includes riparian-based water use rules that embrace hydrologically related groundwater, emphasizes efficient use, sound science and environmental protection. It would prohibit most water diversions outside the basin (but exempt water bottled in containers smaller than 5.7 gallons) and require the basin states to create water conservation programs. According to one commentator, the new Compact creates a new model of "cooperative horizontal federalism" distinct from the allocation model of the Colorado

Mitchell L. Rev. 107 (1990); see also Christine A. Klein, The Environmental Commerce Clause, 27 Harv. Envtl. L. Rev. 1 (2003). Despite the provision, Congress itself has occasionally shown some interest in allowing an increase of diversions at Chicago. See Pittman, supra note 24, at 253.

River Compact (supra pp. 799–808), or the managerial model of the Delaware River Basin Compact (supra pp. 853–858):

> [The approach] relies on common minimum standards for in-basin water uses and protections against diversions, premised on the notion of living within the limits of the watershed. While not explicit, the theory behind the approach is that collective and regional sustainability will result from individual and state compliance with common standards. States retain the flexibility to manage in-basin water uses, but collectively protect against large diversions that threaten total water supply. In administering their individual programs, states have both the benefit of regional resources and the threat of regional enforcement.

Noah Hall, Towards a New Horizontal Federalism: Interstate Water Management in the Great Lakes Region, 77 U. Colo. L. Rev. 405 (2006). More information can be found at the website of the Council of Great Lakes Governors, http://www.cglg.org.

Problems

1. You are a legal advisor to the Governor of Missouri. A severe drought has reduced the flow of the Mississippi River to a point where barge traffic on the river has been halted. Area farmers are facing difficulties in getting their crops to market. Commodity prices for oil and other items that are imported by barge are rising. Assume that, from a hydrologic and engineering standpoint, the Chicago Diversion could, at a reasonable cost and in a short time frame, be increased sufficiently to restore some navigation on the Mississippi. What advice would you give to the Governor about obtaining additional water from the Chicago Diversion? Might it be possible to purchase water from the Sanitary District or other potential sellers? What other approvals might be needed? How is your answer affected by the unique status of the Chicago Diversion, with its genesis in a U.S. Supreme Court decision and its consistent exemption from other, more recently enacted legislation?

2. The facts are the same as in Problem 1. You are legal advisor to the Premier of Ontario who is on record as adamantly opposed to any increase in the Chicago Diversion. What advice would you give to the Premier about Canadian rights under the Treaty and international law more generally? Would your answer change if the 1986 Water Resources Development Act were not on the books?

3. You are mayor of a fast-growing suburb of Cleveland, Ohio, located a few miles from Lake Erie, but across the divide in the Ohio–Mississippi River drainage. Your local water supply of potable water is limited. You want to propose building a pipeline to Lake Erie to tap its waters for your residents. Advise the mayor what water allocation-related approvals might be needed and how best to go about advancing this idea.

Chapter 9

FEDERAL AND INDIAN
WATER RIGHTS

Prior chapters show that the United States government plays an active role in developing water resources and regulating some aspects of their use. It has constructed hundreds of reclamation, navigation, hydroelectric, and flood control projects; its regulation for environmental protection (especially, threatened and endangered species) can have major effects on water diversion and use; and it protects some waterways from development under the Wild and Scenic Rivers Act. Those important areas aside, the impression may be that the United States has left it entirely to the states to establish and define water rights. That is not accurate, especially in the Western United States.

In this Chapter, we first explore "federal reserved water rights," which arise directly from federal law and are largely independent of state water law. Such rights secure water for the benefit of both Indian reservations and various categories of federal lands (which collectively comprise almost one-third of the Nation's land area). After introducing the concept, we address reserved rights in relation to specific categories of federal lands, then look at procedural issues concerning how federal rights may be adjudicated in state courts. A major section follows on federal reserved water rights for Indians. The chapter closes with a brief examination of how the federal government may protect its interests through holding state-created water rights, and how the United States may control water use through its ownership and management of the vast array of federal lands. Cutting across all these issues are questions about the federal and state governments' appropriate roles in shaping water policy. For that reason, these issues have usually been politically charged and hotly contested, in the courts and elsewhere.

A. FEDERAL WATER RIGHTS
BASED ON FEDERAL LAW

A good starting point is to consider the breadth of federal landholdings. Nearly all lands in the West were acquired by the United States from foreign governments by purchase (the Louisiana and Gadsden

Purchases) or by treaty (the Treaty of Guadalupe Hidalgo). The United States Constitution, though drafted in an era in which the federal government was not expected to remain a large landowner, gave Congress broad power to fashion national policy with respect to federal lands, primarily through the so-called "Property Clause" (art. IV, § 3, cl. 2): "The Congress shall have the Power to dispose of and make all needful Rules and Regulations respecting the Territory or other Property belonging to the United States * * *." See generally Kleppe v. New Mexico, 426 U.S. 529 (1976).

The dominant federal lands policy in the 19th century was divestment to promote settlement. Through statehood and railroad land grants, homestead acts, and a variety of other dispositions, the federal government transferred a substantial part of its vast western land holdings into state and private ownership.[1] As the 19th century wore on, however, the federal government's policy changed. Large tracts of federal land were "withdrawn" from disposition and "reserved" for federal purposes. The most familiar of these are Indian and military reservations, national parks and national forests. Hundreds of millions of acres outside these reserved areas also remained in federal ownership, despite being available for divestment under various statutes. The era of large-scale disposition effectively ended in the New Deal era, and in 1976 Congress officially ended (with a few limited exceptions) the divestment policy for these lands by enacting the Federal Land Policy and Management Act (43 U.S.C. §§ 1701–1784).

For water rights purposes, it is important to note that federal land ownership still falls into those two categories: Lands that have been reserved from disposition for particular purposes; and other, residual public domain lands. The reserved lands generally carry with them a reservation of as much of the then-unappropriated water in or on the reserved lands as is needed to fulfill the purposes for which the reservation was made. This reserved water rights doctrine was propounded by the United States Supreme Court in 1908, in the famous *Winters* case immediately below. Federal reserved rights are created and defined by federal law; they are neither appropriative nor riparian rights, and they have a number of features that may pose conflicts with state law water rights regimes.[2]

The first subsection that follows examines the origin and basic nature of the reserved rights doctrine. The next subsection takes up non-

---

1. In 1935, in California Oregon Power Co. v. Beaver Portland Cement Co., supra p. 352, the Supreme Court interpreted several nineteenth century statutes as effectively severing rights to water from rights to public land when it passed into private ownership. Thus those who took title to federal lands under various divestment policies acquired no rights to water under federal law, but instead had to proceed under state water law.

2. Because most federal lands are in the arid west, where prior appropriation is the dominant state law doctrine, all the case law and most academic commentary focus on the relationship between federal reserved rights and prior appropriation. Integrating federal reserved rights with the riparian doctrine is considered briefly infra pp. 927–928.

Indian reserved rights (e.g., for national parks and forests). Succeeding subsections take up process questions in adjudicating and administering such rights and then Indian water rights. The modern Indian cases raise complex issues beyond simple quantification, including the extent to which Indian water rights may be generally used to support tribal economic and cultural development.

1. THE BASIC NATURE OF FEDERAL RESERVED WATER RIGHTS

WINTERS v. UNITED STATES

Supreme Court of the United States, 1908.
207 U.S. 564.

MR. JUSTICE MCKENNA delivered the opinion of the court.

This suit was brought by the United States to restrain appellants and others from constructing or maintaining dams or reservoirs on the Milk River in the State of Montana, or in any manner preventing the water of the river or its tributaries from flowing to the Fort Belknap Indian Reservation.

The allegations of the bill, so far as necessary to state them, are as follows: On the first day of May, 1888, a tract of land, the property of the United States, was reserved and set apart "as an Indian reservation as and for a permanent home and abiding place of the Gros Ventre and Assiniboine bands or tribes of Indians in the State (then Territory) of Montana, designated and known as the Fort Belknap Indian Reservation." The tract has ever since been used as an Indian reservation and as the home and abiding place of the Indians. * * *

It is alleged that "notwithstanding the riparian and other rights" of the United States and the Indians to the uninterrupted flow of the waters of the river the defendants, in the year 1900, wrongfully entered upon the river and its tributaries above the points of the diversion of the waters of the river by the United States and the Indians, built large and substantial dams and reservoirs, and by means of canals and ditches and waterways have diverted the waters of the river from its channel, and have deprived the United States and the Indians of the use thereof. And this diversion of the water, it is alleged, has continued until the present time, to the irreparable injury of the United States, for which there is no adequate remedy at law.

[Defendants answered that they had begun their diversions upstream] without having notice of any claim made by the United States or the Indians that there was any reservation made of the waters of the river or its tributaries for use on said reservation * * * [and acting in the belief that] all of the waters on the [federal] lands open for settlement * * * were subject to appropriation [under federal and state law] in like manner as water on other portions of the public domain [they entered and settled the public lands and acquired title to them under the homestead and desert land laws. They also posted the required notices to establish water rights under state law, and] expended many thousands of dollars in constructing dams, ditches and reservoirs, and in improving said lands, building fences, and other structures * * *. [Defendants also alleged that] if they are deprived of the waters "their lands will be ruined, it will be necessary to abandon their homes, and they will be greatly and irreparably damaged, the extent and amount of which damage cannot now be estimated, but will greatly exceed $100,000" * * *.

The case, as we view it, turns on the agreement of May, 1888, resulting in the creation of Fort Belknap Reservation. In the construction of this agreement there are certain elements to be considered that are prominent and significant. The reservation was a part of a very much larger tract which the Indians had the right to occupy and use and which was adequate for the habits and wants of a nomadic and uncivilized people. It was the policy of the Government, it was the desire of the Indians, to change those habits and to become a pastoral and civilized people. If they should become such the original tract was too extensive, but a smaller tract would be inadequate without a change of conditions. The lands were arid and, without irrigation, were practically valueless. And yet, it is contended, the means of irrigation were deliberately given up by the Indians and deliberately accepted by the Government. The lands ceded were, it is true, also arid; and some argument may be urged, and is urged, that with their cession there was the cession of the waters, without which they would be valueless, and "civilized communities could not be established thereon." And this, it is further contended, the Indians knew, and yet made no reservation of the waters. We realize that there is a conflict of implications, but that which makes for retention of the waters is of greater force than that which makes for their cession. The Indians had command of the lands and the waters— command of all their beneficial use, whether kept for hunting, "and grazing roving herds of stock," or turned to agriculture and the arts of civilization. Did they give up all this? Did they reduce the area of their occupation and give up the waters which made it valuable or adequate? And, even regarding the allegation of the answer as true, that there are springs and streams on the reservation flowing about 2,900 inches of water, the inquiries are pertinent. If it were possible to believe affirmative answers, we might also believe that the Indians were awed by the power of the Government or deceived by its negotiators. Neither view is possible. The Government is asserting the rights of the Indians. But extremes need not be taken into account. By a rule of interpretation of agreements and treaties with the Indians, ambiguities occurring will be resolved from the standpoint of the Indians. And the rule should certainly be applied to determine between two inferences, one of which would support the purpose of the agreement and the other impair or defeat it. On account of their relations to the Government, it cannot be supposed that the Indians were alert to exclude by formal words every inference which might militate against or defeat the declared purpose of themselves and the Government, even if it could be supposed that they had the intelligence to foresee the "double sense" which might some time be urged against them.

Another contention of appellants is that if it be conceded that there was a reservation of the waters of Milk River by the agreement of 1888, yet the reservation was repealed by the admission of Montana into the Union, February 22, 1889, c. 180, 25 Stat. 676, "upon an equal footing with the original States." The language of counsel is that "any reservation in the agreement with the Indians, expressed or implied, whereby the waters of Milk River were not to be subject of appropriation by the citizens and inhabitants of said State, was repealed by the act of admission." But to establish the repeal counsel rely substantially upon the same argument that they advance against the intention of the agreement to reserve the waters. The power of the Government to reserve the waters and exempt them from appropriation under the state laws is not denied, and could not be. United States v. The Rio Grande Dam & Irrig. Co., 174 U.S. 690, 702; United States v. Winans, 198 U.S. 371. That the Government did reserve them we have decided, and for a use which would be necessarily continued through years. This was done May 1, 1888, and it would be extreme to believe that within a year Congress destroyed the reservation and took from the Indians the consideration of their grant, leaving them a barren waste—took from them the means of continuing their old habits, yet did not leave them the power to change to new ones.

Appellants' argument upon the incidental repeal of the agreement by the admission of Montana into the Union and the power over the waters of Milk River which the State thereby acquired to dispose of them under its laws, is elaborate and able, but our construction of the agreement and its effect make it unnecessary to answer the argument in detail. For the same reason we have not discussed the doctrine of riparian rights urged by the Government.

Decree affirmed.

Mr. Justice Brewer dissents.

Notes and Questions

1. This decision established the federal reserved water doctrine, often called the "Winters doctrine." The Court was not writing on an altogether clean slate. It cited two prior decisions. The first, United States v. Rio Grande Dam & Irrigation Co., 174 U.S. 690 (1899), reversed a trial court's dismissal of a suit brought by the United States to stop construction of a private dam across the Rio Grande in the New Mexico Territory. Speaking for a unanimous Court, Justice Brewer found two exceptions to the principle that local law controlled the matter:

> First, that, in the absence of specific authority from Congress, a state cannot by its legislation destroy the right of the United States, as the owner of lands bordering on a stream, to the continued flow of its waters; so far at least as may be necessary for the beneficial

uses of the government property. Second, that it is limited by the superior power of the General Government to secure the uninterrupted navigability of all navigable streams within the limits of the United States.

174 U.S. at 703. The second decision cited in *Winters,* United States v. Winans, 198 U.S. 371 (1905), upheld enforcement of Indian treaties that recognized the right of Indians to fish outside their reservations at "usual and accustomed places." The Court, through Justice McKenna, said that the treaty "was not a grant of rights to the Indians, but a grant of rights from them—a reservation of those not granted." 198 U.S. at 381.

2. How does *Winters* square with the Desert Land Act and related statutes construed by the Supreme Court in *California Oregon Power Company,* supra p. 352? Was *Winters* affected by that later teaching from the Supreme Court?

3. Even though he had authored the Court's *Rio Grande* opinion, Justice Brewer dissented without opinion here. Later Supreme Court decisions on the *Winters* doctrine have sometimes seen the Court divided, but only over questions of application, not foundation. For one historian's assessment of *Winters* in relation to the policy of that era to assimilate the Indians in the larger culture, see Frederick B. Hoxie, A Final Promise: The Campaign to Assimilate the Indians, 1880–1920, at 168–73, 184–87 (1989).

4. How and from whom did defendants obtain their land? Do you suppose their deeds, or the law under which their deeds were provided, said anything about water?

5. Did the 1888 agreement[3] between the Indians and the United States say anything about water? Which way does silence cut? See United States v. Winans, discussed supra Note 1.

6. Is the Court saying the Tribe reserved water in the 1888 agreement, or did the United States reserve it for the Tribe? Compare *Winans,* supra Note 1. Does it make a difference? Recall that common law prior appropriation emphasizes the date of first use. Same result if the non-Indian defendants here had begun appropriating water under state (or territorial) law in, say, 1887? In United States v. Adair, 723 F.2d 1394, 1414 (9th Cir. 1983), the court said the priority date of the Klamath Tribe's water right to support hunting and fishing was time immemorial, on the rationale that the 1864 Treaty with the Tribe merely confirmed the existence of hunting and fishing rights already in being.

7. What result if the United States had not entered into the agreement with the Indians before Montana became a state in 1889? If state law had applied, what result? The non-Indian settlers upstream produced evidence that they began diverting water from the Milk River a few days before the Indian irrigation project began taking water. Winters v. United States, 143 F. 740, 741–42 (9th Cir. 1906); see also Daniel McCool, Command of the

3. Until 1871, nearly all such agreements with Indian tribes entered into by the Executive Branch were treaties submitted to and ratified by the United States Senate. In 1871 the House of Representatives finally balked at being cut out of the action, and thereafter the executive proceeded to deal with tribes by agreement, some of which, as in *Winters,* were ratified by the Congress by statute. See 25 U.S.C. § 71; Paul Gates, The History of Public Land Law Development 370, 453 (1968).

Waters: Iron Triangles, Federal Water Development, and Indian Water 38 (1987). Who would win if prior appropriation principles were applied to these facts?

8. The defendants in *Winters* alleged they had invested $100,000 in their irrigation scheme. To the extent this decision renders their investment (and their state law water rights) worthless, do they have a claim for a taking of their property rights?

9. The *Winters* doctrine has a broad range of potential applications, and has spawned a steady stream of commentary. See, e.g., Todd Fisher, The Winters of Our Discontent: Federal Reserved Water Rights in the Western States, 69 Cornell L. Rev. 1077 (1984). For a historian's view, see Norris Hundley, The Winters Decision and Indian Water Rights: A Mystery Reexamined, 13 W. Hist. Q. 20 (1982); John Shurts, Indian Reserved Water Rights: The Winters Doctrine and its Social and Legal Context, 1880s–1930s (2000). On the interpretive method used by the Court here, see generally Philip P. Frickey, Marshalling Past and Present: Colonialism, Constitutionalism, and Interpretation in Federal Indian Law, 107 Harv. L. Rev. 381 (1993). Somewhat analogous legal doctrines have been found to apply to Pueblos under Spanish and Mexican law and to Native Hawaiians under custom. See Cohen's Handbook of Federal Indian Law §§ 4.07[2][c] & [4] (Nell Newton et al. eds., 2005).

10. How much water are the Indians entitled to, according to this decision? As much as they are now using? Were using in 1888? As much as they might be able to use on their lands? For farming purposes only? Or might the Indians also use the water in other pursuits (e.g., power plants or factories) if they choose? The courts did not address these questions for a long time, as shown in the materials infra pp. 957–996. The water rights of the Fort Belknap Reservation were recently addressed in a compact between Montana and the tribes. See Mt. Code Ann. § 85–20–1001 (2004).

11. Remarkably, the Supreme Court decided only one minor case involving the Winters doctrine between 1908 and 1963. See United States v. Powers, 305 U.S. 527 (1939). Over that time, uncertainty reigned as to the reach and contours of the doctrine. As we shall see, that uncertainty has been only partially abated. The national government's tilt during this era against Indians in favor of non-Indians has come in for serious criticism. See Note 16, infra p. 942.

ARIZONA v. CALIFORNIA

Supreme Court of the United States, 1963.
373 U.S. 546.

[This landmark case, excerpted in Chapter 8 supra p. 821, dealt mostly with the allocation of Colorado River water among the lower basin states of Arizona, California, and Nevada. The United States, however, had intervened and asserted federal reserved water rights for Indian and non-Indian federal reservations along the lower Colorado River. Near the end of its lengthy opinion, the Court briefly addressed these issues, as follows:]

In these proceedings, the United States has asserted claims to waters in the main river and in some of the tributaries for use on Indian

Reservations, National Forests, Recreational and Wildlife Areas and other government lands and works. * * *

The Government, on behalf of five Indian Reservations in Arizona, California, and Nevada, asserted rights to water in the mainstream of the Colorado River. [The reservations were created by a series of Presidential Executive Orders between 1865 and 1907.] The Master found both as a matter of fact and law that when the United States created these reservations or added to them, it reserved not only land but also the use of enough water from the Colorado to irrigate the irrigable portions of the reserved lands. The aggregate quantity of water which the Master held was reserved for all the reservations is about 1,000,000 acre-feet, to be used on around 135,000 irrigable acres of land. * * * Arizona argues that the United States had no power to make a reservation of navigable waters after Arizona became a State; that navigable waters could not be reserved by Executive Orders; that the United States did not intend to reserve water for the Indian Reservations; that the amount of water reserved should be measured by the reasonably foreseeable needs of the Indians living on the reservation rather than by the number of irrigable acres; and, finally, that the judicial doctrine of equitable apportionment should be used to divide the water between the Indians and the other people in the State of Arizona.

The last argument is easily answered. The doctrine of equitable apportionment is a method of resolving water disputes between States. * * * An Indian Reservation is not a State. And while Congress has sometimes left Indian Reservations considerable power to manage their own affairs, we are not convinced by Arizona's argument that each reservation is so much like a State that its rights to water should be determined by the doctrine of equitable apportionment. Moreover, even were we to treat an Indian Reservation like a State, equitable apportionment would still not control since, under our view, the Indian claims here are governed by the statutes and Executive Orders creating the reservations.

Arizona's contention that the Federal Government had no power, after Arizona became a State, to reserve waters for the use and benefit of federally reserved lands rests largely upon statements * * * [in the Court's prior cases that dealt with] only the shores of and lands beneath navigable waters. They do not determine the problem before us and cannot be accepted as limiting the broad powers of the United States to regulate navigable waters under the Commerce Clause and to regulate government lands under Art. IV, § 3, of the Constitution. We have no doubt about the power of the United States under these clauses to reserve water rights for its reservations and property.

Arizona also argues that, in any event, water rights cannot be reserved by Executive Order. Some of the reservations of Indian lands here involved were made almost 100 years ago * * *. In our view, these reservations, like those created directly by Congress, were not limited to land, but included waters as well. * * * We can give but short shrift at this late date to the argument that the reservations either of land or water are invalid because they were originally set apart by the Executive.

Arizona also [argues] * * * that there is a lack of evidence showing that the United States in establishing the reservations intended to reserve water for them; * * * [and] that even if water was meant to be reserved the Master has awarded too much water. We reject both of these contentions. Most of the land in these reservations is and always has been arid. * * * It can be said without overstatement that when the Indians were put on these reservations they were not considered to be located in the most desirable area of the Nation. It is impossible to believe that when [these reservations were created the government was] * * * unaware that most of the lands were of the desert kind—hot, scorching sands—and that water from the river would be essential to the life of the people and to the animals they hunted and the crops they raised. * * *

We also agree with the Master's conclusion as to the quantity of water intended to be reserved. He found that the water was intended to satisfy the future as well as the present needs of the Indian Reservations and ruled that enough water was reserved to irrigate all the practicably irrigable acreage on the reservation. Arizona, on the other hand, contends that the quantity of water reserved should be measured by the Indians' "reasonably foreseeable needs," which, in fact, means by the number of Indians. How many Indians there will be and what their future needs will be can only be guessed. We have concluded, as did the Master, that the only feasible and fair way by which reserved water for the reservations can be measured is irrigable acreage. * * *

The Master ruled that the principle underlying the reservation of water rights for Indian Reservations was equally applicable to other federal establishments such as National Recreation Areas and National Forests. We agree with the conclusions of the Master that the United States intended to reserve water sufficient for the future requirements of the Lake Mead National Recreation Area, the Havasu Lake National Wildlife Refuge, the Imperial National Wildlife Refuge and the Gila National Forest.

Notes and Questions

1. There were no dissents from this portion of the Opinion. What questions left open by *Winters* does this case settle?

2. In connection with the last paragraph in the excerpt, reexamine the rationale for finding a reservation of water for the Indians in *Winters*. Is it obvious that rationale extends to non-Indian federal reservations?

3. Does the *Winters* doctrine contain a notion of appurtenancy? That is, can the federal government reserve waters that are not on, under, or contiguous to federal lands? What is an argument for limiting *Winters* to water appurtenant to federal reservations? For not limiting it? In fact, the reservation of one of the tribes awarded water by the Court's subsequent

decree (376 U.S. at 345–46 (1964)) was not contiguous to the Colorado River. See Cohen's Handbook of Federal Indian Law § 19.03[2][a] (Nell Newton et al. eds., 2005). The same was true for some tracts of land within the Havasu National Wildlife Refuge awarded water in the Court's decree. And see the discussion of waters reserved by the Wild & Scenic Rivers Act, below p. 934.

4. We will take up the many permutations of the quantification standard used here for Indian water rights (the "practicably irrigable acreage" standard, or PIA for short) in the subsection on Indian water rights beginning at p. 957.

CAPPAERT v. UNITED STATES

Supreme Court of the United States, 1976.
426 U.S. 128.

MR. CHIEF JUSTICE BURGER delivered the opinion of the Court.

The question presented in this litigation is whether the reservation of Devil's Hole as a national monument reserved federal water rights in unappropriated water.

Devil's Hole is a deep limestone cavern in Nevada. Approximately 50 feet below the opening of the cavern is a pool 65 feet long, 10 feet wide, and at least 200 feet deep, although its actual depth is unknown. The pool is a remnant of the prehistoric Death Valley Lake System and is situated on land owned by the United States since the Treaty of Guadalupe Hidalgo in 1848, 9 Stat. 922. By the Proclamation of January 17, 1952, President Truman withdrew from the public domain a 40–acre tract of land surrounding Devil's Hole, making it a detached component of the Death Valley National Monument. Proclamation No. 2961. The Proclamation was issued under the American Antiquities Preservation Act, 34 Stat. 225, 16 U.S.C. § 431, which authorizes the President to declare as national monuments "objects of historic or scientific interest that are situated upon the lands owned or controlled by the Government of the United States * * *."

The 1952 Proclamation notes that Death Valley was set aside as a national monument "for the preservation of the unusual features of scenic, scientific, and educational interest therein contained." The Proclamation also notes that Devil's Hole is near Death Valley and contains a "remarkable underground pool." Additional preambulary statements in the Proclamation explain why Devil's Hole was being added to the Death Valley National Monument:

> "WHEREAS the said pool is a unique subsurface remnant of the prehistoric chain of lakes which in Pleistocene times formed the Death Valley Lake System, * * * and

> "WHEREAS the geologic evidence that this subterranean pool is an integral part of the hydrographic history of the Death Valley region is further confirmed by the presence in this pool of a peculiar race of desert fish, and zoologists have demonstrated that this race of fish, which is found nowhere else in the world,

evolved only after the gradual drying up of the Death Valley Lake System isolated this fish population from the original ancestral stock that in Pleistocene times was common to the entire region; and

"WHEREAS the said pool is of such outstanding scientific importance that it should be given special protection, and such protection can be best afforded by making the said forty-acre tract containing the pool a part of the said monument * * *."

The Cappaert petitioners own a 12,000–acre ranch near Devil's Hole, 4,000 acres of which are used for growing Bermuda grass, alfalfa, wheat, and barley; 1,700 to 1,800 head of cattle are grazed. The ranch represents an investment of more than $7 million; it employs more than 80 people with an annual payroll of more than $340,000.

In 1968 the Cappaerts began pumping groundwater on their ranch on land 2 1/2 miles from Devil's Hole; they were the first to appropriate groundwater. The groundwater comes from an underground basin or aquifer which is also the source of the water in Devil's Hole. After the Cappaerts began pumping from the wells near Devil's Hole, which they do from March to October, the summer water level of the pool in Devil's Hole began to decrease. Since 1962 the level of water in Devil's Hole has been measured with reference to a copper washer installed on one of the walls of the hole by the United States Geological Survey. Until 1968, the water level, with seasonable variations, had been stable at 1.2 feet below the copper marker. In 1969 the water level in Devil's Hole was 2.3 feet below the copper washer; in 1970, 3.17 feet; in 1971, 3.48 feet; and, in 1972, 3.93 feet.

When the water is at the lowest levels, a large portion of a rock shelf in Devil's Hole is above water. However, when the water level is at 3.0 feet below the marker or higher, most of the rock shelf is below water, enabling algae to grow on it. This in turn enables the desert fish (cyprinodon diabolis, commonly known as Devil's Hole pupfish), referred to in President Truman's Proclamation, to spawn in the spring. As the rock shelf becomes exposed, the spawning area is decreased, reducing the ability of the fish to spawn in sufficient quantities to prevent extinction.

In April 1970 the Cappaerts, pursuant to Nevada law, applied to the State Engineer for permits to change the use of water from several of their wells. Although the United States was not a party to that proceeding and was never served, employees of the National Park Service learned of the Cappaerts' application through a public notice published pursuant to Nevada law. An official of the National Park Service filed a protest * * *. [A lawyer for the Park Service appeared at a hearing called by the State Engineer and requested that the Cappaerts' application either be denied or a decision postponed until completion of a study commissioned by the United States to determine the extent of the influence of the Cappaerts' wells over the declining water level in Devil's Hole. In December 1970 the State Engineer found there was no federal water right, rejected the Park Service's protest, and granted the application. The National Park Service did not appeal the rejection of its protest to state court.]

In August 1971 the United States * * * sought an injunction in the United States District Court for the District of Nevada to limit, except for domestic purposes, the Cappaerts' pumping from six specific wells and from specific locations near Devil's Hole. The complaint alleged that the United States, in establishing Devil's Hole as part of Death Valley National Monument, reserved the unappropriated waters appurtenant to the land to the extent necessary for the requirements and purposes of the reservation. The complaint further alleged that the Cappaerts had no perfected water rights as of the date of the reservation. * * *

This Court has long held that when the Federal Government withdraws its land from the public domain and reserves it for a federal purpose, the Government, by implication, reserves appurtenant water then unappropriated to the extent needed to accomplish the purpose of the reservation. In so doing the United States acquires a reserved right in unappropriated water which vests on the date of the reservation and is superior to the rights of future appropriators. Reservation of water rights is empowered by the Commerce Clause, Art. I, section 8, which permits federal regulation of navigable streams, and the Property Clause, Art. IV, § 3, which permits federal regulation of federal lands. The doctrine applies to Indian reservations and other federal enclaves, encompassing water rights in navigable and nonnavigable streams.

Nevada argues that the cases establishing the doctrine of federally reserved water rights articulate an equitable doctrine calling for a balancing of competing interests. However, an examination of those cases shows they do not analyze the doctrine in terms of a balancing test. For example, in Winters v. United States, supra, the Court did not mention the use made of the water by the upstream landowners in sustaining an injunction barring their diversions of the water. The "Statement of the Case" in Winters notes that the upstream users were homesteaders who had invested heavily in dams to divert the water to irrigate their land, not an unimportant interest. The Court held that when the Federal Government reserves land, by implication it reserves water rights sufficient to accomplish the purposes of the reservation.

In determining whether there is a federally reserved water right implicit in a federal reservation of public land, the issue is whether the Government intended to reserve unappropriated and thus available water. Intent is inferred if the previously unappropriated waters are necessary to accomplish the purposes for which the reservation was created. See, e.g., Arizona v. California; Winters v. United States. Both the District Court and the Court of Appeals held that the 1952 Proclamation expressed an intention to reserve unappropriated water, and we agree. The Proclamation discussed the pool in Devil's Hole in four of the five preambles and recited that the "pool * * * should be given special protection." Since a pool is a body of water, the protection contemplated is meaningful only if the water remains; the water right reserved by the 1952 Proclamation was thus explicit, not implied.

The implied-reservation-of-water-rights doctrine, however, reserves only that amount of water necessary to fulfill the purpose of the reservation, no more. Here the purpose of reserving Devil's Hole Monument is preservation of the pool. Devil's Hole was reserved "for the preservation of the unusual features of scenic, scientific, and educational interest." The Proclamation notes that the pool contains "a peculiar race of desert fish * * * which is found nowhere else in the world" and that the "pool is of * * * outstanding scientific importance * * *." The pool need only be preserved, consistent with the intention expressed in the Proclamation, to the extent necessary to preserve its scientific interest. The fish are one of the features of scientific interest. The preamble noting the scientific interest of the pool follows the preamble describing the fish as unique; the Proclamation must be read in its entirety. Thus, as the District Court has correctly determined, the level of the pool may be permitted to drop to the extent that the drop does not impair the scientific value of the pool as the natural habitat of the species sought to be preserved. The District Court thus tailored its injunction, very appropriately, to minimal need, curtailing pumping only to the extent necessary to preserve an adequate water level at Devil's Hole, thus implementing the stated objectives of the Proclamation. * * *

No cases of this Court have applied the doctrine of implied reservation of water rights to groundwater. Nevada argues that the implied-reservation doctrine is limited to surface water. Here, however, the water in the pool is surface water. The federal water rights were being depleted because, as the evidence showed, the "(g)roundwater and surface water are physically interrelated as integral parts of the hydrologic cycle." C. Corker, Groundwater Law, Management and Administration, National Water Commission Legal Study No. 6, p. xxiv (1971). Here the Cappaerts are causing the water level in Devil's Hole to drop by their heavy pumping. * * * It appears that Nevada itself may recognize the potential interrelationship between surface and ground water since Nevada applies the law of prior appropriation to both. * * * [W]e hold that the United States can protect its water from subsequent diversion, whether the diversion is of surface or ground water.[7] * * *

We hold, therefore, that as of 1952 when the United States reserved Devil's Hole, it acquired by reservation water rights in unappropriated appurtenant water sufficient to maintain the level of the pool to preserve

---

7. [Cappaert] argues that the effect of applying the implied-reservation doctrine to diversions of groundwater is to prohibit pumping from the entire 4,500 square miles above the aquifer that supplies water to Devil's Hole. First, it must be emphasized that the injunction limits but does not prohibit pumping. Second, the findings of fact in this case relate only to wells within 2 ½ miles of Devil's Hole. No proof was introduced in the District Court that pumping from the same aquifer that supplies Devil's Hole, but a greater distance * * * would significantly lower the level in Devil's Hole. * * * There was testimony from a research hydrologist that substantial pumping 40 miles away "[o]ver a period of perhaps decades [would have] a small effect."

its scientific value and thereby implement Proclamation No. 2961. Accordingly, the judgment of the Court of Appeals is Affirmed.

Notes and Questions

1.   Same result if the underground pool and the pupfish had not been mentioned in the Proclamation reserving Devil's Hole? Does a reservation of federal lands for oil shale development that does not mention water impliedly reserved water rights needed to facilitate the oil extraction and recovery process? See Robert Abrams, Implied Reservation of Water Rights in the Aftermath of Cappaert v. United States, 7 Envtl. L. Rep. 50043, 50053–54 (1977).

2.   Is the determination that the pool in Devil's Hole is really "surface water," albeit underground, convincing? Does it make any difference to the outcome how the water is characterized? If the pool is surface water, then this could be seen as something akin to a typical surface water/groundwater conflict, where different law applies to the different resources, and in this case federal law trumps state law. See Chapter 5 supra pp. 454–468. If the pool is held to be groundwater, then it could be treated as a well interference problem where one pumper's activities injure a neighbor's reliance on groundwater (see supra pp. 468–478). The wrinkle here is that the neighbor (the federal government) is making an *in situ* use of groundwater.

3.   Why was the Supreme Court so seemingly hesitant to award reserved rights to groundwater? (The Court's opinion was unanimous; might avoiding the reserved-right-to-groundwater issue have been the price of unanimity?) Recognition of reserved rights in an aquifer that has a large degree of dependable annual recharge may be little different from a surface water reservation. Recognizing a reserved right in an aquifer with little recharge, however, can give the United States an argument that it has a water right to maintain the water table at a specified level, which could preempt all other use of the aquifer. See footnote 7 in the *Cappaert* opinion. Suppose the aquifer here contained a million acre-feet and was non-recharging, and none of its water was being pumped when the national monument was created in 1952. Did President Truman's proclamation effectively reserve the entire aquifer for the pupfish?

4.   What result if Cappaert had been pumping 1000 acre-feet a year since 1950 (two years before Devils' Hole was reserved by the President), the aquifer contains one million acre-feet, and is non-recharging?

5.   In an amicus brief filed with the Court, the State of Arizona predicted that a decision in favor of the United States would wreak "economic havoc" and make groundwater-dependent cities like Tucson "ghost towns," because by making "virtually all underground water in Arizona subject to [federal reserved rights, s]tate granted water rights will be worthless and Arizona as we know it today will not survive" (quoted in John Leshy & James Belanger, Arizona Law Where Ground and Surface Water Meet, 20 Ariz. St. L.J. 657, 729 (1988)). The prediction of havoc proved false, as anyone who has seen the dramatic growth in Arizona in recent decades can attest.

6.   The late Dean Charles Meyers illuminated some of the important questions left in the wake of *Cappaert* in Federal Groundwater Rights: A

Note on Cappaert v. United States, 13 Land & Water L. Rev. 77 (1978). Among other things, he suggested that "non-Indian federal reservations which have an adequate supply of surface water to satisfy reservation purposes may not have any groundwater right at all." Id. at 385. We will take up the question of whether *Winters* extends to groundwater under Indian reservations further below in connection with the Wyoming Supreme Court's decision in In re General Adjudication of Big Horn River System, infra p. 958.

7. Recall that the Supreme Court in *Arizona v. California* rejected Arizona's argument for "equitable apportionment" between states and tribes in implementing *Winters*. See supra p. 910. Does that suggest anything about how aquifers should be apportioned among Indians or other federal reservations and users of groundwater on state and private land under state law?

8. The decision shut down the Cappaerts' farming operation. A few years later a land developer bought the property and proposed to subdivide it into 20,000 (yes, 20,000) parcels. Land clearing was held up by Endangered Species Act concerns, and in 1984 the land was purchased by The Nature Conservancy and then sold to the federal government where it became part of the Ash Meadows National Wildlife Refuge. Pupfish still exist at Devil's Hole. Ash Meadows contains two refugia populations of pupfish as insurance against a catastrophe at Devil's Hole. We will return later at p. 954 to the procedural issues raised by the appearance of the National Park Service before the Nevada State Engineer to protest the issuance of a state law permit to the Cappaerts.

UNITED STATES v. NEW MEXICO

Supreme Court of the United States, 1978.
438 U.S. 696.

MR. JUSTICE REHNQUIST delivered the opinion of the Court.

The Rio Mimbres rises in the southwestern highlands of New Mexico and flows generally southward, finally disappearing in a desert sink just north of the Mexican border. The river originates in the upper reaches of the Gila National Forest, but during its course it winds more than 50 miles past privately owned lands and provides substantial water for both irrigation and mining. In 1970, a stream adjudication was begun by the State of New Mexico to determine the exact rights of each user to water from the Rio Mimbres. In this adjudication the United States claimed reserved water rights for use in the Gila National Forest. The [state courts] * * * held that the United States, in setting aside the Gila National Forest from other public lands, reserved the use of such water "as may be necessary for the purposes for which [the land was] withdrawn," but that these purposes did not include recreation, aesthetics, wildlife preservation, or cattle grazing. * * * We granted certiorari to consider whether the Supreme Court of New Mexico had applied the correct principles of federal law in determining petitioner's reserved rights in the Mimbres. We now affirm.

I

The question posed in this case—what quantity of water, if any, the United States reserved out of the Rio Mimbres when it set aside the Gila National Forest in 1899—is a question of implied intent and not power. * * * The Court has previously concluded that whatever powers the States acquired over their waters as a result of congressional Acts and admission into the Union, however, Congress did not intend thereby to relinquish its authority to reserve unappropriated water in the future for use on appurtenant lands withdrawn from the public domain for specific federal purposes.

Recognition of Congress' power to reserve water for land which is itself set apart from the public domain, however, does not answer the question of the amount of water which has been reserved or the purposes for which the water may be used. Substantial portions of the public domain *have* been withdrawn and reserved by the United States for use as Indian reservations, forest reserves, national parks, and national monuments. And water is frequently necessary to achieve the purposes for which these reservations are made. But Congress has seldom expressly reserved water for use on these withdrawn lands. If water were abundant, Congress' silence would pose no problem. In the arid parts of the West, however, claims to water for use on federal reservations inescapably vie with other public and private claims for the limited quantities to be found in the rivers and streams. This competition is compounded by the sheer quantity of reserved lands in the Western States, which lands form brightly colored swaths across the maps of these States.[3]

The Court has previously concluded that Congress, in giving the President the power to reserve portions of the federal domain for specific federal purposes, *impliedly* authorized him to reserve "appurtenant water then unappropriated *to the extent needed to accomplish the purpose of the reservation.*" Cappaert, supra, [426 U.S.] at 138 (emphasis added). * * *

Each time this Court has applied the "implied-reservation-of-water doctrine," it has carefully examined both the asserted water right and

---

3. The percentage of federally owned land (excluding Indian reservations and other trust properties) in the Western States ranges from 29.5% of the land in the State of Washington to 86.5% of the land in the State of Nevada, an average of about 46%. Of the land in the State of New Mexico, 33.6% is federally owned. General Services Administration, Inventory Report on Real Property Owned by the United States Throughout the World as of June 30, 1974, pp. 17, 34, and App. 1, table 4. Because federal reservations are normally found in the uplands of the Western States rather than the flat lands, the percentage of water flow originating in or flowing through the reservations is even more impressive. More than 60% of the average annual water yield in the 11 Western States is from federal reservations. The percentages of average annual water yield range from a low of 56% in the Columbia–North Pacific water resource region to a high of 96% in the Upper Colorado region. In the Rio Grande water resource region, where the Rio Mimbres lies, 77% of the average runoff originates on federal reservations. C. Wheatley, C. Corker, T. Stetson, & D. Reed, Study of the Development, Management and Use of Water Resources on the Public Lands 402–406, and table 4 (1969).

the specific purposes for which the land was reserved, and concluded that without the water the purposes of the reservation would be entirely defeated.

This careful examination is required both because the reservation is implied, rather than expressed, and because of the history of congressional intent in the field of federal-state jurisdiction with respect to allocation of water. Where Congress has expressly addressed the question of whether federal entities must abide by state water law, it has almost invariably deferred to the state law. Where water is necessary to fulfill the very purposes for which a federal reservation was created, it is reasonable to conclude, even in the face of Congress' express deference to state water law in other areas, that the United States intended to reserve the necessary water. Where water is only valuable for a secondary use of the reservation, however, there arises the contrary inference that Congress intended, consistent with its other views, that the United States would acquire water in the same manner as any other public or private appropriator.

Congress indeed has appropriated funds for the acquisition under state law of water to be used on federal reservations. Thus in the National Park Service Act of Aug. 7, 1946, 60 Stat. 885, as amended, 16 U.S.C. § 17j–2 (1976 ed.), Congress authorized appropriations for the "[investigation] and establishment of water rights *in accordance with local custom, laws, and decisions of courts*, including the acquisition of water rights or of lands or interests in lands or rights-of-way for use and protection of water rights necessary or beneficial in the administration and public use of the national parks and monuments." (Emphasis added.) The agencies responsible for administering the federal reservations have also recognized Congress' intent to acquire under state law any water not essential to the specific purposes of the reservation.[7] * * *

II

A

The quantification of reserved water rights for the national forests is of critical importance to the West, where, as noted earlier, water is scarce and where more than 50% of the available water either originates

---

7. Before this Court's decisions in FPC v. Oregon, 349 U.S. 435 (1955) and Arizona v. California, recognizing reserved rights outside of Indian reservations, the Forest Service apparently believed that all of its water had to be obtained under state law. "Rights to the use of water for National Forest purposes will be obtained in accordance with State law." Forest Service Manual (1936). While the Forest Service has apparently modified its policy since those decisions, their Service Manual still indicates a policy of deferring to state water law wherever possible. "The right of the States to appropriate and otherwise control the

use of water is recognized, and the policy of the Forest Service is to abide by applicable State laws and regulations relating to water use. When water is needed by the Forest Service either for development of programs, improvements, or other uses, action will be taken promptly to acquire necessary water rights. * * * "Forest Service Manual § 2514 (Feb. 1960). "The rights to use water for national forest purposes will be obtained in accordance with State law. This policy is based on the act of June 4, 1897." Forest Service Manual § 2514.1 (Jan. 1960).

in or flows through national forests. When, as in the case of the Rio Mimbres, a river is fully appropriated, federal reserved water rights will frequently require a gallon-for-gallon reduction in the amount of water available for water-needy state and private appropriators. This reality has not escaped the attention of Congress and must be weighed in determining what, if any, water Congress reserved for use in the national forests.

The United States contends that Congress intended to reserve minimum instream flows for aesthetic, recreational, and fish-preservation purposes. An examination of the limited purposes for which Congress authorized the creation of national forests, however, provides no support for this claim. In the mid and late 1800's, many of the forests on the public domain were ravaged and the fear arose that the forest lands might soon disappear, leaving the United States with a shortage both of timber and of watersheds with which to encourage stream flows while preventing floods. It was in answer to these fears that in 1891 Congress authorized the President to "set apart and reserve, in any State or Territory having public land bearing forests, in any part of the public lands wholly or in part covered with timber or undergrowth, whether of commercial value or not, as public reservations." Creative Act of Mar. 3, 1891, § 24, 26 Stat. 1103, as amended, 16 U.S.C. § 471 (repealed 1976).

The Creative Act of 1891 unfortunately did not solve the forest problems of the expanding Nation. To the dismay of the conservationists, the new national forests were not adequately attended and regulated; fires and indiscriminate timber cutting continued their toll. To the anguish of Western settlers, reservations were frequently made indiscriminately. President Cleveland, in particular, responded to pleas of conservationists for greater protective measures by reserving some 21 million acres of "generally settled" forest land on February 22, 1897. President Cleveland's action drew immediate and strong protest from Western Congressmen who felt that the "hasty and ill considered" reservation might prove disastrous to the settlers living on or near these lands.

Congress' answer to these continuing problems was three-fold. It suspended the President's Executive Order of February 22, 1897; it carefully defined the purposes for which national forests could in the future be reserved; and it provided a charter for forest management and economic uses within the forests. Organic Administration Act of June 4, 1897, 30 Stat. 34, 16 U.S.C. §§ 473 et seq. (1976 ed.). In particular, Congress provided:

> "No national forest shall be established, except to improve and protect the forest within the boundaries, or for the purpose of securing favorable conditions of water flows, and to furnish a continuous supply of timber for the use and necessities of citizens of the United States; but it is not the purpose or intent of these provisions, or of (the Creative Act of 1891), to authorize the inclusion therein of lands more valuable for the mineral therein,

or for agricultural purposes, than for forest purposes." 30 Stat. 35, as codified, 16 U.S.C. § 475 (1976 ed.) (emphasis added).

The legislative debates surrounding the Organic Administration Act of 1897 and its predecessor bills demonstrate that Congress intended national forests to be reserved for only two purposes—"(t)o conserve the water flows, and to furnish a continuous supply of timber for the people."[14] 30 Cong. Rec. 967 (1897) (Cong. McRae). National forests were not to be reserved for aesthetic, environmental, recreational, or wildlife-preservation purposes.

> "The objects for which the forest reservations should be made are the protection of the forest growth against destruction by fire and ax, and preservation of forest conditions upon which water conditions and water flow are dependent. The purpose, therefore, of this bill is to maintain favorable forest conditions, without excluding the use of these reservations for other purposes. They are not parks set aside for nonuse, but have been established for economic reasons." 30 Cong. Rec. 966 (1897) (Cong. McRae).

Administrative regulations at the turn of the century confirmed that national forests were to be reserved for only these two limited purposes.

Any doubt as to the relatively narrow purposes for which national forests were to be reserved is removed by comparing the broader language Congress used to authorize the establishment of national parks. In 1916, Congress created the National Park Service and provided that the:

> "fundamental purpose of the said parks, monuments, and reservations * * * is to conserve the scenery and the natural and historic objects and the wild life therein and to provide for the enjoyment of the same * * * unimpaired for the enjoyment of future generations." National Park Service Act of 1916, 39 Stat. 535, § 1, as amended, 16 U.S.C. § 1 (1976 ed.).

---

14. The Government notes that the Act forbids the establishment of national forests except *"to improve and protect the forest within the boundaries, or* for the purpose of securing favorable conditions of water flows, and to furnish a continuous supply of timber," and argues from this wording that "improvement" and "protection" of the forests form a third and separate purpose of the national forest system. A close examination of the language of the Act, however, reveals that Congress only intended national forests to be established for two purposes. Forests would be created only "to improve and protect the forest within the boundaries," or, *in other words,* "for the purpose of securing favorable conditions of water flows, and to furnish a continuous supply of timber."

This reading of the Act is confirmed by its legislative history. Nothing in the legislative history suggests that Congress intended national forests to be established for three purposes, one of which would be extremely broad. Indeed, it is inconceivable that a Congress which was primarily concerned with limiting the President's power to reserve the forest lands of the West would provide for the creation of forests merely "to improve and protect the forest within the boundaries"; forests would be reserved for their improvement and protection, but only to serve the purposes of timber protection and favorable water supply. * * *

When it was Congress' intent to maintain minimum instream flows within the confines of a national forest, it expressly so directed, as it did in the case of the Lake Superior National Forest:

> "In order to preserve the shore lines, rapids, waterfalls, beaches and other natural features of the region in an unmodified state of nature, no further alteration of the natural water level of any lake or stream * * * shall be authorized." 16 U.S.C. § 577b (1976 ed.).

* * *

B

Not only is the Government's claim that Congress intended to reserve water for recreation and wildlife preservation inconsistent with Congress' failure to recognize these goals as purposes of the national forests, it would defeat the very purpose for which Congress did create the national forest system. * * * Congress authorized the national forest system principally as a means of enhancing the quantity of water that would be available to the settlers of the arid West. The Government, however, would have us now believe that Congress intended to partially defeat this goal by reserving significant amounts of water for purposes quite inconsistent with this goal.

C

In 1960, Congress passed the Multiple–Use Sustained–Yield Act of 1960, 74 Stat. 215, 16 U.S.C. §§ 528 et seq. (1976 ed.), which provides:

> "It is the policy of Congress that the national forests are established and shall be administered for outdoor recreation, range, timber, watershed, and wildlife and fish purposes. The purposes of sections 528 to 531 of this title are declared to be supplemental to, but not in derogation of, the purposes for which the national forests were established as set forth in the [Organic Administration Act of 1897.]"

The Supreme Court of New Mexico concluded that this Act did not give rise to any reserved rights not previously authorized in the Organic Administration Act of 1897. * * * While we conclude that the Multiple–Use Sustained–Yield Act of 1960 was intended to broaden the purposes for which national forests had previously been administered, we agree that Congress did not intend to thereby expand the reserved rights of the United States.[21]

---

21. The United States does not argue that the Multiple–Use Sustained–Yield Act of 1960 reserved additional water for use on the national forests. Instead, the Government argues that the Act confirms that Congress *always* foresaw broad purposes for the national forests and authorized the Secretary of the Interior as early as 1897 to reserve water for recreational, aesthetic, and wildlife-preservation uses. Brief for United States 53–56. As the legislative history of the 1960 Act demonstrates, however, Congress believed that the 1897 Organic Administration Act only authorized the creation of national forests for two purposes— timber preservation and enhancement of water supply—and intended, through the 1960 Act, to *expand* the purposes for which

The Multiple–Use Sustained–Yield Act of 1960 establishes the purposes for which the national forests *"are* established and *shall* be administered." (Emphasis added.) * * * In the administration of the national forests, therefore, Congress intended the Multiple–Use Sustained–Yield Act of 1960 to broaden the benefits accruing from all reserved national forests. The House Report accompanying the 1960 legislation, however, indicates that recreation, range, and "fish" purposes are "to be supplemental to, but not in derogation of, the purposes for which the national forests were established" in the Organic Administration Act of 1897. " * * * Thus, in any establishment of a national forest a purpose set out in the 1897 act must be present but there may also exist one or more of the additional purposes listed in the [1960] bill. * * * " H.R. Rep. No. 1551, 86th Cong., 2d Sess., 4 (1960).

As discussed earlier, the "reserved rights doctrine" is a doctrine built on implication and is an exception to Congress' explicit deference to state water law in other areas. Without legislative history to the contrary, we are led to conclude that Congress did not intend in enacting the Multiple–Use Sustained–Yield Act of 1960 to reserve water for the *secondary* purposes there established.[22] A reservation of additional water could mean a substantial loss in the amount of water available for irrigation and domestic use, thereby defeating Congress' principal purpose of securing favorable conditions of water flow. Congress intended the national forests to be administered for broader purposes after 1960 but there is no indication that it believed the new purposes to be so crucial as to require a reservation of additional water. By reaffirming the primacy of a favorable water flow, it indicated the opposite intent.

III

What we have said also answers the Government's contention that Congress intended to reserve water from the Rio Mimbres for stockwatering purposes. The United States issues permits to private cattle owners to graze their stock on the Gila National Forest and provides for stockwatering at various locations along the Rio Mimbres. The United States contends that since Congress clearly foresaw stockwatering on national forests, reserved rights must be recognized for this purpose. The New Mexico courts disagreed and held that any stockwatering rights must be allocated under state law to individual stockwaterers. We agree.

While Congress intended the national forests to be put to a variety of uses, including stockwatering, not inconsistent with the two principal purposes of the forests, stockwatering was not itself a direct purpose of reserving the land. If stockwatering could not take place in the Gila

the national forests should be administered. See, e.g., H.R. Rep. No. 1551, 86th Cong., 2d Sess., 4 (1960), U.S. Code Cong. & Admin. News 1960, p. 2377. Even if the 1960 Act expanded the reserved water rights of the United States, of course, the rights would be subordinate to any appropriation of water under state law dating to before 1960.

22. We intimate no view as to whether Congress, in the 1960 Act, authorized the subsequent reservation of national forests out of public lands to which a broader doctrine of reserved water rights might apply.

National Forest, Congress' purposes in reserving the land would not be defeated. Congress, of course, did intend to secure favorable water flows, and one of the uses to which the enhanced water supply was intended to be placed was probably stockwatering. But Congress intended the water supply from the Rio Mimbres to be allocated among private appropriators under state law. * * *

IV

Congress intended that water would be reserved only where necessary to preserve the timber or to secure favorable water flows for private and public uses under state law. This intent is revealed in the purposes for which the national forest system was created and Congress' principled deference to state water law in the Organic Administration Act of 1897 and other legislation. The decision of the Supreme Court of New Mexico is faithful to this congressional intent and is therefore Affirmed.

MR. JUSTICE POWELL, with whom MR. JUSTICE BRENNAN, MR. JUSTICE WHITE, and MR. JUSTICE MARSHALL join, dissenting in part.

I agree with the Court that the implied-reservation doctrine should be applied with sensitivity to its impact upon those who have obtained water rights under state law and to Congress' general policy of deference to state water law. I also agree that the Organic Administration Act of 1897, 30 Stat. 11, cannot fairly be read as evidencing an intent to reserve water for recreational or stockwatering purposes in the national forests.[1]

I do not agree, however, that the forests which Congress intended to "improve and protect" are the still, silent, lifeless places envisioned by the Court. In my view, the forests consist of the birds, animals, and fish—the wildlife—that inhabit them, as well as the trees, flowers, shrubs, and grasses. I therefore would hold that the United States is entitled to so much water as is necessary to sustain the wildlife of the forests, as well as the plants. * * *

My analysis begins with the language of the statute. * * * Although the language of the statute is not artful, a natural reading would attribute to Congress an intent to authorize the establishment of national forests for three purposes, not the two discerned by the Court. The New Mexico Supreme Court gave the statute its natural reading in this case when it wrote:

> "The Act limits the purposes for which national forests are authorized to: 1) improving and protecting the forest, 2) secur-

---

1. I express no view as to the effect of the Multiple–Use Sustained–Yield Act of 1960 on the United States' reserved water rights in the national forests that were established either before or after that Act's passage. Although the Court purports to hold that passage of the 1960 Act did not have the effect of reserving any additional water in then-existing forests * * * this portion of the Opinion appears to be dicta. * * * [T]he State has gone so far as to suggest that passage of the 1960 Act may well have expanded the United States' reserved water rights in the national forests, presumably with a priority date for the additional reserved rights of 1960. * * * But there never has been a question in this case as to whether the 1960 Act gave rise to additional reserved water rights with a priority date of 1960 or later in the Gila National Forest.

ing favorable conditions of water flows, and 3) furnishing a continuous supply of timber."

* * * The Court believes that its "reading of the Act is confirmed by its legislative history." * * * The matter is not so clear to me. From early times in English law, the forest has included the creatures that live there. J. Manwood, A Treatise and Discourse of the Laws of the Forrest 1–7 (1598); 1 W. Blackstone, Commentaries 289. [Several passages follow tracing congressional concern for wildlife within the forests.]

One may agree with the Court that Congress did not, by enactment of the Organic Administration Act of 1897, intend to authorize the creation of national forests simply to serve as wildlife preserves. But it does not follow from this that Congress did not consider wildlife to be part of the forest that it wished to "improve and protect" for future generations. It is inconceivable that Congress envisioned the forests it sought to preserve as including only inanimate components such as the timber and flora. Insofar as the Court holds otherwise, the 55th Congress is maligned and the Nation is the poorer, and I dissent.[5]

Notes and Questions

1. Examine the 1897 statute governing forest reservations closely. How does Justice Rehnquist interpret the phrase "improve and protect the forest within the boundaries"? Justice Powell? Does the former lose sight of the forest for the trees, as it were, or did Congress do so in 1897?

2. *New Mexico* remains the leading modern federal reserved rights case and sparked considerable commentary. Consider the opposing views of the decision in Sally Fairfax & A. Dan Tarlock, No Water for the Woods: A Critical Analysis of United States v. New Mexico, 15 Idaho L. Rev. 509 (1979) and Alan Boles & Charles Elliott, United States v. New Mexico and the Course of Federal Reserved Water Rights, 51 U. Colo. L. Rev. 209 (1980). Fairfax and Tarlock maintain that the Supreme Court's reading of the 1891 and 1897 Acts, "is arguably wrong because the reservation of water for instream uses is consistent with the original purpose of the reservations." Boles and Elliott applaud the decision and the protection it affords to existing state law appropriators whose uses might have been displaced by a grant of reserved rights for instream flows. The federal interest, they contend, can be adequately protected by the federal government through condemnation of water rights if reduced flows threaten to harm the forests. Frank Trelease, Uneasy Federalism–State Water Laws and National Water Uses, 55 U. Wash. L. Rev. 751 (1980), sides with Boles and Elliott.

3. In *Cappaert* the water reserved was described as the amount of water necessary to serve the purposes for which the land was reserved. In

---

5. No doubt it will be said that the waterflow necessary to maintain the watershed including the forest will be sufficient for the wildlife. This well may be true in most national forests and most situations. But the Court's opinion, as I read it, recognizes no reserved authority in the Federal Government to protect wildlife itself as a part of the forest, and therefore if and when the need for increased waterflow for this purpose arises the Federal Government would be powerless to act. Indeed, upstream appropriators could be allowed to divert so much water that survival of forest wildlife—including even the fish and other life in the streams—would be endangered.

New Mexico, the adjective "primary" is added as a modifier of "purposes." Does *New Mexico* alter the basic tenets of the reserved rights doctrine, or does it simply read narrowly the purposes behind the creation of the national forest system? For example, does or should the narrow interpretation reflected in *New Mexico* apply to federal reserved rights for Indian reservations? We will return to this issue later in the chapter.

4.   Note that the Court was unanimous in holding that the 1897 Act did not reserve water for stockwatering and recreational uses, even though both are common uses of the national forests. In the absence of congressional action, what options are open to the Forest Service if it wishes to secure water for livestock grazing and campgrounds and other recreational use? For wildlife? Besides condemnation of water rights obtained under state law, the Forest Service can seek to become a state law appropriator, if unappropriated water is available. That and other strategies are considered further infra pp. 996–1008. Also considered below are the application of *Winters* and *New Mexico* to a variety of other federal reservations, including national parks, wildlife refuges, wild and scenic rivers, and wilderness.

The Legal Basis for Federal Reserved Water Rights

The Supreme Court's discussion of the constitutional basis for federal reservations of water consists of a couple of terse sentences in *Arizona v. California* and *Cappaert*, merely asserting that the United States may reserve water under the Commerce and Property clauses of the U.S. Constitution. The most complete explication of the basis for federal water rights was a lengthy opinion by the Department of Justice's Office of Legal Counsel.[1] This Opinion took the view that Congress had broad authority under a number of constitutional provisions to preempt state water law, whether or not in conjunction with a reservation of federal land. Furthermore, it may delegate this power to the executive branch. "[F]ederal reserved rights are not a unique species of federal rights that arise directly out of the reservation of federal lands, so that, absent a reservation of land, no federal water rights can exist. * * * The reserved right doctrine does not rest on any unique constitutional basis." Id. at 363. "Therefore, this power may extend to acquired lands as well as public domain." Id. at 381. "[F]ederal water rights may be asserted without regard to state law to [satisfy] specific congressional directives or authorizations that override inconsistent state law * * * [or to fulfill] primary purposes for the management of federal lands * * * that would be frustrated by the application of state law." Id. See generally John D. Leshy, Water Rights for New Federal Land Conservation Programs: A Turn-of-the-Century Evaluation, 4 U. Denver Water L. Rev. 271 (2001). For an example of Congress reserving water for a national purpose without tying it expressly to federal land, see the Wild & Scenic Rivers Act, discussed infra p. 934. There being little doubt about the power, the important questions are usually whether, in any

---

1.   Federal "Non–Reserved" Water Rights, 6 Op. Off. Legal Counsel 328 (1982). This is sometimes called the "Olson" opinion after the Assistant Attorney General who signed it—Theodore Olson, who later became President George W. Bush's first Solicitor General.

particular situation, Congress or the Executive has reserved water under federal law independent of state law, and if so, how much. These are pursued below.

Federal Reserved Water Rights in Riparian Jurisdictions

The application of the *Winters* doctrine in eastern riparian jurisdictions has not been developed in any reported cases (nor, for that matter, has any case squarely addressed the interface between the doctrine and riparian rights recognized in California). Indeed, an informal survey in the Department of the Interior did not uncover a single instance in which the National Park Service has ever asserted a federal reserved water right in the East, and only one instance where an eastern Indian tribe (the Seminole in Florida) had ever claimed a reserved right (the claim was settled in an agreement involving the State and the South Florida Water Management District[2]). Some original public domain federal land exists in a number of riparian rights states, but most federal lands now found in riparian jurisdictions have been acquired into federal ownership for particular purposes; e.g., national forests, parks, or wildlife refuges. A number of segments of eastern rivers have been designated under the federal Wild & Scenic Rivers Act, which carry water rights with them, as discussed infra p. 934.

The extent to which, in pure riparian jurisdictions, federal reserved water rights may be superior to state law riparian rights (to which federal riparian lands are presumably entitled, see infra p. 997) is not clear. Conceptually, there are some similarities between riparian rights and federal reserved rights. Neither is dependent upon putting water to actual use; both are related to land ownership. But there are some differences. Federal reserved water rights can be quantified on the basis of the amount of water necessary to carry out the purposes for which the federal land is reserved or withdrawn. Riparian rights are more indefinite and inchoate in quantity, being dependent upon comparative reasonableness of all the uses along the stream at any one point in time. In a state like California, where unused state law riparian rights might be effectively eliminated through adjudications (see the *Long Valley* case, supra p. 374), a federal reserved right for use on riparian land should withstand such nullification.

Academic commentary on the subject is growing.[3] A thoughtful recent article lays out several bases for asserting federal water rights in

---

2. See 25 U.S.C. §§ 1772–1772g; Cohen's Handbook of Federal Indian Law § 1901[2] (Nell Newton et al., eds., 2005).

3. See, e.g., Charles Meyers, The Colorado River, 19 Stan. L. Rev. 1, 68–69 (1966); Eva Hanks, Peace West of the 98th Meridian—Solution to Federal–State Conflicts over Western Waters, 23 Rutgers L. Rev. 33, 39–40 n. 25 (1968); Walter Kiechel & Martin Green, Riparian Rights Revisited: Legal Basis For Federal Instream Flow Rights, 16 Nat. Resources J. 969 (1976); Anita Robb, Applying the Reserved Rights Doctrine in Riparian States, 14 N.C. Cent. L.J. 98 (1983); Judith V. Royster, Winters in the East: Tribal Reserved Rights to Water in Riparian States, 25 Wm. & Mary Envtl. L. & Pol'y Rev. 169 (2000); Eric H. Lord, The Obed Wild & and Scenic River of Tennessee: Asserting a Federal Reserved Water Right in a Riparian Jurisdiction, 7 Great Plains Nat. Res. J. 1 (2003).

the east, but concludes that, because they are "too speculative at this juncture to be relied upon," the federal government should generally "comply with regulated riparian requirements to the maximum extent practicable[, declining] ... to do so only when state requirements conflict with federal law, or are reasonably anticipated to interfere with the accomplishment of the federal installation's mission." Jeremy N. Jungreis, "Permit" Me Another Drink: A Proposal for Safeguarding the Water Rights of Federal Lands in the Regulated Riparian East, 29 Harv. Envtl. L. Rev. 369, 419 (2005).

2. NON–INDIAN RESERVED RIGHTS

This subsection briefly explores varieties of reserved rights claims connected with a wide array of non-Indian federal lands and programs, building on the teachings of *Arizona v. California* (which first acknowledged this application of *Winters*), *Cappaert*, and *United States v. New Mexico*.[4] A number of the recent decisions in this area come from the Idaho Supreme Court, which has shown a decidedly hostile attitude toward finding federal reserved rights by implication, taking its cue from Justice Rehnquist's opinion in United States v. New Mexico, supra p. 917. The Idaho decisions are subject to withering criticism in Michael C. Blumm, Reversing the *Winters* Doctrine?: Denying Reserved Water Rights for Idaho Wilderness and Its Implications, 73 U. Colo. L. Rev. 173 (2002).

National Forests

As Justice Rehnquist suggested at the beginning of his opinion in *New Mexico*, the most hotly contested federal non-Indian reserved rights have been in the national forests. This is probably because the national forest system is extensive (comprising nearly two hundred million acres of land) and dominates the headwaters of most important western rivers. *New Mexico* settled some basic questions about national forest reserved water rights, but left a number of other questions open.

For example, what is the precise holding of *New Mexico* regarding the effect of the Multiple Use–Sustained Yield Act of 1960 (MUSYA)? Footnote 21 of the Court's opinion reveals that the United States did not argue that MUSYA created a 1960 reservation of water, but rather that it simply confirmed the 1897 Organic Act's reservation of water for broad purposes. Compare the first footnote in Powell's dissent. Can the United States still argue for reserved rights based on MUSYA alone? For a negative answer, see United States v. City and County of Denver, 656

---

4. In the wake of *New Mexico*, the Solicitor of the Department of the Interior issued a comprehensive Opinion that addressed the reserved rights and other water rights claims of the Interior Department's land managing agencies. 86 Interior Dec. 553 (1979). Some of the material in this note is drawn from that Opinion. For a useful collection of western state perspectives on the scope and nature of non-Indian federal reserved rights claims, both generally and through a state-by-state survey, see D. Craig Bell & James Alder, Federal Non-Indian Claims To Water (Western States Water Council 1999).

P.2d 1, 24–27 (Colo. 1982); United States v. City of Challis, 988 P.2d 1199 (Idaho 1999).

Many of the national parks were created by Congress in areas that had earlier been reserved from the public domain as national forests. If a tract of federal land had been included in a national forest in 1898, and then in a national park in 1930, what is the scope and priority date of the water right associated with those lands? See United States v. City and County of Denver, 656 P.2d 1 (Colo.1982) (holding that the park water right takes the earlier date of the forest reservation "to the extent that the purposes of the national forests and national parks overlap"). See generally Eric Freyfogle, Repairing the Waters of the National Parks: Notes on a Long–Term Strategy, 74 Denv. U. L. Rev. 815 (1997).

Do the national forests have federal reserved rights for water flows to maintain stream channels and associated riparian areas? Note that securing "favorable conditions of water flows" was one of the two 1897 Organic Act purposes *New Mexico* had recognized for the national forest system. The Forest Service has argued that

> recent advances in the science of 'fluvial geomorphology' have shown that strong, recurring instream water flows are necessary to maintain efficient stream channels and to secure favorable conditions of water flows, and that diversions of water within the national forests by private appropriators reduce stream flows and threaten the equilibrium that preserves natural stream channels.

United States v. Jesse, 744 P.2d 491, 498 (Colo. 1987) (paraphrasing the brief for the United States). In the *Jesse* case, the Colorado Supreme Court remanded for a factual trial on such claims. After a lengthy hearing involving many expert witnesses and more than a thousand exhibits, the Colorado trial court ruled that the Forest Service had failed to show that the water rights claimed were necessary to secure favorable water flows. The Forest Service did not appeal, but similar claims have been filed in other Colorado Water Divisions. See generally Wendy Weiss, The Federal Government's Pursuit of Instream Flow Water Rights, 1 U. Den. Water L. Rev. 151, 157–60 (1998).

Questions

1. Should the existence or scope of the reserved water right here determined by the state of scientific knowledge when Congress authorized the reservation of national forests in part to maintain "favorable conditions of water flows," or instead by what modern science shows about the need for scouring flows to maintain ecologically healthy river channels, improve the reliability of flows and reduce downstream flooding?

2. What would be the effect on water management if the Forest Service were to be awarded reserved water rights for channel maintenance? Would it have any adverse effects on downstream junior appropriators? Upstream appropriators? Holders of private inholdings in the national forests, or those

who, with permission of the U.S. Forest Service, make diversions from streams on the national forests?

National Parks

Recall that the Supreme Court's opinion in *United States v. New Mexico* in 1978 compared and contrasted the 1897 Organic Act applying to the national forest system with the counterpart 1916 Organic Act applying to the national park system. See supra p. 921. What water does the 1916 Act implicitly reserve, for what purposes? Instream flows for ecosystem maintenance? Water to sustain natural features like geysers in Yellowstone or Yosemite Falls? What about water for national park employees' residences? Water for campgrounds or service stations for park visitors? Water to grow hay for feeding the horses and mules maintained by national park concessioners? See Solicitor's Opinion, 86 Interior Dec. at 595–96 (1979).

National Park water rights tend not to be so controversial because (1) parks are popular icons (the American cultural equivalent of the cathedrals of Europe, according to historian Alfred Runte in National Parks: The American Experience (2d ed. 1987)); (2) parks are often important contributors to local economies; (3) most park water uses are either nonconsumptive (instream flows for environmental health) or do not consume much (campgrounds, hotels); and (4) many parks are in headwaters or mountainous areas and thus preserve flows for uses downstream.

National Monuments

About one hundred National Monuments (the large majority managed by the National Park Service) have been created by the President, exercising delegated authority from the Congress in the Antiquities Act of 1906 to protect "objects of historic or scientific interest" on federal lands. See 16 U.S.C. § 431; Cappaert v. United States, supra p. 912. If the President creates a national monument encompassing dinosaur remains or an archeological site for scientific study, and the proclamation is silent on water, does it carry with it a reserved water right? For what purpose(s)? Cf. United States v. City and County of Denver, 656 P.2d 1, 27–29 (Colo. 1982); see also Wendy Weiss, The Federal Government's Pursuit of Instream Flow Water Rights, 1 U. Den. Water L. Rev. 151, 161 & nn. 87–88 (1998).

National Recreation and National Conservation Areas

In Arizona v. California, the Supreme Court recognized reserved rights for Lake Mead National Recreation Area (created by statute in 1964, but first reserved by Executive Orders in 1929 and 1930), without elaboration. See supra p. 911. More recently, the Idaho Supreme Court has taken a less charitable view. In 1973 Congress established the Sawtooth National Recreation Area to "assure the preservation and protection of the natural, scenic, historic, pastoral, and fish and wildlife values and to provide for the enhancement of the recreational values associated therewith." 16 U.S.C. § 460aa(a). Does this Act reserve an instream flow for salmon fishery purposes? In State v. United States, 12 P.3d 1284 (Idaho 2000), the court found that the "primary purpose" of the recreation area was to "protect the [area] from the dangers of unrestricted development [from subdividing private inholdings in the area] and mining operations." The statutory reference to protecting fish, the court said, should be understood as merely to protect them "from the dangers associated with unregulated mining operations," which are now being regulated. Because water was not necessary to achieve this purpose, no reservation of water would be implied. Dissenting Justice Silak accused the majority of "ignor[ing] the express legislative language" that defined the purpose of the reservation much more broadly than simply controlling development and mining, which in her view could not be achieved without water.

Statutes may require close reading to determine whether water is reserved. The Hells Canyon National Recreation Area (HCNRA), 16 U.S.C. § 460gg(b), includes "waters" in the area designated, but goes on to say that the Act does not authorize any limitation on "present and future use of the waters of the Snake River and its tributaries *upstream* from the boundaries of" the HCNRA (16 U.S.C. § 460gg–3(a)) (emphasis added), and that "[n]o flow requirement of any kind may be imposed on the waters of the Snake River *below*" the area (16 U.S.C. § 460gg–3(b)) (emphasis added). Does the Act reserve any water under federal law? The Idaho Supreme Court upheld a trial court ruling that the statute was an express reservation of all water "originating in tributaries to the Snake River which are located *within* the HCNRA." Potlatch Corp.v. United States, 12 P.3d 1260, 1270 (Idaho 2000) (emphasis added).

National Wildlife Refuges

The national wildlife refuge system consists of not only refuges but wildlife ranges, game ranges, wildlife management areas, and waterfowl production areas managed by the Fish & Wildlife Service. Many of these areas were originally established by individual Presidential or Secretarial Orders.[5] Most of these orders were silent on water. In Arizona v. California, the Supreme Court found that the United States "intended to reserve water sufficient for the future requirements of" two National Wildlife Refuges. See supra p. 911.

The Deer Flat National Wildlife Refuge was created by Executive Order in 1937. It encompasses some 94 islands along 110 miles of the Snake River in Idaho which are an important component of the Pacific Flyway, used by more than 100 species of birds. The Order referred to the islands as a "sanctuary for migratory birds," designated them "a refuge and breeding ground for migratory birds and other wildlife," but

5. For general background on water for wildlife refuges, see Western Water Policy Review Advisory Commission, Water in the West: Challenge for the Next Century 5–34 (1998). On the National Wildlife Refuge System generally, see Robert Fischman, The National Wildlife Refuges: Coordinating a Conservation System Through Law (2003).

was silent on water rights. Does the Order reserve enough water, expressly or impliedly, to keep the islands as islands, and thus help protect the birds from coyotes and other predators?

The Idaho Supreme Court said no in United States v. State, 23 P.3d 117 (2001). The court said because "there is no standard for the amount of water necessary to have an island," it could be inferred that President Roosevelt had no intent to reserve water for the Refuge. The court determined, on very thin historical evidence, that the original purpose of the Refuge was to provide the birds a sanctuary from hunting only by humans, not by natural predators. Because human hunting is still prohibited in the refuge, the original purpose is being met without a reservation of water. "Even if it were shown that the purpose of the island reservations has evolved over the years to * * * foster isolation from predators, those purposes were not present at the time of the reservations." The court also expressed concern that recognizing a reserved water right for the Refuge might interfere with the operation of federal water projects on the River, and it was "inconceivable that President Roosevelt in 1937 * * * intended to give preference to waterfowl, or any other migratory bird, over people. * * * If nature requires a choice, the recognition of water rights for people will prevail." The United States did not seek review in the U.S. Supreme Court.

The Organic Act for the National Wildlife Refuge System adopted by Congress in 1997 contains several confusing provisions dealing with water rights, including a standard disclaimer like that found in the Wilderness Act, discussed immediately below (16 U.S.C. § 668dd(j)), a provision that the Secretary of the Interior shall "acquire, under State law, water rights that are needed for refuge purposes," 16 U.S.C. § 668dd(a)(4)(G), and a proviso that nothing in the Act "create[s] a reserved water right, express or implied, in the United States for any purpose," or "affect[s] any water right in existence" on the date of enactment, or affects any Federal or State law in existence on the date of enactment "regarding water quality or water quantity." 16 U.S.C. § 668dd(n)(1).[6]

Wilderness Areas

Like most other statutes undergirding federal land reservations, the Wilderness Act of 1964 says very little about water,[7] other than a general disclaimer (also found in several other federal statutes) that nothing in it "shall constitute an express or implied claim or denial on the part of the Federal Government as to exemption from State water laws." 16 U.S.C. § 1133(d)(6).

---

6. The Service's policy manual provisions on water rights (last revised in early 1993) are found at http://www.fws.gov/ policy/403fw1.html.

7. It contains a provision authorizing the President to approve water projects in wilderness areas—areas which are otherwise off limits to development, including roads or other obvious imprints of human activity. See 16 U.S.C. § 1133(d)(4). The legislative history suggests this was to allow "minor" projects, but the provision has never been used even for that purpose. See John Leshy, Water and Wilderness/Law and Politics, 23 Land & Water L. Rev. 389, 402 (1988).

The extent to which federal wilderness areas carry federal water rights with them has been embroiled in sometimes heated controversy for two decades.[8] The reasons for all this fuss are not immediately apparent. Wilderness areas by definition are to be left alone for the forces of nature to operate in them unimpaired. Any water rights they have are to maintain natural flows, i.e., involve no artificial diversion or consumption. These areas are, moreover, usually at high altitudes, at or near the tops of watersheds, which means that protecting their stream-flow usually poses no threat to other, more conventional uses. Finally, since the Wilderness Act was not adopted until 1964, and most wilderness areas were designated by Congress even after that, wilderness water rights have a relatively late priority date.

In 1999 the Idaho Supreme Court held, 3–2, that wilderness designation reserved all the unappropriated water within the wilderness area as of the date of designation. The decision sparked a lively public debate in Idaho, especially because some of the wilderness areas involved were not in headwaters, and some upstream communities voiced concern that their diversions would be threatened. Then the Chief Justice (who had been in the majority) reversed her position and upon rehearing, the Court reversed itself. Potlatch Corp. v. United States, 12 P.3d 1260 (Idaho 2000). While those events were unfolding, the Idaho voters threw another Justice, who wrote the original majority opinion finding a federal reserved water right in wilderness, off the court, after a hard-fought campaign in which her vote in this case was prominently featured. (The Chief Justice would face the voters the following year.) See Michael C. Blumm, Reversing the *Winters* Doctrine?: Denying Reserved Water Rights for Idaho Wilderness and its Implications, 73 U. Colo. L. Rev. 173 (2002). It was not the first time a state Supreme Court Justice had lost reelection over a water rights matter. See Hon. Gregory J. Hobbs, Jr., State Water Politics Versus an Independent Judiciary: The Colorado and Idaho Experiences, 5 U. Denver Water L. Rev. 122 (2001).

The furor over wilderness water rights stems in part from ideology—traditional water users and states' righters don't like federal reserved rights, particularly those that have preservationist purposes. But

---

8. In 1979, the Solicitor of the Department of the Interior concluded that designation of wilderness areas reserves water rights necessary to carry out the preservation-oriented purposes of the Act, including science, education, inspiration and recreation. 86 Interior Dec. at 609–10. After President Reagan took office in 1981, the Forest Service failed to file claims for water rights in twenty-four national forest wilderness areas in an ongoing Colorado adjudication. This led to protracted but ultimately inconclusive litigation brought by environmentalists. See Sierra Club v. Block, 622 F.Supp. 842, 850–51, 862 (D. Colo. 1985), 661 F.Supp. 1490 (D. Colo. 1987), vacated sub nom. Sierra Club v. Yeutter, 911 F.2d 1405 (10th Cir. 1990). In the midst of the litigation, a new Interior Solicitor issued a new opinion, approved by the Justice Department, which reversed the 1979 Opinion. See 96 Interior Dec. 211 (1988). That did not end things. Early in the Clinton Administration, the Attorney General, on advice of the Interior Solicitor and the General Counsel of Agriculture (where the Forest Service is housed), vacated both the 1989 Opinion and the wilderness portion of the 1979 Opinion. See generally Robert Abrams, Water in the Western Wilderness: The Duty to Assert Reserved Water Rights, 1986 U. Ill. L. Rev. 387; John Leshy, Water and Wilderness/Law and Politics, 23 Land & Water L. Rev. 398 (1988); Karin Sheldon, Water for Wilderness, 76 Denver U. L. Rev. 555 (1999).

geography also explains the intensity of the dispute in some places. In Idaho some small communities draw water from streams above wilderness areas. In Colorado, precipitation in the mountains is the source of waters flowing out of the state in all directions, and the State's water establishment has always harbored a deep annoyance that it cannot capture much of that water. Most prominently, it has never been able to develop its full entitlement to the waters of the Colorado River, even though it furnishes most of the River's water. See Chapter 8 supra pp. 802–816. Federal reserved rights to protect water in wilderness, particularly areas in the Colorado River watershed on Colorado's western slope, could make it more difficult for Colorado to develop its entitlement in the traditional ways (high altitude trans-basin diversions from the upper reaches of the less-populated west slope to the megalopolis along the Front Range).

Wild and Scenic Rivers

The Wild and Scenic Rivers Act contains an express, though negatively phrased, assertion of federal reserved water rights:

> *Designation* of any stream or portion thereof as a national wild, scenic or recreational river area *shall* not *be construed as a reservation of the waters of such streams for purposes* other than those specified in this chapter, or *in quantities* greater than *necessary to accomplish these purposes.*[9]

The Act's purpose was to preserve "certain selected rivers" which "possess outstandingly remarkable scenic, recreational, geologic, fish and wildlife, historic, cultural, or other similar values" in their "free-flowing condition," and protect the rivers "and their immediate environments" for the "benefit and enjoyment of present and future generations." 16 U.S.C. § 1271. The water reservation is not tied expressly to any reservation of land, and in fact a number of National Wild & Scenic River corridors have mostly non-federal land. Even the Idaho Supreme Court has agreed that the Act, though "awkwardly stated[,] ... is clear that Congress intended to reserve water to fulfill the purposes of the Act." Potlach Corp. v. United States, 12 P.3d 1256, 1258 (Idaho 2000).

How much water is reserved by this Act? All the natural flows in the designated rivers? If something less than all the flows, how much less? See Solicitor's Opinion, 86 Interior Dec. at 607–09 (1979); Brian Gray, No Holier Temples, Protecting the National Parks Through Wild and Scenic River Designation, 58 U. Colo. L. Rev. 551 (1988).

Bureau of Land Management (BLM) Public Lands

The BLM manages federal lands that, with some exceptions, have not been reserved for specific uses. Instead, most of them are the residual public domain left after disposition into non-federal ownership, or after reservation for specific purposes and transfer for management by other federal agencies like the Forest Service, Park Service, and Fish

9. 16 U.S.C. § 1284(c) (emphasis added).

and Wildlife Service. Unreserved BLM lands are generally regarded as having no federally reserved water rights. In 1976, Congress for the first time gave BLM an organic management statute, the Federal Land Policy and Management Act (FLPMA), 43 U.S.C. §§ 1701 et seq. While this Act set forth broad purposes for which these lands were to be managed, it did not in and of itself reserve water. Sierra Club v. Watt, 659 F.2d 203, 206 (D.C. Cir. 1981). The court in that case expressed "substantial agreement" with the government's argument in its brief:

> Under the controlling decisions of the Supreme Court, the distinction between reservation[s] and unreserved public lands is fundamental. Reserved rights attach only to the former, and then only when water is necessary to fulfill the primary purpose of the reservation. No water is reserved for uses that are merely permissive upon a reservation. *A fortiori*, then, no reserved rights arise under [FLPMA], for no reservation of land is effected.

Id. The court also focused on one of FLPMA's savings clauses, which provides that nothing in FLPMA "shall be construed as * * * *expanding* or diminishing *Federal* or State jurisdiction, responsibility, interests, or *rights in water resources development or control* * * *." FLPMA § 701(g), 90 Stat. 2786 (1976) (emphasis added). The court interpreted the italicized provisions as meaning that no federal water rights were reserved in the statute.

FLPMA essentially calls for BLM public lands to be managed for the same purposes as the national forests: multiple uses including mining, grazing, recreation, timber, and watershed protection, among others. Does it make sense that BLM has no reserved rights for these uses, and the Forest Service does for some of them? Does Congress have to act consistently in directing management of federal lands and associated water?[10]

A 1926 Executive Order (commonly called Public Water Reserve No. 107) reserved lands around every "spring or waterhole" on BLM-managed public lands "for public use." 43 U.S.C. § 300 (repealed prospectively by FLPMA, leaving existing withdrawals intact). The idea behind it was to prevent private monopolization of scarce water sources on the arid western public lands. There has been some debate about how broad "public use" ought to be defined—e.g., whether it includes fish propagation or fire control as well as stockwatering and human consumption.[11]

10. The inconsistency was dramatized in a 1988 statute approving a Forest Service–BLM exchange of management jurisdiction over nearly 700,000 acres of land in Nevada. BLM picked up 23,000 acres of former national forest land, and lost about 662,000 acres to the Forest Service. See Pub. L. 100–550, 102 Stat. 2749 (1988). On the new national forest land, Congress "expressly reserve[d] the minimum quantity of water necessary to achieve the primary purposes" for which national forests were established, with a priority date as of the date of transfer. On the new BLM land, Congress "expressly relinquishe[d] all Federal reserved water rights created by the initial withdrawal from the public domain * * *." Id. § 8.

11. See, e.g., United States v. City and County of Denver, 656 P.2d 1, 31–32 (Colo.

Military Reservations

Military bases and other reservations generally fall within the principles of *Winters*, but there is little reported litigation and commentary on their claims. See William Wilcox, Maintaining Federal Water Rights in the Western United States, Army Lawyer, Oct. 1996, at 3, 10; cf. United States v. Fallbrook Public Util. Dis., 347 F.2d 48, 53 (9th Cir. 1965) (suit involving water rights for Camp Pendleton Marine Base; parties later stipulated it addressed only claims under California law).

Congress Re-enters the Fray: Modern Reserved Water Rights Legislation

In United States v. New Mexico, supra p. 917, the Court said reserved rights claims deserved careful scrutiny because they were for the most part merely *implied* from congressional enactments: "Where Congress has expressly addressed the question of whether federal entities must abide by state water law, it has almost invariably deferred to the state law." 438 U.S. at 696.

Is this accurate? We have already seen numerous cases where Congress has expressly addressed water rights in various federal resource management statutes. Sometimes it has, to be sure, expressly deferred to state water law. But it also has crafted disclaimers, such as the one used in the Wilderness Act of 1964 and several other statutes: "Nothing in this [Act] shall constitute an express or implied claim or denial on the part of the Federal Government as to exemption from State water laws." 16 U.S.C. § 1133(d)(6); see also Wild and Scenic Rivers Act, 16 U.S.C. § 1284(b). What does this language mean? It asserts no *claim* of exemption, yet it also asserts *no denial of a claim* of exemption. Is it calculated, as Yogi Berra supposedly said, to "leave the status quo right where it is"—a status quo that includes the implied reservation of water doctrine? Cf. Potlatch Corp. v. United States, 12 P.3d 1260, 1266 (2000) (the language "neither establishes a federal reserved right nor precludes the recognition of such a right if water is otherwise reserved").

Since United States v. New Mexico was decided, an even more variegated picture has emerged. While sometimes Congress has continued to be silent,[12] sometimes it has specifically addressed water in making changes to the statutory management direction for particular public lands and resources. The result has not, however, been "almost invariabl[e]" deference to state water law. Consider a 1987 statute

1982); 90 Interior Dec. 81 (1983); In re Snake River Basin Adjudication, 131 Idaho 468, 959 P.2d 449 (1998); Angela Liston, Reevaluating the Applicability of the Reservation Doctrine to Public Water Reserve No. 107, 26 Ariz. L. Rev. 127 (1984); James Muhn, Public Water Reserves: The Metamorphosis of a Public Land Policy, 21 J. Land, Res., & Envtl. L. 67 (2001).

12. See, e.g., 114 Stat. 2563 (Las Cienegas National Conservation Area Act of 2000), 114 Stat. 2763 (Black Rock Desert–High Rock Canyon Emigrant Trails National Conservation Area Act of 2000); 114 Stat. 1362 (Santa Rosa and San Jacinto Mountains National Monument Act of 2000); 114 Stat. 1655 (Steens Mountain Cooperative Management and Protection Act of 2000).

establishing a national monument, national conservation area, and wilderness on federal lands in New Mexico:

> Congress expressly reserves to the United States the minimum amount of water required to carry out the purposes [of this Act]. * * * Nothing in this section shall be construed as establishing a precedent with regard to future designations, nor shall it affect the interpretation of any other Act or any designation made pursuant thereto.

101 Stat. 1539, 1549. How should a court go about determining how much water is reserved by this statute? Why do you suppose Congress included the second sentence? Was it to make sure that no negative inference is drawn from the express reservation of water here, when construing whether water is implicitly reserved in another statute that is silent on water?

Consider this 1988 statute designating wilderness areas in national park units in the State of Washington:

> Subject to valid existing rights, within the areas designated as wilderness by this Act, Congress hereby expressly reserves such water rights as necessary, for the purposes for which such areas are so designated. The priority date of such rights shall be the date of enactment of this Act.

102 Stat. 3961, 3968. How much water is reserved? Is groundwater as well as surface water reserved? Because this statute does not use the "minimum amount necessary" language found in the New Mexico statute of a year earlier (quoted in the preceding paragraph), does this statute reserve *more* than the minimum? Does the absence of "no precedent" language (such as was included in the New Mexico statute) allow a court to infer that silence in similar statutes does not imply a reservation of water?[13]

Sometimes Congress has expressly not reserved water, usually going to some lengths to explain why; e.g., in the law creating the Hagerman Fossil Beds National Monument in Idaho in 1988 (102 Stat. 4571, 4576, § 304):

> Congress finds that there are unique circumstances with respect to the water or water-related resources within the Monument designated by this title. The Congress recognizes that there is little or no water or water-related resources that require the protection of a federal reserve [sic] water right. Nothing in this title, nor any action taken pursuant thereto, shall constitute either an expressed or implied reservation of water or water right for any purpose.

See also 114 Stat. 1374, 1378 (§ 6(1) of the Colorado Canyons National Conservation Area and Black Ridge Canyons Wilderness Act of 2000); 116 Stat. 1994, 2003 (§ 203(d) of the Clark County Conservation of

13. Similar language appears in section 706 of the California Desert Protection Act of 1994, 108 Stat. 4471, 4498, although it did include "no precedent" language.

Public Land and Natural Resources Act of 2002); 118 Stat. 2403, 2409–10 (§ 204(d) of the Lincoln County Conservation, Recreation, and Development Act of 2004). Legislation enacted in 2004 expanding Petrified Forest National Park was silent on water. See 118 Stat. 2606. Sometimes Congress has taken a path different from expressly claiming or disclaiming a federal water right. See; e.g., 16 U.S.C. § 460ll–3(d), providing that nothing in 1980 legislation establishing the Rattlesnake National Recreation Area in Montana "shall be construed to permit the [federal land managing agency] to affect or diminish any water right which is vested under either State or Federal law" on the date of enactment. See also the confusing language Congress included in the 1997 National Wildlife Refuge Organic Act, supra p. 932.

Congress has not always in recent years been able to fashion agreement on specific language that addresses water (other than a disclaimer) in legislating on federal land management issues. Where agreement cannot be reached, enactment of legislation may be thwarted even if there is consensus on the rest of it. This was the case in Colorado, where for about a decade Congress could not resolve how to address water in designating new wilderness areas in the State, despite broad agreement over the other features. So long as litigation raged inconclusively over whether already designated wilderness areas in Colorado carried with them reserved water rights (see supra p. 933 n. 8), silence or a disclaimer was not an acceptable option to either wilderness advocates or water developers. The stalemate was finally broken with an agreement enacted into law in the Colorado Wilderness Act of 1993. The compromise expressly rejected the reservation of water in the newly designated areas, but provided an alternative mechanism to protect the water at stake—regulating land access by the federal land managers. See 107 Stat. 756. Controlling water by means of regulating access to federal lands is discussed later in this chapter at pp. 1004–1007.

Because Congress does express itself clearly sometimes on water rights, does that affect how silence in modern legislation ought to be viewed? Should the courts more easily construe silence as a denial of a federal reservation of water? See the exploration of the contemporary meaning of congressional silence in John D. Leshy, Water Rights for New Federal Land Conservation Programs: A Turn-of-the-Century Evaluation, 4 Denver Water L. Rev. 271, 279–82 (2001); and Michael C. Blumm, Reversing the *Winters* Doctrine?: Denying Reserved Water Rights for Idaho Wilderness and its Implications, 73 U. Colo. L. Rev. 173 (2002). A few members of Congress prefer a simpler, more radical solution; see H.R. 2603, 108th Cong. (Rep. Pearce of NM, joined by six other Western Republicans), which among other things would, "[n]otwithstanding any other provision of law," forbid the Secretary of the Interior from claiming "title or other rights to water in a State, other than for Indian reservation lands, absent specific direction of law."

The Executive Branch has also caught the fever of expressly addressing water in new land reservations. President Clinton's 1996 Proclamation creating the nearly two-million-acre Grand Staircase–Escalante

National Monument in southern Utah (the largest in the lower 48 states) says this about water:

> This proclamation does not reserve water as a matter of Federal law. I direct the Secretary to address in the management plan [for the new monument that the proclamation directed be prepared within three years] the extent to which water is necessary for the proper care and management of * * * this monument and the extent to which further action may be necessary pursuant to Federal or State law to assure the availability of water.

Proclamation No. 6920, 61 Fed. Reg. 50223 (1996). What result if the proclamation—which carefully describes the geologic, archeological, and biological "objects of historic or scientific interest" that qualified the area for safeguarding under the Antiquities Act—had been silent on water? Almost all of President Clinton's national monuments expressly addressed water issues, but not in a consistent way. See Leshy, supra, at 278–79.

Settling Non–Indian Federal Reserved Rights

Some non-Indian federal reserved rights claims have been settled by negotiation. An innovative resolution of the water rights claims of Zion National Park in southwestern Utah was executed in December 1996 after five years of negotiation. The Park is on the Virgin River downstream from some water development, and nearby St. George, Utah, is experiencing rapid population growth. The settlement recognizes a federal reserved water right to nearly all unappropriated flows into the Park. A small amount is kept available for future development upstream, but major upstream reservoirs, which had been contemplated, are prohibited. The settlement also includes a groundwater protection zone, restricting wells along the Park's boundaries, and a transfer of federal land to allow construction of a reservoir downstream from the Park. For more detail, see Western Water Policy Review Advisory Commission, Water in the West: Challenge for the Next Century 4–13 (1998). A brief discussion of successful resolution of national park claims in Colorado is found in Wendy Weiss, The Federal Government's Pursuit of Instream Flow Water Rights, 1 U. Den. Water L. Rev. 151, 160–62 (1998).

In Montana in the 1990s, water rights for five National Park Service units (including Yellowstone and Glacier), three National Wildlife Refuges, and a BLM wilderness and Wild and Scenic River unit were all settled by negotiation. A number of these settlements involve variations on the theme employed at Zion National Park: The United States agrees to subordinate its federal reserved rights to some appropriations initiated after the federal reservation, in return for which the state agrees to cap further appropriations and to manage groundwater outside the boundaries of the federal reservation to protect wetlands and other water-dependent resources inside the reservation. In essence, the United States gives up some priority in return for state cooperation, rather than leaving matters to litigation under the *Cappaert* decision. In August 2004, Idaho and the United States reached a settlement quantifying reserved rights claims for 444 miles of Wild & Scenic Rivers and 32 tributary streams and lakes in the Hells Canyon National Recreation Area, decreeing instream flows at various levels in specific time periods, but subordinating the federal water rights to existing water rights and uses and to certain specified future rights and uses. A link to the agreement can be found at http://www.idahorivers.org/news.htm.

As court decisions provide a better fix on the contours of federal reserved rights, federal agencies assemble the information necessary to quantify them, states discover what little threat many of these rights pose to state water right holders, and all continue to suffer from the expense and length of adjudications, the settlement fever may spread.

3. QUANTIFICATION OF FEDERAL RESERVED WATER RIGHTS: STANDARDS AND PROCEDURES

Many federal reserved rights have not yet been formally claimed or adjudicated. Often federally reserved water is being put to use (usually for instream, ecological uses), but there is no need or occasion to claim or adjudicate the right to it; for example, there may no competing claims for the flows, and/or no adjudication has been brought that requires filing the claims. Many federal reservations (such as national parks and national forests) are at the tops of watersheds, where federally reserved instream flows have only positive effects (by preserving the water flows) on downstream diversions. Many other federally reserved uses (for campgrounds in the national parks, for example) are for relatively small amounts of water that may not threaten existing or proposed uses under state law. The only reason the United States filed reserved rights claims in the *New Mexico* case, for example, was because the United States had to file a claim for the right in an ongoing stream adjudication or risk losing it. For more on this, see Nevada v. United States, 463 U.S. 110 (1983), discussed infra pp. 977–978.

In other situations, particularly in the Indian context, federally reserved water may not have yet been put to use. *Winters* rights in the Indian context tend to be larger and involve more consumptive uses than instream flow preservation. Many tribes are exercising some reserved rights, but few are using the full extent of the water they might be entitled to use. Most often, tribal non-use is a function of the tribes' inability to raise sufficient capital to build large water projects to take advantage of their legal entitlements—to convert, as water lawyers put it, "paper rights" into "wet water." For its part, the United States historically has, to put it delicately, lacked the enthusiasm for building Indian water projects (to enable Indians to exercise their *Winters* rights) that it has displayed for cowboy (non-Indian) water projects. See Monique Shay, Promises of a Viable Homeland, Reality of Selective Reclamation: A Study of the Relationship Between the Winters Doctrine and Federal Water Development in the Western United States, 19 Ecology L.Q. 546, 597 (1992).

Whether they are being exercised or not, federal reserved rights can constitute a cloud on water management and administration. Some state law appropriations involve storage or diversions on or above federal reservations, such as those on national forest lands in the Colorado Rockies that feed the growth of crops and people along the Front Range. See United States v. City & County of Denver, 656 P.2d 1, 23 (Colo. 1982). In these cases, federal reserved rights protecting instream flows might disrupt the operation of state law appropriation systems.

Even if unexercised, federal reserved rights that are consumptive in nature, such as tribal reserved rights for irrigation water, may cloud water management. Suppose, for example, that a river with a dependable annual flow of 250,000 acre-feet runs through a large Indian reservation established in 1860. The Tribe's reserved right to water has never been exercised and has not been quantified. There are no state law appropriations before 1860. How much water is available to post–1860 appropriators under state law? The answer is simple but not very helpful: All of it is presently available, but the only dependable supply (if and when the tribe begins to exercise its water right) is that part of the 250,000 acre feet that is not needed to fulfill the purposes of the reservation. How much water is that?

Uncertainty over the answer might be seen as a substantial deterrent to productive investment in water projects. Since *Winters* was decided, however, billions of dollars have been invested in western water projects to benefit non-Indians by federal, state and local governments and the private sector, in the face of unexercised federal reserved rights just like this hypothetical. These investments were made even though water rights for them obtained under state law were junior to the federal reservation, and thus theoretically subject to displacement without compensation if the federal reserved rights were ever exercised.[14] History leaves ample room to doubt, in other words, that the existence of unexercised, unadjudicated federal reserved rights have slowed water development in the West.[15]

14. In practice, as opposed to in theory and political rhetoric, very few if any state law junior appropriators have been displaced by subsequent assertion of senior federal reserved rights. This highly charged issue is discussed more fully below at pp. 990–996.

15. In recent years, however, the Montana Supreme Court has issued a series of decisions enjoining the state water rights agency from issuing state permits to non-Indians to appropriate water on an Indian reservation until the Tribe's reserved water rights have been quantified. See, e.g, Confederated Salish & Kootenai Tribes of the Flathead Reservation v. Stults, 59 P.3d 1093 (Mont. 2002); Matter of Beneficial Water Use Permits (Ciotti), 923 P.2d 1073 (1996). The court reasoned that the state

may not grant a right to something it does not own (if the water has previously been reserved for the Indians). The court has not discussed whether its holding would apply to permits to appropriate water outside of Indian reservations (e.g., upstream) that may be subject to Indian claims under *Winters*. The Court's decisions have set off a brouhaha that led to a tussle between the state legislature and the supreme court that, so far, the court seems to be winning, although one judge said the decisions threaten "a shutdown of the water permitting process in Montana," *Ciotti*, 923 P.2d at 1085 (Turnage, C.J., dissenting), and another has called the matter an "obvious calamity," *Stults*, 59 P.3d at 1102 (Rice, J. concurring and dissenting).

If the uncertainty surrounding federal reserved rights has usually not been a serious impediment to western water development, from the states' point of view the *Winters* doctrine represents a serious intrusion on their authority to manage water resources found within their borders. Nevertheless, for many years the states were unable to force the quantification of the reserved rights because of the federal government's sovereign immunity from suit without its consent. A handful of adjudications purported to settle at least some federal reserved rights in the first half of the twentieth century, but by and large these took place in federal court, with the United States either initiating the suits (as in *Winters* itself) or appearing voluntarily. See, e.g, United States v. Walker River Irrig. Dist., 104 F.2d 334 (9th Cir. 1939). Most of these stemmed from a desire by the United States to quantify Indian water rights as part of efforts to build irrigation projects under the reclamation program primarily to benefit non-Indians,[16] and most were settled by negotiation.[17]

In 1952 Senator Pat McCarran of Nevada succeeded in attaching a "rider" to a Department of Justice appropriations bill that became known as the McCarran *Amendment*.[18] Now codified at 43 U.S.C. § 666 (1970), it provides, in pertinent part:

> Consent is given to join the United States as a defendant in any suit (1) for the adjudication of rights to the use of water of a river system or other source, or (2) for the administration of such rights, where it appears that the United States is the owner of or is in the process of acquiring water rights by appropriation under State law, by purchase, by exchange, or otherwise, and the United States is a necessary party to such suit. * * *

How much of a victory did this seemingly straightforward text give the states? Does it allow the federal government to be joined in a state court proceeding to quantify federal reserved water rights, or just rights sought by the federal government under state law? Does it extend to water rights held on behalf of Tribes? What law must the state court

---

16. Such attempts to quantify Indian water rights were the exception, not the rule. The National Water Commission pointed out that

> [w]ith few exceptions [projects benefitting non-Indians] were planned and built by the Federal Government without any attempt to define, let alone protect, prior rights that Indian tribes might have had in the waters used for the projects. * * * In the history of the United States Government's treatment of Indian tribes, its failure to protect Indian water rights for use on the Reservations it set aside for them is one of the sorrier chapters.

Water Policies for the Future 474–75 (1973). See also Daniel McCool, Command of the Waters: Iron Triangles, Federal Wa-

ter Development, and Indian Water 36–43 (1987).

17. There were also some instances in which the executive branch of the federal government voluntarily appeared in state forums to seek to establish water rights for reclamation projects, which resulted in decrees that are of questionable validity today in adjudicating federal reserved rights. See infra p. 950, Note 8, on whether the McCarran Amendment is retroactive.

18. (Emphasis added), not to be confused with the anti-communist McCarran *Act* of the same era, sponsored by the same Senator. For an account of his colorful career, see Michael Ybarra, Washington Gone Crazy: Senator Pat McCarran and the Great American Communist Hunt (2004).

apply to determine the existence and scope of federal reserved water rights? Does the Amendment allow the state to join the United States in any proceeding that might relate to water rights held by the federal government—e.g., before the state engineer or administrative agency, or just in state court proceedings? May the adjudication scrutinize only federal rights, or does it have to be a general adjudication of all rights on the stream? What geographic area must be covered by such a suit—an entire watershed or only a part thereof? May the adjudication cover only surface water, or must it also cover hydrologically related groundwater?

The Supreme Court has been called upon to interpret the Amendment nearly a dozen times in the four decades since it became law. Its fertility for litigation is due to its imprecision, to the sensitive politics of state-federal relations in water rights, and because the United States, viewing the states as traditionally hostile to Indian and other federal water rights, waged a vigorous but mostly losing campaign to construe the waiver of sovereign immunity as narrowly as possible, in order to avoid litigating federal reserved rights in state fora.

In Dugan v. Rank, 372 U.S. 609 (1963), the first major case on the subject, the Court held that the McCarran Amendment waived federal sovereign immunity only in state court *general* adjudications of water rights. This early win for the federal government was followed by a string of defeats. In 1971, in companion cases arising in Colorado, the Court held that the Amendment's waiver of sovereign immunity covered federal reserved rights, and that the unique Colorado water court system of continuous adjudication met its terms. See United States v. District Court for Eagle County, 401 U.S. 520 (1971); United States v. District Court, 401 U.S. 527 (1971). In the next case the states won their most sweeping McCarran Amendment victory.

COLORADO RIVER WATER CONSERVATION DISTRICT v. UNITED STATES

Supreme Court of the United States, 1976.
424 U.S. 800.

Mr. Justice Brennan delivered the opinion of the Court.

* * * The questions presented by this case concern the effect of the McCarran Amendment upon the jurisdiction of the federal district courts under 28 U.S.C. § 1345 over suits for determination of water rights brought by the United States as trustee for certain Indian tribes and as owner of various non-Indian Government claims. * * *

The reserved rights of the United States extend to Indian reservations, Winters v. United States, * * * and other federal lands, such as national parks and forests, Arizona v. California * * *. The reserved rights claimed by the United States in this case affect waters within Colorado Water Division No. 7. On November 14, 1972, the Government instituted this suit in the United States District Court for the District of Colorado, invoking the court's jurisdiction under 28 U.S.C. § 1345. The

District Court is located in Denver, some 300 miles from Division 7. The suit, against some 1,000 water users, sought declaration of the Government's rights to waters in certain rivers and their tributaries located in Division 7. In the suit, the Government asserted reserved rights on its own behalf and on behalf of certain Indian tribes, as well as rights based on state law. It sought appointment of a water master to administer any waters decreed to the United States. * * *

Shortly after the federal suit was commenced, one of the defendants in that suit filed an application in the state court for Division 7, seeking an order directing service of process on the United States in order to make it a party to proceedings in Division 7 for the purpose of adjudicating all of the Government's claims, both state and federal. On January 3, 1973, the United States was served pursuant to authority of the McCarran Amendment. * * *

We first consider the question of district-court jurisdiction under 28 U.S.C. section 1345. That section provides that the district courts shall have original jurisdiction over all civil actions brought by the Federal Government "(e)xcept as otherwise provided by Act of Congress." It is thus necessary to examine whether the McCarran Amendment is such an Act of Congress excepting jurisdiction under section 1345. * * *

In view of the McCarran Amendment's language and legislative history, controlling principles of statutory construction require the conclusion that the Amendment did not constitute an exception "provided by Act of Congress" that repealed the jurisdiction of district courts under section 1345 to entertain federal water suits. * * *

We turn next to the question whether this suit nevertheless was properly dismissed in view of the concurrent state proceedings in Division 7.

First, we consider whether the McCarran Amendment provided consent to determine federal reserved rights held on behalf of Indians in state court. This is a question not previously squarely addressed by this Court, and given the claims for Indian water rights in this case, dismissal clearly would have been inappropriate if the state court had no jurisdiction to decide those claims. We conclude that the state court had jurisdiction over Indian water rights under the Amendment.

* * * [Prior cases of the Court have held that non-Indian federal reserved rights] were included in those rights where the United States was "otherwise" the owner [in the language of the McCarran Amendment]. * * * [T]he logic of those cases clearly extends to [Indian] rights.

* * * Not only the Amendment's language, but also its underlying policy, dictates a construction including Indian rights in its provisions.

* * * [B]earing in mind the ubiquitous nature of Indian water rights in the Southwest, it is clear that a construction of the Amendment excluding those rights from its coverage would enervate the Amendment's objective.

* * * The Government argues that because of its fiduciary responsibility to protect Indian rights, any state-court jurisdiction over Indian property should not be recognized unless expressly conferred by Congress. * * * The Government has not abdicated any responsibility fully to defend Indian rights in state court, and Indian interests may be satisfactorily protected under regimes of state law. The Amendment in no way abridges any substantive claim on behalf of Indians under the doctrine of reserved rights. * * *

Next, we consider whether the District Court's dismissal was appropriate under the doctrine of abstention. We hold that the dismissal cannot be supported under that doctrine in any of its forms. * * *

Although this case falls within none of the abstention categories, there are principles unrelated to considerations of proper constitutional adjudication and regard for federal-state relations which govern in situations involving the contemporaneous exercise of concurrent jurisdictions, either by federal courts or by state and federal courts. These principles rest on considerations of "(w)ise judicial administration, giving regard to conservation of judicial resources and comprehensive disposition of litigation." * * * Generally, as between state and federal courts, the rule is that "the pendency of an action in the state court is no bar to proceedings concerning the same matter in the Federal court having jurisdiction * * *." As between federal district courts, however, though no precise rule has evolved, the general principle is to avoid duplicative litigation. * * * This difference in general approach between state-federal concurrent jurisdiction and wholly federal concurrent jurisdiction stems from the virtually unflagging obligation of the federal courts to exercise the jurisdiction given them. * * * Given this obligation, and the absence of weightier considerations of constitutional adjudication and state-federal relations, the circumstances permitting the dismissal of a federal suit due to the presence of a concurrent state proceeding for reasons of wise judicial administration are considerably more limited than the circumstances appropriate for abstention. The former circumstances, though exceptional, do nevertheless exist. * * *

Turning to the present case, a number of factors clearly counsel against concurrent federal proceedings. The most important of these is the McCarran Amendment itself. The clear federal policy evinced by that legislation is the avoidance of piecemeal adjudication of water rights in a river system. This policy is akin to that underlying the rule requiring that jurisdiction be yielded to the court first acquiring control of property, for the concern in such instances is with avoiding the generation of additional litigation through permitting inconsistent dispositions of property. This concern is heightened with respect to water rights, the relationships among which are highly interdependent. Indeed, we have recognized that actions seeking the allocation of water essentially involve the disposition of property and are best conducted in unified proceedings. The consent to jurisdiction given by the McCarran Amendment bespeaks a policy that recognizes the availability of comprehensive state systems for adjudication of water rights as the means for achieving these goals. * * *

Beyond the congressional policy expressed by the McCarran Amendment and consistent with furtherance of that policy, we also find significant (a) the apparent absence of any proceedings in the District Court, other than the filing of the complaint, prior to the motion to dismiss, (b) the extensive involvement of state water rights occasioned by this suit naming 1,000 defendants, (c) the 300–mile distance between the District Court in Denver and the court in Division 7, and (d) the existing participation by the Government in Division 4, 5, and 6 proceedings. We emphasize, however, that we do not overlook the heavy obligation to exercise jurisdiction. We need not decide, for example, whether, despite the McCarran Amendment, dismissal would be warranted if more extensive proceedings had occurred in the District Court prior to dismissal, if the involvement of state water rights were less extensive than it is here, or if the state proceeding were in some respect inadequate to resolve the federal claims. But the opposing factors here, particularly the policy underlying the McCarran Amendment, justify the District Court's dismissal in this particular case.

The judgment of the Court of Appeals is reversed and the judgment of the District Court dismissing the complaint is affirmed for the reasons here stated.

MR. JUSTICE STEWART, with whom MR. JUSTICE BLACKMUN and MR. JUSTICE STEVENS concur, dissenting.

The Court says that the United States District Court for the District of Colorado clearly had jurisdiction over this lawsuit. I agree. The Court further says that the McCarran Amendment "in no way diminished" the District Court's jurisdiction. I agree. The Court also says that federal courts have a "virtually unflagging obligation * * * to exercise the jurisdiction given them." I agree. And finally, the Court says that nothing in the abstention doctrine "in any of its forms" justified the District Court's dismissal of the Government's complaint. I agree. These views would seem to lead ineluctably to the conclusion that the District Court was wrong in dismissing the complaint. Yet the Court holds that the order of dismissal was "appropriate." With that conclusion I must respectfully disagree. * * *

The Court's principal reason for deciding to close the doors of the federal courthouse to the United States in this case seems to stem from the view that its decision will avoid piecemeal adjudication of water rights. To the extent that this view is based on the special considerations governing *in rem* proceedings, it is without precedential basis * * *. To the extent that the Court's view is based on the realistic practicalities of this case, it is simply wrong, because the relegation of the Government to the state courts will not avoid piecemeal litigation.

The Colorado courts are currently engaged in two types of proceedings under the State's water-rights law. First, they are processing new claims to water based on recent appropriations. Second, they are integrating these new awards of water rights with all past decisions awarding such rights into one all-inclusive tabulation for each water source. The claims of the United States that are involved in this case have not been adjudicated in the past. Yet they do not involve recent appropriations of water. In fact, these claims are wholly dissimilar to normal state water claims, because they are not based on actual beneficial use of water but rather on an intention formed at the time the federal land use was established to reserve a certain amount of water to support the federal reservations. The state court will, therefore, have to conduct separate proceedings to determine these claims. And only after the state court adjudicates the claims will they be incorporated into the water source tabulations. If this suit were allowed to proceed in federal court the same procedures would be followed, and the federal court decree would be incorporated into the state tabulation, as other federal court decrees have been incorporated in the past. Thus, the same process will occur regardless of which forum considers these claims. * * *

As the Court says, it is the virtual "unflagging obligation" of a federal court to exercise the jurisdiction that has been conferred upon it. Obedience to that obligation is particularly "appropriate" in this case, for at least two reasons.

First, the issues involved are issues of federal law. A federal court is more likely than a state court to be familiar with federal water law and to have had experience in interpreting the relevant federal statutes, regulations, and Indian treaties. Moreover, if tried in a federal court, these issues of federal law will be reviewable in a federal appellate court, whereas federal judicial review of the state courts' resolution of issues of federal law will be possible only on review by this Court in the exercise of its certiorari jurisdiction.

Second, some of the federal claims in this lawsuit relate to water reserved for Indian reservations. It is not necessary to determine that there is no state-court jurisdiction of these claims to support the proposition that a federal court is a more appropriate forum than a state court for determination of questions of life-and-death importance to Indians. This Court has long recognized that "(t)he policy of leaving Indians free from state jurisdiction and control is deeply rooted in the Nation's history." McClanahan v. Arizona State Tax Comm'n, 411 U.S. 164, 168, quoting Rice v. Olson, 324 U.S. 786, 789.

The Court says that "(o)nly the clearest of justifications will warrant dismissal" of a lawsuit within the jurisdiction of a federal court. In my opinion there was no justification at all for the District Court's order of dismissal in this case. * * *

Notes and Questions

1. In a subsequent McCarran Amendment case, the Court repeated a maxim of interpretation the Court has long followed in dozens of past non-water cases—that waivers of sovereign immunity "must be strictly construed in favor of the United States." United States v. Idaho, 508 U.S. 1, 6 (1993).

Did the Court follow that precept here? Is there something special about adjudications of water rights that requires a different, more flexible approach to federal immunity? If so, what? Recall that in *Winters* the Court relied on a principle that ambiguities in the interpretation of agreements and treaties with Indians should be resolved from the standpoint of the Indians. Should that maxim apply to the McCarran Amendment? Is it relevant to the issue here that, when Congress acted to authorize some states to exercise some form of civil jurisdiction over Indians on reservations, it excluded jurisdiction over Indian water rights? See 25 U.S.C. § 1322(b); 28 U.S.C. § 1360(b).

2. Indian Tribes have their own immunity from suit under well-established principles of Indian law. William Canby, American Indian Law in a Nutshell 95–104 (4th ed. 2004). The McCarran Amendment waives federal, not tribal immunity. Tribes therefore have a choice either to participate in state court adjudications to defend their water rights (thereby submitting themselves to the general jurisdiction of the state courts) or to stay out and, being bound by the result, rely upon the United States to vigorously assert and prosecute their water rights claims.

3. A Tribe may bring its own action in federal court to quantify its water rights. If the state thereafter files its own general stream adjudication and joins the U.S. as a defendant, does the *Colorado River Water Conservation District* decision require the federal court to stay the Tribe's suit?

4. In Arizona v. San Carlos Apache Tribe of Arizona, 463 U.S. 545 (1983), the states won another big victory. The constitutions of many western states, including Arizona, include a disclaimer of jurisdiction over lawsuits involving Indian lands, reserving such cases to the "absolute jurisdiction and control" of Congress. The Court in *San Carlos Apache* held that if those states now open their courts to general adjudication suits involving Indian water rights, the rule of federal deference to state proceedings announced in *Colorado River* applies with equal force. The thrust of Justice Brennan's majority opinion was that the problem addressed by the McCarran Amendment did not vary from state to state in the West, and that there was no indication in the Amendment's legislative history that it was intended to be of selective application.

5. A surprising aspect of the Supreme Court's McCarran Amendment jurisprudence is how some of the Court's liberals, especially Justice Brennan, have been so willing to interpret it in favor of state jurisdiction, especially over Indian water rights. In the *San Carlos Apache* case, Justice Brennan wrote:

> We also emphasize, as we did in *Colorado River*, that our decision in no way changes the substantive law by which Indian rights in state water adjudications must be judged. State courts, as much as federal courts, have a solemn obligation to follow federal law. Moreover, any state court decision alleged to abridge Indian water rights protected by federal law can expect to receive, if brought for review before this Court, a particularized and exacting scrutiny commensurate with the powerful federal interest in safeguarding those rights from state encroachment.

463 U.S. at 571.[1] Is it more likely that state (as opposed to federal) judges will misapply federal law, be more biased against Indian claims, or be more politically vulnerable to interests (e.g., non-Indian farmers) who may be most threatened by Indian water rights?[2] State court judges, like federal ones, take an oath to uphold the U.S. Constitution and laws. Does the fight come down to the power of the trial judge over findings of fact, which ordinarily receive much deference on appellate review? See Fed. R. Civ. P. 52(a). What sorts of factual findings control the quantity of water awarded to Indians (or non-Indian federal agencies) claiming federal reserved rights?

6.   How big is a "river system or other source" embraced within the McCarran Amendment? In United States v. District Court for Eagle County, 401 U.S. 520 (1971), the Court firmly rejected the United States' argument that Colorado could not join it in a proceeding to adjudicate only a tributary of the Colorado River. See also Elephant Butte Irr. Dist. v. United States, 849 P.2d 372 (N.M. Ct. App. 1993) (upholding joinder of U.S. in a suit to adjudicate only a portion of the Rio Grande River within New Mexico). On the other hand, the Idaho Supreme Court ruled that a McCarran Amendment adjudication in that state had to include the Snake River and all of its tributaries within Idaho. See In re General Adjudication of Snake River Basin Water System, 764 P.2d 78 (Idaho 1988), cert. denied sub nom., Boise–Kuna Irr. Dist. v. United States, 490 U.S. 1005 (1989). See Thomas H. Pacheco, How Big is Big? The Scope of Water Rights Suits Under the McCarran Amendment, 15 Ecology L.Q. 627 (1988).

7.   The Ninth Circuit rejected a vigorous challenge by the United States that the Oregon general stream adjudication system was neither comprehensive nor judicial enough to meet McCarran's terms. Under that system, the Oregon state water rights agency actually conducts the litigation under minimal judicial supervision, and adjudicates primarily federal water rights, because under the Oregon stream adjudication statute, all other water users merely had to register their water rights, which the court would accept at face value, unless successfully challenged by the United States. Finally, hydrologically related groundwater was not included in the adjudication. The court brushed aside the federal objections, essentially reading the McCarran Amendment as creating a strong presumption in favor of state court adjudications. It also said that, because the features of the Oregon system to which the U.S. objected were all in place when Congress adopted the Amendment in 1952, Congress must have contemplated that the Oregon system met its terms. See United States v. Oregon, 44 F.3d 758 (9th Cir. 1994). Mindful of its dismal track record in the Supreme Court, the United States did not

---

1.   Note that federal court review of alleged errors made in state court adjudications of federal water rights is confined to the discretionary certiorari jurisdiction of the United States Supreme Court under 28 U.S.C. § 1257(3), following exhaustion of all available state appeals.

2.   Brennan's caution did not dissuade the Arizona Republic from editorially crowing that because federal court decisions "generally have been more favorable" to Indians than state courts, the Court's "historic" ruling in San Carlos Apache "indi-

rectly diminishes" the Arizona Tribes' water right claims, and makes "[g]reat amounts of water * * * available to states to accommodate the needs of growth." Ariz. Republic, July 7, 1983, at A6. The Arizona Director of Water Resources responded with a letter complaining that the editorial "only increases the perception by the Indian tribes that they will be treated unfairly in a state court proceeding," and misleads by suggesting that the Court's ruling "create[s] new water." Id., July 20, 1983, at A6.

petition for certiorari. See also In re Rights to Use Water in Gila River, 857 P.2d 1236, 1247–48 (Ariz. 1993) (rejecting a similar U.S. argument that failure to include all hydrologically related groundwater disqualifies an adjudication from the McCarran Amendment waiver). On the other hand, the First Circuit, in approving an injunction against an administrative proceeding brought by the Commonwealth of Puerto Rico contesting the U.S. Navy's right to use water, strictly applied the statutory term "suit," distinguishing the Ninth Circuit's decision. United States v. Puerto Rico, 287 F.3d 212, 218 (1st Cir. 2002). See also *United States v. Morros*, discussed infra p. 1002.

8. In State Engineer v. South Fork of Te–Moak Tribe, 339 F.3d 804 (9th Cir. 2003), a state court adjudication in the 1930s had decreed various water rights in a basin. Some of these rights were appurtenant to ranches later purchased by the federal government to create a reservation for the Te–Moak Tribe of Western Shoshone Indians. The United States owned the ranches and the water rights in trust for the Indians. The state court retained jurisdiction to administer the decree. The Tribe eventually refused to cooperate with state officers administering the decree, and the state began contempt proceedings against it. The United States, joined as a necessary party, removed the action to federal court. The Ninth Circuit held that (a) the McCarran Amendment waived the United States's immunity from suit for administration of water rights, even water rights that vested in the United States before the Amendment was adopted; (b) the Amendment did not repeal the doctrine of prior exclusive jurisdiction that otherwise operated to protect the Nevada state court decree; and (c) therefore the federal court lacked jurisdiction to hear the case after removal. Because in this case the United States acquired water rights already decreed under state law, the court's ruling does not answer all questions about the retroactivity of the McCarran Amendment. Suppose, for example, before the Amendment was enacted, a state court (or even a state administrative agency) purported to adjudicate a federal water right, with the U.S. executive branch officers participating. Is that decree binding on the United States? For an argument that, prior to the McCarran Amendment, state courts lacked subject matter jurisdiction over Indian water rights, see Michael Lieder, Adjudication of Indian Water Rights Under the McCarran Amendment: Two Courts are Better than One, 71 Geo. L. Rev. 1023, 1028–30 (1983).

9. Federal courts retain federal question jurisdiction (concurrent with possible state court jurisdiction under the McCarran Amendment) to decide water allocation disputes involving federal and Indian water rights. See, e.g., South Delta Water Agency v. United States, 767 F.2d 531 (9th Cir. 1985); Kittitas Reclamation Dist. v. Sunnyside Valley Irr. Dist., 763 F.2d 1032 (9th Cir. 1985). United States v. Alpine Land & Reservoir Co., 174 F.3d 1007 (9th Cir. 1999) is a reverse illustration of the doctrine of prior exclusive jurisdiction discussed in Note 8, supra. There, a decree entered into by a federal district court gave that court appellate jurisdiction over decisions of the State Engineer that involved federal water rights confirmed in the decree. The court of appeals held that the trial court had properly enjoined—at the request of the Nevada State Engineer!—a state court proceeding initiated by a county seeking to overturn the State Engineer's decision on a water rights transfer involving the U.S. Fish and Wildlife Service. But see United States

v. City of Las Cruces, 289 F.3d 1170 (10th Cir. 2002) (upholding the federal district court's refusal to exercise jurisdiction over a federal quiet title action covering a portion of the Rio Grande River, in light of an ongoing state stream adjudication).

10. In a rare victory for the United States, the Court held in United States v. Idaho, 508 U.S. 1 (1993) that the McCarran Amendment did not waive the federal government's immunity from paying filing fees in a general stream adjudication (which the government estimated would amount to $10 million in the Snake River Basin Adjudication where the case arose). Justice Rehnquist's opinion noted that the Court is "particularly alert to require a specific waiver of sovereign immunity" before the United States may be held liable for "monetary exactions" in litigation. For a general review of jurisdiction to adjudicate Indian water rights, see Cohen's Handbook of Federal Indian Law (Nell Newton et al. eds., 2005) § 19.05[1].

When Does the Executive Branch Have a Duty to File Reserved Rights Claims in Adjudications?

If Congress intended to create reserved rights and the Executive fails to assert them in a general stream adjudication, is a judicial remedy available? The federal Administrative Procedure Act has been interpreted to create a strong presumption of reviewability of agency action, but one of its exceptions involves matters in which "agency action is committed to agency discretion by law." See 5 U.S.C. § 702(a)(2). The Supreme Court has said that if the statute under which the agency is acting "is drawn so that a court would have no meaningful standard against which to judge the agency's exercise of discretion," the matter is committed to the agency's discretion and not subject to judicial review. Heckler v. Chaney, 470 U.S. 821 (1985); see also Norton v. Southern Utah Wilderness Alliance, 542 U.S. 55 (2004), which interpreted the Administrative Procedure Act's directive that a court shall "compel agency action unlawfully withheld or unreasonably delayed," 5 U.S.C. § 706(l), as empowering a court to order agency action only when the agency fails to take "a *discrete* * * * action that it is *required to take*." 542 U.S. at 64 (emphasis in original).

Like most statutes, treaties or executive orders under which *Winters* claims might be made, the Wilderness Act says nothing about asserting federal reserved water rights. In defending its failure to file water rights claims for wilderness areas against a Sierra Club lawsuit, the federal government argued, among other things, that its action was unreviewable under Heckler v. Chaney. Although the Tenth Circuit ultimately dismissed the Sierra Club's case as not ripe, Sierra Club v. Yeutter, 911 F.2d 1405 (10th Cir. 1990), it seemed to suggest that judicial review was available under certain circumstances because the Wilderness Act

> does provide guidelines the agency must follow: the agency cannot abandon, by action or inaction, the statutory mandate to preserve the wilderness characteristics of the wilderness areas. To the extent the Forest Service's inaction implicates this command of the Wilderness Act, the *Chaney* presumption of

unreviewability is rebutted and we may review the agency's action.

911 F.2d at 1414 n.5. The court concluded that judicial intervention was not warranted on the facts before it because the Sierra Club had not drawn a sufficient connection between the failure to file a claim for a federal reserved right for wilderness areas and harm to "wilderness water values." The court elaborated by noting, first, that "federal reserved water rights, as creatures of federal law, are protected from extinguishment under state law by the Supremacy Clause." Second, even if federal reserved water rights lost their early priority date because they were not timely filed under the rules of the Colorado adjudication, there may be no appropriations under state law that would or even could create adverse impacts on wilderness water values that a federal reserved right for wilderness would prevent. It also acknowledged the Forest Service's argument that "there are either adequate administrative controls in place that will prevent diversions above or within wilderness area or that geographical features render such diversions or projects impractical in areas within or above the wilderness areas." These multiple "contingencies * * * underscore[ ] the speculative and hypothetical nature of this issue." The court left open the possibility of revisiting the matter in the future:

> When and if a water development claim that may threaten wilderness water values is filed, and the Forest Service does not assert a federal reserved water right based on the Wilderness Act, and furthermore such failure to assert the reserved water right is irreconcilable with the Forest Service's duty to protect wilderness characteristics, then the Sierra Club may either intervene in the state water proceeding as appropriate under state law or may seek judicial review of the Forest Service's failure to act in federal court. At that time the record will be more fully developed and the courts can better determine whether the Forest Service's proposed alternatives to the use of wilderness water rights are adequate to reconcile its actions with its obligations under the Act. If the proposed alternatives are not adequate, appropriate corrective orders can be issued.
> * * *

911 F.2d at 1418–19.

Suppose the federal government does not file a claim for a reserved right for a particular wilderness area, and a new appropriation is approved under state law that allows a major diversion upstream which could dewater the wilderness, and the federal government has no regulatory control over the diversion. If the Sierra Club renews its suit against the federal agency, what "appropriate corrective orders" can the court issue? Does the Tenth Circuit require too much vigilance on the part of friends of federal reserved water rights outside the federal agencies?

For another case inconclusively addressing whether federal agencies have a duty to pursue reserved rights claims in litigation, see Sierra Club

v. Andrus, 487 F.Supp. 443, 448–49 (D.D.C. 1980), aff'd sub nom., Sierra Club v. Watt, 659 F.2d 203 (D.C. Cir. 1981). For an illustration of the courts' reluctance to interfere with the judgment of the United States as trustee for Indians in litigation over *Winters* rights, see Shoshone–Bannock Tribes v. Reno, 56 F.3d 1476 (D.C. Cir. 1995).

Congress has sometimes directly addressed the problem of federal agency reluctance to make reserved water rights claims. A 1990 statute designating wilderness areas in Arizona not only expressly reserved water, but directed the Secretary of the Interior "and all other officers of the United States" to "take steps necessary to protect" the federally reserved water rights, including "filing * * * a claim for the quantification of such rights in any present or future appropriate stream adjudication * * *." 104 Stat. 4469, 4473, § 101(g)(2); see also California Desert Protection Act of 1994, 108 Stat. at 4498; San Pedro Riparian National Conservation Area Act of 1988, 102 Stat. 4571, § 102(d). Where these statutes exist, can a federal court order an agency to file a claim?

The Black Canyon of the Gunnison River in Colorado was made a national monument in 1933 by lame-duck President Herbert Hoover.[3] In 1978, the Colorado Water Court decreed the United States a federal reserved water right for the monument, priority date 1933, to carry out the monument purposes (which emphasized preservation of scenic and conservation values), but the court postponed quantifying the right. Shortly before the Clinton Administration left office in January 2001, it filed an application for a 300 cfs base flow and higher peak and shoulder seasonal flows geared to natural runoff. A number of protests were filed. Ultimately the Bush Administration agreed with the state to a decree that gave the national monument a year-round base flow of the lesser of 300 cfs or natural flow, with a priority date of 2003, which could only be enforced by a state agency, the Colorado Water Conservation Board. Conservation interests promptly brought an action in federal court challenging the deal, and they moved for a stay of proceedings in state water court until the federal case is resolved. The water court granted the stay, and the Colorado Supreme Court affirmed. In re Application for Water Rights, 101 P.3d 1072 (Colo. 2004). The court held that the McCarran Amendment does not allow state courts to review federal agencies' decisionmaking as to what kinds of claims to make, and because the federal court is the exclusive forum to hear those claims, the water court acted within its discretion in staying the proceedings. The court noted, among other things, that if the water court were to proceed to quantify the Black Canyon right on the less protective basis the U.S. was now asking for, "res judicata would bar the United States from later claiming a broader reserved right even if the federal court were to decide that the United States violated federal law when it amended its application" to reduce its claim. Justice Hobbs, joined by Justice Kourlis, dissented, reasoning that the federal court would, in ruling on plaintiffs' claims, have to decide what federal law required in the way of water to

---

3. It was made a national park in 1999. 16 U.S.C. § 410fff.

carry out the purposes of the Black Canyon reservation. Because the federal court proceeding "transparently involve[d] quantification" of the national monument water right, the dissent argued it was a matter appropriate for state court jurisdiction under the McCarran Amendment, which "prefers deferral of the federal court to the state court, not the other way around."

Federal Participation in State Administrative Proceedings

Recall that in *Cappaert*, supra p. 912, the National Park Service had appeared before the State Engineer to protest Cappaert's application to change the use of water from its wells. The State Engineer rejected the protest. In the subsequent litigation brought by the U.S. against Cappaert in federal court, the State (an intervenor) sought dismissal on res judicata or collateral estoppel grounds, because the United States had failed to appeal the State Engineer's rejection through the state court system. The Court would have none of it:

> [T]he United States was not made a party to the state administrative proceeding; * * * it did not assert any federal water-rights claims, nor did it seek to adjudicate any claims until the hydrologic studies * * * had been completed. * * * The State Water Engineer's decree explicitly stated it was "subject to existing rights."

426 U.S. at 146–47. In Confederated Salish and Kootenai Tribes of the Flathead Reservation v. Stults, 59 P.3d 1093, 1099–1100 (2002), the Montana Supreme Court noted that the McCarran Amendment waiver of federal sovereign immunity "is limited to comprehensive adjudications," and thus Tribes were not required to participate in a proceeding before a state water administrator to determine whether to issue a water right under state law that the Tribes believed conflicted with their federal reserved water right. See the discussion of this case in footnote 15, supra p. 941.

Can a federal executive branch official waive the sovereign immunity of the United States in proceedings that do not conform to the McCarran Amendment simply by making a general appearance before a State Engineer? Or would that violate the doctrine that the government ordinarily cannot be estopped by the acts of its agents?[4] Could the Nevada State Engineer have demanded that the National Park Service become a formal "party" to the proceeding in order to protest the Cappaert application? Could it have required the Park Service to put on proof of its water rights as a precondition to protest? Could the State Engineer, in the course of deciding whether the Cappaert application would adversely affect the federal water right, determine the scope and quantity of the federal water right? If so, is the federal government bound by that determination unless it appeals it up through the state court system?

---

4. See, e.g., Office of Personnel Management v. Richmond, 496 U.S. 414 (1990).

If a federal appearance before a state agency might bind the United States, federal agencies will be reluctant to participate in such proceedings. If they stay away, state water administrators may not become aware of possible conflicts with federal water rights claims, conflicts which, had they been made aware of them, might have been avoided. Does this suggest that states should allow the federal agencies to make a special appearance without waiving federal immunity, so that the state can learn of the scope of the federal claims and possibly avoid conflicts?

The Conduct of State Court Litigation Involving Federal Reserved Rights

The interface between federal and state law in the conduct of general stream adjudications under the McCarran Amendment gives rise to a number of questions. For example, who has the burden of proof where federal water rights are contested in a state court adjudication? Is that a matter for state or federal law? See In re General Adjudication of the Big Horn River System, 753 P.2d 76, 90 (Wyo. 1988) (applying state law and holding that the burden is on the United States and the Tribes as the claimants); cf. United States v. Washington, 375 F. Supp. 2d 1050, 1076 (W.D.Wash. 2005) (same ultimate result, but determined as a matter of federal law). Another example stems from the well-known maxim of interpretation in federal Indian law that ambiguities in treaties, statutes, and other legal documents pertaining to Indian affairs ought to be resolved in favor of Indians. See, e.g., Bryan v. Itasca County, 426 U.S. 373 (1976). Is a state court bound to follow that canon of construction in adjudicating Indian water rights claims? Is this part of their "solemn obligation to follow federal law" that Justice Brennan referred to in the *San Carlos* case?

To what extent can state courts extinguish federal claims for reserved rights for failure to meet filing deadlines and other procedural requirements of state law? Cf. United States v. Idaho, 508 U.S. 1, 7 (1993) (McCarran Amendment makes the federal government subject to "established state-law rules governing pleading, discovery, and the admissibility of evidence at trial"); see also United States v. Bell, 724 P.2d 631 (Colo. 1986), where the Colorado Supreme Court upheld a water court decision denying the United States the right to relate an amended water rights claim back to the date the original claim was filed, thereby costing the claim several decades of priority.

Is there anything anomalous about a federal failure to follow state procedures defeating federal substantive rights, or is that simply the logical and proper consequence of the McCarran Amendment—the presumed purpose of which was to force the United States to litigate and quantify its claims in state courts just like those of anyone else? On the other hand, what if the Colorado courts would not have enforced the procedural rule involved in *Bell* with equal vigor against a state law appropriator? (How might the United States go about proving that?) Are these issues—when can a state rule defeat a federal right—simply a mirror image of the problems created in diversity jurisdiction cases in federal court, where federal courts apply state substantive law, but follow federal procedures? See Erie R.R. v. Tompkins, 304 U.S. 64 (1938) and its progeny.

The Future of General Stream Adjudications Involving Federal Water Rights

The courts continue to make clear that, though some federal water rights disputes may be handled in federal courts, western states may adjudicate federal water rights in their own courts if they choose to do so. But funny things have happened on the way to state court quantification, bringing to mind the old story of the dog that madly chased after cars until one day it caught one. As noted in Chapter 3 at pp. 314–320, these adjudications can be lengthy and very expensive for states. State efforts to lay some of the cost on the federal treasury were dealt a blow when the Supreme Court ruled that its waiver of sovereign immunity is not broad enough to subject the United States to paying filing fees for its claims. United States v. Idaho, 508 U.S. 1 (1993).

Even more important, and surprising some observers, state law appropriators have not always triumphed over federal reserved rights claims in state court adjudications, because state judges seem to have, for the most part, made a conscientious effort to apply the principles of federal law that govern the *Winters* doctrine.[5] Thus recognition of important federal reserved rights is a possible, perhaps likely, outcome of state court adjudications. Does this suggest the states may be better off living with the uncertainty of unquantified Indian and other federal claims, rather than making strenuous efforts to adjudicate and settle them? Have the states believed too much their own rhetoric about the "need" to adjudicate these rights?

The Administration of Adjudicated Federal Reserved Water Rights in State Systems

Subsection (2) of the McCarran Amendment specifically waives the sovereign immunity of the United States for the "administration" of water rights. In South Delta Water Agency v. United States, 767 F.2d 531, 541 (9th Cir. 1985), the court held that this waiver applies only after rights have first been adjudicated under subsection (1). The decree that results from the adjudication folds these federal-law-based rights in with rights based on state law. Once the decree is entered, the state court has exclusive jurisdiction to enforce its decrees, and the federal courts have no subject-matter jurisdiction. State Engineer v. S. Fork Band of Te–Moak Tribe, 339 F.3d 804, 809–14 (9th Cir. 2003), discussed supra p. 950. A federal reserved right holder is entitled to all of the protections given a state law appropriator. Most fundamentally, the

5. They have been asked to do otherwise. The Colorado Supreme Court in the early 1980s rejected an argument by the City of Denver that captured the theological overtones of these state-federal disputes over water: Denver argued that the Colorado Supreme Court was "not bound to abide by the relevant [*Winters* rights] decisions of the United States Supreme Court because, in Denver's view, they were 'heresy'." United States v. City and County of Denver, 656 P.2d 1, 16 n.25 (1982).

reserved rights holder would be able to call the river in order to assert the rights against juniors, if necessary to vindicate the right. The call would be enforced by state officials acting pursuant to state authority.

Federal reserved rights are not, however, stripped of their federal character as a result of quantification and becoming part of the state priority system. Because federal reserved rights are not lost by non-use, for example, state forfeiture laws may not apply to them under the Supremacy Clause. See *United States v. City & County of Denver*, 656 P.2d 1 (Colo. 1982).[6] Between the two poles of enforcement and forfeiture—where reserved rights are most like and unlike state-created rights—lies a broad range of state water rights administration issues where the precise treatment accorded to federal reserved rights remains uncertain. Consider, for example, the role of state courts when the U.S. proposes to change the use of a decreed federal reserved water right. Suppose a Tribe has a decreed right of 1000 acre-feet for agricultural irrigation, and now wants to use that water for a casino complex. Does it (or the United States as holder of legal title to the right) have to follow state procedures and satisfy state law in making the change of use? These issues of change of use and transferability are most important in the context of Indian reserved rights, and are addressed further infra pp. 972–976.

4. INDIAN RESERVED RIGHTS

The tensions associated with Indian reserved rights are a subset of the general tensions associated with reserved rights, but Indian rights raise several special problems. Most non-Indian federal reserved rights involve instream flows or other uses that are relatively non-consumptive; that is, they tend to preserve the flows for appropriation and reuse by others downstream. Add to this the fact that most federal landholdings are in headwaters areas, and you have a recipe for more accommodation than conflict in meshing state appropriations and federal reserved rights.

While some Indian tribes hold instream flow rights (primarily for fishery purposes, especially if fishing was a mainstay of tribal culture, as in the Pacific Northwest), many Indian rights are quantified on the basis of consumptive purposes; primarily, agricultural irrigation. As both *Winters* and *Arizona v. California* illustrate, most Indian reservations were established in the second half of the nineteenth century with a view to making the Indians farmers. This meant a relatively early priority date, and also led to a standard for quantification—"practicably irrigable acreage," or PIA—that is almost always a larger amount (sometimes much larger) than tribes have historically used. Furthermore, many Indian reservations are not found in headwaters areas. Thus many tribes may have claims to unexercised, large, consumptive, senior, downstream water rights:

---

6. Abandonment might present a closer question, if one assumes the federal government could form an intention to abandon a reserved right if it were no longer needed for a federal purpose.

[W]ater rights claims of the Missouri River basin tribes could total more than 19 million acre-feet, or approximately 40 percent of the average annual flow of the Missouri. As of 1995, there are more than 60 cases in courts involving the resolution of Indian water rights claims. The total amount of water potentially involved in these claims ranges from 45 million to over 65 million acre-feet. * * * [I]n Arizona, for instance, 19 Indian reservations account for 20 million acres (28 percent) of the state's land base. Experts have estimated that the water entitlements of Arizona tribes, many of which remain to be quantified, may surpass the state's water supplies.

Western Water Policy Review Advisory Commission, Water in the West: Challenge for the Next Century 3–48 (1998).

Over the decades since Arizona v. California, many questions about the contours of the *Winters* doctrine in the Indian context remain. This is because there have been relatively few major judicial decisions quantifying Indian water rights, which is surprising for two reasons: First, tribes in the modern era have a much easier time obtaining quality legal representation to assert and protect their water rights. Second, the successes of the States—which are the tribes' usual adversary in water rights—in McCarran Amendment litigation have made state courts generally available to litigants seeking to quantify tribal rights under the *Winters* doctrine. The following case is one of those few decisions, and it addresses a number of important issues. It also illustrates the complexity of modern general stream adjudications, and the glacial pace at which they can unfold. The case took more than a decade to get to the Wyoming Supreme Court. More than 20,000 parties were served; more than 100 attorneys participated; well over one hundred days of testimony were taken, much of it involving expert witnesses; the evidence included 15,000 pages of transcript and more than two thousand exhibits.

IN RE GENERAL ADJUDICATION OF
BIG HORN RIVER SYSTEM

Supreme Court of Wyoming, 1988.
753 P.2d 76.

Before BROWN, C.J., and THOMAS, CARDINE, and MACY, JJ., and HANSCUM, DISTRICT JUDGE.

This appeal is from the district court's order adjudicating rights to use water in the Big Horn River System and all other sources within the State's Water Division No. 3. * * *

Water Division No. 3 is essentially identical with what is known as the Big Horn River drainage basin. It is located in * * * northwestern and west central Wyoming and includes parts of Yellowstone National Park. Other federal entities included are the Wind River Indian Reservation, located in the southeastern portion of the region, consisting of approximately 4,000 square miles of land area. * * *

The history of the Big Horn Basin for purposes of this case begins in the early 1800's when explorers, trappers and traders began traveling into northwestern Wyoming, part of the vast hunting grounds of the peripatetic Shoshone Indians. Neither group encroached on the other and relations were friendly. Nonetheless, in 1865, the United States, hoping to preserve the peace and stability, reached an agreement delineating the area within which the Eastern Shoshone roamed, a 44,672,000 acre region comprising parts of Wyoming, Colorado, and Utah. Following the Civil War, as the westward movement gained momentum, the United States government realized the size of the region set aside for Indians only was unrealistic, and on July 3, 1868, executed the Second Treaty of Fort Bridger with the Shoshone and Bannock Indians, establishing the Wind River Indian Reservation.

During their first years on the reservation, the Shoshone Indians were still dependent on the buffalo as the mainstay of their life, but as the supply rapidly decreased, they began to rely upon an agricultural economy. During the 1870's the Shoshone Indians increased their efforts in both farming and ranching. The Shoshone ceded lands beyond the Popo Agie back to the United States in the 1872 Brunot Agreement. The Arapahoe moved to the reservation in 1878. By the 1880's it was evident that the agricultural economy of the Indians was failing, and by 1895, the Indians on the Wind River Indian Reservation were totally dependent on the government for food, clothing and shelter. These economic misfortunes compelled them to sell more of their land to the United States. The First McLaughlin Agreement, or Thermopolis Purchase, was concluded in 1897; the Big Horn Hot Springs was the main feature of the lands ceded to the United States for cash payment. An additional 1,480,000 acres of reservation land were ceded to the Government in the Second McLaughlin Agreement in 1904–1905. The revenue derived helped to develop the remaining reservation lands (which came to be known as the "diminished reservation"). The United States Government offered the ceded lands for sale to others, under the provisions of the homestead, townsite, coal and mineral land laws, and reimbursed the Tribes or expended for the benefit of the Tribes the money raised by the sales.

The earliest non-Indian settlements in northwestern and north central Wyoming were near the gold and silver fields in the South Pass area of the Wind River Range. These mining camps soon expanded into permanent farming and ranching communities which relied primarily on cattle ranching and dryland or easily-irrigated farming for sustenance. By the mid–1800's, many small communities had been established by settlers who had obtained their land under the Congressional land disposal acts. By the early 1900's most of the best land in the region was occupied by ranches or irrigated farms. Yet the settlers continued to arrive, forcing gradual expansion onto the dry basin floors and prompting the development of many irrigation projects, often sponsored jointly by private citizens and the United States. The arrival of the homesteaders in the Wind River Basin significantly altered the Indian's economic base. As the number of settlers and their farms increased, the number of Indians working their own farms and ranches decreased, and they began to rent and eventually to sell their land while hiring themselves out as laborers.

In 1934, all remaining lands which had been ceded to the United States by the 1904 agreement were reserved from non-Indian settlement. In 1940, the Secretary of [the] Interior began a series of restorations of certain undisposed lands to tribal ownership. These lands again became part of the existing Wind River Reservation. In addition, the United States later reacquired, in trust for the Tribes, additional ceded land and certain lands within the diminished reservation which previously had passed into private ownership. Since 1953, the size of the reservation has remained fairly stable.

* * * The report [of the trial court's special master in this case, former Member of Congress Teno Roncalio] recognized a reserved water right for the Wind River Indian Reservation and determined that the purpose for which the reservation had been established was a permanent homeland for the Indians. A reserved water right for irrigation, stock watering, fisheries, wildlife and aesthetics, mineral and industrial, and domestic, commercial, and municipal uses was quantified and awarded. * * *

* * * Congress intended to reserve water for the Wind River Indian Reservation when it was created in 1868, and we accept the proposition that the amount of water impliedly reserved is determined by the purposes for which the reservation was created.

The special master's finding that the principal purpose for the creation of the reservation was to provide a permanent homeland for the Indians is not a factual determination. * * * The special master found as a matter of law that the treaty was unambiguous and ascertained the purpose for creation of the reservation from the four corners of the treaty, stating:

> "Analyzing the Treaty in its entirety, with specific reference to the above cited provisions, it is not at all unreasonable to conclude that the principal purpose for entering into this Treaty was to provide the Indians with a homeland where they could establish a permanent place to live and to develop their civilization just as any other nation throughout history has been able to develop its civilization."

The district court ascertained the purpose of the reservation from the treaty itself, stating: "On the very face of the Treaty, it is clear that its purpose was purely agricultural." This legal determination is fully reviewable by this court.

* * * Considering the well-established principles of treaty interpretation, the treaty itself, the ample evidence and testimony addressed, and the findings of the district court, we have no difficulty affirming the

finding that it was the intent at the time to create a reservation with a sole agricultural purpose. * * *

Article 7 of the treaty refers to "said agricultural reservations." Article 6 authorizes allotments for farming purposes; Article 8 provides seeds and implements for farmers; in Article 9 "the United States agreed to pay each Indian farming a $20 annual stipend, but only $10 to 'roaming' Indians"; and Article 12 establishes a $50 prize to the ten best Indian farmers. The treaty does not encourage any other occupation or pursuit. The district court correctly found that the reference in Article 4 to "permanent homeland" does nothing more than permanently set aside lands for the Indians; it does not define the purpose of the reservation. Rather, the purpose of the permanent-home reservation is found in Articles 6, 8, 9, and 12 of the treaty. * * *

Although the treaty did not force the Indians to become farmers and although it clearly contemplates that other activities would be permitted (hunting is mentioned in Article 4, lumbering and milling in Article 3, roaming in Article 9), the treaty encouraged only agriculture, and that was its primary purpose. The Court in United States v. Shoshone Tribe of Indians, 304 U.S. 111, discussing the purpose of this treaty, stated:

> "Provisions in aid of teaching children and of adult education in farming, and to secure for the tribe medical and mechanical service, to safeguard tribal and individual titles, when taken with other parts of the treaty, plainly evidence purpose on the part of the United States to help to create an independent permanent farming community upon the reservation." Id., 304 U.S. at 117–118.

The Court, while recognizing that the Tribes were the beneficial owners of the reservation's timber and mineral resources and that it was known to all before the treaty was signed that the Wind River Indian Reservation contained valuable minerals, nonetheless concluded that the purpose of the reservation was agricultural. The fact that the Indians fully intended to continue to hunt and fish does not alter that conclusion. * * *

B. Fisheries

Reserved water rights for fisheries have been recognized where a treaty provision explicitly recognized an exclusive right to take fish on the reservation or the right to take fish at traditional off-reservation fishing grounds, in common with others. United States v. Winans, 198 U.S. 371. * * *

Instream fishery flows have also been recognized where the Indians were heavily, if not totally, dependent on fish for their livelihood. United States v. Adair, 723 F.2d [1394,] 1409 [(9th Cir. 1983)]; Colville Confederated Tribes v. Walton, 647 F.2d [42,] 48 [(9th Cir. 1981)]. In the case at bar, the Tribes introduced evidence showing that fish had always been part of the Indians' diet. The master, erroneously concluding that a reserved right for fisheries should be implied when the tribe is "at least partially dependent upon fishing," awarded an instream flow right for fisheries. The district court, however, finding neither a dependency upon fishing for a livelihood nor a traditional lifestyle involving fishing, deleted the award. The district court did not err. The evidence is not sufficient to imply a fishery flow right absent a treaty provision.

C. Mineral and Industrial

The Tribes were denied a reserved water right for mineral and industrial development. All parties to the treaty were well aware before it was signed of the valuable mineral estate underlying the Wind River Indian Reservation. * * * The question of whether, because the Indians own the minerals, the intent was that they should have the water necessary to develop them must be determined, of course, by the intent in 1868. Neither the Tribes nor the United States has cited this court to any provision of the treaty or other evidence indicating that the parties contemplated in 1868 that a purpose of the reservation would be for the Indians to develop the minerals. The fact that the Tribes have since used water for mineral and industrial purposes does not establish that water was impliedly reserved in 1868 for such uses. The district court did not err in denying a reserved water right for mineral and industrial uses.

D. Municipal, Domestic and Commercial

A reserved water right for municipal, domestic and commercial uses was included within the agricultural reserved water award. Domestic and related use has traditionally been subsumed in agricultural reserved rights. See, e.g., United States ex rel. Ray v. Hibner, 27 F.2d [909,] 911 [(D. Idaho 1928)] (the treaties fixed the rights of the Indians—"to a continuous use of a sufficient amount of water for the irrigation of their lands, and domestic purposes"); United States v. Powers, 305 U.S. [527,] 533 [(1939)] ("waters essential to farming and home making"). Practicably irrigable acreage (PIA) was established as the measure of an agricultural reserved water right in Arizona v. California. The special master there indicated that PIA was the measure of water necessary for agriculture and related purposes. The court properly allowed a reserved water right for municipal, domestic, and commercial use.

E. Livestock

For the reasons stated above, the district court did not err in * * * subsuming livestock use within [the agricultural purpose of the reservation].

F. Wildlife and Aesthetics

The special master awarded 60% of historic flows for wildlife and aesthetic uses, consistent with his determination that the purpose of the reservation was to be a permanent homeland. The district court deleted this award, reciting not only that the purpose was solely agricultural, but that insufficient evidence had been presented to justify an award for these uses. The district court did not err in holding that the Tribes and the United States did not introduce sufficient evidence of a tradition of wildlife and aesthetic preservation which would justify finding this to be a purpose for which the reservation was created and for which water was impliedly reserved.

The district court did not err in finding a sole agricultural purpose in the creation of the Wind River Indian Reservation. The Treaty itself evidences no other purpose, and none of the extraneous evidence cited is sufficient to attribute a broader purpose.

V.   SCOPE OF THE RESERVED WATER RIGHT

A.   *Groundwater*

The logic which supports a reservation of surface water to fulfill the purpose of the reservation also supports reservation of groundwater. See Tweedy v. Texas Company, 286 F. Supp. 383, 385 (D. Mont. 1968) ("whether the (necessary) waters were found on the surface of the land or under it should make no difference"). Certainly the two sources are often interconnected. See § 41–3916, Wyo. Stat. 1977 (where underground and surface waters are "so interconnected as to constitute in fact one source of supply," a single schedule of priorities shall be made); Final Report to the President and to the Congress by the National Water Commission, Water Policies for the Future 233 (1973) (groundwater and surface water "often naturally related"); Cappaert v. United States, 426 U.S. at 142–143 (citing additional authority to this effect).

Acknowledging the above, we note that, nonetheless, not a single case applying the reserved water doctrine to groundwater is cited to us. The ninth circuit indicated that groundwater was reserved in United States v. Cappaert, 508 F.2d 313, 317 (9th Cir. 1974). The United States Supreme Court, however, found the water in the pool reserved for preservation of the pupfish was not groundwater but surface water, protected from subsequent diversions from either surface or groundwater supplies. Nor have the other cases cited to us granted a reserved right in underground water. * * *

The District Court did not err in deciding there was no reserved groundwater right. * * * The State has not appealed the decision that the Tribes may continue to satisfy their domestic and livestock needs (part of the agricultural award) from existing wells at current withdrawal rates; therefore, we do not address that question.

B.   *Exportation*

The district court held that "(t)he Tribes can sell or lease any part of the water covered by their reserved water rights but the said sale or lease cannot be for exportation off of the Reservation." The Tribes did not seek permission to export reserved water, and the United States concedes that no federal law permits the sale of reserved water to non-Indians off the reservation. * * *

VI.   QUANTIFICATION

A.   The Measure

The measure of the Tribes' reserved water right is the water necessary to irrigate the practicably irrigable acreage on the reservation. In Arizona v. California a needs test was rejected as too uncertain, the Court opting instead for practicably irrigable acreage as the measure of a tribal agricultural reserved water right. Two subsequent non-Indian reserved water right cases, Cappaert v. United States and United States v. New Mexico, indicate that necessity is the measure of a reserved water right. And in Washington v. Washington State Commercial Passenger Fishing Vessel Association, 443 U.S. [658,] 686–687 (1979) the Court recognized the propriety of reducing the Indians' proportion of the fish harvest as their needs diminished. Nonetheless, the Court declined the invitation to re-examine the PIA standard in Arizona v. California and reaffirmed the value of the certainty inherent in the practicably irrigable acreage standard. The district court was correct in quantifying the Tribes' reserved water right by the amount of water necessary to irrigate all of the reservation's practicably irrigable acreage.

B.   Future Lands

The Tribes and the United States claimed a reserved water right for lands on the reservation not yet developed for irrigation, but which were in their view, practicably irrigable acreage. Counsel for the State, the Tribes and the United States agreed upon a definition of practicably irrigable acreage: "those acres susceptible to sustained irrigation at reasonable costs." The determination of practicably irrigable acreage involves a two-part analysis, i.e., the PIA must be susceptible of sustained irrigation (not only proof of the arability but also of the engineering feasibility of irrigating the land) and irrigable "at reasonable cost."
* * *

[The court then reviewed at length the methodology used to quantify the tribes' claim. The first issue was how lands would be classified as to their arability. The second issue was engineering feasibility of bringing water to arable land. The third issue was economic feasibility. The net result was that approximately 100,000 acres were determined to be practicably irrigable, which resulted in an award of almost one-half million acre feet per year with a 1868 priority date.]

THOMAS, JUSTICE, dissenting with whom HANSCUM, DISTRICT JUDGE, joins.

* * * The purpose of establishing an Indian reservation, such as the Wind River Indian Reservation, is to provide a homeland for Indian peoples. If one is to assume that, pursuant to the reserved rights doctrine relating to water, there is an implied reservation of those waters essential to accomplish the purpose of the reservation of land, then I cannot agree that the implied reservation of water with respect to the Wind River Indian Reservation should be limited, as the majority has held in approving the judgment of the district court. The fault that I find with such a limitation is that it assumes that the Indian peoples will not

enjoy the same style of evolution as other people, nor are they to have the benefits of modern civilization. I would understand that the homeland concept assumes that the homeland will not be a static place frozen in an instant of time but that the homeland will evolve and will be used in different ways as the Indian society develops. For that reason, I would hold that the implied reservation of water rights attaching to an Indian reservation assumes any use that is appropriate to the Indian homeland as it progresses and develops. The one thing that I would not assume is that using the reserved water as a salable commodity was contemplated in connection with the implied reservation of the water. I would limit its use to the territorial boundaries of the reservation.

Deeming it unnecessary to detail further the formula for allocation of water which involves the concept of practicably irrigable acreage, I am convinced that there has to be some degree of pragmatism in determining practicably irrigable acreage. It is clear from the majority opinion that there was included in quantifying the water reserved to the Indian peoples lands not now irrigable but deemed to be practicably irrigable acreage upon the assumption of the development of future irrigation projects. I would be appalled, as most other concerned citizens should be, if the Congress of the United States, or any other governmental body, began expending money to develop water projects for irrigating these Wyoming lands when far more fertile lands in the midwestern states now are being removed from production due to poor market conditions. I am convinced that, because of this pragmatic concern, those lands which were included as practicably irrigable acreage, based upon the assumption of the construction of a future irrigation project, should not be included for the purpose of quantification of the Indian peoples' water rights. They may be irrigable academically, but not as a matter of practicality, and I would require their exclusion from any quantification.
* * *

HANSCUM, DISTRICT JUDGE, dissenting [and disagreeing with Justice Thomas on one point:]

* * * Justice Thomas would hold that, as a matter of law, marketing water off the reservation never could be appropriate to the progress and development of the Indian homeland.

I disagree. I would go that additional step. I would hold that sale of water off the reservation should be permitted, provided that, as a factual matter, it could be demonstrated that such marketing contributed to the progress and development of the Indian homeland. I can envision a variety of scenarios where such showing could be made successfully. To preclude the opportunity of proving such a nexus unduly would restrict and hamper the prospective development of the Indian homeland in the future.

Notes and Questions

The Standard for Quantification: PIA or Something Else?

1.   The Wyoming decision had an intriguing unofficial subsequent history. The U.S. Supreme Court granted certiorari on a single issue: "[Wheth-

er,] in the absence of any demonstrated necessity for additional water to fulfill Reservation purposes and in the presence of substantial state water rights long in use on the Reservation, may a reserved water right be implied for all practicably irrigable lands within a Reservation?" Following oral argument, the case was affirmed without opinion by an evenly divided Court, Justice O'Connor not participating. See Wyoming v. United States, 492 U.S. 406 (1989). Upon his retirement, Justice Thurgood Marshall deposited his papers in the Library of Congress without restricting access; this led to the discovery the papers included a complete opinion by Justice O'Connor for five Justices in the *Big Horn* case, along with a biting dissent by Justice Brennan. After being assigned the task of writing the opinion for the majority and producing a draft, Justice O'Connor had recused herself only four days before the decision was announced because her family's ranching corporation[7] was, along with several Indian tribes, a party in the Gila River general stream adjudication in Arizona. See Andrew Mergen & Sylvia Liu, A Misplaced Sensitivity: The Draft Opinions in Wyoming v. United States, 68 U. Colo. L. Rev. 683, 685 n.10 (1997).

2. Justice O'Connor's opinion would have read the *New Mexico* decision to create a new "sensitivity doctrine" in quantifying Indian water rights—retreating somewhat from the PIA standard when it threatened other (albeit junior) water rights. (The doctrine's label comes from the first sentence in Justice Powell's partial dissent in that decision, supra p. 924.) The draft majority opinion and draft dissent are both reproduced in an appendix to Mergen & Liu, supra Note 1.

3. How would this opinion have modified the *Winters* doctrine had it become law? How would the tribe at Fort Belknap have fared in *Winters* itself if the Court had applied a "sensitivity analysis" on those facts? Justice Brennan's draft dissent characterized the draft majority opinion as

> propos[ing] in effect, to penalize [tribes] for the lack of Government investment on their reservations by taking from them those water rights that have remained theirs, until now, on paper. * * * I cannot join in such a redistribution of rights at the expense of one of the most disadvantaged groups in American society—on the pretext that the Indians do not "need" the water rights we strip from them.

4. The Supreme Court's failure to produce an opinion in the *Big Horn* case left unsolved a puzzle created by Washington v. Washington State Commercial Passenger Fishing Vessel Ass'n, 443 U.S. 658 (1979). That case upheld an interpretation by lower courts that treaties recognizing the right of Indians in the Northwest to "tak[e] fish * * * in common with all citizens of the Territory" apportioned up to 50% of the harvestable fish to the Indians. The Court, per Justice Stevens, saw Indian water rights cases as analogous:

> As in Arizona v. California and its predecessor cases, the central principle here must be that Indian treaty rights to a natural resource that once was thoroughly and exclusively exploited by the

---

7. Justice O'Connor (with her brother) later published a memoir of growing up on the ranch; LAZY B (2002).

Indians secures so much as, but no more than, is necessary to provide the Indians with a livelihood—that is to say, a moderate living.

443 U.S. at 686. What is a "moderate" living? Was the Court here saying water was reserved for the Indians only in sufficient quantity to make them middle class, but not rich? Does that standard suggest, indeed require, a consideration of the number of Indians now on the reservation? How does this differ from Arizona's argument the Court rejected in Arizona v. California, supra p. 911? The Supreme Court's decree quantifying the Indian water rights along the lower Colorado gave the tribes nearly one million acre-feet of water. Arizona v. California, 376 U.S. 340 (1964). The Fort Mojave Tribe was decreed more than 130,000 acre-feet, even though the reservation was sparsely settled and only a few acres had ever been irrigated.

5. Although there are some dramatic departures from the norm, the experience of the Indians described at the beginning of the *Big Horn* opinion occurred fairly often: First the national government recognized the Indians' right to a vast area. This was followed by reduction in the size of the tribe's[8] land base through a series of treaties or other agreements that opened large areas of formerly tribal land to non-Indian settlement. Eventually the Indian land base was stabilized and perhaps even modestly enlarged. Some reservations were heavily "allotted" under the Dawes Act of 1887 (24 Stat. 388); i.e., tribal lands were broken up and parceled out to individual Indians, who eventually could (and often did) sell (or lose through various means) their lands to non-Indians. Each of these changes may have implications for Indian water rights. The consequences of allotments for water rights is explored in Colville Confederated Tribes v. Walton, infra p. 980.

The Purpose(s) of the Reservation

6. What were the purposes of the Wind River Indian Reservation, according to the special master? According to the trial court and the Wyoming Supreme Court? What difference does it make? Is the Wyoming Supreme Court's approach in *Big Horn* consistent with *Winters*?

7. In Gila River Pima–Maricopa Indian Community v. United States, 684 F.2d 852 (Ct. Cl.1982), the federal Court of Claims addressed the Tribe's claim for damages resulting from the failure of the United States to protect the Tribe's water rights from upstream diversion by non-Indians. The court characterized the friendly Pimas and Maricopas (whose irrigated crops had kept from starving the U.S. soldiers who ventured into the area around the time of the Mexican War) as, at the time their reservation was created in 1859, a "self-sufficient, pastoral people with entrepreneurial abilities." 684 F.2d at 861. It went on to suggest that the purpose of their reservation was "to preserve what they had, not to change their habits from nomadic to pastoral, and this distinction could conceivably make a legal difference." Id. at 864. The case was ultimately resolved on other grounds, but the court's decision suggests the possibility that *Winters* rights might be measured by a reservation-specific inquiry that could lead to dramatically different results from that reached in *Big Horn*. See also Gila River Pima–Maricopa Indian

---

8. Note that on the Big Horn, the Arapaho Tribe was relocated to the reservation initially created for its ancestral adversary, the Shoshone, in 1878.

Community v. United States, 695 F.2d 559 (Fed. Cir. 1982). Is the Court of Claims' analysis consistent with *Winters*? With *Big Horn*? Does *Winters* call for a particularized inquiry into the purposes of individual reservations?

8. Is the Court of Claims in effect suggesting that Indians who were pastoral, entrepreneurial and who cooperated with the invading Europeans are entitled to less water under *Winters* than Indians who were nomadic and hostile? Is that ironic, or logical, or both? Cf. Shoshone Tribe of Indians v. United States, 299 U.S. 476, 486 (1937) (Cardozo, J.) ("The loyalty of the Shoshone tribe to the people of the United States has been conspicuous and unfaltering. A fidelity at least as constant and inflexible was owing in return.").

9. If a conventional PIA standard were used to quantify the rights of the Gila River Pima–Maricopa Indian Community, it might well exceed the entire ordinary flow of the Gila River, the principal on-reservation water source. This is because, among other things, the Community's reservation contains ample amounts of readily irrigable land and the climate is favorable to agriculture. How should that affect the Community's water rights? Should it influence a court's interpretation of the purpose(s) of the reservation, or a court's determination whether to apply the PIA standard to quantify the rights to achieve those purposes, or both?

10. With the support of the United States, tribes generally now seek reserved rights for multiple uses, based on the notion that the single broad purpose for creating Indian reservations was to provide the Indians a "homeland." Does that square with the distinction between "primary purposes" and "secondary uses" drawn by United States v. New Mexico, supra p. 919, in the non-Indian context? Finding "significant differences between Indian and non-Indian reservations," the Arizona Supreme Court rejected that distinction and endorsed the idea that the purpose of every Indian reservation is to provide a "permanent home and abiding place" for Indians, and that the uses of the homeland are not limited to agriculture, as implied by the PIA standard. In re Gila River General Stream Adjudication, 35 P.3d 68, 76–77 (Ariz. 2001). Cf. Dept. of Ecology v. Yakima Res. Irr. Dist., 850 P.2d 1306, 1316–17 (Wash. 1993) (adopting the primary purpose/secondary use approach, but finding more than one primary purpose); United States v. Washington, 375 F. Supp. 2d 1050, 1063–67 (W.D.Wash. 2005) (rejecting the Arizona Supreme Court's "homeland purpose" analysis as contrary to the "primary purpose/secondary use" doctrine, but finding a federal reservation of water for agricultural and domestic purposes, and that enough water was reserved for the latter purpose to make the reservation livable, and not limited by the PIA standard). See also Barbara Cosens, The Measure of Indian Water Rights: The Arizona Homeland Standard, Gila River Adjudication, 42 Nat. Res. J. 835, 863–71 (2003); Cohen's Handbook of Federal Indian Law § 19.03[4] (Nell Newton et al. eds., 2005); Montana v. United States, 450 U.S. 544, 566, n.15 (1981) (characterizing Arizona v. California as holding that tribes "retain rights to river waters necessary to make their reservations livable").

11. Echoing the criticism in Justice Thomas's dissent in *Big Horn*, some have suggested that emphasis on the original purpose of the reservation condemns the tribes to an outmoded, nineteenth century view of water

use that does not allow adaptation to contemporary realities. See, e.g., Walter Rusinek, A Preview of Coming Attractions? Wyoming v. United States and the Reserved Rights Doctrine, 17 Ecology L.Q. 355 (1990); Carla Bennett, Quantification of Indian Water Rights: Foresight or Folly?, 8 U.C.L.A. J. Envtl. L. & Pol'y 267 (1989).

Some Questions on the Practicably Irrigable Acreage (PIA) Standard

12.   Should PIA be measured according to the technology of the date of the reservation? Cropping patterns as of that time? The U. S. Supreme Court has suggested that the determination of PIA is to be based on technology at the time of trial. Arizona v. California, 460 U.S. 605, 625 n.18 (1983).

13.   At one level, applying the PIA standard is somewhat mechanical. Determining how many acres on a reservation can be "practicably" irrigated involves assessing slope and soil type and the engineering and economic feasibility of capturing, storing, and delivering water to the land. A per-acre water duty for crop irrigation can be determined using data on precipitation and growing season and the practices of other irrigators in the region. PIA multiplied by the water duty quantifies the amount of the reserved right. The PIA calculation often turns into a battle of experts—one court described a PIA hearing this way: "[E]xpert hydrologists, geologists, agronomists, economists, and others testified or submitted reports on soil type and quality, climate and growing season, water quantity and quality, market factors and prices, equipment, labor, and financing." New Mexico ex rel. Martinez v. Lewis, 861 P.2d 235, 246 (N.M. Ct. App. 1993).

14.   Should PIA be determined according to the same economic feasibility standards the U. S. government applied to Bureau of Reclamation projects, operated primarily for the benefit of non-Indian farmers? The relatively generous subsidies provided to farmers benefitting from Bureau of Reclamation projects were described in Chapter 7 at pp. 747–750. See H.S. Burness et al., United States Reclamation Policy and Indian Water Rights, 20 Nat. Resources J. 807 (1980). What economic standard did the Wyoming Supreme Court apply in *Big Horn*? In his dissent in *Big Horn*, Wyoming Justice Thomas says he "would be appalled, as most other concerned citizens should be, if the Congress * * * began expending money to develop water projects for irrigating these Wyoming lands when far more fertile lands in the midwestern states are being removed from production due to poor market conditions." A cynic might suggest that few were "appalled" when Congress showered money on the Bureau of Reclamation for such purposes.

15.   What are the consequences for the PIA formula if the economics of irrigation changes dramatically, such as through a decline in the market for farm exports? Over the last few decades, owing to a variety factors, western irrigated agriculture has been shrinking. Economics has played a key role in the application of PIA. For example, in New Mexico ex rel. Martinez v. Lewis, 861 P.2d 235, 246–47 (N.M. Ct. App. 1993), the court upheld the trial court's determination that water projects hypothecated to irrigate reservation land for purposes of calculating PIA could not be built and operated at "reasonable cost."

16. Even if stringent economic criteria were applied to reduce PIA, that standard may still, given the substantial size of many Indian reservations in the West, result in reserved rights awards that are quite large in relation to the available local water supply. Recall that in Arizona v. California, supra p. 909, PIA gave the five tribes along the lower Colorado River about 900,000 acre feet of water to irrigate 135,000 acres of reservation lands. The Court was not deterred by arguments that such an amount dwarfed current uses and the actual needs of the tribes.[9]

17. Assume the only dependable water source contiguous to the Navajo Nation's reservation is the Colorado River, but the irrigable land on the reservation is on a mesa several hundred feet higher than the River, and it is not cost-effective to pump water that far. Moreover, the irrigable land is several thousand feet above sea level, making the growing season very short. Assume further that the reservation was created for the purpose of providing a homeland for the Navajo. Does the Tribe have a *Winters* right in the River? For what quantity? Suppose it would be more cost-effective for the Navajo to divert water from the Colorado River fifty miles upstream from the reservation and bring it to the reservation by gravity flow. Does the *Winters* doctrine allow the Tribe to reach off the reservation that way for water? Some have estimated potential Navajo reserved rights claims at more than two million acre feet. See, e.g., William D. Back & Jeffery S. Taylor, Navajo Water Rights: Pulling The Plug On The Colorado River, 20 Nat. Resources J. 71, 74 (1980); Michael Laird, Water Rights: The Winters Cloud Over the Rockies: Indian Water Rights and the Development of Western Energy Resources, 7 Am. Indian L. Rev. 155 (1980).

18. There is considerable commentary on these and related questions in quantifying Indian water rights. See, e.g., Cohen's Handbook of Federal Indian Law §§ 19.03[4] & [5] (Nell Newton et al. eds., 2005); Sylvia Liu, American Indian Reserved Water Rights: The Federal Obligation to Protect Tribal Water Resources and Tribal Autonomy, 25 Envtl. L. 425 (1995); Judith Royster, A Primer on Indian Water Rights: More Questions Than Answers, 30 Tulsa L.J. 61 (1994); H.S. Burness et al., The "New" Arizona v. California: Practicably Irrigable Acreage and Economic Feasibility, 22 Nat. Resources J. 517 (1982).

Groundwater

19. The Wyoming Supreme Court rejected the idea that federal reserved rights can attach to groundwater. By what reasoning? Is it relevant that technology did not generally exist to pump groundwater when most Indian Reservations were created in the 19th century? Is it relevant that this Indian reservation, like others, was determined (over the objection of the United States) to embrace the minerals underlying the land? See United States v. Shoshone Tribe of Indians, 304 U.S. 111, 117 (1938) (though the

9. The Indian rights involved in Arizona v. California were in litigation for many decades after the landmark 1963 decision, mostly involving previously unresolved issues concerning the precise boundaries of affected Indian reservations which, in turn, affected the amount of irrigable acreage contained within the reservations. In one case, the Court refused to reopen the earlier decree, emphasizing the "strong interest in finality in this case," Arizona v. California, 460 U.S. 605, 620 (1983), but that wasn't the last word; see Arizona v. California, 530 U.S. 392 (2000).

treaty reserving the land for the Indians was silent on minerals, it was made "with knowledge that there were mineral deposits" on the reservation, and ought to be interpreted "in the sense in which naturally the Indians would understand [it]"). Might groundwater be reserved under Indian reservations, but not under National Parks or other non-Indian federal reservations, or vice-versa?

20.   In 1999, the Arizona Supreme Court found the reasoning in *Big Horn* unpersuasive, and ruled that federal reserved rights may extend to groundwater: "The significant question for the purpose of the reserved rights doctrine is not whether the water runs above or below the ground but whether it is necessary to accomplish the purpose of the reservation." In re General Adjudication of Gila River System, 989 P.2d 739 (1999). See E. Brendan Shane, Water Rights and Gila River III: The Winters Doctrine Goes Underground, 4 U. Denver Water L. Rev. 397 (2001). In Confederated Salish and Kootenai Tribes of the Flathead Reservation v. Stults, 59 P.3d 1093, 1098 (2002), the Montana Supreme Court agreed with the Arizona Supreme Court: "[T]he same implications which led the Supreme Court [in *Winters*] to hold that surface waters had been reserved would apply to underground waters as well. The land was arid—water would make it more useful, and whether the waters were found on the surface of the land or under it should make no difference."

21.   If an aquifer is located entirely within the boundaries of a reservation, and the reservation land is all in federal ownership in trust for the Indians, the question may be moot, because non-Indians may not obtain access to the groundwater without federal approval anyway. Commonly, however, non-Indians may own some land within reservation boundaries over an aquifer, and/or aquifers are partially on and partially off a reservation. Even if other federal agencies like the Forest Service control the land bordering the reservation, they may be willing to permit extraction of groundwater from the common aquifer to benefit nearby non-Indian communities.

22.   How does the source of the water relate to the quantification of the tribal right? Suppose a tribe is determined to have a PIA right to 100,000 acre-feet of water, and a stream bordering the reservation has an average flow of 50,000 acre-feet, most of it appropriated upstream by non-Indians under state law after the reservation was made. Lying within the reservation boundaries is an aquifer from which 50,000 acre-feet may be extracted annually without serious long-term mining, or 100,000 acre-feet a year may be extracted annually for 50 years before the aquifer approaches exhaustion, or before its water level drops below the limit of economic retrievability. Does the *Winters* doctrine give the U.S. or the tribe a choice as to how much groundwater versus surface water to tap, or is that a matter for the courts to decide? The Arizona Supreme Court recently suggested that groundwater was the last resort: "A reserved right to groundwater may only be found where other waters are inadequate to accomplish the purpose of a reservation." In re General Adjudication of Gila River System, 989 P.2d 739 (1999). Why should that be? Should the Indians' first claim be to groundwater, and extend to surface water that is being used by junior appropriators under state law only if groundwater is insufficient to accomplish the purpose(s) of the reservation? Would this be an example of how a "sensitivity" doctrine

would work? (See the discussion of Justice O'Connor's phantom opinion in *Big Horn*, supra p. 966, Note 2). Or might the approach vary from reservation to reservation, and depend upon such things as the aquifer's rate of recharge?

23.   One can readily imagine further complications: Suppose the aquifer is half on and half off the reservation, and non-Indians off the reservation rely upon it for irrigating their lands. Does the groundwater doctrine (e.g., American reasonable use, correlative rights, prior appropriation) followed by that particular state make a difference in determining the tribe's rights to groundwater, or their enforceability off the reservation? The possible questions are richly complex; the answers in the decided cases are virtually non-existent.[10] But see In re General Adjudication of Gila River System, 989 P.2d 739 (Ariz. 1999) (holders of federal reserved rights to groundwater should be given broader protection than holders of state law rights to groundwater, if necessary to maintain sufficient water to accomplish the purpose of the reservation). One commentator suggested vesting tribes with a fixed total amount of water to do with as they please—trade, sell or retain for use on the reservation. See Gwendolyn Griffith, Indian Claims to Groundwater: Reserved Rights or Beneficial Interest?, 33 Stan. L. Rev. 103 (1980).

24.   Charles Meyers explored a number of questions concerning Indian reserved groundwater rights in his useful Federal Groundwater Rights: A Note on Cappaert v. United States, 13 Land & Water L. Rev. 377 (1978). Among other things, he argued that intent to reserve groundwater is not the question; rather, Indians gained equitable title to groundwater in "precisely the same manner as title passed to the land and its other resources." Still, he said, a "rule of reason" is "appropriate" in adjudicating Indian claims to groundwater that conflict with uses by neighboring non-Indians, because both Indians and non-Indians have equivalent property interests in the overlying land. Id. at 388, 389.

a. *Changes of Use and Transfers of Indian Water Rights*

If Indian reserved water rights are strictly limited to the type and place of use for which they are quantified—most commonly, agricultural use on practicably irrigable acres—they will probably be far less valuable than they would be if their type and place of use can be changed. This is because agricultural irrigation is, in many parts of the West today, among the lowest valued uses of water. If Indian water rights are not transferable to new uses—and especially new uses outside the boundaries of reservations (such as for municipal use in the West's burgeoning urban areas)—they may never, no matter how large they are, be exercised. This will leave the water subject to the Indians' senior, paper rights available to non-Indian users who have been benefitting from the non-exercise of tribal rights right along. These stark facts make the Tribes' ability to change the type and place of use—and particularly to market water off-reservation—a major battleground.

10.   Similar questions were asked in the non-Indian context in the notes following *Cappaert*, supra pp. 916–917.

The first issue is whether the quantification standard is a limitation on actual use, or whether the use can be changed, and if so, how. This aspect of Indian reserved rights, like many others, has seen relatively little treatment in the courts. The clearest Supreme Court pronouncement on the subject appears, with no explanation, in a provision in a supplemental decree entered in Arizona v. California, 439 U.S. 419, 422 (1979), that provided some further guidance on the rights the Court had awarded tribes in the landmark 1963 decision. The decree provided:

> The foregoing reference to a quantity of water necessary to supply consumptive use required for irrigation [of PIA within the reservations] * * * shall not constitute a restriction of the usage of them to irrigation or other agricultural application. If all or part of the adjudicated water rights of any of the * * * Reservations is used other than for irrigation or other agricultural application, the total consumptive use * * * shall not exceed the consumptive use that would have resulted if the diversions * * * had been used for irrigation of the number of acres specified for that Reservation * * *.

Notes and Questions

1. Suppose the Fort Mojave Tribe has a paper (unexercised) right to 10,000 acre-feet according to the PIA standard. Suppose also that if the tribe irrigated reservation land with this water, there would be return flows to the Colorado River of 4000 acre-feet. The tribe proposes to lease water to Edison International to operate a large coal-fired power plant to be built on the reservation. All the water sent to the power plant would be evaporated, with no return flows. How much water can the tribe sell to Edison under the 1979 decree?

2. Does this 1979 decree essentially borrow, and apply as federal law, the "no-injury" rule that governs transfers and changes of use of water rights in prior appropriation jurisdictions? See Chapter 3, pp. 270–284. Should it make a difference in applying that rule whether a tribe was actually using the water decreed to it? If, as in the hypothetical in ¶ 1, the tribe had not been using the water, might the consumption of any water by Edison International under the lease from the tribe result in actual injury to some other water user? (You may recall from the materials on the lower Colorado River in Chapter 8, at pp. 808–811, that the Metropolitan Water District of Southern California for many years diverted as much of the unused waters of the lower River as its aqueduct would carry. Thus the District would have a credible claim that the tribal lease with Edison would reduce the amount of its diversion in at least some years.)

3. Who (besides the tribal government) must approve such a change in use called for by the decree? The Supreme Court? The federal government? The state? In a later decision of the Supreme Court of Wyoming in the *Big Horn* adjudication, the court by a three to two vote (with five separate opinions being written, none commanding a majority) held that the tribes could not, without the consent of the State Engineer, convert a portion of their PIA-quantified right to an instream flow for fisheries and related purposes. In re General Adjudication of the Big Horn River System, 835 P.2d

273, 278 (Wyo. 1992). See generally Cohen's Handbook of Federal Indian Law § 19.03[6] (Nell Newton et al. eds., 2005).

4. If a tribe has a non-consumptive instream flow water right for fisheries, may it change it to an industrial use that involves consumption, if that injures others? United States v. Adair, 723 F.2d 1394, 1411 (9th Cir. 1983) suggested the answer is no.

5. The transfer of Indian rights to land is limited by operation of a federal law, the Indian Non–Intercourse Act, 25 U.S.C. § 177. This statute dates back to the earliest Congress, and is designed to protect Indians against overreaching by non-Indians. Its core provision states:

> No purchase, grant, lease, or other conveyance of land, or of any title or claim thereto, from any Indian nation or tribe of Indians, shall be of any validity in law or equity, unless the same be made by treaty or convention entered into pursuant to the Constitution.

The last clause is generally understood to mean the consent of Congress is required for such transactions to be effective. For a general discussion of the Act, see Oneida County v. Oneida Indian Nation, 470 U.S. 226 (1985). Although the Act applies to "any title or claim to land", some cases have construed similar references to "land" in statutes of this type to include water. See Holmes v. United States, 53 F.2d 960 (10th Cir. 1931). The statute would plainly come into play with a tribal lease of land and water for a power plant (as in the Edison International hypothetical). There is no authoritative answer to whether the statute extends to the alienation of tribal reserved water rights in transactions independent of land. See Cohen's Handbook of Federal Indian Law § 19.03[7] (Nell Newton et al. eds., 2005). For case studies of tribes leasing water, see Gary Weatherford, Mary Wallace & Lee Herold Storey, Leasing Indian Water: Choices in the Colorado Indian Basin, 26–36 (1988).

6. Assuming the Non–Intercourse Act requires congressional approval for at least some kinds of transfers of Indian water rights, the next question is whether Congress has delegated its authority to approve such transactions to the Executive. One possible delegation is found in 25 U.S.C. § 415, a general statute giving tribes broad authority to lease Indian "lands" with the approval of the Secretary of the Interior. This statute has been interpreted to allow tribes to convey tribal water rights in connection with leases of reservation lands. See Skeem v. United States, 273 Fed. 93 (9th Cir. 1921); 2 Op. Solicitor on Indian Affairs 1930 (Feb. 1, 1964). Two other statutes give the Secretary of the Interior broad authority to supervise and manage Indian affairs, and might also be construed to support agreements between Indians and non-Indians over water. See 25 U.S.C. §§ 2, 9; United States v. Ahtanum, 236 F.2d 321 (9th Cir. 1956).

Off–Reservation Marketing

7. Now for the more difficult case (and more important, given the fact that demand for water will generally be higher off Indian reservations than on them): Suppose the Fort Mohave Tribe wants to lease its paper but decreed water right to San Diego for use in that City, 300 miles from the reservation (with no return flows to the Colorado River). Can the tribe do so? Note that the Wyoming Supreme Court in the *Big Horn* case, supra p.

958, did not squarely address the issue of the transfer of water for use off the reservation, although it noted that the trial court had ruled that the Indians could not export the water awarded, and the two dissenting judges split on the matter.

8. This issue has provoked sometimes heated discussion for decades. To encapsulate the extended debate, some argue that *Winters* rights should be considered akin to riparian rights, not based upon actual diversion and use, but rather deriving from the ownership of, and therefore appurtenant to, land. Just as the riparian rights doctrine frowns on uses off riparian tracts, so should the *Winters* doctrine prohibit off-reservation uses. See, e.g., Jack Palma, Considerations and Conclusions Concerning the Transferability of Indian Water Rights, 20 Nat. Resources J. 91 (1980). Others take the view that the *Winters* doctrine is dynamic and broad, aimed at making tribes self-sustaining political and economic entities in modern American society. See, e.g., Robert Pelcyger, Winters and the Greening of the Reservations, 4 J. Contemp. L. 19 (1977). If a tribe decides that marketing its water rights off-reservation is a path to self-sufficiency, the law should not be interpreted to prohibit it. See, e.g., Susan Williams, Indian Winters Water Rights Administration: Averting New War, 11 Pub. Land L. Rev. 53, 65–66 (1991); Christine Lightenfels, Indian Reserved Water Rights: An Argument for the Right to Export and Sell, 24 Land & Water L. Rev. 131 (1989); David Getches, Management and Marketing of Indian Water: From Conflict to Pragmatism, 58 Colo. L. Rev. 515, 541–42 (1988); Lee Storey, Leasing Indian Water Off the Reservation: A Use Consistent with the Reservation's Purpose, 76 Calif. L. Rev. 179 (1988).

9. Part of the debate is about whether off-reservation transfers are consistent with the purpose(s) of Indian reservations. The problem is, of course, that there is no consensus on what the purpose(s) of reservations are, either in specific cases or more generally. See supra pp. 967–969. There is also an argument that reservation purpose is relevant only to quantifying Indian water rights, and that once quantified, the tribe is entitled to market them just as any water right holder or sovereign might.

10. Where a tribe's water right has been quantified (by a court or Congress), and it has actually put the water to use, the argument that it should be able to market the water off-reservation would seem to be strongest. If the marketing were subject to the no-injury rule, other water users would be protected, so the principal objection would seem to be conceptual, drawing an analogy between a *Winters* and riparian rights.

11. Somewhat more difficult is the case where the tribe's water right has been judicially or legislatively determined, but it has actually not put the water to use. (This is the Fort Mohave Tribe/San Diego hypothetical, supra Note 7.) If the no-injury rule is applied in accordance with the approach of the Supreme Court's 1979 decree in Arizona v. California, supra p. 973—that is, if injury were determined after assuming that the water had been used for agricultural irrigation on-reservation—existing users could still be injured. But their injury would be no greater than if the tribe had put the water to use on-reservation, which it would plainly be entitled to do. See United States v. Orr Water Ditch Co., 309 F. Supp. 2d 1245, 1253–54 (D. Nev. 2004) (injury to junior users from the tribe's proposed on-reservation

shift in the use of its water right from agricultural irrigation to instream flow for fishery is to be measured not against the tribe's existing actual use, but by considering the use the tribe is entitled to make under its decreed right). Once again the primary objection would be based more on the notion that the *Winters* doctrine conceptually ties the water to the reservation.

12.   The most difficult case is where a tribe seeks to market water which it has never used, which has been fully appropriated by non-Indians after the reservation was created, and to which the tribe has only an inchoate, unadjudicated claim (that is, where the tribe's water rights have not been determined by negotiated settlement or by a court of competent jurisdiction). While the tribe may have a credible claim to a senior water right, the fact that it has never used the water suggests that the only way it will ever realize value from its *Winters* claim is to market the water off-reservation. Furthermore, it is difficult to apply a no-injury principle where there has been no determination of the tribe's right to use the water on-reservation.

13.   The Western Water Policy Review Advisory Commission recommended in its final report that the federal government "clarify federal policy regarding marketing of Indian water. Allowing water entitlements of Indian reservations to be leased with no more restrictions than non-Indian rights would facilitate greater efficiencies and flexibility of water use." Water in the West: Challenge for the Next Century 6–10, 11 (1998).

14.   Not all transfers of Indian water rights are accomplished by lease or outright sale. There is also the so-called "forbearance agreement," where a tribe agrees, for consideration, to defer its exercise of reserved rights for a period sufficient to permit other users to recoup their investments in water-dependent activities that could otherwise be eclipsed by the Indians using their reserved rights. The Bonneville Unit of the Central Utah Project was made possible by such an agreement. See Edward Clyde, Special Considerations Involving Indian Rights, 8 Nat. Resources Law. 237 (1975).

15.   Congress may authorize off-reservation marketing, and a number of congressionally approved Indian water rights settlements expressly authorize such transfers. Examples are discussed in connection with negotiated settlements, infra pp. 992–996.

b.   *Indian Rights, the Federal Reclamation Program, Res Judicata, and Conflicts Among Federal Claims*

The United States has sometimes found itself in a conflicted position in asserting Indian water rights as trustee for the Indians, at the same time it promotes reclamation projects that primarily benefit non-Indian farmers. Northern Nevada provided a classic example. The Pyramid Lake Indian Reservation was established for the Paiute Tribe in 1859, five years before Nevada became a state, and about the same time that discovery of the fabled Comstock lode brought thousands of miners into the area. The Reservation surrounds the Lake, which is the terminus of the Truckee River. The United States built one of the first irrigation projects under the Reclamation Act of 1902 in this area of Nevada, which was, not coincidentally, represented in the Senate by the father of the Reclamation Act, Francis Newlands. The eponymous Newlands Project was designed in part to divert flows from the Truckee upstream from the Lake to irrigate the lands of non-Indian farmers, who were organized into the Truckee–Carson Irrigation District, or TCID.

To secure the water rights for the project, the United States brought a general stream adjudication in federal court in 1913. In this litigation the United States represented both the Tribe and the non-Indian farmers in the TCID, even though their interests clashed. The case was eventually settled in 1944 by consent decree (the Orr Ditch decree), which awarded the Tribe enough water to irrigate about 5,900 acres of the 500,000 acre reservation, and awarded the Newlands project enough water to irrigate some 65,000 acres of land. The government did not claim any water rights to sustain the Tribe's traditional fishery in the Lake.

Over the years, the Newlands project's diversion reduced the River's flow and the size of the Lake. The fish and the tribal economy and culture all suffered. In 1973 the United States brought a new action asserting a reserved right for the Indian fishery. The trial court found the 1944 decree was res judicata and binding on the Tribe, because it had been represented by the United States in the litigation. The court of appeals reversed because of the U.S.'s conflict of interest in the earlier proceeding. The Supreme Court unanimously reinstated the trial court decision, explaining:

> Today * * * it may well appear that Congress was requiring the Secretary of the Interior to carry water on at least two shoulders when it delegated to him both the responsibility for the supervision of the Indian tribes and the commencement of reclamation projects in areas adjacent to reservation lands. But Congress chose to do this, and it is simply unrealistic to suggest that the Government may not perform its obligation to represent Indian tribes in litigation when Congress has obliged it to represent other interests as well. In this regard, the Government cannot follow the fastidious standards of a private fiduciary, who would breach his duties to his single beneficiary solely by representing potentially conflicting interests without the beneficiary's consent. The Government does not "compromise" its obligation to one interest that Congress obliges it to represent by the mere fact that it simultaneously performs another task for another interest that Congress has obligated it by statute to do. * * * The United States undoubtedly owes a strong fiduciary duty to its Indian wards. * * * But [here] Congress has imposed upon the United States, in addition to its duty to represent Indian tribes, a duty to obtain water rights for reclamation projects, * * * [and we hold that] the interests of the Tribe and the Project landowners were sufficiently adverse so that both are now bound by the final decree * * *.

Nevada v. United States, 463 U.S. 110, 128, 142–43 (1983).[11]

---

11. The Court observed, in a footnote, that the Tribe had sued the United States   for damages before the Indian Claims Commission in 1951 for failing to receive the

See also In re General Adjudication of Gila River System, 127 P.3d 882 (Ariz. 2006) (1935 decree in prior adjudication in which U.S., but not the tribe, participated held to bind the tribe regarding its *Winters* claims to mainstem of Gila River, but not to the tributaries because the decree was construed as not extending to the tributaries).

The Pyramid Lake history mirrors western water development at large, with non-Indians getting the lion's share of federal aid for water projects, and the United States failing to secure Indian water rights in the process. See the National Water Commission's description of this performance as one of the "sorrier chapters" in the Nation's treatment of Indians; supra p. 942 n.16. See also the final report of the Western Water Policy Review Advisory Commission:

> While tribes share the western landscape, unlike the major beneficiaries of federal water resources development, by and large, they have not shared in the federal government's water largesse from 1902 to the present.

> Federal support for Native American irrigation dates to 1867. During the allotment era (1888–1932), some 150 reservation projects irrigating 362,000 acres were constructed when federal policy was to turn "nomadic" peoples into "pastoral" peoples. An unpublished 1975 Senate Report estimated that $201 million had been expended to irrigate about 648,000 acres and that only 16 Native American projects could be considered major. The gap between Native and non-Native American water expenditures and the difficulties that tribes face in using water for nonirrigation purposes has been a continuing source of frustration to them.

Water in the West: Challenge for the Next Century 4–12 (1998). See also Daniel McCool, Command of the Waters: Iron Triangles, Federal Water Development, and Indian Water 139–42 (1994); Larry A. DiMatteo & Michael J. Meagher, Broken Promises: The Failure of the 1920s Native American Irrigation and Assimilation Policies, 19 U. Hawai'i L. Rev. 1 (1997). By comparison, about ten million acres have been irrigated under the reclamation program; see supra pp. 746–752. What is an appropriate remedy for this maltreatment? Reallocating water from non-Indians to Indians? Cash compensation to the Indians (with which they might seek to buy "wet" water)? The courts have held that, in general, the United States has no duty to develop irrigation facilities for tribes or to deliver irrigation water to Indian allotments. See Cohen's Handbook of Federal Indian Law § 19.06 (Nell Newton et al. eds., 2005), especially the text accompanying nn. 403–404.

water it was entitled to for its fishery. The case had been settled, with the Tribe receiving $8 million. 463 U.S. at 135 n. 14; see also Northern Paiute Tribe v. United States, 30 Ind. Cl. Comm'n 210 (1973).

Conflicts among federal claims in a particular stream adjudication are not limited to those between Indians and reclamation project beneficiaries. An upstream tribe with a large practicably irrigable acreage claim (involving diversion of substantial amounts of water) may be in conflict with a downstream tribe with an instream flow claim for salmon, or a downstream national park or wild and scenic river with an instream flow claim for recreation. Does the Supreme Court's decision in *Nevada v. United States*—by announcing that the courts won't blow the whistle on the executive branch's judgment calls—basically tell the United States to muddle through these situations as best it can? What about a situation where the United States does not make the most aggressive assertion of PIA as a matter of litigation strategy, given the unsettled state of the law? See Fort Mojave Indian Tribe v. United States, 32 Fed. Cl. 29 (1994), aff'd, 64 F.3d 677 (Fed. Cir. 1995). See generally Ann C. Juliano, Conflicted Justice: The Department of Justice's Conflict of Interest in Representing Native American Tribes, 37 Ga. L. Rev. 1307 (2003); Harold Shepherd, Conflict Comes Home to Roost! The Bureau of Reclamation and the Federal Indian Trust Responsibility, 31 Envtl. L. 901 (2001).

c. *Further Applications of Winters, Including the Special Problem of Indian Allotments*

We now take up another case that raises a host of Indian water right issues, but before we do so, a little background is necessary. It is outside our compass to explore in detail the history of federal Indian policy and issues of tribal sovereignty that are important to a full understanding of Indian water rights, but here's a thumbnail sketch: In the young United States, federal policy was to remove Indians to the Indian Territory of the West (what is now Oklahoma). Once the California Gold Rush triggered, in mid-nineteenth-century, a leap of non-Indian settlement across the continent, a movement arose to create Indian reservations. The aim was both to free desirable land for non-Indian settlement and to advance the policy of keeping Indians apart from the larger American culture and economy. Then, in a sharp shift in the latter part of the nineteenth century, Congress adopted a policy of assimilation, which sought to break down tribal culture and the reservation system, to integrate Indians into the mainstream of American social and economic life, and not coincidentally, to continue to free up desirable land for non-Indians.

A central initiative of this assimilationist movement was the allotment policy. Beginning on a tribe-by-tribe basis and culminating in the General Allotment Act of 1887 (24 Stat. 388, now codified at 25 U.S.C. §§ 331–358), it sought to replace traditional Indian communal ownership with grants of reservation lands to individual Indians. To protect the Indians from sharp practices, the land allotted to individual Indians was to be held by the U.S. in trust for a period of years (usually twenty-five) before full fee title was delivered to the allottee. With fee title came the ability of the allottee to alienate the land (which might lead to its passing out of Indian ownership through various means; e.g., foreclosure on loans secured by the land). In some cases, Congress indefinitely extended the trust period for individually allotted land. Lands not allotted to individual Indians were usually deemed surplus and opened to non-Indian purchase.

A half century later, around 1930, the assimilationist reform came to be widely regarded as an abject failure, and further efforts to allot and make Indian lands freely alienable were halted—but not before about 90 million acres of reservation land (out of 140 million reservation acres when the allotment policy was adopted in the 1880s) had passed into non-Indian ownership. Implementation of the allotment policy varied dramatically from reservation to reservation and region to region. Some reservations, particularly in the southwest, were relatively little affected, and have remained mostly in tribal communal ownership. Others now have very complex land patterns—a jumble of lands held by the United States in trust for the tribe, lands held in fee by the tribe, allotted lands held by the United States in trust for individual Indians or by individual Indians in fee, and lands held by non-Indians.

The allotment acts paid scant attention to water rights, not surprising considering the General Allotment Act preceded *Winters* by two decades. But the issues they raise for water rights allocation and regulation can be very important in the modern West. In its only reserved water rights decision between *Winters* in 1908 and Arizona v. California in 1963, the United States Supreme Court held that individual Indian allottees obtained some portion of the tribes' reserved rights by virtue of ownership of allotted lands. United States v. Powers, 305 U.S. 527, 531 (1939). Only in the last quarter century have the courts begun to address a host of challenging questions raised by the intersection of the allotment policy and *Winters* rights, such as the standard for quantification, how water rights are affected when allotted lands are transferred to non-Indians, and whether the reserved water right is defeasible for non-use after allotment and transfer.

COLVILLE CONFEDERATED TRIBES v. WALTON

United States Court of Appeals for the Ninth Circuit, 1981.
647 F.2d 42.

WRIGHT, CIRCUIT JUDGE:

* * * The Colville Confederated Tribes initiated this case a decade ago. They sought to enjoin Walton, non-Indian owner of allotted lands, from using surface and ground waters in the No Name Creek basin. The State of Washington intervened, asserting its authority to grant water permits on reservation lands, and the case was consolidated with a separate suit brought by the United States against Walton.

In 1871 the predecessors of the Colville Confederated Tribes had no treaty with the United States and no reservation. These Indians were contemporaneously described as "good farmers, [who] raise extensive crops, make good improvements, and own stocks of cattle and horses." [1871] Report of the Commissioner of Indian Affairs, 277.

After the Civil War, settlers had begun to encroach on Indian lands. The Farmer in charge at Fort Colville reported that violence was likely unless a reservation was established to protect Indian interests. In response to a request from the Commissioner of Indian Affairs, President Grant created the Colville Reservation. Executive Order of July 2, 1872, reprinted in 1 Kappler, Indian Affairs, Laws and Treaties, 915–16. (2d ed. 1904).[4] Twenty years later, the northern half of the reservation [approximately 1.5 million acres] was taken from the Indians and opened for entry and settlement.

In 1906, Congress ratified an agreement with the Colvilles that provided for distribution of reservation lands to the Indians pursuant to the General Allotment Act of 1887, 24 Stat. 388, and for disposition of the remainder by entry and settlement. The agreement was effectuated by Presidential proclamation in 1916.

In 1917, a row of seven allotments was created in the No Name Creek watershed. Walton, a non-Indian, now owns the middle three, numbers 525, 2371 and 894. He bought them in 1948 from an Indian, not a member of the Tribe, who had begun to irrigate the land by diverting water for 32 acres from No Name Creek. Walton immediately procured a permit from the state to irrigate 65 acres by diverting up to 1 cubic foot per second "subject to existing rights." He now irrigates 104 acres and uses additional water for domestic and stock water purposes.

The United States holds the remaining allotments in trust for the Colville Indians. Allotments 526 and 892 are north of Walton's property and allotments 901 and 903 are south. Allotments 892, 901 and 903 are held for heirs of the original allottees, but the Tribe has a long-term lease. Allotment 526 is beneficially owned by the Tribe. [A map of the area is found at 460 F. Supp. 1335—Eds.]

The No Name Creek is a spring-fed creek flowing south into Omak Lake, which has no outlet and is saline. The No Name hydrological system, consisting of an underground aquifer and the creek, is located entirely on the Colville Reservation.

The aquifer lies under the Indians' northern allotments and the northern tip of Walton's allotment, number 525. No Name Creek originates on the southern tip of the Indians' allotment number [892] and flows through Walton's allotments and the Indians' southern allotments.

Salmon and trout were traditional foods for the Colville Indians, but the salmon runs have been destroyed by dams on the Columbia River. In 1968, the Tribe, with the help of the Department of the Interior, introduced Lahontan cutthroat trout into Omak Lake. The species thrives in the lake's saline water, but needs fresh water to spawn. The

4. Indians who did not live on the land reserved for them were compelled to leave valuable tracts on which they had made extensive improvements and move to the reservation. Report of the Commissioner of Indian Affairs, 62 (1872).

Indians cultivated No Name Creek's lower reach to establish spawning grounds but irrigation use depleted the water flow during spawning season. The federal government has given the Indians fingerlings to maintain the stock of trout.

The trial court found that 1,000 acre feet per year of water were available in No Name Creek Basin in an average year. It calculated the quantity of the Colvilles' reserved water rights on the basis of irrigable acreage. The court excluded the northern-most allotment, number 526, because the evidence showed that it was formerly irrigated with the surface waters of Omak Creek, and the Tribe had not demonstrated that water to irrigate it was required from the No Name System.

The trial court determined the Indians had a reserved right to 666.4 acre feet per year of water from the No Name Creek Basin. It held that Walton was not entitled to share in the Colvilles' reserved water rights. The trial court found, however, that the Colvilles were irrigating only a portion of the irrigable acres included in its calculation.

Under the district court's findings, in an average year there are 333.6 acre feet per year of water not subject to the Indians' reserved right. There are an additional 237.6 acre feet per year of water to which the Indians have a reserved right, but which they are not currently using. This water is available for appropriation by non-Indians, subject to the Indians' superior right. The court held that Walton had a right to irrigate the 32 acres under irrigation at the time he acquired his land, with a priority date of the actual appropriation of water for that use.

The court also held that the Indians were potentially entitled to use water to propagate trout, but refused to award water for that purpose. It concluded that spawning was unnecessary because fingerlings were provided free by the federal government.

By post-trial motion, the Indians sought permission to use some of their irrigation water for trout spawning. The motion was granted and the Tribe has since pumped aquifer water from their wells into No Name Creek during spawning season.

Finally, the court decided that the state could regulate No Name water not reserved for Indian use.

Walton, the Tribe and the State appeal parts of the decision. Colville Confederated Tribes v. Walton, 460 F. Supp. 1320 (E.D. Wash. 1978).

III. THE TRIBE'S WATER RIGHTS

* * * We conclude that, when the Colville reservation was created, sufficient appurtenant water was reserved to permit irrigation of all practicably irrigable acreage on the reservation.

Providing for a land-based agrarian society, however, was not the only purpose for creating the reservation. The Colvilles traditionally fished for both salmon and trout. Like other Pacific Northwest Indians, fishing was of economic and religious importance to them. The Tribe's principal historic fishing grounds on the Columbia River have been destroyed by dams. The Indians have established replacement fishing grounds in Omak Lake by planting a non-indigenous trout.

We agree with the district court that preservation of the tribe's access to fishing grounds was one purpose for the creation of the Colville Reservation. Under the circumstances, we find an implied reservation of water from No Name Creek for the development and maintenance of replacement fishing grounds. * * *

The right to water to establish and maintain the Omak Lake Fishery includes the right to sufficient water to permit natural spawning of the trout. When the Tribe has a vested property right in reserved water, it may use it in any lawful manner. As a result, subsequent acts making the historically intended use of the water unnecessary [because the federal government provided hatchery fingerlings] do not divest the Tribe of the right to the water.

We recognize that open-ended water rights are a growing source of conflict and uncertainty in the West. Until their extent is determined, state-created water rights cannot be relied on by property owners. * * *

Resolution of the problem is found in quantifying reserved water rights, not in limiting their use. * * * Finally, we note that permitting the Indians to determine how to use reserved water is consistent with the general purpose for the creation of an Indian reservation providing a homeland for the survival and growth of the Indians and their way of life. * * *

IV. THE GENERAL ALLOTMENT ACT OF 1887

* * * In determining the nature of the right acquired by non-Indian purchasers [of allotted lands], we consider three aspects of an allottee's right to use reserved waters.

First, the extent of an Indian allottee's right is based on the number of irrigable acres he owns. If the allottee owns 10% of the irrigable acreage in the watershed, he is entitled to 10% of the water reserved for irrigation (i.e., a "ratable share"). This follows from the provision for an equal and just distribution of water needed for irrigation. [25 U.S.C. § 381.]

A non-Indian purchaser cannot acquire more extensive rights to reserved water than were held by the Indian seller. Thus, the purchaser's right is similarly limited by the number of irrigable acres he owns.

Second, the Indian allottee's right has a priority as of the date the reservation was created. This is the principal aspect of the right that renders it more valuable than the rights of competing water users, and therefore applies to the right acquired by a non-Indian purchaser. In the event there is insufficient water to satisfy all valid claims to reserved water, the amount available to each claimant should be reduced proportionately.

Third, the Indian allottee does not lose by non-use the right to a share of reserved water. This characteristic is not applicable to the right acquired by a non-Indian purchaser. The non-Indian successor acquires a right to water being appropriated by the Indian allottee at the time title passes. The non-Indian also acquires a right, with a date-of-reservation priority date, to water that he or she appropriates with reasonable diligence after the passage of title. If the full measure of the Indian's reserved water right is not acquired by this means and maintained by continued use, it is lost to the non-Indian successor.

The full quantity of water available to the Indian allottee thus may be conveyed to the non-Indian purchaser. There is no diminution in the right the Indian may convey. We think Congress would have intended, however, that the non-Indian purchaser, under no competitive disability vis-a-vis other water users, may not retain the right to that quantity of water despite non-use. * * *

V. STATE PERMITS

Finally, we consider Walton's claim to water rights based on state water permits. We hold that the state has no power to regulate water in the No Name System, and the permits are of no force and effect.

State regulatory authority over a tribal reservation may be barred either because it is pre-empted by federal law, or because it unlawfully infringes on the right of reservation Indians to self-government.

* * * A tribe retains the inherent power to exercise civil authority over the conduct of non-Indians on fee lands within its reservation when that conduct threatens or has some direct effect on the health and welfare of the tribe. This includes conduct that involves the tribe's water rights.

A water system is a unitary resource. The actions of one user have an immediate and direct effect on other users. The Colvilles' complaint in the district court alleged that the Waltons' appropriations from No Name Creek imperiled the agricultural use of downstream tribal lands and the trout fishery, among other things.

Regulation of water on a reservation is critical to the lifestyle of its residents and the development of its resources. Especially in arid and semi-arid regions of the West, water is the lifeblood of the community. Its regulation is an important sovereign power. * * * [W]e need not decide whether this power resides exclusively in the tribe or the federal government, or whether it may be exercised by them jointly * * *.

We hold that state regulation of water in the No Name System was pre-empted by the creation of the Colville Reservation. The geographic facts of this case make resolution of this issue somewhat easier than it otherwise might be. The No Name System is non-navigable and is entirely within the boundaries of the reservation. Although some of the water passes through lands now in non-Indian ownership, all of those lands are also entirely within the reservation boundaries.

* * * In a series of Acts culminating in the Desert Lands Act of 1877, ch. 107, 19 Stat. 377, Congress gave the states plenary control of

water on the public domain. Based on this and other legislation, the Supreme Court concluded that Congress almost invariably defers to state water law when it expressly considers water rights.

This deference is not applicable to water use on a federal reservation, at least where such use has no impact off the reservation. * * * Tribal or federal control of No Name waters will have no impact on state water rights off the reservation.

Thus, we conclude that Walton's state permits are of no force and effect. * * *

Notes and Questions

1. On remand, the district court found that Walton had acted with due diligence in using water for 104 of his 170 acres. On appeal, the Ninth Circuit held that Walton's *Winters* rights could not exceed those of his non-Indian predecessors. Because Walton's non-Indian predecessors had for more than twenty years irrigated only 30 acres, reserved rights to use water for more than 30 acres had been lost by non-use. Colville Confederated Tribes v. Walton, 752 F.2d 397 (9th Cir. 1985). The Ninth Circuit relied on Washington state law cases defining standards of non-use in reaching that result. Why should Washington law have any application to the question of whether federal reserved rights have been lost?[32]

2. Further guidance for solving the Rubik's cube of allotment water rights was provided by the Ninth Circuit in United States v. Anderson, 736 F.2d 1358 (9th Cir. 1984), where the results went like this: Reserved water rights for lands that had never left Indian ownership (even if they had been allotted to individual Indians) all retained a priority date of the creation of the reservation. Water rights for lands that had been allotted to individual Indians, had passed into non-Indian ownership, and then been reacquired by the tribe, were reserved rights with a priority as of the date of creation of the reservation unless the reserved water right had been lost by non-use while the land was in non-Indian ownership; in that case, they had a priority as of the date of reacquisition. If reservation lands had been opened to homesteading and passed directly to non-Indians, and then were reacquired by the tribe, they carried with them reserved water rights with a priority as of the date of reacquisition plus whatever state law rights the homesteader had acquired and maintained. See Cohen's Handbook of Federal Indian Law § 19.03[8][c] (Nell Newton et al. eds., 2005).

3. Assume that in some wet years a surplus of water is available for use in the No Name System. How could Walton obtain rights to that water? State law? Federal law? Tribal law? (Tribal water codes are considered further below.) On the question of whether state water law has any place on Indian reservations, compare the 1981 Ninth Circuit decision in *Walton* with United States v. Anderson, 736 F.2d 1358 (9th Cir. 1984). The watershed in *Anderson*, unlike that in *Walton*, was not wholly contained within the reservation. Distinguishing *Walton*, the

---

32. The Wyoming courts are still grappling with *Walton* claims by non-Indian successors of Indian allotments. See In re Big Horn Adjudication, 48 P.3d 1040 (Wyo. 2002).

Ninth Circuit in *Anderson* held that the State of Washington had jurisdiction over non-Indian water users on the reservation, regardless of whether their water rights were obtained under state law or as transferee of Indian reserved water rights. See 736 F.2d at 1365–66.[33]

4. If non-Indians may succeed to Indian allottees' reserved rights, may non-Indian homesteaders who gain title to former reservation land that was "surplused" in the allotment era also claim such rights? The argument goes like this: The original, expansive Indian reservation included reserved water rights. Those rights remained appurtenant to the land once it was taken from the Indians and thrown open for homesteading, and passed with the land to homesteaders, as an exception to the severance doctrine of California Oregon Power Co. v. Beaver Portland Cement, supra p. 352. Such claims, dubbed "super-*Walton* rights," have not been well received; in fact, they sparked rare unanimity of opposition among state, tribal and federal interests, and were rejected by the Wyoming Supreme Court in a later phase of the *Big Horn* litigation, 899 P.2d 848 (1995). See generally Cohen's Handbook of Federal Indian Law § 19.03[8][b] (Nell Newton et al. eds., 2005).

Non–PIA–Based Indian Water Rights—Scope/Quantity/Quality

5. The court in *Walton* recognized a reserved water right to maintain the Omak Lake fishery as a replacement for the destroyed Columbia River fishery. Is this stretching the reserved rights doctrine too far? Should the remedy for any tribal rights in the lost Columbia River fishery simply be cash compensation, which the Indians could, if they chose (and could find willing sellers), use to substitute an Omak Lake fishery by purchasing needed water rights from appropriators in the No Name System? Recall that the Supreme Court of Wyoming did not recognize an independent water right for fishery in the *Big Horn* decision. But see United States v. Adair, 723 F.2d 1394 (9th Cir. 1983), which held that the Klamath Tribe in Oregon had a reserved water right for instream flows to support hunting and fishing with a priority date of "time immemorial." (A senior right, indeed!) See generally Michael C. Blumm, Reserved Water Rights, in 3 Waters and Water Rights § 37.0(c)(3), at 37–39 to 37–42 (R. Beck ed., repl. vol. 2004).

6. The 1985 decision in *Walton* (see Note 1 above) also addressed how reserved rights based on different purposes are to be accommodated with one another. The dependable amount of water in the No Name System was only 1,000 acre feet per year. Even after his *Winters* claim was cut down because of the non-use by his non-Indian predecessors, Walton was still entitled to 120 acre-feet per year (using a water duty of 4 acre-feet per acre). Indian allottees were entitled to 666.4 acre-feet per year and the Omak Lake fishery was awarded 350 acre-feet per year. Because the total of quantified rights exceeded the amount of available water, the Ninth Circuit ruled that the deficit should be shared pro rata, explaining, "since all parties have a priority date as of the creation of the Reservation, each should bear a proportionate share of any adjustment required by shortages of water." 752 F.2d at 405. In a subsequent case, the Ninth Circuit determined that the

---

33. Recall that the Montana Supreme Court has ruled that the state may not issue new water right permits to non-Indi- ans on an Indian reservation until the Indian reserved rights have been quantified. See supra p. 941 n. 15.

priority date for fisheries water was time immemorial (see preceding paragraph), and thus that water right should be satisfied before agricultural water rights. Joint Board of Control of the Flathead, Mission & Jocko Irr. Dist. v. United States, 832 F.2d 1127, 1131 (9th Cir. 1987); see also United States v. Adair, 723 F.2d 1394, 1416 n.25 (9th Cir. 1983).

7.   As decisions like *Walton* show, a number of tribes are being awarded rights to instream flow where it can be shown that their reservation purpose including protecting fishing as a mainstay of tribal culture. Similar arguments are made for water rights necessary to maintain habitats for hunting. Although non-consumptive in nature, Indian reserved rights for instream flows carry the same power to limit upstream diversions as do the wilderness and other federal non-Indian reserved rights previously addressed. See supra pp. 930–934. For an argument that an earlier Supreme Court decision, United States v. Winans (discussed briefly supra p. 908) creates a tribal right to water to preserve an aboriginal way of life not tied to beneficial ownership of land, see Cohen's Handbook of Federal Indian Law § 19.02 (Nell Newton et al. eds., 2005).

8.   A particularly interesting example involves tribal claims to water to support fisheries to realize tribal rights to salmon. Many Pacific Northwest tribes have a treaty right to fish at their "usual and accustomed places" off their reservations in common with all citizens of the region. Does the treaty support an instream flow water right at such places under *Winters* sufficient to sustain a salmon run? Does it support a broader water right, in all waters that are essential habitat or biologically necessary for various fish species to which the treaty right attaches? May a tribe in Idaho claim an instream flow in the downstream state of Washington sufficient to allow the salmon to migrate to the ocean and back? May a Washington tribe with a salmon treaty right claim an instream flow in salmon spawning grounds in tributaries in Idaho and Montana? All salmon spawning grounds, or just some of them? Which ones? Lots of interesting questions, and no answers in the reported cases to date. See Michael C. Blumm, Dale D. Goble, Judith V. Royster & Mary Christina Wood, Judicial Termination of Treaty Water Rights: The Snake River Case, 36 Idaho L.Rev. 449 (2000). In 2004 the Nez Perce Tribe reached a landmark settlement of its water rights in the Snake River Basin Adjudication which also addressed water rights of farmers and ranchers and the needs of endangered fish in the basin. Congress approved the settlement in November 2004, Pub. L. No. 108–447, 118 Stat. 2809. The Idaho Legislature and the Tribe approved it shortly thereafter. Among other things, the complicated settlement (summarized at http://www.doi.gov/news/040515a) gives the tribe instream flow rights on about 170 streams in the Salmon and Clearwater River Basins, to be held by the state for the tribe to protect anadromous fish.

9.   How are fishery water rights to be quantified? By the minimum necessary to protect the fishery, following United States v. New Mexico? How is the "minimum" measured? By the need to keep the fish from becoming endangered? Or to generate sufficient quantities of fish to satisfy tribal subsistence needs? Or to sustain a tribal commercial fishery and provide the Indians with a "moderate living"? In United States v. Adair, 723 F.2d 1394, 1414–15 (9th Cir. 1983), the court said the standard was the amount of water "necessary to support its hunting and fishing rights as

currently exercised to maintain the livelihood of Tribe members, not as these rights once were exercised" at the time of the Treaty. See also United States v. Adair, 187 F. Supp. 2d 1273 (D. Or. 2002) (tribal water right must be sufficient to sustain wetland and forest habitats upon which tribes relied, with possible reduction to a lesser amount sufficient to provide tribes a "moderate living"), vacated as unripe sub nom. United States v. Braren, 338 F.3d 971 (9th Cir. 2003) (staying further proceedings pending completion of the state court general stream adjudication). For a narrow view of a Tribe's claim to a reserved right to water arising from a treaty right to fish, see Skokomish Indian Tribe v. United States, 401 F.3d 979 (9th Cir. 2005) (en banc), relevant part vacated on rehearing, 410 F.3d 506 (9th Cir. 2005).

10.   Some treaties protect a right to hunt game. Do such rights support a water right for game animals? In what water bodies? All sources of water that wildlife may use? Should water consumption by deer or elk be considered de minimis and not worth addressing in a general stream adjudication? Or should the federal reserved right to support hunting embrace a quantity of water sufficient to maintain a healthy habitat for game (which might include enough water sustain an ecosystem)?

11.   Federal reserved water rights may be protected from a material degradation in water quality as a result of actions of junior appropriators upstream. See United States v. Gila Valley Irr. Dist., 117 F.3d 425 (9th Cir. 1997) aff'g 920 F.Supp. 1444 (D. Ariz. 1996), discussed briefly in Chapter 10, infra p. 1014. See generally Michael Blumm & Brett Swift, The Indian Treaty Piscary Profit and Habitat Protection in the Pacific Northwest: A Property Rights Approach, 69 U. Colo. L. Rev. 407 (1998); Cohen's Handbook of Federal Indian Law § 19.03[9] (Nell Newton et al. eds., 2005); Amy Choyce Allison, Extending Winters to Water Quality: Allowing Groundwater for Hatcheries, 77 Wash. L. Rev. 1193 (2002).

Tribal Water Codes and the Water Rights of Indian Allottees

A number of tribal governments regulate water use on their reservations through administrative regimes that have grown in breadth and complexity.[1] The extent to which tribal water codes may regulate water

1. A survey in the mid–1990s by a lawyer in the Department of the Interior's Solicitor's office showed that about three dozen tribes have water codes or are working on them. See Scott Bergstrom, Status of Tribal Water Use and Allocation Codes (1994) (unpublished). See generally Cohen's Handbook of Federal Indian Law § 19.04[4] (Nell Newton et al. eds., 2005); Thomas Clayton, The Policy Choices Tribes Face When Deciding Whether to Enact a Water Code, 17 Am. Indian L. Rev. 523 (1992). Most tribes adopted constitutions in the 1930s under the aegis of the Bureau of Indian Affairs, which was implementing the Indian Reorganization Act, 25 U.S.C. §§ 461 et seq., that ended the allotment era. These constitutions typically required the Secretary of the Interior to approve tribal ordinances such as tribal water codes.

In the last few decades, with the encouragement of the federal government, most tribes deleted the Secretarial approval provision from their constitutions. This means most tribes may adopt tribal water codes and apply them to non-Indians within the limits of federal law, without prior approval of the Secretary. But some tribal constitutions still retain the secretarial approval provision. Since 1975, a Secretarial moratorium on approving tribal water codes has been in effect while the Department of the Interior struggled unsuccessfully to come up with standards for reviewing such codes. See 42 Fed. Reg. 14,885 (1977); 46 Fed. Reg. 944 (1981). Since the moratorium was adopted the Secretary has approved constitutional amendments deleting the secretarial approval requirement altogether, which frees such tribes to adopt water codes.

use by non-Indians is not completely clear. *Walton* recognizes exclusive tribal authority over non-Indian water use on watercourses found wholly with the reservation, but *United States v. Anderson* upheld state regulatory jurisdiction over on-reservation non-Indian water users where the watercourse was not contained within the reservation, leaving open questions of how state and tribal regulatory jurisdiction may interface.

In 1977 the Yakima (now Yakama) Tribe in Washington adopted a code that purported to regulate all water and water users (including non-Indians) found on the reservation. Among other things, the Code gives priority in descending order to tribal use, various classes of tribal members' use, and, finally, to non-Yakama Indians' use. The State of Washington and on-reservation non-Indian water users challenged the tribe's authority to regulate waters in excess of the reserved water rights of the tribe, and eventually prevailed. See Holly v. Confederated Tribes & Bands of Yakima Indian Nation, 655 F.Supp. 557, 558–59 (E.D. Wash. 1985), aff'd sub nom. Holly v. Totus, 812 F.2d 714 (9th Cir. 1987). Applying Supreme Court precedent developed outside the context of water, the trial court determined that the tribe had no regulatory jurisdiction over non-members of the tribe on non-tribal lands, except where the non-members' conduct has a direct effect on the political integrity, economic security or health and welfare of the tribe. Finding no such impacts arising from the use of water outside the scope of the tribe's reserved water rights, the court held that the water code could not be applied to non-members. For general background on the complex (and, from just about every perspective, unsatisfactory) principles the Supreme Court has evolved to govern tribal jurisdiction over non-Indians, see William Canby, American Indian Law in a Nutshell 199–211 (4th ed. 2004); Cohen's Handbook of Federal Indian Law §§ 6.01 et seq. (Nell Newton et al. eds., 2005); Brendale v. Confederated Tribes & Bands of the Yakima Nation, 492 U.S. 408 (1989).

Although the most controversial aspect of tribal water codes concerns regulation of non-Indians or non-tribal members, difficult questions can be raised by tribal regulation of water use by Indian allottees who have their own reserved water rights. The Interior Solicitor addressed these issues in a 1995 Opinion (M–36982—Entitlement to Water under the Southern Arizona Water Rights Settlement Act, March 30, 1995). The Opinion concluded that Indian allottees have a right to a "just and equal distribution" of water for irrigation purposes, quoting a section of the General Allotment Act, 25 U.S.C. § 381, and suggested that it might be a property right protected by the Constitution as well as a statutory one. On the other hand, the Solicitor concluded, the tribe has broad regulatory power over reservation water resources, including those to which allottees have rights. The Opinion also pointed out that tribal authority is constrained by a provision in the Indian Civil Rights Act, 25 U.S.C. § 1302(B), which prohibits tribes from taking any private property for public use without just compensation. The Opinion emphasized that the principles applicable to the distribution of water between tribes and Indian allottees do not affect the standard for quantification of such rights in the first instance. With the understatement that this is a "complex area of law," the Solicitor concluded that it is "inaccurate to speak of either tribal governments or agricultural allottees as having plenary rights in water vis-a-vis each other. Agricultural allottees have rights tribes cannot wholly defeat; at the same time, tribes have regulatory authority over reservation water use from which allottees are not immune."

Notes and Questions

1. Is concurrent tribal and state regulation workable? Is it different in kind or degree from the system of concurrent state and federal regulation that applies to water use in most parts of the United States? A concern sometimes expressed is that non-Indians who may be regulated by tribes don't have a political voice in reservation governments. Is that any different from a resident of Nevada owning and irrigating farmland in California under the supervision of the California State Water Resources Control Board?[2]

2. Both federal statutes and federal common law limit the authority of tribal governments vis-a-vis non-Indians. The Indian Civil Rights Act provides, for example, that "[n]o Indian tribe exercising the powers of self-government shall * * * deny to any person within its jurisdiction the equal protection of its laws or deprive any person of liberty or property without due process of law." 25 U.S.C. § 1302(B). State-law-created water rights would likely be considered property for the purposes of application of the Act. On the other hand, the Supreme Court has held generally that these limits are enforceable only in tribal, not federal court. Santa Clara Pueblo v. Martinez, 436 U.S. 49 (1978); see also Grey v. United States, 21 Cl. Ct. 285 (1990) (Indian allottees with reserved rights must seek enforcement of those rights from the tribe).

3. See generally Cohen's Handbook of Federal Indian Law § 19.03[8] (Nell Newton et al. eds., 2005); Judith Royster, A Primer on Indian Water Rights: More Questions than Answers, 30 Tulsa L.J. 61, 88–91 (1994); Richard Collins, Indian Allotment Water Rights, 20 Land & Water L. Rev. 421 (1985); David Getches, Water Rights on Indian Allotments, 26 S.D. L. Rev. 405 (1981).

Indian Rights Under *Winters*—Some General Questions[3]

As a matter of general policy, should the United States compensate non-Indians whose exercise of state law water rights is limited as a result of honoring *Winters* rights? In considering this question, suppose an Indian reservation was created in 1860. Are the equities different

---

2. We will spare you the additional complexity of tribal government authority over Indians who are members of other tribes; see, e.g., Duro v. Reina, 495 U.S. 676 (1990); William Canby, American Indian Law in a Nutshell 199–201 (4th ed. 2004).

3. Interstate water compacts apportioning waters that traverse Indian reservations typically provide that nothing in the compact is deemed to affect the obligations of the United States to Indians, and some provide that water required to satisfy Indian rights shall be charged against the allocation made to the state where the Indian lands are located. See Cohen's Handbook of Federal Indian Law § 19.06, at p. 1226 (Nell Newton et al. eds., 2005).

among non-Indians who first appropriated water in the area (a) prior to 1908; (b) between 1908 and 1963; and (c) after 1963? Why are these dates arguably relevant in weighing the equities? In its 1973 final report, the National Water Commission recommended compensation for non-Indians who appropriated water prior to 1963, if harmed by the recognition of Indian water rights. See Water Policies for the Future 785 (1973) (Recommendation no. 14–6). Congress has not adopted any generic legislation on the subject.

Is the uncertainty in state-created water rights resulting from the *Winters* doctrine any different from the uncertainty that results from (a) the riparian rights doctrine; (b) unexercised riparian rights in relatively arid states that recognize both appropriative and riparian water rights (cf. *Long Valley*, supra pp. 374–379); (c) uncertainties concerning the right of appropriators to recapture waste or return flows without compensation to a downstream appropriator which had established rights to those flows (cf. Arizona Public Service v. Long, supra p. 201); (d) the public trust doctrine (cf. National Audubon Society v. Superior Court, supra p. 610); or (e) uncertainties created in many jurisdictions by the relationship between groundwater and surface water where the two are hydrologically related (see supra pp. 454–468)? Note that all these other uncertainties are created under state law.

The impact of the Endangered Species Act (ESA, considered in Chapter 6 at pp. 651–668) on the exercise of Indian water rights has attracted considerable attention in recent years. The operation of water projects constructed primarily to benefit non-Indians has often impaired the health of aquatic and riparian habitat to such an extent that species dependent on that habitat have been listed as threatened or endangered under the ESA. Suppose that Indians are now determined to have rights to water superior to those water projects, but in order to realize those rights, new storage and delivery facilities have to be constructed, with federal funds or requiring federal regulatory approval. Section 7 of the ESA requires a consultation before such projects can be implemented, and generally speaking they cannot be implemented if jeopardy to the listed species would result. The regulations implementing the ESA generally provide that, for purposes of section 7 consultation, the proposed action being consulted on must take into account the effects of existing, ongoing action. See, e.g, 50 C.F.R. § 402.02 (definition of "effects of the action"). This creates a conundrum: The ongoing exercise of water rights junior to the Indians' rights in many situations has used up the species' protective cushion, and resulted in the species' listing under the ESA. The listing, in turn, thwarts the construction of projects intended to enable the Indians to realize their senior water rights. This result has been much criticized; see, e.g., Mary Cristina Wood, Fulfilling the Executive's Trust Responsibilities Toward Native Nations on Environmental Issues: A Partial Critique of the Clinton' Administration's Promise and Performance, 25 Envtl. L. 733 (1995); Timothy Vollmann, The Endangered Species Act and Indian Water Rights, 11 Nat. Res. & Environment (Fall 1996); Brian A. Schmidt, Reconciling Section 7 of the

Endangered Species Act with Native American Reserved Water Rights, 18 Stan. Envtl. L.J. 109 (1999). Cohen's Handbook of Federal Indian Law § 19.06, at pp. 1221–23 (Nell Newton et al. eds., 2005). Are the critics right that this unfairly penalizes the Indians? What is the solution to this problem, assuming protection of endangered species remains national policy? The Ninth Circuit has held that the Bureau of Reclamation has the authority to honor senior Indian water rights before serving those who have contracted with it for irrigation water. Klamath Water Users Protective Ass'n v. Patterson, 204 F.3d 1206 (9th Cir. 1999).

Indian Water Rights—A Sample Problem

To bring together numerous threads of Indian reserved rights, to underscore the complexity of the subject, and to set the stage for consideration of negotiated settlements of Indian reserved rights claims, consider the following hypothetical, loosely based on the situation of the Lummi Indian Nation located on Puget Sound north of Seattle: The Lummi Reservation was created by treaty in 1855 as a homeland for the Indians. Hunting and fishing were mentioned in the treaty, as well as the need to train the Indians in agricultural and industrial arts. About 10% of the reservation land is held by the United States in trust for the tribe, most of that purchased from non-Indians who had acquired it after the reservation was allotted early in the twentieth century. The United States holds about 60% of the reservation land in trust for individual Indians. The remaining 30% is owned by non-Indians, a legacy of the allotment era.

The Lummi River, which traverses the reservation, is now usually dry as a result of upstream, non-Indian diversions. Two distinct aquifers underlay the reservation, one wholly within its boundaries and the other extending beyond its borders. Both aquifers recharge, but both are also susceptible to saltwater intrusion as they are pumped down. The safe-yield of both aquifers is a matter of considerable debate. Pumping from wells on subdivisions built by non-Indians on 4% of the reservation land account for about half of the total reservation water use. The other half of reservation water use is tribal, with about half of that (or one quarter of the total) used in a tribal fish hatchery. The state issues permits for some of the non-Indian wells; others are small enough to qualify for exemption from state law. Non–Indian population growth and associated new pumping on the reservation have led to growing fears of saltwater intrusion and conflict with tribal plans for economic expansion.

What claims might the Tribe, its Indian allottees (and/or the United States on behalf of the tribe and its allottees) assert, in what amounts, against whom, and in what forum(s)? For the district court's cut at some of the issues, see United States v. Washington, 375 F. Supp. 2d 1050 (W.D.Wash. 2005).

d. The Cutting Edge: Modern Efforts to Settle Indian Water Rights

The emphasis in Indian water rights in the modern era is not in litigation. The daunting length and expense of general stream adjudications have taxed all participants. The many uncertainties and variables discussed above make the outcome in individual cases something of a crapshoot, despite tribes' credible claims to senior water rights in most situations. From the tribes' perspective, a victory in court might prove hollow. The *Big Horn* litigation is illustrative. The Wyoming Supreme Court's 1988 decision was, in one sense, a dramatic win for the tribes— they emerged with a decreed right of an early priority date for approximately 500,000 acre-feet per year from surface water sources on the reservation. Although the court subsumed other uses in the agriculturally quantified water right, and restricted marketing, the decree still embraced a lot of water. There was one big problem, however; the tribes had no way to readily use it. As of this writing, nearly two decades later, the tribes are no closer to realizing an economic benefit from their decreed water rights than before the adjudication. To enlarge an existing Bureau of Indian Affairs irrigation project on the reservation would take many millions of dollars, and the state, tribes and the federal government have not yet agreed on a formula to share the costs. (Discussions among the state, tribes, and the federal government were ongoing in the spring of 2006 to try to find a way to use the tribe's water rights to reestablish a fishery on the reservation, to provide improved drinking water systems, and to upgrade antiquated irrigation works that benefit non-Indians as well as Indians; as is typical, the more difficult issues revolved around who would pay.) The *Big Horn* saga is a somewhat bitter reminder that court decrees do not necessarily translate into "wet" water.

Powerful motivations for settlement exist among all stakeholders. Non–Indians want to find a way to avoid losing water as the Indian rights are recognized and confirmed. States want to protect and enhance their authority over water uses within their border. Indian tribes are often motivated to seek settlement because it offers them a way to achieve things they cannot obtain through litigation; especially, dollars to build water storage and delivery systems to convert their paper claims into wet water and, sometimes, to gain express authority to lease water off-reservation for cash or other considerations. Environmental factors can be a boost to tribal water rights for fish (as in the Pacific Northwest), or can interfere with tribal plans for projects to bring wet water to reservations, as in the Animas/La Plata Project in southwestern Colorado (where for years endangered species concerns helped stymie implementation of a negotiated settlement of Indian claims).

As noted earlier, relatively few adjudications of Indian water rights have been completed. (This is an important reason why there are practically no examples of non-Indians actually losing water to Indians as a result of application of the *Winters* doctrine.) Instead, major efforts have been made in the last quarter-century to settle Indian water rights claims by negotiation. Successful negotiations usually lead to agreements that are ratified by Congress (and sometimes by state legislatures as well) and then decreed by courts exercising jurisdiction over adjudications. These settlements typically protect—indeed, they may effectively adjudicate—state law water rights held by non-Indian farmers and cities, as well as quantifying Indian and other federal water rights. The principal players in these negotiations are usually the tribes, federal and state governments, and major appropriators under state law.

The Western Water Policy Review Advisory Commission pointed out in its final report:

> [N]egotiated settlements are not an easy solution. They rely on the willingness of parties to negotiate. Delays and political maneuvering are often considerable. Settlements generally must be ratified by the Congress and, in most instances, need judicial recognition to be effective. Most importantly, settlements generally rely on large infusions of federal funds to provide additional water for tribes without damaging the rights of other water users. Federal budgetary concerns will probably restrict funding of new water settlements and project-based solutions. Accordingly, future negotiators will have to be even more creative.

Water in the West: Challenge for the Next Century 3–49 (1998). In the 1980s the Department of the Interior evolved a policy of appointing federal negotiating teams anytime there was a genuine prospect of settlement. These teams operate under guidelines the Department has published in the Federal Register. See 55 Fed. Reg. 9223 (1990).

Amid the litigation and negotiation comes an occasional call for comprehensive legislation to reduce the uncertainty, such as by legislating a quantification standard for Indian reserved rights that limits them to an amount sufficient to meet reasonable present needs and uses. See Belinda Orem, Paleface, Redskin, and the Great White Chiefs In Washington: Drawing Battlelines Over Western Water Rights, 17 San Diego L. Rev. 449 (1980). Other commentators argue congressional quantification is not a palliative. See Charles DuMars & Helen Ingram, Congressional Quantification of Indian Reserved Water Rights: A Definitive Solution or a Mirage?, 20 Nat. Resources J. 17 (1980). One could question the power of Congress to legislate a standard for quantifying Indian rights without raising takings and compensation issues, because these rights may be said to have vested with the creation of Indian reservations a century or more ago. From a somewhat different direction comes a suggestion to decide Indian water rights cases on the basis of equitable apportionment, Robert Abrams, The Big Horn Indian Water Rights Adjudication: A Battle for the Legal Imagination, 43 Okla. L. Rev. 71 (1990), even though the Supreme Court rejected that suggestion by Arizona in Arizona v. California, supra p. 910. For a related approach stressing the economic interests of the tribes and non-Indian water users, see Michael Moore, Native American Water Rights: Efficiency and Fairness, 29 Nat. Resources J. 763 (1989).

Some Issues in Negotiated Settlements
of Reserved Rights Claims

Indian water settlements are rather like snowflakes; they resemble each other but are all different in the details.[4] Well over a dozen Indian water rights settlements have been ratified by Congress in the past two decades.[5] Many of these are in Arizona and Montana[6], although they are also found in California, Colorado, Florida, Idaho, Nevada, New Mexico, Oregon and Utah. Common features of these settlements are (a) a quantification of Indian water rights in a way that does not displace existing non-Indian uses; and (b) creation of a tribal development trust fund, funded mostly or exclusively with dollars from the federal treasury, and often used to build plumbing systems allowing the delivery of some "wet" water to the reservation. Some of the settlements involve some form of marketing of the Indian water, often to a specific transferee (such as a nearby city).

The usual starting point in negotiations is to focus on the quantity of water claimed by Indians through the PIA standard. This can be a battle of the experts, as calculations of PIA can vary rather dramatically depending upon assumptions used. The next step is to consider a host of variables, such as the extent to which the Indian claims, if realized, may displace non-Indian junior uses; the ability of the Indians to use the water claimed on the reservation (and the amount and cost of delivery and distribution systems to enable such use to take place); the interest of the Indians in leasing some of their water to non-Indians; and the availability of federal funds.

Tribal rights recognized in these settlements range from 1500 acre-feet annually[7] to the most recent and the biggest, 655,000 acre-feet to the Gila River Indian Community in Arizona.[8] Federal contributions to tribal economic development funds ranged from $3 million to $125 million. State contributions tend to be zero or a comparatively small

4. See generally Cohen's Handbook of Federal Indian Law § 19.05[2] (Nell Newton et al. eds., 2005) ; n.284 lists 18 settlement acts approved by Congress between 1978 and 2004. Several useful sourcebooks, descriptions of settlements and commentary on the negotiation process are now available. See, e.g., Bonnie G. Colby, John E. Thorson & d Sarah Britton, Negotiating Tribal Water Rights—Fulfilling Promises in the Arid West (2005); Daniel C. McCool, Native Waters: Contemporary Indian Water Settlements and the Second Treaty Era (2002); Peter Sly, Reserved Rights Settlement Manual (Island Press, 1988).

5. Settlements are not entirely a modern phenomenon. Negotiated decrees involving Indian water rights date back to 1910. See Cohen's Handbook of Federal Indian Law § 19.05[2] (Nell Newton et al. eds., 2005).

6. One might ask why Arizona and Montana have been particularly productive of settlement negotiations. In both states massive stream adjudications have long been underway, and the supreme courts in both states have indicated that they will conscientiously apply *Winters* and its progeny. See, e.g., State ex rel. Greely v. Confederated Salish & Kootenai Tribes of the Flathead Reservation, 712 P.2d 754 (1985). In Arizona the federally subsidized Central Arizona Project in effect created a new supply of unallocated water to lubricate settlement discussions, as well as a delivery system to bring the water to or near several reservations. The Montana legislature created a Reserved Water Rights Commission in 1979 to negotiate settlements with all the tribes in Montana, creating an institutional mechanism that removed the negotiation process somewhat from elected politicians.

7. The Yavapai–Prescott Tribe in Arizona, 108 Stat. 4526 (1994).

8. Pub. L. No. 108–451 (2004). The Tohono O'odham Nation south of Tucson is receives 37,800 acre-feet under this legislation.

sum; the largest state contribution in any settlement was $3 million. Thus it seems the burden of compensating the Indians and protecting the non-Indians from being stripped of their water falls almost exclusively on the United States treasury. Is this appropriate?

Does the emergence of marketing provisions and economic development funds as features of Indian water settlements suggest that the impact of the *Winters* doctrine is becoming more financial than anything else? Is there anything wrong with that? In this connection, it might be reasonable to assume that non-Indian interests are willing to recognize larger amounts of water to tribes in these settlements, if the tribes are willing to agree to lease some or all of it back to them.

B. BEYOND RESERVED RIGHTS: OTHER MEANS TO PROTECT FEDERAL INTERESTS IN WATER

1. WATER RIGHTS BASED ON STATE LAW

The Supreme Court said in United States v. New Mexico, supra, that when no federal reserved water right exists to support a desired federal use (such as where water is "only valuable for a secondary use of [a] federal reservation" rather than "necessary to fulfill the very purposes for which a federal reservation was created"), the inference is that "the United States would acquire water in the same manner as any other public or private appropriator." 438 U.S. at 702 (1978). This section will explore what that last clause means. At first blush, the matter seems straightforward: The U.S. would look exclusively to state law for water rights. Federal land on a watercourse in a jurisdiction recognizing riparian rights would have the same rights as its riparian neighbors. In prior appropriation jurisdictions, the U.S. could appropriate water just like all other users. Federal rights to groundwater would also be governed by state law.[9]

But the matter may not be so simple. While the states wield considerable influence in the federal legislature,[10] the converse is not so true. In the politically delicate area of water rights, some states feel, and respond to, pressure to discriminate against federal agencies, especially if doing so would advantage state water users. The United States may also have water needs—for example, to protect endangered species—that may not recognized under state law. These factors may compromise the ability of the United States to obtain, under state law, rights to water it needs. Moreover, as we shall see in the last section of this chapter, the U.S. may be able to control how water is used without perfecting water rights, through its ownership of large tracts of land.

9. Of course, the United States government could, like other sovereign governmental entities, also acquire needed water rights by condemnation or eminent domain.

10. See, e.g, Herbert Wechsler, The Political Safeguards of Federalism—The Role of the States in Composition and Selection of the National Government, 54 Colum. L. Rev. 543 (1954); Larry D. Kramer, Putting the Politics Back into the Political Safeguards of Federalism, 100 Colum. L.Rev. 215 (2000).

The California Supreme Court has addressed the right of the U.S. as landowner to claim riparian water rights under state law. In re Water of Hallett Creek Stream System, 44 Cal.3d 448, 243 Cal.Rptr. 887, 749 P.2d 324 (1988).[11] The United States claimed, on behalf of the U.S. Forest Service, unexercised riparian water rights under state law to be exercised in the future for the "secondary" use of "wildlife enhancement," a use not embraced within the federal reserved water right under the *New Mexico* decision. The court noted that the United States had not heretofore claimed such rights on its reserved lands in California, and the claims could have "far-reaching consequences" because the federal government owned nearly half the land in the Golden State.

The state resisted, arguing, among other things, that Congress had, in nineteenth century federal statutes like the Desert Land Act (as construed in California Oregon Power Co. v. Beaver Portland Cement Co., supra p. 352), "voluntary relinquished all proprietary claims to the western waters, except for reserved water rights." The court rejected the argument, pointing out that the U.S. Supreme Court had there construed the federal statutes as leaving it up to each state "to determine for itself" what water law doctrine to follow. The California Supreme Court then construed its prior decisions like Lux v. Haggin, supra p. 342, as recognizing that "riparian rights exist in federal lands located in California as surely as they inhere in private lands. We have never in California predicated the recognition of riparian water rights on the identity of the riparian owner, and we perceive no principled reason to do so now." 44 Cal.3d at 467, 749 P.2d at 334.

The court went on to address whether unexercised riparian rights held by the U.S. as landowner were subordinate to the rights of appropriators under state law. The court construed the Desert Land Act as answering that question in the affirmative for ordinary public domain lands. But, reversing the lower courts, it held that the Desert Land Act did not apply on federally reserved lands, and thus its provision "subordinating water rights in public domain lands to the vested rights of appropriators established under state law has no effect on riparian rights in federally held reserved lands." 749 P.2d at 336. Therefore, the court concluded, the state law riparian water rights of the U.S. on its reserved national forest lands in California are as fully immune from defeasance as the riparian rights of a private owner. Id. (The federal government's unexercised riparian rights are subject to being subordinated to other rights through a general stream adjudication, however, just like the private owners' riparian rights were in the *Long Valley* case, supra p. 347.)

If the California Supreme Court had come out the opposite way on this point—holding that under California law the U.S. had no riparian water rights on its reserved land—would the U.S. Supreme Court have

---

11. Chapter 4 contains a discussion of California's hybrid system of prior appropriation and riparian rights at pp. 340–349, 374–379. Chapter 5 contains a discussion of California's similar hybrid system, involving on-land and off-land uses of groundwater, under its system of correlative rights, at pp. 429–433, 506–520.

had jurisdiction to take the case and reverse the result? In this connection, consider that, under the *Hallett Creek* decision, state law riparian rights held by the U.S. on its unreserved public domain lands along California streams may in some circumstances be subordinated to state law appropriative rights, even though riparian rights held by persons who acquire those lands from the federal government may not be so subordinated. Is there any legal justification for this discrimination against the federal government in water rights matters? Although there is constitutional authority for limiting the ability of the states to discriminate against the United States in certain matters (see, e.g., Lawrence Tribe, American Constitutional Law 1225 (3d. ed. 2000)), it seems that neither the United States nor its agencies are "persons" protected against state discrimination by the equal protection clause.

STATE v. MORROS

Supreme Court of Nevada, 1988.
104 Nev. 709, 766 P.2d 263.

Per Curiam:

[At issue were State Engineer's decisions on applications by the federal Bureau of Land Management (BLM) for permits to appropriate water under state law for use on BLM-managed federal public land.] * * *

The Blue Lake Application

The Blue Lake application is for a water right to the waters of Blue Lake *in situ,* in place as a natural body of water. The BLM manages the land surrounding the lake and desires this water right to assure maintenance of the pool of Blue Lake for public recreation and fishery purposes. The [Nevada State] Board of Agriculture contends that Nevada water law absolutely requires a physical diversion of water to obtain a water right, and that the district court therefore erred in affirming the state engineer's grant of a right to the water of Blue Lake *in situ.*

[After analyzing Nevada statutes, the court concluded that state law no longer requires a physical diversion in order to appropriate water.] * * * The Board of Agriculture also contends that the grant of a water right for Blue Lake to a United States agency is against the public interest in Nevada and that pursuant to NRS 533.370(3) the state engineer should have denied the application on that basis.[3] We see no threat to the public interest * * *. The BLM manages the land surrounding the lake for recreation and seeks a nonconsumptive water right that will not reduce the amount of water presently available for other uses. Livestock and wildlife retain access to the water of Blue Lake under the district court's order. * * *

---

3. NRS 533.370(3) provides, in pertinent part, that where a proposed appropriation "threatens to prove detrimental to the public interest, the state engineer shall reject the application and refuse to issue the permit asked for."

THE STOCK AND WILDLIFE WATERING PERMIT APPLICATIONS

The district court relied on this court's holding in Prosole v. Steamboat Canal Co., 37 Nev. 154, 140 P. 720 (1914), as authority for reversing the state engineer's grant of permits to the BLM and United States Forest Service to develop new water sources for stock and wildlife watering. In *Prosole,* this court held that the person who "applies the water to the soil", for a beneficial purpose, is the actual appropriator and the owner of the water right, even if someone else, such as a canal company, diverts the water from its natural course.

The BLM and Forest Service intend to provide the water requested in the applications to the livestock of grazing permit holders on federal range lands. Wildlife would also have access to the water. The district court reasoned that since the federal agencies owned no livestock, the United States could not put the water to beneficial use. Rather, the court stated, owners of livestock actually put water appropriated for stockwatering to beneficial use. The district court concluded that therefore under *Prosole* the United States could not appropriate water for stockwatering. The district court applied the same reasoning to wildlife watering. The court noted that the United States does not own the wildlife which is to receive water, because no one "owns" animals in the wild.

We conclude that the district court applied *Prosole* in an excessively rigid fashion. The proposed new water sources are dedicated to providing water to livestock and wildlife. These are beneficial uses of water. Nevada law and longstanding custom recognize stockwatering as a beneficial use of water. * * *

In managing federal grazing lands, the United States acts in a proprietary capacity. The new water sources covered by the applications at issue will permit better use of areas of the public range where grazing is limited by the lack of watering places, a problem recognized by this court. Congress has mandated development of water sources for livestock and wildlife as a component of the federal land management program. See 43 U.S.C. §§ 1751(b) & 1901 to 1904. Thus, the United States acts in its proprietary capacity as a landowner when federal agencies seek to appropriate water under state law for livestock and wildlife watering. Although the United States does not own the livestock and wildlife, it owns the land on which the water is to be put to beneficial use. In addition, the United States benefits as a landowner from the development of new water sources on federal land.

The United States is recognized as a "person" for the purpose of water appropriation in Nevada. NRS 533.010.[4] The district court correctly stated that the United States "is to be treated as a person * * * it is not to be feared, given preferential treatment and certainly not discriminated against." Recently, the California Supreme Court held that the

---

4. NRS 533.010 provides: "As used in this chapter, 'person' includes the United States and this state."

United States could not be denied the same riparian water rights for national forest lands that private riparian landowners enjoy under California water law. *Hallett Creek* supports the principle that the United States is entitled to equal treatment under state water law.

The Board of Agriculture argues that, in addition to the reasons given by the district court, the engineer erred in granting water rights for stock and wildlife watering to the United States because ownership of those water rights by the United States is against the public interest. The Board of Agriculture states that once the water is subject to federal control it will not be available for other uses at a later date. While this may be true, it is inherent in the prior appropriation system of water rights, and we cannot discriminate against the United States on that basis.

Under NRS 533.010, therefore, applications by United States agencies to appropriate water for application to beneficial uses pursuant to their land management functions must be treated on an equal basis with applications by private landowners. Although the United States owns no livestock and does not "own" wildlife, it owns land and may appropriate water for application to beneficial uses on its land. The district court erred in deciding that the United States could not obtain water rights for stockwatering and wildlife watering, and the portion of its order denying those applications is vacated. * * *

Notes and Questions

1. For a similar result, see DeKay v. U.S. Fish & Wildlife Service, 524 N.W.2d 855 (S.D. 1994) (USFWS may appropriate natural springflow under state law to maintain marshes and other waterfowl habitat). Would the result in *Morros* have been the same if the Nevada statute had not defined the U.S. as a "person" for purposes of the state prior appropriation system? Suppose the Nevada state legislature responded to this decision by enacting a statute that only a state agency can appropriate instream flows under state law, even on federal lands. Some states have such laws. See generally Lori Potter, The Public's Role in the Acquisition and Enforcement of Instream Flows, 23 Land & Water L. Rev. 419 (1988).

2. Suppose the state legislature simply did not recognize instream flow appropriations under state law, by anyone. What can BLM do in those states if it wants to protect instream flows or lake levels on federal lands for recreational and fishery purposes? See subsections 2–3, further below.

3. It is unclear whether the second part of *Morros*, that the BLM could hold a water right for stockwatering on federal lands, is still good law in Nevada. A 1995 Nevada statute, enacted in response to new federal rules governing livestock grazing on federal lands, provided that permits to appropriate water for livestock purposes on public lands can only be issued to those "legally entitled to place livestock on the public lands." Nev. Rev. Stat. § 533.503. The Nevada Attorney General advised the State Engineer that this prohibited the issuance of new water appropriations for livestock watering to BLM, and the State Engineer denied nine pending BLM applications in 1997. Upon challenge by the U.S., the Nevada Supreme Court

reversed, interpreting the statute to allow BLM to appropriate water for livestock watering, reasoning that it could issue itself a grazing lease for its own land and then apply for water, and that seemed an unnecessary step. United States v. State Engineer, 27 P.3d 51 (Nev. 2001). After this decision, the state legislature amended the statute to add the criterion that the applicant must have a "legal or proprietary interest in the livestock." Nev. Rev. Stat. § 533.503(1)(a)(1) (2003).

4. The Arizona legislature took the campaign against federal land managers one step further. In 1995 it enacted legislation allowing only ranchers, and not federal land managing agencies like the BLM or the U.S. Forest Service, to hold livestock water appropriations on federal land. Moreover, Arizona sought to apply this rule retroactively—to strip the BLM and the Forest Service of livestock watering appropriations they had previously perfected when state law did not discriminate against the federal government.[1] The Arizona Supreme Court struck down this feature of the law as a violation of the state constitution's due process clause. San Carlos Apache Tribe v. Superior Court, 972 P.2d 179, 189 (Ariz. 1999) ("[l]egislation may not disturb vested substantive rights by retroactively changing the law that applies to completed events"). In Phelps Dodge Corp. v. Ariz. Dept. of Water Resources, 118 P.3d 1110 (Ariz. App. 2005), the court upheld a decision of the state Department of Water Resources awarding the U.S. Forest Service instream flow water rights under state law for fish, wildlife and recreation, rejecting the argument that Arizona water law still required a diversion. The challengers did not question the Forest Service's authority to hold the state law water right.

5. In neither the Nevada nor the Arizona situation did the United States rely on the Supremacy Clause of the U.S. Constitution. One reason for this is that the BLM had adopted a regulation providing that rights to use water for livestock water on public land "shall be acquired, perfected, maintained and administered under the substantive and procedural laws of the State within which such land is located." 43 C.F.R. § 4120.3–9. The regulation went on to provide: "To the extent allowed by the law of the State within which the land is located, any such water right shall be acquired, perfected, maintained and administered in the name of the United States." Id. Suppose this regulation were repealed. Could the U.S. make the argument that, because Congress had authorized BLM to permit livestock grazing on federal lands it manages, the Supremacy Clause trumps state legislation that interferes with this federally authorized use? Cf. Johnson v. Maryland, 254 U.S. 51 (1920) (state licensing requirement invalid as applied to federal employee acting within the scope of federal responsibility). The Supremacy Clause argument is further explored in the next subsection on "federal non-reserved rights," and the relationship between grazing permits and water rights is further explored in the final subsection on controlling access to federal land.

6. States show varying degrees of hostility to water claims by the United States. In State v. United States, 996 P.2d 806 (Idaho 2000), the

---

1. The discrimination was clearly revealed by the fact that the new Arizona law applied only to federal government agen- cies; i.e., it allowed the state to perfect livestock water rights on state-owned lands in the name of the state.

court rejected the U.S. Fish & Wildlife Service's application for an appropriation right under state law for a National Wildlife Refuge, on the ground Idaho law requires a diversion, except for special situations not applicable there. On the other hand, in 1983 California accommodated federal agencies by amending its water code to give them until July 1, 1984, to claim an appropriation of water on reserved federal lands as of right, with a priority as of the first use, so long as (a) the first use was prior to the date of the U.S. Supreme Court's decision in the *New Mexico* case, and (b) the use is "for secondary purposes, other than those for which the federal reservation was created, provided that the priority of right does not impair any existing water use." Cal. Water Code §§ 1227–1227.4.

7. In United States v. Morros, 268 F.3d 695 (9th Cir. 2001), the U.S. Department of Energy filed applications with the state to appropriate water for use in its efforts to build and operate a high level nuclear waste repository at Yucca Mountain. The State Engineer rejected the applications because a state statute made it "unlawful for any person or governmental entity to store high-level radioactive waste in Nevada." The United States sued in federal court, arguing the Nevada statute was preempted by federal law. (It also filed a protective notice of appeal in state court from the State Engineer's decision and moved immediately to stay the action pending resolution of the federal case.) The district court refused to decide the merits, instead abstaining under the principle of *Colorado River* (see supra p. 943). The Ninth Circuit reversed and remanded, finding abstention inappropriate because, among other things, this was "not a comprehensive stream adjudication case to which the McCarran Amendment applies." 268 F.3d at 707.

8. For a discussion of possible state-based Indian water rights, see Barton H. Thompson, Jr., State, Pueblo, and Aboriginal Water Rights, in Indian Water Rights Conference (Stan. L. Sch. & Native American Rights Fund, Sept. 9–10, 1994).

2. FEDERAL NON–RESERVED RIGHTS

Beyond federal reserved water rights and water rights obtained under state substantive and procedural law, is there a "third way" the federal government can satisfy its water needs? In 1978, shortly after the Supreme Court's decision in *New Mexico*, Interior Department Solicitor Leo Krulitz issued an opinion which claimed the existence of "federal non-reserved water rights." As its label suggested, this federal right did not arise from a reservation, but rather from actual use of water to carry out a federal program or purpose. In that respect the right mimicked state law appropriative rights, for its foundation was the application of the water to a beneficial use. But this right was not constrained by how state law defined beneficial use, nor was it subject to state procedural requirements. The Krulitz opinion provided a basis for the U.S. Forest Service or the BLM to claim an instream flow for habitat protection where the *New Mexico* test for a federal reserved right could not be satisfied, and where the state that did not recognize appropriations of instream flows.

The basic legal argument to support federal non-reserved rights goes like this: Congress has delegated its broad power under the Property Clause to federal land managing agencies like the U.S. Forest Service and the Bureau of Land Management. When these agencies act to fulfill their statutorily prescribed federal land management responsibilities, they have, unless Congress provides otherwise, sufficient authority to meet these responsibilities. Therefore, if the requirements of state water law are an obstacle to effective exercise of the federal power, the Supremacy Clause empowers the federal agencies to override state water law.

The Krulitz opinion was not warmly received. See, e.g., Richard Simms, National Water Policy in the Wake of United States v. New Mexico, 20 Nat. Resources J. 1 (1980); Barry Vaughan, Federal Nonreserved Water Rights, 48 U. Chi. L. Rev. 758 (1981); A. Dan Tarlock & Sally Fairfax, Federal Proprietary Rights For Western Energy Development: An Analysis of a Red Herring, 3 J. Energy L. & Pol'y 1 (1982). The most trenchant objection to the Krulitz opinion was not the power it claimed, but that it had not persuasively demonstrated that Congress had actually delegated this power to federal land managing agencies in particular statutes. A key issue was how to construe the water disclaimer in the Federal Land Policy and Management Act, which authorizes a wide variety of uses of the federal lands (such as livestock grazing, fish and wildlife, and recreation). That disclaimer (§ 701(g)-(h); 90 Stat. 2744) is quoted in the discussion of BLM reserved rights supra pp. 934–935.

The Krulitz claim that BLM could claim non-reserved rights on federal public lands was not long-lived[46] A new Solicitor of the Interior rejected it in what came to be known as the Coldiron opinion. See 88 Interior Dec. 1055 (1981). Shortly thereafter the Department of Justice's Office of Legal Counsel addressed the matter in a lengthy opinion signed by Assistant Attorney General Theodore Olson. While Olson found that Congress had not, in FLPMA, given BLM the authority to preempt state water law, he left no doubt that Congress could do so—the key question was "not generally whether Congress has the power to establish federal rights to unappropriated water, but whether it has exercised that power." Federal "Non–Reserved" Water Rights, 6 Op. Off. Legal Counsel 328, 362 (1982), discussed briefly at footnote 1, supra p. 926.

In 2000, Congress adopted a version of a "federal non-reserved right" (though it did not label it as such) in expanding the Great Sand Dunes National Monument in Colorado and converting it to a national park. Scientists had learned that the sand dunes ecosystem was dependent on continuing water flows, and so water became an important issue in the Congress. The legislation authorized the Secretary of the Interior to secure a water right to protect the dunes, to be appropriated through state law processes and in accordance with the state law priority system.

46. The same Solicitor's Opinion also dealt at length with federal reserved water rights of various Interior Department agencies; that portion of the Opinion, discussed earlier in this chapter, has had more staying power.

But the right is to be defined and quantified according to the standard set in the federal statute—namely, whatever unappropriated surface and groundwater is shown to be necessary to protect the dunes ecosystem. And the water right will be held in the name of the National Park Service, even though state law requires a state agency to hold an instream flow water right. See 16 U.S.C. § 410hhh–7(b)(2). For a full discussion and an argument that this "third way" approach has great potential for addressing the legitimate needs of both the states and the federal land management agencies in future federal land conservation designations, see John D. Leshy, Water Rights for New Federal Land Conservation Programs: A Turn-of-the-Century Evaluation, 4 U. Denver Water L. Rev. 273–89 (2001). See also Michael Cianci, Jr., The New National Defense Water Right—An Alternative to Federal Reserved Water Rights for Military Installations, 48 Air Force L. Rev. 159 (2000) (describing Nevada's recognition of a water right for Nellis Air Force Base that incorporated seniority and some flexibility while giving the state the ability to permit and to some extent manage the right); Judith V. Royster, *Winters* in the East: Tribal Reserved Rights to Water in Riparian States, 25 Wm. & Mary Envtl. L. & Pol'y Rev. 168, 101–02 (2000) (discussing the Seminole Indian Compact, 25 U.S.C. § 1772, a congressionally approved settlement of Seminole Tribe's claims which gave the tribe a percentage of water from specified sources in perpetuity in exchange for its complying with certain aspects of the state water law system).

3. CONTROLLING WATER BY REGULATING ACCESS TO FEDERAL LAND

In some circumstances, the federal government may be able to protect water resources found on federal land by controlling land access rather than by claiming water rights. This was the approach used in § 8 of the 1993 Colorado Wilderness Act, 107 Stat. 756, 762. The national forest lands it designated as wilderness were located in headwaters areas with "few, if any, opportunities for diversion, storage, or other uses of water occurring outside such lands that would adversely affect the wilderness values of such lands." Id. § 8(a)(1)(A). Therefore Congress chose to "protect the wilderness values of the lands designated * * * by means other than those based on a Federal reserved water right." Id. § 8(a)(2). The Act said the executive shall not "fund, assist, authorize, or [otherwise permit] * * * the development * * * or enlargement of any water resource facility within the [wilderness] areas" designated by the Act. Id. § 8(c). It protected, within carefully defined limits, access to maintain existing water resource facilities located on the lands. Id. § 8(d)-(f).

Federal law generally gives federal land managing agencies broad power to permit or deny the use of federal lands for water development purposes. The right-of-way provisions of the Federal Land Policy and Management Act, for example, fairly bristle with environmental regulatory power, giving both the BLM and the Forest Service wide power to grant, deny, or condition access to federal lands for various purposes, including water development. 43 U.S.C. §§ 1761–71. It may not be very problematic, politically or legally, to exercise this regulatory authority to prevent *new* non-federal water developments where new, or transfers of existing, appropriations under state law are involved. See, e.g., Washoe County v. United States, 319 F.3d 1320 (Fed. Cir. 2003) (Interior Department's refusal to issue a right-of-way permit across federal lands for a pipeline to facilitate the movement of water secured by a state law water right from a rural to an urban area was not a taking of the water right, because the U.S. neither physically appropriated the water right nor denied the applicant meaningful access to water, and the government had no obligation to assist the holder of the water right in putting the right to its most profitable use).

But it can be controversial for a federal land managing agency to regulate access to federal land in such a way as to limit existing (often longstanding) uses supported by state water rights. The most prominent modern instance has been the so-called "bypass flows" controversy in Colorado. Many years ago non-federal water developers had built, under term-limited Forest Service permits, dams and diversion facilities on national forest land in Colorado's Front Range to supply downstream towns and farms. The developers obtained permanent water appropriations under state law (subject to maintaining beneficial use). When these federal permits expired in the 1970s, the Forest Service, responding to changing public values and a more sophisticated knowledge of environmental health, announced it would renew them only if some flows were restored to natural streams below the diversion facilities. Providing such "bypass flows" reduced the amount of the diversion by as much as 50–80% in dry years, according to the permittees. To the Forest Service, this was environmentally sound land management, and well within its legal authority. To the holders of state law appropriations/federal permits, it was confiscation of their state water rights without compensation.

On the law, the Forest Service had the better of it. See, e.g., Wyoming Wildlife Federation v. U.S. Forest Service, 792 F.2d 981 (10th Cir. 1986); Nevada Land Action Ass'n v. U.S. Forest Service, 8 F.3d 713, 719 (9th Cir. 1993) (upholding federal authority to consider water flows in making decisions about the use of federal lands). Had the Forest Service been able to show that the flows were required to meet the standards of the Clean Water Act or the Endangered Species Act, the case would have been even more compelling. County of Okanogan v. Nat'l Marine Fisheries Serv., 347 F.3d 1081 (9th Cir. 2003) (upholding the exercise of authority reserved in federal rights-of-way permits for irrigation ditches to limit stream diversions to protect endangered species); see also Chapter 6 supra pp. 651–668; cf. P.U.D. No. 1 v. Washington Dept. of Ecology, 511 U.S. 700, 720–21 (1994) (Clean Water Act authorizes regulating flow levels to protect water quality, and such regulation may limit the exercise of water rights obtained under state law).

But politics took a different course. After much brouhaha Congress created a seven-member commission to examine the problem. The Republican leadership in Congress named four members; the Democratic minority and Clinton Administration named three. Predictably, the commission split along party (and developer versus environmentalist) lines, with the majority contesting both the lawfulness and the wisdom of using federal land management authority to protect streamflow on federal lands. Report of the Federal Water Rights Task Force Created Pursuant to Section 389(d)(3) of Pub. L. 104–127 (1997). Meanwhile, state and local water interests insisted that any new settlements of Forest Service reserved water rights claims contain a "poison pill" that would rescind the settlement if the Forest Service requires additional bypass flows on any national forest covered by the agreement. Not surprisingly, the attitudes of the Clinton and Bush Administrations differed markedly, with the former often exercising authority to protect water in renewing permits for private water diversion and storage facilities on national forest lands, and the latter generally shrinking from doing so, and repealing a provision of the Forest Service Handbook (§ 2509.25) that called for requiring bypass flows. The courts may end up resolving the matter in particular cases. See Trout Unlimited v. U.S. Dep't of Agriculture, 320 F. Supp. 2d 1090 (D. Colo. 2004) (Forest Service decision *not* to require bypass flows as a condition to renewal of a right-of-way for a reservoir on federal land is arbitrary and capricious because it does not minimize damage to fish and wildlife habitat and protect the environment as required by the Federal Land Policy & Management Act). Despite the war of words and policies, negotiations have led to some compromise over bypass flows in particular situations. See generally Janet Neuman & Michael Blumm, Water for National Forests: The Bypass Flow Report and the Great Divide in Western Water Law, 18 Stan. Envtl. L.J. 3 (1999); David Gillian, Will There Be Water for the National Forests?, 69 U. Colo. L. Rev. 533 (1998); Thomas Snodgrass, Comment: Bypass Flow Requirements and the Question of Forest Service Authority, 70 U. Colo. L. Rev. 641 (1999); Robert V. Trout, Whose Water? Meeting New Federal Water Demands in Prior Appropriation States, 50 Rocky Mt. Min. L. Inst. 22–1 (2004).

What is the right policy answer here? State law water rights do not insulate appropriators from the need to comply with other laws, such as zoning and environmental statutes. Moreover, the existence of state law water rights, no matter how longstanding, typically do not provide a defense against the application of new zoning or environmental quality standards to the uses made of that water, even if the effect is to reduce water diversions and use. Should federal land permitting requirements be regarded as any different? If federal permission to use federal land is granted for a specific term, but the permittee then perfects a state law water right without a term limit, should the state law water right in effect make that use of federal land permanent? Does it make any difference that the permittee may have a reasonable expectation, grounded in long tolerant federal policy, that it could continue to operate the

project as it always had? That the permittee had a substantial investment in the water project?

Potential collisions between federal land use controls and state law
water rights can be found in many contexts. In the Northern Great
Plains, for example, the U.S. Fish & Wildlife Service has acquired
easements from farmers to preserve so-called "prairie potholes," wetland
areas vital for migratory birds. The easements typically contain a commitment by the farmer to maintain the lands as a waterfowl production
area "by not draining or permitting the draining of any surface water by
ditching or any other means." Assuming these acquired easements do
not create federal reserved rights, and assuming that state law does not
acknowledge *in situ* water rights for such purposes, and/or does not
coordinate groundwater and surface water doctrines, how can the United
States protect itself if the farmer subject to such an easement obtains a
state permit and begins pumping groundwater and draining the wetlands? In United States v. Vesterso, 828 F.2d 1234 (8th Cir. 1987) the
court held that federal law made unlawful the construction of ditches
that drained wetlands protected by federal easements, rejecting the
argument that state water law—pursuant to which the State Water
Commission had permitted the construction to proceed—should control.

If a state law appropriation can no longer be exercised as it custom-
arily has been because of a new but otherwise lawful federal land use
restriction, does the appropriator have a remedy? The U.S. sued to
enjoin Hunter from grazing and watering his cattle within the boundaries of Death Valley, a unit of the National Park System, without a
permit from the National Park Service, which managed the area. One of
Hunter's defenses was that, prior to the area being made part of the
National Park System, he had perfected a valid state law water right at
springs and a stream on the federal land, and these water rights entitled
him to continue to graze cattle there. The Ninth Circuit acknowledged
he had valid water rights, but rejected the defense. It did say, however,
that he "should be allowed a right of way over [Monument] lands to
divert the water * * * elsewhere if he is able;" otherwise, his water right
would simply lapse for non-use. Hunter v. United States, 388 F.2d 148,
154–55 n.4 (9th Cir. 1967). See also W. Douglas Kari, Groundwater
Rights on Public Land in California, 35 Hastings L.J. 1007, 1034–36
(1984). Ranchers with state law water rights to support livestock grazing
on federal land still occasionally argue that their water rights give them
authority over federal land uses, but these claims do not get sympathetic
treatment in the courts. See, e.g., Diamond Bar Cattle Co. v. United
States, 168 F.3d 1209 (10th Cir. 1999); Gardner v. Stager, 103 F.3d 886
(9th Cir. 1996); Colvin Cattle Co. v. United States, 67 Fed. Cl. 568
(2005). A few questions about whether a state law water right has been
taken by the denial of a permit to graze are still in litigation. See Hage v.
United States, 51 Fed. Cl. 570 (2002).

For other examples of how federal agencies might protect water
resources beyond asserting reserved rights, see Eric T. Freyfogle, Repairing the Waters of the National Parks: Notes on a Long Term Strategy,

74 Denv. U. L. Rev. 815, 832–37 (1997) (urging the Park Service, for example, to become involved in water transfers, beneficial use enforcement, water quality and other questions involving state water rights when the parks might benefit); Teresa Rice, Beyond Reserved Rights: Water Resource Protection for the Public Lands, 28 Idaho L. Rev. 715 (1992).

Chapter 10

WATER QUALITY

In one short chapter, we can only begin to investigate the myriad of issues raised by water pollution and the major United States laws designed to control it. A longer, more detailed study is necessarily left for courses in environmental law.

A casebook on water resources, nevertheless, would be incomplete without discussion of water quality. Issues of water quality and water quantity are inherently intertwined. How much, if any, pollution should be discharged into the nation's waters is a question of water allocation much like those discussed in the previous chapters. If the government permits a sewage treatment plant to discharge untreated wastes into a waterway, it is allocating the affected water to waste assimilation rather than to conflicting uses such as domestic consumption or swimming.

Diversions of water for out-of-stream uses also can affect water quality to the detriment of other uses. Irrigation, for example, can leach salt, selenium, and other contaminants into the nation's waters. Significant diversions from rivers and other waterways can increase the salinity of remaining water either by concentrating salt naturally found in the water or, in the case of coastal estuaries, by promoting intrusion of salt water from the ocean.

The law, however, treats water quality quite differently from other allocative decisions. Separate laws and doctrines are generally used to resolve quality and quantity issues. Water pollution, moreover, is far more closely regulated than water consumption. Although administrative oversight is increasing, states still allocate water among competing consumers largely through the traditional water rights systems discussed in Chapters 2 through 5. Pollution discharges, on the other hand, are closely regulated by federal and state environmental agencies acting under detailed water quality statutes.

The differences in legal treatment of quality and quantity issues are diminishing. Due to increasing demands on the nation's waters, pressure is mounting to more closely regulate all water use—not just pollution discharges. Current approaches to regulating water quality thus provide an interesting insight into the potential future management of water diversions and off-stream use. Regulatory approaches currently used to minimize water pollution, for example, may prove useful in regulating the total amount of water that is withdrawn from the country's waterways and aquifers or in dictating the efficiency with which the United States uses water.

A. SURFACE WATER POLLUTION

Surface water is naturally impure—contaminated by such natural pollutants as salt, decaying vegetation, and animal wastes. For centuries, however, the human race has helped pollution along. The pollutants discharged into the nation's waters are diverse. Traditionally concern has centered on potentially harmful bacteria and solids, on nutrients like phosphorous or nitrogen which can stimulate algae growth and accelerate the aging (or "eutrophication") of lakes and reservoirs, and on organic wastes which deplete the oxygen needed by fish and other aquatic life. Recent attention also has focused on discharges of heavy metals and toxic chemicals which can pose acute problems even in small quantities.

There are a number of ways of evaluating the current quality of the nation's waters. In 1997, the national Environmental Protection Agency (EPA) for the first (and so-far only) time attempted a comprehensive review of the state of the nation's surface waters. EPA looked at seven indicators of watershed condition (e.g., pollution levels and fish consumption advisories) and eight indicators of vulnerability (e.g., potential for urban or agricultural runoff). For the nearly three-quarters of the nation's watersheds that EPA was able to assess, only 16% of the watersheds enjoyed good water quality, 36% suffered moderate water quality problems, and another 21% had serious problems. One in every 14 watersheds were vulnerable to further degradation, primarily from urban and rural runoff. U.S. EPA, Index of Watershed Indicators (Oct. 1997).

Up until 2000, EPA also published a biannual report on state water quality information.[1] States unfortunately did not survey all of their waterways during each 2–year reporting cycle. In 2000, for example, states assessed only 19% of all stream miles and 43% of lakes, ponds, and reservoirs. The biannual report, however, provided useful insight into whether waterways were meeting the water quality standards that states themselves set for the waterways. In 2000, 39% of the river miles, 46% of the lake acreage, 78% of the Great Lakes shoreline miles, and 51% of the estuary area had impaired water quality (defined as unable to support one or more of their designated uses). All of these numbers, with the exception of the Great Lakes percentage, were up from just four years earlier. Even though the federal Clean Water Act sought to ensure that all national waterways were fishable and swimable by 1978, over a third

---

1. Since 2000, EPA has provided the state water quality information on-line at http://www.epa.gov. EPA, however, no long- er publishes a report summarizing the data at a national level.

of the assessed river miles failed to fully support aquatic life, and 28% failed to fully support swimming. In 2000, states issued almost 3000 fish consumption advisories warning people not to eat fish from local water bodies. See U.S. EPA, National Water Quality Inventory: 2000 Report to Congress (2002).

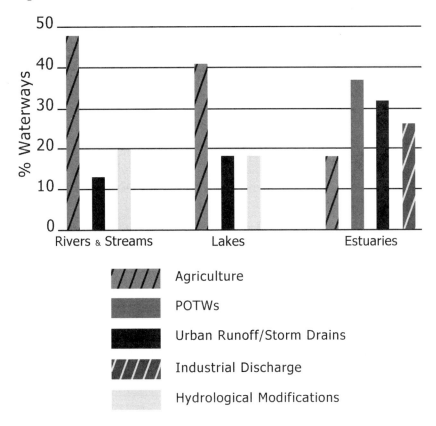

Figure 10–1

Leading U.S. Sources of Water Quality Impairment (2000)

(by percentage of impaired waterways affected)

Source: United States Environmental Protection Agency, National Water Quality Inventory: 2000 Report to Congress, 2002.

Figure 10–1 shows the leading sources of water quality impairment in the United States as of 2000. The national Clean Water Act divides sources of surface water pollution somewhat artificially between "point sources" like factories, which discharge wastes into waters through a confined path such as a pipe or channel, and "nonpoint sources" like most agricultural runoff. When Congress passed the Clean Water Act in

1970, pollution from municipal sewage plants (often called "publicly owned treatment works" or "POTWs") and from industrial factories got the most attention. Reflecting the success of the Clean Water Act's regulation of these point sources, POTWs and industrial facilities no longer rank among the top five contributors of pollution to the nation's rivers, streams, and lakes. In the case of estuaries, however, POTWs remain the major source of pollution, and industrial facilities rank third.

Nonpoint sources are today of greater concern than most point sources—largely because nonpoint sources have not been subject to the same degree of regulation over the last quarter century. As Figure 10–1 shows, agriculture is the major source of pollution in both the nation's rivers and lakes, discharging most of the sediment, nitrogen, phosphorous, and oxygen-consuming organic material. Indeed, agriculture is a source of pollution for over twice as many river miles and lake acreage as the next most important pollution source. Urban runoff from parking lots, streets, and other impervious surfaces, along with storm drains, are a major source of pollution to all types of waterways in the United States.

Highlighting the close connection between quality and quantity, the second most important cause of quality impairment in the nation's rivers and lakes is hydrologic modification of the waterways. Such modifications include reductions and modifications of instream flows, the construction and operation of dams, and the channelization and dredging of waterways.

1. THE COMMON LAW APPROACH

Until well into the twentieth century, courts played the primary role in regulating surface water pollution. In most cases, courts addressed pollution claims through the traditional rules of private or public nuisance. Plaintiffs typically had to be either owners of property affected by the pollution (in the case of private nuisance) or government officials (in the case of public nuisance). In deciding whether particular pollution posed a nuisance, most courts used a reasonableness test and balanced the harm against the economic and social value of the polluting activity. See, e.g., New York v. New Jersey, 256 U.S. 296 (1921) (public nuisance); Taylor Bay Protective Ass'n v. Ruckelshaus, 687 F.Supp. 1319, 1325–29 (E.D. Ark. 1988), aff'd, 884 F.2d 1073 (8th Cir. 1989) (public nuisance); Columbia River Fishermen's Protective Union v. City of St. Helens, 160 Or. 654, 87 P.2d 195 (1939) (private nuisance); Conley v. Amalgamated Sugar Co., 74 Idaho 416, 263 P.2d 705 (1953) (private nuisance); Wilmore v. Chain O'Mines, Inc., 96 Colo. 319, 44 P.2d 1024 (1934) (private nuisance).

Where pollution harmed downstream water uses, water users also could bring claims under their state's water law.[2] In the eastern United

---

2. Indeed pollution disputes served as a principal crucible for the development of the riparian doctrine in the eastern United States. See, e.g., Snow v. Parsons, supra page 42 (dealing with the discharge of spent bark from tanneries).

States, downstream water users often argued that the riparian doctrine barred all pollution that materially damaged their uses, whether or not the pollution was "unreasonable." In Borough of Westville v. Whitney Home Builders, Inc., 40 N.J.Super. 62, 122 A.2d 233 (1956), for example, a city sued a local subdivision for discharging treated sewage into a small stream that emptied into a pond in the city's principal park. The city argued that the natural flow riparian doctrine should apply, entitling the city to a flow of water "in its natural state, not sensibly diminished in quantity or impaired in quality." The court, however, ruled that "the interests of a changing, complex, and technologically mushrooming society" called for application of the reasonable use rule and concluded that the upstream discharge of sewage was not unreasonable:

> [T]he people of Westville cannot be expected to be happy over the continuous presence of sewage effluent in their park pond, no matter how relatively pure. However, * * * it cannot be said that the discharge of treated sewage effluent into a running stream is per se an unreasonable riparian use in today's civilization. Under the reasonable use approach we are called upon to counterweigh social uses and harms. * * * Only two citizens of Westville testified as witnesses, one the borough clerk and the other the borough attorney. Neither gave any evidence of actually lessened use of the park by the citizenry in a recreational sense. * * * On the other scale of the balance, we find the defendant sewerage company, certified as a public utility pursuant to legislation, serving a function plainly essential to the public health * * *.

122 A.2d at 243.

In the west, water users invoked the prior appropriation doctrine to challenge upstream appropriators who polluted the waters. Junior appropriators could not so pollute a waterway as to impair downstream seniors' uses of the water (although the courts permitted some pollution). See, e.g., Atchison v. Peterson, 87 U.S. (20 Wall.) 507, 514–16 (1874); Game & Fish Comm'n v. Farmers Irrig. Co., 162 Colo. 301, 426 P.2d 562 (1967); Wright v. Best, 19 Cal.2d 368, 121 P.2d 702 (1942). A downstream junior, by contrast, took a waterway "subject to its condition as fixed by prior appropriators." State v. California Packing Corp., 105 Utah 182, 141 P.2d 386 (1943). Just as appropriation doctrine proscribes waste and other unreasonable use, however, it also prohibited seniors from *unreasonably* polluting the waters. See id. at 388; Suffolk Gold Mining & Milling Co. v. San Miguel Consol. Mining & Milling Co., 9 Colo.App. 407, 48 P. 828, 832 (1897) (wherever possible, senior is "obligated to so use the water that subsequent locators might * * * receive the balance of the stream unpolluted").

Notes and Questions

1. Can an appropriator complain if *diversions* by upstream juniors lower water quality? In Antioch v. Williams Irrig. Dist., 188 Cal. 451, 205 P. 688 (1922), the California Supreme Court held that an appropriator could

not insist that subsequent appropriators leave a sufficient instream flow to avoid salt water intrusion from San Francisco Bay. The Court admitted that a downstream appropriator would "clearly" be entitled to an injunction if upstream discharges of pollution led to similar contamination. But "all" the defendants in *Antioch* had done was "to deplete the stream by taking out water for irrigation." To require an instream flow sufficient to prevent salt water intrusion "would be extremely unreasonable and unjust to the inhabitants of the valleys above and highly detrimental to the public interests besides." See also Jordan v. City of Santa Barbara, 46 Cal.App.4th 1245, 54 Cal.Rptr.2d 340 (1996) (groundwater users cannot complain of stream diversions that increase groundwater salinity); United States v. State Water Resources Control Bd., 182 Cal.App.3d 82, 227 Cal.Rptr. 161 (1986) (extending *Antioch* to riparian water users). Is the court's argument convincing? Should an appropriator be able to complain of upstream discharges of pollution but not upstream diversions that lead to the same harmful consequences?

2.   In United States v. Gila Valley Irrig. Dist., 920 F.Supp. 1444 (D. Ariz. 1996), aff'd, 117 F.3d 425 (9th Cir. 1997), however, the court held that upstream junior diversions could not materially degrade the quality of water reaching a senior. The case involved agricultural diversions from the Gila River, which is naturally salty, upstream from the San Carlos Apache Reservation. On occasion, farmers would divert the entire flow of the waterway; water arriving back consisted "largely of return flows that [had] absorbed salts from the soils to which the water was applied." Id. at 1451. (The farmers further contributed to the river's salinity by pumping highly saline groundwater and using the groundwater to augment the river.) Because the diversions led to salt concentration levels so high that the Apache Tribe could not irrigate crops, the court held that the diversions violated the tribe's senior priority under a 1935 consent decree. Rather than enjoin the diversions, the court ordered the parties to meet to agree on an order that would limit diversions to a "target flow rate * * * tied in some meaningful way to improving water quality for irrigation purposes." Id. at 1456. As the court noted, flow rate and water pollution are interrelated:

> There are two interrelated aspects of the water quality issue in this case: flow rate and contamination. The contaminant is salt, which prevents the successful cultivation of a variety of crops. The issue of flow rate is, in this case, inseparable from the issue of salt, given the general agreement among the testifying experts that flow rate is a primary factor affecting water quality: at a high level of generalization, the lower the flow rate, the poorer the quality of the water.

Id. at 1449.

Are *Antioch* and *Gila Valley Irrig. Dist.* distinguishable? In *Antioch*, the salt was entirely natural; by contrast, in *Gila Valley Irrig. Dist.*, the farmers' return flow and groundwater pumping were significant sources of salt. But is this relevant? Should it matter whether the source of the contamination is natural, the defendant, or a third party? If the water pollution from a steel mill would not harm a downstream water user absent upstream diversions that concentrate the pollution, does the downstream user have a cause of action against the steel mill? Against the upstream water users? Against both?

3. As you have seen in prior chapters, the negative impacts of water diversions can extend beyond the concentration of any contaminants found in the waterway. By reducing instream flows, for example, diversions can directly harm fish. Why have western states historically recognized greater private and public rights against contamination than against massive diversions of water? Although riparians in western states long have been able to challenge water pollution as a private nuisance, riparians in the West typically cannot complain of diversions that totally dry up streams passing their properties. Pollution that kills fish might be a public nuisance, but diversions that kill fish probably are not. Does the difference reflect a common law bias against remedying purely "aesthetic" or ecological injuries?

2. THE FEDERAL CLEAN WATER ACT

The common law still plays a role in regulating pollution. See, e.g., Springer v. Joseph Schlitz Brewing Co., 510 F.2d 468, 470 (4th Cir. 1975); Hale v. Colorado River Muni. Water Dist., 818 S.W.2d 537 (Tex. App. 1991); Birchwood Lakes Colony Club v. Borough of Medford Lakes, 90 N.J. 582, 449 A.2d 472 (1982). As pollution increased in the twentieth century, however, concerns grew that the common law could not effectively protect the nation's surface waters. The concerns were multifold:[3]

1. Courts could not act until after suit was brought. Potential plaintiffs typically did not file lawsuits unless and until pollution was critical. Once lawsuits were filed, moreover, courts were dependent on the quality of the parties' presentations (which often did not fully reflect the public interest in pollution control).

2. Courts were also hampered in ensuring that their orders were obeyed. Absent an administrative staff to monitor for and police infractions, courts had to rely on plaintiffs to discover injunction violations and bring contempt actions. Plaintiffs, however, often did not have the authority or resources to monitor the defendant's emissions, and contempt actions were expensive and time consuming to pursue.

3. Because the common law addressed pollution on a case by case basis, it often ignored the cumulative impact of numerous pollution sources. Pollution from a particular source might appear reasonable in isolation, but contribute to unacceptably poor water quality when combined with the effluents of numerous other sources.

4. Common law doctrines were often difficult to apply to waterways with multiple sources of pollution. Injuries frequently could not be traced to particular sources.

5. Pollution cases also typically involved complex scientific and technical issues that the courts were not adequately trained to resolve.

---

3. For a discussion of the failings of the common law in controlling water pollution, see James Salzman & Barton H. Thompson, Jr., Environmental Law and Policy 41–43 (2003); William Hines, Nor Any Drop to Drink: Public Regulation of Water Quality, 52 Iowa L. Rev. 186, 195–201 (1966).

6. Many judicial critics also complained that the common law did not adequately reflect the strong public interest in water quality. Private citizens often could not bring public nuisance actions. Most courts refused to recognize purely "aesthetic" injuries. Finally, numerous defenses and exceptions permitted many pollution operations to continue despite adverse impacts on water quality.

Administrative regulation therefore has slowly but almost completely displaced the common law. By 1930, most states had vested state agencies with regulatory authority, but the authority was generally quite weak. States were reticent to impose the expense of better sewage treatment on local governments and feared driving industry elsewhere if they clamped down on industrial discharges. In the 1965 Water Quality Act, Congress directed the states to classify their interstate waters by intended use (e.g., drinking, swimming and fishing, or agriculture), adopt water quality standards for each stretch of water to ensure the intended use, and then formulate plans to achieve the standards. Congress, however, failed to provide any effective enforcement mechanism. States, moreover, found it difficult to identify the pollution sources that needed to be controlled on any given waterway and then to translate the broad quality standards into specific effluent limitations for each source.

By the first Earth Day in 1970, the country was beset by major water pollution problems. Many sewage systems continued to dump raw, untreated sewage into the nation's waters; less than 10 percent of the municipal sewer works treated their wastes by other than filters and settling tanks. Slightly less than a third of all industrial wastewater was being treated before being dumped in the nation's waterways. Observers believed that some waterways, like Lake Erie, were already beyond restoration, and the nation's other surface waters were quickly deteriorating.

In 1972, Congress responded to these problems by passing the Clean Water Act by overwhelming margins.[4] Unlike prior legislation, the Clean Water Act aggressively attacked water pollution by imposing technology-based limitations on the discharge of effluents by point sources, strengthening the requirement that states set and implement water quality standards, and subsidizing new public treatment facilities. The Act's tenor was set by the "national goals" that Congress laid out in section 101.[5] The Act was to "provide for the protection and propagation of fish, shellfish, and wildlife" and for "recreation in and on the water" by July 1, 1983, and to eliminate *all* discharge of pollutants into the nation's waters by 1985.[6]

Notes and Questions

1. Do the reasons for questioning the common law's ability to protect water quality also suggest a need for stronger administrative regulation of water consumption?

2. Most water allocation issues have traditionally been left to state government. What justifies regulating water pollution at a national level? Several arguments have been made. Faced by heavy regulation in one state,

---

4. The Clean Water Act is codified at 33 U.S.C. §§ 1251 et seq.

5. 33 U.S.C. § 1251(a).

6. Clean Water Act §§ 101(a)(1)-(2), 33 U.S.C. §§ 1251(a)(1)-(2).

industry and other pollution sources may simply move to another state. States, in turn, may compete for industry and population by adopting lax pollution standards. Given the interstate character of many of the nation's waterways, water pollution in one state will also almost inevitably affect water quality in other states. Finally, given the scientific and technical complexity of water pollution, national regulation enjoys economies of scale and scope. Most states simply cannot afford the expertise and personnel necessary to fully evaluate and regulate water quality.

Do these arguments also call for a greater federal role in water allocation issues? Should the federal government, for example, enact legislation to control groundwater overdraft? To encourage water conservation? To preserve minimum instream flows? Western members of Congress strenuously oppose such federal regulation, and have opposed including any requirements in the Clean Water Act that might be read as interfering with allocation decisions.

3. While adopting a national pollution control program, Congress has avoided totally federalizing the field. States are free to adopt stricter quality control laws where they wish. See, e.g., Clean Water Act § 510, 33 U.S.C. § 1370. While setting the overall goals and approach, moreover, the Clean Water Act permits states to implement and enforce the federal program if they have the necessary resources and legislative authority.

4. In retrospect at least, Congress' goal of eliminating all manmade water pollution by 1985 was unrealistic. Of waters surveyed in 2000, over a third of the nation's rivers, streams, lakes, and estuaries did not meet water quality goals; 78 percent of the Great Lakes shoreline was quality impaired. See U.S. Environmental Protection Agency, National Water Quality Inventory: 2000 Report to Congress (2002).

Does the elimination of all water pollution make sense as a legislative goal? Why permit people to withdraw and consume water but never to use water for pollution disposal? Consider the views of the National Water Commission in the early 1970s:

> The Commission believes adoption of "no discharge" as a national goal for water quality management is no more sound than would be the establishment of a "no development" goal for controlling land use. * * * [T]he no discharge policy assumes that restoration and preservation of natural water quality is of higher value than any other use of the resource. * * * Adoption of a no discharge policy * * * amounts to the imputation of an extravagant social value to an abstract concept of water purity; a value that the Commission is convinced the American people would not endorse if the associated costs and effect on other resources were fully appreciated and the policy alternatives clearly understood.

National Water Commission, Final Report: Water Policies for the Future 69–70 (1973).

Congress apparently recognized that "the zero-discharge goal was 'not enforceable,' not based on refined cost estimates, and quite possibly 'beyond the ability of the American people to absorb the cost.' " National Wildlife Federation v. Gorsuch, 693 F.2d 156, 181 (D.C. Cir. 1982). Why then did

Congress set a no-discharge goal? Is it wise policy to set unachievable goals? See John Dwyer, The Pathology of Symbolic Legislation, 17 Ecology L.Q. 233 (1990); Charles Meyers, "Good Laws" and Bad Societies, in Approaches to Controlling Air Pollution 65 (A. Friedlander, ed. 1978).

5. If zero discharge is an inappropriate goal, what should be the nation's goal for water quality? The National Water Commission suggested that the "goal of the control program should be to regulate [human discharges] to achieve and maintain a quality sufficient to sustain the uses people wish to make of the water now or in the future." National Water Commission, supra Note 4, at 70. Does even this more modest goal fail to consider the *costs* of pollution control? Should costs be considered? To what degree? Compare William Baxter, People or Penguins (1974) (arguing that costs must be a factor in any rational public policy) with the views of Senator Edmund Muskie, the principal sponsor of the Clean Water Act:

> Can we afford clean water? Can we afford rivers and lakes and streams and oceans which continue to make possible life on this planet? Can we afford life itself? Those questions were never asked as we destroyed the waters of our Nation, and they deserve no answers as we finally move to restore and renew them. These questions answer themselves.

S. Rep. No. 1, 93–1, at 164 (1973).

Is the Commission's proposed goal too anthropocentric? Does humanity have any obligation to reduce pollutants beyond its own needs? See James Salzman & Barton H. Thompson, Jr., Environmental Law and Policy 26–39 (2003) (setting out various frameworks, including biocentric and ecocentric perspectives, for setting environmental goals).

6. What water quality goals would the court that decided National Audubon Society v. Superior Court, supra p. 610, set? Recall that in deciding that the public trust doctrine does not limit all appropriative rights, the *National Audubon* court emphasized that California's population and economy depend on some water uses that are inconsistent with the public trust. In the court's view this required a balancing of the value of such uses against the public trust. Is a similar balance required in the case of water pollution?

a. *Technology–Based Effluent Limitations*

The strictures of the Clean Water Act depend on the source of the pollution. For example, the Act regulates point sources of pollution such as factories and power plants in a radically different fashion than it treats nonpoint sources such as agriculture or construction sites. The Act also regulates factories that discharge their pollution directly into rivers or streams differently than factories that empty their waste into sewage systems, where the waste is hopefully treated to at least some degree by a POTW. Figure 10–2 illustrates the principal pollution sources for purposes of the Clean Water Act. In the materials that follow, always ask yourself why Congress chose to differentiate among various types of pollution sources and whether the differences make sense.

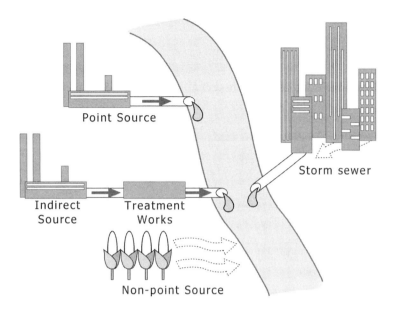

Figure 10–2

Sources of Water Pollution

Until recently, the Clean Water Act's major focus has been regulating the discharges from POTWs and other point sources. All point sources must obtain a permit under the National Pollutant Discharge Elimination System (NPDES) before discharging wastes into the nation's surface waters.[7] Nonpoint sources, by contrast, are largely unregulated as discussed infra p. 1023.

States, if qualified, can issue NPDES permits subject to federal requirements—and about three quarters of the states have qualified; EPA issues the permits in the remaining states. Permits are generally issued for five-year periods and are subject to modification or revocation for cause. The most important parts of the permit are the "effluent limitations" which restrict the amount of specific pollutants that the source can discharge into the nation's waters. The limitations are set by EPA based on technological standards established by the Act. These standards (which have unfortunately given birth to a confusing new vocabulary of acronyms) vary depending on whether the point source is a POTW, an existing source other than a POTW, or a new non-POTW source.

Publicly Owned Treatment Works. Engineers often talk of three different levels of sewage treatment. Primary treatment relies on filters and gravity to separate out solid wastes. Secondary treatment uses biochemical processes to neutralize organic matter. Tertiary treatment

---

7. Clean Water Act §§ 301 & 402, 33 U.S.C. §§ 1311 & 1342.

refers to a wide variety of processes for removing yet additional pollutants.

The Clean Water Act originally required that effluent limitations for POTWs be based on secondary treatment no later than 1977,[8] and on the "best practicable waste treatment technology over the life of the works" by 1983. To help defray the considerable expense of upgrading POTWs, Congress also provided for direct federal grants of up to 85 percent of the cost.[9]

By 1977, many cities had still not begun using secondary treatment, and costs were running higher than expected. As a result, Congress eliminated the 1983 standard and provided for waivers of even the secondary treatment standard in some settings where municipal sewage is dumped into coastal waters.[10] Faced by budgetary problems and by criticism that the construction-grants program was not cost effective, Congress has also phased out federal grants—replacing them with a revolving loan program.[11]

Other Existing Point Sources. Congress has also loosened the effluent limitations that it originally expected other *existing* point sources to meet. Initially, effluent limitations for other existing point sources were to reflect the "best practicable control technology currently available" (or "BPT") by 1977,[12] and the "best available technology economically achievable" (or "BAT") by 1983.[13] Although the standards might sound similar on first reading, Congress contemplated that BAT would be a much more stringent standard than BPT. EPA was to balance costs and benefits in determining BPT, for example, but not BAT. The Act also originally ordered EPA to set separate health-based effluent limitations for toxic pollutants.

Over time, however, Congress delayed the BAT standard and eliminated it entirely for some pollutants. The exact technological standard required today depends on the type of pollutant involved.

> *Toxic Pollutants:* The Act still requires effluent limitations to reflect BAT in the case of "toxic pollutants"—but Congress abandoned the health-based standards as unworkable, and ultimately pushed back the BAT deadline six years to 1989.[14] Toxic pollutants include a list of 126 chemical substances specified by Congress, as well as any other pollutants that EPA determines to be toxic based on the pollutant's toxicity, persistence, degradability, and impact on organisms.[15]

8. Id. § 301(b)(1)(B), 33 U.S.C. § 1311(b)(1)(B).

9. Id. §§ 201–217, 33 U.S.C. §§ 1281–1297.

10. The coastal variance provisions are found in section 301(h) of the Act, 33 U.S.C. § 1311(h).

11. Id. §§ 601–604, 33 U.S.C. §§ 1381–1384.

12. Id. § 301(b)(1)(A), 33 U.S.C. § 1311(b)(1)(A).

13. Id. § 301(b)(2)(A), 33 U.S.C. § 1311(b)(2)(A).

14. Id. §§ 301(a)(2) (C) & (D), 33 U.S.C. § 1311(a)(2)(C) & (D).

15. Id. § 307(a), 33 U.S.C. § 1317(a).

Conventional Pollutants: Congress abandoned the BAT requirement entirely for "conventional pollutants"—i.e., biological oxygen demand, total suspended solids, pH, fecal coliform bacteria, oil, and grease. In place of the BAT standard, the Act requires effluent limitations for conventional pollutants to reflect the "best conventional pollutant control technology" (or "BCT")—which Congress saw as lying somewhere between BPT and BAT, and which EPA has in most cases equated to BPT.[16]

Nonconventional Pollutants: Finally, Congress provided that EPA could, based either on cost or on the quality of the receiving water, modify or waive the BAT requirement for certain "nonconventional pollutants"—ammonia, chloride, color, iron, nitrate, and other pollutants that EPA determines should be treated as nonconventional and nontoxic.[17]

New Direct Point Sources. The Act requires *new* point sources to meet a higher standard than existing sources. New sources must meet effluent standards reflecting

the greatest degree of effluent reduction which the Administrator determines to be achievable through application of the best available control technology, processes, operating methods, or other alternatives, including, where practicable, a standard permitting no discharge of pollutants.[18]

Note that this standard (often referred to as "BACT") reflects the possibility of using not only control technology to reduce discharges, but also process and operation changes, and does not specifically consider cost. Why should new sources be subject to a higher standard than existing sources? Or, looked at the other way around, why should existing sources enjoy a relaxed standard? Congress set a higher standard for new sources presumably for at least two reasons: (1) new sources have greater flexibility in controlling pollution, and (2) existing sources were a potent lobbying force, while future sources by nature raised largely hypothetical concerns. Congress also assumed that companies ultimately would replace their old facilities, so that over time the standard for new sources would become the most important standard.

Was Congress wise in making effluent limitations the central focus of the Clean Water Act? Many economists and other policy analysts have criticized the Act's use of effluent limitations as costly and inefficient. The Act requires all facilities in the same industry to meet the exact same technology-based standard, even though pollution from one facility might not be as harmful as the pollution from another (either because the waterway in which the pollution is discharged is already highly polluted or because the waterway has a greater assimilative capacity) and even though one facility might find it far more expensive to meet the standard. Industries that cause little environmental harm, moreover,

---

16. Id. § 301(b)(2)(E), 33 U.S.C. § 1311(b)(2)(E).

17. Id. § 301(g), 33 U.S.C. § 1311(g).

18. Id. § 306, 33 U.S.C. § 1316.

might have to meet a higher standard than industries that cause substantial harm. Rather than focusing on technological feasibility as the Clean Water Act does, economists would concentrate on those industries that can reduce the most harmful pollution at the lowest cost.

Some environmentalists also have criticized the Clean Water Act's reliance on technology-based standards, but for different reasons. The complex technical studies and judgments needed to implement technology-based standards have often slowed the development and revision of the standards. EPA sometimes has taken years to develop or revise the standards and often has missed statutory deadlines for their issuance. The technology-based standards, moreover, have focused EPA officials on engineering questions rather than the overall state of the nation's waterways and the effect of pollution on human and aquatic health.

So why use technology-based standards? The primary answer is that they work effectively in reducing pollution. As noted earlier, Congress' initial efforts to regulate pollution under the 1965 Water Quality Act by focusing on overall water quality proved technically daunting. Congress therefore purposefully focused on an issue that it hoped would be far less complex: what degree of pollution reduction is technologically feasible? Setting standards based on the relative costs and benefits of limiting particular discharges, as many economists propose, would only increase the complexity and cost of implementation and would give polluters another ground for challenging effluent limitations. Technology-based standards, moreover, are relatively easy to enforce.

Notes and Questions

1. For discussions of the pros and cons of technology-based effluent limitations, see Drew Caputo, A Job Half Finished: The Clean Water Act After 25 Years, 27 Envtl. L. Rep. 10574 (1997); William Pederson, Turning the Tide on Water Quality, 15 Ecology L.Q. 69 (1988); Bruce Ackerman & Richard Stewart, Reforming Environmental Law, 37 Stan. L. Rev. 1333, 1336–37 (1985); Howard Latin, Ideal Versus Real Regulatory Efficiency: Implementation of Uniform Standards and "Fine–Tuning" Regulatory Reforms, 37 Stan. L. Rev. 1267 (1985).

2. Should technology-based standards be used to address other water issues? Consider, for example, setting limits on the amounts of water that various users can withdraw or consume from a river or aquifer based on the best available conservation methods and technology. The Arizona Groundwater Management Act of 1980, noted supra p. 487, adopts this approach in part; industrial users, for example, are required to use "the latest commercially available conservation technology consistent with reasonable economic return." Ariz. Rev. Stat. § 45–564. The "water duties" that many appropriation states impose on agricultural users (see supra p. 159) are also a primitive version of such an approach. Should states that face water shortages or groundwater overdraft impose more rigorous technology-based water duties on all users? If states fail to do so, should the federal government?

3. The cost of complying with the Clean Water Act's effluent limitations encourages industry, where it can, to discharge wastes into POTWs

rather than directly into waterways. A large amount of such waste either passes through POTWs untreated to waterways or endangers the POTWs' operations (e.g., by increasing the risk of fire or explosion, or by interfering with the process by which the POTW treats domestic wastes); over a third of the toxins that pollute the nation's waters come from such indirect sources.

To help protect water quality from these discharges, the Act imposes both "prohibited discharge standards" and "categorical pretreatment standards" on indirect sources. Under the former, indirect sources are prohibited from discharging a pollutant into a POTW that will interfere with the proper operation of the POTW or pass through untreated. Clean Water Act §§ 307(b)-(e), 33 U.S.C. §§ 1317(b)-(e). The categorical pretreatment standards require all indirect sources to meet BAT standards for discharges of toxic wastes into POTWs—unless the POTW has proven that it can effectively treat the pollutants. Id. § 307(b), 33 U.S.C. § 1317(b).

4. Congress consciously designed the NPDES program to permit relatively straightforward enforcement. Each holder of an NPDES permit must report discharges on a regular, usually monthly, basis to both EPA and the state. The reports permit easy comparison of permitted and actual discharges and are admissible in court as proof of a violation. Where the federal and state governments fail to pursue violations, environmental groups have found it relatively simple to use the reports as the basis for citizen suits. See Barton H. Thompson, Jr., The Continuing Evolution of Citizen Enforcement, 2000 U. Ill. L. Rev. 185, 199–200.

b. *Nonpoint Pollution*

One might expect that the Clean Water Act would use the same technology-based approach to regulate water pollution from agriculture, the major source of water pollution in the United States today. In 1973, EPA issued regulations exempting farms of less than 3000 acres, as well as animal feedlots and silviculture, from the NPDES permit requirements, even if they otherwise constituted point sources. According to EPA, it would be administratively infeasible to apply the NPDES requirements to such sources. "An effluent limitation must be a precise number in order for it to be an effective regulatory tool; both the discharger and the regulatory agency need to have an identifiable standard upon which to determine whether the facility is in compliance."[1] EPA also argued that the exempt sources numbered in the hundreds of thousands and, if subject to NPDES requirements, would overwhelm the agency.

In 1977, the D.C. Circuit disagreed and invalidated the regulations. Natural Resources Defense Council v. Costle, 568 F.2d 1369 (D.C. Cir. 1977). According to the court, permit terms could be adjusted to meet the unique characteristics of the sources, and EPA could reduce the sheer numerical burden by issuing "general permits" for various classes of polluters. The court's decision as to agricultural operations, however, was short lived. Only a few months later, Congress amended the defini-

---

1. The language is from an EPA memorandum quoted in Natural Resources De- fense Council v. Costle, 568 F.2d 1369, 1378 (D.C. Cir. 1977).

tion of point source to exclude return flows from irrigated agriculture.[2] Congress also banned EPA from requiring an NPDES permit for "discharges composed entirely of return flow from irrigated agriculture," or "directly or indirectly, requir[ing] any State to require such a permit."[3]

Although the Clean Water Act emphasizes the importance of regulating non-point pollution from agriculture and other activities, it primarily leaves the policy decisions of whether, to what degree, and how up to states and local governments. Section 208 of the Act requires states to designate local agencies to coordinate pollution control efforts in areas with "substantial water quality problems."[4] These agencies in turn must prepare "areawide waste treatment management plans," including procedures and methods to control "to the extent feasible" pollution from agriculture, silviculture, mining, and construction.[5] Valuable in theory, section 208 is toothless. Although waste treatment management plans must be submitted to EPA for approval, EPA is not authorized to impose its own plan if a state or local agency fails to comply with section 208 or submits an inadequate plan. Left on their own to confront agricultural, mining, and construction interests, most local agencies and states have avoided any serious regulation of nonpoint sources under section 208.

In 1987, numerous members of Congress urged a "renewed commitment to the cleanup of nonpoint sources of pollution." 133 Cong. Rec. S744 (Jan. 14, 1987) (Sen. Baucus). The principal result was the addition of section 319 which requires each state to implement a "nonpoint source management program." Under section 319, each state was to prepare, by August 1988, a report identifying those categories of nonpoint sources that were preventing the attainment of the state's water quality standards, and describing measures to "reduce, to the maximum extent practicable, the level of pollution" from such sources.[6] During the same period, each state was to prepare a management plan describing how the state would implement its proposed nonpoint control program over the first four years—including a schedule of annual milestones.[7] Central to section 319 is the mandate that states require nonpoint sources to use "best management practices ['BMPs'] * * * at the earliest practicable date."[8]

---

2. Clean Water Act § 502(14), 33 U.S.C. § 1362(14). While exempting most agricultural operations, Congress chose to explicitly include concentrated animal feeding operations (CAFOs) in the definition of point sources. Id.

3. Id. § 402(l)(1), 33 U.S.C. § 1342(l)(1).

4. Clean Water Act § 208(a), 33 U.S.C. § 1288(a).

5. Id. § 208(b), 33 U.S.C. § 1288(b).

6. Clean Water Act § 319(a), 33 U.S.C. § 1329(a).

7. Id. § 319(b), 33 U.S.C. § 1329(b).

8. Id. § 319(b)(2)(C), 33 U.S.C. § 1329(b)(2)(C). "The term [BMP] encom-

passes a broad array of management practices that can be undertaken, alone or in combination, to reduce nonpoint sources of pollution. For example, in soil conservation programs over forty BMP's have been identified, including conservation tillage, grassed waterways, cover crops, undisturbed field perimeters near waterways, and terracing. * * * Simple and cost-free changes in agricultural practices, such as careful scheduling and application of fertilizer and pesticides, may reduce runoff of these pollutants, thereby resulting in cost savings to the farmer." S. Rep. No. 98–282, at 7 (1983).

If a state fails to prepare the first report, EPA must prepare a report for the state identifying those categories of nonpoint sources that need to be addressed. EPA is not given authority to identify control measures for the state, however; nor is EPA empowered to adopt a management plan for any state. These omissions were intentional. According to Senator George Mitchell, section 319 does not require a state to control nonpoint pollution. "If a State decides that it does not want a program to control nonpoint pollution, that is it."[9]

Notes and Questions

1. For recent discussions of the problems of and possible solutions to nonpoint pollution, see Environmental Law Institute, Enforceable State Mechanisms for the Control of Nonpoint Source Water Pollution (1997); Robin Curtis Craig, Local or National? The Increasing Federalization of Nonpoint Source Pollution, 15 J. Envtl. L. & Litig. 179 (2000); Scott Anderson, Watershed Management and Nonpoint Source Pollution, 26 B.U. Envtl. Aff. L. Rev. 339 (1999); Gabriel Calvo, Voluntary Public–Private Nonpoint Source Pollution Projects: A Welcome Response to Regulatory Shortcomings Under the Clean Water Act, 3 Great Plains Nat. Resources J. 159 (1999).

2. Proponents of the agricultural exemption from the NPDES system have argued that agricultural operations are too diverse to be controlled through uniform national standards, that the diffuse, non-point character of agricultural return flow makes numeric standards difficult to set and enforce, and that the huge number of farms in the United States would bury EPA and the states in NPDES applications. Could the practical difficulties of controlling the quality of agricultural return flow be mitigated by regulating water districts rather than individual farms?

John Davidson has suggested that regulation of water districts would carry several advantages: EPA would be faced with a manageable number of NPDES permits; districts often have collective drainage systems that could be monitored much as the outfall of a POTW or other point source; and the decision how to meet the quality standards would be left to the district itself.

> Special water districts are well suited to the unique function that nonpoint source control requires. Organized locally and along the lines of natural watersheds, they are, by purpose and experience, the experts in local water management. * * * How the district chooses to meet permit requirements can be addressed flexibly by the people who know the land best—the district members. By demanding performance, but leaving the solution to the district members, it may be possible to achieve a middle ground between voluntariness and coercion.

John Davidson, Commentary: Using Special Water Districts to Control Nonpoint Sources of Water Pollution, 65 Chicago–Kent L. Rev. 503, 515, 517 (1989). See also Terry Young & Chelsea Congdon, Plowing New Ground: Using Economic Incentives to Control Water Pollution from Agriculture

---

9. 133 Cong. Rec. S1968 (Feb. 4, 1987).

(Envtl. Def. Fund 1994) (proposing a market-based system for controlling agricultural water pollution that would rely on local districts for administration).

In 1989, a committee of the National Academy of Sciences recommended that Congress repeal the NPDES exemption of agricultural return flow. See National Research Council, Irrigation–Induced Water Quality Problems: What Can Be Learned from the San Joaquin Valley Experience (1989). For further discussion of agriculture and the Clean Water Act, see John H. Davidson, Factory Fields: Agricultural Practices, Polluted Water and Hypoxic Oceans, 9 Great Plains Nat. Resources J. 1 (2004); Robert W. Adler, Water Quality and Agriculture: Assessing Alternative Futures, 25 Environs Envtl. L. & Pol'y J. 77 (2002).

3. Do states have a public trust responsibility to protect water quality from nonpoint pollution? In People v. Gold Run Ditch & Mining Co., 66 Cal. 138, 4 P. 1152 (1884), the California Supreme Court invoked the public trust doctrine to protect inland waters from non-point pollution that affected navigation. For decades, the hydraulic mining industry had used high velocity water cannons to break down hillsides from which it could recover gold. An unfortunate byproduct of hydraulic mining was 5,000 cubic yards of boulders, gravel, and sand that washed into the state's waterways every day. The beds of some rivers rose dramatically, in some cases from six to 12 feet, seriously impairing navigation. Although the hydraulic mining industry annually generated $10 million of gold, the court enjoined discharges of the mining tailings into navigable waterways, effectively ending hydraulic mining in California. According to the court, "the rights of the people in the navigable rivers of the State are paramount and controlling." While the state can grant the soils underlying navigable waterways to private individuals, it "cannot grant the rights of the people to the use of navigable waters flowing over it; these are inalienable."

Can *Gold Run Ditch & Mining Co.* be paired with other cases such as the *Mono Lake* opinion, supra p. 610, that recognize public trust interests in the environment to forge a more general legal approach for successfully attacking non-point pollution? See generally Ralph Johnson, Water Pollution and the Public Trust Doctrine, 19 Envtl. L. 485 (1989).

4. Attempts to limit nonpoint pollution may affect water quantity. An oft-suggested solution to irrigation-induced quality problems is to reduce water use by irrigators in areas where return flow is prone to contamination by salt, selenium, or other pollutants. See National Research Council, Irrigation–Induced Water Quality Problems: What Can Be Learned from the San Joaquin Valley Experience 65 (1989). Other potential solutions to irrigation-induced quality problems include better irrigation management, evaporation ponds, disposal of drainage in the ocean or other less sensitive waterways, and deep-well injection—all of which could reduce the amount of return flow available to downstream water users. Could a downstream user object if a farmer wished voluntarily to undertake such a solution? If the state imposed such a solution, would a downstream user be entitled to compensation under the Constitution?

c. *Hydrologic Modifications*

Hydrologic modifications are one of the major sources of water quality impairment in the nation. See Figure 10–3. Diversions of water from rivers and streams can concentrate downstream pollutants, whether natural pollutants like salt or human-added pollutants. Dams and other water projects can change the amount of dissolved oxygen in downstream waters (either reducing the oxygen and its ability to break down organic materials and other pollutants, or "supersaturating" it and killing fish), add various minerals and other harmful nutrients, or raise or lower downstream water temperatures. Such hydrologic modifications are the second most important source of water quality impairment in rivers, streams, and lakes and the sixth greatest source of impairment in estuaries.

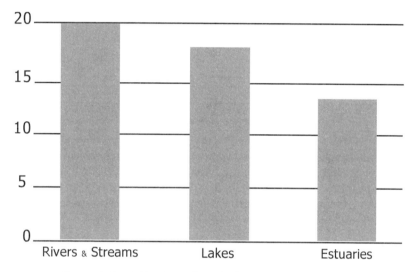

Percent Contribution of Hydrologic Modifications

Figure 10–3

Given the importance of hydrologic modifications, a recurring question has been whether hydrologic modifications ever constitute point sources of pollution subject to the NPDES permit system and technology-based standards.

NATIONAL WILDLIFE FEDERATION v. GORSUCH

United States Court of Appeals for the D.C. Circuit, 1982.
693 F.2d 156.

WALD, CIRCUIT JUDGE

The National Wildlife Federation petitioned the district court for a declaration that the Administrator of the Environmental Protection

Agency (EPA) has a nondiscretionary duty to require dam operators to apply for pollutant discharge permits under § 402(a) of the Clean Water Act, 33 U.S.C. § 1342(a) * * *.

I. BACKGROUND

A. *Dam–Induced Water Quality Changes*

Dams cause a variety of interrelated water quality problems, both in reservoirs and in river water downstream from a dam. * * *

Water released from a reservoir through a dam into downstream water may be low in dissolved oxygen. The river below the dam will remain oxygen-depleted for some distance, although the river will gradually become re-aerated through wind mixing as it flows downstream. If the oxygen level is too low, fish cannot survive. Also, a river low in oxygen has limited ability to break down pollutants and other organic matter. * * *

The record does not indicate the number of dams for which discharge of low-oxygen water is a significant problem, nor the cost of the various methods of mechanical aeration.[8] But the problem is serious for at least some dams, and the cure is apparently expensive. * * *

If dissolved oxygen is totally depleted from the [lower (or "hypolimnion") layer of water in a reservoir], a further problem develops. A number of minerals and plant nutrients, insoluble under normal "aerobic" conditions, are soluble in zero-oxygen "anaerobic" water. These compounds—including iron, manganese, and phosphates—therefore tend to be leached from bottom muds into the reservoir. High concentrations of these minerals and nutrients, released into the downstream river, can harm fish, make the water unpalatable for drinking, and foster undesirable plant growth. * * *

In a thermally stratified reservoir, the lower layer will generally be colder than the upstream river, while the upper [or "epilimnion"] layer will be warmer. Some species of fish can survive only in warm water; others can survive only in cold water. Thus, cold hypolimnion water, even if fully oxygenated, will harm or kill warm water fish but benefit cold water fish; conversely, warm epilimnion water will harm or kill cold water fish and benefit warm water fish. * * * In short, dams cause changes in the temperature of downstream water, and some of the time, but not all of the time, those changes are undesirable. * * *

When water plunges at high velocity from the reservoir into the downstream river, it becomes mixed with air. Depending on the velocity and turbulence of the falling water and the depth of the receiving basin, this can cause downstream water to become "supersaturated"—aerated

---

8. * * * The only quantitative data in the record is an EPA report indicating that in 1977, 15% of water basins in the country experienced some sort of water quality problem caused by dams. Environmental Protection Agency, National Water Quality Inventory: 1977 Report to Congress 15–19 (Oct. 1978).

in excess of normal concentration. Supersaturated water does not harm people and is suitable for most uses, but can be fatal to fish; documented fish kills have occurred at a number of dams. * * *

B. Legal Issue Presented

The issue in this case is one of statutory construction—which if any of the water quality changes caused by dams must be regulated under the National Pollutant Discharge Elimination System (NPDES) established by § 402 of the Clean Water Act, 33 U.S.C. § 1342. Under § 402(a), "the Administrator may, after opportunity for public hearing, issue a permit for the discharge of any pollutant." Unless the Administrator issues an NPDES permit, "the discharge of any pollutant by any person [is] unlawful." Id. § 301(a), 33 U.S.C. § 1311(a). Section 502(12), 33 U.S.C. § 1362(12), defines the key phrase "discharge of a pollutant" as "any addition of any pollutant to navigable waters from any point source." Thus, for dams to require NPDES permits, five elements must be present: (1) a pollutant must be (2) added (3) to navigable waters (4) from (5) a point source.

The parties agree that a dam can, in some circumstances, be a "point source" * * *. They dispute whether low dissolved oxygen, cold, and supersaturation are "pollutants" and whether any of the disputed water quality problems constitute the "addition" of a pollutant "from" a point source. * * *

EPA argues * * * that for addition of a pollutant from a point source to occur, the point source must introduce the pollutant into navigable water from the outside world; dam-caused pollution, in contrast, merely passes through the dam from one body of navigable water (the reservoir) into another (the downstream river). Also, while conceding that all adverse water quality changes are "pollution"—broadly defined in § 502(19), 33 U.S.C. § 1362(19), as "the man-made or man-induced alteration of the chemical, physical, biological, and radiological integrity of water"—EPA argues that low dissolved oxygen, cold, and supersaturation are not included in the narrower statutory term "pollutant," defined in § 502(6), 33 U.S.C. § 1362(6) as:

> dredged spoil, solid waste, incinerator residue, sewage, garbage, sewage sludge, munitions, chemical wastes, biological materials, radioactive materials, heat, wrecked or discarded equipment, rock, sand, cellar dirt and industrial, municipal, and agricultural waste discharged into water.

* * *

III. THE REASONABLENESS OF EPA'S INTERPRETATION

* * * If we conclude that EPA's interpretation is inconsistent with the language of the Clean Water Act, as interpreted in light of the legislative history, or if it "frustrate[s] the policy that Congress sought to implement," no amount of deference can save it. * * * But if the agency's construction neither contradicts the language of the statute nor

frustrates congressional policy, our inquiry is a limited one. The agency's construction must be upheld if, in light of the appropriate degree of deference, it is "sufficiently reasonable," even if it is not "the only reasonable one or even the reading the court would have reached" on its own. * * *

A. *Specific Substantive Provisions*

* * *

1. *"Pollutant"*

Low dissolved oxygen, cold, and supersaturation do not plainly fall within the statutory list of pollutants in § 502(b) * * *. These dam-induced changes are water conditions, not substances added to water. Section 502(6), however, primarily lists substances; "heat" is the only listed water condition. Moreover, the wording of § 506(6) makes us cautious in adding new terms to the definition. Congress used restrictive phrasing—"[t]he term 'pollutant' means dredged spoil, [etc.]"—rather than the looser phrase "includes," used elsewhere in the Act. * * *[56]

2. *"Addition" of a Pollutant "from" a Point Source*

The Act does not define what constitutes the "addition" of a pollutant. The parties agree that water quality problems that occur within a reservoir (e.g., dissolved minerals) are nonpoint pollution, for lack of a point source. The Wildlife Federation argues, however, that the statutorily necessary "addition * * * from a point source" occurs when (1) a dam causes pollutants to enter the reservoir and (2) the polluted water subsequently passes through the dam—the point source—into the formerly unpolluted river below. EPA responds that addition from a point source occurs only if the point source itself physically introduces a pollutant into water from the outside world. * * * As for supersaturation, which does not exist in the reservoir, EPA argues that it occurs downstream, after the water is released from the dam. * * *

In our view, the language of the statute permits either construction. The legislative history does not provide much help either. Throughout its

---

56. We do not decide in this case whether the statutory list necessarily excludes low dissolved oxygen, cold, and supersaturation, only whether EPA can reasonably so interpret it. Several factors suggest that the list does not necessarily exclude unlisted water conditions. The list includes one condition—heat. Also, one court has found that a substance—gasoline—is a pollutant even though it was not clearly listed. United States v. Hamel, 551 F.2d 107, 110–11 (6th Cir. 1977). And EPA admits that "sediment" is a pollutant, although not clearly listed. Moreover, the haphazard nature of the listed pollutants, as specific as "cellar dirt" (but not "dirt" as such) and as general as "industrial, municipal, and agricultur-

al wastes," together with places in the statute where Congress did not pay careful attention to its own definition, makes us reluctant to conclude that Congress intended to preclude EPA from adding unlisted items to the definition. * * *

Finally, we can imagine circumstances where EPA might want to treat low dissolved oxygen as a pollutant. Suppose an industrial facility, rather than discharging oxygen-demanding organic waste directly into a river, instead diverts river water, discharges the organic waste into the diverted water, waits for the waste to decompose, and then returns the oxygen-depleted water to the river. * * *

consideration of the Act, Congress' focus was on traditional industrial and municipal wastes; it never considered how to regulate facilities such as dams which indirectly cause pollutants to enter navigable upstream water and then convey these polluted waters downstream. * * *

3. *The Primacy of § 402 on the Legislative Scheme*

The Wildlife Federation also argues that the definitions of "pollutant" and "addition" should be read broadly because the NPDES permit program is Congress' preferred method of water pollution control and would have been applied to all sources of pollution had Congress thought that it was technologically feasible to do so. There is indeed some basis in the legislative history for the position that Congress viewed the NPDES program as its most effective weapon against pollution. * * *

Nonetheless, it does not appear that Congress wanted to apply the NPDES system wherever feasible. Had it wanted to do so, it could easily have chosen suitable language, e.g., "all pollution released through a point source." Instead, as we have seen, the NPDES system was limited to "addition" of "pollutants" "from" a point source. * * * In 1972, the Congress made a clear and precise distinction between point sources, which would be subject to direct Federal regulation, and nonpoint sources, control of which was specifically reserved to State and local governments * * *.

B. *The Purposes of the Act*

* * * The district court, in giving "pollutant" and "addition" a broad reading, relied heavily on the "purposes" section of the Act [which sets out Congress' goals of fishable-swimmable waters by 1983 and no discharges by 1985].

Undeniably, Congress' strong statement of its objective must color EPA's and our interpretation of specific provisions of the Act. But, as any student of the legislative process soon learns, it is one thing for Congress to announce a grand goal, and quite another for it to mandate full implementation of that goal. Read as a whole, the Clean Water Act shows not only Congress' determined effort to clean up our polluted lakes and rivers, but also its practical recognition of the economic, technological, and political limits on total elimination of all pollution from all sources. The Act contains numerous requirements that cost be taken into account in establishing effluent limits, as well as assorted exemptions from those limits. * * *

In addition to our general doubts, expressed above, about how heavily to rely on the broad goals of the Act, we find specific indication in the Act that Congress did not want to interfere any more than necessary with state water management, of which dams are an important component. Section 101(g), 33 U.S.C. § 1251(g), states:

> It is the policy of Congress that the authority of each State to allocate quantities of water within its jurisdiction shall not be superseded, abrogated, or otherwise impaired by this [Act].

In light of its intent to minimize federal control over state decisions on water quantity, Congress might also, if confronted with the issue, have decided to leave control of dams insofar as they affect water quality to the states. * * *

3. *Policy Considerations*

* * * [D]am-caused pollution is unique because its severity depends partly on whether other sources have polluted the upstream river. The NPDES program, however, requires EPA to issue nationally uniform standards, and thus would not allow the agency to take full account of the interrelationship between dam-caused pollution and other pollution sources. Moreover, dams are a major component of state water management, providing irrigation, drinking water, flood protection, etc. In light of these complexities, which the NPDES program was not designed to handle, it may well be that state * * * plans are the better regulatory tool.

Also, the severity of dam-caused pollution is highly site-specific. Common forms of NPDES limits (x% reduction in biochemical oxygen demand (BOD) or y pounds of BOD per ton of industrial output) would entail major costs at one dam, and only minor costs at another. Thus, it would be difficult at best for EPA to determine what level of reduction is obtainable by using the "best available technology economically achievable" for each "category or class" of polluter. Control that is economically feasible at one site may be infeasible at another. Conversely, major expenditures might be required for dams where, say, dissolved oxygen levels are slightly reduced immediately below the dam, but not enough to harm fish, and the river is fully re-aerated within a few miles. * * *

SOUTH FLORIDA WATER MANAGEMENT DIST. v. MICCOSUKEE TRIBE

Supreme Court of the United States, 2004.
541 U.S. 95.

JUSTICE O'CONNOR delivered the opinion of the Court.

Petitioner South Florida Water Management District operates a pumping facility that transfers water from a canal into a reservoir a short distance away. Respondents Miccosukee Tribe of Indians and the Friends of the Everglades brought a citizen suit under the Clean Water Act contending that the pumping facility is required to obtain a discharge permit under the National Pollutant Discharge Elimination System. The District Court agreed and granted summary judgment to respondents. A panel of the United States Court of Appeals for the Eleventh Circuit affirmed. Both the District Court and the Eleventh Circuit rested their holdings on the predicate determination that the canal and reservoir are two distinct water bodies. For the reasons explained below, we vacate and remand for further development of the factual record as to the accuracy of that determination.

I

A

The Central and South Florida Flood Control Project (Project) consists of a vast array of levees, canals, pumps, and water impoundment areas in the land between south Florida's coastal hills and the Everglades. Historically, that land was itself part of the Everglades, and its surface and groundwater flowed south in a uniform and unchanneled sheet. Starting in the early 1900's, however, the State began to build canals to drain the wetlands and make them suitable for cultivation. These canals proved to be a source of trouble; they lowered the water table, allowing salt water to intrude upon coastal wells, and they proved incapable of controlling flooding. Congress established the Project in 1948 to address these problems. It gave the United States Army Corps of Engineers the task of constructing a comprehensive network of levees, water storage areas, pumps, and canal improvements that would serve several simultaneous purposes, including flood protection, water conservation, and drainage. These improvements fundamentally altered the hydrology of the Everglades, changing the natural sheet flow of ground and surface water. The local sponsor and day-to-day operator of the Project is the South Florida Water Management District (District).

Five discrete elements of the Project are at issue in this case. One is a canal called "C–11." C–11 collects groundwater and rainwater from a 104 square-mile area in south central Broward County. The area drained by C–11 includes urban, agricultural, and residential development, and is home to 136,000 people. At the western terminus of C–11 is the second Project element at issue here: a large pump station known as "S–9." When the water level in C–11 rises above a set level, S–9 begins operating and pumps water out of the canal. The water does not travel far. Sixty feet away, the pump station empties the water into a large undeveloped wetland area called "WCA–3," the third element of the Project we consider here. WCA–3 is the largest of several "water conservation areas" that are remnants of the original South Florida Everglades. The District impounds water in these areas to conserve fresh water that might otherwise flow directly to the ocean, and to preserve wetlands habitat.

Using pump stations like S–9, the District maintains the water table in WCA–3 at a level significantly higher than that in the developed lands drained by the C–11 canal to the east. Absent human intervention, that water would simply flow back east, where it would rejoin the waters of the canal and flood the populated areas of the C–11 basin. That return flow is prevented, or, more accurately, slowed, by levees that hold back the surface waters of WCA–3. Two of those levees, L–33 and L–37, are the final two elements of the Project at issue here. The combined effect of L–33 and L–37, C–11, and S–9 is artificially to separate the C–11 basin from WCA–3; left to nature, the two areas would be a single wetland covered in an undifferentiated body of surface and ground water flowing slowly southward.

B

As the above description illustrates, the Project has wrought large-scale hydrologic and environmental change in South Florida, some deliberate and some accidental. Its most obvious environmental impact has been the conversion of what were once wetlands into areas suitable for human use. But the Project also has affected those areas that remain wetland ecosystems.

Rain on the western side of the L–33 and L–37 levees falls into the wetland ecosystem of WCA–3. Rain on the eastern side of the levees, on the other hand, falls on agricultural, urban, and residential land. Before it enters the C–11 canal, whether directly as surface runoff or indirectly as groundwater, that rainwater absorbs contaminants produced by human activities. The water in C–11 therefore differs chemically from that in WCA–3. Of particular interest here, C–11 water contains elevated levels of phosphorous, which is found in fertilizers used by farmers in the C–11 basin. When water from C–11 is pumped across the levees, the phosphorous it contains alters the balance of WCA–3's ecosystem (which is naturally low in phosphorous) and stimulates the growth of algae and plants foreign to the Everglades ecosystem.

The phosphorous-related impacts of the Project are well known and have received a great deal of attention from state and federal authorities for more than 20 years. A number of initiatives are currently under way to reduce these impacts and thereby restore the ecological integrity of the Everglades. Respondents Miccosukee Tribe of Indians and the Friends of the Everglades (hereinafter simply Tribe), impatient with the pace of this progress, brought this Clean Water Act suit in the United States District Court for the Southern District of Florida. They sought, among other things, to enjoin the operation of S–9 and, in turn, the conveyance of water from C–11 into WCA–3.

C

Congress enacted the Clean Water Act (Act) in 1972. Its stated objective was "to restore and maintain the chemical, physical, and biological integrity of the Nation's waters." 33 U.S.C. § 1251. To serve those ends, the Act prohibits "the discharge of any pollutant by any person" unless done in compliance with some provision of the Act. § 1311(a). The provision relevant to this case, § 1342, establishes the National Pollutant Discharge Elimination System, or "NPDES." Generally speaking, the NPDES requires dischargers to obtain permits that place limits on the type and quantity of pollutants that can be released into the Nation's waters. The Act defines the phrase " 'discharge of a pollutant' " to mean "any addition of any pollutant to navigable waters from any point source." § 1362(12). A " 'point source,' " in turn, is defined as "any discernible, confined and discrete conveyance," such as a pipe, ditch, channel, or tunnel, "from which pollutants are or may be discharged." § 1362(14).

According to the Tribe, the District cannot operate S–9 without an NPDES permit because the pump station moves phosphorous-laden water from C–11 into WCA–3. The District does not dispute that phosphorous is a pollutant, or that C–11 and WCA–3 are "navigable waters" within the meaning of the Act. The question, it contends, is whether the operation of the S–9 pump constitutes the "discharge of [a] pollutant" within the meaning of the Act. * * *

II

The District and the Federal Government, as *amicus*, advance three separate arguments, any of which would, if accepted, lead to the conclusion that the S–9 pump station does not require a point source discharge permit under the NPDES program. Two of these arguments involve the application of disputed contentions of law to agreed-upon facts, while the third involves the application of agreed-upon law to disputed facts. For reasons explained below, we decline at this time to resolve all of the parties' legal disagreements, and instead remand for further proceedings regarding their factual dispute.

A

In its opening brief on the merits, the District argued that the NPDES program applies to a point source "only when a pollutant originates from the point source," and not when pollutants originating elsewhere merely pass through the point source. This argument mirrors the question presented in the District's petition for certiorari: "Whether the pumping of water by a state water management agency that adds nothing to the water being pumped constitutes an 'addition' of a pollutant 'from' a point source triggering the need for a National Pollutant Discharge Elimination System permit under the Clean Water Act." Although the Government rejects the District's legal position, it and the Tribe agree with the factual proposition that S–9 does not itself add any pollutants to the water it conveys into WCA–3.

This initial argument is untenable, and even the District appears to have abandoned it in its reply brief. A point source is, by definition, a "discernible, confined, and discrete *conveyance*." § 1362(14) (emphasis added). That definition makes plain that a point source need not be the original source of the pollutant; it need only convey the pollutant to "navigable waters," which are, in turn, defined as "the waters of the United States." § 1362(7). Tellingly, the examples of "point sources" listed by the Act include pipes, ditches, tunnels, and conduits, objects that do not themselves generate pollutants but merely transport them. § 1362(14). In addition, one of the Act's primary goals was to impose NPDES permitting requirements on municipal wastewater treatment plants. See, e.g., § 1311(b)(1)(B) (establishing a compliance schedule for publicly owned treatment works). But under the District's interpretation of the Act, the NPDES program would not cover such plants, because they treat and discharge pollutants added to water by others. We therefore reject the District's proposed reading of the definition of

" 'discharge of a pollutant' " contained in § 1362(12). That definition includes within its reach point sources that do not themselves generate pollutants.

B

Having answered the precise question on which we granted certiorari, we turn to a second argument, advanced primarily by the Government as *amicus curiae* in merits briefing and at oral argument. For purposes of determining whether there has been "any addition of any pollutant to navigable waters from any point source," ibid., the Government contends that all the water bodies that fall within the Act's definition of " 'navigable waters' " (that is, all "the waters of the United States, including the territorial seas," § 1362(7)) should be viewed unitarily for purposes of NPDES permitting requirements. Because the Act requires NPDES permits only when there is an addition of a pollutant "to navigable waters," the Government's approach would lead to the conclusion that such permits are *not* required when water from one navigable water body is discharged, unaltered, into another navigable water body. That would be true even if one water body were polluted and the other pristine, and the two would not otherwise mix. See Catskill Mountains Chapter of Trout Unlimited, Inc. v. New York, 273 F.3d 481, 492 (2nd Cir. 2001); Dubois v. United States Dep't of Agric., 102 F.3d 1273 (1st Cir. 1996). Under this "unitary waters" approach, the S–9 pump station would not need an NPDES permit.

The "unitary waters" argument focuses on the Act's definition of a pollutant discharge as "any addition of any pollutant to navigable waters from any point source." § 1362(12). The Government contends that the absence of the word "any" prior to the phrase "navigable waters" in § 1362(12) signals Congress' understanding that NPDES permits would not be required for pollution caused by the engineered transfer of one "navigable water" into another. It argues that Congress intended that such pollution instead would be addressed through local nonpoint source pollution programs. Section 1314(f)(2(F), which concerns nonpoint sources, directs the Environmental Protection Agency (EPA) to give States information on the evaluation and control of "pollution resulting from . . . changes in the movement, flow, or circulation of any navigable waters or ground waters, including changes caused by the construction of dams, levees, channels, causeways, or flow diversion facilities."

We note, however, that § 1314(f)(2)(F) does not explicitly exempt nonpoint pollution sources from the NPDES program if they *also* fall within the "point source" definition. And several NPDES provisions might be read to suggest a view contrary to the unitary waters approach. For example, under the Act, a State may set individualized ambient water quality standards by taking into consideration "the designated uses of the navigable waters involved." 33 U.S.C. § 1313(c)(2)(A). Those water quality standards, in turn, directly affect local NPDES permits; if standard permit conditions fail to achieve the water quality goals for a given water body, the State must determine the total pollutant load that the water body can sustain and then allocate that load among the permit-holders who discharge to the water body. § 1313(d). This approach suggests that the Act protects individual water bodies as well as the "waters of the United States" as a whole.

The Government also suggests that we adopt the "unitary waters" approach out of deference to a longstanding EPA view that the process of "transporting, impounding, and releasing navigable waters" cannot constitute an " 'addition' " of pollutants to " 'the waters of the United States.' " But the Government does not identify any administrative documents in which EPA has espoused that position. Indeed, an *amicus* brief filed by several former EPA officials argues that the agency once reached the opposite conclusion. See Brief for Former Administrator Carol M. Browner et al. as *Amici Curiae* 17 (citing *In re Riverside Irrigation Dist.*, 1975 WL 23864 (Off. Gen. Couns., June 27, 1975) (irrigation ditches that discharge to navigable waters require NPDES permits even if they themselves qualify as navigable waters)). The "unitary waters" approach could also conflict with current NPDES regulations. For example, 40 CFR § 122.45(g)(4) (2003) allows an industrial water user to obtain "intake credit" for pollutants present in water that it withdraws from navigable waters. When the permit holder discharges the water after use, it does not have to remove pollutants that were in the water before it was withdrawn. There is a caveat, however: EPA extends such credit "only if the discharger demonstrates that the intake water is drawn from the same body of water into which the discharge is made." The NPDES program thus appears to address the movement of pollutants among water bodies, at least at times.

Finally, the Government and numerous *amici* warn that affirming the Court of Appeals in this case would have significant practical consequences. If we read the Clean Water Act to require an NPDES permit for every engineered diversion of one navigable water into another, thousands of new permits might have to be issued, particularly by western States, whose water supply networks often rely on engineered transfers among various natural water bodies. See Brief for Colorado et al. as *Amici Curiae* 2–4. Many of those diversions might also require expensive treatment to meet water quality criteria. It may be that construing the NPDES program to cover such transfers would therefore raise the costs of water distribution prohibitively, and violate Congress' specific instruction that "the authority of each State to allocate quantities of water within its jurisdiction shall not be superseded, abrogated or otherwise impaired" by the Act. § 1251(g). On the other hand, it may be that such permitting authority is necessary to protect water quality, and that the States or EPA could control regulatory costs by issuing general permits to point sources associated with water distribution programs. Indeed, that is the position of the one State that *has* interpreted the Act to cover interbasin water transfers. See Brief for Pennsylvania Department of Environmental Protection as *Amicus Curiae* 11–18.

Because WCA–3 and C–11 are both "navigable waters," adopting the "unitary waters" approach would lead to the conclusion that the District may operate S–9 without an NPDES permit. But despite its relevance here, neither the District nor the Government raised the unitary waters approach before the Court of Appeals or in their briefs respecting the petition for certiorari. (The District adopted the position as its own in its reply brief on the merits.) Indeed, we are not aware of any reported case that examines the unitary waters argument in precisely the form that the Government now presents it. As a result, we decline to resolve it here. Because we find it necessary to vacate the judgment of the Court of Appeals with respect to a third argument presented by the District, the unitary waters argument will be open to the parties on remand.

C

In the courts below, as here, the District contended that the C–11 canal and WCA–3 impoundment area are not distinct water bodies at all, but instead are two hydrologically indistinguishable parts of a single water body. The Government agrees with the District on this point, claiming that because the C–11 canal and WCA–3 "share a unique, intimately related, hydrological association," they "can appropriately be viewed, for purposes of Section 402 of the Clean Water Act, as parts of a single body of water." The Tribe does not dispute that if C–11 and WCA–3 are simply two parts of the same water body, pumping water from one into the other cannot constitute an "addition" of pollutants. As the Second Circuit put it in *Trout Unlimited*, "[i]f one takes a ladle of soup from a pot, lifts it above the pot, and pours it back into the pot, one has not 'added' soup or anything else to the pot." 273 F.3d at 492. What the Tribe disputes is the accuracy of the District's factual premise; according to the Tribe, C–11 and WCA–3 are two pots of soup, not one.

The record does contain information supporting the District's view of the facts. Although C–11 and WCA–3 are divided from one another by the L–33 and L–37 levees, that line appears to be an uncertain one. Because Everglades soil is extremely porous, water flows easily between ground and surface waters, so much so that "[g]round and surface waters are essentially the same thing." C–11 and WCA–3, of course, share a common underlying aquifer. Moreover, the L–33 and L–37 levees continually leak, allowing water to escape from WCA–3. This means not only that any boundary between C–11 and WCA–3 is indistinct, but also that there is some significant mingling of the two waters; the record reveals that even without use of the S–9 pump station, water travels as both seepage and groundwater flow between the water conservation area and the C–11 basin.

The parties also disagree about how the relationship between S–9 and WCA–3 should be assessed. At oral argument, counsel for the Tribe focused on the differing "biological or ecosystem characteristics" of the respective waters, while counsel for the District emphasizes the close hydrological connections between the two. Despite these disputes, the District Court granted summary judgment to the Tribe. It applied a test that neither party defends; it determined that C–11 and WCA–3 are distinct "because the transfer of water or its contents from C–11 into the

Everglades would not occur naturally." The Court of Appeals for the Eleventh Circuit endorsed this test.

We do not decide here whether the District Court's test is adequate for determining whether C–11 and WCA–3 are distinct. Instead, we hold only that the District Court applied its test prematurely. Summary judgment is appropriate only where there is no genuine issue of material fact. The record before us leads us to believe that some factual issues remain unresolved. The District Court certainly was correct to characterize the flow through the S–9 pump station as a non-natural one, propelled as it is by diesel-fired motors against the pull of gravity. And it also appears true that if S–9 were shut down, the water in the C–11 canal might for a brief time flow *east*, rather than west, as it now does. But the effects of shutting down the pump might extend beyond that. The limited record before us suggests that if S–9 were shut down, the area drained by C–11 would flood quite quickly. That flooding might mean that C–11 would no longer be a "distinct body of navigable water," but part of a larger water body extending over WCA–3 and the C–11 basin. It also might call into question the Eleventh Circuit's conclusion that S–9 is the cause in fact of phosphorous addition to WCA–3. Nothing in the record suggests that the District Court considered these issues when it granted summary judgment. Indeed, in ordering later emergency relief from its own injunction against the operation of the S–9 pump station, the court admitted that it had not previously understood that shutting down S–9 would "literally ope[n] the flood gates."

We find that further development of the record is necessary to resolve the dispute over the validity of the distinction between C–11 and WCA–3. After reviewing the full record, it is possible that the District Court will conclude that C–11 and WCA–3 are not meaningfully distinct water bodies. If it does so, then the S–9 pump station will not need an NPDES permit. In addition, the Government's broader "unitary waters" argument is open to the District on remand. Accordingly, the judgment of the United States Court of Appeals for the Eleventh Circuit is vacated, and the case is remanded for further proceedings consistent with this opinion.

It is so ordered.

[The concurring and dissenting opinion of Justice Scalia is omitted.]

Notes and Questions

1. Both *Gorsuch* and *Miccosukee Tribe* raise the question of whether and when the Clean Water Act requires water projects such as dams and canals to obtain NPDES permits when they negatively affect water quality. Are there good reasons to exempt dams, canals, and other water projects from the NPDES program? To what extent can the federal government avoid intruding into state water management while still protecting water quality from the harmful effects of dams, canals, and other water projects? For interesting discussions of the applicability of the Clean Water Act to hydrological modifications, see Steven G. Davison, Defining "Addition" of a Pollutant Into Navigable Waters from a Point Source Under the Clean

Water Act: The Questions Answered—And Those Not Answered—By *South Florida Water Management District v. Miccosukee Tribe of Indians*, 16 Fordham Envtl. L.J. 1 (2004); Robert A. Adler, The Two Lost Books in the Water Quality Trilogy: The Elusive Objectives of Physical and Biological Integrity, 33 Envtl. L. 29 (2003).

2. What is the relevance to the issues in *Gorsuch* and *Miccosukee Tribe* of the Wallop Amendment to the Clean Water Act, § 101(g), 33 U.S.C. § 1251(g), which provides that it "is the policy of Congress that the authority of each State to allocate quantities of water within its jurisdiction shall not be superseded, abrogated, or otherwise impaired" by the provisions of the Act? How do the D.C. Circuit and the Supreme Court differ in their treatment of the Wallop Amendment?

3. The United States Supreme Court in *Miccosukee Tribe* ultimately does not decide when, if ever, hydrological modification requires an NPDES permit. What are the pros and cons of the federal government's "unitary waters" approach? If the question is whether water from one waterbody is being emptied into the waters of a "distinct" waterbody, how should courts determine whether the two bodies of water are "meaningfully distinct" rather than "hydrologically indistinguishable parts of a single water body"? Why should it matter? Should the inquiry simply be whether the hydrological modification leads to deteriorated water quality in some area of a waterway?

4. In deciding whether the diversion of water from one waterway to another requires an NPDES permit, does the source of the "pollution" matter? Should it? New York City draws water from a number of watersheds, and the waters often end up becoming mixed as they are brought to the city's residents. In Catskill Mtns. Chapter of Trout Unlimited v. City of New York, 273 F.3d 481 (2nd Cir. 2001), environmentalists argued that the city needed to obtain an NPDES permit before taking water from Schoharie Reservoir, which was high in suspended solids, turbidity, and heat, and discharging the waters into the "naturally clearer and cooler" waters of Esopus Creek. The Court of Appeals agreed. In response to the city's argument that Congress in the Wallop Amendment sought to leave water management to the states, the court noted that

> like many complex statutes (and the CWA is among the most complex), the CWA balances a welter of consistent and inconsistent goals. In contrast with the policies cited by the City, the CWA also expressly includes a broad and uncompromising policy of "restoring and maintaining the chemical, physical, and biological integrity of the Nation's waters." 33 U.S.C. § 1251(a). Artificially transferring water and pollutants between watersheds as the City has done here might well interfere with that integrity, as Catskill has alleged.

5. Courts have consistently rejected arguments that dams should obtain NPDES permits—even when they discharge entrained fish. In addition to *Gorsuch*, see National Wildlife Federation v. Consumers Power Co., 862 F.2d 580 (6th Cir. 1988); United States ex rel. TVA v. Tennessee Water Quality Control Bd., 717 F.2d 992 (6th Cir. 1983); Missouri ex rel. Ashcroft v. Department of the Army, 672 F.2d 1297 (8th Cir. 1982). For criticism of the *Gorsuch* and *Missouri* decisions, see John Attey & Drew Liebert, Clean

Water, Dirty Dams: Oxygen Depletion and the Clean Water Act, 11 Ecology L.Q. 703 (1984).

6. Merely withdrawing water from a waterway can lead to saltwater intrusion downstream or further concentrate existing salinity or other pollution. Does the Clean Water Act require states to limit such diversions? Section 208 requires states and local agencies, as part of their waste treatment management plans, to

> (i) identify, if appropriate, salt water intrusion into rivers, lakes, and estuaries resulting from reduction of fresh water flow from any cause, including irrigation, obstruction, ground water extraction, and diversion, and (ii) set forth procedures and methods to control such intrusion to the extent feasible

but only "where such procedures and methods are *otherwise a part* of the waste treatment plan." 33 U.S.C. § 1288(b)(1)(I) (emphasis added). The latter qualifier, which is not found elsewhere in section 208, suggests that whether to limit water diversions is totally up to the states. This is also consistent with the Wallop Amendment. See Colorado Wild, Inc. v. United States Forest Service, 122 F. Supp. 2d 1190 (D. Colo. 2000) (withdrawal of water from the Snake River, although concentrating pollution, "is not a discharge of pollution" and does not violate the Act); United States v. State Water Resources Control Bd., 182 Cal.App.3d 82, 227 Cal.Rptr. 161, 172–73 (1986) (Act requires states to set quality standards for salinity but provides no means of implementing the standards).

Should water withdrawals be treated differently than other "sources" of contamination under the Clean Water Act? As originally proposed in 1972, the Clean Water Act would have included stringent controls on saltwater intrusion. According to Stuart Somach, Water Quality/Water Quantity Conflicts in California, Nat. Resources & Env't, Fall 1986, at 39, the controls were removed "as a result of the stated concern of the California State Water Resources Control Board that such regulation would divest the Board of control over its water resource development program."

7. Reversing the state's common law rule (see Antioch v. Williams Irrig. Dist., supra p. 1013), California nevertheless has chosen under its water quality legislation to regulate diversions where necessary to limit saltwater intrusion. As discussed in Chapter 6 at page 628, diversions from the San Joaquin and Sacramento river systems have permitted salt water to invade the delta of the two rivers. In 1971, and again in 1978, the State Water Resources Control Board issued decisions requiring the federal Central Valley Project and the California State Water Project to release additional water into the delta in an effort to reduce the salt water intrusion. In United States v. State Water Resources Control Bd., supra Note 6, the California Court of Appeal not only upheld the board's authority to issue such orders but concluded that the board should have also considered curtailing diversions by other water users. 227 Cal.Rptr. at 177–81. For discussions of the many interesting issues raised by the court's decision, see supra pp. 628–639; Brian Gray, The Modern Era in California Water Law, 45 Hastings L.J. 249, 267–70 (1994); Ronald Robie, The Delta Decisions: The Quiet Revolution in California's Water Rights, 19 Pac. L.J. 1111 (1988).

d. Ambient Water Quality Standards

The Clean Water Act's emphasis on technology-based effluent limitations reflects Congress' disillusionment in 1972 with the water quality approach of the 1965 Water Quality Act. As noted earlier, the 1965 Act tried to reduce interstate water pollution by requiring each state to adopt water quality standards and then develop plans to achieve those standards.

The approach failed for several reasons. First, states did not have the political willpower to reduce discharges by a sufficient margin to achieve their standards. Second, the water quality approach proved technically challenging. Scientific information was often inadequate to determine the specific quality standard needed to allow a particular use of a waterway such as fishing or swimming. Models designed to translate standards into workable effluent limits for particular sources were complicated—yet did not come close to representing the complex process by which effluents mix and affect water quality. Polluters often used the scientific uncertainty to argue that their discharges were not the source of water quality problems. For an interesting discussion of the history of the 1965 Act's water quality approach, see Oliver Houck, TMDLs: The Resurrection of Water Quality Standards–Based Regulation Under the Clean Water Act, 27 Envtl. L. Rep. 10329 (1997) (hereinafter TMDLs I).

In light of these reported difficulties, the Senate in 1972 proposed totally abandoning quality standards. At the House of Representatives' insistence, however, Congress chose to retain water quality standards as a supplement to the technology-based effluent limitations. The principal requirements are set out in section 303 of the Clean Water Act.[1] Each state begins by designating specific beneficial uses for each of its waterways. Examples of typical beneficial uses include fish consumption (requiring water sufficiently clean that fish caught from the waters pose no health risk to consumers) and drinking water supply. States next establish water quality standards needed to support the designated uses. Typically the standards are quantitative (e.g., no more than 8 milligrams per liter of a particular contaminant); standards for toxic pollutants *must* be quantitative.[2] Except in limited settings, the quality standards must provide at least for the "protection and propagation of fish, shellfish, and wildlife" and for "recreation in and on the water"—thus supporting the Act's "interim" 1983 goal of "fishable and swimmable" waters—and must protect against any degradation of current water quality.[3] To help states set the standards, EPA prepares water quality criteria, based on the latest scientific information, showing the minimum physical, chemical, and biological parameters required to support various designated uses of a waterway.[4] States must review and, if appropriate, revise their standards at least every three years.[5] If a state fails to set

1. 33 U.S.C. § 1313.

2. Clean Water Act § 303(c)(2)(B), 33 U.S.C. § 1313(c)(2)(B).

3. Id. §§ 303(c)(2)(A) & (d)(4), 33 U.S.C. §§ 1313(c)(2)(A) & (d)(4).

4. Id. § 304(a), 33 U.S.C. § 1314(a).

5. Id. § 303(C), 33 U.S.C. § 1313(C).

adequate water standards, the federal government can set its own standards for the state.[6]

The Act also requires states to identify those waterways where the technology-based effluent limitations are insufficient to attain the water quality standards. For such "quality-limited" waterways, states must determine the "Total Maximum Daily Load" (or TMDL) of pollutants that can be discharged while achieving "the applicable water quality standards with seasonal variations and a margin of safety which takes into account any lack of knowledge concerning the relationship between effluent limitations and water quality."[7]

For the Act's first quarter century, however, most states failed to comply with these requirements. And EPA looked the other way, focusing instead on the Act's technology-based effluent limitations. Congress encouraged this neglect. Senator Edmund Muskie, who was the principal Senate author of the Clean Water Act, instructed EPA to "assign secondary priority" to the water quality standards. Houck, TMDLs I, supra, at 10338. Nor was it clear what EPA could do if a state failed to identify quality impaired waterways and set TMDLs. The Act requires states to submit lists of quality impaired waterways and TMDLs to EPA, which can then approve or disapprove the lists; if EPA disapproves the list, EPA must then prepare its own list.[8] But the Act says nothing explicitly about what happens if a state does not submit a list at all. For discussions of EPA's and the states' initial neglect of the water quality provisions, see Houck, TMDLs I, supra; Oliver Houck, TMDLs, Are We There Yet?: The Long Road Toward Water Quality–Based Regulation Under the Clean Water Act, 27 Envtl. L. Rep. 10391 (1997) (hereinafter TMDLs II).

A series of lawsuits in the 1980s and 1990s, however, has forced EPA to take seriously the Act's requirements for water quality standards. In 1984, a Court of Appeals held that the "prolonged failure" of a state to file a list of quality-impaired waterways could constitute a "constructive submission" of no TMDLs, triggering EPA's duty to prepare its own TMDLs. Scott v. City of Hammond, 741 F.2d 992 (7th Cir. 1984). Then in 1996, a District Court found EPA's approval of a list omitting waters the state previously had identified as impaired to be arbitrary and capricious. Idaho Sportsmen's Coalition v. Browner, 951 F.Supp. 962 (W.D. Wash. 1996). The message was clear: both states and EPA must comply with the Clean Water Act's water quality requirements.

Two important questions remained open when this casebook went to press in 2006. First, do TMDLs apply to non-point sources, or only point sources? Second, what happens if a state properly prepares TMDLs but then does not implement them? What, if any, authority does EPA have

---

6. Id. §§ 303(b) & (c)(3)-(4), 33 U.S.C. §§ 1313(b) & (c)(3)-(4).

7. Id. § 303(d)(1), 33 U.S.C. § 1313(d)(1).

8. Clean Water Act, § 303(d)(2), 33 U.S.C. § 1313(d)(2).

to implement TMDLs? As Professor Oliver Houck explains in the following excerpt from his excellent series of articles on TMDLs, the answer to this latter question is far from clear.

> Once [states have prepared lists of quality-impaired waterways and prepared TMDLs], the language of § 303(d) ends. Section 303(e) proceeds to require a "continuing planning process" (CPP) with "plans" that "include" § 303(d)'s TMDLs. While these sections authorize EPA to approve or disapprove a CPP on the basis, inter alia, of TMDLs, they do not authorize the Agency to implement them. The question is, at this point, has the statute run its string? Does all the work of TMDLs and their load allocations wind up as references in state plans, implemented if and as the states may wish? Or does the TMDL itself have to include the means of its own implementation in order to receive EPA's approval? EPA's authority to review and reject TMDLs may succeed in securing the inclusion of those steps and commitments necessary to implement them, retaining some meaningful outcome for the process. Further, if these measures are inadequate, EPA may reject a TMDL and may then promulgate measures of its own in a federal TMDL. But then what? For point sources, the Agency may ensure that those additional limitations imposed by a TMDL are actually implemented through its supervision of discharge permits under the NPDES program. But for nonpoint sources, here is the rub: there are no federal controls over nonpoint sources under the Clean Water Act. For these sources, the § 303(d) program leads, ultimately, to a state prerogative. If it is found to cover [nonpoint] sources at all.

Houck, TMDL II, supra, at 10399. See also Oliver Houck, TMDLs III: A New Framework for the Clean Water Act's Ambient Standards Program, 28 Envtl. L. Rep. 10415 (1998).

Courts to date have consistently concluded that the water quality standards of the Clean Water Act do not require states to regulate nonpoint pollution causing violations of the ambient water quality standards. "While the CWA requires states to designate water standards and identify bodies of water that fail to meet these standards, 'nothing in the CWA demands that a state adopt a regulatory system for nonpoint sources.' " Defenders of Wildlife v. United States EPA, 415 F.3d 1121, 1124 (10th Cir. 2005), quoting American Wildlands v. Browner, 260 F.3d 1192, 1197 (10th Cir. 2001).

Notes and Questions

1. Given that EPA cannot force states to regulate non-point sources of pollution, must states list waterbodies that are impaired solely by nonpoint sources of pollution and develop TMDLs for such waterbodies? See Pronsolino v. Nastri, 291 F.3d 1123 (9th Cir. 2002) (section 303 applies fully to such waters).

2. Is there any reason to believe that the TMDL requirements will work any better than the water quality approach of the 1965 Clean Water Act? According to Professor Houck, a supporter of TMDLs:

> Pollution control science based on ambient standards have always relied more on science than science can deliver. They are looking for numbers, thresholds, and fixed limits. They require proof of causes and effects that, arguably, come from other causes and have other effects, and pinning the tail on the right donkey has plagued air, water, and toxic programs from their inception * * *.

Oliver Houck, TMDLs IV: The Final Frontier, 29 Envtl. L. Rep. 10469, 10475 (1999).

3. Indeed, could the increased emphasis on TMDLs be counterproductive? According to Professor Houck, farms and other nonpoint sources have responded to the TMDL threat by convincing states to list only those waterways that scientists unhesitatingly conclude are impaired. "[Many states have actually cut their § 303(d) lists in half since 1996, relegating hundreds of waters to such categories as 'further study,' 'insufficient information,' and only 'moderately impaired.' " Id. at 10476. In an effort to avoid the impact of tight TMDLs, moreover, sources of pollution also have urged states to lower their applicable water quality standards by changing the designated use to a less quality-sensitive purpose. Id.

4. Section 304(l) of the Clean Water Act, which deals with toxic pollutants, provides a success story for water quality standards. In amending the Act in 1987, Congress required all states to submit to EPA a list of waterways not meeting quality standards because of toxic pollutants. The lists were to identify the specific point sources responsible for the quality shortfall, the amount of toxics discharged by each such source, and "an individual control strategy" for each source designed to achieve water quality standards. Prodded by EPA, states ultimately identified nearly 600 toxic waterways and implemented more than 675 individual control strategies. See Oliver Houck, TMDLs: The Resurrection of Water Quality Standards–Based Regulation Under the Clean Water Act, 27 Envtl. L. Rep. 10329 (1997).

5. The question remains whether the new emphasis on TMDLs is worth it. "All the money and effort spend in calibrating loads and 'proving' impacts could be better spent developing explicit technology-based best management practices, sweetening them through financial incentives, and enforcing them through the same permit mechanisms that have proven so successful in the CWA and other laws." Houck, TMDLs IV, supra note 2, at 10485. Professor Houck, nonetheless, believes that TMDLs should be embraced because they "provide both a bottom line and their own reason to get there, a reason that everybody can understand. * * * We are not 'treating for treatment sake' * * *; we are treating for something tangible that we all drink, fish, swim in, and simply look at with the pleasure of knowing that it is alive and well." Id.

6. Efforts to implement water quality standards inevitably highlight the linkage between water quality and water quantity because water quality can be improved either by reducing pollution or increasing stream flow. The following case involves EPA's veto of an NPDES permit that proposed

meeting water quality standards by augmenting the flow rather than reducing the discharge.

FORD MOTOR CO. v. ENVIRONMENTAL PROTECTION AGENCY

United States Court of Appeals for the Sixth Circuit, 1977.
567 F.2d 661.

WEICK, CIRCUIT JUDGE.

[In late 1974 Ford obtained an NPDES permit for discharges from its Monroe, Michigan stamping plant into the Raisin River. In July 1975, Michigan proposed modifying the permit at Ford's request to allow Ford to meet the state water quality standards by augmenting the river's flow with water from Lake Erie; the additional water would dilute Ford's effluents sufficiently to meet the quality standards.]

The proposed modification was succinctly stated by Jeffrey G. Miller, EPA Deputy Assistant Administrator for Water Enforcement:

> The relevant facts are that the best practicable technology will achieve necessary reduction in pounds of pollutants discharged but that the resulting concentration in the volume of process effluent is still greater than concentration limits specified in the Michigan Water Quality Standards. The State proposes to allow flow augmentation (dilution) to meet the water quality standard concentration limitations. Monitoring for compliance with the BPT [effluent] limitations is to be done prior to dilution. Monitoring for compliance with the water quality standards concentration limitations is to be done at [a point approximately 900 feet below the point of discharge].

[EPA, however, vetoed the proposal on the ground that flow augmentation was inconsistent with the in-stream concentration limits of Michigan's water quality standards.]

[T]he EPA Administrator has authority to refuse a NPDES permit proposed by the State if the Administrator, within ninety days of the State's transmittal of the proposed permit, objects to it in writing "as being outside the guidelines and requirements" of the [Clean Water Act]. § 402(d)(2)(B).

Ford argues that EPA objected to the use of low-flow augmentation to meet water quality standards under the [Act] solely upon EPA's own ad hoc policy determination * * *. Ford further contends that there are no published regulations, guidelines or specific statutory requirements under the [Act] prohibiting the use of low-flow augmentation to meet water quality standards. Ford concludes, therefore, that EPA exceeded its veto authority when it denied Ford the permit modification because § 402(d)(2)(B) allows EPA to object only to the issuance of NPDES permits which are outside the guidelines and requirements of the [Act], and not upon the EPA's private policy determination. In fact, Ford maintains that EPA's action in the present case denied Ford, as a permittee, its statutory right to a hearing on the issues related to the permit. Ford argues that although § 402(b)(3) provides the permittee a right to a hearing under a state's permit program, EPA in effect renders this statutory right to a hearing a nullity when it declines to issue a NPDES permit for any policy reason, rather than upon "previously promulgated generic guidelines." We believe that the main thrust of Ford's argument is well taken.

It is clear from the record in this appeal that EPA had no prior well-established agency policy which prohibited the use of low-flow augmentation to meet water quality standards. * * * An examination of the various statutory provisions of the [Act] indicates that Congress, among other things, directed EPA to publish guidelines and regulations setting forth the effluent limitations applicable to point sources. * * * The absence of such regulations and guidelines, as well as the lack of specific statutory requirements under the Act relating to the use of flow augmentation to meet water quality standards, precludes EPA's denial of a modification on a NPDES permit as to flow augmentation under § 402(d)(2)(B) because such modification is not "outside the guidelines and requirements" of the Act. * * *

ENGEL, CIRCUIT JUDGE, dissenting.

I respectfully dissent. The practical effect of the majority opinion is to hold that if a pollution discharge is not expressly forbidden by the [Clean Water Act], EPA regulations or state-adopted water quality standards, it is permitted. * * *

In my view it is precisely because flow augmentation is not specifically authorized as a means of achieving concentrations under Michigan's water quality standards that the EPA is justified in intervening. * * *

While it is not necessary to hold that flow augmentation is implicitly forbidden by the [Clean Water Act], there is much within the Act and its history to support such a view. Congress chose the phrase "effluent *limitation*" to describe the means for obtaining water quality.[5] * * * The goals and policy of Congress, as declared in the statute itself, include the prevention, reduction and elimination of pollutants from the nation's water. The statute, needless to say, does not speak in terms of dilution. It is significant, however, that the Conference Committee replaced the words "abate" and "abatement" with "reduction" and "elimination" in Sections 101 and 102.[a] S. Conf. Rep. 92–1236, 92d Cong., 2d Sess. (1972), reprinted in 2 U.S. Code Cong. & Admin. News at 3778 (1972). Flow augmentation, it is agreed, simply reduces the concentration of pollu-

---

5. In addition, the nationwide system of discharge permits, which governs Ford's Monroe plant and thousands of other point sources, is formally entitled the National Pollution Discharge *Elimination* System.

a. Section 101 contains Congress' declaration of goals and policies and, as already noted, states a "national goal that the discharge of pollutants into the navigable wa-

ters be *eliminated* by 1985." Clean Water Act § 101(a)(1), 33 U.S.C. § 1251(a)(1) (emphasis added). Section 102 requires EPA to develop comprehensive programs with other governmental agencies "for preventing, reducing, or eliminating" water pollution. Id. § 102(a), 33 U.S.C. § 1252(a).—Eds.

tants introduced into a body of water. It does not, however, eliminate or reduce the quantity of the pollution.

A further indication of national policy is to be gleaned from Section 102(b)(1) of the Act, 33 U.S.C. § 1252(b)(1), which states:

> In the survey or planning of any reservoir by the Corps of Engineers, Bureau of Reclamation, or other Federal agency, consideration shall be given to inclusion of storage for regulation of streamflow, except that *any such storage and water releases shall not be provided as a substitute for adequate treatment or other methods of controlling waste at the source.* (Emphasis added).

The flow augmentation contemplated by Section 102(b)(1) involves the release of impounded waters at a time of low flow. The Act notes that such augmentation shall not be a substitute for "adequate treatment or other methods of controlling waste at the source."

The Conference Committee Report noted with respect to Section 102(b)(1):

> *The Conference substitute specifically bans pollution dilution as an alternative to waste treatment.* At the same time it recognizes that *steam flow augmentation may be useful as a means of reducing the environmental impact of runoff from nonpoint sources.* The Conference substitute also recognizes that stream flow augmentation may be useful for recreational, navigation, and other purposes. Finally, section 102(b) specifically sets forth that any calculation for the need for and value of stream flow augmentation to reduce the impact of pollution must be determined by the Administrator of the Environmental Protection Agency. (Emphasis added).

S. Conf. Rep. No. 92–1236, 92d Cong., 2d Sess. (1972), reprinted in 2 U.S. Code Cong. & Admin. News at 3778–79 (1972).

> Without question, Ford's Monroe plant is a "point source," as defined in [the Act], and is thus not within the qualified exception recognized in the Conference Committee Report. The conclusion is inescapable that the drafters of the [Act] did not intend industrial dischargers of waste materials from point sources such as Ford's Raisin River plant to achieve statutory compliance by using dilution as a substitute for waste treatment. * * *

Notes and Questions

1. EPA subsequently has issued regulations concerning flow augmentation:

> Technology-based treatment requirements cannot be satisfied through the use of "non-treatment" techniques such as flow augmentation and in-stream mechanical aerators. However, these techniques can be considered as a method of achieving water quality standards on a case-by-case basis when:

(1) The technology-based treatment requirements applicable to the discharge are not sufficient to achieve the standards;

(2) The discharger agrees to waive any opportunity to request a variance [from the technology-based effluent limitations]; and

(3) The discharger demonstrates that such a technique is the preferred environmental and economic method to achieve the standards after consideration of alternatives such as advanced waste treatment, recycle and reuse, land disposal, changes in operating methods, and other available methods.

40 C.F.R. § 125.3(f).

2. Why shouldn't a factory be permitted to meet water quality standards by increasing the flow of the river either by importing water or by curtailing current upstream diversions? If it is cheaper to increase streamflow than to install additional pollution control equipment, isn't society better off by permitting flow augmentation? According to Professor William Rodgers, flow augmentation is a complex quality tool that, if not carefully planned and managed, can easily fail. 2 William Rodgers, Environmental Law 366–67 (1986). In addition,

It is a pollution dilution strategy that serves to forgive or mask the wrongful discharges of the offender. The policy is wrong morally because it allows the polluter to entertain options other than cessation of discharge. It is worse hydrologically because it invites engineering excesses by manipulating the stream to accommodate the discharge rather than the other way around. And it is worse than worse morally and economically if the augmentation is done at government expense so as to subsidize continuing pollution discharges.

Id. at 366. To help avoid against the latter possibility, the Clean Water Act provides that water releases from federal water projects "shall not be provided as a substitute for adequate treatment or other methods of controlling waste at the source." Clean Water Act § 102(b)(1), 33 U.S.C. § 1252(b)(1). The value of providing extra storage in a federal project for purposes of flow augmentation, moreover, is to be determined by EPA, not the sponsoring agency. Id. § 102(b)(3), 33 U.S.C. § 1252(b)(3).

3. As Judge Engel notes, Congress suggested that flow augmentation should not be an alternative to waste treatment, but could serve "as a means of reducing the environmental impact of runoff from non-point sources." Why should flow augmentation be an adequate alternative to controlling nonpoint contamination, but not point pollution?

4. State water agencies are increasingly opposed to the use of water for pollution dilution. In the view of some agencies, pollution dilution is ordinarily a less valuable use of water than alternative out-of-stream uses. See Anne Squier, Water Quality Under Western Water Law: Water Quality, Water Quantity: The Reluctant Marriage, 21 Envtl. L. 1081, 1083 (1991). Justice Gregory Hobbs of the Colorado Supreme Court also has objected that devoting water to pollution dilution "is nothing more than a back door way

of imposing the natural flow theory of riparian water law on prior appropriation states." Id. at 1084.

5. Should the Clean Water Act bar a state from permitting new water diversions or changes in existing diversions that would, by removing diluting flow, lead to a downstream violation of water quality standards? Can the federal government issue a section 404 permit for a water project that would lead to such a diversion? Look again at the relevant language of section 404, quoted supra pp. 646–647. According to EPA, a section 404 permit cannot issue if it would lead to a violation of water quality standards, *unless* additional nonpoint or point restrictions are imposed to compensate. See EPA, Questions and Answers on Antidegradation 11 (Aug. 1985).

CITY OF THORNTON v. BIJOU IRRIGATION CO.

Supreme Court of Colorado, 1996.
926 P.2d 1.

JUSTICE LOHR delivered the Opinion of the Court.

[Faced by deteriorating local water quality and a growing population, the city of Thornton, Colorado, embarked on an ambitious water project to import 50,000 acre-feet of water per year from the Cache La Poudre River. As part of this project, Thornton applied to the Colorado water court to transfer certain water rights to its service area, to "exchange" new diversions for the elimination of existing water uses, and to appropriate yet additional water. Numerous objections were filed, including by the Eastman Kodak Company. Kodak complained that Thornton's diversions of water from the Cache La Poudre River might require Kodak to meet more stringent effluent standards.]

Kodak's discharge of treated wastewater is conducted under a wastewater discharge permit issued by the Colorado Department of Health Water Quality Control Division (Water Quality Division or Division). Pursuant to this permit, Kodak's discharge must meet or remain below certain effluent limits for various chemicals, including ammonia. These effluent limits are based in part on an average low-flow value in the river in the vicinity of Kodak's discharge point,[80] and Kodak has consistently met these current limitations through operation of its existing treatment facility.

Thornton's proposed Poudre River exchange will have a negative, if indirect, impact on Kodak's waste treatment operations. The exchange proposed by Thornton contemplates the diversion of water from the

---

80. Discharge permits regulate discharges through effluent limits, which set forth the permissible concentrations of pollutants in the discharged wastewater. The effluent limits are calculated to ensure that water quality standards developed by the Water Quality Commission will be met in each relevant area of the stream. One controlling variable in calculating effluent limits is the volume of water in the stream just upstream of the discharge point. The volume of water is measured as a statistically determined, biologically based average low flow, termed the 30 E 3 flow. Should a detrimental change in stream flow occur, the Division is authorized to impose stricter effluent limits to maintain the water quality standards. Thus, a reduction in average low-flow conditions in a stream may result in stricter effluent limits in a discharge permit.

Poudre River above the location of Kodak's plant and return of the substitute supply into the Poudre below the plant. The water being exchanged upon is not water necessary to satisfy Kodak's appropriative rights—i.e., the amount of water remaining in the river after the exchange diversion will be sufficient to allow Kodak to divert the full amount of its appropriative right. Furthermore, as a consequence of the location of the point chosen for return of the substitute supply, none of the substituted water even passes by the Kodak facility. The effect of the exchange about which Kodak complains, however, is the substantial depletion of Poudre River flows at Kodak's plant. Kodak presented evidence that this depletion in flow will affect the average low-flow rates on which Kodak's effluent limits are based and result in stricter union-ized ammonia limits on Kodak's discharged water. Kodak alleges that such more stringent standards would require the construction of an entirely new treatment facility at a cost of between nine and twelve million dollars. Kodak objected to Thornton's exchange, seeking imposi-tion by the water court of unspecified terms and conditions to protect the company against these negative impacts on its treatment operations.

In its Memorandum of Decision, the trial court interpreted Kodak's request for protective terms and conditions as a request for a minimum instream flow right for waste dilution purposes, and held that it was forbidden to decree such a right except as specifically authorized by statute. The court noted that "issues relating to water quality are primarily the concern of the appropriate federal and state administrative agencies." The court ultimately approved the exchange subject to various conditions designed to provide protection of water quality. However, these conditions assure that the substitute supply to be introduced into the river below Kodak's plant will meet statutory standards and do not provide any relief to Kodak. Accordingly, Kodak appeals the trial court's decision to approve the Poudre River exchange without specifically addressing the impact of the exchange on Kodak's water treatment operations.

1. RELATION BETWEEN APPROPRIATION DOCTRINE AND QUALITY ISSUES

From the earliest cases, Colorado courts have given at least some recognition to water quality concerns, holding, for example, that a water right does not include the right to discharge pollutants that detrimental-ly affect downstream users. However, beyond recognition of this general prohibition on unreasonable discharges, the system of water quality regulation in Colorado reflects a continued conflict with and subordina-tion to the prior appropriation system. Rather than consolidating the power to regulate water quantity and water quality in the same body, Colorado divides responsibilities for these matters between two very distinct entities. The prior appropriation system, embodied in the adjudi-cation of appropriative rights to water, is presided over by the judiciary in general and the water court in particular. Operating under the constitutional and statutory policy of maximum beneficial use, the water court reviews applications for adjudication of appropriative rights and evaluates compliance with the statutorily mandated components of diversion and beneficial use. Although the water court must consider the effects on other water users when a water right owner seeks a change of water right, water court protection of such other users has traditionally been limited to ensuring that they do not suffer a decrease in the quantity of water available through exercise of their rights. See, e.g., In re Application for Water Rights in Las Animas Consol. Canal Co., 688 P.2d 1102 (Colo. 1984); City of Colo. Springs v. Bender, 148 Colo. 458, 366 P.2d 552 (1961). The court is explicitly required to consider water quality issues only in the case of an exchange whereby water is being actively substituted into the stream for the use of other appropriators. The water court's primary concern is thus limited to aspects of appropriations unrelated to water quality.

In the Colorado Water Quality Control Act, Colo. Rev. Stat. §§ 25–8–101 to –703, the legislature delegated authority over water quality regulation to the Water Quality Control Commission and the Water Quality Division. These agencies were created to develop and enforce water quality standards across the state. Although these agencies exercise considerable authority over water users, the legislature made clear its intention that this authority cannot be exercised in a manner that significantly compromises the appropriative rights of present or future water users. The Water Quality Control Act states in pertinent part:

> No provision of this article shall be interpreted so as to supersede, abrogate, or impair rights to divert water and apply water to beneficial uses in accordance with the provisions of sections 5 and 6 of article XVI of the constitution of the state of Colorado, compacts entered into by the state of Colorado, or the provisions of articles 80 to 93 of title 37, Colo. Rev. Stat., or Colorado court determinations with respect to the determination and administration of water rights.

> Nothing in this article shall be construed, enforced, or applied so as to cause or result in material injury to water rights.

§ 25–8–104(1). Water quality regulation that affects water rights without causing material injury or impairment is not necessarily prohibited. However, section 25–8–104(1) serves notice that despite the importance of water quality regulation, the legislature's primary emphasis in enacting this scheme is to maximize beneficial use and to minimize barriers to further beneficial appropriation. The result of this policy decision is essentially to focus water quality regulation on uses culminating in unreasonable discharges, as such discharges are not part of any appropriative right under common law.

For better or worse, this dual system limits the ability of both the water court and the water quality control agencies to address certain water quality issues. The plight of appropriators in Kodak's situation, who allege quality impacts as a result of appropriative depletion rather than substandard discharge or supply water, is a prime example of the limitations of the present system to provide remedies for all types of injuries. * * *

2. Relation Between Quality and Cognizable Injury

Kodak argues, however, that [the rule that prohibits water transfers and exchanges that will injure other water users required the trial court to impose] terms and conditions necessary to ensure that operation of the exchange will not "injuriously affect" Kodak's water rights. * * *

Kodak does not allege that operation of the Poudre River exchange will reduce the quantity of water available in the river to a volume less than the amount of its appropriative right. Kodak also cannot contend that the substitute supply provided by Thornton in the Poudre River exchange will affect the quality of the water diverted to its plant. The sole negative impact of the Poudre River exchange on Kodak's treatment operations results from a diminution in the flow of excess river water— i.e., water that would otherwise flow by Kodak's plant but that is in excess of the amount that can be diverted under Kodak's water right. Because the volume of water in a stream just upstream of the discharge point is a controlling variable in the formula to set effluent limits, Kodak contends that diminution in flow caused by operation of the exchange will necessarily result in more stringent effluent limits for Kodak. However, to avoid this impact on Kodak's treatment operations, the trial court would have had to impose conditions that required maintenance of sufficient volume in the stream to preserve the average low-flow values that determine Kodak's effluent limits. Despite Kodak's arguments to the contrary, such protection would necessarily require the imposition of conditions creating a private instream flow right for Kodak for the purpose of waste dilution or assimilation.

3. Relation Between Quality and Minimum Stream Flow

The legislature expressed a clear intent to prohibit private parties from adjudicating instream flow rights. Pursuant to section 37–92– 102(3), the General Assembly vested exclusive authority in a state entity, the Colorado Water Conservation Board (CWCB), to appropriate minimum stream flows and limited the purpose for these appropriations to "preserv[ation of] the environment to a reasonable degree." See City of Thornton v. City of Fort Collins, 830 P.2d 915, 930 (1992); Board of County Comm'rs v. Collard, 827 P.2d 546, 551 n.10 (Colo. 1992). The same provision reinforces this exclusivity with the following prohibition:

> In the adjudication of water rights pursuant to this article and other applicable law, no other person or entity shall be granted a decree adjudicating a right to water or interests in water for instream flows in a stream channel between specific points * * * for any purpose whatsoever.

§ 37–92–102(3). The meaning of this exclusive delegation of authority is clear—the judiciary is without authority to decree an instream flow right to any private entity.

The legislature similarly prohibited the Colorado Water Quality Commission and the Water Quality Division from imposing minimum instream flows in the course of their water quality protection activities. These agencies must perform their duties subject to the following restriction: "Nothing in this article shall be construed to allow the commission or the division to require minimum stream flows * * *." § 25–8–104(1). This language reinforces the legislative intent expressed in the water right adjudication provisions that minimum stream flows are not a valid tool for protecting water quality.

Even in the absence of a specific legislative prohibition, the type of right sought by Kodak is inconsistent with Colorado law and policy concerning appropriations. Kodak currently diverts the full amount of its appropriative right, * * * and the company does not argue that Thornton's exchange will affect its future ability to divert its maximum appropriated amount. Instead, Kodak claims an additional amount of water, above that amount which it can lawfully divert, to ensure the less expensive exercise of its right. Because this additional water exceeds the amount to which Kodak is entitled under its water right, Kodak cannot claim such water as part of its original appropriation. See Rominiecki v. McIntyre Livestock Corp., 633 P.2d 1064, 1067 (Colo. 1981) (appropriative right is limited to amount of water actually diverted and put to beneficial use). Without an appropriative right or otherwise established beneficial use, Kodak is not entitled to protection of its incidental use of this water against lawful appropriations by other users. See Colo. Const. art XVI, § 6 ("The right to divert the unappropriated water of any natural stream to beneficial uses shall never be denied."); see also *Bender*, 148 Colo. at 462, 366 P.2d at 555 ("[An appropriator] is not entitled to command the whole or a substantial flow of the stream merely to facilitate his taking the fraction of the whole flow to which he is entitled.") (citing Schodde v. Twin Falls Water Co., 224 U.S. 107, 119 (1911)). Absent a new appropriation, Kodak cannot establish a protected right to waters in excess of its current appropriation. We decline Kodak's invitation to avoid the effect of the specific prohibition on private instream flow rights by creating such a right in the guise of a condition imposed on the lawful appropriations of others. Under the current system, with its emphasis on maximum beneficial use, Kodak's reliance on unappropriated water in excess of its appropriative right is subject to the risk that a lawful appropriator will appropriate that excess water.

4. CONCLUSION

We are not unaware of the interrelationship between water quantity and water quality concerns or to the specific impact that Thornton's exchange will have on Kodak's operations. However, exchanges in the nature of Thornton's proposal are innovative methods of increasing the beneficial use of the state's waters. Under the current legislative scheme, the impact of which Kodak complains is tolerated as a consequence of the policy of maximum beneficial use. The decision whether further to integrate the consideration and administration of water quality concerns into the prior appropriation system is the province of the General Assembly or the electorate. Thus, we affirm the trial court's decision not to include conditions in the final decree designed to protect Kodak's waste treatment operations. * * *

Notes and Questions

1. Could Kodak avoid a tightening of its discharge standards by buying out upstream diversions? Would this be impermissible flow augmentation in violation of the EPA regulations discussed above?

2. Given that water quality and instream flow levels are inherently connected, should Congress require the states to maintain certain instream flows and perhaps even give EPA the power to set them where a state fails to do so? In 1977, the United States Water Resources Council recommended that Congress enact such legislation to protect the assimilative capacity of streams as well as fish, wildlife, recreation, and aesthetics. Congress responded by passing the Wallop Amendment, supra p. 650, Note 2, and requiring EPA to study the relationship between water quality and water allocation. A 1979 draft of EPA's study, which suggested that "minimum flows in themselves may be necessary to meet the objectives of the Clean Water Act," was withdrawn after western officials severely criticized it. See EPA, Draft Water Quality/Water Allocation Coordination Study (Aug. 28, 1979).

In the late 1990s, EPA considered developing optimum flow guidance that states could use in addressing instream flows. "EPA never actually produced flow guidance or criteria, however, probably due in large part to the opposition of traditional western water users and their allies." Reed D. Benson, Pollution Without Solution: Flow Impairment Problems Under Clean Water Act Section 303, 24 Stan. Envtl. L.J. 199 (2005).

3. Most states explicitly prohibit their environmental agencies from preventing diversions of surface water in order to protect water quality. See, e.g., Ariz. Rev. Stat. § 49–206 (Water Quality Control Act shall not be interpreted as preventing exercise of surface water rights); Nev. Rev. Stat. § 445.351 (Water Pollution Control Law does not amend or supersede water allocation laws); N.M. Stat. § 74–6–12(A) (Water Quality Control Commission cannot take away or modify water rights); Rev. Code Wash. § 90.48.422(3) (Department of Ecology cannot "abrogate, supersede, impair, or condition the ability of a water right holder to fully divert or withdraw water").

4. In 1967, California placed decisionmaking responsibility for both water allocation and water quality in the same administrative agency. The State Water Resources Control Board has ultimate responsibility for the state's water quality standards and can subject appropriations to whatever terms and conditions are necessary to meet the standards. Appropriation permits, moreover, expressly allow future modification where necessary to maintain those standards. At the same time, however, the Board functions to a considerable degree as if quantity and quality management are separate tasks.

Doesn't the inherent relationship between allocation and quality call for such joint management? Is there any disadvantage to integrating quality and allocation functions in one agency? According to one study of environmental laws, a "serious, seemingly permanent, drawback to integration is that tying water-quantity management more closely to that of water quality makes it more difficult to integrate water-quality programs with air and solid-waste regulation. Ending management fragmentation in one problem area may often cause it in another." Conservation Foundation, State of the Environment: An Assessment at Mid-Decade 382 (1984).

5. Where a waterway fails to meet water quality standards due to flow impairment, must the state list the waterway under section 303 and develop TMDLs for that waterway? Noting that flow impairment is not a "pollutant" and that TMDLs are designed to limit pollutants, EPA has rejected arguments that such waterways must be listed under section 303. See Benson, supra Note 2, at 236.

6. For valuable discussions of the relationships between water quality and quantity, see Benson, supra Note 2; Gregory Hobbs & Bennett Raley, Water Quality Versus Water Quantity: A Delicate Balance, 34 Rocky Mtn. Min. L. Inst. 24–1 (1989).

e. Section 401 Certification

PUD NO. 1 v. WASHINGTON DEPARTMENT OF ECOLOGY

Supreme Court of the United States, 1994.
511 U.S. 700.

JUSTICE O'CONNOR delivered the opinion of the Court.

Petitioners, a city and a local utility district, want to build a hydroelectric project on the Dosewallips River in Washington State. We must decide whether respondent state environmental agency (hereinafter respondent) properly conditioned a permit for the project on the maintenance of specific minimum stream flows to protect salmon and steelhead runs.

I

This case involves the complex statutory and regulatory scheme that governs our Nation's waters, a scheme that implicates both federal and state administrative responsibilities. The Federal Water Pollution Control Act, commonly known as the Clean Water Act, is a comprehensive water quality statute designed to "restore and maintain the chemical, physical, and biological integrity of the Nation's waters." 33 U.S.C. § 1251(a). The Act also seeks to attain "water quality which provides for the protection and propagation of fish, shellfish, and wildlife." § 1251(a)(2). * * *

The State of Washington has adopted comprehensive water quality standards intended to regulate all of the State's navigable waters. * * * As required by the Act, EPA reviewed and approved the State's water quality standards. Upon approval by EPA, the state standard became

only ensure that the project complies with "any applicable effluent limitations and other limitations, under [33 U.S.C. §§ 1311, 1312]" or certain other provisions of the Act, "and with any other appropriate requirement of State law." The State asserts that the minimum stream flow requirement was imposed to ensure compliance with the state water quality standards adopted pursuant to § 303 of the Clean Water Act. We agree with the State that ensuring compliance with § 303 is a proper function of the § 401 certification. Although § 303 is not one of the statutory provisions listed in § 401(d), the statute allows States to impose limitations to ensure compliance with § 301 of the Act [33 U.S.C. § 1311]. Section 301 in turn incorporates § 303 by reference. As a consequence, state water quality standards adopted pursuant to § 303 are among the "other limitations" with which a State may ensure compliance through the § 401 certification process. * * * Moreover, limitations to assure compliance with state water quality standards are also permitted by § 401(d)'s reference to "any other appropriate requirement of State law." We do not speculate on what additional state laws, if any, might be incorporated by this language. But at a minimum, limitations imposed pursuant to state water quality standards adopted pursuant to § 303 are "appropriate" requirements of state law. Indeed, petitioners appear to agree that the State's authority under § 401 includes limitations designed to ensure compliance with state water quality standards.

B

Having concluded that, pursuant to § 401, States may condition certification upon any limitations necessary to ensure compliance with state water quality standards or any other "appropriate requirement of State law," we consider whether the minimum flow condition is such a limitation. Under § 303, state water quality standards must "consist of the designated uses of the navigable waters involved and the water quality criteria for such waters based upon such uses." In imposing the minimum stream flow requirement, the State determined that construction and operation of the project as planned would be inconsistent with one of the designated uses of Class AA water, namely "salmonid [and other fish] migration, rearing, spawning, and harvesting." The designated use of the river as a fish habitat directly reflects the Clean Water Act's goal of maintaining the "chemical, physical, and biological integrity of the Nation's waters." 33 U.S.C. § 1251(a). Indeed, the Act defines pollution as "the man-made or man induced alteration of the chemical, physical, biological, and radiological integrity of water." § 1362(19). Moreover, the Act expressly requires that, in adopting water quality standards, the State must take into consideration the use of waters for "propagation of fish and wildlife." § 1313(c)(2)(A).

Petitioners * * * assert more generally that the Clean Water Act is only concerned with water "quality," and does not allow the regulation of water "quantity." This is an artificial distinction. In many cases, water quantity is closely related to water quality; a sufficient lowering of the water quantity in a body of water could destroy all of its designated uses, be it for drinking water, recreation, navigation or, as here, as a fishery. In any event, there is recognition in the Clean Water Act itself that reduced stream flow, i.e., diminishment of water quantity, can constitute water pollution. First, the Act's definition of pollution as "the man-made or man induced alteration of the chemical, physical, biological, and radiological integrity of water" encompasses the effects of reduced water quantity. 33 U.S.C. § 1362(19). This broad conception of pollution—one which expressly evinces Congress' concern with the physical and biological integrity of water—refutes petitioners' assertion that the Act draws a sharp distinction between the regulation of water "quantity" and water "quality." Moreover, § 304 of the Act expressly recognizes that water "pollution" may result from "changes in the movement, flow, or circulation of any navigable waters * * *, including changes caused by the construction of dams." 33 U.S.C. § 1314(f). This concern with the flowage effects of dams and other diversions is also embodied in the EPA regulations, which expressly require existing dams to be operated to attain designated uses. 40 C.F.R. § 131.10(g)(4) (1992).

Petitioners assert that two other provisions of the Clean Water Act, §§ 101(g) and 510(2), exclude the regulation of water quantity from the coverage of the Act. Section 101(g) provides "that the authority of each State to allocate quantities of water within its jurisdiction shall not be superseded, abrogated or otherwise impaired by this chapter." 33 U.S.C. § 1251(g). Similarly, § 510(2) provides that nothing in the Act shall "be construed as impairing or in any manner affecting any right or jurisdiction of the States with respect to the waters * * * of such States." 33 U.S.C. § 1370. In petitioners' view, these provisions exclude "water quantity issues from direct regulation under the federally controlled water quality standards authorized in § 303."

This language gives the States authority to allocate water rights; we therefore find it peculiar that petitioners argue that it prevents the State from regulating stream flow. In any event, we read these provisions more narrowly than petitioners. Sections 101(g) and 510(2) preserve the authority of each State to allocate water quantity as between users; they do not limit the scope of water pollution controls that may be imposed on users who have obtained, pursuant to state law, a water allocation. * * *

IV

Petitioners contend that we should limit the State's authority to impose minimum flow requirements because FERC has comprehensive authority to license hydroelectric projects pursuant to the FPA. In petitioners' view, the minimum flow requirement imposed here interferes with FERC's authority under the FPA.

The FPA empowers FERC to issue licenses for projects "necessary or convenient * * * for the development, transmission, and utilization of power across, along, from, or in any of the streams * * * over which Congress has jurisdiction." § 797(e). The FPA also requires FERC to consider a project's effect on fish and wildlife. §§ 797(e), 803(a)(1). In California v. FERC, 495 U.S. 490 (1990), we held that the California Water Resources Control Board, acting pursuant to state law, could not impose a minimum stream flow which conflicted with minimum stream flows contained in a FERC license. We concluded that the FPA did not "save" to the States this authority. No such conflict with any FERC licensing activity is presented here. FERC has not yet acted on petitioners' license application, and it is possible that FERC will eventually deny petitioners' application altogether. Alternatively, it is quite possible, given that FERC is required to give equal consideration to the protection of fish habitat when deciding whether to issue a license, that any FERC license would contain the same conditions as the state § 401 certification. Indeed, at oral argument the Deputy Solicitor General stated that both EPA and FERC were represented in this proceeding, and that the Government has no objection to the stream flow condition contained in the § 401 certification.

Finally, the requirement for a state certification applies not only to applications for licenses from FERC, but to all federal licenses and permits for activities which may result in a discharge into the Nation's navigable waters. For example, a permit from the Army Corps of Engineers is required for the installation of any structure in the navigable waters which may interfere with navigation, including piers, docks, and ramps. See Rivers and Harbors Appropriation Act of 1899, § 10, 33 U.S.C. § 403. Similarly, a permit must be obtained from the Army Corps of Engineers for the discharge of dredged or fill material, and from the Secretary of the Interior or Agriculture for the construction of reservoirs, canals, and other water storage systems on federal land. See Clean Water Act § 404, 33 U.S.C. §§ 1344(a), (e); 43 U.S.C. § 1761. We assume that a § 401 certification would also be required for some licenses obtained pursuant to these statutes. Because § 401's certification requirement applies to other statutes and regulatory schemes, and because any conflict with FERC's authority under the FPA is hypothetical, we are unwilling to read implied limitations into § 401. If FERC issues a license containing a stream flow condition with which petitioners disagree, they may pursue judicial remedies at that time.

In summary, we hold that the State may include minimum stream flow requirements in a certification issued pursuant to § 401 of the Clean Water Act insofar as necessary to enforce a designated use contained in a state water quality standard. The judgment of the Supreme Court of Washington, accordingly, is affirmed.

[The concurring opinion of Justice Stevens and the dissenting opinion of Justices Thomas and Scalia are omitted.]

Notes and Questions

1. Note that section 401 requires a state certification of any applicant for a federal license or permit seeking to engage in an activity "which may result in any *discharge* into the navigable waters." Does this include activities that may result in non-point discharges? Reversing a lower court

decision that had held that applicants for federal grazing permits must obtain a section 401 certification, the Ninth Circuit Court of Appeals has concluded that section 401 applies only to point sources. See Oregon Natural Desert Ass'n v. Dombeck, 172 F.3d 1092 (9th Cir. 1998). See also Colorado Wild, Inc. v. United States Forest Service, 122 F. Supp. 2d 1190 (D. Colo. 2000) (section 401 inapplicable to permits for water withdrawals that do not discharge pollution but merely reduce the dilution of existing pollution).

2. Must a dam operator obtain a section 401 certification if it seeks federal permission to *reduce* discharges from the dam? North Carolina v. Federal Energy Regulatory Comm'n, 112 F.3d 1175 (D.C. Cir. 1997), was one of the most recent chapters in Virginia Beach's efforts to obtain a new water supply from the Roanoke River. See supra pp. 88–101. Because Virginia Beach's intake structure will be located within the boundaries of a federally licensed power project, the operator of the project applied to FERC for a license amendment permitting the water diversion. North Carolina, within whose borders the dam itself is located, argued that the operator must obtain a section 401 certification from the North Carolina water control agency. The Court of Appeals disagreed:

> We recognize that the withdrawal of water from Lake Gaston will reduce the volume of water passing through the dam turbines. But neither the withdrawal of water from the Lake nor the reduction in the volume of water passing through the dam turbines "results in a discharge" for purposes of Section 401(a)(1). * * * [T]he word "discharge" contemplates the addition, not the withdrawal, of a substance or substances.

Id. at 1187. Judge Wald dissented, noting that "even alterations of existing discharges that do not 'add' any 'substance or substances' to the water may yet affect the water's 'movement, flow, or circulation,' " and thus constitute pollution. Id. at 1197.

3. For thoughts on the potential implications of the Supreme Court's decision in *PUD No. 1* for state instream flow policies, see David Baron, Water Quality Standards for Rivers and Lakes: Emerging Issues, 27 Ariz. St. L.J. 559, 581–88 (1995).

3. INTERSTATE POLLUTION ISSUES

a. *The Legal Regime*

As the Supreme Court has observed, "Interstate waters have been a font of controversy since the founding of the Nation." Arkansas v. Oklahoma, 503 U.S. 91, 98 (1992). Surprisingly, therefore, the Clean Water Act pays scant attention to interstate pollution. Section 103 of the Act requires the EPA Administrator to encourage "cooperative activities by the States * * * and, so far as practicable, uniform State laws relating to the prevention, reduction, and elimination of pollution."[1] The same section sanctions interstate compacts concerning water pollution.[2] Sections 401 and 402 of the Act provide states with notice and an opportunity to be heard before NPDES permits are issued for discharges

1. 33 U.S.C. § 1253(a).   2. 33 U.S.C. § 1253.

into an interstate waterway from neighboring states.[3] "Significantly, however, an affected State does not have the authority to block the issuance of the permit if it is dissatisfied with the proposed standards. An affected State's only recourse is to apply to the EPA Administrator, who then has the discretion to disapprove the permit if he concludes that the discharges will have an undue impact on interstate waters." International Paper Co. v. Ouellette, 479 U.S. 481, 490 (1987).

Recall that section 301 of the Clean Water Act requires point sources to achieve emission limitations "necessary to meet water quality standards." To what degree must emission limitations protect the water quality standards of downstream states? In Arkansas v. Oklahoma, 503 U.S. 91 (1992), Oklahoma objected to EPA's issuance of an NPDES permit authorizing a POTW in Arkansas to discharge sewage effluent into the Illinois River 39 miles upstream from the Oklahoma border. (EPA issued the permit because Arkansas had not qualified to administer the NPDES program.) In issuing the permit, EPA looked to see whether the discharge would cause an "actual detectable or measurable" impairment of Oklahoma's water quality and concluded that the discharge would not. Because the Illinois River was already out of compliance with Oklahoma's water quality standards, Oklahoma argued that the Clean Water Act prohibited *any* discharge that would reach Oklahoma waters. The Supreme Court concluded that EPA has the authority to consider downstream states' water quality standards in issuing NPDES permits, but rejected Oklahoma's argument that no discharge was permitted. The Court did not reach the question of whether EPA (or an issuing state) *must* consider the water quality standards of downstream states in issuing an NPDES permit.

Prior to passage of the Clean Water Act, the Supreme Court held that a state could sue under a "federal common law" of nuisance to abate pollution resulting from operations in another state. Illinois v. Milwaukee, 406 U.S. 91 (1972). Almost a decade later in what has become known as the *Milwaukee II* decision, however, the Court held that the Clean Water Act had preempted such federal common law actions. City of Milwaukee v. Illinois, 451 U.S. 304 (1981).

> Congress has not left the formulation of appropriate federal standards to the courts through application of often vague and indeterminate nuisance concepts and maxims of equity jurisprudence, but rather has occupied the field through the establishment of a comprehensive regulatory program supervised by an expert administrative agency. * * * There is * * * no question that the problem of effluent limitations has been thoroughly addressed through the administrative scheme established by Congress, as contemplated by Congress. This being so there is no basis for a federal court to impose more stringent limitations than those imposed under the regulatory regime by reference to federal common law * * *.

3.   33 U.S.C. §§ 1341(a)(2) & 1342(b).

Id. at 317, 320. In International Paper Co. v. Ouellette, 479 U.S. 481 (1987), moreover, the Court held that a Vermont resident could not invoke Vermont nuisance law to enjoin discharges in New York. "The inevitable result of such suits would be that Vermont and other States could do indirectly what they could not do directly—regulate the conduct of out-of-state sources." Aggrieved plaintiffs, however, can bring a nuisance action pursuant to the law of the source state.

b. *Salinity and the Colorado River*

The Colorado River presents both interstate and international salinity problems.[4] As one travels downstream on the Colorado River, the water gets saltier. The mountain streams that feed the upper reaches of the Colorado contain as little as 50 mg/l of total dissolved salt (or "TDS"); by the time the Colorado reaches the Imperial Dam just north of the Mexican border, salinity has risen to over 700 mg/l. With increased salinity comes added expenses and damages. The salinity has so far not proved a public health problem because communities receiving Colorado River water dilute it with other water to bring the salinity level down to drinking water standards. The high levels of salinity, however, have caused corrosion damage, forced industries to install expensive water treatment equipment, and taken a toll on plumbing and water appliances. Crop yields, moreover, have fallen, and longterm soil productivity has declined as salt has built up in the soil. Recent estimates put the total cost to the economy of the increased salinity at close to $1 billion annually. See Dale Pontius, Colorado River Basin Study: Report to the Western Water Policy Review Advisory Commission 67 (1998).

There are a number of causes of the salinity buildup. Almost half of the salinity results from natural sources. Many stretches of the Colorado River pass over soils and rocks laden with soluble salts that the water picks up. Many of the streams that feed the Colorado are also naturally saline. Blue Springs, which empties into the Little Colorado River in Arizona, for example, contributes 550,000 tons of salt every year. Another third of the Colorado's salinity comes from irrigation return flow. A not insignificant amount of salinity also results from reservoir evaporation and exports. As water evaporates from reservoirs, the remaining water increases in salinity. The diversion by upper basin states of water that is relatively low in salt, and that would thus tend to reduce the river's salinity, also increases the downstream salt content.

TAYLOR MILLER, GARY WEATHERFORD, & JOHN THORSON, THE SALTY COLORADO

25–31 (1986).

[In the 1960s, the] Colorado River salinity problem ranked high among the many water quality issues that attracted national attention.

---

4. As discussed in Chapter 8, the Colorado River Basin includes portions of seven different states and Mexico. See Figure 8–1, supra p. 803.

It was the subject of seven interstate conferences convened by the federal government between 1960 and 1972.

In 1965 Congress had passed the Water Quality Act, calling for states to establish water-quality standards and plans. As part of the implementation of this mandate, the states of the Colorado River basin were given until 1969 to develop salinity standards including numeric criteria for total dissolved solids (TDS). Citing unresolved scientific questions, the states opposed the setting of numeric criteria for TDS, chlorides, sulfates, and sodium in the Colorado River. In 1968 the federal government backed off, committing the subject to study.

A report issued in 1971 by the newly created [EPA] advised the basin states to take the steps necessary to establish a numeric objective for salinity concentration. The states supported the concept of maintaining salinity at 1972 levels but still argued that not enough was known about salinity control to justify adoption of numeric criteria. They also reiterated their view that salinity should be regarded as a "basin-wide problem that needs to be solved to maintain lower basin water salinity at or below present levels while the upper basin continues to develop its compact-apportioned water, recognizing that salinity levels may rise until control measures are made effective."

* * * In December 1974 EPA published a regulation [under the Clean Water Act] requiring the basin states to adopt numeric criteria that, together with an implementation plan for their achievement, would maintain salinity at or below the flow-weighted annual average for 1972 in the Colorado's lower main stem. EPA's general counsel interpreted the [Clean Water Act] to require each state in the basin to adopt salinity standards, and for a short time agency policy called for setting of standards at state lines.

The basin states adamantly opposed state-line standards, arguing instead for a basin-wide approach. They finally prevailed in 1976, when EPA and the states agreed [on numeric standards to apply at three lower-basin locations: below Hoover Dam, below Parker Dam, and Imperial Dam.] The standards also included an implementation plan that described actions to be taken to achieve the numeric criteria.

The numeric criteria approximated the flow-weighted average salinity for 1972 at the three measuring points. They generally conformed to EPA's policy but were not based on any analyses of what criteria were needed to protect beneficial uses or the economic and environmental trade-offs of higher or lower figures. * * * Interestingly, the salinity level at Imperial Dam in 1972 was about as high as at any previous time, before or since. The lower-basin states seem to have opted for a policy that recognized some damage would occur at this level but at least established a ceiling limiting future increases.

The Clean Water Act requires states and EPA review of water-quality standards at least once every three years. These reviews are coordinated in the basin states by the [Colorado River Basin Salinity

Control Forum, which the basin states formed in 1972 to oversee the development of salinity criteria.] * * *

EPA's 1974 regulation included a paragraph stating: "Salinity levels in the lower main stem may temporarily rise above the 1972 levels if control measures to offset the increases are included in the control plan. However, compliance with the 1972 levels shall be a primary consideration." The Salinity Control Forum's 1984 review noted that temporary increases in salinity above the numeric criteria may result from completion of water development projects before salinity control projects are brought on line. * * * The forum review document also stated that the numeric criteria might be exceeded because of below-normal river flows and resulting unfavorable reservoir conditions. Such increases will be deemed in conformance with the standards as long as they are "temporary." * * *

How is a true violation of the standards to be distinguished from a temporary increase "deemed to be in conformance"? Assuming a violation is somehow established, how would the standards actually be enforced?

These questions do not yield easy answers, but exploring them reveals some important differences from other water-quality problems addressed by the Clean Water Act. Federal water-quality standards for salinity may in fact best serve as tools to stimulate coordinated and active efforts by states and federal agencies to deal with the salt problem, rather than as the basis for decisive enforcement in the event of future salinity increases.

Returning to the first question: How can a violation be established? Given the forum's interpretation permitting temporary increases, establishing a violation requires that a case be made that high salinity is not caused either by low flows or by the outpacing of salinity control by water development * * *. A cause other than low flow or new water development is, of course, hard to imagine. Even if it were conceptually possible, it would be even harder to prove, given the complexities of the interactions of water use, basin hydrology, and geologic features.

With regard to the second question concerning methods of enforcement, the Clean Water Act does provide a range of civil and criminal enforcement remedies * * *. But a number of imposing obstacles arise here as well.

First, who can be held responsible for a violation of the lower-stem criteria. Who would the defendants be? One or more of the upstream states (for permitting new diversions or uses)? One or more water districts (for a new diversion or expansion of a service area)? Individual users (for the salt contributed by their particular uses and practices)? One or more of the federal agencies (for failing to implement needed control programs)? Congress (for failing to appropriate the money needed to undertake salinity control projects)?

Second, what relief could be obtained in an action brought under the act? Criminal or civil penalties against government officials remain remote or nonexistent possibilities. An injunction might be obtained, but what is the recourse if it is violated? The standard remedy of contempt of court has seldom been used against government and is unavailable in particular to force Congress to appropriate funds for salinity control.

Notes and Questions

1. In a 1996 report, the Colorado River Basin Salinity Control Forum (CRBSCF) estimated that, by 2015, approximately 1.5 million tons of salt will need to be removed annually from the Colorado River in order to maintain salinity levels at the 1972 levels. When the river is fully developed, the CRBSCF estimates that 1.8 million tons of salt will need to be removed. See CRBSCF, Triennial Review Report (1996).

2. In the Colorado River Basin Salinity Control Act of 1974 (CRBSCA), 43 U.S.C. §§ 1592 et seq., Congress provided federal funding for a variety of salinity control projects needed to achieve the desired salt levels. Many projects involve reducing water use and improving irrigation techniques in basin farming communities by, for example, carefully timing irrigation to avoid overapplication. The government also has purchased and retired some farm land, but state and local interests have vigorously opposed extensive buyouts. In some projects, the government intercepts saline water, for example by pumping it from saline aquifers, before the water reaches the Colorado. If as a result a downstream appropriator no longer receives sufficient water, is the appropriator constitutionally entitled to compensation?

3. The basin states' implementation plan draws largely on the projects funded through the CRBSCA. The Environmental Defense Fund challenged the implementation plan in the early 1980s on the grounds that it "was based upon unrealistic assumptions, relied upon insufficient control measures, and contained 'patently' ineffective provisions." The plan was upheld, however, in Environmental Defense Fund v. Costle, 657 F.2d 275 (D.C. Cir. 1981).

4. Who should pay the costs of the various salinity control projects? What portion should be borne by water users in the lower basin states who currently suffer salinity damage? By the farmers and upper basin water users who contribute to the salinity problem? By federal taxpayers? By taxpayers of the Colorado basin states? Currently the federal government pays from 70 to 75 percent of all costs. In the case of irrigation improvements sponsored by the Department of Agriculture, farmers generally pay the remaining costs. For other projects in the Lower Basin, a levy on sales of hydroelectric power from Hoover Dam covers the remaining costs.

Congress reduced its funding for the salinity control projects in the late 1990s, leading to concerns whether the 1972 numeric criteria will be met. See Dale Pontius, Colorado River Basin Study: Report to the Western Water Policy Review Advisory Commission 65–66 (1998).

5. As noted in Chapter 8, there is also an international dimension to the Colorado River's salinity problems. See supra p. 808. As a result of

federally subsidized irrigation in the lower basin (and more particularly the Wellton–Mohawk Irrigation District), the saline content of Colorado river water flowing across the Mexican border in 1961 reached 2,700 mg/l of TDS. Following over a decade of negotiations, the United States and Mexico agreed to salinity standards for Colorado River water delivered to Mexico. See Permanent and Definitive Solution to the International Problem of the Salinity of the Colorado River, IBWC Minute No. 242, Mex.–U.S., Aug. 30, 1973, 24 U.S.T. 1971.

The CRBSCA authorized various projects to help meet the United States' obligation to Mexico, including the construction of a desalting plant near Yuma, Arizona. The federal government finished building the plant in 1992 at a cost of $258 million. Because salinity levels have been low enough since 1992 to meet the United States' obligations to Mexico without operating the plant, the plant has stood idle. To maintain the plant in "ready reserve," however, the federal government spends almost $7 million annually. If the plant ever operates, each desalted acre-foot will cost almost $400, not including capital costs. See Pontius, supra Note 4, at 68.

Economists have estimated that far cheaper means of meeting the United States' obligation to Mexico would be to retire farmland that contributes to the salinity problem or to purchase water rights for dilution. Water in the region sells for less than $40 per acre foot. According to Allen Kneese, these solutions were rejected because of opposition in the Colorado basin states to losing any drop of water to Mexico. See Allen Kneese, Environmental Stress and Political Conflicts: Salinity in the Colorado River, Transboundary Resources Rep., Summer 1990, at 1. See also David Getches, From Ashkabad to Wellton–Mohawk, to Los Angeles: The Drought in Water Policy, 64 U. Colo. L. Rev. 523, 532–34 (1993) (recommending the purchase of low-value farm land as the best means of addressing the salinity problem). The federal government has assumed the entire cost of meeting the United States' obligation to Mexico. Who *should* bear the cost?

B. GROUNDWATER POLLUTION

Concerns over groundwater contamination are of relatively recent origin.[1] As an increasingly large percentage of the United States comes to rely on groundwater for domestic drinking needs, however, the threat to public health posed by groundwater contamination escalates. Current estimates indicate that roughly half of all Americans (and 95 percent of rural domestic households) rely on groundwater for potable drinking water—and the percentage continues to increase.

Until recently, it was commonly believed that the soil filtered out most dangerous contaminants before they could befoul groundwater. Today we know that is often not the case. Information concerning the extent of groundwater contamination in the United States is still sketchy—both because of the difficulty of testing for groundwater con-

---

1. For comprehensive discussions of the topic, see Ruth Patrick, Emily Ford, & John Quarles, Groundwater Contamination in the United States (2d ed. 1987); Conservation Foundation, Groundwater Protection (1987); Robert Glicksman & George Coggins, Groundwater Pollution I: The Problem and the Law, 35 U. Kan. L. Rev. 75 (1986).

tamination and the absence of any truly comprehensive testing requirements. However, thousands of groundwater wells (affecting millions of Americans) have been closed due to contamination. The available test data, moreover, suggests a trend toward increasing pollution.[2]

The problems of surface and groundwater pollution differ in a number of respects. Intentional point discharges, for example, are only a minor contributor to groundwater contamination. According to reports from 37 states, three sources of groundwater contamination are the leading contributors:

> • *Leaking underground storage tanks.* Leaking underground storage tanks (USTs) were cited as the highest priority contaminant source of concern to States. The primary causes of leakage in USTs are faulty installation and corrosion of tanks and pipelines. As of March 1996, more than 300,000 releases from USTs had been confirmed. EPA estimates that nationally 60% of these leaks have impacted ground water quality and, in some States, the percentage is as high as 90%.

> • *Landfills.* Landfills were cited by States as the second highest contaminant source of concern. Landfills are used to dispose of sanitary (municipal) and industrial wastes. * * * States indicate that the most common contaminants associated with landfills were metals, halogenated solvents, and petroleum compounds. To a lesser extent, organic and inorganic pesticides were also cited as a contaminant of concern.

> • *Septic systems.* Septic systems were cited by 29 out of 37 States as a potential source of ground water contamination. Ground water may be contaminated by releases from septic systems when the systems are poorly designed (tanks are installed in areas with inadequate soils or shallow depth to ground water), poorly constructed; have poor well seals; are improperly used, located, or maintained; or are abandoned. Typical contaminants from domestic septic systems include bacteria, nitrates, viruses, phosphates from detergents, and other chemicals that might originate from household cleaners.[3]

Other major sources of groundwater contamination identified by at least a quarter of the reporting states are hazardous waste sites and surface impoundments.

Groundwater contamination also is not as easy to spot as surface pollution. Years often pass before groundwater contamination is discovered and its source located; by that time, contamination can be extensive. Groundwater quality, moreover, is much more difficult to restore than is surface water quality. Surface waters tend to cleanse themselves by breaking down pollutants through agitation, aeration, evaporation, or

---

2. For more data on the extent and nature of groundwater contamination in the United States, see U.S. EPA, National Water Quality Inventory: 1996 Report to Congress (1997).

3. Id. at I–32.

sedimentation. Most groundwater pollutants, by contrast, remain volatile and do not decompose. There are important exceptions: the leaching process that occurs in the zone of aeration, for example, is successfully used in septic fields to treat human wastes. Nevertheless, it is a fair generalization that pollutants introduced into groundwater often stay there. And methods to limit the spread of groundwater pollution and to clean already contaminated water are imperfect and expensive.

1. COMMON LAW ACTIONS AGAINST GROUNDWATER CONTAMINATION

Courts have long used common law principles to address groundwater contamination. Unlike in the surface water context, however, courts have seldom used groundwater allocation rules to resolve contamination issues. A 1974 study of 203 groundwater contamination cases found only two cases decided under groundwater allocation rules. Most of the cases were decided under either nuisance or negligence rules. See Peter Davis, Groundwater Pollution: Case Law Theories For Relief, 39 Mo. L. Rev. 117, 120–21 (1974). See also Tom Kuhnle, The Rebirth of Common Law Actions for Addressing Hazardous Waste Contamination, 15 Stan. Envtl. L.J. 187 (1996) (discussing the use of nuisance and negligence law to address contamination of groundwater and other property by hazardous waste).

Several factors have steered courts toward nuisance and negligence doctrine. Because groundwater contamination results more from negligent operation of surface activities than from intentional discharges into aquifers, tort law seems a more logical legal tool to control groundwater contamination than doctrines designed to allocate groundwater among competing users. Several of the eastern groundwater doctrines, moreover, would arguably place little, if any, constraints on groundwater pollution. The English absolute ownership rule, or the rule of capture (supra p. 415), provides little or no protection to users of groundwater from the polluting activities of others, and the American reasonable use rule (supra p. 415) would at best limit polluting activities only when they are "unreasonable" and cause "unreasonable" harm to groundwater users.

Even negligence and nuisance actions, however, are imperfect tools with which to combat groundwater contamination. The foreseeability of contamination is almost always a bitterly fought issue in negligence cases, and the defendant is often aided by the alleged vagaries of hydrology. Both nuisance and negligence actions, moreover, have historically required some showing of injury. Once an aquifer is contaminated and injury has occurred, clean up is generally a difficult, if not impossible task.

The common law has evolved to help meet these difficulties. Courts have grown more willing, for example, to hold groundwater polluters liable in strict liability.[4] See, e.g., Sterling v. Velsicol Chemical Corp., 855

---

4. Courts also have applied strict liability in cases of surface water pollution. See, e.g., Cities Service Co. v. State, 312 So.2d 799 (Fla. Ct. App. 1975). But see Fortier v.

F.2d 1188 (6th Cir. 1988); Branch v. Western Petroleum, Inc., 657 P.2d 267, 272–75 (Utah 1982). Some courts also have held that an activity can be enjoined as a "prospective nuisance" when it is highly probable that contamination will occur, thus eliminating the problem of having to wait until an aquifer is already contaminated. See, e.g., Village of Wilsonville v. SCA Services, Inc., 86 Ill.2d 1, 426 N.E.2d 824 (1981); Gonzalez v. Whitaker, 97 N.M. 710, 643 P.2d 274 (App. 1982). For many of the reasons discussed in connection with surface water pollution (supra pp. 1015–1016), however, the common law remains a highly imperfect system for controlling groundwater contamination, and legislation has emerged to fill the void.

Do groundwater users have a cause of action against surface water diversions that, by reducing the recharge to an aquifer, lead to salt water intrusion into the aquifer? Relying on Antioch v. Williams Irrigation Dist., supra p. 1013, a California court has concluded no. See Jordan v. City of Santa Barbara, 46 Cal.App.4th 1245, 54 Cal.Rptr.2d 340 (1996). Assuming no overdraft, should a groundwater user have a cause of action against other nearby groundwater withdrawals that contribute to salt water intrusion? Is there any reason to treat groundwater withdrawals that lead to salt water intrusion differently than surface water withdrawals that lead to salt water intrusion?

2. FEDERAL PREVENTION OF GROUNDWATER CONTAMINATION

The federal government again has taken the legislative lead in both protecting groundwater and cleaning up contaminated aquifers. Federal protection efforts have centered on ensuring the safe storage and disposal of waste and hazardous substances. As EPA has commented, "The sage adage that 'An ounce of prevention is worth a pound of cure' is being borne out in the field of ground water protection. Studies evaluating the cost of prevention versus the cost of cleaning up contaminated ground water have found that there are real cost advantages to promoting protection." U.S. EPA, National Water Quality Inventory: 1996 Report to Congress I–44 (1997).

Resource Conservation and Recovery Act

The major protective statute is the Resource Conservation and Recovery Act (RCRA).[5] Under RCRA, EPA has developed a comprehensive regulatory program for underground storage tanks (USTs) storing petroleum or certain other hazardous substances. All USTs must have both leak detection and leak prevention components.

RCRA also provides for the comprehensive regulation of waste disposal. RCRA's most detailed requirements focus on hazardous waste.

Flambeau Plastics Co., 164 Wis.2d 639, 476 N.W.2d 593 (Ct. App. 1991) (declining to apply strict liability).

5. RCRA is codified at 42 U.S.C. §§ 6921 et seq.

First, RCRA mandates safety standards for all the handlers of hazardous waste—generators; transporters; and treatment, storage, and disposal facilities (often nicknamed TSDFs).[6] In the case of TSDFs, RCRA imposes a number of "minimum technological requirements," requires extensive groundwater monitoring, and bans the disposal of certain untreated wastes on land or in deep injection wells unless EPA concludes that such disposal is safe to human health and the environment.[7] The minimum technological requirements prescribe liners, leachate collection systems, and other precautions to prevent wastes from leaching into the soil and groundwater. To help enforce the TSDF requirements, RCRA prohibits the treatment, longterm storage, or disposal of hazardous wastes except by a facility that has received a permit from EPA or an authorized state.[8]

RCRA also establishes a "cradle-to-grave" manifest system to track hazardous waste from its generation to ultimate disposal.[9] Before releasing hazardous waste for transportation to a TSDF, a generator must prepare a manifest identifying the waste and its characteristics. The manifest must then accompany the waste to its final destination; transporters and TSDFs must check the accuracy of the manifest and, if they discover any discrepancy, report the discrepancy immediately to EPA and the local state.

Safe Drinking Water Act

The Safe Drinking Water Act (SDWA)[10] also protects against groundwater contamination. The SDWA requires EPA to set national drinking water standards and takes a number of steps to protect the quality of aquifers used to supply drinking water. First, the SDWA requires states to establish an EPA-approved permit program for underground injection of wastes and to prohibit any underground injection for which a permit has not been received.[11] State permit systems must ensure that injection wells comply with a series of technical safety requirements (such as maximum injection pressures, casing and cementing standards, and groundwater monitoring).[12] No permit can be issued for a well that may contaminate groundwater that is a current or potential source of drinking water.[13]

The SDWA also establishes a "sole source aquifer" program. If EPA finds, on its own initiative or on the petition of any interested party, that an aquifer is the sole or principal source of drinking water for an area and that contamination of the aquifer could create a significant hazard to public health, EPA must so designate the aquifer.[14] Thereafter, the

6. RCRA §§ 3002–3004, 42 U.S.C. §§ 6922–6924.

7. Id. § 3004, 42 U.S.C. § 6924.

8. Id. §§ 3005–3006, 42 U.S.C. §§ 6925–6926.

9. See id. § 3002(a)(5), 42 U.S.C. § 6922(a)(5); 45 Fed. Reg. 12,728 (Feb. 26, 1980).

10. The Safe Drinking Water Act is codified at 42 U.S.C. §§ 300f et seq.

11. SDWA § 1421, 42 U.S.C. § 300h.

12. 40 C.F.R. pt. 144.

13. SDWA §§ 1421(b)(1) & (d)(2), 42 U.S.C. §§ 300h(b)(1) & (d)(2).

14. Id. § 1424(e), 42 U.S.C. § 300h–3(e).

federal government cannot provide financial assistance for any project that EPA concludes may contaminate the aquifer and endanger public health.[15] State governments, moreover, may apply for federal financial assistance to develop and implement demonstration programs to protect those portions of a sole or principal source aquifer that EPA designates a Critical Aquifer Protection Area based on vulnerability to contamination and various other criteria.[16] As of January 2000, EPA had designated 70 sole source aquifers.

Finally, the SDWA requires all states to adopt "wellhead protection programs" to protect from contamination the surface and subsurface area surrounding well fields furnishing public drinking water. As in other areas, Congress gave EPA no power to impose a wellhead protection program on a state, but provided financial assistance for states in the form of grants covering 50 to 90 percent of the implementation costs.

An Evaluation of Federal Protection Statutes

ROBERT GLICKSMAN & GEORGE COGGINS, GROUNDWATER POLLUTION I: THE PROBLEM AND THE LAW

35 U. KAN. L. REV. 75, 138–39 (1986).

Despite the plethora of federal laws * * *, the Office of Technology Assessment [OTA] concluded recently that "[t]here is no explicit comprehensive national legislative mandate to protect groundwater from contamination." Federal efforts to protect groundwater quality are fragmented among a number of federal agencies * * *. Even within the EPA, numerous divisions are responsible for different groundwater-related activities. While specialization has virtues, the component parts have not been integrated into a larger whole. * * *

As the OTA points out, significant gaps in federal regulatory coverage remain. Some known groundwater contaminants are not regulated adequately or at all under the federal laws. The EPA has established [drinking water standards] for only a handful of substances, although recent amendments to the SDWA require the Agency to regulate many more substances in the next few years. The number of chemicals covered by regulations under the [Toxic Substances Control Act] and the [Federal Insecticide, Fungicide, and Rodenticide Act] is even more limited. Further, not all bodies of groundwater are protected. Certain aquifers, for example, may be exempt from [underground injection control] programs under the SDWA, leaving underground injection into those aquifers uncontrolled. Some known contamination sources are not covered at all by federal law. The OTA cites as examples surface impoundments, waste piles, materials stockpiles, tanks and pipelines used to contain or store non-hazardous waste, and noncoal mining activities on private land.

---

15. Id.   **16.** Id. § 1427, 42 U.S.C. § 300h–6.

Even where regulatory coverage exists, it is sometimes minimal or inadequate. Not all sources of groundwater contamination are regulated to the same extent. Perhaps they should not be, but, according to the OTA, the differences in regulatory treatment "often have little relation to the potential for a source to cause contamination." Thus, point sources generally are subject to much more extensive and stringent controls than are nonpoint sources * * * even though such nonpoint sources as pesticide runoff from agricultural activities are significant contributors to groundwater pollution. Several sources are not required to engage in groundwater monitoring under any federal law [including] irrigation, fertilizer application, pipelines, and activities causing salt water [or brackish water] intrusion * * *. Finally, mandatory preventive mechanisms such as design and operating requirements have not been established for all groundwater pollution sources.

Notes and Questions

1. How large of a role should the federal government play in protecting groundwater quality? Many observers have argued that states should play the principal role and that the task of the federal government should be to encourage and aid state regulation. See EPA, Ground–Water Protection Strategy (Aug. 1984). Groundwater is far more localized than surface water and many of the sources of contamination, such as runoff, do not lend themselves to uniform national solutions. Land use controls, which have traditionally rested with state and local governments, are likely to play a major role in any protection strategy.

2. States have not been inactive. A sizable number of states have adopted comprehensive statewide strategies that, depending on the state, classify aquifers according to likely use, set groundwater quality standards, monitor groundwater quality, and/or employ land use planning and best management practices to help protect aquifers. More common is source-specific legislation designed to help protect groundwater from particular pollution sources or contaminants. Over half of the states, for example, have enacted legislation to regulate underground storage tanks (largely in response to a RCRA requirement that states adopt programs to detect, prevent, and correct leaking underground storage tanks). About the same number have enacted legislation to regulate agricultural chemicals and prevent their migration into groundwater. For descriptions of various state legislation, see Larry Morandi, State Groundwater Protection Policies: A Legislator's Guide (1989); John Davidson, South Dakota Groundwater Protection Law, 40 S.D. L. Rev. 1 (1995).

3. Can any groundwater quality program be effective if it does not address groundwater withdrawals? Groundwater pumping can increase contamination in several ways. As noted in Chapter 5, excessive pumping from coastal aquifers can lead to salt water intrusion. Where an aquifer is already partly contaminated, moreover, groundwater pumping can also cause or hasten the migration of the contaminated water into areas from which drinking water is drawn. See, e.g., Conservation Foundation, State of the Environment: An Assessment at Mid–Decade 377 (1984) (describing how

groundwater pumping encouraged the spread of TCE in the aquifer underlying Tucson, Arizona).

Why should the federal government regulate waste management techniques but not the overpumping of coastal aquifers? Should Congress give EPA the power to limit pumping where the pumping is likely to draw contaminated water toward the well and endanger a drinking water source?

4. Under the Clean Water Act, a state cannot set a water quality standard that permits a waterway to degrade below its current condition. Clean Water Act § 303(d)(4)(B), 33 U.S.C. § 1313(d)(4)(B); 40 C.F.R. § 35.131.12. Groundwater quality provisions such as the SDWA's wellhead protection program, by contrast, appear to contemplate that some, but not all aquifers should be protected from degradation. Should there be a national antidegradation requirement for all groundwater aquifers?

5. Despite the interrelationships between groundwater quality and quantity, even fewer states have integrated quality and allocation management for groundwater than for surface water. Minnesota took one of the earliest steps toward integration by creating a Groundwater Protection Strategy Work Group comprised of officials from a number of federal, state, and local agencies. See Conservation Foundation, supra Note 3, at 381.

3. GROUNDWATER CLEANUP

Due to the years when potential groundwater contaminants went largely unregulated and the regulatory gaps that still exist today, many aquifers are contaminated and in need of cleanup. Unfortunately, although several cleanup methods are available, they are imperfect. One relatively straightforward, but expensive and inefficient method is to remove and then clean the contaminated groundwater. The groundwater is pumped from the aquifer; cleansed through settling pools, filtration, or a number of other processes; and finally reinjected into the aquifer.

A promising avenue for groundwater clean-up is the use of injected catalysts that react with and neutralize the hazardous contaminants. At the present, such in situ techniques are limited, often experimental, and frequently difficult to apply. Nevertheless, they are increasingly being used and have tremendous promise for providing cost-effective remedies.

Trapping the contaminated materials—by constructing impervious barriers, for example—is an almost hopeless task. Once the contaminant has spread into the groundwater, any attempt to limit its movement entails building barriers around all four sides, the bottom, and perhaps the top of the contaminated portion of the aquifer. The barrier building process will inevitably intersect the water table, making construction of the barrier exceedingly difficult. An alternative to barriers is leachate control, in which migration is limited by controlling subsurface flows. This too is a difficult and, in most instances, imperfect remedy.

Several of the federal acts designed to avoid groundwater contamination also permit the federal government to order the cleanup of aquifers. Where the federal government has evidence that past or present hazardous waste operations "may present an imminent and substantial endangerment to health or the environment," RCRA permits the government to seek a judicial order requiring any person who has handled, stored, treated, transported, or disposed of the waste to take cleanup action.[17] Similarly where EPA has evidence that a contaminant threatens an underground source of drinking water and "may present an imminent and substantial endangerment to the health of persons," and state and local authorities are not taking adequate action, the SDWA permits EPA to either issue an administrative order or seek judicial relief.[18] RCRA also requires TSDFs to monitor nearby groundwater and, if contamination is detected in sufficient amounts, take corrective actions.[19]

In response to Love Canal and similar incidents of toxic contamination, Congress in 1980 decided to enact legislation directed explicitly at the cleanup of sites contaminated by hazardous substances. The Comprehensive Environmental Response, Compensation, & Liability Act (also known as "CERCLA" and "Superfund")[20] provides the government with three methods of cleaning up contaminated sites (including polluted aquifers):

1. Federal Cleanup & Cost Recovery. First, the government can clean up the site itself drawing upon federal funds—and then sue to recover its costs from parties responsible for the contamination. CERCLA established a "superfund" in 1980 specifically to pay for clean-ups, supported through taxes imposed on a broad range of American industry, but with most money coming from the petroleum and chemical industries. Congress, however, permitted the tax to expire in 1995, and the fund has now run out of money. As a result, federal cleanups today must compete for funding from the federal fisc. To set standards and priorities for cleanups, CERCLA requires EPA to prepare a National Contingency Plan (or NCP). Pursuant to the NCP, EPA has created a National Priority List (NPL) of those sites in greatest need of federal cleanup; as of May 2006, there were over 1200 sites on the NPL (and over 300 deleted sites). Thousands of other sites, although not dangerous enough to make it on the NPL, also require cleanup.

Under section 107 of CERCLA, the government can recover its costs from four broad sets of "potentially responsible parties" (or PRPs): (i) current owners and operators of the contaminated site, (ii) anyone who owned or operated the site at the time hazardous wastes were disposed of, (iii) generators of the waste or others who "arranged for disposal or treatment" of the waste, and (iv) transporters of the waste who selected where to take it. The government need not show negligence or culpability; liability is strict. In most cases, moreover, PRPs can be held jointly and severally liable, meaning that the government can seek its expenses from one or all of the PRPs. Except for someone who innocently acquired a site without contributing to or knowing of the waste problem, PRPs

17. RCRA § 7003, 42 U.S.C. § 6973.

18. SDWA § 1431, 42 U.S.C. § 300i.

19. RCRA §§ 3004(u)-(v), 42 U.S.C. §§ 6924(u)-(v).

20. 42 U.S.C. §§ 9601 et seq.

have only a few, exceptionally limited defenses. Even innocent purchasers of a hazardous waste site often have difficulty escaping liability.

Generally the federal government uses section 107 liability as a stick to negotiate an agreement with PRPs providing for cleanup of the site by the PRPs under the government's supervision. The government typically prefers PRP cleanups because they can be undertaken faster and do not drain limited federal funds. PRPs favor them because they have greater control over the process and can frequently clean up the site for less money than the government.

2. *PRP Cleanup.* CERCLA also gives the federal government power to order PRPs to clean up a site. If the government believes that a contaminated site may pose an "imminent and substantial endangerment" to public health or the environment, it can seek a judicial order requiring PRPs to take whatever steps "may be necessary to abate such danger or threat."[21] More importantly, EPA can issue an administrative order requiring cleanup whenever "necessary to protect public health and welfare and the environment."[22] If a PRP fails to obey such an order, CERCLA provides for fines of up to $25,000 per day,[23] and if the government is forced to clean up the site, the government can collect punitive damages of up to triple its costs.[24]

3. *Non-federal Cleanup.* Finally, state or local governments, Indian tribes, and private parties can clean up a site and then, assuming that the cleanup is consistent with CERCLA and the cleanup standards of the NCP, sue PRPs for their costs.[25]

CERCLA also provides that the federal or state governments can sue PRPs for "injury to, destruction of, or loss of natural resources, including the reasonable costs of assessing such injury, destruction, or loss resulting from such a release."[26] In providing for natural resource damage actions, Congress

> intended to expand and strengthen a state government's role as trustee of natural resources. By extending the geographical reach of the public trust doctrine [beyond navigable waters to all resources] and by adopting a comprehensive measure of natural resource damages, CERCLA's natural resource damages provisions establish a powerful cause of action that authorizes a state government to act on behalf of the environment and the public if a release of hazardous substances injures natural resources.

21. CERCLA § 106(a), 42 U.S.C. § 9606(a).

22. Id.

23. Id. § 106(b), 42 U.S.C. § 9606(b).

24. Id. § 107(c)(3), 42 U.S.C. § 9607(c)(3).

25. Id. §§ 107(a)(A)-(B), 42 U.S.C. §§ 9607(a)(A)-(B). For cases recognizing a right of recovery in a private party, see Wickland Oil Terminals v. Asarco, Inc., 792 F.2d 887 (9th Cir. 1986); Chemical Waste Management, Inc. v. Armstrong World Industries, Inc., 669 F.Supp. 1285 (E.D. Pa. 1987).

26. CERCLA §§ 107(a)(4)(C) & (f), 42 U.S.C. §§ 9607(a)(4)(C) & (f).

Note, CERCLA's Natural Resource Damage Provisions: A Comprehensive and Innovative Approach to Protecting the Environment, 45 Wash. & Lee L. Rev. 1417, 1436–37 (1988).

Notes and Questions

1. Absent CERCLA, would a state government have a right to sue under the public trust doctrine for natural resource damages resulting from the contamination of either surface water or groundwater? Commonwealth of Puerto Rico v. SS Zoe Colocotroni, 628 F.2d 652 (1st Cir. 1980), dealt with a pre-CERCLA suit by the Commonwealth of Puerto Rico to recover natural resource damages to mangrove trees and various species of marine organisms from an oil spill. The district court held that the commonwealth had a cause of action for natural resource damages as the "trustee of the public trust in these resources." Id. at 670. "[T]he flora and fauna were part of a trust held for the people by the Commonwealth of Puerto Rico. Perforce, the Commonwealth must have the ability to have the corpus of said public trust reimbursed for the diminution attributable to the wrongdoers." Id. at 662. On appeal, the Second Circuit found it unnecessary to decide the "difficult question" of whether the public trust provided an independent cause of action because a Commonwealth statute authorized the Commonwealth's Environmental Quality Board to bring such actions. Id. at 671. See also Carter Strickland, The Scope of Authority of Natural Resource Trustees, 20 Colum. J. Envtl. L. 301, 313–14 (1995) (arguing that the public trust doctrine provides a cause of action for damages to trust resources); Cynthia Carlson, Making CERCLA Natural Resource Regulations Work: The Use of the Public Trust Doctrine and Other State Remedies, 18 Envtl. L. Rep. 10299 (1988) (same).

If the public trust doctrine permits an action for damages to trust resources, do private parties have a right to sue for the natural resource damages? See Marks v. Whitney, supra p. 597 (recognizing private standing to enforce public trust obligations); Carlson, supra, at 10306 (urging that private parties should be able to sue for damages to trust resources).

2. Where a surface waterway or groundwater aquifer is polluted by hazardous waste, do state governments have a public-trust *obligation* to sue for natural resource damages?

3. Under section 107 of CERCLA, a municipal or other water supplier whose groundwater source has been contaminated by hazardous waste can recover the costs of alternative water supplies. See Lutz v. Chromatex Inc., 718 F.Supp. 413, 419 (M.D. Pa. 1989); Artesian Water Co. v. Government of New Castle County, 659 F.Supp. 1269, 1287–91 (D. Del. 1987), aff'd, 851 F.2d 643 (3d Cir. 1988). Can a water supplier sue for the cost of cleaning up an aquifer if that cost is greater than the estimated expense of obtaining alternative water supplies? If the cost of cleaning up the aquifer is more than the estimated value of the water that is lost? See Ohio v. United States Dept. of Interior, 880 F.2d 432 (D.C. Cir. 1989) (holding that restoration is the presumptively correct remedy for injury to natural resources); Utah v. Kennecott Corp., 801 F.Supp. 553 (D. Utah 1992).

4. Could a state or municipality also recover natural resource damages for the non-use value of a contaminated aquifer? Does an aquifer have a non-

use value? In other contexts (e.g., pollution of a coastal estuary), courts have suggested that governments can recover for various non-use values such as option value (the value of having the opportunity to use a resource even if you never use it) and existence value (the value of simply knowing that a resource exists). See, e.g., Ohio v. United States Dept. of Interior, 880 F.2d 432 (D.C. Cir. 1989). Does an aquifer have the same type of non-use values as an estuary, beach, or national park? In Utah v. Kennecott Corp., 801 F.Supp. 553 (D. Utah 1992), the court rejected a proposed consent decree settling a claim for natural resource damages to an aquifer, in part because the state "failed to assess the non-consumptive use values of the aquifer, i.e., option and existence value." In a footnote, the court added: "Although the aquifer is unlike most other natural resources such as lakes, eagles or seals which have more obvious existence and option values, its existence value should have been considered in the settlement given the fact that people who live in a desert most likely would assign substantial value in just knowing that an aquifer exists."

If an aquifer has a non-use value, how should a court determine that value? The principal method suggested by economists, the Contingent Valuation (CV) method, surveys members of the public to find out how much they would pay to protect the resource. For a small taste of the controversy that has swirled around the CV approach, see Valuing Natural Assets: The Economics of Natural Resource Damage Assessment (Raymond Kopp & Kerry Smith eds., 1993); Judith Robinson, The Role of Nonuse Values in Natural Resource Damages: Past, Present, and Future, 75 Tex. L. Rev. 189 (1996); Daniel Levy & David Friedman, The Revenge of the Redwoods? Reconsidering Property Rights and the Economic Allocation of Natural Resources, 61 U. Chi. L. Rev. 493 (1994).

*

Appendix

GLOSSARY OF COMMON WATER RESOURCE TERMS

These definitions are designed to help law students understand the materials in this book. They do not purport to be scientifically acceptable. Water measurements are discussed in greater detail at pages 17–19 of Chapter 1.

ACRE–FOOT	The quantity of water required to cover 1 acre to a depth of 1 foot, or 325,851 gallons.
AQUIFER	A porous water-bearing geologic formation. The term is used to describe any underground area which serves as a common supply of water obtained by pumping.
ARTESIAN WELL	A well that taps a confined aquifer. The aquifer often has sufficient pressure to create a natural flow of water.
CALLING THE RIVER	The action taken by a senior appropriator to curtail junior diversions when necessary to permit the senior to take her full entitlement.
CONFINED AQUIFER	An aquifer that is enclosed between impermeable materials.
CONJUNCTIVE USE	The coordinated use of surface water and groundwater to maximize the value of both resources.
CONSUMPTIVE USE	The amount of water consumed by a particular use and thus unavailable for further use.
CONVEYANCE LOSS	The loss of water from a ditch, canal, or other conduit due to evaporation, leakage, seepage, or transpiration.

CUBIC FOOT PER SECOND

The quantity of water flowing at a velocity of one foot per second through a box one foot wide and one foot deep. Usually abbreviated "cfs," it is equivalent to 448.8 gallons per minute or slightly more than 646,000 gallons per day.

DITCH

An artificial open channel or waterway constructed through earth or rock, for the purpose of carrying water. A ditch is smaller than a canal, although the line of demarcation between the two is indefinite. A ditch usually has sharper curvature in its alignment, is not constructed to such refinement of uniformity of grade or cross section, and may or may not be lined with impervious material to prevent seepage.

DIVERSION

The extraction of water from its natural source, usually into a ditch or canal, for ultimate use on land, in industry, or for domestic purposes.

DIVIDE

A high point on land which separates two river basins or drainage basins.

DRAINAGE BASIN

The area drained by a river and its tributaries. The land area from which water drains into the Colorado River and its tributaries, for example, comprises the Colorado River basin. Also called a "catchment area" "watershed," or "river basin."

EFFICIENCY

The ratio of (1) the quantity of water *consumed* by a particular use to (2) the volume of water *diverted* for the use. Sometimes defined as the ratio of the quantity consumed to the volume of water *delivered* for the use.

EFFLUENT

The water, usually polluted, which is discharged into a stream from sewers, industrial plants, or other pollution sources.

FLOOD PLAIN

That portion of a river valley which is covered with water when the river overflows its banks at flood stage.

GROUNDWATER

Subsurface water from which wells and springs are fed. In a strict sense the term applies only to water below the water table.

GROUNDWATER BASIN

A physiographic or geologic unit containing at least one aquifer of significant areal extent.

HEADGATE

A device to control water flow, placed at the entrance to a conduit such as a pipeline, or canal. The point at which water is diverted from a river into an irrigation ditch.

HEADWATERS

The place where a river originates.

IMPERMEABLE

Material that does not permit the passage of water or other fluids.

INSTREAM USE

Water uses that do not require a diversion—e.g., fishing or transportation.

LATERAL

A minor ditch that branches off a main ditch or canal and is used to transport water onto the land where it will be used.

LEACHING

The removal of salts and alkali from soils by abundant irrigation combined with drainage.

LITTORAL RIGHTS

The equivalent of riparian rights for those who border a lake rather than a flowing stream.

MINER'S INCH

An obsolescent term measuring the rate of flow of water. A variable measure equal to between 0.02 and 0.029 cfs depending on the state.

MOUTH OF A RIVER

The place where a river empties into another river, or into the sea.

NONCONSUMPTIVE USE

Any water use that does not reduce the supply of water available for other uses—e.g., hunting and swimming.

PHREATOPHYTE

A water-loving plant. Usually describes vegetation such as cottonwood trees which line the banks of a stream and soak up water sought to be used to irrigate agricultural crops.

RECHARGE, GROUNDWATER

The flow of water into an aquifer.

RETURN FLOW

Any flow which returns to a stream channel after diversion for use. In irrigation, water applied to an area which is not consumed in evaporation or transpiration, and returns

	to a surface stream or groundwater aquifer.
RIVER BASIN	See "Drainage Basin."
SAFE YIELD	Definitions vary. Generally the amount of water that can be extracted each year from an aquifer on a renewable basis.
SEEPAGE	(1) The water lost from canals, ditches, reservoirs, agricultural fields, etc., by infiltration into the soil. Also (2) the slow movement of water through soil and other materials into or out of a body of surface water or groundwater.
UNCONFINED AQUIFER	An aquifer having no layer of impermeable material above it.
WATER, DUTY OF	In irrigation, the quantity of water required to satisfy the irrigation water requirements of land. It is expressed either as the rate of flow required per unit area of land, the area which can be served by a unit, or the total volumetric quantity of water in terms of depth of water, required during the irrigation season or given portion thereof.
WATERSHED	See "Drainage Basin."
WATER TABLE	The highest elevation, at or below the surface of the earth, under which the ground is saturated with water. A well, for example, must be dug down to the water table in order to make the pumping of water effective.

Index

References are to Pages

1085

References are to Pages

References are to Pages

†